EXCESS ALCOHOL

The legal limits are:

Breath: 35 microgrammes per 100 millilitres

Blood: 80 milligrammes per 100 millilitres

Urine: 107 milligrammes per 100 millilitres

Between 40 and 52 microgrammes per 100 millilitres of breath the suggested fine is £480 and disqualification for 12 months. For amounts in excess of 52 microgrammes (breath) or 120 milligrammes (blood) or 160 milligrammes (urine) then refer to the chart below and read off a datum or entry point for your deliberations.

For breath: take the reading on the left hand side of the chart and go to the diagonal line. Where the reading meets the diagonal, drop vertically to the base line and read off the associated fine and disqualification.

For blood: above 210, go to the the right of the diagonal, drop vertically and read off fine and disqualification. Below 210, go left and proceed as above.

For urine: take the reading on the right hand side of the chart and go left to the diagonal line. Where the reading meets the diagonal, drop vertically to the base line and read off fine and disqualification.

IMPORTANT: This only provides a starting point. Always apply circumstances to increase or decrease fine or disqualification.

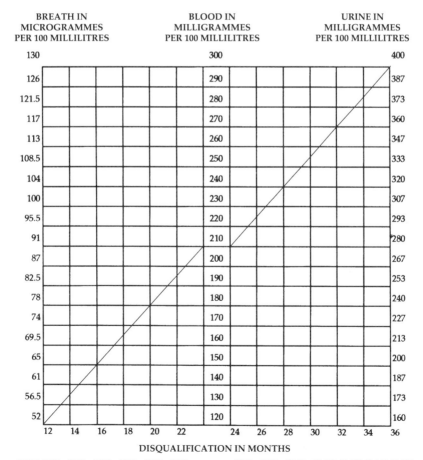

BREATH IN MICROGRAMMES PER 100 MILLILITRES	BLOOD IN MILLIGRAMMES PER 100 MILLILITRES	URINE IN MILLIGRAMMES PER 100 MILLILITRES
130	300	400
126	290	387
121.5	280	373
117	270	360
113	260	347
108.5	250	333
104	240	320
100	230	307
95.5	220	293
91	210	280
87	200	267
82.5	190	253
78	180	240
74	170	227
69.5	160	213
65	150	200
61	140	187
56.5	130	173
52	120	160

12 14 16 18 20 22 24 26 28 30 32 34 36

DISQUALIFICATION IN MONTHS

FINE £480 £540 £600 £660 £720 £780 £840 £900 £960 £1,020 £1,080 £1,140 £1,200
.... CONSIDER CUSTODY ....

REFUSING BREATH BLOOD OR URINE SPECIMENS (DRIVING ETC.) – £720 AND DISQUALIFY 18 MONTHS

AUSTRALIA
The Law Book Company
Brisbane ● Sydney ● Melbourne ● Perth

CANADA
Carswell
Ottawa ● Toronto ● Calgary ● Montreal ● Vancouver

Agents:
Steimatzky's Agency Ltd, Tel Aviv
N.M. Tripathi (Private) Ltd, Bombay
Eastern Law House (Private) Ltd, Calcutta
M.P.P. House, Bangalore
Universal Book Traders, Delhi
Aditya Books, Delhi
MacMillan Shuppan KK, Tokyo
Pakistan Law House, Karachi, Lahore

ROAD TRAFFIC
LAW
AND
PRACTICE

ROAD TRAFFIC LAW AND PRACTICE THIRD EDITION

BY

Linda P. Dobbs, B.SC., LL.M.,
PH.D. (LOND.)
Of Gray's Inn, Barrister

AND

Mark Lucraft, B.A. (KENT)
Of the Inner Temple, Barrister

LONDON
SWEET & MAXWELL

First Edition 1993
Second Edition 1994
Third Edition 1995

Published in 1995 by
Sweet & Maxwell Limited of
South Quay Plaza, 183 Marsh Wall,
London E14 9FT
Phototypeset by
MFK Information Services Ltd., Hitchin, Herts.,
and printed and bound in Great Britain by Hartnolls Ltd., Bodmin

**A catalogue reference for this book is available from
The British Library**

ISBN 0–421 54220 9

INTRODUCTION

This new edition arrives one year after the last. We have come to the conclusion that it is necessary to cope with the legislative changes and wealth of authority in Road Traffic law. It is not for us to comment on the volume of legislation in the past decade but practitioners and academics alike would welcome a period of stability to allow the police and the courts time to absorb the developments.

We are still determined to resist the temptation to expand into two volumes. The aim remains the same as before: one portable and accessible volume incorporating all essential aspects of Road Traffic law and practice. Whereas the extent of the information available in the previous edition has been fully augmented, it is now published in a new and significantly cheaper form.

We have also taken the opportunity to introduce a new feature at the front of the book: the *Quick Access Summary*, which provides the hard-pressed practitioner with a short, clear and authoritative overview of each chapter. We are also conscious of the fact that the realities of trials, particularly in the lower courts, often involve the need to consult a text in the heat of battle. These Summaries provide an immediate answer, and avoid the need for agonised fumblings through the index.

We have incorporated the existing law, particularly the new Criminal Justice and Public Order Act 1994, indicating provisions in force as well as those yet to appear. We have also reflected society's increasing concern with vehicular crime by dealing comprehensively with the new crimes and penalties introduced by the government.

We have as always an immense debt to our friends and colleagues within the legal and publishing worlds. We have also been most gratified by the friendly and constructive letters we have received from our readers. In this edition we wish to give particular thanks to Alisdair Williamson and – an old friend of this book – David Etherington. Errors and omissions which remain are, of course, our responsibility alone.

The law is stated as of March 1995.

5 King's Bench Walk   L.D.
Temple   M.L.
London EC4Y 7DN.

March 2, 1995.

ACKNOWLEDGMENT

The Magistrates' Association Sentencing Guidelines are reproduced with the kind permission of the Magistrates' Association.

Contents

PART A OFFENCES

Contents

CHAPTER 3 PRELIMINARY BREATH TESTS AND ROADSIDE PROCEDURE

Contents

Contents

Contents

Contents

Contents

Contents

Contents

Chapter 14 Disqualification, Endorsement and Penalty Points

Contents

CHAPTER 15 SPECIAL REASONS

CHAPTER 16 MITIGATING CIRCUMSTANCES

Contents

PART B STATUTES

Contents

PART C STATUTORY INSTRUMENTS

Contents

PART D APPENDICES

Contents

TABLE OF CASES

PARA.

PARA.

TABLE OF STATUTES

Table of Statutes

xlix

1

TABLE OF STATUTORY INSTRUMENTS

(f) **R.T.A. 1988, s.175**: issuing false documents.

Similar time limits apply under the **Vehicle Excise and Registration Act 1994 (s.47)**:

    (a) using and keeping a vehicle without an excise licence (**s.29**);
    (b) using a trade licence in breach of its conditions (**s.34**).

The summons

Must contain details of the defendant, the court, the hearing, the information and the informant. For summary only offences service is treated as proved if it was posted by registered or recorded post to his last known address; otherwise, it must be proved that the summons came to the defendant's knowledge: **Magistrates' Courts Rules 1981, r.99.** If the defendant fails to attend the court may adjourn (**M.C.A. 1980, s.10**), proceed in his absence (**s.11**) or issue a warrant for his arrest (**s.13** – only where the defendant is a juvenile, the offence is imprisonable or the court proposed to disqualify having already convicted). There is also a power to issue a warrant under the **M.C.A., s.1**.   A1–09

Notice of intended prosecution

The **R.T.O.A. 1988, s.1** provides that a person shall not be convicted of one of the offences below unless he was warned at the time of the danger of prosecution, or within 14 days he was served with a summons, or a notice of intended prosecution was served on him, or the registered keeper of the vehicle (if appropriate). Notice is deemed to have been served if it was sent by registered or recorded post. This requirement does not apply if at the time of the offence, or immediately after, an accident occurs due to the presence on a road of the vehicle; **R.T.O.A. 1988, s.2(1)**, nor does it apply if a Fixed Penalty Notice has been issued, or a notice to produce documents at a police station **R.T.O.A. 1988, s.2(2)**. This is not a total bar to conviction as **section 2(3)** provides that the court may convict if satisfied that the name and address could not with reasonable diligence be ascertained within the time limits or that the accused contributed to the failure. **A1–10, A1–11**
The offences are under the **R.T.A. 1988**:

    (a) dangerous driving and causing death thereby (**ss.2 and 1**);
    (b) careless driving (**s.3**);
    (c) leaving a vehicle in a dangerous position (**s.22**);

Chapter 1

PROCEDURE

Most road traffic matters are initiated by the laying of an information, although the defendant may instead be charged at the police station. A summons is issued on an information laid before a magistrate or a magistrates' court clerk.

The information

May be oral or written but must include details of an offence known to law which it is alleged was committed by the named person within the jurisdiction of the court (usually the county). The information must be laid by a named informant who has authority to prosecute the matter and it must detail the provisions of the Act which it is alleged have been breached. **A1–03**

Time limits

An information for a summary only offence must be laid within six months of the commission of the offence. The **R.T.O.A. 1988, s.6** creates time limits for certain offences by which proceedings must be brought within six months from the prosecutor having sufficient information, in his opinion, to warrant prosecution. In any event, no proceedings may be brought more than three years after their commission. These offences are:

(a) **R.T.A. 1988, s.94**: failure to notify of onset or deterioration of disability;

(b) **R.T.A. 1988, s.99**: failure to surrender licence and give correct particulars when these have changed;

(c) **R.T.A. 1988, s.103**: obtaining a licence or driving when disqualified;

(d) **R.T.A. 1988, s.143**: using a motor vehicle or causing or permitting it to be used while uninsured;

(e) **R.T.A. 1988, s.174(1) or (5)** making false statements in connection with licences, registration as an approved driving instructor, or insurance certificates;

[1]

QUICK ACCESS SUMMARY

(d) careless cycling and dangerous cycling (**ss. 29** and **28**);
(e) failure to comply with traffic signs (**ss. 35** and **36**).

LEGAL AID   A1–14

The granting of legal aid is governed by the **Legal Aid Act 1988**. As well as taking into account the defendant's means, the interests of justice are also considered. Their definition has made it more difficult in less serious road traffic matters for legal aid to be obtained. The interests of justice test is set out in **section 22(2) L.A.A. 1988**:

(a) the applicant stands to lose his liberty or livelihood or suffer serious damage to his reputation;
(b) the case may involve consideration of a substantial point of law;
(c) the accused may be unable to understand the proceedings or state his case because of his inadequate knowledge of English, mental illness or physical disability;
(d) the nature of the defence will require the tracing and interviewing of witnesses or expert cross-examination of the prosecution witnesses;
(e) it is in the interests of a third party that the accused be represented.

Appeal from the decision of the magistrate, the court or the clerk is to the area criminal legal aid committee.   **A1–15**

THE HEARING   A1–17

The bench

Summary trials should be conducted in open court before a bench of two to seven lay magistrates (three being the norm) or one stipendiary magistrate; a retrial should be ordered if they are equally divided. The same bench should return to continue to hear a matter adjourned part heard although a different bench may sentence the defendant. Committal proceedings should be held in open court (unless it is in the interests of justice not to do so (**M.C.A., s.4(2)**) before one or more examining justices.   **A1–18**

Presence of the defendant

In many minor cases it may be expeditious for the defendant to "plead guilty by post". This may be done where the defendant is an adult, the offence is a summary one with a maximum of three months' imprisonment and the court is not considering disqualification. Before accepting the plea, the prosecution statement of facts and the defendant's mitigation must be read out. The court may only order endorsement and the imposition of penalty points. The defendant may also be absent during trial if:

(a) he has unreasonably failed to appear in response to a summons; or

(b) he appeared before on an adjourned hearing.

The defendant must be present during committal unless ill, consenting and legally represented. **A1–20**

Chapter 2

DEFINITIONS

Driver

Based on the concept of degree of control, therefore, if control of the vehicle is shared, more than one person may be the driver of the same vehicle, *e.g.* one steers and the other operates the pedals (*Tyler v. Whatmore* [1976] R.T.R. 83). The passenger may be charged with aiding and abetting if appropriate on the facts. **A2–02**

Driving

Starting point is General L.J. in *Ames v. MacLeod*, 1969 S.C. (J.): was the defendant in a substantial sense controlling the movement and direction of the vehicle? It does not matter how the motion is produced, by pushing or otherwise. **A2–04**

Automatism

The courts are not ready to accept the defence of automatism. The question of how the state arose is central. Any condition, act or omission which one knows, or ought to know, will result in incapacity, will defeat the defence of automatism. If some of the actions during driving are voluntary, and not automatic, the defence will fail. **A2–07**

Attempted driving

Must be more than merely preparatory and sufficiently proximate to the full offence; *n.b.* Criminal Attempts Act 1981 does not apply to purely summary offences, therefore definition of the summary offence must incorporate an attempt. Whether attempt or the full offence probably depends on whether the vehicle was in motion.   **A2–10**

In charge

Undefined in the Acts, it is therefore a question of fact: *R. v. Harnett* [1955] Crim. L. R. 793, C.C.A.   **A2–11**

Test: Remain in charge of vehicle until demonstrate relinquishing control, *e.g.* by handing keys to another or by abandoning it: *Haines v. Roberts* [1953] 1 W.L.R. 309; *R. v. Short, The Times*, December 10,1955.

Test too severe? *Woodage v. Jones (No. 2)* [1975] R.T.R. 119. Does not necessitate proof of likelihood of defendant driving the vehicle: *D.P.P. v. Watkins* [1989] Q.B. 821.   **A2–12**

Where, however, defendant is not the lawful possessor of the vehicle but is involved with the vehicle the question is whether he has assumed control of it. Factors include possession of key, actions of defendant and others, evidence of intention to assert control by driving or otherwise. Burden on defendant to show no likelihood of driving while unfit, once shown to be unfit. *D.P.P. v. Watkins* (supra).

Statutory defences

The defendant to prove on balance of probabilities there was no likelihood of driving while over the limit or unfit. Immobilising the car will not suffice (*Saycell v. Bool* [1948] 2 All E. R. 83), but having it immobilised by clamping may; *Drake v. D.P.P.* [1994] R.T.R. 411: **R.T.A. 1988, s.4(3), 5(2)**.

Motor vehicle

"[A] mechanically propelled vehicle intended or adapted for use on the roads". The section sets out the classes of motor vehicle. Invalid carriages are subject to special provisions, as are electrically assisted pedal cycles: **R.T.A. 1988, s.185(1)**.   **A2–16**

Mechanically propelled

The vehicle must be mechanically propelled (whether petrol, oil or even steam, etc.). A common question is whether a broken down vehicle can still be said to be mechanically propelled.

Test: whether there is no reasonable prospect of the vehicle ever being made mobile again: *Blinks v. Department of the Environment* [1975] R.T.R. 318.　　　　　　　　　　　　　　　　　**A2–17**

"Intended or adapted" for use on the roads

Test is objective and does not depend on intention of anyone: would the reasonable man looking at the vehicle say that one of its users would be a road user: *Burns v. Currell* [1963] 2 Q.B. 433.　　　**A2–18**

Road

Any highway and any other road to which the public has access, and includes bridges over which a road passes: *Horizon v. Hill* [1932] J.C. 13;

> "any road may be regarded as a road to which the public have access upon which members of the public are to be found who have not obtained access either by overcoming a physical obstruction or in defiance of a prohibition express or implied."

The prosecution must show that it is the general public and not a restricted class who have access: **R.T.A. 1988, s.192**.　　　**A2–19**

Other public place

Drink/driving cases can be committed on a road or other public place as can offences under **R.T.A. 1988, ss. 1–3** as amended by **R.T.A. 1991**.　　　　　　　　　　　　　　　　　　　　　**A2–23**

Question of fact for prosecution to prove; similar considerations apply as above. Private land to which the public have access by invitation, express or implied, or by toleration may be a public place.

Accident

Undefined in the Act. No hard and fast definition.

Test: "would an ordinary man in the circumstances of the case say there had been an accident?" This includes deliberate acts. *Chief Constable of West Midlands Police v. Billingham* [1979] 1 W.L.R. 747; *Chief Constable of Staffordshire v. Lees* [1981] R.T.R. 506.　　　**A2–24**

A constable in uniform

Member of any police force in the jurisdiction, including special constables: **Police Act 1964, s.19**; *Richards v. West* [1980] R.T.R. 215. The prosecution must prove the fact that the constable was in uniform; if no evidence but unchallenged, the court may assume was in uniform: *Cooper v. Rowlands* [1971] R.T.R. 265. A constable not wearing his helmet was still in uniform: *Wallwork v. Giles* [1970] R.T.R. 118.   **A3–02**

Chapter 3

PRELIMINARY BREATH TESTS

SCREENING BREATH TESTS   **A3–01**

Where a person has been, or is, driving or attempting to drive, or is, or has been, in charge of a motor vehicle and a constable in uniform has reasonable cause to *suspect* that that person has, or had and continues to have, alcohol in their body and/or a moving traffic offence has been committed, the constable may require the driver to provide a specimen for a breath test (unless that person is in hospital – see **A3–24** – a breath test may not be required at a hospital. Blood or urine may only be required after the defendant's medical practitioner in the case has been consulted): **R.T.A. 1988, s.6(1)**.

The requirement may also be made under **section 6(2)** when a constable (not necessarily in uniform) has reasonable cause to *believe*:

> "where there has been an accident due to the presence of a motor vehicle on a road or other public place, that the person was driving or attempting to drive or in charge of the vehicle at the time of the accident."

The requirement need not be in any special form of words so long as it is made clear what the requirement is.   **A3–09**

Reasonable cause to suspect/believe

Belief is higher than suspicion, which will not therefore suffice for **subsection(2)**. The prosecution must prove whether the constable had reasonable grounds: *Griffiths v. Willet* [1979] R.T.R. 195.   **A3–03**

The power to stop – random tests

The police have several powers to stop vehicles including the general one contained in **R.T.A. 1988, s.163** and those in **PACE (A3–07)**. To that extent they may stop vehicles randomly. However, they may not move to breathalyse unless they have reasonable grounds for suspicion/belief, otherwise any arrest may be unlawful and the result of the test excluded: *D.P.P. v. Godwin* [1991] R.T.R. 303 D.C., **A3–04**. This suspicion may arise before or after the vehicle has been stopped; nor need it be a suspicion that the alcohol level is in excess of the limit: *Blake v. Pope* [1986] 1 W.L.R. 1152.

The constable does not need to state his grounds for suspicion: *Williams v. Jones* [1972] R.T.R. 4, **A3–05**. The grounds may be based on information from others depending on source and contemporaneity: *Erskine v. Hollin* [1971] R.T.R. 199; *Monaghan v. Corbett, The Times,* June 23, 1983. **A3–06**

"Accident" and "traffic offence"

Prosecution must prove that an accident actually took place. There need be no other vehicle involved: *R. v. Pico* [1971] R.T.R. 500, C.A., nor conversely need the defendant's vehicle be involved in the accident, but there must be a direct causal connection between the vehicle's presence on the road and the accident: *M. (A Minor) v. Oxford* [1981] R.T.R. 246, D.C.: **R.T.A. 1988, s.6(2)**. **A3–08**

The breath test

Must be carried out at or near the place where the requirement is made (**subsection (3)**) by an approved device (**section 6**) the assembly of which has been carried out in accordance with the manufacturer's instructions: *R. v. Coates* [1971] R.T.R. 74, C.A. Failure will not be fatal unless it can be shown to invalidate the result: *Att.-Gen.'s Reference (No. 1 of 1978)* [1978] R.T.R. 377. **A3–10**

The officer may ask for a second test where he believes the first to be unreliable, even though the officer could have arrested on the result of the first test: *Sparrow v. Bradley* [1985] R.T.R. 122, D.C.; *R. v. Broomhead* [1975] R.T.R. 558.

FAILURE TO PROVIDE A ROADSIDE SPECIMEN

Section 6(4) R.T.A. 1988 creates the offence of failure without reasonable excuse to provide a specimen of breath for a breath test when required to do so. The word fail includes refuse: (**section 11(2)**). *Fox v. Chief Constable of Gwent* [1985] 1 W.L.R. 1126: a person cannot be convicted if the police officer was a trespasser. *Gull v. Scarborough* [1987] R.T.R. 261: a person cannot be convicted under this section if there has been an unlawful arrest. **A3–13**

"Failure"

There is failure when a person has been given the opportunity to do something and does not do it: *R. v. Ferguson* [1970] 1 W.L.R. 1246. Refusing to wait for a breath-test machine to arrive may be a failure, as may the refusal to stop eating mints: *R. v. Wagner* [1970] R.T.R. 422; *R. v. Mackey* [1977] R.T.R. 146. The test of waiting is what was reasonable in the circumstances: *Ely v. Marle* [1977] R.T.R. 412. Deliberate or inadvertent failure to comply with the instructions given may on the facts amount to refusal: *R. v. Littell* [1981] 1 W.L.R. 1146; *Mallows v. Harris* [1979] Crim.L.R. 3220, D.C. **A3–15**

"Reasonable excuse"

Burden to raise the issue on the defendant then the prosecution must prove that the defendant had no reasonable excuse. *R. v. Lennard* [1973] 1 W.L.R. 483; a reasonable excuse must arise out of a physical or mental inability to provide a specimen or a substantial risk to health. It is important that person understands what is required. **A3–16**

It is no excuse that the person was not the driver at the time and that the constable was not acting in good faith; or that the police officer had no power to make the requirement: *McGrath v. Vipas* [1984] R.T.R. 58; *R. v. Reid* [1973] 1 W.L.R. 1283.

Powers of arrest and entry   A3–20

Penalties   A3–28

Failure to provide a roadside specimen is a summary-only offence and is punishable with a level 3 fine. It is endorsable with discretionary disqualification also: Code DR70. **A3–28**

Chapter 4

DRIVING WHILST UNFIT

THE OFFENCES: A4–08

Section 4 R.T.A. 1988 as amended by **R.T.A. 1991, s.46**. It is an offence to drive, attempt to drive, or be in charge of a mechanically propelled vehicle on a road or other public place when under the influence of drink or drugs.

Common also to charge **section 5**; plea to one will usually be accepted.

Section 15 R.T.O.A. 1988. The evidence of analyses of blood or urine, or the statement and certificate of the breath test tendered in respect of **section 5** are admissible under **section 4**.

Evidence of Impairment

The prosecution must prove not only the influence of drink or drugs but also that proper control of the vehicle is impaired: *R. v. Hawkes* (1931) 22 Cr.App.R. 172. This may be shown by evidence of:

(a) manner of driving;
(b) the driver's physical condition;
(c) a specimen.

It must be shown that the impairment was caused by the drink or drugs.   **A4–09**

Powers of Arrest

Conviction does not depend on lawful arrest: **section 4(6) R.T.A. 1988**.   **A4–10**

Medical Examination

A person may not be examined against their will, but there is nothing to stop the doctor observing him and drawing certain conclusions.   **A4–11**

DEFENCES: **A4–13**

The section 4(3) defence

Deemed not to have been in charge if defendant proves on the balance of probabilities that at the material time the circumstances were such that there was no likelihood of his driving so long as he remained unfit. The court may disregard any injury to him and any damage to the vehicle: **section 4(4)**.

The section 15(3) defence

It is assumed that the proportion of alcohol in the defendant's breath, blood or urine at the time of the alleged offence was not less than the specimen. The assumption shall not be made if the defendant proves:

(a) that he consumed alcohol after he had ceased to drive, attempt

to drive or be in charge of a motor vehicle on a road or other public place and before he had provided the specimen; and
(b) that had he not done so the proportion of alcohol in his breath, blood or urine would not have been such as to impair his ability to drive properly: **section 15(3) R.T.O.A. 1988.**   **A4–14**

It will usually be necessary to call expert evidence to show the back calculation: *Dawson v. Lunn* [1986] R.T.R. 234.

Other defences

Depending on the facts the prosecution may be put to strict proof on a number of matters. Examples include (a) that the person was not in charge; (b) that they were not unfit; (c) that the impairment was not through drink or drugs.

Penalties   A4–416

Summary only. Driving or attempting to drive whilst unfit; level 5 fine and/or six months' imprisonment. Disqualification and endorsement are obligatory unless there are special reasons. See also Chapters 14 and 16. Code drink DR20, drugs DR80.
     Section 24 R.T.A. 1991: section 4(2) "being in charge" alternative verdict to **section 4(1)** "driving or attempting to drive".
     Being in charge: level 4 fine and/or three months' imprisonment. Endorsable unless special reasons. Discretionary disqualification. Code drink DR50, drugs DR90.

Riding a cycle while unfit   A4–18

Chapter 5

ABOVE THE PRESCRIBED LIMIT

THE OFFENCE   A5–01

Section 5 R.T.A. 1988. It is an offence if a person drives, attempts to drive or is in charge of a motor vehicle on a road or other public place after consuming so much alcohol that the proportion of it in his breath, blood or urine exceeds the prescribed limit.
     Section 11(2) R.T.A. 1988. The limits are:

(a) 35 microgrammes of alcohol in 100 ml of breath;
(b) 80 milligrammes of alcohol in 100 ml of blood;
(c) 107 milligrammes of alcohol in 100 ml of urine.

Section 15(2) R.T.O.A. 1988. Assume proportion of alcohol at time of offence not less than the specimen. *D.P.P. v. Johnson, The Times,* March 15, 1994: "consuming" not limited to intake by mouth.   **A5–02**

Aiding and Abetting The Offence

The prosecution has to prove that the principal offender had committed the offence, that the defendant was aware, or was reckless whether, the principal offender had consumed excessive alcohol and that the defendant had aided, abetted, counselled or procured the principal to commit the offence. (*D.P.P. v. Anderson* [1990] R.T.R. 269, D.C.). *Blakely v. D.P.P.* [1991] R.T.R. 405, D.C. suggests that recklessness will not suffice for a charge of procuring.   **A5–03**

Breath specimens: the approved device   **A5–06**

BREATH SPECIMENS:
THE POWER TO REQUIRE SPECIMENS   **A5–11**

Section 7 R.T.A. 1988. In the course of an investigation into whether an offence under **sections 4** or **5** has occurred a constable at a police station may require two (one will not suffice for prosecution) specimens of breath for analysis. Lawful arrest is not a condition precedent.

The warning

When requiring a specimen of breath, blood or urine, the officer must warn the defendant that failure to provide the specimen may render him liable to prosecution: **section 7(7)**. If there is no warning then the requirement is negatived: *Simpson v. Spalding* [1978] R.T.R. 221. It also affords a reasonable excuse for failing to provide a specimen: *R. v. Dolan* [1970] R.T.R. 43.   **A5–30**

Blood and urine specimens

If the constable reasonably believes that there are medical (**A5–15**) or mechanical reasons (**A5–17**) why a breath specimen should not be taken or the constable is advised by a medical practitioner that the defendant's condition may be due to drugs then a specimen of blood or urine may be required at a police station or at a hospital (**section 7(3)**). The driver also has an option (**section 8(2)**) where the lower breath reading was below 50 microgrammes to request that specimen be replaced by one of blood or urine (that choice still being the officer's). If the option is exercised the breath specimen may not be used in evidence. *Archbold v. Jones* [1986] R.T.R. 178.   **A5–15; A5–17**

Procedure

The procedure in any event is strict (*D.P.P. v. Warren* [1992] 3 W.L.R. 884, H.L.; *Williams v. D.P.P., D.P.P. v. Nesbitt* [1994] R.T.R. 241). Deviation from it may be fatal. The officer is required by **section 7(4)** to inform the driver that the specimen is to be of blood or urine and that it is for the constable to decide which. There is no requirement to invite the driver to express his preference; that if the officer intends to require a specimen of blood, the driver is to be given the right to object on medical grounds to be determined by a medical practitioner or, if the requirement has been made under **section 7(3)**, for some other reason affording a "reasonable excuse" within **section 7(6)**.   **A5–14; A5–23**

The provision of blood   A5–27

The provision of urine   A5–29

Detention at the police station

A defendant can be detained until he is fit to drive (**section 10(1)**) or the officer is satisfied that there is no likelihood of him driving (**section 10(2)**).   **A5–31**

Chapter 6

EXCESS ALCOHOL EVIDENCE AND PENALTIES

*E*VIDENCE

Section 16(1) provides that evidence of alcohol proportion in a specimen may be given by the production of (a) the machine printout and a certificate from the officer that the printout relates to the defendant's specimen at the date and time shown; or (b) a certificate signed by an authorised analyst.   **A6–01, A6–03, A6–06**

The prosecution may also give this evidence by other means, *e.g.*

oral evidence of the officer as to the reading and calibration readings: *Owen v. Chesters* [1985] R.T.R. 191.   **A6–02**

The prosecution may not rely on the printout or certificate where;

(a) a copy was not handed to the defendant at the time or served on him at least seven clear days before the hearing at which evidence is to be given: **section 16(3)**; or   **A6–10**
(b) the defendant gives at least three clear days notice to the prosecutor that he requires the attendance of the signatory: **section 16(4)**; or   **A6–03**
(c) the defendant at the time asked for a portion of his blood sample and he was not given it: **section 15(5)**.

Any other document is inadmissible unless a copy had been served on the defendant at least seven clear days before the hearing: **section 16(3)(b)**. Admissibility: procedural pre-requirements.   **A6–10**

The printout: cases on admissibility

The printout may not be relied on where the defendant has exercised his option to provide blood or urine. Nor can it be relied on if the self-calibration check is outside the limits: *R. v. Kingston-upon-Thames Justices, ex p. Khanna* [1986] R.T.R. 364, D.C. The printout may, however, be relied on where the defendant frustrates the proper exercise of the option or, indeed, tampers with his option specimen: *D.P.P. v. Poole* [1992] R.T.R. 177; *Yhnell v. D.P.P.* [1989] R.T.R. 250.   **A6–04**

The certificate: cases on admissibility

Continuity is vital. Minor faults will not render the evidence inadmissible in the presence of other evidence that the specimen is that of the defendant: *Dickson v. Atkins* [1972] R.T.R. 209. Both points on continuity and contamination will only succeed where they cast doubt on the reliability of the prosecution evidence. Under **section 16(2)** the sample of blood must have been taken with the defendant's consent, otherwise the result of analysis will be inadmissible.   **A6–07, A6–08**

The irrebuttable statutory assumption and back calculation

The prosecution may rely on the irrebuttable statutory assumption (**section 15(2)**) to prove that the defendant's alcohol level at the time of the offence was the same as in his specimen or they may back calculate to show that it was higher: *Smith v. Geraghty* [1986] R.T.R. 222. This is so even where the specimen alcohol proportion is below the limit and it is back calculation which takes the defendant over the limit: *Gumbley v. Cunningham; Gould v. Castle* [1987] 3 All E.R. 733. Back calculation is, however, both judicially and medically discouraged due to the inherently unreliable nature of the calculation and should not be relied on unless the evidence is straightforward and would place the defendant clearly over the limit at the time of the offence: *Gumbley v. Cunningham*.   **A6–17; A6–19**

PENALTIES   A6–21

Driving or attempt while over the limit

Summary only; level 5 fine and/or 6 months' imprisonment. Disqualification obligatory for a minimum of 12 months unless there are special reasons not to, or to do so for a shorter period. Endorsement is obligatory. Code DR10. **Section 5(1)(a)**.

Previous convictions

If in the preceding 10 years the defendant has been convicted of driving or attempting to drive while unfit (**section 4(1)**) or with excess alcohol (**section 5(1)**) or of failure to provide a specimen (**section 7(6)**) then the minimum period of disqualification is three years: **R.T.O.A. 1988, s.34**.

Alternative verdict

Being in charge with excess alcohol (**section 5(1)(b)**) may be an alternative verdict: **R.T.O.A. 1988, s.24** (**R.T.A. 1991, s.24**). Summary only: 3 months imprisonment and/or level 4 fine. Disqualification discretionary; endorsement is obligatory unless there are special reasons. Code DR50.

Sentencing

Varies around the country but Magistrates' Association suggests start of £480 and 12 months' disqualification.   **A6–22**

Breath/Alcohol	Disqualification Period
65	18 months
88	2 yrs (danger custody)
110	3 yrs (danger custody)

Chapter 7

EXCESS ALCOHOL DEFENCES

The Statutory Defence   A7–01

The "hip flask" defence

Section 15(3) R.T.O.A. 1988 is available for a charge of driving with excess alcohol (**R.T.A. 1988, s.5**) as it is for a charge of driving whilst unfit (**section 4**). It has the effect that the statutory assumption shall not be made if the defendant proves on the balance of probabilities:

    (a) that he consumed alcohol after he had ceased to drive, attempting to drive or be in charge of a motor vehicle on a road or other public place and before he provided the specimen; and

    (b) that had he not done so the proportion of alcohol in his breath, blood or urine would not have exceeded the prescribed limit.

Unless the matter would be obvious to a lay-person, the defence should call expert evidence which the prosecution should subject to cross-examination: *Dawson v. Lunn* [1986] R.T.R. 234; *Lloyd v. Knight, The Times*, February 13, 1985.

    Under **section 5** once the defence has been proved, it is not open to convict on another limb, *e.g.* being in charge: *Rynsard v. Spalding* [1986] R.T.R. 303.

No likelihood of driving

It is a defence to **section 5(1)(b)**, being in charge, for the defendant to prove on the balance of probabilities that there was no likelihood of him driving while above the limit. This can be found where the car has been clamped: *Drake v. D.P.P.* [1994] R.T.R. 411, D.C.

Attacking the Intoximeter   A7–03

General

The House of Lords has held that there are no restrictions on the kind of evidence that can be called to challenge the printout: *Cracknell v. Willis* [1988] A.C. 450. The reality, however, for the defence is somewhat less boundless. The Divisional Court has rejected "fishing expeditions" where the defence has tried to compel the production of documents to challenge the reliability of the device: *R. v. Tower Bridge Magistrates' Court, ex p. D.P.P.* (1988) 86 Cr.App.R. 257. Unreliability which appears to have been favourable to the defendant will not, seemingly, result in the evidence being excluded: *Wright v. Taplin (Note)* [1986] R.T.R. 388, D.C. The presumption that the device is working properly is very difficult to rebut: *D.P.P. v. Hill* [1991] R.T.R. 351.

Ways and means

(a) Wide discrepancy in the readings: would seem to suggest that the machine is faulty but the court's approach seems to have been that if both readings are above the limit then conviction will follow; *Lloyd v. Morris* [1986] R.T.R. 299; *Gordon v. Thorpe* [1986] R.T.R. 358.   **A7–06**

(b) A modified machine. If there is evidence that the machine has been modified then it may no longer qualify as an approved device: *Young v. Flint* [1987] R.T.R. 300.   **A7–09**

(c) Procedure: points on the printout not complying with **section 16 R.T.O.A. 1988** may render it inadmissible but the prosecution may cure this by other evidence.   **A7–10**

(d) Calibration: calibrations outside 32–37 for the Intoximeter and 32–38 for the Camic should result in the admissibility of the printout being challenged.   **A7–11**

(e) Non-compliance with manufacturer's instructions and purging: it seems some prejudice to the defendant would have to be shown: *Black v. Bickmore* [1982] R.T.R. 167, D.C.   **A7–12**

Acetone

If acetone is detected by the Intoximeter expert advice should be sought if the defendant is unaware of any condition he has which may result in acetone expiration. Conversely, if the defendant knows that acetone may be found in his breath and the Intoximeter fails to show any, the reliability of the machine should be challenged.   **A7–14**

Duress and necessity

Duress is a difficult defence to raise. It has been emphasised, in two drink/driving cases, that the fear which must obtain is that of fear for life or of serious injury. The fear must be immediate and operating from a reasonable belief which is good cause for that fear: *D.P.P. v. Davis; D.P.P. v. Pittaway* [1994] Crim.L.R. 600. It is also clear that the course of driving should not continue beyond that which is necessary to escape the danger: *D.P.P. v. Jones* [1990] R.T.R. 33.

Chapter 8

FAILURE TO PROVIDE

THE OFFENCE   A8–01

Section 7(6) R.T.A. 1988. A person who without reasonable excuse, fails to provide a specimen when required to do so in pursuance of this section is guilty of an offence.

The requirement

The specimen in question is the evidential rather than screening specimen. The procedure must be followed but it is not a condition precedent that there has been a lawful arrest, only that there is an investigation into an offence under **sections 3A, 4** or **5**: *Bunyard v. Hayes* [1985] R.T.R. 348. The prosecution must prove that the requirement was properly made and that the warning was given.   **A8–02**

More than one person may be required to give a specimen in respect of the same offence: *Pearson v. Commissioner of Police of the Metropolis* [1988] R.T.R. 276, D.C.

The section creates only one offence although it may arise in two ways; an investigation into an offence under **section 4** or under **section 5**: *Butterworth v. D.P.P.* [1994] R.T.R. 181.

"Fails"

It is arguable that once the specimen(s) has been physically handed over to the officer, the requirement is fulfilled. Thus stealing the sample back was not failure but dropping it in the process of handing it over was: *R. v. Rothery* [1976] R.T.R. 550; *Ross v. Hodges* [1975] R.T.R. 55. Moreover, an initial refusal followed by later agreement is still failure (*Procaj v. Johnstone* [1970] Crim.L.R. 110), as is only providing one specimen when two are required, even though the first was below the limit: *Stepniewski v. Commissioner of Police of the Metropolis* [1985] R.T.R. 330. The printout is admissible to show failure: *Castle v. Cross* [1984] 1 W.L.R. 1372.   **A8–04**

REASONABLE EXCUSE   **A8–05**

The defendant has an evidential burden to raise the issue. Whether the facts are capable of amounting to a reasonable excuse is a question of law. Once raised, the burden is on the prosecution to prove beyond reasonable doubt that there is no reasonable excuse. It is a question of fact and degree whether there is a reasonable excuse.

"Reasonable excuse" is undefined in the Act but it has been held that it must arise, "out of a physical or mental inability to provide [a specimen] or a substantial risk to health in its provision.": *R. v. Lennard* [1973] 1 W.L.R. 483. Expert evidence would normally be required (*D.P.P. v. Crofton* [1994] R.T.R. 279) though the justices may decide without it: *D.P.P. v. Pearman* [1992] R.T.R. 407.

Physical inability

It is expected that medical evidence would be called. In *R. v. Harding* [1974] R.T.R. 325, Lord Widgery C.J. said that no fear short of a medically recognised phobia and supported by medical evidence would excuse the failure. Genuine but unreasonable phobias may still, however, be accepted: *DeFreitas v. D.P.P.* [1993] R.T.R. 98.   **A8–06**

There is conflict of authority on whether it is uncumbent upon the defendant to inform the officer of any inability (what of the effect of the caution?): *Teape v. Godfrey* [1986] R.T.R. 213; *D.P.P. v. Kinnersley* [1993] R.T.R. 105. There is also conflict on whether "trying as hard as one can" may amount to a reasonable excuse.   **A8–07**

Non-comprehension

It is vital that the requirement and warning are comprehended by the defendant. It was held to be a reasonable excuse that the defendant was unable to understand what was said to him due to his limited grasp of English: *Beck v. Sager* [1979] Crim.L.R. 257. It may be the case that self-induced intoxication such that one cannot comprehend the requirement is a reasonable excuse: *Spalding v. Laskaraina Paine* [1985] Crim.L.R. 673.   **A8–08**

For miscellaneous successful and unsuccessful excuses see **A8–09**, *et seq.*

Excess alcohol when driving or attempting to; ability to drive

When the specimen was required to investigate whether the defendant was over the limit when driving or attempting to or when it was required to investigate ability to drive, the penalties are 6 months' imprisonment and/or level 5 fine. Endorsement and a minimum 12 months' disqualification are obligatory unless there are special reasons. Code DR30.

Previous convictions

A conviction for a similar offence in the preceding 10 years will result in the minimum disqualification being three years.

Other failures

Where the investigation was not into the above then the penalties are three months and/or level 4 fine. In the absence of special reasons, endorsement is obligatory. Disqualification is discretionary. Code DR60.

Chapter 9

DANGEROUS DRIVING

THE OFFENCES A9–03

Section 2 R.T.A. 1988
"A person who drives a mechanically propelled vehicle dangerously on a road or other public place is guilty of an offence."

Section 1 R.T.A. 1988
"A person who causes the death of another person by driving a mech-

anically propelled vehicle dangerously on a road or other public place is guilty of an offence."

Dangerous defined

Dangerous is defined in **section 2A R.T.A. 1988** (as amended by **R.T.A. 1991, s.1**) as essentially a two-stage test:

   (a) Did the driving fall far below that of a careful and competent driver? An objective test taking into account those circumstances of which the defendant could be expected to be aware and also those shown to be within his knowledge.
   (b) If so, would it be obvious to a competent and careful driver that driving in such a way would be dangerous? The danger is of injury to any person or serious damage to property.

Driving a vehicle in a dangerous state is also included.   **A9–04**

Causes the death of another person

The driving need not be the sole or main cause but merely a cause which is above the *de minimis* principle: *R. v. Hennigan* [1971] 3 All E.R. 133.   **A9–21**

Evidence

One has to look at the particular facts of each case, the manner and speed of driving, the road conditions, the state of the vehicle, any explanation offered and the condition and knowledge of the driver. Breaches of the Highway Code are not *per se* offences but are good evidence of dangerous or careless driving: **section 38(7) R.T.A. 1988.**   **A9–10**
   Although evidence of impairment due to intoxication is subject to the usual rules on admissibility, it will nearly always be the case that its probative value outweighs its prejudicial effect. The question is whether the intoxication was such as to impair control: *R. v. McBride* [1962] 2 Q.B. 167; *R. v. Griffiths (Gordon)* [1990] R.T.R. 224; *R. v. Woodward, The Times,* December 7, 1994.

The course of driving

The court may be entitled to look at the manner of the defendant's driving in the period leading up to the incident. Where there is only one place named in the information or the indictment, the time gap and the distance from the actual scene will be factors determining the evidence's admissibility: *Coles v. Underwood, The Times*, November 2, 1983. **A9–12**

PARTICULAR DEFENCES

Emergencies

"Rescuers" are not exempt from prosecution and the emergency services are subject to the same standard and duty of care as civilians: *Marshall v. Osmond* [1983] Q.B. 1034. Such matters would go to the questions of special reasons and mitigation. **A9–25**

Necessity or duress

Duress by circumstance has been accepted as a defence: *D.P.P. v. Bell* [1992] R.T.R. 335. If the defence fails the facts may still amount to special reasons. **A9–26**

Self-defence

The Court of Appeal has accepted that self-defence could be raised successfully against a charge of reckless driving: *R. v. Renouf* [1986] 1 W.L.R. 522. **A9–27**

THE PENALTIES

Dangerous driving

Triable either way. On indictment two years and/or unlimited fine.

Summary trial 6 months and/or maximum statutory fine. An alternative verdict is careless driving (**R.T.A. 1988, s.3**), see **section 24 R.T.O.A. 1988** on alternative verdicts. **A9–03**

Causing death

Indictable only. 10 years after August 16, 1993, five if committed before. Alternative verdicts are dangerous or careless driving or causing bodily harm by furious driving. **A9–19**

Sentencing

Unless there are special reasons, obligatory disqualification for minimum one year (two for causing death) and endorsement with 3–11 points. Obligatory re-take of driving test: **section 36 R.T.O.A. 1988**. *R. v. Boswell* [1984] 1 W.L.R. 1047, C.A. set out the guidelines and aggravating features. Speed, drugs and drink, length and distance of driving, and previous similar convictions may all be taken into account. Generally custody will become appropriate when one or more aggravating features are present. Racing and drinking may mean a starting point of 5 years; *R. v. Sheppard, R. v. Wernet, The Times*, December 27, 1993. **A9–16**

Chapter 10

CARELESS DRIVING

THE OFFENCE   A10–02

Section 3 R.T.A. 1988
"If a person drives a mechanically propelled vehicle on a road or other public place without due care and attention, or without reasonable consideration for other persons using the road or place, he is guilty of an offence."

Test

This creates one offence in two forms (without due care and without consideration) but the same objective test applies to both: "was the defendant exercising the degree of care and attention that a reasonable and prudent driver would in the circumstnaces?" *Simpson v. Peat*

[1952] 2 Q.B. 447, D.C. If the second limb is charged, however, some evidence of inconveniencing others must be shown: *Dilks v. Bowman Shaw* [1981] R.T.R. 4, D.C. Excessively slow driving may satisfy the test. **A10–03, A10–08**

Evidence

The same factors as for dangerous driving may be relied on. The whole set of circumstances should be examined. In the case of careless driving, several breaches of the Highway Code will be strong evidence of falling below ordinary and prudent driving standards: *Trentham v. Rowlands* [1974] R.T.R. 164. It may be easier for the prosecution to rely on *res ipsa loquitor* with a careless driving charge than with a dangerous one. **A10–06**

DEFENCES   A10–09

Duress

In a case which considered the application of the defence to careless driving, it was said that while it would be anomalous for the defence to be available for dangerous and not careless driving, in the particular situation of "jumping" red lights any defence of necessity was contained within **reg. 33** of the **Traffic Signs Regulations and General Direction 1994**; *D.P.P. v. Harris, The Times*, March 16, 1994. **A10–09; C29–36**

Automatism

Discussed above. Difficult to raise and requires all the driver's actions during the period in question to be involuntary; *Broome v. Perkins* [1987] R.T.R. 321. **A10–10**

Mechanical defect

No provision as to the state of the vehicle is made, unlike dangerous driving. Therefore, if the defect is one of which the defendant is unaware, he may be entitled to a defence. If he was aware of it, it may be evidence of carelessness: *R. v. Spurge* [1961] 2 Q.B. 205.

SECTION 3A R.T.A. 1988

Causing death by careless driving when under the influence

The elements of the offence are that:

(a) The death was caused as a result of the defendant having driven without due care and attention or without reasonable consideration for other persons using the road or place, and

(b) (i) at the time of driving the defendant was unfit to drive through drink or drugs; or

(ii) that the defendant had consumed so much alcohol that he exceeded the prescribed limit; or

(iii) the defendant was required within 18 hours after the driving to provide a specimen in pursuance of the Act but failed to do so without reasonable excuse.   **A10–12**

THE PENALTIES   **A10–15**

Careless driving

The offence varies widely in its turpitude and so, therefore, do the penalties. Where the truth of the matter is lapse of concentration the court should be urged not to stick slavishly to guidelines. Summary only, level 4 fine, discretionary disqualification and obligatory endorsement (3–9).

Causing death under the influence

Indictable only. Ten years and/or unlimited fine, obligatory two year minimum disqualification, endorsement (3–11) and compulsory re-testing. For alternative verdicts see **R.T.O.A. 1988, s.24**.   **A10–13**

Chapter 11

GENERAL DRIVING OFFENCES

Speeding

The speed limit on a road depends on the type of road and the class of vehicle that is being driven. The offences are contained in the **Road Traffic Regulation Act 1984, ss. 81–89**. Restricted roads are ones which are so designated or which have an adequate system of street lighting of lamps not more than 200 yards apart (**A11–03**) and they will, in built-up areas, have a general speed limit of 30 m.p.h. (see table **A11–03**). Unrestricted roads have their speed limits designated by statutory instrument under **R.T.R.A. 1984, s.88**.   **A11–01**

Corroboration

A person may not be convicted solely on the opinion evidence of one person: **R.T.R.A. 1984, s.82(2)**. Corroboration is not required for overall speeding offences on motorways (**R.T.R.A. 1984, s.17(4)**) or where there is a speed restriction, not limit, in force (*e.g.* roadworks). Nor is corroboration required for photographic evidence from speed cameras (**R.T.O.A. 1988, s.20**). Corroboration may come from another witness, a speedometer, accident damage, speed check equipment, Vascar or from photos. Where reliance is to be placed on an automatic camera, a copy of the evidence must be served on the defence 7 days before the hearing (**R.T.O.A. 1988, s.20(8)**).   **A11–05, A11–08**

Temporary/variable speed limits

Section 88(1) of the **R.T.R.A. 1984** allows the Secretary of State to impose both maximum and minimum speed limits in the interests of safety or the movement of traffic. **Sections 14–16 R.T.R.A.** permit any highway authority to impose a temporary speed restriction on a road because of roadworks or danger to the public. Local authorities are empowered to vary speed limits within their areas; **R.T.R.A. 1984, s.84**.   **A11–09**

Penalties

Except for temporary speed restrictions or minimum speed limits these offences are endorsable with 3 to 6 points unless dealt with by a Fixed Penalty of 3 points.

Motorways

Motorways have several offences particular to them as set out in the **Motor Vehicles (Speed Limits on Motorways) Regulations 1973, Motor Traffic (England and Wales) Regulations 1982** and **R.T.R.A. 1984, s.17**. The most common offences are:

(a) Driving in the wrong direction (**M.T.R. 1982, reg. 6(3)**)
(b) Making a U-turn (**M.T.R. 1982, reg. 6(5)(a),(b)**)
(c) Driving an excluded class of vehicle (**R.T.R.A. 1984, s.17(4)**)
(d) Exceeding the overall limit (**R.T.R.A. 1984, s.17**).

Signs and signals

Failure to comply with the direction given by a sign (of the prescribed size, colour, etc) or by a constable is an offence (**R.T.A. 1988, ss. 36, 35** respectively). The two offences are similar and only differ in that the former is an absolute offence whereas if it can be shown that the defendant did not see the constable's signal and was not at fault then the defendant is not guilty of the latter offence. Failure to comply with a stop sign, a double white line, a red traffic light or a police constable is endorsable with 3 points and carries discretionary disqualification. Other signs are not endorsable.   **A11–15, A11–19**

Obstruction

Obstruction may be caused in two ways for which there are three offences. It may be (i) physical obstruction caused by blocking other vehicles (which is a plain matter of fact); and (ii) by the unreasonable use of the right of stopping (in which case what is reasonable in the circumstances falls to be considered *Nagy v. Weston* [1965] 1 W.L.R. 280). The three offences are:

(a) **section 137** of the **Highways Act 1980** – wilfully obstructing the free passage of a highway ("all ways over which members of the public are entitled to pass");
(b) **Regulation 3** of the **Road Vehicles (Construction and Use) Regulations 1986** – causing or permitting a motor vehicle or trailer to stand on a road so as to cause any unnecessary obstruction of the road; and
(c) **section 28** of the **Town Police Clauses Act 1847** – wilfully causing an obstruction in any public footpath or public thoroughfare.

These offences are punishable by way of a fine, in addition the latter carries a potential term of imprisonment of 14 days.   **A11–20**

Parking offences

These are by their nature local orders. Offences may be committed against parking meter restrictions (**R.T.R.A. 1984, ss. 45–56, Road Traffic Regulation (Parking) Act 1986**), "no waiting" streets (**R.T.R.A., ss. 1–8, section 5(1), section 8(1)** and **Schedule 2 R.T.O.A. 1988**). **Section 22 R.T.A. 1988** makes it an offence to leave a vehicle in a dangerous position. These offences are usually dealt with by the fixed penalty system. **A11–22**

Taking a vehicle without the owners consent

Section 12 Theft Act 1968 states that it shall be an offence if a person, without the consent of the owner or other lawful authority, takes any conveyance for his own, or another's use *or* who, knowing that any such conveyance has been taken without such authority, drives it or allows himself to be carried in or on it. There must be a movement, however small, by which the vehicle is used as a conveyance but it need not be driven. Passengers may be aiders and abettors, etc if they act together with the principal and/or were carried in it knowing of the unlawful taking: *R. v. Stally* [1959] 3 All E.R. 814. **A11–28, A11–31**

Belief (not necessarily reasonable) by a defendant that he had lawful authority or would have had the owner's consent constitutes a statutory "defence" under **section 12(6)**. This offence is summary only; 6 months' imprisonment and/or level 5 fine. Obligatory 8 points and discretionary disqualification. **A11–33**

Aggravated vehicle-taking

Section 12A of the Act provides that a person is guilty of the aggravated offence where the basic offence (above) is committed, and before the vehicle is recovered, the vehicle was driven, or injury or damage was caused in one of more of the following circumstances; **section 12A(2)**:

(a) The vehicle was driven dangerously on a road or other public place;
(b) owing to the driving of the vehicle, an accident occurred by which injury was caused to any person;
(c) owing to the driving of the vehicle, an accident occurred by which damage was caused to any property, other than the vehicle;

(d) damage was caused to the vehicle.   **A11–38**

Mode of trial

When **section 46** of the **Criminal Justice and Public Order Act 1994**
comes into force, the entitlement of the defendant to elect trial by jury
will be affected. Where the aggravation is related to damage only, the
offence will be considered for mode of trial on the same basis as criminal damage and therefore damage under £5000 will only be triable
summarily.

Defences

The above defences are available, in addition there is the defence contained in **section 12A(3)** where the defendant proves that the relevant
driving, injury or damage occurred before he committed the basic
offence or that he was neither in, on nor in the vicinity of the vehicle
when that driving, injury or damage occurred.   **A11–43**

Penalties

On indictment two years' imprisonment and an unlimited fine except
for **section 12A(4)** where a personal injury accident resulting in the
death of the victim occurred, in which case the maximum is five years.
When tried summarily, six months' imprisonment and/or the maximum fine. Obligatory disqualification and endorsement, where
special reasons are found for not disqualifying, of 3–11 points. **A11–44**

Interference with vehicles

Section 9 Criminal Attempts Act 1981 provides that a person is guilty
of an offence if he interferes with a motor vehicle or trailer with the
intention that one of the following offences shall be committed by him
or another; (a) theft of the motor vehicle or trailer or part of it; (b) theft
of anything carried in or on the motor vehicle or trailer; and (c) an
offence under **section 12(1) Theft Act 1968**.   **A11–47A**

Construction and use regulations

There are numerous regulations covering the construction and use of domestic vehicles for which recourse should be had to the text and the regulations made under **sections 41** and **54 R.T.A. 1988**. In particular, **section 40A R.T.A. 1988** provides:

"A person is guilty of an offence if he uses, or causes, or permits another to use, a motor vehicle or trailer on a road when—

(a) the condition of the motor vehicle or trailer, or of its accessories or equipment, or

(b) the purpose for which it is used, or

(c) the number of passengers carried by it, or the manner in which they are carried, or

(d) the weight, position or distribution of its load, or the manner in which it is secured,

is such that the use of the motor vehicle or trailer involves a danger of injury to any person."

Level 4 fine unless adapted to carry 8 or more passengers in which case it is a level 5 fine; endorsement with 3 points and discretionary disqualification. The latter two may be avoided if the defendant proves that he did not know, and had no reasonable cause to suspect that the use of the vehicle involved a danger of injury.   **A11–47**

Failing to stop/report

Section 170 R.T.A. 1988 requires that where an accident occurs involving personal injury or damage, the driver is under a duty to stop and if required to do so, give his name and address. If the driver does not give these details he must report the accident at a police station or to a constable as soon as is reasonably practicable and, in any case, within 24 hours of the accident. It is possible to be convicted of both the offences which the section creates; *Roper v. Sullivan* [1978] R.T.R. 181. The offences carry obligatory endorsement with 5 to 10 points and discretionary disqualification.

Chapter 12

DRIVING WHILE DISQUALIFIED

Section 103 R.T.A. 1988

"(1) A person is guilty of an offence if, while disqualified for holding or obtaining a licence, he:

(a) obtains a licence, or

(b) drives a motor vehicle on a road."

The licence is the one issued under Part III of the Act, *i.e.* that granted on passing a driving test. It should be noted that neither an attempt to drive (as the offence is now summary only) nor being in charge will suffice for liability under the section.   **A12–09**

Proof of disqualification

May be proved in several ways;

(a) under **section 73 PACE**
(b) under **r. 68 Magistrates' Courts Rules 1981**
(c) by a Certificate of Disqualification
(d) by the licence on which particulars of disqualification have been endorsed
(e) by defence admission.   **A12–06**

Effect of disqualification

The defendant's licence is revoked. He should therefore apply for a new licence once the period of disqualification is over; once that application has been received he may drive (**section 88 R.T.A. 1988**). Otherwise he may be committing offences of obtaining a licence while disqualified (**section 103(a) R.T.A. 1988**), making a false statement to obtain a licence (**section 174 R.T.A. 1988**) or driving without a licence (**section 87(1) R.T.A. 1988**). If a defendant obtains a licence while disqualified, that licence is of no effect: **section 103(2)**.   **A12–07**

Power of arrest

Section 103(3): where a constable in uniform has reasonable grounds to suspect that a person who is driving a motor vehicle on a road is disqualified from so doing he may arrest without warrant.   **A12–11**

Defences

The offence is an absolute one requiring no *mens rea*; *R. v. Bowsher* [1973] R.T.R. 202. Points that may be taken therefore are limited to ones such as the place was not a road or the defendant was not driving and/or disqualified. It is possible that necessity may form a defence *in extremis*: *R. v. Martin* [1989] R.T.R. 63. No proceedings may be brought more than three years after the commission of the offence: **section 180 M.C.A. 1980.** **A12–10**

Penalties

An offence under **section 103(1)(a)** level 3 fine; under **s.103(1)(b)** level 5 fine and/or 6 months' imprisonment.

Reference should be made to the text for offences committed before the coming into force of the **Criminal Justice Act 1988** and also for the provisions relating to the trial at Crown Court of summary only offences.

A12–13

RELATED OFFENCES

Driving without a licence

Section 87(1) R.T.A. 1988. It must be shown that the driver was driving the particular motor vehicle on a road. The burden is then on the defence to show that he held a licence: *Tynan v. Jones* [1975] R.T.R. 465. **Section 87(2)** causing or permitting the foregoing: see below. **A12–16**

Provisional licences

The **Motor Vehicle (Driving Licences) Regulations 1987** require that a provisional licence holder must be accompanied by a full licence holder when driving a motor vehicle on a road (**reg. 9(1)(a)**). The vehicle must also display two "L-plates" (**reg. 9(1)(b)**). Summary only, level 3 fine, obligatory 2 points and discretionary disqualification. **A12–17**

Driving without insurance

Once the prosecution has shown that the defendant used the vehicle (not limited to driving; thus the owner may be using when not driving: *Cobb v. Williams* [1973] R.T.R. 113) on a road, it is for the defendant to prove that there was a valid policy of insurance in force for the vehicle which covered the use to which it was being put: *Philcox v. Carberry*

[1960] Crim.L.R. 563, D.C. Level 4 fine and 6 to 8 points and discretionary disqualification. **A12–19**

Using a vehicle with no M.O.T.

Three years from first being registered the vehicle becomes subject to the annual testing scheme. It is an offence to use a vehicle which requires a test certificate and for which there is none: **section 47(1) R.T.A. 1988**. Roadside tests may also be carried out by an authorised examiner: **section 67 R.T.A. 1988**. Vehicle excise offences. **A12–24, A12–28, A12–29**

Causing or permitting

In both cases it must be shown that the causer or permitter knew of the facts which rendered the use unlawful. "Cause" requires a command or direction: *Redhead Freight Ltd v. Shulman* [1988] Crim.L.R. 696. "Permission" may be expressly given or inferred from conduct; it requires the fulfilment of any conditions attached to the permission (*Newbury v. Davis* [1974] R.T.R. 367). **A12–33**

Chapter 13

FIXED PENALTIES

Notices in general

Procedure varies according to whether the driver is present or the Fixed Penalty Offence (FPO) is endorsable or not. In general Fixed Penalty Notices (FPNs) must give sufficient particulars of the alleged offence to give reasonable information about the offence: **section 52(2) R.T.O.A. 1988**. It must also contain the period for payment, the amount and the court to which payment should be made: **section 52(3) R.T.O.A. 1988**. **A13–03**

Endorsable offences

Where a constable in uniform has reason to believe that a FPO is or has been committed and he is satisfied on inspecting the driver's surrendered licence (either at the scene or within 7 days at a police station after issue of a notice **section 54(4),(5))** that the driver would not thereby be liable to disqualification as a "totter", then he may issue a FPN to the driver: **section 54 R.T.O.A. 1988.**   A13–04

Once the FPN is issued no proceedings may be brought within 28 days. The driver will either request a court hearing, in which case the matter proceeds as usual, or he pays, the matter is concluded and his licence endorsed. Where neither occurs the penalty plus half as much again may be registered against that person for enforcement as a fine. This will not avoid endorsement of the licence: **section 55 R.T.O.A. 1988.**

Endorsable offence, driver not present

Where the FPN is not given or attached to the vehicle, a conditional FPN may be sent to the driver. It contains the same details as a FPN; it is dated, and time runs, from its issue: **section 75 R.T.O.A. 1988.**   A13–05

Non-endorsable offences

The procedure is the same except that sight of the licence is not required (**section 54(3) R.T.O.A. 1988**) and the power is exercisable by an authorised traffic warden (**section 95(5) R.T.R.A. 1984**).   A13–06

Driver not present

The constable or warden may affix the FPN to the vehicle (**section 62(1) R.T.O.A. 1988**); it is an offence to interfere with that notice unless the driver, owner or person liable (**section 62(2)**). Otherwise the procedure is broadly similar with the exception that where the fine is not paid a notice containing the details above may be sent but with the addition that it must also state that if the fine is not paid then the person who appears to be the owner will be asked for a statutory declaration as to ownership. In other words if the person proves that they are not the owner they are released from liability; or they may provide a statement of facts whereby another person purports to be the driver and wishes to give notice requesting a hearing of the matter. A13–07

The practitioner should consult the body of the text for the rules governing the various statutory declarations that may be made as the provisions are complex but of the essence where a mistake has been made.

Chapter 14

DISQUALIFICATION, ENDORSEMENT AND PENALTY POINTS

Parts I and **II** to **Schedule 2** of the **R.T.O.A. 1988** contain a near comprehensive list of penalties.

Endorsement

Any licence issued under **Part III** of the **R.T.O.A. 1988** (not international, foreign, HGV or PSV licences) upon conviction for an endorsable offence may be endorsed with the particulars of the offence, disqualification and points (if appropriate) unless there are special reasons (**section 44(1) R.T.O.A. 1988**). Where the driver does not hold an endorsable licence, the DVLA will be informed and any endorsable licence issued to the driver during the currency of the penalty will be so endorsed.   **A14–02**

Which offences?

Areas not covered in **Schedule 2** include:

(a) Conditional and absolute discharges; although usually not seen as sentences, they will be endorsed in the usual way: **section 46(2) R.T.O.A. 1988**. Probation orders are now considered as sentences and thereby endorsable.
(b) Deferment of sentence; endorsement is also deferred.
(c) Attempts; where indictable only or either way then endorsable as the full offence would be: **Criminal Attempts Act 1981, s.4(1)(b),(c)**.
(d) Aiding and abetting; as per the full offence. Where the substantive offence carries obligatory disqualification the abettor is liable to have 10 points endorsed: **section 28(2) R.T.O.A. 1988**.
(e) T.I.C.'s; no endorsement or points may be ordered in respect of TICs.

Penalty points

It is vital to remember that 12 points over a three year period will activate a penalty points disqualification and that the court may take into account any penalties that are already on the licence when considering what to impose on this occasion. Where more than one offence is committed on the same occasion the court is restricted to imposing the highest number that could be imposed in respect of one of those offences even where sentencing takes place on different occasions. The court has a power, however, to derogate from this: **section 28(6) R.T.O.A. 1988.**   **A14–09**

When are points not endorsed?

When there are special reasons or the driver is disqualified. In the latter case although not endorsed, the points may still count towards a subsequent penalty points disqualification; the fact of disqualification is still endorsed: **sections 28(1)** and **44(1) R.T.O.A. 1988.**

DISQUALIFICATION   A14–16

Obligatory disqualification

Unless there are special reasons not to disqualify or to do so for a shorter period, the court must disqualify for the minimum period or upwards, whatever view it takes of the case. It should be remembered that in those cases where a previous conviction in the preceding 10 years will lead to a longer period of disqualification, the 10 years runs from the date of conviction to the date of commission.

N.B. being drunk in charge or being in charge with excess alcohol will not trigger the extended disqualification.

Discretionary disqualification

The Magistrates' Association issues guidelines and the decision will rest upon the facts of the case. Speeds in excess of 100 m.p.h. on the motorway or 30 m.p.h. in excess of a speed limit, driving the wrong way on a motorway and serious failure to report an accident are all examples of likely disqualification. All courts also have the power to disqualify where a vehicle is used to assault a person: **section 44 P.C.C.A. 1973.**   **A14–19**

Penalty points disqualification

Unless there are *mitigating factors* the court shall order a disqualification for a minimum of 6 months where the defendant has accumulated 12 or more points in the three years preceding the commission of the offence. This minimum rises to 12 months and two years respectively where the driver has been previously disqualified one or more times. **A14–21**

Approved drink driver courses

Where they operate they may result in the reduction of the driver's sentence by 3 months or one quarter if the driver attends. **A14–22**

Disqualification until extended re-test

Obligatory in cases of manslaughter, dangerous driving and causing death by dangerous driving: **section 36 R.T.O.A. 1988.** **A14–23**

Procedure

Where disqualification is to be ordered the defendant must be present or have been given an opportunity to attend (**section 11(4) M.C.A. 1980**); where this is done and the defendant does not attend, the court may proceed or issue a warrant for arrest. The attendance of a legal representative will sometimes suffice (**section 122 M.C.A.**). **A14–26**

Disqualification may be ordered on its own or with any other sentence (including discharges). Consecutive periods of disqualification may not be ordered but the order may be suspended pending appeal.

Chapter 15

SPECIAL REASONS

Special reasons should not be confused with mitigating circumstances or with general mitigation. They apply to obligatory disqualification or endorsement and are by their nature peculiar to the offence (not the offender) and the courts will be loath to find them where the offence is a serious example of its type or where the defendant should have been "on enquiry" as to the circumstances which form the special reason. In any event the court is free to find special reasons but nonetheless refuse to exercise the discretion that special reasons give rise to: *R. v. Newton* [1974] R.T.R. 451. The prosecution should be notified in advance if special reasons are to be run.

[37]

Definition

There is no statutory definition, but the accepted definition is that in *R. v. Crossen* [1939] N.I. 106 as approved in *Whittall v. Kirby* [1946] 2 All E.R. 552 and interpreted in *R. v. Wickens* (1958) 42 Cr.App.R. 236. From this four points emerge:

    (a) It must be a mitigating or extenuating circumstance;

    (b) it must not amount in law to a defence;

    (c) it must be directly connected with the commission of the offence;

    (d) it must be a matter which the court ought properly to take into account when considering sentence. **A15–03**

It is rare to find them successful in one of the three main breathalyser offences and almost never will they succeed where the blood/alcohol level exceeds 100 mg per 100 ml of blood: *Scobie v. Graham* [1970] R.T.R. 358.

Caselaw

The text contains summaries of cases in the main areas in which special reasons occur but as special reasons are peculiar to the offence both the text and the relevant cases should be examined carefully. What follows is a guide to drink/driving, the text should be consulted for other areas such as speeding and insurance cases which carry endorsement rather than disqualification.

Drink/driving

There are three groups of circumstance in respect of drink driving:

    (a) Circumstances explaining how the driver:

        (i) came to be unfit to drive; or

        (ii) had excess alcohol in his body. **A15–07**

These cover the situations where the defendant is on medication, had his drink laced or was drinking a stronger drink than he realised. The courts take the view that the defendant should have been "on enquiry" either through the fact that he knew he was on medication or from observing that he was suffering the effects of alcohol such that he may be unfit to drive.

    (b) Explanations why the defendant drove. There are three main areas here:

        (i) The emergency principle; the discretion will only be exercised where the emergency was acute and there was no alternative means of dealing with it. As with duress, the course of driving should not exceed what the situation demands, *Taylor v. Rajan* [1974] R.T.R. 304.

(ii) Police instructions.

(iii) Shortness of distance driven; factors include whether at the instigation of a third party, likelihood of contact with other road users, danger, manner of driving, state of vehicle, the reason for driving and whether the driver intended to go further, *Chatters v. Burke* [1986] R.T.R. 396.

(c) Miscellaneous; these are mainly limited to old cases on pre-breathalyser blood specimens and failure to provide a specimen. Only the latter is considered here.

Care should be taken as what may appear to be a special reason for failing to provide may in fact be a reasonable excuse and therefore where the defence of reasonable excuse has failed, special reasons are unlikely to be found.

Chapter 16

MITIGATING CIRCUMSTANCES

Section 35(1) R.T.O.A. 1988: "Where - (a) a person is convicted of an offence involving obligatory or discretionary disqualification, and (b) the number of penalty points to be taken into account on that occasion number 12 or more; the court must order him to be disqualified for not less than the minimum period unless the court is satisfied, having regard to all the circumstances, that there are grounds for mitigating the normal consequences of conviction and thinks fit to order him to be disqualified for a shorter period or not order him to be disqualified."

It should be remembered that the period of three years (in which points have been accumulated) runs up to the date of commission of the offence and that a disqualification under **section 35 R.T.O.A. 1988** will have had the effect of wiping the licence clean. Mandatory disqualification under **section 34** may or may not wipe the licence.

A16–03

It may be better to argue for a short period of discretionary disqualification for the offence in hand than the imposition of points which would leave the client with the prospect of "totting" disqualification for 6 months hanging over his head.

Mitigating circumstance?

Section 35(4) R.T.O.A. 1988 clearly excludes some matters from the purview of mitigation:

(a) "any circumstances that are alleged to make the offence or any of the offences not a serious one"; this includes arguing that previous points impositions were not serious offences. One may still look to this aspect, though, for special reasons;

(b) "hardship other than exceptional hardship." This includes hardship to others than the defendant *e.g.*
  (i) Loss of employment to the driver or others dependant on the defendant's driving;
  (ii) hardship to the defendant's employer or employees;
  (iii) hardship to the defendant's family.
  Exceptional hardship may arise from the offences being dealt with in such a manner that the defendant is open to disqualification for a greater period than is merited by any individual offence or than would have occurred if the offences were dealt with in a different order;

(c) "any circumstances, which within the three years immediately preceding the conviction, have been taken into account under that subsection in ordering the offender to be disqualified for a shorter period or not ordering him to be disqualified" *i.e.* A previously successful argument cannot be used again, though an unsuccessful one may be.   **A16–05, A16–07**

It should be remembered that mitigating circumstances are wider than special reasons and the court may consider any unexcluded matter. As a matter of policy a term of disqualification which exceeds any term of imprisonment should not be imposed upon a young offender: *R. v. Thomas* [1983] 3 All E.R. 756.

Chapter 17

OTHER PENALTIES

CUSTODIAL SENTENCES   A17–01

The imposition of custodial sentences is governed by the **Criminal Justice Act 1991** as amended by the **C.J.A. 1993** and supplemented by the **Criminal Justice and Public Order Act 1994**. The basic proposition is that custody may only be ordered where the "custody threshold" is passed whereby the offence is so serious only custody is justified (**C.J.A. 1991, s.1**). Custody may also be imposed where the offender has refused his consent to a community sentences order or where the offence is a violent or sexual one and the public require protection from serious harm by the offender. Road traffic matters do not usually fall into the latter. The **1994 Act** has altered the requirements on the court to obtain a pre-sentence report for matters triable either-way where it is considering custody. The length of sentence shall be commensurate with seriousness of the offence and in determining this the court may have regard to the defendant's previous convictions, whether this offence was committed while the defendant was on bail (**C.J.A. 1991, s.29**) and the prevalence of the offence; *R. v. Cox (David Geoffrey)* [1993] 1 W.L.R. 188. The **1994 Act** has also placed on a statutory footing the discount for an early plea of guilty. **A17–02, A17–04A**

Young offenders

The minimum age for imprisonment is 21. Offenders under 21 can be sentenced to a period of detention in a young offender institution, and once the provisions of the **C.J.P.O.A. 1994** are in force, offenders aged 12, 13, and 14 may be sentenced to a period on a Secure Training Order. **A17–04**

Suspended sentences

Suspended sentences may only be considered for adults where the custody threshold has been passed and the court would impose a term of imprisonment of 2 years or less but for the fact that there are "exceptional circumstances": **section 22(2) P.C.C.A. 1973**. It has been made clear that exceptional circumstances are just that – exceptional, and should not be confused with standard mitigation: *R. v. Okinikan* [1993] 1 W.L.R. 173. The court should consider whether to also impose a fine or the making of a compensation order (**s.22(2A)**), it may not however combine a suspended sentence with sentences of imprisonment or probation for other offences dealt with on the same occasion. **A17–05, A17–06**

FINES   A17–07

Fines for offences dealt with summarily have an upper limit of £5000 and decrease from that in 5 levels. There is no maximum fine for offences which are dealt with on indictment. Unit fines have been abolished. The court has to inquire into the financial means of the offender and the fine must reflect the seriousness of the offence: **C.J.A. 1991, s.18**. The court may make a financial circumstances order to inquire into the defendants means before sentencing: **C.J.A. 1991, s.20**. The parents or guardians of a young offender may be ordered to pay the fine should the defendant default: **section 127 C.J.A. 1988**.

There is a similar community sentence threshold by which the court has to be satisfied that the offence was serious enough to warrant such a sentence; **section 6(1) C.J.A. 1991**. Community sentences are defined to include probation orders, community service orders, combination orders, curfew orders, supervision orders and attendance centre orders. The court is required to obtain a pre-sentence report where either a probation order with additional requirements, a community service order, a combination order or a supervision order are being considered: **sections 6** and **7 C.J.A. 1991**. Refusing to consent to, or being in breach of a community sentence may result in imprisonment: **C.J.A. 1991, Sched. 2**.

Probation orders

Probation orders are now sentences and can therefore be combined with other disposals. They can be made in respect of any offence (except murder) on any offender over 16 who consents. The order is for a minimum of 6 months and a maximum of 3 years and is imposed where it is desirable in the interests of the offender's rehabilitation or to protect the public; **sections 2 – 6 P.C.C.A. 1973**.

Community service orders

These may be made in respect of any imprisonable offence committed by an offender who consents to its imposition. The number of hours range from 40–240 and must be able to be fulfilled within 1 year. The order may be combined with other forms of sentence and have ancillary orders as to costs or compensation attached to it: **sections 14–17 P.C.C.A. 1973**. This order may be combined with probation in a separate order known as a "Combination order" which is limited to a period on probation of one to three years and community service of 40 to 100 hours.   **A17–16**

COMPENSATION   A17–18

Compensation in respect of any personal injury, loss or damage may be ordered on its own or in combination with any other sentence: **section 35 P.C.C.A. 1973**. With regard to road traffic accidents the powers of compensation are limited to damages flowing from an offence under the **Theft Act 1968** or where the defendant is uninsured: **section 104 C.J.A. 1988**.

FORFEITURE   A17–20

Section 43 P.C.C.A. Allows a court to order that any property in the offender's possession which was used in the commission of the offence to be forfeited. **Section 43(1B)** provides that for offences of driving or attempting to drive or being in charge of a vehicle, failing to provide a breath specimen or failing to stop/report, that the vehicle shall be regarded as having been used for the commission of the offence. **Section 43(1C)** applies this section to any offence under the **R.T.A. 1988** which is punishable with imprisonment.

Chapter 18
APPEALS AND REMOVALS

Appeals to the Crown Court from the magistrates

On giving written notice to the justices' clerk and the prosecution within 21 days of the conclusion of the case a defendant may appeal against conviction (by way of rehearing before a judge and two lay justices, who may hear fresh evidence from either side) or sentence (procedure as for guilty plea) or both. The Crown Court may in either case increase the sentence passed. The Crown Court may confirm, reverse, vary, remit for reconsideration the magistrates' decision or pass any order it sees fit but it may not exceed the penalties imposable by magistrates: **sections 108–110 M.C.A. 1980, Crown Court Rules 1982, rr. 6–11**.   A18–02

Appeals to the Divisional Court by case stated

The Divisional Court may review the decision of a magistrates' court, or a Crown Court considering an appeal from a magistrates' court, only on the grounds that it was wrong in law or in excess of jurisdiction. The magistrates may only refuse to state a case for the Divisional Court if they find it to be frivolous (this decision may in turn be appealed to the High Court). Written notice setting out the error must

[43]

have been given within 21 days of the decision (or sentence if later). The draft statement, once agreed between the parties, is sent to the applicant to be lodged with the High Court within 10 days of receipt. The High Court will not hear evidence but only argument on the point of law, after which it may confirm, vary, reverse or remit the decision: **section 111 M.C.A.** and **R.S.C. Ord. 56.**   A18–07

N.B. Appeal should be made to the Crown Court first as an appeal to the Divisional Court precludes a subsequent appeal to the Crown Court. Bear in mind that the prosecution may also appeal to the Divisional Court.

Applications for judicial review

Similar to Case Stated, only available from the Crown Court when it is seized of an appeal from the magistrates' court. The case is only reviewable on grounds of natural justice or a matter of law which arises before the conclusion of the case. Where there is difficulty in establishing the facts the proper avenue is by way of case stated. Application is in writing, setting out the grounds and relief, and is initially for leave *ex parte* before a single High Court judge; the application must be supported by affidavit. The decision of the single judge may be appealed to the full court.   A18–12

Appeals to the criminal division of the Court of Appeal

Appeals against conviction or sentence from a matter tried on indictment or from a committal for sentence to the Crown Court follow the standard criminal route of appeal from the Crown Court to the Court of Appeal. The leave of the Crown Court judge or a single High Court judge is required unless the matter is one of pure law. Notice and Grounds of Appeal must be lodged within 28 days of the conclusion of the matter.   A18–15

It should be remembered that the prosecution now have the right to appeal an unduly lenient sentence by way of the Attorney-General to the Court of Appeal; **sections 35, 36** and **Schedule 3 Criminal Justice Act 1988.** Otherwise the Court of Appeal has no power to increase the sentence passed.

APPLICATION FOR REMOVAL OF DISQUALIFICATION   A18–20

A defendant who has been disqualified for more than two years may apply to have his disqualification removed early. Those who are disqualified for a lesser period or who are subject to a disqualification until they have passed a re-test may not so apply: **section 42 R.T.O.A. 1988.**   **A18–20**

When?

Only after expiration of the relevant period from the date of the order, excluding any period of suspension, that is:

(a) two years, if the disqualification is for less than four years;
(b) Half the period of disqualification if for less than 10 years but for four or more years;
(c) In any other case five years; **section 42(3) R.T.O.A. 1988.**   **A18–21**

Grounds

In any event it will be the more difficult, the more serious the original offence was. The court:
   "... shall have regard to the character of the person disqualified and his conduct subsequent to the order, the nature of the offence, and any other circumstances of the case..."
Evidence should be called to support the application.   **A18–23**

The application

Is made by way of complaint for summons from the original convicting court to the Chief Officer of Police for the area. Once an application is refused, another may not be made until 3 months have passed: **section 42(4)**. The court may grant the application or order it to take effect from a future date or refuse the application. If granted then the licence of the defendant should be endorsed to that effect.   **A18–24**

(b) **R.T.A. 1988, s.99**: driving licence holder failing, when his particulars become incorrect, to surrender licence and give particulars;

(c) **R.T.A. 1988, s.103,** substituted by **R.T.A. 1991, s.19**: obtaining a driving licence while disqualified and driving while disqualified;

(d) **R.T.A. 1988, s.143**: using a motor vehicle or causing or permitting it to be used while uninsured or unsecured against third party risks;

(e) **R.T.A. 1988, s.174(1)** or **(5)**: making false statements in connection with licences under the Act and with registration as an approved driving instructor; or making false statement or withholding material information in order to obtain the issue of insurance certificates;

(f) **R.T.A. 1988, s.175**: issuing false documents.

Similar time limits to those under **section 6** of the **R.T.O.A. 1988**   **A1–06** apply by virtue of **section 47** of the **Vehicle Excise and Registration Act 1994**. The time limits apply to a number of offences including:

(a) **section 29**: using and keeping an unlicensed vehicle;

(b) **section 34**: using a trade licence in breach of its conditions;

(c) **section 44**: forging, issuing and making false statements relating to driving licences, insurance certificates, test certificates, etc.

When computing the time, the date of the offence is not included. Therefore, if the date of the offence is January 1, an information may be laid up to and including July 1.

In practice most informations are in writing. Bundles of infor-   **A1–07** mations can be considered by a Justice or by a clerk to the Justices and thereafter authority may be given for others to affix the signature of the person who has considered the informations and authorised the issue of the summonses. The task of signing the summons can be performed vicariously by use of a facsimile signature on a rubber stamp in order to comply with **rule 98** of the **Magistrates' Courts Rules 1981:** *R. v. Brentford Justices, ex p. Catlin* [1975] Q.B. 455.

Summons: points to note

The following points should be noted: **A1–08**

(a) A magistrate or clerk may refuse to issue a summons if he has reasonable grounds to do so. It is a matter of discretion, which is open to judicial review if he has acted unreasonably. (See *R. v. Tower Bridge Metropolitan Stipendiary Magistrate, ex p. Chaudry* [1994] R.T.R. 113 for an example of a magistrate refusing to issue a summons upon information laid by a private person against a defendant already facing proceedings brought by the Crown Prosecution Service for less serious charges);

(b) a summons may be refused if the information appears frivolous or vexatious or if there appears to be an abuse of process. For example, it may be an abuse of process if the prosecutor lays an information without having decided whether or not to prosecute and the justices may later decline jurisdiction: *R. v. Brentford Justices, ex p. Wong* [1981] Q.B. 445. Another example of abuse of the process was a case where an information was laid which was ambiguous in its terms and no further details were given clarifying the situation before the time limits expired. The prosecution was stopped: *R. v. Newcastle-upon-Tyne Justices, ex p. Hindle* [1984] 1 All E.R. 770;

(c) before issuing a summons the magistrate(s) or the clerk may enquire into the reasons for any delay, if it appears to them that there has been substantial delay, even though the information is within the statutory period: *R. v. Clerk to the Medway Justices, ex p. Department of Health and Social Security* [1986] Crim.L.R. 686. Where the delay is found to be unjustifiable and the defendant shows on the balance of probabilities that owing to the delay he will suffer serious prejudice to the extent that no fair trial can be held, then the proceedings must be stayed: *Att.-Gen.'s Reference (No. 1 of 1990)* [1992] 1 Q.B. 630.

(d) If a person appears in person to lay an information, the justices or the clerk may question the person. The accused person may even be given the opportunity to oppose the issue of a summons, but he has no right to be heard: *R. v. West London Stipendiary Magistrate, ex p. Klahn* [1979] 1 W.L.R. 933. This probably is unlikely in a road traffic case;

(e) a magistrate or magistrates' court clerk cannot reconsider an application which has been rejected by a colleague: *R. v. Worthing Justices, ex p. Norvell* [1981] W.L.R. 413.

Summons: form and service

A1–09   The summons orders the defendant to attend the magistrates' court on a date specified in order to answer the information(s) that have been laid against him. The summons should have details of the defendant's name and address, the name and address of the court, the date and time of hearing, the details of the information and the name and address of the informant.

The **Magistrates' Courts Rules 1981, r. 99** lays down the conditions of service. Service may be carried out by delivering the summons in person to the defendant or posting it to his last known address or by leaving it with some person at his last known address. If the offence is purely a summary one, service is treated as proved if it was sent by recorded delivery or registered. Otherwise, it must be shown that the summons came to the knowledge of the defendant. If the defendant fails to attend and service is proved, then the court may adjourn the matter to another date, or if a reasonable time has elapsed between service and the date of hearing, then they may hear the case in his absence. (**Magistrates' Courts Act 1980, ss.10** and **11**). There is a third alternative under **section 13**. The court may adjourn the case and issue a warrant if (a) it is proved that the summons has been served a reasonable time before the hearing, (b) the information was substantiated on oath and (c) either the accused was a juvenile, or the offence alleged is punishable with imprisonment, or the defendant has been convicted in his absence and the court proposes to disqualify him from driving.

There is also a power for a warrant to be issued on a sworn information in writing being laid under **Magistrates' Court Act 1980, s.1**. A warrant may not be issued for the arrest of a person of 17 years upwards unless the offence is indictable, triable either way or punishable by imprisonment, or the person's address is not sufficiently ascertained in order for a summons to be served on him: **Magistrates' Courts Act 1980, s.1(4)**.

Notice of intended prosecution: provisions

Under the **Road Traffic Offenders Act 1988 (R.T.O.A. 1988), s.1** (as   **A1–10** amended by **R.T.A. 1991, Sched. 4, para. 80**):

"a person shall not be convicted of an offence to which this section applies unless:
  (a) he was warned at the time the offence was committed that the question of prosecuting him for some one or other offence to which the section applies would be considered, or
  (b) within fourteen days of the commission of the offence a summons for the offence was served on him, or
  (c) within fourteen days of the commission of the offence a notice of intended prosecution specifying the nature of the alleged offence and the time and place where it is alleged to have been committed, was—
       (i) in the case of an offence under section 28 [substituted by **section 7 R.T.A. 1991**] or 29 of the Road Traffic Act 1988 (cycling offences), served on him,
       (ii) in the case of any other offence, served on him or on the person, if any, registered as the keeper of the vehicle at the time of the commission of the offence."

A notice is deemed to have been served for these purposes if it was sent by registered post or recorded delivery service addressed to him, at his last known address, notwithstanding that the notice was returned as undelivered or was for any other reason not received by him. Personal service may be effected by service to the defendant or to some other person authorised to receive letters on his behalf. There is a strong inference that a wife living with her husband is an authorised receiver: *Hosier v. Goodall* [1962] 2 Q.B. 401.

Supplementary provisions

A1–11   Under the **R.T.O.A. 1988, s.2(1)**, the requirement of **section 1(1)** does not apply in relation to an offence if, at the time of the offence or immediately after it, an accident occurs owing to the presence on a road of the vehicle in respect of which the offence was committed. But see *Bentley v. Dickinson* [1983] R.T.R. 356, where the accident was so trivial that it was unknown to the driver. This potential loophole has been addressed in *D.P.P. v. Pidhajeckyi* [1991] R.T.R. 136. In this case, the defendant was involved in a serious road traffic accident. He was unconscious for five days and in intensive care for eight days. He had no recollection of the accident. No notice of intended prosecution was given or attempted to be given to him within the required 14 days. He was charged with driving without due care and attention. The justices dismissed the information. The Divisional Court allowed the appeal brought by the prosecutor. It was held that since the defendant was involved in a serious accident and in the light of **section 179(3A) R.T.A. 1972**, as inserted, the prosecutor was under no duty to serve a notice of intended prosecution.

In addition the requirement does not apply in relation to an offence in respect of which a fixed penalty notice has been given or fixed (see **Part 3** of the Act), nor if a notice has been given under **section 54(4)** of the Act (notice to produce driving licence at a police station): **R.T.O.A. 1988, s.2(2).**

If the conditions of **section 1(1)** are not satisfied, it is not necessarily a bar to conviction, because **section 2(3)** provides that the court may convict where it is satisfied:

    (a) that neither the name and address of the accused nor the name and address of the registered keeper, if any, could with reasonable diligence have been ascertained in time for a summons to be served or for a notice to be served or sent in compliance with the requirement or

    (b) that the accused by his own conduct contributed to the failure.

There is also provision to convict on a lesser charge in certain circumstances without the requirement being satisfied: **section 2(4) R.T.O.A. 1988** (as amended by **R.T.A. 1991, Sched. 4, para. 81**). (See Chapter 9, § A9–02 *et seq.*)

The relevant offences

A1–12   Section 1 applies to the following offences under the **R.T.A. 1988** as amended by **R.T.A. 1991** (See **R.T.O.A. 1988, Sched. 1** as amended by **R.T.A. 1991, Sched. 1**):

    (a) Dangerous driving (reckless driving) (**section 2**);

    (b) causing death by dangerous driving (causing death by reckless driving) (**section 1**);

(c) careless and inconsiderate driving (**section 3**);
(d) leaving vehicles in dangerous positions (**section 22**);
(e) dangerous cycling (**section 28**);
(f) careless and inconsiderate cycling (**section 29**);
(g) failing to comply with traffic signs (**sections 35** and **36**).

R.T.A. 1991, Sched. 1, paras. 1 and **2** amend **R.T.O.A. 1988, Sched. 1** by adding to the list offences of speeding, including temporary speed restrictions associated with road works, speeding on motorways, temporary speed limits and speeding generally under **sections 14, 16, 17, 88** and **89** of the **Road Traffic Regulation Act 1984 (R.T.R.A. 1984)**.

Section 1: points to note

(a) See above for service of summons;   **A1–13**
(b) the notice must be in writing and be served as outlined in the subsection. Service can be accepted by someone authorised to accept letters on the defendant's behalf: *Layton v. Shires* [1960] 2 Q.B. 294, *Burt v. Kircaldy* [1965] 1 W.L.R. 474;
(c) the notice must be posted within such a time that it will arrive within the 14 days in the ordinary course of post: *Stewart v. Chapman* [1951] 2 K.B. 792;
(d) service to a registered office of a company is valid service if the company is the registered keeper;
(e) if there is an error in the notice, then the court has to decide as a matter of fact to what extent the defendant has been misled. The object of the notice is that the defendant is not taken unawares weeks after the alleged offence. Mistakes as to time and place may be material and each case will depend on its facts;
(f) there is a presumption that the requirements have been complied with unless the contrary is shown (**section 1(3)**). The defence has to raise the issue and has to discharge the onus of proof on the balance of probabilities: *Offen v. Ranson* [1980] R.T.R. 484. This may well involve calling not only the defendant, but also the registered keeper if he is not the defendant. It may be worth obtaining a formal admission from the prosecution that notice was not served on one or the other as the case may be, to avoid calling unnecessary witnesses;
(g) the warning may be oral or written. The decision as to whether a warning was given at the time will be a matter of fact and degree: *R. v. Okike* [1978] R.T.R. 489, C.A. Several hours elapsing after the offence will probably not suffice: *Cuthbert v. Hollis* [1958] Crim.L.R. 814. The defendant has to raise the issue that the delay rendered the warning unreasonable: *R. v. Okike, supra*. The cautioning and charging of an accused is sufficient compliance: *Lindsay v. Smith* [1990] S.C.C.R. 581.
(h) there is no form of words for the warning and it will be a matter of common sense as to whether the warning was effective. It is a matter of fact to be decided in any event if challenged. The

burden will be on the defendant to show that the warning was not effective: *Gibson v. Dalton* [1980] R.T.R. 410, D.C. The same principles apply to this aspect as do to arrest and warnings given under the drink driving legislation;

(i) it is submitted that a defendant must be aware that an accident, however slight, has taken place for the section to apply. This was the situation under the **1972 Act** and there is no reason why this principle should have changed. It is the same principle as that applicable to failing to stop after an accident. See: *Bentley v. Dickinson* [1983] R.T.R. 356.

Legal aid: general provisions

A1–14   The granting of legal aid is governed by the **Legal Aid Act 1988**. Under **section 20(5)** there is provision for a "through" legal aid order to the Crown Court. There is a prescribed form to be filled out, which includes a statement of means. It may be considered by a court, a justices' clerk or a single magistrate. It may be granted if they are satisfied that the applicant's means are such that he required assistance in meeting the legal costs of the case and that it is in the interests of justice that legal aid should be granted. The means of the applicant are examined. If the person is unemployed, then he is deemed to have no income and is entitled in principle to legal aid without a contribution. If the person is in employment, then the net weekly income will be looked at and deductions made for expenses, then calculations made to determine if there should be a contribution, and if so what that contribution should be. How does one define the interests of justice?

A1–15   The following criteria were laid down by the Departmental Committee on Legal Aid when considering the grant of legal aid and are also laid out in **section 22** of the **Legal Aid Act 1988**. They are:

(a) Where the charge is one where the applicant stands to lose his liberty or livelihood or suffer serious damage to his reputation if convicted;

(b) where there is a substantial question of law involved;

(c) where the applicant will be at a disadvantage by reason of his mental condition, physical disability or inadequate command of English;

(d) where it will be necessary to trace and interview witnesses or where expert cross-examination of prosecution witnesses will be involved;

(e) where it may be in the interests of a third party that the applicant be given proper legal advice as to his plea.

If a person had his application refused by the magistrates' court (including the clerk), application could be made to the area criminal legal aid committee for the matter to be reviewed. This was under the **Legal Aid Act 1974** as amended. It is intended that this right of appeal should continue. There are provisions under **section 21(10) Legal Aid Act 1988** for regulations to provide for an appeal against the refusal of a magistrates' court to grant representation (**S.I. 1989 No. 344; S.I. 1990 No. 459; S.I. 1991 No. 637**). Certain criteria had to be satisfied before such an application could be considered. There had to be an indictable offence charged, the application must have been refused on the ground of "interests of justice" (see above), and the original application for legal aid must have been made no later than 21 days before the date fixed for trial or committal proceedings, assuming that such a date had been fixed. This meant in practice that most road traffic offences did not qualify under the criteria laid down for a review.

Legal aid: road traffic cases

It seems that legal aid is becoming increasingly difficult to obtain for road traffic offences. The criteria laid out above were laid down by the Widgery Committee in 1966 and are now embodied in **section 22(2)** of the **Legal Aid Act 1988**. **A1–16**

The factors to be taken into account in determining whether it is in the interests of justice that representation be granted for the purposes of the proceedings include:

(a) the offence is such if proved, it is likely that the court would impose a sentence which would deprive the accused of his liberty or lead to loss of his livelihood or serious damage to his reputation;

(b) the determination of the case may involve consideration of a substantial question of law;

(c) the accused may be unable to understand the proceedings or to state his case because of his inadequate knowledge of English, mental illness or physical disability;

(d) the nature of the defence is such as to involve the tracing and interviewing of witnesses or expert cross-examination of a witness for the prosecution;

(e) it is in the interests of someone other than the accused that the accused be represented.

If one looks at them closely, for the run-of-the-mill road traffic case, it can be seen that it will be difficult to come within them. The most common headings that such cases would come under would be in the category of loss of liberty or livelihood, or expert cross-examination of prosecution witnesses and allied to this a substantial question of law involved. The most common reason in practice is probably the risk of losing one's livelihood if convicted and disqualified from driving. It is important, therefore, right at the outset, to try and identify if these criteria apply and in particular if an expert will be required, because this will give much greater weight to the application.

The hearing: points to note

A1–17   In the following paragraphs a number of aspects of the hearing will be considered. They are points which are likely to be encountered during any proceedings. It must be emphasised that for full details of points of procedure and evidence, access should be had to the many specialist books on the topics.

The court and constitution of the Bench

A1–18   When magistrates hold a summary trial or committal proceedings, generally, these should be in open court: **section 121 Magistrates' Courts Act 1980**. There are various statutory exceptions not relevant to this book. In committal proceedings, there is a power for the examining magistrates to take depositions, not in open court, if it appears to them that the ends of justice would not be served by sitting in open court: **section 4(2) Magistrates' Courts Act 1980**. The bench is usually composed of three justices (although up to seven may sit in a magistrates' court) or alternatively, a stipendiary magistrate. At least two magistrates must sit to try a case summarily, but one justice can act as an examining justice. Where a Bench is equally divided, then there can be a retrial before a separate bench. A Bench which adjourns a case part heard should come back to finish the case. A new Bench may sentence a person, however, once he has been convicted and the matter has been adjourned for sentence. It is desirable, whenever practicable, for the same Bench to carry out this function, having heard all the evidence and seen the witnesses.

Reporting of court proceedings

A1–19   Subject to certain exceptions, the press may report all legal proceedings conducted in open court: **Contempt of Court Act 1981, s.4(1)**. The exceptions which may affect road traffic matters are:

   (a) Juveniles. An order can be made under **section 39** of the **Children and Young Persons Act 1933,** that the press do not reveal the name or address or other particulars which could lead to the identification of a juvenile in any proceedings, be he witness or defendant.
   (b) Committal proceedings. The following may be reported: the court, the names, addresses and occupations of the parties in the case, the charges, the names of legal representatives, the charges on which the defendant is committed and to which court the committal is made and questions of legal aid, and bail. Application can be made for reporting restrictions on other matters to be removed.

(c) Matters withheld from the public during proceedings in court. An order will be made under **section 11** of the **Contempt of Court Act 1981** and must be specific in its ambit.

(d) There is a power to postpone publication of reports of court proceedings where it is necessary in the administration of justice to avoid a substantial risk of prejudice.

Presence of the defendant

In a large number of road traffic cases, the presence of the defendant is not required. This is particularly so for minor offences and much time and money is saved by the defendant not having to attend. **Section 12** of the **Magistrates' Courts Act 1980 (M.C.A. 1980)** makes provision for pleas of guilty to be accepted by the court without the defendant attending in person. This relates to summary offences only which carry a maximum sentence of three months imprisonment. In addition, it only applies to adults and not juveniles. There is a special format, which lays out the statement of facts (Form 903 in London) and there is provision for mitigating circumstances to be filled out by the defendant which will be considered by the court before sentence. The defendant must also be informed of Unit Fines (**C.J.A. 1991, s.18, M.C.A. 1980, s.12(1)(a)** as amended). A company or a corporation may also enter a plea of guilty by post.

A1–20

If a person has intimated a plea of guilty by letter but wishes to withdraw it and appear in person at the hearing, he may do so as long as written notice is given to the clerk to the justices. As the clerk will already have informed the prosecutor of the guilty plea, he will inform the prosecution of the change. If this plea is withdrawn then the court will hear the case in the usual way: **section 12(3)**.

Before accepting the plea of guilty, the statement of facts and anything that the defendant has said in mitigation must be read out. It often happens that in mitigation the accused raises a defence or the plea is equivocal. In these circumstances the case must be adjourned to allow the attendance of the defendant. Only the statement of facts may be read out on behalf of the prosecution and no other statements: **section 12(5)**.

The statement of facts will be read out by the clerk of the court. This means that such cases can be dealt with even if a prosecutor is not present. The court may order the defendant's licence to be endorsed and penalty points imposed under the procedure of guilty plea by post, but if disqualification is to be considered, then the defendant must be given an opportunity to attend court: **section 11(4) M.C.A. 1980**. Generally speaking the court cannot try a defendant in his absence unless it is satisfied that either the summons was properly served within a reasonable time to give the defendant an opportunity to appear or that he appeared on a previous hearing when the case was adjourned. The defendant must appear in person for committal proceedings unless prevented by illness, is legally represented and gives his consent: **section 4(4) M.C.A. 1980**. This also applies in the case where he indulges in unruly behaviour and the court orders him to be excluded from the hearing.

Charges: mode of trial

A1–21 Most road traffic offences are summary only, so the mode of trial provision is less frequently used than in other areas of the criminal law. This is particularly so now that the offences of driving whilst disqualified and taking and driving away have become summary only offences under **section 37** of the **Criminal Justice Act 1988**. If a person is charged with an offence triable either way, then mode of trial proceedings have to take place. The magistrates must first decide if they consider themselves able to deal with the matter. This is usually decided after a brief thumbnail sketch of the allegation has been given by the prosecution, who may make representations as to mode of trial. The defence may also make such representations. If the magistrates decline jurisdiction, then the matter will be committed to the Crown Court. If they accept jurisdiction, then the defendant is asked to make his election where he wishes to be tried. He must be told that if at the end of the case, the justices feel that their powers of sentence are inadequate, they may commit him to the Crown Court for sentence. The defendant will then elect the mode of trial.

If an offence is triable either way, then the defendant is now entitled to advance disclosure of the case against him, prior to consideration of mode of trial. Such disclosure may be either in the form of the witness statements, the interview of the defendant or a summary. There are certain circumstances where disclosure may be withheld, such as fear of intimidation of witnesses but there must be notice in writing of the decision to withhold disclosure. When advance information has been disclosed, then the court may be asked to grant an adjournment to the defence for its consideration if the matter is complex. If a case is adjourned in the defendant's absence, then reasonable notice must be given to him of the adjourned hearing see: **section 10(2) M.C.A. 1980** and the **Magistrates' Courts Rules** as mentioned above regarding service.

Charges: separate or together?

A1–22 Generally speaking, in past years, the principle that operated in the magistrates' court was that a defendant would only face one information at a time, unless he consented to more than one information being tried at the same hearing. This practice has moved more into line with trial on indictment and the principles governing joinder in the indictment. In the case of *Clayton v. Chief Constable of Norfolk* [1983] 2 A.C. 473, it was said that trial in the magistrates' court in this respect should follow the principles as enunciated in the case of *R. v. Assim* [1966] 2 Q.B. 249 by Sachs J. This related to a trial of a number of defendants together. The principle is that if the evidence is so related by time or other factors and the interests of justice are best served by trying them together, then they should be tried together subject to the court's discretion. It would be a common sense approach in a case such as using and permitting use of the same vehicle on the same occasion with no insurance.

When considering whether to try a number of charges or infor- **A1–23** mations against one defendant, the court will have regard to the same principles that apply in a trial on indictment. In general terms, there should be sufficient nexus between the offences, they must be part of a series of the same or similar offences or may be founded on the same set of facts. The defence will normally apply for charges or informations to be tried separately if they relate to different dates and there is force in such an application. Where a number of offences are alleged to be based on the same set of facts then the application is likely to be rejected. At the end of the day, it is a question for the magistrates' discretion, and if it is shown that the magistrates considered the matter and exercised their discretion as a result of their deliberations against the defendant, an attempt to review their decision will not be received favourably: *R. v. Sandwich Justices, ex p. Berry* [1982] R.T.R. 332. But see also *R. v. Liverpool City Justices, ex p. Topping* [1983] 1 W.L.R. 119.

Chapter 2

DEFINITIONS

Introduction

The terms defined in this chapter represent the most common ones likely to be encountered in this book. The outlines refer to the general use of the terms and are summarised by means of guidance only. Any special uses of a term will be referred to in the relevant chapter. In addition, although the terms "cause, permit, use" will feature in later chapters, they are not to be defined in this chapter. The terms refer very largely to construction, use and employer/employee liability, an area which will receive scant attention in this book. These definitions will be dealt with in Chapter 12. **A2–01**

It is not an automatic reaction to consider whether or not a point may be taken which involves looking at a definition. It is important to give consideration to this aspect. Was the defendant driving in fact? Was the car driven on a road or other public place? Questions to similar effect should always be considered just in case it is possible to mount an argument along those lines. Recourse may even be needed to the local authority, special maps or similar sources of reference in cases which may involve argument as to the nature of the road, highway, etc. Never assume anything at the initial stage; take thorough instructions; and, if necessary, visit the scene so that any possible argument can be prepared properly. The following terms will be covered in this chapter: driver; driving; attempted driving; in charge; motor vehicle; road; other public place; accident.

Driver

Section 192 of the **R.T.A. 1988** deals with general interpretation provisions and says in relation to the term driver: **A2–02**

> " 'driver', where a separate person acts as steersman of a motor vehicle, includes (except for the purposes of section 1 of this Act) that person as well as any other person engaged in the driving of the vehicle, and 'drive' shall be construed accordingly."

In practical terms this can mean that two people may be found to be driving at the same time. This is illustrated by the case of *Tyler v. Whatmore* [1976] R.T.R. 83 where the occupant of the passenger seat was held to be driving when she had both hands on the steering wheel, directing the car and able to reach the handbrake and ignition. The occupant of the driver's seat, who had an obstructed view due to the other person leaning across, was controlling the motion of the car but not the direction. This was also held to be driving. It will be a matter of fact in each case, depending on the element of control: *D.P.P. v. Hastings* [1993] R.T.R. 205, D.C. In this case, the defendant who was the front-seat passenger, leant across and pulled the steering wheel in order to make the vehicle veer towards the pavement, the aim being to scare a friend. A conviction for reckless driving was quashed as it was held that the actions amounted to an interference with the driving of the vehicle and not driving. In *Jones v. Pratt* [1983] R.T.R. 54, D.C. a passenger who took hold of the steering wheel very briefly causing the car to veer off the road was found not to be driving in the ordinary meaning of the word and therefore was not the driver.

Driving instructors who give lessons in dual control vehicles may well find themselves classed as drivers and, even where the car does not have dual control, the instructor may be the driver depending on the nature of his actions: *Langman v. Valentine* [1952] 2 All E.R. 803 (here the instructor had his hand on the steering wheel and the handbrake). Compare with *Evans v. Walkden* [1956] 1 W.L.R. 1019 where the instructor was a passive spectator. The instructor could also face a charge of aiding and abetting the driver: *Carter v. Richardson* [1974] R.T.R. 314.

A2–03   In a case under **section 6** of the **R.T.A. 1972** (excess alcohol), the prosecution were unable to prove which of two occupants of the car (both of whom were over the legal limit) was the driver. They were both charged as participants to a joint enterprise of the principal offence, and it was held that it was unnecessary for the prosecution to establish which person drove the vehicle and which aided and abetted the driving, provided it could be proved that each occupant was guilty either because he was driving or because he aided and abetted the driving. In this case, however, it was necessary for the prosecution to establish that both occupants knew or were reckless that the other was unfit to drive: *Smith v. Mellors* [1987] R.T.R. 210.

The question of liability as an accomplice is considered in an interesting article by David Lanham where different situations are discussed with reference to past cases and liability assessed under the "control principle" in the context of the use of vehicles: "Drivers, Control and Accomplices" [1982] Crim.L.R. 419. Where there is an issue of whether the defendant was the driver, it must be proved by the prosecution to the criminal standard and it is not sufficient to show that the defendant was the registered owner of the vehicle: *Clarke v. D.P.P.* (1992) 156 J.P. 605.

Driving

A2–04   The case of *R. v. McDonagh* [1974] Q.B. 448 laid down guidelines on the meaning of driving. They can be summarised as follows:

18

(a) The essence of driving is the use of the driver's controls in order to direct the movement of the vehicle however the movement is produced.
(b) There must be a distinction between pushing and driving. This would depend on the extent and degree to which the defendant was relying on the controls.
(c) It matters not, however, that the vehicle is not moving under its own power, nor that it is driven by the force of gravity nor whether it is being pushed by other people.
(d) The ordinary meaning of the word drive could not extend to the facts of the case in question, the appellant was not in the car, had both feet on the road and made no use of the controls apart from an occasional adjustment of the steering wheel.

The court did go on to say that the facts of the case were on the borderline and might have been decided differently if, for instance, the motorist had had one foot in the car in order to make effective use of the controls. The court agreed with the test adopted by the Lord Justice General in the case of *Ames v. MacLeod*, 1969 S.C. (J.) 1 that the question of driving turned on whether the defendant was "in a substantial sense controlling the movement and direction of the car" but added that they did not think that the test was exhaustive.

Examples of driving

Some examples of cases where the defendant was held to be driving are as follows: **A2–05**

Burgoyne v. Phillips [1983] R.T.R. 49, in which the defendant, sitting in the driver's seat, under the misapprehension that the ignition keys were in the ignition, released the brake and let the car roll forward in order to drive off. On realising the key was not in the ignition he immediately put the brake on. The car rolled on a further 30 feet and collided with another vehicle and although the steering wheel was locked and the engine off, the Divisional Court held that the defendant was driving. This decision is not on all fours with the definition in *McDonagh* as the defendant had no control of the movement of the car due to the steering lock being engaged. It is felt that the decision must have been influenced, wrongly, it is submitted, by the fact that the defendant intended to drive and would have done so had the keys been in the ignition. The court's rationale was that by sitting in the driver's seat and setting the car in motion, the defendant was seeking to control the movement of the car. See the commentary to this case in [1983] Crim.L.R. 265.

The Divisional Court emphasised in the case of *Rowan v. Chief Constable of Merseyside, The Times*, December 10, 1985, that what constituted "driving" depended on the facts of each particular case. In this case, the defendant had knelt on the driving seat of the vehicle, released the handbrake and then attempted to re-apply the handbrake to stop the movement of the vehicle. It was held that this amounted to driving.

If a person is being towed and is able to steer the car and apply the brakes if necessary then that person will be driving:

McQuaid v. Anderton [1981] 1 W.L.R. 154; *Caise v. Wright* [1981] R.T.R. 49, D.C.

In *McKoen v. Ellis* [1987] R.T.R. 26 a defendant who had been standing astride a motorcycle and had for some distance pushed and steered the bike whilst still astride with the ignition and lights on was held to be driving. This was followed in *Selby v. D.P.P.* [1994] R.T.R. 157. A defendant who pedals a moped where the engine is out of action will be driving: *R. v. Tahsin* [1970] R.T.R. 88.

In *Gunnell v. D.P.P.* [1994] R.T.R. 151, the defendant was on the driveway of a house sitting astride a moped, trying to kick-start it. He was not wearing a crash helmet. The engine did not start. He set the moped in motion by sitting astride it and propelling it with his feet down the drive and for some 60 yards down the road and back. The engine did not start nor were the lights on. He controlled the movement and direction of the moped with his hands on the handlebars. He was held to be driving.

Under **section 5** of the **R.T.A. 1988** (excess alcohol), an admission by the defendant that he has driven the vehicle is enough to warrant a conviction: *Patterson v. Charlton District Council* [1986] R.T.R. 18, D.C.

Examples of cases of "not driving"

A2–06 The following are examples of cases where the defendant has been held not to be driving:

R. v. Roberts (No. 2) [1965] 1 Q.B. 85 was a case where the handbrake of a lorry which was parked on a hill was released with the consequence of the lorry travelling down the hill. This was held not to be driving.

Pushing a motor scooter was held not to be driving: *R. v. Munning* [1961] Crim.L.R. 555; nor was accidental contact with the controls: *Blayney v. Knight* [1975] R.T.R. 279.

See: *D.P.P. v. Hastings, supra*. A motorist sitting in the driver's seat starting the engine and placing hands on the steering wheel was held not to be driving: *Leach v. D.P.P.* [1993] R.T.R. 161.

Automatism

A2–07 The courts, by their decisions, can be seen to be loath to accept the defence of automatism. It would have to be shown that if the vehicle operated as a result of the defendant's movements, that those movements were completely unconnected with the defendant's conscious will: *Watmore v. Jenkins* [1962] 2 Q.B. 572. The cases have been unsuccessful in the main because the court has been able to find, to give some examples, that, although the defendant's mind was in a state of "hysterical fugue," his mind was working sufficiently purposefully in order to drive away from an accident: *R. v. Isitt* [1978] R.T.R. 211.

A man who was a diabetic, and drove although he felt a diabetic coma coming on, was found by a court to have failed to take precautions necessary to the condition: *Moses v. Winder* [1981] R.T.R. 37.

The case of *R. v. Quick* [1973] Q.B. 910 illustrates the court's attitude. Lord Justice Lawton in the case said (at p. 922):

> "A self-induced capacity will not excuse … nor will one which could have been reasonably foreseen as a result of either doing, or omitting to do something, as, for example, taking alcohol against medical advice after using certain prescribed drugs, or failing to have regular meals while taking insulin. From time to time difficult cases are likely to arise."

It was found that only external factors were capable of leading to automatism. This has been further defined by the Court of Appeal in *R. v. Hennessy* [1989] 1 W.L.R. 287 where their Lordships thought that to qualify, the "external elements" must be novel or accidental. By way of example, stress, anxiety and depression failed to pass the test, as they were more than transitory and thus better categorised as part of Mr Hennessy's mental state whereas an injection (*Quick, supra*) did qualify.

Medical evidence will have to be called if any defence such as automatism is to be raised. It appears however, that even this kind of evidence will not always assist the defendant. In *Broome v. Perkins* [1987] R.T.R. 321, the defendant was charged with driving without due care and attention. He was a diabetic and during his journey home had an accident having driven the car erratically. He did not appear to an eye witness to be in control of his faculties. The defendant remembered setting off on his journey and being at home. Medical evidence was called to show that this was compatible with a hypoglycaemic state. It was also accepted that he could not have foreseen the onset of the attack and, in addition, that he was very familiar with the route so that he could follow it in a state of automatism. The prosecution appealed. The Divisional Court remitted the case back to the magistrates with a direction to convict on the basis that if, during some of the driving the actions were voluntary and not automatic, then the defence would fail. See the commentary in [1987] Crim.L.R. 271. **A2–08**

In another case the defendant called evidence to show that he was suffering from "highway hypnosis" at the time of an accident where he crashed into the back of another car killing the two occupants. The expert Dr Ivan Brown, an adviser to the Department of Transport, and assistant director of the Medical Research Council's applied psychology unit at Cambridge, said that the defendant Miller had been hypnotised by the familiarity of the motorway and had fallen into a "trance-like" state. The defendant was convicted (*The Times*, September 29, 1988). This case was referred to the Court of Appeal under **section 36** of the **Criminal Justice Act 1972** where it was held that driving without awareness was not as a matter of law a state capable of founding a defence of automatism: *Att.-Gen.'s Reference (No. 2 of 1992)* [1994] Crim.L.R. 692.

Epilepsy and insanity

A2–09　If a person commits an offence whilst having an epileptic fit, it seems the verdict of the jury should be not guilty by reason of insanity: *R. v. Sullivan* [1984] A.C. 156. However, if this condition is one which is known to the driver, it should have been declared and would no doubt come under the comments quoted in *Quick* if indeed the person was allowed to hold a licence.

　In the *Att.-Gen.'s Reference (No. 2 of 1992), supra*, the Court of Appeal considered the authorities drawing a distinction between insane automatism and non-insane automatism. The effect of the decision was that if the defence of automatism was said to arise from internal causes so as to bring the defendant within the McNaughton Rules, then if it succeeded, the verdict should be not guilty by reason of insanity. An epileptic seizure (*Sullivan*), stress disorder or accident (*Hennessy* [1989] 1 W.L.R. 287) and sleepwalking (*Burgess* [1991] 2 Q.B. 92) were all regarded as internal causes.

Attempted driving

A2–10　The usual principles which apply to the law of attempt will apply to attempted driving. The act in question has to be more than merely preparatory and sufficiently proximate to the full offence. The following cases refer to summary cases which have a provision of attempted driving because it should be noted that the **Criminal Attempts Act 1981** applies to indictable offences and not apparently purely summary ones:

　In *Kelly v. Hogan* [1982] R.T.R. 352, D.C., the defendant, who was unfit to drive, sat in the driver's seat trying to insert various keys in the ignition although he had no ignition key. He was convicted of attempting to drive.

　In *R. v. Farrance* [1978] R.T.R. 225, it was said that if a person sits in the driving seat of the car attempting to start it, or putting it in gear or applying the accelerator to make the car move, then that is an attempt to drive despite the fact that due to some mechanical failure the car was unable to be driven. The question of whether there is an attempt or the full offence will most probably turn on whether the vehicle was in motion. Going to fetch keys or carrying keys approaching the vehicle are not sufficient to amount to an attempt: *Harman v. Wardrop* [1971] R.T.R. 127.

In charge

A2–11　The **R.T.A. 1988** does not define the words "in charge." Each case has to be looked at on its merits as it is a question of fact whether a person is "in charge": *R. v. Harnett* [1955] Crim.L.R. 793, C.C.A. There is a divergence between the approach adopted by the Scottish courts and that of the English courts. In Scotland the question is whether there is a sufficiently close link between the defendant and his position to take and exercise control of the vehicle. In England on the other hand, the presumption is that a person is prima facie in charge if he has the keys to the vehicle: *Blayney v. Knight* [1975] R.T.R. 279. The test was laid down in *Haines v. Roberts* [1953] 1 W.L.R. 309 when Goddard L.C.J. said:

> "It may be that if a man goes to a public house and leaves his car outside or in the car park and getting drunk asks a friend to go and look after the car for him or take the car home, he has put it in charge of somebody else, but if he has not put the car in charge of somebody else he is in charge of it until he does so. His car is away from home on the road ... and he is in charge."

The test was criticised as being too severe in the case of *Woodage v. Jones (No. 2)* [1975] R.T.R. 119.

In the case of *R. v. Short, The Times*, December 10, 1955, it was said   **A2–12** that "somebody must be in charge of a car when it is on the road unless it has been abandoned altogether." In order to show that a person is not in charge he must have handed the keys over to someone or demonstrated that he was relinquishing control over the keys and with it the vehicle.

In *Ellis v. Smith* [1962] 1 W.L.R. 1486, a bus driver was held to be in charge of a bus because he had not put his vehicle in anybody else's charge although he was off duty.

In *Woodage v. Jones (supra)*, a driver had been stopped by other motorists and his car pulled off the road onto the forecourt of a garage. On hearing that the police were to be called, he walked away. He was arrested half a mile from his car and was held to be "in charge" of it as he had not given over his keys to anyone else.

In the case of *D.P.P. v. Watkins* [1989] Q.B. 821, the Divisional Court said that the phrase "in charge" necessitated a close connection between the defendant and the control of a motor vehicle but did not necessitate proof of the likelihood of the defendant driving the vehicle. Taylor L.J. (at p. 831) identified two distinct classes of case. The first class of case where the driver is the owner or lawful possessor of the car to which the rule in *Haines v. Roberts* was directed, where it will be a question for the court whether he has relinquished charge. The second class of case is where the defendant is not the owner nor lawful possessor but is sitting in the vehicle or otherwise involved with it and the question will be has he assumed being in charge of it. He will be in charge if he is voluntarily in *de facto* control of the vehicle. The factors to be considered include:

(i) whether and where he was in the vehicle or how far he is from it;
(ii) what he is doing at the relevant time;

    (iii) whether he is in possession of a key which fits the ignition;

    (iv) whether there is evidence of an intention to take or assert control of the car by driving or otherwise;

    (v) whether any other person is in, at or near the vehicle and if so, the like particulars in respect of that person.

The prosecution had to establish that the person was prima facie in charge whilst unfit, but in order to do so there was no need to show likelihood of driving while still unfit. The burden was on the defendant, once there was a prima facie case, to show that there was no such likelihood. The court went on to say that the following factors might be relevant:

    (a) Whether and where he was in the vehicle or how far he was from it.

    (b) What he was doing at the relevant time.

    (c) Whether he was in possession of keys that fitted the ignition.

    (d) Whether there was any evidence of an intention to take or assert control of the car by driving or otherwise.

    (e) Whether any person was in, at or near the vehicle and, if so, the like particulars in respect of that person.

A2–13 In the case of *D.P.P. v. Webb* [1988] R.T.R. 374, D.C., the defendant had parked his car in road A. Later, having consumed alcohol, he was seen tampering with a different car in road B, which was some two-tenths of a mile distant from road A. He was arrested under **section 5(2) R.T.A. 1972** (in charge while unfit). He was charged with being in charge of a motor vehicle at road B while unfit to drive. He was convicted at the magistrates' court, appealed to the Crown Court where at the close of the prosecution case the matter was dismissed. The Divisional Court dismissed the prosecution's appeal. It was said that, albeit in every case it was a matter of fact and degree whether a person was in charge of the vehicle, **section 5(2)** made the geographic place critically the place where the motor vehicle was and not where the defendant was; so that, the defendant's car not being at road B but road A, the geographic location was flawed.

Driving instructors

A2–14 What is the situation regarding driving instructors and those who are supervising learner drivers? As was pointed out earlier (§ A2–02), a driving instructor can be held to be the driver in certain circumstances, in particular when exercising control over the car's functions. It may be said that the instructor is in charge of the vehicle in any event if not driving it, and it would be hard for him if charged under **sections 4** or **5** of the **R.T.A. 1988** to avail himself of the statutory defences (which will be discussed below) if he was taking a learner driver out for a lesson. See generally *Sheldon v. Jones* [1970] Crim.L.R. 38, D.C.; *Crampton v. Fish* [1970] Crim.L.R. 235.

The statutory defence

Sections 4(3) and **5(2) R.T.A. 1988** provide statutory defences to the   **A2–15**
charges of being "in charge" whilst unfit or with excess alcohol. The
defendant has to show, and the burden of proof is on him on the balance of probabilities, that there was no likelihood of his driving whilst
likely to be over the limit or unfit. This will be dealt with in more detail
in the relevant chapter, but suffice it to say here that a mere statement
by the defendant that he did not intend to drive will probably not be
enough, nor will merely immobilising the car: *Saycell v. Bool* [1948] 2
All E.R. 83.

Motor vehicle

Section 185(1) R.T.A. 1988 defines motor vehicle for the purposes of   **A2–16**
the Act. It is defined as "a mechanically propelled vehicle intended or
adapted for use on the roads." This is subject to special provisions
about invalid carriages to be found in **section 20** of the **Chronically
Sick and Disabled Persons Act 1970**. The various classes of motor
vehicles are laid down in **section 185(1)**. They are:

(a) Heavy locomotive;
(b) heavy motor car;
(c) invalid carriage;
(d) light locomotive;
(e) motor car;
(f) motor cycle;
(g) motor tractor.

It is advisable to look at the definitions carefully as some of them carry
specifications as to weight and function. It is noteworthy that an electrically assisted pedal cycle does not come within the definition of a
motor vehicle. Its provisions can be found in **section 189**.

Mechanically propelled

The first requirement under the section is that the vehicle be mechan-   **A2–17**
ically propelled. This can mean that it is petrol or oil driven or even
electrically or steam driven. The question that frequently arises in the
courts is whether a broken down or cannibalised vehicle can be said to
be still mechanically propelled. The test to be applied is "whether
there is no reasonable prospect of the vehicle ever being made mobile
again": *Binks v. Department of the Environment* [1975] R.T.R. 318. The
following cases illustrate the point in question.

In *Newberry v. Simmonds* [1961] 2 Q.B. 345 a car which had no engine was still held to be mechanically propelled as there was a possibility that the engine would be replaced within a reasonable time. In
McRachan v. Hurst [1978] R.T.R. 462, the defendant was pedalling a

moped, the engine of which was not working nor was there petrol in the tank. It was held that this was a mechanically propelled vehicle as that is what it had been constructed as.

In an earlier case it had been stated that the test was "is the vehicle constructed so that it can be mechanically propelled?": *R. v. Tahsin* [1970] R.T.R. 88.

A case which was successful was *Smart v. Allan* [1963] 1 Q.B. 291. Here the vehicle had no gearbox and was in such a condition that there was no prospect of it being made mobile. The onus is on the prosecution to show that the vehicle had not gone beyond the point of no return: *Reader v. Bunyard* (1987) 85 Cr.App.R. 185.

"Intended or adapted" for use on roads

A2–18   The guidelines on whether a vehicle was intended or adapted for use on roads were laid down in *Burns v. Currell* [1963] 2 Q.B. 433. The test is an objective one and depends neither on the intention of the user nor on the intention of the manufacturer, wholesaler or retailer. The test is whether "the reasonable man looking at the vehicle would say that one of its users would be a road user." See also *O'Brien v. Anderton* [1979] R.T.R. 388.

In the case of *Chief Constable of Avon and Somerset v. F.* [1987] 1 All E.R. 318, it was said by way of guidance that once it was established that the vehicle as manufactured was intended or adapted for use on a road, it would require a very substantial, indeed, a dramatic alteration for it to be said no longer to be a motor vehicle. Whether the detachment of parts required to be on a vehicle in order to comply with road traffic regulations would turn the vehicle in question into one which any reasonable person would say was no longer intended or adapted for road use was a question of fact for the justices.

Road

A2–19   The courts will now be concerned with the wider question of whether the offence took place on a road *or* in a public place as a result of the **R.T.A. 1991**.

A "road" for the purposes of the Act is "any highway and any other road to which the public has access, and includes bridges over which a road passes": **R.T.A. 1988, s.192**.

There will generally be no difficulty if the case involves an incident on a highway. The problem arises when it is a question of whether it is (a) a road and (b) whether the public has access to it. The burden is on the prosecution to establish the above propositions: *R. v. Shaw* [1974] R.T.R. 225. In most cases the operative question is whether the public has access. See: *Oxford v. Austin* [1981] R.T.R. 416, D.C. There are a number of questions to be considered:

(a) Is the location in fact within the ordinary meaning of the word "road," *i.e.* a definite way between two points where a vehicle can pass?

(b) Does the general public have access to the road?

(c) In the case of (b) above it may be necessary to go one step further and show that the general public have access at least by tolerance of the owner: *Deacon v. A.T. (A Minor)* [1976] R.T.R. 244.

In this and other cases the dictum of Lord Sands in the case of *Harrison* **A2–20**
v. Hill (1932) J.C. 13 has been approved and applied. It was said that "any road may be regarded as a road to which the public have access upon which members of the public are to be found who have not obtained access either by overcoming a physical obstruction or in defiance of prohibition express or implied." The prosecution must show that the general public and not a restricted class of people have access: *Harrison v. Hill*; *Deacon v. A.T., supra*.

In *D.P.P. v. Vivier* [1991] R.T.R. 205 the situation arose where those seeking entry were only allowed to do so if they had a pass. The test outlined by the court was:

" ... do those admitted pass through the screening process for a reason, or on account of some characteristic, personal to themselves? Or are they in truth merely members of the public who are being admitted as such and processed simply so as to make them subject to payment and whatever other conditions the landowner might choose to impose."

On the facts, the campers and caravaners did not possess personal characteristics to differentiate them, they merely bought a licence. *Vivier* was approved in *Selby v. D.P.P.* [1990] 154 J.P.N. 508.

Examples of a "road"

The following cases are examples of where the place has been held to **A2–21**
be a road. In *Harrison v. Hill, supra*, a road to a farmhouse which was maintained by the farmer without a gate was held to be a road as it was also used by people who were not on farm business.

D.P.P. v. Coulman [1993] R.T.R. 230: a ferry lane.

In *Bass v. Boynton* [1960] Crim.L.R. 497 a cul-de-sac was held to be a road. This will not necessarily be the case with all cul-de-sacs and will depend very much on the use. The road need not even be made up or maintained.

Houghton v. Scholfield [1973] R.T.R. 239 was another case where a cul-de-sac was held to be a road because members of the public used it and there was no sign to show that it had restricted use.

What about private residential estates? In the case of *Adams v. Commissioner of Police of the Metropolis* [1980] R.T.R. 289, a private road in a private residential estate was found to be a road within the meaning of the Act as the public had access both as pedestrians and drivers.

Car parks have been held to fall into the definition:

Bowman v. D.P.P. [1991] R.T.R. 263: no barrier into a public car park (NCP).

Capell v. D.P.P. [1991] 155 J.P.N. 139: parking bay not separated from the highway.

A partly privately-owned pavement has been held to be a road: *Price v. D.P.P.* [1990] R.T.R. 413.

Roads at Heathrow Airport which were subject to various restrictions, which had signs saying "no entry except for access" but which had no barriers or obstructions to deny access, where short cuts to the airport were not allowed but which were open to sightseers and regular use was made of them, were held to be roads to which the public had access. Consideration whether the roads were maintainable at public expense (see **Article 1(1)** of **Council Regulation 3820/85** of December 20, 1985) could not be introduced into the definition: *D.P.P. v. Cargo Handling Ltd.* [1992] R.T.R. 318.

Examples of "no road"

A2–22 *Harrison v. Hill* (1932) J.C. 13 was distinguished in the case of *R. v. Beaumont* [1964] Crim.L.R. 665. Here a road which led to a farm and a caravan site and which also gave access to a river used by anglers with the farmer's permission was held not to be a road, as there was no evidence that the road was used other than by a particular class of persons with the farmer's authority.

Alston v. O'Brien, 1992 S.L.T. 856 (a Scottish case): a road to a farmyard used only by visitors and delivery vehicles although no sign saying "private."

An example involving a cul-de-sac is the case of *Knaggs v. Elson* (1965) 109 S.J. 596. In this case the cul-de-sac gave access to a number of houses. There was a "private property" sign but there was no evidence to show that it was used regularly by the general public. It was not a road within the definition. There has to be some obstruction or express or implied prohibition to members of the general public for a road or lane not to fall within the definition.

Young v. Carmichael, 1991 S.C.C.R. 332 (a Scottish case): a car park attached to private flats that had a sign saying "no entry," "private property" and "residents only".

Other public place

A2–23 Drink/driving offences can be committed on a road "or other public place" as are offences under **R.T.A. 1988, ss.1–3**, as amended by **R.T.A. 1991**. Here again the prosecution must prove that the location was an "other public place." "It is a question of fact. Private land to which the public were invited to watch a sporting event has come within the definition: *R. v. Collinson* (1931) 23 Cr.App.R. 49. A car park attached to a public house may be considered a public place during licensing hours but not necessarily outside these hours: *Sandy v. Martin* [1974] R.T.R. 263. An area other than the defined parking area by an inn used by the public to park in was held to be a public place. *Elkins v. Cartlidge* [1947] 1 All E.R. 829. The car park of a private club cannot be regarded as a public place unless there is evidence to show that the car park is used by the general public: *Pugh v. Knipe* [1972] R.T.R. 286.

In *Havell v. D.P.P.* [1993] Crim.L.R. 621, the Divisional Court, applying the principles in *Vivier* (*supra*) held that the appellant who had parked in the community centre car park was within a category separate to and different from the general public as he was a member of the centre and was using the car park in exercise of that membership.

In *Edwards v. D.P.P.* March 10 1994, (unreported) E was convicted of **A2–24** driving with excess alcohol. The issue in the case was whether a car park next to a nightclub was a public place. The car park was owned by a limited company which had not used it as a staff car park for about two years. The company had given the nightclub, the local school and a taxi firm permission to use it. The nightclub held a deed allowing the owner, his employees and licensees the right to use the car park between certain hours in connection with use of the nightclub. The car park was regularly used by members of the local community. The company was aware of this fact. At the time of E's arrest at 2 a.m. on a Saturday, the car park was three-quarters full. There were no signs or notices or barriers prohibiting use.

It was argued on behalf of the appellant that the deed gave the nightclub the right to use the car park between certain hours and therefore, the justices could not have held that it was a public place during those hours. It was held by the Divisional Court that this was irrelevant. It was not essential for the purpose of a car park being a public place that members of the public should have rights (enforceable in law if need be) to go to that place. The question was whether, as a matter of fact, they did use it with sufficient regularity so that it had become *de facto* a public place even though if the owners of the land had sought to enforce their rights they could have stopped its use in that manner. The appeal was dismissed.

Accident

There is no definition of this word in the Act and the courts have been **A2–25** reluctant to lay down any hard and fast definition.

Indeed in the case of *Chief Constable of West Midlands Police v. Billingham* [1979] 1 W.L.R. 747, the court expressed its reluctance to define the word and suggested that the approach a court should take is to ask the question, "Would an ordinary man in the circumstances of the case say there had been an accident?" This would include a deliberate act as in *Billingham* where a police vehicle was put in motion, and on its downhill journey collided with a telegraph pole.

The principle of this case was followed in the case of *Chief Constable of Staffordshire v. Lees* [1981] R.T.R. 506, 510, where it was noted:

"It would be an insult to commonsense if a collision involving a motor car arising from some careless and inadvertent act entitled a constable to exercise his powers under the Act but a similar result caused by a deliberate anti-social act did not. Previous cases have made it clear that one should look at the ordinary meaning of the word 'accident', and it is relevant to note that in the *Oxford English Dictionary*, among other meanings, is to be found an 'unfortunate event, a mishap', which definition, it seems to me, is wide enough to include an event not occurring in the ordinary course, of such a nature as in this case."

In the instant case the defendant deliberately drove at a locked kissing-gate and smashed it. As can be seen from the above two cases there is no need for any other vehicle or person to be involved.

Chapter 3

PRELIMINARY BREATH TESTS AND ROADSIDE PROCEDURE

Preliminary breath tests

Under **section 6(1)** of the **R.T.A. 1988**, where a constable in uniform   A3–01
has reasonable cause to suspect:

(a) That a person driving or attempting to drive or in charge of a motor vehicle on a road or other public place has alcohol in his body or has committed a traffic offence whilst the vehicle was in motion, or

(b) that a person has been driving or attempting to drive or been in charge of a motor vehicle on a road or other public place with alcohol in his body and that that person still has alcohol in his body, or

(c) that a person has been driving or attempting to drive or been in charge of a motor vehicle on a road or other public place and has committed a traffic offence whilst the vehicle was in motion;

he may, subject to the protection for hospital patients, require the person to provide a specimen for a breath test. This test is often known as the "screening breath test," as opposed to the "evidential breath test," which will be covered in Chapter 5. Additionally under **subsection 2**, if an accident occurs owing to the presence of a motor vehicle on a road or other public place, the constable may make the requirement if he has reasonable cause to believe that the person was driving or attempting to drive or in charge of the vehicle at the time of the accident. Please note the use of the word "suspect" under **subsection 1** and "believe" in **subsection 2**. There are three situations identified: (i) the presence of alcohol in the body; (ii) a moving traffic offence; (iii) an accident.

A constable in uniform

A constable is a member of any police force in the jurisdiction and this   A3–02
includes special constables: **section 19** of the **Police Act 1964**; *Richards v. West* [1980] R.T.R. 215. The prosecution must prove that the constable was in uniform. This is a question of fact. The officer will usually give evidence that he was in uniform, but it appears that if the officer has failed to give that evidence and the matter has not been chal-

lenged, then the court is entitled to assume that he was in uniform: *Cooper v. Rowlands* [1971] R.T.R. 291. The operative time for the constable being in uniform is at the time the requirement is made: *Taylor v. Baldwin* [1976] R.T.R. 265. If the issue comes to light as a result of the defendant's statement or what other witnesses say, it should be raised during the evidence, as the prosecution must prove this element. A constable not wearing a helmet is still in uniform: *Wallwork v. Giles* [1970] R.T.R. 118. A police officer who was in uniform with a raincoat over it and in a private car was held to be in uniform: *Taylor v. Baldwin*.

Reasonable cause to suspect/believe

A3–03   The question whether a constable had reasonable grounds to suspect or believe is a question of fact and will depend on all the circumstances of the case. These circumstances should be explored closely as the prosecution must adduce cogent evidence to prove the grounds: *Griffiths v. Willett* [1979] R.T.R. 195. The court should not assume that reasonable grounds for suspicion existed merely by virtue of the fact that a person was asked to give a specimen of breath: *Siddiqui v. Swain* [1979] R.T.R. 454. There is, as noted earlier (§ A3–01), a difference in the requirements between the two subsections. Belief is higher than suspicion, so mere suspicion will not suffice for **subsection (2)**. But if the officer uses the wrong term it may not render the requirement invalid provided that the evidence exists to found the grounds: *Johnson v. Whitehouse* [1984] R.T.R. 38, D.C.

The manner of driving may indicate both a traffic offence and presence of alcohol in the body. The moving traffic offence may be easier to prove because judgment may not be so much in issue. A constable's suspicion about alcohol need not arise until he has stopped the vehicle, nor need the suspicion be that the driver's level of alcohol is above the prescribed limit: *Blake v. Pope* [1986] 1 W.L.R. 1152. In the case of *Mulcaster v. Wheatstone* [1980] R.T.R. 190, a driver was stopped due to the manner of driving which did not necessarily support the inference of alcohol in the body. The officer smelled drink and the driver admitted drinking two pints. The police were entitled therefore to go through the roadside and subsequent procedures.

In *Winter v. Barlow* [1980] R.T.R. 209, the defendant was followed in his car by two police officers, who on stopping and speaking to him suspected him of having alcohol in his body. The justices found that the police had no reasonable cause to suspect the defendant of drinking or of a moving traffic offence but they were of the opinion that the police had power under the **R.T.A. 1972, s.159** to stop the car and once having formed a suspicion were entitled to carry out the procedures. His convictions for failure to supply a roadside specimen and excess alcohol were upheld.

In *Such v. Ball* [1982] R.T.R. 140 a police officer followed and stopped a driver. On speaking to him he smelled drink and required a breath test. The conviction was upheld in the absence of mala fides.

In *D.P.P. v. McGladrigan* [1991] R.T.R. 297, the defendant stalled his   **A3–04**
car whilst manoeuvring it out of a car park. A police officer stopped
the defendant, who confirmed that he had previously consumed
alcohol. He provided a positive breath test and later specimens of
breath for analysis. He was charged under **section 5(1) R.T.A. 1988**.
The justices were of the opinion that the constable had no reasonable
grounds to suspect that he had alcohol in his body at the time of driving, and took the view therefore that he was unlawfully arrested. The
Divisional Court held that since the defendant on being stopped confirmed that he had consumed alcohol, the constable then had both
reasonable cause to suspect that the defendant had alcohol in his body
and a complete basis for requiring a breath test.

In *D.P.P. v. Godwin* [1991] R.T.R. 303, D.C., the defendant was stopped by a constable on routine traffic stop checks. The constable asked
the defendant if he had been drinking and he replied he had not. The
defendant failed to provide a specimen of breath for a breath test and
was arrested. He provided two specimens of breath for analysis which
revealed a reading of 96 microgrammes in 100 millilitres of breath. He
was charged under section 5. The justices were of the opinion that, in
the absence of evidence to the contrary, the constable had no reasonable cause to suspect alcohol in the defendant's body before the
request for him to take a breath test and therefore the arrest was
unlawful. They exercised their discretion under **section 78 Police and
Criminal Evidence Act 1984 (P.A.C.E. 1984)** to exclude the evidence of
the breath analysis and the charge was dismissed. The Divisional
Court did not interfere with their findings.

The police officer does not need to state the grounds for his sus-   **A3–05**
picions: *Williams v. Jones* [1972] R.T.R. 4; *Atkinson v. Walker* [1976]
R.T.R. 117. However, where the grounds for the requirement are not
made out, the court should not convict the defendant on an alternative
ground if there is no evidence to support alternative grounds: *Clem-
ents v. Dams* [1978] R.T.R. 206. If there is evidence of an alternative
ground (*e.g.* evidence of a moving traffic offence and the original
reason was suspicion of alcohol) and the court in considering convicting on that basis, then the defendant should be given an opportunity
to deal with the grounds, including being granted an adjournment if
necessary: *Morriss v. Lawrence* [1977] R.T.R. 205.

Can an officer form his suspicions before the driving begins? The
answer must be in the affirmative. Obvious cases would be when the
officer saw a driver coming out of a public house or observed a person's gait or the smell of alcohol on his breath prior to his entering the
vehicle: *R. v. Furness* [1973] Crim.L.R. 759, C.A.

Are there reasonable grounds for suspicion on the basis of infor-   **A3–06**
mation from others? This will depend on the source of the information. The courts have found that information from one police
officer to another is sufficient: *Erskine v. Hollin* [1971] R.T.R. 199; *R. v.
Evans* [1974] R.T.R. 232. Information from neighbours may be sufficient but must relate to the day in question and not be based on
reports of the person's drinking habits: *Monaghan v. Corbett, The Times,*
June 23, 1983.

In *D.P.P. v. Wilson* [1991] R.T.R. 284, an anonymous phone call was made to the police station about the defendant. A police officer lay in wait for over an hour, saw the defendant and stopped him. He smelled alcohol on his breath. There had been no moving traffic offence. The breath test was positive. The justices excluded evidence under **section 78 P.A.C.E. 1984** as they felt that the police officer had laid a trap, that his suspicion was not based on the manner of driving and therefore, he had acted with mala fides. On appeal by the prosecutor, the Divisional Court held *inter alia*, that; (a) a constable was entitled to act on anonymously provided information and that an acceptable basis for reasonable suspicion within **section 6(1)(a) R.T.A. 1988** existed where a constable smelled alcohol on the breath of a driver who had been stopped in the course of driving; and (b) a constable had a duty to act on information passed to him and to act appropriately when an offence was committed.

Police powers to stop vehicles

A3–07   Under **section 163** of the **R.T.A. 1988** the police have a general power to stop motor vehicles including motorcycles, and failure to stop when required to do so is an offence. If a police officer stops a car at random and then suspects the presence of alcohol in the body, then this is within the law. The authority on this aspect is the case of *Chief Constable of Gwent v. Dash* [1986] R.T.R. 41. In this case the police were stopping cars at random in order for a junior officer to gain experience of the breath test procedure under the supervision of a senior officer. The court said that provided there was no malpractice, capricious or oppressive behaviour on the part of the officer, then there is no restriction on the random stopping of motorists in order to establish whether they have alcohol in their breath.

However, random tests are not permissible! In other words, if a person is stopped at random and the police do not smell alcohol and the driver denies drinking then it would appear that they cannot do a "random" test. In *Lodwick v. Sanders* [1985] 1 W.L.R. 382 it was said that **section 159** of the **R.T.A. 1972** (now **section 163**) gave the police the power to stop a vehicle and once they did so they could exercise any other power they were entitled to exercise.

Under **P.A.C.E. 1984, ss.1** and 2, police constables have the power to stop and search vehicles and their occupants for stolen or prohibited items and under **section 4** there is power to set up road checks for up to seven days in a specified area for purposes of ascertaining whether a vehicle is carrying a person who has committed or who is intending to commit or is a witness to a serious arrestable offence. Thus a person could be stopped under these provisions and find themselves subject to breath tests.

"Accident" and "traffic offence"

A3–08   Under **section 6(2) R.T.A. 1988** the prosecution must prove that there has been an accident. It is not sufficient that the officer suspected or believed that an accident had taken place: *Chief Constable of the West Midlands Police v. Billingham* [1979] 1 W.L.R. 747. Reference can be made to Chapter 2 for the definition of "accident," but the following points can be noted. There need be no other vehicle involved: *R. v. Pico* [1971] R.T.R. 500, C.A. There is no necessity for the defendant's vehicle to be physically involved in the accident, but there must be a direct causal connection between the presence of the defendant's vehicle on the road and the accident: *Quelch v. Phipps* [1955] 2 Q.B. 107; *Redman v. Taylor* [1975] Crim.L.R. 348, D.C.; *M. (A Minor) v. Oxford* [1981] R.T.R. 246, D.C. It should be noted that where a breath test is required after an accident the constable need not be in uniform. The test is "reasonable cause to believe" that the person was driving, attempting to drive or in charge of the vehicle at the time of the accident.

Under **section 6**, a traffic offence means an offence under any provision of the **R.T.A. 1988** with the exception of **Part 5**, any provision under **Part 2** of the **Public Passenger Vehicles Act 1981**, any provision of the **Road Traffic Regulation Act 1984**, and any provision of the **R.T.O.A. 1988** except **Part 3**.

The requirement

The requirement needs no particular form of words, so long as it is **A3–09** made clear what the requirement is: *Atkinson v. Walker* [1976] R.T.R. 117. Again, it is a question of fact, where there is a challenge that the request was made: *R. v. O'Boyle* [1973] R.T.R. 445, C.A. If the requirement is made in good faith by the police officer who believes that the defendant has heard, it is valid even though the defendant may not have heard or understood: *R. v. Nicholls* [1972] 1 W.L.R. 502.

The breath test

Under **subsection 3** the test should be carried out "at or near the place **A3–10** where the requirement is made." Again this will be a matter of fact for the courts to consider. The breath test must be carried out on an approved device. For the purposes of **section 6** the devices approved by the Secretary of State are the Alcotest®80 and 80A, the Alcolyser, the Lion Alcometer SL-2A and the Alert. It is not often that points are taken on the reliability of these devices although they could be more susceptible to such an approach as the manufacturers make no claims that the instruments are of exacting precision. The constable must comply with the manufacturer's instructions concerning assembly of the device, and if he fails to do so, the test is invalid: *R. v. Coates* [1971] R.T.R. 74, C.A.; *Price v. Davies* [1979] R.T.R. 204, D.C.

The House of Lords considered the screening breath test procedure in the case of *D.P.P. v. Carey* [1970] A.C. 1072. They commented that the manufacturer's instructions did not form part of the device as approved, but that the instructions as to assembly had to be complied with. Where there was bona fide use of the device by the officer, but he failed to comply with other instructions, this in itself would not render the breath test invalid. The only relevance that non-compliance with the manufacturer's instructions could have, would be in establishing whether there was any mala fides on the part of the police officer.

A3–11   If the officer realises that the equipment is faulty, or that he has assembled the equipment incorrectly, he may ask for a second test on another device or may re-assemble the device: *Sparrow v. Bradley* [1985] R.T.R. 122, D.C. The officer has a discretion to ask for a second test where, for instance, he thinks that the motorist may be confused as to his instructions or anxious and that the test was consequently carried out unsatisfactorily. This is even so where he could have arrested the motorist on the result of the first test: *R. v. Broomhead* [1975] R.T.R. 558; *Revel v. Jordan* [1983] R.T.R. 497.

One or two points in relation to some of the manufacturers' instructions need to be considered. One of the instructions for the Alcotest®80 states that the measuring bag should be fully inflated by a single breath in not less than 10 and no more than 20 seconds. It has been held, that a direction by an officer to take a deep breath and blow is sufficient. The officers themselves should be able to judge the time scale and whether or not the bag is fully inflated. Non-compliance with the instructions will not be fatal unless it can be shown to have invalidated the result. (See *D.P.P. v. Carey* [1970] A.C. 1072; *Walker v. Lovell* [1975] 1 W.L.R. 1141; *Att.-Gen.'s Reference (No. 1 of 1978)* [1978] R.T.R. 377 for further guidance on this aspect.)

A3–12   Another instruction for the same device relates to smoking. There should be no smoking during or immediately prior to the test. The effect of a high concentration of tobacco smoke is that it may lead to discolouration of the reagent. Any challenge on the basis of smoking during or prior to the test can only be relevant if it is to be suggested that discolouration did take place or that the result was unclear: *Butcher v. Catterall* [1975] R.T.R. 436. See also for smoking and its effects: *Watkinson v. Barley* [1975] 1 W.L.R. 70; *R. v. Callum* [1975] R.T.R. 415; *Att.-Gen.'s Reference (No. 2 of 1974)* [1975] 1 W.L.R. 328.

The other point relates to the consumption of alcohol. The instructions for the Alcotest®80 state that "it is essential that at least 20 minutes should elapse between the drinking of alcohol and the use of the device." This also includes the taking of aromatic drinks or the use of mouth sprays. What happens if the suspect has had a drink within 20 minutes prior to the test? If the constable knew this to be the situation, then the point should be argued. This would be an argument pointing to mala fides, because if such information is available to him, then he should wait: *D.P.P. v. Carey*. However the constable is under no obligation to make enquiry: *Jeffrey v. MacNeil* (1976) J.C. 134. Where alcohol had been consumed in the 20 minutes prior to the test, but the constable was unaware of the fact, and had no reasonable cause to suspect this, then any breath test taken will not be rendered invalid: *D.P.P. v. Carey*.

For further details of the manufacturers' instructions, please refer to the appendices.

Failure to provide a roadside specimen: the offence

Under **section 6(4) R.T.A. 1988**, it is an offence to fail without reason- **A3–13** able excuse to provide a specimen of breath for a breath test when required to do so. The word "fail" includes "refuse": **section 11(2)**. In order for a conviction to stand under this section the prosecution must prove the proper procedure has been followed. Therefore, if the test is incorrectly administered, or the grounds for the requirement are not made out, then a number of points can be raised in relation to unlawful arrest, the bona fides of the police officer and also whether or not any of these matters can amount to reasonable excuse for failure. A person cannot be convicted under this section if the police officer was a trespasser: *Fox v. Chief Constable of Gwent* [1985] 1 W.L.R. 1126. Nor can the person be convicted under this section if it is found that there has been an unlawful arrest: *Gull v. Scarborough* [1987] R.T.R. 261.

Definition of failure

Whether or not a person has failed to provide a specimen is a question **A3–14** of fact. What does failure mean? In the case of *R. v. Ferguson* [1970] 1 W.L.R. 1246, the court held that there was a failure once a person had been given an opportunity to do something and did not do it. Where a person refuses to wait until the breath-testing device arrives, this may amount to a failure. It would depend on the circumstances of the case and failure may be inferred from the defendant's conduct: *R. v. Miles* [1979] R.T.R. 509, C.A. In the case of *R. v. Wagner* [1970] R.T.R. 422, C.A., a motorist who pushed an officer and told him he would not wait for the device to arrive was held to have refused the test. The test of waiting is: what is reasonable in the circumstances?: *Ely v. Marle* [1977] R.T.R. 412. In this case 10 minutes was held not to be an unreasonable time. It would be a failure where a person refused to wait until 20 minutes had elapsed since alcohol was last consumed: *R. v. Auker-Howlett* [1974] R.T.R. 109; *Horton v. Twells, The Times*, December 9, 1983, D.C. Where a driver, on being required to give a specimen of breath, began eating mints – this was held to be a refusal as he refused to stop eating the mints: *R. v. Mackey* [1977] R.T.R. 146.

Failure: some examples

The above cases are more concerned with aspects of refusal. How else **A3–15** can the test be failed? The most common reason for failure is failure to follow the instructions given either deliberately or inadvertently. Failure can be due to insufficiency of breath. This may arise because a person has purposely made insufficient effort, or inadvertently failed to blow hard enough, or as a result of a physical or medical condition, he was unable to blow hard enough. This last point will be dealt with under "reasonable excuse." If the test is positive then it matters not what the quantity of breath was: *Corp v. Dalton* [1983] R.T.R. 160.

Where the driver fails to comply with the instructions and the test is negative, then it is a question of degree on the facts as to whether there has been a failure. In *R. v. Littell* [1981] 1 W.L.R. 1146, the defendant inflated the bag by several short puffs and produced a negative result and this was held to amount to a failure. It also does not matter that the failure is not deliberate: *Mallows v. Harris* [1979] Crim.L.R. 320, D.C.

Reasonable excuse

A3–16   Once it has been proved that the defendant has failed to provide a specimen of breath, then the prosecution must go on to prove that this was without reasonable excuse. The prosecution must negative any excuse advanced. This is a mixed issue of law and fact. First, it has to be determined as a matter of law whether the facts are capable of amounting to a reasonable excuse and secondly, as a matter of fact, whether in the circumstances it was a reasonable excuse: *Rowland v. Thorpe* [1970] R.T.R. 406; *R. v. Harling* [1970] R.T.R. 441. The burden of raising the issue is on the defendant, but once this is raised, it is incumbent on the prosecution to negative it and prove beyond reasonable doubt that the defendant had no reasonable excuse.

Reasonable excuse: definition

A3–17   What is a reasonable excuse? There is no definition of this phrase in the Act. In the case of *R. v. Lennard* [1973] 1 W.L.R. 483 it was held that a reasonable excuse must arise out of a physical or mental inability to provide a specimen or a substantial risk to health in its provision. It is important that the person understands what is required of him. This is relevant of course in the case of those who have difficulty in comprehending English. This is a double-edged sword, because if a person has managed to pass the driving test it will be assumed by the court that there is nothing wrong with that person's power of comprehension! See *Beck v. Sager* [1979] R.T.R. 475, a case on this aspect. If a person is in a hysterical or highly emotional state, it may be that they fail to understand what is required of them: *Spalding v. Laskaraina Paine* [1985] Crim.L.R. 673.

No reasonable excuse

A3–18   The following cases are examples of situations which have been held not to amount to reasonable excuse. It is no excuse that a person thought that he had not committed a moving traffic offence: *R. v. Downey* [1970] R.T.R. 257; nor that the person was not the driver at the time and the constable was not acting in good faith: *McGrath v. Vipas* [1984] R.T.R. 58. It is no excuse that the police officer had no power to make the requirement: *R. v. Reid* [1973] 1 W.L.R. 1283. The principle of ignorance of the law is also no excuse. As a general principle, unless there is evidence of a physical disability or other medical complaint, it will be no reasonable excuse that the person tried as hard as he could: *Dawes v. Taylor* [1986] R.T.R. 81, D.C.

Reasonable excuse: physical or mental inability

In order to raise the issue of reasonable excuse due to physical or mental inability, or a substantial risk to health, there must be cogent evidence before the court, usually in the form of a statement from an expert. It may be that the expert will have to give the evidence live if there is some dispute as to the condition or its possible effects. The disability must be serious: *Rowland v. Thorpe* [1970] R.T.R. 406. The person involved should inform the constable who requires the specimen, of any medical condition which may affect his ability to comply with the requirement: *Teape v. Godfrey* [1986] R.T.R 213, D.C. (Compare with the case of *Denneny v. Harding* [1986] R.T.R. 350.) (See also observations made about *Teape* in case of *D.P.P. v. Kinnersley* [1993] R.T.R. 105. See Chapter 8, §A8–07.) A bronchitic condition may be a reasonable excuse: *Hirst v. Wilson* [1970] 1 W.L.R. 47; *Burridge v. East* [1986] R.T.R. 328. A permanent tracheotomy may be a reasonable excuse: *R. v. Kelly* [1972] R.T.R. 447. In relation to this particular case it was said that this would not be a reasonable excuse under the old **section 8** (now **section 7**) specimens other than breath being available. Pain and confusion may be a reasonable excuse: *Scobie v. Graham* [1970] R.T.R. 358. It is not a reasonable excuse however, that a person is unable to breathe through the nose: *Woolman v. Lenton* [1985] Crim.L.R. 516, D.C.

A3–19

Powers of arrest and entry

The powers of arrest for drink/driving offences are contained in **sections 4** and **6** of the **R.T.A. 1988. Section 4(6) R.T.A. 1988** confers a power of arrest without warrant where a constable has reasonable cause to suspect that a person is or has been committing an offence under the section (driving or in charge whilst unfit). In addition, in order to effect the arrest, the constable may enter (if need be by force) any place where that person is or where the constable with reasonable cause suspects him to be.

Under **section 6(5)** the circumstances where a constable may arrest a person (although he is not obliged to do so) are:

(a) If as a result of a breath test he has reasonable cause to suspect that the proportion of alcohol in that person's breath or blood exceeds the prescribed limit;

A3–20

    (b) if that person has failed to provide a specimen of breath for a
        breath test when required to do so under the section and the
        constable has reasonable cause to suspect that he has alcohol in
        his body.

The power of arrest cannot be exercised when the person is at hospital
as a patient (see hospital procedure §A3–24). As indicated earlier, the
constable need not arrest the motorist and can exercise his discretion
whether to arrest or not. In practice however, the arrest is invariably
carried out.

Arrest

A3–21   The purpose of the arrest is to take the suspect to a police station so
that he can be detained in order for the evidential breath test procedure to be carried out. It also allows the police to detain that person
until such time as he is fit to drive and under the legal limit. One point
to remember is that a valid arrest is not a precondition to a conviction
under **section 5** of the Act: *Fox v. Chief Constable of Gwent* [1985] 1
W.L.R. 1126; *Anderton v. Royle* [1985] R.T.R. 91; (cases under **section 6
R.T.A. 1972**) nor under **section 7(6)** of the Act: *Bunyard v. Hayes* [1985]
R.T.R. 348 (case under **section 8(7) R.T.A. 1972**).

    When a motorist is arrested, he must be told the reason for the
arrest, unless it is impracticable to do so: *Christie v. Leachinsky* [1974]
A.C. 573. As long as the arrest is carried out in good faith, it is not
rendered invalid by the mere fact that the suspect may not have heard
or did not understand: *Wheatley v. Lodge* [1971] 1 W.L.R. 29.

Entry

A3–22   The constable has a power of entry in the following situations:

    (a) Under **section 4** as mentioned above;
    (b) where he has reasonable cause to suspect (where an accident
        owing to the presence of a motor vehicle on a road or other pub-
        lic place has taken place) that the accident involved injury to
        another person and he wishes to require a specimen of breath;
    (c) where he wishes to arrest a person under his powers of arrest
        under **section 6(5)** (see § A3–21).

Points to note are:

    (a) That there must have been an accident. It is not enough for the
        constable to have reasonable cause to believe that there has
        been an accident;
    (b) that there must have been injury to a person other than the
        suspect;
    (c) that the place entered by the constable must be the place where
        the person is or where the constable with reasonable cause sus-
        pects him to be;
    (d) the constable may use force to effect entry if needs be, but the

use of force must be justified and must be no more than is reasonable in the circumstances: *Swales v. Cox* [1981] Q.B. 849.

Other than the statutory powers of entry, a constable is entitled to   **A3–23** enter private property to require a breath test only with the occupier's consent. There are a number of points in relation to this. Police officers, like other members of the public who are on lawful business (*i.e.* postmen) have an implied licence to enter on private property. This implied licence stands until it is expressly revoked: *Snook v. Mannion* [1982] R.T.R. 321, D.C. An invitation to enter may be implied by conduct and need not be by words: *Faulkner v. Willetts* [1982] R.T.R. 159. The case of *R. v. Jones* [1970] R.T.R. 56 said that a driver cannot escape liability by driving off a road in order to avoid taking a breath test. In other words a constable may administer a test off the road provided he is not trespassing on the driver's property.

The case of *Fox* (*supra*) involved police officers who went to the defendant's home after he had been involved in an accident. There was no evidence from which the officers could form any suspicion of injury to another person. They entered the house as trespassers in order to require a specimen of breath. The defendant refused, was arrested and taken to the police station. At the station he provided specimens which were above the legal limit. He was charged with offences under **section 6** (now **s.5**) and **section 7(4)** (now **s.6(4)**). The case went to the House of Lords which said that proof of a **section 6** offence was no longer dependent on a valid arrest. However, it was established that it was not possible to secure a conviction under **section 7** in those circumstances, as the police officers were trespassers. This was under the principle in *Morris v. Beardmore* [1981] A.C. 446 (see the commentary in [1986] Crim.L.R. 60). It would seem therefore, that convictions under **sections 5, 6** and **8(7)** (now **ss.4, 5**, and **7(6)**) will stand even if the police have been trespassers on the defendant's property.

Hospital procedure

Where a suspect is at hospital as a patient, **section 9** provides that he   **A3–24** cannot be required to provide a breath test or specimen for analysis until the medical practitioner in immediate charge of his case has been notified of the proposal to make the requirement; and

  (a) if the requirement is then made, it shall be for the provision of a specimen at the hospital; but
  (b) if the medical practitioner objects on the ground that
       (i) the requirement, or
       (ii) the provision of a specimen, or
       (iii) in the case of a specimen of blood or urine the warning

required under **section 7(7) R.T.A. 1988** would be prejudicial to the proper care and treatment of the patient, then the requirement shall not be made.

The case of *D.P.P. v. Warren* [1993] R.T.R. 58, whilst laying down the procedure for requesting specimens at a police station under **sections 7(4)** and **8(2) R.T.A. 1988**, did not deal with hospital procedure. This was considered in the case of *Duffy v. D.P.P.* [1994] R.T.R. 241, 261. In this case, D who was involved in an accident, was taken to hospital. A constable obtained permission from a medical practitioner in charge of the case to give the statutory warning and obtain a specimen of blood. A registrar also confirmed that there was no medical reason why a specimen of blood should not be taken. The constable did not inform the driver however, that a specimen of breath could not be required as it could only be taken at a police station. In addition, the constable did not ask whether there was any reason why a specimen of blood could not or should not be taken from him by a medical practitioner. It was held by the Divisional Court, that due to the two omissions, the appropriate procedure had not been complied with.

By contrast, in the case of *R. v. Burton upon Trent Magistrates' Court, ex p. Woolley, The Times*, November 17, 1994, the Divisional Court observed, that the case of *Warren* was not a "hospital" case and that Lord Bridge did not specifically address the particular requirements that existed in such cases. It was also noted that the court in *Duffy*, saw itself as applying the general requirements identified by Lord Bridge to the example of hospital cases, without seeking to add of its own motion to the elements found within Lord Bridge's speech. Delivering the judgment, Buxton J. said that in hospital cases, there was no obligation for the constable to inform the driver why a specimen of breath could not be taken, but that at some stage during the process at the hospital, the constable had to ask whether there was any reason why a specimen of blood should not be taken. There was no obligation for the constable to ask specifically whether there was any reason based on **medical** grounds.

"In hospital as a patient"

A3–25   **Section 11(2) R.T.A. 1988** defines a hospital as an institution which provides medical or surgical treatment for in-patients or out-patients. This would be a question of fact. It would cover hospitals in the public and private sector. A person is deemed to be in a hospital if he is anywhere in the precincts of a hospital: *Att.-Gen.'s Reference (No. 1 of 1976)* [1977] 1 W.L.R. 646. Whether a person is at a hospital as a patient is a matter of fact. Naturally a person ceases to be a patient once he is discharged and in those circumstances the constable can exercise whatever powers are available to him: *Bourlet v. Porter* [1973] 1 W.L.R. 866. In addition the *Attorney General's Reference* also says that once a person's treatment for that particular visit is completed, he then ceases to be a patient even though there may be follow-up appointments. A case under the old law has held that a person in an ambulance on the way to a hospital is not a patient: *Hollingsworth v. Howard* [1974] R.T.R. 58. In *Askew v. D.P.P.* [1988] R.T.R. 303, the defendant who was involved in a road accident was taken to hospital and X-rayed. He was given painkillers and sent home. In fact he was suffering from a serious injury. Police officers investigating the accident administered the breath test just outside the hospital. He was later convicted of excess alcohol. He appealed on the basis that he was still a patient at the hospital at the time the test was taken. The appeal was dismissed.

"Medical practitioner in immediate charge of the case has been notified"

In practice, the medical practitioner in immediate charge of the case   **A3–26** will be the doctor on duty in casualty. The prosecution does not need to produce a list of practitioners to prove this aspect: *Jones v. Brazil* [1970] R.T.R. 449, D.C. The doctor does not have to be called, and unless it is challenged, the evidence of the police officer concerning the medical practitioner will generally be accepted. It must be shown that the medical practitioner was notified before any request is made. This is a question of fact, as is the question of whether he objected. It may be in certain circumstances that the defence may have to call the doctor to say that he was not notified/did not consent if the matter is in issue and the prosecution have called only the police officer to establish the fact. A police officer is able to give evidence in court to the effect that the medical practitioner was notified and made no objection: *Burn v. Kernohan* [1973] R.T.R. 82. The patient need not be absent when the notification is given: *Oxford v. Lowton* [1978] R.T.R. 237; nor need the constable notify the medical practitioner of his intention to give the **section 7(7)** warning: *Baker v. Foulkes* [1975] 1 W.L.R. 1551. If a requirement is to be made, then the choice of specimen will normally be made after medical advice.

The doctor may not consent to the requirement or the provision of a   **A3–27** specimen. On the other hand he may consent to the requirement, the provision of a specimen and the warning at the same time, although of course, he may wish to arrive at his decisions in stages, depending on the circumstances of the case: *Ratledge v. Oliver* [1974] R.T.R. 394. If consent is given to the taking of a particular specimen (*i.e.* blood) then a specimen of urine cannot be taken: *R. v. Green* [1970] R.T.R. 193. Once consent is given then the constable is free to carry out the requirement. If the patient fails, once required, to provide a specimen of breath, then an offence is committed, but the officer cannot arrest the patient whilst still at hospital. In fact it would appear from **section 7** that an officer may require a specimen of blood or urine without having gone through the screening breath test procedure. Once consent is given the normal procedure will be followed. Where the proforma is used and given to the doctor, the document may be used in court by the constable and the doctor as a memory refreshing document: *Taylor v. Armand* [1975] R.T.R. 225.

Penalties

A3–28   Failure to provide a roadside specimen is triable summarily only. It is punishable with a fine of level 3. It is endorsable and carries discretionary disqualification. The code is DR 70.

Approach

A3–29   The questions which follow may assist when dealing with cases under this chapter. The key is the taking of thorough, detailed and precise instructions or statements. It is all too easy to take certain matters for granted, which can have the effect of missing a legal point or of being insufficiently prepared for the conduct of the case. This can cause delay and add to expense.

Preliminary breath test

A3–30   (a) Are the grounds for the officer's suspicions or belief sufficiently made out? If not, then the resulting arrest will be unlawful. A lawful arrest is a precondition to an offence under **section 6**.
(b) Was the officer in uniform?
(c) What reason has been given for stopping the vehicle?
(d) Is there admissible evidence that an accident has occurred?
(e) Is there evidence of injury or any grounds for the officer to have reasonable cause to suspect that injury has been suffered by a third party?
(f) What were the circumstances of the requirement for a specimen of breath? Was a requirement made?
(g) Take full details of the breath test procedure. Was it properly carried out? Is there any question that the equipment was faulty, or that the test was negative? Did the defendant have a medical condition which could have affected his ability to give a specimen? If so, was this communicated to the officer? Has there been a 20-minute gap between the last drink and the test?

Failure to provide a specimen

A3–31   (a) What were the circumstances of the failure? Was it failure or refusal?
(b) What are the reasons advanced for the failure? Can it amount to a reasonable excuse?
(c) If the failure is due to a medical condition, then expert evidence must be called, detailing the problem and the effect this would have on a breath test.
(d) If the reason advanced is lack of comprehension, cover the point about the obtaining of a full driving licence!

(e) Remember that once reasonable excuse is raised, the pros- **A3–31**
ecution must negative this: *Dawes v. Taylor* [1986] R.T.R. 81,
D.C.

Arrest and entry

A3–32

(a) Check the circumstances to see if the arrest is lawful.
(b) Is there any evidence of mala fides?
(c) Was the reason for the arrest communicated to the defendant?
(d) Is there evidence of accident or injury to a third party (where appropriate)?
(e) In the case of entry, was the entry under the statutory provisions? If not, did the defendant consent to the officers entering or were they trespassers?

Hospital procedure

(a) Has the procedure been complied with? **A3–33**
(b) Is there any dispute as to what may have been said by the doctor? Is it necessary to require the doctor's attendance at court?
(c) If consent was given by the doctor for a specimen to be taken, which specimen was stated?

Chapter 4

DRIVING OR IN CHARGE WHILST UNFIT

Alcohol and its absorption

Before embarking on the law in respect of this offence, it seems useful   **A4–01**
to look at questions relating to the effect of alcohol, the rate of absorption and other matters which may contribute to the effect alcohol may
have on the driver. To a lesser extent, the area of drugs and their effects
will be considered, but it must be emphasised, that this is by way of
rough and ready guidance and for in-depth study reference should be
made to the numerous works which exist on the subjects. The summaries which follow represent a distillation of the data available and
an attempt to lay down some basic principles as simply as possible.

When a person drinks alcohol, it passes through to the stomach.
About 20 per cent. of it is absorbed straight away into the bloodstream
via the stomach wall. The rest moves on into the duodenum (small
intestine) via the pyloric valve, and from there it is absorbed into the
bloodstream. Once in the bloodstream, the alcohol circulates around
the body. The liver slowly breaks down the alcohol. In an average
man, this is broken down at a rate of about one unit an hour. A unit is
roughly the equivalent of a glass of wine, sherry or port, a pub measure of spirits, or half a pint of ordinary strength lager or bitter.

There are a number of factors which affect the absorption of alcohol   **A4–02**
into the blood. As two-thirds of the body's weight is water, then the
larger the person, the lower will be the final concentration of alcohol in
the blood. Fat absorbs less alcohol than water, so a fatter person will
reach a higher blood/alcohol level than a muscular person. It is generally accepted that women carry more fat than men, making them more
susceptible to reaching higher blood/alcohol levels.

A factor which affects the rate of absorption of alcohol, is whether or
not alcohol is taken on a full or empty stomach. If the stomach is empty
when alcohol is consumed, it will enter the bloodstream more quickly.
This is so in the case of most drinks. In the case of neat spirits however,
they may inhibit the pyloric valve from opening and thus absorption
becomes slower. If the stomach is full, then the alcohol will take longer
to be absorbed into the bloodstream.

Another factor influencing the absorption of alcohol into the blood,
is the kind of alcohol consumed. It seems that the higher the percentage of alcohol in the drink, the faster it is absorbed, except in the case of
neat spirits, as mentioned earlier. Additionally, it is generally accepted
that alcohol is absorbed more quickly in the case of "sparkling" drinks,

such as sparkling wines and spirits or wine with mixers. This does not apply to beer and cider which have a fairly slow rate of absorption.

Alcohol and its effects

A4–03   What effect does alcohol have on the drinker's functions? It is a common misconception that alcohol is a stimulant. It is not. It is a depressant. Why does it appear to be a stimulant? The reason advanced is that, when alcohol reaches the brain, it initially affects the "higher" centres of the brain which control inhibition and this has the effect of releasing the inhibition. Numerous studies have produced tables to show what effect a certain level of alcohol can have on a person and his behaviour. It must be borne in mind that these tables are only rough guides. There are many factors which affect how quickly a person will get drunk, including sex, age, weight, build, rate of drinking and drinking habits.

Blood/alcohol level	Effect
50 and under	No obvious effects. Feelings of well-being and relaxation.
80 (legal limit)	Feelings of well-being but reactions beginning to slow down. Statistics indicate one is twice as likely to have an accident.
100-140	Lack of coordination becoming more obvious. Poor perception. More emotional responses likely. Between four and six times more likely to have an accident.
150	Drunk. Speech slurred. Ten times more likely to have an accident.
200	Staggering gait. Speech incoherent. Poor recent memory. Twenty times more likely to have an accident.
300	Danger level. Could pass out.
400	Death a possibility, coma a probability.
450-500	Death probable.

Blood/alcohol levels

A4–04   Blood/alcohol levels are expressed in milligrammes of alcohol per 100 millilitres of blood. The legal limit for drink/driving is 80mg. This level will be achieved by a man drinking between about three-and-a-half to five units within an hour and in the case of women, depending on size, it can be as little as two-and-a-half units within the hour. The table represents the likely effects of alcohol on a person and his or her behaviour.

Drugs and their effects

The first matter for consideration is what constitutes a drug? The case   **A4–05**
of *Armstrong v. Clark* [1957] 2 Q.B. 391 said that a drug meant a medic-
ament or medicine—something given to cure, alleviate or assist an ail-
ing body. A more recent case, *Bradford v. Wilson* [1984] R.T.R. 116, held
that a substance taken into the body which was not drink and not tak-
en as food, which affected the control of the human body, was capable
of being a drug. **Section 11** of the **R.T.A. 1988** defines a drug as "any
intoxicant other than alcohol." Insulin is a drug: *Armstrong* (*supra*).
Toluene inhaled when glue-sniffing is a drug: *Bradford v. Wilson*
(*supra*).

Types of drug

For our purposes, drugs can be divided into two main categories: **A4–06**
legally-prescribed drugs and illegal drugs. Under prescribed drugs
the most common are:

   (a) Tranquillisers: these may have side effects of drowsiness, con-
       fusion, blurred vision and possible dizziness.
   (b) Sedatives (sleeping pills): similar effects to alcohol.
   (c) Anti-depressants: similar to tranquillisers.
   (d) Anti-histamines: drowsiness and other effects.
   (e) Drugs used for asthma, high blood pressure and slimming
       tablets: may also affect driving ability.

Illegal drugs such as cannabis, cocaine, heroin and amphetamines can
all seriously affect a person's driving ability. For the different effects,
recourse should be had to the specialist books on the subject.

Evidential problems

There are a number of problems that arise when considering a charge   **A4–07**
involving drugs, the question of proof being the most central! As cases
under this heading are less frequently brought, there is less experience
in the analysis of substances in the body fluids than there is with

alcohol. Although there is documentation on the effects of certain levels of drugs, this is generally in relation to the prescription of drugs. Before the observation can be made on the extent of the effect of the drug on the person, the drug itself must be identified, then measured, then a decision taken on whether it is the cause of the impairment.

In the case of *R. v. Ealing Magistrates' Court, ex p. Woodman*, [1994] R.T.R. 189, W, a diabetic, having taken his normal dose of insulin some 12 hours earlier, suffered a hypoglycaemic attack whilst driving and crashed his car. He was charged with driving whilst unfit through drugs. Expert evidence was called to say that W's very low blood-sugar level at the time of the accident could have been produced by an excessive injection of insulin or by insufficient food intake after normal dosage. W was convicted on the basis that his unfitness to drive was caused by insulin. Quashing the conviction, the Divisional Court noted that whilst a prosecution of a diabetic could be pursued under **section 4(1) R.T.A. 1988**, it would only be apt if it could be shown clearly that unfitness to drive as a result of hypoglycaemic attack was the direct consequence of an insulin injection. In this case, there was no evidence showing whether the insulin or part of it still remained in W's body at the time of the accident so as to produce the blood-sugar imbalance.

If there is a combination of drink and drugs in a person's system, it will be difficult to ascribe the impairment to one or the other unless the results are very clear cut. As drugs in general are more potent than alcohol, a person may be affected by only a small amount of drugs. This obviously makes analysis more difficult. In addition, there are many different drugs which are being prescribed on a daily basis.

In practice it would seem that a case would only be pursued if:

(a) There is no evidence of alcohol, so there would have to be another explanation for the impairment;

(b) if the driver admitted having taken some kind of drug or there was evidence of drugs found on the defendant or in his possession;

(c) if there were a fairly low alcohol reading but the evidence of impairment was very markedly over the above what would be expected for the alcohol reading.

It may be, however, that impairment occurs in a person who is suffering from withdrawal symptoms; this, it is thought, could not found a charge under the section if no drugs were in the system. However, there may be an argument for saying that a person was under the influence of drugs when exhibiting withdrawal symptoms since, if there had been no taking of drugs in the first place, there could be no withdrawal symptoms due to the lack of drugs.

The offences

A4–08   Under **section 4** of the **R.T.A. 1988** as amended by **section 4** of the

R.T.A. 1991, it is an offence to drive, attempt to drive, or be in charge of a mechanically propelled vehicle on a road or other public place when under the influence of drink or drugs. It is not unusual for a person to be charged with this offence and the offence under **section 5** (excess alcohol) as often the person will have been required to take an evidential breath test when enquiry is being made into impairment. If a plea is tendered to one of the charges it is not normal for the other charge to be pursued. Under **section 15** of the **R.T.O.A. 1988**, the evidence of analyses of blood or urine, or the statement and certificate of the breath test usually tendered in respect of **section 5**, are admissible under **section 4**.

Evidence of impairment

A person is unfit to drive if his ability to drive properly is for the time being impaired. The prosecution must prove not only the influence of drink or drugs but also that the proper control of the vehicle is impaired: *R. v. Hawkes* (1931) 22 Cr.App.R. 172. Impairment can be shown by adducing evidence of: **A4–09**

   (a) The manner of driving;
   (b) the driver's physical condition;
   (c) a specimen.

Often the case will be proved by a combination of some or all of these matters.

There must be evidence of drink or drugs and there must be a causal connection between the impairment and the drink or drugs. Observation of driving alone may not be sufficient. It is a matter of fact for the court to determine what inferences can be drawn from the evidence. It may be that a person driving too slowly rather than too fast is unfit to drive: *R. v. McCall* [1974] R.T.R. 216. In *R. v. Hunt* [1980] R.T.R. 29 C.A., the driver collided with a stationary vehicle. He was acquitted of driving with excess alcohol (hip flask defence) but nevertheless convicted of driving while unfit.

Powers of arrest

Under **section 4(6)** a constable may arrest a person without a warrant if he has reasonable cause to suspect that the person is or has been committing an offence under the section. Additionally, for the purpose of arresting the person under the section, the constable may enter (if need be by force) any place where the person is or where the constable with reasonable cause suspects him to be. Two points need to be made. Conviction of the offence does not depend any longer on the requirement of a lawful arrest. In addition, the power of arrest is no longer confined to a person who "is committing" an offence. The constable's suspicions can arise after the person has ceased driving or attempting to drive. **A4–10**

Medical examination

A4–11   If a person is arrested under this section, there will normally need to be a medical examination and, in certain cases, the taking of samples. The detained person should be informed by the police surgeon of what is proposed and his consent should be obtained. In the case of *R. v. Payne* [1963] 1 W.L.R. 637, the defendant was told before consenting to an examination that the results would not be given in evidence. It was said that those results should not be admitted. It may well be that a different approach might be taken today in the absence of mala fides. A person may not be examined against his will, but there is nothing to stop the doctor observing him and drawing certain conclusions from his condition and behaviour. Where a person was not told of his right to refuse such an examination, the results of the examination were excluded: *R. v. Urech* [1962] C.L.Y. 587. Before a specimen of blood can be taken under **section 7(3)(c) R.T.A. 1988**, a doctor must give his opinion that a possible cause of the defendant's condition may be drugs: *Cole v. D.P.P.* [1988] R.T.R. 224. It is not enough that the officer thinks that the possible cause may be drugs.

Evidence

A4–12   What is the status of witnesses and their observations?

It was said in the case of *R. v. Nowell* [1948] 1 All E.R. 794 that the evidence of a police doctor should be regarded as "that of a professional man giving independent expert evidence with no other desire than to assist the court." In *R. v. Lanfear* [1968] 2 Q.B. 77 it was said that the court should not be directed that his evidence ought not, therefore, to be accepted in the absence of reasons for rejecting them. That would give a false impression of the weight to be attached to it. Invariably it will be the case that a doctor will not examine a person until some time after he has been driving. Consequently, the evidence will relate to the time of examination and not to the time of driving. However, the courts are reluctant to overlook such evidence unless the question is raised by the defence, usually establishing grounds to cast doubt on the examination. In the case of *Dryden v. Johnson* [1961] Crim.L.R. 551, it was held that a charge should not have been dismissed just because the doctor's evidence related to half an hour after the arrest and not the time of arrest.

A non-expert witness can give evidence as to whether the driver had been drinking but the question of fitness is one for the court: *R. v. Davies (No. 2)* [1962] 1 W.L.R. 1111. The observations of an experienced driver were allowed in the case of *R. v. Neal* [1962] Crim.L.R. 698, the rationale being that the court was entitled to convict on his evidence having disregarded the evidence of opinion of fitness to drive!

The section 4(3) defence

There are defences available to a charge under this section by virtue of **A4–13** **section 4(3) R.T.A. 1988** and also **section 15(3) R.T.O.A. 1988**. The defence under **section 4(3)** relates to a person who is in charge of a motor vehicle. A person under this subsection is deemed not to have been in charge of a motor vehicle if he proves that, at the material time, the circumstances were such that there was no likelihood of his driving so long as he remained unfit to drive through drink or drugs. In determining whether there was such a likelihood, the court may disregard any injury to him and any damage to the vehicle: **section 4(4)**. The burden of proof is on the defendant on the balance of probabilities: *Morton v. Confer* [1963] 1 W.L.R. 763; *R. v. Rivers* [1974] R.T.R. 31.

The court will have to look at all the circumstances as they will no doubt operate on the prima facie presumption that the defendant was in charge. It will normally be the case that evidence in the form of the evidential breath test or a blood test will be produced by the prosecution. It means therefore that expert evidence will normally be required to show that the person would cease to be unfit within a certain period of time. It may be that it is obvious where, for instance, the person says that there was no likelihood of his driving for two days. It must be borne in mind also that, in cases where the result of a blood test is relied on by the prosecution, there may be an appreciable time lapse between the time of the alleged offence and the time of the medical examination and the taking of the specimen.

The section 15(3) defence

Under **section 15(3) R.T.O.A. 1988**, it is assumed that the proportion of **A4–14** alcohol in the defendant's breath, blood or urine at the time of the alleged offence was not less than the specimen. Where, however, in a case under this section, the defendant is alleged to have been unfit through drink, the assumption shall not be made if the defendant proves:

"(a) that he consumed alcohol after he had ceased to drive, attempt to drive or be in charge of a motor vehicle on a road or other public place and before he had provided the specimen; and

(b) that had he not done so the proportion of alcohol in his breath, blood or urine would not have been such as to impair his ability to drive properly."

The burden is on the defendant to raise and prove the matter on the balance of probabilities. It must be shown therefore:

(a) That drink has been consumed by the defendant since driving, attempting to drive or being in charge;

(b) that the quantity of drink must be accurately ascertainable;

(c) that the drink taken subsequently was of such an amount that the drink consumed before driving would not have been sufficient to impair his ability to drive properly.

Again it will be necessary in most cases to call expert evidence to show the back calculation and evidence as to the effect of the drink taken: *Dawson v. Lunn* [1986] R.T.R. 234.

Other defences

A4–15 Apart from the statutory defences, the prosecution case can be challenged and the prosecution put to proof on a number of matters depending on the facts of the case. Such areas include:

(a) That the person was not in charge.

This would probably involve the calling of evidence, for instance, of the person in whose charge the defendant put the vehicle (see Chapter 2);

(b) That the defendant was not unfit.

Here the situation is more difficult. It involves challenging the evidence that is put before the court. If, for instance, there is evidence of manner of driving plus evidence of some alcohol or drugs, the form of challenge could be twofold. There could be independent evidence of an eyewitness to contradict the officer's evidence, and secondly, evidence of alcohol or drugs and their effects. If the prosecution rely on the findings of the police doctor then, were the defendant to have had the presence of mind to be examined immediately by an independent doctor, contradictory evidence could be presented;

(c) That the impairment was not through drink or drugs.

Again this would be a difficult area requiring the consideration of an expert. It may be that a person's driving has been impaired due to sudden illness although some alcohol may have been consumed. If it could be shown that the illness was the cause of the impairment and not the alcohol or drugs, then the defendant would be entitled to an acquittal.

Penalties

A4–16 The offences are triable summarily only. For driving or attempting to drive whilst unfit the fine is level 5 and/or six months' imprisonment. Disqualification is obligatory, as is endorsement, unless there are special reasons found for not so doing. See Chapter 14 on penalties for the periods of disqualification and penalty points to be endorsed if disqualification is not ordered. See Chapter 16 on special reasons for the circumstances where disqualification need not be ordered. The Endorsement code is DR 20 for drink and DR 80 for drugs. **Section 24**

R.T.O.A. 1988 as substituted by **section 24 R.T.A. 1991** provides that **section 4(2)** "being in charge" is an alternative verdict to **section 4(1)** "driving or attempting to drive" whilst unfit.

The offence of being in charge carries a level 4 fine and/or three months' imprisonment. The offence is endorsable unless special reasons for not endorsing are found. Disqualification is discretionary. The code is DR 50 for drink and DR 90 for drugs.

Approach

(a) Check the charge. Which offence is alleged? Does the evidence support the charge?   **A4–17**

(b) If the case is not to be contested are there special reasons which can be advanced for not disqualifying or endorsing? (See Chapter 16 on special reasons for approach.) What points can be put forward in mitigation? If it is a case of being "in charge" prepare argument for why the court should exercise its discretion in the defendant's favour and not disqualify.

(c) If the case is to be defended, on what basis? Identify the possible defences.

(d) Is there a challenge to the prosecution case as to the ingredients to be proved? If so, is there independent evidence available, or is expert evidence required?

(e) Is the defence a statutory one? If so, again the question of independent evidence or expert evidence should be considered.

(f) If there is a medical/technical aspect to the defence, instruct an expert immediately for a preliminary opinion. Expert evidence is not always favourable and the approach or indeed the plea may be affected by the expert's findings.

(g) Was the defendant on medication? If so what and in what doses?

(h) Was the defendant suffering from any illness which could explain the manner of driving?

(i) Take statements from any witnesses as soon as possible. If the defence is under **section 15(3)** then accuracy and consistency as to consumption are vital.

(j) Where relevant, have the defendant's specimen of blood analysed.

(k) If the expert evidence can be agreed by both prosecution and defence then much time, inconvenience and money will be saved.

Riding a cycle whilst unfit

Section 30(1) R.T.A. 1988 makes it an offence for a person to ride a   **A4–18**

bicycle, tricycle or cycle having four or more wheels, not being a motor vehicle on a road (which includes a bridleway and footpaths or foot-ways forming part of a road) or other public place whilst being unfit to ride through drink or drugs.

"Unfit to ride" means being under the influence of drink or drugs to such an extent as to be incapable of having proper control.

There is no specific power of arrest under the statute nor does the police officer have power to request a specimen. *Quaere*, the admissibility of any specimen obtained by a police officer, knowing that he does not have the power to request a specimen from the cyclist. There is a power of arrest under **section 25 P.A.C.E. 1984** afforded to a police constable if he has reasonable grounds for believing that the arrest is necessary in order to prevent the cyclist from causing physical injury to himself or others.

The offence is punishable with a level 3 fine.

Chapter 5

DRIVING OR IN CHARGE ABOVE THE PRESCRIBED LIMIT

The offence: section 5 of the Road Traffic Act 1988

Under **section 5** it is an offence if a person drives, attempts to drive or
is in charge of a motor vehicle on a road or other public place after
consuming so much alcohol that the proportion of it in his breath,
blood or urine exceeds the prescribed limit. The prescribed limit is laid
down in **section 11(2)** of the **R.T.A. 1988**. The limit is:

    A5–01

   (a) 35 microgrammes of alcohol in 100 millilitres of breath;
   (b) 80 milligrammes of alcohol in 100 millilitres of blood; or
   (c) 107 milligrammes of alcohol in 100 millilitres of urine.

That means prosecutions can follow with readings of 36, 81 and 108
respectively. However, in the Home Office Circular 46/83, it is said
that the police will not proceed against those with a result less than 40.
This allowance is comparable with the allowance currently subtracted
from specimens analysed in the laboratory. In practice this circular is
followed by police forces.

    The prosecution need only prove that the alcohol content exceeded
the limit, so that where there is a difference in readings but the experts
agree that the reading could not be below the prescribed limit then a
conviction will be upheld: *Gordon v. Thorpe* [1986] R.T.R. 358.

    A5–02

    In *Oswald v. D.P.P.* [1989] R.T.R. 360, D.C., it was held that although
it might be the practice of analysis to deduct 6 milligrammes from a
particular result in order to allow for a margin of error which might
otherwise occur, that approach was not necessarily appropriate when
a whole range of results was produced by analysis. (The prosecution
analyses all exceeded 86 milligrammes of alcohol in blood, the average
being 88.2, and the defence analyses all exceeding 85, the average
being 86.2.)

    Section 15(2) of the **R.T.O.A. 1988** provides that evidence of the pro-
portion of alcohol or any drug in a specimen of breath, blood or urine
provided by the accused shall, in all cases, be taken into account and,
subject to the statutory defence of post driving consumption, it shall
be assumed that the proportion of alcohol at the time of the alleged
offence was not less than the specimen. This section has the effect of
passing the burden on to the defendant to prove that he was not above
the limit when driving: *Patterson v. Charlton District Council* [1986]

R.T.R. 18. This aspect will be covered when the question of defences is considered.

"Consuming" is not limited to drinking. Entry into the body other than by mouth is included: *D.P.P. v. Johnson* [1995] R.T.R. 9.

Aiding and abetting the offence

A5–03 As noted in Chapter 2, a driving instructor can be convicted of aiding and abetting a driver. But liability does not just lie with driving instructors or those acting in a supervisory capacity.

In the case of *D.P.P. v. Anderson* [1990] R.T.R. 269, the question of aiding, abetting, counselling or procuring driving with excess alcohol was considered. In that case, the defendant, a pillion passenger on a motor cycle with an engine capacity of 50cc. was charged with contravening **section 44(1)** of the **Magistrates' Courts Act 1980,** in that he aided and abetted, counselled or procured the motor cyclist, a provisional licence holder aged 16, to drive with excess alcohol. At the hearing the defendant did not appear, but was represented by his solicitor who admitted that the driver had been convicted of excess alcohol. Unchallenged evidence was adduced by the prosecution of an admission by the defendant that he knew that the driver had consumed half a bottle of wine, half a bottle of cider and a mixed spirit drink and a further admission that it was irresponsible of him (the defendant) to encourage the driving, but he had had a lot to drink and never thought about telling the motorcyclist not to drive. The justices took the view that the case was not made out as the defendant was not acting in a supervisory role and was merely a passenger. They did not consider the wider aspect of whether the aider and abetter knew or was reckless whether the principal had consumed excessive alcohol.

A5–04 Allowing the appeal by the prosecution, the Divisional Court held, that in order to establish the defendant had committed the offence as charged, the prosecution had to prove that the principal offender had committed the offence, that the defendant was aware, or was reckless whether, the principal offender had consumed excessive alcohol and that the defendant had aided, abetted, counselled or procured the principal to commit the offence. On the unchallenged evidence before the justices, they were bound to find the defendant guilty. The case was remitted with a direction to convict.

In *Blakely v. D.P.P.* [1991] R.T.R. 405, the two defendants laced the drink of one Mr Taft. They did so in the hope that he would not drive home to see his wife. At the end of the evening Taft went to the lavatory and left the hotel without speaking to the defendants. He was arrested driving on his way home. The defendants were convicted at the magistrates' court and their appeal to the Crown Court was dismissed. The defence case was that they did not intend Taft to drive; on the contrary they intended that he should not drive. The offence of procuring could only be committed by someone who knowingly sets out to cause another to commit an offence; shutting one's eyes to the obvious risk did not suffice.

The prosecution contention was that the offence was committed if the defendants deliberately caused Taft to consume excess alcohol or were reckless as to whether the amount consumed by him was over the prescribed limit and were reckless as to whether he would then drive.

The questions for the opinion of the Divisional Court were: **A5–05**

(i) Whether the offence of procuring could be committed by someone who brought it about, not intending that the offence should be committed but reckless as to whether it be committed or not; and

(ii) if so, whether the meaning of recklessness in such a case was that given to it by Lord Diplock in *R. v. Lawrence* [1982] A.C. 510.

The convictions were quashed, the court having reviewed the authorities with particular reference to the *Att.-Gen.'s Reference (No. 1 of 1975)* [1975] Q.B. 773 where it was strongly suggested in the judgment of Widgery C.J. that in order to procure, it is necessary to prove that the accused intended to bring about the principal offence without any reference to the question of recklessness. The answers to the questions were as follows:

(i) The use of the word recklessness is best avoided when considering the *mens rea* of someone accused with procuring the commission of a substantive offence;

(ii) in so far as the correct approach to that *mens rea* accords with the concept of recklessness, no.

In a New Zealand case, it was decided that where an owner of a vehicle is aware of all the circumstances and in particular how much alcohol the driver had consumed, he could be convicted of aiding and abetting an excess alcohol offence although he did not know the precise breath or blood alcohol concentration: *Cooper v. Ministry of Transport* [1991] 2 N.Z.L.R. 693.

Breath specimens: the approved device

In the course of an investigation into whether a person has committed **A5–06** an offence under **section 4** or **5** of the **1988 Act** a constable, subject to certain exceptions, may require the person to provide two evidential specimens of breath on a device of a type approved by the Secretary of State. Under this section the two devices which have been approved are the Camic Breath Analyser and the Lion Intoximeter 3000. They were approved by the Home Secretary in the **Breath Analysis Devices (Approval) Order 1983**. Either device can be used in England and Wales, but in practice the Lion Intoximeter is used throughout most of England. The Camic is used in some parts of England, largely confined to the North, and in Scotland. Both devices are automatic measuring devices and measure alcohol by the infra-red absorption of its vapour, but they do this in slightly different ways. As the Lion Intoximeter is the more common device, attention will be focused on this machine and its function with occasional reference to the Camic.

The Lion Intoximeter: the background to its introduction

A5–07   The prescribed limit offence dates back to the **Road Safety Act 1967**. The limit under the Act was 80 milligrammes of alcohol in 100 milli-litres of blood, or 107 milligrammes of alcohol in 100 millilitres of urine. Blood was the usual specimen provided. This, of course, involves calling out doctors to take the blood, a procedure which entails cost and delay. A strong influence in the decision to impose a prescribed limit for drink/driving was the Grand Rapids study, which was published in 1964 in the USA. This study found that alcohol/ blood levels in excess of 80 milligrammes substantially increased the risk of being involved in an accident. The initial impact of the legis-lation was fairly dramatic, but a decade later the effects were wearing off. A Departmental Committee was set up in 1974 under Mr Blenner-hassett Q.C. to review the laws relating to drinking and driving. Infor-mation about the practices abroad was obtained, and it was found that other countries were using breath samples as being accurate and more cost effective. The Committee, in its report on "Drinking and Driving" in 1976, recommended the introduction of substantive breath testing devices to be used countrywide. The result of this recommendation was that a group of scientists formed into the Blennerhassett Group in order to evaluate a number of machines that were submitted to them for testing. They selected three machines for use in field trials conduc-ted at police stations between December 1977 and June 1978. Arrested drivers who had already supplied the necessary specimen of blood or urine were invited to supply a specimen of breath which was com-pared with the blood or urine analysis. Further trials were carried out in 1981 and 1982 and as a result, approval was given to the Camic and the Lion Intoximeter. When the Lion Intoximeter was approved there was much disquiet as to its accuracy and reliability with ex-employees of Lion casting doubt on its reliability. This aspect will be covered in the section dealing with assumptions about the reliability of the device.

The Lion Intoximeter: background data

A5–08   The Lion Intoximeter uses infra-red analysis to determine the concen-tration of alcohol in expired breath, as does the Camic. This breath is deep lung breath. There has to be a minimum volume of breath which has been set at 1.5 litres. The subject has to breathe continuously and light up a series of bars on the display panel. If the subject does not manage to light up at least two or three bars or if he sucks in air or stops blowing, then the machine will abort. Three minutes are allowed to supply a breath sample. Up to five attempts can be made before the instrument will register "No sample." Both the Lion and the Camic have a device to check calibration. Air is pumped through an external simulator which contains an alcohol solution of a given strength. The solution is heated by the simulator and kept at a level of 34°C, so that, when the air is pumped through, the vapour generated will contain 35 microgrammes per 100 millilitres of alcohol vapour. This standard vapour is used to check the calibration of the instrument both before and after analysis of the subject's samples. The readings of the calibration check should be between 32 and 37 on the Intoximeter and between 32 and 38 on the Camic. It is claimed by the manufacturers of the Intoximeter that, if the readings are outside those limits, then the machine will automatically close down and not accept breath samples for analysis. The two machines are said to compensate automatically for the presence of acetone and this is shown on the printout in the case of the Intoximeter. Both machines operate to Greenwich Mean Time.

The Lion Intoximeter: operating instructions

The instructions for the breath test programme on the Intoximeter are laid out in 18 stages: **A5–09**

(1) Press "start" button;
(2) Enter operator's name;
(3) Enter operator's code (N.B. only trained and approved operators can use the machine, in practice usually the duty sergeant at the police station);
(4) Enter the subject's name;
(5) Enter the subject's date of birth (from this point until the final printout the keyboard is de-activated from the instrument);
(6) Stand-by. If less than 30 minutes have elapsed since the instrument was last used this step will be by-passed;
(7) Purge and blank cycle. Fresh air is pumped through the sampling system and air flow lines to purge out any residual alcohol. When the machine is satisfied that the system is free of alcohol it carries out a blank check. This is signified by "BLK." This must show a reading of 0. See appendices for examples of the printout;
(8) First calibration check. Air is now pumped through the external simulator and a sample of the standard alcohol vapour generated is analysed. The reading will be shown and, as mentioned earlier, must be between 32–37. The programme can proceed no further if the reading is outside these figures;
(9) Purge and blank cycle. Step 7 is repeated to clear the alcohol vapour from the breath sampling system and flow lines;
(10) Attach mouthpiece. A new mouthpiece is fitted for each test, then the subject should be told what to do to complete the test procedure satisfactorily;

(11) Subject's first breath sample. Once the purge and blank cycle has been carried out satisfactorily the display will show "Blow until star." The subject has three minutes in which to provide a sample. He must be told to take a deep breath and blow through the mouthpiece until told to stop. He must blow hard enough and long enough to cause a series of bars to illuminate and for the flashing star to illuminate. If the subject does not blow hard enough or sucks back before the star flashes then the display will show "Aborted." The machine will carry out a purge and blank cycle and, if this happens within the three minutes the subject can try again. If three minutes elapse before the star flashes, then the printout will show "No Sample";

(12) Purge and blank cycle. If the subject has provided a satisfactory breath sample, a further purge and blank cycle will be carried out to clear the alcohol from the infra-red chamber and air flow lines;

(13) Subject's second breath sample;

(14) Purge and blank cycle. The mouthpiece will be removed and discarded. The same mouthpiece must not be used again;

(15) Second calibration check. The result of this calibration is displayed and printed and, if it is outside the acceptable tolerance band, the value will be accompanied by the word "High" or "Low" as appropriate;

(16) Printout. As soon as the second standard value is displayed, the printer is activated to produce the pre-defined number of test record copies. If the second calibration check is outside the specified range this will be shown on the printout, alongside the actual result, and the time will be omitted from this line to indicate an invalid test programme;

(17) Tear off, sign and fix test records;

(18) Postscript. Instructions to check the instrument.

The Lion Intoximeter: assumptions regarding the reliability of the device

A5–10 When the Lion Intoximeter first came into use there were many challenges mounted on the basis that the machine was unreliable. There have been various criticisms of the device by scientists and even ex-employees of Lion Laboratories. In 1984, as a result of two ex-employees of Lion Laboratories releasing certain confidential documents to the *Daily Express*, Lion Laboratories initially obtained an injunction against the *Daily Express* preventing publication. This injunction was subsequently lifted and the documents printed. The documents showed that there had been problems with the machines and that the machines were certified in 1982 as complying with Home Office requirements by the head of the calibration laboratory when in fact they were imperfectly calibrated. (See: *Lion Laboratories v. Evans* [1985] Q.B. 526.) Despite these revelations however, there is a presumption that the machine is in order unless the defence calls evidence to rebut the presumption in order to challenge the reliability of the device at the material time: *R. v. Skegness Magistrates' Court, ex p. Cardy* [1985] R.T.R. 49; *Anderton v. Waring* [1986] R.T.R. 74.

There is no right to discovery of documents with a view to searching for material which might support a submission that the device in question was defective at the relevant time. Witness summonses have been quashed in cases where they were issued with a view to compelling the production of documents relating to the machine in order to support a challenge to the reliability of the device: *R. v. Coventry Magistrates' Court, ex p. Perks* [1985] R.T.R. 74.

Numerous articles have been written by scientists to question the reliability of various aspects of the machine (see in particular work by Professor Marks of Surrey University, *e.g.* in the *Law Society Gazette* 1984, p. 86). There is nothing to stop a challenge being mounted as to the reliability of the particular device used to carry out the defendant's breath test, but in practice it is very difficult to raise such a challenge without access for instance to the maintenance log or other documents. These aspects will be considered in detail in the following chapter.

Breath specimens: the power to require specimens

Under **section 7** of the **R.T.A. 1988**, in the course of an investigation **A5–11** into whether a person has committed an offence under **section 4** or **5** of the Act a constable may, subject to certain exceptions, require him to provide two specimens of breath for analysis on an approved device or to provide a specimen of blood or urine for a laboratory test. The specimens of blood and urine will be dealt with in the following paragraphs. Investigation means "an enquiry into": *Graham v. Albert* [1985] R.T.R. 352, D.C. There are a number of points to note about this section:

(a) The defendant does not need to be arrested, therefore an unlawful arrest will not invalidate any results in proceedings under **sections 4** and **5**. However, it must be remembered that there is a discretion to exclude the evidence under **section 78 P.A.C.E. 1984**. In the case of *Hawes v. D.P.P.* [1993] R.T.R. 116, the defendant drove his car in a car park of a public house which was being used as a car park for officials at a nearby function. He was arrested and charged with driving in a public place whilst unfit, and failing to provide specimens of breath. The prosecution withdrew the first charge taking the view that the car park was not a public place at the material time. On appeal against conviction for the **section 7** offence on the basis that the defendant had not committed an offence under **section 4** or **5**, it was held, dismissing the appeal, that the court was merely concerned with whether or not there was a bona fide investigation into the question of whether the offence had been commmitted under **sections 4** or **5**.

A5–12   (b) The specimen required at the police station will be breath unless one of three situations applies: **section 7(3)**. These are:

        (i) If the constable making the requirement has reasonable cause to believe that for medical reasons a specimen of breath cannot be provided or should not be required, or

       (ii) at the time the requirement is made a device, or a reliable device of the type approved is not available at the police station, or it is then for any other reason not practicable to use such a device there, or

     (iii) the suspected offence is one under section 4 of the Act and the constable making the requirement has been advised by a medical practitioner that the condition of the person required to provide the specimen might be due to some drug.

   (c) Specimens of breath for analysis can be obtained only at a police station.

   (d) Specimens of blood or urine for analysis can be obtained only at a police station or a hospital. (See Chapter 3, § A3–24, Hospital Procedure.)

   (e) Although the operation of the breath test device is limited to a number of trained operators, there is nothing in the Act which appears to restrict the requirement being made only by those operators, so it would appear to be in order if the arresting officer for example made the requirement.

Specimens of breath

A5–13   Under **section 8**, of the two specimens of breath provided by the defendant, the specimen with the lower reading shall be used and the other specimen will be disregarded. If both readings are the same, then of course either reading is admissible: *Clarke v. Hegarty, The Times*, May 19, 1986. It means that if one reading is over 35 but the other is below 35, then the defendant will not be proceeded against. If the defendant were to supply one specimen only, he cannot be convicted on it: *Cracknell v. Willis* [1988] A.C. 450, overruling *Duddy v. Gallagher* [1985] R.T.R. 401, D.C. Twenty minutes must have elapsed since the suspect last consumed alcohol before the breath test can be administered.

Where a police officer wrongly requests a third specimen of breath, only evidence of the first two specimens are admissible and the higher reading of the first two readings will be disregarded: *Howard v. Hallett* [1984] R.T.R. 353; *Chief Constable of Avon and Somerset v. Creech* [1986] R.T.R. 87; *Wakely v. Hyams* [1987] R.T.R. 49.

In *Durdan v. Chief Officer Metropolitan Police*, July 28, 1994 (unreported) following a roadside breath test, the appellant was taken to the police station. There, the breath test procedure was carried out by a Police Sergeant. During the procedure, the appellant complained of stomach pains and said that he had ulcers. Each time he was asked a question he complained that he felt ill. He was asked twice to provide a specimen of breath and made no reply on each occasion. The officer taking the view that there was reasonable cause to believe that for medical reasons a specimen of breath could not be given, then asked for a specimen of blood. The appellant made no reply to this request.

A doctor was called who confirmed that the appellant was suffering from stomach ulcers, but that his pain was not continuous and that a specimen of breath could be obtained in between spasms. The doctor advised the appellant that the breath test only lasted 10 seconds and that he could give a specimen of breath in the gap between the pain period. The appellant was asked to provide a specimen of breath and he said he could not. He was charged.

The question was whether it was lawful to request a further specimen of breath, having requested one previously and follow that request by a request for a specimen of blood. The second question was if the second request for breath was lawful, should a request for blood not have followed it?

Dismissing the appeal, the Divisional Court could find nothing in the statutory requirements which precluded the sergeant from asking on a second occasion for a specimen of breath. They found therefore that it was lawful for the officer to demand a further specimen of breath for analysis. The second question before the court was held to be irrelevant in the light of their Lordships' findings.

Specimens of blood or urine: general provisions

A person may be required to provide a specimen of blood or urine at a   **A5–14** police station if one of the situations outlined in § A5–11 above apply. He may be asked to provide an alternative specimen even though he may already have provided two specimens of breath (**section 7(3)**). Under **section 7(4)**, the question whether the specimen shall be blood or urine falls to be decided by the constable making the requirement. If a medical practitioner is of the opinion that for medical reasons a specimen of blood cannot or should not be taken, the specimen shall be a specimen of urine. Invariably, the practice has been that a specimen of blood will be requested, but the constable making the requirement must now tell the motorist about the choice of specimen before he makes any decision on which specimen to require: *D.P.P. v. Gordon, D.P.P. v. Griggs* [1990] R.T.R. 71. Decisions concerning the obligation of the constable to inform the motorist of the choice of specimen prior to this case had concerned the motorist's option to replace a breath test showing a reading of no higher than 50 microgrammes per 100 milli-litres of breath. (See §§ A5–22 *et seq.*, on the option.)

The procedure to be followed under **section 7(4)** has been laid down by the House of Lords in the case of *D.P.P. v. Warren* [1993] A.C. 319, H.L. The constable must tell the driver why breath specimens cannot be taken or used, tell him in those circumstances that he is required to give a specimen of blood or urine but that it is for the constable to decide which, warn him that failure to provide a specimen may render him liable to prosecution, and then, if the constable decided he required blood, ask him if there are any reasons why a specimen can-not or should not be taken from him by a doctor. Provided the driver has an opportunity to raise any objection he might have to give blood on medical grounds or for any other reason which might afford "a reasonable excuse," there was nothing in the language of the statute which would justify a procedural requirement that the driver be invited to express his own preference for giving blood or urine.

In *Edge v. D.P.P.* [1993] R.T.R. 146, as a result of a reliable device not being available, the defendant was required to provide a specimen of blood or urine. He was given the warning. He was asked, "Will you provide such a specimen?" He agreed. The constable said, "I have decided that it should be a specimen of blood." This was provided. Allowing the appeal, it was held that he should have been asked if there were any reasons why a specimen of blood could not or should not be taken by a doctor.

In *Meade v. D.P.P.* [1993] R.T.R. 151, the defendant was asked by the constable if he would supply a specimen of blood to a doctor. The warning was given and he was told the decision as to blood or urine would be the officer's. The doctor asked if he was agreeable to supply-ing blood and a sample was taken. The Divisional Court, quashing the conviction, held that the words spoken by the officer and the doctor did not give the defendant the right to object to the giving of blood for medical reasons.

It is apparent now from the cases that have come before the Div-isional Court since the decision in *Warren*, that failure to comply with the procedure as set out by Lord Bridge could be fatal to a conviction: *Williams v. D.P.P.; D.P.P. v. Nesbitt* [1994] R.T.R. 241; *Whelan v. D.P.P. July 28, 1994* (unreported).

Blood or urine: reasonable cause to believe a specimen of breath cannot be provided

A5–15   As indicated in § A5–12, one of the situations in which the constable may require an alternative specimen is if he has reasonable cause to believe that for medical reasons a specimen of breath cannot be pro-vided or should not be required. The constable, not being an expert, has to make a decision on the information before him, usually assertions by the motorist, and make a value judgment. He has to decide whether any problem raised is capable of being a condition which gives him reasonable cause to believe that a specimen of breath should not be provided or required see: *Dempsey v. Catton* [1986] R.T.R. 194, D.C. (agoraphobia) and *Horrocks v. Binns* (Note) [1986] R.T.R. 202 (cuts to head and bruises) on this aspect. Intoxication has been held to be a medical reason within **section 7(3)(a)**: *Young v. D.P.P.* [1992] R.T.R. 388. Taking tablets was held to be capable of being a medical reason: *Wade v. D.P.P., The Times*, February 14, 1995. In *Webb v. D.P.P.* [1992] R.T.R. 299, the defendant indicated that she did not suffer from any medical problem and was blowing as hard as she could, but the sergeant took the view that there was reasonable cause to believe that for medical reasons a specimen of breath could not be provided because the defendant was of slight build, in shock and in a distressed condition. It was argued on the defendant's behalf that this could not amount to a medical reason and thus the specimen of blood provided was inadmissible. The Divisional Court dismissed the appeal, saying that "reasonable cause" was a matter of fact to be objectively determined by the justices, that the sergeant was to be treated as a layman on medical matters, and the medical reasons put before him related to the physical or mental capacity of the defendant to provide a breath specimen and that the matters noted by the sergeant were capable of amounting to a medical condition within **section 7(3)(a)**. *Quaere*, would this amount to reasonable excuse for failure to provide a specimen?

If the sergeant does have reasonable cause to believe that for a medical reason a specimen of breath should not be required or provided he should not require it: *Woolman v. Lenton* [1985] Crim.L.R. 516, D.C.

Relating this to the decision in *Gordon and Griggs*, it would appear **A5–16** now that the constable may have to go through similar considerations when deciding whether the alternative specimen should be blood or urine. Previously, apart from the opinion of a medical practitioner that for medical reasons a specimen cannot or should not be taken, the constable was not under a duty to evaluate the circumstances when making his decision: *Grix v. Chief Constable of Kent* [1987] R.T.R. 193. In *Davis v. D.P.P.* [1988] Crim.L.R. 249, D.C., it was held that what is or is not "reasonable cause to believe" is a matter of fact to be determined by the justices and does not depend on the officer's actual belief. See also *White v. Proudlock* [1988] R.T.R. 163, D.C. In other words, whether on the facts known to the police officer he had reasonable cause to believe that for medical reasons a specimen of breath could not be provided or should not be required. The issue is one for the court: *Davies v. D.P.P.* [1989] R.T.R. 391.

Although there is no legal obligation on the motorist to inform the police about any medical condition suffered, failure to do so may be something the justices will take into account in any evidence or argument advanced by the defendant or on his behalf.

Blood or urine: reliable device not available

Under **section 7(3)(b)** the alternative specimens may be required **A5–17** when, at the time the requirement is made, a device or reliable device is not available at the police station or it is for any other reason not practicable to use such a device there. Here again the constable has to make an essentially subjective decision, as only the trained operator is expert in the functioning of the device. The test will be of the constable's reasonable belief: *Thompson v. Thynne* [1986] R.T.R. 293. The Divisional Court in the case of *D.P.P. v. Dixon* [1993] R.T.R. 22 approved the subjective test laid down in *Thompson v. Thynne*. The question of reliability has been discussed in § A5–10 above and will be considered in following paragraphs on evidence in drink/driving cases. There have been several cases in this area and a number of propositions can be drawn from them. Where the calibration check reading is not within the limits laid down then the machine cannot be regarded as reliable: *Waite v. Smith* [1986] Crim.L.R. 405, D.C.

There seems to be nothing preventing the breath test being taken at a nearby police station if a reliable device is not available at the first station: *Denny v. D.P.P.* [1990] R.T.R. 417. However, where a request was made for blood and the defendant was taken to another police station for the specimen to be taken, and the latter police station had a reliable device available, this was held to be no bar to the specimen of blood being taken, as the request for it had been lawfully made at the first police station: *Chief Constable of Kent v. Berry* [1986] R.T.R. 321.

A5–18   To what do the words "at the time of the requirement" refer? They refer to the time when the requirement for blood or urine is made: *Cotter v. Kamil* [1984] R.T.R. 371. This is supported by *Oxford v. Baxendale* [1987] R.T.R. 247 where it was not realised that the machine was not working properly until some time after the specimens of breath had been provided. Two conflicting cases on this subject exist, although it was sought to distinguish them. In the case of *Morgan v. Lee* [1985] R.T.R. 409, the defendant gave two specimens of breath but the printout did not issue from the machine due to the paper being tangled up inside. The police officer had been able to see the readings and the calibration checks on the screen, and it was held that there was nothing to show that the machine was unreliable, as the police officer could have given oral evidence of the readings. In *Haghigat-Kou v. Chambers* [1988] R.T.R. 95, the printout mechanism was not working, so the officer at the outset formed the view that the machine was not reliable and requested a specimen of blood. The defendant was convicted and appealed. The appeal was dismissed on the basis that as the fault was known to the officer at the outset, and as the test was a subjective one (*i.e.* the officer's reasonable belief) there was evidence to support his belief and therefore the requirement for blood was legally made, thus distinguishing *Morgan v. Lee*.

A5–19   The effect of the subjective approach means that it will be more difficult to challenge such requests for the alternative specimen. It must be proved in court that a reliable device was not available and this must be by means of admissible evidence: *Hughes v. McConnell* [1986] 1 All E.R. 268. Where evidence that "the sergeant said that no reliable device was available" was relied on, it did not satisfy the criteria of admissibility as to that fact: *Dye v. Manns* [1987] R.T.R. 90. In *Slender v. Boothby* (Note) [1986] R.T.R. 385 a machine which did not make provision for a leap year was held not to be reliable.

In *Badkin v. Chief Constable of South Yorkshire* [1987] Crim.L.R. 830 the defendant gave two breath specimens but no printout was produced. The officer decided that the device might be unreliable and required blood. The result of the analysis was not disclosed to the defendant. It was said that no prosecution could be based on the breath specimens once blood was required. See Chapter 6 for further cases on this point.

In *Jones v. D.P.P.* [1991] R.T.R. 41, after providing two breath speci-   **A5–20** mens for analysis, the readings were 50 and 45. The defendant was offered the option. The defendant chose to provide a specimen of urine due to a fear of needles. The sergeant noticing that there was no printout after a breath test, took the view that the machine was unreliable. He then made the requirement under **section 7(1)(b)** and **(3) (b)** for blood or urine. The defendant agreed to provide urine. After he had provided a specimen, the Lion Intoximeter produced a printout. He was charged with having excess alcohol in his urine. It was contended on behalf of the defence that the officer's decision with regard to the machine being unreliable was unreasonable (he had failed to carry out the basic check of flicking the switch) and that the **section 7(1)** and **(3)** procedure should be disregarded and that the certificate was inadmissible due to the choice under **section 8.** The justices took the view that as the defendant had agreed to provide urine under **section 8(2)** its analysis was not rendered inadmissible by the provision having followed a second different and more onerous requirement by the sergeant under **section 7(1)** and **(3)** and they convicted the defendant. This was upheld by the Divisional Court.

There must be grounds for the officer forming the view that a reliable device is not available and this must be established in evidence before the court: *Stokes v. Sayers* [1988] R.T.R. 89.

The second limb to this subsection allows for an alternative specimen to be required when "it is for any other reason not practicable to use such a device there." This will apply in most cases where there is no trained operator at the police station to use the machine. In *Chief Constable of Avon and Somerset v. Kelliher* [1987] R.T.R. 305 it was said that the police do not have to take steps to find a trained operator from other police stations before being able to make the requirement for the specimen of blood.

Blood or urine: condition due to drugs

Section 7(3)(c) will operate in cases where there has been an examin-   **A5–21** ation by a medical practitioner, in practice relating to an offence under **section 4**. There must be a clear statement by the medical practitioner that he believes that drugs are a possible cause of the defendant's condition before a request can be made for the alternative specimen: *Cole v. D.P.P.* [1988] R.T.R. 224. See Chapter 4 for further reference.

Section 8(2): the option

Under **section 8(2)** of the **R.T.A. 1988** if the breath specimen with the   **A5–22** lower proportion of alcohol contains no more than 50 microgrammes of alcohol in 100 millilitres of breath, the person who provided it may claim that it should be replaced by such specimen as may be required (blood or urine) and if he then provides such a specimen, then neither breath specimen shall be used. The courts are concerned with the actual reading of the specimen and not with the possibility that it may be two or three microgrammes out, thus putting a motorist with a reading of 51 within the option: *Reeves v. Enstone, The Times,* February 15, 1985. The choice of specimen will be the officer's, but the defendant must be told of the choice: *Hobbs v. Clark* [1988] R.T.R. 36 followed in *D.P.P. v. Magill* [1988] R.T.R. 337 and approved in *D.P.P. v. Gordon; D.P.P. v. Griggs, supra.*

In *Regan v. D.P.P.* [1990] R.T.R. 102, it was held that to ask a motorist in the relevant circumstances if he intended to provide a sample of blood rather than requiring blood or urine was sufficient to discharge the duty. *Hobbs v. Clark* was the starting point of a number of cases which dealt with the question of driver preference in relation to the choice of specimen. It was stated that the driver had to be given an opportunity to express his preference of replacement specimen. (See *D.P.P. v. Byrne* [1991] R.T.R. 119 and *Renshaw v. D.P.P.* [1992] R.T.R. 186).

A5–23   Recently however, the cases following *Hobbs v. Clark,* in particular the case of *Byrne* have been overturned. The House of Lords, in the case of *D.P.P. v. Warren, supra,* allowed an appeal by the prosecution from the Divisional Court's decision that a police officer had not made a valid requirement for a specimen of blood from the defendant. (This case, although concerned with **section 7(3)(b)** has ramifications for the exercise of the option.)

Lord Bridge said that there was no ground whatever on the face of the statute why, in a **section 8(2)** case, the driver should be invited to state whether he preferred to give blood or urine or to state any reasons for his preference. The driver could give a replacement specimen of whichever kind the constable required of him subject only to his right to object to giving blood on medical grounds and if accepted by the doctor, to give urine instead.

In a case where a driver claims to have the breath specimen replaced under **section 8(2)**, the constable must fully explain to him the nature of the options open to him and what would be involved if he exercises it, *i.e.* that he is entitled to have the specimen of breath replaced by a specimen of blood or urine if he wishes, but that if he does so, it will be for the constable to decide whether the replacement specimen is to be of blood or urine and that if the constable requires a specimen of blood it will be taken by a doctor, unless the doctor considers that there are medical reasons for not taking blood, when urine may be given instead.

It is apparent from the recent cases that the courts are following faithfully the procedure laid down by Lord Bridge. See: *Ogburn v. D.P.P.; Williams v. D.P.P.; D.P.P. v. Duffy; D.P.P. v. Nesbitt* [1994] R.T.R. 241; *Brennan v. D.P.P.; Noscoe v. D.P.P.,* October 13, 1994 (unreported).

However, some caution was urged by the Divisional Court in the following cases: *D.P.P. v. Charles; D.P.P. v. Kukadia; Ruxton v. D.P.P.;*

Reavley v. D.P.P.; Healy v. D.P.P.; McKean v. D.P.P.; Edge v. D.P.P., May 27, 1994 (unreported).

The seven appeals by way of case stated had a common feature, namely that they concerned drivers of motor vehicles arrested on suspicion of driving or being in charge with excess alcohol. In each case the drivers gave breath tests which were in excess of the prescribed limit, and at least one sample contained between 40 and 50 microgrammes of alcohol in 100 millilitres breath so the situation came within the scope of **section 8(2)** of the **R.T.A. 1988** ("the option"). In each case, the driver did not offer a replacement specimen.

In each case not all the points were laid down by Lord Bridge in *D.P.P. v. Warren*, but it was argued by the Crown that each driver received enough information to understand his or her rights. On behalf of the defence, it was contended that what Lord Bridge said had to be followed to the letter and that the information had to be given at the outset.

The Divisional Court concluded that in each of the seven cases, the failure of the constable to comply in every particular with the *Warren* formula was immaterial as:

  (a) the driver in each case having elected not to provide a replacement specimen, the prosecution relied upon the analysis of the original specimen of breath which was untainted by the later breach of the Warren formula and

  (b) in no case was there any evidence to suggest that the constable's failure to give the full formula deprived the driver of the opportunity to exercise the option, or caused them to exercise it in a way that he or she would not have done had everything been said.

It was noted that although it was important to comply with the statutory provisions as interpreted by the House of Lords, it was important to have regard to the overall intention of Parliament when the statute was enacted. The relevant provisions were intended to enable a driver to provide a replacement specimen in a situation where he faces conviction on the specimen already provided. The provisions were not intended to provide a series of hazards for police officers which, if not skilfully negotiated with complete precision, would enable drivers to escape conviction entirely.

In an earlier case the issue was raised when the defendant said that **A5–24** he did not like needles, having fainted years earlier after a blood test. He was offered only blood and it was held that the officer had usurped the function of the medical practitioner by holding that it was not valid: *Johnson v. West Yorkshire Metropolitan Police* [1986] R.T.R. 167.

In *Andrews v. D.P.P.* [1992] R.T.R. 1 the defendant indicated that he wished to give a specimen of urine as he was terrified of needles. A hospital casualty doctor told the officer that this did not amount to a medical reason for not supplying blood. This information was communicated to the defendant, who declined to provide a specimen of blood so the prosecutor relied on the certificate. Dismissing the defendant's appeal the Divisional Court said that **section 7(4)** required a medical opinion to be obtained and whether the doctor's opinion was right or wrong was irrelevant. The court drew attention to the possibility of the defence placing reliance on **section 78** of **P.A.C.E. 1984** in instances where there was an irrational medical opinion or where the doctor or police officer were acting in bad faith. In *R. v. Epping Justices, ex p. Quy*, April 7 [1993] Crim.L.R. 970, Q having been arrested, provided specimens of breath with readings of 43 and 46. He was offered the option. He offered to provide urine, indicating that he was terrified of needles. The officer insisted on blood. It was held that this was capable of being a medical reason and thus the officer was not entitled to insist on blood without more enquiry.

A5–25   If the reading falls within the limits of the subsection then the defendant must be told of the option: *Anderton v. Lythgoe* [1985] 1 W.L.R. 222. Failure to do so may render the breath specimen inadmissible because of the failure to carry out the procedure.

Where a motorist refused to listen to the officer explaining the option, it was held that (a) the officer was under a duty to take reasonable steps to explain the options, but (b) where the defendant by reason of his own actions frustrated the performance of that duty, he was not entitled to be acquitted of the charge: *D.P.P. v. Poole* [1992] R.T.R. 177.

The option is a right and not a duty and therefore the defendant may not be required to give a specimen of blood: *Wakely v. Hyams* [1987] R.T.R. 49.

If the defendant exercises his rights to choose an option, then the breath specimen readings shall not be used in evidence: **section 8(2)**, *Smith v. Geraghty* [1986] R.T.R. 222.

If the defendant exercises his option but the specimen is subsequently lost or cannot be used, then the breath specimen cannot be used in evidence: *Archbold v. Jones* [1986] R.T.R. 178. Where a defendant elects for the option and is asked to give a specimen of blood, he must give his unconditional consent to the taking of blood (the onus is on him to show that he gave such consent) otherwise the evidence of the breath test may be given in evidence if the doctor has not taken a specimen of blood believing that the defendant did not give his unconditional consent: *Rawlins v. Brown* [1987] R.T.R. 238.

A5–26   If the defendant declines to exercise his rights under the option, or fails to provide a specimen, then the breath specimen may be used in evidence against him. In addition, if the defendant, having agreed to provide a specimen under the option, then changes his mind, he had to take the consequences that the prosecutor would be able to rely on the breath analysis result: *Hope v. D.P.P.* [1992] R.T.R. 305.

In *D.P.P. v. Winstanley* [1993] R.T.R. 222, the defendant, having exercised his option to provide a replacement specimen, was asked to provide a specimen of blood. When it became apparent that no doctor was available, the officer asked for a specimen of urine. The defendant agreed but was unable to provide a specimen. In the Divisional Court it was submitted that the police officer, having asked for a specimen of blood, could not then ask for a specimen of urine. The Divisional Court disagreed. Further, it was held that the prosecution could rely on the breath specimen to prove its case. There is no duty, nor need, to give the statutory warning under **section 7(7)** in "option" cases: *Hayes v. D.P.P.* [1993] Crim.L.R. 966.

Under **section 8(3)** the Secretary of State may by regulations, substitute another proportion of alcohol in breath for the 50 microgrammes level.

The provision of blood

A person may be required to give blood at a police station or a hospital. A person provides a specimen of blood if, and only if, he consents to its being taken by a medical practitioner and if it is so taken: **section 11(4)**. (See also **section 15(4)** of the **R.T.O.A. 1988** and *Rawlins v. Brown*, above.) **A5–27**

In *Friel v. Dickson* [1992] R.T.R. 366, the defendant was injured in an accident. He was taken to hospital. He had been given a number of drugs which resulted in a reduction of consciousness and breathing difficulties when requested by the officer to consent to the taking of a specimen of blood. The defendant, without speaking, but moving his head, indicated assent. The police surgeon, who knew nothing of his condition and medication, arrived and asked the defendant if he consented. He said nothing but held out his arm. The defendant was later charged with excess alcohol. The defendant was acquitted on the basis that the Crown had failed to prove that the defendant had consented to provide the specimen to the police surgeon. This finding was upheld on appeal where it was noted that the question whether consent was given was a matter of fact for the tribunal.

The defendant cannot direct where the blood is to be taken from; this is for the medical practitioner to decide: *Solesbury v. Pugh* [1969] 1 W.L.R. 1114, nor can he direct the kind of blood to be taken (capillary as opposed to intravenous): *Rushton v. Higgins* [1972] R.T.R. 456. If the issue is raised that the sample was not properly taken, then it is for the prosecution to prove that the sample was properly taken: *Rowlands v. Harper* [1972] R.T.R. 469. Where the defendant guided the syringe into his vein because the doctor could not find it, it was still held that the sample had been taken by the doctor: *R. v. Burdekin* [1976] R.T.R. 27. A driver has no general right to insist that the specimen of blood be taken by his own medical practitioner: *D.P.P. v. Smith, The Times*, June 1, 1993.

There is no requirement as under the old legislation that the officer has to inform the defendant of his right to be given part of the specimen of blood. However, where the defendant does ask to be provided with a specimen, then it must be divided into two parts at the time of its provision and one part given to the defendant. If this is not done, the specimen cannot be used in evidence: **section 15(5) R.T.O.A. 1988**. In *D.P.P. v. Snook* [1993] Crim.L.R. 883, S provided two specimens of breath. The lower reading was 44. He therefore elected to give blood. S was given his part of the sample which had been divided into two parts. He was told he would be reported and the outcome depending on the analysis might be a prosecution. He was given a brown envel- **A5–28** ope but the sample was not put in it. After a conversation with an employee in the office of the analyst, S formed the view that as the sample had to be sealed in the envelope at the time of being taken, the sample would be of little evidential value in court. The sample was never analysed. At court the defence took the point that the proper procedure was not followed. The Divisional Court held that what is called "the brown envelope routine" is not part of the requirement of the statutory provisions laid down. All that is necessary is that the person be given his sample so he can make up his mind whether to have it analysed. The fact that the part specimen was wrongly labelled did not mean it was not supplied for the purposes of the section: *Butler v. D.P.P.* [1990] R.T.R. 377. The request for a sample must be made at the time of the provision of the specimen and not afterwards: *R. v. Jones* [1974] R.T.R. 117.

A specimen, whether it be blood or urine, must be sufficient to enable the analysis to be carried out. This means that the part given to the defendant must also fulfil that criterion: *Smith v. Cole* [1971] 1 All E.R. 200. The part given to the defendant must be capable of remaining suitable for analysis within a reasonable time: *R. v. Wright* [1975] R.T.R. 193. The sample must not be mixed with any previous sample however minimal the contamination: *Dear v. D.P.P.* [1988] R.T.R. 148. Whether the sample is sufficient and suitable will be a question of fact.

The provision of urine

A5–29   Under **section 7(5)** a specimen of urine shall be provided within one hour of the requirement for its provision being made and after the provision of a previous specimen of urine. Once an analysis is made of the alcohol level in the urine, there is no need for the analyst to go further and equate it with the blood or breath equivalents: *McGarry v. Chief Constable of Bedfordshire* [1983] R.T.R. 172. This would appear to be obvious, as there are conversion charts available to the courts. If a specimen is taken after the expiry of an hour after the requirement is made, it is still admissible in evidence: *Roney v. Matthews* [1975] R.T.R. 273. The relevance of the hour goes to the question of whether or not there has been a failure to provide a specimen. A specimen of urine does not need to be taken by a medical practitioner and is usually taken by the police officer making the requirement. There is no right for an officer to require another specimen if by mistake he discards the specimen: *Poole v. Lockwood* [1981] R.T.R. 285. If the specimen is spilled or lost before being handed over to the officer then there is no provision: *Ross v. Hodges* [1975] R.T.R. 55.

What time should elapse between the giving of the first and second specimen? In *Over v. Musker* [1985] R.T.R. 84 the defendant gave two specimens within a minute of each other. This was held to be two distinct specimens. This can be contrasted with *Prosser v. Dickeson* [1982] R.T.R. 96 where the officer told the defendant to stop urinating, took a specimen and then told him to continue. It was found that this was a single specimen and therefore the analysis was inadmissible.

It matters not which specimen is sent up for analysis as long as one is sent up: *Nugent v. Ridley* [1987] R.T.R. 412.

Evidence of a correctly taken specimen of urine is not rendered inadmissible by a prior invalid and unproductive request for a specimen of blood: *D.P.P. v. Garrett, The Times,* February 3, 1995.

The warning

When requiring a specimen of breath, blood or urine, the officer must **A5–30** warn the defendant that failure to provide the specimen may render him liable to prosecution: **section 7(7)**. If there is no warning then the requirement is negatived: *Simpson v. Spalding* [1987] R.T.R. 221. It would also afford a reasonable excuse for failing to provide a specimen: *R. v. Dolan* [1970] R.T.R. 43.

In *Murray v. D.P.P.* [1993] R.T.R. 209, it was emphasised that the warning was an essential part of the breath test procedure. It went on to say that specimens obtained without the warning were inadmissible in evidence, despite the fact that no prejudice had been caused to the motorist.

Detention at the police station

A person required to provide a specimen of breath, blood or urine may **A5–31** afterwards be detained at a police station until it appears to a constable that, were the person to drive or attempt to drive a motor vehicle on a road, he would not be committing an offence under **section 4** or **5** of the Act: **section 10(1)**. However he shall not be detained if it appears to the constable that there is no likelihood of his driving or attempting to drive a motor vehicle whilst his ability to drive is impaired or whilst the proportion of alcohol in his breath, blood or urine exceeds the limit: **section 10(2)**. The constable must consult a medical practitioner if there is a question of the person's ability being impaired through drugs and he must act on the medical practitioner's advice. In practice a person is usually released into the custody of a friend, relative or taxi driver to be driven home, the car remaining at the police station. **Section 10(2)** would seem to envisage this situation.

The Transport and Works Act 1992

The **Transport and Works Act 1992** embodies offences for certain per- **A5–32** sons working on transport systems similar to the drink/driving provisions under **R.T.A. 1988**. The offences are:

    (a) carrying out work while unfit through drink or drugs **section 27(1)**;

(b) carrying out work after having consumed alcohol in excess of the prescribed limit **section 27(2)**;

(c) offences by operators of the transport system **section 28**.

The penalties for the above are a level 5 fine and/or 6 months' imprisonment.

(d) Failure to take a breath test **section (5)**.

This attracts a level 3 fine.

(e) Failure to give a sample for analysis **section 31(8)**.

The penalty is a level 5 fine and/or 6 months' imprisonment.

Chapter 6

EXCESS ALCOHOL: EVIDENCE AND PENALTIES

Evidence: section 16 of the Road Traffic Offenders Act 1988

Sections 15 and 16 of the **R.T.O.A. 1988** provide for the use of speci-   **A6–01**
mens in proceedings for offences under **sections 4** and **5** of the **R.T.A.
1988. Section 16(1)** provides that:

"Evidence of the proportion of alcohol or a drug in a specimen of
breath, blood or urine may, subject to **subsections (3)** and **(4)** below
and to **section 15(5)** of this Act, be given by the production of a
document or documents purporting to be whichever of the following is appropriate, that is to say—

(a) a statement automatically produced by the device by
which the proportion of alcohol in a specimen of breath
was measured and a certificate signed by a constable
(which may but need not be contained in the same document as the statement) that the statement relates to a specimen provided by the accused at the date and time shown in
the statement, and

(b) a certificate signed by an authorised analyst as to the proportion of alcohol or any drug found in a specimen of
blood or urine identified in the certificate."

It should be noted that the section does not limit the way in which the
prosecution can prove the reading. For example, oral evidence may be
given of the Intoximeter reading by the officer, but only if this evidence includes the breath alcohol reading and the device's calibration
readings: *Owen v. Chesters* [1985] R.T.R. 191; *Morgan v. Lee* [1985] R.T.R.
409; *Denneny v. Harding* [1986] R.T.R. 350; *Mayon v. D.P.P.* [1988]
R.T.R. 281; *Thom v. D.P.P.* [1994] R.T.R. 11; *Greenaway v. D.P.P.* [1994]
R.T.R. 17. The importance of this of course, goes to the reliability of the
device and, in certain circumstances, the credit of the officer.

In the case of *Chief Constable of Avon and Somerset v. Creech* [1986]   **A6–02**
R.T.R. 87, having accepted that oral evidence could be given of the
readings of the Intoximeter, the court went on to say that if the
printout had been mislaid and the officer could offer no adequate
explanation for its loss, then this would be relevant to his credit overall, and consequently also the evidence he had given about the
readings.

In *D.P.P. v. Hutchings* [1991] R.T.R. 380, a set of three printouts were produced by the machine. One was handed to the defendant and the other two placed on the table from where they ultimately disappeared. The officer obtained another printout from the test. It was sought to put this second printout in evidence, the officer having explained what took place at the police station. The defence objected on the basis that it was not an original document and there was no evidence to show that the Lion Intoximeter had a memory capable of producing a second printout. The justices dismissed the information. The Divisional Court, allowing the appeal by the prosecutor, held that the second printout was just as much an original as the first one and was admissible providing the necessary evidence as to the reliability of the device was given. Nor was it in fact necessary for the second printout to be used as the officer had given oral evidence of the result of the breath test and testified that the machine was in working order. Once this was proved there was no need for the prosecution to adduce specific proof that the device had a memory bank.

The printout and certificate

A6–03 Evidence of the reading from the evidential breath-testing machine is generally given in the form of the certified printout. It must be noted however that under **section 16(4)** of the above Act:

> "... a document purporting to be a certificate (or so much of a document as purports to be a certificate) is not so admissible if the accused, not later than three days before the hearing or within such further time as the court may in special circumstances allow, has served notice on the prosecutor requiring the attendance at the hearing of the person by whom the document purports to be signed."

This means that if the defendant requires the attendance of the certifying witness, then the document cannot be led in evidence.

A case which attempted ultimately (unsuccessfully) to make use of this provision under the **1972 Act (section 10(5))** was *Temple v. Botha* [1985] Crim.L.R. 517. The defence had served notice on the prosecutor requiring the attendance of the operator. They then argued successfully in front of the magistrates that the printout could not be used alone to prove the prosecution case and the operator was not allowed to hand in the printout on the basis that he was proving the certificate and its contents. The justices relying on *Gaimster v. Marlow* [1984] Q.B. 218 came to the view that once objection was taken under **section 10(5)**, then the printout was automatically inadmissible. The appeal by the prosecutor was allowed. It was said that the justices had misunderstood the decision in *Gaimster v. Marlow*.

One purpose of **section 10(5)** was to ensure the attendance of a witness for cross-examination. Only in the circumstances outlined in **section 10(5)** was the printout inadmissible. Following a guilty plea however, the original printout need not be produced: *R. v. Tower Bridge Magistrates' Court, ex p. D.P.P.* [1989] R.T.R. 118.

The certificate: some cases on admissibility

The printout may not be used where the result is under 50 micro-grammes and the defendant has exercised his right to provide a specimen of blood or urine. If the self calibration check is outside the permitted limits then the printout should not be used in evidence: *R. v. Kingston-upon-Thames Justices, ex p. Khanna* [1986] R.T.R. 364, D.C. There are two unusual cases in which the printout has been held to be admissible despite exercise of the option.

   In the case of *Smith v. D.P.P.* [1989] R.T.R. 159, the defendant declined to exercise the option when invited to, but an hour later having consulted with his solicitor changed his mind and provided a specimen of blood. It was held that the justices were entitled to find that the statutory procedure had ended when the defendant firmly rejected the option; so that they were correct in law to admit the evidence of the breath specimen.

   Where a defendant frustrated the officers attempts to explain the option, the prosecution was entitled to rely on the printout: *D.P.P. v. Poole* [1992] R.T.R. 177.

   In *Yhnell v. D.P.P.* [1989] R.T.R. 250, there was evidence that the defendant, having exercised the option and provided blood, had injected his sample with alcohol-free blood thus lowering the reading. It was held that the justices had not erred in admitting the evidence of the breath analysis, for they had accepted the evidence that the defendant had falsified the lower blood analysis reading.

   If the printout contains errors in spelling which can be laid at the door of the operator and does not put into question the reliability of the machine, then it is admissible: *Toovey v. Chief Constable of Northumbria* [1986] Crim.L.R. 475, D.C.; *Burditt v. Roberts (Note)* [1986] R.T.R. 391.

   In a case where the police officer had altered the printout to show times in British Summer Time and not Greenwich Mean Time, it was still held to be a document within the Act and the defendant was held to have received the copy within the meaning of the Act: *Beck v. Scammell* [1986] R.T.R. 162.

   During British Summer Time it is perfectly acceptable for the printout from the Lion Intoximeter to show the time when a breath test is taken in terms of Greenwich Mean Time (GMT): *Parker v. D.P.P.* [1993] R.T.R. 283.

   In *Garner v. D.P.P.* [1990] R.T.R. 208, it was held that the justices had properly admitted the printout of the Intoximeter as real evidence, notwithstanding that it had not been signed by the officer conducting the test.

   This can be contrasted to some extent with the case of *R. v. Medway Magistrates' Court, ex p. Goddard*, May 16, 1994 (unreported), where the officer responsible for signing the standard form and certificate had

A6–04

A6–05

failed to do so. The Divisional Court observed that the certificate is designed to make admissible the evidence adduced by the Intoximeter and act as affirmative evidence that the computer was working properly. No oral evidence had been called to prove the elements. Quoting the case of *R. v. Shephard* [1993] 2 W.L.R. 102, the court said that it was beyond doubt that the prosecution could not simply rely on the presumption that the device was working normally.

In the case of *Van Flute v. D.P.P.*, June 9, 1994 (unreported) the certificate was not produced and the officer gave evidence of the readings and calibration but not of the date and time of the test. The Divisional Court held that although there was no direct evidence of the time of the test, there was evidence by inference and therefore the omission was not fatal to conviction.

In the case of *Hasler v. D.P.P.* [1989] R.T.R. 148 the police officer in charge of the case stated in evidence that the printout was available in court. It was not produced. After rejection of a submission of no case, the printout was handed to the justices and the defendant was convicted. On appeal, it was held that the printout not having been adduced in evidence and the justices, therefore, not having been able to take information on it into account, the prosecutor had failed to establish a case against the defendant at the close of his submissions; and that it was not open to the prosecutor to contend that the justices admitted the evidence as a matter of discretion after rejecting the submission of no case to answer. The conviction was quashed. Where a motorist provided two specimens of breath and the device was then found to be faulty, he could lawfully be requested to furnish two further specimens of breath (in this case at a different police station) instead of being called on to provide blood or urine, and the subsequent printout would be admissible: *Denny v. D.P.P.* [1990] R.T.R. 417.

The above are just some examples of cases on this topic: see also Chapter 7 for cases where the admissibility of the printout has been challenged.

The analyst's certificate

A6–06   A certificate signed by an authorised analyst which speaks to the proportion of alcohol or drugs found in the specimen of blood or urine is admissible as evidence of the facts so certified, subject to the provisions of **section 16(4)** of the **R.T.O.A. 1988** (see §§ A6–01 *et seq.*). An authorised analyst means:

> "... any person possessing the qualifications prescribed by regulations made under **section 76** of the **Food Act 1984** or **section 57** of the **Food and Drugs (Scotland) Act 1956** as qualifying for appointment as public analysts under those Acts, and any other person authorised by the Secretary of State to make analyses for the purposes of this section" (**R.T.O.A. 1988, s.16(7)**).

It should be noted that the subsection only requires that the certificate be signed by an authorised analyst and does not require analysis by an authorised analyst: *R. v. Rutter* [1977] R.T.R. 105, C.A. In practice, though, it would be expected that the person who signed the certificate would be a person who had some dealings with the analysis; if not, what is the point of being able to require the attendance of the signatory to the analysis if he cannot actually speak to the analysis and its circumstances?

Evidence of a certificate signed by an authorised analyst, where the analysis procedure was carried out at his laboratory under his control and supervision was held to be admissible: *R. v. Kershberg* [1976] R.T.R. 526.

The analyst's certificate: cases on admissibility

Continuity of the specimen is important. The prosecution must establish that the specimen taken from the defendant was sent for analysis, and that the certificate of the analysis relates to the same defendant's specimen. It does not matter that, for instance, the certificate or the label has typing errors, if there is other evidence that the specimen is that of the defendant: *Dickson v. Atkins* [1972] R.T.R. 209. **A6–07**

Not every step of continuity need be established by the prosecution if it can be shown that the sample was taken and sealed and the analyst received the sealed container: *Tremlett v. Fawcett* (1984) 1 R.T.L.B. 68.

In *Braddock v. Whittaker* [1970] Crim.L.R. 112, the defendant was held to be properly convicted although the sample produced in court was not identified by the doctor and the cups into which the specimen was placed contained undetermined crystals which the doctor merely assumed were anti-coagulants.

One of the points on appeal in the case of *Paterson v. D.P.P.* [1990] R.T.R. 329, was that there was insufficient evidence that the blood analysed was that of the defendant. The defendant was arrested and tested at Charles Street police station, but the specimen was put in an envelope labelled as coming from Asfordby Street station. The Divisional Court said that the correct method of proof must be followed, that the proof of analysis was unsatisfactory and that the defendant was entitled to have the benefit of any lack of correct procedure having been followed. **A6–08**

Evidence of analysis of blood carried out by means of gas chromatography on a computer, the results being produced by means of a graph without satisfying the requirements of **section 69** of **P.A.C.E. 1984**, is admissible: *Sophocleous v. Ringer* [1987] Crim.L.R. 422.

Under **section 16(2)** a sample of blood must be taken with the defendant's consent, otherwise the result will be inadmissible. If there is challenge to the certificate, then the defence must serve notice on the prosecution to require the witness's attendance. If this is not done, then any expert evidence sought to be adduced by the defendant to contradict the prosecution will not be admitted: *Thomas v. Henderson* [1983] R.T.R. 293, D.C.

Even where there is a challenge to the prosecution's analysis (*i.e.* the defence analysis being lower) the justices are entitled to find the evidence of one expert preferable to the other: *Stephenson v. Clift* [1988] R.T.R. 171, D.C. In this case there were different results from the analysis of the defendant's specimen of blood. The justices found that the method used by the prosecution expert (gas chromatography) was more accurate and modern than that used by the defence expert (I.C.M.A.).

A6–09   In *Dear v. D.P.P.* [1988] R.T.R. 148, it was held that the obtaining of the blood sample had to comply strictly with the statutory provisions for the analysis to be admitted. In this case the portion of the sample handed to the defendant contained a minimal quantity of an earlier sample. The portion retained by the police and its analysis were held to be inadmissible.

Dear was considered in the case of *D.P.P. v. Elstob* [1992] R.T.R. 45, where it was held that the justices were wrong in deciding that the blood sample analysis was inadmissible because the division of the sample did not take place in front of the defendant. Compliance with the Act did not require the presence of the defendant. They added however, that it was desirable that, wherever possible, division should take place in front of the accused.

A string of cases came before the Divisional Court on the same point. They applied for judicial review to quash convictions based on analyses of blood specimens taken by police surgeons in the Greater Manchester area from February 1987 and December 1988 where the standard kits had been replaced by "Medi-prep" swabs containing ethanol which contaminated the blood and increased the alcohol level by a small but significant amount. The applications were granted because:

(i) The mischief arose from a failure by the police to exercise ordinary care by ascertaining whether, having regard to the use for which the swabs were intended, Medi-prep swabs were a suitable alternative to alcohol-free swabs, and that the police and the Crown Prosecution Service collectively were the prosecution.

(ii) Judicial review by way of certiorari to quash the convictions would be granted on the grounds analogous to fraud or collusion; that an analyst's certificate based on a false premise that a sample was unadulterated contained hidden untruths and their admission in evidence was akin to perjury albeit unwittingly committed; and that, since the prosecution had unfairly corrupted the process leading to conviction by giving the motorist no proper opportunity to decide how to plead, and wrongly denying him a complete defence to the charge, the prosecution's conduct was analogous to fraud, collusion or perjury and the convictions would be quashed: *R. v. Bolton Magistrates' Court, ex p. Scally* [1991] 1 Q.B. 537.

Procedural preconditions for the admissibility of documents

Section 16(3) of the **Road Traffic Offenders Act 1988** states:

> "...subject to subsection (4) below—
>   (a) a document purporting to be such a statement or such a certificate (or both such a statement and such a certificate) as is mentioned in subsection (1)(a) above is admissible in evidence on behalf of the prosecution in pursuance of this section only if a copy of it either has been handed to the accused when the document was produced or has been served on him not later than seven days before the hearing, and
>   (b) any other document is so admissible only if a copy of it has been served on the accused not later than seven days before the hearing."

A6–10

The statutory procedure must be complied with fully in order for the documents to be admissible. Can there be waiver of the right to object to admissibility when there is non-compliance? In *Anderton v. Kinnard* [1986] R.T.R. 11 it was held that, where the documents had not been properly served, there had been waiver by two actions on behalf of the defence:

   (a) A letter from the defendant's solicitors to the prosecution, and
   (b) no objection having been taken at trial to the admissibility of the documents.

This case can be contrasted with *Tobi v. Nicholas* [1988] R.T.R. 343. In this case counsel for the appellant accepted, before the magistrate, copies of the analyst's and the medical practitioner's certificates which had not been served in accordance with the legislation. He then successfully argued in the Divisional Court that service was a prerequisite for the admissibility of the documents and no purported waiver by him could render them inadmissible.

A6–11

In *Williams v. D.P.P.* [1991] R.T.R. 214, it was held that the requirement for the analyst's certificate to be served on the defendant not later than seven days before the hearing, meant the hearing at which the evidence would be given and not necessarily the defendant's first appearance.

"Copy ... handed to"

It has been held that the fact that a copy is not signed, does not prevent it from being a copy within the meaning of the section: *Chief Constable of Surrey v. Wickens* [1985] R.T.R. 277. Manuscript alterations of GMT to show BST do not bring the document outside the meaning of the section: *Beck v. Scammell, supra.*

A6–12

In general "handed to" means delivery of the copy by hand into the defendant's possession or hands. In *Walton v. Rimmer* [1986] R.T.R. 31, D.C., three copies of statements from an approved device were placed in front of the defendant for signature. He signed two copies, but not the third. It was held that the third copy had not been handed to the defendant and the printout was therefore inadmissible.

Service

A6–13   The statements or certificates may be served on the defendant but not later than seven days before the hearing. This means seven clear days between the date of service and the date of the hearing. Service can be effected personally or sent by registered post or recorded delivery. By **section 7** of the **Interpretation Act 1978** service is deemed to be effected when it would have arrived in the normal course of post. Service need not necessarily be made on the defendant, an agent may suffice. In certain cases therefore, counsel may accept service but may decline if he so wishes: *Penman v. Parker* [1986] 1 W.L.R. 882. A solicitor has authority to accept service on behalf of the defendant: *Anderton v. Kinnard* [1986] R.T.R. 11; *Penman v. Parker, supra*. It is generally assumed that a wife has authority to accept service on behalf of her husband: *Burt v. Kirkaldy* [1965] 1 W.L.R. 474.

What happens if the defendant disputes service? Normally there is little challenge on the question of service as, where possible, these documents are served on the defendant's legal representative either at court or at their offices. This, of course, assumes that the defendant is legally represented. In *Hawkins v. D.P.P.* [1988] R.T.R. 380, the defendant disputed having received copies of the analyst's and medical practitioner's certificates which had been sent by post. The Divisional Court dismissed his appeal, holding that there was sufficient proof for service to have been deemed to be made within **rule 67(2)** of the **Magistrates' Courts Rules 1981**. It was open to the defendant in accordance with **section 7** of the **Interpretation Act 1978** to satisfy the justices that the certificate had not been served. Since he had failed to do so, the justices were therefore entitled to find that the certificates were admissible.

Any points on service and admissibility should be taken at the earliest opportunity during the prosecution case, for failure to challenge evidence of a certificate which was not served may have the effect of leaving the evidence in: *R. v. Banks* [1972] 1 W.L.R. 346. If the requirements of the subsection are not fulfilled, then it seems that the prosecution may call the witness in person to give the evidence.

Section 78 P.A.C.E. and the discretion to exclude

A6–14   As the opportunities to challenge the breath test procedures have diminished, so the courts have been asked increasingly to exercise their discretion to exclude the evidence under **section 78 P.A.C.E. 1984**. The following represent the kind of cases where such applications have been made, both successfully and unsuccessfully. Fuller facts of these cases can be found in the relevant chapters.

Procedure under sections 7 and 8 R.T.A. 1988

Under P.A.C.E. 1984, these procedures do not constitute an interview.   **A6–15**
See *D.P.P. v. Billington* [1988] R.T.R. 231; *D.P.P. v. Rous, D.P.P. v. D. (A juvenile)* [1992] R.T.R. 246, *R. v. Epping Justices, ex p. Quy*, April 7, 1993, (unreported c.o. 093792). Compare with the case of *Hudson v. D.P.P.* [1992] R.T.R. 27 (see Chapter 8 for facts).

Mala fides

In *Matto v. Wolverhampton Crown Court* [1987] R.T.R. 337, it was found   **A6–16**
that the police had acted in bad faith by remaining on private property, when their implied licence to remain had been revoked, in order to request a sample of breath. The Divisional Court held that the behaviour at the scene was relevant and affected the subsequent procedure at the police station.

An absence of bad faith by the police does not prevent the justices from exercising their discretion under **section 78**: *D.P.P. v. McGladrigan* [1991] R.T.R. 297; *D.P.P. v. Godwin* [1991] R.T.R. 303; *Andrews v. D.P.P.* [1992] R.T.R. 1. Compare with *D.P.P. v. Wilson* [1991] R.T.R. 284 and *Thomas v. D.P.P.* [1991] R.T.R. 292.

It was noted in *Andrews, supra*, that **section 78** gives protection to a defendant in any case where good faith is missing, either because the constable does not recount the facts fully and fairly to the doctor, or the doctor gives an opinion that he knows the constable wants rather than one based on a firm medical assessment. (See Chapter 5 for facts.)

The statutory assumption as to alcohol levels

Section 15(2) of the **Road Traffic Offenders Act 1988** states: **A6–17**

"Evidence of the proportion of alcohol or any drug in a specimen of breath, blood or urine provided by the accused shall, in all cases, be taken into account and, subject to **subsection (3)** below, it shall be assumed that the proportion of alcohol in the accused's breath, blood or urine at the time of the alleged offence was not less than the specimen."

This assumption has the effect of preventing the defendant from challenging the results of the analysis on the grounds that he had recently drunk alcohol and the analysis was too high due to his alcohol level having risen since being stopped or driving. This does not apply to alcohol consumed after driving (see Chapter 7).

Back calculation

A6–18   The statutory assumption also allows the prosecution to call evidence
to show that the defendant's alcohol level was in fact higher at the time
of the commission of the offence than shown in the reading. This, of
course, could be something that would be relevant to the question of
sentence. This principle of back calculation to establish the alcohol
level at an earlier period in time has been approved to some extent in
Smith v. Geraghty [1986] R.T.R. 222 but with a note of caution introduced. Glidewell J., in summary, noted that the practice of back calculation was permissible but only practicable in cases where there is
clear, straightforward and simple evidence to illustrate it. "The justices," he warned, "should not be drawn into any detailed scientific
calculations."

A6–19   In *Gumbley v. Cunningham; Gould v. Castle* [1987] 3 All E.R. 733, the
Divisional Court confirmed that **section 10(2)** of the **R.T.A. 1972** (now
section 15(2) of the **R.T.O.A. 1988**) does not preclude the admission of
evidence, other than the specimen itself, to show a higher alcohol level
than revealed by the specimen. This means therefore that, even if the
specimen contains less than the legal limit, but it can be shown by back
calculation that the driver had excess alcohol at the time of the offence,
then a conviction will follow. Mann J. emphasised, however, that the
prosecution should not seek to rely on such evidence except and
unless the evidence was "easily understood and clearly persuasive of
the presence of excess alcohol at the time when the accused person
was driving."

Moreover, justices must be very careful, especially where there is
conflicting evidence, not to convict unless the scientific and other evidence which they found safe to rely on was such that they were sure
that an excess of alcohol was in the defendant's body when he was
actually driving as charged.

The appeal in the case of *Gumbley* was dismissed as the court found
that the justices had been sure, but in the second case (*Gould v. Castle*)
the appeal was allowed as the prosecution evidence was, that it was
likely that the defendant had between 43 and 65 microgrammes at the
time of driving. This was not sufficient to warrant the court saying it
was sure. The decision of the Divisional Court in *Gumbley v. Cunningham* was upheld by the House of Lords: [1989] R.T.R. 49.

The presumption created by **section 15** is irrebuttable and the
defendant is not entitled to call evidence to show that at the time of
driving the reading may have been lower than at the time of the test.
This is in the case of pre-driving consumption of alcohol: *Beauchamp-
Thompson v. D.P.P.* [1989] R.T.R. 54; *Millard v. D.P.P.* [1990] R.T.R. 201.
However, this is always subject to any challenge on the reliability of
the analysis/machine.

In *D.P.P. v. Hill* [1991] R.T.R. 351, the justices accepted evidence of
the defendant and two witnesses that the defendant had only drunk
half a pint. The Divisional Court allowing the appeal by the prosecutor
noted that this finding had some very surprising consequences that

the two machines were faulty and that there was some other explanation for the defendant's glazed vision as observed by the officer. The case was remitted with a direction to convict.

Back calculation: some guidelines

The kind of information on which back calculations are based will generally include: **A6–20**

    (i) The analysis of the specimen in question;
    (ii) the time the specimen was taken;
    (iii) the time alcohol was consumed (if the information is available to the prosecution);
    (iv) the amount of alcohol consumed; the probable time of "peaking" and assumptions as to the rate that alcohol levels drop.

The last two items are estimates and there is variation in rates between different individuals and under different circumstances. Although tables and charts dealing with average rates of alcohol elimination are available, they must be treated with caution by the courts and by the reader. For our purposes here, they are only used by way of guidance. An expert must be consulted to deal with the individual case.

As far back as 1965, a report of a Special Committee of the British Medical Association, although giving certain guidelines as to the period of time it takes for alcohol to reach a peak concentration in the blood (between 15–90 minutes, usually little more than 30 minutes) urged the courts not to indulge in back calculation because the rate of elimination of alcohol, both between different individuals and in the same individual at different times, varies to some extent. In their opinion, an exercise of this kind could not be justified. The absorption of alcohol was considered and explained in Chapter 4. What needs to be considered in addition now is the elimination of alcohol. It may be recalled that when the alcohol reaches the duodenum it becomes absorbed into the bloodstream. As the blood travels from the duodenum, it passes through the liver where the alcohol is continuously removed in small quantities. Elimination is a slow process. If the person continues drinking, then their alcohol level will be rising faster than the rate of elimination. The average rate of elimination, assuming a healthy liver, is between 6–9 microgrammes per hour or the blood equivalent is 15–20 milligrammes per hour. Figures of 11–20 milligrammes have also been quoted. As stated the figures are guidelines only and it has been said that the courts are not entitled to look at extracts of elimination rates in the British Medical Journal to form their conclusions: *Dawson v. Lunn* [1986] R.T.R. 234.

Penalties

Where a person is convicted of driving or attempting to drive a motor   **A6–21** vehicle on a road or other public place whilst over the prescribed limit, the maximum penalty is six months' imprisonment and/or a fine on level 5. The offences are triable summarily only. The offences carry obligatory disqualification unless special reasons can be found for not disqualifying or disqualifying for a shorter period than the minimum 12 months. The minimum period is three years if the person has been convicted for an offence under **section 4(1)** of driving or attempting to drive while unfit, **section 5(1)** of driving or attempting to drive with excess alcohol and **section 7(6)** of failing to provide a specimen, within the 10 years immediately preceding the commission of the present offence: **section 34 R.T.O.A. 1988.** Endorsement is obligatory. The endorsement code is DR10.

An alternative verdict to **section 5(1)(a)** under **section 24 R.T.O.A. 1988** as substituted by **section 24 R.T.A. 1991** is **section 5(1)(b)** "being in charge" with excess alcohol.

For being in charge with excess alcohol the maximum sentence is three months' imprisonment and/or a level 4 fine. Disqualification is discretionary. Endorsement is obligatory unless special reasons for not endorsing are found. The endorsement code is DR50.

Sentencing

A6–22   Sentencing in drink/driving cases, as in other offences, varies throughout the country from those magistrates' courts which hand out custodial sentences for a first drink/driving offence to those which pass fines on offenders with a number of similar previous convictions. For an offence of driving with excess alcohol (no doubt a first offence), the Magistrates' Association's suggestions are a fine starting at £480 and 12 months' disqualification. The higher the reading, the higher the suggested fine and disqualification. Under the Magistrates' Association's suggestions a reading of over 65 (breath/alcohol) will attract disqualification for 18 months, two years for a reading of over 88 (breath/alcohol) and three years for a reading of over 110 (breath/alcohol). These periods of disqualification and longer have been upheld by the Court of Appeal.

A short custodial sentence is considered with breath specimen readings of over 88 microgrammes. A custodial sentence for a first drink/driving offence has been held not to be wrong in principle: *R. v. Nokes* [1978] R.T.R. 101. This case, however, had many features considered to be aggravating, such as a high reading, speeding and bad driving record. Whilst a high reading on its own may not justify an immediate custodial sentence, other factors taken together, in particular a past history of drink/driving or bad driving, may attract such a sentence. Any considerations of custodial sentences now will be subject to the provisions of the **Criminal Justice Act 1991**, as amended.

Rehabilitation courses for drink/drive offenders

In early 1993, the government introduced into 28 petty sessions areas **A6–23**
an experimental scheme for convicted drink/drivers. Magistrates in
those specified areas can now offer offenders the chance of a reduced
period of disqualification in return for attendance on a rehabilitation
course.

The progress of the scheme will be the subject of a three-year study,
after which it is hoped that the scheme will be extended nationwide.

The law

Section 30 of the **Road Traffic Act 1991** inserts **ss.34A–C** in the **Road** **A6–24**
Traffic Act 1988. This provides for the court to offer the opportunity to
drink/drivers to attend special courses. It is not part of the penalty
and is voluntary. Successful completion on the course leads to a
reduced period of disqualification. The offences to which this section
applies are:

(i) Causing death by careless driving when under the influence of
drink or drugs (it is not yet in force in respect of this offence);
(ii) driving or being in charge when under the influence of drink or
drugs;
(iii) driving or being in charge with excess alcohol and
(iv) failing to provide an evidential breath specimen.

Under **section 34A** the minimum period of reduction is three months
and not more than one-quarter of the period of disqualification not
subject to reduction.

There are certain conditions which must be fulfilled:

(i) There must be a place available on a course;
(ii) the offender must be over the age of 17;
(iii) the court must explain the effect of the order, the cost and
requirements of the course;
(iv) the offender must consent to the order.

Following successful completion a certificate of completion is sent to
the court in order for the reduced period to come into effect. There are
provisions concerning the "non issue" of a certificate by the course
organiser which allows the offender to apply to the court for a declaration that the organiser has defaulted in his obligations. If such a declaration is made, then it has the effect of the certificate being issued
(**section 34B(7), (9)**).

The courses are educative. They seek to teach offenders about
alcohol in general and specifically as to the effect it can have on driving. Each area designs its own course. These courses are based upon
the guidelines issued in a press release by the Department of Transport on December 3, 1992. These guidelines state that the courses are to
include:

- basic facts about drink, its alcohol content and what effect this can have upon the body;
- the effects of alcohol on driving;
- analysis of drink-driving offences;
- the alternatives to drinking in public places and driving.

The Department of Transport recommends that the courses should run for between 16 and 30 hours and the fees, to be set by the organising bodies, are to be between £50 and £200.

Concerns about the scheme

A6–25　Concern has been expressed by a number of persons about potential problems which may arise from the system in its present form. The areas of concern can be divided into the following headings:

    (1) Cost;
    (2) Disparity in sentencing;
    (3) Lack of sanction;
    (4) Other concerns.

(1) Cost

As noted above, course fees should range between £50–£200. This has to be paid by the offender in advance of being accepted on the course. This means in effect that those who are unemployed or on a low income will be unable to afford such a course. It is likely that most courses will set fees at the higher level of the recommended figures.

Additionally, although a person may have been able to afford the cost of the course, if coupled with a fine (which is the probable sentence in most first time cases), a person is likely to think twice before accepting a place on a course, unless the early return of the licence is imperative.

(2) Disparity in sentencing

A6–26　There are at present no guidelines as to the criteria that magistrates should employ when considering the offer to an offender of a place on a course. The North Report envisaged the courses being suitable for first time offenders under a certain alcohol limit. The legislation has imposed no limit, therefore both the re-offender and the person with a high alcohol reading can be given the opportunity to reduce their periods of disqualification.

This leads to the concern over the possible disparity in sentencing. This is a potential problem for two reasons. First, as there are no limits on what kind of offender is eligible for such a scheme, the potential for inconsistency in approach from area to area is high.

Secondly, the period of reduction in disqualification for sentences of above 12 months is at the court's discretion and thus subject to differences from court to court.

(3) Lack of sanctions

Another concern expressed about the scheme, is that there are no sanctions for failure to complete the course. Albeit the offender does not get a reduced period of disqualification, it does mean that there is potential for abuse. Already it has been found that persons are agreeing to undertake the course and then failing to do so.

(4) Other concerns

With the lack of guidance available, it may be that some courts will want pre-sentence reports before offering someone a place on the course. This has been indicated to us by a number of magistrates. The result could be an additional burden on an already overworked service and will add considerably to costs.

The procedure for challenge to the organiser's refusal to issue a certificate of completion is an area which is uncharted. What form will this dispute take? Will the prosecution need to attend? Indeed will they have any *locus standi*? Will a person who was eligible for legal aid be covered by it to have their case argued? No doubt some formula will be evolved, but firm guidance would prevent waste of time and money.

Does a person have a right to challenge the decision of the magistrates not to offer a course to a drink/driver if he indicates his willingness to attend? The appropriate section says that magistrates "may" offer a person a place on a course. Is there more room for further litigation? The issuing of guidelines would be of great assistance.

(5) Research to date

The Transport Research Laboratory has now produced their first report on the extent to which these courses have been successful in changing participants attitudes to, and awareness of, the effects of alcohol, particularly on driving ability. In the courts in the experimental areas, there were a total of 11,275 drink/drive offenders since referrals under the scheme began. A total of 4,206 of those offenders were referred to the courses. Of those, a total of 1,254 offenders took part in the courses and by January 1995, 944 had successfully completed their courses. The conclusion reached by the research is that the courses have largely achieved their initial objectives with the majority of participants showing a positive shift in their attitude to drinking and driving by the end of the courses. As the overall objective of the courses is to reduce the incidence of reoffending, the long term effectiveness of the courses is to be measured by monitoring driver records from DVLA to compare the rates of reconviction in the designated courts, with the rates of conviction in the matched control courts where the rehabilitation courses are not available.

High risk offenders

The problem of "high risk offenders" has been one which has taxed the courts for years. As from June 1990, a person will be considered to be a high risk offender if he falls into any of the following groups:

(i) Those disqualified from driving having a reading of two-and-a-half times over the prescribed limit;

(ii) those who have been disqualified on more than one occasion within 10 years;

(iii) those disqualified by virtue of a conviction for failing to supply a specimen for analysis.

(See **regulation 8** of the **Motor Vehicles (Driving Licences) (Amendment) Regulations 1990, S.I. 1990 No. 842.**)

The effect of coming within one of these groups is that on expiry of the disqualification and application for the licence, a decision will be made whether the conviction indicated a medical condition or problem and, if so, whether this disability has been overcome. To this end, before the expiry of the disqualification a letter is sent to the offender together with the application form for a licence. The letter explains that he has to satisfy the Secretary of State that there is no drink problem before a licence can be renewed.

A6–28   On application for renewal, the person is invited to attend a special examination centre where he is interviewed and undergoes a medical examination. A blood sample is also taken from him. From these results, the decision whether or not to renew the licence will be determined. The Secretary of State, in any event, has power to revoke or refuse a licence under **sections 92** and **93** of the **R.T.A. 1988.** Under **section 92**, if it appears from the applicant's declaration, or if on inquiry, the Secretary of State is satisfied from other information, that the applicant is suffering from a relevant disability, he must, subject to certain provisions, refuse to grant a licence.

"Disability" includes disease. "Relevant disability" means any prescribed disability (see the **Motor Vehicles (Driving Licences) Regulations 1987** set out at §§C16–01, *et seq.*) and any other disability likely to cause the driving of a vehicle by him in pursuance of a licence to be a source of danger to the public. It would be under the latter definition that the persistent drinker would fall.

Any appeal against a decision made under **sections 92** and **93** of the Act can be brought in the magistrates' court, by virtue of **section 100 R.T.A. 1988.** Any order made by the court is binding on the Secretary of State.

Chapter 7

EXCESS ALCOHOL: DEFENCES

The statutory defence

The statutory assumption shall not be made under **section 5** of the   **A7–01**
R.T.A. 1988 if the accused proves:

(a) That he consumed alcohol after he had ceased to drive, attempt-
    ing to drive or be in charge of a motor vehicle on a road or other
    public place and before he provided the specimen, and
(b) that had he not done so the proportion of alcohol in his breath,
    blood or urine would not have exceeded the prescribed limit
    (**section 15(3) R.T.O.A. 1988**).

The burden of proof is on the defendant on the balance of probabilities. An observation was made that, in the last resort, the prosecution
must discharge the general burden of proof; in other words negative
the live issue. If they fail to do this then the accused should be acquitted: *Thynne v. Hindle* [1984] R.T.R. 231.

The statutory defence: general points

Applying the principle in *Pugsley v. Hunter* [1973] 1 W.L.R. 578, the   **A7–02**
court noted in *Dawson v. Lunn* [1986] R.T.R. 234 that, unless it was
obvious to the layman that post-driving consumption explained the
excess, the defendant should call the necessary expert evidence to
show that he would not have been over the prescribed limit but for the
subsequent drinking. See also *D.P.P. v. Singh* [1988] R.T.R. 209, D.C.
The defendant will need to show generally that an ascertainable
amount of alcohol was consumed after ceasing to drive (attempting to
drive or being in charge) and that this specific amount would reduce
the reading to below the prescribed limit.

Once justices had been given clear evidence from an expert as to the
amount of alcohol necessary to cause a particular driver to exceed the
legal limit and had been given plausible evidence as to the quantity
consumed after the occurrence of an accident, it was then open to
them, in spite of that fact that apparent discrepancies remained unex-
plained, to find that the defendant had discharged the burden necessary under **section 15(3)**: *D.P.P. v. Lowden, The Times*, April 10, 1992.

The report of a forensic scientist dealing with the effect of intoxicating liquor on breath alcohol is admissible: *Lloyd v. Knight, The Times*, February 13, 1985. This case however contains a caution to prosecutors to think carefully before they consent to reports being read rather than subjecting the expert to cross-examination. In this case, the defence report was agreed by the prosecution and it seems likely that, if the expert had been called and cross-examined, a different light might have been shed on the evidence.

In section 5, the offences are disjunctive. This means, therefore, that, if charged with driving with excess alcohol, a defendant who shows that he was under the limit when he ceased to drive must be acquitted even though he may have consumed more alcohol since then which would make him in charge with excess alcohol: *Rynsard v. Spalding* [1986] R.T.R. 303.

Attacking the Intoximeter: general matters

A7–03   There are a number of approaches to attacking the Intoximeter and its printout. One has to work from the general principle that there is a presumption that the device was in order when it was used. It is, therefore, always open to the defendant to rebut the presumption by calling evidence to throw doubt on the reliability of the device at the time: *R. v. Skegness Magistrates' Court, ex p. Cardy* [1985] R.T.R. 49. This, as mentioned earlier, is a very difficult task in practice and produces a situation where the defendant is at a great disadvantage.

When the issue is raised by a defendant and he or his legal representatives wish to explore the avenues to establish if there is any merit in the point raised, nothing lies ahead but obstacles. In past cases, solicitors have tried to compel the production of documents relating to the machine in question, in order to see if there are grounds for challenging the reliability of the device. In the main, any summonses which have been issued have been quashed by the Divisional Court. See for example *R. v. Coventry Magistrates' Court, ex p. Perks* [1985] R.T.R. 74; *R. v. Tower Bridge Magistrates' Court, ex p. D.P.P.* [1988] 86 Cr.App.R. 257. The Divisional Court seems to regard this exercise as a "fishing expedition" and one which should not be allowed. Unless there is evidence to the contrary, however, it is assumed that the machine was working properly: *Anderton v. Waring* [1986] R.T.R. 74.

A7–04   This is the obstacle the defence has to overcome on every occasion it is sought to challenge the reliability of the device. It would seem, however, that even where expert evidence has been heard that the Intoximeter was working erratically, but the effect was to be favourable to the defendant (*i.e.* the reading was very low), the printout will be relied on by the magistrates and a conviction will be upheld: *Wright v. Taplin (Note)* [1986] R.T.R. 388, D.C. A person cannot challenge the printout on the basis of a negative screening breath test provided only minutes before the evidential breath test: *Snelson v. Thompson* [1985]

R.T.R. 220, D.C. Readings of the printout are conclusive unless there is evidence of malfunction.

In *D.P.P. v. Hill* [1991] R.T.R. 351 the defendant was involved in an accident after leaving the nightclub where he worked. He failed a roadside test and it was noted that his eyes were glazed and his breath smelled of alcohol. The result of the specimen of breath provided at the police station was in excess of the prescribed limit. The justices accepted the evidence of the defendant and two witnesses who said that the defendant had only consumed half a pint of beer. They acquitted. The Divisional Court, allowing the prosecutor's appeal, said that it was possible to rebut the presumption, but that it was not an easy thing to do. If that were the case here, it would mean that both breath testing devices were faulty and that there was some other explanation for the defendant's glazed vision. The case was remitted with a direction to convict.

Ways of attacking the Intoximeter

There are a number of ways to challenge the evidence produced by the **A7–05** Intoximeter, and they will be dealt with in turn. It must be remembered that each individual case will turn on its own facts, and the aspects considered below, although under the umbrella of defences, are not all defences in the proper sense of the word, but in many cases merely amount to putting the prosecution to proof or challenging the basis of their evidence. In *Cracknell v. Willis* [1988] A.C. 450 the House of Lords said that there were no restrictions on the kind of evidence that can be called to challenge the printout and went on to say that the cases of *Hughes v. McConnell* [1985] R.T.R. 244, D.C., and *Price v. Nicholls* [1986] R.T.R. 155, D.C., were wrongly decided. In these two cases it was held that only direct evidence of the machine malfunctioning was admissible, and that it was not open to the defendant to challenge the reliability of the machine by giving oral evidence of what alcohol he had consumed. It is with the case of *Cracknell* in mind that the points to follow are put forward as ways of challenging the Intoximeter.

Wide discrepancy in readings

If there is a wide discrepancy in the readings (more than 20 per cent.) **A7–06** then it is submitted that the printout should be investigated and, where necessary, expert evidence called to challenge the readings. Having said this, it must be made clear that to date this approach has not been met with much sympathy from the courts.

In *Lloyd v. Morris* [1986] R.T.R. 299, the readings were 88 and 76 microgrammes. It was held that there was no evidence justifying the justices' dismissal of the case. In *Gordon v. Thorpe* [1986] R.T.R. 358 the readings were 110 and 94. Expert evidence was called on both sides and the experts disagreed as to the effects of the disparity. They did agree, however, that the breath alcohol level could be no less than 40 microgrammes. As the prosecution only has to prove that the defendant's breath/alcohol level was above the prescribed limit and not a particular figure, the ensuing conviction is not so surprising.

A7–07 In the Lion Laboratories Fact Sheet No. 1 on "Breath Samples and Differences in Readings," it is said that any variation in the breath readings is the result of a variation in the alcohol concentration in the breath sample. In effect this means that if the machine is operating within the Home Office specifications, it cannot be the machine that is responsible for the difference in readings. Some examples are given of situations where different readings may appear. The first reason advanced is that if a person with a large lung capacity blows into the instrument and fully expels the air in his lungs then the reading will be higher than if he merely satisfies the minimum 1.5 litre requirement. This operates in the motorist's favour (says the fact sheet), as the higher reading represents the true concentration of alcohol whereas it is the lower reading that is used in evidence.

A second example given to explain differences in readings is if the person artificially and very temporarily reduces his breath alcohol concentration to a small degree by hyperventilating immediately before blowing into the instrument. They do note, however, that a person trying this would be prevented by the police from doing so and may find themselves charged with failing to supply a specimen. As this undoubtedly would be the case, one wonders why it is advanced as an explanation for differences in readings, since in practice what is being challenged are specimens properly given. See also for cases on this aspect: *Maharaj v. Solomon* [1987] R.T.R. 295; *Lodge v. Chief Constable of Greater Manchester* [1988] Crim.L.R. 533. Convictions were upheld with readings of 81 and 67, 52 and 64 microgrammes respectively.

In a case where the driver sought to challenge the reliability of the Intoximeter by asserting that he had only drunk a certain quantity of alcohol, the Divisional Court held that it was open to the prosecution to seek to rebut that assertion by any relevant evidence, including the roadside breath test: *Lafferty v. D.P.P.*, March 11, 1994 (unreported).

Differences in readings between the printout and the blood or urine analysis

A7–08 In cases where the defendant has exercised his right to a blood or urine test after having given a specimen of breath, and after conversion the results are widely disparate then, in particular if the option reading is lower than the printout, the printout may be challenged. One must remember to take into account the time that the different specimens were taken and the usual considerations of back calculation. See *Lucking v. Forbes* [1986] R.T.R. 97.

A modified machine

The machine on which the test is taken must conform with the Home **A7–09**
Office specifications. There is always a possibility, faint it is conceded,
that the machine has been modified in some way and therefore is not
within the scope of the Approval Order. Again, as stated before, this
would be difficult to investigate. It would involve compelling the production of documents or compelling the attendance of an engineer
and, in addition, inspection of the machine. These facilities are not
generally available to the defence. See *Young v. Flint* [1987] R.T.R. 300,
D.C.

Section 16 Road Traffic Offenders Act 1988

A challenge can be made on the basis that the printout does not com- **A7–10**
ply with **section 16** of the **R.T.O.A. 1988**. Points may be taken if the
printout is inaccurate in its record of the time, date or even that it does
not relate to the defendant. It should be signed in the appropriate
places by the officer and the defendant. If there is such a challenge, it
may be appropriate to give notice to require the attendance of the
certifying officer.

In *McKeown v. D.P.P.; Jones v. D.P.P.* [1995] Crim.L.R. 69, the clock on
the Intoximeter in both cases was inaccurate. The argument successfully advanced in *McKeown* was that the inaccuracy of the timing
mechanism rendered documents produced by the Intoximeter
inadmissible.

In the case of *Jones* it was found that the device was not reliable and
therefore the defendant should not have been convicted of failure to
provide a specimen of breath.

Calibration readings

The calibration readings must be within the prescribed limits (32–37 **A7–11**
for the Intoximeter and 32–38 for the Camic). If they are not, then the
admissibility of the printout should be challenged.

The purge and blank cycle

If the purge result does not register zero then this would appear to **A7–12**
show that the machine was not functioning properly and, by impli-
cation, not purging the residual alcohol properly. The operator's
handbook does not assist as to whether it is impossible for the procedure to be carried out if the purge is not satisfactory. As a matter of
logic it may appear to be so but, as experience has shown, machines
can do funny things!

Non-compliance with the manufacturers' instructions

That the manufacturers' instructions have not been complied with, **A7–13** should afford a basis for challenging the printout. Again there would be problems for the defence in seeking to establish this point. For such a challenge to succeed, it would seem that some prejudice to the defendant would have to be shown or that the result was unduly helpful to the prosecution: *Black v. Bickmore* [1982] R.T.R. 167, D.C. Also it would be incumbent on the defence to show non-compliance: *Att.-Gen.'s Reference (No. 1 of 1978)* [1978] R.T.R. 377.

Acetone: medical conditions which could affect the readings

A7–14   The Lion Intoximeter has a second alcohol/acetone detector in order to detect the presence of acetone in the breath sample. Although most people do not generate acetone in their breath, there are some people who do so for various reasons. The most common reasons are diabetes persons on high protein/low carbohydrate diets, fasting, shock and people who take excessive exercise without a sufficient intake of carbohydrates. There are other conditions which are thought to contribute to the body generating acetone. These are:

   (a) Anaesthesia or surgical operation;
   (b) Van Gierkes disease;
   (c) Throtoxicosis;
   (d) severe infection;
   (e) vomiting in early pregnancy;
   (f) alcohol abuse.

Acetone can be ingested. Some drugs contain acetone and certain drink mixers convert into acetone in the body. Acetone can be inhaled where, for example, solvent is used in the working environment.

   Some medications could also cause high readings, such as mouthwash.

Acetone and the Intoximeter

A7–15   In the Intoximeter, once the sample of breath has been analysed in the infra-red cell, a small sample passes to the acetone detector and if acetone is detected a correction should be made to the reading of the infra-red cell. If acetone is found in the breath, its presence will be indicated on the display as "trace acetone", "moderate acetone", and "large acetone."

   One of the confidential documents leaked by Dr Jones (an ex-employee of Lion Laboratories) in the *Daily Express* case was an internal memo dated December 20, 1983. This memo revealed that recent tests carried out by the Home Office showed that the great majority of machines at the time had little or no acetone compensation, the reason for this being that the instruments were not set up correctly according to the laid-down procedure.

This begs the question: can we be sure that each machine is correctly set up today? In addition one has to bear in mind the problem in calling evidence tending to show that the machine was not correctly set up.

The question then arises: can there be a challenge to the Intoximeter on the grounds of the presence of acetone? It is submitted that in extreme cases there can be a challenge, the success of which, of course, is perhaps doubtful, given the courts' attitude to these matters.

There are two approaches. If there is a reading for acetone and there **A7–16** is no medical explanation for it, then an immediate examination by a doctor would be required and the calling of expert evidence to found the challenge. The opposite situation should also apply. If the machine detects no acetone but the person has such a medical condition that acetone should be shown, then this could cast doubt on the reliability of the machine.

The answer provided by Lion Laboratories is that, as the two systems are separate, and different principles and techniques are used, if the acetone system is over-sensitive, the alcohol readings are reliable inasmuch as they do not over-reflect the subject's breath/alcohol concentration. If the system is over-sensitive, it has the effect of reducing the alcohol reading to a small extent. The question of under-sensitivity is not dealt with though.

The second point made by the company is that, even with severe conditions, the excess would rarely be above 3 microgrammes. These arguments should be taken into account when consulting an expert but should not, it is submitted, deter a defendant from investigating the issue where there are strong grounds for so doing.

Duress and necessity

There have been some cases in the past which have considered the **A7–17** defences of duress and necessity, but they have been in the main concerned with the manner of driving. In recent years there have been cases which have been concerned specifically with drink/driving offences.

In the case of *D.P.P. v. Jones* [1990] R.T.R. 33, the defendant had been drinking in a public house. He was struck on the head in the car park by another man. In an attempt to evade the other man, the defendant ran around his car several times, got into it and locked himself in. The other man hit and kicked the car, shouted abuse, whereupon the defendant decided that his only means of escape was to drive out of the car park, which he did. He did not check to see if he was being pursued and drove home some two miles away. At trial he submitted that he had a defence akin to duress. The justices found that the defence of necessity was open to him and dismissed the information.

The appeal by the prosecutor was allowed, as the defendant had not ascertained if he was being pursued, whether on foot, in a vehicle, or otherwise, and that the defence of necessity did not avail him driving all the way home in his car.

A7–18   In *D.P.P. v. Bell* [1991] R.T.R. 335, the Crown Court on appeal found that the defendant (driver) and three friends had been to various public houses and finally to a club where the defendant got into an argument and was forced to beat a hasty retreat. The defendant admitted that he had intended to carry on driving. At the time of driving off, the defendant was in terror of being caused serious personal injury and drove off in that belief. The Crown Court being of that opinion allowed the appeal. The prosecution asserted that the defence was not available to a person whose material actions would have been the same if the threatening circumstances had not occurred.

The Divisional Court held that where the defence of duress was raised in relation to an illegal course of action, the point at which that course of action ceased to be legitimised was a matter for the tribunal of fact and it was not open to them on appeal on a question of law to investigate whether the facts found could amount to duress.

A7–19   The defence of duress rarely succeeds. In two more recent cases, the Divisional Court, allowing appeals by the prosecution against magistrates' decisions to acquit on the grounds of duress, emphasised that the magistrates had to consider the objective limb of the test which they had failed to do in the present cases.

In the first case, Davis who was twice the legal limit at the time of the incident, said that he had driven off from the flat of a male acquaintance after he had become the object of unwelcome homosexual advances by the acquaintance.

In the second case, Pittaway, who was recently divorced from a violent husband, went to a party with her boyfriend. The boyfriend became jealous of another man who spoke to her and he became abusive. There were no specific threats. Fearing violence, she waited outside in her car for some minutes and then drove off. She was stopped by the police and found to be two times over the legal limit. The two cases were remitted back to the magistrates court with directions to convict as neither defendant on the facts was in immediate fear of death or serious injury: *D.P.P. v. Davis; D.P.P. v. Pittaway* [1994] Crim.L.R. 600.

A7–20   It is a defence to an allegation of being "in charge" with excess alcohol to show on the balance of probabilities, that, at the material time, there was no likelihood of the defendant driving whilst the proportion of alcohol in his breath, blood or urine remained likely to exceed the prescribed limit: **section 5(2) R.T.A. 1988.** Following the comments in *D.P.P. v. Frost* [1989] R.T.R. 11, expert evidence will invariably be needed to establish that at the time when the defendant next intended to drive, he would have been below the limit.

In the case of *Drake v. D.P.P.* [1994] R.T.R. 411, the appellant was convicted of being in charge of a motor vehicle with excess alcohol. He had left his car in a British Rail car park without paying the parking fee and thus his car was clamped. He returned later to the car and there then ensued a heated argument with the subcontractors who refused to take the clamp off until the £35 fee was paid. The appellant took a claw hammer from his boot and attempted to remove the clamp. A plain clothes police man arrived and told Drake to put the hammer away. Uniformed officers then arrived and he was arrested. At the police station he provided two specimens of breath on the Intoximeter which were above the prescribed limit.

The appellant's case at the Crown Court, was that any offence must have been committed between his returning to the car and the time of his arrest, but as his car was clamped there was no likelihood of him driving it.

In the Divisional Court it was also argued that, as the car was immobile the appellant could not be in charge. The Divisional Court found that (a) the appellant was in charge of the car, but (b) that there was no likelihood of him driving at the material time. The appeal was allowed.

Defence checklist

(a) Examine the printout carefully: **A7–21**
    (i) Check the correctness of the date, the officer's name, the defendant's name and the time;
    (ii) do the signatures appear in the right portion of the printout, and is the printout signed?;
    (iii) check the STD figures. Are they between 32 and 37 or 32 and 38 for the Lion Intoximeter and the Camic respectively?;
    (iv) check the BLK readings and the times between each reading. Longer than a few seconds may reveal some evidence of problems with the machine;
    (v) check the readings. If there is a large difference in the readings consider further steps;
    (vi) is there a reading for acetone? If so, investigate further;
    (vii) was it served within seven days of the hearing?
(b) If the defendant provided a second specimen under the option, ensure it is analysed. Is there a large discrepancy in the result? If so, seek expert advice.
(c) If the reading was up to 50, check that the option was offered. If so, was he told of the option to provide blood or urine?
(d) Remember to check:
    (i) Whether the driver had been drinking within 20 minutes of the test;
    (ii) whether he had taken a mouthwash, breath freshener or aniseed just before the test;
    (iii) whether he had vomited just before the test; and
    (iv) whether he had been smoking just before the test.
(e) If necessary, obtain full medical history from the defendant or preferably his doctor.
(f) Remember, if post-offence consumption is raised, then expert

evidence is needed. Take full instructions dealing with the matters laid out in § A7–02.

(g) Remember that the constable must be in uniform for an arrest under **section 6** of the **R.T.A. 1988**. For example a constable is still in uniform when not wearing his helmet: *Wallwork v. Giles* [1970] R.T.R. 118.

(h) Did the constable have reasonable cause to suspect an offence was being, or had been committed or that alcohol had been consumed? Look at the circumstances carefully.

(i) If the motorist is requested to take an alternative specimen, check the circumstances. Do they fall within the exceptions under **section 7(3)** of the **R.T.A. 1988**.

(j) Remember the principles of the exclusion of illegally or unfairly obtained evidence. Have in mind **section 78 P.A.C.E. 1984** (exclusion of unfair evidence). See: *Matto v. Wolverhampton Crown Court* [1987] R.T.R. 337.

(k) Check the current state of the law, especially on appeal. In *Stokes v. Sayers* [1988] R.T.R. 89, it was said that lawyers in breathalyser cases should be alert to ensure that new legal developments had not made a pending appeal unnecessary before it came on for hearing.

(l) If the defence are not accepting the evidence of the printout, notice must be served on the prosecution in order for the officer to give evidence as to the operation of the breath test. Use the operator's handbook as a basis for testing in cross examination whether the officer is trained upon the device.

Chapter 8

FAILURE TO PROVIDE A SPECIMEN

The offence

Section 7(6) of the **R.T.A. 1988** provides: A8–01

"A person who without reasonable excuse, fails to provide a specimen when required to do so in pursuance of this section is guilty of
an offence."

The section refers to the provision of a specimen for analysis.

A person can be charged and tried on two charges under **section
7(6)** in respect of the same facts and factual situation: *R. v. Chichester
Justices, ex p. D.P.P.* [1994] R.T.R. 175.

The requirement

The power to require a specimen to be provided is laid down in **sec-**   A8–02
tion 7(1). The proper procedure must be followed. One point to note in
relation to this section is that there only needs to be an investigation
into whether a person has committed an offence under **sections 4** or **5**
before the constable may require a specimen for analysis. The fact that
a person has attended a police station voluntarily (in other words not
under arrest) or has been arrested lawfully or unlawfully, is immaterial: *Bunyard v. Hayes* [1985] R.T.R. 348. The prosecution must show
that the requirement was properly made and also that the warning of
the consequences of failure was given.

Can a constable require more than one person to provide a specimen
for analysis in respect of the same offence? The case of *Pearson v. Commissioner of Police of the Metropolis* [1988] R.T.R. 276, D.C., answered
this point in the affirmative. In this case there were three persons who
had been drinking. The officer did not know which of them had been
driving or in charge. They were all required to provide a specimen. On
appeal, it was argued that as only one person could be guilty of the
offence, the officer had to establish who was the driver and could not
require more than one person to provide a specimen. The argument
was rejected and the convictions upheld.

A charge that a motorist, in the course of an investigation as to   A8–03
whether he had committed an offence under **section 4** or **5** of **R.T.A.
1988**, did without reasonable excuse fail to provide a specimen of
breath for analysis in pursuance of a requirement by a constable under

the provisions of the Act contrary to **section 7(6)**, was held to be bad for duplicity: *D.P.P. v. Corcoran* [1992] R.T.R. 289. This case has now been held to be erroneous and reached *per incuriam*. The section does not create two separate offences: *Shaw v. D.P.P.* [1993] R.T.R. 2.

The conflict between the decisions in *Corcoran* and *Shaw* has been resolved by the House of Lords in the case of *Butterworth v. D.P.P.* [1994] R.T.R. 181. Their Lordships took the view that only one offence was created by the section and thus endorsed the decision in *Shaw*.

The root of the problem lay in the conflict between the two House of Lords cases of *Commissioner of Police for the Metropolis v. Curran* [1976] 1 W.L.R. 87 and *R. v. Courtie* [1984] 1 A.C. 463. In the former Lord Diplock stated that similar provisions in the **R.T.A. 1972** created *one* offence committed independently of the defendant's guilt of the offence in connection with which the specimen was requested. In the latter, a case concerning buggery, Lord Diplock held that where a statute prescribes different maximum penalties dependant on a particular factual ingredient, two distinct offences are created. The latter was relied on in *Corcoran* (which said that an information for failing to supply a specimen must specify whether the police were investigating an offence under **sections 4** or **5(1)(a)** (driving or attempting to drive) or under **section 5(1)(b)** (being in charge)) and the former in *Shaw*.

In the last edition, the authors took the view that the *Shaw* and *Curran* line of authority best upheld the spirit and function of **section 7(6)**, because on the face of the section, one offence is created. During the course of an investigation into any of the offences mentioned above, the defendant may be required to give a specimen. He is guilty of an offence if he fails to do so without reasonable excuse, irrespective of a subsequent disposal the offence being investigated. This is supported by the courts' interpretation of "reasonable excuse" under **section 7(6)** as restricted to physical or mental inability (*R. v. Lennard* [1973] 1 W.L.R. 483). The mischief at which **section 7(6)** is aimed, fairly or not, is the simple refusal to cooperate during the course of an investigation. The definition of the offence under **section 7(6)** does not involve different factual ingredients in the way envisaged in *Courtie*.

Two points can be noted in passing. There is no bar to the investigating officer under the **section 7** procedure carrying out some of the functions of the custody officer as laid out in **P.A.C.E. 1984**. In addition, the **section 7** procedure does not constitute an interview for the purposes of the **Code on Detention and Treatment** (para. 6c Notes for Guidance).

"Fails"

A8–04 The word "failure" includes a failure, an inability or a refusal to comply with the requirement made. Where a person supplied a specimen of urine but later stole it, it was held that he could not be convicted of failure to supply a specimen: *R. v. Rothery* [1976] R.T.R. 550. Where a specimen was provided but the jar containing the specimen dropped out of the suspect's hand when handing it to the police officer, there was failure to provide a specimen: *Ross v. Hodges* [1975] R.T.R. 55. The court will work from the assumption that the Intoximeter was in working order when the requirement was made if there is a "no sample" record: *Anderton v. Waring* [1986] R.T.R. 74. A person who later changes his mind and agrees to give a specimen will nonetheless be convicted of failure to provide a specimen: *Procaj v. Johnstone* [1970] Crim.L.R. 110. It is not sufficient to provide one specimen of breath; there must be two within the specified period: *Cracknell v. Willis* [1988] A.C. 450.

If the suspect provides one specimen and it is less than the prescribed limit, he is still guilty of the offence if he fails to give a second specimen: *Stepniewski v. Commissioner of Police of the Metropolis* [1985] R.T.R. 330. An observation was made in relation to future cases of this sort – that the court should mitigate any penalty in such circumstances and that the prosecuting authorities should give serious consideration about prosecuting similar cases. The evidence of failure should be in admissible form: *Bermudez v. Chief Constable of Avon and Somerset* [1988] Crim.L.R. 452, D.C. The printout is admissible to show failure: *Castle v. Cross* [1984] 1 W.L.R. 1372. It is not, however, a prerequisite: *Teape v. Godfrey* [1986] R.T.R. 213.

There is argument for the exclusion of the printout in a case where one specimen has been provided, when there is dispute between the prosecution and defence about the procedure, on the grounds of the prejudicial effect of introducing the analysis when the issue is the failure: *Oldfield v. Anderton* [1986] R.T.R. 314.

Reasonable excuse

The defendant has to raise the issue of reasonable excuse, but once this is done the onus is on the prosecution to disprove it: *Rowland v. Thorpe* [1970] 3 All E.R. 195. The question of whether the facts are capable of amounting to a reasonable excuse is a matter of law, but once this hurdle is overcome, then it is a question of fact and degree whether it is a reasonable excuse, but the burden is still on the prosecution to show that there is no reasonable excuse: *Law v. Stephens* [1971] R.T.R. 358, D.C. **A8–05**

The prosecution must prove there is no reasonable excuse to the criminal standard, *i.e.* beyond reasonable doubt: *R. v. Harling* [1970] R.T.R. 441. See the case of *R. v. Hunt* [1987] A.C. 352, where the House of Lords considered the question of reverse burdens. There is no definition in the Act of "reasonable excuse," but it was stated in the case of *R. v. Lennard* [1973] 1 W.L.R. 483 that the reasonable excuse "must arise out of a physical or mental inability to provide one or a substantial risk to health in its provision." Given the requirements of the breath test machines for a minimum pressure of breath to provide a satisfactory specimen, lack of lung capacity may well provide a reasonable excuse if it is backed up by medical evidence.

In *D.P.P. v. Curtis* [1993] R.T.R. 72, it was held that justices were not entitled to act upon material which was beyond the evidence before them; that whilst they could, where appropriate use their knowledge of a particular subject, they should be wary of using their knowledge of a physical or mental condition which was not supported by evidence before them. (The justices concluded that the defendant had suffered an asthma attack as a result of fear and anxiety and, therefore, could not give a second specimen although the defendant had complained only of a cold and the medical evidence was that she had a low anxiety threshold and she had been treated for nervous asthma.) See also *D.P.P. v. Radford* [1995] R.T.R. 86.

Reasonable excuse: some successful cases on physical inability

A8–06 A physical inability to provide a specimen due to some physical incapacity may be a reasonable excuse. In the case of *R. v. Harding* [1974] R.T.R. 325, it was said that a fear of a hypodermic needle may have had the effect of making the defendant incapable of providing a specimen of blood. It is submitted that there would have to be some supporting medical evidence for this defence to succeed. In fact, it is expected that, if a medical reason is being advanced, medical evidence on the condition will need to be called. Indeed Lord Widgery C.J. said in *Harding* that:

> "No fear short of a phobia recognised by medical science to be as strong and inhibiting as, for instance, claustrophobia can be allowed to excuse failure to provide a specimen for a laboratory test, and most if not all cases where the fear of providing it is claimed to be invincible the claim will have to be supported by medical evidence."

A genuine but unreasonable phobia of contracting AIDS has been found to be a reasonable excuse: *DeFreitas v. D.P.P.* [1993] R.T.R. 98. (Contrast with *D.P.P. v. Fountain, infra.*)

A8–07 The courts are being discouraged from accepting the word of the defendant alone: *Sykes v. White* [1983] R.T.R. 419, D.C. This case was followed in *Alcock v. Read* [1980] R.T.R. 71 which involved a "genuine invincible repugnance" to needles. In the case of *Teape v. Godfrey* [1986] R.T.R. 213 it was said that, if a suspect knows that he suffers from a medical condition which prevents him from providing sufficient breath to satisfy the requirement, he must inform the constable of this fact. If this is done, then the constable would have to consider the situation and may ask for an alternative specimen or insist on a breath specimen. The constable, if he insists on the breath test, runs the risk of the case being dismissed at court if medical evidence is then called by the defence as to the medical condition.

The court in the case of *D.P.P. v. Kinnersley* [1993] R.T.R. 105, disagreed with the view expressed in *Teape* that there was a duty to inform the police officer of any medical condition, commenting that the view was clearly *obiter* and that the effect of the caution had not been considered.

This case also says that the suspect must additionally show that he tried as hard as he could to provide a specimen. In *Cotgrove v. Cooney* [1987] R.T.R. 124, the justices found that there was a reasonable excuse when a person tried as hard as he could to provide a specimen. This can be contrasted with the case of *Grady v. Pollard* [1988] R.T.R. 316 and other more recent cases in which it was held that the fact that the person tried as hard as he could was not a reasonable excuse. The court declined to state that *Cotgrove* had been wrongly decided so the issue remains open. The case of *Dempsey v. Catton* [1986] R.T.R. 194, D.C., raised the question of phobia of machines but the issue was not resolved. The Divisional Court has warned justices not to be gullible and accept a defence argument that a defendant was too stressed following an accident to provide a specimen of breath. If this was an automatic reasonable excuse, the whole purpose of the Act would be defeated: *D.P.P. v. Eddowes* [1991] R.T.R. 35.

Justices were entitled, without having heard any medical evidence, to find that shock combined with inebriation which rendered a defendant physically incapable of providing a breath specimen for analysis, could amount to a reasonable excuse: *D.P.P. v. Pearman* [1992] R.T.R. 407.

See also: *D.P.P. v. Crofton* [1994] R.T.R. 279, where the findings of the magistrates were upheld in the Divisional Court. They found that breathlessness caused by pre-existing depression which was not self-precipitated had caused the defendant's failure to provide two specimens of breath. There was no medical evidence to support the contention, just evidence from the defendant alone which had been accepted. The Divisional Court referring to the case of *Pearman* noted that although medical evidence would normally be required, the justices had believed the defendant on the important matters such as the evidence of mental or physical inability and the causative link between the conditions, and the failure to provide the specimen.

Reasonable excuse: successful cases on non-comprehension

It is essential that the requirement and the warning are communicated **A8–08** effectively to the suspect for it may afford a defence that the person failed to comprehend what was being communicated. In the case of *Beck v. Sager* [1979] Crim.L.R. 257, it was held to be a reasonable excuse that the defendant was unable to understand what was said to him due to his limited grasp of English. The same finding was made in the case of *Chief Constable of Avon and Somerset v. Singh* [1988] R.T.R. 107 where it was held that if a warning was given but not understood by the defendant, then it was not an adequate warning within **section 8(8)** of the **1972 Act**. The statutory procedure was not properly complied with, and the defendant was entitled to be acquitted. In the case of *R. v. Dolan* [1969] 1 W.L.R. 1479, it was held to be a reasonable excuse if the defendant did not understand the statutory warning as to the consequences of failure.

An unusual case was *Spalding v. Laskaraina Paine* [1985] Crim.L.R. 673. In this case the defendant was found in a car with half a bottle of whisky. At the police station she repeatedly stated that she wished to die. The magistrates found a reasonable excuse due to her emotional distress. The acquittal was upheld by the Divisional Court which said that this came under a "mental inability" to provide a specimen. The court did go on to distinguish the situation of self-induced intoxication which would make the defendant unable to appreciate the requirement being made.

Reasonable excuse: successful cases – miscellaneous

A8–09   If the defendant's doctor happens to be present at the police station at the appropriate time then it will not be a refusal (failure) if the defendant insists on the specimen being taken by his own doctor: *Bayliss v. Thames Valley Police* [1978] R.T.R. 328. Where a defendant insisted on reading the consent form before signing it, he was held not to have refused (failed), although the police thought he was indulging in delaying tactics: *Hier v. Read* [1978] R.T.R. 114, D.C. In *R. v. Harling* [1970] R.T.R. 441, the doctor made three unsuccessful attempts to take blood. The defendant lost confidence in the doctor's competence and it was stated that this may have been a reasonable excuse.

No reasonable excuse: physical inability

A8–10   The following cases are examples of physical disabilities held not to amount to reasonable excuse:

(a) Unspecified medical grounds: *D.P.P. v. Boden* [1988] R.T.R. 188, D.C.;

(b) a mere dislike of the sight of blood not amounting to a phobia: *Sykes v. White* [1983] R.T.R. 419, D.C.;

(c) a fear of blood such as to make the defendant so light-headed that he had to sit down: *Sykes v. White, supra*;

(d) a fear of contracting AIDS through the use of needles: *D.P.P. v. Fountain* [1988] Crim.L.R. 123;

(e) an offer that blood to be taken from a different part of the body or in a different way from ordinary medical practice: *Solesbury v. Pugh* [1969] 1 W.L.R. 1114; *Rushton v. Higgins* [1972] Crim.L.R. 440;

(f) difficulty in breathing through the nose: *Woolman v. Lenton* [1985] Crim.L.R. 516, D.C.;

(g) making every effort by blowing as hard as able but being unable to provide a specimen: *Grady v. Pollard* [1988] R.T.R. 316; *D.P.P. v. Daley* [1992] R.T.R. 155; *Smith v. D.P.P.* [1992] R.T.R. 413;

(h) the defendant's self-induced intoxication which had rendered him unable to understand the procedure: *D.P.P. v. Beech* [1992] R.T.R. 239;

(i) stress caused by self-precipitated agitation. Almost invariably medical evidence would be required for such a defence: *D.P.P. v. Ambrose* [1992] R.T.R. 285.

No reasonable excuse: miscellaneous

Most of the cases in this section relate to ignorance of law, making con-   **A8–11**
sent conditional and other procedural matters:

(a) A wish to see a solicitor first before providing a specimen: *D.P.P. v. Billington* [1988] R.T.R. 231; *Grennan v. Westcott* [1988] R.T.R. 253, D.C.; *Francis v. Chief Constable of Avon and Somerset Constabulary* [1988] R.T.R. 250, D.C.; *Dickinson v. D.P.P.* [1989] Crim.L.R. 741, D.C.; *Salter v. D.P.P.* [1992] R.T.R. 386. But see *Hudson v. D.P.P.* [1992] R.T.R. 27 where the defendant refused to provide a specimen of breath until after he had seen a solicitor having been provided with a form on his arrival at the police station stating he had a right to see a solicitor "at any time." The Divisional Court said that in this particular case it was not possible to say that there was no material upon which the court could have exercised its discretion under **section 78 P.A.C.E. 1984** to exclude the evidence of the defendant's refusal;

(b) agreement to provide a specimen on condition that solicitor is   **A8–12**
present: *Pettigrew v. Northumbria Police Authority* [1976] R.T.R. 177; *Payne v. Diccox* [1980] R.T.R. 83;

(c) desire to wait for diplomatic representative: *R. v. Seaman* [1971] R.T.R. 456;

(d) religious belief: *R. v. Najran* [1973] R.T.R. 451, C.A.; *R. v. John* [1974] 1 W.L.R. 624;

(e) being in a confused state: *Chief Constable of Avon and Somerset v. O'Brien* [1987] R.T.R. 182;

(f) a belief that no offence was committed: *R. v. Downey* [1970] R.T.R. 257; *Williams v. Osborne* [1975] R.T.R. 181; *Daniels v. D.P.P.* [1992] R.T.R. 140;

(g) believing the officer had no power to make the requirement: *R. v. Reid* [1973] R.T.R. 536;

(h) believing that the officer was acting in bad faith: *McGrath v. Vipas* [1984] R.T.R. 58;

(i) post-driving consumption: *R. v. Lennard* [1973] 1 W.L.R. 483;

(j) the first specimen of breath was under the prescribed limit: *R. v. Stepniewski* [1985] R.T.R. 330;

(k) refusal to give blood and sign consent form: *R. v. McAllister*   **A8–13**
[1974] R.T.R. 408;

(l) where several persons suspected of being the driver, no excuse that defendant was not in fact the driver: *Pearson v. Commissioner of Police of the Metropolis* [1988] R.T.R. 276;

(m) failure to reply following caution when requested to provide a specimen of breath: *Campbell v. D.P.P.* [1989] R.T.R. 256;

(n) right to read the Codes of Practice not an excuse to delay test: *D.P.P. v. Skinner, D.P.P. v. Cornwall* [1990] R.T.R. 254; *D.P.P. v. Whalley* [1991] R.T.R. 161;

(o) a previous unlawful arrest was irrelevant to subsequent procedures and could not amount to a reasonable excuse: *Thomas v. D.P.P.* [1991] R.T.R. 292;

(p) it was not a prerequisite and therefore no reasonable excuse that an offence under **sections 4** or **5** had been committed: *Hawes v. D.P.P.* [1993] R.T.R. 116 (driving on private land);

(q) the defendant was not told that he had to provide the second specimen within three minutes: *D.P.P. v. Thomas, The Times,* July 10, 1992;

(r) insisting on having one's own doctor to take the specimen: *D.P.P. v. Smith,* May 11, 1993 (unreported).

Penalties

A8–14 The maximum penalty for this offence depends on which offence was being investigated. Where the specimen was required to ascertain ability to drive or the proportion of alcohol at the time the offender was driving or attempting to drive, then the maximum penalty is six months' imprisonment and/or a level 5 fine. Endorsement and disqualification are obligatory unless special reasons exist. Twelve months is the minimum disqualification or three years if there has been a similar conviction within the previous 10 years. In any other case, the maximum is three months and/or a level 4 fine. Disqualification is discretionary and endorsement is obligatory unless special reasons apply. The code is DR30 where there is obligatory disqualification and DR60 in any other case.

In *Crampsie v. D.P.P., The Times,* February 18, 1993 it was emphasised that justices should make clear on what basis they are sentencing when dealing with cases under **section 7**.

Checklist

A8–15
(1) Did the driver at the time suffer from any physical disability to affect capacity to carry out the test, *i.e.* lung complaint? If so, obtain expert evidence.

(2) What was the driver's physical and mental condition at the time of the test?

(3) Was the warning given? If so, was it understood?

Chapter 9

DANGEROUS AND RECKLESS DRIVING

Introduction

This chapter deals with the offences of dangerous driving and causing   **A9–01**
death by dangerous driving introduced by the **R.T.A. 1991**. As there
are still some cases under the old law, the previous offences of reckless
driving and causing death by reckless driving are also dealt with.
Some other offences, for example wanton and furious driving are also
considered.
   The offence of careless driving is dealt with in Chapter 10.

Dangerous and reckless driving

The **R.T.A. 1991** replaced the offences of causing death by reckless   **A9–02**
driving and reckless driving by substituting for them causing death by
dangerous driving and dangerous driving.

Dangerous driving

Section 2 of the **R.T.A. 1991** provides that: **A9–03**

> "A person who drives a mechanically propelled vehicle danger-
> ously on a road or other public place is guilty of an offence."

This offence is an "either way" offence; on indictment it carries a maximum sentence of two years and/or an unlimited fine and on summary
conviction of six months and/or a fine subject to the statutory maximum. As a result of other changes brought about by the R.T.A. 1991,
the offence also carries obligatory disqualification for a period of not
less then 12 months and the offender's licence must be endorsed with
points in the range of three to eleven. In addition, there must be an
order that the driver be ordered to take an "appropriate driving test":
section 36 R.T.O.A. 1988 as substituted by **section 32 R.T.A. 1991**.
   The offence of dangerous driving is not new to the statute books.
Dangerous driving was abolished in 1977 with the passing of the
Criminal Law Act 1977 and was replaced with reckless driving. Since
the passing of the **1977 Act**, there had been considerable criticism of
the offence, and in particular of the word "recklessly". There was no

111

definition of recklessly in the Act and, in practice, it had proved to be a difficult concept for courts to deal with. The **1991 Act** seeks to address this problem in defining the term "dangerous".

How is dangerous defined?

A9–04 **Section 1** of the **1991 Act** substitutes a new **section 2A** to the **R.T.A. 1988**:

> **"Meaning of dangerous driving**
>   2A. – (1) For the purposes of sections 1 and 2 above a person is to be regarded as driving dangerously if (and, subject to subsection (2) below, only if)
>   (a) the way he drives falls far below what would be expected of a competent and careful driver, and
>   (b) it would be obvious to a competent and careful driver that driving in that way would be dangerous.
>   (2) A person is also to be regarded as driving dangerously for the purposes of sections 1 and 2 above if it would be obvious to a competent and careful driver that driving the vehicle in its current state would be dangerous.
>   (3) In subsections (1) and (2) above 'dangerous' refers to danger either of injury to any person or of serious damage to property; and in determining for the purposes of those subsections what would be expected of, or obvious to, a competent and careful driver in a particular case, regard shall be had not only to the circumstances of which he could be expected to be aware but also to any circumstances shown to have been within the knowledge of the accused.
>   (4) In determining for the purposes of subsection (2) above the state of a vehicle, regard may be had to anything attached to or carried on it or in it and to the manner in which it is attached or carried."

A9–05 There are essentially two stages to go through in deciding in each case whether the driving constitutes dangerous driving:

(a) Did the driving fall far below that of a careful and competent driver? An objective test of the standard of driving – taking into account those circumstances of which the defendant could be expected to be aware and also those shown to be within his knowledge, and if so

(b) would it be obvious to a competent and careful driver that driving in such a way would be dangerous – that is driving causing danger either of injury to any person, or of serious damage to property.

Other changes in the offence

A9–06 The other changes to note are that the scope of the offence has been widened to include "mechanically propelled vehicles" rather than just motor vehicles, and road has been substituted with "road or other public place." Prior to this change, the definition of motor vehicle given in **section 185** of the **R.T.A. 1988** had only included mechanically propelled vehicles intended or adapted for use on roads and had excluded various categories of vehicles, for example, go-karts. By also extending the scope of the offence to other public places, the driver of, for example, a stock car driving it in a public place, although he may not be a licensed driver, will be subject to the provisions of this new offence. Similar changes have been made to cover the offences of causing death by dangerous driving and careless driving offences.

The only exception from the effect of the newly defined offences appears to be motoring events authorised by regulations made by the Secretary of State: **section 13A** of the **R.T.A. 1988** as substituted by **section 5** of the **R.T.A. 1991**.

Reckless driving

Prior to the passing of the **R.T.A. 1991**, **section 2** of the **R.T.A. 1988** provided that: **A9–07**

> "a person who drives a motor vehicle on a road recklessly shall be guilty of an offence."

The offence was an "either way" offence, on indictment it carried a maximum sentence of two years and/or a fine and on summary conviction six months and/or a fine of level 5.

How has reckless driving been defined?

The leading case on the definition of recklessness is the House of Lords decision in *R. v. Lawrence* [1982] A.C. 510. The House of Lords decided that recklessness consisted of driving a vehicle in such a manner so as to create an obvious and serious risk of harmful consequences, where the driver failed to give any thought to there being any possibility of any such risk, or, having recognised that there was such a risk, nevertheless went on to take that risk. Lord Diplock gave, as part of his judgment, a model direction on recklessness based on the outline given above. He said: **A9–08**

> "[The jury] must be satisfied of two things: *First*, that the defendant was in fact driving the vehicle in such a manner as to create an *obvious and serious risk* of causing physical injury to some other person who might happen to be using the road, or doing substantial damage to property; *and second*, that in driving in that manner the defendant *did so without having given any thought to the possibility of there being any such risk or, having recognised that there was some risk involved, had nonetheless gone on to take it.*" [Emphasis added.]

Recklessness was also considered in the Scottish case of *Allan v. Pat-* **A9–09** *terson* [1980] R.T.R. 97. The High Court of Justiciary set out the test of recklessness as they saw it. The **R.T.A. 1988**, and its predecessors, applies to Scotland as well as to England and Wales, and it is interesting to note the differences in interpretation and of explanation. It is also interesting to note the similarities between the definition of reckless as set out in this judgment and the definition of dangerous driving set out in the **1991 Act**. The test set out in *Allan v. Patterson* requires an objective judgment of a course of driving to see whether the driving has "the grave quality of recklessness." This is further defined as driving:

> "... falling far below the standard of driving expected of the competent and careful driver and that it occurred either in the face of obvious and material dangers which were or should have been observed, appreciated and guarded against, or in circumstances which showed a complete disregard for any potential dangers which might result from the way the vehicle was being driven."

Parts of the judgment of this case may be of particular use to the practitioner who is faced with a case of reckless driving, dangerous driving or a case of careless driving, as useful comparisons are made between the standards. Reckless driving is said to mean:

> "... a piece of driving which, judged objectively, is eloquent of a high degree of negligence – much more than a mere want of due care and attention – and supports the inference that material risks were deliberately courted or that these risks which ought to have been obvious to any observant and careful driver were not noticed by reason of gross inattention. Driving 'recklessly' accordingly, is driving which demonstrates a gross degree of carelessness in the face of evident dangers."

Evidence of dangerousness/recklessness

A9–10   In considering whether a course of driving is dangerous or reckless, one must look at the whole of the particular incident; whether a particular course of driving amounts to dangerous or reckless driving will depend on the particular facts of the case. It is particularly important to look at the manner of the driving, the speed of the driving, the road conditions and what explanations the defendant is able to put forward about his driving. The condition of the vehicle involved is also important. In relation to dangerous driving, the **1991 Act** makes specific reference to the state of the vehicle and that a driver is to be regarded as driving dangerously, if it would be obvious to a competent and careful driver that driving the vehicle in the state it is would be dangerous: **section 2A(2)**. In considering this particular issue, anything attached to or carried on the vehicle and the manner in which it is attached or carried can be looked at. Also in relation to this consideration, and the question of dangerously as a whole, the **1991 Act** specifically sets out that "regard shall be had not only to the circumstances of which he could be expected to be aware but also to any circumstances shown to have been within the knowledge of the accused": **section 2A(3)**. The position was essentially the same under the old law, for example, it was held in the case of *R. v. Millar (Contractors) Ltd.* [1970] 2 Q.B. 54 that a driver who drove whilst aware of a defect could be convicted of reckless driving (see also *R. v. Crossman* [1986] R.T.R. 49).

The other important factor is the condition of the defendant: **A9–11** whether he is suffering from any impairment or disability which he knows of and which could result in creating an obvious and serious risk. The disability or impairment may take the form of an illness, drink or drugs. Where, for example, there is evidence of the consumption of alcohol, whether or not the defendant has been charged with an offence of driving under the influence of drink, and the amount consumed is such that it is likely to adversely affect the driver, then such evidence is clearly of some weight. There is no general hard and fast rule that all evidence of the consumption of alcohol is admissible although, in most cases, it will be admissible as it is highly probative. There is a general discretion to exclude such evidence where the prejudicial effect of the evidence outweighs the probative value of that evidence: see *R. v. McBride* [1962] 2 Q.B. 167.

The test of whether evidence of consumption is admissible or not, is whether the evidence tends to show that the amount of drink consumed was such that it would adversely affect a driver or that the driver was adversely affected by having consumed that alcohol: *R. v. Thorpe* [1972] 1 W.L.R. 342. In the case of *R. v. Griffiths (Gordon)* [1990] R.T.R. 224, Parker L.J. said:

> "The result of *Reg. v. Lawrence* and the earlier cases is as follows: (1) if the first limb of the test is satisfied and there is nothing more, the jury may convict; (2) if the prosecution wish to strengthen the inference which may be drawn from the fact that the first limb is satisfied or to displace any explanation advanced by the driver, they can do so by any evidence which is admissible; and (3) evidence of alcoholic consumption sufficient to impair control is admissible for this purpose."

(See also *R. v. Clarke (Andrew)* [1990] R.T.R. 248 and *R. v. Welburn* [1992] R.T.R. 391.) In the case of *R. v. Woodward, The Times*, December 7, 1994, C.A., the construction of **1988 Act, s.2A** and a defective driver was considered. They referred to the fact that the consumption of a large quantity of alcohol are within the driver's knowledge.

The course of driving

In certain circumstances there may be evidence of the defendant's **A9–12** driving some time before the actual incident which is the subject of the charge. In certain cases, the charge or indictment may be worded in such a manner so as to include several roads that it is alleged the defendant drove along **dangerously or recklessly**. Where there is only one place named in the information or indictment, it may be arguable whether evidence of earlier driving is admissible. The time gap and the distance from the actual scene will obviously be important factors in determining whether the evidence is admissible or not: *Coles v. Underwood, The Times*, November 2, 1983.

A9–13   *The Highway Code*

Although a breach of a provision of the Highway Code will not of itself lead to a criminal charge (**section 38(7) R.T.A. 1988**), it is often seen as a good guide in determining what amounts to dangerous, reckless or careless driving. Reference should always be made to the terms of the Highway Code when considering any case of dangerous, reckless or careless driving as a failure to observe the code may be relied upon as a factor in proving the allegation.

A9–14   *Other evidence that may show dangerousness or recklessness*

As mentioned above, it will be necessary to consider all the facts of the particular case. The speed of the vehicle, the speed limit in force on the particular road, the general traffic conditions and the condition of the road are all important factors. Driving at excessive speed in a built-up area near a school will be very strong evidence of dangerousness or recklessness.

A number of cases where the driving has been held to be reckless:

  (i) *R. v. Bannister* [1991] R.T.R. 1: driver drove behind another car on a motorway with his headlights on full beam, overtook the other car and pulled in front of him, he then braked sharply, forcing the other car to overtake him and then he followed feet behind the other car for some time. When the other car increased speed he pulled out and collided with the other car.

  (ii) *R. v. Steel* [1992] Crim.L.R. 904: driver drove along a dual carriageway where there was a 30 m.p.h. limit. He overtook one car on the offside, and then accelerated and overtook on the nearside another vehicle which was in the outside lane. In doing this, he lost control of his car, which hit the central reservation, rose into the air and landed in the opposite carriageway where it collided with a motorcycle.

  (iii) *R. v. Avellano* [1990] Crim.L.R. 121, C.A.: driver drove along the North Circular Road at 4 a.m. at 70 m.p.h. weaving from side to side, and going through three red traffic lights.

Procedure and alternative verdicts

A9–15   As stated at the start of this chapter, dangerous driving and the old offence of reckless driving are both either way offences. Both the old and new offences are closely associated with the offence of driving without due care and attention and a driver charged with an offence of dangerous driving or reckless driving can be convicted of driving without due care and attention. **Section 24 R.T.O.A. 1988**, as substituted by **section 24 R.T.A. 1991**, sets out the position in relation to alternative verdicts generally for road traffic offences. For example, a defendant who is charged with an offence of dangerous driving and is found not guilty of that offence may be convicted of careless driving.

For offences where the old law is still relevant, the position is that for an offence of reckless driving a defendant may, as an alternative, be found guilty of careless driving when he is acquitted by a jury of the main offence: **section 24 R.T.O.A. 1988**. Equally, where the Crown Court is considering an appeal against a charge of reckless driving, it can direct that a charge of careless driving is preferred where it allows an appeal: **section 24 R.T.O.A. 1988**. Where a charge under section 2 is to be tried at the Crown Court, and at committal the magistrates find that there is no case to answer on reckless driving, the court can go on to consider a charge of a lesser offence arising from the same facts (for example a **section 3** offence) – where the defendant has been summonsed in respect of that lesser offence or where he waives service of the summons. Where a defendant is tried at the magistrates' court in respect of an allegation of reckless driving, the magistrates can direct that a charge of careless driving is to be preferred if they find that the offence of reckless driving is not proved: **section 24 R.T.O.A. 1988**. This is different from the position on indictment, as it is not a finding of guilt on the lesser charge put simply the preferment of the lesser charge and, once the charge is preferred, the normal summary trial procedure is followed.

Sentencing: dangerous and reckless driving, causing death by dangerous driving or reckless driving

It is convenient to consider the question of sentencing for these offences together as the factors that will affect sentence are very broadly similar. **A9–16**

Dangerous driving and reckless driving carry a maximum sentence of two years' imprisonment and/or an unlimited fine if tried on indictment, and six months and/or a fine subject to the statutory maximum if tried summarily. There are some differences in the question of disqualification. In relation to the offence of dangerous driving there is a minimum disqualification period of 12 months, unless special reasons can be shown. For situations where reckless driving applies, the position is that disqualification is normally discretionary but, if the offence is committed within three years of a conviction for an offence of reckless driving or causing death by reckless driving, disqualification is obligatory. If there is no order of disqualification, the driver's licence will be endorsed with 10 penalty points (see Appendix E).

Causing death by dangerous driving, and the old offence of causing death by reckless driving, are triable only on indictment. The **C.J.A. 1993** has increased the maximum sentence for offences of causing death by dangerous driving, and for causing death by careless driving whilst under the influence of alcohol, from five years to 10 years' imprisonment. Disqualification is obligatory in all cases – for causing death by dangerous driving for a period of not less than two years unless the court finds that there are special reasons. For causing death by dangerous driving, the offender's licence must be endorsed with penalty points in the range of three to eleven.

A9–17   For offences of dangerous driving and causing death by dangerous driving where the offender is disqualified from driving, the court must also order the driver to take an appropriate test, and to be disqualified until the test is passed: **section 36 R.T.O.A. 1988** as substituted by **section 32 R.T.A. 1991**.

In the case of *R. v. Boswell* [1984] 1 W.L.R. 1047, the Court of Appeal issued guidelines for the sentencing of offences of reckless driving and causing death by reckless driving. Clearly the same principles will apply to causing death by dangerous driving and dangerous driving. As part of the judgment, the Lord Chief Justice indicated the various factors that would aggravate the offence and thereby increase the sentence, and also those factors that would mitigate the offence and the sentence. The main aggravating features were said to be:

(a) The consumption of drink or drugs;
(b) grossly excessive speed or racing;
(c) disregard of warnings;
(d) other related offences also committed at the same time;
(e) length and distance of the particular driving complained of, and whether the driving was deliberate;
(f) previous convictions for similar offences particularly offences involving the consumption of alcohol;
(g) more than one death resulting from the driving (*R. v. Rodenhurst* [1989] R.T.R. 333, appears to restrict this to continuous bad driving rather than multiple deaths in one car);
(h) the general nature of the defendant's behaviour at the time of the incident: failing to stop, or taking steps to escape;
(i) reckless driving or causing death by reckless driving during the course of trying to avoid apprehension.

A9–18   So far as the mitigating factors are concerned, the main ones were said to be:

(a) good driving record;
(b) a one-off piece of bad driving: a momentary lapse;
(c) good character;
(d) the effect the offence has had on the defendant: whether he has shown remorse for the offence.

Following on from these guidelines, it was said that generally, where there were no aggravating features present, then a non-custodial sentence might be appropriate, but where one or more of the aggravating features were present, then there would generally be a custodial sentence. An example of the application of these guidelines can be found in the case of *R. v. Janes* (1985) 7 Cr.App.R.(S.) 170. The appellant was a young man of 21. He pleaded guilty to two counts of causing death by reckless driving. He left a party driving a car with four passengers. He drove at high speed, despite protests from the passengers and lost control of the car, which then collided with a lamp-post. Two of the passengers in the car were killed. The appellant had a high blood alcohol level, he had no insurance, only held a provisional licence and the car was in a poor condition. He was sentenced to three-and-a-half years' imprisonment and disqualified from driving for 10 years. On appeal, his sentence was reduced to two years. The reduction was said to be as a result of the appellant's remorse and the effect on him of the death of a close friend. Also see *R. v. Marshall* (1988) 10 Cr.App.R.(S.) 246 where a police officer pleaded guilty to causing death by reckless driving. He had spent several hours drinking and then drove at high speed colliding with a cyclist who died. The driver's breath alcohol level was 135 microgrammes per 100 millilitres of breath. His sentence was reduced from four years to two-and-a-half. Auld J. said:

> "In our view, the circumstances here justify a substantial sentence, after allowing for the appellant's good record, the particular penalties that he will suffer as a result of being discharged from the police, his genuine remorse and his plea of guilty."

In relation to dangerous and reckless driving the general factors as outlined in *Boswell* will clearly be relevant. An example of the application of the principles is given in the case of *R. v. Gibbon* (1991) 13 Cr.App.R.(S.) 479, where the appellant pleaded guilty to taking a vehicle without consent and reckless driving. The appellant was seen driving at high speed through four sets of traffic lights with police officers giving chase. The appellant eventually crashed into a van coming in the opposite direction. He was sentenced to 18 months in respect of the reckless driving which was upheld on appeal.

See also the case of *R. v. Bannister* [1991] R.T.R. 1 a sentence of three months' imprisonment was imposed in respect of a driver who drove aggressively along a motorway (for the facts see § A9–14 above). See also the case of *R. v. Duncan* [1994] R.T.R. 93, C.A.

In the cases of *R. v. Shepherd; R. v. Wernet (Att.-Gen.'s References Nos. 14 and 24 of 1993)* [1994] R.T.R. 49), the Court of Appeal with the Lord Chief Justice presiding, considered how sentences would be effected by the increase in the maximum sentence for causing death by dangerous driving and also how offences of careless driving causing death having consumed alcohol ought to be dealt with. In dealing with the first point, the court indicated that the examples of aggravating and mitigating circumstances still stood. The court went on to say that in cases where drivers indulge in racing or are driving without regard for others having consumed alcohol, they will lose their liberty for upwards of five years. In the very worst cases, if contested, sentences would be in the higher range of those now permitted by Parliament. On the second point, the general principles of *Boswell* apply to offences of careless driving causing death having consumed alcohol. The Lord Chief points out that the first aggravating factor in *Boswell* was drink, and so where a driver is over the limit and kills someone as a result of his careless driving, a prison sentence would ordinarily be appropriate. The length of any sentence would depend on the aggravating and mitigating circumstances in the particular case.

Causing death by dangerous driving and causing death by reckless driving

A9–19   Section 1 of the **R.T.A. 1991** substitutes a new **section 1** of the **R.T.A. 1988** and creates the new offence of causing death by dangerous driving. The section provides that;

> "A person who causes the death of another person by driving a mechanically propelled vehicle dangerously on a road or other public place is guilty of an offence."

The offence is triable only on indictment and carries a maximum sentence of 10 years for offences committed on or after August 16, 1993. For offences committed prior to that date the maximum sentence is one of five years.

Section 1 of the **R.T.A. 1988** before it was altered provided that:

> "... a person who causes the death of another person by driving a motor vehicle on the road recklessly shall be guilty of an offence."

The offence was also one that could only be tried on indictment and it carried a maximum sentence of five years' imprisonment.

The changes are as for those in relation to dangerous driving – the extension of the scope of the offence to include mechanically propelled vehicles and other public places.

In certain circumstances, causing death by driving may be charged as manslaughter rather than under **section 1** of the **R.T.A. 1991**. Manslaughter is triable only on indictment and carries a maximum sentence of life imprisonment, and as such would only be used in the most serious of cases. In the case of *Jennings v. United States Government* [1983] 1 A.C. 624, Lord Roskill said that manslaughter should only be used in "a very grave case." It may be the case that the driving is particularly serious or the circumstances or the nature of the death warrant the more serious charge.

Manslaughter was also a useful alternative to causing death by reckless driving where the incident leading to the death of another person takes place other than on a road, as there is nothing in the definition of manslaughter to restrict it to offences taking place on a road as there is with reckless driving.

In *R. v. Rayner; R. v. Wing (Att. Gen.'s References (Nos. 24 and 32 of 1994))* *The Times*, October 31, 1994, the Court of Appeal increased sentences of 18 months for causing death by dangerous driving and causing death by driving without due care and attention having consumed so much alcohol that the proportion of it at the time exceeded the prescribed limit, to four years in each case. The Lord Chief Justice again reiterated that each case had to be looked at and the criminality of the defendant assessed, and that the court would not be persuaded by campaigns or clamour in cases involving death by driving to pass extremely long sentences where the criminality of the offenders did not justify them. See also *Att.-Gen.'s Reference (No. 22 of 1994) (R. v. Nevison), The Times*, November 10, 1994.

In the case of *R. v. Jordan, The Times*, November 10, 1994, the question of sentencing in cases of driving with fatal consequences where amphetamines had been consumed were considered. The Court of Appeal said that the guidelines in cases of alcohol were not useful. The appellant had consumed a quantity of an unlawful drug which there was clear evidence to show was likely to have, and did have an adverse effect on his driving. It was said that the driving did not constitute a persistent course of bad driving, but that the appellant had made a bad misjudgment. His sentence was reduced from three years' imprisonment to two years.

Manslaughter: sentencing

As mentioned above, manslaughter is reserved for the most grave **A9–19A**
cases (see § A9–19 above). In the case *R. v. Pimm* [1994] R.T.R. 391, C.A., the question of sentencing for an offence of manslaughter involving a van driver trying to escape apprehension by the deceased was considered. The appellant was 17. He and another youth were observed trying to steal a car. A man asked his wife to call a neighbour for help, and chased the youths to a van, which they had stolen earlier. The appellant tried to start the van. The neighbour arrived and stood in front of the van with his arms outstretched. When the engine started suddenly, and was put into gear, it leapt forwards forcing the neighbour to jump onto the van. The van accelerated and the neighbour was thrown onto the roof. The windscreen cracked and when the van swerved from side to side, the neighbour was thrown from the van. He fell onto the road, striking his head. He died some six days later. Pimm admitted he was quite drunk, pleaded guilty to manslaughter and was sentenced to nine years. His appeal was dismissed. The court held that sentencing powers of the court for manslaughter were not limited by relation to the maximum sentence for the offence of causing death by reckless driving. The court also held that the more grave offence should only be charged where on the facts there was a very high risk of death, as there had been here. Additionally, the court went on to state that the conduct of Pimm in the present case was appalling as it combined theft, excess alcohol, attempts to escape apprehension and a gross disregard for human life.

Elements of the offences

In order to prove an allegation of causing death by dangerous driving, **A9–20**
it must be shown that (i) the driving was dangerous, (ii) the offence took place on a road or other public place and the vehicle involved was a mechanically propelled vehicle, and (iii) that the driving was the

cause of death of another person. Similarly, to establish death by reckless driving the elements are: (i) that the driving was reckless, (ii) the offence took place on a road and that the vehicle involved was a motor vehicle, and (iii) the driving was a cause of the death of another person.

Most of these elements in relation to dangerous and reckless driving are discussed above in relation to the offences of dangerous and reckless driving and the same principles apply. Definitions of what constitutes a road, other public place and motor vehicle and mechanically propelled vehicle are dealt with in Chapter 2. The particular element that we need to consider in this chapter is the third – causing the death of another.

"Causes the death of another person"

A9–21 The basic proposition is that the cause of death must be shown to be connected with the driving of the defendant. Whether the driving needs to be the only cause of death was considered in the case of *R. v. Hennigan* [1971] 3 All E.R. 133. The Court of Appeal held in that case that it need not be the sole or main cause of death, but a cause something more than *de minimis*. The case actually concerned an allegation of causing death by dangerous driving under the pre-1977 law rather than by reckless driving or the new dangerous driving, but it appears still to be good law and the principle has been applied in more recent cases dealing with reckless driving. (See *R. v. Paget*, *The Times*, February 4, 1983 and *R. v. Mitchell* [1983] Crim.L.R. 549.) In *R. v. Crossman* [1986] R.T.R. 49, the Court of Appeal held that where a driver, who was driving a lorry with a heavy load, knew that there was a serious risk the load might fall off and kill or injure another road user and it did in fact fall off and kill a pedestrian, then he was guilty of causing death by reckless driving as there was the necessary causal link between his driving and the death. In the case of *R. v. Bennett* [1992] R.T.R. 397 the trial judge said:

> "You may find that he drove recklessly if you are sure that the defendant had taken alcohol in such quantities that he knew – or must have known – that his ability to drive safely was substantially impaired, because there would then be the creation of an obvious and serious risk of him causing injury to some body or doing damage to property. If knowing that he has had alcohol in such quantities he drives, then he creates that risk and takes it and, of course, if he thereby causes the death of one of his passengers, that is this offence."

A9–22 On appeal Taylor L.J. (as he then was) said:

> "The effect of that passage was to suggest that a conviction is justified if the driver knows he has taken enough alcohol to impair substantially his driving ability and whilst he is driving a fatal accident

occurs. What is missing is the need to prove the manner of his driving created an obvious and serious risk. Foolishly, and in the ordinary sense recklessly, to drink to excess and then drive is not in itself enough. It is no doubt possible that someone with far too much alcohol in his blood may be involved whilst driving in a fatal accident which is wholly the fault of another."

The "other person" can be another road user, a passenger in the defendant's car or a pedestrian. The section simply requires that the driver causes the death of another person. In a recent Scottish case *McCluskey v. Her Majesty's Advocate* [1989] R.T.R. 182, the question arose as to whether the defendant could be charged with causing the death by reckless driving where the death was that of a child of 35 weeks' gestation, born after injury *in utero*. The High Court of Justiciary held that the defendant could be charged under **section 1** of the **R.T.A. 1972**:

"... it is impossible to find, in the enactment of section 1 in a U.K. statute, that the words 'the death of another person' must relate only to the death of a person in life at the time of the act of reckless driving ..."

Coroner's inquests

In situations where a death takes place in a road accident there may **A9–23** well be a coroner's inquest. Were there to be an inquest and a charge under **section 1** of the **R.T.A. 1988**, or a charge of murder, manslaughter, infanticide or aiding and abetting a suicide has been preferred, or if there is a specific request from the D.P.P., the inquest will be adjourned pending the outcome of the criminal matter. The coroner will normally be notified by the clerk to the magistrates' court that a charge has been preferred and the outcome of committal proceedings. The coroner will also be notified of the eventual disposal of the case by the appropriate authorities (**Coroners Act 1988, ss.16 and 17**).

Alternative verdicts

A jury trying a case involving an allegation of causing death by **A9–24** dangerous driving may convict the defendant of one of a number of alternative offences if they are not sure of the main elements of the allegation, *i.e.* they are not satisfied that the driving was a cause of the death, or that the manner of the driving was dangerous. The alternatives are:

   (i) dangerous driving: **section 2**;
   (ii) causing bodily harm by furious driving: **section 35** of the **Offences against the Person Act 1861** (see § A9–29);

(iii) careless or inconsiderate driving: **section 3** (see **section 24 R.T.O.A. 1988**).

Particular defences

A9–25   In addition to the general defences applicable to all criminal charges, a few words need to be said about two particular defences that may arise.

Emergencies

There is no general exemption from prosecution for an offence of dangerous, reckless or careless driving, where the driver is a member of the emergency services responding to an emergency. Police officers or drivers of fire engines or ambulances are subject to the same standard of driving. It has been held in several cases that a police officer owes the same duty of care as a civilian driver to the public: *Wood v. Richards* [1977] R.T.R. 201 and *Marshall v. Osmond* [1983] Q.B. 1034. Although a policeman or other similar person is charged with an offence of this nature, he may not escape prosecution or indeed conviction, but the fact that he was driving in such a manner so that he could attend at an emergency is clearly a matter which will affect the question of special reasons and mitigation generally.

Necessity or duress

A9–26   Where there is evidence that the defendant drove as he did under duress or out of necessity, the defendant may be able to rely on that fact as a defence. The case of *R. v. Willer* [1987] R.T.R. 22 established that necessity could be a defence to a charge of reckless driving where the defendant could show "duress of circumstances". In *Willer* the facts relied upon to show that the defendant drove under duress were that a group of youths were shouting out "I'll kill you", and also that one of the group had actually got into the car to fight with a passenger. In *R. v. Conway* [1989] R.T.R. 35, the defendant, when approached by police officers, drove his car at speed to get away from them at the instigation of a passenger in the car, a man called Tonna. Tonna was wanted by the police. The defendant was aware that, on an earlier occasion, this same person had been in a car when somebody had been shot. The reason the defendant gave for driving at speed on this occasion was to prevent another potentially fatal attack. A further example of the principle is given by the case of *R. v. Murray, The Times,* June 24, 1994 where it was held that the knowledge of the previous convictions of another driver in a two-car incident might have assisted the jury in determining whether the defendant had acted under duress. In that case the trial judge had excluded the evidence, and the exclusion was held to be a material irregularity. The same question has arisen in a number of cases on driving with excess alcohol. In *D.P.P. v. Bell* [1992] R.T.R. 335, the case concerned a driver who had been drinking with three friends throughout an evening. He left the club where they had been drinking in the early hours of the morning intending to drive himself and friends. The defendant spoke to some people in a coach and trouble broke out on the coach. The defendant retreated, pursued by others. His friends came to his assistance but they were outnumbered. The defendant and one of his friends got into the car and drove off. The defendant was arrested a short time later and found to be over the limit. His defence of duress of circumstances was not accepted by the magistrates, but the Crown Court found that at the time he drove, he was in terror of being caused serious personal injury and drove off with that belief. Additionally, they found that he had driven no further than was necessary to escape the danger. See also *D.P.P. v. Davis*: *D.P.P. v. Pittaway* [1994] Crim.L.R. 600.

Self defence

In the case of *R. v. Renouf* [1986] 1 W.L.R. 522, the Court of Appeal **A9–27** agreed that self-defence could be raised as a defence to a charge of reckless driving. The facts of the case were that the appellant was working on a garage forecourt when a car pulled up and the people in the car threw objects at the appellant and caused him some injury. His reaction was to telephone the police and then to give pursuit in his own car. By the manner of his driving, he forced them on to a verge at the side of the road and was subsequently charged with reckless driving. The appellant claimed that his actions amounted to reasonable force for the purpose of assisting in the arrest of the offenders. The court decided that this defence ought to have been left to the jury.

Related offences

There are several offences which are similar to the offences covered in **A9–28** this chapter and it is relevant to deal with some of the most common at this stage.

Causing bodily harm by furious driving

Section 35 of the **Offences against the Person Act 1861** states that: **A9–29**

"Whosoever having the charge of any carriage or vehicle, shall, by *wanton* or *furious driving* or *racing*, or other *wilful misconduct*, or by *wilful neglect*, do or cause to be done any *bodily harm* to *any person whatsoever* shall be guilty of an offence and being convicted thereof shall be liable, at the discretion of the court to be imprisoned for any term not exceeding two years ..." [Emphasis added.]

The scope of this offence is very wide in that it applies not just to mechanically propelled vehicles, but also to cycles and other carriages, *e.g.* horse-drawn vehicles. Although the section is drafted in these wide terms, the use of the section has been limited to those situations where for one reason or another, reckless driving could not be used. In particular where the driving complained of did not take place on a road or other public place as it is not restricted to driving on a road. (See *R. v. Cooke* [1971] Crim.L.R. 44.)

The section sets out various offences or rather the same offence that can take several different forms. Wanton driving, furious driving, racing, other wilful misconduct, or wilful neglect really means evidence of a positive lack of care or something of a negative nature: *R. v. Burdon* (1927) 20 Cr.App.R. 60.

Racing on highways

A9–30 **Sections 12** and **13** of the **R.T.A. 1988** create several offences which deal with motor racing and motoring events on public ways. **Section 12** makes it an offence to promote or take part in a race or trial of speed between motor vehicles on a public way – and public way is defined so as to include a public highway. **Section 13** makes it an offence to promote or take part in a competition or trial (other than in the situations covered by **section 12**) involving the use of motor vehicles on a public way unless the competition or trial is authorised by the Secretary of State. Following the terms of these offences, there must be more than one vehicle involved to constitute the offence. Where only one vehicle is involved, although it may be racing, it would not be covered by this section. Both of these offences are triable summarily only. (See also **section 33** of the **R.T.A. 1988** which deals with the use of motor vehicles in trials away from roads.)

Dangerous and reckless cycling

A9–31 **Section 7** of the **R.T.A. 1991** substitutes a new **section 28** of the **R.T.A. 1988** and creates an offence of dangerous cycling. The section provides that:

> "(1) A person who rides a cycle on a road dangerously is guilty of an offence.
> (2) For the purposes of subsection (1) above a person is to be regarded as riding dangerously if (and only if) –
> > (a) the way he rides falls far below what would be expected of a competent and careful cyclist, and
> > (b) it would be obvious to a competent and careful cyclist that riding in that way would be dangerous."

Dangerous is defined in the same terms as for the driving offences (see §§ A9–04 *et seq.*). It is interesting to note that the offence is restricted to offences which take place on a road. Dangerous cycling on a footpath would not appear to be an offence under this section. The offence is a summary only offence subject to a fine of level 4. This new offence replaces reckless cycling. **Section 28** of the **R.T.A. 1988** before the change provided that "A person who rides a cycle on a road recklessly is guilty of an offence."

The terms of the offence are very similar to the offence of reckless driving and the authorities on the cases referring to cars apply equally to cycling. There is one difference to the definition of road in that the section specifically includes bridleways in the definition. **A9–32**

Cycle is defined in **section 192** of the **1988 R.T.A.** as meaning bicycles, tricycles and cycles having four or more wheels, not being in any case a motor vehicle. If the cycle has a motor fitted to it, but the motor is not used all the time the cycle is in motion, it may still be counted as a motor vehicle, but if all the essential mechanical parts have been removed then it may count as a cycle: *Lawrence v. Howlett* [1952] 2 All E.R. 74. This offence is also a summary only offence. One other offence that ought to be mentioned is the offence of promoting or taking part in a race or trial of speed on a highway – a similar offence to **section 12**, above, which concerns motor vehicles. **Section 31** of the **1988 R.T.A.** makes such trials of speed or races offences, unless they are authorised and conducted in accordance with the conditions imposed by the Secretary of State.

Chapter 10

DRIVING WITHOUT DUE CARE AND ATTENTION

Introduction

This chapter deals with the offences of driving without due care and **A10–01** attention or careless driving, causing death by careless driving when under the influence of drink or drugs, and related offences. As with the previous chapter, as some matters may still be subject to the pre-1991 legislation, both situations are considered.

Driving without due care and attention

Section 2 of the **R.T.A. 1991** substitutes a new **section 3** of the **R.T.A.** **A10–02** **1988**. The section provides that:

"If a person drives a mechanically propelled vehicle on a road or other public place without due care and attention, or without reasonable consideration for other persons using the road or place, he is guilty of an offence."

Driving without due care and attention careless driving may take one of two different forms, *i.e.* driving without due care and attention or driving without reasonable consideration. The changes to the new offence from the **1988 Act** are that, as for the offences of causing death by dangerous driving and dangerous driving, "mechanically propelled vehicles" has replaced "motor vehicle," and "road or other public place" has replaced "road" thereby extending the scope of the section.

The offence is a summary only offence and carries a maximum penalty of a fine of level 4 (£2,500 as from October 1992), discretionary disqualification and is endorsable with a number of points in the range three to nine. (For offences committed prior to March 1, 1989 the range is two to five.)

As stated above, the offence may take one of two different forms but **A10–03** the same test applies to both limbs. The test is to ask, "was the defendant exercising the degree of care and attention that a reasonable and prudent driver would in the circumstances?": *Simpson v. Peat* [1952] 2 Q.B. 447, D.C.

It has been said that this standard is:

"... an objective standard, impersonal and universal, fixed in relation to the safety of other users of the highway. It is in no way related to the degree of proficiency or degree of experience attained by the individual driver": *McCrone v. Riding* [1938] 1 All E.R. 157.

The key to any allegation of driving without due care and attention or of driving without reasonable consideration, as with dangerous or reckless driving considered in the last chapter, is a careful analysis of the particular facts of the individual case. It will be difficult to appeal the decision of a bench of magistrates or of a jury on the facts alone, unless the decision is perverse, as the first court will be considered to have been in the best position to assess the facts.

It is often said that the best guide as to whether a driver has departed from the proper standard of driving is the Highway Code. As with dangerous or reckless driving, a breach of a provision in the Code will not of itself lead to a prosecution, but the fact that the driver failed to observe the Code may well be relied upon: **section 38(7) R.T.A. 1988**. In cases where there are several breaches of the Highway Code, the fact of the breaches will be strong evidence that the driving fell below the standard of ordinary and prudent driving: *Trentham v. Rowlands* [1974] R.T.R. 164.

The distinction between dangerous or reckless driving and careless driving?

A10–04   The enactment of the **Criminal Justice Act 1977** left two standards of driving that were the subject of offences in that Act – careless and reckless. The **1991 Act** also provides for two standards – dangerous and careless. Dangerous is defined in the **1991 Act**, careless is not. In considering what amounts to careless driving, it is useful to refer back to the leading case on recklessness *R. v. Lawrence* [1982] A.C. 510. The distinction between the two standards is considered. It was held that reckless driving involved driving which created an obvious and serious risk of causing physical injury or damage. Careless driving, however, involved any driving which was below the standard of an ordinary prudent and competent driver. Unlike reckless driving, it was not necessary to show that the driver was conscious of the consequences of his actions, just that he knew what he was doing. Lord Diplock made the following comment about careless driving:

"... an *absolute* offence in the sense in which that term is commonly used to denote an offence for which the only mens rea needed is simply that the prohibited physical act done by the accused was directed by a mind that was conscious of what his body was doing, it being *unnecessary* to show that his mind was also conscious of the possible consequences of his doing it. So section 3 takes care of this kind of *inattention or misjudgement* to which the ordinary careful motorist is occasionally subject without its necessarily involving any moral turpitude, although it causes inconvenience and annoyance to other users of the road." [Emphasis added.]

What has to be proved to establish careless driving?

The evidence must show that the driving of the defendant fell below   **A10–05**
the standard of driving of an ordinary and competent driver in all the circumstances of the particular case. It is a question of fact for the magistrates or, in rare cases, the jury, to decide on the evidence before them – was the defendant driving reasonably in the circumstances?

Careless driving is very wide in its scope ranging from the merest bump to the near catastrophe. In many cases there will be overlapping charges arising out of the same incident. For example a charge of driving without due care and attention, and a charge of failing to stop at a red light. It may be said that failing to stop at a red light of itself is careless driving as indeed, speeding may be in a busy built-up area – it will depend on the facts of the particular case. If the other offences really do not add anything to the allegation, the normal course is to try the careless driving matter first, and if the defendant is convicted, not to pursue the other matters any further. Where the additional charges do add to the picture then all the offences may be tried together.

Evidence of what may amount to carelessness

In the last chapter, several matters were considered which may go to   **A10–06**
show dangerous or reckless driving: drink, drugs and speed (see §§ A9–10 *et seq.*). These factors apply equally to careless driving. Similarly, the following factors may apply equally to dangerous driving (or reckless driving) as well as to careless driving.

Res ipsa loquitor

This doctrine is often quoted in civil pleadings arising out of road   **A10–07**
traffic accidents, and it may well be that the facts of a particular case really do "speak for themselves." If the charge of careless driving arises out of an accident, any evidence of skidmarks on the road showing the path of the vehicles, their speed, the point of impact and the general road conditions may well be evidence which on its own is capable of proving that the defendant must have been driving carelessly in the particular circumstances. Equally evidence that the defendant was driving with excess alcohol, too fast for the road conditions or in excess of the speed limit may well be evidence that "speaks for itself."

In many cases there will not be any eye-witness accounts of the defendant's driving and all that can be said is that there was a collision and the defendant's vehicle ended up off the road. Clearly in such a case any explanation by the defendant will be of great importance; for example, that he suddenly lost control of the car through no fault of his own when the brakes failed to work. If the explanation is not reasonable, or the prosecution are able to disprove it, then the defendant will probably be convicted. Where the explanation put forward is credible, the prosecution must both disprove it and prove the charge beyond reasonable doubt to obtain a conviction.

What is the difference between the two limbs of the offence?

A10–08   The two forms of the offence are:

(a) driving without due care and attention, and
(b) driving without reasonable consideration for other persons using the road or place.

So far as the first limb (a) is concerned, the evidence must show that the defendant's driving fell below the required standard, in that he was not displaying the proper care and attention of a reasonable and competent and prudent driver. For the second limb, the evidence must show that other road users were inconvenienced by the inconsiderate driving of the defendant.

In the case of *Dilks v. Bowman Shaw* [1981] R.T.R. 4, D.C., the defendant was the driver of a car which was in the outside lane of a motorway. There were two cars in front of him and in order to get past them, he overtook on the inside. He got caught on the inside and pulled out between the two vehicles. The drivers of the two cars he was overtaking gave evidence to the effect that they had not been inconvenienced by his manoeuvre and, as he had been charged with this particular limb of the offence, he was acquitted. It may well be the case that overtaking on the inside on a motorway or other major road could amount to careless driving in any event but, where the case is put on the basis of inconveniencing others, there must be evidence of actual inconvenience.

Driving at slow speed may be said to cause inconvenience to others as in the situation of a man who was driving at 18–20 m.p.h. in a 30 m.p.h. zone at the head of a two-mile traffic jam. He was convicted by magistrates of driving without reasonable consideration for other road users. However, in relation to slow speeds, one must consider paragraphs 54–56 of the Highway Code and the principle that speed limits are maximum speeds for the particular roads and not set speeds.

Defences

In Chapter 9 possible defences of necessity and duress were con-   **A10–09**
sidered. Most of the cases mentioned dealt specifically with reckless
driving. In the case of *D.P.P. v. Harris, The Times,* March 16, 1994 the
question of the application of the defence to careless driving was considered. The case involved a police officer driving an unmarked police
car, covertly following a vehicle carrying persons believed to be plan-
ning to carry out an armed robbery. As part of the covert operation the
officer had followed the car, driven through a red light and collided
with another vehicle. It was held that there was no scope for the doctrine of necessity of circumstances in the situation as here. Such
defence of necessity as existed was set out in **regulation 33** of the **Traffic Signs Regulations and General Directions 1994** (see § C29–36).
The wider consideration as to the scope of the defence to careless driving was not decided. In the course of his judgment Mr. Justice
Curtis advanced the proposition that it was a defence to careless driving in circumstances other than the present, as the offence was an
alternative verdict to reckless and dangerous driving and the non-
availability of necessity as a defence to the section 3 charge would be
anomalous.

Automatism

The mental element of the offence of careless or inconsiderate driving   **A10–10**
only requires the prosecution to prove that the defendant was conscious of what was going on (*i.e.* that the act was a voluntary act) and,
once it is shown that the defendant was in the driving seat, it is reasonable to infer that he was driving the vehicle. If the defendant can show
that at the time he was in a state where he was not actually driving (*e.g.*
he was having an epileptic fit at the time), then he may be able to rely
on the defence of automatism. Automatism is also relevant to a charge
of dangerous or reckless driving as again, if it can be shown that the
acts of the defendant were not voluntary, then an essential element of
the charge will not have been proved.

For automatism to be considered, there must be some evidence that
can be put before the court on which the defence can be based. In the
case of *Hill v. Baxter* [1958] 1 Q.B. 227, it was held that the evidence
must show at least a prima facie case before the defence of automatism
can be considered. Once this hurdle is overcome the prosecution must
show that the act was indeed a voluntary one.

The scope of automatism as a defence is very narrow. In the case of
Bratty v. Att.-Gen. for N. Ireland [1963] A.C. 386 Lord Denning said that
it is to be confined to involuntary movement of the body or limbs. In
Broome v. Perkins [1987] R.T.R. 321, the defendant was in a hypoglycaemic state whilst he was driving. He was in a position to exercise
some degree of control over the car from time-to-time: he steered the
car away from possible collisions. He was convicted of driving with-

out due care and attention and his conviction was held to be correct by the Divisional Court.

Mechanical defect

A10–11   In relation to offences of dangerous driving or causing death by dangerous driving, the 1991 Act has made specific provision that a driver is to be "regarded as driving dangerously if it would be obvious to a competent and careful driver that driving the car in its current state would be dangerous." (See § A9–10.) No similar provision is included within the **1991 Act** for careless driving. The position is, therefore, that where it can be shown that there was a material defect with the vehicle the defendant was driving, and of which he was unaware, the situation is rather similar to a defence of automatism; the effect of the defence is the same, "I was not really in control of the vehicle." Where the defect is one of which the defendant was aware, or ought reasonably to have been aware, then not only can he not rely on the defect as a defence, but it may also be evidence to prove careless driving or reckless driving: *R. v. Spurge* [1961] 2 Q.B. 205.

Causing death by careless driving when under the influence of drink or drugs

A10–12   **Section 3** of the **1991 Act** creates a new offence to be substituted into the **R.T.A. 1988** before **section 4.** The section provides:

> "3A. – (1) If a person causes the death of another person by driving a mechanically propelled vehicle on a road or other public place without due care and attention, or without reasonable consideration for other persons using the road or place, and —
>
>> (a) he is, at the time when he is driving, unfit to drive through drink or drugs, or
>>
>> (b) he has consumed so much alcohol that the proportion of it in his breath, blood or urine exceeds the prescribed limit, or
>>
>> (c) he is, within 18 hours after that time, required to provide a specimen in pursuance of section 7 of this Act, but without reasonable excuse fails to provide it, he is guilty of an offence.
>
> (2) For the purposes of this section a person shall be taken to be unfit to drive at any time when his ability to drive properly is impaired.
>
> (3) Subsection (1)(b) and (c) above shall not apply in relation to a person driving a mechanically propelled vehicle other than a motor vehicle."

A10–13   This is an important new offence. The **Road Traffic Law Review Report (the North Report)** considered the question of death by careless driving very carefully. From the report, it is clear that strong representations were made to the committee that "bad drivers who have been drinking and who cause death are frequently dealt with too leniently" (p. 83). The offence is an indictable only offence and is punishable in the same way as causing death by dangerous driving. The maximum sentence is one of 10 years for those offences committed on or after August 16, 1993. There are a number of alternative verdicts open to a jury, if they are not satisfied that the offence is made out. If the jury was not satisfied that the death was caused by careless driving they may convict of careless driving (**section 3**). If the jury was not satisfied that there was careless driving, they may convict of driving whilst unfit through drink or drugs; driving with alcohol in excess of the prescribed limit or; failing to provide a specimen for analysis: **section 24 R.T.O.A.,** as substituted by **section 24 R.T.A. 1991**.

Elements of the offence

There are the following elements to the offence:　　　　　　　**A10–14**

(a) The death has been caused as a result of defendant having driven without due care and attention or without reasonable consideration for other persons using the road or place, and

(b)　　(i) at the time of driving the defendant was unfit to drive through drink or drugs; *or*

(ii) that the defendant had consumed so much alcohol that the proportion of it in his breath, blood or urine at the time exceeds the prescribed limit; *or*

(iii) where the defendant is within 18 hours after the driving, required to provide a specimen in pursuance of the Act, but fails without reasonable excuse to provide it.

The same considerations as to evidence of carelessness set out above apply equally to this offence, as do the matters of driving whilst unfit or with excess alcohol covered in Chapter 6. Where it cannot be proven that the death was caused by the careless driving of the defendant, or although the death was caused by the careless driving the defendant was under the limit, then this offence would not be made out.

Sentencing for careless driving

As the offence of careless driving covers a whole range of driving, the　**A10–15** penalties imposed also vary widely. The court has a broad discretion as to the number of points to impose in respect of the offence (three to nine) and it can impose a fine of up to level 4.

In assessing the penalty, the court will have to consider the facts of the particular case and where it falls in the scale of seriousness. In the case of *R. v. Krawec* (1984) 6 Cr.App.R.(S.) 367, the Court of Appeal considered the general approach that should be adopted. The appellant had been convicted of careless driving and acquitted of causing death by reckless driving. The court held that the relevant factor was the quality of the driving and not the consequences of it. Lord Lane C.J. said, "We do not think that the fact that the unfortunate man died was relevant on this charge."

A10–16   The Court of Appeal mentioned that, in the particular case, the defendant had failed to keep a proper lookout, had failed to notice that the lights had changed and had not seen the pedestrian until the last moment, and these were all relevant matters to sentence. In the case of *R. v. Sanders* (1987) 9 Cr.App.R.(S.) 390 the defendant pleaded guilty to driving without due care and attention on an indictment for reckless driving. He had driven his car at excessive speed and had lost control of the car on a bridge colliding with a car travelling in the opposite direction. The driver of the other car sustained severe injuries. He was sentenced to a fine of £750 and disqualified for 12 months. On appeal, this disqualification was reduced to six months. Russell L.J. made the following observations on the guidelines of the Magistrates' Association:

> "Our attention has been drawn by counsel to certain guidelines which are applied in the magistrates' court, where of course offences of driving without due care and attention have to be dealt with from day to day. Just as on previous occasions this court has taken account of those guidelines, so we do, but we remind ourselves that they are no more than guidelines and that each individual case has to be considered upon its individual merits."

As the range of conduct concluded within this charge is so wide, it is important that those defending the case of the mere lapse of concentration urge the court not to stick slavishly to the list of penalties recommended by the Magistrates' Association.

The sentencing guidelines for offences under **section 3A** are covered in Chapter 9 at §§ A9–16—A9–18.

Related offences

Causing danger to road users

A10–17   **Section 6** of the **R.T.A 1991** creates a new offence of causing danger to road users by inserting **section 22A** into the **R.T.A. 1988**. The section provides that:

> **"Causing danger to road-users**
> 22A. – (1) A person is guilty of an offence if he intentionally and without lawful authority or reasonable cause—
>   (a) causes anything to be on or over a road, or
>   (b) interferes with a motor vehicle, trailer or cycle, or

(c) interferes (directly or indirectly) with traffic equipment, in such circumstances that it would be obvious to a reasonable person that to do so would be dangerous."

The offence is an either way offence. On summary trial it is subject to six months imprisonment and/or a fine subject to the statutory maximum, and on indictment to seven years imprisonment and/or an unlimited fine.

The offence is designed to cater for those instances where danger is caused by the commission of some deliberate act aimed at obstructing traffic. It is the act itself which must be intentional rather than an intention that danger be caused.

Careless or inconsiderate cycling

Section 29 of the **R.T.A. 1988** provides that;   **A10–18**

"If a person rides a cycle on a road without due care and attention, or without reasonable consideration for other persons using the road he is guilty of an offence."

The offence is a summary offence with a maximum penalty of a fine of level 3. It is interesting to note that this offence has not been amended in the same way as careless driving – the offence can only be committed on a road. Road for the purposes of this section includes a bridleway – as indeed it does for reckless cycling where that offence still applies. Careless or inconsiderate have the same meaning as they do for driving and reference should be made to the appropriate paragraphs above.

Chapter 11

GENERAL DRIVING OFFENCES

This chapter covers a number of different areas – from speeding, parking and obstruction to failing to stop and failing to report.

Speed limits

The speed limit applicable to a particular road depends on the nature **A11–01** of that road and the type or class of vehicle that is being driven. On a restricted road the limit may be 30, 40, or 50 m.p.h. and on a motorway the limit will normally be 70 m.p.h. In considering speed limits, it is important to consider the restriction that applies to the road as well as any restriction that applies to the class of vehicle.

Speeding offences

The **Road Traffic Regulation Act 1984 (R.T.R.A. 1984)** sets out a num- **A11–02** ber of different offences of exceeding the speed limit. The offences can be divided into five categories:

(1) Exceeding the limit on a restricted road;
(2) exceeding the limit applicable to the class of the vehicle being driven;
(3) exceeding the limit on a motorway;
(4) exceeding a temporary speed limit: see § A11–09;
(5) exceeding the limit imposed by local authorities: see § 11–09.

The offences are contained in the **R.T.R.A. 1984, ss.81–89** as amended.

(1) Restricted roads

Section 82 R.T.R.A. 1984 defines a restricted road as a road which has **A11–03** a system of street lighting with the lamps placed not more than 200 yards apart, or a road which has been designated as a restricted road even though there is no street lighting. Where there are street lights and signs displayed, it is no defence to say that you failed to see the signs (*Hood v. Lewis* [1976] R.T.R. 99). It must be shown that there were signs or street lights and it will be a question of fact for the justices to decide whether the signs or street lighting are adequate where the issue is raised. (See *Spittle v. Kent County Constabulary* [1986] R.T.R. 142.) (**Section 85(3)** states that a person cannot be convicted if there are no signs or street lights.) Although the section does not state that the street lamps must be in working order, where they are not illuminated the court may find that there is no adequate system of street lamps and the defendant could not be expected to see the lamp-posts. Where signs are used to indicate the speed, the signs must comply with the regulations governing the size and colour of those signs (see **Traffic Signs (Speed Limits) Regulations and General Directions 1994**). If the signs do not comply with these regulations then the defendant is entitled to be acquitted.

(2) Class of vehicle

There are restrictions on speed for certain classes of vehicle on all types of road. The limits are helpfully set out in the Highway Code:

Table of Speed Limits

Type of vehicle:	Built-up areas	Elsewhere		Motorway
		Single carriageway	Dual carriageway	
Car	30	60	70	70
Cars towing caravans or trailers	30	50	60	60
Buses and coaches	30	50	60	70
Goods vehicles (up to 7.5 tonnes laden)	30	50	60	70
H.G.V.	30	40	50	60

A "goods vehicle" is defined in **section 192(1)** of the **R.T.A. 1988** (same meaning for the **R.T.R.A. 1984**) as a "motor vehicle constructed or adapted for use for the carriage of goods, or a trailer so constructed or adapted." "Goods" is also defined in the same section as including "goods or burden of any description."

(3) Exceeding the speed limit on a motorway

The table set out above gives the limits applicable to the various classes of vehicle on "special roads" (see § A11–12). The overall limit is 70 m.p.h. and only where there is a different overall limit in force is it necessary for signs to be displayed (**section 17(2)** and **section 85(6) R.T.R.A. 1984**).

Evidence of speed and the need for corroboration

A11–04   Section 89(2) of the **R.T.R.A. 1984** provides that where a person is prosecuted for an offence of exceeding the speed limit, he is not liable to be convicted solely on the evidence of one witness to the effect that in the opinion of that witness, the defendant was driving in excess of the limit. (There is a similar requirement for corroboration for temporary speed limit offences set out in **section 88(7)** of the same Act.) The requirement for corroboration does not extend to those offences contrary to **section 17(4) R.T.R.A. 1984** covering overall speed limits for motorways, nor does it apply to cases where reliance is placed on a photograph produced by a camera installed for the purpose of detecting speed or other offences (see §A11–08).

Corroboration

Evidence which is capable of amounting to corroboration may take a number of different forms: **A11–05**

(a) Another witness

Another person (*e.g.* another police officer) may be able to give evidence of the speed of the vehicle. The evidence must relate to the same moment in time. It would not be sufficient to say that a second person had seen the defendant driving at a different place on the same road: *Brighty v. Pearson* [1938] 4 All E.R. 127.

(b) Speedometers

A police officer who is following a driver who is speeding may use the reading of the speedometer of the vehicle which he is driving to corroborate his evidence as to the speed of the defendant's vehicle: *Nicholas v. Penny* [1950] 2 All E.R. 89; *Swain v. Gillet* [1974] R.T.R. 446.

(c) Skidmarks/accident damage

It may be possible to tell the speed of a vehicle from any marks left on the road surface or from the impact damage. Where this is possible, or where it is possible to reconstruct the accident, this evidence may amount to corroboration: *Crossland v. D.P.P.* [1988] R.T.R. 417.

(d) Speed check equipment

In the vast majority of cases some form of radar equipment will be used to ascertain the speed of a particular vehicle. **Section 20** of the **R.T.O.A. 1988** states that any evidence provided by means of a radar machine is only admissible where the device is one which has been approved by the Secretary of State. **A11–06**

There are currently six devices which have received the necessary approval:

Kustom HR4	Muniquip T3
Kustom HR8	Gatso Mini Radar Mk3
MPH K15	Gatso Mini Radar Mk4

The various devices all work on the same basic principle (the "Doppler Effect") and record the speed of a target car as it passes the machine. Where evidence from one of these machines is placed before the court it is obviously strong evidence. However, there is a significant "human factor" element in the correct operation of these machines and it will ultimately be a matter for the court as to whether reliance can be placed on the evidence provided by the machine. In the case of *Kent v. Stamps* [1982] R.T.R. 273 it was said:

> "The reading on the machine is, as I have said before, strong and should in most cases be conclusive evidence of the fact that the vehicle was travelling at a speed in excess of the limit. The Justices would be, and should be, extremely reluctant to reject that finding, although there must be situations in which they are entitled to doubt it. They will be few and far between, and the Justices must be very careful not to allow somebody to run away with their judgment on these matters."

The court should be satisfied that the machine is accurate and that it was operated properly by the police constable. Some devices are hand-held and some are static. They can be extremely accurate but, if affected by other factors, such as other cars, metal objects or radio interference they can give false readings. The Home Office issues guidelines on the recommended procedure for the use of radar equipment in order to try and establish its accuracy during use. Where a driver is seeking to challenge the reading, particular attention should be paid to the procedure adopted at the time. For example, the operator should be asked:

(i) Was the machine pointed towards the sky to make sure that there was no interference?
(ii) Was the machine pointed at a vehicle driving at a known speed?
(iii) Was any radio equipment anywhere near the machine?
(iv) Were there any other vehicles in the area – parked or moving?

(e) Vascar (Visual Average Speed Computer & Recorder)

A11–07   This is a device for ascertaining the speed of a vehicle. It is mounted in the police vehicle and is extremely accurate. Like the other devices mentioned above, it relies on the accuracy of the user as well as the machine. The machine records the speed as averaged by the vehicle over a known distance rather than, as in the case of some of the other devices, recording the speed for the fraction of a second it takes for the vehicle to pass through the radar beam.

(f) Photographic evidence

A11–08   Automatic cameras for detecting speeding and traffic light offences have now been in operation for over two years following the implementation of the **Road Traffic Offenders (Prescribed Devices) (No. 2) Order 1992**. The order, in force since July 1, 1992, defines one of the latest "prescribed devices" for detecting traffic offences approved by the Secretary of State under **section 20(9)** of the **R.T.O.A. 1988** (as amended by **section 23** of the **R.T.A. 1991**).

The new prescribed device is the "Gatso" camera, named after its inventor, Maurice Gatsonides, the Dutch former racing driver. Each camera contains a cassette with 800 frames of colour film which can detect a total of 400 offences through its 35mm lens (each vehicle number plate is photographed twice at a one-second interval). The cameras themselves are attached to 10 feet high structures placed in demarcated areas on fixed or mobile sites alongside both roads and motorways.

A11–09

The statutory implementation of technological devices in the detection of road traffic offences owes much to the recommendations of the 1988 **Road Traffic Law Review** (the North Report). The recommendations, which drew much of their impetus from examples of the successful combining of automatic speed-sensing devices with camera surveillance in mainland Europe, were broadly transformed into legislative form in the shape of the **R.T.A. 1991**. In terms of camera surveillance, **section 40(1)** of the **1991 Act** inserts a new **section 95A** into the **Highways Act 1980** allowing a highway authority to install "structures and equipment for the detection of traffic offences" on or near a highway, and generally amends **section 20** of the **R.T.O.A. 1988** to streamline the procedure for admitting evidence of road traffic offences caught on camera.

The obvious aim of camera surveillance is to secure evidence sufficient **in itself** to prosecute offences of speeding and non-compliance with red light signals (**R.T.O.A. section 20(2)**). Currently under **section 20(6)** of the **1988 Act**, evidence of the record of an approved device which is signed by a constable (or other police authorised person) is prima facie admissible to prove an offence. The record is deemed to be authentic, unless this presumption is rebutted by the defence. **Section 20(8)** specifies that the record must be served on the defendant not less than seven days before the hearing. The defence can then request that the signatory of the record attend court if they serve notice to this effect not less than three days before trial. The main purpose of the updated section, however, is to allow the prosecution to proceed without requiring the corroboration of a live prosecution witness.

The probative value of photographs of vehicle number plates taken by an approved camera under the **Road Traffic Offenders (Prescribed Devices) (No. 2) Order 1992** must necessarily be high. Whether such evidence is completely failsafe has yet to be tested. It is, however, submitted that still of relevance is the *dictum* of Omrod L.J. in *Kent v. Stamps* [1982] R.T.R. 273 (a case concerning speed sensing radar) that the reading of such a device is "very cogent evidence", but should not necessarily be accepted as "absolutely accurate and true no matter what."

A11–10   The impact of the **1992 Order** on the prosecution of road traffic offences has been enormous. According to Home Office statistics, during the second half of 1992, automatic cameras accounted for the prosecution of an unprecedented 11,678 traffic light offences, along with the issue of 6,100 £40 fixed penalties, across 12 police authorities. Two hundred and ninety speeding prosecutions were also mounted during the same period as a result of photographic evidence from automatic cameras. The Home Office has not finished collating statistics for 1993 but their provisional figures suggest that the number of prosecutions and fixed penalties for traffic light offences for the equivalent period has more than doubled. The number of speeding prosecutions is thought to have risen by a factor of 20.

The London Metropolitan area now has 150 fixed and mobile camera sights, with 113 in the Thames Valley area. Since the end of 1992, a further five police authorities have adopted the use of automatic cameras in prosecutions. As a result, by mid-1994 an estimated 6000 motorists *per week* were being prosecuted for speeding offences captured on automatic camera. The consequent effect on road safety has been considerable. During its first year in operation in Oxfordshire, Thames Valley police estimate that speeding in some 30 m.p.h. zones reduced by half. In London, one stretch of the A316 has seen speeding reduced by as much as 96 per cent while Westminster Council has reported 30 per cent drop in accidents in zones where cameras have been installed. In Liverpool, a single fixed site camera led to the number of vehicles exceeding 50 m.p.h. in a 30 m.p.h. limit dropping from an average 2604 to 249 a week. Accidents have also decreased noticeably in the relevant areas.

A11–11   The only factor inhibiting the immediate spread of automatic cameras across the remaining 50 per cent of police authorities not already using them is their cost. Each camera costs £27,000 itself plus a further £6,000 for setting up the site. It also costs £100 to process every 30 metres of film, along with the ancillary costs of paying police civilian staff to examine the negatives for offences committed. For these reasons police authorities have been known to take pragmatic views in cases where the breach of the speed limit is not excessive. On motorways many cameras are only triggered where the speed exceeds 90 m.p.h., while on other roads a lee-way of 10 m.p.h. over the speed limit is normally tolerated. In some areas "dummy" cameras have been installed which only flash at motorists without actually taking photographs.

These cameras have obviously had a great deterrent effect. Police forces and local authorities around the country would like to see more widespread use of the cameras. The problem, as identified above, is the question of cost. An estimated £1m per month is collected by way of fines which goes straight to the Treasury. A senior police officer is quoted as saying: "If police forces and local authorities were allowed to use the money to spend on more speed cameras and cameras at traffic lights, then road deaths and injuries would decline more rapidly." Judging from the figures, he is most probably right.

Temporary/variable speed limits

Section 88(1)(a) and (b) R.T.R.A 1984 allow an order to be made by the   **A11–12**
Secretary of State to impose temporary maximum and minimum
speed limits where he is of the opinion that it is in the interests of
safety or for facilitating the movement of traffic.

(a) Maximum speeds

The **70 m.p.h., 60 m.p.h. and 50 m.p.h. (Temporary Speed Limit)
Order 1977** is the present order which applies to all roads other than
motorways in England, Wales and Scotland. The effect of this order is
that on all unrestricted dual carriageways the speed limit is 70 m.p.h.,
and for unrestricted single carriageways the limit is 60 m.p.h. There is
only the need to display signs indicating the limit where a lower limit
applies to the particular stretch of road: **section 88(5) R.T.R.A. 1984**.

(b) Minimum speeds

Section 88(1)(b) R.T.R.A. 1984 permits minimum speed orders to be   **A11–13**
made and where such an order has been made in respect of a particular road then signs must be displayed indicating that speed: **section
88(5) R.T.R.A. 1984**.

(c) Road works

Sections 14 to 16 of the **R.T.R.A. 1984** permit any highway authority to
impose a temporary speed restriction on a road because of road works
on or near to the road or because of the likelihood of danger to the
public. The restriction applies only for three months unless it is
approved by the Secretary of State. It should be noted that this is not a
speed limit, but a speed restriction and there is no requirement for corroboration: **section 16 R.T.R.A. 1984**.

(d) Local authority variation of speed limits

Section 45 of the **R.T.A. 1991** amends **section 84** of the **R.T.R.A. 1984**
to enable local authorities to vary speed limits within their areas. This
was passed to allow local authorities to decrease speed limits to 20
m.p.h. in the immediate vicinity of certain discrete areas. The
amended section allows local authorities to impose speed restrictions
on particular local roads temporarily or permanently or even during
certain times of day, *e.g.* at times when children are entering/leaving
schools.

Penalties

All the speeding offences covered in this chapter with the exception of   **A11–14**
exceeding a temporary speed restriction for road works or minimum
speed limit offences are endorsable with penalty points in the range of

three to six, except where the matter is dealt with by way of a fixed penalty when it is three points. Many courts work on the basis that where the offence involves driving at a speed of more than 30 m.p.h. in excess of the speed limit a period of disqualification will be imposed.

Motorways

A11–15   In addition to the general driving offences covered in this book, there are a number of offences which apply solely to the use of motor vehicles on roads designated as motorways. A motorway is otherwise known as a "special road" and various regulations govern the use of special roads. The most important regulations govern the speed limits and which classes of vehicle may use the special road. The road must be designated a special road before the regulations are applicable.

Specific motorway offences

A11–16   The **Motor Vehicles (Speed Limits on Motorways) Regulations 1973** and the **Motorways Traffic (England and Wales) Regulations 1982 (M.T.R. 1982)** together with **section 17** of the **R.T.R.A. 1984** set out the various specific motorway offences. The two sets of Regulations contain numerous prohibitions, but only a few are dealt with here. Reference should be made to the Regulations themselves for matters not within the scope of this book. The most common offences are the following:

(a) Driving in the wrong direction on a motorway (**M.T.R. 1982, reg. 6(3)**);
(b) making a U-turn (**M.T.R. 1982, reg. 6(5)(a), (b)**);
(c) driving an excluded class of motor vehicle on a motorway (**R.T.R.A. 1984, s.17(4)**);
(d) exceeding the overall limit for a motorway (**R.T.R.A. 1984, s.17 (4)**). (See § A11–12, above.)

The offences really speak for themselves: what must be proved is that the road was a special road and that the defendant committed the particular breach complained of.

Penalties

A11–17   All the specific motorway offences are summary only offences. All, bar the offence of unlawfully stopping on the hard shoulder (see *Mawson v. Chief Constable of Merseyside* [1987] R.T.R. 398), are endorsable and carry penalty points and discretionary disqualification.

Signs and signals

The Highway Code sets out a multitude of different signs indicating   **A11–18**
various features about the road and also giving directions to the
driver. In certain instances, the traffic may be controlled by a constable
rather than by fixed signs – but in either case the driver is under a duty
to obey the signs that are displayed. A failure to comply with the direction given by a fixed sign or by a constable may be an offence, but it
may also be evidence of careless or dangerous driving.

Failing to comply with a sign

Section 36(1) of the **R.T.A. 1988** provides that where a traffic sign of   **A11–19**
the size, colour and type prescribed or authorised by the Secretary of
State under powers in the **R.T.R.A. 1984** is lawfully placed on or near a
road, any person who drives or propels a vehicle and who fails to comply with the indication given by the sign, is guilty of an offence. For the
purposes of this section, it is deemed that a traffic sign is of the prescribed size, colour and type and that it has been lawfully placed
unless the contrary is proved (**section 36(3) R.T.A. 1988**). In certain
situations, vehicles may be exempt from complying with the direction
that is given: for example, an emergency vehicle responding to an
emergency call may "go through" a red light. Where the sign does not
comply with the requirements of the Regulations as to size, colour and
type, the defendant ought to be acquitted (*Davies v. Heatley* [1971]
R.T.R. 145) except where there is only a trivial departure from the
requirements (*Cotterill v. Chapman* [1984] R.T.R. 73).

Which signs are covered by Road Traffic Act 1988, s.36?

The section covers signs indicating a statutory prohibition, restriction   **A11–20**
or requirement or those signs which are said to be subject to this section by or under any provision of the traffic acts: **section 36(2)**. **Regulation 10** of the **Traffic Signs Regulations and General Directions
1994 (S.I. 1994 No. 1519)** sets out the signs to which **section 36** applies,
e.g. stop signs at major road junctions, red traffic lights and "no entry"
signs. Other traffic signs not included within this section may be covered by **section 5(1)** of the **R.T.R.A. 1984**, *e.g.* no waiting signs, bus lane
signs and box junction signs. **Section 5(1)** covers the use, or causing or
permitting the use, of a vehicle in contravention of a "Traffic Regulation Order." Signs that are included within **section 5(1)** will have
been placed on the authority of a Traffic Regulation Order and the
defence is entitled to ask that the relevant Order is produced.

The **Traffic Signs Regulations and General Directions 1994** came
into force on August 12, 1994. The regulations consolidate with various amendments the **Traffic Signs Regulations and General Direc-**

tions 1981 and all subsequent amending instruments. The regulations set out over some 350 pages the requirements as to size, colour and allowable variations for most of the traffic signs and markings. The regulations also set out the deadlines on the replacement of signs which are rendered obsolete. The substantive text of these regulations is set out at §§ C23–01 *et seq.* The traffic signs have not been reproduced.

Neglecting or refusing to comply with a sign

A11–21   Section 35 of the **R.T.A. 1988** contains a provision whereby, if a constable is engaged in the regulation of traffic on a road and directs a person to stop his vehicle or make his vehicle proceed, and that person fails to comply with the direction, the person commits an offence. This offence is really a companion to the **section 36** offence and covers those situations where the traffic is being controlled by a police officer rather than fixed traffic signs. The directions given by the constable have to be to stop the vehicle or to make it proceed or to keep to a particular line of traffic and the constable must be acting in the execution of his duty at the time the direction is given (see *Johnson v. Phillips* [1976] R.T.R. 170). It does not matter whether the constable is in uniform or not (although presumably the prosecution must show that the defendant was aware that the person was a constable). It also applies to special constables acting in the area for which they are appointed and also to traffic wardens: **section 96 R.T.R.A. 1984.** A wider power is given to constables in uniform to stop any vehicle on a road by virtue of **section 163 R.T.A. 1988.** The constable need not be in the execution of his duty or involved in directing traffic; he can simply require the vehicle to stop. Whether the stop is lawful may be challenged in due course: *Lodwick v. Saunders* [1985] 1 W.L.R. 382.

Mens rea and defences

A11–22   An offence under **section 36** is an absolute offence and no *mens rea* is required. All that need be shown is that the defendant failed to comply with the sign: see *Hill v. Baxter* [1958] 1 All E.R. 193. So far as **section 35** is concerned, the offence is committed by neglecting or refusing to comply with the direction given, rather than simply failing to comply. It must be shown that the defendant actually saw the direction. Where the defendant says he did not see the direction and was neither negligent nor at fault then that would amount to a defence to the charge: see *Harding v. Price* [1948] 1 All E.R. 283 and *Leicester v. Pearson* [1952] 2 All E.R. 71.

Penalties

Some differentiation is made between various traffic signs when it **A11–23** comes to penalties. A failure to comply with a stop sign, a double white line, a red traffic light or a police constable (**section 35**) is endorsable with three penalty points and carries with it the discretionary power to disqualify, whereas the failure to comply with a "give way" sign is not endorsable and so there is no power to disqualify (see Appendix A).

Obstruction

Obstruction can be caused in two ways; (1) physical obstruction **A11–24** caused by blocking other vehicles; or (2) by the unreasonable use of the right of stopping, making it more difficult for other vehicles to pass. Whether in either of these two types of situation there is in fact an obstruction will be a matter of fact in each case. In the first situation, it may be perfectly clear where there is evidence of other road users being blocked, but in the second case whether something amounts to an unreasonable user of the right to stop will depend on the local situation, the time at which the vehicle is stopped and the duration of the stopping. In the case of *Nagy v. Weston* [1965] 1 W.L.R. 280 Lord Parker said:

> "... there must be proof that the use in question was an unreasonable use. Whether or not the user amounting to an obstruction is or is not an unreasonable use of the highway is a question of fact. It depends upon all the circumstances. ..."

This test of "reasonableness" has been applied in a number of cases since: see *Lewis v. Dickson* [1976] R.T.R. 431, D.C. and *Nelmes v. Rhys Howells Transport Ltd.* [1977] R.T.R. 266. An example of what may amount to an unreasonable user is given in the case of *Waltham Forest London Borough Council v. Mills* [1980] R.T.R. 201 where it was held that the selling of snacks from a parked mobile snack bar placed in a lay-by constituted an obstruction under what is now **section 137** of the **Highways Act 1980**. Other examples include *Worth v. Brooks* [1959] Crim.L.R. 885, where a car parked on a grass verge between a footpath and a wall for five hours was held to be an unnecessary obstruction and *Police v. O'Connor* [1957] Crim.L.R. where it was said not to be an unreasonable use of the highway to park a large vehicle outside the driver's own home which was in a cul-de-sac.

Obstruction offences

Having considered what may amount to obstruction, there are three **A11–25** offences of obstruction which may be used depending on the particular conditions and facts:

(a) **Section 137** of the **Highways Act 1980** creates the offence of wilfully obstructing the free passage of a highway. A highway is defined in the Act as "all ways over which all members of the public are entitled to pass". An act is done wilfully if it is done with the intention of obstructing. It is no defence to say that it was done in the belief of genuine authority if there is no actual lawful authority or reasonable excuse: *Arrowsmith v. Jenkins* [1963] Q.B. 561.

(b) **Regulation 3** of the **Road Vehicles (Construction and Use) Regulations 1986** creates the offence of causing or permitting a motor vehicle or trailer to stand on a road so as to cause any unnecessary obstruction of the road ("road" is defined in Chapter 2).

(c) **Section 28** of the **Town Police Clauses Act 1847** creates an offence of wilfully causing an obstruction in any public footpath or public thoroughfare. The section actually requires that any obstruction is an obstruction annoyance or danger to residents or passengers in the street.

In each of these possible charges, applying the principles set out in § A11–24 whether something is an obstruction or not will be a matter of fact for the court on the evidence.

Parking offences

A11–26 Parking restrictions are by their very nature local orders and in all cases it will be necessary to consider the local order to see what is permitted. The parking may be controlled by means of meters (**see sections 45–56 R.T.R.A. 1984** and the **Road Traffic Regulation (Parking) Act 1986**) or a road may be a "no waiting" street.

Parking meters

A11–27 The general rule applying to parking meters is that a driver, on placing the appropriate fee into the meter, may park for a specified time, but no longer. If the vehicle remains in the parking place longer than the specified time an excess charge is payable. If the vehicle remains in the place for an additional length of time an offence is committed. Further money cannot normally be inserted to extend the time period once the period has commenced. It is normally the case that the fee becomes payable as soon as the car is left in the parking place and a driver is not normally permitted to go and find money to pay the fee: see *Strong v. Dawtry* [1961] 1 All E.R. 926. The actual terms of the local order should be scrutinised as there are many differences in the orders from area to area.

"No waiting" streets

An order may be made under **sections 1** to **8** of the **R.T.R.A. 1984** des- **A11–28**
ignating a road or a part of a road a "no waiting" area. Under **sections
5(1), 8(1)** and **Schedule 2** to the **R.T.O.A. 1988**, it is an offence to wait
where such an order is in existence. Normally the restriction is shown
by a yellow line or double yellow lines sign detailing the particular
restrictions and any exemptions. For example, the restriction may only
apply on certain days or may exempt loading or unloading during certain times and reference should be made to the particular restrictions.
Where there are no signs or the signs do not comply with the requirements of the regulations made under **section 64 R.T.R.A. 1984,** then no
offence is committed: *Macleod v. Hamilton* [1965] S.L.T. 305.

Leaving a vehicle in a dangerous position

Section 22 of the **R.T.A. 1988** makes it an offence for a person in charge **A11–29**
of a vehicle to:

> "... cause or permit that vehicle or a trailer drawn by it to remain on
> a road or in such a position or in such a condition or in such circum-
> stances as to be likely to cause danger to other persons using the
> road ..."

It has to be shown that danger is likely to other persons using the road:
a danger to persons using buildings nearby would not be sufficient.

Removal of illegally parked vehicles

Sections 99 to **102** of the **R.T.R.A. 1984** give the police the power to **A11–30**
remove motor vehicles which are illegally parked. The power to
remove a vehicle is wide and includes those vehicles which have
broken down, vehicles which are causing an obstruction and those
which are a danger. Where a vehicle is removed the police or local
authority are entitled to charge a fee and retain the custody of that
vehicle until the fee is paid: **section 102(4) R.T.R.A. 1984. Section 101
(5A)** of the **R.T.R.A. 1984** states that the authority must pay over the
proceeds of sale of a vehicle, less costs, if the vehicle has been sold
within one year of it being impounded.

Penalties

The vast majority of parking offences are dealt with by means of the **A11–31**
fixed penalty system (see Chapter 13) and only in a limited number of
cases will the court be considering the penalty. Appendix A sets out
the general offences and the penalties. So far as obstruction offences

are concerned, the offences covered in this chapter are not endorsable, they simply carry a fine. In the case of offences contrary to **section 28 Town and Police Clauses Act 1847** there is the power to impose a period of imprisonment of up to 14 days.

Taking a vehicle without the owner's consent

A11–32   This offence, contrary to **section 12** of the **Theft Act 1968**, is now a summary only offence (**section 12(2) Theft Act 1968** as amended by **Criminal Justice Act 1988, s. 37**).

The offence

A11–33   A person commits an offence under **section 12** if, without the consent of the owner or other lawful authority, he takes any conveyance for his own, or another's use *or* who, knowing that any such conveyance has been taken without such authority, drives it or allows himself to be carried in or on it.

The offence is complete if the defendant "takes" and not "takes and drives away" the vehicle. Further, the conveyance must be constructed or adapted for the carrying of a "person." In *R. v. Bogacki* [1973] 1 Q.B. 832 it was held that "take" was not equivalent to "use." To constitute an offence, there must be an unauthorised taking of possession or control of the conveyance adverse to the rights of the owner or person entitled to possession, coupled with a movement, however small. In *R. v. Bow* [1977] R.T.R. 6 it was held that entering a vehicle and coasting it out of the way to effect an escape was an offence under **section 12**, though pushing the vehicle out of the way would not have been an offence as the vehicle would not have been used as a conveyance.

Where a vehicle is taken without the owner's consent or other lawful authority and then abandoned, a subsequent such taking also constitutes an offence within **section 12(1)**: *D.P.P. v. Spriggs* [1994] R.T.R. 1.

"Driving away"

A11–34   *Shimmell v. Fisher* [1951] 2 All E.R. 672 held that releasing the brake of a lorry so that it ran downhill, driverless, is not taking and driving away as there would be no control over it. It is submitted that it cannot constitute "taking" the vehicle either.

Passengers

A11–35   Passengers are aiders, abettors, counsellors and procurers of the offence by the driver if they act together in taking the conveyance. The passenger must be carried in the conveyance whilst it is in motion *R. v.*

Diggin [1981] R.T.R. 83. To convict a passenger of taking, there must be some evidence to show that each accused was a party to the taking or knew of the unlawful taking. Entering a car after it had been taken, without evidence that the passenger was a party to or knew of the taking is not enough *R. v. Stally* [1959] 3 All E.R. 814.

Pedal cycles

These are covered by **section 12(5) Theft Act** and **section 12(1)** does not apply to them, even though they are "conveyances."   **A11–36**

Defences

(1) Statutory defence

Belief by a defendant that he had lawful authority or would have had the owner's consent had the owner known of his action and the circumstances of it, constitutes a statutory "defence" under **section 12(6)**, although, where the issue is raised, the onus is on the prosecution to establish lack of belief to the criminal standard of proof. The belief of the accused that he had authority need not be reasonable, and may indeed be completely fantastic, but if the Prosecution cannot disprove it, it would appear to be a defence.   **A11–37**

(2) Consent of the owner

Consent obtained by intimidation is not "consent" (*R. v. Hogdon* [1962] Crim.L.R. 563, C.C.A.). Consent obtained by false pretences, as long as it is not a fundamental misrepresentation, is no offence under **section 12**.   **A11–38**

Attempts

As the offence is now a summary only offence, the **Criminal Attempts Act 1981** no longer applies to it. Prior to this change, in *R. v. Cook* [1964] Crim.L.R. 56 it was held that a man caught in the front seat of a car fiddling with the ignition who admitted that, had he not been caught he would have got away "within another minute", was properly convicted of attempting to take the vehicle. Equivocal acts done by a defendant can amount to an attempt, though the court should take into account any evidence of the defendant's actual intention (*Jones v. Brooks* (1968) 52 Cr.App.R. 614).   **A11–39**

Penalties

On conviction the maximum sentence is one of six months' imprisonment, or a fine up to level 5 or both. Disqualification is discretionary, though the licence must be endorsed with eight points.   **A11–40**

Aggravated vehicle-taking

A11–41   **Section 1** of the **Aggravated Vehicle-Taking Act 1992** amends the **Theft Act 1968** by inserting **section 12A**. The Act was passed in something of a hurry to fill what was perceived as a lacuna in the sentencing powers of courts to deal with "joyriders" since the offence of taking without consent was made a summary only offence by the **Criminal Justice Act 1988** (see § B1–02).

The offence

A11–42   **Section 12A** of the Act provides that, subject to subsection (3): A person is guilty of the aggravated taking of a vehicle if he commits an offence under section 12(1) (in this section referred to as a "basic offence") (taking without consent or driving or allowing oneself to be carried in a taken vehicle) in relation to a mechanically propelled vehicle and it is proved that, at any time after the vehicle was taken (whether by him or another) and before it was recovered, the vehicle was driven, or injury or damage was caused, in one or more of the circumstances set out in paragraphs (a) to (d) of subsection (2).

A11–43   The circumstances in **section 12A(2)** are:

(a) That the vehicle was driven dangerously on a road or other public place;
(b) that, owing to the driving of the vehicle, an accident occurred by which injury was caused to any person;
(c) that, owing to the driving of the vehicle, an accident occurred by which damage was caused to any property, other than the vehicle;
(d) that damage was caused to the vehicle.

The aggravating features

A11–44   (a) Dangerous driving is defined by **section 12A(7)** of the **Theft Act 1968** as "driven in a way which falls below what would have been expected of a competent and careful driver; and it would be obvious to a competent and careful driver that driving the vehicle in that way would be dangerous." (See §§ A9–04 *et seq.* above for further details of dangerous driving). As this aggravating feature can only occur on a road or public place it is narrower than the injury and damage aggravations and the section 12 basic offence;
(b) refers to the driving only and "injury" is to any person (including, presumably the defendant driver or passenger);
(c) refers to the driving only and "property" would include another vehicle, a domestic animal and any other property;

(d) refers to damage to the vehicle itself, but it must be caused *after* the taking. This implies that the aggravating element cannot arise from damage to the vehicle in the course of the initial taking, such as damage to effect entry. A vehicle is recovered, for the purpose of this section when retrieved by the police or on their behalf (see § B1–02). In the case of *Dawes v. D.P.P.,* [1994] R.T.R. 209, the defendant had entered a car parked in the street and driven it away. The car had been adapted so that when the door was opened the police were alerted, and after it had been driven a short distance, the engine cut out and the doors locked. When this occurred the defendant was locked inside the car. He broke a window to escape. The police arrived and arrested the defendant. The Divisional Court dismissed his appeal. The court held that his arrest was not unlawful, and since he had broken the window in order to escape from arrest, damage within **section 12A** had taken place before the vehicle was recovered.

Mode of trial

Where the aggravation relates to damage only, and the value of the damage is small, the aggravated offence is assimilated to the criminal damage provisions in the **Magistrates' Courts Act 1980** and is triable summarily in accordance with **section 22** of the 1980 Act. **A11–45**

Section 46 of the **Criminal Justice and Public Order Act 1994** when it comes into force, will affect the entitlement of a defendant to elect trial by jury in relation to aggravated vehicle-taking as well as criminal damage. The value of damage will be increased from £2,000 to £5,000.

Application of the offence

The new offence applies to anyone who has committed a "basic offence" under **section 12(1)** in the aggravated form, including passengers as well as drivers, even though neither was involved in the original taking. **A11–46**

This introduces stringent punishments on passengers not hitherto available under the old legislation (see below for penalties).

Attempts

The **Criminal Attempts Act 1981** makes it impossible to attempt to commit a summary offence. **Section 12** of the **Theft Act 1968** is now a summary only offence. **Section 12A**, however is an indictable offence. It is difficult, though, to imagine an attempted taking coupled with aggravation as the aggravating features all imply completion. It is easier to imagine an attempted **section 12(1)** driving offence, knowing the vehicle to have been taken, coupled with aggravation. **A11–47**

However, under the wording of **section 12A**, it is necessary for a

section 12 (summary only offence) to have been committed as well and strictly this is impossible under the **Criminal Attempts Act**. Until a higher court takes a different, and more robust, view, logic would dictate that it is impossible to attempt to commit an aggravated offence.

Defences

A11–48   As the aggravated offence is part of **section 12** of the **Theft Act 1968**, the defence under **section 12(6)** is available, *i.e.* the defence of belief that the defendant has lawful authority or the belief that he would have had the owner's consent if the owner had known of his doing it, and the circumstances of it.

There is a further defence under **section 12A(3)** open to all offenders, whether drivers or passengers, where the defendant proves that either the relevant driving, injury or damage occurred before he committed the basic offence or that he was neither in, on nor in the immediate vicinity of, the vehicle when that driving, injury or damage occurred. The burden of proving this defence rests on the defendant and the standard will, accordingly be the balance of probabilities.

Penalties

A11–49   It should be pointed out that the penal consequences below depend not on the culpability of the defendant but on the consequential results of the driving. Where the offence is charged in the aggravated form, it will only be possible to sentence for the single offence under the 1992 Act and this will cover the taking, the dangerous driving and the damage as the facts relate. Ironically, a higher total punishment could be used by charging separately under the alternative "basic offences."

The maximum penalty on indictment for the aggravated offence will be two years' imprisonment, or under **section 12A(4)** if, owing to the driving of the vehicle, a personal injury accident was caused resulting in the death of the victim, five years' imprisonment. There will also be an unlimited fine. Where a defendant is convicted of aggravated vehicle-taking where death results from the use of the vehicle, unless the indictment alleges the offence of causing death by aggravated vehicle-taking, a court may not pass a sentence in excess of two years' imprisonment: *R. v. Sherwood and Button*, October 7, 1994 (unreported).

The maximum penalty in a summary jurisdiction is six months' immediate imprisonment, or a fine up to the statutory maximum or both. In the same way as under the old law, with **section 12(1)** offences, magistrates will have the power to impose consecutive sentences amounting to 12 months in all, where there is more than one offence.

The aggravated offence will carry a *compulsory* disqualification of a minimum of 12 months and endorsement (**section 3(1) R.T.A. 1991**). Penalty points and totting-up are restored for the aggravated offence, in that if there are special reasons found for not disqualifying but an endorsement is ordered, that aggravated offence will carry between three and eleven penalty points.

An example of sentencing for this new offence is given in the case of *R. v. Bird* (1992) 14 C.App.R. (S.) 343. The case involved a 17 year-old who took a car from the driveway of the owner's home and then picked up three others. There was a chase with the police for 20 miles when the vehicle was driven dangerously. Eventually it went out of control and there was a collision. The Court of Appeal dealt with the aggravating features of the offence – they would be primarily the over-all culpability of the driving; how bad it was and for how long, and, to a lesser extent, how much injury or damage was caused. Drink would affect the dangerousness of the driving, but where it was a major factor, it would be the subject of a separate charge. A guilty plea showing contrition would be a mitigating feature, but the youth of the defendant would be less significant in this type of case than others, as the Act was aimed at young offenders. The Court of Appeal reduced the sentence from 15 months' detention in a young offender institution to 12 months as that was the maximum sentence which could be passed under the **Criminal Justice Act 1991** on a 17 year-old, although that Act did not apply to the particular case.

Special reasons

A person convicted of a **section 12A** offence will not be allowed to put forward as a special reason for not being compulsorily disqualified under **section 34 R.T.O.A. 1988**, the fact that he did not drive the vehicle in question at any particular time or at all: **section 3(2)**.   **A11–50**

Alternative verdicts

Under **section 12A(5)**, an alternative verdict of guilty of the basic **section 12(1)** offence is open to both Crown and magistrates' courts where the person is found not guilty of the aggravated offence.   **A11–51**

A magistrates' court, unlike a Crown Court now has power, however, to alternatively convict of dangerous driving, etc., even though established.

Interference with vehicles

Section 9 of the **Criminal Attempts Act 1981** provides that a person is guilty of interfering with a motor vehicle or trailer (or anything carried on or in a motor vehicle or trailer) if he interferes with the intention that one of the following offences shall be committed by him or some other person. The offences are set out in **section 9(2)**:   **A11–52**
   (a) theft of the motor vehicle or trailer or part of it;
   (b) theft of anything carried in or on the motor vehicle or trailer; and
   (c) an offence under **section 12(1)** of the **Theft Act 1968**.

Section 9(2) also states that it does not matter that it cannot be shown which of the offences should be committed, it is sufficient to show that one of those was intended.

This offence is a summary offence and there is a maximum penallty of 3 months imprisonment, a fine or level 4 or both.

There are two elements to the offence: interference and intention. Interference is not defined in the Act. In the case of *Renolds v. Metropolitan Police* [1982] Crim.L.R. 831, it was said that interference was more than just looking into cars or touching them. If there had been evidence of the opening of car doors or applying pressure to car door handles then that might have been sufficient. Evidence of intention will in most cases, be the evidence of the circumstances in which the defendant was interfering with the motor vehicle, for example the time of day, what was actually done to the motor vehicle and whether there were items in the car which could have been stolen.

Construction and Use Regulations

A11–53 The regulations governing the standards for construction, maintenance and safe use of motor vehicles in this country are many and varied. There are additional regulations to cover goods vehicles and heavy goods vehicles. These regulations are too voluminous to be covered in depth in this book. However, the general principles can be considered.

Section 8 of the **R.T.A. 1991** inserted three offences into the **1988 R.T.A.** The first of the offences inserted is **section 40A**. This section creates an offence of using a vehicle in a dangerous condition, and is set out below.

"**40A.** A person is guilty of an offence if he uses, or causes or permits another to use, a motor vehicle or trailer on a road when:
(a) the condition of the motor vehicle or trailer, or of its accessories or equipment, or
(b) the purpose for which it is used, or
(c) the number of passengers carried by it, or the manner in which they are carried, or
(d) the weight, position or distribution of its load, or the manner in which it is secured,
is such that the use of the motor vehicle or trailer involves a danger of injury to any person."

A11–54 **Section 41A** creates an offence in relation to the construction and use requirements as to brakes, steering-gear or tyres (see § A12–49), and **section 41B** creates an offence in relation to the requirements as to weights. **Section 40A** is a broad provision which will cover a number of situations from a dangerous part on a vehicle to a dangerous load. It will cover those matters not dealt with in the specific sections which follow. The common element is that there must be a danger of injury to a person – presumably including the offender himself. A breach of this new section carries a fine of level 4, unless it involves a goods vehicle or a vehicle adapted to carry eight or more passengers in which case the fine is of level 5. The offender's licence must be endorsed with three penalty points and there is discretionary power to disqualify. A new **section 48** is inserted in to the **R.T.O.A. 1988** by **Schedule 4, para. 101** of the **R.T.A. 1991** which provides that, in the case of an offence under **section 40A**, the offender must not be disqualified nor must his licence be endorsed if he proves on the balance of probabilities that he did not know, and had no reasonable cause to suspect that the use of the vehicle involved a danger of injury to any person.

Construction and Use Regulations: domestic vehicles

There are two sources of regulations: **A11–55**

   (a) **Regulations. Section 41** of the **R.T.A. 1988** permits the Secretary of State to make regulations as to the use of motor vehicles and trailers on roads as well as their construction. The section sets out certain specific areas where regulations can be made, *e.g.* brakes (see **section 41(2), (3)** and **(4)**), lighting equipment and appliances fitted to vehicles. A failure to comply with any of the regulations made pursuant to this section is an offence: section **42 R.T.A. 1988**. The main regulations are contained in the **Motor Vehicles (Construction and Use) Regulations 1986** as amended **(M.V.(C.&U.) Regs. 1986)**.

   (b) **"Type approval" requirements.** The "type approval" scheme is a scheme whereby vehicles and components are tested and approved and then marked to show that they comply with a common EC standard. The EC, through harmonisation directives and regulations, sets out the various standards, and **section 54** of the **R.T.A. 1988** enables the Secretary of State to prescribe the requirements as set out by the EC by regulation. The regulation will follow the EC directive or regulation. In due course the "type approval" scheme will replace the construction part of the Construction and Use Regulations. The use, or the causing or permitting the use, of a vehicle which does not comply with any of the type approval requirements which have been prescribed by regulation is an offence: **section 63(1) R.T.A. 1988**.

Certain examples of the Construction and Use Regulations

Brakes (Regulations 15–18 of the M.V.(C.&U.) Regulations 1986) as amended

Section 8(2) R.T.A. 1991 substitutes for section **42 R.T.A. 1988** a new **A11–56**
section 41A which creates a substantive offence relating to brakes,

steering gear and tyres. It is an offence to contravene or fail to comply with such a requirement. It is also an offence to cause or permit a vehicle or trailer so to be used, or to use a vehicle or trailer on a road which does not comply with such a requirement. It may be irrelevant that the overall effect of the system is efficient where one of the brakes is badly worn: see *Kennet v. British Airports Authority* [1975] R.T.R. 164. The duty to maintain the brakes in good and efficient working order is an absolute duty and it is no defence to say that the brakes have been serviced regularly: see *Haynes v. Swain* [1975] R.T.R. 40 and *Hawkins v. Holmes* [1974] R.T.R. 436. In order to establish a breach of the regulation it will be necessary for the prosecution to prove beyond reasonable doubt a breach of the particular regulation relied upon. For example in the case of *Cole v. Young* [1938] 4 All E.R. 39, the failure of a braking system to work on one occasion did not prove that the system had been constructed improperly. Whether the brakes are in good order will be a question of fact for the court to decide. It is normal for the prosecution to call evidence as to the state of the braking system from a qualified vehicle examiner but this is not always required: see *Stoneley v. Richardson* [1973] R.T.R. 229.

Tyres: Regulation 27 of the Construction and Use Regulations 1986

A11–57   This regulation sets out the requirements as to tyres. There are a number of requirements as to the condition of tyres, for example dealing with tread depths, inflation pressure, lumps or bulges, and exposed ply or cord. It is important that the correct subparagraph of the regulation is chosen: *Renouf v. Franklin* [1971] R.T.R. 469. From January 1992, tyres have to comply with stricter requirements as to tread depth. The requirement is that grooves of the tread pattern must be of a depth of at least 1.6 mm throughout a continuous band situated in the central three-quarters of the breadth of the tread and round the entire circumference of the tyre. Separate informations are required where there is more than one tyre which falls foul of the regulations: *Saines v. Woodhouse* [1970] 1 W.L.R. 961. As in the case of brakes, evidence will normally be given by a police officer as to an examination of the tyre or tyres and the findings: see *Phillips v. Thomas* [1974] R.T.R. 28.

Construction and Use: a checklist

A11–58
(1) In most cases it will be necessary to examine the particular regulation which it is alleged that the defendant has breached. Many of the regulations are detailed and careful consideration should be given to the wording of the regulation.
(2) **Regulation 3** of the **R.V.(C.&U.) Regs. 1986** as amended contains the definitions for the Regulations, but some other definitions are also found in the 1988 Act.
(3) Some regulations only apply to vehicles first registered after a certain date, other regulations apply to all vehicles.

(4) Certain vehicles are exempt from the regulations: see **section 44** of the 1988 Act.

(5) **Sections 42** and **63** only apply to the use of vehicles on a road: see Chapter 2.

(6) The summons setting out the offence should state that the offence is contrary to **section 41(A)** or **section 63(1)** and also state the regulation.

(7) For "Use" offences, it is not necessary for the prosecution to show *mens rea*, apart from proving knowledge that the defendant was using the vehicle, unless the regulation is worded in such a way that the exercise of proper care or the absence of knowledge are defences: *James and Son v. Smee* [1955] 1 Q.B. 78. For "causing or permitting" offences, it is normally necessary for the prosecution to prove prior knowledge of the unlawful use on the person causing or permitting the use: see *Ross Hillman Ltd. v. Bond* [1974] R.T.R. 279 and Chapter 12. It is usually safer for the court to have the substantive offence proved before going on to consider the case of "causing or permitting."

Penalties

A breach of the 1986 Regulations (**section 41A** of the **R.T.A. 1988**) **A11–59** relating to domestic or non-goods vehicles carries a fine of level 4 (level 5 for goods vehicles). In addition, the offence may be endorsable and carry the additional penalty of discretionary disqualification. The powers of endorsement and disqualification are set out in **Schedule 2** of the **R.T.O.A. 1988** as amended. Offences under **section 40A** or **41A** carry obligatory endorsement with three penalty points and discretionary disqualification. Breaches of other construction and use requirements dealt with under **section 42** do not carry endorsement or discretionary disqualification.

Rectification schemes

Vehicle Defect Rectification Schemes (V.D.R.S.) are non-statutory **A11–60** schemes operated by the police which allow for a vehicle which is found not to comply with the Construction and Use Regulations to be rectified or scrapped within a certain time limit, on the basis that the driver will not then be charged with the offence. When the vehicle is stopped and a defect is found, the driver is given the option of taking part in the scheme. If the driver has the necessary repair work carried out or he has the vehicle scrapped, and he is in a position to satisfy the police of that fact, then the police will not prosecute him. There are a number of different schemes in existence throughout the country but the basic concept is the same. The main differences that do exist concern the offences which are covered and the time limit for having the repair done or the vehicle scrapped.

Failing to stop/failing to report

A11–61   **Section 170** of the **R.T.A. 1988** requires that where an accident occurs involving personal injury or damage, the driver is under a duty to stop and, if required to do so, give his name and address. If the driver does not give his name or address he must report the accident at a police station or to a constable as soon as is reasonably practicable and, in any case, within 24 hours of the accident. The section creates two offences – failing to stop and failing to report – and it is possible that a driver can be convicted of both: *Roper v. Sullivan* [1978] R.T.R. 181.

Definitions

Failing to stop

A11–62   **Section 170(1) R.T.A. 1988** provides that where:

"... owing to the presence of a motor vehicle on a road, an accident occurs by which—
   (a) personal injury is caused to a person other than the driver of that motor vehicle, or
   (b) damage is caused....
   (2) The driver of the motor vehicle must stop and, if required to do so by any person having reasonable grounds for so requiring, give his name and address and also the name and address of the owner and the identification marks of the vehicle."

It was held in the case of *Quelch v. Phillips* [1955] 2 All E.R. 302 that there must be some direct link between the presence of the defendant's vehicle on the road and the accident. **Section 170(1)(b)** sets out the nature of the damage that will be covered.

The duty to stop extends to requiring the driver to remain at the scene for such period of time as is appropriate in the circumstances (*Lee v. Knapp* [1966] 3 All E.R. 961), and also to supplying his name, address, the name of the owner of the vehicle and his address and the identification marks of the vehicle to any person who has reasonable grounds for requiring that information of him. It is important to note that both stopping and giving particulars are required and a failure to do one or the other will result in this offence: *North v. Gerrish* (1959) 123 J.P. 313. See also *D.P.P. v. Bennett* [1993] R.T.R. 175.

Failing to report

A11–63   **Section 170(3)** states that:

"If for any reason the driver of a motor vehicle does not give his name and address under subsection (2) above, he must report the accident."

The precise duties involved in reporting an accident are set out in subsection (6). The driver is required to report the accident at a police station or to a constable as soon as is reasonably practicable and, in any case, within 24 hours of the accident. The duty cannot be discharged by the driver telephoning the police station (*Wisdom v. MacDonald* [1983] R.T.R. 186) nor is it sufficient for the driver to tell a friend who happens to be a police constable. It must be to the constable in the course of his duties: *Mutton v. Bates (No. 1)* [1984] R.T.R. 256, D.C.

Mens rea

The duty to stop and the duty to report only arise where the driver of **A11–64** the vehicle concerned is aware of the accident: see *Harding v. Price* [1948] 1 All E.R. 283. The prosecution must prove that an accident involving the defendant's vehicle took place and that that accident caused injury or damage. Once the prosecution has proved that, it is for the defendant to establish, on the balance of probabilities, that he was unaware of the accident. See *Selby v. Chief Constable of Somerset* [1988] R.T.R. 216 and *R. v. Carr-Briant* [1943] 2 All E.R. 156.

Penalties

Both offences are summary only offences. They carry obligatory en- **A11–65** dorsement with five to 10 points. (Offences of failing to stop committed prior to March 1, 1989, carried five to nine points and failing to report offences four to nine). In relation with both offences, there is the power to disqualify. Whether a particular case will warrant disqualification will depend on the facts of the individual case. However, where the offence is a "hit and run" or where both offences are committed, it is quite likely that disqualification will follow.

Chapter 12

DRIVING WHILST DISQUALIFIED AND RELATED MATTERS

Driving whilst disqualified is, by its very nature, regarded as one of the more serious driving offences. The driver is normally in breach of an order of the court. He is also inevitably driving whilst uninsured, and so is putting other road users and pedestrians at risk should an accident result from his driving. This chapter deals with the offence of driving whilst disqualified, as well as the related offences of driving whilst uninsured and driving without holding a driving licence, M.O.T. certificate or vehicle excise licence.

A12–01

The **Criminal Justice Act 1988** made several important changes to the law relating to the offence of driving whilst disqualified – most importantly making it a summary only offence. The relevant provisions of the Act are dealt with in § A12–13 below, together with the general provisions that affect road traffic offences.

A12–02

Driving whilst disqualified

A new **section 103 R.T.A. 1988** has been substituted by **section 19 R.T.A. 1991**. The section creates a new offence of obtaining a licence or driving a motor vehicle on a road while disqualified for holding or obtaining a licence. **Section 103(1)** states:

A12–03

"(1) A person is guilty of an offence if, while disqualified for holding or obtaining a licence, he:
(a) obtains a licence, or
(b) drives a motor vehicle on a road."

Section 103(4) makes it clear that this provision, unlike its forerunner does not apply to those disqualified by virtue of **section 101** – under-age drivers. An under-age driver will have to be dealt with under **section 87(1)** (see §A12–16).

The elements of the offence

The essential elements of the offence are:

A12–04

(a) (i) That a motor vehicle,
   (ii) was driven (it is not sufficient to show that a person was merely in charge of the vehicle without any attempt on their part at driving the vehicle),

    (iii) on a road,
    (iv) by a person who was disqualified for holding or obtaining a licence, or
  (b) (i) a person who was disqualified for holding or obtaining a licence,
    (ii) obtains a licence.

Definitions of the terms "motor vehicle," "driving" and "road" are dealt with in Chapter 2. We need to concentrate our attention on the last element, namely, disqualified for holding or obtaining a licence.

Disqualified for holding or obtaining a licence

A12–05   **Section 108** of the **R.T.A. 1988** is the general definition section of Part III of the Act. "Licence" is defined as "a licence to drive a motor vehicle granted under [Part III] of the Act." A licence granted under Part III of the Act is that granted on the passing of a test of competence to drive.

    Part III of the R.T.A. applies only to England, Wales and Scotland. A person disqualified by reason of an order of a court in Great Britain, or by reason of his age, commits an offence if he drives in Great Britain. The position if he drives in another country may be different. Whether or not he can drive abroad without committing an offence will depend on the law of the particular country, *e.g.* is there a provision in the law of the particular country to prohibit a driver disqualified in this country from driving? Does the driver hold a separate licence or permit for that country?

    It is also the case that a person who is disqualified by a court outside Great Britain does not commit an offence contrary to **section 103(b)** if he drives in Great Britain, but may be committing an offence of driving without holding a valid driving licence.

Proof of disqualification

A12–06   A disqualification imposed by a court may be proved in one of a number of different ways:

    (a) Under **section 73** of **P.A.C.E. 1984**;
    (b) in the magistrates' court under **rule 68** of the **Magistrates' Courts Rules 1981**;
    (c) by the production of the Certificate of Disqualification from the records of the court that made the order;
    (d) by producing the defendant's licence in which the particulars of the disqualification have been endorsed, together with some evidence as to the identification of the defendant; and
    (e) by a written or oral admission by the defendant that he was disqualified at the time the offence took place, for example an admission under **section 10** of the **Criminal Justice Act 1967**.

The certificate or form of the evidence should normally be restricted to the relevant offence for which the defendant was disqualified: *Stone v. Bastick* [1965] 3 All E.R. 713.

Where there is an error of law in the decision to disqualify the defendant which has found its way on to the record, and that is the only evidence of the earlier decision, then the court is bound by that decision. A situation such as this arose in the case of *Holland v. Phipp* [1982] 1 W.L.R. 1150. The defendant was disqualified from driving for a period of five years. On the same occasion, he was also disqualified for a period of two-and-a-half years under the provisions in **section 93(3)** of the **R.T.A. 1972**. The court order showed that the two periods were to run concurrently, rather than consecutively as was the intention of the court. The defendant drove after the five years had elapsed and was charged with driving whilst disqualified. It was held that the magistrates could only act on the evidence that was before them, which showed that the defendant had ceased to be disqualified at the time he was actually driving.

The effect of disqualification

The effect of ordering the disqualification of a driver is to revoke the licence he holds: **section 37** of the **R.T.O.A. 1988**. This revocation takes effect from the start of the period of disqualification and, before the driver can drive again, he must apply for a licence. If he drives after the end of the disqualification period without making an application for a licence, he is driving without holding a licence authorising him to drive and is committing an offence contrary to **section 87(1)** of the **R.T.A. 1988**. (See § A12–16.)   **A12–07**

A disqualified driver who has held a licence in the past, and is entitled to hold a similar licence when the period of disqualification is at an end, can drive quite legally immediately the period of disqualification is at an end, even though he does not physically hold a licence, provided that an application for a licence has been received by the appropriate authorities and the applicant fulfills the general requirements as to the grant of licences under the 1988 Act. For the conditions, see **section 88** of the **R.T.A. 1988**.

Where an application for the issue of a licence to operate during the currency of a period of disqualification is made, the application may fall foul of the provisions of **section 174** of the **R.T.A. 1988** by knowingly making a false statement to obtain a driving licence, in addition to the provisions of **section 103(*a*)** of the Act which make it an offence to obtain a licence whilst disqualified.

Mens rea

It is not necessary to prove that the driver knows of the disqualification. Driving whilst disqualified is an absolute offence not requiring proof of *mens rea*. There are a number of authorities on this point. In *R. v. Bowsher* [1973] R.T.R. 202, the defendant was disqualified from driving for a period of six months by two different courts in respect of dif-   **A12–08** ferent offences that occurred on the same date. The minute of the court imposing the second period of disqualification was incorrect. The licensing authority allowed the defendant to recover his licence. He resumed driving and was charged with driving whilst disqualified on the basis that the two orders of disqualification were consecutive and not concurrent to each other. It was argued on his behalf that *mens rea* on his part was not established; he had an honest belief in his entitlement to drive and his licence had been returned to him. His appeal was refused. In the case of *R. v. Lynn* [1971] R.T.R. 369, it was held that even though a conviction which imposed a period of disqualification was quashed subsequently on appeal, a person may still commit the offence of driving whilst disqualified if he drives pending a successful appeal. See also *Taylor v. Keynon* [1952] 2 All E.R. 726 and *R. v. Miller* [1975] R.T.R. 479.

Attempting to drive whilst disqualified

A12–09   As the offence of driving whilst disqualified is now a summary only offence, the **Criminal Attempts Act 1981** no longer applies to it. However, it will apply to those offences committed prior to **section 37** of the **Criminal Justice Act 1988** coming into force.

Defences

A12–10   As stated above, the offence is one of strict liability. Once it is shown that the defendant is disqualified and is driving, that is sufficient. There are limits to the defences available in most cases – either that the defendant was not the driver, the place where the driving took place was not a road, or the driver was not disqualified. The defendant may be able to rely on necessity as a defence in extreme cases. In the case of *R. v. Martin* [1989] R.T.R. 63, the defence was that the reason the defendant drove when he was disqualified was because his wife had threatened to commit suicide if he did not drive their son to work. The son was late for work and was at risk of losing his job. The wife had a history of suicide attempts and there was evidence to the effect that she may well have carried out the threat had the defendant not acted upon it. The Court of Appeal held that, where the defence of necessity was open to the accused on his account of the facts, the issue should be left to the jury for them to decide.

Power of arrest

A12–11   **Section 103(3)** of the **R.T.A. 1988** as amended gives a constable in uniform the power to arrest, without a warrant, a person who is driving a motor vehicle on a road where he has reasonable grounds to suspect that the person is disqualified from driving. Since the **Criminal Justice Act 1988**, there is no power of arrest for attempting to commit the offence: **Schedule 16 Criminal Justice Act 1988**. This power does not apply to those disqualified under **section 101 R.T.A. 1988**.

Proceedings

As driving whilst disqualified is now a summary offence, proceedings **A12–12**
may be brought at any time within six months from the time that sufficient evidence of the commission of the offence has come to the
notice of the prosecutor. However, no proceedings may be brought
more than three years after the commission of the offence: **section 180
M.C.A. 1980**. Offences of driving whilst disqualified committed prior
to the coming into force of the **Criminal Justice Act 1988** are still dealt
with as offences triable either way and proceedings for such offences
may be instituted at any time.

The effect of the Criminal Justice Act 1988

Until **section 37** of the Act came in to force on October 10, 1988, driving **A12–13**
whilst disqualified was an either way offence and the defendant had
the right to elect trial at the Crown Court. However, the provisions in
sections 40 and **41** of the Act permit trial at the Crown Court of the
summary only offences in certain limited circumstances:

(a) where the offence is founded on the same facts or evidence as a
count charging an indictable offence; or
(b) it is part of a series of offences of the same or similar character as
an indictable offence which is also charged, and the facts or evidence relating to the offence were disclosed on the committal
papers,

then a count charging what is otherwise a summary offence may be
included in the indictment.

If the matter is included in the indictment, the Crown Court tries the
matter as if it were an indictable offence but, if he is convicted, may
only deal with him in a manner in which the magistrates could have
dealt with him. **Section 40** enables the Crown Court to deal with an
otherwise summary offence, rather than grant any greater rights to a
defendant.

Section 41 enables the magistrates' court to commit a defendant for
trial on certain summary offences when committing the defendant in
respect of offences triable either way. The summary offence must be
one that:

"(a) is punishable with imprisonment or involves obligatory or discretionary disqualification from driving; and
(b) arises out of circumstances which appear to the court to be the
same as or connected with those giving rise to the offence, or
one of the offences, triable either way,
whether or not evidence relating to that summary offence
appears on the depositions or written statements in the case.
..."

Where the magistrates decide to exercise this power they must give
notice to the defendant and the Crown Court to that effect. In situ-

ations where the defendant is committed for trial but the summary offence is not part of the indictment then the Crown Court can deal with the matter only on a guilty plea, or the prosecution offer no evidence: **section 41(7) Criminal Justice Act 1988**.

Obtaining a licence whilst disqualified

A12–14 **Section 103 R.T.A. 1988** as set out above (see § A12–03) creates two offences. **Section 103(1)(a)** makes it an offence to obtain a licence whilst disqualified. To establish a case on this limb of section 103, it must be shown that the defendant obtained a licence whilst he was the subject of a period of disqualification. This offence covers some of the same ground as **section 174 R.T.A. 1988** where the obtaining of the licence is by the making of a false statement.

If the defendant actually obtains a licence whilst he is disqualified, **section 103(2)** states that such a licence is of no effect.

Penalties

A12–15 The penalties for offences under **section 103** are as follows:

  (a) section 103(1)(*a*): a fine of level 3 (there is no power to order endorsement, disqualification or penalty points);
  (b) section 103(1)(*b*): a fine of level 5 or six months' imprisonment or both.

Offences of driving whilst disqualified carry six penalty points. Endorsement is obligatory unless the court finds special reasons for not endorsing. Disqualification is discretionary.

Driving without holding a driving licence

A12–16 **Section 87(1)** of the **R.T.A. 1988**, as amended by **section 17 R.T.A. 1991**, makes it an offence to drive a motor vehicle on a road otherwise than in accordance with a licence authorising him to drive a motor vehicle of that class. This offence as it has been amended is aimed at covering the situations where the person driving the vehicle is not subject to a disqualification, or is under the appropriate age, but simply does not hold a licence. It may be the case that the driver has not passed a test of competence to drive (**section 89 R.T.A. 1988**) or because he is a driver from abroad who does not hold a licence or permit authorising him to drive.

To prove the charge, it must be shown that the driver was driving the particular motor vehicle on a road. It is then for the driver to show that, at the time, he held a licence authorising him to drive: *John v. Humphreys* [1955] 1 All E.R. 793 and *Tynan v. Jones* [1975] R.T.R. 465.

There are certain exceptions to this section (see **section 88 R.T.A. 1988**), the most important of which relates to disqualified drivers who have re-applied for their licences: see § A12–07, above.

Section 87(2) as amended by **section 17 R.T.A. 1991** creates a further offence:

> "(2) It is an offence for a person to cause or permit another person to drive on a road a motor vehicle of any class otherwise than in accordance with a licence authorising that other person to drive a motor vehicle of that class."

The phrase which needs consideration is to "cause or permit." It is a phrase which is common to several offences covered in this chapter – driving licences, M.O.T. certificates, and insurance: see § A12–33, below.

Provisional licences

A driver who has not passed a test of competence to drive, but who holds a provisional licence granted under **section 97(3)** of the **R.T.A. 1988**, may only drive a motor vehicle on a road if he is accompanied by a person who does hold a full driving licence. If not so accompanied, he commits an offence contrary to **Motor Vehicles (Driving Licences) Regulations 1987, reg. 9(1)(a). Regulation 9(1)(b)** requires that the vehicle that the provisional licence holder is driving has two L-plates displayed on the vehicle. Both of these offences are summary only offences and they carry a maximum fine of level 3, obligatory endorsement with two penalty points and discretionary disqualification.

A12–17

The role of the supervising driver

The qualified driver who is present with the learner driver must hold a full driving licence and exercise such care as can be expected of a person who is supervising the acts of another: see *Rubie v. Faulkener* [1940] 1 All E.R. 185. It is possible that, where the learner is charged with driving without due care and attention, the supervisor may be charged with aiding and abetting where he has not acted to prevent the learner from acting carelessly: for example, by allowing the learner to drive after having consumed sufficient alcohol to put the learner over the limit: see *Carter v. Richardson* [1974] R.T.R. 314.

A12–18

Driving without insurance

Section 143(1) and **(2)** of the **R.T.A. 1988** make it compulsory for all "users" (see § A12–21) of motor vehicles on roads to be insured or secured against third-party risks. If a person uses or causes or permits the use of a motor vehicle where there is not at least third-party insurance, he commits an offence. The offence is one of absolute liability. This applies equally to situations where the defendant is said to

A12–19

have used the vehicle or caused or permitted its use: *Tapsell v. Maslen* [1967] Crim.L.R. 53.

Conditions of the insurance

A12–20   **Section 145(3)** sets out the requirements in respect of policies of insurance. The most important requirement is that the policy must insure the driver and those specified in the policy in respect of any liability which may be incurred by him or them, in respect of the death of or bodily injury to any person or damage to property caused by, or arising out of, the use of the vehicle on a road in Great Britain.

The policy of insurance must be one that is granted by an "authorised insurer" (see **section 145(2) and (5) R.T.A. 1988**) and, for the insurance to have effect, a "certificate of insurance" in the prescribed form and containing such particulars of any conditions to which the policy is subject must be delivered to the insured: **section 147(1) R.T.A. 1988**.

In order to establish whether the defendant was in fact covered by his policy of insurance at the time of the offence, reference must be made to the individual policy for the details of the cover, any restrictions on driving it may contain, or as to liability. If the defendant's use of the vehicle falls outside that covered by the policy, he may be committing an offence.

Definition of "use": insurance offences

A12–21   The word "use" means in this context, some degree of controlling, managing or operating the particular vehicle as a vehicle. The actual owner of a vehicle may be using the vehicle even when he is not actually driving it himself: *Cobb v. Williams* [1973] R.T.R. 113 and *Crawford v. Haughton* [1972] R.T.R. 125, *F.E. Charman v. Clow* [1974] 1 W.L.R. 1384 and *Bennett v. Richardson* [1980] R.T.R. 358. **Section 143** does not require that the vehicle is actually driven just that there is evidence of its use.

What has to be shown to prove the charge?

A12–22   Once the prosecution has shown that the defendant used the vehicle on a road, it is for the defendant to prove that at the time there was a valid policy of insurance in force for the vehicle: see *Philcox v. Carberry* [1960] Crim.L.R. 563, D.C.

Penalties

A12–23   Using or causing or permitting the use of a motor vehicle without insurance carries a fine of level 4 and six to eight penalty points. (For offences committed before March 1, 1989, the range of points is four to eight.) The offence also carries discretionary disqualification. The main concern of the court in assessing the appropriate penalty to impose will be whether the use was deliberate or unintentional. If the former, the court will normally consider some period of disqualification to be appropriate.

Using a motor vehicle without an M.O.T. certificate

Sections 45 to **48** of the **R.T.A. 1988** contain provisions relating to test   **A12–24**
certificates for vehicles. **Section 47** of the **1988 Act** requires every motor vehicle first registered more than three years before the time that it is being used on a road, to have passed a test under **section 45**. Annual tests of the condition and construction of the vehicle are then required. The use or causing or permitting the use of a vehicle which requires a test certificate and for which there is no valid certificate in force is an offence: **section 47(1)**.

It is important to note that the offences created by this part of the Act only arise from the use of a vehicle on a road, or the causing or permitting of the use on a road without a valid test certificate, and not from the failure actually to submit the vehicle for testing.

The main exception to the three-year rule relates to certain vehicles used for carrying more than eight passengers, taxis and ambulances. These vehicles have to be tested every year from registration.

The test procedure

The test procedure, requirements and the definitions of its scope are   **A12–25**
covered by the **Motor Vehicles (Tests) Regulations 1981** as amended. Any vehicle first registered more than three years ago which is in use on the roads of Great Britain, must have a valid test certificate. Except for temporarily imported vehicles, it does not matter where the vehicle was manufactured or when it has been registered. All that is important is its use on the road. Where a vehicle is temporarily in Great Britain, and less than 12 months has elapsed since it was last brought in to Great Britain, then the vehicle does not require a test certificate for use during a period of 12 months since that import.

Issue of certificates

Test certificates issued under **section 45** are annual. If a vehicle is ret-   **A12–26**
ested within the last month of an existing test certificate, **section 48(2)** allows the new certificate to expire on the anniversary of the expiry of the old certificate. The certificates are only available from approved centres where the test is carried out by an "authorised examiner." If a test certificate is refused, then the tester is required to issue a notice of the refusal stating the grounds of refusal and a person aggrieved may appeal to the Secretary of State: **section 45(4)**. Any appeal is by fresh examination, by a person approved by the Secretary of State who will decide whether to grant the certificate or not.

Goods vehicles

A12–27 There are similar requirements for the testing of goods vehicles and the issue of test certificates (**sections 49–53** of the **R.T.A. 1988**). The offences are also similar (**section 53**). The main difference with goods vehicles is that the testing is carried out on behalf of the Secretary of State at government testing stations.

Roadside tests

A12–28 **Section 67** of the **R.T.A. 1988** enables an authorised examiner to carry out a roadside test of a motor vehicle. Such a test is for the purpose of determining whether the requirements as to brakes, silencer, steering gear, tyres, prevention or reduction of noise, smoke, fumes or vapour, lighting equipment, reflectors are being complied with. An "authorised examiner" may include both a constable appointed as such by his chief constable and a person appointed by his police authority for the purposes of this section. The driver may elect for the test to be deferred unless the constable thinks that the vehicle is so defective that the test should be carried out straightaway or that the vehicle has caused an accident: **section 67(6), (7)** and **(8)**. The option for the test to be deferred is that of the driver and not the owner. The examiner need not inform the driver that he has this option and so its use is somewhat limited: *Brown v. Mclindoe*, 1963 S.L.T. 237.

Vehicle excise licence offences

A12–29 The **Vehicle Excise and Registration Act 1994** which received the Royal Assent on July 5, 1994, and came into force on September 1, 1994, is intended to consolidate all past enactments relating to vehicle excise duty and the registration of vehicles. The vast majority of the Act is derived from the provisions of the **Vehicles (Excise) Act 1971** and the numerous subsequent amendments and additions to the law contained mostly in the various Finance Acts dating back to 1976. In the main there are no substantive changes to the law in this area, the primary purpose being to tidy up the existing law and unify the relevant principles within one Act. The principal offences under the **1971 Act** are found intact, although they are sometimes expressed in a slightly altered form. The sentences for the principal offences remain as per the provisions of the **1971 Act**.

Using or keeping a motor vehicle without a licence

A12–30 **Section 29** of the **Vehicle Excise and Registration Act 1994** re-creates **section 6** of the **Vehicles (Excise) Act 1971**. The section makes it an offence to use, or keep on a public road, a vehicle which is not an exempt vehicle, which is unlicensed. The offence is complete even if the vehicle is not actually driven on a road; all that has to be established is that the vehicle is kept on a public road. Public road is defined in **section 62** (for England, Wales and Northern Ireland) as a road which is repairable at the public expense. The offence carries a maximum fine of level 3 or five times the duty chargeable whichever is the greater. **Section 30** of the **1994 Act** provides that additional liability will be payable in respect of back duty for any period where there was no licence in force. The amount is assessed as one-twelfth of the annual rate of vehicle excise duty appropriate to the vehicle for each month, or part of the month for the "relevant period". The "relevant period" is defined in **section 31** of the **1994 Act** as ending on the date the offence was committed and starting on the date of acquisition of the vehicle, or expiry of the last licence in force for the vehicle, whichever is the later.

Failing to fix and exhibit an excise licence

Section 33 of the **Vehicle Excise and Registration Act 1994** re-creates **section 12(4)** of the **Vehicles (Excise) Act 1971**. The section creates the offence of failing to fix and exhibit an excise licence on a vehicle, when that vehicle is used or kept on a public road. The offence is similar to that discussed above, but this section requires that the licence is actually displayed. The evidence must show simply that there was no licence displayed in the vehicle, whether or not there was a licence in force: see *Stowager v. John* [1974] R.T.R. 124.   **A12–31**

Fraudulent use of a vehicle excise licence

Section 44 of the **Vehicle Excise and Registration Act 1994** re-enacts **section 26(1)** of the **Vehicles (Excise) Act 1971**. The section makes it an offence to forge, fraudulently alter, use, lend or allow to be used by another person a vehicle licence, trade licence, a registration document or registration mark (**section 44(2)**). The offence is triable either way. On summary conviction there is a maximum penalty of a fine of £2,000 and, where the matter is tried on indictment, there is a maximum sentence of two years' imprisonment, a fine or both.   **A12–32**

What has to be shown to prove the offence?

The evidence must show that there is some act of forgery, an act done with the intention of deceiving or that an act was done to avoid paying the duty payable. "Fraudulently" has been held to include an intention to deceive a police officer into believing that the vehicle was properly licensed: see *Welham v. D.P.P.* [1961] A.C. 103 and *R. v. Terry* [1984] A.C. 374. In the case of *R. v. Manner-Astley* [1967] 1 W.L.R. 1505 it was held that fraudulently meant with intent to avoid payment of the proper fee, and where on the evidence the vehicle was not mechanically propelled so as to attract tax and require a licence there was no offence.   **A12–33**

Causing or permitting

A12–34 As indicated above, there are several offences considered in this chapter which can be committed either by the use of a vehicle or by a person causing or permitting the use of a vehicle. The former, in the context of the offences in this chapter, needs no proof of *mens rea*, except where the offence includes the word "fraudulently." However, causing or permitting will require such proof in that it must be shown that the person causing or permitting use had knowledge of the facts which rendered the use unlawful. In the situation where the "person" who causes the use is a company, the guilty knowledge must be that of someone who is directing the company's affairs: see the cases of *James and Son Ltd v. Smee* [1955] 1 Q.B. 78 and *Lowery and Sons Ltd v. Wark* [1975] R.T.R. 45. In the more recent case of *Redhead Freight Ltd v. Shulman* [1988] Crim.L.R. 696, the word "causing" was considered as it applied to tachograph offences. The Divisional Court held that knowledge of the facts was required in order to prove the case. The appellants were a limited company and, on the evidence before the magistrates, there was no doubt that the appellants either knew or deliberately shut their eyes to what was going on, although there was no evidence of any command or direction from the company to their employee to do the act complained of. It was held that "causing" required a command or direction to do the act on the part of the company to be established, which had not been done in this case.

The position is therefore, that, in order to show a person is guilty of causing the use of a vehicle, there has to be proof of their knowledge of the facts of the particular case. "Permitting" is a more vague term. Permission may be expressly given or inferred from the conduct of the person who allows another to use the vehicle. Permitting still requires the proof of guilty knowledge on the part of the person who is giving the permission in the context of the offences covered in this chapter. If a person gives their permission to another, subject to a condition which is not fulfilled, then that does not count as being a permission: *Newbury v. Davis* [1974] R.T.R. 367. See also *D.P.P. v. Fisher* [1992] R.T.R. 93. In the case of *Baugh v. Crago* [1975] R.T.R. 453 it was held that where the owner permitted another to drive his car in the honest but mistaken belief that the other was the holder of a driving licence, and the insurance therefore did not cover him, permission had been granted and the owner was therefore guilty of the offence.

Chapter 13
FIXED PENALTIES

Introduction

In the White Paper "The Road User and the Law" (1989 Cm. 576), fig-   **A13–01**
ures are given for the number of motoring offences in Great Britain in
1987 which resulted in formal action. The total figure is 8.9 million
offences and of that figure 6.3 million (71 per cent) were dealt with by
means of the fixed penalty procedure.

The fixed penalty procedure gives a defendant the opportunity of
discharging any liability to conviction for the offence to which the
fixed penalty notice refers, by allowing him to pay a fixed penalty: **section 52(2) R.T.O.A. 1988**. The present penalty is £40 for offences
involving obligatory endorsement and £20 in other cases: **section 53(2)
R.T.O.A. 1988**. The benefit to the defendant is that the procedure cuts
out any court hearing and the expense that may involve, and the fixed
penalty will almost certainly be less than any fine that may be imposed
by a court upon conviction. For the police it is also a saving in financial
terms and so far as their time is concerned. The driver's licence can be
endorsed for an endorsable offence without the need for a court order:
section 57(1) R.T.O.A. 1988.

The first form of fixed penalty procedure was introduced in 1960 in   **A13–02**
the **Road Traffic and Roads Improvement Act**. This Act confined the
operation of fixed penalties to parking offences, lighting offences and
offences relating to stationary vehicles. The number of offences incorporated within the scheme has increased over the years and the
scheme has been altered in order to iron out earlier difficulties. The last
major changes were implemented as a result of the report of the Inter-
Departmental Committee on Road Traffic Law. This report suggested
various improvements to the scheme to cover inconsistencies in
approach and also procedural difficulties. As a result of the findings of
this report, **Part III** of the **Transport Act 1982** was enacted and brought
into force in April 1986. The legislation covering fixed penalties is now
contained in **sections 51–90** of the **R.T.O.A. 1988** as amended by **section 34** of the **R.T.A. 1991**. The effect of the latest Act is to standardise
procedure throughout Great Britain.

The fixed penalty scheme now extends to cover the most common
motoring offences – speeding, provisional licence conditions and the
Construction and Use Regulations.

The procedure in outline

A13–03   There are important differences in procedure depending on whether the vehicle is occupied at the time and whether the offence is endorsable or not. However, there are also common features throughout the fixed penalty procedure and most of these concern the fixed penalty notice itself. It "... must give such particulars of the circumstances alleged to constitute the offence to which it relates as are necessary for giving reasonable information about the offence": **section 52(2) R.T.O.A. 1988.** The notice must also contain certain other information about the period within which the person issued with the notice must pay the fixed penalty (the "suspended enforcement period") the amount of the fixed penalty and the court to which payment should be made: **section 52(3) R.T.O.A. 1988.**

The procedure for endorsable offences

Driver present

A13–04   Where a uniformed constable has reason to believe that a fixed penalty offence is or has been committed, he may give the person concerned a fixed penalty notice: **section 54(1) and (2) R.T.O.A. 1988.** In relation to endorsable offences, the constable may only give a fixed penalty notice at the time if the driver is able to produce his driving licence, surrenders the licence to the constable and the constable is satisfied on inspecting the licence that the driver would not be liable to be disqualified as a "totter" if convicted of the offence: **section 54(3) R.T.O.A. 1988.** There is also a provision to cater for those persons who are not able to produce their licences at the time. In such a situation the constable may issue a notice allowing seven days for the production of the licence together with the notice to a constable or authorised person at a police station. If the person is able to produce the licence within the time allowed and surrender it at the police station and the points for the offence would not make him a "totter," then the person may be issued with a fixed penalty notice: **section 54(4) and (5).**

Once the fixed penalty notice has been issued, there follows a period of 28 days during which no proceedings can be brought in respect of the offence. This period is referred to as the "suspended enforcement period." If, during the course of that 28-day period, the person who has been issued with the notice gives notice of a request for a court hearing in respect of that offence, then proceedings will follow in the normal way for that particular offence: **section 55 R.T.O.A. 1988.** If the person pays the fixed penalty within the 28 days then that is the end of the matter. The driver will have his licence endorsed with the particulars of the offence, together with the appropriate number of penalty points and the licence will be returned to him. Where the person does not give notice of a request for a hearing and the fixed penalty has not been paid, then the penalty plus half as much again may be registered against that person for enforcement as a fine: **section 55(3) R.T.O.A. 1988**. In such a situation, where the penalty is registered as a fine, the licence will still be endorsed with the necessary particulars and penalty points.

When the penalty is registered as a fine, the clerk to the justices for the particular area must give a notice of registration to the defaulter. The notice must specify the amount of the sum which has been registered, together with information about the offence and the authority to register the penalty: **section 71(6) R.T.O.A. 1988**. The effect of this section, together with the following section (**section 72**) is to permit the recipient of the notice of registration to make and serve a statutory declaration stating that either he was not the person who was given the fixed penalty notice or that, before the expiry of the 28-day suspended enforcement period, he gave notice requesting a court hearing: **section 72(2) R.T.O.A. 1988**.

Driver not present

Section 54 R.T.O.A. 1988, which governs the issue of fixed penalty **A13–05** notices in respect of endorsable offences, requires that the driver is present at the time the offence has been, or is being, committed, who can produce to the police constable a driving licence (**section 54(3)**), or who can produce it within seven days at the police station (**section 54(4) and (5)**). However, the fixed penalty procedure can also now be used for endorsable offences when the driver is not present where a constable has reason to believe that a fixed penalty offence has been committed but no notice is either given or attached to the vehicle at the time: **section 75 R.T.O.A. 1988** as substituted by **section 34 R.T.A. 1991**. The purpose of this amendment would appear to be to deal with offences detected by means of speed and traffic junction cameras. Prior to this amendment the normal procedure of reporting the offence would have been the only option.

A notice issued in circumstances such as these is referred to as a "conditional notice". The notice is sent to the registered owner, and must set out such circumstances alleged to constitute the offence as are necessary for giving reasonable information about the offence. The notice must also state the amount of the fixed penalty and that proceedings cannot be brought for 28 days following the date of issue of the "conditional offer".

Once the notice is issued the procedure is the same as above in relation to the driver being present.

The procedure for non-endorsable offences

Driver present

The procedure governing the issue of a fixed penalty notice for non- **A13–06** endorsable offences is broadly similar to the situation for endorsable offences save for the one major exception that the constable in uniform does not need to have sight of the driving licence before he issues the fixed penalty notice: **section 54(3) R.T.O.A. 1988**. One other difference is that the power to issue a fixed penalty notice in such a situation may be exercised by a traffic warden if the warden is so authorised: **section 95(5) R.T.R.A. 1984** (and see **section 86 R.T.O.A. 1988**).

Driver not present

A13–07   In relation to non-endorsable offences, a constable (or an authorised traffic warden):

> "... who has reason to believe in the case of any stationary vehicle that a fixed penalty offence is being or has on that occasion been committed in respect of it, he may fix a fixed penalty notice in respect of the offence to the vehicle ...": **section 62(1) R.T.O.A. 1988**.

Section 62(2) makes it an offence to remove or interfere with any notice fixed to the vehicle unless the person removing the notice is the owner, the driver or the person who is liable for the fixed penalty.

A notice issued under the authority of **section 62** also has a suspended enforcement period of 28 days. If the fixed penalty is paid within the 28 days then that is an absolute bar to any proceedings being brought against the person issued with the notice. If the fixed penalty has not been paid, a notice may be served on the person who appears to be the owner of the vehicle: **section 63(2) R.T.O.A. 1988**. The notice to the owner must give particulars of the offence, the penalty concerned, the period that is allowed for payment and it must also state that if the fixed penalty is not paid within the period, the person issued with the notice is asked to provide a statutory statement of ownership of the vehicle. The reason for this requirement of a notice to the owner is that, as the vehicle was unoccupied at the time of the offence, the owner may wish to contest the penalty on the basis that he was not in charge of the vehicle at the time. **Section 63(4), (5)** and **(6)** govern the other information that must be relayed to the owner of the vehicle: that the person may request a court hearing of the matter, or alternatively provide a statutory statement of ownership and a statement of facts where another person purports to be the driver at the time and wishes to give notice requesting a hearing of the matter.

Where the person who is served with the notice to the owner was not in fact the owner at the material time, and provides a statutory statement to that effect in the time allowed, then he will escape any liability: **section 64(4) R.T.O.A. 1988**.

Where there is no response at all to the notice to owner, the penalty plus one-half may be enforced as a fine against the person who was served with the notice: **section 64(2) R.T.O.A. 1988**.

In relation to non-endorsable offences, a "conditional offer" of fixed penalty may also be issued: **section 75 R.T.O.A. 1988** as substituted by **section 34 R.T.A. 1991** (see § A13–06 above).

Miscellaneous points

Mistakes

In relation to endorsable offences, the penalty points attributable to **A13–08** the offence have to be added to the points already present on the driver's licence to see if the person will be a "totter" before a fixed penalty notice can be issued. It is possible that mistakes can occur in the calculation of the number of points and that fixed penalty notices will be issued where they should not have been. The Act makes provision for errors of this sort to be rectified by the fixed penalty clerk. If he spots that there is an error, then the licence is sent to the police, who have six months from the date that the fixed penalty notice was issued to commence proceedings for the offence covered in the notice: **section 61 R.T.O.A. 1988**. There is no provision allowing for mistakes in calculation that result in the person being reported for the offence when in fact the fixed penalty procedure was applicable, and the only way of dealing with the matter would appear to be to mitigate on that basis.

The other main area where mistakes are most likely to occur is the completion of statutory declarations. Often mistakes will occur due to the rather complicated nature of the statutory provisions and, in case there are errors which only surface once the notice of registration in default is served, **sections 72** and **73** of the **R.T.O.A. 1988** provide some safety for those affected.

Section 72 applies in the situation where a fixed penalty notice has **A13–09** been given to a person on-the-spot or at the police station. The section permits the person who receives a notice of registration of a penalty as a fine to complete a statutory declaration to the effect that either (a) he was not the person to whom the fixed penalty notice was given, or (b) that he gave notice of a request for a court hearing in respect of the offence within the permitted time. If the person is in the position of being able to make a declaration along the lines of (a), the effect of the declaration is to render void the fixed penalty notice, any endorsement of the driving licence, the registration and any proceedings taken to enforce the fine. In the case of a declaration along the lines of (b) above, the effect of the declaration is to render as void the registration, any endorsement of the driving licence and any proceedings taken to enforce the fine. What will happen in such a case (under (b) above) is that there will follow a hearing in respect of the offence.

Section 73 applies to those cases where the fixed penalty notice was affixed to the vehicle when the driver was not present. Where the person can state that either (a) he did not know of the fixed penalty or any notice issued in respect of that notice until he received the notice of registration; or (b) that he was not the owner of the vehicle at the time of the alleged offence and he has a reasonable excuse for failing to comply with the notice to owner; or (c) that he gave notice requesting a court hearing in good time then, depending on which category he falls into, the notice to the owner and of registration may be void. In cases (a) and (b) above, the effect of such a declaration is to render as void the notice to the owner, the registration of the penalty as a fine and any enforcement proceedings. In (c) the effect is to prevent any proceedings for enforcing payment of the sum registered being brought for a period of 21 days. A further notice to the owner may be issued in either (a) or (c) and, if one is served, matters will take their normal course under the general procedure.

Other offences committed on the same occasion

A13–10   It is quite possible that a driver may be dealt with by means of the fixed penalty procedure for one or more offences and also be reported in the normal way for offences not contained within the ambit of the fixed penalty procedure and dealt with by summary prosecution. Where a person is convicted of an endorsable offence, and his licence has been endorsed by a fixed penalties clerk in respect of a fixed penalty offence (or offences) committed on the same occasion, the number of points for the offence he is convicted of is treated as being reduced by the number of points endorsed in respect of the connected fixed penalty offence: **section 30 R.T.O.A. 1988**.

Hire vehicles

A13–11   **Section 66 R.T.O.A. 1988** provides some protection for hire firms where a fixed penalty notice has been affixed to a hire vehicle and they are served with a notice to owner. If the hire firm is able to show that at the time of the offence the vehicle was let to another person under a hiring agreement, and it can supply a copy of the hiring agreement, a copy of the statement of liability signed by the hirer under that agreement and a statement signed by or on behalf of the firm stating that the vehicle was hired under a hiring agreement, then the hire firm may escape liability to the fixed penalty.

Conclusion

A13–12   The fixed penalty procedure is clearly important to the practitioner as the vast majority of offences are dealt with in this way (see § 13–03) and a working knowledge of the system is required. The system is particularly complicated in the area of statutory declarations as the rules differ depending on whether the fixed penalty notice was given to the person or simply affixed to the vehicle. The other factor to be borne in mind is that the decision whether or not to initiate the procedure and issue a fixed penalty notice or a "conditional offer" of fixed penalty or not in the first place, is that of the constable present at the time. **Section 87** of the Act obliges the Secretary of State to issue guidance to the chief officers of police for all areas covered by the Act to work towards uniformity of implementation, but there are still differences in approach.

Chapter 14

DISQUALIFICATION, ENDORSEMENT AND PENALTY POINTS

Introduction

This chapter is concerned with the main penalties that may be imposed in respect of road traffic offences and which are exclusive to road traffic offences and other offences involving motor vehicles. The offences to be considered fall into three categories: **A14–01**

(a) those offences which carry obligatory endorsement and obligatory disqualification;

(b) those which carry obligatory endorsement and discretionary disqualification; and

(c) others which carry neither endorsement nor disqualification.

We shall consider each of the three areas of endorsement, penalty points and disqualification in turn.

Endorsement

The vast majority of road traffic offences considered in this book are summary offences. A high proportion of those offences are "endorsable" offences, *i.e.* the court, upon conviction, will order that the particulars of the offence are to be endorsed on the defendant's licence unless the court finds that there are special reasons for not endorsing: **section 44(1) R.T.O.A. 1988**. **A14–02**

What is endorsed on the licence?

The endorsement to the licence will give the particulars of any disqualification that has been ordered or, where there has been no order of disqualification, the particulars of the offence or offences, including the date the offence was committed and the penalty points attributable to the offence. **A14–03**

What types of licence can be endorsed?

A14–04 Any licence that comes within the provisions of **section 44** of the **R.T.A. 1988**, *i.e.* any licence that has been issued under the provisions of **Part III** of the **1988 R.T.A.** can be ordered to be endorsed. This does not, however, include international driving permits, foreign driving licences, heavy goods vehicle licences or public service vehicle licences.

In the situation where the driver does not hold a British licence, and any licence that he does hold cannot be endorsed, then D.V.L.A. at Swansea is informed of the particulars of the offence and the details of the driver. If, in the future, the driver applies for a British licence, the endorsement or endorsements will appear on the licence issued to him unless the application is outside the period when endorsements may be removed from the licence.

Which offences are endorsable?

A14–05 Road traffic offences are often categorised according to the powers of punishment available to the courts. **Parts I** and **II** to **Schedule 2** of the **R.T.A. 1988** contain most of the information on the prosecution and punishment of the offences included within the Traffic Acts and as well as those not within the Traffic Acts. Certain situations are not covered in this Schedule, but, by and large, it forms a comprehensive list. The most important situations not covered by the Schedule are:

(a) Conditional and absolute discharges

Although in normal situations, where one of these orders is made, it is not seen as a conviction for the offence, **section 46(2)** of the **R.T.O.A. 1988** provides that, where such an order is made for an endorsable offence, the endorsement will be ordered in the normal way. Probation orders were also covered by **section 46(2)** but they are now considered as a sentence (see § A17–15).

(b) Deferment of sentence

Where a court decides to exercise its power to defer sentence for a period of up to six months (**section 1 Powers of Criminal Courts Act 1973 (P.C.C.A. 1973)**) then all aspects of the sentencing process, including endorsement, are deferred.

(c) Attempts

A14–06 Attempting to commit a road traffic offence is endorsable in the same

way as the full offence would be only where that offence is an indictable or an either way offence: **Criminal Attempts Act 1981, s. 4(1)(b)**
and **(c).**

(d) Aiding and abetting

Offences of aiding, abetting, counselling or procuring the commission
of an endorsable offence carry the same penalties as the full offence
and, therefore, they are endorsable in the same way as the full offence:
section 44 M.C.A. 1980. Section 28(2) of the **R.T.O.A. 1988**, as substituted by **section 27** of the **R.T.A. 1991**, provides that where a person is
convicted of aiding, abetting, counselling or procuring, or inciting the
commission of an offence involving obligatory disqualification, he is
liable to have 10 points endorsed on his licence.

(e) Offences to be taken into consideration

The general rule governing any offences to be taken into consideration
by a court in passing sentence is that the offences must be of a similar
nature to the offence or offences with which the defendant is charged:
R. v. Simons [1953] 2 All E.R. 599. Offences involving disqualification
or endorsement should not, therefore, be taken into consideration
when sentence is being passed on dissimilar offences. Where there are
offences to be taken into consideration that are similar, it is worth considering the penalty points position. No endorsement or penalty
points will be ordered in respect of offences taken into consideration,
and in certain situations this may save the defendant from a penalty
points disqualification.

What is the effect of endorsement?

Section 42(2) of the **R.T.O.A. 1988** states: A14–07

> "... where a court orders the endorsement of any licence held by a
> person, it may, and if the court orders him to be disqualified, must,
> send the licence, on its being produced to the court, to the Secretary
> of State; and if the court orders endorsement but does not send the
> licence to the Secretary of State it must send him notice of the
> endorsement."

D.V.L.A. in Swansea will, therefore, be notified of any endorsements
on a driver's licence and in most situations the driver's licence or a
form D 20 (see below) will be sent to them. The endorsement is then
recorded by D.V.L.A. and, if it also has the licence, the endorsement
will be printed on to the licence before it is returned to the driver.

A form D 20 is a computer form and its use avoids the need for a
driver's licence to be sent away to D.V.L.A. The particulars of the
endorsement are typed on at court and the licence returned to the
driver straightaway. This method is particularly useful in situations

where the driver knows that he will be needing his licence in the near future. A good example is a driver who is travelling abroad within the next fortnight.

Fixed penalties and endorsements

A14–08　On October 1, 1986, **Part III** of the **Transport Act 1985** came into force. The effect of the provisions contained within this part of the Act was radically to alter the law in relation to fixed penalties. Fixed penalties could be offered for endorsable offences and licences could be endorsed without the need for a court to be involved. These changes are now incorporated in **Part III** of the **R.T.O.A. 1988**. (See Chapter 13.)

Which offences are included?

Fixed penalty offences are defined in **section 51** and **Schedule 3** of the **R.T.O.A. 1988**. See Chapter 13.

Penalty points

A14–09　The present system of penalty points was introduced by the **Transport Act 1981** which came into force on November 1, 1982. The provisions are now contained in **Part II** of the **R.T.O.A. 1988**. The aim of the system was to try and discriminate between offences of differing severity by "attaching" to offences a number of points that would be endorsed on the driver's licence. Previously, all endorsements counted equally whatever the offence. Now that the penalty points system is in force, all endorsable offences carry a particular number or range of penalty points – for example speeding carries between three and six points (except when it is dealt with by means of a fixed penalty when only three points can be given), and driving without due care and attention a range of points from three to nine. These points are endorsed on the driver's licence in all situations where a court orders the driving licence to be endorsed and does not disqualify. As we will see later, the number of points actually endorsed can be vitally important and it must be remembered that, when considering penalty points, 12 points over a three-year period will activate a penalty points disqualification.

Number of points to be endorsed

A14–10　There are some offences that carry a fixed number of points and there are other offences which carry a range of points. It is either the fixed number or a number within the range of points for the offence that is endorsed on the driver's licence: **section 28(1) R.T.O.A. 1988**. The particular number or range of points in respect of all endorsable offences is shown in **Parts I** and **II** of **Schedule 2** of the **R.T.O.A. 1988** (Appendix A).

Offences carrying a fixed number of penalty points

The vast majority of endorsable offences fall into this category. The   **A14–11**
court dealing with offences of this nature has no discretion whatsoever as to the number of points to be endorsed on the licence. Assuming that there are no special reasons for not endorsing, and that the driver is not disqualified from driving, the fixed number of points for the offence will be endorsed on the licence.

Offences carrying a range of penalty points

There are a number of offences that carry a range of penalty points. For   **A14–12**
example:

Offence	Penalty points
No insurance	6–8
Driving without due care and attention or driving without reasonable consideration	3–9
Failing to stop after an accident	5–10
Failing to report an accident	5–10

In relation to these offences, the courts do have a discretion as to the number of points that can be imposed. The number must be within the particular range for the offence. Although the Act does not provide any guidance as to the principles to be applied in deciding the correct number of points to be endorsed for any particular offence, by stating a range of points for these offences the guiding principle must be the gravity of the particular offence. The court will have to consider all the facts of the particular case and attribute a certain number of points to the offence. The number of points which the court decides to impose will be particularly relevant where the driver is at risk of a penalty points disqualification, *i.e.* he already has a number of points on his licence and any additional points – say, more than seven, would make him liable for a "totting-up" disqualification. In such a situation, it is obviously vitally important to try and argue that the offence is not so serious as to require that number of points to be endorsed. It should be remembered that the court determining the issue as to the number of points to be endorsed will have seen the driving licence by the time this argument is put before them, as the driver is required to produce his licence to the court when he is convicted of an offence involving obligatory endorsement and, where the driver cannot produce a driving licence, the court will have before it a printout from D.V.L.A. in Swansea: **section 27 R.T.O.A. 1988**. The court, in deciding the number of points to be imposed, can take into account any conviction or disqualification and penalty points that are on the licence: **section 31 R.T.O.A. 1988**.

The effect of **sections 27** and **31** is important since, although the primary consideration of the court must be to impose the number of points that are warranted by the gravity of the particular offence, the previous driving record of the driver may have some effect on the decision of the court.

Offences committed on the same occasion

A14–13   In some situations, the driver will face more than one charge arising from the same incident: for example, driving without due care and attention and failing to stop after an accident. Where he is convicted of more than one offence committed on the same occasion involving obligatory endorsement, the total number of points to be endorsed on the licence is the highest number of points that would be attributed on conviction of one of them: **section 28(4) R.T.O.A. 1988**. In the situation where a defendant is dealt with on separate occasions for offences committed on the same occasion, the effect of this subsection is to restrict the latter court as to the number of points that can be awarded. The **1991 Act** also introduces a further power for the court to depart from this rule:

> "28.—(5) In a case where (apart from this subsection) subsection (4) above would apply to two or more offences, the court may if it thinks fit determine that that subsection shall not apply to the offences (or, where three or more offences are concerned, to any one or more of them.)"

Should a court decide to make use of this power then the reasons for so doing must be stated in open court and entered on to the register: **section 28(6) R.T.O.A. 1988**.

This rule relates only to offences committed on the same occasion and not to offences that may have been committed on different occasions but are dealt with on the same occasion by the court. In the case of *Johnson v. Finbow* [1983] 1 W.L.R. 879, the defendant had been charged with the offences of failing to stop after an accident and failing to report the same accident. The Divisional Court held that both offences arose from the same accident. Although there was a time difference between the commission of the offences, they should have been dealt with as being on the same occasion. The Divisional Court formed a similar view in the case of *Johnston v. Over* [1985] R.T.R. 240. The case involved two offences of using vehicles without insurance. The defendant had two motor vehicles on a public road and was in the process of stripping parts from one to put on the other. The court indicated that the question to be decided (*i.e.* whether the offences occurred on the same occasion) is one of fact and not of law.

A14–14   In practical terms, where the offences which the driver faces are all offences which carry a fixed number of penalty points, the number of points to be endorsed on his licence is easily determined. The particulars of all the offences are endorsed but only one will have the points endorsed by it – the highest number or, if they are all the same, then that number. The court must decide which offence actually has the points endorsed by it – presumably the most serious aspect of the particular case.

Where the charges which the driver faces include one or more offences that carry a range of penalty points, then the situation is a little more complicated. The most sensible method for the court to adopt is to consider the offence or offences that carry a range of points first and determine the most serious offence. Having considered what is the most serious aspect, the court should then decide how many points to impose in respect of that offence. Take for example the situation of a driver who is charged with driving without due care and attention and no insurance. The court will have to consider the facts of the case as a whole and determine the most serious aspect of it (in our example, say perhaps the driving without due care and attention) and then determine the number of points attributable to that offence, assuming that the number of points they decide on is the highest number that can be imposed in respect of one of the offences (in our example six points is the minimum number of points that could be imposed) that number of points will be endorsed on the licence.

When are points not endorsed on the licence?

As was stated in § 14–02 above, penalty points are always endorsed on   **A14–15**
a driving licence when the court orders the licence to be endorsed except, when on the same occasion the driver is disqualified, or the court finds special reasons for not endorsing the licence. If the driver is disqualified, the particulars of the offence, or offences, are endorsed but no points are printed on the licence: **sections 28(1)** and **44(1)** of the **R.T.O.A. 1988**. Although the points are not endorsed on the licence, they can still be "counted" towards the magic figure of 12 points if the driver is at risk of a penalty points disqualification. (For Special Reasons see Chapter 15.)

Disqualification

Disqualification of a driver can arise in a number of different ways: **A14–16**

   (a) The offence is one which involves obligatory disqualification;
   (b) there is a discretion to disqualify in respect of the offence;
   (c) the defendant is liable to a penalty points disqualification.

Offences involving obligatory disqualification

Offences under this heading fall into three different groups: **A14–17**

   (1) Causing death by dangerous driving; causing death by reckless

driving; reckless driving; causing death by careless driving while unfit; manslaughter by the driver of a motor vehicle; dangerous driving and reckless driving where it is committed within three years of a previous conviction for either causing death by reckless driving or reckless driving.

(2) Driving or attempting to drive with excess alcohol in breath, blood or urine; driving or attempting to drive while unfit or failing to provide a specimen after driving or attempting to drive.

(3) Motor racing and speed trials on highways.

In respect of these offences obligatory disqualification means that, unless the court finds special reasons for not disqualifying the defendant (see Chapter 15), it must disqualify for not less than the minimum period set out in **Schedule 2** to the **1988 Act: section 34(1) R.T.O.A. 1988**. This obligation was highlighted in the case of *Owen v. Imes* [1972] R.T.R. 489. The court held that, in the absence of special reasons, the disqualification must follow from the conviction whatever view the magistrates may have formed of the case and regardless of the decision to impose an absolute discharge.

Length of the disqualification

A14–18   The minimum period of the obligatory disqualification, assuming that the court does not find special reasons for shortening the period, is either 12 months or two years, depending on the offence. For offences of manslaughter, causing death by dangerous driving and causing death by careless driving whilst unfit the minimum is two years (subject to **section 34(3)**) for other offences it is one year. **Section 34(4)** provides that the period is also to be two years where more than one period of disqualification for a period of 56 days or more has been imposed on the driver within the three years immediately preceding the commission of the present offence. In the case of *Learmont v. D.P.P.* [1994] R.T.R. 286, the Divisional Court considered this provision. In that case the driver pleaded guilty to dangerous driving in November 1992. In January 1990, he had been sentenced for driving with excess alcohol and was disqualified for 18 months. At that time four notional points were added to those shown as existing against him, and he was further disqualified as a "totter" for six months. The magistrates dealing with the dangerous driving offence were of the opinion that he was within **section 34(4)(b)** and had disqualified for two years. On appeal, it was held that they were in error on this. They should not have treated is as two disqualifications. Now double disqualifications for one offence will not arise (see § A14–30).

In certain circumstances, there is provision for the minimum period of disqualification to be extended from 12 months to three years. This applies in situations where a person convicted of causing death by careless driving while under the influence of drink or drugs, driving or attempting to drive while unfit, driving or attempting to drive with excess alcohol, or failing to provide a specimen involving obligatory disqualification has committed a similar offence within the last 10 years. It is important to remember that where there has been a previous conviction for an offence of being drunk in charge, or being in charge with excess alcohol within the previous 10 years, there is no mandatory disqualification for three years. The 10-year period runs from the date of the disqualification to the date of the commission of the latest offence: **section 34(3) R.T.O.A. 1988**. The important word in **section 34(3) R.T.O.A. 1988** is "conviction," and so it does not matter that, on the previous occasion, the defendant was not actually disqualified, for example, because of special reasons.

The three-year period is the minimum period that must be ordered by the court, the actual length of the disqualification will depend on the facts of the present offence, the facts of the previous offence and the length of time between the offences.

In the case of *R. v. Ealing Justices, ex p. Scrafield* [1994] R.T.R. 195 a disqualification for 10 years following a third drink driving offence within a two year period. There was also a three month sentence of imprisonment for the offence of driving whilst disqualified. It was said on the appeal to the Divisional Court (see also Chapter 18) that the period of disqualification could not be regarded as harsh bearing in mind the flagrant disregard of the drinking and driving laws and the potential risk to other road users. See also *Tucker v. D.P.P.* [1994] R.T.R. 203.

Occasionally disqualifications for life are imposed. In the case of *R. v. Henry* (1992) Cr.App.R.(S.) 668 it was held following the case of *R. v. Russell* (December 3, 1990, unreported), that the court in considering the length of the disqualification to be imposed should have regard to the effect of an order and its length in two respects on the defendant: first, insofar as it might enhance the likelihood on release from his custodial sentence of further transgression of the road traffic rules. "Secondly, and most importantly, the adverse effect a lengthy period of disqualification would have on the defendant's prospects of effective rehabilitation upon his release from custody." See also the case of *R. v. Lark* (1992) 14 Cr.App.R.(S.).

Discretionary disqualification

The offences falling under this heading are essentially all the other   **A14–19** endorsable offences, not covered under the last heading, where the court has the power to order the defendant to be disqualified in respect of the particular offence: **section 34(2) R.T.O.A. 1988** as substituted by **section 29 R.T.A. 1991**. For example, with the offence of speeding, the court has the power to order the defendant to be disqualified and may disqualify the defendant for a short period of time where he was driving at more than 100 m.p.h. on a motorway, or was driving at more than 50 m.p.h. in a 30 m.p.h. zone.

The factors affecting the decision to disqualify or not will probably be the same as those affecting a decision to disqualify for a period over and above the statutory minimum in respect of offences involving obligatory disqualification. The primary factor will be the facts of the particular case: the gravity of the offence or offences.

When to disqualify?

A14–20 Most magistrates' courts will have their own policy on when they will consider disqualifying in respect of offences involving discretionary disqualification which will reflect the seriousness of the offence. The Magistrates' Association makes various suggestions as to occasions when disqualification should be ordered or considered. In particular, they comment that disqualification should be considered in cases of failing to stop, or of failing to report where the facts are serious. Presumably where they are considering both matters the likelihood of disqualification will be far greater. In relation to driving without insurance, the suggestion is that if the commission of the offence is deliberate then the court should disqualify. They also suggest that consideration be given to disqualification in relation to offences speeding at more than 30 m.p.h. over the prescribed limit, and driving in the wrong direction on a motorway. In the case of *R. v. Krawec* [1985] R.T.R. 1 these suggestions were considered. It was held that the suggestions did not constitute a standard where divergence from the standard would constitute grounds of appeal. Clearly there are offences which are more likely to result in disqualification than others, and the decision whether to disqualify or not will turn on the particular facts of the case, but more and more courts do treat no insurance cases very seriously, because of the potential hazards for innocent victims.

Penalty points disqualifications

A14–21 As stated above in § A14–09, where a driver accumulates 12 or more points on his licence in a three-year period, then he is at risk of a penalty points or "totting-up" disqualification: **section 35 R.T.O.A. 1988**. The only exception to this section taking effect is if the court finds that there are mitigating circumstances for not ordering the driver to be disqualified or for shortening the length of the disqualification (see Chapter 16). Where the driver has accumulated 12 or more points on his licence within the three years immediately preceding the commission of the latest offence, and the court does not find that there are mitigating circumstances, then the length of the disqualification is a minimum of six months. This minimum period is increased, where the driver has been disqualified on a previous or more than one previous occasion, to 12 months and two years respectively.

The considerations that will affect the actual period of the disqualification ordered in these circumstances will be the same as those considered in relation to obligatory and discretionary disqualifications above.

Section 29 of the **R.T.O.A. 1988** as substituted by **section 28** of the **1991 R.T.A.** sets out the provisions relating to the penalty points to be taken into account on conviction for offences involving obligatory endorsement.

Reduced periods of disqualification for attending approved courses for drink drivers

Section 30 of the **R.T.A. 1991** introduces a new **section 3A** into the **R.T.O.A. 1988** which makes provision for those who are convicted of, and disqualified in respect of, drink driving offences to have the period of disqualification reduced if they satisfactorily complete a rehabilitation course. The court cannot compel the defendant to attend but the effect of successfully completing the course is to reduce the period of disqualification that would otherwise be served. The amount of the reduction will be between three months and one-quarter of the original period. For a driver subject to a 12-month disqualification this will mean a reduction of three months. The rehabilitation courses are being run on an experimental basis at the moment. They are only available in certain areas, but where available and applicable they ought to be dealt with in mitigation. There are a number of conditions to be satisfied before an order under the section can be made: **section 34A(4) 1988 R.T.O.A.**

A14–22

Disqualification until a test is passed

Section 32 of the **R.T.A. 1991** has introduced a new **section 36** into the **R.T.O.A. 1988**. The effect of the new section is to require a court in certain instances to order that a defendant must be disqualified from driving until he has passed an approved driving test. The section currently applies to those defendants convicted of either manslaughter by the driver of a vehicle, causing death by dangerous driving or dangerous driving, and the requirement is that they pass an extended driving test: **section 36(5)**. There is also a power within the section for the Secretary of State to extend the scope of mandatory retesting to drivers disqualified under **sections 34** or **35 R.T.O.A. 1988**, or those convicted of offences involving obligatory endorsement. In addition a court now has the discretion to disqualify, until a test is passed, any driver who has been convicted of an offence involving mandatory endorsement of his licence: **section 36(4). Section 36(6)** states that in determining whether to make an order under **subsection (4)** the court shall have regard to the safety of other road users.

A14–23

Interim disqualification

A14–24 Where a magistrates' court commits an offender to the Crown Court under **section 56 Criminal Justice Act 1967** for sentence, or remits an offender to another magistrates' court under **section 39 M.C.A. 1980**, in respect of an offence involving either obligatory or discretionary disqualification, then it may order that he be disqualified until he is dealt with by that other court for the offence. There is a similar power for the magistrates' court or the Crown Court where either sentence is deferred or sentence is adjourned: **section 26 R.T.O.A. 1988** as amended by **section 25 R.T.A. 1991**. If an order is made, the licence is not endorsed but the Secretary of State must be notified. Under this section there is a maximum period of disqualification of six months. In effect what happens is that if the hearing has not taken place within six months of the order being made, the order will cease to have effect: **section 26(4)**. If at the subsequent hearing no disqualification is ordered, then notice must be given to the Secretary of State. If a period of disqualification is ordered then any period imposed will be reduced by the period disqualified under **section 26**.

Disqualification where a vehicle is used for assault

A14–25 **Section 38 R.T.A. 1991** has amended **section 44** of the **P.C.C.A. 1973** by extending the power to any court (not just the Crown Court as before) to disqualify a person who is convicted of common assault or any other offence involving an assault where the court is satisfied that the assault was committed by the driver of a motor vehicle. The power given is to disqualify for such period as the court thinks fit: **section 38 R.T.A. 1991**.

Disqualification: procedural points

Presence of the defendant

A14–26 In all situations the defendant must be present, or have been given the opportunity to be present, when an order to disqualify him is to be made: **section 11(4) M.C.A. 1980**. In certain circumstances, a court may accept that the defendant is deemed present through the presence of his legal representative: **section 122 M.C.A. 1980** but it is clearly desirable that the defendant himself is present when an order is to be made for two reasons: first, it gives him or his representative the opportunity to address the court on the question of the disqualification and the length of the order, and secondly, it ensures that the defendant is aware of the fact that he has actually been disqualified from driving.

In the situation where the defendant is not present when he is convicted of an offence where disqualification is a possibility, the case will normally be adjourned for him to attend. If the case has been adjourned for the defendant to attend, and he fails to attend, the court has the power to issue a warrant for his arrest: **section 13 M.C.A. 1980**. A warrant should only be issued where the court determines that it is undesirable by virtue of the gravity of the offence to proceed in the accused's absence: **section 13(5) M.C.A. 1980**. The procedure, when the defendant is not present at conviction, is for the court to issue a notice upon the defendant informing him that the court is considering disqualification, giving him the opportunity to attend and to make any representations he wishes to. If the defendant does not attend, the court can either proceed in his absence or issue a warrant.

Disqualification and other forms of sentence

Disqualification can be combined with any other form of sentence, except that a court cannot impose penalty points on the same occasion as it disqualifies: *R. v. Kent* [1983] 3 All E.R. 1. Disqualification can be ordered alongside a conditional or absolute discharge, contrary to the normal situation that such orders are not convictions (**section 1C(1) P.C.C.A. 1973** as inserted by **C.J.A. 1991, s.8** and **Sched. 1**), the defendant is treated as if he had been convicted for the purposes of endorsement and disqualification: **section 46(1) R.T.O.A. 1988**. Disqualification can also be ordered in respect of young offenders in exactly the same way as for adults. Disqualification is not a sentence on its own, but is an ancillary order: *R. v. Nottingham Justices, ex p. Nottingham Corporation* [1964] Crim.L.R. 827. In *R. v. Bignell* [1967] Crim.L.R. 711 it was held that the failure to impose a proper sentence in addition to an order of disqualification does not invalidate the disqualification itself.

A14–27

Effect of disqualification

The defendant who is disqualified from driving is disqualified from the announcement of the order and any licence that he held prior to the announcement is revoked: **section 103(2) R.T.A. 1988**. In certain circumstances, the order of disqualification can be suspended pending appeal (see Chapter 18 on Appeals) and, where such an application is made and granted, the operation of the order is postponed until the appeal is heard: *Taylor v. Commissioner of Police for the Metropolis* [1987] R.T.R. 118. Clearly, where the appeal is successful in respect of the disqualification, it would not take effect at all.

A14–28

Consecutive periods of disqualification

Periods of disqualification must start on the day that the order is announced. **Section 34** of the **R.T.O.A. 1988** provides that consecutive periods of disqualification are not permissible. In the case of *R. v. Bain* [1973] R.T.R. 213 it was decided that orders made on the same occasion

A14–29

to run consecutively were wrongly made, and in *R. v. Johnston* [1973] R.T.R. 403, an order was held to be wrong when it purported to be specified to take effect consecutive to a previous disqualification.

Obligatory disqualifications and penalty points

A14–30 When an order of disqualification is made under **section 34(1) R.T.O.A. 1988**, no penalty points are endorsed on the defendant's licence. Prior to the passing of the 1991 Act "notional points" would be added to the licence of an offender in order to ascertain whether the defendant was also to be disqualified under the totting-up procedure (see § A 14–21, above). The new provision for calculating penalty points (**Section 29(1)(a) R.T.A. 1991**) has abolished the old system of notional penalty points and it is no longer possible to impose two orders of disqualification as a result of the same conviction. (See *Learmont v. D.P.P., The Times*, March 1, 1994, at § A14–18.)

Endorsement and disqualification checklist

A14–31
    (a) Is the offence endorsable?
    (b) Can special reasons be argued?
    (c) If the offence is endorsable, how many points are to be endorsed?
    (d) Does the driver have any relevant points on his licence?
    (e) Is there a risk of a "totting" disqualification?
    (f) Can mitigating circumstances be put forward?
    (g) Does the driver have a good or bad driving record?
    (h) Is there going to be a mandatory three-year ban?
    (i) Is it better to be subject to a short ban now and wipe the slate clean, rather than have additional points endorsed on the licence?

Chapter 15

SPECIAL REASONS

Introduction

The terms "special reasons," "mitigating circumstances" and "miti- **A15–01**
gation" are often confused in practice. This chapter is devoted to
special reasons. A court may refrain from disqualifying in cases
involving obligatory disqualification, or not endorsing in respect of
endorsable offences, if it finds certain facts proved which are capable
in law of amounting to a special reason for not disqualifying or
endorsing.

Mitigating circumstances, the subject-matter of the following chapter covers those situations where the court has a wide discretion not to
disqualify under the penalty points system.

Mitigation in general is aimed at the overall picture, including
matters such as how the offence came to be committed, the offender's
background, means and antecedents. This is directed at sentence as a
whole. This will also be covered later in the book in Chapter 17.

Statutory provisions governing special reasons

Section 34 of the **R.T.O.A. 1988** states that in cases that carry obliga- **A15–02**
tory disqualification:

"... the court shall order him to be disqualified for such period not
less than twelve months as the court thinks fit unless the court for
special reasons thinks fit to order him to be disqualified for a shorter
period or not to order him to be disqualified."

From this it follows that the court may not disqualify at all or, if it
feels that some disqualification is merited, it can disqualify for a
period shorter than the statutory minimum. A person is liable to
obligatory disqualification when he is convicted of:

(a) Driving or attempting to drive with an alcohol concentration
above the prescribed limit;
(b) driving or attempting to drive whilst unfit through drink or
drugs;
(c) failing to provide a specimen if driving or attempting to drive;
(d) manslaughter arising from the use of a motor vehicle;

(e) causing death by dangerous driving;
(f) causing death by careless driving whilst unfit;
(g) dangerous driving;
(h) motor racing and speed trials on the highways.

Disqualification is for no less than 12 months in the case of (a), (b), (c), (g) and (h), and two years under (d), (e) and (f) above. If, in the 10 years immediately preceding the commission of the offence under (a), (b), (c) and (f) above, he has been convicted of any such offence then the minimum period is three years: **section 34(3), (4)** as amended by **section 29 R.T.A. 1991**.

Definition of special reasons

A15–03 There is no statutory definition of special reasons, but the accepted definition is to be found in the case of *R. v. Crossen* [1939] N.I. 106 as approved in *Whittall v. Kirby* [1946] 2 All E.R. 552:

> "A special reason within the exception is one which is special to the facts of the particular case, that is special to the facts which constitute the offence. It is in other words, a mitigating or extenuating circumstance, not amounting in law to a defence to the charge, yet directly connected with the commission of the offence and one which the court ought properly to take into consideration when imposing punishment. A circumstance peculiar to the offender as distinguished from the offence is not a special reason within the exception."

Despite the last sentence in the definition, cases often come before the court in which special reasons are sought to be raised but where the facts relied on relate to the offender and not to the offence. It may be that the words in the definition "mitigating or extenuating circumstances" serve to confuse.

A15–04 The following are examples of cases where special reasons were unsuccessfully advanced and which can be seen in fact to relate principally to mitigation:

(i) Disqualification is too severe a measure for the offence: *Glendinning v. Batty* [1973] R.T.R. 405;
(ii) disqualification is unfair: *Denneny v. Harding* [1986] R.T.R. 408;
(iii) the person relies on his vehicle for transport: *R. v. Hart, R. v. Jackson* [1970] R.T.R. 165;
(iv) disqualification will cause serious hardship on the family: *Taylor v. Austin* [1969] 1 W.L.R. 264; *Reynolds v. Roche* [1972] R.T.R. 282;
(v) the defendant is a professional driver: *Whittall v. Kirby* [1946] 2 All E.R. 552;
(vi) the defendant has driven for years without complaint: *Lines v. Hersom* [1951] 2 All E.R. 650;

(vii) the excess was minimal: *R. v. Anderson* [1972] R.T.R. 113;
(viii) a mile before a positive test the defendant had given a negative one: *D.P.P. v. White* [1988] R.T.R. 267;
(ix) ignorance of the overnight effect of alcohol on breath-alcohol level: *D.P.P. v. O'Meara* [1989] R.T.R. 24.

Guidelines

Four criteria drawn from the above definition were laid down in the **A15–05** case of *R. v. Wickens* (1958) 42 Cr.App.R. 236. These criteria must be satisfied for special reasons to be found:

(a) It must be a mitigating or extenuating circumstance;
(b) it must not amount in law to a defence;
(c) it must be directly connected with the commission of the offence;
(d) it must be a matter which the court ought properly to take into account when considering sentence.

One word of warning. Although the court may find that special reasons exist, nevertheless, they may decide not to exercise their discretion in the defendant's favour: *R. v. Newton* [1974] R.T.R. 451. As is clear from this case it is a two stage process:

(i) To determine if special reasons exist, and if so
(ii) whether the justices in their discretion should not disqualify or disqualify for less than 12 months.

There are considerations which the court can and should take into account in the exercise of its discretion, matters such as: should the defendant have realised he was not in a fit state to drive?: *Pridige v. Grant* [1985] R.T.R. 196. The general rule of thumb is that the exercise of discretion should be used only in "clear and compelling cases": *Vaughan v. Dunn* [1984] R.T.R. 376 following *Taylor v. Rajan* [1974] R.T.R. 304.

It has been observed by the courts that it will be only in rare circum- **A15–06** stances that the court may properly refrain from disqualifying in one of the three main breathalyser offences and, in any event, the court should rarely if ever exercise its discretion in favour of the defendant if the blood/alcohol content exceeds 100 milligrams per 100 millilitres of blood: *Scobie v. Graham* [1970] R.T.R. 358; *Taylor v. Rajan*.

Cases where the facts were found to be capable of amounting to special reasons will be looked at and contrasted with some unsuccessful cases. The point to note when consulting these cases is that a special reason is one which is special to the facts of each particular case and, therefore, these cases should be used by way of guidance only. It will be seen that cases with similar facts often have different outcomes, so it is wise to read the case itself if presented with facts that appear similar to the very brief resumé that will follow.

Drink/driving cases: general points on special reasons

A15–07 Three groups of circumstances have been identified in relation to
drink/driving offences:

   (a) Circumstances explaining how the driver came to be unfit to
       drive or had excess alcohol in his body;
   (b) those explaining why the defendant drove;
   (c) miscellaneous.

Explanations why the driver was unfit to drive

A15–08 These cases in the main relate to a combination of drink and medical
conditions involving prescribed drugs. The cases are fairly old ones,
and it is thought that nowadays the courts would not be so sympath-
etic in similar cases given the warnings that now exist on prescriptions
and a general awareness that one should not drink alcohol when taking medication. The following cases could well be decided differently
today:

   (a) *Chapman v. O'Hagan* [1949] All E.R. 690: drug taken for pain in
       injured leg, unaware that he would be affected by drinking
       alcohol.
   (b) *R. v. Holt* [1962] Crim.L.R. 565: the defendant was given a pre-
       scription for tablets by his doctor who failed to warn him of the
       effects of alcohol.

These two cases fall into the category of the defendant being misled
into committing the offence. This aspect is a common thread throughout the cases which have been successful in the past: in other words,
the intervention of a third party. However, the attitude of the courts
today is much more along the lines that the defendant should have
been "on enquiry" especially if he has a medical condition and is taking medication for it.

   (c) *R. v. Wickens* (1958) 42 Cr.App.R. 236 was a case where ignor-
       ance of a medical condition was successful, the defendant was
       unaware that he was a diabetic and drank beer.
   (d) *Archer v. Woodward* [1959] Crim.L.R. 461: by way of contrast,
       found that unfitness due to lack of food could not amount to a
       special reason.
   (e) *Williams v. Neale* [1971] R.T.R. 149, where the defendant hon-
       estly thought he was drinking a soft drink but it was laced with
       alcohol. This was a successful laced drink case.

The court, in addition to looking at the explanation as to why the
defendant was unfit, is entitled to look at other matters when considering whether to exercise their discretion. Factors to be considered may
be: how he was driving; his ability to drive; what he was drinking and
his tolerance for alcohol; should he have realised that he was not fit to
drive. See *D.P.P. v. Barker* [1990] R.T.R. 1.

Why the defendant had excess alcohol in his body

Here two different situations are distinguished. The first is what is **A15–09** commonly known as the laced drink situation – that is, the defendant does not know he is drinking alcohol. The second situation is that the defendant knows he is drinking alcohol, but he is misled as to the nature of the drink. In the case of the laced drink, it was said that the court was entitled to find special reasons where it can be established that:

(a) The defendant's drink was laced, and
(b) that he did not know nor suspect that fact, and
(c) had it not been laced he would not have been above the legal limit: *Pugsley v. Hunter* [1973] R.T.R. 284; *D.P.P. v. Frost* [1989] R.T.R. 11.

Expert evidence is needed to establish the excess unless it would be very obvious to the layman. The courts have gone further to say that magistrates have a discretion to hear "back calculation" evidence in considering special reasons: *Smith v. Geraghty* [1986] R.T.R. 222.

In *Smith v. D.P.P.* [1990] R.T.R. 17, the defendant had consumed one- **A15–10** and-a-half pints of lager and then went on to consume a fruit drink which he was unaware contained a measure of vodka. The specimen showed a blood/alcohol reading of 86 milligrammes: just over the legal limit. No medical evidence was called and the Crown Court held, following *Pugsley*, that it was not prepared to speculate on the dissipation rate and enter into detailed calculations, and therefore the defendant had failed to show the laced drink was responsible for the limit. This was upheld in the Divisional Court.

A number of laced drinks cases were considered together in the Divisional Court which gave some guidance for the conduct of such cases: *D.P.P. v. O'Connor* [1992] R.T.R. 66. Reviewing the cases before the court, it was noted that justices were not always sufficiently conscious of the relevance of expert evidence with regard to credibility. Normally, where the defendant sought to rely on special reasons, justices would expect to receive help from expert evidence to determine the case except in obvious cases such as in the case of a defendant whose blood alcohol level was just above the prescribed limit. However, each case turned on its own facts.

Observations were made about the procedure. Where the defendant intends to call evidence to prove facts or medical opinion in support of special reasons, it is desirable that notice is given to the prosecution in sufficient time before the hearing, to enable the prosecution to be prepared to deal with the evidence. In such cases it should be possible for the prosecution to make available expert evidence which it was to be hoped that, in the interests of costs, the defence may be able to agree. (If the defence has given such notice, it is quite likely that they have already obtained a report from an expert, which once served could be agreed by the prosecution!) The solution might be in a case where the defendant had not informed the prosecution of his intention to rely on

201

special reasons, the prosecution might elicit that fact in the course of cross-examination so that the justices could consider whether the defendant's failure to give notice reflects on his bona fides.

Where special reasons are established, it does not follow that disqualification is automatically avoided: *Donahue v. D.P.P.* [1993] R.T.R. 156. Where the motorist drives erratically or the excess of alcohol is substantial, justices will wish to consider whether he should have appreciated that he was not in a condition in which he should have driven.

A15–11   Following *D.P.P. v. Anderson* [1990] R.T.R. 269, it is open to the prosecution in appropriate cases to bring proceedings against the person responsible for lacing the drinks.

It must be pointed out, therefore, that if a defendant proposes to call evidence in a "laced drink" case in the form of the person who laced the drink, then that person should be warned that he could be in danger of being charged with procuring the commission of a criminal offence: *Att.-Gen.'s Reference (No. 1 of 1975)* [1975] Q.B. 773.

Cases in the second category, of being misled as to the nature of the drink, are fairly old and it is questionable whether the courts would take such a generous view today:

> *R. v. Shippam* [1971] R.T.R. 209. The defendant genuinely thought he was drinking lager and lime but it contained vodka.

> *Alexander v. Latter* [1972] R.T.R. 447. Diabetic lager was supplied by the barman with no warning that it was double strength.

> *R. v. Krebbs* [1977] R.T.R. 406. The defendant had drunk Harp lager and then was given Lowenbrau which was much stronger.

A15–12   In both categories special reasons were found under the principle of the defendant being misled. They need to be contrasted with:

> *Adams v. Bradley* [1975] R.T.R. 233. The defendant drank strong lager unaware of its strength, the principle here being that he didn't ask. Beer drinkers may be a little sceptical about the cases, given the difference in specific gravity and taste between ordinary strength and strong lagers.

In the case of *R. v. Messom* [1973] R.T.R. 140, the defendant asked for a small whisky and a large ginger ale, he was given a large brandy with a small ginger ale. Special reasons were found to exist here. Again, it is difficult in practice to see how one could have been misled.

But see *D.P.P. v. Younas* [1990] R.T.R. 22, the defendant drank almost two pints of lager both of which were laced with a double rum. The breath/alcohol reading was 72 microgrammes, double the legal limit. Evidence of this was given by the defendant's friend. No medical evidence was called. The justices found special reasons for not disqualifying him. The prosecution appealed and the appeal was dismissed. It was held that each case depended on its own facts and the decision of the justices could not be said to be perverse.

A15–13   The above cases should be contrasted with the following unsuccessful cases:

> *Goldsmith v. Laver* [1970] R.T.R. 162: the defendant was aware of his diabetic condition.

R. v. Scott [1970] R.T.R. 173: the defendant took sleeping tablets and alcohol after an accident.

Newnham v. Trigg [1970] R.T.R. 107: the defendant was given an unknown amount of whisky and ginger for a cold.

R. v. Jackson and *R. v. Hart* [1970] R.T.R. 165: the fact that a liver condition caused retention of alcohol for a longer period was held not to be capable of amounting to a special reason.

R. v. David Newton [1974] R.T.R. 451: this was an unsuccessful case although it was a laced drink situation. The defendant's drink had been laced with vodka. The view of the court was that it was not sufficient for the defendant to make no enquiry as to the nature of his drink and, even if special reasons could be found, the court was bound to consider when exercising its discretion whether he should have realised he was not fit to drive.

In *Beauchamp-Thompson v. D.P.P.* [1989] R.T.R. 54 it was held that the defendant should have been able to distinguish between a lighter Riesling wine and a heavier Chardonnay and therefore special reasons were not found.

In *R. v. Cambridge Magistrates' Court, ex p. Wong* [1992] R.T.R. 382 the defendant had consumed some wine and two doses of cough linctus.

A specimen of breath analysed gave a reading of 40 microgrammes. The defendant pleaded guilty. Evidence was called to show that the linctus taken would account for 1.6 microgrammes. The defendant gave evidence that he was unaware that the linctus contained alcohol. As it was not the practice of the prosecution to prosecute below the figure of 40 microgrammes, special reasons existed for not disqualifying. This was rejected by the justices, who found against the defendant as a matter of law. The Divisional Court found that they had fallen into error and that the facts were capable of amounting to special reasons. An order of mandamus requiring the justices to continue the hearing was made.

Explanations why the defendant drove

There are three main headings covering explanations as to why the defendant drove. These are: **A15–14**

(a) The emergency principle;
(b) police instructions;
(c) the distance driven was very short.

Emergency principle

Explanations in successful cases have been largely in the nature of an **A15–15** emergency or on police instructions. The situation would arise only where a person had been drinking not intending to drive and a sudden, but unexpected, situation arose which compelled him to drive. *Brown v. Dyerson* [1969] 1 Q.B. 45 lays down the principle that driving due to a sudden medical emergency was capable of amounting to a special reason. This principle was acknowledged in *Taylor v. Rajan* [1974] R.T.R. 304, but the case failed on the facts as the defendant drove after the emergency was dealt with. It was made clear that the discretion would be exercised only in the case where the emergency was acute and there was no alternative means of dealing with it. This principle is reflected in the cases dealt with below.

R. v. Baines [1970] R.T.R. 455, *Evans v. Bray* [1977] R.T.R. 24 and *Jacobs v. Reed* [1974] R.T.R. 81 were all cases of emergencies, but alternative methods of transport had not been considered and therefore were unsuccessful. *Jacobs* lays down the general principles relating to emergencies. They are:

(a) The degree and character of the emergency which arose and whether it was acute enough to justify taking out the car;
(b) the extent to which alternative means of transport might be employed;
(c) the other means of dealing with the emergency.

A15–16   In *D.P.P. v. Bird*, February 24, 1994 (unreported), B pleaded guilty to driving with excess alcohol. He was almost three times over the limit. They found special reasons based on the emergency principle and did not disqualify him.

The facts on which the decision was based are, that B was woken up at 9.30 p.m. by a close friend who was sobbing. She said that she did not want to live any more. She had indicated suicidal tendencies in the past. B had not had anything alcoholic to drink nor had he eaten since breakfast. He drove to her house. On arrival, the friend was very distressed. They talked for hours, during which time she gave him gin and Coca Cola to drink. He did not realise how much alcohol he had drunk. By 3.30 a.m. the friend had got into a state of extreme anger and refused to let B stay as he had anticipated. She also threatened to take an overdose. She would not let him call a taxi and ordered him to leave. He did so. He lived 6 miles away and there was no public transport at that time of the morning, so he drove his car. A few hundred yards down the road, he was stopped by the police.

Allowing the appeal by the D.P.P., the Divisional Court held, that the justices were wrong to find that special reasons existed, noting that B could have hidden the pills; that the area was more urban than described by the justices, and that he could have gone to a house or a phone box to call a taxi.

A15–17   The following two cases give an indication of the types of situations that the courts would regard as genuine emergencies.

In *D.P.P. v. Upchurch* [1994] R.T.R. 366, the defendant had left a restaurant on foot when he and his friends were innocently caught up in a serious disturbance which resulted in his friends suffering head injuries. The defendant sought the assistance of a police officer to call an ambulance but was told no ambulances were available. He and his friends walked home, but as his friends seemed seriously unwell, the defendant rang for a taxi. The taxi would not come out due to the disturbance. He decided to drive his friends three miles to the hospital.

He was stopped by a police officer who noted that he was driving twice the speed limit but otherwise properly. He was breathalysed and was found to have a reading of 45 microgrammes of alcohol in 100 millilitres of breath. The prosecutor appealed against the justices' decision not to disqualify the defendant. The Divisional Court held that on the evidence it *was* open to the justices to find that the circumstances amounted to an emergency and any other decision would have been perverse.

In *D.P.P. v. Knight* [1994] R.T.R. 374, the defendant, who had been the recipient of threatening phone calls, left her baby at home with the 14-year-old babysitter and went by car to the public house. She phoned home to check all was well and found out that there had been a number of telephone calls in which the caller had threatened to use a knife. The babysitter begged the defendant to return home. The defendant who had consumed one-and-a-half-pints of cider, had not intended to drive home. She tried to get a taxi unsuccessfully and also tried, again unsuccessfully to contact friends who could take her home. She then decided to drive herself and was stopped by a police officer. She was breathalysed and found to have a reading of 44 microgrammes of alcohol in 100 millilitres of breath. The justices found special reasons to exist and did not disqualify. On dismissing the appeal by the prosecution, the Divisional Court stated that the case was, on the facts found by the justices, as clear and compelling an example as could be contemplated of an emergency and that there was no evidence that the driving was exceptionable, and the amount of alcohol was not much over the limit.

The safety of the public was of paramount importance so the manner of the defendant's driving would be relevant as would whether he acted responsibly. **A15–18**

Park v. Hicks [1979] R.T.R. 259. The defendant drove his wife away from a party where there had been some trouble in the fear that, as she had had a brain haemorrhage in the past, there was a risk of repetition as a result of the trouble. It was found that the evidence was not of a satisfactory nature for the magistrates to find special reasons.

Powell v. Gliha [1979] R.T.R. 126. A wife drove her paraplegic husband home from a party in order that he could use his special facility toilet. It was found that she should have given thought to his needs before she set off for the party.

Holroyd v. Berry [1973] R.T.R. 145. Here the defendant was a doctor in an area where there was difficulty in getting doctors and also an area where he needed his car to make calls. This was not found to be sufficient.

D.P.P. v. Walker [1989] R.T.R. 112. The Divisional Court remitted the case back to the magistrates' court with a direction to impose the statutory disqualification, as it was held that there was a distinct difference in a situation presented to a driver on an outward journey on the way to an emergency and on the homeward journey when the emergency had been dealt with. The justices had erred in finding special reasons.

A similar finding was made in the case of *D.P.P. v. Feeney, The Times,* December 13, 1988.

In *Williams v. Tierney* [1988] R.T.R. 118, it was held that fear of imminent attack was sufficient an emergency to amount to special reasons for not disqualifying someone for driving with excess alcohol.

A15–19 In *D.P.P. v. Doyle, The Times,* December 29, 1992, the defendant had been assaulted by her boyfriend. She drove to a friend's house and called the police. She also consumed some brandy and drove home. She was breathalysed. The justices found that special reasons did exist as she was in genuine fear of her personal safety, and her unwillingness to abandon her car and use alternative transport was reasonable. Allowing the appeal by the prosecutor, the Divisional Court, adopting the prosecutor's argument said, that the emergency had begun before she had made the decision deliberately to drink and that where a driver had deliberately taken that decision knowing he would or probably would drive, it was not open to the justices to find special reasons.

Police instructions

A15–20 Two successful cases in this area are:

R. v. McIntyre [1976] R.T.R. 330. The defendant moved his car a short distance in the genuine but mistaken belief that he had been instructed to do so by the police. This case succeeded no doubt by virtue of the fact that he only drove a very short distance.

R. v. Gravelling, Daily Telegraph, September 15, 1983. The defendant, who was the keyholder of premises, was called out by the police to effect entry.

The case of *De Munthe v. Stewart* [1982] R.T.R. 27 can be contrasted. Although the defendant moved his car at the police request, he had already been driving immediately prior to the request.

Shortness of distance driven

A15–21 If the defendant has driven the car for a short distance only and it was at the instigation or because of a third party, then providing he would have been unlikely to come into contact with other road users, nor have been a danger on the road, special reasons may be found.

James v. Hall [1972] R.T.R. 228: the defendant drove a few yards from the road into a drive.

R. v. Agnew [1969] Crim.L.R. 152: the defendant, a passenger in the car, was asked by the owner to move the car a matter of some six feet.

Redmond v. Parry [1986] R.T.R. 146: a more recent case, acknowledged that shortness of distance driven was a matter which should be properly considered as it can amount to a special reason.

Nevertheless, the Divisional Court in the case of *Chatters v. Burke* [1986] R.T.R. 396 set out matters which should be taken into account when determining if special reasons exist which go beyond the mere question of shortness of distance driven. They are:

(a) How far the vehicle is driven in fact;
(b) the manner in which it was driven;
(c) the state of the vehicle;
(d) whether the driver intended to drive any further;
(e) the road and traffic conditions at the time;
(f) whether there was any possibility of danger by contact with other road users;
(g) the reason the vehicle was driven.

In that particular case, the defendant, who had been a passenger, after the car had rolled over from the road into a field, drove the car from the field to the road and left it there. It was held that special reasons existed.

In *Coombs v. Kehoe* [1972] R.T.R. 224 the defendant drove only 200 **A15–22** yards but had collided with other vehicles in the process. The Divisional Court warned that the case of *James v. Hall* was a very special case on its facts. The inference to be drawn is that heavy reliance may not be placed on the case. This was also confirmed in *Haime v. Walkett* [1983] R.T.R. 512, where the defendant reversed his car ready to drive it some 200 yards to park it for the night. It was said that the fact that the defendant was merely parking his car was not by itself capable of being a special reason. The defendant in reversing had stalled the car and mounted the pavement twice! Another unsuccessful case was *R. v. Shaw* [1974] R.T.R. 225: the defendant drove his car a short distance down a private lane where the public had access.

In *D.P.P. v. Corcoran* [1991] R.T.R. 329, the defendant, intending to drive only some 40 yards to park the car, drove the car with no danger to other road users. The justices found special reasons for not disqualifying or endorsing his licence. The prosecution appealed on the question whether a reasonable Bench could find special reasons for not disqualifying or endorsing. Dismissing the appeal, the Divisional Court answered in the affirmative.

Miscellaneous circumstances

Cases not falling under the previous heading have tended to relate to **A15–23** specimens of blood and failure to provide a specimen. The cases regarding specimens of blood are mainly under the old pre-breathalyser machines legislation and such cases will be rare nowadays.

Specimens

R. v. Anderson [1972] R.T.R. 113 is a case that probably stands on its own as the Court of Appeal stressed that it was a very unusual situation and unlikely to be repeated. Here the defendant had been told that he would not be prosecuted so he destroyed his sample of blood. The prosecution analysis was 81 milligrammes. Special reasons were found to exist. Contrast with: *Doyle v. Leroux* [1981] R.T.R. 438 where the defendant kept his sample for some weeks and then destroyed it on receipt of a letter from the police saying that he would not be prosecuted. He made no attempt during the period to have the sample analysed and the prosecution reading was 168 milligrammes.

   Harding v. Oliver [1973] R.T.R. 497: the defendant's sample was lost at the laboratory where he sent it for analysis. No special reasons were found.

   Lodwick v. Brow [1984] R.T.R. 394: the defendant could not remember having provided a sample due to temporary amnesia and when informed about it could not find the sample. No special reasons were found.

   D.P.P. v. Phillips, June 22, 1994 (unreported): unhappiness causing one to drink to excess nor the necessity to keep one's licence in order to visit a spouse in hospital were not sufficient to amount to special reasons.

Failure to provide a specimen

A15–24   Care has to be taken in this particular area. Reasons which are put forward based on the circumstances of the offence may well amount to the defence of reasonable excuse rather than special reasons. It would seem that if there is no reasonable excuse on the facts, then there are no special reasons, see *D.P.P. v. Daley (No. 2)* [1994] R.T.R. 107. Generally, therefore, defendants in this area do not meet with much success. Two cases can be distinguished from the others:

   White (Arvin) v. Metropolitan Police Commissioner [1984] Crim.L.R. 687 – special reasons were found to exist to reduce a three year disqualification to 12 months. The first breath test reading was 27 microgrammes and the defendant refused to supply a second sample on the basis that he was under the legal limit, as the lower figure is the one to be produced in court.

   McCormick v. Hitchins [1988] R.T.R. 182 the defendant was in charge of a parked car which was damaged by others. He refused to give a specimen. It was found that there was no intent to drive and special reasons were found for not endorsing 10 penalty points, when not driving nor attempting to drive.

   In *Sutch v. C.P.S.*, unreported, January 30, 1987: the defendant was seen walking towards his crashed car, he was arrested and taken to the police station. He had not been the driver of the car at the time of the crash and had no intention of driving. He refused to give a specimen of breath. Special reasons were found for not endorsing his licence with the obligatory number of penalty points.

   In *Daniels v. D.P.P.* [1992] R.T.R. 140 it was held that the fact that at the time the defendant was asked to provide a specimen, he was still preoccupied with a charge of theft against him of which he was in fact innocent; and although he understood the request he was distracted by the more serious charge; that if he had been told the charge was no longer being explored he might have taken a different view of the request; that was something which a court was entitled to take into account as possibly providing special reasons for not disqualifying.

In *D.P.P. v. Kinnersley* [1993] R.T.R. 105, it was held that a fear of **A15–25** AIDS could amount to a special reason. Before the justices, the fear of AIDS had been run as a reasonable excuse for not providing a specimen. The justices convicted but found special reasons to exist. The prosecution argument on appeal was that (a) the justices had confused the circumstances which were connected with the offence with the circumstances connected with the offender and (b) that the defendant was under a duty to draw to the police officers attention any circumstances which were special to him which prevented him providing a specimen and that if he did not do so special reasons could not succeed. The Divisional Court disagreed. There was no duty on a driver to give an explanation, but a failure to give an early explanation might reflect on the bona fides of the defendant.

In the case of *Crawford v. D.P.P.* (No. CO-725-93), October 14, 1993, D.C., C was observed by members of the public driving erratically and as a result he was met by the police upon his return home. Once inside, the defendant consumed alcohol. He refused to give a specimen both at home and at the police station. Having pleaded guilty to reckless driving, failure to provide a specimen at home and having been found guilty of failure to provide a sample at the station, C then proceeded to successfully argue the existence of special reasons. They were established on the grounds that he was irrational and traumatised at the time when requested to give a specimen and that he was never over the limit when driving. Medical evidence was called in support of the second ground.

The Crown appealed by way of case stated and applied for the matter to be remitted to the Justices for amendment, arguing that the findings of fact upon which the magistrates stated the case were incomplete. Kennedy L.J. agreed in repsect of the evidence surrounding the number of drinks consumed by C once inside the house. The case was therefore remitted for amendment on that basis.

The court expressed concern at the procedure adopted in special reasons hearings, emphasising that the Justices must scrutinise thoroughly all evidence given.

In the following cases special reasons were found not to exist: **A15–26**

Hosein v. Edmunds [1970] R.T.R. 51: the defendant refused to supply a sample before having consulted with his solicitor.

R. v. Seaman [1971] R.T.R. 456: the defendant refused a test until he had received advice from the Australian Consulate.

R. v. Harding [1974] R.T.R. 325: a fear of needles which fell short of phobia was not sufficient.

Anderton v. Anderton [1977] R.T.R. 385: the defendant was driving to hospital for urgent treatment and refused to give a specimen.

> *Courtman v. Masterson* [1978] R.T.R. 457: a case of post-accident con-
> sumption. No special reasons, even though there would have
> been a defence to drink/driving.
> *Grix v. Chief Constable of Kent* [1987] R.T.R. 193: the defendant offered
> to supply urine instead of blood.

D.P.P. v. Williams, June 22, 1994 (unreported): shortness of distance
driven was not directly connected with the offence of failure to provide a specimen and thus could not amount to a special reason.

Other offences and special reasons

A15–27 These cases in the main are concerned with the endorsement of penalty points as opposed to the statutory disqualification that has been
discussed, and they cover the manner of driving, the speed of driving
and driving without insurance.

Driving: sections 1, 2 and 3 of the Road Traffic Act 1988

A15–28 These sections include the following offences: death by dangerous
driving, dangerous driving and careless and inconsiderate driving,
causing death by careless driving when under the influence of drink or
drugs (originally death by reckless driving, reckless driving and careless driving).

> *R. v. Lundt-Smith* [1964] 3 All E.R. 225. This comes under the emerg-
> ency principle. It was a charge of death by dangerous driving.
> The defendant was an ambulanceman who crossed a red light
> and collided with a motor cyclist who was killed. He pleaded
> guilty but was not disqualified.
> *Wood v. Richards* [1977] R.T.R. 210: the defendant was a police officer
> responding to an emergency call. The magistrate found special
> reasons for not endorsing on a charge of driving without due
> care and attention.
> *Agnew v. D.P.P.* [1991] R.T.R. 144: the defendant, engaged in a police
> driver training exercise, collided slightly with another vehicle.
> He pleaded guilty to driving without due care and attention,
> but appealed the endorsement of his licence to the Crown
> Court arguing that being engaged in a police training exercise
> should be capable of amounting to special reasons for not
> endorsing. The Crown Court rejected the argument. Whilst not
> supporting that argument, the Divisional Court held in any
> event that the particular case was not one where it would have
> been appropriate to exercise the discretion not to endorse. The
> discretion should be used in favour of the driver "only in clear
> and compelling circumstances."

Where a motorist does a U-turn across the central reservation of a
motorway the court can find special reasons for not endorsing because

the motorway was blocked with stationary traffic on the motorist's side and none on the other side: *Fruer v. D.P.P., Siba v. D.P.P., Ward v. D.P.P.* [1989] R.T.R. 29.

Speeding

Police v. Humphreys [1970] Crim.L.R. 234: an articled clerk was **A15–29** speeding to get to court in time after having been delayed on the way.

Marks v. West Midlands Police [1981] R.T.R. 471: the defendant unintentionally exceeded the motorway limit by 10 m.p.h. as he was worried that his passenger who was 80 years old and incontinent might become ill and was hurrying to the nearest service area. The fact that the limit was exceeded by a few miles was not a consideration but the other facts were.

Two cases can be contrasted:

Burgess v. West [1982] R.T.R. 269. The defendant came from a 40 m.p.h. area to a 30 m.p.h. area but there were no signs to denote the 30 m.p.h. limit. Special reasons were found in this case, but not in *Walker v. Rawlinson* [1976] R.T.R. 94: ignorance of the fact that a 30 m.p.h. area is usually designated by street lights at certain intervals was not accepted.

In *Robinson v. D.P.P.* [1989] R.T.R. 42 no special reasons were found for not endorsing a solicitor's licence who was rushing to a potentially serious disturbance. The situation was defused before the arrival of the solicitor.

Insurance cases

There are a number of cases in this area. They are also characterised in **A15–30** the main by the fact that the defendant was misled in some way. The earlier cases dealt with disqualification, as prior to 1965 the offence of no insurance carried obligatory disqualification. Now, of course, it carries penalty points.

Labrum v. Williamson [1947] 1 All E.R. 824: the defendant applied for full cover but was provided with a named driver policy and was not informed of this.

Lyons v. May [1948] 2 All E.R. 1062: a lorry owner asked the garage proprietor to deliver his lorry back to his premises assuming the garage proprietor was insured. He was not insured and failed to tell the lorry owner.

Reay v. Young [1949] 1 All E.R. 1102 is unusual on its facts and relates to the shortness of distance driven. The defendant held the wheel of a car for 150 yards on open moorland where there was no traffic. This can be contrasted with *Gott v. Chisholm* (1950) 114 J.P. 212 where an unsupervised learner driver drove a short distance but caused an accident.

If, by looking at a policy, it would appear to the layman that the vehicle was covered then this can amount to a special reason: *Carlton v. Garrity* [1964] Crim.L.R. 146.

A15–31   More recent cases deal with endorsement:

> *East v. Bladen* [1987] R.T.R. 291. The owner of a car who had been severely injured allowed another to drive the car thinking that the policy covered himself and other drivers. It was held that ignorance as a general principle was not capable of amounting to a special reason, but that here there were special circumstances which justified the decision of the magistrates. These circumstances seem to have been that his injuries had such an effect, so as to reduce his ability to be aware of the policy's provisions.

> *Barnett v. Fieldhouse* [1987] R.T.R. 266. Here special reasons were found for not endorsing in respect of causing or permitting uninsured use of a motor vehicle. In this case the car was used uninsured on several occasions constituting separate offences. It was found that, had the defendant been aware of the offence on the first occasion, then future offences might have been avoided and thus there were special reasons for not endorsing his licence.

The general principle that ignorance of the law cannot be a special reason can be found in *Swell v. McKechnie* [1956] Crim.L.R. 523 and that an honest though groundless belief that a policy covers a particular use is no reason: *Rennison v. Knowler* [1947] 1 All E.R. 302. This case was distinguished in *East v. Bladen*.

Approach

A15–32   To summarise, what principles can be gleaned from the cases and how can they help in approaching a case in hand?

Ignorance cannot be put forward as a special reason nor can the triviality of the offence; these are matters which may go to mitigation. The courts are increasingly reluctant to exercise their discretion and therefore the case has to be looked at carefully to see if it is a proper case for advancing special reasons. Here are some guidelines as to approach:

(a) Look carefully to see if the case falls into the definition and criteria laid down in §§ A15–03 – A15–06;

(b) if so, look at the relevant cases to get some guidance as to prospects of success or failure. It is best to read the case itself if it is similar on the facts;

(c) ask the following questions: did the defendant have an alternative course of action open to him? Should he have been on notice or on inquiry as to certain facts? If the answer to either is yes, then the chances are slim;

(d) even if the case would seem to be strong for the defendant, go   **A15–33**
   one step further and consider whether there are any other circumstances, over and above the facts upon which the special
   reasons are based, to persuade the court to exercise its discretion in the defendant's favour. Or are there any features
   where, although the court may find special reasons proved, it
   nevertheless may decide not to exercise its discretion? An
   example would be a high reading: see *Taylor v. Rajan* where
   Lord Widgery said that, if the alcohol content exceeds 100 milligrammes per 100 millilitres of blood, the magistrates should
   rarely if ever exercise their discretion in the defendant's favour;

(e) remember expert evidence will need to be called if seeking to
   establish a case under the laced drink heading and, in some
   cases, to explain why the defendant was unfit;

(f) the onus of establishing special reasons is on the defendant and
   the standard is the balance of probabilities: *Pugsley v. Hunter*
   [1973] 1 W.L.R. 578;

(g) the defendant must call evidence to establish the case: *Jones v.
   English* [1951] 2 All E.R. 853;

(h) the evidence cannot be hearsay, but only admissible evidence:
   Flewitt v. Horvath [1972] R.T.R. 121; *James v. Morgan* [1988]
   R.T.R. 85;

(i) the prosecution should be notified in advance if it is proposed
   to raise special reasons *Pugsley v. Hunter*. The prosecution may,
   if they choose, place evidence before the court to contradict or
   put a different complexion on the evidence called by the
   defence. Serious consideration should be given to any possible
   deficiencies in the defence case;

(j) whether the facts are capable of amounting to special reasons is
   a matter of law and may well be the subject of argument in
   court. It is worth discussing the matter with the court clerk if in
   doubt.

Chapter 16

MITIGATING CIRCUMSTANCES

Introduction

This chapter deals exclusively with mitigating circumstances. It covers those situations where, upon a plea of guilty to any of the endorsable driving offences involving either obligatory or discretionary disqualification, or a finding of guilty on any such offences, the defendant faces a penalty points disqualification because he has accumulated 12 points on his licence as a result of this latest matter and other points endorsed on other occasions within three years of the last offence. Where such a penalty points disqualification arises, the court has a discretion not to disqualify the defendant at all or to disqualify for a shorter period than the statutory minimum period, if the court finds that there are circumstances such that the normal consequences of the conviction can be mitigated.

A16–01

Mitigating circumstances: the statutory provisions and definition

Section 19 of the **Transport Act 1981** introduced a system of penalty points that were to be endorsed on a driver's licence upon conviction for endorsable driving offences involving either obligatory or discretionary disqualification. In respect of any of these offences the court has the power to order a period of disqualification. However, if no period of disqualification was ordered for the individual offence and penalty points were endorsed on the driver's licence, the driver may have been caught by the provisions of **section 19(2)** of the 1981 Act. **Section 19** of the **Transport Act 1981** was re-enacted in **section 35** of the **R.T.O.A. 1988**.

A16–02

The effect of **section 35(2)** is that where a driver has accumulated 12 or more points in a three-year period then he is liable to a period of disqualification. The only way of avoiding a penalty points disqualification, assuming special reasons for not endorsing the driving licence in respect of the present offence are not found (see Chapter 15), is to satisfy the court that there are circumstances for "mitigating the normal consequences of conviction."

Section 35(1) of the **R.T.O.A. 1988** states that:

"**35.**—(1) Where—

   (a) a person is convicted of an offence involving obligatory or
       discretionary disqualification, and

   (b) the number of penalty points to be taken into account on
       that occasion number twelve or more,

the court must order him to be disqualified for not less than the
minimum period unless the court is satisfied, having regard to all
the circumstances, that there are grounds for mitigating the normal
consequences of the conviction and thinks fit to order him to be disqualified for a shorter period or not order him to be disqualified."

As in the case for special reasons, it follows that if the court finds that
there are mitigating circumstances, it may exercise its discretion and
make no order of disqualification, or disqualify for a shorter period
than the statutory minimum.

Penalty points to be taken into account

A16–03   Twelve points is the number of points that will attract a "totting-up"
disqualification. In calculating whether the driver has accumulated 12
points, the court will include those points for the present offence or
offences, disregarding any offence where an order under **section 34
R.T.O.A. 1988** is made, together with points ordered on any previous
occasion within three years of the date of the present offence, unless
there has been a period of disqualification under **section 35 R.T.O.A.
1988** in the meantime. If there has been a period of disqualification
imposed under **section 35**, this has the effect of "wiping" the licence
clean and, consequently there will not be any points to be taken into
account. Where a period of disqualification is ordered under **section
34** (offences involving mandatory disqualification), the penalty points
on the licence at the time that order is made, if any are not "wiped"
from the licence as a result of the disqualification, will be taken into
account in deciding whether the defendant is a "totter": **section
29(1)(b) R.T.O.A. 1988**.

   It should be noted that the relevant time period is the three-year
period up to the date of commission of the latest offence, not the date
of the hearing.

   It should also be noted that in certain circumstances a short period
of disqualification may be more beneficial to a driver than the addition
to his licence of some more points. Take the example of a driver who
has eight points on his licence and who is to be dealt with on a speeding matter. Rather than argue that he ought not to be disqualified for
the present offence but simply have just the minimum of three points
endorsed on his licence, it may be a better argument for him to be disqualified for a short period of a few weeks now than carry 11 points on
his licence and then face the prospect of a six-month disqualification as
a "totter" if he were to commit another minor offence.

Minimum period of disqualification: section 35(2)

If a driver has 12 points on his licence and there has been no previous   **A16–04**
period of disqualification imposed within three years immediately
preceding the commission of the latest offence, then the minimum period of disqualification is six months. In situations where there has
been a previous period of disqualification within three years, then the
minimum period of disqualification is increased. It becomes one year
where there has been one previous period of disqualification in the
three years and two years where more than one period of disqualification has been ordered. It is important to note that the relevant
three-year period runs from the date of the imposition of the disqualification on the previous matter to the date of the commission of the
latest offence, and not the date of hearing.

What is excluded from consideration as a mitigating circumstance?

Section 35(4) R.T.O.A. 1988 makes it clear that certain matters are   **A16–05**
excluded and a court is not entitled to take them into account when
considering whether circumstances exist for mitigating the normal
consequences of conviction. There are three exclusions:

*"(a) any circumstances that are alleged to make the offence or any
of the offences not a serious one"*

From this it is clear that it cannot be argued as a mitigating circumstance that the number of points endorsed on an earlier occasion
within the relevant three years, or the number of points to be endorsed
on this occasion, if there is no period of disqualification, are not justified on the facts of the offences. It may still be open to argue "special
reasons" for not endorsing the driver's licence on the basis of the facts
of the particular offence, thereby avoiding this particular problem, as
no points would then be endorsed on the driver's licence.

"(b) hardship other than exceptional hardship"

There is no definition of "exceptional hardship" in the Act, nor are   **A16–06**
there any guidelines to assist a court to determine whether any particular hardship is exceptional. It is simply a question of fact for the
court to determine on the circumstances of the case. By using the word
"exceptional," Parliament clearly intended that the circumstances be
unusual or peculiar in some way to take the case beyond the normal

hardship consequential on the disqualification of any driver. Exceptional hardship suffered by a person himself or by other persons directly or indirectly, as a result of the disqualification, can be argued to be a mitigating circumstance.

There follow a few examples of what may amount to exceptional hardship:

(i) Loss of employment to the driver or others dependant upon the driver being able to drive;

(ii) hardship to the driver's employer or employees;

(iii) hardship to the members of the family of the driver;

(iv) hardship to other innocent third parties.

It almost goes without saying that, where the true victim of the order disqualifying the driver is not the driver himself, but some other person, then that will weigh much more heavily upon the minds of the court, particularly where the other person is at risk of losing his employment.

A16–07 *Owen v. Jones* [1988] R.T.R. 102, is an example of a court finding exceptional hardship to exist. The matter was before the Divisional Court on the question of whether it was necessary for the justices to hear evidence about mitigating circumstances before deciding not to disqualify the defendant. The court held that the justices were entitled to rely on their own knowledge which they had gathered over the course of time and did not need evidence to be called before them. It was argued that it would be an exceptional hardship on the defendant to be disqualified as he was a serving police officer and was likely to lose both his job and his home if he was disqualified. That corresponded with the justices belief that it was the policy of the local police to dismiss any officer who was disqualified. They relied on their own belief and did not disqualify him.

Apart from the examples outlined above, other rather different circumstances may also be argued to come within the meaning of exceptional hardship. For example, a driver who has committed a number of offences on different dates. If the defendant is before a court and is disqualified for an offence which occurred later in time, before an earlier matter had been dealt with, any penalty points imposed would not be "wiped off" the licence as they would have been had the matters been dealt with chronologically. That may well amount to exceptional hardship, except where the delay has been caused by the defendant without good cause.

In the situation where a driver has been disqualified under **section 35(2)** of the **R.T.O.A. 1988** and **section 36** of the **R.T.O.A. 1988** (disqualification until he passes a test of competence to drive) on the same occasion, if he then reaches 12 points subsequently, he would be liable to a minimum period of disqualification of two years (even where the two disqualifications relate to the same offence). A court may well regard this as amounting to exceptional hardship and disqualify for a period of less than the two years. As the driver will have a period of disqualification to be taken into account, it would seem that the court could not refrain from disqualifying altogether, but it could reduce the period to not less than one year.

"(c) any circumstances which, within the three years immediately preceding the conviction, have been taken into account under that subsection in ordering the offender to be disqualified for a shorter period or not ordering him to be disqualified"

The effect of this provision is that where any mitigating circumstances **A16–08** were successfully argued on a previous occasion, within the three-year period, then the same circumstances cannot be taken into account on any subsequent occasion within the three-year period. This does not prevent a fresh argument on the circumstances unsuccessfully argued on a previous occasion in the hope of being lucky second time around, even where mitigating circumstances were found on an earlier occasion on a different ground. It is for the defendant to show that the mitigating circumstances are not the same as previously taken into account where that issue arises: *R. v. Sandbach Justices, ex p. Prescund* (1983) 5 Cr.App.R.(S.) 177.

Establishing that the grounds are different from those taken into account on an earlier occasion may create an evidential problem for the defendant. However, a court finding mitigating circumstances for not disqualifying a defendant, or for disqualifying for a shorter period than the minimum, is required to state the grounds for the finding in open court and those grounds should be entered on the court register: **section 47 R.T.O.A. 1988**. The best proof of what circumstances were found by the court on the previous occasion is to obtain from the court a certified extract of the register detailing the circumstances found to exist and then ensure that the certified extract is produced for the court dealing with the present offence. Failing that, it will be necessary to try to establish the grounds by calling other evidence.

Other mitigating circumstances

Almost invariably the mitigating circumstances that a court will be **A16–09** asked to find will centre on some aspect of exceptional hardship as discussed above which will be suffered by the defendant, or others, if the defendant is disqualified. However, it should be emphasised that a court is entitled to take into account any circumstance, which is not excluded by reason of the statutory provisions, that relates to the offence or to the offender.

Examples of other mitigating circumstances

R. v. Thomas [1983] 3 All E.R. 756, was a case where the Court of Appeal **A16–10** held that the general policy of imposing a long period of disqualification on a young offender which continued beyond his release date from prison was counter-productive and contrary to public interest by inviting him to commit further motoring offences. It was a ground for mitigating the normal consequences of conviction. (The editor of the *Criminal Law Review* points out that this argument will be caught by the provisions of **section 35(4)(c)** and could only be argued once in three years in the case of particularly persistent offenders).

R. v. Preston [1986] R.T.R. 136, was a case where the defendant pleaded *inter alia* to theft of a motor car. His licence was endorsed with eight penalty points and he was disqualified under **section 35(2)** for six months. He was also sentenced to nine months' imprisonment suspended for two years. The court held that **section 35(2)** gives the court a wider discretion than is allowed when special reasons not to disqualify have to be argued. The offence was one which had not involved bad driving, nor irresponsible use of a motor car on the road. There had been no transgression of any of the provisions of the Road Traffic Act. The defendant was employed in a position which involved regular driving and this was the first occasion he had abused his position as hirer of a motor car. The court allowed his appeal and quashed the order disqualifying him. The court also dealt with the question of hardship and the rehabilitation of the offender. The offences that he had committed were committed in part due to the lack of funds. The court stated that in not disqualifying the driver, they were increasing the chances of rehabilitation.

Mitigating circumstances and special reasons: a checklist for preparation prior to the hearing

A16–11 Some of these points have been covered in the last chapter but it does no harm for them to be reiterated.

(a) Consider the facts of the case with care. Do the facts constitute a plea of guilty to the charge and a submission on those facts that special reasons or mitigating circumstances apply? Do the facts fall within the relevant definitions and criteria? If so, consider the strength of the application. Do the circumstances constitute special reasons, mitigating circumstances or are they matters which go to mitigation generally?

(b) If special reasons are to be argued, notify the prosecution.

(c) Will it be necessary to call expert evidence? Where it is sought to establish a case under the "laced drinks" line of cases or to explain why the defendant was unfit, it will be necessary to call an expert. As soon as it becomes apparent that an expert will have to be instructed, he should be instructed (having obtained the go-ahead from the legal aid fund) and the court and the prosecution notified.

(d) In cases where it is hoped to be able to explain why the defendant drove, what evidence can be obtained to support the defendant's account of events?

(e) Where mitigating circumstances have been successfully argued on a previous occasion, within three years of the present offence, and are to be argued on this occasion, obtain an extract of the court register to see if the circumstances are the same.

A checklist for the procedure at the hearing on a plea of guilty to the charge and submission of special reasons or mitigating circumstances as appropriate

(a) Charge/s put to the defendant and pleas taken.   **A16–12**

(b) Facts of the offence opened to the court by the prosecution.

(c) Defence indicates to the court that it is seeking to show that special reasons or mitigating circumstances can be found in this case and give a brief outline to the court of what the reasons or circumstances are.

(d) Evidence in support of the application is called by the defence. Those witnesses may be cross-examined by the prosecution.

(e) Any evidence the prosecution intends to place before the court to contradict the evidence called in support of the submission is called and can be cross-examined.

(f) Defence makes its closing submissions.

(g) The prosecution has the right to address the court on matters of law.

(h) The court considers whether it finds special reasons or mitigating circumstances to exist, and if so, whether it will exercise its discretion and not disqualify/endorse.

(i) If the court finds special reasons or mitigating circumstances to exist, then those reasons must be given in open court and entered on the court register.

Chapter 17

OTHER PENALTIES AND MITIGATION

Custodial sentences

There are a number of road traffic offences which carry the possibility **A17–01** of a custodial sentence, *e.g.* dangerous driving, driving whilst disqualified and drink/driving offences. The imposition of such a sentence is now governed by the **Criminal Justice Act 1991 (C.J.A. 1991)**, as amended by the **Criminal Justice Act 1993 (C.J.A. 1993.)** The act creates a statutory framework within which courts will be required to work when imposing custodial sentences. A court is not permitted to pass a custodial sentence unless it is of the opinion that:

"(a) ... the offence, or the combination of the offence and one or more offences associated with it, was so serious that only such a sentence can be justified for the offence; or

(b) where the offence, is a violent or sexual offence, that only such a sentence would be adequate to protect the public from serious harm from him." (**C.J.A. 1991, s.1.**, as amended).

In relation to road traffic matters it is clearly subsection (a) which is of relevance. Where a custodial sentence is passed, the length of the sentence has to be "commensurate with the seriousness of the offence, or the combination of the offence and one or more offences associated with it." For offences of a violent or sexual nature the sentence shall be "for such longer term as in the opinion of the court is necessary to protect the public from serious harm from the offender": **section 2(2) C.J.A. 1991** (as amended).

The only exceptions to these rules are where the sentence is fixed by **A17–02** law, or where an offender refuses to give his consent to a community sentence proposed by the court and which requires the consent of the offender: **section 1(1) and (3)**.

In considering the statutory requirements, the court is required to take into account certain things, and to do certain things, namely:

(a) To obtain and consider a pre-sentence report before forming an opinion on custody, except where the offence or any other offence associated with it is triable only on indictment and the court is of the opinion that it is unnecessary to obtain a pre-sentence report; and

(b) to take into account all the information about the circumstances of the offence or (as the case may be) of the offence or offences

223

associated with it as is available to the court – including the aggravating and mitigating factors; and

(c) where **sections 1(2)(b)** or **2(2)(b)** are concerned it may take into account any information about the offender which is before it: **section 3 C.J.A. 1991**; and

(d) to take into account the rule of law as to the totality of sentences: **section 28 C.J.A. 1991**.

Paragraph 39 of Schedule 9 to the **Criminal Justice and Public Order Act 1994** when it comes into force, will make an important change to the obligation to obtain and consider a pre-sentence report in all courts save youth courts. A court will be able to pass a custodial sentence on an either way offence without first obtaining and considering a report, if in the circumstances of the case, the court is of the opinion that it is unnecessary to do so. The new act does not amend **section 3(1)** but creates an exception to the rule and gives the court a greater discretion to pass a custodial sentence than previously.

The phrase "so serious that only such a sentence can be justified for the offence" is not defined in the Act. In the case of *R. v. Cox (David Geoffrey)* [1993] 1 W.L.R. 188 the Court of Appeal adopted the formulation given by Lawton L.J. in the case of *R. v. Bradbourn* (1985) Cr.App.R.(S.) 180 that the phrase meant, "The kind of offence which when committed by a young person would make right-thinking members of the public, knowing all the facts, feel that justice had not been done by the passing of any sentence other than a custodial one" and was of general application rather than being just applicable to young persons. The court went on to hold that the prevalence of a particular class of offences, and public concern about them, was relevant to the seriousness of an instant offence. However, a court was not required to pass such a sentence even though such offences were prevalent. **Section 28 C.J.A. 1991** was also referred to by the court, and it was said that the court was still required to consider whether such a sentence was appropriate having regard to the mitigating factors available and relevant to the offender, as opposed to such factors as were relevant to the offence. See also *R. v. Baverstock* (1993) 14 Cr.App.R.(S.) 471.

A17–03 If a court decides to impose a custodial sentence, it is required to state in open court that either or both **section 1(2)(a)** or **(b)** applies and why it has formed that view, unless custody is being imposed as a result of the offender's refusal to consent to a community sentence. In addition, the court is also required to explain to the offender in open court and in "ordinary language" why it is imposing a custodial sentence upon him: **section 1(4)** and **(5)**.

So far as previous convictions are concerned, **section 29 C.J.A. 1991** as amended by **section 66 of the C.J.A. 1993** provides that:

"(1) In considering the seriousness of any offence, the court may take into account any previous convictions of the offender or any failure of his to respond to previous sentences.

(2) In considering the seriousness of any offence committed while the offender was on bail, the court shall treat the fact that it was committed in those circumstances as an aggravating factor."

The **1993 Act** appears to have considerably altered the **1991 Act**. Prior to this change, the Act prohibited sentencers from regarding an offence as more serious simply because the offender had previous convictions. Now previous convictions, failures to respond to previous sentences and offences committed whilst on bail can all be taken into account in assessing seriousness.

Young offenders

The minimum age for imprisonment is 21. Offenders under 21 can be **A17–04** sentenced to a period of detention in a young offender institution, and once the provisions of the **Criminal Justice and Public Order Act 1994** (**C.J.P.O.A. 1994**) are in force offenders aged 12, 13 and 14 may be sentenced to a period on a Secure Training Order.

The statutory framework for all custodial sentences is now broadly the same regardless of the age of the offender and is set out above. The **C.J.A. 1991** made important changes to the range of sentences available to young offenders. The minimum age for detention in a young offender institution is 15 and there is no distinction between the sexes. The minimum term for those aged 15 or 16 is two months and the maximum is currently 12 months. **Section 17** of the **C.J.P.O.A. 1994** when it comes into force will increase the maximum period to two years.

A new form of sentence is to be introduced by the **C.J.P.O.A. 1994** when it comes into force, for offenders aged 12, 13 and 14. The Secure Training Order has two elements to it: a period of detention followed by a period of supervision. The combined period must not be less than six months and must not exceed two years. The period that is served in detention must be half that specified in the order. It will only be possible to pass an order of this kind if the following conditions are met:

(i) the offender is aged between 12 and 15 and has been convicted of an imprisonable offence;

(ii) the offender was 12 or over at the time of commission of the offence;

(iii) the offender has been convicted of three or more imprisonable offences; and

(iv) has on the occasion of sentence or on a previous occasion either been found to be in breach of a supervision order, or to have been convicted of an offence whilst subject to a supervision order.

The sentence is a custodial sentence for the purposes of the **sections 1** to **4** of the **C.J.A. 1991** and therefore the general requirements of those sections must be satisfied: **section 1(6) C.J.P.O.A. 1994**.

Discounts in sentence for an early plea of guilty

A17–04A **Section 48** of the **C.J.P.O.A. 1994** when it comes into force will make the following provision:

"(1) In determining what sentence to pass on an offender who has pleaded guilty to an offence in proceedings before that court or another court a court shall take into account—

    (a) the stage in the proceedings for the offence at which the offender indicated his intention to plead guilty; and

    (b) the circumstances in which the indication was given.

(2) If, as a result of taking into account any matter referred to in subsection (10) above, the court imposes a punishment on the offender which is less severe than it would otherwise have imposed, it shall state in open court that it has done so."

This provision appears to put onto a statutory footing what has been common practice. What is clear is that there is an obligation upon a court to take into account the stage at which the defendant enters his plea, and if that has made an impact on the sentence to state that reason in open court.

Suspended sentences

A17–05 **Section 22** of the **Powers of Criminal Courts Act 1973 (P.C.C.A. 1973)** as amended by **section 5** of the **C.J.A. 1991**, allows a court, when passing a sentence of imprisonment of two years or less, to suspend that sentence for a period of between one and two years. Suspended sentences can only be passed on sentences of imprisonment and therefore do not apply to offenders under 21. **Section 22(2)** makes it clear that a suspended sentence can only be passed in those situations where a sentence of immediate imprisonment would have been appropriate but for the power allowing the court to suspend the sentence, and that there are exceptional circumstances to justify the passing of it. If a court is considering a suspended sentence, **section 22(2A) P.C.C.A. 1973**, as amended, requires the court to consider whether the circumstances of the case are such as to warrant, in addition, the imposition of a fine or the making of a compensation order. In the case of *R. v. Okinikan* [1993] 1 W.L.R. 173 the question of what amounts to exceptional circumstances for imposing a suspended sentence was considered. The court did not lay down a definition, but said that it would depend on the facts of each individual case. Good character, youth and an early plea, either together or alone, were said not to be exceptional circumstances justifying a suspended sentence. They were said to be features common to many cases, and could amount to mitigation sufficient to persuade a court that a custodial sentence should not be passed or to reduce its length. In *R. v. Robinson* (1993) 14 Cr.App.R.(S.) 559 Taylor L.C.J., in giving the judgment of the Court of Appeal, said that since the commencement of the **1991 Act** "the instances in which a suspended sentence will be appropriate will be few and far between". See also the cases of *R. v. Lowery* (1993) 14 Cr.App.R.(S.) 485 and *R. v. Bradley* (1994) 15 Cr.App.R.(S.) 597.

Suspended sentences should not be combined with sentences of immediate imprisonment or probation orders for other offences dealt with on the same occasion. If the court wishes there to be some form of supervision during the operation of the suspended sentence, **section 26 P.C.C.A. 1973** allows the court to make a suspended sentence supervision order where the length of the sentence is not more than six months.

If an offender is convicted of an offence punishable with imprisonment committed during the period of suspension, he will be at risk of having the suspended sentence activated in full or in part. The court has the power to make the offender serve the sentence concurrently or consecutively to any other period of imprisonment imposed in respect of the new offences.

Partially suspended sentences

As a result of the passing of the **C.J.A. 1991**, the power to impose partially suspended sentences and extended sentences has been abolished. **A17–06**

Fines

The penalty common to all road traffic offences is the power to impose a fine. The level of that fine differs according to the gravity of the offence. There are five levels of fine to cover all the summary offences and offences triable either way that are dealt with summarily. The levels range from £200 to £5,000 and denote the maximum fine in respect of the relevant offence (see Appendix F). Offences which are triable on indictment, or either way offences dealt with on indictment, may also result in the imposition of a fine but of unlimited amount as the crown court is not restricted by the maximum levels. **A17–07**

When should a fine be imposed?

The **C.J.A. 1991** introduced a "unit fine" system. The aim of the scheme was to try and deal with variations in levels of fines imposed by magistrates in different areas. The system was heavily criticised in practice and was abolished by the **C.J.A. 1993**. New **sections 18** and **20** were brought into force. The provisions abolishing the unit fine system came into force on September 20, 1993, and apply to offenders sentenced on or after that date irrespective of the date of the offence. The new provisions apply to the fixing of levels of fine by both the Crown Court and magistrates' court. **A17–08**

Section 18 C.J.A. 1991 (as amended) sets out a framework for the court to follow in deciding the appropriate level of fine. The court has to inquire into the financial circumstances of the offender (**section 18(1)**) and the amount of any fine has to reflect the court's opinion of the seriousness of the offence (**section 18(2)**). **Section 18(3) C.J.A. 1903**.

A17–09   When assessing the appropriate level of the fine, the magistrates' court will have regard to the levels suggested in the Magistrates' Association's suggested penalties. The suggestions are stated not to be a tariff, but they are to be used as a starting point, with an allowance of about one-third for timely guilty plea.

The new provisions appear to put into statutory form the effect of cases such as *R. v. Fairbairn* [1981] Crim.L.R. 190 and *R. v. Ashmore* [1974] Crim.L.R. 375. The aims of the earlier reforms to try and iron out regional variations in sentencing seem to have been forgotten, as although the new provisions are means related to an extent, the assessment of means and the level of fine are left flexible.

Section 20 of the **C.J.A.** (as inserted by the **C.J.A. 1993, section 65**) empowers a court to make a financial circumstances order before sentencing. The order requires the relevant person to give to the court a statement of his financial circumstances. Where the person before the court, or where it is a young person, his parent or guardians, fail to supply sufficient information or failed to cooperate in the court's inquiries, the court may make such order as it thinks fit: **section 18(4) C.J.A. 1991** as amended.

A17–10   A fine is often seen as an alternative to a sentence of imprisonment in more serious cases and, where the offence is serious, it is clearly not right for a person of substantial means to be able to buy their way out of a prison sentence, nor is it right for a person with little, if any, means to go to prison just because he cannot pay a fine. See *R. v. Markwick* (1953) 37 Cr.App.R. 125 and *R. v. Reeves* (1972) 56 Cr.App.R. 366.

The totality principal on sentencing is incorporated within **section 28** of the **C.J.A. 1991**. A court is permitted to mitigate the sentence by taking into account any relevant matters. The overall impact of fines was considered in the case of *R. v. Chelmsford Crown Court, ex p. Birchall* (1989) 11 Cr.App.R.(S.) 510. This was a case where the defendant pleaded guilty before the magistrates' court to ten offences of using a goods vehicle when the gross weight was exceeded. Parker L.J. said (at p. 84).

> "It appears that what the justices have done, and what the Crown Court have upheld, is to apply a rigid formula to each offence without regard to each offence without regard to the past record of the applicant, the period over which the offences took place and without regard to the question whether it was within his capacity to pay, either at all or by the instalments provided ... It must be remembered, and I stress, that the application of a rigid formula is not right, even for one offence. To take a rigid formula and apply it to each of 10 offences and then add it up is plainly wrong. A formula is justifiable as a base, but in each case, and even if there is only one offence, the justices and the Crown Court have to consider all the circumstances and apply the principles of sentencing which are well known."

Once a fine is imposed, time to pay is normally allowed. However, if the offender's means result in instalments continuing for more than two years, or in exceptional circumstances, three years, the level of the fine may be regarded as excessive. (See *R. v. Olliver and Olliver* (1989) 11 Cr.App.R.(S.) 10.)

Enforcement of fines

The powers of the magistrates' court to enforce fines are dealt with in the **Magistrates' Courts Act 1980** as amended. It may be that the fine can be deducted from the income of an offender under regulations drawn up by the Secretary of State under **section 24 C.J.A. 1991**. In most cases, it will be necessary for the magistrates to hold a means enquiry before an offender can be committed to prison for non-payment. An exception is where the person is unlikely to remain at a fixed address long enough for a payment order to be enforced, and therefore a period of imprisonment in default will be ordered at the same time the fine is imposed. **A17–11**

Fines on young persons

There is no lower age limit on fines – offenders of all ages can be fined. When an order fining a young person is made, the order may be on the parent or guardian to pay the sum if the young person defaults, unless that would be unreasonable, or the parent or guardian cannot be found: **section 127 C.J.A. 1988**. Where the young person has reached the age of 16, the duty on the parent to pay the fine has been amended to take the form of a power: **section 57 C.J.A. 1991**. The effect of this provision is that where the parent is ordered to pay the fine, the fine will be based on the parents' means, and where the young person is ordered to pay, it will be based on their means. **A17–12**

Community sentences

The imposition of non-custodial penalties is also covered by the **C.J.A. 1991**. As for custodial sentences, the circumstances in which a court can pass what is termed as a "community sentence" are set out in the Act. There is a similar "seriousness" threshold for community sentences of which a court has to be satisfied before a community sentence can be passed. **Section 6(1)** provides that: **A17–13**

> "A court shall not pass on an offender a community sentence, that is to say, a sentence which consists of or includes one or more community orders, unless it is of the opinion that the offence, or the combination of the offence and one or more offences associated with it, was serious enough to warrant such a sentence."

Community orders are defined as including probation orders, community service orders, combination orders, curfew orders, supervision orders and attendance centre orders: **section 6(4)**.

A17–14   **Sections 6** and **7** set out the procedural requirements on a court considering the imposition of a community order. These requirements are similar to those in relation to custodial sentences.

The court is required in considering sentence:

(a) To take into account all information about the circumstances of the offence or (as the case may be) of the offence and the offence or offences associated with it including any aggravating or mitigating factors available to it, and

(b) to obtain and consider a pre-sentence report where either a probation order with additional requirements, a community service order, a combination order or a supervision order are being considered.

In addition, there are the general provisions as to the totality principle and previous convictions as set out for custodial sentences.

Some community sentences require the consent of the offender, *e.g.* a probation order. If the offender refuses to give that consent a court may impose a custodial sentence: **section 1(3)**. If an offender is in breach of a community sentence then that may amount to a refusal on his part to consent to it, and a court may impose a custodial sentence: **C.J.A. 1991, Sched. 2**.

A breach of a community order, as opposed to the commission of an additional offence during the currency of an order, may result in the issue of a summons by a justice of the peace requiring the offender to appear before the magistrates' court, or the issue of a warrant for the offender's arrest. The magistrates' court may then impose a fine, make a community service order, make an attendance centre order, or revoke the order and deal with him in any manner it could have done if he had just been convicted by the court: **Schedule 2, para. 3(1)**. The magistrates' court may decide to commit the offender to the Crown Court if the order was originally made by the Crown Court. The magistrates' court has to take into account the extent to which the offender has complied with the order and "may assume, in the case of an offender who has wilfully and persistently failed to comply with those requirements, that he has refused to give his consent to a community sentence which has been proposed by the court and requires that consent": **Sched. 2, para. 3(2)**. A Crown Court dealing with a breach has similar powers to the magistrates' court: **Sched. 2, para. 4**.

Probation orders

A17–15   Probation orders can be made in respect of any offence (except those fixed by law) and of any offender who is aged 16 or over and who consents to such an order being made. The imposition and general requirements of probation orders are governed by **sections 2** to **6** of the **P.C.C.A. 1973**, as amended by the **C.J.A. 1991**. As a result of the amendments made by the **C.J.A.** a probation order is now a sentence and it can be combined with other disposals, for example, a fine. **Sec-**

tion 2(1) P.C.C.A. as amended sets out that a probation order may be made where the court is of the opinion that the supervision of the offender by a probation order is desirable in the interests of:

"(a) securing the rehabilitation of the offender; or
(b) protecting the public from harm from him or preventing the commission by him of further offences."

The Act requires that a probation order be for a minimum of six months and the maximum term of three years. The offender must comply with supervision provided by the probation service, and any additional requirements specified in the order: for example, a requirement to reside at a probation hostel for a period of time.

The court is also required to explain to an offender the effect of the order and that, should the offender breach the conditions of the order or re-offend during the period of the order, what may happen to him, and additionally that the court has the power to review the order. Probation orders made under the new provisions are now deemed to count as convictions unlike those made under the previous legislation: **section 8(2), C.J.A. 1991**.

Community service orders

Sections 14 to **17** of the **P.C.C.A. 1973** as amended by the **C.J.A. 1991** **A17–16** deal with the imposition of community service orders. In dealing with any offender who is aged 16 or over, for an imprisonable offence, the court may order that the offender carry out some form of unpaid work for the community, usually in the offender's local area. The number of hours of work is specified when making the order within the limits of 40–240. The number of hours should reflect the seriousness of the offence and it should be possible to complete the order within a year.

The following conditions must be fulfilled before such an order is made:

(1) The offender must consent to the order being made;
(2) there must be a community service scheme in the area where the offender lives;
(3) the offender is a suitable person to undertake community service;
(4) the offender must be at least 16; and
(5) that provision for him to perform work under such an order can be made under such orders which exist in the petty sessions area where he resides: **section 14(2) P.C.C.A. 1973** as amended.

A community service order can be combined with other forms of sentence for the same offence: **section 14(1) P.C.C.A. 1973** as amended, and the court can make ancillary orders as to costs or compensation: **section 14(8) P.C.C.A. 1973**. A court is empowered as a result of the changes brought about by the **C.J.A. 1991**, to make what is termed a "combination order." Again a pre-sentence report is required to assess the offender's suitability: **section 7(3) C.J.A. 1991**. The order combines probation and community service. The probation part must be for not less than 12 months, or more than three years, and the community service part for not less than 40 hours and not more than 100 hours. The offender must be over 16 and must have been convicted of an offence punishable with imprisonment. Such an order may be made where the court is of the opinion that the making of such an order is desirable in the interests of either securing his rehabilitation or of protecting the public from harm from him or preventing the commission by him of other offences: **section 11 C.J.A. 1991**. The same test applies to probation orders.

Absolute and conditional discharges

A17–17   In situations where a court is of the opinion that "... having regard to all the circumstances including the nature of the offence and the character of the offender, that it is inexpedient to inflict punishment ..." the court may make an order discharging the offender either conditionally or absolutely. The "condition" of the former is that the offender does not re-offend during the period of the order which commences as soon as it is made and must not exceed three years. A breach of the condition can result in the offender being resentenced for the original offence afresh: **sections 1A – 1C P.C.C.A. 1973** as substituted by **C.J.A. 1991, Sched. 1, Pt. I.**

A court cannot combine a fine for the same offence when ordering either of the discharges, but can make compensation and/or costs orders.

An absolute discharge is, as its name suggests, absolute and there are no strings attached. Together with a conditional discharge, it is not regarded as a conviction except for the proceedings when the order is made: **section 1C** of the **P.C.C.A. 1973**. An absolute discharge is appropriate for the disposal of a purely technical offence, with no moral turpitude involved, *e.g.* driving without insurance where the defendant had paid his premium to the broker but the broker had failed to pay the insurance company in time.

The other main requirement when either a conditional discharge or an absolute discharge order is made is that the court explain the effect of the order it is making to the offender.

Compensation

A17–18   Section 35 of the **P.C.C.A. 1973** (as amended) gives a court the power to order that the offender pay compensation. The order may be imposed alongside any other order of the court on sentence, or it can be imposed on its own. A payment of compensation may be in respect of any personal injury, loss or damage which results from the commission of the offence. **Section 104** of the **C.J.A. 1988** has widened the scope of the courts' powers to allow payments to cover funeral expenses or bereavement in respect of a death for offences other than deaths resulting from road traffic accidents. In addition, **section 104(2)** of the **C.J.A. 1988** amends the **P.C.C.A. 1973** to allow compensation to be ordered where injury, loss or damage resulted from a road traffic accident in a limited number of cases:

> "(a) it is in respect of damage which is treated by subsection (2) above as resulting from an offence under the Theft Act 1968; or
> (b) it is in respect of injury, loss or damage as respects which—
>   (i) the offender is uninsured in relation to the use of the vehicle; and
>   (ii) compensation is not payable under any arrangements to which the Secretary of State is a party;
> and, where a compensation order is made in respect of injury, loss or damage due to such an accident, the amount to be paid may include an amount representing the whole or part of any loss or reduction in preferential rates of insurance attributable to the accident."

It is not necessary for there to be a formal application before the court for it to make a compensation order against the offender. In fact, the court is under a duty to give reasons for not imposing a compensation order where it has the power to make an order: **section 104(1) C.J.A. 1988**.

The amount of compensation

Section 35(1A) of the **P.C.C.A. 1973** requires that the amount of compensation that is ordered to be paid is an amount that is considered to be appropriate, with regard to any evidence and any representations made to the court by the parties. Where there is a clear dispute on the evidence as to the amount of the compensation, or whether there is indeed anything owing, it is not appropriate for the court to make an order but, if any party wishes to pursue the matter, they can do so through the civil courts: *R. v. Inwood* (1975) 60 Cr.App.R. 70 and *R. v. Amey* [1983] 1 W.L.R. 346. Where the court is minded to make a compensation order, it must have regard to the means of the offender. Where there is a fine and a compensation order, and the means of the offender are limited, then preference should be given to compensation in stipulating the respective amounts. The aggrieved party without any or adequate compensation may succeed in the civil courts, but the civil damages will be reduced by any compensation paid: **P.C.C.A. 1973, section 38**.

The maximum amount of compensation that can be ordered by the magistrates' court is £5,000 in respect of any one offence: **section 40 M.C.A. 1980** as amended by **C.J.A. 1991**. The Crown Court is not subject to this maximum.

A17–19

Forfeiture

A17–20   **Section 69** of the **C.J.A. 1988**, which came into force on September 29, 1988, substituted a new **section 43** to the **P.C.C.A. 1973**. This section now provides a power to order that any property in the offender's possession which was used in the commission of the offence for which he is before the court to be forfeited.

The court must be satisfied that the property was used for the purpose of committing or facilitating the commission of the offence, or was intended to be so used: **section 69(1)**. The property must have been lawfully seized from the defendant or was in his possession or control at the time of his arrest or when the summons was issued. If these conditions are not met, the court has no power to order that the property be forfeited.

Section 36 R.T.A. 1991 inserts a new **section 43(1B)** into the **P.C.C.A. 1973** and provides that for offences of driving or attempting to drive or being in charge of a vehicle, failing to provide a breath specimen or failing to stop and give information or to report an accident, that the vehicle shall be regarded as having been used for the commission of the offence.

Section 43(1C) applies this section to any offence under the **R.T.A. 1988** which is punishable with imprisonment.

A17–21   When considering such an order, which can be made alongside any other order, the court must also have regard to the value of the property and what effect the order will have on the defendant. This is particularly important where the court is considering other financial penalties.

Section 107 of the **C.J.A. 1988** added a new **section 43A** to the **P.C.C.A. 1973** which enables a court, when making a forfeiture order in relation to an offence which resulted in a person suffering injury, loss or damage, also to order that the proceeds of sale of the property forfeited be paid to the benefit of the victim.

As for compensation orders, a forfeiture order should not be made where there is a dispute as to the value of the property, nor should such an order be made where there are complications over ownership: *R. v. Maidstone Crown Court, ex p. Gill* [1986] 1 W.L.R. 1405.

Costs

Prosecution costs

A17–22   **Section 18** of the **Prosecution of Offences Act 1985 (P.O.A. 1985)** makes provision for the payment of the prosecution costs by defendants where they are convicted by the magistrates' court, the Crown

Court, or where the Crown Court dismisses an appeal from the magistrates' court. The court may make such order as it considers to be "just and reasonable."

The **P.O.A. 1985** allows only private prosecutors to apply under **sections 16** and **17** for their costs to be paid out of central funds, so ending applications by public authority prosecutors.

Defence costs

Sections **16** and **17** of the **P.O.A. 1985** provides that a court may make   **A17–23**
an order out of central funds in respect of any application for the costs of a defendant. The order is referred to as a "defendant's costs order," and is defined by **section 16(6) P.O.A. 1985** as an order for the payment out of central funds of such amount as the court considers is appropriate to compensate him for any expenses properly incurred by him in the proceedings.

Expenses incurred in the proceedings

Section 21(1) of the Act provides that the term proceedings does include all proceedings in any court below the court that is asked to make the order.

Expense incurred by the defendant

The wording of the section is such that the court may make an order in   **A17–24**
favour of the "accused": **section 16(3)**. However **section 16(6)** talks about an order being in favour of the person who is named in the order. Whether an order can be made in favour of a third party who has paid the defendant's costs is debateable.

General mitigating features

Most pleas in mitigation can be divided into two parts: those features   **A17–25**
which go to the facts of the case, and those which go to the personal circumstances of the defendant. So far as the facts are concerned, it may be very important to try and play down the seriousness of the conduct of the defendant where, for example, he is at risk of being disqualified. In other cases, it may be the case that the defendant's acts following the commission of an offence are of importance – for example where there has been an accident and the defendant alerted the emergency services and went to the aid of an injured party.

Turning to features which relate to the defendant personally, his general driving record will be a crucial factor. If the defendant is of previous good character, and holds a "clean" driving licence, it will be strong mitigation. Conversely a bad driving record and numerous disqualifications will be strong grounds for considering some form of custodial sentence or lengthy disqualification.

One of the main factors to affect sentence is a plea of guilty at an early stage of the proceedings. This is particularly true in the more serious cases – dangerous driving and causing death by dangerous driving. A plea of guilty is often given a greater discount by the Crown Court than by the magistrates' court and hence it is a factor when considering mode of trial on matters triable either way.

Chapter 18

APPEALS AND APPLICATIONS FOR REMOVAL OF DISQUALIFICATION

Appeals from the magistrates' courts

A defendant has the general right to appeal any decision of the magis-   **A18–01**
trates' court to the Crown Court. There is also the right of the defendant or the prosecutor to appeal a decision of the magistrates to the
High Court on a point of law.

Appeals to the Crown Court

The defendant has the right of appeal to the Crown Court against the   **A18–02**
decision of the magistrates' court whether his appeal is against sentence or conviction. The only exception to this general rule is where
the defendant has pleaded guilty and, therefore, has no right of appeal
against conviction unless it can be shown that his plea was equivocal:
section 108(1) Magistrates' Courts Act 1980 (M.C.A. 1980).

Appeals to the Crown Court are governed by **sections 108–110** of
the **M.C.A. 1980** and **rules 6–11** of the **Crown Court Rules 1982
(C.C.R. 1982)** which require that notice of appeal be given within 21
days of the decision of the magistrates' court and that the notice is
given in writing to the clerk to the magistrates and to the prosecution.
This time period runs from the conclusion of the case and not from the
date of conviction, although in most cases this will in fact be the same
date. The notice need not state the grounds on which the appeal is to
be based, although they can be included. All that need be stated is
whether the appeal is against conviction, sentence or both. Where
notice is not given within the 21 day period **rule 7(5) C.C.R. 1982** gives
the Crown Court a general discretion to allow notice to be given out of
time.

An appeal before the Crown Court takes the form of a re-hearing of
the case following the same procedure as for a summary trial. An
appeal to the Crown Court is more appropriate where it is felt that an
incorrect decision as to fact has been found by the magistrates or
where it is considered that the evidence did not come out as it was
expected. The court hearing the case should normally comprise a
Crown Court judge (or a recorder) sitting with two magistrates:
Supreme Court Act 1981, s.74(1).

Appeals against conviction

A18–03   The evidence relating to the matter against which the defendant is appealing, will be called before the Crown Court as at the magistrates' court. The defendant, or for that matter the prosecutor, may call evidence additional to that called in the court below or decide not to call evidence that was called in the magistrates' court.

In considering an appeal against conviction, the Crown Court has no power to amend the information upon which the defendant was convicted: *Garfield v. Maddocks* [1974] Q.B. 7 2 All E.R. 303, and *Fairgrieve v. Newman* [1986] Crim.L.R. 47, D.C.

Appeals against sentence

A18–04   An appeal against sentence follows the same procedure as a plea. The court hears a summary of the facts of the matter, the defendant's convictions (if any) and mitigation before considering sentence.

Powers of the Crown Court

A18–05   **Section 48** of the **Supreme Court Act 1981**, sets out the extensive powers of the Crown Court in deciding appeals from the magistrates' court. It can either confirm, reverse or vary the decision of the magistrates. The Crown Court can also remit the matter to the magistrates' court for them to reconsider or make such other order which the court thinks fit.

Section 48 gives the Crown Court the power to increase the sentence of the magistrates' court where appropriate, which can discourage frivolous appeals. The power to increase sentence can be exercised whether the appeal is against sentence or against conviction but, where the sentence is increased, it must still remain within the penalty limits of the magistrates' court: **section 48(4)**. It is right to say, however, that the power to increase sentence is rarely exercised.

Miscellaneous points

A18–06   An appellant may abandon his appeal by giving notice to the court and to the prosecution. The notice should be given at least three days before the hearing date or the defendant may be ordered to pay the costs of the prosecution of the appeal. A magistrates' court may suspend any period of disqualification pending an appeal to the Crown Court. However, there is no similar appeal for the Crown Court pending an appeal to the Court of Appeal.

Appeals to the Divisional Court by case stated

A18–07   Appeals by way of case stated are appeals to the High Court by either the prosecution or defence, where they feel aggrieved by a decision of the magistrates' court (or the Crown Court) on a matter of law. The points of law to be considered by the High Court are set out in the "case" drawn-up by the clerk to the magistrates' and the magistrates themselves.

The procedure

The procedure for appeals by case stated is governed by **section 111** of the **M.C.A. 1980** and **Rules of the Supreme Court (R.S.C.) Ord. 56**. An appeal can only be based on one of two points: either it is wrong in law, or it is in excess of jurisdiction: **section 111 M.C.A. 1980**. For example, the appeal may be based on the point that evidence was admitted where it should not have been, or on the basis that the finding of the court was not supported by the evidence and no reasonable tribunal could have reached the decision that was made: *Bracegirdle v. Oxley* [1947] K.B. 349. If the defendant feels that his grievance falls within either of these two divisions, then an application can be made to the magistrates to state a case. **A18–08**

Notice of appeal by case stated must be given in writing within 21 days of the decision (21 days of sentence if that is a later date). The period of 21 days cannot be extended. *Michael v. Gowland* [1977] 1 W.L.R. 296. The notice must set out the error of law or of jurisdiction that the court is being asked to state: **M.C.R. 1981, r. 76**. The magistrates will consider the application and, if they view it as frivolous, they may refuse to comply with the application. The applicant then may seek an order of mandamus from the High Court ordering them to comply with his application: **section 111(6) M.C.A. 1980**.

If the magistrates do not find the application frivolous, they must state the case, *i.e.* set out their findings of fact, the charges the defendant faced and any representations made by the parties present on matters of law. The draft statement is then shown to the interested parties and, after any necessary alterations have been made and agreed, the case statement is sent to the applicant. Within 10 days of receiving the statement, the applicant must lodge it with the High Court: **R.S.C. Ord. 56, r. 6**.

The appeal hearing

The appeal in the Divisional Court of the Queen's Bench Division of the High Court takes the form of argument on the matters of law raised in the case stated, and no evidence is called. The Divisional Court may either alter, reverse, affirm or amend the finding of the magistrates' court or remit the matter to the magistrates' court with their opinion on the case. This may have a considerable impact on a defendant whose case was dismissed by the magistrates' court as the Divisional Court may remit the matter to the magistrates' court with a direction to convict. **A18–09**

Case stated from the Crown Court

Appeals by way of case stated can be made from the Crown Court **A18–10** where, on an appeal from the magistrates' court, the Crown Court makes a decision which is either wrong in law or in excess of jurisdiction: **section 28 Supreme Court Act 1981**. (Other decisions of the Crown Court are normally appealed to the Court of Appeal and are dealt with below at § A18–15.) The same general considerations apply to the Crown Court as apply to applications in respect of the magistrates' court.

Miscellaneous points

A18–11 It is important to remember that an appeal by case stated to the Divisional Court prevents a defendant from appealing a decision to the Crown Court. However, if the defendant appeals first to the Crown Court, he can then appeal the matter to the Divisional Court where the Crown Court makes an error on the law or acts in excess of its jurisdiction: *James v. Chief Constable of Kent, The Times*, June 7, 1986.

In *Tucker v. D.P.P. (Note: 1991)* [1994] R.T.R. 203 a sentence passed by magistrates was appealed by way of case stated. The Divisional Court held that the sentence passed was not truly astonishing, it was severe but not wrong in law or in excess of jurisdiction. Woolf L.J. said that for those convicted by justices who wish to appeal sentence, in all but the most exceptional cases, the appropriate course to adopt is to appeal to the Crown Court. This principle was upheld in *R. v. Ealing Justices, ex p. Scrafield* [1994] R.T.R. 195.

Applications for judicial review

A18–12 Applications for judicial review seek to establish that the magistrates have failed to exercise their jurisdiction, or they should be prevented from exercising a jurisdiction that they do not have. The appeal goes to the fairness of the proceedings of the magistrates' court: *R. v. Chief Constable of North Wales Police, ex p. Evans* [1982] 1 W.L.R. 1155.

The effect of an appeal by case stated and an application for judicial review is similar in that the applicant is seeking to have the decision set aside, and there is some overlap between the two in so far that the defendant may be able to appeal by either of these avenues. It was decided in the case of *R. v. Ipswich Crown Court, ex p. Baldwin* (Note) [1981] 1 All E.R. 596 that the applicant who has the choice may use the avenue which is more convenient but, where there is difficulty in establishing the facts, the proper avenue is by way of case stated.

The main areas where judicial review is considered are where it is argued that there has been a breach of the natural rules of justice (for example the prosecution failing to inform the defence of potential witnesses who may assist the defence), or where there has not been a final determination of a case but a matter of law arises (for example an application for certiorari to quash a committal for sentence).

The procedure

Section 31 of the **Supreme Court Act 1981** and **R.S.C. Ord. 53** set out   **A18–13**
the detailed procedure for applications for judicial review, which is
broadly similar whether seeking an order of certiorari (an order to
quash the earlier decision), mandamus (an order compelling the
magistrates' court to carry out its functions), or prohibition (an order
to prevent the magistrates' court from acting unlawfully).

The application, which is made in writing, must set out the grounds
of the application and the relief sought. This initial application is for
leave to apply for judicial review and is made *ex parte* before a High
Court judge. On considering the application together with a supporting affidavit, the judge may determine the matter without a hearing
and, if leave is refused, the applicant may renew the application before
the full court. If leave is granted, the applicant then makes the application proper by way of originating motion to the Divisional Court.
The hearing takes the form of evidence, normally presented in the
form of affidavits, and arguments from parties interested in the matter
which may include the magistrates who made the earlier decision, as
they have a right to be represented.

Applications for judicial review from the Crown Court

Applications for judicial review can only be made in cases where the   **A18–14**
Crown Court is exercising its powers in considering appeals from the
magistrates' court, and cannot be made where the Crown Court is
exercising its jurisdiction in relation to matters on indictment: **section
29(3)** of the **Supreme Court Act 1981**.

Appeals from the Crown Court

Where a defendant wishes to appeal against his conviction on indict-   **A18–15**
ment, or the sentence that was passed upon him by the Crown Court
for a matter tried on indictment or by way of a committal for sentence,
the appeal is to the Court of Appeal, Criminal Division.

Appeals by way of case stated or by way of an application for
judicial review arise where the appeal is against the decision of the
Crown Court in its determination of an appeal from the magistrates'
court and are dealt with in §§ A18–10 and A18–14 above.

The procedure for appeal

The applicant has 28 days from the conclusion of the matter in the   **A18–16**
Crown Court to lodge his notice and Grounds of Appeal. Unless the
appeal is on a matter of pure law, or the Crown Court judge has
granted a certificate that the case involves a matter to be considered by
the Court of Appeal, leave to appeal will be required. If the appeal is
against sentence leave is always required. Leave is determined by a

single High Court judge on the basis of the grounds before him and any transcripts of the trial with which he is provided. If the single judge refuses leave, the applicant can apply to the full court of the Court of Appeal for leave.

Appeals against conviction

A18–17   Once the applicant has obtained leave to appeal, where required, the matter is listed before the full court. The appeal takes the form of argument on the basis of the grounds submitted together with the transcripts of the Crown Court proceedings.

Section 2(1) of the **Criminal Appeal Act 1968 (C.A.A. 1968)** gives the Court of Appeal the power either to:

(a) Set aside the conviction of the defendant on the basis that it is unsafe or unsatisfactory; or

(b) decide that the trial judge made a wrong decision on a question of law; or

(c) decide that there was a material irregularity during the course of the trial.

Examples of appeals that may fall within these headings are where the indictment is bad for duplicity, or where evidence was admitted which should not have been admitted, or where the trial judge failed to give a proper direction to the jury during the course of his summing-up.

The court in considering the appeal may apply the proviso, *i.e.* decide that, although the appellant has a point, no actual miscarriage of justice actually occurred.

Appeals against sentence

A18–18   The Court of Appeal, on an appeal against sentence, may replace the order made in the Crown Court with any order that it thinks fit. The Court of Appeal will normally only reduce a sentence if it considers that passed by the Crown Court was wrong in principle or was manifestly excessive (*R. v. Gumbs* (1926) 19 Cr.App.R. 74), having considered the mitigating features that were before the judge as well as the facts of the individual case.

By virtue of **sections 35** and **36** together with **Schedule 3** of the **Criminal Justice Act 1988** the Court of Appeal can also consider cases appealed by the Attorney-General on the basis that the sentence passed was unduly lenient. The power applies to offences triable on indictment together with offences triable either way as specified by statutory instrument. The Court of Appeal is empowered to impose such sentence as they think fit for such cases. Except for this rather limited area of appeals, for which the Attorney-General acts as a filter, the Court of Appeal has no power to increase sentence. However, it should be remembered that the Court of Appeal can direct that any time spent in custody pending the outcome of the appeal should not count towards the sentence that was passed on the defendant: **section 29 C.A.A. 1968**.

Appeal checklist

(1) Which avenues of appeal are open?   **A18–19**

Notes	Defence	Prosecution
(A) From the magistrates' court:		
to (*a*) Crown Court	yes	no
(*b*) Divisional Court – case stated	yes	yes
(*c*) High Court – judicial review	yes	yes
(B) From the Crown Court:		
to (*a*) Court of Appeal	yes	yes (over-lenient sentence)
(*b*) Divisional Court – case stated	yes	yes
(*c*) High Court	yes	yes
(B) (*b*) and (*c*) only arise where the Crown Court is dealing with an appeal from the magistrates' court.		

(2) Is the appeal against conviction or sentence or is it on a point of law?

(3) If the appeal is by the prosecution, only points of law can be appealed to the High Court – except over lenient sentences through the Attorney-General.

(4) Is it necessary to apply for leave to appeal?

(5) What is the time limit for appeal? Normally 21 days from the magistrates' court and 28 days from the Crown Court.

(6) What are the chances of success? Is there any new evidence that can be put before the court on appeal? How strong is the evidence? What are the grounds of the appeal?

Application for removal of disqualification

Subject to the provisions of **section 42** of the **R.T.O.A. 1988**, a disquali-   **A18–20**
fied driver may apply to the court that disqualified him for the disqualification to be removed. The court hearing the application may either remove the disqualification immediately, remove it from a future date or refuse the application. The application can be made

only if certain conditions are fulfilled which relate primarily to the period of disqualification that must be served before an application can be made.

Relevant periods

A18–21   An application can only be made at the expiration of the relevant period from the date of order of disqualification. The relevant periods are:

(a) Two years, if the disqualification is for less than four years;
(b) one-half of the period of disqualification, if it is for less than 10 years but not less than four years;
(c) in any other case, five years: **section 42(3) R.T.O.A. 1988.**

The period starts on the date of the order and, in ascertaining the date of expiration, "any time after the conviction during which the disqualification was suspended, or he was not disqualified shall be disregarded": **section 42(3) R.T.O.A. 1988.**

Once the relevant proportion of the total period has expired, application may be made. A driver who is disqualified for two years or less cannot apply, as he does not fall within the requirements of **section 42(3)(a)**, and therefore can only appeal his sentence to the Crown Court in the hope that the period of disqualification will be reduced.

Disqualification until having passed another driving test

A18–22   Section 42(6) of the **R.T.O.A. 1988** excludes applications for the removal of disqualifications imposed under **section 36** of the Act (as substituted by **section 32** of the **R.T.A. 1991**) – disqualifications until a driving test has been passed. *R. v. Nuttall* [1971] R.T.R. 279 was a situation where the defendant had been disqualified from driving for a period of five years and also disqualified until such time as he passed a driving test. The court decided that it had power to remove the disqualification despite **section 42(6)** and the application was in fact granted.

On what grounds will the application be decided?

A18–23   Section 42(2) sets out the matters on which the court hearing the application has to decide. The court:

"... shall have regard to the character of the person disqualified and his conduct subsequent to the order, the nature of the offence, and any other circumstances of the case ..."

Where the offence for which the applicant was originally disqualified was a very serious matter, or the period of disqualification arose from repeated drink/driving offences, then the application is less likely to succeed than a case where the disqualification was a discretionary order of the court. In almost all cases, it will be necessary to call evidence in support of the application: for example, evidence from an employer to show the defendant's conduct since the order was made, the effect the order has had on the employer's business, on the defendant's promotion prospects and home life. There is no further statutory definition of the grounds upon which applications are to be decided; each case will depend on its own facts. When considering an application, the court will be interested in the facts which were before the court that ordered the disqualification in the first place, and the gravity of the offence. Where the offence is particularly grave, careful consideration will have to be given by the court before it permits the defendant prematurely to resume driving.

The application

An application is made to the magistrates' court by way of complaint   **A18–24**
for a summons to be issued to the Chief Officer of Police for the area to show cause why an order should not be made removing the disqualification: **M.C.R. 1981, r. 101.** The complaint is made to a justice of the peace or a justices' clerk for a summons to be issued. Provided that the application falls within the basic requirements of **section 42**, the summons must be issued. The complaint can be made prior to the expiry of the relevant period providing the application is not heard before the period has expired; for example, it is possible for a driver who has been disqualified for a period of three years to time matters so that his application can be heard on the day the two-year period expires.

Previous applications

Section 42(4) prohibits a fresh application for removal of disquali-   **A18–25**
fication being made within three months of refusal of an earlier application. The effect of this section is to prevent multiple applications. Where an application is refused, a further complaint for a summons to be issued can be made within the three months so long as the application is not heard within that period.

To which court should the application be made?

The Act specifies that the application shall be made to the court which   **A18–26**
made the original order. In the case of the magistrates' court that does not mean the actual persons sitting on the occasion when the order was made, but a court of summary jurisdiction for the same Petty Sessional Division. Where an order of disqualification is upheld or varied on appeal from the magistrates' court to the Crown Court, the order

will have the same effect as if it had been made by the magistrates' court: **section 110 M.C.A. 1980**. If the original order of disqualification was made by the Crown Court, then again the application need not be heard by the same judge, but the application is made to and heard by the Crown Court sitting for that area: *Practice Direction* [1971] 1 W.L.R. 1535.

The court's powers

A18–27   The court hearing the application may either remove the disqualification straight away, or from a future date, or it may refuse the application. The order of disqualification cannot be varied in any other way, for example by requiring an applicant to pass a driving test. In the case of *R. v. Bentham* [1982] R.T.R. 357, an application for the removal of a disqualification was made to the Crown Court. The judge made an order reducing the order of disqualification to a period of 12 months as from the date of the application, and imposed a condition that the driver, when eligible, should take a driving test in order to obtain a licence. The Court of Appeal held that such a condition could not be imposed and the whole of the sentence of the Crown Court was invalid. (See also *R. v. Cottrell (No. 2)* [1956] 1 All E.R. 751 and *R. v. Manchester Justices, ex p. Gaynor* [1956] 1 All E.R. 610.)

Endorsing the licence

A18–28   **Section 42(5)** of the Act requires the court, if it grants the application, to endorse the particulars of the order on the licence that was held prior to the period of disqualification. The court must also inform the Department of Transport of the terms of the order made under **section 42**.

Appeals

A18–29   Following an unsuccessful application for the removal of disqualification, there is no right of appeal save for an appeal to the High Court on a point of law. The only option open to most applicants is to make a fresh application once three months has elapsed.

Costs

A18–30   **Section 42(5)** of the Act gives the court deciding the application, the power to order the applicant to pay the whole or any part of the costs of the application even where the application succeeds. This is clearly something to be taken in to account when considering the merits of any application.

Legal aid may be granted to pursue an application for the removal of a disqualification. An application of this kind is included in the definition of "criminal proceedings" in the Legal Aid Act 1988 (section 19(5)): *R. v. Recorder of Liverpool, ex p. McCann, The Times*, May 4, 1994.

THEFT ACT 1968
(1968 c. 60)

Taking motor vehicle or other conveyance without authority

12.—(1) Subject to subsections (5) and (6) below, a person shall be guilty of an offence if, without having the consent of the owner or other lawful authority, he takes any conveyance for his own or another's use or, knowing that any conveyance has been taken without such authority, drives it or allows himself to be carried in or on it. **B1–01**

(2) A person guilty of an offence under subsection (1) above shall be liable on summary conviction to a fine not exceeding level 5 on the standard scale, to imprisonment for a term not exceeding six months, or to both.

(3) [...]

(4) If on the trial of an indictment for theft the jury are not satisfied that the accused committed theft, but it is proved that the accused committed an offence under subsection (1) above, the jury may find him guilty of the offence under subsection (1) and if he is found guilty of it, he shall be liable as he would have been liable under subsection (2) above on summary conviction.

(5) Subsection (1) above shall not apply in relation to pedal cycles; but, subject to subsection (6) below, a person who, without having the consent of the owner or other lawful authority, takes a pedal cycle for his own or another's use, or rides a pedal cycle knowing it to have been taken without such authority, shall on summary conviction be liable to a fine not exceeding level 3 on the standard scale.

(6) A person does not commit an offence under this section by anything done in the belief that he has lawful authority to do it or that he would have the owner's consent if the owner knew of his doing it and the circumstances of it.

(7) For purposes of this section—
- (a) "conveyance" means any conveyance constructed or adapted for the carriage of a person or persons whether by land, water or air, except that it does not include a conveyance constructed or adapted for use only under the control of a person not carried in or on it, and "drive" shall be construed accordingly; and
- (b) "owner", in relation to a conveyance which is the subject of a hiring agreement or hire-purchase agreement, means the person in possession of the conveyance under that agreement.

Aggravated vehicle-taking

12A.—(1) Subject to subsection (3) below, a person is guilty of aggravated taking of a vehicle if— **B1–02**
- (a) he commits an offence under section 12(1) above (in this section referred to as a "basic offence") in relation to a mechanically propelled vehicle; and
- (b) it is proved that, at any time after the vehicle was unlawfully taken

249

(whether by him or another) and before it was recovered, the vehicle was driven, or injury or damage was caused, in one or more of the circumstances set out in paragraphs (a) to (d) of subsection (2) below.

(2) The circumstances referred to in subsection (1)(b) above are—

(a) that the vehicle was driven dangerously on a road or other public place;

(b) that, owing to the driving of the vehicle, an accident occurred by which injury was caused to any person;

(c) that, owing to the driving of the vehicle, an accident occurred by which damage was caused to any property, other than the vehicle;

(d) that damage was caused to the vehicle.

(3) A person is not guilty of an offence under this section if he proves that, as regards any such proven driving, injury or damage as is referred to in subsection (1)(b) above, either—

(a) the driving, accident or damage referred to in subsection (2) above occurred before he committed the basic offence; or

(b) he was neither in nor on nor in the immediate vicinity of the vehicle when that driving, accident or damage occurred.

(4) A person guilty of an offence under this section shall be liable on conviction on indictment to imprisonment for a term not exceeding two years or, if it is proved that, in circumstances falling within subsection (2)(b) above, the accident caused the death of the person concerned, five years.

(5) If a person who is charged with an offence under this section is found not guilty of that offence but it is proved that he committed a basic offence, he may be convicted of the basic offence.

(6) If by virtue of subsection (5) above a person is convicted of a basic offence before the Crown Court, that court shall have the same powers and duties as a magistrates' court would have had on convicting him of such an offence.

(7) For the purposes of this section a vehicle is driven dangerously if—

(a) it is driven in a way which falls far below what would be expected of a competent and careful driver; and

(b) it would be obvious to a competent and careful driver that driving the vehicle in that way would be dangerous.

(8) For the purposes of this section a vehicle is recovered when it is restored to its owner or to other lawful possession or custody; and in this subsection "owner" has the same meaning as in section 12 above.

Going equipped for stealing, etc.

25.—(1) A person shall be guilty of an offence if, when not at his place of abode, he has with him any article for use in the course of or in connection with any burglary, theft or cheat.

(2) A person guilty of an offence under this section shall on conviction on indictment be liable to imprisonment for a term not exceeding three years.

(3) Where a person is charged with an offence under this section, proof that he had with him any article made or adapted for use in committing a burglary, theft or cheat shall be evidence that he had it with him for such use.

(4) Any person may arrest without warrant anyone who is, or whom he, with reasonable cause, suspects to be, committing an offence under this section.

(5) For purposes of this section an offence under section 12(1) of this Act of

taking a conveyance shall be treated as theft, and "cheat" means an offence under section 15 of this Act.

CIVIL EVIDENCE ACT 1968

(1968 c. 64)

10.—(1) In this Part of this Act— **B2–01**
"computer" has the meaning assigned by section 5 of this Act;
"document" includes, in addition to a document in writing—

    (a) any map, plan, graph or drawing;

    (b) any photograph;

    (c) any disc, tape, sound track or other device in which sounds or other data (not being visual images) are embodied so as to be capable (with or without the aid of some other equipment) of being reproduced therefrom; and

    (d) any film, negative, tape or other device in which one or more visual images are embodied so as to be capable (as aforesaid) of being reproduced therefrom;

"film" includes a microfilm;
"statement" includes any representation of fact, whether made in words or otherwise.

(2) In this Part of this Act any reference to a copy of a document includes—

    (a) in the case of a document falling within paragraph (c) but not (d) of the definition of "document" in the foregoing subsection, a transcript of the sounds or other data embodied therein;

    (b) in the case of a document falling within paragraph (d) but not (c) of that definition, a reproduction or still reproduction of the image or images embodied therein, whether enlarged or not;

    (c) in the case of a document falling within both those paragraphs, such a transcript together with such a still reproduction; and

    (d) in the case of a document not falling within the said paragraph (d) of which a visual image is embodied in a document falling within that paragraph, a reproduction of that image, whether enlarged or not,

and any reference to a copy of the material part of a document shall be construed accordingly.

(3) For the purposes of the application of this Part of this Act in relation to any such civil proceedings as are mentioned in section 18(1)(a) and (b) of this Act, any rules of court made for the purposes of this Act under section 99 of the Supreme Court of Judicature (Consolidation) Act 1925 shall (except in so far as their operation is excluded by agreement) apply, subject to such modifications as may be appropriate, in like manner as they apply in relation to civil proceedings in the High Court.

Provided that in the case of a reference under section 92 of the County Courts Act 1959 this subsection shall have effect as if for the references to the said section 99 and to civil proceedings in the High Court there were substituted respectively references to section 102 of the County Courts Act 1959 and to proceedings in a county court.

(4) If any question arises as to what are, for the purposes of any such civil proceedings as are mentioned in section 18(1)(a) or (b) of this Act, the appropriate modifications of any such rule of court as is mentioned in subsection (3)

above, that question shall, in default of agreement, be determined by the tribunal or the arbitrator or umpire, as the case may be.

CHRONICALLY SICK AND DISABLED PERSONS ACT 1970

(1970 c. 44)

Use of invalid carriages on highways

B3–01   **20.**—(1) In the case of a vehicle which is an invalid carriage complying with the prescribed requirements and which is being used in accordance with the prescribed conditions—

    (a) no statutory provision prohibiting or restricting the use of footways shall prohibit or restrict the use of that vehicle on a footway;

    (b) if the vehicle is mechanically propelled, it shall be treated for the purposes of the Road Traffic Regulation Act 1984 and the Road Traffic Act 1988, except section 22A of that Act (causing danger to road users by interfering with motor vehicles etc.), and the Road Traffic Offenders Act 1988 as not being a motor vehicle and sections 1 to 4, 163, 170 and 181 of the Road Traffic Act 1988 shall not apply to it; and

    (c) whether or not the vehicle is mechanically propelled, it shall be exempted from the requirements of section 83 of the Road Traffic Act 1988.

(2) In this section—

    "footway" means a way which is a footway, footpath or bridleway within the meaning of the Highways Act 1980; and in its application to Scotland means a way over which the public has a right of passage on foot only or a bridleway within the meaning of section 47 of the Countryside (Scotland) Act 1967;

    "invalid carriage" means a vehicle, whether mechanically propelled or not, constructed or adapted for use for the carriage of one person, being a person suffering from some physical defect or disability;

    "prescribed" means prescribed by regulations made by the Minister of Transport;

    "statutory provision" means a provision contained in, or having effect under, any enactment.

(3) Any regulations made under this section shall be made by statutory instrument, may make different provision for different circumstances and shall be subject to annulment in pursuance of a resolution of either House of Parliament.

Badges for display on motor vehicles used by disabled persons

B3–02   **21.**—(1) There shall be a badge of a prescribed form to be issued by local authorities for motor vehicles driven by, or used for the carriage of, disabled persons; and—

    (a) subject to the provisions of this section, the badge so issued for any vehicle or vehicles may be displayed on it or on any of them either inside or outside the area of the issuing authority; and

(b) any power under Part III of Schedule 9 to the Road Traffic Regulation Act 1984 to make regulations requiring that orders under the Act shall include exemptions shall be taken to extend to requiring that an exemption given with reference to badges issued by one authority shall be given also with reference to badges issued by other authorities.

(2) A badge may be issued to a disabled person of any prescribed description resident in the area of the issuing authority for one or more vehicles driven by him or used by him as a passenger.

(4) A badge may be issued to an institution concerned with the care of the disabled for any motor vehicle or, as the case may be, for each motor vehicle kept in the area of the issuing authority and used by or on behalf of the institution to carry disabled persons of any prescribed description;

(4A) A badge issued under this section may be displayed only in such circumstances and in such manner as may be prescribed.

(4B) A person who drives a motor vehicle on a road (within the meaning of the Road Traffic Act 1988) at a time when a badge of a form prescribed under this section is displayed on the vehicle is guilty of an offence unless the badge is issued under this section and displayed in accordance with regulations made under it.

(4C) A person guilty of an offence under subsection (4B) above shall be liable on summary conviction to a fine not exceeding level 3 on the standard scale.

(5) A local authority shall maintain a register showing the holders of badges issued by the authority under this section, and the vehicle or vehicles for which each of the badges is held.

(6) A badge issued under this section shall remain the property of the issuing authority, shall be issued for such period as may be prescribed, and shall be returned to the issuing authority in such circumstances as may be prescribed.

(7) Anything which is under this section to be prescribed shall be prescribed by regulations made by the Minister of Transport and Secretary of State by statutory instrument, which shall be subject to annulment in pursuance of a resolution of either House of Parliament; and regulations so made may make provision—

(a) as to the cases in which authorities may refuse to issue badges, and as to the fee (if any) which an authority may charge for the issue or re-issue of a badge; and

(b) as to the continuing validity or effect of badges issued before the coming into force of this section in pursuance of any scheme having effect under section 29 of the National Assistance Act 1948 or any similar scheme having effect in Scotland; and

(c) as to any transitional matters, and in particular the application to badges issued under this section of orders made before the time when it comes into force and operating with reference to any such badges as are referred to in paragraph (b) above (being orders made, or at that time having effect as if made, under the Road Traffic Regulations Act 1967).

(7A) Where the prescribed conditions are met in the case of any person, then—

(a) if he applies to a local authority for the issue of a badge under this section, the authority may by notice refuse the application; and

(b) if he holds a badge issued under this section by the authority, the authority may by notice require him to return the badge to them.

The conditions that may be prescribed for the purposes of this subsection are conditions relating to the misuse of badges issued under this section.

(7B) A notice under subsection (7A) above may be given by post.

(7C) A person whose application is refused under subsection (7A) above or who is required to return his badge under that subsection may, within the prescribed time, appeal to the Secretary of State who may confirm or reverse the decision of the local authority; and if he reverses it, the authority shall issue a badge accordingly or, as the case may be, the requirement to return the badge shall cease to have effect.

(7D) A badge which is required to be returned to the issuing authority by virtue of subsection (6) above may not be displayed on any vehicle; and a badge which is required to be so returned by virtue of a notice under subsection (7A) above shall be returned within the prescribed time and may not be displayed on any vehicle after that time.

(7E) Regulations under this section may provide for the procedure to be followed in connection with appeals under subsection (7C) above; but the Secretary of State shall consult with the Council on Tribunals before making regulations that so provide.

(8) The local authorities for purposes of this section shall be the common council of the City of London, the council of a county or metropolitan district in England or of a London borough, the council of a Welsh county or county borough, and in relation to Scotland, a council constituted under section 2 of the Local Government etc. (Scotland) Act 1994; and in this section "motor vehicle" has the same meaning as in the Road Traffic Regulation Act 1984.

(9) This section shall come into operation on such date as the Minister of Transport and Secretary of State may by order made by statutory instrument appoint.

NOTE: There is no longer a subsection (3) in this section: Road Traffic Act 1991, s.35(2).

VEHICLES (EXCISE) ACT 1971

(1971 c. 10)

NOTE: Readers should note that this statute has been repealed by the Vehicle Excise and Registration Act 1994, relevant sections of which have been reproduced at §§ B23–01 *et seq.* The sections reproduced here have been retained for readers' ease of reference.

Exemptions from duty of certain descriptions of vehicle

B4–01   4.—(1) No duty shall be chargeable under this Act in respect of mechanically propelled vehicles of any of the following descriptions, that is to say—

(aa) electrically propelled vehicles;

(a) fire engines;

(b) vehicles kept by a local authority while they are used or kept on a road for the purposes of their fire brigade service;

(c) ambulances;

(ca) veterinary ambulances;

(cb) vehicles used solely as mine rescue vehicles or for the purpose of conveying or drawing emergency winding-gear at mines;

(d) road rollers;

(e) vehicles used on tram lines;

(f) vehicles used or kept on a road for no purpose other than the haulage of lifeboats and the conveyance of the necessary gear of the lifeboats which are being hauled;

(g) vehicles (including cycles with an attachment for propelling them by mechanical power) which do not exceed ten hundredweight in weight unladen and are adapted, and used or kept on a road, for invalids;

(h) road construction vehicles used or kept on a road solely for the conveyance of built-in road construction machinery (with or without articles or material used for the purposes of that machinery);

(i) vehicles constructed or adapted, and used, solely for the conveyance of machinery for spreading material on roads to deal with frost, ice or snow or for the conveyance of such machinery and articles and material used for the purposes of that machinery;

(j) local authority's watering vehicles;

(k) tower wagons used solely by a street lighting authority, or by any person acting in pursuance of a contract with such an authority, for the purpose of installing or maintaining materials or apparatus for lighting streets, roads or public places;

(ka) vehicles neither constructed nor adapted for use nor used for the carriage of a driver or passenger;

(kb) vehicles (other than ambulances) used for the carriage of disabled persons by bodies for the time being recognised for the purposes of this paragraph by the Secretary of State;

(l) vehicles which are made available by the Secretary of State to any person, body or local authority in pursuance of section 11 or section 13 of the National Health Service Reorganisation Act 1973 and which are used in accordance with the terms on which they are so made available.

(1A) The Secretary of State shall recognise a body for the purposes of subsection (1)(kb) above if, on application made to him in such manner as he may specify, it appears to him that the body is concerned with the care of disabled persons.

(1B) The issue by the Secretary of State of a nil licence in respect of a mechanically propelled vehicle shall be treated, where the document is issued by virtue of paragraph (kb) of subsection (1) above, as recognition by him for the purposes of that paragraph of the body by reference to whose use of the vehicle the document is issued.

(1C) The Secretary of State may withdraw recognition of a body for the purposes of subsection (1)(kb) above if it appears to him that the body is no longer concerned with the care of disabled persons.

(1D) The reference in subsection (1B) above to the issue by the Secretary of State of a nil licence is a reference to the issue by him in accordance with regulations under this Act of a document which—

(a) is in the form of a vehicle licence, and

(b) has the word "NIL" marked in the space provided for indicating the amount of duty payable.

(2) In this section—

"fire engine" means a vehicle—

(a) constructed or adapted for use for the purpose of fire fighting, salvage or both, and

(b) used solely for the purposes of a fire brigade (whether or not one maintained under the Fire Services Act 1947);

"ambulance" means a vehicle which—

(a) is constructed or adapted for, and used for no other purpose than, the carriage of sick, injured or disabled persons to or from welfare centres or places where medical or dental treatment is given; and

(b) is readily identifiable as a vehicle used for the carriage of such persons by virtue of being marked "Ambulance" on both sides;

"disabled person" means a person suffering from a physical or mental defect or disability;

"veterinary ambulance" means a vehicle which—

(a) is used for no other purpose than the carriage of sick or injured animals to or from places where veterinary treatment is given; and

(b) is readily identifiable as a vehicle used for the carriage of such animals by virtue of being marked "Veterinary Ambulance" on both sides;

"weight unladen" shall be construed in accordance with section 190(2) of the Road Traffic Act 1988;

"road construction vehicle" means a vehicle constructed or adapted for use for the conveyance of built-in road construction machinery and not constructed or adapted for the conveyance of any other load except articles and material used for the purposes of that machinery;

"road construction machinery" means a machine or contrivance suitable for use for the construction or repair of roads and used for no purpose other than the construction or repair of roads at the public expense;

"built-in road construction machinery", in relation to a vehicle, means road construction machinery built in as part of the vehicle or permanently attached thereto;

"local authority's watering vehicle" means a vehicle used solely within the area of a local authority by that local authority, or by any person acting in pursuance of a contract with that local authority, for the purpose of cleansing or watering roads or cleansing gulleys;

"tower wagon" means a goods vehicle—

(a) into which there is built, as part of the vehicle, any expanding or extensible contrivance designed for facilitating the erection, inspection, repair or maintenance of overhead structures or equipment, and

(b) which is neither constructed nor adapted for use nor used for the conveyance of any load other than—

(i) such a contrivance and articles used in connection therewith, and

(ii) articles used in connection with the installation or maintenance, by means of such a contrivance, of materials or apparatus for lighting streets, roads or public places;

"street lighting authority" means any local authority or Minister having power under any enactment to provide or maintain materials or apparatus for lighting streets, roads or public places.

(3) In its application to Northern Ireland, this section shall have effect as if—

(a) in paragraph (b) of subsection (1) for "a local authority" there were substituted "the Fire Authority for Northern Ireland" and for "their" there were substituted "its";

(b) in paragraph (j) of that subsection for "local authority's" there were substituted "district council's";

(c) in subsection (2)—
    (i) in the definition of "fire engine", for "the Fire Services Act 1947" there were substituted "the Fire Services (Northern Ireland) Order 1984";
    (ii) in the definition of "weight unladen", for "section 190(2) of the Road Traffic Act 1988" there were substituted "Article 2(3) of the Road Traffic (Northern Ireland) Order 1981";
    (iii) in the definition of "local authority's watering vehicle", for "local authority's" there were substituted "district council's" and for the words "local authority", in each place where they occur, there were substituted "district council"; and
    (iv) in the definition of "street lighting authority", for "local authority or Minister" there were substituted "Northern Ireland department".

Exemptions from duty in connection with vehicle testing, etc.

5.—(1) A mechanically propelled vehicle shall not be chargeable with any **B4–02** duty under this Act by reason of its use on public roads—
  (a) solely for the purpose of submitting it by previous arrangement for a specified time on a specified date for, or bringing it away from, a compulsory test; or
  (b) in the course of a compulsory test, solely for the purpose of taking it to, or bringing it away from, any place where a part of the test is to be or, as the case may be, has been carried out, or of carrying out any part of the test, the person so using it being an authorised person; or
  (c) where the relevant certificate is refused on a compulsory test, solely for the purpose of delivering it by previous arrangement for a specified time on a specified date at a place where work is to be done on it to remedy the defects on the ground of which the certificate was refused, or bringing it away from a place where work has been done on it to remedy such defects.

(2) In paragraph (c) above the reference to work done or to be done on the vehicle to remedy the defects there mentioned is, in a case where the relevant certificate which is refused is a test certificate, a reference to work done or to be done to remedy those defects for a further compulsory test and includes, in a case where the relevant certificate which is refused is a goods vehicle test certificate, type approval certificate or Minister's approval certificate, a reference to work done or to be done to alter the vehicle in some aspect of design, construction, equipment or marking on account of which the certificate was refused.

(3) In this section—
    "compulsory test" means an examination under section 45 of the Road Traffic Act 1988 with a view to obtaining a test certificate without which a vehicle licence cannot be granted for the vehicle under this Act or, in the case of a goods vehicle for which by virtue of section 66(3) of that Act a vehicle licence cannot be so granted, an examination under regulations under section 49 or for the purposes of sections 54 to 58 of that Act (examinations as to a goods vehicle's compliance with construction and use or type approval requirements respectively) or an examination under regulations under section 61(2)(a) of that Act (in connection with alterations to goods vehicles subject to type approval requirements) or for the purposes of section 60 of that Act (appeals);

"the relevant certificate" means a test certificate as defined in subsection (2) of the said section 45, a goods vehicle test certificate as defined in the said section 49, a type approval certificate or a Minister's approval certificate as defined in the said sections 54 to 58;

"authorised person" in the case of a compulsory test under the said section 45 means a person who is, or is acting on behalf of, an examiner or inspector entitled to carry out examinations for the purposes of that section or a person acting under the personal direction of such a person as aforesaid; and in the case of any other compulsory test means a vehicle examiner or a person carrying out the test under his direction or a person driving the vehicle in pursuance of a requirement to do so under regulations under which the compulsory test is carried out;

"vehicle examiner" means an examiner appointed under section 66A of the Road Traffic Act 1988.

(4) In its application to Northern Ireland, this section shall have effect as if—

(a) in subsection (2) for the word "Minister's" there were substituted "Department's"; and

(b) for subsection (3) there were substituted the following subsection—

"(3) In this section—

"authorised person" means an inspector of vehicles within the meaning of Article 2(2) of the Road Traffic (Northern Ireland) Order 1981;

"compulsory test" means an examination to obtain a vehicle test certificate under Article 33 of the Road Traffic (Northern Ireland) Order 1981 without which a vehicle licence cannot be obtained for the vehicle under this Act, or an examination to obtain a goods vehicle certificate, public service vehicle licence or certificate of inspection under Article 53, 60(1) or 67 respectively of that Order;

"the relevant certificate" means a vehicle test certificate, a goods vehicle certificate, a public service vehicle licence (those expressions having the same meanings as they have in the Road Traffic (Northern Ireland) Order 1981) a certificate of inspection within the meaning of Article 67(2) of that Order, a type approval certificate within the meaning of Article 31A of that Order or a Department's approval certificate within the meaning of that Article."

Exemptions from duty in respect of vehicles acquired by overseas residents

6.—(1) A mechanically propelled vehicle shall not be chargeable with any duty under this Act if it has been supplied to the person keeping it by a taxable person within the meaning of section 2(2) of the Value Added Tax Act 1983 and the supply has been zero-rated in pursuance of subsection (7) of section 16 of the Act; but if, at any time, the value added tax that would have been chargeable on the supply but for the zero-rating becomes payable under subsection (9) of that section, or would have become so payable but for any authorisation or waiver under that subsection, then the provisions of subsection (3) below shall apply in relation to that vehicle.

(2) [...]

(3) Where under subsection (1) above the provisions of this subsection are to apply in relation to a vehicle, the vehicle shall be deemed never to have been exempted from duty under the said subsection (1) and, without prejudice to the provisions of section 9 of this Act, unless, or except to the extent that, the

Secretary of State sees fit to waive payment of the whole or part of the duty, there shall be recoverable by the Secretary of State as a debt due to him—
  (a) from the person by whom the vehicle was acquired from its manufacturer, the duty in respect of the whole period since the registration of the vehicle; or
  (b) from any other person who is for the time being the keeper of the vehicle, the duty in respect of the period since the vehicle was first kept by that other person,
other than any part of that period by reference to which there was calculated an amount ordered to be paid by the person in question in respect of the vehicle in pursuance of section 9(1) of this Act.

Miscellaneous exemptions from duty

7.—(1) If an applicant for a vehicle licence satisfies the Secretary of State that **B4–04** the vehicle is intended to be used on public roads—
  (a) only in passing from land in his occupation to other land in his occupation, and
  (b) for distances not exceeding in the aggregate six miles in any calendar week,
then, with the consent of the Treasury, the Secretary of State may exempt the vehicle from the duty chargeable under this Act in respect of the use of the vehicle on roads; but if a vehicle so exempted is used on public roads otherwise than for the purpose or to the extent specified above, the vehicle shall cease to be exempted.

(2) A mechanically propelled vehicle shall not be chargeable with any duty under this Act by reason of its use by or for the purposes of a person ("a disabled person") suffering from a physical defect or disability or by reason of its being kept for such use if—
  (a) it is registered under this Act in the name of that person; and
  (b) he has obtained, or is eligible for, a grant under paragraph 2 of Schedule 2 to the National Health Service Act 1977 or section 46(3) of the National Health Service (Scotland) Act 1978 or Article 30(3) of the Health and Personal Social Services (Northern Ireland) Order 1972 in relation to that vehicle or is in receipt of a disability living allowance by virtue of entitlement to the mobility component at the higher rate or a mobility supplement; and
  (c) no other vehicle registered in his name under this Act is exempted from duty under this subsection, subsection (2C) below, or section 7 of the Finance Act 1971;
and for the purposes of this subsection a vehicle shall be deemed to be registered in the name of a disabled person in receipt of a disability living allowance by virtue of such entitlement or of a mobility supplement if it is registered in the name of an appointee or in the name of a person nominated for the purposes of this subsection by the disabled person or by an appointee.
(2A) In subsection (2) above—
    "mobility supplement" means a mobility supplement under—
      (a) a scheme made under the Personal Injuries (Emergency Provisions) Act 1939, or
      (b) an Order in Council made under section 12 of the Social Security (Miscellaneous Provisions) Act 1977,
      or any payment appearing to the Secretary of State to be of a simi-

lar kind and specified by him by order by statutory instrument; and

"appointee" means—

(i) a person appointed pursuant to regulations under the Social Security Act 1975 or the Social Security (Northern Ireland) Act 1975 to exercise any of the rights or powers of a person in receipt of a mobility allowance, or

(ii) a person to whom a mobility supplement is paid for application for the benefit of another person in receipt of the supplement.

(2B) An order under subsection (2A) above may provide that it shall be deemed to have come into force on any date after 20th November 1983.

(2C) A mechanically propelled vehicle suitable for use by persons having a particular disability that so incapacitates them in the use of their limbs that they have to be driven and cared for by a full-time constant attendant and registered in the name of such a disabled person under this Act shall not be chargeable with any duty under this Act by reason of its use by or for the purposes of that disabled person or by reason of its being kept for such use where—

(a) the disabled person is sufficiently disabled to be eligible under the Health and Personal Social Services (Northern Ireland) Order 1972 for an invalid tricycle but too disabled to drive it; and

(b) no vehicle exempted from duty under subsection (2) above is (or by virtue of that subsection is deemed to be) registered in his name under this Act.

(2D) Subsection (2C) above applies only in relation to Northern Ireland.

(3) A mechanically propelled vehicle shall not be chargeable with any duty under this Act by reason of its use for clearing snow from public roads by means of a snow plough or similar contrivance, whether forming part of the vehicle or not, or by reason of its being kept for such use or by reason of its use for the purpose of going to or from the place where it is to be used for clearing snow from public roads by those means.

(3A) Regulations under this Act may provide that, in such cases, subject to such conditions and for such period as may be prescribed, a mechanically propelled vehicle shall not be chargeable with any duty under this Act if it has been imported by—

(a) a person for the time being appointed to serve with any body, contingent or detachment of the forces of any prescribed country, being a body, contingent or detachment which is for the time being present in the United Kingdom on the invitation of Her Majesty's Government in the United Kingdom, or

(b) a member of any country's military forces, except Her Majesty's United Kingdom forces, who is for the time being appointed to serve in the United Kingdom under the orders of any prescribed organisation, or

(c) a person for the time being recognised by the Secretary of State as a member of a civilian component of such a force as is mentioned in paragraph (a) above or as a civilian member of such an organisation as is mentioned in paragraph (b) above, or

(d) any prescribed dependant of a person falling within paragraph (a), paragraph (b) or paragraph (c) above.

(4) [...]

(4A) A mechanically propelled vehicle shall not be chargeable with any duty under this Act at a time when it is used or kept on a road by a health service body, as defined in section 60(7) of the National Health Service and Community Care Act 1990 or a National Health Service trust established under Part I of that Act or the National Health Service (Scotland) Act 1978 or a health and social services body, as defined in Article 7(6) of the Health and Personal Social Services (Northern Ireland) Order 1991 or a Health and Social Services Trust established under that Order.

(5) [...]

Using and keeping vehicles without a licence

8.—(1) If any person uses or keeps on a public road any mechanically pro-   **B4–05**
pelled vehicle for which a licence is not in force, not being a vehicle exempted from duty under this Act by virtue of any enactment (including any provision of this Act), he shall be liable to the greater of the following penalties, namely—

(a) an excise penalty of level 3 on the standard scale; or
(b) an excise penalty equal to five times the amount of the duty chargeable in respect of the vehicle.

(2) In any proceedings for an offence under this section it shall be a defence to prove that—

(a) while an expired vehicle licence for the vehicle was in force an application was duly made for a further vehicle licence for the vehicle to take effect from or before the expiration of the expired licence and for a period including the time in question; and
(b) the expired licence was at that time fixed to and exhibited on the vehicle in the manner prescribed in pursuance of section 12(4) of this Act; and
(c) the period between the expiration of the expired licence and that time did not exceed fourteen days.

For the purposes of paragraph (a) above an application for a further licence is made when the application is received by the Secretary of State.

(3) For the purposes of this section—

(a) where a vehicle for which a vehicle licence is in force is transferred by the holder of the licence to another person, the licence shall be treated as no longer in force unless it is delivered to that other person with the vehicle;
(b) the amount of the duty chargeable in respect of a vehicle shall be taken to be an amount equal to the annual rate of duty applicable to the vehicle at the date on which the offence was committed or, where in the case of a vehicle kept on a public road that rate differs from the annual rate by reference to which the vehicle was at that date chargeable under section 1 of this Act in respect of the keeping thereof, equal to the last mentioned rate.

For the purposes of paragraph (b) above the offence shall, in the case of a conviction for a continuing offence, be taken to have been committed on the date or latest date to which the conviction relates.

Additional liability for keeping unlicensed vehicle

9.—(1) Where a person convicted of an offence under section 8 of this Act is   **B4–06**

the person by whom the vehicle in respect of which the offence was committed was kept at the time it was committed, the court shall, in addition to any penalty which it may impose under that section, order him to pay an amount calculated in accordance with subsections (2) to (4) below.

(2) The said amount shall, subject to subsection (3) below, be an amount equal to one three-hundred-and-sixty-fifth of the annual rate of duty appropriate to the vehicle in question for each day in the relevant period, and the relevant period shall be one ending with the date of the offence and beginning—

> (a) if the person convicted has before that date notified the Secretary of State of his acquisition of the vehicle in accordance with regulations under this Act, with the date on which the notification was received by the Secretary of State or, if later, with the expiry of the vehicle licence last in force for the vehicle, or
> (b) in any other case, with the expiry of the vehicle licence last in force for the vehicle before the date of the offence or, if there has not at any time before that date been a vehicle licence in force for the vehicle, with the date on which the vehicle was first kept by that person:

Provided that, where the person convicted has been ordered to pay an amount under this section on the occasion of a previous conviction in respect of the same vehicle, and the offence then charged was committed after the date specified above for the beginning of the relevant period, that period shall begin instead with the day following that on which the former offence was committed.

(3) Where the person convicted proves—

> (a) that throughout any day comprised in the relevant period the vehicle in question was not kept by him, or
> (b) [...]
> (c) [...]
> (d) that he has paid duty in respect of the vehicle for any such day, whether or not on a licence,

the said amount shall be calculated as if that day were not comprised in the relevant period.

(3A) Where an order has previously been made against a person under section 26A of this Act to pay an amount for a month or part of a month in the case of a vehicle, the amount which he is ordered to pay under this section in the case of the vehicle shall be calculated as if no part of that month were comprised in the relevant period.

(4) In relation to any day comprised in the relevant period, the reference in subsection (2) above to the annual rate of duty appropriate to the vehicle in question is a reference to the annual rate applicable to it on that day; and, except so far as it is proved to have fallen within some other description for the whole of any such day, a vehicle shall be taken for the purposes of this section to have belonged throughout the relevant period to that description of vehicle to which it belonged for the purposes of duty at the date of the offence or, if the prosecution so elect, the date when a vehicle licence for it was last issued.

(5) Where, on a person's conviction of an offence under section 8 of this Act, an order is made under section 1C of the Powers of Criminal Courts Act 1973 or the Probation Act (Northern Ireland) 1950 discharging him absolutely or conditionally, the foregoing provisions of this section shall apply as if the conviction were deemed to be a conviction for all purposes.

(6) In the foregoing provisions of this section any reference to the expiry of a vehicle licence includes a reference to its surrender, and to its being treated as no longer in force for the purposes of section 8 of this Act by virtue of subsection (3)(a) of that section; and in the case of a conviction for a continuing

offence, the offence shall be taken for the purposes of those provisions to have been committed on the date or latest date to which the conviction relates.

(7) The foregoing provisions of this section shall have effect subject to the provisions (applying with the necessary modifications) of any enactment relating to the imposition of fines by magistrates' courts, other than one conferring a discretion as to their amount; and any sum payable by virtue of an order under this section shall be treated as a fine, and the order as a conviction, for the purposes of Part III of the Magistrates' Courts Act 1952 (including any enactment having effect as if contained in that Part) and of any other enactment relating to the recovery or application of sums ordered to be paid by magistrates' courts.

(8) In its application to Scotland, this section shall have effect as if for subsections (5) and (7) there were substituted the following subsections respectively:—

"(5) Where a person is charged before a court of summary jurisdiction with, an offence under section 8 of this Act, and an order is made under the Criminal Justice (Scotland) Act 1949 discharging him absolutely or placing him on probation, the foregoing provisions of this section shall apply as if the making of the order by the court of summary jurisdiction were a conviction."

"(7) The foregoing provisions of this section shall have effect subject to the provisions (applying with the necessary modifications) of any enactment relating to the imposition of fines by courts of summary jurisdiction, other than one conferring a discretion as to their amount; and any sum payable by virtue of an order under this section shall be treated as a fine, and the order as a conviction, for the purposes of any enactment relating to the recovery or application of sums ordered to be paid by courts of summary jurisdiction."

(9) In its application to Northern Ireland, this section shall have effect as if for subsection (7) there were substituted the following subsection—

"(7) A sum payable by virtue of any order made under this section by a court shall be recoverable as a sum adjudged to be paid by a conviction and treated for all purposes as a fine within the meaning of section 20 of the Administration of Justice Act (Northern Ireland) 1954."

Continuous liability for duty

10.—(1) Subject to the provisions of this section and of section 11 of this Act, **B4–07** a person who for any period keeps a vehicle in respect of which duty under this Act has at any time become chargeable shall, whether or not it is still a mechanically propelled vehicle, be liable to pay duty under this Act in respect of the vehicle for that period.

(2) Subject as aforesaid, a person shall not be liable by virtue of subsection (1) above to pay duty under this Act in respect of a vehicle—

(a) for any period for which duty under this Act in respect of the vehicle has been paid and has not been repaid in consequence of the surrender of a licence;

(b) for any period in respect of which he has, in accordance with regulations under section 11 of this Act, given notice to the Secretary of State that the vehicle will not be used or kept on a public road;

(c) for any period when the vehicle is not a mechanically propelled vehicle and a notice stating that it has ceased to be such a vehicle has, in accordance with regulations under section 11 of this Act, been given to the Secretary of State and not revoked in pursuance of subsection (2) of that section;

(d) for any period when the vehicle is exempt from duty by virtue of section 4 or 6 or section 7 (except subsection (3)) of this Act;

(e) for any period when he keeps the vehicle solely for the purpose of selling or supplying it in the course of his business as a motor dealer or using it under the authority of a trade licence in the course of his business as a motor trader within the meaning of section 16 of this Act;

(f) [...]

(g) for any period by reference to which there was calculated an amount ordered to be paid by him in respect of the vehicle in pursuance of section 9(1) of this Act.

(3) A person shall not by virtue of subsection 2(b) above be exempt from his liability for any period under subsection (1) above in respect of a vehicle if—

(a) at any time during that period he or any other person with his consent uses or keeps the vehicle on a public road and no vehicle licence is in force for the vehicle at that time; or

(b) after he has given notice under the said subsection (2)(b) in relation to the vehicle in respect of that period he applies for a vehicle licence for the vehicle to have effect on any day included in the first thirty days of that period;

and for the purposes of paragraph (a) above the consent there mentioned shall be presumed to have been given unless the contrary is shown, but any use or keeping of the vehicle in question as respects which the vehicle is exempt by virtue of any enactment for the time being in force from duty under this Act shall be disregarded.

(4) Sums payable in pursuance of this section by way of duty in respect of a vehicle shall accrue due from day to day at one three-hundred-and-sixty-fifth of the annual rate of duty applicable to the vehicle on that day.

(5) Without prejudice to any other mode of recovering sums payable by virtue of this section, where an application for a vehicle licence for twelve months or four months for a vehicle is made by a person by whom such sums are payable in respect of the vehicle and a vehicle licence other than a temporary licence is to be issued in pursuance of the application, the licence shall, if the Secretary of State so directs but subject to subsection (6) below, be made to have effect for a shorter period specified in the direction, being a period which is not less than thirty days and is such that the difference between the amount tendered in connection with the application and the amount chargeable upon the licence for the specified period does not exceed the aggregate amount of the sums aforesaid; and the amount so chargeable shall be equal to the number of days in the specified period multiplied by—

(a) where the application is for a licence for twelve months, one three-hundred-and-sixty-fifth of the annual rate of duty under this Act payable in respect of the vehicle on the date of the application; and

(b) where the application is for a licence for four months, eleven three-thousand-six-hundred-and-fiftieths of that rate;

and where a licence is made to have effect for a specified period in pursuance of this subsection the aggregate amount of the sums aforesaid shall be treated as reduced by the difference aforesaid.

(6) A person to whom a licence is issued for a period specified in a direction under subsection (5) above may appeal to the county court, or in Scotland by way of summary application to the sheriff, on the ground that the Secretary of State was not authorised by that subsection to give the direction.

Provisions supplementary to s.10

11.—(1) For the purposes of section 10 of this Act a vehicle in respect of   **B4–08**
which a vehicle licence has been issued and sums are payable by virtue of that
section for any period shall, except so far as it is shown to have been a mechanically propelled vehicle of some other description during that period, be
deemed to have belonged throughout that period to the description to which
it belonged on the date when the last such licence was issued in respect of it.

(2) When a vehicle in respect of which a notice has been given in pursuance
of subsection 2(c) of section 10 of this Act becomes a mechanically propelled
vehicle, its keeper for the time being shall forthwith give to the Secretary of
State a further notice revoking the first-mentioned notice; and where a person
required to give such a further notice does not do so, then—

(a) if he knowingly fails to give it he shall be liable on summary conviction
to a fine not exceeding level 3 on the standard scale; and

(b) in a case where he became the keeper of the vehicle after the first-mentioned notice was given it shall be deemed to have been revoked on the
date when he became the keeper of the vehicle, and in any other case
the first-mentioned notice shall be deemed not to have been given.

(3) The Secretary of State may by regulations make such provision as he
considers appropriate for the purposes of section 10(2)(b) or (c) of this Act or
subsection (2) above including, without prejudice to the generality of the
power conferred by this subsection, provision—

(a) as to the form of and particulars to be included in a notice under those
provisions, the manner of giving such a notice and the time at which it
is to be treated as being given;

(b) for securing that notice under the said paragraph (b) is not given in
respect of a period of less than thirty days or more than twelve months;

(c) as to the mode of calculating the period in respect of which notice under the said paragraph (b) is to be treated as given;

(d) with respect to the mode of proving the giving of notice;

(e) for deeming notice to have been given in relation to a vehicle in respect
of any period or at any time if in the circumstances of any particular
case the Secretary of State considers it reasonable to do so.

Issue and exhibition of licences

12.—(1) Every person applying for a vehicle licence shall make such a decla-   **B4–09**
ration and furnish such particulars with respect to the vehicle for which the
licence is to be taken out or otherwise as may be prescribed.

(2) Every vehicle licence shall be issued for the vehicle specified in the application for the licence and shall not entitle the person to whom it is issued to
use or keep any other vehicle.

(3) The Secretary of State shall not be required to issue any vehicle licence
for which application is made unless he is satisfied—

(i) that the licence applied for is the appropriate licence for the vehicle
specified in the application; and

(ii) in the case of an application for a licence for a vehicle purporting to be
the first application for a licence for the vehicle, that a licence has not
previously been issued for that vehicle.

(4) Subject to the provisions of regulations under this Act, and without
prejudice to section 8 thereof, any person who uses or keeps on a public road
any mechanically propelled vehicle on which duty under this Act is chargeable without there being fixed to and exhibited on that vehicle in the pre-

scribed manner a licence for, or in respect of the use of, that vehicle issued under this Act and for the time being in force shall be liable on summary conviction to a fine not exceeding level 1 on the standard scale.

(5) In any proceedings for an offence under subsection (4) above it shall be a defence to prove that—

    (a) while an expired vehicle licence for the vehicle was in force an application was duly made for a further vehicle licence for the vehicle to take effect from or before the expiration of the expired licence and for a period including the time in question; and

    (b) the expired licence was at that time fixed to and exhibited on the vehicle in the manner prescribed in pursuance of subsection (4) above; and

    (c) the period between the expiration of the expired licence and that time did not exceed fourteen days.

For the purposes of paragraph (a) above an application for a further licence is made when the application is received by the Secretary of State.

(6) Regulations under this Act may provide for the issue of new licences in the place of licences which may be lost or destroyed, and for the fee to be paid on the issue of a new licence.

(7) Any vehicle licence may be transferred in the prescribed manner.

Alteration of vehicle or of its use

18.—(1) Subject to the provisions of this section, where a vehicle licence has been taken out for a vehicle at any rate under this Act and the vehicle is at any time while the licence is in force used in an altered condition or in a manner or for a purpose which brings it within, or which if it was used solely in that condition or in that manner or for that purpose would bring it within, a description of vehicle to which a higher rate of duty is applicable under this Act, duty at that higher rate shall become chargeable in respect of the licence for the vehicle.

(2) Where duty at a higher rate becomes chargeable under subsection (1) above in respect of any vehicle licence, the licence may be exchanged for a new vehicle licence, for the period beginning with the date on which the higher rate of duty becomes chargeable and expiring at the end of the period for which the original vehicle licence was issued, on payment of the appropriate proportion of the difference between—

    (a) the amount payable under this Act on the original vehicle licence; and

    (b) the amount payable under this Act on a vehicle licence taken out for the period for which the original licence was issued but at the higher rate of duty, that amount being calculated, if that rate has been changed since the issue of the original licence, as if that rate had been in force at all material times at the level at which it is in force when it becomes chargeable.

(3) For the purposes of subsection (2) above the appropriate proportion is the proportion which the number of days in the period beginning when the higher rate of duty becomes chargeable and ending with the end of the period for which the original licence was issued bears to the number of days in the whole of the last-mentioned period, that period being treated as 365 days in the case of a licence for twelve months and 120 days in the case of a licence for four months.

(4) Where a vehicle licence has been taken out for a vehicle, and by reason of

the vehicle being used as mentioned in subsection (1) above, a higher rate of duty becomes chargeable and duty at the higher rate was not paid before the vehicle was so used, the person so using the vehicle shall be liable to the greater of the following penalties, namely—

(a) an excise penalty of level 3 on the standard scale; or

(b) an excise penalty of an amount equal to five times the difference between the duty actually paid on the licence and the amount of the duty at that higher rate.

(5) Where a vehicle licence has been taken out for a vehicle of a certain description, duty at a higher rate applicable to vehicles of some other description shall not become chargeable in respect of the vehicle by reason of the vehicle being used as mentioned in subsection (1) above, unless the vehicle as used while the said licence is in force satisfies all the conditions which must be satisfied in order to bring the vehicle for the purposes of the charge of duty under this Act into the said other description of vehicles.

(6) Where duty has been paid in respect of a vehicle at a rate applicable under Schedule 4 to this Act, then, so long as the vehicle is to a substantial extent being used for the conveyance of goods or burden belonging to a particular person (whether the person keeping the vehicle or not), duty at a higher rate shall not become chargeable in respect of the vehicle by reason only that it is used for the conveyance without charge in the course of their employment of employees of the person aforesaid.

(7) Where duty has been paid in respect of a vehicle at a rate applicable to farmers' goods vehicles under Schedule 4 to this Act, duty at a higher rate shall not become chargeable in respect of the vehicle by reason only that, on an occasion when the vehicle is being used by the person in whose name it is registered under this Act for the purpose of the conveyance of the produce of, or of articles required for the purposes of, the agricultural land which he occupies, it is also used for the conveyance for some other person engaged in agriculture of the produce of, or of articles required for the purposes of, the agricultural land occupied by that other person, if it is shown—

(a) that the vehicle is so used only occasionally;

(b) that the goods conveyed for that other person represent only a small proportion of the total amount of goods which the vehicle is conveying on that occasion; and

(c) that no payment or reward of any kind is, or is agreed to be, made or given for the conveyance of the goods of that other person.

(8) Where duty has been paid in respect of a vehicle at a rate applicable to farmers' goods vehicles under Schedule 4 to this Act, duty at a higher rate shall not become chargeable in respect of the vehicle by reason only that, during such periods and in such areas as may be specified by order of the Treasury made by statutory instrument, it is used, whether or not by the person in whose name it is registered under this Act, for any such purpose as is specified in the order.

An order under this subsection may be revoked or varied by a subsequent order of the Treasury.

(9) Subsection (8) above shall continue in force until such date as Her Majesty may by Order in Council determine.

(10) In its application to Northern Ireland, this section shall have effect as if—

(a) for subsection (8) there were substituted the following subsection—

"(8) Where duty has been paid under this Act in respect of a vehicle either—

(a) as an agricultural tractor under Schedule 3, or

(b) as a farmer's goods vehicle under Schedule 4,
duty at a higher rate shall not become chargeable in respect of that
vehicle by reason only that it is used by the person in whose name it is
registered for conveying to or from any agricultural land in his occupation livestock owned by him in connection with the agricultural
activities carried on by him on that land; but this subsection shall not
have effect in relation to a vehicle used for conveying any livestock
which for the time being is part of the stock in trade of a dealer in cattle
and is conveyed in the course of his business as such dealer."; and
(b) subsection (9) were omitted.

Additional liability in relation to alteration of vehicle or its use

B4–11 18A.—(1) Where a person convicted of an offence under section 18 of this
Act is the person by whom the vehicle in respect of which the offence was
committed was kept at the time it was committed, the court shall, in addition
to any penalty which it may impose under that section, order him to pay an
amount (the "additional duty") calculated in accordance with this section.

(2) The additional duty shall, subject to subsections (7) and (8) below, be an
amount equal to one three-hundred-and-sixty-fifth of the appropriate annual
rate of duty for each day in the relevant period.

(3) The following Cases are referred to in subsections (5) and (6) below—

CASE A

Where—
(a) at the time of the offence the vehicle in question had a plated weight
(the "higher plated weight") which exceeds the plated weight (the
"previous plated weight") which it had when the current licence was
taken out; and
(b) the current licence was taken out at the rate of duty applicable to the
previous plated weight.

CASE B

Where—
(a) the vehicle in question is a tractor unit (within the meaning of paragraph 15 of Schedule 4 to this Act);
(b) the current licence was taken out at a rate of duty applicable to the use
of the vehicle only with semi-trailers having not less than two axles or,
as the case may be, only with semi-trailers having not less than three
axles; and
(c) the offence consisted in using the vehicle with a semi-trailer with a
smaller number of axles than that mentioned in paragraph (b) above.

CASE C

Where—
(a) the current licence was taken out at the rate of duty applicable, by virtue of paragraph 8 of Schedule 4 to this Act, to a weight lower than the
plated weight of the vehicle in question; and
(b) the offence consisted in using the vehicle in contravention of a condition imposed by virtue of paragraph 8(3) of Schedule 4.

CASE D

Where the current licence was taken out at a rate of duty lower than that applicable to the vehicle in question by reference to its plated weight and the circumstances of the case do not bring it within Case A, B or C.

CASE E

Where the current licence was taken out at a rate of duty lower than that at which duty was chargeable in respect of that condition or manner of use of the vehicle which constituted the offence and the circumstances of the case do not bring it within Case A, B, C or D.

(4) In this section "current licence" means the licence in relation to which the offence was committed.

(5) In this section "appropriate annual rate of duty" means the difference between the rate of duty at which the current licence was taken out and—

    (a) in Case A, the rate which would have been applicable had the current licence been taken out by reference to the higher plated weight;

    (b) in Case B, the rate which would have been applicable had the current licence been taken out by reference to that use of the vehicle which constituted the offence;

    (c) in Case C, the rate which would have been applicable had the current licence been taken out by reference to the plated weight of the vehicle;

    (d) in Case D, the rate which would have been applicable had the current licence been taken out by reference to the plated weight of the vehicle; and

    (e) in Case E, the rate which would have been applicable had the current licence been taken out by reference to that condition or use of the vehicle which constituted the offence.

(6) In this section "relevant period" means the period ending with the day on which the offence was committed and beginning—

    (a) in relation to Case A, with the day on which the vehicle in question was plated with the higher plated weight; and

    (b) in relation to each of the other Cases, with the day on which the current licence first took effect.

(7) Where the person convicted proves—

    (a) that throughout any day comprised in the relevant period he was not the keeper of the vehicle in question; or

    (c) that he had, before his conviction, paid the higher of the two rates of duty referred to in the relevant paragraph of subsection (5) above in respect of the vehicle for any such day, whether or not on a licence

the additional duty shall be calculated as if that day were not comprised in the relevant period.

(8) Where a person is convicted of more than one contravention of section 18 of this Act in respect of the same vehicle (whether or not in the same proceedings) the court shall, in calculating the additional duty payable in respect of any one of those offences, reduce the amount calculated in accordance with the preceding provisions of this section in relation to a particular period by the amount of the additional duty ordered to be paid under this section in relation to that period in respect of the other offence or, as the case may be, offences.

(9) Except so far as it is proved to have fallen within some other description for the whole of any day comprised in the relevant period, the vehicle in question shall be taken for the purposes of this section to have belonged throughout the relevant period to that description of vehicle to which it belonged for the purposes of duty at the date of the offence.

(10) Where, on a person's conviction of an offence under section 18 of this Act, an order is made under Part I of the Powers of Criminal Courts Act 1973

or the Probation Act (Northern Ireland) 1950 placing him on probation or discharging him absolutely or conditionally, this section shall apply as if the conviction were deemed to be a conviction for all purposes.

(11) This section shall have effect subject to the provisions (applying with the necessary modifications) of any enactment relating to the imposition of fines by magistrates' courts, other than one conferring a discretion as to their amount; and any sum payable by virtue of an order under this section shall be treated as a fine, and the order as a conviction, for the purposes of Part III of the Magistrates' Courts Act 1980 (including any enactment having effect as if contained in that Part) and of any other enactment relating to the recovery or application of sums ordered to be paid by magistrates' courts.

(12) In its application to Scotland, this section shall have effect as if for subsections (10) and (11) there were substituted the following subsections—

"(10) Where a person is convicted on indictment of, or is charged before a court of summary jurisdiction with, an offence under section 18 of this Act, and an order is made under section 182 or 383 of the Criminal Procedure (Scotland) Act 1975 discharging him absolutely, or under section 183 or 384 of that Act placing him on probation, this section shall apply as if the making of the order were a conviction for all purposes.

(11) Any sum payable by virtue of an order under this section shall be treated as a fine imposed by a court of summary jurisdiction."

(12A) In its application to Northern Ireland, this section shall have effect as if—

(a) in subsections (3) and (5) for "plated weight", in each place, there were substituted "relevant maximum weight or, as the case may be, relevant maximum train weight";

(b) in subsection (6) for "plated with the higher plated weight" there were substituted "rated at the higher relevant maximum weight or, as the case may be, the higher relevant maximum train weight"; and

(c) for subsection (11) there were substituted the following subsections—

"(11) A sum payable by virtue of any order made under this section by a court shall be recoverable as a sum adjudged to be paid by a conviction and treated for all purposes as a fine within the meaning of section 20 of the Administration of Justice Act (Northern Ireland) 1954.

(11A) In this section "relevant maximum weight" and "relevant maximum train weight" have the same meaning as in Schedule 4 to this Act."

(13) This section is subject to Schedule 7 to this Act.

Failure to fix, and obscuration of, marks and signs

22.—(1) If any mark to be fixed or sign to be exhibited on a vehicle in accordance with section 19 or 21 of this Act is not so fixed or exhibited, the person driving the vehicle, or, where the vehicle is not being driven, the person keeping the vehicle, shall be guilty of an offence.

Provided that it shall be a defence for a person charged under this subsection with failing to fix a mark on a vehicle to prove—

(a) that he had no reasonable opportunity of registering the vehicle under this Act and that the vehicle was being driven on a public road for the purpose of being so registered; or

(b) in a case where the charge relates to a vehicle to which section 47 of the Road Traffic Act 1988 applies by virtue of subsection (2)(b) thereof (vehicles manufactured before the prescribed period and used before registration), that he had no reasonable opportunity of so registering the vehicle and that the vehicle was being driven on a road

for the purposes of or in connection with its examination under section 45 of the said Act of 1988 (examinations for test certificates) in circumstances in which its use is exempted from the said section 47(1) by regulations under section 47(6) thereof.

(2) If any mark fixed or sign exhibited on a vehicle as aforesaid is in any way obscured or rendered or allowed to become not easily distinguishable, the person driving the vehicle, or, where the vehicle is not being driven, the person keeping the vehicle, shall be guilty of an offence:

Provided that it shall be a defence for a person charged with such an offence to prove that he took all steps reasonably practicable to prevent the mark or sign being obscured or rendered not easily distinguishable.

(3) Any person guilty of an offence under this section shall be liable on summary conviction to a fine not exceeding level 3 on the standard scale.

(4) In its application to Northern Ireland, subsection (1) above shall have effect as if for paragraph (b) of the proviso there were substituted the following paragraph—

"(b) in a case where the charge relates to a vehicle to which Article 34 of the Road Traffic (Northern Ireland) Order 1981 applies by virtue of paragraph (2)(b) thereof, that he had no opportunity of so registering the vehicle and that the vehicle was driven on a road for the purposes of or in connection with its examination under Article 33 of the said Order of 1981 in circumstances in which its use is exempted from paragraph (1) of the said Article 34 by regulations under paragraph (5) thereof."

Forgery and false information

26.—(1) If any person forges or fraudulently alters or uses, or fraudulently   **B4–13**
lends or allows to be used by any other person—
    (a) any mark to be fixed or sign to be exhibited on a mechanically propelled vehicle in accordance with section 19 or 21 of this Act; or
    (b) any trade plates or replacements such as are mentioned in section 23(c) of this Act; or
    (c) any licence or registration document under this Act,
he shall be liable on summary conviction to a fine not exceeding the prescribed sum or on conviction on indictment to imprisonment for a term not exceeding two years.

(2) Any person who—
    (a) in connection with an application for a licence or for the allocation of temporary licences or registration marks makes a declaration which to his knowledge is false or in any material respect misleading; or
    (b) being required by virtue of this Act to furnish particulars relating to, or to the keeper of, any vehicle, furnishes any particulars which to his knowledge are false or in any material respect misleading,
shall be liable on summary conviction to a fine not exceeding the prescribed sum or on conviction on indictment to imprisonment for a term not exceeding two years.

Dishonoured cheques: additional liability in certain cases

B4–14   26A.—(1) Where a person has been convicted of an offence under section 102 of the Customs and Excise Management Act 1979 (payment for licence by dishonoured cheque) in relation to a licence issued under this Act, the court shall, in addition to any penalty which it may impose under that section, order him to pay an amount equal to one twelfth of the appropriate annual rate of duty for each month or part of a month in the relevant period.

(2) The relevant period for the purposes of this section is the period which—

(a) begins with the first day of the period for which the licence was applied for or, if it is later, the day on which the licence first was to have effect, and

(b) ends with whichever is the earliest of the following, namely—

(i) the end of the month in which the order is made;

(ii) the date on which the licence was due to expire;

(iii) the end of the month during which the licence was delivered up; and

(iv) the end of the month preceding that in which a new licence for the licensed vehicle first had effect.

(3) The appropriate annual rate of duty for the purposes of this section is the annual rate of duty which, at the beginning of the relevant period, was appropriate to a vehicle of the description specified in the application.

(4) Where an order has previously been made against a person under section 9 of this Act to pay an amount for a month or part of a month in the case of a vehicle, the amount which he is ordered to pay under this section in the case of the vehicle shall be calculated as if no part of that month were comprised in the relevant period.

Duty to give information

B4–15   27.—(1) Where it is alleged that a mechanically propelled vehicle has been used or kept in contravention of section 8, 16(7) or 18(4) of this Act—

(a) the person keeping the vehicle shall give such information as he may be required by or on behalf of a chief officer of police or the Secretary of State to give as to the identity of the person or persons concerned and, if he fails to do so, shall be guilty of an offence unless he shows to the satisfaction of the court that he did not know and could not with reasonable diligence have ascertained the identity of the person or persons concerned;

(b) any other person shall, if required as aforesaid, give such information as it is in his power to give and which may lead to the identification of any of the persons concerned and, if he fails to do so, shall be guilty of an offence; and

(c) in a case where it is alleged that the vehicle has been used at any time in contravention of the said section 8, the person who is alleged to have so used the vehicle shall, if required as aforesaid, give such information as it is in his power to give as to the identity of the person by whom the vehicle was kept at that time and, if he fails to do so, shall be guilty of an offence.

(2) The following persons shall be treated for the purposes of subsection (1)(a) and (b) above as persons concerned, that is to say—

(a) in relation to an alleged offence of using a vehicle in contravention of

272

section 8, 16(7) or 18(4) of this Act, both the driver and any person using the vehicle;

(b) in relation to an alleged offence of keeping the vehicle in contravention of the said section 8, the person keeping the vehicle.

(3) A person guilty of an offence under subsection (1) of this section shall be liable on summary conviction to a fine not exceeding level 3 on the standard scale.

(4) In its application to Northern Ireland, subsection (1)(a) above shall have effect as if for "a chief officer of police" there were substituted "the Chief Constable of the Royal Ulster Constabulary".

Institution and conduct of proceedings in England and Wales

28.—(1) Subject to the provisions of this section, summary proceedings for **B4–16** an offence under section 8, 11(2), 16(7), 18(4) or 26(1) or (2) of this Act or under regulations made in pursuance of this Act may be instituted in England and Wales by the Secretary of State or a constable (in this section severally referred to as "the authorised prosecutor") at any time within six months from the date on which evidence sufficient in the opinion of the authorised prosecutor to warrant the proceedings came to his knowledge; but no proceedings for any offence shall be instituted by virtue of this subsection more than three years after the commission of the offence.

(2) No proceedings for an offence under section 8, 16(7) or 18(4) of this Act shall be instituted in England and Wales except by the authorised prosecutor; and no proceedings for such an offence shall be so instituted by a constable except with the approval of the Secretary of State.

(3) A certificate stating—

(a) the date on which such evidence as is mentioned in subsection (1) above came to the knowledge of the authorised prosecutor; or

(b) that the Secretary of State's approval is given for the institution by a constable of any proceedings specified in the certificate,

and signed by or on behalf of the authorised prosecutor or, as the case may be, the Secretary of State shall for the purposes of this section be conclusive evidence of the date or approval in question; and a certificate purporting to be given in pursuance of this subsection and to be signed as aforesaid shall be deemed to be so signed unless the contrary is proved.

(4) In a magistrates' court or before the registrar of a county court any proceedings by or against the Secretary of State under this Act may be conducted on behalf of the Secretary of State by a person authorised by him for the purposes of this subsection.

(5) Section 145 of the Customs and Excise Management Act 1979 (which restricts the bringing of proceedings under that Act) and section 146A of that Act (which extends the time for bringing such proceedings) shall not apply to proceedings in England and Wales for offences under this Act.

Admissibility of records as evidence

31.—(1) A statement contained in a document purporting to be— **B4–17**

(a) a part of the records maintained by the Secretary of State in connection with any functions exercisable by the Secretary of State by virtue of this Act; or

(b) a copy of a document forming part of those records; or

(c) a note of any information contained in those records,

and to be authenticated by a person authorised in that behalf by the Secretary of State shall be admissible in any proceedings as evidence of any fact stated therein to the same extent as oral evidence of that fact is admissible in those proceedings.

(2) In subsection (1) above "document" and "statement" have the same meanings as in subsection (1) of section 10 of the Civil Evidence Act 1968, and the reference to a copy of a document shall be construed in accordance with subsection (2) of that section; but nothing in this subsection shall be construed as limiting to civil proceedings the references to proceedings in subsection (1) above.

(3) Nothing in the foregoing provisions of this section shall enable evidence to be given with respect to any matter other than a matter of the prescribed description.

(4) In its application to Scotland this section shall have effect as if—

    (a) in subsection (1), for the words from "as evidence" onwards there were substituted the words "as sufficient evidence of any fact stated therein, so however that nothing in this subsection shall be deemed to make such a statement evidence in any proceedings except where oral evidence to the like effect would have been admissible in those proceedings"; and

    (b) in subsection (2), for the references to subsections (1) and (2) of section 10 of the Civil Evidence Act 1968 there were substituted references to subsections (3) and (4) respectively of section 17 of the Law Reform (Miscellaneous Provisions) (Scotland) Act 1968.

(5) In its application to Northern Ireland, this section shall have effect as if in subsection (2) for "subsection (1) of section 10 of the Civil Evidence Act 1968" there were substituted "subsection (1) of section 6 of the Civil Evidence Act (Northern Ireland) 1971".

Evidence of admissions in certain proceedings

32.—(1) Where in any proceedings in England and Wales for an offence under section 8 or section 16(7) of this Act—

    (a) it is proved to the satisfaction of the court, on oath or in manner prescribed by rules made under section 15 of the Justices of the Peace Act 1949, that a requirement under section 27(1)(a) or (b) of this Act to give information as to the identity of the driver of, or the person using or keeping, a particular vehicle on the particular occasion on which the offence is alleged to have been committed has been served on the accused by post; and

    (b) a statement in writing is produced to the court purporting to be signed by the accused that the accused was the driver of, or the person using or keeping that vehicle on that occasion,

the court may accept the statement as evidence that the accused was the driver of, or the person using or keeping, that vehicle on that occasion.

(2) Subsection (1) above shall apply in Northern Ireland as if—

    (a) for the words "England and Wales" there were substituted "Northern Ireland"; and

    (b) for the words from "rules" to "1949" there were substituted "magistrates' courts rules as defined in Article 2(3) of the Magistrates' Courts (Northern Ireland) Order 1981".

Burden of proof in certain proceedings

33. If in any proceedings under section 8, 16(7) or 26(2) of this Act any question arises—   **B4–19**
(a) as to the number of mechanically propelled vehicles used, or
(b) as to the character, weight, horse-power or cylinder capacity of any mechanically propelled vehicle, or
(c) as to the number of persons for which a mechanically propelled vehicle has seating capacity, or
(d) as to the purpose for which any mechanically propelled vehicle has been used,
the burden of proof in respect of the matter in question shall lie on the defendant.

Fixing of amount payable under s.9 on pleas of guilty by absent accused

34.—(1) Where in pursuance of section 12(2) of the Magistrates' Courts Act   **B4–20**
1980 a person is convicted in his absence of an offence under section 8 of this Act, or under section 102 of the Customs and Excise Management Act 1979 in relation to a licence issued under this Act, and it is proved to the satisfaction of the court, on oath or in the manner prescribed by rules made under section 144 of the Magistrates' Courts Act 1980 that there was served on the accused with the summons a notice stating that, in the event of his being convicted of the offence, it will be alleged that an order requiring him to pay an amount specified in the notice falls to be made by the court in pursuance of section 9(1) or, as the case may be, 26A(1) of this Act then, unless in the notification purporting to be given by or on behalf of the accused in pursuance of the said section 12(2) it is stated that the amount so specified is inappropriate, the court shall proceed in pursuance of the said section 9(1) or, as the case may be, 26A(1) as if that amount had been calculated as required by that subsection.
(2) In its application to Northern Ireland, subsection (1) above shall have effect as if—
(a) for "section 12(2) of the Magistrates' Courts Act 1980" and "the said section 12(2)" there were substituted "Article 24(2) of the Magistrates' Courts (Northern Ireland) Order 1981" and "the said Article 24(2)" respectively; and
(b) for the words from "or in" to "1980" there were substituted "or by affidavit or in the manner prescribed by magistrates' courts rules as defined by Article 2(3) of the Magistrates' Courts (Northern Ireland) Order 1981".

Interpretation

38.—(1) In this Act unless the context otherwise requires—   **B4–21**
"community bus" means a vehicle used on public roads solely in accordance with a community bus permit (within the meaning of section 22 of the Transport Act 1985), and not used for providing a

275

service under an agreement providing for service subsidies (within the meaning of section 63(10)(b) of that Act);

"conditional sale agreement" means an agreement for the sale of a vehicle under which the purchase price or part of it is payable by instalments, and the property in the vehicle is to remain in the seller (notwithstanding that the buyer is to be in possession of the vehicle) until such conditions as may be specified in the agreement are fulfilled;

"gas" means any fuel which is wholly gaseous at a temperature of 60 degrees Fahrenheit under a pressure of 30 inches of mercury;

"hackney carriage" means a mechanically propelled vehicle standing or plying for hire and includes any mechanically propelled vehicle bailed or (in Scotland) hired under a hire agreement by a person whose trade it is to sell such vehicles or bail or hire them under hire agreements but does not include a community bus;

"hire agreement" means an agreement for the bailment or (in Scotland) the hiring of a vehicle which is not a hire-purchase agreement;

"hire-purchase agreement" means an agreement, other than a conditional sole agreement, under which—

(a) a vehicle is bailed or (in Scotland) hired in return for periodical payments by the person to whom it is bailed or hired, and

(b) the property in the vehicle will pass to that person if the terms of the agreement are complied with and one or more of the following occurs—

  (i) the exercise of an option to purchase by that person,

  (ii) the doing of any other specified act by any party to the agreement,

  (iii) the happening of any other specified event;

"licence" means a vehicle licence or a trade licence;

"motor dealer" means a person carrying on the business of selling or supplying mechanically propelled vehicles;

"prescribed" means prescribed by regulations made by the Secretary of State;

"public road" means a road which is repairable at the public expense except that in Scotland it has the same meaning as in the Roads (Scotland) Act 1984;

"temporary licence" has the meaning assigned to it by section 13(1) of this Act;

"trade licence" means a licence issued under section 16(1) of this Act; and

"transfer date" has the same meaning as in the Vehicle and Driving Licences Act 1969, that is to say, such date as the Secretary of State may by order appoint for the purposes of section 1(1) of that Act;

"vehicle licence" means a licence under this Act for a mechanically propelled vehicle.

(2) For the purposes of any provision of this Act and any subsequent enactment relating to the keeping of mechanically propelled vehicles on public roads, a person keeps such a vehicle on a public road if he causes it to be on such a road for any period, however short, when it is not in use there.

(3) A mechanically propelled vehicle shall not be treated as an electrically propelled vehicle for the purposes of this Act unless the electrical motive power is derived either from a source external to the vehicle or from any electrical storage battery which is not connected to any source of power when the vehicle is in motion.

(4) […]

(5) The unit of horse-power or cylinder capacity for the purposes of any rate of duty under this Act shall be calculated in accordance with regulations under this Act.

(6) References in this Act to any enactment shall be construed, unless the context otherwise requires, as references to that enactment as amended by or under any other enactment.

POWERS OF CRIMINAL COURTS ACT 1973

(1973 c. 62)

Power to deprive offender of property used, or intended for use, for purposes of crime

43.—(1) Subject to the following provisions of this section, where a person is convicted of an offence and—   **B5–01**

  (a) the court by or before which he is convicted is satisfied that any property which has been lawfully seized from him or which was in his possession or under his control at the time when he was apprehended for the offence or when a summons in respect of it was issued—
    (i) has been used for the purpose of committing, or facilitating the commission of, any offence; or
    (ii) was intended by him to be used for that purpose; or
  (b) the offence, or an offence which the court has taken into consideration in determining his sentence, consists of unlawful possession of property which—
    (i) has been lawfully seized from him; or
    (ii) was in his possession or under his control at the time when he was apprehended for the offence of which he has been convicted or when a summons in respect of that offence was issued,

the court may make an order under this section in respect of that property, and may do so whether or not it also deals with the offender in respect of the offence in any other way and without regard to any restrictions or forfeiture in an enactment contained in an Act passed before the Criminal Justice Act 1988.

(1A) In considering whether to make such an order in respect of any property a court shall have regard—
  (a) to the value of the property; and
  (b) to the likely financial and other effects on the offender of the making of the order (taken together with any other order that the court contemplates making).

(1B) Where a person commits an offence to which this subsection applies by—
  (a) driving, attempting to drive, or being in charge of a vehichle, or
  (b) failing to comply with a requirement made under section 7 of the Road Traffic Act 1988 (failure to provide a specimen for analysis or laboratory test) in the course of an investigation into whether the offender

277

had committed an offence while driving, attempting to drive or being in charge of a vehicle, or

(c) failing, as the driver of a vehicle, to comply with subsection (2) or (3) of section 170 of the Road Traffic Act 1988 (duty to stop and give information or report accident),

the vehicle shall be regarded for the purposes of subsection (1)(a) above (and subsection (4)(b) below) as used for the purpose of committing the offence (and for the purpose of committing any offence of aiding, abetting, counselling or procuring the commission of the offence).

(1C) Subsection (1B) above applies to—

(a) an offence under the Road Traffic Act 1988 which is punishable with imprisonment,

(b) an offence of manslaughter, and

(c) an offence under section 35 of the Offences against the Person Act 1861 (wanton and furious driving).

(2) Facilitating the commissioning of an offence shall be taken for the purposes of this section and section 44 of this Act to include the taking of any steps after if has been committed for the purpose of disposing of any property to which it relates or of avoiding apprehension or detection, and references in this or that section to an offence punishable with imprisonment shall be construed without regard to any prohibition or restriction imposed by or under any enactment on the imprisonment of young offenders.

(3) An order under this section shall operate to deprive the offender of his rights, if any, in the property to which it relates, and the property shall (if not already in their possession) be taken into the possession of the police.

(4) The Police (Property) Act 1897 shall apply, with the following modifications, to property which is in the possession of the police by virtue of this section—

(a) no application shall be made under section 1(1) of that Act by any claimant of the property after the expiration of six months from the date on which the order in respect of the property was made under this section; and

(b) no such application shall succeed unless the claimant satisfies the court either that he had not consented to the offender having possession of the property or, where an order is made under subsection 1(a) above, that he did not know, and had no reason to suspect, that the property was likely to be used for the purpose mentioned in that paragraph.

(5) In relation to property which is in the possession of the police by virtue of this section, the power to make regulations under section 2(1) of the Police (Property) Act 1897 (disposal of property in cases where the owner of the property has not been ascertained and no order of a competent court has been made with respect thereto) shall include power to make regulations for disposal in cases where no application by a claimant of the property has been made within the period specified in subsection (1)(a) above or no such application has succeeded.

Driving disqualification where vehicle used for purposes of crime

B5–02   **44.**—(1) This section applies where a person is convicted before the Crown Court of an offence punishable on indictment with imprisonment for a term of two years or more or, having been convicted by a magistrates' court of such an offence, is committed under section 38 of the Magistrates' Courts Act 1980 to the Crown Court for sentence.

(1A) This section also applies where a person is convicted by or before any court of common assault or of any other offence involving an assault (including an offence of aiding, abetting, counselling or procuring, or inciting to the commission of, an offence).

(2) If in a case to which this section applies by virtue of subsection (1) above the Crown Court is satisfied that a motor vehicle was used (by the person convicted or by anyone else) for the purpose of committing, or facilitating the commission of, the offence in question (within the meaning of section 43 of this Act), the court may order the person convicted to be disqualified, for such period as the court thinks fit, from holding or obtaining a licence to drive motor vehicle granted under Part III of the Road Traffic Act 1988.

(2A) If in a case to which this section applies by virtue of subsection (1A) above the court is satisfied that the assault was committed by driving a motor vehicle, the court may order the person convicted to be disqualified, for such period as the court thinks fit, from holding or obtaining such a licence.

(3) A court which makes an order under this section disqualifying a person for holding or obtaining any such licence as is mentioned in subsection (2) above shall require him to produce any such licence held by him.

JUSTICES OF THE PEACE ACT 1979

(1979 c. 55)

Petty sessions areas

4.—(1) The following areas outside Greater London are petty sessions areas, **B6–01** that is to say—

(a) every non-metropolitan county which is not divided into petty sessional divisions;

(b) every petty sessional division of a non-metropolitan county;

(c) every metropolitan district which is not divided into petty sessional divisions; and

(d) every petty sessional division of a metropolitan district.

(1A) In subsection (1) above, any reference to a non-metropolitan county is to be construed in relation to Wales, as a reference to a preserved county.

(2) In the following provisions of this Act "petty sessions area" means any of the following, that is to say—

(a) any of the areas outside Greater London specified in subsection (1) above;

(b) the inner London area if it is not divided into petty sessional divisions;

(c) any petty sessional division of the inner London area;

(d) any outer London borough which is not divided into petty sessional divisions;

(e) any petty sessional divisional of an outer London borough; and

(f) the City of London.

MAGISTRATES' COURTS ACT 1980

(1980 c. 43)

Notices to employer

B7–01   **11.**—(1) Subject to the provisions of this Act, where at the time and place appointed for the trial or adjourned trial of an information the prosecutor appears but the accused does not, the court may proceed in his absence.

(2) Where a summons has been issued, the court shall not begin to try the information in the absence of the accused unless either it is proved to the satisfaction of the court, on oath or in such other manner as may be prescribed, that the summons was served on the accused within what appears to the court to be a reasonable time before the trial or adjourned trial or the accused has appeared on a previous occasion to answer to the information.

(3) A magistrates' court shall not in a person's absence sentence him to imprisonment or detention in a detention centre or make a secure training order or an order under section 23 of the Powers of Criminal Courts Act 1973 that a suspended sentence passed on him shall take effect.

(4) A magistrates' court shall not in a person's absence impose any disqualification on him, except on resumption of the hearing after an adjournment under section 10(3) above; and where a trial is adjourned in pursuance of this subsection the notice required by section 10(2) above shall include notice of the reason for the adjournment.

Non-appearance of accused: plea of guilty

B7–02   **12.**—(1) This section shall apply where—
    (a) a summons has been issued requiring a person to appear before a magistrates' court, other than a youth court, to answer to an information for a summary offence, not being—
        (i) an offence for which the accused is liable to be sentenced to be imprisoned for a term exceeding 3 months; or
        (ii) an offence specified in an order made by the Secretary of State by statutory instrument; and
    (b) the clerk of the court is notified by or on behalf of the prosecutor that the documents mentioned in subsection (3) below have been served upon the accused with the summons.

(2) The reference in subsection (1)(a) above to the issue of a summons requiring a person to appear before a magistrates' court other than a youth court includes a reference to the issue of a summons requiring a person who has attained the age of 16 at the time when it is issued to appear before a youth court.

(3) The documents referred to in subsection (1)(b) above are—
    (a) a notice containing such statement of the effect of this section as may be prescribed;
    (b) a concise statement in the prescribed form of such facts relating to the charge as will be placed before the court by or on behalf of the prosecutor if the accused pleads guilty without appearing before the court; and

(c) if any information relating to the accused will or may, in those circumstances, be placed before the court by or on behalf of the prosecutor, a notice containing or describing that information.

(4) Where the clerk of the court receives a notification in writing purporting to be given by the accused or by a legal representative acting on his behalf that the accused desires to plead guilty without appearing before the court—

(a) the clerk of the court shall inform the prosecutor of the receipt of the notification; and

(b) the following provisions of this section shall apply.

(5) If at the time and place appointed for the trial or adjourned trial of the information—

(a) the accused does not appear; and

(b) it is proved to the satisfaction of the court, on oath or in such manner as may be prescribed, that the documents mentioned in subsection (3) above have been served upon the accused with the summons,

the court may, subject to section 11(3) and (4) above and subsections (6) to (8) below, proceed to hear and dispose of the case in the absence of the accused, whether or not the prosecutor is also absent, in like manner as if both parties had appeared and the accused had pleaded guilty.

(6) If at any time before the hearing the clerk of the court receives an indication in writing purporting to be given by or on behalf of the accused that he wishes to withdraw the notification—

(a) the clerk of the court shall inform the prosecutor of the withdrawal; and

(b) the court shall deal with the information as if the notification had not been given.

(7) Before accepting the plea of guilty and convicting the accused under subsection (5) above, the court shall cause the following to be read out before the court by the clerk of the court, namely—

(a) the statement of facts served upon the accused with the summons;

(b) any information contained in a notice so served, and any information described in such a notice and produced by or on behalf of the prosecutor;

(c) the notification under subsection (4) above; and

(d) any submission received with the notification which the accused wishes to be brought to the attention of the court with a view to mitigation of sentence.

(8) If the court proceeds under subsection (5) above to hear and dispose of the case in the absence of the accused, the court shall not permit—

(a) any other statement with respect to any facts relating to the offence charged; or

(b) any other information relating to the accused,

to be made or placed before the court by or on behalf of the prosecutor except on a resumption of the trial after an adjournment under section 10(3) above.

(9) If the court decides not to proceed under subsection (5) above to hear and dispose of the case in the absence of the accused, it shall adjourn or further adjourn the trial for the purpose of dealing with the information as if the notification under subsection (4) above had not been given.

(10) In relation to an adjournment on the occasion of the accused's conviction in his absence under subsection (5) above or to an adjournment required by subsection (9) above, the notice required by section 10(2) above shall include notice of the reason for the adjournment.

(11) No notice shall be required by section 10(2) above in relation to an adjournment—

(a) which is for not more than 4 weeks; and

(b) the purpose of which is to enable the court to proceed under subsection (5) above at a later time.

(12) No order shall be made under subsection (1) above unless a draft of the order has been laid before and approved by resolution of each House of Parliament.

(13) Any such document as is mentioned in subsection (3) above may be served in Scotland with a summons which is so served under the Summary Jurisdiction (Process) Act 1881.

Application of section 12 where accused appears

B7–02A   12A.—(1) Where the clerk of the court has received such a notification as is mentioned in subsection (4) of section 12 above but the accused nevertheless appears before the court at the time and place appointed for the trial or adjourned trial, the court may, if he consents, proceed under subsection (5) of that section as if he were absent.

(2) Where the clerk of the court has not received such a notification and the accused appears before the court at that time and place and informs the court that he desires to plead guilty, the court may, if he consents, proceed under section 12(5) above as if he were absent and the clerk had received such a notification.

(3) For the purposes of subsections (1) and (2) above, subsections (6) to (11) of section 12 above shall apply with the modifications mentioned in subsection (4) or, as the case may be, subsection (5) below.

(4) The modifications for the purposes of subsection (1) above are that—

(a) before accepting the plea of guilty and convicting the accused under subsection (5) of section 12 above, the court shall afford the accused an opportunity to make an oral submission with a view to mitigation of sentence; and

(b) where he makes such a submission, subsection (7)(d) of that section shall not apply.

(5) The modifications for the purposes of subsection (2) above are that—

(a) subsection (6) of section 12 above shall apply as if any reference to the notification under subsection (4) of that section were a reference to the consent under subsection (2) above;

(b) subsection (7)(c) and (d) of that section shall not apply; and

(c) before accepting the plea of guilty and convicting the accused under subsection (5) of that section, the court shall afford the accused an opportunity to make an oral submission with a view to mitigation of sentence.

"Magistrates' court"

B7–03   148.—(1) In this Act the expression "magistrates' court" means any justice or justices of the peace acting under any enactment or by virtue of his or their commission or under the common law.

(2) Except where the contrary is expressed, anything authorised or required by this Act to be done by, to or before the magistrates' court by, to or before which any other thing was done, or is to be done, may be done by, to or before any magistrates' court acting for the same petty sessions area as that court.

CRIMINAL ATTEMPTS ACT 1981

(1981 c. 47)

Attempting to commit an offence

1.—(1) If, with intent to commit an offence to which this section applies, a **B8–01** person does an act which is more than merely preparatory to the commission of the offence, he is guilty of attempting to commit the offence.

(1A) Subject to section 8 of the Computer Misuse Act 1990 (relevance of external law), if this subsection applies to an act, what the person doing it had in view shall be treated as an offence to which this section applies.

(1B) Subsection (1A) above applies to an act if—

(a) it is done in England and Wales; and

(b) it would fall within subsection (1) above as more than merely preparatory to the commission of an offence under section 3 of the Computer Misuse Act 1990 but for the fact that the offence, if completed, would not be an offence triable in England and Wales.

(2) A person may be guilty of attempting to commit an offence to which this section applies even though the facts are such that the commission of the offence is impossible.

(3) In any case where—

(a) apart from this subsection a person's intention would not be regarded as having amounted to an intent to commit an offence; but

(b) if the facts of the case had been as he believed them to be, his intention would be so regarded,

then, for the purposes of subsection (1) above, he shall be regarded as having had an intent to commit that offence.

(4) This section applies to any offence which, if it were completed, would be triable in England and Wales as an indictable offence, other than—

(a) conspiracy (at common law or under section 1 of the Criminal Law Act 1977 or any other enactment);

(b) aiding, abetting, counselling, procuring or suborning the commission of an offence;

(c) offences under section 4(1) (assisting offenders) or 5(1) (accepting or agreeing to accept consideration for not disclosing information about an arrestable offence) of the Criminal Law Act 1967.

Interference with vehicles

9.—(1) A person is guilty of the offence of vehicle interference if he inter- **B8–02** feres with a motor vehicle or trailer or with anything carried in or on a motor vehicle or trailer with the intention that an offence specified in subsection (2) below shall be committed by himself or some other person.

(2) The offences mentioned in subsection (1) above are—

(a) theft of the motor vehicle or trailer or part of it;

(b) theft of anything carried in or on the motor vehicle or trailer; and

(c) an offence under section 12(1) of the Theft Act 1968 (taking and driving away without consent);

and, if it is shown that a person accused of an offence under this section intended that one of those offences should be committed, it is immaterial that it cannot be shown which it was.

(3) A person guilty of an offence under this section shall be liable on summary conviction to imprisonment for a term not exceeding three months or to a fine not exceeding £500 or to both.

(4) A constable may arrest without warrant anyone who is or whom he with reasonable cause suspects to be guilty of an offence under this section.

(5) In this section "motor vehicle" and "trailer" have the meanings assigned to them by section 190(1) of the Road Traffic Act 1972.

CRIMINAL JUSTICE ACT 1982

(1982 c. 48)

The standard scale of fines for summary offences

B9–01   **37.**—(1) There shall be a standard scale of fines for summary offences, which shall be known as "the standard scale".

(2) The standard scale is shown below—

Level on the scale	Amount of fine
1	£200
2	£500
3	£1,000
4	£2,500
5	£5,000

(3) Where any enactment (whether contained in an Act passed before or after this Act) provides—

   (a) that a person convicted of a summary offence shall be liable on conviction to a fine or a maximum fine by reference to a specified level on the standard scale; or

   (b) confers power by subordinate instrument to make a person liable on conviction of a summary offence (whether or not created by the instrument) to a fine or maximum fine by reference to a specified level on the standard scale,

it is to be construed as referring to the standard scale for which this section provides as that standard scale has effect from time to time by virtue either of this section or of an order under section 143 of the Magistrates' Courts Act 1980.

ROAD TRAFFIC REGULATION ACT 1984

(1984 c. 27)

Temporary prohibition or restriction on roads

B10–01   **14.**—(1) If the traffic authority for a road are satisfied that traffic on the road should be restricted or prohibited—

   (a) because works are being or are proposed to be executed on or near the road; or

   (b) because of the likelihood of danger to the public, or of serious damage to the road, which is not attributable to such works; or

(c) for the purpose of enabling the duty imposed by section 89(1)(a) or (2) of the Environmental Protection Act 1990 (litter clearing and cleaning) to be discharged,

the authority may by order restrict or prohibit temporarily the use of the road, or of any part of it, by vehicles, or vehicles of any class, or by pedestrians, to such extent and subject to such conditions or exceptions as they may consider necessary.

(2) The traffic authority for a road may at any time by notice restrict or prohibit temporarily the use of the road, or of any part of it, by vehicles, or vehicles of any class, or by pedestrians, where it appears to them that it is—

(a) necessary or expedient for the reason mentioned in paragraph (a) or the purpose mentioned in paragraph (c) of subsection (1) above; or

(b) necessary for the reason mentioned in paragraph (b) of that subsection,

that the restriction or prohibition should come into force without delay.

(3) When considering the making of an order or the issue of a notice under the foregoing provisions an authority shall have regard to the existence of alternative routes suitable for the traffic which will be affected by the order or notice.

(4) The provision that may be made by an order or notice under the foregoing provisions is—

(a) any such provision as is mentioned in section 2(1), (2) or (3) or 4(1) of this Act; or

(b) any provision restricting the speed of vehicles;

but no such order or notice shall be made or issued with respect to any road which would have the effect of preventing at any time access for pedestrians to any premises situated on or adjacent to the road, or to any other premises accessible for pedestrians from, and only from, the road.

(5) Where any such order or notice is made or issued by an authority (in this subsection referred to as the "initiating authority") any such provision as is mentioned in subsection (4) above may be made as respects any alternative road—

(a) if that authority is the traffic authority for the alternative road, by an order made by the initiating authority or by that notice;

(b) if the initiating authority is not the traffic authority for the alternative road, by an order made by the initiating authority with the consent of the traffic authority for the alternative road.

(6) Section 3(1) and (2) of this Act shall apply to the provisions that may be made under subsection (5) above as they apply to the provisions of a traffic regulation order.

(7) An order or notice made or issued under this section may—

(a) suspend any statutory provision to which this subsection applies; or

(b) for either of the reasons or for the purpose mentioned in subsection (1) above suspend any such provision without imposing any such restriction or prohibition as is mentioned in subsection (1) or (2) above.

(8) Subsection (7) above applies to—

(a) any statutory provision of a description which could have been contained in an order or notice under this section;

(b) an order under section 32(1)(b), 35, 45, 46 or 49 of this Act or any such order as is mentioned in paragraph 11(1) of Schedule 10 to this Act; and

(c) an order under section 6 of this Act so far as it designates any parking places in Greater London.

(9) In this section "alternative road", in relation to a road as respects which

an order is made under subsection (1) or a notice is issued under subsection (2) above, means a road which—

(a) provides an alternative route for traffic diverted from the first-mentioned road or from any other alternative road; or

(b) is capable of providing such an alternative route apart from any statutory provision authorised by subsection (7) above to be suspended by an order made or notice issued by virtue of subsection (5) above.

Duration of orders and notices under s.14

15.—(1) Subject to subsections (2), (3) and (5) below, an order under section 14 of this Act shall not continue in force—

(a) if it is in respect of a footpath, bridleway, cycle track or byway open to all traffic, for more than six months; and

(b) in any other case, for more than eighteen months,

from the date on which it comes into force.

(2) The time-limit of eighteen months in subsection (1) above shall not apply to an order made for the reason mentioned in section 14(1)(a) of this Act if the authority making it are satisfied, and it is stated in the order that they are satisfied, that the execution of the works in question will take longer; but in any such case the authority shall revoke the order as soon as the works are completed.

(3) Where an order subject to the time-limit of eighteen months in subsection (1) above (in this subsection referred to as "the temporary order") has not ceased to be in force and the Secretary of State is satisfied that—

(a) an order which the authority that made the temporary order proposes to make under any other provision of this Act has the sole effect of reproducing the provisions of the temporary order and continuing them in force; and

(b) in consequence of the procedure required to be followed in connection with the making of the proposed order that authority would be unable to make it so that it would come into operation before the temporary order ceases to be in force,

the Secretary of State may, subject to subsection (4) below, from time to time direct that the temporary order shall continue in force for a further period not exceeding six months from the date on which it would otherwise cease to be in force.

(4) Where the Secretary of State is not himself the authority that made the temporary order he shall not give a direction under subsection (3) above except at the request of that authority.

(5) The Secretary of State may, at the request of an authority that has made an order subject to the time-limit of six months in subsection (1) above, from time to time direct that the order shall continue in force for a further period from the date on which it would otherwise cease to be in force.

(6) Where the Secretary of State refuses a request under subsection (5) above in respect of an order no further order to which that subsection applies shall be made in respect of any length of road to which the previous order related unless the Secretary of State has consented to the making of the further order or at least three months have expired since the date on which the previous order ceased to be in force.

(7) A notice under section 14 of this Act shall not continue in force—

(a) if issued for the reason mentioned in paragraph (a) or the purpose mentioned in paragraph (c) of subsection (1) of that section, for more than five days from the date of the notice;

(b) if issued for the reason mentioned in paragraph (b) of that subsection, for more than twenty-one days from that date;

but the Secretary of State may by regulations alter the number of days for the time being specified in this subsection.

(8) Provided that no restriction or prohibition imposed under section 14 of this Act in respect of any length of road remains in force for more than the period applicable to an order in respect of the road under subsection (1) above (except by virtue of subsection (2), (3) or (5) above and subject to subsection (6) above)—

    (a) a restriction or prohibition imposed by an order under that section may be continued by a further order or further orders under that section; and

    (b) a restriction or prohibition imposed by a notice under that section may be continued—

        (i) by an order under that section; or

        (ii) if the notice was issued for the reason mentioned in subsection (1)(b) of that section, by one (but not more than one) further notice under that section.

(9) In the application of this section to England and Wales—

    (a) "footpath" does not include a highway over which the public have a right of way on foot only which is at the side of a public road;

    (b) "cycle track" has the same meaning as in the Highways Act 1980; and

    (c) "byway open to all traffic" means a highway over which the public have a right of way for vehicular and all other kinds of traffic but which is used by the public mainly for the purpose for which footpaths and bridleways are used.

(10) In the application of this section to Scotland "footpath" and "cycle track" have the same meaning as in the Roads (Scotland) Act 1984.

Supplementary provisions as to orders and notices under s.14

16.—(1) A person who contravenes, or who uses or permits the use of a vehicle in contravention of, a restriction or prohibition imposed under section 14 of this Act shall be guilty of an offence. **B10–03**

(2) The Secretary of State may make regulations with respect to the procedure to be followed in connection with the making of orders and the issue of notices under section 14 of this Act including provision for notifying the public of the exercise, or proposed exercise, of the powers conferred by that section and of the effect of orders and notices made or issued in the exercise of those powers.

(2A) Without prejudice to the generality of subsection (2) above, the Secretary of State may by regulations under that subsection make, in relation to such orders as he thinks appropriate, provision—

    (a) for the making and consideration of objections to a proposed order; and

    (b) for any of the matters mentioned in paragraph 22(1) of Schedule 9 to this Act;

and paragraph 25 of that Schedule shall apply to regulations under that subsection as it applies to regulations under Part III of that Schedule, taking references to orders as including both orders and notices.

    (3) […]

    (4) […]

Prohibition or restriction on roads in connection with certain events

B10–04   **16A.**—(1) In this section "relevant event" means any sporting event, social event or entertainment which is held on a road.

(2) If the traffic authority for a road are satisfied that traffic on the road should be restricted or prohibited for the purpose of—

(a) facilitating the holding of a relevant event,

(b) enabling members of the public to watch a relevant event, or

(c) reducing the disruption to traffic likely to be caused by a relevant event,

the authority may by order restrict or prohibit temporarily the use of that road, or any part of it, by vehicles or vehicles of any class or by pedestrians, to such extent and subject to such conditions or exceptions as they may consider necessary or expedient.

(3) Before making an order under this section the authority shall satisfy themselves that it is not reasonably practicable for the event to be held otherwise than on a road.

(4) An order under this section—

(a) may not be made in relation to any race or trial falling within subsection (1) of section 12 of the Road Traffic Act 1988 (motor racing on public ways);

(b) may not be made in relation to any competition or trial falling within subsection (1) of section 13 of that Act (regulation of motoring events on public ways) unless the competition or trial is authorised by or under regulations under that section; and

(c) may not be made in relation to any race or trial falling within subsection (1) of section 31 of that Act (regulation of cycle racing on public ways) unless the race or trial is authorised by or under regulations made under that section.

(5) An order under this section may relate to the road on which the relevant event is to be held or to any other road.

(6) In the case of a road for which the Secretary of State is the traffic authority, the power to make an order under this section is also exercisable, with his consent, by the local traffic authority or by any local traffic authority which is the traffic authority for any other road to which the order relates.

(7) In the case of a road for which a local traffic authority is the traffic authority, the power to make an order under this section is also exercisable, with the consent of that local traffic authority, by a local traffic authority which is the traffic authority for any other road to which the order relates.

(8) When considering the making of an order under this section, an authority shall have regard to the safety and convenience of alternative routes suitable for the traffic which will be affected by the order.

(9) The provision that may be made by an order under this section is—

(a) any such provision as is mentioned in section 2(1), (2) or (3) or 4(1) of this Act;

(b) any provision restricting the speed of vehicles; or

(c) any provision restricting or prohibiting—

(i) the riding of horses, or

(ii) the leading or driving of horses, cattle, sheep or other animals,

but no such order shall be made with respect to any road which would have the effect of preventing at any time access for pedestrians to any premises situated on or adjacent to the road, or to any other premises accessible for pedestrians from, and only from, the road.

(10) An order under this section may—

(a) suspend any statutory provision to which this subsection applies; or

(b) for any of the purposes mentioned in subsection (2) above, suspend any such provision without imposing any such restriction or prohibition as is mentioned in that subsection.

(11) Subsection (10) above applies to—

(a) any statutory provision of a description which could have been contained in an order under this section;

(b) an order under section 32(1)(b), 35, 45, 46 or 49 of this Act or any such order as is mentioned in paragraph 11(1) of Schedule 10 to this Act; and

(c) an order under section 6 of this Act so far as it designates any parking places in Greater London.

Restrictions on orders under s.16A

16B.—(1) An order under section 16A of this Act shall not continue in force for a period of more than three days beginning with the day on which it comes into force unless—   **B10–05**

(a) the order is made by the Secretary of State as the traffic authority for the road concerned; or

(b) before the order is made, he has agreed that it should continue in force for a longer period.

(2) Where an order under section 16A of this Act has not ceased to be in force and the relevant event to which it relates has not ended, the Secretary of State may, subject to subsections (4) and (5) below, from time to time direct that the order shall continue in force for a further period not exceeding three days beginning with the day on which it would otherwise cease to be in force.

(3) A direction under subsection (2) above may relate to all the roads to which the order under section 16A of this Act relates or only to specified roads.

(4() Where an order under section 16A of the Act relates only to roads for which the Secretary of State is not himself the traffic authority, he shall not give a direction under subsection (2) above except at the request of the traffic authority for any road to which the order relates.

(5) Where an order under section 16A of this Act relates to any road for which the Secretary of State is not himself the traffic authority, he shall not give a direction under subsection (2) above affecting that road except with the consent of the traffic authority for that road.

(6) Where an order has been made under section 16A of this Act in any calendar year, no further order may be made under that section in that year so as to affect any length of road affected by the previous order, unless the further order—

(a) is made by the Secretary of State as the traffic authority for the road concerned; or

(b) is made with his consent.

(7) For the purposes of subsection (6) above, a length of road is affected by an order under section 16A of this Act if the order contains provisions—

(a) prohibiting or restricting traffic on that length of road; or

(b) suspending any statutory provision applying to traffic on that length of road.

Supplementary provisions as to orders under s.16A

16C.—(1) A person who contravenes, or who uses or permits the use of a   **B10–06**

vehicle in contravention of, a restriction or prohibition imposed by an order under section 16A of this Act shall be guilty of an offence.

(2) The Secretary of State may make regulations with respect to the procedure to be followed in connection with the making of orders under section 16A of this Act including provision for notifying the public of the exercise or proposed exercise of the powers conferred by that section and of the effect of orders made in the exercise of those powers.

(3) Without prejudice to the generality of subsection (2) above, the Secretary of State may by regulations under that subsection make, in relation to such orders as he thinks appropriate, provision—

(a) for the making and consideration of representations relating to a proposed order; and

(b) for any of the matters mentioned in paragraph 22(1)(a), (c), (d) or (e) of Schedule 9 to this Act;

and paragraph 25 of that Schedule shall apply to regulations under that subsection as it applies to regulations under Part III of that Schedule.

(2) In Part I or Schedule 2 to the Road Traffic Offenders Act 1988 (prosecution and punishment of offences), after the entry relating to section 16(1) of the Road Traffic Regulation Act 1984 there shall be inserted—

"RTRA section 16C(1).	Contravention of prohibition or restriction relating to relevant event.	Summarily.	Level 3 on the standard scale.	—	—	—"

Traffic regulation on special roads

17.—(1) A special road shall not be used except by traffic of a class authorised to do so—

(a) in England and Wales, by a scheme made, or having effect as if made, under section 16 of the Highways Act 1980 or by virtue of paragraph 3 of Schedule 23 to that Act, or

(b) in Scotland, by a scheme made, or having effect as if made, under section 7 of the Roads (Scotland) Act 1984.

(2) The Secretary of State may make regulations with respect to the use of special roads. Such regulations may, in particular—

(a) regulate the manner in which and the conditions subject to which special roads may be used by traffic authorised to do so;

(b) authorise, or enable such authority as may be specified in the regulations to authorise, the use of special roads on occasion or in an emergency or for the purpose of crossing, or for the purpose of securing access to premises abutting on or adjacent to the roads, by traffic other than that described in paragraph (a) above:

(c) relax, or enable any authority so specified to relax, any prohibition or restriction imposed by the regulations;

(d) include provisions having effect in such places, at such times, in such manner or in such circumstances as may for the time being be indicated by traffic signs in accordance with the regulations.

(3) Regulations made under subsection (2) above may make provision with respect to special roads generally, or may make different provision with respect to special roads provided for the use of different classes of traffic, or may make provision with respect to any particular special road.

(4) If a person uses a special road in contravention of this section or of regulations under subsection (2) above, he shall be guilty of an offence.

(5) The provisions of this section and of any regulations under subsection (2) above do not apply in relation to a road, or part of a road, until the date declared by the traffic authority, by notice published in the prescribed manner, to be the date on which the road or part is open for use as a special road.

This does not prevent the making of regulations under subsection (2) above before that date, so as to come into force in relation to that road or part on that date.

(6) In this section "use", in relation to a road, includes crossing.

Pedestrian crossing regulations

25.—(1) The Secretary of State may make regulations with respect to the precedence of vehicles and pedestrians respectively, and generally with respect to the movement of traffic (including pedestrians), at and in the vicinity of crossings.   **B10–08**

(2) Without prejudice to the generality of subsection (1) above, regulations under that subsection may be made—
  (a) prohibiting pedestrian traffic on the carriageway within 100 yards of a crossing, and
  (b) with respect to the indication of the limits of a crossing, or of any other matter whatsoever relating to the crossing, by marks or devices on or near the roadway or otherwise, and generally with respect to the erection of traffic signs in connection with a crossing.

(3) Different regulations may be made under this section in relation to different traffic conditions, and in particular (but without prejudice to the generality of the foregoing words) different regulations may be made in relation to crossings in the vicinity of, and at a distance from, a junction of roads, and in relation to traffic which is controlled by the police, and by traffic signals, and by different kinds of traffic signals, and traffic which is not controlled.

(4) Regulations may be made under this section applying only to a particular crossing or particular crossings specified in the regulations.

(5) A person who contravenes any regulations made under this section shall be guilty of an offence.

(6) In this section "crossing" means a crossing for pedestrians established—
  (a) by a local authority under section 23 of this Act, or
  (b) by the Secretary of State in the discharge of the duty imposed on him by section 24 of this Act,
and (in either case) indicated in accordance with the regulations having effect as respects that crossing; and, for the purposes of a prosecution for a contravention of the provisions of a regulation having effect as respects a crossing, the crossing shall be deemed to be so established and indicated unless the contrary is proved.

Stopping of vehicles at school crossings

28.—(1) When between the hours of eight in the morning and half-past five in the afternoon a vehicle is approaching a place in a road where children on their way to or from school, or from one part of a school to another, are crossing or seeking to cross the road, a school crossing patrol wearing a uniform approved by the Secretary of State shall have power, by exhibiting a prescribed sign, to require the person driving or propelling the vehicle to stop it.   **B10–09**

(2) When a person has been required under subsection (1) above to stop a vehicle—

    (a) he shall cause the vehicle to stop before reaching the place where the children are crossing or seeking to cross and so as not to stop or impede their crossing, and

    (b) the vehicle shall not be put in motion again so as to reach the place in question so long as the sign continues to be exhibited.

(3) A person who fails to comply with paragraph (a) of subsection (2) above, or who causes a vehicle to be put in motion in contravention of paragraph (b) of that subsection, shall be guilty of an offence.

(4) In this section—

    (a) "prescribed sign" means a sign of a size, colour and type prescribed by regulations made by the Secretary of State or, if authorisation is given by the Secretary of State for the use of signs of a description not so prescribed, a sign of that description;

    (b) "school crossing patrol" means a person authorised to patrol in accordance with arrangements under section 26 of this Act;

and regulations under paragraph (a) above may provide for the attachment of reflectors to signs or for the illumination of signs.

(5) For the purposes of this section—

    (a) where it is proved that a sign was exhibited by a school crossing patrol, it shall be presumed, unless the contrary is proved, to be of a size, colour and type prescribed, or of a description authorised, under subsection (4)(b) above, and, if it was exhibited in circumstances in which it was required by the regulations to be illuminated, to have been illuminated in the prescribed manner;

    (b) where it is proved that a school crossing patrol was wearing a uniform, the uniform shall be presumed, unless the contrary is proved, to be a uniform approved by the Secretary of State; and

    (c) where it is proved that a prescribed sign was exhibited by a school crossing patrol at a place in a road where children were crossing or seeking to cross the road, it shall be presumed, unless the contrary is proved, that those children were on their way to or from school or from one part of a school to another.

Designation of paying parking places on highways

B10–10   **45.**—(1) A local authority may by order designate parking places on highways or, in Scotland, roads in their area for vehicles or vehicles of any class specified in the order; and the authority may make charges (of such amount as may be prescribed under section 46 below) for vehicles left in a parking place so designated.

The exercise of this power by a local authority outside Greater London in relation to a highway or road for which they are not the traffic authority is subject to obtaining the consent of the traffic authority.

(2) An order under this section may designate a parking place for use (either at all times or at times specified in the order) only by such persons or vehicles, or such persons or vehicles of a class specified in the order, as may be authorised for the purpose by a permit from the authority operating the parking place or both by such persons or vehicles or classes of persons or vehicles and also, with or without charge and subject to such conditions as to duration of parking or times at which parking is authorised, by such other persons or vehicles, or persons or vehicles of such other class, as may be specified; and

(a) in the case of any particular parking place and any particular vehicle, or any vehicle of a particular class, the authority operating the parking place may issue a permit for that vehicle to be left in the parking place while the permit remains in force, either at all times or at such times as may be specified in the permit, and

(b) except in the case of a public service vehicle, may make such charge in connection with the issue or use of the permit, of such amount and payable in such manner, as the authority by whom the designation order was made may by order prescribe.

(3) In determining what parking places are to be designated under this section the authority concerned shall consider both the interests of traffic and those of the owners and occupiers of adjoining property, and in particular the matters to which that authority shall have regard include—

(a) the need for maintaining the free movement of traffic;

(b) the need for maintaining reasonable access to premises; and

(c) the extent to which off-street parking accommodation, whether in the open or under cover, is available in the neighbourhood or the provision of such parking accommodation is likely to be encouraged there by the designation of parking places under this section.

(4) The exercise by an authority of functions under this section shall not render the authority subject to any liability in respect of the loss of or damage to any vehicle in a parking place or the contents or fittings of any such vehicle.

(5) Nothing in this section shall affect the operation of section 6 or 32 of this Act.

(6) Subject to Parts I to III of Schedule 9 to this Act, where it appears to the authority concerned to be expedient to do so having regard to any objections duly made in respect of proposals made by that authority for a designation order they may, if they think fit, make an interim order pursuant to the proposals or application in respect of any one or more of the sites affected, or in respect of any part of any of those sites, and postpone for further consideration the making of any further order in pursuance of the proposals or application.

(7) In this section and in sections 46 to 55 of this Act, "local authority"—

(a) in England means the council of a county, metropolitan district, or London borough or the Common Council of the City of London;

(b) in Wales, means the council of a county or of a district; and

(c) in Scotland, means a council constituted under section 2 of the Local Government etc. (Scotland) Act 1994,

and "the local authority", in relation to a parking place or proposed parking place on any site, in England or Scotland means the local authority (as defined above) in whose area the site is and in Wales means each of the two councils (of the county and the district respectively) in whose area the site is.

General provisions as to traffic signs

64.—(1) In this Act "traffic sign" means any object or device (whether fixed **B10–11** or portable) for conveying, to traffic on roads or any specified class of traffic, warnings, information, requirements, restrictions or prohibitions of any description—

(a) specified by regulations made by the Ministers acting jointly or

(b) authorised by the Secretary of State,

and any line or mark on a road for so conveying such warnings, information, requirements, restrictions or prohibitions.

(2) Traffic signs shall be of the size, colour and type prescribed by regulations made as mentioned in subsection (1)(a) above except where the Secretary of State authorises the erection or retention of a sign of another character; and for the purposes of this subsection illumination, whether by lighting or by the use of reflectors or reflecting material, or the absence of such illumination, shall be part of the type or character of a sign.

(3) Regulations under this section may be made so as to apply either generally or in such circumstances only as may be specified in the regulation.

(4) Except as provided by this Act, no traffic sign shall be placed on or near a road except—

(a) a notice in respect of the use of a bridge;

(b) a traffic sign placed, in pursuance of powers conferred by a special Act of Parliament or order having the force of an Act, by the owners or operators of a tramway, light railway or trolley vehicle undertaking, a dock undertaking or a harbour undertaking; or

(c) a traffic sign placed on any land—

(i) by a person authorised under the following provisions of this Act to place the sign on a road, and

(ii) for a purpose for which he is authorised to place it on a road.

(5) Regulations under this section, or any authorisation under subsection (2) above, may provide that section 36 of the Road Traffic Act 1988 (drivers to comply with traffic directions) shall apply to signs of a type specified in that behalf by the regulations or, as the case may be, to the sign to which the authorisation relates.

(6) References in any enactment (including any enactment contained in this Act) to the erection or placing of traffic signs shall include references to the display of traffic signs in any manner, whether or not involving fixing or placing.

General speed limit for restricted roads

B10–12   **81.**—(1) It shall not be lawful for a person to drive a motor vehicle on a restricted road at a speed exceeding 30 miles per hour.

(2) The Ministers acting jointly may by order made by statutory instrument and approved by a resolution of each House of Parliament increase or reduce the rate of speed fixed by subsection (1) above, either as originally enacted or as varied under this subsection.

What roads are restricted roads

B10–13   **82.**—(1) Subject to the provisions of this section and of section 84(3) of this Act, a road is a restricted road for the purposes of section 81 of this Act if—

(a) in England and Wales, there is provided on it a system of street lighting furnished by means of lamps placed not more than 200 yards apart;

(b) in Scotland, there is provided on it a system of carriageway lighting furnished by means of lamps placed not more than 185 metres apart and the road is of a classification or type specified for the purposes of this subsection in regulations made by the Secretary of State.

(2) The traffic authority for a road may direct—

(a) that the road which is a restricted road for the purposes of section 81 of this Act shall cease to be a restricted road for those purposes, or

(b) that the road which is not a restricted road for those purposes shall become a restricted road for those purposes.

(3) A special road is not a restricted road for the purposes of section 81 on or after the date declared by the traffic authority, by notice published in the prescribed manner, to be that date on which the special road, or the relevant part of the special road, is open for use as a special road.

Provisions as to directions under s.82(2)

83.—(1) A direction under section 82(2) by the Secretary of State shall be given by means of an order made by the Secretary of State after giving public notice of his intention to make an order.   **B10–14**

(2) A direction under section 82(2) by a local traffic authority shall be given by means of an order made by the authority.

(3) Section 68(1)(c) of this Act shall apply to any order made under subsection (2) above.

Speed limits on roads other than restricted roads

84.—(1) An order made under this subsection as respects any road may prohibit—   **B10–15**

(a) the driving of motor vehicles on that road at a speed exceeding that specified in the order,

(b) the driving of motor vehicles on that road at a speed exceeding that specified in the order during periods specified in the order, or

(c) the driving of motor vehicles on that road at a speed exceeding the speed for the time being indicated by traffic signs in accordance with the order.

(1A) An order made by virtue of subsection (1)(c) above may—

(a) make provision restricting the speeds that may be indicated by traffic signs or the periods during which the indications may be given, and

(b) provide for the indications to be given only in such circumstances as may be determined by or under the order;

but any such order must comply with regulations made under subsection (1B) below, except where the Secretary of State authorises otherwise in a particular case.

(1B) The Secretary of State may make regulations governing the provision which may be made by orders of local authorities under subsection (1)(c) above, and any such regulations may in particular—

(a) prescribe the circumstances in which speed limits may have effect by virtue of an order,

(b) prescribe the speed limits which may be specified in an order, and

(c) make transitional provision and different provision for different cases.

(2) The power to make an order under subsection (1) is exercisable by the traffic authority, who shall before exercising it in any case give public notice of their intention to do so.

(3) While an order made by virtue of subsection (1)(a) above is in force as respects a road, that road shall not be a restricted road for the purposes of section 81 of this Act.

(4) This section does not apply to any part of a special road which is open for use as a special road.

(5) Section 68(1)(c) of this Act shall apply to any order made under subsection (1) above.

(6) Any reference in a local Act to roads subject to a speed limit shall, unless the contrary intention appears, be treated as not including a reference to roads subject to a speed limit imposed only by virtue of subsection (1)(b) or (c) above.

Traffic signs for indicating speed restrictions

B10–16   **85.**—(1) For the purpose of securing that adequate guidance is given to drivers of motor vehicles as to whether any, and if so what, limit of speed is to be observed on any road, it shall be the duty of the Secretary of State, in the case of a road for which he is the traffic authority, to erect and maintain traffic signs in such positions as may be requisite for that purpose.

(2) In the case of any other road, it is the duty of the local traffic authority—

    (a) to erect and maintain traffic signs in such positions as may be requisite in order to give effect to general or other directions given by the Secretary of State for the purpose mentioned in subsection (1) above, and

    (b) to alter or remove traffic signs as may be requisite in order to give effect to such directions, either in consequence of the making of an order by the Secretary of State or otherwise.

(3) If a local traffic authority makes default in executing any works required for the performance of the duty imposed on them by subsection (2) above, the Secretary of State may himself execute the works; and the expense incurred by him in doing so shall be recoverable by him from the local authority and, in England or Wales, shall be so recoverable summarily as a civil debt.

(4) Where no such system of street or carriageway lighting as is mentioned in section 82(1) is provided on a road, but a limit of speed is to be observed on the road, a person shall not be convicted of driving a motor vehicle on the road at a speed exceeding the limit unless the limit is indicated by means of such traffic signs as are mentioned in subsection (1) or subsection (2) above.

(5) In any proceedings for a contravention of section 81 of this Act, where the proceedings relate to driving on a road provided with such a system of street or carriageway lighting, evidence of the absence of traffic signs displayed in pursuance of this section to indicate that the road is not a restricted road for the purposes of that section shall be evidence that the road is a restricted road for those purposes.

(6) Where by regulations made under section 17(2) of this Act a limit of speed is to be observed, then, if it is to be observed—

    (a) on all special roads, or

    (b) on all special roads provided for the use of particular classes of traffic, or

    (c) on all special roads other than special roads of such description as may be specified in the regulations, or

    (d) as mentioned in paragraph (a), (b) or (c) above except for such lengths of special road as may be so specified,

this section shall not apply in relation to that limit (but without prejudice to its application in relation to any lower limit of maximum speed or, as the case may be, any higher limit of minimum speed, required by any such regulations to be observed on any specified length of any specified special road).

(7) The power to give general directions under subsection (2) above shall be exercisable by statutory instrument.

Speed limits for particular classes of vehicles

86.—(1) It shall not be lawful for a person to drive a motor vehicle of any **B10–17**
class on a road at a speed greater than the speed specified in Schedule 6 to this
Act as the maximum speed in relation to a vehicle of that class.

(2) Subject to subsections (4) and (5) below, the Secretary of State may by
regulations vary, subject to such conditions as may be specified in the regulations, the provisions of that Schedule.

(3) Regulations under this section may make different provision as respects
the same class of vehicles in different circumstances.

(4) [...]

(5) The Secretary of State shall not have power under this section to vary the
speed limit imposed by section 81 of this Act.

(6) The Secretary of State shall not have power under this section to impose
a speed limit, as respects driving on roads which are not restricted roads for
the purposes of section 81 of this Act, on a vehicle which—

   (a) is constructed solely for the carriage of passengers and their effects;

   (b) is not adapted to carry more than 8 passengers exclusive of the driver;

   (c) is neither a heavy motor car nor an invalid carriage;

   (d) is not drawing a trailer; and

   (e) is fitted with pneumatic tyres on all its wheels.

Exemption of fire brigade, ambulance and police vehicles from speed limits

87. No statutory provision imposing a speed limit on motor vehicles shall **B10–18**
apply to any vehicle on an occasion when it is being used for fire brigade,
ambulance or police purposes, if the observance of that provision would be
likely to hinder the use of the vehicle for the purpose for which it is being used
on that occasion.

Temporary speed limits

88.—(1) Where it appears to the Secretary of State desirable to do so in the **B10–19**
interests of safety or for the purpose of facilitating the movement of traffic, he
may, after giving public notice of his intention to do so, by order prohibit, for a
period not exceeding 18 months, the driving of motor vehicles—

   (a) on all roads, or on all roads in any area specified in the order, or on all
      roads of any class so specified, or on all roads other than roads of any
      class so specified, or on any road so specified, at a speed greater than
      that specified in the order, or

   (b) on any road specified in the order, at a speed less than the speed speci-
      fied in the order, subject to such exceptions as may be so specified.

(2) Any prohibition imposed by an order under subsection (1) above may be
so imposed either generally, or at times, on days or during periods specified in
the order; but the provisions of any such order shall not, except in so far as
may be provided by the order, affect the provisions of sections 81 to 84 of this
Act.

(3) For the purposes of an order under subsection (1)(a) above, roads may be
classified by reference to any circumstances appearing to the Secretary of State
to be suitable for the purpose, including their character, the nature of the traffic to which they are suited or the traffic signs provided on them.

(4) The provisions of any order under subsection (1) above may be continued, either indefinitely or for a specified period, by an order of the Secretary of State made by statutory instrument, which shall be subject to annulment in pursuance of a resolution of either House of Parliament.

(5) Where by virtue of an order under this section a speed limit is to be observed, then—

    (a) if it is to be observed on all roads, on all roads of any class specified in the order or on all roads other than roads of any class so specified, section 85 of this Act shall not apply in relation to that limit;

    (b) if it is to be observed on all roads in any area and, at all points where roads lead into the area, is indicated as respects the area as a whole by means of such traffic signs as are mentioned in subsection (1) or subsection (2) of section 85 of this Act, the limit shall, for the purposes of subsection (4) of that section, be taken as so indicated with respect to all roads in the area.

(6) This section does not apply to any part of a special road which is open for use as a special road.

(7) If a person drives a motor vehicle on a road in contravention of an order under subsection (1)(b) above, he shall be guilty of an offence; but a person shall not be liable to be convicted of so driving solely on the evidence of one witness to the effect that, in the opinion of the witness, he was driving the vehicle at a speed less than that specified in the order.

(8) The first order to be made under subsection (1)(b) above shall not be made until a draft of the order has been laid before Parliament and approved by a resolution of each House of Parliament.

Speeding offences generally

B10–20   89.—(1) A person who drives a motor vehicle on a road at a speed exceeding a limit imposed by or under any enactment to which this section applies shall be guilty of an offence.

(2) A person prosecuted for such an offence shall not be liable to be convicted solely on the evidence of one witness to the effect that, in the opinion of the witness, the person prosecuted was driving the vehicle at a speed exceeding a specified limit.

(3) The enactments to which this section applies are—

    (a) any enactment contained in this Act except section 17(2);

    (b) section 2 of the Parks Regulation (Amendment) Act 1926; and

    (c) any enactment not contained in this Act, but passed after 1st September 1960, whether before or after the passing of this Act.

(4) If a person who employs other persons to drive motor vehicles on roads publishes or issues any time-table or schedule, or gives any directions, under which any journey, or any stage or part of any journey, is to be completed within some specified time, and it is not practicable in the circumstances of the case for that journey (or that stage or part of it) to be completed in the specified time without the commission of such an offence as is mentioned in subsection (1) above, the publication or issue of the time-table or schedule, or the giving of the directions, may be produced as prima facie evidence that the employer procured or (as the case may be) incited the persons employed by him to drive the vehicles to commit such an offence.

Immobilisation of vehicles illegally parked

104.—(1) Subject to sections 105 and 106 of this Act, where a constable finds on a road a vehicle which has been permitted to remain at rest there in contravention of any prohibition or restriction imposed by or under any enactment, he may—

    (a) fix an immobilisation device to the vehicle while it remains in the place in which he finds it; or

    (b) move it from that place to another place on the same or another road and fix an immobilisation device to it in that other place;

or authorise another person to take under his direction any action he could himself take by virtue of paragraph (a) or (b) above.

(2) On any occasion when an immobilisation device is fixed to a vehicle in accordance with this section the constable or other person fixing the device shall also affix to the vehicle a notice—

    (a) indicating that such a device has been fixed to the vehicle and warning that no attempt should be made to drive it or otherwise put it in motion until it has been released from that device;

    (b) specifying the steps to be taken in order to secure its release; and

    (c) giving such other information as may be prescribed.

(3) A vehicle to which an immobilisation device has been fixed in accordance with this section may only be released from that device by or under the direction of a person authorised to give such a direction by the chief officer of police within whose area the vehicle in question was found.

(4) Subject to subsection (3) above, a vehicle to which an immobilisation device has been fixed in accordance with this section shall be released from that device on payment in any manner specified in the notice affixed to the vehicle under subsection (2) above of such charge in respect of the release as may be prescribed.

(5) A notice affixed to a vehicle under this section shall not be removed or interfered with except by or under the authority of the person in charge of the vehicle or the person by whom it was put in the place where it was found by the constable; and any person contravening this subsection shall be guilty of an offence.

(6) Any person who, without being authorised to do so in accordance with this section, removes or attempts to remove an immobilisation device fitted to a vehicle in accordance with this section shall be guilty of an offence.

(7) Where a vehicle is moved in accordance with this section before an immobilisation device is fixed to it, any power of removal under regulations for the time being in force under section 99 of this Act which was exercisable in relation to that vehicle immediately before it was so moved shall continue to be exercisable in relation to that vehicle while it remains in the place to which it was so moved.

(8) In relation to any vehicle which is removed in pursuance of any such regulations or under section 3 of the Refuse Disposal (Amenity) Act 1978 (duty of local authority to remove abandoned vehicles) from a place to which it was moved in accordance with this section, references in the definition of "person responsible" in section 102(8) of this Act and section 5 of the said Act of 1978 mentioned above (recovery from person responsible of charges and expenses in respect of vehicles removed) to the place from which the vehicle was removed shall be read as references to the place in which it was immediately before it was moved in accordance with this section.

(9) In this section "immobilisation device" means any device or appliance designed or adapted to be fixed to a vehicle for the purpose of preventing it

from being driven or otherwise put in motion, being a device or appliance of a type approved by the Secretary of State for use for that purpose in accordance with this section.

(10) [...]

(11) Any sum received by virtue of subsection (4) above shall be paid into the police fund.

(12) Regulations under subsection (2) or (4) above may make different provision for different cases or classes of case or in respect of different areas.

(12A) For the purposes of this section, the suspension under section 13A or 49 of this Act of the use of a parking place is a restriction imposed under this Act.

Exemptions from s.104

B10–22   **105.**—(1) Subject to the following provisions of this section, section 104(1) of this Act shall not apply in relation to a vehicle found by a constable in the circumstances mentioned in that subsection if either—

  (a) a current disabled person's badge is displayed on the vehicle; or
  (b) the vehicle is in a meter bay within a parking place designated by a designation order.

(2) The exemption under subsection (1)(b) above shall not apply in the case of any vehicle if—

  (a) the meter bay in which it was found was not authorised for use as such at the time when it was left there (referred to below in this section as the time of parking); or
  (b) an initial charge was not duly paid at the time of parking; or
  (c) there has been since that time any contravention in relation to the relevant parking meter of any provision made by virtue of section 46(2) (c) of this Act; or
  (d) more than two hours have elapsed since the end of any period for which an initial charge was duly paid at the time of parking or (as the case may be) since the end of any unexpired time in respect of another vehicle available on the relevant parking meter at the time of parking.

(3) For the purposes of subsection (2)(a) above, a meter bay in a parking place designated by a designation order is not authorised for use as such at any time when—

  (a) by virtue of section 49(1)(a) of this Act the parking place is treated for the purposes of sections 46 and 47 of this Act as if it were not designated by that order; or
  (b) the use of the parking place or of any part of it that consists of or includes that particular meter bay is suspended [...].

(4) In relation to any vehicle found in a meter bay within a parking place designated by a designation order, references in subsection (2) above to an initial charge are references to an initial charge payable in respect of that vehicle under section 45 or 50 of this Act.

(5) In any case where section 104(1) of this Act would apply in relation to a vehicle but for subsection (1)(a) above, the person guilty of contravening the prohibition or restriction mentioned in section 104(1) is also guilty of an offence under this subsection if the conditions mentioned in subsection (6) below are met.

(6) Those conditions are that at the time when the contravention occurred—

(a) the vehicle was not being used [in accordance with regulations under] section 21 of the Chronically Sick and Disabled Persons Act 1970 (badges for display on motor vehicles used by disabled persons); and

(b) he was not using the vehicle in circumstances falling within section 117(1)(b) of this Act.

(7) In this section, "meter bay" means a parking space equipped with a parking meter; and the references in subsection (2) above to the relevant parking meter are references to the parking meter relating to the meter bay in which the vehicle in question was found.

Liability of vehicle owner in respect of excess parking charge

107.—(1) This section applies where—

(a) an excess charge has been incurred in pursuance of an order under sections 45 and 46 of this Act;

(b) notice of the incurring of the excess charge has been given or affixed as provided in the order; and

(c) the excess charge has not been duly paid in accordance with the order; and in the following provisions of this Part of this Act "the excess charge offence" means the offence under section 47 of this Act of failing duly to pay the excess charge.

(2) Subject to the following provisions of this section—

(a) for the purposes of the institution of proceedings in respect of the excess charge offence against any person as being the owner of the vehicle at the relevant time, and

(b) in any proceedings in respect of the excess charge offence brought against any person as being the owner of the vehicle at the relevant time,

it shall be conclusively presumed (notwithstanding that that person may not be an individual) that he was the driver of the vehicle at that time and, accordingly, that acts or omissions of the driver of the vehicle at that time were his acts or omissions.

(3) Subsection (2) above shall not apply in relation to any person unless, within the period of 6 months beginning on the day on which the notice of the incurring of the excess charge was given or affixed as mentioned in subsection (1)(b) above, a notice under section 108 of this Act has been served on him—

(a) by or on behalf of the authority which is the local authority for the purposes of sections 45 and 46 of this Act in relation to the parking place concerned, or

(b) by or on behalf of the chief officer of police.

(4) If the person on whom a notice under section 108 of this Act is served in accordance with subsection (3) above was not the owner of the vehicle at the relevant time, subsection (2) above shall not apply in relation to him if he furnishes a statutory statement of ownership to that effect in compliance with the notice.

(5) The presumption in subsection (2) above shall not apply in any proceedings brought against any person as being the owner of the vehicle at the relevant time if, in those proceedings, it is proved—

(a) that at the relevant time the vehicle was in the possession of some other person without the consent of the accused, or

(b) that the accused was not the owner of the vehicle at the relevant time and that he has a reasonable excuse for failing to comply with the notice under section 108 of this Act served on him in accordance with subsection (3) above.

Notice in respect of excess parking charge

B10–24   **108.**—(1) A notice under this section shall be in the prescribed form, shall give particulars of the excess charge and shall provide that, unless the excess charge is paid before the expiry of the appropriate period, the person on whom the notice is served—

(a) is required, before the expiry of that period, to furnish to the authority or chief officer of police by or on behalf of whom the notice was served a statutory statement of ownership (as defined in Part I of Schedule 8 to this Act), and

(b) is invited, before the expiry of that period, to furnish to that authority or chief officer of police a statutory statement of facts (as defined in Part II of that Schedule).

(2) If, in any case where—

(a) a notice under this section has been served on any person, and

(b) the excess charge specified in the notice is not paid within the appropriate period,

the person so served fails without reasonable excuse to comply with the notice by furnishing a statutory statement of ownership he shall be guilty of an offence.

(3) If, in compliance with or in response to a notice under this section any person furnishes a statement which is false in a material particular, and does so recklessly or knowing it to be false in that particular, he shall be guilty of an offence.

(4) Where a notice under this section has been served on any person in respect of any excess charge—

(a) payment of the charge by any person before the date on which proceedings are begun for the excess charge offence, or, as the case may be, for an offence under subsection (2) above in respect of a failure to comply with the notice, shall discharge the liability of that or any other person (under this or any other enactment) for the excess charge offence or, as the case may be, for the offence under subsection (2) above;

(b) conviction of any person of the excess charge offence shall discharge the liability of any other person (under this or any other enactment) for that offence and the liability of any person for an offence under subsection (2) above in respect of a failure to comply with the notice; and

(c) conviction of the person so served of an offence under subsection (2) above in respect of a failure to comply with the notice shall discharge the liability of any person for the excess charge offence;

but, except as provided by this subsection, nothing in section 107 of this Act or this section shall affect the liability of any person for the excess charge offence.

Modifications of ss.107 and 108 in relation to hired vehicles

B10–25   **109.**—(1) This section shall apply where—

(a) a notice under section 108 of this Act has been served on a vehicle-hire firm, and

(b) at the relevant time the vehicle in respect of which the notice was served was let to another person by the vehicle-hire firm under a hiring agreement to which this section applies.

(2) Where this section applies, it shall be a sufficient compliance with the notice served on the vehicle-hire firm if the firm furnishes to the chief officer of police or local authority by or on behalf of whom the notice was served a statement in the prescribed form, signed by or on behalf of the vehicle-hire firm, stating that at the relevant time the vehicle concerned was hired under a hiring agreement to which this section applies, together with—

(a) a copy of that hiring agreement, and

(b) a copy of a statement of liability in the prescribed form, signed by the hirer under that hiring agreement;

and accordingly, in relation to the vehicle-hire firm on whom the notice was served, the reference in section 108(2) of this Act to a statutory statement of ownership shall be construed as a reference to a statement under this subsection together with the documents specified in paragraphs (a) and (b) above.

(3) If, in a case where this section applies, the vehicle-hire firm has complied with the notice served on the firm by furnishing the statement and copies of the documents specified in subsection (2) above, then sections 107 and 108 of this Act shall have effect as if in those provisions—

(a) any reference to the owner of the vehicle were a reference to the hirer under the hiring agreement, and

(b) any reference to a statutory statement of ownership were a reference to a statutory statement of hiring.

(4) Where, in compliance with a notice under section 108 of this Act, a vehicle-hire firm has furnished copies of a hiring agreement and statement of liability as mentioned in subsection (2) above, a person authorised in that behalf by the chief officer of police or local authority to whom the documents are furnished may, at any reasonable time within 6 months after service of that notice, and on production of his authority, require the production by the firm of the originals of those documents; and if, without reasonable excuse, a vehicle-hire firm fails to produce the original of a document when required to do so under this subsection, the firm shall be treated as not having complied with the notice under section 108 of this Act.

(5) This section applies to a hiring agreement, under the terms of which the vehicle concerned is let to the hirer for a fixed period of less than 6 months (whether or not that period is capable of extension by agreement between the parties or otherwise); and any reference in this section to the currency of the hiring agreement includes a reference to any period during which, with the consent of the vehicle-hire firm, the hirer continues in possession of the vehicle as hirer, after the expiry of the fixed period specified in the agreement, but otherwise on terms and conditions specified in it.

(6) In this section "statement of liability" means a statement made by the hirer under a hiring agreement to which this section applies to the effect that the hirer acknowledges that he will be liable, as the owner of the vehicle, in respect of any excess charge which, during the currency of the hiring agreement, may be incurred with respect to the vehicle in pursuance of an order under sections 45 and 46 of this Act.

(7) In this section—

"hiring agreement" refers only to an agreement which contains such particulars as may be prescribed and does not include a hire-purchase agreement within the meaning of the Consumer Credit Act 1974, and "vehicle-hire firm" means any person engaged in hiring vehicles in the course of a business.

Time for bringing and evidence in, proceedings for certain offences

B10–26   110.—Proceedings in England or Wales for an offence under section 108(3) of this Act may be brought within a period of six months from the date on which evidence sufficient in the opinion of the prosecutor to warrant the proceedings came to his knowledge; but no such proceedings shall be brought by virtue of this section more than 3 years after the commission of the offence.

(2) Proceedings in Scotland for an offence to which subsection (1) above applies shall not be commenced after the expiry of the period of 3 years from the commission of the offence; but, subject to the foregoing limitation, and notwithstanding anything in section 331 of the Criminal Procedure (Scotland) Act 1975, any such proceedings may be commenced at any time within 6 months after the date on which evidence sufficient in the opinion of the Lord Advocate to justify the proceedings came to his knowledge or, where such evidence was reported to him by a local authority, within 6 months after the date on which it came to their knowledge; and subsection (3) of the said section 331 shall apply for the purposes of this subsection as it applies for the purposes of that section.

(3) For the purposes of subsections (1) and (2) above a certificate signed by or on behalf of the prosecutor or, as the case may be, the Lord Advocate or the local authority, and stating the date on which evidence such as is mentioned in the subsection in question came to his or their knowledge, shall be conclusive evidence of that fact; and a certificate stating that matter and purporting to be so signed shall be deemed to be so signed unless the contrary is proved.

(4) Where any person is charged with the offence of failing to pay an excess charge, and the prosecutor produces to the court any of the statutory statements in Schedule 8 to this Act or a copy of a statement of liability (within the meaning of section 109 of this Act) purporting—

   (a) to have been furnished in compliance with or in response to a notice under section 108 of this Act, and

   (b) to have been signed by the accused,

the statement shall be presumed, unless the contrary is proved, to have been signed by the accused and shall be evidence (and, in Scotland, sufficient evidence) in the proceedings of any facts stated in it tending to show that the accused was the owner, the hirer or the driver of the vehicle concerned at a particular time.

Supplementary provisions as to excess charges

B10–27   111.—(1) The provisions of Schedule 8 to this Act shall have effect for the purposes of sections 107 to 109 of this Act (in this section referred to as "the specified sections").

(2) In the specified sections—

   "appropriate period", in relation to a notice under section 108 of this Act, means the period of 14 days from the date on which the notice is served, or such longer period as may be specified in the notice or as may be allowed by the chief officer of police or authority by or on behalf of whom the notice is served;

304

"driver", in relation to an excess charge and in relation to an offence of failing duly to pay such a charge, means the person driving the vehicle at the time when it is alleged to have been left in the parking place concerned;

"relevant time", in relation to an excess charge, means the time when the vehicle was left in the parking place concerned, notwithstanding that the period in respect of which the excess charge was incurred did not begin at that time.

(3) For the purposes of the specified sections the owner of a vehicle shall be taken to be the person by whom the vehicle is kept; and for the purpose of determining, in the course of any proceedings brought by virtue of the specified sections, who was the owner of the vehicle at any time, it shall be presumed that the owner was the person who was the registered keeper of the vehicle at that time.

(4) Notwithstanding the presumption in subsection (3) above, it shall be open to the defence in any proceedings to prove that the person who was the registered keeper of a vehicle at a particular time was not the person by whom the vehicle was kept at that time, and it shall be open to the prosecution to prove that the vehicle was kept by some other person at that time.

(5) A notice under section 108 of this Act may be served on any person—

(a) by delivering it to him or by leaving it at his proper address, or

(b) by sending it to him by post;

and, where the person on whom such a notice is to be served is a body corporate, it shall be duly served if it is served on the secretary or clerk of that body.

(6) For the purposes of subsection (5) above and of section 7 of the Interpretation Act 1978 (references to service by post) in its application to that subsection, the proper address of any person on whom such a notice is to be served—

(a) shall, in the case of the secretary or clerk of a body corporate, be that of the registered or principal office of that body or the registered address of the person who is the registered keeper of the vehicle concerned at the time of service, and

(b) shall in any other case be the last known address of the person to be served.

(7) References in this section to the person who was or is the registered keeper of a vehicle at any time are references to the person in whose name the vehicle was or is at that time registered under the Vehicle Excise and Regulation Act 1994; and, in relation to any such person, the reference in subsection (6)(a) above to that person's registered address is a reference to the address recorded in the record kept under that Act with respect to that vehicle as being that person's address.

(8) For the purposes of sections 1(2) and 2(1) of the Magistrates' Courts Act 1980 (power to issue summons or warrant and jurisdiction to try offences), any offence under subsection (2) of section 108 of this Act shall be treated as committed at any address which at the time of service of the notice under that section to which the offence relates was the accused's proper address (in accordance with subsection (6) above) for the service of any such notice as well as at the address to which any statutory statement furnished in response to that notice is required to be returned in accordance with the notice.

Information as to identity of driver or rider

112.—(1) This section applies to any offence under any of the foregoing provisions of this Act except— **B10–28**

(a) sections 43, 52, 88(7), 104, 105 and 108;

(b) the provisions of subsection (2) or (3) of section 108 as modified by subsections (2) and (3) of section 109; and

(c) section 35A(5) in its application to England and Wales.

(2) Where the driver of a vehicle is alleged to be guilty of an offence to which this section applies—

(a) the person keeping the vehicle shall give such information as to the identity of the driver as he may be required to give—

(i) by or on behalf of a chief officer of police, or

(ii) in the case of an offence under section 35A(1) or against section 47 of this Act, by or on behalf of a chief officer of police or, in writing, by or on behalf of the local authority for the parking place in question; and

(b) any other person shall, if required as mentioned in paragraph (a) above, give any information which it is in his power to give and which may lead to the identification of the driver.

(3) In subsection (2) above, references to the driver of a vehicle include references to the person riding a bicycle or tricycle (not being a motor vehicle); and—

(a) [...]

(b) in relation to an offence under section 61(5) of this Act, subsection (2) (a) above shall have effect as if, for sub-paragraphs (i) and (ii), there were substituted the words "by a notice in writing given to him by a local authority in whose area the loading area in question is situated", and in subsection (2)(a) above, as modified by paragraph (b) of this subsection, "local authority" means any of the following, that is to say, a county council, [...] a district council, a London borough council and the Common Council of the City of London.

(4) Except as provided by subsection (5) below, a person who fails to comply with the requirements of subsection (2)(a) above shall be guilty of an offence unless he shows to the satisfaction of the court that he did not know, and could not with reasonable diligence have ascertained, who was the driver of the vehicle or, as the case may be, the rider of the bicycle or tricycle; and a person who fails to comply with the requirements of subsection (2)(b) above shall be guilty of an offence.

(5) As regards Scotland, subsection (4) above shall not apply where the offence of which the driver of the vehicle is alleged to be guilty is an offence under section 61(5) of this Act.

Mishandling of parking documents and related offences

B10–29   115.—(1) A person shall be guilty of an offence who, with intent to deceive,—

(a) uses, or lends to, or allows to be used by, any other person,—

(i) any parking device or apparatus designed to be used in connection with parking devices;

(ii) any ticket issued by a parking meter, parking device or apparatus designed to be used in connection with parking devices;

(iii) any authorisation by way of such a certificate, other means of identification or device as is referred to in any of sections 4(2), 4(3), 7(2) and 7(3) of this Act; or

(iv) any such permit or token as is referred to in section 46(2)(i) of this Act;

(b) makes or has in his possession anything so closely resembling any such thing as is mentioned in paragraph (a) above as to be calculated to deceive; or

(c) in Scotland, forges or alters any such thing as is mentioned in that paragraph.

(2) A person who knowingly makes a false statement for the purpose of procuring the grant or issue to himself or any other person of any such authorisation as is mentioned in subsection (1) above shall be guilty of an offence.

(2A) In any proceedings for an offence under this section it shall be assumed, unless the contrary is shown, that any such device as is referred to in section 35(3B) or, as the case may be, section 51(4) of this Act, or any apparatus designed to be used in connection with parking devices, is of a type and design approved by the Secretary of State.

(3) Summary proceedings in Scotland for an offence under this section may be brought—

(a) within a period of 6 months from the date of the commission of the alleged offence, or

(b) within a period which exceeds neither 3 months from the date in which it came to the knowledge of the procurator fiscal that the offence had been committed nor one year from the date of the commission of the offence,

whichever period is the longer.

Provisions supplementary to s.115

116.—(1) If any person authorised in that behalf by or under a designation order has reasonable cause to believe that a document or article carried on a vehicle, or by the driver or person in charge of a vehicle, is a document or article in relation to which an offence has been committed under subsection (1) of section 115 of this Act (so far as that subsection relates to such authorisations as are referred to in it) or under subsection (2) of that section, he may detain that document or article, and may for that purpose require the driver or person in charge of the vehicle to deliver up the document or article; and if the driver or person in charge of the vehicle fails to comply with that requirement, he shall be guilty of an offence.

B10–30

(2) When a document or article has been detained under subsection (1) above and—

(a) at any time after the expiry of 6 months from the date when that detention began no person has been charged since that date with an offence in relation to the document or article under subsection (1) or (2) of section 115 of this Act, and

(b) the document or article has not been returned to the person to whom the authorisation in question was issued or to the person who at that date was the driver or person in charge of the vehicle,

then, on an application made for the purpose to a magistrates' court (or, in Scotland, on a summary application made for the purpose to the sheriff court), the court shall make such order respecting disposal of the document or article and award such costs (or, in Scotland, expenses) as the justice of the case may require.

(3) Any of the following, but no other, persons shall be entitled to make an application under subsection (2) above with respect to a document or article, that is to say—

(a) the person to whom the authorisation was issued;

(b) the person who, at the date when the detention of the document or article began, was the driver or person in charge of the vehicle; and

(c) the person for the time being having possession of the document or article.

Wrongful use of disabled person's badge

B10–31   117.—(1) A person who at any time acts in contravention of, or fails to comply with, any provision of an order under this Act relating to the parking of motor vehicles is also guilty of an offence under this section if at that time—

(a) there was displayed on the motor vehicle in question a badge of a form prescribed under section 21 of the Chronically Sick and Disabled Persons Act 1970, and

(b) he was using the vehicle in circumstances where a disabled person's concession would be available to a disabled person's vehicle,

but he shall not be guilty of an offence under this section if the badge was issued under that section and displayed in accordance with regulations made under it.

(3) In this section—

[…]; and

"disabled person's concession" means—

(a) an exemption from an order under this Act given by reference to disabled persons' vehicles; or

(b) a provision made in any order under this Act for the use of a parking place by disabled persons' vehicles.

Meaning of "motor vehicle" and other expressions relating to vehicles.

B10–32   136.—(1) In this Act, subject to section 20 of the Chronically Sick and Disabled Persons Act 1970 (which makes special provision with respect to invalid carriages), "motor vehicle" means a mechanically propelled vehicle intended or adapted for use on roads, and "trailer" means a vehicle drawn by a motor vehicle.

(2) In this Act "motor car" means a mechanically propelled vehicle, not being a motor cycle or an invalid carriage, which is constructed itself to carry a load or passengers and of which the weight unladen—

(a) if it is constructed solely for the carriage of passengers and their effects, is adapted to carry not more than 7 passengers exclusive of the driver, and is fitted with tyres of such type as may be specified in regulations made by the Secretary of State, does not exceed 3050 kilograms;

(b) if it is constructed or adapted for use for the conveyance of goods or burden of any description, does not exceed 3050 kilograms (or 3500 kilograms if the vehicle carries a container or containers for holding, for the purposes of its propulsion, any fuel which is wholly gaseous at 17·5 degrees Celsius under a pressure of 1·013 bar or plant and materials for producing such fuel); or

(c) In a case falling within neither of the foregoing paragraphs, does not exceed 2540 kilograms.

(3) In this Act "heavy motor car" means a mechanically propelled vehicle, not being a motor car, which is constructed itself to carry a load or passengers and of which the weight unladen exceeds 2540 kilograms.

(4) In this Act (except for the purposes of section 57) "motor cycle" means a

mechanically propelled vehicle (not being an invalid carriage) with fewer than 4 wheels, of which the weight unladen does not exceed 410 kilograms.

(5) In this Act "invalid carriage" means a mechanically propelled vehicle of which the weight unladen does not exceed 254 kilograms and which is specially designed and constructed, and not merely adapted, for the use of a person suffering from some physical default or disability and is used solely by such a person.

(6) In this Act "motor tractor" means a mechanically propelled vehicle which is not constructed itself to carry a load, other than excepted articles, and of which the weight unladen does not exceed 7370 kilograms.

(7) In this Act "light locomotive" and "heavy locomotive" mean a mechanically propelled vehicle which is not constructed itself to carry a load, other than excepted articles, and of which the weight unladen—

(a) in the case of a light locomotive, exceeds 7370 but does not exceed 11690 kilograms, and

(b) in the case of a heavy locomotive, exceeds 11690 kilograms.

(8) In subsections (6) and (7) above "excepted articles" means any of the following, that is to say, water, fuel, accumulators and other equipment used for the purpose of propulsion, loose tools and loose equipment.

Supplementary provisions relating to s.136

137.—(1) A sidecar attached to a motor vehicle shall, if it complies with such conditions as may be specified in regulations made by the Secretary of State, be regarded as forming part of the vehicle to which it is attached and not as being a trailer. **B10–33**

(2) For the purposes of section 136 of this Act, in a case where a motor vehicle is so constructed that a trailer may by partial superimposition be attached to the vehicle in such a manner as to cause a substantial part of the weight of the trailer to be borne by the vehicle, that vehicle shall be deemed to be a vehicle itself constructed to carry a load.

(3) For the purposes of that section, in the case of a motor vehicle fitted with a crane, dynamo, welding plant or other special appliance or apparatus which is a permanent or essentially permanent fixture, the appliance or apparatus shall not be deemed to constitute a load or goods or burden of any description, but shall be deemed to form part of the vehicle.

(4) The Secretary of State may by regulations vary any of the maximum or minimum weights specified in section 136 of this Act: and such regulations may have effect—

(a) either generally or in the case of vehicles of any class specified in the regulations, and

(b) either for the purposes of this Act and of all regulations made under it or for such of those purposes as may be so specified.

(5) Nothing in section 86 of this Act shall be construed as limiting the powers conferred by subsection (4) above.

Certain vehicles not to be treated as motor vehicles

140.—(1) For the purposes of this Act— **B10–34**

(a) a mechanically propelled vehicle which is an implement for cutting grass, is controlled by a pedestrian and is not capable of being used or adapted for any other purpose;

(b) any other mechanically propelled vehicle controlled by a pedestrian which may be specified by regulations made by the Secretary of State for the purposes of this section and of section 189 of the Road Traffic Act 1988; and

(c) an electrically assisted pedal cycle of such class as may be prescribed by regulations so made,

shall be treated as not being a motor vehicle.

(2) In this section "controlled by a pedestrian" means that the vehicle either—

(a) is constructed or adapted for use only under such control, or

(b) is constructed or adapted for use either under such control or under the control of a person carried on it, but is not for the time being in use under, or proceeding under, the control of a person carried on it.

B10–35 **Section 86** SCHEDULE 6

SPEED LIMITS FOR VEHICLES OF CERTAIN CLASSES

PART I

VEHICLES FITTED WITH PNEUMATIC TYRES ON ALL WHEELS

(see application provisions below the following Table)

TABLE

1	2	3		
Item No.	Class of Vehicle	Maximum speed (in miles per hour) while vehicle is being driven on:		
		(a) Motorway	(b) Dual carriageway road not being a motorway	(c) Other road
1.	A passenger vehicle, motor caravan or dual-purpose vehicle not drawing a trailer being a vehicle with an unladen weight exceeding 3·05 tonnes or adapted to carry more than 8 passengers:			
	(i) if not exceeding 12 metres in overall length	70	60	50
	(ii) if exceeding 12 metres in overall length	60	60	50
2.	An invalid carriage	not applicable	20	20
3.	A passenger vehicle, motor caravan, car-derived van or dual-purpose vehicle drawing one trailer	60	60	50
4.	A passenger vehicle, motor caravan, car-derived van or dual-purpose vehicle drawing more than one trailer	40	20	20

1	2	3		
Item No.	Class of Vehicle	Maximum speed (in miles per hour) while vehicle is being driven on:		
		(a) Motorway	(b) Dual carriageway road not being a motorway	(c) Other road
5.	(1) A goods vehicle having a maximum laden weight not exceeding 7·5 tonnes and which is not— (a) an articulated vehicle, or (b) drawing a trailer, or (c) a car-derived van	70	60	50
	(2) A goods vehicle which is— (a) (i) an articulated vehicle having a maximum laden weight not exceeding 7·5 tonnes, or (ii) a motor vehicle, other than a car-derived van, which is drawing one trailer where the aggregate maximum laden weight of the motor vehicle and the trailer does not exceed 7·5 tonnes	60	60	50
	(b) (i) an articulated vehicle having a maximum laden weight exceeding 7·5 tonnes, (ii) a motor vehicle having a maximum laden weight exceeding 7·5 tonnes and not drawing a trailer, or (iii) a motor vehicle drawing one trailer where the aggregate maximum laden weight of the motor vehicle and the trailer exceeds 7.5 tonnes	60	50	40
	(c) a motor vehicle, other than a car-derived van, drawing more than one trailer	40	20	20
6.	A motor tractor (other than an industrial tractor), a light locomotive or a heavy locomotive— (a) if the provisions about springs and wings as specified in paragraph 3 of Part IV of this Schedule are complied with, and the vehicle is not drawing a trailer, or if those provisions are complied with and the vehicle is drawing one trailer, which also complies with those provisions	40	30	30
	(b) in any other case	20	20	20
7.	A works truck	18	18	18
8.	An industrial tractor	not applicable	18	18
9.	An agricultural motor vehicle	40	40	40

Application

This Part applies only to motor vehicles, not being track-laying vehicles, every wheel of which is fitted with a pneumatic tyre and to such vehicles drawing one or more trailers, not being track-laying vehicles, every wheel of which is fitted with a pneumatic tyre.

1	2	3
Item No.	Class of Vehicle	Maximum Speed (in miles per hour) while vehicle is being driven on a road
3.	A vehicle specified in item 1 above drawing one or more trailers any one of which is either— (a) a track-laying vehicle not fitted with springs and resilient material as mentioned in that item, or (b) not a track-laying vehicle and at least one wheel of which is not fitted with either a pneumatic tyre or a resilient tyre	5
4.	A motor vehicle being a track-laying vehicle which is not fitted with springs and resilient material as mentioned in item 1 above, whether drawing a trailer or not	5
5.	A motor vehicle not being a track-laying vehicle, which is drawing one or more trailers any one or more of which is a track-laying vehicle— (a) if every wheel of the motor vehicle and of any non-track-laying trailer is fitted with a pneumatic tyre or with a resilient tyre, and every trailer which is a track-laying vehicle is fitted with springs and resilient material as mentioned in item 1	20
	(b) in any other case	5

Application

This part applies to—
(a) a motor vehicle which is a track-laying vehicle, and
(b) a motor vehicle of any description which is drawing one or more trailers any one or more of which is a track-laying vehicle.

PART IV

APPLICATION AND INTERPRETATION

1. This Schedule does not apply to a vehicle which is being used for the purpose of experiments or trials under section 6 of the Road Improvements Act 1925 or section 283 of the Highways Act 1980.

2. In this Schedule—

"agricultural motor vehicle," "articulated vehicle," "dual-purpose vehicle," "industrial tractor," "passenger vehicle," "pneumatic tyre," "track-laying," "wheel" and "works truck" have the same meanings as are respectively given to those expressions in Regulation 3(1) of the Motor Vehicles (Construction and Use) Regulations 1978;

"car-derived van" means a goods vehicle which is constructed or adapted as a derivative of a passenger vehicle and which has a maximum laden weight not exceeding 2 tonnes;

"construction and use requirements" has the same meaning as in section 41(7) of the Road Traffic Act 1988;

"dual-carriageway road" means a road part of which consists of a central reservation to separate a carriageway to be used by vehicles proceeding in one direction from a carriageway to be used by vehicles proceeding in the opposite direction;

"goods vehicle" has the same meaning as in section 192(1) of the Road Traffic Act 1988;

"maximum laden weight" in relation to a vehicle or a combination of vehicles means—

(a) in the case of a vehicle, or combination of vehicles, in respect of which a gross weight not to be exceeded in Great Britain is specified in construction and use requirements, that weight;

(b) in the case of any vehicle, or combination of vehicles, in respect of which no such weight is specified in construction and use requirements, the weight which the vehicle, or combination of vehicles, is designed or adapted not to exceed when in normal use and travelling on a road laden;

"motor caravan" has the same meaning as in Regulation 2(1) of the Motor Vehicles (Type Approval) (Great Britain) Regulations 1979;

"motorway" has the same meaning as in Regulation 3(1) of the Motorways Traffic (England and Wales) Regulations 1982, as regards England and Wales, and Regulation 2(2) of the Motorways Traffic (Scotland) Regulations 1964, as regards Scotland; and

"resilient tyre" means a tyre, not being a pneumatic tyre, which is soft or elastic.

3. The specification as regards springs and wings mentioned in item 6 of Part I of this Schedule is that the vehicle—

(i) is equipped with suitable and sufficient springs between each wheel and the frame of the vehicle, and

(ii) unless adequate protection is afforded by the body of the vehicle, is provided with wings or other similar fittings to catch, so far as practicable, mud or water thrown up by the rotation of the wheels.

4. A vehicle falling in two or more classes specified in Part I, II or III of this Schedule shall be treated as falling within the class for which the lower or lowest speed limit is specified.

SCHEDULE 8

STATUTORY STATEMENTS (EXCESS CHARGES)

PART I

STATUTORY STATEMENT OF OWNERSHIP OR HIRING

1. For the purposes of the specified sections, a statutory statement of own-   **B10–36**

ership is a statement in the prescribed form, signed by the person furnishing it and stating—

    (a) whether he was the owner of the vehicle at the relevant time; and

    (b) if he was not the owner of the vehicle at the relevant time, whether he ceased to be the owner before, or became the owner after, the relevant time, and, if the information is in his possession, the name and address of the person to whom, and the date on which, he disposed of the vehicle or, as the case may be, the name and address of the person from whom, and the date on which, he acquired it.

2. For the purposes of the specified sections, a statutory statement of hiring is a statement in the prescribed form, signed by the person furnishing it, being the person by whom a statement of liability was signed and stating—

    (a) whether at the relevant time the vehicle was let to him under the hiring agreement to which the statement of liability refers; and

    (b) if it was not, the date on which he returned the vehicle to the possession of the vehicle-hire firm concerned.

PART II

STATUTORY STATEMENT OF FACTS

3. For the purposes of the specified sections, a statutory statement of facts is a statement which is in the prescribed form and which—

    (a) states that the person furnishing it was not the driver of the vehicle at the relevant time;

    (b) states the name and address at the time when the statement is furnished of the person who was the driver of the vehicle at the relevant time; and

    (c) is signed both by the person furnishing it and by the person stated to be the driver of the vehicle at the relevant time.

PART III

INTERPRETATION

4. In this Schedule "the specified sections" has the meaning assigned to it by subsection (1) of section 111 of this Act.

5. Subsections (2) to (4) of that section shall have effect for the purposes of Parts I and II of this Schedule as they have effect for the purposes of the specified sections.

6. In paragraph 2 above "statement of liability", "hiring agreement" and "vehicle-hire firm" have the same meanings as in section 109 of this Act.

PART VI

VALIDITY OF CERTAIN ORDERS

35. If any person desires to question the validity of, or of any provision contained in, an order to which this Part of this Schedule applies, on the grounds—

(a) that it is not within the relevant powers, or

(b) that any of the relevant requirements has not been complied with in relation to the order,

he may, within 6 weeks from the date on which the order is made, make an application for the purpose to the High Court or, in Scotland, to the Court of Session.

36.—(1) On any application under this Part of this Schedule the court—

(a) may, by interim order, suspend the operation of the order to which the application relates, or of any provision of that order, until the final determination of the proceedings; and

(b) if satisfied that the order, or any provision of the order, is not within the relevant powers, or that the interests of the applicant have been substantially prejudiced by failure to comply with any of the relevant requirements, may quash the order or any provision of the order.

(2) An order to which this Part of this Schedule applies, or a provision of any such order, may be suspended or quashed under sub-paragraph (1) above either generally or so far as may be necessary for the protection of the interests of the applicant.

37. Except as provided by this Part of this Schedule, an order to which this Part of this Schedule applies shall not, either before or after it has been made, be questioned in any legal proceedings whatever.

SCHEDULE 10

Transitional Provisions and Savings

General

1.—(1) In this Schedule "the 1967 Act" means the Road Traffic Regulation   **B10–37**
Act 1967.

(2) For the purposes of any provision of this Schedule which refers—

(a) to an enactment repealed by this Act, or to the repeal by this Act of any enactment, and

(b) to the commencement of this Act,

the commencement of this Act shall be taken to be the date on which the repeal by this Act of that enactment takes effect.

2. Where any enactment or document refers, whether specifically or by means of a general description, to an enactment repealed by and re-enacted (with or without modification) in this Act, or is to be construed as so referring, the reference shall, except where the context otherwise requires, be construed as, or as including, a reference to the corresponding provision of this Act.

3. Any reference in this Act (whether express or implied) to a thing done or required or authorised to be done, or omitted to be done, or deemed to have been done, or to an event which has occurred, under or by virtue of or for the purposes of, or by reference to, any provision of this Act includes (except where the context otherwise requires) a reference to the corresponding thing done, or having effect as if done, or required or authorised to be done, or omitted to be done, or deemed to have been done, or to the corresponding event which has occurred, as the case may be, under or by virtue of or for the purposes of or by reference to, the corresponding enactment repealed by this Act.

4.—(1) Without prejudice to paragraph 3 above, any reference in this Act (whether express or implied) to a thing done by the Secretary of State, a local authority or any other authority under a provision of this Act includes (except where the context otherwise requires) a reference to the corresponding thing done, or having effect as if done, by a predecessor authority under the corresponding provision repealed by this Act.

(2) In sub-paragraph (1) above "predecessor authority"—

    (a) in relation to the Secretary of State, means the Minister of Transport or other Minister exercising the relevant function before the transfer of the function to the Secretary of State, and

    (b) in relation to a council, means the authority exercising the relevant function before it vested in the council under the Local Government Act 1972, the London Government Act 1963, the Local Government (Scotland) Act 1973 or any other enactment.

(3) In sub-paragraph (2) above any reference to the Minister or authority exercising a function includes a reference to a Minister or authority exercising that function for particular purposes only or in relation only to a particular part of Great Britain.

5. Without prejudice to paragraphs 3 and 4 above, any power which, under an enactment repealed by this Act, was exercisable by the Secretary of State, a local authority or other authority immediately before the commencement of this Act by reference (whether express or implied) to anything done before the commencement of this Act may be exercised by the Secretary of State or that authority, as the case may be, under the corresponding provision of this Act.

6. Where a period of time specified in an enactment repealed by this Act is current at the commencement of this Act, this Act shall have effect as if the corresponding provision of this Act had been in force when that period began to run.

Traffic regulation byelaws in Scotland

7. Any byelaw made under section 104 of the Roads and Bridges (Scotland) Act 1878 or paragraph (1) or (3) of section 385 of the Burgh Police (Scotland) Act 1892 which—

    (a) was in force immediately before the commencement of the 1967 Act and by virtue of paragraph 6 of Schedule 8 to that Act had effect as if it were an order made under section 1 of that Act; and

    (b) continues so to have effect immediately before the commencement of this Act,

shall have effect as if it were an order under section 1 of this Act.

Meaning of "heavy commercial vehicle"

8.—(1) The following are the provisions referred to in subsection (7) of section 138 of this Act which, by virtue of that subsection, are to have effect for the purpose specified in that subsection during a transitional period; and the transitional period referred to in that section is the period beginning with 28th October 1982 and ending with 31st December 1989.

(2) Subject to sub-paragraphs (3) to (6) below, for the purpose and during the transitional period referred to in sub-paragraph (1) above "heavy commercial vehicle" means any vehicle, whether mechanically propelled or not, which is constructed or adapted for the carriage of goods and has an unladen weight exceeding 3 tons.

(3) The Secretary of State may by regulations amend sub-paragraph (2) above in either or both of the following ways, that is to say—

    (a) by substituting, for the reference to unladen weight, a reference to such other description of weight as may be specified in the regulations;

    (b) by substituting, for the reference to 3 tons, a reference to such other weight as may be so specified.

    (4) Different regulations may be made under sub-paragraph (3) above for the purposes of different provisions of this Act and as respects different classes of vehicles or as respects the same class of vehicles in different circumstances and as regards different times of the day or night and as respects roads in different localities.

    (5) Regulations under sub-paragraph (3) above shall not so amend sub-paragraph (2) above that there is in any case in which a vehicle whose unladen weight does not exceed 3 tons is, by virtue of this paragraph, a heavy commercial vehicle for the purposes of any of the provisions of this Act.

    (6) In the application of sub-paragraphs (2) to (5) above to a vehicle drawing one or more trailers, the drawing vehicle and the trailer or trailers shall be treated as one vehicle.

Pedestrian crossings

    9.—(1) Subsections (2) and (3) of section 23 of this Act shall apply in relation to the alteration and removal of crossings established, or having effect as if established, under section 21 of the 1967 Act (whether as that section had effect at any time before the commencement of the Local Government, Planning and Land Act 1980 or as it had effect by virtue of that Act) as they apply in relation to the alteration and removal of crossings established under section 23 of this Act.

    (2) Section 25(6) of this Act shall apply in relation to a crossing established, or having effect as if established—

    (a) by a local authority under section 21 of the 1967 Act (whether as that section had effect at any time before the commencement of the said Act of 1980 or as it had effect by virtue of that Act), or

    (b) by a Minister under section 22 of the 1967 Act,

as it applies in relation to a crossing established by a local authority under section 23 or by the Secretary of State under section 24 of this Act.

Parking places

    10.—(1) The power conferred on a local authority by section 33(7) of this Act shall have effect in relation to an off-street parking place provided by the authority under section 81 of the Road Traffic Act 1960, or under that section as applied by virtue of section 82 of that Act, or under the corresponding provisions of the enactments repealed by that Act, as well as (by virtue of any of the provisions of the Interpretation Act 1978) it has effect in relation to an off-street parking place provided by the authority under section 28 of the 1967 Act.

    (2) Any arrangements for collecting and retaining charges as mentioned in section 33(7) of this Act which were made in respect of any parking place provided under any of the provisions referred to in sub-paragraph (1) above, and which are in force immediately before the commencement of this Act, shall continue to have effect after the repeal by this Act of section 29(9) of the 1967 Act, as if they were arrangements made under section 33(7) of this Act.

    11.—(1) The repeal of this Act of Schedule 8 to the 1967 Act shall not affect the operation of paragraph 9 of that Schedule in relation to orders made before 1st January 1963 under the enactments mentioned in that paragraph (which saved such orders from the effect of the repeal of those enactments by that Act) except that the power to revoke or vary any such order shall be exercisable by an order under section 46 or 49 of this Act.

    (2) Without prejudice to the power of revocation conferred by sub-para-

graph (1) above, an order made by a Minister before 1st January 1963 under section 86 or 87 of the Road Traffic Act 1960 may be revoked by an order of the Secretary of State.

(3) The power to make an order under sub-paragraph (2) above shall be exercisable by statutory instrument which shall be subject to annulment in pursuance of a resolution of either House of Parliament.

12. [. . .]

13. Nothing in [subsections (1) to (38) of section 3B or subsections (1) to (4) of section 35A] of this Act shall affect the Restriction of Ribbon Development (Power to Provide Parking Places) Order 1936, so far as it applies to the City of London, or shall apply to any byelaws having effect as respects the City of London by virtue of that Order; and that Order, so far as it so applies, shall continue to have effect by virtue of this paragraph.

Speed limits

14.—(1) A direction in an order made under section 1 of the Road Traffic Act 1934 that a length of road is to be deemed to be, or not to be, a road in a built-up area, if—

    (a) by virtue of paragraph 10 of Schedule 8 to the 1967 Act it had effect as a direction that that length of road was to become, or (as the case may be) was to cease to be, a restricted road for the purposes of section 71 of that Act, and

    (b) the direction continues so to have effect immediately before the commencement of this Act,

shall have the like effect for the purposes of section 81 of this Act.

(2) Any reference in any provision of an Act, or of any instrument (other than such an order as is mentioned in sub-paragraph (1) above) made under an enactment repealed by the Road Traffic Act 1960, to a road in a built-up area, if the provision is in force immediately before the commencement of this Act, shall be construed as a reference to a restricted road for the purposes of section 81 of this Act.

15. Any limit of speed which was in force on 1st November 1962 by virtue of any direction, order or regulation given or made by an authority under section 19(2), 26 or 34 of the Road Traffic Act 1960, if—

    (a) by virtue of paragraph 12 of Schedule 8 to the 1967 Act it was deemed to have been imposed by an order made by that authority under section 74(1) of the 1967 Act, and

    (b) it continues to be in force immediately before the commencement of this Act

shall be deemed to have been imposed by an order made by that authority under section 84(1) of this Act and may be revoked or varied accordingly.

16.—(1) This paragraph applies to any road which—

    (a) would have become a restricted road for the purposes of section 71 of the 1967 Act on 1st November 1982 as a result of the repeal of section 72(2) of the 1967 Act by section 61 of the Transport Act 1982; but

    (b) by reason of section 61(2) of that Act was taken to have ceased to be a restricted road before that day by virtue of a direction duly given under section 72(3) of the 1967 Act and still in force at the beginning of that day; and

    (c) did not become a restricted road at any time between the beginning of that day and the commencement of this Act.

(2) At the commencement of this Act, any road to which this paragraph applies shall be treated as if it were the subject of a direction duly given under section 82(2)(a) of this Act.

(3) Nothing in sub-paragraph (2) above prevents a direction under section 82(2)(b) of this Act being given in respect of any road to which this paragraph applies.

Saving for agreements and incidental matters

17.—(1) The repeal of this Act by any enactment shall not affect any agreement which, immediately before the commencement of this Act, has effect in pursuance of the enactment, notwithstanding that the enactment is not re-enacted in this Act; and any provision conferring a power to determine disputes or other provision incidental to any such agreement which, immediately before the commencement of this Act, has effect in connection with the agreement shall continue to have effect notwithstanding the repeal.

(2) Without prejudice to the operation of sub-paragraph (1) above in relation to any agreement under subsection (8) of section 34 of the Transport (London) Act 1969 (which relates to agreements consequential upon the transfer of traffic signs and related property and rights to the Greater London Council under subsection (6) of that section), the repeal by this Act of that section (and in particular of subsection (9)) shall not cause that council to be treated for the purposes of the Public Utilities Street Works Act 1950 as the highway authority for any highway for which they would not be the highway authority apart from any such transfer.

(3) Sub-paragraphs (1) and (2) above shall have effect without prejudice to the operation of the preceding provisions of this Schedule, or of any provisions of the Interpretation Act 1978, in relation to an enactment repealed by this Act which is re-enacted in it, with or without modification.

Offences relating to disabled persons' concessions

18. The repeal by this Act of section 2 of the Disabled Persons Act 1981 shall not affect the operation of subsection (2) of that section (which precludes subsection (1) of that section from applying to offences committed before the commencement of that Act) in relation to offences committed before 27th October 1981.

References to "foot passengers" in subordinate legislation

19. For the purposes of the application of any provisions of the Interpretation Act 1978, or of paragraphs 2 to 5 of this Schedule, in relation to any subordinate legislation made, or having effect as if made, under any enactment consolidated by this Act, "foot passengers" shall be taken to have the same meaning as "pedestrians"; and any reference in any such subordinate legislation to foot passengers or to foot passenger traffic shall be construed accordingly.

Statutory statement of facts

20.—(1) Sub-paragraph (2) below shall have effect until the coming into operation of paragraph 3 of Schedule 8 to this Act as if that sub-paragraph were contained in Part II of Schedule 8.

(2) For the purposes of sections 107 to 109 of this Act, a statutory statement of facts is a statement which is in the prescribed form and which either—

    (a) states that the person furnishing it was the driver of the vehicle at the relevant time and is signed by him; or

    (b) states that that person was not the driver of the vehicle at the relevant time, states the name and address at the time the statement is furnished of the person who was the driver of the vehicle at the relevant time and is signed both by the person furnishing it and by the person stated to be the driver of the vehicle at the relevant time.

POLICE AND CRIMINAL EVIDENCE ACT 1984

(1984 c. 60)

Power of constable to stop and search persons, vehicles etc.

B11–01   1.—(1) A constable may exercise any power conferred by this section—

(a) in any place to which at the time when he proposes to exercise the power the public or any section of the public has access, on payment or otherwise, as of right or by virtue of express or implied permission; or

(b) in any other place to which people have ready access at the time when he proposes to exercise the power but which is not a dwelling.

(2) Subject to subsection (3) to (5) below, a constable—

(a) may search—

(i) any person or vehicle;

(ii) anything which is in or on a vehicle,

for stolen or prohibited articles; and

(b) may detain a person or vehicle for the purpose of such a search.

(3) This section does not give a constable power to search a person or vehicle or anything in or on a vehicle unless he has reasonable grounds for suspecting that he will find stolen or prohibited articles.

(4) If a person is in a garden or yard occupied with and used for the purposes of a dwelling or on other land so occupied and used, a constable may not search him in the exercise of the power conferred by this section unless the constable has reasonable grounds for believing—

(a) that he does not reside in the dwelling; and

(b) that he is not in the place in question with the express or implied permission of a person who resides in the dwelling.

(5) If a vehicle is in a garden or yard or other place occupied with and used for the purposes of a dwelling or on other land so occupied and used, a constable may not search the vehicle or anything in or on it in the exercise of the power conferred by this section unless he has reasonable grounds for believing—

(a) that the person in charge of the vehicle does not reside in the dwelling; and

(b) that the vehicle is not in the place in question with the express or implied permission of a person who resides in the dwelling.

(6) If in the course of such a search a constable discovers an article which he has reasonable grounds for suspecting to be a stolen or prohibited article, he may seize it.

(7) An article is prohibited for the purposes of this Part of this Act if it is—

(a) an offensive weapon; or

(b) an article—

(i) made or adapted for use in the course of or in connection with an offence to which this sub-paragraph applies; or

(ii) intended by the person having it with him for such use by him or by some other person.

(8) The offences to which subsection (7)(b)(i) above applies are—

320

(a) burglary;

(b) theft;

(c) offences under section 12 of the Theft Act 1968 (taking motor vehicle or other conveyance without authority); and

(d) offences under section 15 of that Act (obtaining property by deception).

(8A) This subsection applies to any article in relation to which a person has committed, or is committing or is going to commit an offence under section 139 of the Criminal Justice Act 1988.

(9) In this Part of this Act—

"offensive weapon" means any article—

(a) made or adapted for use for causing injury to persons; or

(b) intended by the person having it with him for such use by him or by some other person.

Provisions relating to search under s.1 and other powers

2.—(1) A constable who detains a person or vehicle in the exercise   **B11–02**

(a) of the power conferred by section 1 above; or

(b) of any other power—

(i) to search a person without first arresting him; or

(ii) to search a vehicle without making an arrest,

need not conduct a search if it appears to him subsequently—

(i) that no search is required; or

(ii) that a search is impracticable.

(2) If a constable contemplates a search, other than a search of an unattended vehicle, in the exercise—

(a) of the power conferred by section 1 above; or

(b) of any other power, except the power conferred by section 6 below and the power conferred by section 27(2) of the Aviation Security Act 1982—

(i) to search a person without first arresting him; or

(ii) to search a vehicle without making an arrest,

it shall be his duty, subject to subsection (4) below, to take reasonable steps before he commences the search to bring to the attention of the appropriate person—

(i) if the constable is not in uniform, documentary evidence that he is a constable; and

(ii) whether he is in uniform or not, the matters specified in subsection (3) below,

and the constable shall not commence the search until he has performed that duty.

(3) The matters referred to in subsection (2)(ii) above are—

(a) the constable's name and the name of the police station to which he is attached;

(b) the object of the proposed search;

(c) the constable's grounds for proposing to make it; and

(d) the effect of section 3(7) or (8) below, as may be appropriate.

(4) A constable need not bring the effect of section 3(7) or (8) below to the attention of the appropriate person if it appears to the constable that it will not be practicable to make the record in section 3(1) below.

(5) In this section "the appropriate person" means—

(a) if the constable proposes to search a person, that person; and

(b) if he proposes to search a vehicle, or anything in or on a vehicle, the person in charge of the vehicle.

(6) On completing a search of an unattended vehicle or anything in or on such a vehicle in the exercise of any such power as is mentioned in subsection (2) above a constable shall leave a notice—

  (a) stating that he has searched it;

  (b) giving the name of the police station to which he is attached;

  (c) stating that an application for compensation for any damage caused by the search may be made to that police station; and

  (d) stating the effect of section 3(8) below.

(7) The constable shall leave the notice inside the vehicle unless it is not reasonably practicable to do so without damaging the vehicle.

(8) The time for which a person or vehicle may be detained for the purposes of such a search is such time as is reasonably required to permit a search to be carried out either at the place where the person or vehicle was first detained or nearby.

(9) Neither the power conferred by section 1 above nor any other power to detain and search a person without first arresting him or to detain and search a vehicle without making an arrest is to be construed—

  (a) as authorising a constable to require a person to remove any of his clothing in public other than an outer coat, jacket or gloves; or

  (b) as authorising a constable not in uniform to stop a vehicle.

(10) This section and section 1 above apply to vessels, aircraft and hover-craft as they apply to vehicles.

Duty to make records concerning searches

3.—(1) Where a constable has carried out a search in the exercise of any such power as is mentioned in section 2(1) above, other than a search—

  (a) under section 6 below; or

  (b) under section 27(2) of the Aviation Security Act 1982,

he shall make a record of it in writing unless it is not practicable to do so.

  (2) If—

  (a) a constable is required by subsection (1) above to make a record of a search; but

  (b) it is not practicable to make the record on the spot,

he shall make it as soon as practicable after the completion of the search.

(3) The record of a search of a person shall include a note of his name, if the constable knows it, but a constable may not detain a person to find out his name.

(4) If a constable does not know the name of a person whom he has searched, the record of the search shall include a note otherwise describing that person.

(5) The record of a search of a vehicle shall include a note describing the vehicle.

(6) The record of a search—

  (a) shall state—

    (i) the object of the search;

    (ii) the grounds for making it;

    (iii) the date and time when it was made;

    (iv) the place where it was made;

    (v) whether anything, and if so what, was found;

    (vi) whether any, and if so what, injury to a person or damage to property appears to the constable to have resulted from the search; and

(b) shall identify the constable making it.

(7) If a constable who conducted a search of a person made a record of it, the person who was searched shall be entitled to a copy of the record if he asks for one before the end of the period specified in subsection (9) below.

(8) If—

(a) the owner of a vehicle which has been searched or the person who was in charge of the vehicle at the time when it was searched asks for a copy of the record of the search before the end of the period specified in subsection (9) below; and

(b) the constable who conducted the search made a record of it, the person who made the request shall be entitled to a copy.

(9) The period mentioned in subsections (7) and (8) above is the period of 12 months beginning with the date on which the search was made.

(10) The requirements imposed by this section with regard to records of searches of vehicles shall apply also to records of searches of vessels, aircraft and hovercraft.

Road checks

4.—(1) This section shall have effect in relation to the conduct of road checks   **B11–04** by police officers for the purpose of ascertaining whether a vehicle is carrying—

(a) a person who has committed an offence other than a road traffic offence or a vehicle excise offence;

(b) a person who is a witness to such an offence;

(c) a person intending to commit such an offence; or

(d) a person who is unlawfully at large.

(2) For the purposes of this section a road check consists of the exercise in a locality of the power conferred by section 163 of the Road Traffic Act 1988 in such a way as to stop during the period for which its exercise in that way in that locality continues all vehicles or vehicles selected by any criterion.

(3) Subject to subsection (5) below, there may only be such a road check if a police officer of the rank of superintendent or above authorises it in writing.

(4) An officer may only authorise a road check under subsection (3) above—

(a) for the purpose specified in subsection (1)(a) above, if he has reasonable grounds—

(i) for believing that the offence is a serious arrestable offence; and

(ii) for suspecting that the person is, or is about to be, in the locality in which vehicles would be stopped if the road check were authorised;

(b) for the purpose specified in subsection (1)(b) above, if he has reasonable grounds for believing that the offence is a serious arrestable offence;

(c) for the purpose specified in subsection (1)(c) above, if he has reasonable grounds—

(i) for believing that the offence would be a serious arrestable offence; and

(ii) for suspecting that the person is, or is about to be in the locality in which vehicles would be stopped if the road check were authorised;

(d) for the purpose specified in subsection (1)(d) above, if he has reasonable grounds for suspecting that the person is, or is about to be, in that locality.

(5) An officer below the rank of superintendent may authorise such a road check if it appears to him that it is required as a matter of urgency for one of the purposes specified in subsection (1) above.

(6) If an authorisation is given under subsection (5) above, it shall be the duty of the officer who gives it—

(a) to make a written record of the time at which he gives it; and

(b) to cause an officer of the rank of superintendent or above to be informed that it has been given.

(7) The duties imposed by subsection (6) above shall be performed as soon as it is practicable to do so.

(8) An officer to whom a report is made under subsection (6) above may, in writing, authorise the road check to continue.

(9) If such an officer considers that the road check should not continue, he shall record in writing—

(a) the fact that it took place; and

(b) the purpose for which it took place.

(10) An officer giving an authorisation under this section shall specify the locality in which vehicles are to be stopped.

(11) An officer giving an authorisation under this section, other than an authorisation under subsection (5) above—

(a) shall specify a period, not exceeding seven days, during which the road check may continue; and

(b) may direct that the road check—

(i) shall be continuous; or

(ii) shall be conducted at specified times, during that period.

(12) If it appears to an officer of the rank of superintendent or above that a road check ought to continue beyond the period for which it has been authorised he may, from time to time, in writing specify a further period, not exceeding seven days, during which it may continue.

(13) Every written authorisation shall specify—

(a) the name of the officer giving it;

(b) the purpose of the road check; and

(c) the locality in which vehicles are to be stopped.

(14) The duties to specify the purposes of a road check imposed by subsections (9) and (13) above include duties to specify any relevant serious arrestable offence.

(15) Where a vehicle is stopped in a road check, the person in charge of the vehicle at the time when it is stopped shall be entitled to obtain a written statement of the purpose of the road check, if he applies for such a statement not later than the end of the period of twelve months from the day on which the vehicle was stopped.

(16) Nothing in this section affects the exercise by police officers of any power to stop vehicles for purposes other than those specified in subsection (1) above.

Arrest without warrant for arrestable and other offences

24.—(1) The powers of summary arrest conferred by the following subsections shall apply—

(a) to offences for which the sentence is fixed by law;

(b) to offences for which a person of 21 years of age or over (not previously convicted) may be sentenced to imprisonment for a term of five years (or might be sentenced but for the restrictions imposed by section 33 of the Magistrates' Courts Act 1980); and

   (c) to the offences to which subsection (2) below applies,

and in this Act "arrestable offence" means any such offence.

  (2) The offences to which this subsection applies are—

   (a) offences for which a person may be arrested under the customs and excise Acts, as defined in section 1(1) of the Customs and Excise Management Act 1979;

   (b) offences under the Official Secrets Act 1920 that are not arrestable offences by virtue of the term of imprisonment for which a person may be sentenced in respect of them;

 (bb) offences under any provision of the Official Secrets Act 1989 except section 8(1), (4) or (5);

   (c) offences under section 22 (causing prostitution of women) or 23 (procuration of girl under 21) of the Sexual Offences Act 1956;

   (d) offences under section 12(1) (taking motor vehicle or other conveyance without authority etc.) or 25(1) (going equipped for stealing etc.) of the Theft Act 1968; and

   (e) any offence under the Football (Offences) Act 1991.

   (f) an offence under the Obscene Publications Act 1959 (publication of obscene matter);

   (g) an offence under section 1 of the Protection of Children Act 1978 (indecent photographs and pseudo-photographs of children);

   (h) an offence under section 166 of the Criminal Justice and Public Order Act 1994 (sale of tickets by unauthorised persons);

   (i) an offence under section 19 of the Public Order Act 1986 (publishing, etc. material intended or likely to stir up racial hatred);

   (j) an offence under section 167 of the Criminal Justice and Public Order Act 1994 (touting for car hire services).

  (3) Without prejudice to section 2 of the Criminal Attempts Act 1981, the powers of summary arrest conferred by the following subsections shall also apply to the offences of—

   (a) conspiring to commit any of the offences mentioned in subsection (2) above;

   (b) attempting to commit any such offence other than an offence under section 12(1) of the Theft Act 1968;

   (c) inciting, aiding, abetting, counselling or procuring the commission of any such offence,

and such offences are also arrestable offences for the purposes of this Act.

  (4) Any person may arrest without a warrant—

   (a) anyone who is in the act of committing an arrestable offence;

   (b) anyone whom he has reasonable grounds for suspecting to be committing such an offence.

  (5) Where an arrestable offence has been committed, any person may arrest without a warrant—

   (a) anyone who is guilty of the offence;

   (b) anyone whom he has reasonable grounds for suspecting to be guilty of it.

  (6) Where a constable has reasonable grounds for suspecting that an arrestable offence has been committed, he may arrest without a warrant anyone whom he has reasonable grounds for suspecting to be guilty of the offence.

  (7) A constable may arrest without a warrant—

   (a) anyone who is about to commit an arrestable offence;

(b) anyone whom he has reasonable grounds for suspecting to be about to commit an arrestable offence.

General arrest conditions

B11–06 **25.**—(1) Where a constable has reasonable grounds for suspecting that any offence which is not an arrestable offence has been committed or attempted, or is being committed or attempted, he may arrest the relevant person if it appears to him that service of a summons is impracticable or inappropriate because any of the general arrest conditions is satisfied.

(2) In this section, "the relevant person" means any person whom the constable has reasonable grounds to suspect of having committed or having attempted to commit the offence or of being in the course of committing or attempting to commit it.

(3) The general arrest conditions are—

(a) that the name of the relevant person is unknown to, and cannot be readily ascertained by, the constable;

(b) that the constable has reasonable grounds for doubting whether a name furnished by the relevant person as his name is his real name;

(c) that—

(i) the relevant person has failed to furnish a satisfactory address for service; or

(ii) the constable has reasonable grounds for doubting whether an address furnished by the relevant person is a satisfactory address for service;

(d) that the constable has reasonable grounds for believing that arrest is necessary to prevent the relevant person—

(i) causing physical harm to himself or any other person;

(ii) suffering physical injury;

(iii) causing loss of or damage to property;

(iv) committing an offence against public decency; or

(v) causing an unlawful obstruction of the highway;

(e) that the constable has reasonable grounds for believing that arrest is necessary to protect a child or other vulnerable person from the relevant person.

(4) For the purposes of subsection (3) above an address is a satisfactory address for service if it appears to the constable—

(a) that the relevant person will be at it for a sufficiently long period for it to be possible to serve him with a summons; or

(b) that some other person specified by the relevant person will accept service of a summons for the relevant person at it.

(5) Nothing in subsection (3)(d) above authorises the arrest of a person under sub-paragraph (iv) of that paragraph except where members of the public going about their normal business cannot reasonably be expected to avoid the person to be arrested.

(6) This section shall not prejudice any power of arrest conferred apart from this section.

Repeal of statutory powers of arrest without warrant or order

B11–07 **26.**—(1) Subject to subsection (2) below, so much of any Act (including a local Act) passed before this Act as enables a constable—

(a) to arrest a person for an offence without a warrant; or

(b) to arrest a person otherwise than for an offence without a warrant or an order of a court,

shall cease to have effect.

(2) Nothing in subsection (1) above affects the enactments specified in Schedule 2 to this Act.

Arrest for further offence

31. Where—   **B11–08**
    (a) a person—
        (i) has been arrested for an offence; and
        (ii) is at a police station in consequence of that arrest; and
    (b) it appears to a constable that, if he were released from that arrest, he would be liable to arrest for some other offence,

he shall be arrested for that other offence.

Limitations on police detention

34.—(1) A person arrested for an offence shall not be kept in police deten-   **B11–09**
tion except in accordance with the provisions of this Part of this Act.

(2) Subject to subsection (3) below, if at any time a custody officer—
    (a) becomes aware, in relation to any person in police detention, that the grounds for the detention of that person have ceased to apply; and
    (b) is not aware of any other grounds on which the continued detention of that person could be justified under the provisions of this Part of this Act,

it shall be the duty of the custody officer, subject to subsection (4) below, to order his immediate release from custody.

(3) No person in police detention shall be released except on the authority of a custody officer at the police station where his detention was authorised or, if it was authorised at more than one station, a custody officer at the station where it was last authorised.

(4) A person who appears to the custody officer to have been unlawfully at large when he was arrested is not to be released under subsection (2) above.

(5) A person whose release is ordered under subsection (2) above shall be released without bail unless it appears to the custody officer—
    (a) that there is need for further investigation of any matter in connection with which he was detained at any time during the period of his deten-tion; or
    (b) that proceedings may be taken against him in respect of any such matter,

and if it so appears, he shall be released on bail.

(6) for the purposes of this Part of this Act a person arrested under section 6(5) of the Road Traffic Act 1988 is arrested for an offence.

(7) For the purposes of this Part of this Act a person who returns to a police station to answer to bail or is arrested under section 46A below shall be treated as arrested for an offence and the offence in connection with which he was granted bail shall be deemed to be that offence.

Custody officers at police stations

36.—(1) One or more custody officers shall be appointed for each desig-   **B11–10**
nated police station.

327

(2) A custody officer for a designated police station shall be appointed—

(a) by the chief officer of police for the area in which the designated police station is situated; or

(b) by such other police officer as the chief officer of police for that area may direct.

(3) No officer may be appointed a custody officer unless he is of at least the rank of sergeant.

(4) An officer of any rank may perform the functions of a custody officer at a designated police station if a custody officer is not readily available to perform them.

(5) Subject to the following provisions of this section and to section 39(2) below, none of the functions of a custody officer in relation to a person shall be performed by an officer who at the time when the function falls to be performed is involved in the investigation of an offence for which that person is in police detention at that time.

(6) Nothing in subsection (5) above is to be taken to prevent a custody officer—

(a) performing any function assigned to custody officers—

(i) by this Act;

(ii) by a code of practice issued under this Act;

(b) carrying out the duty imposed on custody officers by section 39 below;

(c) doing anything in connection with the identification of a suspect; or

(d) doing anything under sections 7 or 8 of the Road Traffic Act 1988.

(7) Where an arrested person is taken to a police station which is not a designated police station, the functions in relation to him which at a designated police station would be the functions of a custody officer shall be performed—

(a) by an officer who is not involved in the investigation of an offence for which he is in police detention, if such an officer is readily available; and

(b) if no such officer is readily available, by the officer who took him to the station or any other officer.

(8) References to a custody officer in the following provisions of this Act include references to an officer other than a custody officer who is performing the functions of a custody officer by virtue of subsection (4) or (7) above.

(9) Where by virtue of subsection (7) above an officer of a force maintained by a police authority who took an arrested person to a police station is to perform the functions of a custody officer in relation to him, the officer shall inform an officer who—

(a) is attached to a designated police station; and

(b) is of at least the rank of inspector,

that he is to do so.

(10) The duty imposed by subsection (9) above shall be performed as soon as it is practicable to perform it.

Duties of custody officer before charge

B11–11   37.—(1) Where

(a) a person is arrested for an offence—

(i) without a warrant; or

(ii) under a warrant not endorsed for bail, or

(b) [*Repealed.*]

(2) If the custody officer determines that he does not have such evidence before him, the person arrested shall be released either on bail or without bail,

unless the custody officer has reasonable grounds for believing that his detention without being charged is necessary to secure or preserve evidence relating to an offence for which he is under arrest or to obtain such evidence by questioning him.

(3) If the custody officer has reasonable grounds for so believing, he may authorise the person arrested to be kept in police detention.

(4) Where a custody officer authorises a person who has not been charged to be kept in police detention, he shall, as soon as is practicable, make a written record of the grounds for the detention.

(5) Subject to subsection (6) below, the written record shall be made in the presence of the person arrested who shall at that time be informed by the custody officer of the grounds for his detention.

(6) Subsection (5) above shall not apply where the person arrested is, at the time when the written record is made—

(a) incapable of understanding what is said to him;

(b) violent or likely to become violent; or

(c) in urgent need of medical attention.

(7) Subject to section 41(7) below, if the custody officer determines that he has before him sufficient evidence to charge the person arrested with the offence for which he was arrested, the person arrested—

(a) shall be charged; or

(b) shall be released without charge, either on bail or without bail.

(8) Where—

(a) a person is released under subsection (7)(b) above, and

(b) at the time of his release a decision whether he should be prosecuted for the offence for which he was arrested has not been taken,

it shall be the duty of the custody officer so to inform him.

(9) If the person arrested is not in a fit state to be dealt with under subsection (7) above, he may be kept in police detention until he is.

(10) The duty imposed on the custody officer under subsection (1) above shall be carried out by him as soon as practicable after the person arrested arrives at the police station or, in the case of a person arrested at the police station, as soon as practicable after the arrest.

(15) In this Part of this Act—

"arrested juvenile" means a person arrested with or without a warrant who appears to be under the age of 17...

"endorsed for bail" means endorsed with a direction for bail in accordance with section 117(2) of the Magistrates' Courts Act 1980.

Limits on period of detention without charge

41.—(1) Subject to the following provisions of this section and to sections 42 and 43 below, a person shall not be kept in police detention for more than 24 hours without being charged.   **B11–12**

(2) The time from which the period of detention of a person is to be calculated (in this Act referred to as "the relevant time")—

(a) in the case of a person to whom this section applies, shall be—

(i) the time at which that person arrives at the relevant police station, or

(ii) the time 24 hours after the time of that person's arrest, whichever is the earlier;

(b) in the case of a person arrested outside England and Wales, shall be

(i) the time at which that person arrives at the first police station to

which he is taken in the police area in England or Wales in which the offence for which he was arrested is being investigated; or
  (ii) the time 24 hours after the time of that person's entry into England and Wales, whichever is the earlier.
(c) in the case of a person who—
  (i) attends voluntarily at a police station; or
  (ii) accompanies a constable to a police station without having been arrested,
and is arrested at the police station, the time of his arrest;
  (d) in any other case, except when subsection (5) below applies, shall be the time at which the person arrested arrives at the first police station to which he is taken after his arrest.
(3) Subsection (2)(a) above applies to a person if—
  (a) his arrest is sought in one police area in England and Wales;
  (b) he is arrested in another police area; and
  (c) he is not questioned in the area in which he is arrested in order to obtain evidence in relation to an offence for which he is arrested,
and in sub-paragraph (i) of that paragraph "the relevant police station" means the first police station to which he is taken in the police area in which his arrest was sought.
(4) Subsection (2) above shall have effect in relation to a person arrested under section 31 above as if every reference in it to his arrest or his being arrested were a reference to his arrest or his being arrested for the offence for which he was originally arrested.
(5) If—
  (a) a person is in police detention in a police area in England and Wales ("the first area"); and
  (b) his arrest for an offence is sought in some other police area in England and Wales ("the second area"); and
  (c) he is taken to the second area for the purposes of investigating that offence, without being questioned in the first area in order to obtain evidence in relation to it,
the relevant time shall be—
  (i) the time 24 hours after he leaves the place where he is detained in the first area; or
  (ii) the time at which he arrives at the first police station to which he is taken in the second area,
whichever is the earlier.
(6) When a person who is in police detention is removed to hospital because he is in need of medical treatment, any time during which he is being quest- ioned in hospital or on the way there or back by a police officer for the purpose of obtaining evidence relating to an offence shall be included in any period which falls to be calculated for the purposes of this Part of this Act, but any other time while he is in hospital or on his way there or back shall not be so included.
(7) Subject to subsection (8) below, a person who at the expiry of 24 hours after the relevant time is in police detention and has not been charged shall be released at that time either on bail or without bail.
(8) Subsection (7) above does not apply to a person whose detention for more than 24 hours after the relevant time has been authorised or is otherwise permitted in accordance with section 42 or 43 below.
(9) A person released under subsection (7) above shall not be rearrested without a warrant for the offence for which he was previously arrested unless new evidence justifying a further arrest has come to light since his release; but this does not prevent an arrest under section 46A below.

Access to legal advice

58.—(1) A person arrested and held in custody in a police station or other   **B11–13**
premises shall be entitled if he so requests, to consult a solicitor privately at
any time.

(2) Subject to subsection (3) below, a request under subsection (1) above and
the time at which it was made shall be recorded in the custody record.

(3) Such a request need not be recorded in the custody record of a person
who makes it at a time while he is at a court after being charged with an
offence.

(4) If a person makes such a request, he must be permitted to consult a solicitor as soon as is practicable except to the extent that delay is permitted by this
section.

(5) In any case he must be permitted to consult a solicitor within 36 hours
from the relevant time, as defined in section 41(2) above.

(6) Delay in compliance with a request is only permitted—

    (a) in the case of the person who is in police detention for a serious arres-
        table offence; and

    (b) if an officer of at least the rank of superintendent authorises it.

(7) An officer may give an authorisation under subsection (6) above orally
or in writing but, if he gives it orally, he shall confirm it in writing as soon as is
practicable.

(8) Subject to section 8A below an officer may only authorise delay where he
has reasonable grounds for believing that the exercise of the right conferred by
subsection (1) above at the time when the person detained desires to exercise
it—

    (a) will lead to interference with or harm to evidence connected with a
        serious arrestable offence or interference with or physical injury to
        other persons; or

    (b) will lead to the alerting of other persons suspected of having commit-
        ted such an offence but not yet arrested for it; or

    (c) will hinder the recovery of any property obtained as a result of such an
        offence.

(8A) An officer may also authorise delay where the serious arrestable
offence is a drug trafficking offence or an offence to which Part VI of the
Criminal Justice Act 1988 applies and the officer has reasonable grounds for
believing—

    (a) where the offence is a drug trafficking offence, that the detained per-
        son has benefited from drug trafficking and that the recovery of the
        value of that person's proceeds of drug trafficking will be hindered by
        the exercise of the rights conferred by subsection (1) above; and

    (b) where the offence is one to which Part VI of the Criminal Justice Act
        1988 applies, that the detained person has benefited from the offence
        and that the recovery of the value of the property obtained by that per-
        son from or in connection with the offence or of the pecuniary advan-
        tage derived by him from or in connection with it will be hindered by
        the exercise of the right conferred by subsection (1) above.

(9) If delay is authorised—

    (a) the person in police detention shall be told the reason for it; and

    (b) the reason shall be noted on his custody record.

(10) The duties imposed by subsection (9) above shall be performed as soon
as is practicable.

(11) There may be no further delay in permitting the exercise of the right
conferred by subsection (1) above once the reason for authorising delay ceases
to subsist.

(12) The reference in subsection (1) above to a person arrested includes a reference to a person who has been detained under the terrorism provisions.

(13) In the application of this section to a person who has been arrested or detained under the terrorism provisions—

    (a) subsection (5) above shall have effect as if for the words from "within" onwards there were substituted the words "before the end of the period beyond which he may no longer be detained without the authority of the Secretary of State";

    (b) subsection (6)(a) above shall have effect as if for the words "for a serious arrestable offence" there were substituted the words "under the terrorism provisions"; and

    (c) subsection (8) above shall have effect as if at the end there were added "or

    (d) will lead to interference with the gathering of information about the commission, preparation or instigation of acts of terrorism; or

    (e) by alerting any person, will make it more difficult—

        (i) to prevent an act of terrorism; or

        (ii) to secure the apprehension, prosecution or conviction of any person in connection with the commission, preparation or instigation of an act of terrorism."

(14) If an officer of appropriate rank has reasonable grounds for believing that, unless he gives a direction under subsection (15) below, the exercise by a person arrested or detained under the terrorism provisions of the right conferred by subsection (1) above will have any of the consequences specified in subsection (8) above (as it has effect by virtue of subsection (13) above), he may give a direction under that subsection.

(15) A direction under this subsection is a direction that a person desiring to exercise the right conferred by subsection (1) above may only consult a solicitor in the sight and hearing of a qualified officer of the uniformed branch of the force of which the officer giving the direction is a member.

(16) An officer is qualified for the purpose of subsection (15) above if—

    (a) he is of at least the rank of inspector; and

    (b) in the opinion of the officer giving the direction he has no connection with the case.

(17) An officer is of appropriate rank to give a direction under subsection (15) above if he is of at least the rank of Commander or Assistant Chief Constable.

(18) A direction under subsection (15) above shall cease to have effect once the reason for giving it ceases to subsist.

Confessions

76.—(1) In any proceedings a confession made by an accused person may be given in evidence against him in so far as it is relevant to any matter in issue in the proceedings and is not excluded by the court in pursuance of this section.

(2) If, in any proceedings where the prosecution proposes to given in evidence a confession made by an accused person, it is represented to the court that the confession was or may have been obtained—

    (a) by oppression of the person who made it; or

    (b) in consequence of anything said or done which was likely, in the circumstances existing at the time, to render unreliable any confession which might be made by him in consequence thereof,

the court shall not allow the confession to be given in evidence against him except in so far as the prosecution proves to the court beyond reasonable doubt that the confession (notwithstanding that it may be true) was not obtained as aforesaid.

(3) In any proceedings where the prosecution proposes to give in evidence a confession made by an accused person, the court may of its own motion require the prosecution, as a condition of allowing it to do so, to prove that the confession was not obtained as mentioned in subsection (2) above.

(4) The fact that a confession is wholly or partly excluded in pursuance of this section shall not affect the admissibility in evidence—

    (a) of any facts discovered as a result of the confession; or

    (b) where the confession is relevant as showing that the accused speaks, writes or expresses himself in a particular way, of so much of the confession as is necessary to show that he does so.

(5) Evidence that a fact to which this subsection applies was discovered as a result of a statement made by an accused person shall not be admissible unless evidence of how it was discovered is given by him or on his behalf.

(6) Subsection (5) above applies—

    (a) to any fact discovered as a result of a confession which is wholly excluded in pursuance of this section; and

    (b) to any fact discovered as a result of a confession which is partly so excluded, if that fact is discovered as a result of the excluded part of the confession.

(7) Nothing in Part VII of this Act shall prejudice the admissibility of a confession made by an accused person.

(8) In this section "oppression" includes torture, inhuman or degrading treatment, and the use or threat of violence (whether or not amounting to torture).

Confessions by mentally handicapped persons

77.—(1) Without prejudice to the general duty of the court at a trial on   **B11–15** indictment to direct the jury on any matter on which it appears to the court appropriate to do so, where at such a trial—

    (a) the case against the accused depends wholly or substantially on a confession by him; and

    (b) the court is satisfied—

        (i) that he is mentally handicapped; and

        (ii) that the confession was not made in the presence of an independent person,

the court shall warn the jury that there is special need for caution before convicting the accused in reliance on the confession, and shall explain that the need arises because of the circumstances mentioned in paragraphs (a) and (b) above.

(2) In any case where at the summary trial of a person for an offence it appears to the court that a warning under subsection (1) above would be required if the trial were on indictment, the court shall treat the case as one in which there is a special need for caution before convicting the accused on his confession.

(3) In this section—

      "independent person" does not include a police officer or a person employed for, or engaged on, police purposes;

      "mentally handicapped", in relation to a person, means that he is in a state of arrested or incomplete development of mind which includes significant impairment of intelligence and social functioning; and "police purposes" has the meaning assigned to it by section 64 of the Police Act 1964.

Exclusion of unfair evidence

B11–16   78.—(1) In any proceedings the court may refuse to allow evidence on which the prosecution purposes to rely to be given if it appears to the court that, having regard to all the circumstances, including the circumstances in which the evidence was obtained, the admission of the evidence would have such an adverse effect on the fairness of the proceedings that the court ought not to admit it.

(2) Nothing in this section shall prejudice any rule of law requiring a court to exclude evidence.

Time for taking accused's evidence

B11–17   79. If at the trial of any person for an offence—
   (a) the defence intends to call two or more witnesses to the facts of the case; and
   (b) those witnesses include the accused,
the accused shall be called before the other witnesses unless the court in its discretion otherwise directs.

Interpretation of Part VIII

B11–18   82.—(1) In this Part of this Act—
   "confession" includes any statement wholly or partly adverse to the person who made it, whether made to a person in authority or not and whether made in words or otherwise;
   "court-martial" means a court-martial constituted under the Army Act 1955, the Air Force Act 1955 or the Naval Discipline Act 1957 or a disciplinary court constituted under section 50 of the said Act of 1957;
   "proceedings" means criminal proceedings, including—
      (a) proceedings in the United Kingdom or elsewhere before a court-martial constituted under the Army Act 1955 or the Air Force Act 1955;
      (b) proceedings in the United Kingdom or elsewhere before the Courts-Martial Appeal Court—
         (i) on an appeal from a court-martial so constituted or from a court-martial constituted under the Naval Discipline Act 1957; or
         (ii) on a reference under section 34 of the Courts Martial (Appeals) Act 1968; and
      (c) proceedings before a Standing Civilian Court; and
   "Service court" means a court-martial or a Standing Civilian Court.
(2) In this Part of this Act references to conviction before a Service court are references—
   (a) as regards a court-martial constituted under the Army Act 1955 or the

Air Force Act 1955, to a finding of guilty which is, or falls to be treated as, a finding of the court duly confirmed;
(b) as regards—
   (i) a court-martial; or
   (ii) a disciplinary court,
constituted under the Naval Discipline Act 1957, to a finding of guilty which is, or falls to be treated as, the finding of the court;
and "convicted" shall be construed accordingly.

(3) Nothing in this Part of this Act shall prejudice any power of a court to exclude evidence (whether by preventing questions from being put or otherwise) at its discretion.

Meaning of "serious arrestable offence"

116.—(1) This section has effect for determining whether an offence is a seri-   **B11–19**
ous arrestable offence for the purposes of this Act.

(2) The following arrestable offences are always serious—
(a) an offence (whether at common law or under any enactment) specified in Part I of Schedule 5 to this Act; and
(b) an offence under an enactment specified in Part II of that Schedule; and
(c) any of the offences mentioned in paragraphs (a) to (f) of section 1(3) of the Drug Trafficking Act 1994.

(3) Subject to subsections (4) and (5) below, any other arrestable offence is serious only if its commission—
(a) has led to any of the consequences specified in subsection (6) below; or
(b) is intended to lead to any of those consequences.

(4) An arrestable offence which consists of making a threat is serious if carrying out the threat would be likely to lead to any of the consequences specified in subsection (6) below.

(5) An offence under section 2, 8, 9, 10 or 11 of the Prevention of Terrorism (Temporary Provisions) Act 1989 is always a serious arrestable offence for the purposes of section 56 or 58 above, and an attempt or conspiracy to commit any such offence is also always a serious arrestable offence for those purposes.

(6) The consequences mentioned in subsections (3) and (4) above are—
(a) serious harm to the security of the State or to public order;
(b) serious interference with the administration of justice or with the investigation of offences or of a particular offence;
(c) the death of any person;
(d) serious injury to any person;
(e) substantial financial gain to any person; and
(f) serious financial loss to any person.

(7) Loss is serious for the purposes of this section if, having regard to all the circumstances, it is serious for the person who suffers it.

(8) In this section "injury" includes any disease and any impairment of a person's physical or mental condition.

SCHEDULE 5

PART II

OFFENCES MENTIONED IN SECTION 116(2)(*b*)

Explosive Substances Act 1883 (*c.* 3)

B11–20 1. Section 2 (causing explosion likely to endanger life or property).

Sexual Offences Act 1956 (*c.* 69)

2. Section 5 (intercourse with a girl under the age of 13).

Firearms Act 1968 (*c.* 27)

3. Section 16 (possession of firearm with intent to injure).
4. Section 17(1) (use of firearms and imitation firearms to resist arrest).
5. Section 18 (carrying firearms with criminal intent).

Road Traffic Act 1972 (*c.* 20)

6. [Repealed by the Road Traffic (Consequential Provisions) Act 1988, Sched. 1.]

Taking of Hostages Act 1982 (*c.* 28)

7. Section I (hostage-taking).

Aviation Security Act 1982 (*c.* 36)

8. Section I (hijacking).

Criminal Justice Act 1988 (*c.* 33)

9. Section 134 (torture).

Road Traffic Act 1988 (*c.* 52)

10. Section 1 (causing death by dangerous driving).
    Section 3A (causing death by careless driving when under the influence of drink or drugs).

Aviation and Maritime Security Act 1990 (*c.* 31)

11. Section 1 (endangering safety at aerodromes).
12. Section 9 (hijacking of ships).
13. Section 10 (seizing or exercising of control of fixed platforms).

Protection of Children Act 1978 (*c.* 37)

14. Section 1 (indecent photographs and pseudo-photographs of children).

Obscene Publications Act 1959 (*c.* 66)

15. Section 2 (publication of obscene matter).

PROSECUTION OF OFFENCES ACT 1985

(1985 c. 23)

Functions of the Director

3.—(1) The Director shall discharge his functions under this or any other 　**B12–01**
enactment under the superintendence of the Attorney General.

(2) It shall be the duty of the Director, subject to any provisions contained in
the Criminal Justice Act 1967—

(a) to take over the conduct of all criminal proceedings, other than specified proceedings, instituted on behalf of a police force (whether by a
member of that force or by any other person);

(b) to institute and have the conduct of criminal proceedings in any case
where it appears to him that—

(i) the importance or difficulty of the case makes it appropriate that
proceedings should be instituted by him; or

(ii) it is otherwise appropriate for proceedings to be instituted by him;

(c) to take over the conduct of all binding over proceedings instituted on
behalf of a police force (whether by a member of that force or by any
other person);

(d) to take over the conduct of all proceedings begun by summons issued
under section 3 of the Obscene Publications Act 1959 (forfeiture of
obscene articles);

(e) to give, to such extent as he considers appropriate, advice to police
forces on all matters relating to criminal offences;

(f) to appear for the prosecution, when directed by the court to do so, on
any appeal under—

(i) section 1 of the Administration of Justice Act 1960 (appeal from
the High Court in criminal cases);

(ii) Part I or Part II of the Criminal Appeal Act 1968 (appeals from the
Crown Court to the criminal division of the Court of Appeal and
thence to the House of Lords); or

(iii) section 108 of the Magistrates' Courts Act 1980 (right of appeal to
Crown Court) as it applies, by virtue of subsection (5) of section 12
of the Contempt of Court Act 1981, to orders made under section
12 (contempt of magistrates' courts); and

(g) to discharge such other functions as may from time to time be assigned
to him by the Attorney General in pursuance of this paragraph.

(3) In this section—

"the court" means—

(a) in the case of an appeal to or from the criminal division of the
Court of Appeal, that division;

(b) in the case of an appeal from a Divisional Court of the Queen's
Bench Division, the Divisional Court; and

(c) in the case of an appeal against an order of a magistrates' court,
the Crown Court;

"police force" means any police force maintained by a police authority
under the Police Act 1964 and any other body of constables for the
time being specified by order made by the Secretary of State for the
purposes of this section; and

"specified proceedings" means proceedings which fall within any category for the time being specified by order made by the Attorney General for the purposes of this section.

(4) The power to make orders under subsection (3) above shall be exercisable by statutory instrument subject to annulment in pursuance of a resolution of either House of Parliament.

Defence costs

16.—(1) Where—

(a) an information laid before a justice of the peace of any area, charging any person with an offence, is not proceeded with;

(b) a magistrates' court determines not to transfer for trial proceedings for an indictable offence;

(c) a magistrates' court dealing summarily with an offence dismisses the information;

the court or, in a case falling within paragraph (a) above, a magistrates' court for that area, may make an order in favour of the accused for a payment to be made out of central funds in respect of his costs (a "defendant's costs order").

(2) Where—

(a) any person is not tried for an offence for which he has been indicted or in respect of which proceedings against him have been transferred for trial; or

(aa) a notice of transfer is given under a relevant transfer provision but a person in relation to whose case it is given is not tried on a charge to which it relates; or

(b) any person is tried on indictment and acquitted on any count in the indictment;

the Crown Court may make a defendant's costs order in favour of the accused.

(3) Where a person convicted of an offence by a magistrates' court appeals to the Crown Court under section 108 of the Magistrates' Courts Act 1980 (right to appeal against conviction or sentence) and, in consequence of the decision on appeal—

(a) his conviction is set aside; or

(b) a less severe punishment is awarded;

the Crown Court may make a defendant's costs order in favour of the accused.

(4) Where the Court of Appeal—

(a) allows an appeal under Part I of the Criminal Appeal Act 1968 against—

(i) conviction;

(ii) a verdict of not guilty by reason of insanity; or

(iii) a finding under section 4 of the Criminal Procedure (Insanity) Act 1964 that the appellant is under disability;

(aa) directs under section 8(1B) of the Criminal Appeal Act 1968 the entry of a judgment and verdict of acquittal;

(b) on an appeal under that Part against conviction—

(i) substitutes a verdict of guilty of another offence;

(ii) in a case where a special verdict has been found, orders a different conclusion on the effect of that verdict to be recorded; or

(iii) is of the opinion that the case falls within paragraph (a) or (b) of section 6(1) of that Act (cases where the court substitutes a finding of insanity or unfitness to plead); or

(c) on an appeal under that Part against sentence, exercises its powers under section 11(3) of that Act (powers where the court considers that the

appellant should be sentenced differently for an offence for which he was dealt with by the court below);
the court may make a defendant's costs order in favour of the accused.

(4A) The court may also make a defendant's cost order in favour of the accused on an appeal under section 9(11) of the Criminal Justice Act 1987 (appeals against orders or rulings at preparatory hearings).

(5) Where—

   (a) any proceedings in a criminal cause or matter are determined before a Divisional Court of the Queen's Bench Division;
   (b) the House of Lords determines an appeal, or application for leave to appeal, from such a Divisional Court in a criminal cause or matter;
   (c) the Court of Appeal determines an application for leave to appeal to the House of Lords under Part II of the Criminal Appeal Act 1968; or
   (d) the House of Lords determines an appeal, or application for leave to appeal, under Part II of that Act;

the court may make a defendant's costs order in favour of the accused.

(6) A defendant's costs order shall, subject to the following provisions of this section, be for the payment out of central funds, to the person whose favour the order is made, of such amount as the court considers reasonably sufficient to compensate him for any expenses properly incurred by him in the proceedings.

(7) Where a court makes a defendant's costs orders but is of the opinion that there are circumstances which make it inappropriate that the person in whose favour the order is made should recover the full amount mentioned in subsection (6) above, the court shall—

   (a) assess what amount would, in its opinion, be just and reasonable; and
   (b) specify that amount in the order.

(8) [...]

(9) Subject to subsection (7) above, the amount to be paid out of central funds in pursuance of a defendant's costs order shall—

   (a) be specified in the order, in any case where the court considers it appropriate for the amount to be so specified and the person in whose favour the order is made agrees the amount; and
   (b) in any other case, be determined in accordance with regulations made by the Lord Chancellor for the purposes of this section.

(10) Subsection (6) above shall have effect, in relation to any case falling within subsection (1)(a) or (2)(a) above, as if for the words "in the proceedings" there were substituted the words "in or about the defence".

(11) Where a person ordered to be retried is acquitted at his retrial, the costs which may be ordered to be paid out of central funds under this section shall include—

   (a) any costs which, at the original trial, could have been ordered to be so paid under this section if he had been acquitted; and
   (b) if no order was made under this section in respect of his expenses on appeal, any sums for the payment of which such an order could have been made.

(12) In subsection (2)(aa) "relevant transfer provision" means—

   (a) section 4 of the Criminal Justice Act 1987, or
   (b) section 53 of the Criminal Justice Act 1991.

Prosecution costs

17.—(1) Subject to subsection (2) below, the court may—   **B12–03**

(a) in any proceedings in respect of an indictable offence; and

(b) in any proceedings before a Divisional Court of the Queen's Bench Division or the House of Lords in respect of a summary offence;

order the payment out of central funds of such amount as the court considers reasonably sufficient to compensate the prosecutor for any expenses properly incurred by him in the proceedings.

(2) No order under this section may be made in favour of—

(a) a public authority; or

(b) a person acting—

(i) on behalf of a public authority; or

(ii) in his capacity as an official appointed by such an authority.

(3) Where a court makes an order under this section but is of the opinion that there are circumstances which make it inappropriate that the prosecution should recover the full amount mentioned in subsection (1) above, the court shall—

(a) assess what amount would, in its opinion, be just and reasonable; and

(b) specify that amount in the order.

(4) Subject to subsection (3) above, the amount to be paid out of central funds in pursuance of an order under this section shall—

(a) be specified in the order, in any case where the court considers it appropriate for the amount to be so specified and the prosecutor agrees the amount; and

(b) in any other case, be determined in accordance with regulations made by the Lord Chancellor for the purposes of this section.

(5) Where the conduct of proceedings to which subsection (1) above applies is taken over by the Crown Prosecution Service, that subsection shall have effect as if it referred to the prosecutor who had the conduct of the proceedings before the intervention of the Service and to expenses incurred by him up to the time of intervention.

(6) In this section "public authority" means—

(a) a police force within the meaning of section 3 of this Act;

(b) the Crown Prosecution Service or any other government department;

(c) a local authority or other authority or body constituted for purposes of—

(i) the public service or of local government; or

(ii) carrying on under national ownership any industry or undertaking or part of an industry or undertaking; or

(d) any other authority or body whose members are appointed by Her Majesty or by any Minister of the Crown or government department or whose revenues consist wholly or mainly of money provided by Parliament.

Award of costs against accused

18.—(1) Where—

(a) any person is convicted of an offence before a magistrates' court;

(b) the Crown Court dismisses an appeal against such a conviction or against the sentence imposed on that conviction; or

(c) any person is convicted of an offence before the Crown Court;

the court may make such order as to the costs to be paid by the accused to the prosecutor as it considers just and reasonable.

(2) Where the Court of Appeal dismisses—

(a) an appeal or application for leave to appeal under Part I of the Criminal Appeal Act 1968; or

   (b) an application by the accused for leave to appeal to the House of Lords under Part II of that Act;

   (c) an appeal or application for leave to appeal under section 9(11) of the Criminal Justice Act 1987;

it may make such order as to the costs to be paid by the accused, to such person as may be named in the order, as it considers just and reasonable.

   (3) The amount to be paid by the accused in pursuance of an order under this section shall be specified in the order.

   (4) Where any person is convicted of an offence before a magistrates' court and—

   (a) under the conviction the court orders payment of any sum as a fine, penalty, forfeiture or compensation; and

   (b) the sum so ordered to be paid does not exceed £5;

the court shall not order the accused to pay any costs under this section unless in the particular circumstances of the case it considers it right to do so.

   (5) Where any person under the age of eighteen is convicted of an offence before a magistrates' court, the amount of any costs ordered to be paid by the accused under this section shall not exceed the amount of any fine imposed on him.

   (6) Costs ordered to be paid under subsection (2) above may include the reasonable cost of any transcript of a record of proceedings made in accordance with rules of court made for the purposes of section 32 of the Act of 1968.

Provisions for orders as to costs in other circumstances

   19.—(1) The Lord Chancellor may by regulations make provision   **B12–05** empowering magistrates' courts, the Crown Court and the Court of Appeal, in any case where the court is satisfied that one party to criminal proceedings has incurred costs as a result of an unnecessary or improper act or omission by, or on behalf of, another party to the proceedings, to make an order as to the payment of those costs.

   (2) Regulationss made under subsection (1) above may, in particular—

   (a) allow the making of such an order at any time during the proceedings;

   (b) make provision as to the account to be taken, in making such an order, of any other order as to costs ... which has been made in respect of the proceedings which has been made under the Legal Aid Act 1988;

   (c) make provision as to the account to be taken of any such order in the making of any other order as to costs in respect of the proceedings; and

   (d) contain provisions similar to those in section 18(4) and (5) of this Act.

   (3) The Lord Chancellor may by regulations make provision for the payment out of central funds, in such circumstances and in relation to such criminal proceedings as may be specified, of such sums as appear to the court to be reasonably necessary—

   (a) to compensate any witness in the proceedings for the expense, trouble or loss of time properly incurred in or incidental to his attendance;

   (b) to cover the proper expenses of an interpreter who is required because of the accused's lack of English;

   (c) to compensate a duly qualified medical practitioner who—

     (i) makes a report otherwise than in writing for the purpose of section 30 of the Magistrates' Court Act 1980 (remand for medical examination); or

     (ii) makes a written report to a court in pursuance of a request to which section 32(2) of the Criminal Justice Act 1967 (report by medical practitioner on medical condition of offender) applies;

for the expenses properly incurred in or incidental to his reporting to the court.

(3A) In subsection (3)(a) above "attendance" means attendance at the court or elsewhere.

(4) The Court of Appeal may order the payment out of central funds of such sums as appear to it to be reasonably sufficient to compensate an appellant who is not in custody and who appears before it on, or in connection with, his appeal under Part I of the Criminal Appeal Act 1968.

(5) The Lord Chancellor may by regulations provide that any provision made by or under this Part which would not otherwise apply in relation to any category of proceedings in which an offender is before a magistrates' court or the Crown Court shall apply in relation to proceedings of that category, subject to any specified modifications.

Interpretation, etc.

B12–06   21.—(1) In this Part—
> "defendant's costs order" has the meaning given in section 16 of this Act;
> "legally assisted person", in relation to any proceedings, means a person to whom representation under the Legal Aid Act 1988 has been granted for the purposes of the proceedings.
> "proceedings" includes—
>> (a) proceedings in any court below; and
>> (b) in relation to the determination of an appeal by any court, any application made to that court for leave to bring the appeal; and
> "witness" means any person properly attending to give evidence, whether or not he gives evidence or is called at the instance of one of the parties or of the court, but does not include a person attending as a witness to character only unless the court has certified that the interests of justice required his attendance.

(2) Except as provided by or under this Part no costs shall be allowed on the hearing or determination of, or of any proceedings preliminary or incidental to, an appeal to the Court of Appeal under Part I of the Criminal Appeal Act 1968.

(3) Subject to rules of court made under section 53(1) of the Supreme Court Act 1981 (power by rules to distribute business of Court of Appeal between its civil and criminal divisions), the jurisdiction of the Court of Appeal under this Part, or under regulations made under this Part, shall be exercised by the criminal division of that Court; and references in this Part to the Court of Appeal shall be construed as references to that division.

(4) For the purposes of sections 16 and 17 of this Act, the costs of any party to proceedings shall be taken to include the expense of compensating any witness for the expense, trouble or loss of time properly incurred in or incidental to his attendance.

(4A) Where one party to any proceedings is a legally assisted person then
> (a) for the purposes of sections 16 and 17 of this Act, his costs shall be taken not to include either the expenses incurred on his behalf by the Legal Aid Board or the Lord Chancellor or, if he is liable to make a contribution under section 23 of the Legal Aid Act 1988, any sum paid or payable by way of contribution; and
> (b) for the purposes of sections 18 and 19 of this Act, his costs shall be taken to include the expenses incurred on his behalf by the Legal Aid

Board or the Lord Chancellor (without any deduction on account of any contribution paid or payable under section 23 of the Legal Aid Act 1988) but, if he is liable to make such a contribution his costs shall be taken not to include any sum paid or payable by way of contribution,

(5) Where, in any proceedings in a criminal cause or matter or in either of the cases mentioned in subsection (6) below, an interpreter is required because of the accused's lack of English, the expenses properly incurred on his employment shall not be treated as costs of any party to the proceedings.

(6) The cases are—

(a) where an information charging the accused with an offence is laid before a justice of the peace for any area but not proceeded with and the expenses are incurred on the employment of the interpreter for the proceedings on the information; and

(b) where proceedings against the accused are transferred to the Crown Court for trial but the accused is not tried and the expenses are incurred on the employment of the interpreter for the proceedings in the Crown Court.

CRIMINAL JUSTICE ACT 1988

(1988 c. 33)

Certain either way offences relating to motor vehicles to be summary offences

37.—(1) In section 12 of the Theft Act 1968 (taking motor vehicle or other conveyance without authority etc.)— **B13–01**

(a) in subsection (2), for the words "on conviction on indictment be liable to imprisonment for a term not exceeding three years" there shall be substituted the words "be liable on summary conviction to a fine not exceeding level 5 on the standard scale, to imprisonment for a term not exceeding six months, or to both."; and

(b) at the end of subsection (4) there shall be added the words "and if he is found guilty of it, he shall be liable as he would have been liable under subsection (2) above on summary conviction.".

(2) [. . .]

Power to join in indictment count for common assault etc.

40.—(1) A count charging a person with a summary offence to which this section applies may be included in an indictment if the charge— **B13–02**

(a) is founded on the same facts or evidence as a count charging an indictable offence; or

(b) is part of a series of offences of the same or similar character as an indictable offence which is also charged,

but only if (in either case) the facts or evidence relating to the offence were disclosed in the documents sent with the copy of a notice of the prosecution case to the Crown Court.

(2) Where a count charging an offence to which this section applies is included in an indictment, the offence shall be tried in the same manner as if it

were an indictable offence; but the Crown Court may only deal with the offender in respect of it in a manner in which a magistrates' court could have dealt with him.

(3) The offences to which this section applies are—

    (a) [*Omitted*];

    (aa) [*Omitted*];

    (ab) [*Omitted*];

    (b) an offence under section 12(1) of the Theft Act 1968 (taking motor vehicle or other conveyance without authority etc.);

    (c) an offence under section 103(1)(b) of the Road Traffic Act 1988 (driving a motor vehicle while disqualified);

    (d) [*Omitted*];

    (e) any summary offence specified under subsection (4) below.

(4) The Secretary of State may by order made by statutory instrument specify for the purposes of this section any summary offence which is punishable with imprisonment or involves obligatory or discretionary disqualification from driving.

(5) A statutory instrument containing an order under this section shall be subject to annulment in pursuance of a resolution of either House of Parliament.

Power of Crown Court to deal with summary offence where person committed for either way offence

B13–03 41.—(1) Where a magistrates' court transfers to the Crown Court for trial proceedings against a person for an offence triable either way or a number of such offences, it may also transfer to the Crown Court for trial proceedings against a person for any summary offence with which he is charged and which—

    (a) is punishable with imprisonment or involves obligatory or discretionary disqualification from driving; and

    (b) arises out of circumstances which appear to the court to be the same as or connected with those giving rise to the offence, or one of the offences, triable either way,

whether or not evidence relating to that summary offence was sent to the person charged with the notice of the transfer of the proceedings; and the trial of the information charging the summary offence shall then be treated as if the magistrates' court had adjourned it under section 10 of the Magistrates' Courts Act 1980 and had not fixed the time and place for its resumption.

(2) Where a magistrates' court transfers to the Crown Court for trial proceedings against a person for a number of offences triable either way and exercises the power conferred by subsection (1) above in respect of a summary offence, the magistrates' court shall give the Crown Court and the person in respect of whom proceedings are transferred for trial a notice stating which of the offences triable either way appears to the court to arise out of circumstances which are the same as or connected with those giving rise to the summary offence.

(3) A magistrates' court's decision to exercise the power conferred by subsection (1) above shall not be subject to appeal or liable to be questioned in any court.

(4) The transfer for trial of proceedings against a person under this section in respect of an offence to which section 40 above applies shall not preclude the exercise in relation to the offence of the power conferred by that section;

but where he is tried on indictment for such an offence, the functions of the Crown Court under this section in relation to the offence shall cease.

(5) If he is convicted on the indictment, the Crown Court shall consider whether the conditions specified in subsection (1) above were satisfied.

(6) If it considers that they were satisfied, it shall state to him the substance of the summary offence and ask him whether he pleads guilty or not guilty.

(7) If he pleads guilty, the Crown Court shall convict him, but may deal with him in respect of that offence only in a manner in which a magistrates' court could have dealt with him.

(8) If he does not plead guilty, the powers of the Crown Court shall cease in respect of the offence except as provided by subsection (9) below.

(9) If the prosecution inform the Court that they would not desire to submit evidence on the charge relating to the summary offence, the Court shall dismiss it.

(10) The Crown Court shall inform the clerk of the magistrates' court of the outcome of any proceedings under this section.

(11) Where the Court of Appeal allows an appeal against conviction of an offence triable either way which arose out of circumstances which were the same as or connected with those giving rise to a summary offence of which the appellant was convicted under this section—

(a) it shall set aside his conviction of the summary offence and give the clerk of the magistrates' court notice that it has done so; and

(b) it may direct that no further proceedings in relation to the offence are to be undertaken;

and the proceedings before the Crown Court in relation to the offence shall thereafter be disregarded for all purposes.

(12) A notice under subsection (11) above shall include particulars of any direction given under paragraph (b) of that subsection in relation to the offence.

(13) The references to the clerk of the magistrates' court in this section are to be construed in accordance with section 141 of the Magistrates' Courts Act 1980.

Amendments relating to committal for sentence

42.—(1) Section 56 of the Criminal Justice Act 1967 shall be amended as follows. **B13–04**

(2) In subsection (1), for the words "offence triable either way" there shall be substituted the words "indictable offence".

(3) In subsection (2), for the words from "and sections 8(6)" to the end there shall be substituted the words ", section 8(6) of the Powers of Criminal Courts Act 1973 (probationer convicted of subsequent offence) and section 24(2) of that Act and paragraph 2(2)(a) of Schedule 9 to the Criminal Law Act 1977 (committal to be dealt with in respect of a wholly or partly suspended sentence)".

Forfeiture general

69.—(1) The following subsections shall be substituted for section 43(1) of the Powers of Criminal Courts Act 1973— **B13–05**

"(1) Subject to the following provisions of this section, where a person is convicted of an offence and—

(a) the court by or before which he is convicted is satisfied that any prop-

erty which has been lawfully seized from him or which was in his possession or under his control at the time when he was apprehended for the offence or when a summons in respect of it was issued—
  (i) has been used for the purpose of committing, or facilitating the commission of, any offence; or
  (ii) was intended by him to be used for that purpose; or
  (b) the offence, or an offence which the court has taken into consideration in determining his sentence, consists of unlawful possession of property which—
    (i) has been lawfully seized from him; or
    (ii) was in his possession or under his control at the time when he was apprehended for the offence of which he has been convicted or when a summons in respect of that offence was issued,
the court may make an order under this section in respect of that property, and may do so whether or not it also deals with the offender in respect of the offence in any other way and without regard to any restrictions on forfeiture in an enactment contained in an Act passed before the Criminal Justice Act 1988.

(1A) In considering whether to make such an order in respect of any property a court shall have regard—
  (a) to the value of the property;
  (b) to the likely financial and other effects on the offender of the making of the order (taken together with any other order that the court contemplates making)."

(2) At the end of section 12(4) of that Act (which authorises a court, on making a probation order in respect of an offender or discharging an offender absolutely or conditionally, to order him to pay costs or compensation) there shall be added the words "or to make an order under section 43 below".

Compensation orders

B13–06   104.—(1) At the end of subsection (1) of section 35 of the Powers of Criminal Courts Act 1973 there shall be added the words "or to make payments for funeral expenses or bereavement in respect of a death resulting from any such offence, other than a death due to an accident arising out of the presence of a motor vehicle on a road; and a court shall give reasons, on passing sentence, if it does not make such an order in a case where this section empowers it to do so".

(2) The following subsections shall be substituted for subsection (3) of that section—

"(3) A compensation order may only be made in respect of injury, loss or damage (other than loss suffered by a person's dependants in consequence of his death) which was due to an accident arising out of the presence of a motor vehicle on a road, if—
  (a) it is in respect of damage which is treated by subsection (2) above as resulting from an offence under the Theft Act 1968; or
  (b) it is in respect of injury, loss or damage as respects which—
    (i) the offender is uninsured in relation to the use of the vehicle; and
    (ii) compensation is not payable under any arrangements to which the Secretary of State is a party;
and, where a compensation order is made in respect of injury, loss or damage due to such an accident, the amount to be paid may include an amount representing the whole or part of any loss of or reduction in preferential rates of insurance attributable to the accident.

(3A) A vehicle the use of which is exempted from insurance by section 144 of the Road Traffic Act 1972 is not uninsured for the purposes of subsection (3) above.

(3B) A compensation order in respect of funeral expenses may be made for the benefit of anyone who incurred the expenses.

(3C) A compensation order in respect of bereavement may only be made for the benefit of a person for whose benefit a claim for damages for bereavement could be made under section 1A of the Fatal Accidents Act 1976.

(3D) The amount of compensation in respect of bereavement shall not exceed the amount for the time being specified in section 1A(3) of the Fatal Accidents Act 1976."

Enforcement of compensation orders

105.—The following sections shall be substituted for sections 36 to 38 of the Powers of Criminal Courts Act 1973. **B13–07**

"Enforcement and appeals

36.—(1) A person in whose favour a compensation order is made shall not be entitled to receive the amount due to him until (disregarding any power of a court to grant leave to appeal out of time) there is no further possibility of an appeal on which the order could be varied or set aside.

(2) Rules under section 144 of the Magistrates' Courts Acts 1980 may make provision regarding the way in which the magistrates' court for the time being having functions (by virtue of section 41(1) of the Administration of Justice Act 1970) in relation to the enforcement of a compensation order is to deal with money paid in satisfaction of the order where the entitlement of the person in whose favour it was made is suspended.

(3) The Court of Appeal may by order annul or vary any compensation order made by the court of trial, although the conviction is not quashed; and the order, if annulled, shall not take effect and, if varied, shall take effect as varied.

(4) Where the House of Lords restores a conviction, it may make any compensation order which the court of trial could have made.

(5) Where a compensation order has been made against any person in respect of an offence taken into consideration in determining his sentence—

(a) the order shall cease to have effect if he successfully appeals against his conviction of the offence or, if more than one, all the offences, of which he was convicted in the proceedings in which the order was made;

(b) he may appeal against the order as if it were part of the sentence imposed in respect of the offence or, if more than one, any of the offences, of which he was so convicted.

Review of compensation orders

37.—At any time before the person against whom a compensation order has been made has paid into court the whole of the compensation which the order requires him to pay, but at a time when (disregarding any power of a court to grant leave to appeal out of time) there is no further possibility of an appeal on which the order could be varied or set aside, the magistrates' court for the time being having functions in relation to the enforcement of the order may, on the application of the person against whom it was made, discharge the order, or reduce the amount which remains to be paid, if it appears to the court—

(a) that the injury, loss or damage in respect of which the order was made has been held in civil proceedings to be less than it was taken to be for the purposes of the order; or

(b) in the case of an order in respect of the loss of any property, that the property has been recovered by the person in whose favour the order was made; or

(c) that the means of the person against whom the order was made are insufficient to satisfy in full both the order and a confiscation order under Part VI of the Criminal Justice Act 1988 made against him in the same proceedings; or

(d) that the person against whom the order was made has suffered a substantial reduction in his means which was unexpected at the time when the compensation order was made, and that his means seem unlikely to increase for a considerable period;

but where the order was made by the Crown Court, a magistrates' court shall not exercise any power conferred by this section in a case where it is satisfied as mentioned in paragraph (c) or (d) above unless it has first obtained the consent of the Crown Court.

Effect of compensation order on subsequent award of damages in civil proceedings

38.—(1) This section shall have effect where a compensation order has been made in favour of any person in respect of any injury, loss or damage and a claim by him in civil proceedings for damages in respect of the injury, loss of damage subsequently falls to be determined.

(2) The damages in the civil proceedings shall be assessed without regard to the order; but the plaintiff may only recover an amount equal to the aggregate of the following—

(a) any amount by which they exceed the compensation; and

(b) a sum equal to any portion of the compensation which he fails to recover,

and may not enforce the judgment, so far as it relates to a sum such as is mentioned in paragraph (b) above, without the leave of the court."

Discretion of Crown Court to specify extended period of imprisonment in default of payment of compensation

B13–08   **106.**—The following subsections shall be substituted for section 41(8) of the Administration of Justice Act 1970—

"(8) Subject to subsection (8A) below, where in the case specified in paragraph 10 of Schedule 9 to this Act the Crown Court thinks that the period for which the person subject to the order is liable apart from this subsection to be committed to prison for default under the order is insufficient, it may specify a longer period for that purpose; and then, in the case of default—

(a) the specified period shall be substituted as the maximum for which the person may be imprisoned under section 76 of the Magistrates' Courts Act 1980; and

(b) paragraph 2 of Schedule 4 to the Act shall apply, with any necessary modifications, for the reduction of the specified period where, at the time of the person's imprisonment, he has made part payment under the order.

(8A) The Crown Court may not specify under subsection (8) above a period of imprisonment longer than that which it could order a person to undergo on imposing on him a fine equal in amount to the sum required to be paid by the order."

Power to make order applying proceeds of sale of property forfeited by offender for benefit of victim

107.—(1) The following section shall be inserted after section 43 of the Powers of Criminal Courts Act 1973—   **B13–09**

"Application of proceeds of forfeited party

43A.—(1) Where a court makes an order under section 43 above in a case where—

    (a) the offender has been convicted of an offence which has resulted in a person suffering personal injury, loss or damage; or

    (b) any such offence is taken into consideration by the court in determining sentence, the court may also make an order that any proceeds which arise from the disposal of the property and which do not exceed a sum specified by the court shall be paid to that person.

(2) The court may only make an order under this section if it is satisfied that but for the inadequacy of the means of the offender it would have made a compensation order under which the offender would have been required to pay compensation of an amount not less than the specified amount.

(3) An order made under this section has no effect—

    (a) before the end of the period specified in section 43(4)(a) above; or

    (b) if a successful application under section 1(1) of the Police (Property) Act 1897 has been made."

LEGAL AID ACT 1988

(1988 c. 34)

Scope of this Part

19.—(1) This Part applies to criminal proceedings before any of the following—   **B14–01**

    (a) a magistrates' court;

    (b) the Crown Court;

    (c) the criminal division of the Court of Appeal or the Courts-Martial Appeal Court; and

    (d) the House of Lords in the exercise of its jurisdiction in relation to appeals for either of those courts;

and representation under this Part shall be available to any person subject to and in accordance with sections 21, 22, 23, 24 and 25.

(2) Representation under this Part for the purposes of the proceedings before any court extends to any proceedings preliminary or incidental to the proceedings, including bail proceedings, whether before that or another court.

(3) Representation under this Part for the purposes of the proceedings before a magistrates' court extends to any proceedings before a youth court or other magistrates' court to which the case is remitted.

(4) In subsection (2) above in its application to bail proceedings, "court" has the same meaning as in the Bail Act 1976, but that subsection does not extend representation to bail proceedings before a judge of the High Court exercising the jurisdiction of that Court.

(5) In this Part—

"competent authority" is to be construed in accordance with section 20;

"Court of Appeal" means the criminal division of that Court;

"criminal proceedings" includes proceedings for dealing with an offender for an offence or in respect of a sentence or as a fugitive offender and also includes proceedings instituted under section 115 of the Magistrates' Courts Act 1980 (binding over) in respect of an actual or apprehended breach of the peace or other misbehaviour and proceedings for dealing with a person for a failure to comply with a condition of a recognizance to keep the peace or be of good behaviour and also includes proceedings under section 15 of the Children and Young Persons Act 1969 (variation and discharge of supervision orders) and section 16(8) of that Act (appeals in such proceedings);

"proceedings for dealing with an offender as a fugitive offender" means proceedings before a metropolitan stipendiary magistrate under section 9 of the Extradition Act 1870, section 7 of the Fugitive Offenders Act 1967 or section 6 of the Criminal Justice Act 1988; and

"remitted", in relation to a youth court, means remitted under section 56(1) of the Children and Young Persons Act 1933;

and any reference, in relation to representation for the purposes of any proceedings, to the proceedings before a court includes a reference to any proceedings to which representation under this Part extends by virtue of subsection (2) or (3) above.

Competent authorities to grant representation under this Part

20.—(1) Subject to any provision made by virtue of subsection (10) below, the following courts are competent to grant representation under this Part for the purposes of the following proceedings, on an application made for the purpose.

(2) The court before which any proceedings take place, or are to take place, is always competent as respects those proceedings, except that this does not apply to the House of Lords; and, in the case of the Court of Appeal and the Courts-Martial Appeal Court, the reference to proceedings which are to take place includes proceedings which may take place if notice of appeal is given or an application for leave to appeal is made.

(3) The Court of Appeal or, as the case may be, the Courts-Martial Appeal Court is also competent as respects proceedings on appeal from decisions of theirs to the House of Lords.

(4) The magistrates' court—

  (a) which commits a person for sentence or to be dealt with in respect of a sentence,

 (aa) which proceeds with a view to transferring proceedings to the Crown Court for trial,

  (b) which has been given a notice of transfer under section 4 of the Criminal Justice Act 1987 (transfer of serious fraud cases) or section 53 of the Criminal Justice Act 1991 (transfer of certain cases involving children);

(bb) which has been given a notice of transfer under Part I of the schedule to the War Crimes Act 1991;

(c) from which a person appeals against his conviction or sentence, is also competent as respects the proceedings before the Crown Court.

(5) The magistrates' court inquiring into an offence as examining justices is also competent, before it decides whether or not to commit the person for trial, as respects any proceedings before the Crown Court on his trial.

(6) The Crown Court is also competent as respects applications for leave to appeal and proceedings on any appeal to the Court of Appeal under section 9(11) of the Criminal Justice Act 1987 (appeals against orders or rulings at preparatory hearings).

(7) On ordering a retrial under section 7 of the Criminal Appeal Act 1968 (new trials ordered by Court of Appeal or House of Lords on fresh evidence) the court ordering the retrial is also competent as respects the proceedings before the Crown Court.

(8) Any magistrates' court to which, in accordance with regulations, a person applies for representation when he has been arrested for an offence but has not appeared or been brought before a court is competent as respects the proceedings in relation to the offence in any magistrates' court.

(9) In the event of the Lord Chancellor making an order under section 3(4) as respects the function of granting representation under this Part for the purposes of proceedings before any court, the Board shall be competent as respects those proceedings, on an application made for the purpose.

(10) An order under section 3(4) may make provision restricting or excluding the competence of any court mentioned in any of subsections (2) to (8) above and may contain such transitional provisions as appear to the Lord Chancellor necessary or expedient.

Availability of representation under this Part

21.—(1) Representation under this Part for the purposes of any criminal **B14–03** proceedings shall be available in accordance with this section to the accused or convicted person but shall not be available to the prosecution except in the case of an appeal to the Crown Court against conviction or sentence, for the purpose of enabling an individual who is not acting in an official capacity to resist the appeal.

(2) Subject to subsection (5) below, representation may be granted where it appears to the competent authority to be desirable to do so in the interests of justice; and section 22 applied for the interpretation of this subsection in relation to the proceedings to which that section applies.

(3) Subject to subsection (5) below, representation must be granted—

(a) where proceedings against a person who is charged with murder are transferred to the Crown Court for trial, for that person's trial;

(b) where the prosecutor appeals or applies for leave to appeal to the House of Lords, for the proceedings on the appeal;

(c) where a person charged with an offence before a magistrates' court—
  (i) is brought before the court in pursuance of a remand in custody when he may be again remanded or committed in custody; and
  (ii) is not, but wishes to be, legally represented before the court (not having been legally represented when he was so remanded), for so much of the proceedings as relates to the grant of bail; and

(d) where a person—
  (i) is to be sentenced or otherwise dealt with for an offence by a magistrates' court or the Crown Court; and

(ii) is to be kept in custody to enable enquiries or a report to be made to assist the court,

for the proceedings on sentencing or otherwise dealing with him.

(4) Subject to any provision made under section 3(4) by virtue of section 20(10), in a case falling within subsection (3)(a) above, it shall be for the magistrates' court which transfers the proceedings against the person for trial, and not for the Crown Court, to make the grant of representation for his trial.

(5) Representation shall not be granted to any person unless it appears to the competent authority that his financial resources are such as, under regulations, make him eligible for representation under this Part.

(6) Before making a determination for the purposes of subsection (5) above in the case of any person, the competent authority shall, except in prescribed cases, require a statement of his financial resources in the prescribed form to be furnished to the authority.

(7) Where a doubt arises whether representation under this Part should be granted to any person, the doubt shall be resolved in that person's favour.

(8) Where an application for representation for the purposes of an appeal to the Court of Appeal or the Courts-Martial Appeal Court is made to a competent authority before the giving of notice of appeal or the making of an application for leave to appeal, the authority may, in the first instance, exercise its power to grant representation by making a grant consisting of advice on the question whether there appear to be reasonable grounds of appeal and assistance in the preparation of an application for leave to appeal or in the giving of a notice of appeal.

(9) Representation granted by a competent authority may be amended or withdrawn, whether by that or another authority competent to grant representation under this part.

(10) Regulations may provide for an appeal to lie to a specified court or body against any refusal by a magistrates' court to grant representation under this Part and for that other court or body to make any grant of representation that could have been made by the magistrates' court.

(11) Subsection (3) above shall have effect in its application to a person who has not attained the age of eighteen as if the reference in paragraphs (c) and (d) to remand in custody and to bring remanded or kept in custody included references to being committed under section 23 of the Children and Young Persons Act 1969 to the care of a local authority or a remand centre.

Criteria for grant of representation for trial proceedings

B14–04 22.—(1) This section applies to proceedings by way of a trial by or before a magistrates' court or the Crown Court or on an appeal to the Crown Court against a person's conviction.

(2) The factors to be taken into account by a competent authority in determining whether it is in the interests of justice that representation be granted for the purposes of proceedings to which this section applies to an accused shall include the following—

(a) the offence is such that if proved it is likely that the court would impose a sentence which would deprive the accused of his liberty or lead to loss of his livelihood or serious damage to his reputation;

(b) the determination of the case may involve consideration of a substantial question of law;

(c) the accused may be unable to understand the proceedings or to state his own case because of his inadequate knowledge of English, mental illness or other mental or physical disability;

(d) the nature of the defence is such as to involve the tracing and interviewing of witnesses or expert cross-examination of a witness for the prosecution;

(e) it is in the interests of someone other than the accused that the accused be represented.

(3) The Lord Chancellor may, by order, vary the factors listed in subsection (2) above by amending factors in the list or by adding new factors to the list.

Reimbursement of public funds by contributions

23.—(1) Where representation under this Part is granted to any person **B14–05** whose financial resources are such as, under regulations, make him liable to make a contribution, the competent authority shall order him to pay a contribution in respect of the costs of his being represented under this Part.

(2) Where the legally assisted person has not attained the age of sixteen, the competent authority may, instead of or in addition to ordering him to make a contribution, order any person—

(a) who is an appropriate contributor in relation to him, and

(b) whose financial resources are such as, under regulations, make him liable to make a contribution,

to pay a contribution in respect of the costs of the representation granted to the legally assisted person.

(3) Regulations may authorise the making of a contribution order under subsection (1) or (2) above after the grant of representation in prescribed circumstances.

(4) The amount of the contribution to be required under subsection (1) or (2) above by the competent authority shall be such as is determined in accordance with the regulations.

(5) A legally assisted person or appropriate contributor may be required to make his contribution in one sum or by instalments as may be prescribed.

(6) Regulations may provide that no contribution order shall be made in connection with a grant of representation under this Part for the purposes of proceedings in the Crown Court, the Court of Appeal or the House of Lords in a case where a contribution order was made in connection with a grant of such representation to the person in question in respect of proceedings in a lower court.

(7) Subject to subsection (8) below, if the total contribution made in respect of the costs of representing any person under this Part exceeds those costs, the excess shall be repaid—

(a) where the contribution was made by one person only, to him; and

(b) where the contribution was made by two or more persons, to them in proportion to the amounts contributed by them.

(8) Where a contribution has been made in respect of the costs of representing any person under this Part in any proceedings and an order for costs is made in favour of that person in respect of those proceedings, then, where sums due under the order for costs are paid to the Board or the Lord Chancellor under section 20(2) of the Prosecution of Offences Act 1985 (recovery regulations)—

(a) if the costs of the representation do not exceed the sums so paid, subsection (7) above shall not apply and the contribution shall be repaid;

(b) if the costs of the representation do not exceed the sums so paid, subsection (7) above shall apply as if the costs of the representation were equal to the excess.

(9) References in subsection (8) above to the costs of representation include any charge or fee treated as part of those costs by section 26(2).

(10) In this Part—

"appropriate contributor", means a person of a description prescribed under section 34(2)(c); and

"contribution order" means an order under subsection (1) or (2) above.

Contribution orders: supplementary

B14–06   **24.**—(1) Where a competent authority grants representation under this Part and in connection with the grant makes a contribution order under which any sum is required to be paid on the making of the order, it may direct that the grant of representation shall not take effect until that sum is paid.

(2) Where a legally assisted person fails to pay any relevant contribution when it is due, the court in which the proceedings for the purposes of which he has been granted representation are being heard may, subject to subsection (3) below, revoke the grant.

(3) A court shall not exercise the power conferred by subsection (2) above unless, after affording the legally assisted person an opportunity of making representations in such manner as may be prescribed, it is satisfied—

(a) that he was able to pay the relevant contribution when it was due; and

(b) that he is able to pay the whole or part of it but has failed or refused to do so.

(4) In subsection (2) above "relevant contribution", in relation to a legally assisted person, means any sum—

(a) which he is required to pay by a contribution order made in connection with the grant to him or representation under this Part, and

(b) which falls due after the making of the order and before the conclusion of the proceedings for the purposes of which he has been granted such representation.

(5) Regulations with respect to contribution orders may—

(a) provide for their variation or revocation in prescribed circumstances;

(b) provide for their making in default of the prescribed evidence of a person's financial resources;

(c) regulate their making after the grant of representation;

(d) authorise the remission or authorise or require the repayment in prescribed circumstances of sums due or paid under such orders; and

(e) prescribe the court or body by which any function under the regulations is to be exercisable.

(6) Schedule 3 to this Act, shall have effect with respect to the enforcement of contribution orders.

Payment of costs of representation under this Part

B14–07   **25.**—(1) Where representation under this Part has been granted to any person the costs of representing him shall be paid—

(a) by the Lord Chancellor, or

(b) by the Board,

as the Lord Chancellor may direct.

(2) Subject to regulations, the costs of representing any person under this Part shall include sums on account of the fees payable to his legal representative and disbursements reasonably incurred by his legal representative for or in connection with his representation.

(3) The costs required by this section to be paid in respect of representing him shall not include any sum in respect of allowances to witnesses attending to give evidence in the proceedings for the purposes of which he is represented in any case where such allowances are payable under any other enactment.

Payment for advice or assistance where representation under this Part is subsequently granted

26.—(1) This section has effect where— **B14–08**

    (a) advice or assistance under Part III is given to a person in respect of any matter which is or becomes the subject of criminal proceedings against him; and

    (b) he is subsequently granted representation under this Part for the purposes of those proceedings.

(2) If the legal representative acting for the person under the grant of representation is the one who gave him the advice or assistance, any charge or fee in respect of the advice or assistance which, apart from this section, would fall to be secured, recovered or paid as provided by section 11 shall instead be paid under section 25 as if it were part of the costs of representation.

(3) If a contribution order is made in connection with the grant of representation under this Part to him—

    (a) any sum which he is required by virtue of section 9(6) or (7) to pay in respect of the advice or assistance (whether or not already paid) shall be credited against the contribution to be made by him under the contribution order; and

    (b) section 25 shall have effect in a case to which subsection (2) above applies as if the charges and fees properly chargeable in respect of the advice or assistance were part of the costs of the representation under this Part and as if any such sum as is mentioned in paragraph (a) above which he has paid were part of the contribution made under the contribution order.

ROAD TRAFFIC ACT 1988

(1988 c. 52)

Causing death by dangerous driving

1. A person who causes the death of another person by driving a mechanically propelled vehicle dangerously on a road or other public place is guilty of an offence. **B15–01**

Dangerous driving

B15–02   2. A person who drives a mechanically propelled vehicle dangerously on a road or other public place is guilty of an offence.

Meaning of dangerous driving

B15–03   2A.—(1) For the purposes of sections 1 and 2 above a person is to be regarded as driving dangerously if (and, subject to subsection (2) below, only if)—

    (a) the way he drives falls far below what would be expected of a competent and careful driver, and

    (b) it would be obvious to a competent and careful driver that driving in that way would be dangerous.

(2) A person is also to be regarded as driving dangerously for the purposes of sections 1 and 2 above if it would be obvious to a competent and careful driver that driving the vehicle in its current state would be dangerous.

(3) In subsections (1) and (2) above "dangerous" refers to danger either of injury to any person or of serious damage to property; and in determining for the purposes of those subsections what would be expected of, or obvious to, a competent and careful driver in a particular case, regard shall be had not only to the circumstances of which he could be expected to be aware but also to any circumstances shown to have been within the knowledge of the accused.

(4) In determining for the purposes of subsection (2) above the state of a vehicle, regard may be had to anything attached to or carried on or in it and to the manner in which it is attached or carried.

Careless, and inconsiderate, driving

B15–04   3. If a person drives a mechanically propelled vehicle on a road or other public place without due care and attention, or without reasonable consideration for other persons using the road or place, he is guilty of an offence.

Causing death by careless driving when under influence of drink or drugs

B15–05   3A.—(1) If a person causes the death of another person by driving a mechanically propelled vehicle on a road or other public place without due care and attention, or without reasonable consideration for other persons using the road or place, and—

    (a) he is, at the time when he is driving, unfit to drive through drink or drugs, or

    (b) he has consumed so much alcohol that the proportion of it in his breath, blood or urine at that time exceeds the prescribed limit, or

    (c) he is, within 18 hours after that time, required to provide a specimen in pursuance of section 7 of this Act, but without reasonable excuse fails to provide it,

he is guilty of an offence.

(2) For the purposes of this section a person shall be taken to be unfit to drive at any time when his ability to drive properly is impaired.

(3) Subsection (1)(b) and (c) above shall not apply in relation to a person driving a mechanically propelled vehicle other than a motor vehicle.

Driving, or being in charge, when under influence of drink or drugs

4.—(1) A person who, when driving or attempting to drive a mechanically   **B15–06**
propelled vehicle on a road or other public place, is unfit to drive through
drink or drugs is guilty of an offence.

(2) Without prejudice to subsection (1) above, a person who, when in charge
of a mechanically propelled vehicle which is on a road or other public place, is
unfit to drive through drink or drugs is guilty of an offence.

(3) For the purposes of subsection (2) above, a person shall be deemed not to
have been in charge of a mechanically propelled vehicle if he proves that at the
material time the circumstances were such that there was no likelihood of his
driving it so long as he remained unfit to drive through drink or drugs.

(4) The court may, in determining whether there was such a likelihood as is
mentioned in subsection (3) above, disregard any injury to him and any damage to the vehicle.

(5) For the purposes of this section, a person shall be taken to be unfit to
drive if his ability to drive properly is for the time being impaired.

(6) A constable may arrest a person without warrant if he has reasonable
cause to suspect that that person is or has been committing an offence under
this section.

(7) For the purpose of arresting a person under the power conferred by subsection (6) above, a constable may enter (if need be by force) any place where
that person is or where the constable, with reasonable cause, suspects him to
be.

(8) Subsection (7) above does not extend to Scotland, and nothing in that
subsection affects any rule of law in Scotland concerning the right of a constable to enter any premises for any purpose.

Driving or being in charge of a motor vehicle with alcohol concentration above prescribed limit

5.—(1) If a person—   **B15–07**
  (a) drives or attempts to drive a motor vehicle on a road or other public
    place, or
  (b) is in charge of a motor vehicle on a road or other public place,
after consuming so much alcohol that the proportion of it in his breath, blood
or urine exceeds the prescribed limit he is guilty of an offence.

(2) It is a defence for a person charged with an offence under subsection
(1)(b) above to prove that at the time he is alleged to have committed the
offence the circumstances were such that there was no likelihood of his driving the vehicle whilst the proportion of alcohol in his breath, blood or urine
remained likely to exceed the prescribed limit.

(3) The court may, in determining whether there was such a likelihood as is
mentioned in subsection (2) above, disregard any injury to him and any damage to the vehicle.

Breath tests

6.—(1) Where a constable in uniform has reasonable cause to suspect—   **B15–08**
  (a) that a person driving or attempting to drive or in charge of a motor
    vehicle on a road or other public place has alcohol in his body or has
    committed a traffic offence whilst the vehicle was in motion, or

(b) that a person has been driving or attempting to drive or been in charge of a motor vehicle on a road or other public place with alcohol in his body and that that person still has alcohol in his body, or

(c) that a person has been driving or attempting to drive or been in charge of a motor vehicle on a road or other public place and has committed a traffic offence whilst the vehicle was in motion,

he may, subject to section 9 of this Act, require him to provide a specimen of breath for a breath test.

(2) If an accident occurs owing to the presence of a motor vehicle on a road or other public place, a constable may, subject to section 9 of this Act, require any person who he has reasonable cause to believe was driving or attempting to drive or in charge of the vehicle at the time of the accident to provide a specimen of breath for a breath test.

(3) A person may be required under subsection (1) or subsection (2) above to provide a specimen either at or near the place where the requirement is made or, if the requirement is made under subsection (2) above and the constable making the requirement thinks fit, at a police station specified by the constable.

(4) A person who, without reasonable excuse, fails to provide a specimen of breath when required to do so in pursuance of this section is guilty of an offence.

(5) A constable may arrest a person without warrant if—

(a) as a result of a breath test he has reasonable cause to suspect that the proportion of alcohol in that person's breath or blood exceeds the pre-scribed limit, or

(b) that person has failed to provide a specimen of breath for a breath test when required to do so in pursuance of this section and the constable has reasonable cause to suspect that he has alcohol in his body,

but a person shall not be arrested by virtue of this subsection when he is at a hospital as a patient.

(6) A constable may, for the purpose of requiring a person to provide a specimen of breath under subsection (2) above in a case where he has reason-able cause to suspect that the accident involved injury to another person or of arresting him in such a case under subsection (5) above, enter (if need be by force) any place where that person is or where the constable, with reasonable cause, suspects him to be.

(7) Subsection (6) above does not extend to Scotland, and nothing in that subsection shall affect any rule of law in Scotland concerning the right of a constable to enter any premises for any purpose.

(8) In this section "traffic offence" means an offence under—

(a) any provision of Part II of the Public Passenger Vehicles Act 1981,

(b) any provision of the Road Traffic Regulation Act 1984,

(c) any provision of the Road Traffic Offenders Act 1988 except Part III, or

(d) any provision of this Act except Part V.

Provision of specimens for analysis

B15–09   7.—(1) In the course of an investigation into whether a person has commit-ted an offence under section 3A, 4 or 5 of this Act a constable may, subject to the following provisions of this section and section 9 of this Act, require him—

(a) to provide two specimens of breath for analysis by means of a device of a type approved by the Secretary of State, or

(b) to provide a specimen of blood or urine for a laboratory test.

(2) A requirement under this section to provide specimens of breath can only be made at a police station.

(3) A requirement under this section to provide a specimen of blood or urine can only be made at a police station or at a hospital; and it cannot be made at a police station unless—

    (a) the constable making the requirement has reasonable cause to believe that for medical reasons a specimen of breath cannot be provided or should not be required, or

    (b) at the time the requirement is made a device or a reliable device of the type mentioned in subsection (1)(a) above is not available at the police station or it is then for any other reason not practicable to use such a device there, or

    (c) the suspected offence is one under section 3A or 4 of this Act and the constable making the requirement has been advised by a medical practitioner that the condition of the person required to provide the specimen might be due to some drug;

but may then be made notwithstanding that the person required to provide the specimen has already provided or been required to provide two specimens of breath.

(4) If the provision of a specimen other than a specimen of breath may be required in pursuance of this section the question whether it is to be a specimen of blood or a specimen of urine shall be decided by the constable making the requirement, but if a medical practitioner is of the opinion that for medical reasons a specimen of blood cannot or should not be taken the specimen shall be a specimen of urine.

(5) A specimen of urine shall be provided within one hour of the requirement for its provision being made and after the provision of a previous specimen of urine.

(6) A person who, without reasonable excuse, fails to provide a specimen when required to do so in pursuance of this section is guilty of an offence.

(7) A constable must, on requiring any person to provide a specimen in pursuance of this section, warn him that a failure to provide it may render him liable to prosecution.

Choice of specimens of breath

8.—(1) Subject to subsection (2) below, of any two specimens of breath provided by any person in pursuance of section 7 of this Act that with the lower proportion of alcohol in the breath shall be used and the other shall be disregarded.   **B15–10**

(2) If the specimen with the lower proportion of alcohol contains no more than 50 microgrammes of alcohol in 100 millilitres of breath, the person who provided it may claim that it should be replaced by such specimen as may be required under section 7(4) of this Act and, if he then provides such a specimen, neither specimen of breath shall be used.

(3) The Secretary of State may by regulations substitute another proportion of alcohol in the breath for that specified in subsection (2) above.

Protection for hospital patients

9.—(1) While a person is at a hospital as a patient he shall not be required to provide a specimen of breath for a breath test or to provide a specimen for a   **B15–11**

laboratory test unless the medical practitioner in immediate charge of his case has been notified of the proposal to make the requirement; and—

> (a) if the requirement is then made, it shall be for the provision of a specimen at the hospital, but
> (b) if the medical practitioner objects on the ground specified in subsection (2) below, the requirement shall not be made.

(2) The ground on which the medical practitioner may object is that the requirement or the provision of a specimen or, in the case of a specimen of blood or urine, the warning required under section 7(7) of this Act, would be prejudicial to the proper care and treatment of the patient.

Detention of persons affected by alcohol or a drug

B15–12   10.—(1) Subject to subsections (2) and (3) below, a person required to provide a specimen of breath, blood or urine may afterwards be detained at a police station until it appears to the constable that, were that person then driving or attempting to drive a mechanically propelled vehicle on a road, he would not be committing an offence under section 4 or 5 of this Act.

(2) A person shall not be detained in pursuance of this section if it appears to a constable that there is no likelihood of his driving or attempting to drive a mechanically propelled vehicle whilst his ability to drive properly is impaired or whilst the proportion of alcohol in his breath, blood or urine exceeds the prescribed limit.

(3) A constable must consult a medical practitioner on any question arising under this section whether a person's ability to drive properly is or might be impaired through drugs and must act on the medical practitioner's advice.

Interpretation of sections 4 to 10

B15–13   11.—(1) The following provisions apply for the interpretation of sections 3A to 10 of this Act.

(2) In those sections—

> "breath test" means a preliminary test for the purpose of obtaining, by means of a device of a type approved by the Secretary of State, an indication whether the proportion of alcohol in a person's breath or blood is likely to exceed the prescribed limit,
> "drug" includes any intoxicant other than alcohol,
> "fail" includes refuse,
> "hospital" means an institution which provides medical or surgical treatment for in-patients or out-patients,
> "the prescribed limit" means, as the case may require—
> > (a) 35 microgrammes of alcohol in 100 millilitres of breath,
> > (b) 80 milligrammes of alcohol in 100 millilitres of blood, or
> > (c) 107 milligrammes of alcohol in 100 millilitres of urine,
> or such other proportion as may be prescribed by regulations made by the Secretary of State.

(3) A person does not provide a specimen of breath for a breath test or for analysis unless the specimen—

> (a) is sufficient to enable the test or the analysis to be carried out, and
> (b) is provided in such a way as to enable the objective of the test or analysis to be satisfactorily achieved.

(4) A person provides a specimen of blood if and only if he consents to its being taken by a medical practitioner and it is so taken.

Motor racing on public ways

12.—(1) A person who promotes or takes part in a race or trial of speed   **B15–14**
between motor vehicles on a public way is guilty of an offence.

(2) In this section "public way" means, in England and Wales, a highway
and, in Scotland, a public road.

Regulation of motoring events on public ways

13.—(1) A person who promotes or takes part in a competition or trial (other   **B15–15**
than a race or trial of speed) involving the use of motor vehicles on a public
way is guilty of an offence unless the competition or trial—

    (a) is authorised, and

    (b) is conducted in accordance with any conditions imposed,

by or under regulations under this section.

(2) The Secretary of State may by regulations authorise, or provide for authorising, the holding of competitions or trials (other than races or trials of
speed) involving the use of motor vehicles on public ways either—

    (a) generally, or

    (b) as regards any area, or as regards any class or description of compe-
        tition or trial or any particular competition or trial,

subject to such conditions, including conditions requiring the payment of fees,
as may be imposed by or under the regulations.

(3) Regulations under this section may—

    (a) prescribe the procedure to be followed, and the particulars to be given,
        in connection with applications for authorisation under the regu-
        lations, and

    (b) make different provision for different classes or descriptions of com-
        petition or trial.

(4) In this section "public way" means, in England and Wales, a highway
and, in Scotland, a public road.

Disapplication of sections 1 to 3 for authorised motoring events

13A.—(1) A person shall not be guilty of an offence under sections 1, 2 or 3   **B15–16**
of this Act by virtue of driving a vehicle in a public place other than a road if he
shows that he was driving in accordance with an authorisation for a motoring
event given under regulations made by the Secretary of State.

(2) Regulations under this section may in particular—

    (a) prescribe the persons by whom, and limit the circumstances in which
        and the places in respect of which, authorisations may be given under
        the regulations;

    (b) specify conditions which must be included among those incorporated
        in authorisations;

    (c) provide for authorisations to cease to have effect in prescribed
        circumstances;

    (d) provide for the procedure to be followed, the particulars to be given,
        and the amount (or the persons who are to determine the amount) of
        any fees to be paid, in connection with applications for authorisations;

(e) make different provisions for different cases.

Seat belts: adults

B15–17   **14.**—(1) The Secretary of State may make regulations requiring, subject to such exceptions as may be prescribed, persons who are driving or riding in motor vehicles on a road to wear seat belts of such description as may be prescribed.

(2) Regulations under this section—

(a) may make different provision in relation to different classes of vehicles, different descriptions of persons and different circumstances,

(aa) may, for the purpose of implementing the seat belt Directive, authorise the wearing of a seat belt approved under the law of a member state other than the United Kingdom.

(b) shall include exceptions for—

(i) the users of vehicles constructed or adapted for the delivery of goods or mail to consumers or addressees, as the case may be, while engaged in making local rounds of deliveries,

(ii) the drivers of vehicles while performing a manoeuvre which includes reversing,

(iii) any person holding a valid certificate signed by a medical practitioner to the effect that it is inadvisable on medical grounds for him to wear a seat belt,

(bb) shall, for the purpose of implementing the seat belt Directive, include an exception for any person holding a certificate to the like effect as that mentioned in paragraph (b)(iii) above which was issued in a member state other than the United Kingdom and which, under the law of that state, is valid for purposes corresponding to those of this section.

(c) may make any prescribed exceptions subject to such conditions as may be prescribed, and

(d) may prescribe cases in which a fee of a prescribed amount may be charged on an application for any certificate required as a condition of any prescribed exception.

(3) A person who drives or rides in a motor vehicle in contravention of regulations under this section is guilty of an offence; but, notwithstanding any enactment or rule of law, no person other than the person actually committing the contravention is guilty of an offence by reason of the contravention.

(4) If the holder of any such certificate as is referred to in subsection (2)(b) or (bb) above is informed by a constable that he may be prosecuted for an offence under subsection (3) above, he is not in proceedings for that offence entitled to rely on the exception afforded to him by the certificate unless—

(a) it is produced to the constable at the time he is so informed, or

(b) it is produced—

(i) within seven days after the date on which he is so informed, or

(ii) as soon as is reasonably practicable,

at such police station as he may have specified to the constable, or

(c) where it is not produced at such police station, it is not reasonably practicable for it to be produced there before the day on which the proceedings are commenced.

(5) For the purposes of subsection (4) above, the laying of the information or, in Scotland, the service of the complaint on the accused shall be treated as the commencement of the proceedings.

(6) Regulations under this section requiring the wearing of seat belts by persons riding in motor vehicles shall not apply to children under the age of fourteen years.

(7) In this section, "the seat belt Directive" means the Directive of the Council of the European Communities, dated 16th December 1991 (No. 91/671/ EEC) on the approximation of the laws of the member states relating to compulsory use of safety belts in vehicles of less than 3·5 tonnes.

Restriction on carrying children not wearing seat belts in motor vehicles

15.—(1) Except as provided by regulations, where a child under the age of **B15–18** fourteen years is in the front of a motor vehicle, a person must not without reasonable excuse drive the vehicle on a road unless the child is wearing a seat belt in conformity with regulations.

(2) It is an offence for a person to drive a motor vehicle in contravention of subsection (1) above.

(3) Except as provided by regulations, where a child under the age of fourteen years is in the rear of a motor vehicle and any seat belt is fitted in the rear of that vehicle, a person must not without reasonable excuse drive the vehicle on a road unless the child is wearing a seat belt in conformity with regulations.

(3A) Except as provided by regulations, where—
- (a) a child who is under the age of 12 years and less than 150 centimetres in height is in the rear of a passenger car,
- (b) no seat belt is fitted in the rear of the passenger car, and
- (c) a seat in the front of the passenger car is provided with a seat belt but is not occupied by any person,

a person must not without reasonable excuse drive the passenger on a road.

(4) It is an offence for a person to drive a motor vehicle in contravention of subsection (3) or (3A) above.

(5) Provision may be made by regulations—
- (a) excepting from the prohibition in subsection (1), (3) or (3A) above children of any prescribed description, vehicles of a prescribed class or the driving of vehicles in such circumstances as may be prescribed,
- (b) defining in relation to any class of vehicle what part of the vehicle is to be regarded as the front of the vehicle for the purposes of subsection (1) or (3A) above or as the rear of the vehicle for the purposes of subsection (3) or (3A) above,
- (c) prescribing for the purposes of subsection (1) or (3) above the descriptions of seat belt to be worn by children of any prescribed description and the manner in which such seat belt is to be fixed and used.

(5A) Without prejudice to the generality of subsection (5) above, regulations made by virtue of paragraph (c) of that subsection may, for the purpose of implementing the seat belt Directive—
- (a) make different provision in relation to different vehicles and different circumstances,
- (b) authorise the wearing of a seat belt approved under the law of any member state other than the United Kingdom.

(6) Regulations made for the purposes of subsection (3) or (3A) above—
- (a) shall include an exemption for any child holding a valid certificate signed by a medical practitioner to the effect that it is inadvisable on medical grounds for him to wear a seat belt, and
- (b) shall, for the purpose of implementing the seat belt Directive, include

an exemption for any child holding a certificate to the like effect which was issued in any member state, other than the United Kingdom and which, under the law of that state, is valid for purposes corresponding to those of this section,

but such regulations may, for the purpose of implementing that Directive, make either of those exemptions subject to such conditions as may be prescribed.

(6) Regulations made for the purposes of subsection (3) above shall include an exemption for any child holding a valid certificate signed by a medical practitioner to the effect that it is inadvisable on medical grounds for him to wear a seat belt.

(7) If the driver of a motor vehicle is informed by a constable that he may be prosecuted for an offence under subsection (4) above, he is not in proceedings for that offence entitled to rely on an exception afforded to a child by a certificate referred to in subsection (6) above unless—

    (a) it is produced to the constable at the time he is so informed, or

    (b) it is produced—

        (i) within seven days after the date on which he is so informed, or

        (ii) as soon as is reasonably practicable,

    at such police station as he may have specified to the constable, or

    (c) where it is not produced at such police station, it is not reasonably practicable for it to be produced there before the day on which the proceedings are commenced.

(8) For the purposes of subsection (7) above, the laying of the information or, in Scotland, the service of the complaint on the accused shall be treated as the commencement of the proceedings.

(9) In this section—

    "maximum laden weight" has the meaning given by Part IV of Schedule 6 to the Road Traffic Regulation Act 1984;

    "passenger car" means a motor vehicle which—

        (a) is constructed or adapted for use for the carriage of passengers and is not a goods vehicle,

        (b) has no more than eight seats in addition to the driver's seat,

        (c) has four or more wheels,

        (d) has a maximum design speed exceeding 25 kilometres per hour, and

        (e) has a maximum laden weight not exceeding 3·5 tonnes,

    "regulations" means regulations made by the Secretary of State under this section, and

    "seat belt" includes any description of restraining device for a child and any reference to wearing a seat belt is to be construed accordingly.

    "the seat belt Directive" has the same meaning as in section 14.

Safety equipment for children in motor vehicles

B15–19   **15A.**—(1) The Secretary of State may make regulations prescribing (by reference to shape, construction or any other quality) types of equipment of any description to which this section applies that are recommended as conducive to the safety in the event of accident of prescribed classes of children in prescribed classes of motor vehicles.

(2) Regulations under this section may make provision for securing that

when equipment of a type prescribed by the regulations is sold or offered for sale as equipment which is so conducive—

    (a) appropriate information is provided in relation to it in such manner as may be prescribed, and

    (b) inappropriate information is not provided in relation to it.

(3) Except in such circumstances as may be prescribed, if a person sells, or offers for sale, equipment of any description for which a type is prescribed under this section as equipment which is so conducive and that equipment—

    (a) is not of a type so prescribed; or

    (b) is sold or offered for sale in contravention of regulations under this section,

he is, subject to subsection (5) below, guilty of an offence.

(4) Except in such circumstances as may be prescribed, if a person sells, or offers for sale, equipment of any description for which a type is prescribed under this section as equipment conducive to the safety in the event of accident—

    (a) of children not of a class prescribed in relation to equipment of that type; or

    (b) of children in motor vehicles not of a class prescribed in relation to equipment of that type,

he is, subject to subsection (5) below, guilty of an offence.

(5) A person shall not be convicted of an offence under this section in respect of the sale or offer for sale of equipment if he proves that it was sold or, as the case may be, offered for sale for export from Great Britain.

(6) The provisions of Schedule 1 to this Act shall have effect in relation to contraventions of this section.

(7) Regulations under this section may make different provision in relation to different circumstances.

(8) This section applies to equipment of any description for use in a motor vehicle consisting of—

    (a) a restraining device for a child or for a carry-cot; or

    (b) equipment designed for use by a child in conjunction with any description of restraining device.

(9) Reference in this section to selling or offering for sale include respectively references to letting on hire and offering to let on hire.

Wearing of protective headgear

16.—(1) The Secretary of State may make regulations requiring, subject to   **B15–20**
such exceptions as may be specified in the regulations, persons driving or riding (otherwise than in side-cars) on motor cycles of any class specified in the regulations to wear protective headgear of such description as may be so specified.

(2) A requirement imposed by regulations under this section shall not apply to any follower of the Sikh religion while he is wearing a turban.

(3) Regulations under this section may make different provision in relation to different circumstances.

(4) A person who drives or rides on a motor cycle in contravention of regulations under this section is guilty of an offence; but notwithstanding any enactment or rule of law no person other than the person actually committing the contravention is guilty of an offence by reason of the contravention unless the person actually committing the contravention is a child under the age of sixteen years.

Authorisation of head-worn appliances for use on motor cycles

B15–21   **18.**—(1) The Secretary of State may make regulations prescribing (by reference to shape, construction or any other quality) types of appliance of any description to which this section applies as authorised for use by persons driving or riding (otherwise than in sidecars) on motor cycles of any class specified in the regulations.

(2) Regulations under this section—

(a) may impose restrictions or requirements with respect to the circumstances in which appliances of any type prescribed by the regulations may be used, and

(b) may make different provision in relation to different circumstances.

(3) If a person driving or riding on a motor cycle on a road uses an appliance of any description for which a type is prescribed under this section and that appliance—

(a) is not of a type so prescribed, or

(b) is otherwise used in contravention of regulations under this section,

he is guilty of an offence.

(4) If a person sells, or offers for sale, an appliance of any such description as authorised for use by persons on or in motor cycles, or motor cycles of any class, and that appliance is not of a type prescribed under this section as authorised for such use, he is, subject to subsection (5) below, guilty of an offence.

(5) A person shall not be convicted of an offence under this section in respect of the sale or offer for sale of an appliance if he proves that it was sold or, as the case may be, offered for sale for export from Great Britain.

(6) The provisions of Schedule 1 to this Act shall have effect in relation to contraventions of subsection (4) above.

(7) This section applies to appliances of any description designed or adapted for use—

(a) with any headgear, or

(b) by being attached to or placed upon the head,

(as, for example, eye protectors or earphones).

(8) References in this section to selling or offering for sale include respectively references to letting on hire and offering to let on hire.

Prohibition of parking of HGVs on verges, central reservations and footways

B15–22   **19.**—(1) Subject to subsection (2) below, a person who parks a heavy commercial vehicle (as defined in section 20 of this Act) wholly or partly—

(a) on the verge of a road, or

(b) on any land situated between two carriageways and which is not a footway, or

(c) on a footway,

is guilty of an offence.

(2) A person shall not be convicted of an offence under this section in respect of a vehicle if he proves to the satisfaction of the court—

(a) that it was parked in accordance with permission given by a constable in uniform, or

(b) that it was parked in contravention of this section for the purpose of saving life or extinguishing fire or meeting any other like emergency, or

(c) that it was parked in contravention of this section but the conditions specified in subsection (3) below were satisfied.

(3) The conditions mentioned in subsection (2)(c) above are—

(a) that the vehicle was parked on the verge of a road or on a footway for the purpose of loading or unloading, and

(b) that the loading or unloading of the vehicle could not have been satisfactorily performed if it had not been parked on the footway or verge, and

(c) that the vehicle was not left unattended at any time while it was so parked.

(4) In this section "carriageway" and "footway," in relation to England and Wales, have the same meanings as in the Highways Act 1980.

Definition of "heavy commercial vehicle" for the purposes of section 19

20.—(1) In section 19 of this Act, "heavy commercial vehicle" means any goods vehicle which has an operating weight exceeding 7.5 tonnes. **B15–23**

(2) The operating weight of a goods vehicle for the purposes of this section is—

(a) in the case of a motor vehicle not drawing a trailer or in the case of a trailer, its maximum laden weight,

(b) in the case of an articulated vehicle, its maximum laden weight (if it has one) and otherwise the aggregate maximum laden weight of all the individual vehicles forming part of that articulated vehicle, and

(c) in the case of a motor vehicle (other than an articulated vehicle) drawing one or more trailers, the aggregate maximum laden weight of the motor vehicle and the trailer or trailers attached to it.

(3) In this section "articulated vehicle" means a motor vehicle with a trailer so attached to it as to be partially superimposed upon it; and references to the maximum laden weight of a vehicle are references to the total laden weight which must not be exceeded in the case of that vehicle if it is to be used in Great Britain without contravening any regulations for the time being in force under section 41 of this Act.

(4) In this section, and in the definition of "goods vehicle" in section 192 of this Act as it applies for the purposes of this section, "trailer," means any vehicle other than a motor vehicle.

(5) The Secretary of State may by regulations amend subsections (1) and (2) above (whether as originally enacted or as previously amended under this subsection)—

(a) by substituting weights of a different description for any of the weights there mentioned, or

(b) in the case of subsection (1) above, by substituting a weight of a different description or amount, or a weight different both in description and amount, for the weight there mentioned.

(6) Different regulations may be made under subsection (5) above as respects different classes of vehicles or as respects the same class of vehicles in different circumstances and as respects different times of the day or night and as respects different localities.

(7) Regulations under subsection (5) above shall not so amend subsection (1) above that there is any case in which a goods vehicle whose operating weight (ascertained in accordance with subsection (2) above as originally enacted) does not exceed 7.5 tonnes is a heavy commercial vehicle for any of the purposes of section 19 of this Act.

Leaving vehicles in dangerous positions

B15–24 22. If a person in charge of a vehicle causes or permits the vehicle or a trailer drawn by it to remain at rest on a road in such a position or in such condition or in such circumstances as to involve a danger of injury to other persons using the road, he is guilty of an offence.

Causing danger to road-users

B15–25 22A.—(1) A person is guilty of an offence if he intentionally and without lawful authority or reasonable cause—
  (a) causes anything to be on or over a road, or
  (b) interferes with a motor vehicle, trailer or cycle, or
  (c) interferes (directly or indirectly) with traffic equipment,
in such circumstances that it would be obvious to a reasonable person that to do so would be dangerous.

  (2) In subsection (1) above "dangerous" refers to danger either of injury to any person while on or near a road, or of serious damage to property on or near a road; and in determining for the purposes of that subsection what would be obvious to a reasonable person in a particular case, regard shall be had not only to the circumstances of which he could be expected to be aware but also to any circumstances shown to have been within the knowledge of the accused.

  (3) In subsection (1) above "traffic equipment" means—
  (a) anything lawfully placed on or near a road by a highway authority;
  (b) a traffic sign lawfully placed on or near a road by a person other than a highway authority;
  (c) any fence, barrier or light lawfully placed on or near a road—
    (i) in pursuance of section 174 of the Highways Act 1980, or section 65 of the New Roads and Street Works Act 1991 (which provide for guarding, lighting and signing in streets where works are undertaken), or
    (ii) by a constable or a person acting under the instructions (whether general or specific) of a chief officer of police.

  (4) For the purposes of subsection (3) above anything placed on or near a road shall unless the contrary is proved be deemed to have been lawfully placed there.

  (5) In this section "road" does not include a footpath or bridleway.

  (6) This section does not extend to Scotland.

Restriction of carriage of persons on motor cycles

B15–26 23.—(1) Not more than one person in addition to the driver may be carried on a motor bicycle.

  (2) No person in addition to the driver may be carried on a motor bicycle otherwise than sitting astride the motor cycle and on a proper seat securely fixed to the motor cycle behind the driver's seat.

  (3) If a person is carried on a motor cycle in contravention of this section, the driver of the motor cycle is guilty of an offence.

Tampering with motor vehicles

25. If, while a motor vehicle is on a road or on a parking place provided by a **B15–27**
local authority, a person—
    (a) gets on to the vehicle, or
    (b) tampers with the brake or other part of its mechanism,
without lawful authority or reasonable cause he is guilty of an offence.

Holding or getting on to vehicle in order to be towed or carried

26.—(1) If, for the purpose of being carried, a person without lawful auth- **B15–28**
ority or reasonable cause takes or retains hold of, or gets on to a motor vehicle
or trailer while in motion on a road he is guilty of an offence.

(2) If, for the purpose of being drawn, a person takes or retains hold of a
motor vehicle or trailer while in motion on a road he is guilty of an offence.

Dangerous cycling

28.—(1) A person who rides a cycle on a road dangerously is guilty of an **B15–29**
offence.

(2) For the purposes of subsection (1) above a person is to be regarded as
riding dangerously if (and only if)—
    (a) the way he rides falls far below what would be expected of a com-
        petent and careful cyclist, and
    (b) it would be obvious to a competent and careful cyclist that riding in
        that way would be dangerous.

(3) In subsection (2) above "dangerous" refers to danger either of injury to
any person or of serious damage to property; and in determining for the purposes of that subsection what would be obvious to a competent and careful
cyclist in a particular case, regard shall be had not only to the circumstances of
which he could be expected to be aware but also to any circumstances shown
to have been within the knowledge of the accused.

Careless, and inconsiderate, cycling

29. If a person rides a cycle on a road without due care and attention, or **B15–30**
without reasonable consideration for other persons using the road, he is guilty
of an offence.

Cycling when under influence of drink or drugs

30.—(1) A person who, when riding a cycle on a road or other public place, **B15–31**
is unfit to ride through drink or drugs (that is to say, is under the influence of
drink or a drug to such an extent as to be incapable of having proper control of
the cycle) is guilty of an offence.

(2) In Scotland a constable may arrest without warrant a person committing
an offence under this section.

Regulation of cycle racing on public ways

B15–32   **31.**—(1) A person who promotes or takes part in a race or trial of speed on a public way between cycles is guilty of an offence, unless the race or trial—

(a) is authorised, and

(b) is conducted in accordance with any conditions imposed,

by or under regulations under this section.

(2) The Secretary of State may by regulations authorise, or provide for authorising, for the purposes of subsection (1) above, the holding on a public way other than a bridleway—

(a) of races or trials of speed of any class or description, or

(b) of a particular race or trial of speed,

in such cases as may be prescribed and subject to such conditions as may be imposed by or under the regulations.

(3) Regulations under this section may—

(a) prescribe the procedure to be followed, and the particulars to be given, in connection with applications for authorisation under the regulations, and

(b) make different provision for different classes or descriptions of race or trial.

(4) Without prejudice to any other powers exercisable in that behalf, the chief officer of police may give directions with respect to the movement of, or the route to be followed by, vehicular traffic during any period, being directions which it is necessary or expedient to give in relation to that period to prevent or mitigate—

(a) congestion or obstruction of traffic, or

(b) danger to or from traffic,

in consequence of the holding of a race or trial of speed authorised by or under regulations under this section.

(5) Directions under subsection (4) above may include a direction that any road or part of a road specified in the direction shall be closed during the period to vehicles or to vehicles of a class so specified.

(6) In this section "public way" means, in England and Wales, a highway, and in Scotland, a public road but does not include a footpath.

Prohibition of driving motor vehicles elsewhere than on roads

B15–33   **34.**—(1) Subject to the provisions of this section, if without lawful authority a person drives a motor vehicle—

(a) on to or upon any common land, moorland or land of any other description, not being land forming part of a road, or

(b) on any road being a footpath or bridleway,

he is guilty of an offence.

(2) It is not an offence under this section to drive a motor vehicle on any land within fifteen yards of a road, being a road on which a motor vehicle may lawfully be driven, for the purpose only of parking the vehicle on that land.

(3) A person shall not be convicted of an offence under this section with respect to a vehicle if he proves to the satisfaction of the court that it was driven in contravention of this section for the purpose of saving life or extinguishing fire or meeting any other like emergency.

(4) It is hereby declared that nothing in this section prejudices the operation of—

(a) section 193 of the Law of Property Act 1925 (rights of the public over commons and waste lands), or

(b) any byelaws applying to any land,

or affects the law of trespass to land or any right or remedy to which a person may by law be entitled in respect of any such trespass or in particular confers a right to park a vehicle on any land.

Drivers to comply with traffic directions

35.—(1) Where a constable is for the time being engaged in the regulation of **B15–34** traffic in a road, a person driving or propelling a vehicle who neglects or refuses—

   (a) to stop the vehicle, or

   (b) to make it proceed in, or keep to, a particular line of traffic,

when directed to do so by the constable in the execution of his duty is guilty of an offence.

   (2) Where—

   (a) a traffic survey of any description is being carried out on or in the vicinity of a road, and

   (b) a constable gives to a person driving or propelling a vehicle a direction—

      (i) to stop the vehicle,

      (ii) to make it proceed in, or keep to, a particular line of traffic, or

      (iii) to proceed to a particular point on or near the road on which the vehicle is being driven or propelled,

   being a direction given for the purposes of the survey (but not a direction requiring any person to provide any information for the purposes of a traffic survey),

the person is guilty of an offence if he neglects or refuses to comply with the direction.

   (3) The power to give such a direction as is referred to in subsection (2) above for the purposes of a traffic survey shall be so exercised as not to cause any unreasonable delay to a person who indicates that he is unwilling to provide any information for the purposes of the survey.

Drivers to comply with traffic signs

36.—(1) Where a traffic sign, being a sign— **B15–35**

   (a) of the prescribed size, colour and type, or

   (b) of another character authorised by the Secretary of State under the provisions in that behalf of the Road Traffic Regulation Act 1984,

has been lawfully placed on or near a road, a person driving or propelling a vehicle who fails to comply with the indication given by the sign is guilty of an offence.

   (2) A traffic sign shall not be treated for the purposes of this section as having been lawfully placed unless either—

   (a) the indication given by the sign is an indication of a statutory prohibition, restriction or requirement, or

   (b) it is expressly provided by or under any provision of the Traffic Acts that this section shall apply to the sign or to signs of a type of which the sign is one;

and, where the indication mentioned in paragraph (a) of this subsection is of the general nature only of the prohibition, restriction or requirement to which the sign relates, a person shall not be convicted of failure to comply with the indication unless he has failed to comply with the prohibition, restriction or requirement to which the sign relates.

(3) For the purposes of this section a traffic sign placed on or near a road shall be deemed—

(a) to be of the prescribed size, colour and type, or of another character authorised by the Secretary of State under the provisions in that behalf of the Road Traffic Regulation Act 1984, and

(b) (subject to subsection (2) above) to have been lawfully so placed,

unless the contrary is proved.

(4) Where a traffic survey of any description is being carried out on or in the vicinity of a road, this section applies to a traffic sign by which a direction is given—

(a) to stop a vehicle,

(b) to make it proceed in, or keep to, a particular line of traffic, or

(c) to proceed to a particular point on or near the road on which the vehicle is being driven or propelled,

being a direction given for the purposes of the survey (but not a direction requiring any person to provide any information for the purposes of the survey).

(5) Regulations made by the Secretary of State for Transport, the Secretary of State for Wales and the Secretary of State for Scotland acting jointly may specify any traffic sign for the purposes of column 5 of the entry in Schedule 2 to the Road Traffic Offenders Act 1988 relating to offences under this section (offences committed by failing to comply with certain signs involve discretionary disqualification).

Directions to pedestrians

B15–36   **37.** Where a constable in uniform is for the time being engaged in the regulation of vehicular traffic in a road, a person on foot who proceeds across or along the carriageway in contravention of a direction to stop given by the constable in the execution of his duty, either to persons on foot or to persons on foot and other traffic, is guilty of an offence.

The Highway Code

B15–37   **38.**—(1) The Highway Code shall continue to have effect, subject however to revision in accordance with the following provisions of this section.

(2) Subject to the following provisions of this section, the Secretary of State may from time to time revise the Highway Code by revoking, varying, amending or adding to the provisions of the Code in such manner as he thinks fit.

(3) Where the Secretary of State proposes to revise the Highway Code by making any alterations in the provisions of the Code (other than alterations merely consequential on the passing, amendment or repeal of any statutory provision) he must lay the proposed alterations before both Houses of Parliament and must not make the proposed revision until after the end of a period of forty days beginning with the day on which the alterations were so laid.

(4) If within the period mentioned in subsection (3) above either House

resolves that the proposed alterations be not made, the Secretary of State must not make the proposed revision (but without prejudice to the laying before Parliament of further proposals for alteration in accordance with that subsection).

(5) Before revising the Highway Code by making any alterations in its provisions which are required by subsection (3) above to be laid before Parliament, the Secretary of State must consult with such representative organisations as he thinks fit.

(6) The Secretary of State must cause the Highway Code to be printed and may cause copies of it to be sold to the public at such price as he may determine.

(7) A failure on the part of a person to observe a provision of the Highway Code shall not of itself render that person liable to criminal proceedings of any kind but any such failure may in any proceedings (whether civil or criminal, and including proceedings for an offence under the Traffic Acts, the Public Passenger Vehicles Act 1981 or sections 18 to 23 of the Transport Act 1985) be relied upon by any party to the proceedings as tending to establish or negative any liability which is in question in those proceedings.

(8) In this section "the Highway Code" means the code comprising directions for the guidance of persons using roads issued under section 45 of the Road Traffic Act 1930, as from time to time revised under this section or under any previous enactment.

(9) For the purposes of subsection (3) above—

(a) "statutory provision" means a provision contained in an Act or in subordinate legislation within the meaning of the Interpretation Act 1978 (and the reference to the passing or repeal of any such provision accordingly includes the making or revocation of any such provision),

(b) where the proposed alterations are laid before each House of Parliament on different days, the later day shall be taken to be the day on which they were laid before both Houses, and

(c) in reckoning any period of forty days, no account shall be taken of any time during which Parliament is dissolved or prorogued or during which both Houses are adjourned for more than four days.

Drivers of motor vehicles to have driving licences

87.—(1) It is an offence for a person to drive on a road a motor vehicle of any class otherwise than in accordance with a licence authorising him to drive a motor vehicle of that class.   **B15–38**

(2) It is an offence for a person to cause or permit another person to drive on a road a motor vehicle of any class otherwise than in accordance with a licence authorising that other person to drive a motor vehicle of that class.

Exceptions

88.—(1) Notwithstanding section 87 of this Act, a person may drive or cause or permit another person to drive a vehicle of any class if—   **B15–39**

(a) the driver has held—

(i) a licence under this Part of this Act to drive vehicles of that or a corresponding class, or

(ii) a Northern Ireland licence to drive vehicles of that or a corresponding class, or

  (iii) a British external licence or British Forces licence to drive vehicles of that or a corresponding class, or

  (iv) an exchangeable licence to drive vehicles of that or a corresponding class, and

 (b) either—

  (i) a qualifying application by the driver for the grant of a licence to drive vehicles of that class for a period which includes that time has been received by the Secretary of State, or

  (ii) a licence to drive vehicles of that class granted to him has been revoked or surrendered in pursuance of section 99(3) or (4) of this Act otherwise than by reason of a current disqualification or of its having been granted in error, and

 (c) any conditions which by virtue of section 97(3) or 98(2) of this Act apply to the driving under the authority of the licence of vehicles of that class are complied with.

(1A) An application for the grant of a licence to drive vehicles of any class is a qualifying application for the purposes of subsection (1)(b)(i) above if—

 (a) the requirements of paragraphs (a), (b) so far as it relates to initial evidence and (c) of section 97(1) of this Act have been satisfied;

 (b) the applicant—

  (i) is not subject to a current disqualification which is relevant to the licence he applies for, and

  (ii) is not prevented from obtaining it by section 89 of this Act; and

 (c) the declaration made in pursuance of section 92(1) of this Act indicates that he is not suffering from a relevant disability.

(1B) A disqualification is relevant to a licence for which a person makes an application if—

 (a) in the case of an application made by virtue of any provision of subsection (1)(a) above, the disqualification subsists under or by virtue of any provision of the Road Traffic Acts and relates to vehicles of the class to which his application relates;

 (b) in the case of an application made by virtue of subsection (1)(a)(ii) above, the disqualification subsists under or by virtue of any provision of the law of Northern Ireland and relates to vehicles of the class, or of a class corresponding to the class, to which his application relates;

 (c) in the case of an application made by virtue of subsection (1)(a)(iii) above, the disqualification subsists under or by virtue of any provision of the relevant external law or, as the case may be, is a disqualification for holding or obtaining a British Forces licence and relates to vehicles of the class, or of a class corresponding to the class, to which his application relates; and

 (d) in the case of an application made by virtue of subsection (1)(a)(iv) above, the disqualification subsists under or by virtue of any provision of the law of the member State or country or territory under which the licence which he held was granted and relates to vehicles of the class, or of a class corresponding to the class, to which his application relates;

but a disqualification which does not prevent the person disqualified from obtaining a provisional licence or, as the case may be, a licence corresponding to a provisional licence is relevant to a full licence but not to a provisional licence.

(2) The benefit of subsection (1) above does not extend—

 (a) beyond the date when a licence is granted in pursuance of the application mentioned in subsection (1)(b) above or (as the case may be) in pursuance of section 99(7) of this Act in consequence of the revocation or surrender so mentioned, or

(b) in a case where a licence is not in fact so granted, beyond the expiration of the period of one year or such shorter period as may be prescribed, beginning on the date of the application or (as the case may be) the revocation or surrender mentioned in subsection (1)(b) above, or

(c) in a case where a licence is refused under section 92(3) of this Act, beyond the day on which the applicant receives notice of the refusal.

(3) The Secretary of State may by regulations provide that subsection (1) above shall also apply (where the requirements of that subsection are otherwise met) in the case of a person who has not previously held a licence to drive vehicles of the relevant class.

(4) Regulations made by virtue of subsection (3) above shall, if not previously revoked, expire at the end of the period of one year beginning with the day on which they came into operation.

(5) Regulations may provide that a person who becomes resident in Great Britain shall, during the prescribed period after he becomes so resident, be treated for the purposes of section 87 of this Act as the holder of a licence authorising him to drive motor vehicles of the prescribed classes if—

(a) he satisfies the prescribed conditions, and

(b) he is the holder of a permit of the prescribed description authorising him to drive vehicles under the law of a country outside the United Kingdom.

(6) Regulations made by virtue of subsection (5) above may provide for the application of any enactment relating to licences, counterparts of licences or licence holders, with or without modifications, in relation to any such permit and its holder respectively.

(7) Notwithstanding section 87 of this Act—

(a) a person who is not a holder of a licence may act as steersman of a motor vehicle, being a vehicle on which a speed limit of five miles per hour or less is imposed by or under section 86 of the Road Traffic Regulation Act 1984, under the orders of another person engaged in the driving of the vehicle who is licensed in that behalf in accordance with the requirements of this Part and Part IV of this Act, and

(b) a person may cause or permit another person who is not the holder of a licence so to act.

(8) In this Part of this Act—

"British external licence" means a licence granted in the Isle of Man or any of the Channel Islands under the relevant external law;

"British Forces licence" means a licence granted in the Federal Republic of Germany by the British authorities to members of the British Forces or of the civilian components of those Forces or their dependants; and

"relevant external law" means the law for the time being in force in the Isle of Man or any of the Channel Islands which corresponds to this Part of this Act.

Tests of competence to drive

89.—(1) A licence authorising the driving of motor vehicles of any class shall not be granted to any person unless he satisfies the Secretary of State—   **B15–40**

(a) that at some time during the period of two years ending with the date the application is made but not earlier than the appointed day he has passed—

(i) the test of competence to drive prescribed by virtue of subsection (3) below, or

(ii) a Northern Ireland test of competence to drive which corresponds to such a test, or

(iii) a test of competence which under subsection (6) below is a sufficient test;

or that, if it is available to him, he satisfies the alternative requirement of section 89A of this Act; or

(b) that at some time not earlier than the appointed day he has held—

    (i) a full licence authorising the driving of vehicles of that class, or

    (ii) a full Northern Ireland licence authorising the driving of vehicles of that or a corresponding class;

or that, if it is available to him, he satisfies the alternative requirement of section 89A of this Act; or

(c) that at some time during the period of two years ending with the date the application is made he has passed a test of competence to drive vehicles of that or a corresponding class conducted under any relevant external law or for the purpose of obtaining a British Forces licence; or

(d) that at some time not earlier than the appointed day he has held a full British external licence or a full British Forces licence to drive vehicles of that or a corresponding class or that, if it is available to him, he satisfies the alternative requirement of section 89A of this Act; or

(e) that at some time during the period of two years ending with the date the application is made he has passed a test of competence to drive vehicles of that or a corresponding class conducted under the law of another member State or of Gibraltar or a designated country or territory; or

(f) that, at the time of the application for the licence—

    (i) he holds an exchangeable licence authorising the driving of vehicles of that or a corresponding class, and

    (ii) he is normally resident in Great Britain or (where the exchangeable licence is a Community licence) the United Kingdom but has not been so resident for more than the prescribed period.

This subsection is subject to the provisions of this Part of this Act as to provisional licences and to the provisions of any regulations made by virtue of section 105(2)(f) of this Act.

(2) For the purposes of subsection (1) above—

(a) a licence which has been revoked under section 99(3) of this Act or any corresponding provision of the law of Northern Ireland or under any corresponding provision of the relevant external law as a licence granted in error shall be disregarded for the purposes of paragraph (b) or, as the case may be, paragraph (d) of that subsection;

(b) a test of competence to drive any class of goods vehicle or any class of passenger-carrying vehicle conducted under a relevant external law is to be disregarded for the purposes of paragraph (c) of that subsection unless the Secretary of State, by order made by statutory instrument, designates that law as one which makes satisfactory provision for tests of competence to drive such vehicles;

(c) a British external licence to drive any class of goods vehicle or any class of passenger-carrying vehicle is to be disregarded for the purposes of paragraph (d) of that subsection unless the Secretary of State, by order made by statutory instrument, designates the relevant external law under which it is granted as one which makes satisfactory provision for the granting of such licences.

(2A) Except as provided under subsection (5A) below, no person submitting himself for a test of competence to drive a motor bicycle shall be permitted to take the test unless he furnishes the prescribed certificate of completion by him of an approved training course for motor cyclists either with his application for an appointment for a test or to the person who is to conduct the test.

(3) Regulations may make provision with respect to—
- (a) the nature of tests of competence to drive for the purposes of this section and section 36 of the Road Traffic Offenders Act 1988 (disqualification),
- (b) the qualifications, selection and appointment of persons by whom they may be conducted and the revocation of any appointment,
- (c) evidence of the results of such tests,

and generally with respect to such tests.

(4) In particular, regulations may, without prejudice to the generality of subsection (3) above, provide—
- (a) for requiring a person submitting himself for a test to provide a vehicle for the purposes of the test, in the case of prescribed classes of goods vehicle, loaded or unloaded as may be prescribed and, if requirements as respects loading are prescribed, loaded in accordance with the requirements,
- (b) for requiring a fee, of such amount as may be specified in the regulations or, in such cases as may be prescribed, specified by such person as may be prescribed, to be paid by a person who submits himself for a test or applies for an appointment for a test,
- (c) for ensuring that a person submitting himself for a test and failing to pass that test shall not be eligible to submit himself for another test by the same or any other person before the expiration of a period specified in the regulations, except under an order made by a court or sheriff under the power conferred by section 90 of this Act,

and different regulations may be made with respect to tests of competence to drive different classes of vehicles.

(5) If regulations make provision for a test of competence to drive to consist of separate parts, they may make for each part—
- (a) any provision that could be made for a test not consisting of separate parts, and
- (b) provision for the supply by the Secretary of State of forms for certificates evidencing the results and for charges to be made for the supply.

(5A) Regulations may prescribe cases in which persons are exempt from the requirement imposed by subsection (2A) above; and the regulations may—
- (a) limit the exemption to persons in prescribed circumstances;
- (b) limit the exemption to a prescribed period;
- (c) attach conditions to the exemption; and
- (d) regulate applications for, and the issue and form of, certificates evidencing a person's exemption from that requirement.

(6) For the purposes of subsection (1)(a)(iii) above or section 89A(2)(b)(iii) below, a test of competence shall be sufficient for the granting of a licence authorising the driving of—
- (a) vehicles of any class, if at the time the test was passed it authorised the granting of a licence to drive vehicles of that class,
- (b) vehicles of all classes which are designated by regulations as a group for the purposes of subsection (1)(a) above, if at the time the test was passed it authorised the granting of a licence to drive vehicles of any class included in the group, and
- (c) vehicles of all classes included in another such group, if a person passing the test is treated by virtue of regulations made for the purposes of

this paragraph as competent also to drive vehicles of a class included in that other group.

(7) If vehicles of any classes are designated by regulations as a group for the purposes of subsection (1)(b) above, a licence authorising the driving of vehicles of a class included in the group shall be deemed for the purposes of subsection (1)(b)(i) above or section 89A(4)(a) below to authorise the driving of—

(a) vehicles of all classes included in the group, and

(b) vehicles of all classes included in another such group, if a person holding the licence is treated by virtue of regulations as competent also to drive vehicles of a class included in that other group.

The reference in this subsection to a licence does not include a licence which has been revoked in pursuance of section 99(3) of this Act.

(8) For the purposes of this section and section 88(1) of this Act, an exchangeable licence issued in respect of a member State, country or territory shall not be treated as authorising a person to drive a vehicle of any class if—

(a) the licence is not for the time being valid for that purpose, or

(b) it was issued in respect of that class for a purpose corresponding to that mentioned in section 97(2) of this Act.

(9) A test of competence falling within paragraphs (a)(ii), (c) or (e) of subsection (1) above shall be sufficient for the granting of a licence authorising the driving of—

(a) vehicles of all classes designated by regulations as a group for the purposes of subsection (1)(a) above, if at the time the test was passed it authorised the granting of a licence to drive vehicles of any class included in the group, or of any class corresponding to a class included in the group, and

(b) vehicles of all classes included in another such group, if a person passing a test of competence authorising the granting of a licence to drive vehicles of a class included in the group mentioned in paragraph (a) above is treated by virtue of regulations as competent also to drive vehicles of a class included in that other group.

(10) A full Northern Ireland licence, a full British external licence, a full British Forces licence or an exchangeable licence shall be treated for the purposes of paragraphs (b)(ii), (d) or (f) (as the case may be) of subsection (1) above as authorising the driving of—

(a) vehicles of all classes designated by regulations as a group for the purposes of subsection (1)(b) above, if the licence authorises the driving of vehicles of any class included in the group, or any class corresponding to a class included in the group, and

(b) vehicles of all classes included in another such group, if by virtue of regulations a person holding a licence authorising him to drive vehicles of any class included in the group mentioned in paragraph (a) above is treated as competent also to drive vehicles of a class included in that other group.

(11) In this section "designated country or territory" means a country or territory designated under section 108(2) of this Act for the purposes of the definition of exchangeable licence and in this section and section 89A "the appointed day" means the day appointed for the coming into force of section 1 of the Road Traffic (Driver Licensing and Information Systems) Act 1989.

The alternative requirements to those in section 89

89A.—(1) The alternative requirements referred to in section 89(1) of this **B15–41**
Act are the following.

(2) The requirement which is alternative to that specified in section 89(1)(a)
on an application by a person for a licence authorising the driving of motor
vehicles of any class other than any class of goods vehicle or passenger-carrying vehicle prescribed for the purposes of subsection (3) below—

    (a) is available to that person if the application is made within the period
        of ten years beginning with the appointed day, and

    (b) is that at some time before the appointed day and during the period of
        ten years ending with the date the application is made he has passed—

        (i) the test of competence to drive prescribed by virtue of section
           89(3) of this Act or a test of competence to drive which corre-
           sponds to such a test, or

        (ii) a Northern Ireland test of competence to drive which corre-
           sponds to any test falling within (i) above, or

        (iii) a test of competence which under section 89(6) of this Act is a suf-
           ficient test or a test of competence to drive which corresponds to
           such a test.

(3) The requirement which is alternative to that specified in section 89(1)(a)
on an application by a person for a licence authorising the driving of any class
of goods vehicle or passenger-carrying vehicle prescribed for the purposes of
this subsection—

    (a) is available to that person if the application is made within the period
        of five years beginning with the appointed day, and

    (b) is that at some time before the appointed day and during the period of
        five years ending with the date the application is made he has
        passed—

        (i) a test of competence to drive a heavy goods vehicle or public ser-
           vice vehicle of a class corresponding to the class of vehicle to
           which his application relates, or

        (ii) a corresponding Northern Ireland test of competence to drive a
           heavy goods vehicle or public service vehicle of a class which cor-
           responds to the class of goods vehicle or passenger-carrying
           vehicle to which his application relates.

(4) The requirement which is alternative to that specified in section 89(1)(b)
on an application by a person for a licence authorising the driving of motor
vehicles of any class other than any class of goods vehicle or passenger-carrying vehicle prescribed for the purposes of subsection (5) below is that at some
time before the appointed day but not earlier than January 1, 1976 he has
held—

    (a) a full licence authorising the driving of vehicles of a class correspond-
        ing to the class of motor vehicle to which his application relates, or

    (b) a full Northern Ireland licence authorising the driving of vehicles of a
        class corresponding to the class of motor vehicle to which his appli-
        cation relates.

(5) The requirement which is alternative to that specified in section 89(1)(b)
on an application by a person for a licence authorising the driving of any class
of goods vehicle or passenger-carrying vehicle prescribed for the purposes of
this subsection is that at some time before the appointed day but not earlier
than the beginning of the period of five years ending with the appointed day
he has held—

    (a) a full heavy goods vehicle or a public service vehicle driver's licence authorising the driving of vehicles of a class corresponding to the class of vehicle to which his application relates, or

(b) a full Northern Ireland licence to drive heavy goods vehicles of a class corresponding to the class of vehicle to which his application relates or a Northern Ireland licence to drive public service vehicles of a class corresponding to the class of vehicle to which his application relates.

(6) The requirement which is alternative to that specified in section 89(1)(d) on an application by a person for a licence authorising the driving of motor vehicles of any class—

(a) is available to that person if the application is made within the period of ten years beginning with the appointed day, and

(b) is that at some time before the appointed day and during the period of ten years ending with the date the application is made he has held a full British external licence or a full British Forces licence to drive vehicles of that or a corresponding class.

(7) In this section "heavy goods vehicle" and "public service vehicle" have the same meaning as they had for the purposes of Part IV of this Act or section 22 of the Public Passenger Vehicles Act 1981 before their repeal by section 1 of the Road Traffic (Driver Licensing and Information Systems) Act 1989.

Review of conduct of test

B15–42   **90.**—(1) On the application of a person who has submitted himself for a test of competence to drive—

(a) a magistrates' court acting for the petty sessions area in which he resides, or

(b) in Scotland, the sheriff within whose jurisdiction he resides, may determine whether the test was properly conducted in accordance with regulations.

(2) The court or, as the case may be, sheriff may, if it appears that the test was not so conducted—

(a) order that the applicant shall be eligible to submit himself for another test before the expiration of the period specified for the purposes of section 89(4)(c) of this Act, and

(b) order that any fee payable by the applicant in respect of the test shall not be paid or, if it has been paid, shall be repaid.

(3) If regulations make provision for a test of competence to drive to consist of separate parts, this section applies in relation to each part as well as in relation to the whole of the test.

Requirements as to physical fitness of drivers

B15–43   **92.**—(1) An application for the grant of a licence must include a declaration by the applicant, in such form as the Secretary of State may require, stating whether he is suffering or has at any time (or, if a period is prescribed for the purposes of this subsection, has during that period) suffered from any relevant disability or any prospective disability.

(2) In this Part of this Act—

"disability" includes disease,

"relevant disability" in relation to any person means—

(a) any prescribed disability, and

380

(b) any other disability likely to cause the driving of a vehicle by him in pursuance of a licence to be a source of danger to the public, and

"prospective disability" in relation to any person means any other disability which—

(a) at the time of the application for the grant of a licence or, as the case may be, the material time for the purposes of the provision in which the expression is used, is not of such a kind that it is a relevant disability, but

(b) by virtue of the intermittent or progressive nature of the disability or otherwise, may become a relevant disability in course of time.

(3) If it appears from the applicant's declaration, or if on inquiry the Secretary of State is satisfied from other information, that the applicant is suffering from a relevant disability, the Secretary of State must, subject to the following provisions of this section, refuse to grant the licence.

(4) The Secretary of State must not by virtue of subsection (3) above refuse to grant a licence—

(a) on account of any relevant disability which is prescribed for the purposes of this paragraph, if the applicant has at any time passed a relevant test and it does not appear to the Secretary of State that the disability has arisen or become more acute since that time or was, for whatever reason, not disclosed to the Secretary of State at that time,

(b) on account of any relevant disability which is prescribed for the purposes of this paragraph, if the applicant satisfies such conditions as may be prescribed with a view to authorising the grant of a licence to a person in whose case the disability is appropriately controlled,

(c) on account of any relevant disability which is prescribed for the purposes of this paragraph, if the application is for a provisional licence.

(5) Where as a result of a test of competence to drive or of information obtained under the relevant powers the Secretary of State is satisfied that the person who took the test or in relation to whom the information was obtained is suffering from a disability such that there is likely to be a danger to the public—

(a) if he drives any vehicle, or

(b) if he drives a vehicle other than a vehicle of a particular class,

the Secretary of State must serve notice in writing to that effect on that person and must include in the notice a description of the disability.

(6) Where a notice is served in pursuance of subsection (5)(a) above, then—

(a) if the disability is not prescribed under subsection (2) above, it shall be deemed to be so prescribed in relation to the person who took the test, and

(b) if the disability is prescribed for the purposes of subsection (4)(c) above it shall be deemed not to be so prescribed in relation to him.

(7) Where a notice is served in pursuance of subsection (5)(b) above, any licence granted to the person who took the test shall be limited to vehicles of the particular class specified in the notice and, if the Secretary of State so directs in the notice, his entitlement to drive other classes of vehicles by virtue of section 98(2) of this Act shall be limited as specified in the notice.

(7A) If he considers it appropriate to do so the Secretary of State may, after serving a notice in pursuance of subsection (5)(a) above, serve a notice in pursuance of subsection (5)(b) above or, after serving a notice in pursuance of subsection (5)(b) above, serve a notice in pursuance of subsection (5)(a) above or a further notice in pursuance of subsection (5)(b) above; and on his serving a further notice under any of those provisions the notice previously served shall cease to have effect and any limited licence previously granted shall be revoked by the subsequent notice.

(7B) In subsection (5) above the references to a test of competence to drive and to information obtained under the relevant powers are references respectively to a test of competence prescribed for the purposes of section 89 or so much of such a test as is required to be taken in pursuance of section 94(5)(c) of this Act and to information obtained in pursuance of section 94(5)(a) or (b) of this Act.

(7C) A person whose licence is revoked by virtue of subsection (7A) above must deliver the licence and its counterpart to the Secretary of State forthwith after the revocation and a person who, without reasonable excuse, fails to do so is guilty of an offence.

(8) In this section "relevant test," in relation to an application for a licence, means any such test of competence as is mentioned in section 89 of this Act or a test as to fitness or ability in pursuance of section 100 of the Road Traffic Act 1960 as originally enacted, being a test authorising the grant of a licence in respect of vehicles of the classes to which the application relates.

(9) Without prejudice to subsection (8) above, for the purposes of subsection (4)(a) above—

    (a) an applicant shall be treated as having passed a relevant test if, and on the day on which, he passed a test of competence to drive which—

        (i) under a provision of the law of Northern Ireland or a relevant external law corresponding to subsections (3) and (4) or (6) of section 89 of this Act, either is prescribed in relation to vehicles of classes corresponding to the classes to which the application relates or is sufficient under that law for the granting of a licence authorising the driving of vehicles of those classes, or

        (ii) is sufficient for the granting of a British Forces licence authorising the driving of vehicles of those classes, and

    (b) in the case of an applicant who is treated as having passed a relevant test by virtue of paragraph (a) above, disclosure of a disability to his licensing authority shall be treated as disclosure to the Secretary of State.

(10) A person who holds a licence authorising him to drive a motor vehicle of any class and who drives a motor vehicle of that class on a road is guilty of an offence if the declaration included in accordance with subsection (1) above in the application on which the licence was granted was one which he knew to be false.

Revocation of licence because of disability or prospective disability

B15–44   **93.**—(1) If the Secretary of State is at any time satisfied on inquiry—

    (a) that a licence holder is suffering from a relevant disability, and

    (b) that the Secretary of State would be required by virtue of section 92(3) or (7) of this Act to refuse an application for the licence made by him at that time.

the Secretary of State may serve notice in writing on the licence holder revoking the licence with effect from such date as may be specified in the notice, not being earlier than the date of service of the notice.

(2) If the Secretary of State is at any time satisfied on inquiry that a licence holder is suffering from a prospective disability, the Secretary of State may—

    (a) serve notice in writing on the licence holder revoking the licence with effect from such date as may be specified in the notice, not being earlier than the date of service of the notice, and

(b) on receipt of the licence so revoked and its counterpart and of an application made for the purposes of this subsection, grant to the licence holder, free of charge, a new licence for a period determined by the Secretary of State under section 99(1)(b) of this Act.

(3) A person whose licence is revoked under subsection (1) or (2) above must deliver up the licence and its counterpart to the Secretary of State forthwith after the revocation and a person who, without reasonable excuse, fails to do so is guilty of an offence.

(4) Where a person whose licence is revoked under subsection (1) or (2) above—

(a) is not in possession of his licence or its counterpart in consequence of the fact that he has surrendered them to a constable or authorised person (within the meaning of Part III of the Road Traffic Offenders Act 1988) on receiving a fixed penalty notice given to him under section 54 of that Act but

(b) delivers them to the Secretary of State immediately on their return,

he is not in breach of the duty under subsection (3) above.

Provision of information, etc. relating to disabilities

94.—(1) If at any time during the period for which his licence remains in force, a licence holder becomes aware— **B15–45**

(a) that he is suffering from a relevant or prospective disability which he has not previously disclosed to the Secretary of State, or

(b) that a relevant or prospective disability from which he has at any time suffered (and which has been previously so disclosed) has become more acute since the licence was granted,

the licence holder must forthwith notify the Secretary of State in writing of the nature and extent of his disability.

(2) The licence holder is not required to notify the Secretary of State under subsection (1) above if—

(a) the disability is one from which he has not previously suffered, and

(b) he has reasonable grounds for believing that the duration of the disability will not extend beyond the period of three months beginning with the date on which he first becomes aware that he suffers from it.

(3) A person who fails without reasonable excuse to notify the Secretary of State as required by subsection (1) above is guilty of an offence.

(3A) A person who holds a licence authorising him to drive a motor vehicle of any class and who drives a motor vehicle of that class on a road is guilty of an offence if at any earlier time while the licence was in force he was required by subsection (1) above to notify the Secretary of State but has failed without reasonable excuse to do so.

(4) If the prescribed circumstances obtain in relation to a person who is an applicant for, or the holder of, a licence or if the Secretary of State has reasonable grounds for believing that a person who is an applicant for, or the holder of, a licence may be suffering from a relevant or prospective disability, subsection (5) below applies for the purpose of enabling the Secretary of State to satisfy himself whether or not that person may be suffering from that or any other relevant or prospective disability.

(5) The Secretary of State may by notice in writing served on the applicant or holder—

(a) require him to provide the Secretary of State, within such reasonable time as may be specified in the notice, with such an authorisation as is mentioned in subsection (6) below, or

(b) require him, as soon as practicable, to arrange to submit himself for examination—

    (i) by such registered medical practitioner or practitioners as may be nominated by the Secretary of State, or

    (ii) with respect to a disability of a prescribed description, by such officer of the Secretary of State as may be so nominated,

for the purpose of determining whether or not he suffers or has at any time suffered from a relevant or prospective disability, or

(c) except where the application is for, or the licence held is, a provisional licence, require him to submit himself for such a test of competence to drive as the Secretary of State directs in the notice.

(6) The authorisation referred to in subsection (5)(a) above—

(a) shall be in such form and contain such particulars as may be specified in the notice by which it is required to be provided, and

(b) shall authorise any registered medical practitioner who may at any time have given medical advice or attention to the applicant or licence holder concerned to release to the Secretary of State any information which he may have, or which may be available to him, with respect to the question whether, and if so to what extent, the applicant or licence holder concerned may be suffering, or may at any time have suffered, from a relevant or prospective disability.

(7) If he considers it appropriate to do so in the case of any applicant or licence holder, the Secretary of State—

(a) may include in a single notice under subsection (5) above requirements under more than one paragraph of that subsection, and

(b) may at any time after the service of a notice under that subsection serve a further notice or notices under that subsection.

(8) If any person on whom a notice is served under subsection (5) above—

(a) fails without reasonable excuse to comply with a requirement contained in the notice, or

(b) fails any test of competence which he is required to take as mentioned in paragraph (c) of that subsection,

the Secretary of State may exercise his powers under sections 92 and 93 of this Act as if he were satisfied that the applicant or licence holder concerned is suffering from a relevant disability which is not prescribed for the purposes of any paragraph of section 92(4) of this Act or, if the Secretary of State so determines, as if he were satisfied that the applicant or licence holder concerned is suffering from a prospective disability.

(9) Except where the requirement is made in the circumstances prescribed for the purposes of subsection (5) above, it shall be for the Secretary of State (and not for any other person) to defray any fees or other reasonable expenses of a registered medical practitioner in connection with—

(a) the provision of information in pursuance of an authorisation required to be provided under subsection (5)(a) above, or

(b) any examination which a person is required to undergo as mentioned in subsection (5)(b) above.

Driving after refusal or revocation of licence

B15–46   **94A.**—(1) A person who drives a motor vehicle of any class on a road otherwise than in accordance with a licence authorising him to drive a motor vehicle of that class is guilty of an offence if—

(a) at any earlier time the Secretary of State has in accordance with section 92(3) of this Act refused to grant such a licence, or has under section 93(1) or (2) revoked such a licence, and

(b) he has not since that earlier time held such a licence.

(2) Section 88 of this Act shall apply in relation to subsection (1) above as it applies in relation to section 87.

Notification of refusal of insurance on grounds of health

95.—(1) If an authorised insurer refuses to issue to any person such a policy **B15–47** of insurance as complies with the requirements of Part VI of this Act on the ground that the state of health of that person is not satisfactory, or on grounds which include that ground, the insurer shall as soon as practicable notify the Secretary of State of that refusal and of the full name, address, sex and date of birth of that person as disclosed by him to the insurer.

(2) In subsection (1) above "authorised insurer" means a person or body of persons carrying on insurance business within Group 2 in Part II of Schedule 2 to the Insurance Companies Act 1982 and being a member of the Motor Insurers' Bureau (a company limited by guarantee and incorporated under the Companies Act 1929 on 14th June 1946).

Driving with uncorrected defective eyesight

96.—(1) If a person drives a motor vehicle on a road while his eyesight is **B15–48** such (whether through a defect which cannot be or one which is not for the time being sufficiently corrected) that he cannot comply with any requirement as to eyesight prescribed under this Part of this Act for the purposes of tests of competence to drive, he is guilty of an offence.

(2) A constable having reason to suspect that a person driving a motor vehicle may be guilty of an offence under subsection (1) above may require him to submit to a test for the purpose of ascertaining whether, using no other means of correction than he used at the time of driving, he can comply with the requirement concerned.

(3) If that person refuses to submit to the test he is guilty of an offence.

Form of licence

98.—(1) A licence shall be in such form as the Secretary of State may deter- **B15–49** mine and shall—

(a) state whether, apart from subsection (2) below, it authorises its holder to drive motor vehicles of all classes or of certain classes only and, in the latter case, specify those classes,

(b) specify the restrictions on the driving of vehicles of any class in pursuance of the licence to which its holder is subject by virtue of the provisions of section 101 of this Act, and

(c) in the case of a provisional licence, specify the conditions subject to which it is granted.

(2) Subject to subsections (3), (4) and (4A) below, a person who holds a

licence which authorises its holder to drive motor vehicles of certain classes only (not being—

(a) a provisional licence, or

(b) any other prescribed description of licence)

may drive motor vehicles of all other classes subject to the same conditions as if he were authorised by a provisional licence to drive motor vehicles of those other classes.

(3) Subsection (2) above does not authorise a person to drive—

(a) a vehicle of a class for the driving of which he could not, by reason of the provisions of section 101 of this Act, lawfully hold a licence, or

(b) unless he has passed a test of competence to drive, a motor bicycle without a side-car which, by virtue of section 97(3)(d) of this Act, a provisional licence would not authorise him to drive before he had passed that test, or

(c) unless he has passed a test of competence to drive, a motor bicycle on a road in circumstances in which, by virtue of section 97(3)(e) of this Act, a provisional licence would not authorise him to drive it before he had passed that test.

(4) In such cases or as respects such classes of vehicles as the Secretary of State may prescribe, the provisions of subsections (2) and (3) above shall not apply or shall apply subject to such limitations as he may prescribe.

(4A) Subsection (2) above does not authorise a person on whom a notice under section 92(5)(b) of this Act has been served to drive motor vehicles otherwise than in accordance with the limits specified in the notice.

Duration of licences

B15–50 99.—(1) In so far as a licence authorises its holder to drive motor vehicles of classes other than any prescribed class of goods vehicle or any prescribed class of passenger-carrying vehicle, it shall, unless previously revoked or surrendered, remain in force, subject to subsection (2) below—

(a) except in a case falling within paragraph (b) or (c) of this subsection, for the period ending on the seventieth anniversary of the applicant's date of birth or for a period of three years, whichever is the longer,

(b) except in a case falling within paragraph (c) of this subsection, if the Secretary of State so determines in the case of a licence to be granted to a person appearing to him to be suffering from a relevant or prospective disability, for such period of not more than three years and not less than one year as the Secretary of State may determine, and

(c) in the case of a licence granted in exchange for a subsisting licence and in pursuance of an application requesting a licence for the period authorised by this paragraph, for a period equal to the remainder of that for which the subsisting licence was granted, and any such period shall begin with the date on which the licence in question is expressed to come into force.

(1A) In so far as a licence authorises its holder to drive any prescribed class of goods vehicle or passenger-carrying vehicle, it shall, unless previously revoked, suspended or surrendered, remain in force—

(a) except in a case falling within paragraph (c) or (d) of this subsection—

(i) for the period ending on the forty-fifth anniversary of the applicant's date of birth or for a period of five years, whichever is the longer, or

     (ii) where the applicant's age at the date on which the licence is to come into force will exceed forty-five but not sixty-five years, for the period ending on the sixty-sixth anniversary of the applicant's date of birth or for a period of five years, whichever is the shorter,

  (b) except in a case falling within paragraph (d) of this subsection, where the applicant's age at that date will exceed sixty-five years, for a period of one year,

  (c) except in a case falling within paragraph (b) or (d) of this subsection, if the Secretary of State so determines in the case of a licence to be granted to a person appearing to him to be suffering from a relevant or prospective disability, for such period of not more than three years and not less than one year as the Secretary of State may determine, and

  (d) in the case of a licence granted in exchange for a subsisting licence and in pursuance of an application requesting a licence for the period authorised by this paragraph, for a period equal to the remainder of that for which the subsisting licence was granted.

and any such period shall begin with the date on which the licence in question is expressed to come into force.

(2) To the extent that a provisional licence authorises the driving of a motor cycle of a prescribed class it shall, unless previously surrendered or revoked, remain in force—

  (a) for such period as may be prescribed, or

  (b) if the licence is granted to the holder of a previous licence which was surrendered, revoked or treated as being revoked—

     (i) for the remainder of the period for which the previous licence would have authorised the driving of such a motor cycle, or

     (ii) in such circumstances as may be prescribed, for a period equal to that remainder at the time of surrender or revocation.

(3) Where it appears to the Secretary of State—

  (a) that a licence granted by him to any person was granted in error or with an error or omission in the particulars specified in the licence, or

  (aa) that the counterpart of a licence granted by him to any person is required to be endorsed in pursuance of any enactment or was issued with an error or omission in the particulars specified in the counterpart or required to be so endorsed on it, or

  (b) that the particulars specified in a licence granted by him to any person or in its counterpart do not comply with any requirement imposed since the licence was granted by any provision made by or having effect under any enactment,

the Secretary of State may serve notice in writing on that person revoking the licence and requiring him to surrender the licence and its counterpart forthwith to the Secretary of State and it shall be the duty of that person to comply with the requirement.

(4) Where the name or address of the licence holder as specified in a licence ceases to be correct, its holder must forthwith surrender the licence and its counterpart to the Secretary of State and provide him with particulars of the alterations falling to be made in the name or address and, in the case of a provisional licence as respects which the prescribed conditions are satisfied, with a statement of his sex and date of birth.

(5) A person who without reasonable excuse fails to comply with the duty under subsection (3) or (4) above is guilty of an offence.

(6) Where a person who has a duty under this section to surrender his licence and its counterpart is not in possession of them in consequence of the

fact that he has surrendered them to a constable or authorised person (within the meaning of Part III of the Road Traffic Offenders Act 1988) on receiving a fixed penalty notice given to him under section 54 of that Act, he does not fail to comply with the duty if he surrenders the licence and its counterpart to the Secretary of State immediately on their return.

(7) On the surrender of a licence and its counterpart by any person in pursuance of subsection (3) or (4) above, the Secretary of State—

    (a) must, except where the licence was granted in error or the licence and its counterpart are surrendered in pursuance of subsection (3) above in consequence of an error or omission appearing to the Secretary of State to be attributable to that person's fault or in consequence of a current disqualification, and

    (b) may in such an excepted case which does not involve a current disqualification,

grant to that person free of charge a new licence for such period (subject to subsection (8) below) that it expires on the date on which the surrendered licence would have expired had it not been surrendered.

(8) Where the period for which the surrendered licence was granted was based on an error with respect to the licence holder's date of birth such that, if that error had not been made, that licence would have been expressed to expire on a different date, the period of the new licence shall be such that it expires on that different date.

Appeals relating to licences

B15–51   **100.**—(1) A person who is aggrieved by the Secretary of State's—

    (a) refusal to grant or revocation of a licence in pursuance of section 92 or 93 of this Act, or

    (b) determination under section 99(1)(b) of this Act to grant a licence for three years or less, or

    (c) revocation of a licence in pursuance of section 99(3) of this Act,

or by a notice served on him in pursuance of section 92(5) of this Act may, after giving to the Secretary of State notice of his intention to do so, appeal to a magistrates' court acting for the petty sessions area in which he resides or, in Scotland, to the sheriff within whose jurisdiction he resides.

(2) On any such appeal the court or sheriff may make such order as it or he thinks fit and the order shall be binding on the Secretary of State.

(3) It is hereby declared that, without prejudice to section 90 of this Act, in any proceedings under this section the court or sheriff is not entitled to entertain any question as to whether the appellant passed a test of competence to drive if he was declared by the person who conducted it to have failed it.

Disqualification of persons under age

B15–52   **101.**—(1) A person is disqualified for holding or obtaining a licence to drive a motor vehicle of a class specified in the following Table if he is under the age specified in relation to it in the second column of the Table.

TABLE

Class of motor vehicle	Age (in years)
1. Invalid carriage	16
2. Motor cycle	16
3. Small passenger vehicle or small goods vehicle	17
4. Agricultural tractor	17
5. Medium-sized goods vehicle	18
6. Other motor vehicles	21

(2) The Secretary of State may by regulations provide that subsection (1) above shall have effect as if for the classes of vehicles and the ages specified in the Table in that subsection there were substituted different classes of vehicles and ages or different classes of vehicles or different ages.

(3) Subject to subsection (4) below, the regulations may—
  (a) apply to persons of a class specified in or under the regulations,
  (b) apply in circumstances so specified,
  (c) impose conditions or create exemptions or provide for the imposition of conditions or the creation of exemptions,
  (d) contain such transitional and supplemental provisions (including provisions amending section 108, 120 or 183(5) of this Act) as the Secretary of State considers necessary or expedient.

(4) For the purpose of defining the class of persons to whom, the class of vehicles to which, the circumstances in which or the conditions subject to which regulations made by virtue of subsection (2) above are to apply where an approved training scheme for drivers is in force, it is sufficient for the regulations to refer to a document which embodies the terms (or any of the terms) of the scheme or to a document which is in force in pursuance of the scheme.

(5) In subsection (4) above—
  "approved" means approved for the time being by the Secretary of State for the purpose of the regulations,
  "training scheme for drivers" means a scheme for training persons to drive vehicles of a class in relation to which the age which is in force under this section (but apart from any such scheme) is 21 years,
but no approved training scheme for drivers shall be amended without the approval of the Secretary of State.

Obtaining licence, or driving, while disqualified

103.—(1) A person is guilty of an offence if, while disqualified for holding or obtaining a licence, he—   **B15–53**
  (a) obtains a licence, or
  (b) drives a motor vehicle on a road.

(2) A licence obtained by a person who is disqualified is of no effect (or, where the disqualification relates only to vehicles of a particular class, is of no effect in relation to vehicles of that class).

(3) A constable in uniform may arrest without warrant any person driving a motor vehicle on a road whom he has reasonable cause to suspect of being disqualified.

(4) Subsections (1) and (3) above do not apply in relation to disqualification by virtue of section 101 of this Act.

(5) Subsections (1)(b) and (3) above do not apply in relation to disqualification by virtue of section 102 of this Act.

(6) In the application of subsections (1) and (3) above to a person whose disqualification is limited to the driving of motor vehicles of a particular class by virtue of—

    (a) section 102 or 117 of this Act, or

    (b) subsection (9) of section 36 of the Road Traffic Offenders Act 1988 (disqualification until test is passed),

the references to disqualification for holding or obtaining a licence and driving motor vehicles are references to disqualification for holding or obtaining a licence to drive and driving motor vehicles of that class.

Interpretation

108.—(1) In this Part of this Act—

    "agricultural tractor" means a tractor used primarily for work on land in connection with agriculture,

    "articulated goods vehicle" means a motor vehicle which is so constructed that a trailer designed to carry goods may by partial superimposition be attached to it in such manner as to cause a substantial part of the weight of the trailer to be borne by the motor vehicle, and "articulated goods vehicle combination" means an articulated goods vehicle with a trailer so attached,

    "British external licence" and "British Forces licence" have the meanings given by section 88(8) of this Act,

    "Community licence" means a document issued in respect of a member State other than the United Kingdom by an authority of that or another member State (including the United Kingdom) authorising the holder to drive a motor vehicle, not being—

    (a) a document containing a statement to the effect that that or a previous document was issued in exchange for a document issued in respect of a State other than a member State, or

    (b) a document in any of the forms for an international driving permit annexed to the Paris Convention on Motor Traffic of 1926, the Geneva Convention on Road Traffic of 1949 or the Vienna Convention on Road Traffic of 1968,

    "disability" has the meaning given by section 92 of this Act,

    "disqualified" means disqualified for holding or obtaining a licence (or, in cases where the disqualification is limited, a licence to drive motor vehicles of the class to which the disqualification relates) and "disqualification" is to be interpreted accordingly,

    "exchangeable licence" means a Community licence or a document which would be a Community licence if—

    (a) Gibraltar, and

    (b) each country or territory within this paragraph by virtue of an order under subsection (2) below,

    were or formed part of a member State other than the United Kingdom,

    "full licence" means a licence other than a provisional licence,

    "licence" (except where the context otherwise requires) means a licence to drive a motor vehicle granted under this Part of this Act and "counterpart," in relation to a licence, means a document in such

form as the Secretary of State may determine, issued with the licence,
containing such information as he determines and designed for the
endorsement of particulars relating to the licence,

"maximum gross weight," in relation to a motor vehicle or trailer,
means the weight of the vehicle laden with the heaviest load which it
is constructed or adapted to carry,

"maximum train weight," in relation to an articulated goods vehicle
combination, means the weight of the combination laden with the
heaviest load which it is constructed or adapted to carry,

"medium-sized goods vehicle" means a motor vehicle which is constructed or adapted to carry or to haul goods and is not adapted to
carry more than nine persons inclusive of the driver and the permissible maximum weight of which exceeds 3.5 but not 7.5 tonnes,

"Northern Ireland driving licence" or "Northern Ireland licence"
means a licence to drive a motor vehicle granted under the law of
Northern Ireland,

"passenger-carrying vehicle" has the meaning given by section 121(1)
of this Act,

"permissible maximum weight," in relation to a goods vehicle (of
whatever description), means—

(a) in the case of a motor vehicle which neither is an articulated
goods vehicle nor is drawing a trailer, the relevant maximum
weight of the vehicle,

(b) in the case of an articulated goods vehicle—

(i) when drawing only a semi-trailer, the relevant maximum
train weight of the articulated goods vehicle combination,

(ii) when drawing a trailer as well as a semi-trailer, the aggregate of the relevant maximum train weight of the articulated
goods vehicle combination and the relevant maximum
weight of the trailer,

(iii) when drawing a trailer but not a semi-trailer, the aggregate
of the relevant maximum weight of the articulated goods
vehicle and the relevant maximum weight of the trailer,

(iv) when drawing neither a semi-trailer nor a trailer, the relevant maximum weight of the vehicle,

(c) in the case of a motor vehicle (not being an articulated goods
vehicle) which is drawing a trailer, the aggregate of the relevant
maximum weight of the motor vehicle and the relevant maximum weight of the trailer,

"prescribed" means prescribed by regulations,

"prospective disability" has the meaning given by section 92 of this
Act,

"provisional licence" means a licence granted by virtue of section 97(2)
of this Act,

"regulations" means regulations made under section 105 of this Act,

"relevant disability" has the meaning given by section 92 of this Act,

"relevant external law" has the meaning given by section 88(8) of this
Act,

"relevant maximum weight," in relation to a motor vehicle or trailer,
means—

(a) in the case of a vehicle to which regulations under section 49 of
this Act apply which is required by regulations under section 41
of this Act to have a maximum gross weight for the vehicle
marked on a plate issued by the Secretary of State under regu-

lations under section 41, the maximum gross weight so marked on the vehicle,

(b) in the case of a vehicle which is required by regulations under section 41 of this Act to have a maximum gross weight for the vehicle marked on the vehicle and does not also have a maximum gross weight marked on it as mentioned in paragraph (a) above, the maximum gross weight marked on the vehicle,

(c) in the case of a vehicle on which a maximum gross weight is marked by the same means as would be required by regulations under section 41 of this Act if those regulations applied to the vehicle, the maximum gross weight so marked on the vehicle,

(d) in the case of a vehicle on which a maximum gross weight is not marked as mentioned in paragraph (a), (b) or (c) above, the notional maximum gross weight of the vehicle, that is to say, such weight as is produced by multiplying the unladen weight of the vehicle by the number prescribed by the Secretary of State for the class of vehicle into which that vehicle falls,

"relevant maximum train weight," in relation to an articulated goods vehicle combination, means—

(a) in the case of an articulated goods vehicle to which regulations under section 49 of this Act apply which is required by regulations under section 41 of this Act to have a maximum train weight for the combination marked on a plate issued by the Secretary of State under regulations under section 41, the maximum train weight so marked on the motor vehicle,

(b) in the case of an articulated goods vehicle which is required by regulations under section 41 of this Act to have a maximum train weight for the combination marked on the vehicle and does not also have a maximum train weight marked on it as mentioned in paragraph (a) above, the maximum train weight marked on the motor vehicle,

(c) in the case of an articulated goods vehicle on which a maximum train weight is marked by the same means as would be required by regulations under section 41 of this Act if those regulations applied to the vehicle, the maximum train weight so marked on the motor vehicle,

(d) in the case of an articulated goods vehicle on which a maximum train weight is not marked as mentioned in paragraph (a), (b) or (c) above, the notional maximum gross weight of the combination, that is to say, such weight as is produced by multiplying the sum of the unladen weights of the motor vehicle and the semi-trailer by the number prescribed by the Secretary of State for the class of articulated goods vehicle combination into which that combination falls,

"semi-trailer," in relation to an articulated goods vehicle, means a trailer attached to it in the manner described in the definition of articulated goods vehicle,

"small goods vehicle" means a motor vehicle (other than a motor cycle or invalid carriage) which is constructed or adapted to carry or to haul goods and is not adapted to carry more than nine persons inclusive of the driver and the permissible maximum weight of which does not exceed 3.5 tonnes,

"small passenger vehicle" means a motor vehicle (other than a motor cycle or invalid carriage) which is constructed solely to carry passengers and their effects and is adapted to carry not more than nine persons inclusive of the driver, and

"test of competence to drive" means such a test conducted under section 89 of this Act,

"approved training course for motor cyclists" and, in relation to such a course, "prescribed certificate of completion" means respectively any course of training approved under, and the certificate of completion prescribed in, regulations under section 97(3A) of this Act.

(2) If the Secretary of State is satisfied that satisfactory provision for the granting of licences to drive motor vehicles is made by the law of a country or territory which neither is nor forms part of a member State, he may by order made by statutory instrument designate that country or territory as a country or territory within paragraph (b) of the definition of exchangeable licence in subsection (1) above.

(3) Before making any order under subsection (2) above, the Secretary of State shall consult with such representative organisations as he thinks fit.

Licensing of drivers of large goods vehicles and passenger-carrying vehicles

110.—(1) Licences under Part III of this Act to drive motor vehicles of classes which include large goods vehicles or passenger-carrying vehicles or large goods vehicles or passenger-carrying vehicles of any class shall be granted by the Secretary of State in accordance with this Part of this Act and shall, in so far as they authorise the driving of large goods vehicles or passenger-carrying vehicles, be otherwise subject to this Part of this Act in addition to Part III of this Act. **B15–55**

(2) In this Part of this Act—

"large goods vehicle driver's licence" means a licence under Part III of this Act in so far as it authorises a person to drive large goods vehicles of any class; and

"passenger-carrying vehicle driver's licence" means a licence under Part III of this Act in so far as it authorises a person to drive passenger-carrying vehicles of any class.

Driving instruction for payment to be given only by registered or licensed persons

123.—(1) No paid instruction in the driving of a motor car shall be given unless— **B15–56**

(a) the name of the person giving the instruction is in the register of approved instructors established in pursuance of section 23 of the Road Traffic Act 1962 (in this Part of this Act referred to as "the register"), or

(b) the person giving the instruction is the holder of a current licence granted under this Part of this Act authorising him to give such instruction.

(2) No paid instruction in the driving of a motor car shall be given unless there is fixed to and exhibited on that motor car in such manner as may be prescribed by regulations either—

(a) a certificate in such form as may be so prescribed that the name of the person giving the instruction is in the register, or

(b) a current licence granted under this Part of this Act authorising the person giving the instruction to give such instruction.

(3) For the purposes of subsection (1) and (2) above, instruction is paid instruction if payment of money or money's worth is, or is to be, made by or in respect of the person to whom the instruction is given for the giving of the instruction and for the purposes of this subsection instruction which is given—

(a) free of charge to a person who is not the holder of a current licence to drive a motor vehicle granted under Part III of this Act (other than a provisional licence),

(b) by, or in pursuance of arrangements made by, a person carrying on business in the supply of motor cars, and

(c) in connection with the supply of a motor car in the course of that business,

shall be deemed to be given for payment of money by the person to whom the instruction is given.

(4) Where instruction is given in contravention of subsection (1) above—

(a) the person by whom it is given, and

(b) if that person is employed by another to give that instruction, that other, as well as that person,

is guilty of an offence.

(5) In proceedings against a person for an offence under subsection (4) above it shall be a defence for him to prove that he did not know, and had no reasonable cause to believe, that his name or, as the case may be, that of the person employed by him, was not in the register at the material time.

(6) If instruction is given in contravention of subsection (2) above, the person by whom it is given is guilty of an offence.

(7) Any reference in this Part of this Act to a current licence is a reference to a licence which has not expired and has not been cancelled, revoked or suspended.

(8) In this section "provisional licence" has the same meaning as in Part III of this Act.

Users of motor vehicles to be insured or secured against third-party risks

B15–57   143.—(1) Subject to the provisions of this Part of this Act—

(a) a person must not use a motor vehicle on a road unless there is in force in relation to the use of the vehicle by that person such a policy of insurance or such a security in respect of third party risks as complies with the requirements of this Part of this Act, and

(b) a person must not cause or permit any other person to use a motor vehicle on a road unless there is in force in relation to the use of the vehicle by that other person such a policy of insurance or such a security in respect of third party risks as complies with the requirements of this Part of this Act.

(2) If a person acts in contravention of subsection (1) above he is guilty of an offence.

(3) A person charged with using a motor vehicle in contravention of this section shall not be convicted if he proves—

(a) that the vehicle did not belong to him and was not in his possession under a contract of hiring or of loan,

(b) that he was using the vehicle in the course of his employment, and

  (c) that he neither knew nor had reason to believe that there was not in force in relation to the vehicle such a policy of insurance or security as is mentioned in subsection (1) above.

(4) This Part of this Act does not apply to invalid carriages.

Requirements in respect of policies of insurance

145.—(1) In order to comply with the requirements of this Part of this Act, a **B15–58** policy of insurance must satisfy the following conditions.

(2) The policy must be issued by an authorised insurer.

(3) Subject to subsection (4) below, the policy—

  (a) must insure such person, persons or classes of persons as may be specified in the policy in respect of any liability which may be incurred by him or them in respect of the death of or bodily injury to any person or damage to property caused by, or arising out of, the use of the vehicle on a road in Great Britain, and

  (aa) must, in the case of a vehicle normally based in the territory of another member state, insure him or them in respect of any civil liability which may be incurred by him or them as a result of an event related to the use of the vehicle in Great Britain if—

    (i) according to the law of that territory, he or they would be required to be insured in respect of a civil liability which would arise under that law as a result of that event if the place where the vehicle was used when the event occurred were in that territory, and

    (ii) the cover required by that law would be higher than that required by paragraph (a) above, and

  (b) must, in the case of a vehicle normally based in Great Britain insure him or them in respect of any liability which may be incurred by him or them in respect of the use of the vehicle and of any trailer, whether or not coupled, in the territory other than Great Britain and Gibraltar of each of the member States of the Communities according to

    (i) the law on compulsory insurance against civil liability in respect of the use of vehicles of the state in whose territory the event giving rise to the liability occurred; or

    (ii) if it would give higher cover, the law which would be applicable under this Part of this Act if the place where the vehicle was used when that event occurred were in Great Britain; and

  (c) must also insure him or them in respect of any liability which may be incurred by him or them under the provisions of this Part of this Act relating to payment for emergency treatment.

(4) The policy shall not, by virtue of subsection (3)(a) above, be required—

  (a) to cover liability in respect of the death, arising out of and in the course of his employment, of a person in the employment of a person insured by the policy or of bodily injury sustained by such a person arising out of and in the course of his employment, or

  (b) to provide insurance of more than £250,000 in respect of all such liabilities as may be incurred in respect of damage to property caused by, or arising out of, any one accident involving the vehicle, or

  (c) to cover liability in respect of damage to the vehicle, or

  (d) to cover liability in respect of damage to goods carried for hire or reward in or on the vehicle or in or on any trailer (whether or not coupled) drawn by the vehicle, or

    (e) to cover any liability of a person in respect of damage to property in his custody or under his control, or

    (f) to cover any contractual liability.

    (4A) In the case of a person—

    (a) carried in or upon a vehicle, or

    (b) entering or getting on to, or alighting from, a vehicle,

the provisions of paragraph (a) of subsection (4) above do not apply unless cover in respect of the liability referred to in that paragraph is in fact provided pursuant to a requirement of the Employers' Liability (Compulsory Insurance) Act 1969.

    (5) In this Part of this Act "authorised insurer" means a person or body of persons carrying on insurance business within Group 2 in Part II of Schedule 2 to the Insurance Companies Act 1982 and being a member of the Motor Insurers' Bureau (a company limited by guarantee and incorporated under the Companies Act 1929 on 14th June 1946).

    (6) If any person or body of persons ceases to be a member of the Motor Insurers' Bureau, that person or body shall not by virtue of that cease to be treated as an authorised insurer for the purposes of this Part of this Act—

    (a) in relation to any policy issued by the insurer before ceasing to be such a member, or

    (b) in relation to any obligation (whether arising before or after the insurer ceased to be such a member) which the insurer may be called upon to meet under or in consequence of any such policy or under section 157 of this Act by virtue of making a payment in pursuance of such an obligation.

Avoidance of certain exceptions to policies or securities

    148.—(1) Where a certificate of insurance or certificate of security has been delivered under section 147 of this Act to the person by whom a policy has been effected or to whom a security has been given, so much of the policy or security as purports to restrict—

    (a) the insurance of the persons insured by the policy, or

    (b) the operation of the security,

(as the case may be) by reference to any of the matters mentioned in subsection (2) below shall, as respects such liabilities as are required to be covered by a policy under section 145 of this Act, be of no effect.

    (2) Those matters are—

    (a) the age or physical or mental condition of persons driving the vehicle,

    (b) the condition of the vehicle,

    (c) the number of persons that the vehicle carries,

    (d) the weight or physical characteristics of the goods that the vehicle carries,

    (e) the time at which or the areas within which the vehicle is used,

    (f) the horsepower or cylinder capacity or value of the vehicle,

    (g) the carrying on the vehicle of any particular apparatus, or

    (h) the carrying on the vehicle of any particular means of identification other than any means of identification required to be carried by or under the Vehicle Excise and Registration Act 1994.

    (3) Nothing in subsection (1) above requires an insurer or the giver of a security to pay any sum in respect of the liability of any person otherwise than in or towards the discharge of that liability.

    (4) Any sum paid by an insurer or the giver of a security in or towards the

discharge of any liability of any person which is covered by the policy or security by virtue only of subsection (1) above is recoverable by the insurer or giver of the security from that person.

(5) A condition in a policy or security issued or given for the purposes of this Part of this Act providing—

(a) that no liability shall arise under the policy or security, or

(b) that any liability so arising shall cease,

in the event of some specified thing being done or omitted to be done after the happening of the event giving rise to a claim under the policy or security, shall be of no effect in connection with such liabilities as are required to be covered by a policy under section 145 of this Act.

(6) Nothing in subsection (5) above shall be taken to render void any provision in a policy or security requiring the person insured or secured to pay to the insurer or the giver of the security any sums which the latter may have become liable to pay under the policy or security and which have been applied to the satisfaction of the claims of third parties.

(7) Notwithstanding anything in any enactment, a person issuing a policy of insurance under section 145 of this Act shall be liable to indemnify the persons or classes of persons specified in the policy in respect of any liability which the policy purports to cover in the case of those persons or classes of persons.

Avoidance of certain agreements as to liability towards passengers

149.—(1) This section applies where a person uses a motor vehicle in cir- **B15–60** cumstances such that under section 143 of this Act there is required to be in force in relation to his use of it such a policy of insurance or such a security in respect of third-party risks as complies with the requirements of this Part of this Act.

(2) If any other person is carried in or upon the vehicle while the user is so using it, any antecedent agreement or understanding between them (whether intended to be legally binding or not) shall be of no effect so far as it purports or might be held—

(a) to negative or restrict any such liability of the user in respect of persons carried in or upon the vehicle as is required by section 145 of this Act to be covered by a policy of insurance, or

(b) to impose any conditions with respect to the enforcement of any such liability of the user.

(3) The fact that a person so carried has willingly accepted as his the risk of negligence on the part of the user shall not be treated as negativing any such liability of the user.

(4) For the purposes of this section—

(a) references to a person being carried in or upon a vehicle include references to a person entering or getting on to, or alighting from, the vehicle, and

(b) the reference to an antecedent agreement is to one made at any time before the liability arose.

Insurance or security in respect of private use of vehicle to cover use under car-sharing arrangements

150.—(1) To the extent that a policy or security issued or given for the pur- **B15–61** poses of this Part of this Act—

   (a) restricts the insurance of the persons insured by the policy or the operation of the security (as the case may be) to use of the vehicle for specified purposes (for example, social, domestic and pleasure purposes) of a non-commercial character, or

   (b) excludes from that insurance or the operation of the security (as the case may be)—

      (i) use of the vehicle for hire or reward, or

      (ii) business or commercial use of the vehicle, or

      (iii) use of the vehicle for specified purposes of a business or commercial character,

then, for the purposes of that policy or security so far as it relates to such liabilities as are required to be covered by a policy under section 145 of this Act, the use of a vehicle on a journey in the course of which one or more passengers are carried at separate fares shall, if the conditions specified in subsection (2) below are satisfied, be treated as falling within that restriction or as not falling within that exclusion (as the case may be).

   (2) The conditions referred to in subsection (1) above are—

   (a) the vehicle is not adapted to carry more than eight passengers and is not a motor cycle,

   (b) the fare or aggregate of the fares paid in respect of the journey does not exceed the amount of the running costs of the vehicle for the journey (which for the purposes of this paragraph shall be taken to include an appropriate amount in respect of depreciation and general wear), and

   (c) the arrangements for the payment of fares by the passenger or passengers carried at separate fares were made before the journey began.

   (3) Subsections (1) and (2) above apply however the restrictions or exclusions described in subsection (1) are framed or worded.

   (4) In subsections (1) and (2) above "fare" and "separate fares" have the same meaning as in section 1(4) of the Public Passenger Vehicles Act 1981.

Power of police to stop vehicles

B15–62   **163.**—(1) A person driving a mechanically propelled vehicle on a road must stop the vehicle on being required to do so by a constable in uniform.

   (2) A person riding a cycle on a road must stop the cycle on being required to do so by a constable in uniform.

   (3) If a person fails to comply with this section he is guilty of an offence.

Power of constables to require production of driving licence and in certain cases statement of date of birth

B15–63   **164.**—(1) Any of the following persons—

   (a) a person driving a motor vehicle on a road,

   (b) a person whom a constable or vehicle examiner has reasonable cause to believe to have been the driver of a motor vehicle at a time when an accident occurred owing to its presence on a road,

   (c) a person whom a constable or vehicle examiner has reasonable cause to believe to have committed an offence in relation to the use of a motor vehicle on a road, or

   (d) a person—

      (i) who supervises the holder of a provisional licence while the holder is driving a motor vehicle on a road, or

(ii) whom a constable or vehicle examiner has reasonable cause to believe was supervising the holder of a provisional licence while driving, at a time when an accident occurred owing to the presence of the vehicle on a road or at a time when an offence is suspected of having been committed by the holder of the provisional licence in relation to the use of the vehicle on a road,

must, on being so required by a constable or vehicle examiner, produce his licence and its counterpart for examination, so as to enable the constable or vehicle examiner to ascertain the name and address of the holder of the licence, the date of issue, and the authority by which they were issued.

(2) A person required by a constable under subsection (1) above to produce his licence must in prescribed circumstances, on being so required by the constable, state his date of birth.

(3) If—

(a) the Secretary of State has—

    (i) revoked a licence under section 93 or 99 of this Act, or

    (ii) revoked or suspended a large goods vehicle driver's licence or a passenger-carrying vehicle driver's licence under section 115 of this Act, and

(b) the holder of the licence fails to deliver it and its counterpart to the Secretary of State or the traffic commissioner, as the case may be in pursuance of section 93, 99 or 118 (as the case may be),

a constable or vehicle examiner may require him to produce the licence and its counterpart, and upon their being produced may seize them and deliver them to the Secretary of State.

(4) Where a constable has reasonable cause to believe that the holder of a licence, or any other person, has knowingly made a false statement for the purpose of obtaining the grant of the licence, the constable may require the holder of the licence to produce it and its counterpart to him.

(4A) Where a constable to whom a provisional licence has been produced by a person driving a motor bicycle has reasonable cause to believe that the holder was not driving it as part of the training being provided on a training course for motor cyclists, the constable may require him to produce the prescribed certificate of completion of a training course for motor cyclists.

(5) Where a person has been required under section 26 or 27 of the Road Traffic Offenders Act 1988 or section 44 of the Powers of Criminal Courts Act 1973 or section 223A or 436A of the Criminal Procedure (Scotland) Act 1975 to produce a licence and its counterpart to the court and fails to do so, a constable may require him to produce them and, upon their being produced, may seize them and deliver them to the court.

(6) If a person required under the preceding provisions of this section to produce a licence and its counterpart or state his date of birth or to produce his certificate of completion of a training course for motor cyclists fails to do so he is, subject to subsections (7) to (8A) below, guilty of an offence.

(7) Subsection (6) above does not apply where a person required on any occasion under the preceding provisions of this section to produce a licence and its counterpart—

(a) produces on that occasion a current receipt for the licence and its counterpart issued under section 56 of the Road Traffic Offenders Act 1988 and, if required to do so, produces the licence and its counterpart in person immediately on their return at a police station that was specified on that occasion, or

(b) within seven days after that occasion produces such a receipt in person at a police station that was specified by him on that occasion and, if required to do so, produces the licence and its counterpart in person immediately on their return at that police station.

(8) In proceedings against any person for the offence of failing to produce a licence and its counterpart it shall be a defence for him to show that—

- (a) within seven days after the production of his licence and its counterpart was required he produced them in person at a police station that was specified by him at the time their production was required, or
- (b) he produced them in person there as soon as was reasonably practicable, or
- (c) it was not reasonably practicable for him to produce them there before the day on which the proceedings were commenced,

and for the purposes of this subsection the laying of the information or, in Scotland, the service of the complaint on the accused shall be treated as the commencement of the proceedings.

(8A) Subsection (8) above shall apply in relation to a certificate of completion of a training course for motor cyclists as it applies in relation to a licence.

(9) Where in accordance with this section a person has stated his date of birth to a constable, the Secretary of State may serve on that person a notice in writing requiring him to provide the Secretary of State—

- (a) with such evidence in that person's possession or obtainable by him as the Secretary of State may specify for the purpose of verifying that date, and
- (b) if his name differs from his name at the time of his birth, with a statement in writing specifying his name at that time,

and a person who knowingly fails to comply with a notice under this subsection is guilty of an offence.

(10) A notice authorised to be served on any person by subsection (9) above may be served on him by delivering it to him or by leaving it at his proper address or by sending it to him by post; and for the purposes of this subsection and section 7 of the Interpretation Act 1978 in its application to this subsection the proper address of any person shall be his latest address as known to the person giving the notice.

(11) In this section "licence", "counterpart" and "provisional licence" and "training course for motor cyclists" and, in relation to such a course, "the prescribed certificate of completion" have the same meanings as in Part III of this Act and "vehicle examiner" means an examiner appointed under section 66A of this Act.

Power of constables to obtain names and addresses of drivers and others, and to require production of evidence of insurance or security and test certificates

165.—(1) Any of the following persons—

- (a) a person driving a motor vehicle (other than an invalid carriage) on a road, or
- (b) a person whom a constable or vehicle examiner has reasonable cause to believe to have been the driver of a motor vehicle (other than an invalid carriage) at a time when an accident occurred owing to its presence on a road, or
- (c) a person whom a constable or vehicle examiner has reasonable cause to believe to have committed an offence in relation to the use on a road of a motor vehicle (other than an invalid carriage),

must, on being so required by a constable or vehicle examiner, give his name and address and the name and address of the owner of the vehicle and produce the following documents for examination.

(2) Those documents are—

(a) the relevant certificate of insurance or certificate of security (within the meaning of Part VI of this Act), or such other evidence that the vehicle is not or was not being driven in contravention of section 143 of this Act as may be prescribed by regulations made by the Secretary of State,

(b) in relation to a vehicle to which section 47 of this Act applies, a test certificate issued in respect of the vehicle as mentioned in subsection (1) of that section, and

(c) in relation to a goods vehicle the use of which on a road without a plating certificate or goods vehicle test certificate is an offence under section 53(1) or (2) of this Act, any such certificate issued in respect of that vehicle or any trailer drawn by it.

(3) Subject to subsection (4) below, a person who fails to comply with a requirement under subsection (1) above is guilty of an offence.

(4) A person shall not be convicted of an offence under subsection (3) above by reason only of failure to produce any certificate or other evidence if in proceedings against him for the offence he shows that—

(a) within seven days after the date on which the production of the certificate or other evidence was required it was produced at a police station that was specified by him at the time when its production was required, or

(b) it was produced there as soon as was reasonably practicable, or

(c) it was not reasonably practicable for it to be produced there before the day on which the proceedings were commenced,

and for the purposes of this subsection the laying of the information or, in Scotland, the service of the complaint on the accused shall be treated as the commencement of the proceedings.

(5) A person—

(a) who supervises the holder of a provisional licence granted under Part III of this Act while the holder is driving on a road a motor vehicle (other than an invalid carriage), or

(b) whom a constable or vehicle examiner has reasonable cause to believe was supervising the holder of such a licence while driving, at a time when an accident occurred owing to the presence of the vehicle on a road or at a time when an offence is suspected of having been committed by the holder of the provisional licence in relation to the use of the vehicle on a road,

must, on being so required by a constable or vehicle examiner, give his name and address and the name and address of the owner of the vehicle.

(6) A person who fails to comply with a requirement under subsection (5) above is guilty of an offence.

(7) In this section "owner," in relation to a vehicle which is the subject of a hiring agreement, includes each party to the agreement and "vehicle examiner" means an examiner appointed under section 66A of this Act.

Failure to give, or giving false, name and address in case of reckless or careless or inconsiderate driving or cycling

168. Any of the following persons— **B15–65**

(a) the driver of a mechanically propelled vehicle who is alleged to have committed an offence under section 2 or 3 of this Act, or

 (b) the rider of a cycle who is alleged to have committed an offence under section 28 or 29 of this Act,

who refuses, on being so required by any person having reasonable ground for so requiring, to give his name or address, or gives a false name or address, is guilty of an offence.

Duty of driver to stop, report accident and give information or documents

B15–66 **170.**—(1) This section applies in a case where, owing to the presence of a mechanically propelled vehicle on a road, an accident occurs by which—

 (a) personal injury is caused to a person other than the driver of that mechanically propelled vehicle, or

 (b) damage is caused—

  (i) to a vehicle other than that mechanically propelled vehicle or a trailer drawn by that mechanically propelled vehicle, or

  (ii) to an animal other than an animal in or on that mechanically propelled vehicle or a trailer drawn by that mechanically propelled vehicle, or

  (iii) to any other property constructed on, fixed to, growing in or otherwise forming part of the land on which the road in question is situated or land adjacent to such land.

(2) The driver of the mechanically propelled vehicle must stop and, if required to do so by any person having reasonable grounds for so requiring, give his name and address and also the name and address of the owner and the identification marks of the vehicle.

(3) If for any reason the driver of the mechanically propelled vehicle does not give his name and address under subsection (2) above, he must report the accident.

(4) A person who fails to comply with subsection (2) or (3) above is guilty of an offence.

(5) If, in a case where this section applies by virtue of subsection (1)(a) above, the driver of a motor vehicle does not at the time of the accident produce such a certificate of insurance or security, or other evidence, as is mentioned in section 165(2)(a) of this Act—

 (a) to a constable, or

 (b) to some person who, having reasonable grounds for so doing, has required him to produce it,

the driver must report the accident and produce such a certificate or other evidence.

This subsection does not apply to the driver of an invalid carriage.

(6) To comply with a duty under this section to report an accident or to produce such a certificate of insurance or security, or other evidence, as is mentioned in section 165(2)(a) of this Act, the driver—

 (a) must do so at a police station or to a constable, and

 (b) must do so as soon as is reasonably practicable and, in any case, within twenty-four hours of the occurrence of the accident.

(7) A person who fails to comply with a duty under subsection (5) above is guilty of an offence, but he shall not be convicted by reason only of a failure to produce a certificate or other evidence if, within seven days after the occurrence of the accident, the certificate or other evidence is produced at a police station that was specified by him at the time when the accident was reported.

(8) In this section "animal" means horse, cattle, ass, mule, sheep, pig, goat or dog.

Duty to give information as to identity of driver etc. in certain circumstances

172.—(1) This section applies—
    (a) to any offence under the preceding provisions of this Act except—
        (i) an offence under Part V, or
        (ii) an offence under section 13, 16, 51(2), 61(4), 67(9), 68(4), 96 or 120, and to an offence under section 178 of this Act,
    (b) to any offence under sections 25, 26 or 27 of the Road Traffic Offenders Act 1988,
    (c) to any offence against any other enactment relating to the use of vehicles on roads, except an offence under paragraph 8 of Schedule 1 to the Road Traffic (Driver Licensing and Information Systems) Act 1989, and
    (d) to manslaughter, or in Scotland culpable homicide, by the driver of a motor vehicle.

(2) Where the driver of a vehicle is alleged to be guilty of an offence to which this section applies—
    (a) the person keeping the vehicle shall give such information as to the identity of the driver as he may be required to give by or on behalf of a chief officer of police, and
    (b) any other person shall if required as stated above give any information which it is in his power to give and may lead to identification of the driver.

(3) Subject to the following provisions, a person who fails to comply with a requirement under subsection (2) above shall be guilty of an offence.

(4) A person shall not be guilty of an offence by virtue of paragraph (a) of subsection (2) above if he shows that he did not know and could not with reasonable diligence have ascertained who the driver of the vehicle was.

(5) Where a body corporate is guilty of an offence under this section and the offence is proved to have been committed with the consent or connivance of, or to be attributable to neglect on the part of, a director, manager, secretary or other similar officer of the body corporate, or a person who was purporting to act in any such capacity, he, as well as the body corporate, is guilty of that offence and liable to be proceeded against and punished accordingly.

(6) Where the alleged offender is a body corporate, or in Scotland a partnership or an unincorporated association, or the proceedings are brought against him by virtue of subsection (5) above or subsection (11) below, subsection (4) above shall not apply unless, in addition to the matters there mentioned, the alleged offender shows that no record was kept of the persons who drove the vehicle and that the failure to keep a record was reasonable.

(7) A requirement under subsection (2) may be made by written notice served by post; and where it is so made—
    (a) it shall have effect as a requirement to give the information within the period of 28 days beginning with the day on which the notice is served, and
    (b) the person on whom the notice is served shall not be guilty of an offence under this section if he shows either that he gave the information as soon as reasonably practicable after the end of that period or that it has not been reasonably practicable for him to give it.

(8) Where the person on whom a notice under subsection (7) above is to be served is a body corporate, the notice is duly served if it is served on the secretary or clerk of that body.

(9) For the purposes of section 7 of the Interpretation Act 1978 as it applies for the purposes of this section the proper address of any person in relation to the service on him of a notice under subsection (7) above is—

(a) in the case of the secretary or clerk of a body corporate, that of the registered or principal office of that body or (if the body corporate is the registered keeper of the vehicle concerned) the registered address, and

(b) in any other case, his last known address at the time of service.

(10) In this section—

"registered address", in relation to the registered keeper of a vehicle, means the address recorded in the record kept under the Vehicle Excise and Registration Act 1994 with respect to that vehicle as being that person's address, and

"registered keeper", in relation to a vehicle, means the person in whose name the vehicle is registered under that Act;

and references to the driver of a vehicle include references to the rider of a cycle.

(11) Where, in Scotland, an offence under this section is committed by a partnership or by an unincorporated association other than a partnership and is proved to have been committed with the consent or connivance or in consequence of the negligence of a partner in the partnership or, as the case may be, a person concerned in the management or control of the association, he (as well as the partnership or association) shall be guilty of the offence.

Forgery of documents, etc.

173.—(1) A person who, with intent to deceive—

(a) forges, alters or uses a document or other thing to which this section applies, or

(b) lends to, or allows to be used by, any other person a document or other thing to which this section applies, or

(c) makes or has in his possession any document or other thing so closely resembling a document or other thing to which this section applies as to be calculated to deceive,

is guilty of an offence.

(2) This section applies to the following documents and other things—

(a) any licence under any Part of this Act, or, in the case of a licence to drive, any counterpart of such a licence,

(b) any test certificate, goods vehicle test certificate, plating certificate, certificate of conformity or Minister's approval certificate (within the meaning of Part II of this Act),

(c) any certificate required as a condition of any exception prescribed under section 14 of this Act,

(cc) any seal required by regulations made under section 41 of this Act with respect to speed limiters,

(d) any plate containing particulars required to be marked on a vehicle by regulations under section 41 of this Act or containing other particulars required to be marked on a goods vehicle by sections 54 to 58 of this Act or regulations under those sections,

(dd) any document evidencing the appointment of an examiner under section 66A of this Act,

(e) any records required to be kept by virtue of section 74 of this Act,

   (f) any document which, in pursuance of section 89(3) of this Act, is issued as evidence of the result of a test of competence to drive,
  (ff) any certificate provided for by regulations under section 97(3A) of this Act relating to the completion of a training course for motor cyclists,
   (g) any badge or certificate prescribed by regulations made by virtue of section 135 of this Act,
   (h) any certificate of insurance or certificate of security under Part VI of this Act,
   (j) any document produced as evidence of insurance in pursuance of Regulation 6 of the Motor Vehicles (Compulsory Insurance) (No. 2) Regulations 1973,
   (k) any document issued under regulations made by the Secretary of State in pursuance of his power under section 165(2)(a) of this Act to prescribe evidence which may be produced in lieu of a certificate of insurance or a certificate of security,
   (l) any international road haulage permit and
  (m) a certificate of the kind referred to in section 34B(1) of the Road Traffic Offenders Act 1988.

   (3) In the application of this section to England and Wales "forges" means makes a false document or other thing in order that it may be used as genuine.

   (4) In this section "counterpart," in relation to a licence to drive under Part III of this Act, has the same meaning as in that Part.

False statements and withholding material information

   174.—(1) A person who knowingly makes a false statement for the   **B15–69**
purpose—
   (a) of obtaining the grant of a licence under any Part of this Act to himself or any other person, or
   (b) of preventing the grant of any such licence, or
   (c) of procuring the imposition of a condition or limitation in relation to any such licence, or
   (d) of securing the entry or retention of the name of any person in the register of approved instructors maintained under Part V of this Act, or
   (e) of obtaining the grant of an international road haulage permit to himself or any other person,
is guilty of an offence.

   (2) A person who, in supplying information or producing documents for the purposes either of sections 53 to 60 and 63 of this Act or of regulations made under sections 49 to 51, 61, 62 and 66(3) of this Act—
   (a) makes a statement which he knows to be false in a material particular or recklessly makes a statement which is false in a material particular, or
   (b) produces, provides, sends or otherwise makes use of a document which he knows to be false in a material particular or recklessly produces, provides, sends or otherwise makes use of a document which is false in a material particular,
is guilty of an offence.

   (3) A person who—
   (a) knowingly produces false evidence for the purposes of regulations under section 66(1) of this Act, or

   (b) knowingly makes a false statement in a declaration required to be made by the regulations,

is guilty of an offence.

   (4) A person who—

   (a) wilfully makes a false entry in any record required to be made or kept by regulations under section 74 of this Act, or

   (b) with intent to deceive, makes use of any such entry which he knows to be false,

is guilty of an offence.

   (5) A person who makes a false statement or withholds any material information for the purpose of obtaining the issue—

   (a) of a certificate of insurance or certificate of security under Part VI of this Act, or

   (b) of any document issued under regulations made by the Secretary of State in pursuance of his power under section 165(2)(a) of this Act to prescribe evidence which may be produced in lieu of a certificate of insurance or a certificate of security,

is guilty of an offence.

Meaning of "motor vehicle" and other expressions relating to vehicles

B15–70   **185.**—(1) In this Act—

"heavy locomotive" means a mechanically propelled vehicle which is not constructed itself to carry a load other than any of the excepted articles and the weight of which unladen exceeds 11690 kilograms,

"heavy motor car" means a mechanically propelled vehicle, not being a motor car, which is constructed itself to carry a load or passengers and the weight of which unladen exceeds 2540 kilograms,

"invalid carriage" means a mechanically propelled vehicle the weight of which unladen does not exceed 254 kilograms and which is specially designed and constructed, and not merely adapted, for the use of a person suffering from some physical defect or disability and is used solely by such a person,

"light locomotive" means a mechanically propelled vehicle which is not constructed itself to carry a load other than any of the excepted articles and the weight of which unladen does not exceed 11690 kilograms but does exceed 7370 kilograms,

"motor car" means a mechanically propelled vehicle, not being a motor cycle or an invalid carriage, which is constructed itself to carry a load or passengers and the weight of which unladen—

   (a) if it is constructed solely for the carriage of passengers and their effects, is adapted to carry not more than seven passengers exclusive of the driver and is fitted with tyres of such type as may be specified in regulations made by the Secretary of State, does not exceed 3050 kilograms,

   (b) if it is constructed or adapted for use for the conveyance of goods or burden of any description, does not exceed 3050 kilograms, or 3500 kilograms if the vehicle carries a container or containers for holding for the purposes of its propulsion any fuel which is wholly gaseous at 17.5 degrees Celsius under a pressure of 1.013 bar or plant and materials for producing such fuel,

   (c) does not exceed 2540 kilograms in a case not falling within subparagraph (a) or (b) above, "motor cycle" means a mechanically propelled vehicle, not being an invalid carriage, with less than four wheels and the weight of which unladen does not exceed 410 kilograms,

"motor tractor" means a mechanically propelled vehicle which is not constructed itself to carry a load, other than the excepted articles, and the weight of which unladen does not exceed 7370 kilograms,

"motor vehicle" means, subject to section 20 of the Chronically Sick and Disabled Persons Act 1970 (which makes special provision about invalid carriages, within the meaning of that Act), a mechanically propelled vehicle intended or adapted for use on roads, and

"trailer" means a vehicle drawn by a motor vehicle.

(2) In subsection (1) above "excepted articles" means any of the following: water, fuel, accumulators and other equipment used for the purpose of propulsion, loose tools and loose equipment.

Supplementary provisions about those expressions

186.—(1) For the purposes of section 185 of this Act, a side car attached to a   **B15–71** motor vehicle, if it complies with such conditions as may be specified in regulations made by the Secretary of State, is to be regarded as forming part of the vehicle to which it is attached and as not being a trailer.

(2) For the purposes of section 185 of this Act, in a case where a motor vehicle is so constructed that a trailer may by partial super-imposition be attached to the vehicle in such a manner as to cause a substantial part of the weight of the trailer to be borne by the vehicle, that vehicle is to be deemed to be a vehicle itself constructed to carry a load.

(3) For the purposes of section 185 of this Act, in the case of a motor vehicle fitted with a crane, dynamo, welding plant or other special appliance or apparatus which is a permanent or essentially permanent fixture, the appliance or apparatus is not to be deemed to constitute a load or goods or burden of any description, but is to be deemed to form part of the vehicle.

(4) The Secretary of State may by regulations vary any of the maximum or minimum weights specified in section 185 of this Act.

(5) Regulations under subsection (4) above may have effect—
  (a) either generally or in the case of vehicles of any class specified in the regulations, and
  (b) either for the purposes of the provisions of the Road Traffic Acts and of all regulations made under those provisions or for such of those purposes as may be so specified.

(6) Nothing in section 86 of the Road Traffic Regulation Act 1984 limits the powers conferred by subsection (4) above.

General interpretation of Act

192.—(1) In this Act—   **B15–72**
  "bridleway" means a way over which the public have the following, but no other, rights of way: a right of way on foot and a right of way on horseback or leading a horse, with or without a right to drive animals of any description along the way,
  "carriage of goods" includes the haulage of goods,
  "cycle" means a bicycle, a tricycle, or a cycle having four or more wheels, not being in any case a motor vehicle,

"driver", where a separate person acts as a steersman of a motor vehicle, includes (except for the purposes of section 1 of this Act) that person as well as any other person engaged in the driving of the vehicle, and "drive" is to be interpreted accordingly,

"footpath", in relation to England and Wales, means a way over which the public have a right of way on foot only,

"goods" includes goods or burden of any description,

"goods vehicle" means a motor vehicle constructed or adapted for use for the carriage of goods, or a trailer so constructed or adapted,

"highway authority", in England and Wales, means—

(a) in relation to a road for which he is the highway authority within the meaning of the Highways Act 1980, the Secretary of State, and

(b) in relation to any other road, the council of the county, metropolitan district or London borough, or the Common Council of the City of London, as the case may be;

"international road haulage permit" means a licence, permit, authorisation or other document issued in pursuance of a Community instrument relating to the carriage of goods by road between member States or an international agreement to which the United Kingdom is a party and which relates to the international carriage of goods by road,

"owner", in relation to a vehicle which is the subject of a hiring agreement or hire-purchase agreement, means the person in possession of the vehicle under that agreement,

"petty sessions area" has the same meaning as in the Magistrates' Courts Act 1980,

"prescribed" means prescribed by regulations made by the Secretary of State,

"road",

(a) in relation to England and Wales, means any highway and any other road to which the public has access, and includes bridges over which a road passes, and

(b) in relation to Scotland, means any road within the meaning of the Roads (Scotland) Act 1984 and any other way to which the public has access, and includes bridges over which a road passes,

"the Road Traffic Acts" means the Road Traffic Offenders Act 1988, the Road Traffic (Consequential Provisions) Act 1988 (so far as it reproduces the effect of provisions repealed by that Act) and this Act,

"statutory", in relation to any prohibition, restriction, requirement or provision, means contained in, or having effect under, any enactment (including any enactment contained in this Act),

"the Traffic Acts" means the Road Traffic Acts and the Road Traffic Regulation Act 1984,

"traffic sign" has the meaning given by section 64(1) of the Road Traffic Regulation Act 1984,

"tramcar" includes any carriage used on any road by virtue of an order under the Light Railways Act 1896, and

"trolley vehicle" means a mechanically propelled vehicle adapted for use on roads without rails under power transmitted to it from some external source (whether or not there is in addition a source of power on board the vehicle).

(1A) In this Act—

(a) any reference to a county shall be construed in relation to Wales as including a reference to a county borough; and

(b) section 17(4) and (5) of the Local Government (Wales) Act 1994 (references to counties and districts to be construed generally in relation to Wales as references to counties and county boroughs) shall not apply.

(2) In this Act—
"carriageway"
"footway"
"local roads authority"
"public road"
"roads authority"
"special road" and
"trunk road",

in relation to Scotland, have the same meanings as in the Roads (Scotland) Act 1984, and "footpath", in relation to Scotland, means a way over which the public have a right of way on foot only (whether or not associated with a carriageway).

(3) References in this Act to a class of vehicles are to be interpreted as references to a class defined or described by reference to any characteristics of the vehicles or to any other circumstances whatsoever and accordingly as authorising the use of "category" to indicate a class of vehicles, however defined or described.

Sections 17 and 18   SCHEDULE 1

SUPPLEMENTARY PROVISIONS IN CONNECTION WITH PROCEEDINGS FOR OFFENCES UNDER SECTION 15A, 17 AND 18(4)

Proceedings in England and Wales

1.—(1) A person against whom proceedings are brought in England and   **B15–73**
Wales for an offence under section 15A, 17 or 18(4) of this Act is, upon information duly laid by him and on giving the prosecution not less than three clear days' notice of his intention, entitled to have any person to whose act or default he alleges that the contravention of that section was due brought before the court in the proceedings.

(2) If, after the contravention has been proved, the original accused proves that the contravention was due to the act or default of that other person—
(a) that other person may be convicted of the offence, and
(b) if the original accused further proves that he has used all due diligence to secure that section 15A, 17 or, as the case may be, 18(4) was complied with, he shall be acquitted of the offence.

(3) Where an accused seeks to avail himself of the provisions of sub-paragraphs (1) and (2) above—
(a) the prosecution, as well as the person whom the accused charges with the offence, has the right to cross-examine him, if he gives evidence, and any witness called by him in support of his pleas, and to call rebutting evidence, and
(b) the court may make such order as it thinks fit for the payment of costs by any party to the proceedings to any other party to the proceedings.

2.—(1) Where—
(a) it appears that an offence under section 15A, 17 or 18(4) of this Act has been committed in respect of which proceedings might be taken in England and Wales against some person (referred to below in this paragraph as "the original offender"), and

(b) a person proposing to take proceedings in respect of the offence is reasonably satisfied—
  (i) that the offence of which complaint is made was due to an act or default of some other person, being an act or default which took place in England and Wales, and
  (ii) that the original offender could establish a defence under paragraph 1 of this Schedule,

the proceedings may be taken against that other person without proceedings first being taken against the original offender.

(2) In any such proceedings the accused may be charged with, and on proof that the contravention was due to his act or default be convicted of, the offence with which the original offender might have been charged.

3.—(1) Where proceedings are brought in England and Wales against a person (referred to below in this paragraph as "the accused") in respect of a contravention of section 15A, 17 or 18(4) of this Act and it is proved—
  (a) that the contravention was due to the act or default of some other person, being an act or default which took place in Scotland, and
  (b) that the accused used all due diligence to secure compliance with that section,

the accused shall, subject to the provisions of this paragraph, be acquitted of the offence.

(2) The accused is not entitled to be acquitted under this paragraph unless within seven days from the date of the service of the summons on him—
  (a) he has given notice in writing to the prosecution of his intention to rely upon the provisions of this paragraph, specifying the name and address of the person to whose act or default he alleges that the contravention was due, and
  (b) he has sent a like notice to that person.

(3) The person specified in a notice served under this paragraph is entitled to appear at the hearing and to give evidence and the court may, if it thinks fit, adjourn the hearing to enable him to do so.

(4) Where it is proved that the contravention of section 15A, 17 or 18(4) of this Act was due to the act or default of some person other than the accused, being an act or default which took place in Scotland, the court must (whether or not the accused is acquitted) cause notice of the proceedings to be sent to the Secretary of State.

Proceedings in Scotland

4.—(1) Where a contravention of section 15A, 17 or 18(4) of this Act committed by a person in Scotland (referred to in this sub-paragraph as "the original offender") was due to the act or default of any other person, being an act or default which took place in Scotland then, whether or not proceedings are taken against the original offender, that other person may be charged with and convicted of the contravention and shall be liable on conviction to the same punishment as might have been inflicted on the original offender if he had been convicted of the contravention.

(2) Where a person (referred to in this sub-paragraph as "the accused") who is charged in Scotland with a contravention of section 15A, 17 or 18(4) of this Act proves to the satisfaction of the court—
  (a) that he used all due diligence to secure that the provision in question was complied with, and
  (b) that the contravention was due to the act or default of some other person,

the accused shall be acquitted of the contravention.

Proceedings in Great Britain

5.—(1) Subject to the provisions of this paragraph, in any proceedings (whether in England and Wales or Scotland) for an offence under section 17 or 18(4) of this Act it shall be a defence for the accused to prove—

(a) that he purchased the helmet or appliance in question as being of a type which—

    (i) in the case of section 17, could be lawfully sold or offered for sale under that section, and

    (ii) in the case of section 18(4), could be lawfully sold or offered for sale under section 18 as authorised for use in the manner in question, and with a written warranty to that effect, and

(b) that he had no reason to believe at the time of the commission of the alleged offence that it was not of such a type, and

(c) that it was then in the same state as when he purchased it.

(1A) Subject to the provisions of this paragraph, in any proceedings (whether in England and Wales or Scotland) for an offence under section 15A of this Act it shall be a defence for the accused to prove—

(a) if the offence is under subsection (3)(a) of that section—

    (i) that he purchased the equipment in question as being of a type which could be lawfully sold or offered for sale as conducive to the safety in the event of accident of prescribed classes of children in prescribed classes of motor vehicles and with a written warranty to that effect;

    (ii) that he had no reason to believe at the time of the commission of the alleged offence that it was not of such a type; and

    (iii) that it was then in the same state as when he purchased it;

(b) if the offence is under subsection (3)(b) of that section, he provided information in relation to the equipment and it is alleged that it did not include appropriate information or included or consisted of inappropriate information—

    (i) that the information provided by him was information which had been provided to him with a written warranty to the effect that it was the information required to be provided by him under section 15A of this Act; and

    (ii) that he had no reason to believe at the time of the commission of the alleged offence that the information provided by him was not the information required to be provided under that section; or

(c) if the offence is under subsection (3)(b) of that section, he provided information in relation to the equipment and it is alleged that it was not provided in the manner required under that section—

    (i) that the information provided by him had been provided to him either with a written warranty to the effect that it was provided to him in the manner in which it was required to be provided by him under that section or with instructions as to the manner in which the information should be provided by him and with a written warranty to the effect that provision in that manner would comply with regulations under that section;

    (ii) that he had no reason to believe at the time of the commission of the alleged offence that he was not providing the information in the manner required under that section; and

    (iii) that the information was then in the same state as when it was provided to him or, as the case may be, that it was provided by him in accordance with the instructions given to him.

(2) A warranty is only a defence in any such proceedings if—

    (a) the accused—
        (i) has, not later than three clear days before the date of the hearing, sent to the prosecutor a copy of the warranty with a notice stating that he intends to rely on it and specifying the name and address of the person from whom he received it, and
        (ii) has also sent a like notice of his intention to that person, and
    (b) in the case of a warranty given by a person outside the United Kingdom, the accused proves that he had taken reasonable steps to ascertain, and did in fact believe in, the accuracy of the statement contained in the warranty.

(3) Where the accused is a servant of the person who purchased the equipment, helmet or appliance in question under a warranty, or to whom the information in question was provided under a warranty, he is entitled to rely on the provisions of this paragraph in the same way as his employer would have been entitled to do if he had been the accused.

(4) The person by whom the warranty is alleged to have been given is entitled to appear at the hearing and to give evidence and the court may, if it thinks fit, adjourn the hearing to enable him to do so.

6.—(1) An accused who in any proceedings for an offence under section 15A, 17 or 18(4) of this Act wilfully applies to equipment, information, a helmet or, as the case may be, an appliance a warranty not given in relation to it is guilty of an offence.

(2) A person who, in respect of equipment, a helmet or an appliance sold by him, or information provided by him, being equipment, a helmet, an appliance or information in respect of which a warranty might be pleaded under paragraph 5 of this Schedule, gives to the purchaser a false warranty in writing, is guilty of an offence, unless he proves that when he gave the warranty he had reason to believe that the statements or description contained in it were accurate.

(3) Where the accused in a prosecution for an offence under section 15A, 17 or 18(4) of this Act relies successfully on a warranty given to him or his employer, any proceedings under sub-paragraph (2) above in respect of the warranty may, at the option of the prosecutor, be taken before a court having jurisdiction in the place—
    (a) where the equipment, helmet or appliance, or any of the equipment, helmets or appliances, to which the warranty relates was procured,
    (b) where the information, or any of it, to which the warranty relates was provided, or
    (c) where the warranty was given.

7. In this Schedule, "equipment" means equipment to which section 15A of this Act applies and "appliance" means an appliance to which section 18 of this Act applies.

ROAD TRAFFIC OFFENDERS ACT 1988

(1988 c. 53)

Requirement of warning etc. of prosecutions for certain offences

B16–01   **1.**—(1) Subject to section 2 of this Act, a person shall not be convicted of an offence to which this section applies unless—

   (a) he was warned at the time the offence was committed that the question of prosecuting him for some one or other of the offences to which this section applies would be taken into consideration, or

   (b) within fourteen days of the commission of the offence a summons (or, in Scotland, a complaint) for the offence was served on him, or

   (c) within fourteen days of the commission of the offence a notice of the intended prosecution specifying the nature of the alleged offence and the time and place where it is alleged to have been committed, was—

      (i) in the case of an offence under section 28 or 29 of the Road Traffic Act 1988 (cycling offences), served on him,

      (ii) in the case of any other offence, served on him or on the person, if any, registered as the keeper of the vehicle at the time of the commission of the offence.

(2) A notice shall be deemed for the purposes of subsection (1)(c) above to have been served on a person if it was sent by registered post or recorded delivery service addressed to him at his last known address, notwithstanding that the notice was returned as undelivered or was for any other reason not received by him.

(3) The requirement of subsection (1) above shall in every case be deemed to have been complied with unless and until the contrary is proved.

(4) Schedule 1 to this Act shows the offences to which this section applies.

Requirements of warning etc: supplementary

  2.—(1) The requirement of section 1(1) of this Act does not apply in relation   **B16–02** to an offence if, at the time of the offence or immediately after it, an accident occurs owing to the presence on a road of the vehicle in respect of which the offence was committed.

(2) The requirement of section 1(1) of this Act does not apply in relation to an offence in respect of which—

   (a) a fixed penalty notice (within the meaning of Part III of this Act) has been given or fixed under any provision of that Part, or

   (b) a notice has been given under section 54(4) of this Act.

(3) Failure to comply with the requirement of section 1(1) of this Act is not a bar to the conviction of the accused in a case where the court is satisfied—

   (a) that neither the name and address of the accused nor the name and address of the registered keeper, if any, could with reasonable diligence have been ascertained in time for a summons or, as the case may be, a complaint to be served or for a notice to be served or sent in compliance with the requirement, or

   (b) that the accused by his own conduct contributed to the failure.

(4) Failure to comply with the requirement of section 1(1) of this Act in relation to an offence is not a bar to the conviction of a person of that offence by virtue of the provisions of—

   (a) section 24 of this Act, or

   (b) any of the enactments mentioned in section 24(6);

but a person is not to be convicted of an offence by virtue of any of those provisions if section 1 applies to the offence with which he was charged and the requirement of section 1(1) was not satisfied in relation to the offence charged.

Exemption from Licensing Act offence

  5. A person liable to be charged with an offence under section 3A, 4, 5, 7 or   **B16–03**

30 of the Road Traffic Act 1988 (drink and drugs) is not liable to be charged under section 12 of the Licensing Act 1872 with the offence of being drunk while in charge, on a highway or other public place, of a carriage.

Time within which summary proceedings for certain offences must be commenced

B16–04   6.—(1) Subject to subsection (2) below, summary proceedings for an offence to which this section applies may be brought within a period of six months from the date on which evidence sufficient in the opinion of the prosecutor to warrant the proceedings came to his knowledge.

(2) No such proceedings shall be brought by virtue of this section more than three years after the commission of the offence.

(3) For the purposes of this section, a certificate signed by or on behalf of the prosecutor and stating the date on which evidence sufficient in his opinion to warrant the proceedings came to his knowledge shall be conclusive evidence of that fact.

(4) A certificate stating that matter and purporting to be so signed shall be deemed to be so signed unless the contrary is proved.

(5) In relation to proceedings in Scotland, subsection (3) of section 331 of the Criminal Procedure (Scotland) Act 1975 (date of commencement of proceedings) shall apply for the purposes of this section as it applies for the purposes of that.

(6) Schedule 1 to this Act shows the offences to which this section applies.

Mode of trial

B16–05   9. An offence against a provision of the Traffic Acts specified in column 1 of Part I of Schedule 2 to this Act or regulations made under such a provision (the general nature of which offence is indicated in column 2) shall be punishable as shown against the offence in column 3 (that is, on summary conviction or on indictment or in either one way or the other).

Evidence by certificate as to driver user or owner

B16–06   11.—(1) In any proceedings in England and Wales for an offence to which this section applies, a certificate in the prescribed form, purporting to be signed by a constable and certifying that a person specified in the certificate stated to the constable—

   (a) that a particular mechanically propelled vehicle was being driven or used by, or belonged to, that person on a particular occasion, or
   (b) that a particular mechanically propelled vehicle on a particular occasion was used by, or belonged to, a firm and that he was, at the time of the statement, a partner in that firm, or
   (c) that a particular mechanically propelled vehicle on a particular occasion was used by, or belonged to, a corporation and that he was, at the time of the statement, a director, officer or employee of that corporation,

shall be admissible as evidence for the purpose of determining by whom the vehicle was being driven or used, or to whom it belonged, as the case may be, on that occasion.

(2) Nothing in subsection (1) above makes a certificate admissible as evidence in proceedings for an offence except in a case where and to the like extent to which oral evidence to the like effect would have been admissible in those proceedings.

(3) Nothing in subsection (1) above makes a certificate admissible as evidence in proceedings for an offence—

(a) unless a copy of it has, not less than seven days before the hearing or trial, been served in the prescribed manner on the person charged with the offence, or

(b) if that person, not later than three days before the hearing or trial or within such further time as the court may in special circumstances allow, serves a notice in the prescribed form and manner on the prosecutor requiring attendance at the trial of the person who signed the certificate.

(4) In this section "prescribed" means prescribed by rules made by the Secretary of State by statutory instrument.

(5) Schedule 1 to this Act shows the offences to which this section applies.

Proof, in summary proceedings, of identity of driver of vehicle

12.—(1) Where on the summary trial in England and Wales of an infor- **B16–07** mation for an offence to which this subsection applies—

(a) it is proved to the satisfaction of the court, on oath or in manner prescribed by rules made under section 144 of the Magistrates' Courts Act 1980, that a requirement under section 172(2) of the Road Traffic Act 1988 to give information as to the identity of the driver of a particular vehicle on the particular occasion to which the information relates has been served on the accused by post, and

(b) a statement in writing is produced to the court purporting to be signed by the accused that the accused was the driver of that vehicle on that occasion,

the court may accept that statement as evidence that the accused was the driver of that vehicle on that occasion.

(2) Schedule 1 to this Act shows the offences to which subsection (1) above applies.

(3) Where on the summary trial in England and Wales of an information for an offence to which section 112 of the Road Traffic Regulation Act 1984 applies—

(a) it is proved to the satisfaction of the court, on oath or in manner prescribed by rules made under section 144 of the Magistrates' Courts Act 1980, that a requirement under section 112(2) of the Road Traffic Regulation Act 1984 to give information as to the identity of the driver of a particular vehicle on the particular occasion to which the information relates has been served on the accused by post, and

(b) a statement in writing is produced to the court purporting to be signed by the accused that the accused was the driver of that vehicle on that occasion,

the court may accept that statement as evidence that the accused was the driver of that vehicle on that occasion.

(4) In summary proceedings in Scotland for an offence to which section 20(2) of this Act applies, where—

(a) it is proved to the satisfaction of the court that a requirement under section 172(2) of the Road Traffic Act 1988 to give information as to the identity of a driver on a particular occasion to which the complaint relates has been served on the accused by post, and

(b) a statement in writing is produced to the court, purporting to be signed by the accused, that the accused was the driver of the vehicle on that occasion, that statement shall be sufficient evidence that the accused was the driver of the vehicle on that occasion.

Use of specimens in proceedings for an offence under section 4 or 5 of the Road Traffic Act

B16–08 **15.**—(1) This section and section 16 of this Act apply in respect of proceedings for an offence under section 3A, 4 or 5 of the Road Traffic Act 1988 (driving offences connected with drink or drugs); and expressions used in this section and section 16 of this Act have the same meaning as in sections 3A to 10 of that Act.

(2) Evidence of the proportion of alcohol or any drug in a specimen of breath, blood or urine provided by the accused shall, in all cases (including cases where the specimen was not provided in connection with the alleged offence), be taken into account and, subject to subsection (3) below, it shall be assumed that the proportion of alcohol in the accused's breath, blood or urine at the time of the alleged offence was not less than in the specimen.

(3) That assumption shall not be made if the accused proves—

(a) that he consumed alcohol before he provided the specimen and—

(i) in relation to an offence under section 3A, after the time of the alleged offence, and

(ii) otherwise, after he had ceased to drive, attempt to drive or be in charge of a vehicle on a road or other public place, and

(b) that had he not done so the proportion of alcohol in his breath, blood or urine would not have exceeded the prescribed limit and, if it is alleged that he was unfit to drive through drink, would not have been such as to impair his ability to drive properly.

(4) A specimen of blood shall be disregarded unless it was taken from the accused with his consent by a medical practitioner.

(5) Where, at the time a specimen of blood or urine was provided by the accused, he asked to be provided with such a specimen, evidence of the proportion of alcohol or any drug found in the specimen is not admissible on behalf of the prosecution unless—

(a) the specimen in which the alcohol or drug was found is one of two parts into which the specimen provided by the accused was divided at the time it was provided, and

(b) the other part was supplied to the accused.

Documentary evidence as to specimens in such proceedings

B16–09 **16.**—(1) Evidence of the proportion of alcohol or a drug in a specimen of breath, blood or urine may, subject to subsections (3) and (4) below and to section 15(5) of this Act, be given by the production of a document or documents purporting to be whichever of the following is appropriate, that is to say—

(a) a statement automatically produced by the device by which the proportion of alcohol in a specimen of breath was measured and a certificate signed by a constable (which may but need not be contained in the same document as the statement) that the statement relates to a specimen provided by the accused at the date and time shown in the statement, and

(b) a certificate signed by an authorised analyst as to the proportion of alcohol or any drug found in a specimen of blood or urine identified in the certificate.

(2) Subject to subsections (3) and (4) below, evidence that a specimen of blood was taken from the accused with his consent by a medical practitioner may be given by the production of a document purporting to certify that fact and to be signed by a medical practitioner.

(3) Subject to subsection (4) below—

(a) a document purporting to be such a statement or such a certificate (or both such a statement and such a certificate) as is mentioned in subsection (1)(a) above is admissible in evidence on behalf of the prosecution in pursuance of this section only if a copy of it either has been handed to the accused when the document was produced or has been served on him not later than seven days before the hearing, and

(b) any other document is so admissible only if a copy of it has been served on the accused not later than seven days before the hearing.

(4) A document purporting to be a certificate (or so much of a document as purports to be a certificate) is not so admissible if the accused, not later than three days before the hearing or within such further time as the court may in special circumstances allow, has served notice on the prosecutor requiring the attendance at the hearing of the person by whom the document purports to be signed.

(5) In Scotland—

(a) a document produced in evidence on behalf of the prosecution in pursuance of subsection (1) or (2) above and, where the person by whom the document was signed is called as a witness, the evidence of that person, shall be sufficient evidence of the facts stated in the document, and

(b) a written execution purporting to be signed by the person who handed to or served on the accused or the prosecutor a copy of the document or of the notice in terms of subsection (3) or (4) above, together with, where appropriate, a post office receipt for the registered or recorded delivery letter shall be sufficient evidence of the handing or service of such a copy or notice.

(6) A copy of a certificate required by this section to be served on the accused or a notice required by this section to be served on the prosecutor may be served personally or sent by registered post or recorded delivery service.

(7) In this section "authorised analyst" means—

(a) any person possessing the qualifications prescribed by regulations made under section 27 of the Food Safety Act 1990 as qualifying persons for appointment as public analysts under those Acts, and

(b) any other person authorised by the Secretary of State to make analyses for the purposes of this section.

Speeding offences etc.: admissibility of certain evidence

20.—(1) Evidence (which in Scotland shall be sufficient evidence) of a fact **B16–10** relevant to proceedings for an offence to which this section applies may be given by the production of—

(a) a record produced by a prescribed device, and

(b) (in the same or another document) a certificate as to the circumstances in which the record was produced signed by a constable or by a person authorised by or on behalf of the chief officer of police for the police area in which the offence is alleged to have been committed;

but subject to the following provisions of this section.

(2) This section applies to—

(a) an offence under section 16 of the Road Traffic Regulation Act 1984 consisting in the contravention of a restriction on the speed of vehicles imposed under section 14 of that Act;

(b) an offence under subsection (4) of section 17 of that Act consisting in the contravention of a restriction on the speed of vehicles imposed under that section;

(c) an offence under section 88(7) of that Act (temporary minimum speed limits);

(d) an offence under section 89(1) of that Act (speeding offences generally);

(e) an offence under section 36(1) of the Road Traffic Act 1988 consisting in the failure to comply with an indication given by a light signal that vehicular traffic is not to proceed.

(3) The Secretary of State may by order amend subsection (2) above by making additions to or deletions from the list of offences for the time being set out there; and an order under this subsection may make such transitional provision as appears to him to be necessary or expedient.

(4) A record produced or measurement made by a prescribed device shall not be admissible as evidence of a fact relevant to proceedings for an offence to which this section applies unless—

(a) the device is of a type approved by the Secretary of State, and

(b) any conditions subject to which the approval was given are satisfied.

(5) Any approval given by the Secretary of State for the purposes of this section may be given subject to conditions as to the purposes for which, and the manner and other circumstances in which, any device of the type concerned is to be used.

(6) In proceedings for an offence to which this section applies, evidence (which in Scotland shall be sufficient evidence)—

(a) of a measurement made by a device, or of the circumstances in which it was made, or

(b) that a device was of a type approved for the purposes of this section, or that any conditions subject to which an approval was given were satisfied,

may be given by the production of a document which is signed as mentioned in subsection (1) above and which, as the case may be, gives particulars of the measurement or of the circumstances in which it was made, or states that the device was of such a type or that, to the best of the knowledge and belief of the person making the statement, all such conditions were satisfied.

(7) For the purposes of this section a document purporting to be a record of the kind mentioned in subsection (1) above, or to be a certificate or other document signed as mentioned in that subsection or in subsection (6) above, shall be deemed to be such a record, or to be so signed, unless the contrary is proved.

(8) Nothing in subsection (1) or (6) above makes a document admissible as evidence in proceedings for an offence unless a copy of it has, not less than seven days before the hearing or trial, been served on the person charged with the offence; and nothing in those subsections makes a document admissible as evidence of anything other than the matters shown on a record produced by a

prescribed device if that person, not less than three days before the hearing or trial or within such further time as the court may in special circumstances allow, serves a notice on the prosecutor requiring attendance at the hearing or trial of the person who signed the document.

(9) In this section "prescribed device" means device of a description speci-fied in an order made by the Secretary of State.

(10) The powers to make orders under subsections (3) and (9) above shall be exercisable by statutory instrument, which shall be subject to annulment in pursuance of a resolution of either House of Parliament.

Proceedings in which evidence of one witness sufficient in Scotland

21.—(1) In any proceedings in Scotland for an offence to which this subsec-tion applies the accused may be convicted on the evidence of one witness.   **B16–11**

(2) Subsection (1) above applies to any offence created by or under an enact-ment and punishable on summary conviction, being an offence committed in respect of a vehicle—

   (a) by its being on a road during the hours of darkness without the lights or reflectors required by law, or

   (b) by its obstructing a road, or waiting, or being left or parked, or being loaded or unloaded, in a road, or

   (c) by the non-payment of a charge made at a street parking place, or

   (d) by its being used in contravention of any provision of an order made or having effect as if made under section 1 or 9 of the Road Traffic Regulation Act 1984, being a provision—

      (i) as to the route to be followed by vehicles of the class to which that vehicle belongs, or

      (ii) as to roads or parts of carriageways which are not to be used for traffic by such vehicles, or

      (iii) as to the places where such vehicles may not turn so as to face in the opposite direction to that in which they were proceeding or as to the conditions under which such vehicles may so turn, or

(3) Subsection (1) above also applies to any offence under section 35, 36 or 172 of the Road Traffic Act 1988.

(4) In subsection (2) above—

     "hours of darkness" means the time between half-an-hour after sunset and half-an-hour before sunrise, and

     "street parking place" means a parking place on land which forms part of a road.

(5) References in subsection (2) above to a class of vehicles are to be inter-preted as references to a class defined or described by reference to any charac-teristics of the vehicles or to any other circumstances whatsoever.

Alternative verdicts: general

24.—(1) Where—   **B16–12**

   (a) a person charged with an offence under a provision of the Road Traffic Act 1988 specified in the first column of the Table below (where the general nature of the offences is also indicated) is found not guilty of that offence, but

   (b) the allegations in the indictment or information (or in Scotland complaint) amount to or include an allegation of an offence under one or more of the provisions specified in the corresponding entry in the second column,

he may be convicted of that offence or of one or more of those offences.

Offence charged	Alternative
Section 1 (causing death by dangerous driving)	Section 2 (dangerous driving)
	Section 3 (careless, and inconsiderate, driving)
Section 2 (dangerous driving)	Section 3 (careless, and inconsiderate, driving)
Section 3A (causing death by careless driving when under influence of drink or drugs)	Section 3 (careless, and inconsiderate, driving)
	Section 4(1) (driving when unfit to drive through drink or drugs)
	Section 5(1)(a) (driving with excess alcohol in breath, blood or urine)
	Section 7(6) (failing to provide specimen)
Section 4(1) (driving or attempting to drive when unfit to drive through drink or drugs)	Section 4(2) (being in charge of a vehicle when unfit to drive through drink or drugs)
Section 5(1)(a) (driving or attempting to drive with excess alcohol in breath, blood or urine)	Section 5(1)(b) (being in charge of a vehicle with excess alcohol in breath, blood or urine)
Section 28 (dangerous cycling)	Section 29 (careless, and inconsiderate, cycling)

(2) Where the offence with which a person is charged is an offence under section 3A of the Road Traffic Act 1988, subsection (1) above shall not authorise his conviction of any offence of attempting to drive.

(3) Where a person is charged with having committed an offence under section 4(1) or 5(1)(a) of the Road Traffic Act 1988 by driving a vehicle, he may be convicted of having committed an offence under the provision in question by attempting to drive.

(4) Where by virtue of this section a person is convicted before the Crown Court of an offence triable only summarily, the court shall have the same powers and duties as a magistrates' court would have had on convicting him of that offence.

(5) Where, in Scotland, by virtue of this section a person is convicted under solemn procedure of an offence triable only summarily, the penalty imposed shall not exceed that which would have been competent on a conviction under summary procedure.

(6) This section has effect without prejudice to section 6(3) of the Criminal Law Act 1967 (alternative verdicts on trial on indictment), sections 61, 63, 64, 312 and 457A of the Criminal Procedure (Scotland) Act 1975 and section 23 of this Act.

Interim disqualification

26.—(1) Where a magistrates' court—

    (a) commits an offender to the Crown Court under subsection (1) of section 56 of the Criminal Justice Act 1967, or any enactment to which that section applies, or

   (b) remits an offender to another magistrates' court under section 39 of the Magistrates' Courts Act 1980,

to be dealt with for an offence involving obligatory or discretionary disqualification, it may order him to be disqualified until he has been dealt with in respect of the offence.

(2) Where a court in England and Wales—

   (a) defers passing sentence on an offender under section 1 of the Powers of Criminal Courts Act 1973 in respect of an offence involving obligatory or discretionary disqualification, or

   (b) adjourns after convicting an offender of such an offence but before dealing with him for the offence,

it may order the offender to be disqualified until he has been dealt with in respect of the offence.

(3) Where a court in Scotland—

   (a) adjourns a case under section 179 or section 380 of the Criminal Procedure (Scotland) Act 1975 (for inquiries to be made or to determine the most suitable method of dealing with the offender);

   (b) remands a person in custody or on bail under section 180 or section 381 of the Criminal Procedure (Scotland) Act 1975 (to enable a medical examination and report to be made);

   (c) defers sentence under section 219 or section 432 of the Criminal Procedure (Scotland) Act 1975;

   (d) remits a convicted person to the High Court for sentence under section 104 of the Criminal Procedure (Scotland) Act 1975,

in respect of an offence involving obligatory or discretionary disqualification, it may order the accused to be disqualified until he has been dealt with in respect of the offence.

(4) Subject to subsection (5) below, an order under this section shall cease to have effect at the end of the period of six months beginning with the day on which it is made, if it has not ceased to have effect before that time.

(5) In Scotland, where a person is disqualified under this section where section 219 or section 432 of the Criminal Procedure (Scotland) Act 1975 (deferred sentence) applies and the period of deferral exceeds 6 months, subsection (4) above shall not prevent the imposition under this section of any period of disqualification which does not exceed the period of deferral.

(6) Where a court orders a person to be disqualified under this section ("the first order"), no court shall make a further order under this section in respect of the same offence or any offence in respect of which an order could have been made under this section at the time the first order was made.

(7) Where a court makes an order under this section in respect of any person it must—

   (a) require him to produce to the court any licence held by him and its counterpart, and

   (b) retain the licence and counterpart until it deals with him or (as the case may be) cause them to be sent to the clerk of the court which is to deal with him.

(8) If the holder of the licence has not caused it and its counterpart to be delivered, or has not posted them, in accordance with section 7 of this Act and does not produce the licence and counterpart as required under subsection (7) above, then he is guilty of an offence.

(9) Subsection (8) above does not apply to a person who—

   (a) satisfies the court that he has applied for a new licence and has not received it, or

   (b) surrenders to the court a current receipt for his licence and its counterpart issued under section 56 of this Act, and produces the licence and counterpart to the court immediately on their return.

(10) Where a court makes an order under this section in respect of any person, sections 44(1) and 47(2) of this Act and section 109(3) of the Road Traffic Act 1988 (Northern Ireland drivers' licences) shall not apply in relation to the order, but—

    (a) the court must send notice of the order to the Secretary of State, and

    (b) if the court which deals with the offender determines not to order him to be disqualified under section 34 or 35 of this Act, it must send notice of the determination to the Secretary of State.

(11) A notice sent by a court to the Secretary of State in pursuance of subsection (10) above must be sent in such manner and to such address and contain such particulars as the Secretary of State may determine.

(12) Where on any occasion a court deals with an offender—

    (a) for an offence in respect of which an order was made under this section, or

    (b) for two or more offences in respect of any of which such an order was made,

any period of disqualification which is on that occasion imposed under section 34 or 35 of this Act shall be treated as reduced by any period during which he was disqualified by reason only of an order made under this section in respect of any of those offences.

(13) Any reference in this or any other Act (including any Act passed after this Act) to the length of a period of disqualification shall, unless the context otherwise requires, be construed as a reference to its length before any reduction under this section.

(14) In relation to licences which came into force before June 1, 1990 the references in this section to counterparts of licences shall be disregarded.

Production of licence

27.—(1) Where a person who is the holder of a licence is convicted of an offence involving obligatory or discretionary disqualification, and a court proposes to make an order disqualifying him or an order under section 44 of this Act, the court must, unless it has already received them, require the licence and its counterpart to be produced to it.

(2) [. . .]

(3) If the holder of the licence has not caused it and its counterpart to be delivered, or posted it and its counterpart, in accordance with section 7 of this Act and does not produce it and its counterpart as required under this section or section 44 of the Powers of Criminal Courts Act 1973, or section 223A or 436A of the Criminal Procedure (Scotland) Act 1975 then, unless he satisfies the court that he has applied for a new licence and has not received it—

    (a) he is guilty of an offence, and

    (b) the licence shall be suspended from the time when its production was required until it and its counterpart are produced to the court and shall, while suspended, be of no effect.

(4) Subsection (3) above does not apply where the holder of the licence—

    (a) has caused a current receipt for the licence and its counterpart issued under section 56 of this Act to be delivered to the clerk of the court not later than the day before the date appointed for the hearing, or

    (b) has posted such a receipt, at such time that in the ordinary course of post it would be delivered not later than that day, in a letter duly addressed to the clerk and either registered or sent by the recorded delivery service, or

(c) surrenders such a receipt to the court at the hearing,

and produces the licence and its counterpart to the court immediately on their return.

Penalty points to be attributed to an offence

28.—(1) Where a person is convicted of an offence involving obligatory endorsement, then, subject to the following provisions of this section, the number of penalty points to be attributed to the offence is— **B16–15**

(a) the number shown in relation to the offence in the last column of Part I or Part II of Schedule 2 to this Act, or

(b) where a range of numbers is shown, a number within that range.

(2) Where a person is convicted of an offence committed by aiding, abetting, counselling or procuring, or inciting to the commission of, an offence involving obligatory disqualification, then, subject to the following provisions of this section, the number of penalty points to be attributed to the offence is ten.

(3) Where both a range of numbers and a number followed by the words "(fixed penalty)" is shown in the last column of Part I of Schedule 2 to this Act in relation to an offence, that number is the number of penalty points to be attributed to the offence for the purposes of sections 57(5) and 77(5) of this Act; and, where only a range of numbers is shown there, the lowest number in the range is the number of penalty points to be attributed to the offence for those purposes.

(4) Where a person is convicted (whether on the same occasion or not) of two or more offences committed on the same occasion and involving obligatory endorsement, the total number of penalty points to be attributed to them is the number or highest number that would be attributed on a conviction of one of them (so that if the convictions are on different occasions the number of penalty points to be attributed to the offences on the later occasion or occasions shall be restricted accordingly).

(5) In a case where (apart from this subsection) subsection (4) above would apply to two or more offences, the court may if it thinks fit determine that that subsection shall not apply to the offences (or, where three or more offences are concerned, to any one or more of them).

(6) Where a court makes such a determination it shall state its reasons in open court and, if it is a magistrates' court, or in Scotland a court of summary jurisdiction, shall cause them to be entered in the register (in Scotland, record) of its proceedings.

(7) The Secretary of State may by order made by statutory instrument—

(a) alter a number or range of numbers shown in relation to an offence in the last column of Part I or Part II of Schedule 2 to this Act (by substituting one number or range for another, a number for a range, or a range for a number),

(b) where a range of numbers is shown in relation to an offence in the last column of Part I, add or delete a number together with the words "(fixed penalty)", and

(c) alter the number of penalty points shown in subsection (2) above;

and an order under this subsection may provide for different numbers or ranges of numbers to be shown in relation to the same offence committed in different circumstances.

(8) Where the Secretary of State exercises his power under subsection (7)

above by substituting or adding a number which appears together with the words "(fixed penalty)", that number shall not exceed the lowest number in the range shown in the same entry.

(9) No order shall be made under subsection (7) above unless a draft of it has been laid before and approved by resolution of each House of Parliament.

Penalty points to be taken into account on conviction

B16–16   29.—(1) Where a person is convicted of an offence involving obligatory endorsement, the penalty points to be taken into account on that occasion are (subject to subsection (2) below)—

   (a) any that are to be attributed to the offence or offences of which he is convicted, disregarding any offence in respect of which an order under section 34 of this Act is made, and

   (b) any that were on a previous occasion ordered to be endorsed on the counterpart of any licence held by him, unless the offender has since that occasion and before the conviction been disqualified under section 35 of this Act.

(2) If any of the offences was committed more than three years before another, the penalty points in respect of that offence shall not be added to those in respect of the other.

(3) In relation to licences which came into force before 1st June 1990, the reference in subsection (1) above to the counterpart of a licence shall be construed as a reference to the licence itself.

Court may take particulars endorsed on licence into consideration

B16–17   31.—(1) Where a person is convicted of an offence involving obligatory or discretionary disqualification and his licence and its counterpart are produced to the court—

   (a) any existing endorsement on the counterpart of his licence is prima facie evidence of the matters endorsed, and

   (b) the court may, in determining what order to make in pursuance of the conviction, take those matters into consideration.

(2) This section has effect notwithstanding anything in sections 311(5) and 357(1) of the Criminal Procedure (Scotland) Act 1975 (requirements as to notices of penalties and previous convictions).

Fine and imprisonment

B16–18   33.—(1) Where a person is convicted of an offence against a provision of the Traffic Acts specified in column 1 of Part I of Schedule 2 to this Act or regulations made under any such provision, the maximum punishment by way of fine or imprisonment which may be imposed on him is that shown in column 4 against the offence and (where appropriate) the circumstances or the mode of trial there specified.

(2) Any reference in column 4 of that Part to a period of years or months is to be construed as a reference to a term of imprisonment of that duration.

Disqualification for certain offences

B16–19   34.—(1) Where a person is convicted of an offence involving obligatory disqualification, the court must order him to be disqualified for such period not less than twelve months as the court thinks fit unless the court for special reasons thinks fit to order him to be disqualified for a shorter period or not to order him to be disqualified.

(1A) Where a person is convicted of an offence under section 12A of the Theft Act 1968 (aggravated vehicle-taking), the fact that he did not drive the vehicle in question at any particular time or at all shall not be regarded as a special reason for the purposes of subsection (1) above.

(2) Where a person is convicted of an offence involving discretionary disqualification, and either—

(a) the penalty points to be taken into account on that occasion number fewer than twelve, or

(b) the offence is not one involving obligatory endorsement,

the court may order him to be disqualified for such period as the court thinks fit.

(3) Where a person convicted of an offence under any of the following provisions of the Road Traffic Act 1988, that is—

(aa) section 3A (causing death by careless driving when under the influence of drink or drugs),

(a) section 4(1) (driving or attempting to drive while unfit),

(b) section 5(1)(a) (driving or attempting to drive with excess alcohol), and

(c) section 7(6) (failing to provide a specimen) where that is an offence involving obligatory disqualification,

has within the ten years immediately preceding the commission of the offence been convicted of any such offence, subsection (1) above shall apply in relation to him as if the reference to twelve months were a reference to three years.

(4) Subject to subsection (3) above, subsection (1) above shall apply as if the reference to twelve months were a reference to two years—

(a) in relation to a person convicted of—

(i) manslaughter, or in Scotland culpable homicide, or

(ii) an offence under section 1 of the Road Traffic Act 1988 (causing death by dangerous driving), or

(iii) an offence under section 3A of that Act (causing death by careless driving while under the influence of drink or drugs), and

(b) in relation to a person on whom more than one disqualification for a fixed period of 56 days or more has been imposed within the three years immediately preceding the commission of the offence.

(4A) For the purposes of subsection (4)(b) above there shall be disregarded any disqualification imposed under section 26 of this Act or section 44 of the Powers of Criminal Courts Act 1973 or section 223A or 436A of the Criminal Procedure (Scotland) Act 1975 (offences committed by using vehicles) and any disqualification imposed in respect of an offence of stealing a motor vehicle, an offence under section 12 or 25 of the Theft Act 1968, an offence under section 178 of the Road Traffic Act 1988, or an attempt to commit such an offence.

(5) The preceding provisions of this section shall apply in relation to a conviction of an offence committed by aiding, abetting, counselling or procuring, or inciting to the commission of, an offence involving obligatory disqualification as if the offence were an offence involving discretionary disqualification.

(6) This section is subject to section 48 of this Act.

Reduced disqualification period for attendance on courses

B16–20   34A.—(1) This section applies where—

(a) a person is convicted of an offence under section 3A (causing death by careless driving when under influence of drink or drugs), 4 (driving or being in charge when under influence of drink or drugs), 5 (driving or being in charge with excess alcohol) or 7 (failing to provide a specimen) of the Road Traffic Act 1988, and

(b) the court makes an order under section 34 of this Act disqualifying him for a period of not less than twelve months.

(2) Where this section applies, the court may make an order that the period of disqualification imposed under section 34 shall be reduced if, by a date specified in the order under this section, the offender satisfactorily completes a course approved by the Secretary of State for the purposes of this section and specified in the order.

(3) The reduction made by an order under this section in a period of disqualification imposed under section 34 shall be a period specified in the order of not less than three months and not more than one quarter of the unreduced period (and accordingly where the period imposed under section 34 is twelve months, the reduced period shall be nine months).

(4) The court shall not make an order under this section unless—

(a) it is satisfied that a place on the course specified in the order will be available for the offender,

(b) the offender appears to the court to be of or over the age of 17,

(c) the court has explained the effect of the order to the offender in ordinary language, and has informed him of the amount of the fees for the course and of the requirement that he must pay them before beginning the course, and

(d) the offender has agreed that the order should be made.

(5) The date specified in an order under this section as the latest date for completion of a course must be at least two months before the last day of the period of disqualification as reduced by the order.

(6) An order under this section shall name the petty sessions area (or in Scotland the sheriff court district or, where an order has been made under this section by a stipendiary magistrate, the commission area) in which the offender resides or will reside.

Certificates of completion of courses

B16–21   34B.—(1) An offender shall be regarded for the purposes of section 34A of this Act as having completed a course satisfactorily if (and only if) a certificate that he has done so is received by the clerk of the supervising court before the end of the period of disqualification imposed under section 34.

(2) If the certificate referred to in subsection (1) above is received by the clerk of the supervising court before the end of the period of disqualification imposed under section 34 but after the end of the period as it would have been reduced by the order, the order shall have effect as if the reduced period ended with the day on which the certificate is received by the clerk.

(3) The certificate referred to in subsection (1) above shall be a certificate in such form, containing such particulars, and given by such person, as may be prescribed by, or determined in accordance with, regulations made by the Secretary of State.

(4) A course organiser shall give the certificate mentioned in subsection (1)

above to the offender not later than fourteen days after the date specified in the order as the latest date for completion of the course, unless the offender fails to make due payment of the fees for the course, fails to attend the course in accordance with the organiser's reasonable instructions, or fails to comply with any other reasonable requirements of the organiser.

(5) Where a course organiser decides not to give the certificate mentioned in subsection (1) above, he shall give written notice of his decision to the offender as soon as possible, and in any event not later than fourteen days after the date specified in the order as the latest date for completion of the course.

(6) An offender to whom a notice is given under subsection (5) above may, within such period as may be prescribed by rules of court, apply to the supervising court for a declaration that the course organiser's decision not to give a certificate was contrary to subsection (4) above; and if the court grants the application section 34A of this Act shall have effect as if the certificate had been duly received by the clerk of the court.

(7) If fourteen days after the date specified in the order as the latest date for completion of the course the course organiser has given neither the certificate mentioned in subsection (1) above nor a notice under subsection (5) above, the offender may, within such period as may be prescribed by rules of court, apply to the supervising court for a declaration that the course organiser is in default; and if the court grants the application section 34A of this Act shall have effect as if the certificate had been duly received by the clerk of the court.

(8) A notice under subsection (5) above shall specify the ground on which it is given, and the Secretary of State may by regulations make provision as to the form of notices under that subsection and as to the circumstances in which they are to be treated as given.

(9) Where the clerk of a court receives a certificate of the kind referred to in subsection (1) above, or a court grants an application under subsection (6) or (7) above, the clerk or court must send notice of that fact to the Secretary of State; and the notice must be sent in such manner and to such address, and must contain such particulars, as the Secretary of State may determine.

Provisions supplementary to sections 34A and 34B

34C.—(1) The Secretary of State may issue guidance to course organisers, or **B16–22** to any category of course organiser as to the conduct of courses approved for the purposes of section 34A of this Act; and—

    (a) course organisers shall have regard to any guidance given to them under this subsection, and

    (b) in determining for the purposes of section 34B(6) whether any instructions or requirements of an organiser were reasonable, a court shall have regard to any guidance given to him under this subsection.

(2) In sections 34A and 34B and this section—

    "course organiser", in relation to a course, means the person who, in accordance with regulations made by the Secretary of State, is responsible for giving the certificates mentioned in section 34B(1) in respect of the completion of the course;

    "petty sessions area" has the same meaning as in the Magistrates' Courts Act 1980;

    "supervising court", in relation to an order under section 34A, means—

        (a) in England and Wales, a magistrates' court acting for the petty sessions area named in the order as the area where the offender resides or will reside;

(b) in Scotland, the sheriff court for the district where the offender resides or will reside or, where the order is made by a stipendiary magistrate and the offender resides or will reside within his commission area, the district court for that area,

and any reference to the clerk of a magistrates' court is a reference to the clerk to the justices for the petty sessions area for which the court acts.

(3) Any power to make regulations under section 34B or this section—

(a) includes power to make different provisions for different cases, and to make such incidental or supplemental provision as appears to the Secretary of State to be necessary or expedient;

(b) shall be exercisable by statutory instrument, which shall be subject to annulment in pursuance of a resolution of either House of Parliament.

Disqualification for repeated offences

　　35.—(1) Where—

(a) a person is convicted of an offence to which this section applies, and

(b) the penalty points to be taken into account on that occasion number twelve or more,

the court must order him to be disqualified for not less than the minimum period unless the court is satisfied, having regard to all the circumstances, that there are grounds for mitigating the normal consequences of the conviction and thinks fit to order him to be disqualified for a shorter period or not to order him to be disqualified.

(1A) Subsection (1) above applies to

(a) an offence involving discretionary disqualification and obligatory endorsement, and

(b) an offence involving obligatory disqualification in respect of which no order is made under section 34 of this Act.

(2) The minimum period referred to in subsection (1) above is—

(a) six months if no previous disqualification imposed on the offender is to be taken into account, and

(b) one year if one, and two years if more than one, such disqualification is to be taken into account;

and a previous disqualification imposed on an offender is to be taken into account if it was for a fixed period of 56 days or more and was imposed within the three years immediately preceding the commission of the latest offence in respect of which penalty points are taken into account under section 29 of this Act.

(3) Where an offender is convicted on the same occasion of more than one offence to which subsection (1) above applies—

(a) not more than one disqualification shall be imposed on him under subsection (1) above,

(b) in determining the period of the disqualification the court must take into account all the offences, and

(c) for the purposes of any appeal any disqualification imposed under subsection (1) above shall be treated as an order made on the conviction of each of the offences.

(4) No account is to be taken under subsection (1) above of any of the following circumstances—

(a) any circumstances that are alleged to make the offence or any of the offences not a serious one,

(b) hardship, other than exceptional hardship, or

(c) any circumstances which, within the three years immediately preceding the conviction, have been taken into account under that subsection in ordering the offender to be disqualified for a shorter period or not ordering him to be disqualified.

(5) References in this section to disqualification do not include a disqualification imposed under section 26 of this Act or section 44 of the Powers of Criminal Courts Act 1973 or section 223A or 436A of the Criminal Procedure (Scotland) Act 1975 (offences committed by using vehicles) or a disqualification imposed in respect of an offence of stealing a motor vehicle, an offence under section 12 or 25 of the Theft Act 1968, an offence under section 178 of the Road Traffic Act 1988, or an attempt to commit such an offence.

(5A) The preceding provisions of this section shall apply in relation to a conviction of an offence committed by aiding, abetting, counselling, procuring, or inciting to the commission of, an offence involving obligatory disqualification as if the offence were an offence involving discretionary disqualification.

(6) In relation to Scotland, references in this section to the court include the district court.

(7) This section is subject to section 48 of this Act.

Endorsement of licences

44.—(1) Where a person is convicted of an offence involving obligatory endorsement, the court must order there to be endorsed on the counterpart of any licence held by him particulars of the conviction and also—   **B16–24**

(a) if the court orders him to be disqualified, particulars of the disqualification, or

(b) if the court does not order him to be disqualified—

(i) particulars of the offence, including the date when it was committed, and

(ii) the penalty points to be attributed to the offence.

(2) Where the court does not order the person convicted to be disqualified, it need not make an order under subsection (1) above if for special reasons it thinks fit not to do so.

(3) In relation to Scotland, references in this section to the court include the district court.

(4) This section is subject to section 48 of this Act.

Combination of disqualification and endorsement with probation orders and orders for discharge

46.—(1) Notwithstanding anything in section 1C(3) of the Powers of Criminal Courts Act 1973 (conviction of offender discharged to be disregarded for the purposes of enactments relating to disqualification), a court in England and Wales which on convicting a person of an offence involving obligatory or discretionary disqualification makes—   **B16–25**

(a) a probation order, or

(b) an order discharging him absolutely or conditionally,

may on that occasion also exercise any power conferred, and must also discharge any duty imposed, on the court by sections 34, 35, 36 or 44 of this Act.

(2) A conviction—

(a) in respect of which a court in England and Wales has ordered a person to be disqualified, or

(b) of which particulars have been endorsed on the counterpart of any licence held by him,

is to be taken into account, notwithstanding anything in section 1C(1) of the Powers of Criminal Courts Act 1973 (conviction of offender discharged to be disregarded for the purpose of subsequent proceedings), in determining his liability to punishment or disqualification for any offence involving obligatory or discretionary disqualification committed subsequently.

(3) Where—

(a) a person is charged in Scotland with an offence involving obligatory or discretionary disqualification, and

(b) the court makes an order in respect of the offence under section 182 or 383 (absolute discharge) or 183 or 384 (probation) of the Criminal Procedure (Scotland) Act 1975,

then, for the purposes of sections 34, 35, 36, 44 and 45 of this Act, he shall be treated as if he had been convicted of an offence of the kind in question and section 191 or, as the case may be, section 392 of that Act shall not apply.

Offender escaping consequences of endorseable offence by deception

B16–26   **49.**—(1) This section applies where in dealing with a person convicted of an offence involving obligatory endorsement a court was deceived regarding any circumstances that were or might have been taken into account in deciding whether or for how long to disqualify him.

(2) If—

(a) the deception constituted or was due to an offence committed by that person, and

(b) he is convicted of that offence,

the court by or before which he is convicted shall have the same powers and duties regarding an offer for disqualification as had the court which dealt with him for the offence involving obligatory endorsement but must, in dealing with him, take into account any order made on his conviction of the offence involving obligatory endorsement.

Fixed penalty offences

B16–27   **51.**—(1) Any offence in respect of a vehicle under an enactment specified in column 1 of Schedule 3 to this Act is a fixed penalty offence for the purposes of this Part of this Act, but subject to subsection (2) below and to any limitation or exception shown against the enactment in column 2 (where the general nature of the offence is also indicated).

(2) An offence under an enactment so specified is not a fixed penalty offence for those purposes if it is committed by causing or permitting a vehicle to be used by another person in contravention of any provision made or restriction or prohibition imposed by or under any enactment.

(3) The Secretary of State may by order provide for offences to become or (as the case may be) to cease to be fixed penalty offences for the purposes of this Part of this Act, and may make such modifications of the provisions of this Part of this Act as appear to him to be necessary for the purpose.

Fixed penalty notices

52.—(1) In this Part of this Act "fixed penalty notice" means a notice offer-   **B16–28**
ing the opportunity of the discharge of any liability to conviction of the
offence to which the notice relates by payment of a fixed penalty in accordance
with this Part of this Act.

(2) A fixed penalty notice must give such particulars of the circumstances
alleged to constitute the offence to which it relates as are necessary for giving
reasonable information about the alleged offence.

(3) A fixed penalty notice must state—
   (a) the period during which, by virtue of section 78(1) of this Act, proceed-
       ings cannot be brought against any person for the offence to which the
       notice relates, being the period of twenty-one days following the date
       of the notice or such longer period (if any) as may be specified in the
       notice (referred to in this Part of this Act as the "suspended enforce-
       ment period"),
   (b) the amount of the fixed penalty, and
   (c) the justices' clerk or, in Scotland, the clerk of court to whom and the
       address at which the fixed penalty may be paid.

(4) A fixed penalty notice given under section 54(2) of this Act in respect of
an offence committed in Scotland must be in the prescribed form.

Amount of fixed penalty

53.—(1) The fixed penalty for an offence is—   **B16–29**
   (a) such amount as the Secretary of State may by order prescribe, or
   (b) one-half of the maximum amount of the fine to which a person com-
       mitting that offence would be liable on summary conviction,
whichever is the less.

(2) Any order made under subsection (1)(a) may make different provision
for different cases or classes of case or in respect of different areas.

Notices on-the-spot or at a police station

54.—(1) This section applies where in England and Wales on any occasion a   **B16–30**
constable in uniform has reason to believe that a person he finds is committing
or has on that occasion committed a fixed penalty offence.

(2) Subject to subsection (3) below, the constable may give him a fixed penalty notice in respect of the offence.

(3) Where the offence appears to the constable to involve obligatory
endorsement, the constable may only give him a fixed penalty notice under
subsection (2) above in respect of the offence if—
   (a) he produces his licence and its counterpart for inspection by the
       constable,
   (b) the constable is satisfied, on inspecting the licence and its counterpart,
       that he would not be liable to be disqualified under section 35 of this
       Act if he were convicted of that offence, and
   (c) he surrenders his licence and its counterpart to the constable to be
       retained and dealt with in accordance with this Part of this Act.

(4) Where—
   (a) the offence appears to the constable to involve obligatory endorse-
       ment, and

(b) the person concerned does not produce his licence and its counterpart for inspection by the constable,

the constable may give him a notice stating that if, within seven days after the notice is given, he produces the notice together with his licence and its counterpart in person to a constable or authorised person at the police station specified in the notice (being a police station chosen by the person concerned) and the requirements of subsection (5)(a) and (b) below are met he will then be given a fixed penalty notice in respect of the offence.

(5) If a person to whom a notice has been given under subsection (4) above produces the notice together with his licence and its counterpart in person to a constable or authorised person at the police station specified in the notice within seven days after the notice was so given to him and the following requirements are met, that is—

(a) the constable or authorised person is satisfied, on inspecting the licence and its counterpart, that he would not be liable to be disqualified under section 35 of this Act if he were convicted of the offence, and

(b) he surrenders his licence and its counterpart to the constable or authorised person to be retained and dealt with in accordance with this Part of this Act,

the constable or authorised person must give him a fixed penalty notice in respect of the offence to which the notice under subsection (4) above relates.

(6) A notice under subsection (4) above shall give such particulars of the circumstances alleged to constitute the offence to which it relates as are necessary for giving reasonable information about the alleged offence.

(7) A licence and a counterpart of a licence surrendered in accordance with this section must be sent to the fixed penalty clerk.

(8) [. . .]

(9) In this Part of this Act "authorised person," in relation to a fixed penalty notice given at a police station, means a person authorised for the purposes of this section by or on behalf of the chief officer of police for the area in which the police station is situated.

(10) In determining for the purposes of subsections (3)(b) and (5)(a) above whether a person convicted of an offence would be liable to disqualification under section 35, it shall be assumed, in the case of an offence in relation to which a range of numbers is shown in the last column of Part I of Schedule 2 to this Act, that the number of penalty points to be attributed to the offence would be the lowest in the range.

Effect of fixed penalty notice given under section 54

B16–31   55.—(1) This section applies where a fixed penalty notice relating to an offence has been given to any person under section 54 of this Act, and references in this section to the recipient are to the person to whom the notice was given.

(2) No proceedings shall be brought against the recipient for the offence to which the fixed penalty notice relates unless before the end of the suspended enforcement period he has given notice requesting a hearing in respect of that offence in the manner specified in the fixed penalty notice.

(3) Where—

(a) the recipient has not given notice requesting a hearing in respect of the offence to which the fixed penalty notice relates in the manner so specified, and

(b) the fixed penalty has not been paid in accordance with this Part of this Act before the end of the suspended enforcement period,

a sum equal to the fixed penalty plus one-half of the amount of that penalty may be registered under section 71 of this Act for enforcement against the recipient as a fine.

Licence receipts

56.—(1) A constable or authorised person to whom a person surrenders his licence and its counterpart on receiving a fixed penalty notice given to him under section 54 of this Act must issue a receipt for the licence and its counterpart under this section.   **B16–32**

(2) The fixed penalty clerk may, on the application of a person who has surrendered his licence and its counterpart in those circumstances, issue a new receipt for them.

(3) A receipt issued under this section ceases to have effect—

    (a) if issued by a constable or authorised person, on the expiration of the period of one month beginning with the date of issue or such longer period as may be prescribed, and

    (b) if issued by the fixed penalty clerk, on such date as he may specify in the receipt,

or, if earlier, on the return of the licence and its counterpart to the licence holder.

Endorsement of licences without hearings

57.—(1) Subject to subsection (2) below, where a person (referred to in this section as "the licence holder") has surrendered his licence and its counterpart to a constable or authorised person on the occasion when he was given a fixed penalty notice under section 54 of this Act, the counterpart of his licence may be endorsed in accordance with this section without any order of a court.   **B16–33**

(2) The counterpart of a person's licence may not be endorsed under this section if at the end of the suspended enforcement period—

    (a) he has given notice, in the manner specified in the fixed penalty notice, requesting a hearing in respect of the offence to which the fixed penalty notice relates, and

    (b) the fixed penalty has not been paid in accordance with this Part of this Act.

(3) On the payment of the fixed penalty before the end of the suspended enforcement period, the fixed penalty clerk must endorse the relevant particulars on the counterpart of the licence and return it together with the licence to the licence holder.

(4) Where any sum determined by reference to the fixed penalty is registered under section 71 of this Act for enforcement against the licence holder as a fine, the fixed penalty clerk must endorse the relevant particulars on the counterpart of the licence and return it together with the licence to the licence holder—

    (a) if he is himself the clerk who registers that sum, on the registration of that sum, and

    (b) in any other case, on being notified of the registration by the clerk who registers that sum.

(5) References in this section to the relevant particulars are to—

(a) particulars of the offence, including the date when it was committed, and

(b) the number of penalty points to be attributed to the offence.

(6) On endorsing the counterpart of a person's licence under this section the fixed penalty clerk must send notice of the endorsement and of the particulars endorsed to the Secretary of State.

Effect of endorsement without hearing

B16–34   58.—(1) Where the counterpart of a person's licence is endorsed under section 57 of this Act he shall be treated for the purposes of sections 13(4), 28, 29 and 45 of this Act and of the Rehabilitation of Offenders Act 1974 as if—

(a) he had been convicted of the offence,

(b) the endorsement had been made in pursuance of an order made on his conviction by a court under section 44 of this Act, and

(c) the particulars of the offence endorsed by virtue of section 57(5)(a) of this Act were particulars of his conviction of that offence.

(2) In relation to any endorsement of the counterpart of a person's licence under section 57 of this Act—

(a) the reference in section 45(4) of this Act to the order for endorsement, and

(b) the references in section 13(4) of this Act to any order made on a person's conviction,

are to be read as references to the endorsement itself.

Notification of court and date of trial in England and Wales

B16–35   59.—(1) On an occasion when a person is given a fixed penalty notice under section 54 of this Act in respect of an offence, he may be given written notification specifying the magistrates' court by which and the date on which the offence will be tried if he gives notice requesting a hearing in respect of the offence as permitted by the fixed penalty notice.

(2) Subject to subsections (4) and (5) below, where—

(a) a person has been notified in accordance with this section of the court and date of trial of an offence in respect of which he has been given a fixed penalty notice, and

(b) he has given notice requesting a hearing in respect of the offence as permitted by the fixed penalty notice,

the provisions of the Magistrates' Courts Act 1980 shall apply as mentioned in subsection (3) below.

(3) Those provisions are to have effect for the purpose of any proceedings in respect of that offence as if—

(a) the allegation in the fixed penalty notice with respect to that offence were an information duly laid in accordance with section 1 of that Act, and

(b) the notification of the court and date of trial were a summons duly issued on that information by a justice of the peace for the area for which the magistrates' court notified as the court of trial acts, requiring the person notified to appear before that court to answer to that information and duly served on him on the date on which the notification was given.

(4) If, in a case within subsection (2) above, notice is served by or on behalf

of the chief officer of police on the person who gave notice requesting a hearing stating that no proceedings are to be brought in respect of the offence concerned, that subsection does not apply and no such proceedings are to be brought against the person who gave notice requesting a hearing.

(5) Section 14 of that Act (proceedings invalid where accused did not know of them) is not applied by subsection (2) above in a case where a person has been notified in accordance with this section of the court and date of trial of an offence.

Fixed penalty notice mistakenly given: exclusion of fixed penalty procedures

61.—(1) This section applies where, on inspection of a licence and its **B16–36** counterpart sent to him under section 54(7) of this Act, it appears to the fixed penalty clerk that the person whose licence it is would be liable to be disqualified under section 35 of this Act if he were convicted of the offence in respect of which the fixed penalty notice was given.

(2) The fixed penalty clerk must not endorse the counterpart of the licence under section 57 of this Act but must instead send it together with the licence to the chief officer of police.

(3) Nothing in this Part of this Act prevents proceedings being brought in respect of the offence in respect of which the fixed penalty notice was given where those proceedings are commenced before the end of the period of six months beginning with the date on which that notice was given.

(4) Where proceedings in respect of that offence are commenced before the end of that period, the case is from then on to be treated in all respects as if no fixed penalty notice had been given in respect of the offence.

(5) Accordingly, where proceedings in respect of that offence are so commenced, any action taken in pursuance of any provision of this Part of this Act by reference to that fixed penalty notice shall be void (including, but without prejudice to the generality of the preceding provision—

    (a) the registration under section 71 of this Act of any sum, determined by reference to the fixed penalty for that offence, for enforcement against the person whose licence it is as a fine, and

    (b) any proceedings for enforcing payment of any such sum within the meaning of sections 73 and 74 of this Act (defined in section 74(5))).

(6) In determining for the purposes of subsection (1) above whether a person convicted of an offence would be liable to disqualification under section 35, it shall be assumed, in the case of an offence in relation to which a range of numbers is shown in the last column of Part I of Schedule 2 to this Act, that the number of penalty points to be attributed to the offence would be the lowest in the range.

Fixing notices to vehicles

62.—(1) Where on any occasion a constable has reason to believe in the case **B16–37** of any stationary vehicle that a fixed penalty offence is being or has on that occasion been committed in respect of it, he may fix a fixed penalty notice in respect of the offence to the vehicle unless the offence appears to him to involve obligatory endorsement.

(2) A person is guilty of an offence if he removes or interferes with any

notice fixed to a vehicle under this section, unless he does so by or under the authority of the driver or person in charge of the vehicle or the person liable for the fixed penalty offence in question.

Service of notice to owner if penalty not paid

B16–38   **63.**—(1) This section applies where a fixed penalty notice relating to an offence has been fixed to a vehicle under section 62 of this Act.

(2) Subject to subsection (3) below, if at the end of the suspended enforcement period the fixed penalty has not been paid in accordance with this Part of this Act, a notice under this section may be served by or on behalf of the chief officer of police on any person who appears to him (or to any person authorised to act on his behalf for the purposes of this section) to be the owner of the vehicle.

Such a notice is referred to in this Part of this Act as a "notice to owner."

(3) Subsection (2) above does not apply where before the end of the suspended enforcement period—

(a) any person has given notice requesting a hearing in respect of the offence in the manner specified in the fixed penalty notice, and

(b) the notice so given contains a statement by that person to the effect that he was the driver of the vehicle at the time when the offence is alleged to have been committed.

That time is referred to in this Part of this Act as the "time of the alleged offence."

(4) A notice to owner—

(a) must give particulars of the alleged offence and of the fixed penalty concerned,

(b) must state the period allowed for response to the notice, and

(c) must indicate that, if the fixed penalty is not paid before the end of that period, the person on whom the notice is served is asked to provide before the end of that period to the chief officer of police by or on whose behalf the notice was served a statutory statement of ownership (as defined in Part I of Schedule 4 to this Act).

(5) For the purposes of this Part of this Act, the period allowed for response to a notice to owner is the period of twenty-one days from the date on which the notice is served, or such longer period (if any) as may be specified in the notice.

(6) A notice to owner relating to any offence must indicate that the person on whom it is served may; before the end of the period allowed for response to the notice, either—

(a) give notice requesting a hearing in respect of the offence in the manner indicated by the notice, or

(b) if—

(i) he was not the driver of the vehicle at the time of the alleged offence, and

(ii) a person purporting to be the driver wishes to give notice requesting a hearing in respect of the offence,

provide, together with a statutory statement of ownership provided as requested in that notice, a statutory statement of facts (as defined by Part II of Schedule 4 to this Act) having the effect referred to in paragraph 3(2) of that Schedule (that is, as a notice requesting a hearing in respect of the offence given by the driver).

(7) In any case where a person on whom a notice to owner relating to any

offence has been served provides a statutory statement of facts in pursuance of subsection (6)(b) above—

(a) any notice requesting a hearing in respect of the offence that he purports to give on his own account shall be of no effect, and

(b) no sum may be registered for enforcement against him as a fine in respect of the offence unless, within the period of two months immediately following the period allowed for response to the notice to owner, no summons or, in Scotland, complaint in respect of the offence in question is served on the person identified in the statement as the driver.

Enforcement or proceedings against owner

64.—(1) This section applies where—   **B16–39**

(a) a fixed penalty notice relating to an offence has been fixed to a vehicle under section 62 of this Act,

(b) a notice to owner relating to the offence has been served on any person under section 63(2) of this Act before the end of the period of six months beginning with the day on which the fixed penalty notice was fixed to the vehicle, and

(c) the fixed penalty has not been paid in accordance with this Part of this Act before the end of the period allowed for response to the notice to owner.

(2) Subject to subsection (4) below and to section 63(7)(b) of this Act, a sum equal to the fixed penalty plus one-half of the amount of that penalty may be registered under section 71 of this Act for enforcement against the person on whom the notice to owner was served as a fine.

(3) Subject to subsection (4) below and to section 65 of this Act, proceedings may be brought in respect of the offence against the person on whom the notice to owner was served.

(4) If the person on whom the notice to owner was served—

(a) was not the owner of the vehicle at the time of the alleged offence, and

(b) provides a statutory statement of ownership to that effect in response to the notice before the end of the period allowed for response to the notice,

he shall not be liable in respect of the offence by virtue of this section nor shall any sum determined by reference to the fixed penalty for the offence be so registered by virtue of this section for enforcement against him as a fine.

(5) Subject to subsection (6) below—

(a) for the purposes of the institution of proceedings by virtue of subsection (3) above against any person on whom a notice to owner has been served, and

(b) in any proceedings brought by virtue of that subsection against any such person,

it shall be conclusively presumed (notwithstanding that that person may not be an individual) that he was the driver of the vehicle at the time of the alleged offence and, accordingly, that acts or omissions of the driver of the vehicle at that time were acts or omissions.

(6) That presumption does not apply in any proceedings brought against any person by virtue of subsection (3) above if, in those proceedings, it is proved that at the time of the alleged offence the vehicle was in the possession of some other person without the consent of the accused.

(7) Where—

(a) by virtue of subsection (3) above proceedings may be brought in respect of an offence against a person on whom a notice to owner was served, and

(b) section 74(1) of this Act does not apply,

section 127(1) of the Magistrates' Courts Act 1980 (information must be laid within six months of time offence committed) and section 331(1) of the Criminal Procedure (Scotland) Act 1975 (proceedings must be commenced within six months of that time) shall have effect as if for the reference to six months there were substituted a reference to twelve months.

Restrictions on proceedings against owner and others

B16–40   **65.**—(1) In any case where a notice to owner relating to an offence may be served under section 63 of this Act, no proceedings shall be brought in respect of the offence against any person other than a person on whom such a notice has been served unless he is identified as the driver of the vehicle at the time of the alleged offence in a statutory statement of facts provided in pursuance of section 63(6)(b) of this Act by a person on whom such a notice has been served.

(2) Proceedings in respect of an offence to which a notice to owner relates shall not be brought against the person on whom the notice was served unless, before the end of the period allowed for response to the notice, he has given notice, in the manner indicated by the notice to owner, requesting a hearing in respect of the offence.

(3) Proceedings in respect of an offence to which a notice to owner relates may not be brought against any person identified as the driver of the vehicle in a statutory statement of facts provided in response to the notice if the fixed penalty is paid in accordance with this Part of this Act before the end of the period allowed for response to the notice.

(4) Once any sum determined by reference to the fixed penalty for an offence has been registered by virtue of section 64 of this Act under section 71 for enforcement as a fine against a person on whom a notice to owner relating to that offence has been served, no proceedings shall be brought against any other person in respect of that offence.

Hired vehicles

B16–41   **66.**—(1) This section applies where—

(a) a notice to owner has been served on a vehicle-hire firm,

(b) at the time of the alleged offence the vehicle in respect of which the notice was served was let to another person by the vehicle-hire firm under a hiring agreement to which this section applies, and

(c) within the period allowed for response to the notice the firm provides the chief officer of police by or on whose behalf the notice was served with the documents mentioned in subsection (2) below.

(2) Those documents are a statement on an official form, signed by or on behalf of the firm, stating that at the time of the alleged offence the vehicle concerned was hired under a hiring agreement to which this section applies, together with—

(a) a copy of that hiring agreement, and

(b) a copy of a statement of liability signed by the hirer under that hiring agreement.

(3) In this section a "statement of liability" means a statement made by the hirer under a hiring agreement to which this section applies to the effect that

the hirer acknowledges that he will be liable, as the owner of the vehicle, in respect of any fixed penalty offence which may be committed with respect to the vehicle during the currency of the hiring agreement and giving such information as may be prescribed.

(4) In any case where this section applies, sections 63, 64 and 65 of this Act shall have effect as if—

(a) any reference to the owner of the vehicle were a reference to the hirer under the hiring agreement, and

(b) any reference to a statutory statement of ownership were a reference to a statutory statement of hiring,

and accordingly references in this Part of this Act (with the exceptions mentioned below) to a notice to owner include references to a notice served under section 63 of this Act as it applies by virtue of this section.

This subsection does not apply to references to a notice to owner in this section or in section 81(2)(b) of or Part I of Schedule 4 to this Act.

(5) In any case where this section applies, a person authorised in that behalf by the chief officer of police to whom the documents mentioned in subsection (2) above are provided may, at any reasonable time within six months after service of the notice to owner (and on the production of his authority) require the firm to produce the originals of the hiring agreement and statement of liability in question.

(6) If a vehicle-hire firm fails to produce the original of a document when required to do so under subsection (5) above, this section shall thereupon cease to apply (and section 64 of this Act shall apply accordingly in any such case after that time as it applies in a case where the person on whom the notice to owner was served has failed to provide a statutory statement of ownership in response to the notice within the period allowed).

(7) This section applies to a hiring agreement under the terms of which the vehicle concerned is let to the hirer for a fixed period of less than six months (whether or not that period is capable of extension by agreement between the parties or otherwise); and any reference in this section to the currency of the hiring agreement includes a reference to any period during which, with the consent of the vehicle-hire firm, the hirer continues in possession of the vehicle as hirer, after the expiry of the fixed period specified in the agreement, but otherwise on the terms and conditions so specified.

(8) In this section—

"hiring agreement" refers only to an agreement which contains such particulars as may be prescribed and does not include a hire-purchase agreement within the meaning of the Consumer Credit Act 1974, and

"vehicle-hire firm" means any person engaged in hiring vehicles in the course of a business.

False statements in response to notices to owner

67. A person who, in response to a notice to owner, provides a statement which is false in a material particular and does so recklessly or knowing it to be false in that particular is guilty of an offence. **B16–42**

"Owner," "statutory statement" and "official form"

68.—(1) For the purposes of this Part of this Act, the owner of a vehicle shall **B16–43**

be taken to be the person by whom the vehicle is kept; and for the purposes of determining, in the course of any proceedings brought by virtue of section 64(3) of this Act, who was the owner of a vehicle at any time, it shall be presumed that the owner was the person who was the registered keeper of the vehicle at that time.

(2) Notwithstanding the presumption in subsection (1) above, it is open to the defence in any proceedings to prove that the person who was the registered keeper of a vehicle at a particular time was not the person by whom the vehicle was kept at that time and to the prosecution to prove that the vehicle was kept by some other person at that time.

(3) References in this Part of this Act to statutory statements of any description are references to the statutory statement of that description defined in Schedule 4 to this Act; and that Schedule shall also have effect for the purpose of requiring certain information to be provided in official forms for the statutory statements so defined to assist persons in completing those forms and generally in determining what action to take in response to a notice to owner.

(4) In this Part of this Act "official form," in relation to a statutory statement mentioned in Schedule 4 to this Act or a statement under section 66(2) of this Act, means a document supplied by or on behalf of a chief officer of police for use in making that statement.

Payment of penalty

B16–44   **69.**—(1) Payment of a fixed penalty under this Part of this Act must be made to such justices' clerk or, in Scotland, clerk of court as may be specified in the fixed penalty notice relating to that penalty.

(2) Without prejudice to payment by any other method, payment of a fixed penalty under this Part of this Act may be made by properly addressing, prepaying and posting a letter containing the amount of the penalty (in cash or otherwise) and, unless the contrary is proved, shall be regarded as having been made at the time at which that letter would be delivered in the ordinary course of post.

(3) A letter is properly addressed for the purposes of subsection (2) above if it is addressed to the fixed penalty clerk at the address specified in the fixed penalty notice relating to the fixed penalty as the address at which the fixed penalty may be paid.

(4) References in this Part of this Act (except in sections 75 to 77), in relation to any fixed penalty or fixed penalty notice, to the fixed penalty clerk are references to the clerk specified in accordance with subsection (1) above in the fixed penalty notice relating to that penalty or (as the case may be) in that fixed penalty notice.

Registration certificates

B16–45   **70.**—(1) This section and section 71 of this Act apply where by virtue of section 55(3) or 64(2) of this Act a sum determined by reference to the fixed penalty for any offence may be registered under section 71 of this Act for enforcement against any person as a fine.

In this section and section 71 of this Act—

   (a) that sum is referred to as a "sum payable in default", and
   (b) the person against whom that sum may be so registered is referred to as the "defaulter".

(2) Subject to subsection (3) below, the chief officer of police may in respect

of any sum payable in default issue a certificate (referred to in this section and section 71 as a "registration certificate") stating that the sum is registrable under section 71 for enforcement against the defaulter as a fine.

(3) Where the fixed penalty notice in question was given to the defaulter under section 54 in respect of an offence committed in Scotland—

(a) subsection (2) above does not apply, but

(b) the fixed penalty clerk must, unless the defaulter appears to him to reside within the jurisdiction of the court of summary jurisdiction of which he is himself the clerk, issue a registration certificate in respect of the sum payable in default.

(4) Where the chief officer of police or the fixed penalty clerk issues a registration certificate under this section, he must—

(a) if the defaulter appears to him to reside in England and Wales, cause it to be sent to the clerk to the justices for the petty sessions area in which the defaulter appears to him to reside, and

(b) if the defaulter appears to him to reside in Scotland, cause it to be sent to the clerk of a court of summary jurisdiction for the area in which the defaulter appears to him to reside.

(5) A registration certificate issued under this section in respect of any sum payable in default must—

(a) give particulars of the offence to which the fixed penalty notice relates,

(b) indicate whether registration is authorised under section 55(3) or 64(2) of this Act, and

(c) state the name and last known address of the defaulter and the amount of the sum payable in default.

Registration of sums payable in default

71.—(1) Where the clerk to the justices for a petty sessions area receives a **B16–46** registration certificate issued under section 70 of this Act in respect of any sum payable in default, he must, subject to subsection (4) below, register that sum for enforcement as a fine in that area by entering it in the register of a magistrates' court acting for that area.

(2) Where the clerk of a court of summary jurisdiction receives a registration certificate issued under section 70 of this Act in respect of any sum payable in default, he must, subject to subsection (4) below, register that sum for enforcement as a fine by that court.

(3) Where—

(a) the fixed penalty notice in question was given to the defaulter under section 54 of this Act in respect of an offence committed in Scotland, and

(b) the defaulter appears to the fixed penalty clerk to reside within the jurisdiction of the court of summary jurisdiction of which he is himself the clerk,

the fixed penalty clerk must register the sum payable in default for enforcement as a fine by that court.

(4) Where it appears to the clerk receiving a registration certificate issued under section 70 of this Act in respect of any sum payable in default that the defaulter does not reside in the petty sessions area or (as the case may be) within the jurisdiction of the court of summary jurisdiction in question—

(a) he is not required by subsection (1) or (2) above to register that sum, but

(b) he must cause the certificate to be sent to the appropriate clerk,

and subsection (1) or, as the case may be, (2) above shall apply accordingly on receipt by the appropriate clerk of the certificate as it applies on receipt by the clerk to whom it was originally sent.

(5) For the purposes of subsection (4) above, the appropriate clerk—

    (a) if the defaulter appears to the clerk receiving the registration certificate to reside in England and Wales, is the clerk to the justices for the petty sessions area in which the defaulter appears to him to reside, and

    (b) if the defaulter appears to the clerk receiving the registration certificate to reside in Scotland, is the clerk of a court of summary jurisdiction for the area in which the defaulter appears to him to reside.

(6) On registering any sum under this section for enforcement as a fine, the clerk to the justices for a petty sessions area or, as the case may be, the clerk of a court of summary jurisdiction must give to the defaulter notice of registration—

    (a) specifying the amount of that sum, and

    (b) giving the information with respect to the offence and the authority for registration included in the registration certificate by virtue of section 70(5)(a) and (b) of this Act or (in a case within subsection (3) above) the corresponding information.

(7) On the registration of any sum in a magistrates' court or a court of summary jurisdiction by virtue of this section any enactment referring (in whatever terms) to a fine imposed or other sum adjudged to be paid on the conviction of such a court shall have effect in the case in question as if the sum so registered were a fine imposed by that court on the conviction of the defaulter on the date of the registration.

(8) Accordingly, in the application by virtue of this section of the provisions of the Magistrates' Courts Act 1980 relating to the satisfaction and enforcement of sums adjudged to be paid on the conviction of a magistrates' court, section 85 of that Act (power to remit a fine in whole or in part) is not excluded by subsection (2) of that section (references in that section to a fine not to include any other sum adjudged to be paid on a conviction) from applying to a sum registered in a magistrates' court by virtue of this section.

(9) For the purposes of this section, where the defaulter is a body corporate, the place where that body resides and the address of that body are either of the following—

    (a) the registered or principal office of that body, and

    (b) the address which, with respect to the vehicle concerned, is the address recorded in the record kept under the Vehicle Excise and Registration Act 1994 as being that body's address.

Notices on-the-spot or at a police station: when registration and endorsement invalid

B16–47   72.—(1) This section applies where—

    (a) a person who has received notice of the registration, by virtue of section 55(3) of this Act, of a sum under section 71 of this Act for enforcement against him as a fine makes a statutory declaration to the effect mentioned in subsection (2) below, and

    (b) that declaration is, within 21 days of the date on which the person making it received notice of the registration, served on the clerk of the relevant court.

(2) The statutory declaration must state—

    (a) that the person making the declaration was not the person to whom the relevant fixed penalty notice was given, or

442

(b) that he gave notice requesting a hearing in respect of the alleged offence as permitted by the fixed penalty notice before the end of the suspended enforcement period.

(3) In any case within subsection (2)(a) above, the relevant fixed penalty notice, the registration and any proceedings taken before the declaration was served for enforcing payment of the sum registered shall be void.

(4) Where in any case within subsection (2)(a) above the person to whom the relevant fixed penalty notice was given surrendered a licence and its counterpart held by the person making the declaration, any endorsement of that counterpart made under section 57 of this Act in respect of the offence in respect of which that notice was given shall be void.

(5) In any case within subsection (2)(b) above—

(a) the registration, any proceedings taken before the declaration was served for enforcing payment of the sum registered, and any endorsement, in respect of the offence in respect of which the relevant fixed penalty notice was given, made under section 57 of this Act before the declaration was served, shall be void, and

(b) the case shall be treated after the declaration is served as if the person making the declaration had given notice requesting a hearing in respect of the alleged offence as stated in the declaration.

(6) The clerk of the relevant court must—

(a) cancel an endorsement of the counterpart of a licence under section 57 of this Act that is void by virtue of this section on production of the licence and its counterpart to him for that purpose, and

(b) send notice of the cancellation to the Secretary of State.

(7) References in this section to the relevant fixed penalty notice are to the fixed penalty notice relating to the fixed penalty concerned.

Notices fixed to vehicles: when registration invalid

73.—(1) This section applies where— **B16–48**

(a) a person who has received notice of the registration, by virtue of section 64(2) of this Act, of a sum under section 71 of this Act for enforcement against him as a fine makes a statutory declaration to the effect mentioned in subsection (2) below, and

(b) that declaration is, within twenty-one days of the date on which the person making it received notice of the registration, served on the clerk of the relevant court.

(2) The statutory declaration must state either—

(a) that the person making the declaration did not know of the fixed penalty concerned or of any fixed penalty notice or notice to owner relating to that penalty until he received notice of the registration, or

(b) that he was not the owner of the vehicle at the time of the alleged offence of which particulars are given in the relevant notice to owner and that he has a reasonable excuse for failing to comply with that notice, or

(c) that he gave notice requesting a hearing in respect of that offence as permitted by the relevant notice to owner before the end of the period allowed for response to that notice.

(3) In any case within subsection (2)(a) or (b) above—

(a) the relevant notice to owner,

(b) the registration, and

(c) any proceedings taken before the declaration was served for enforcing payment of the sum registered,

shall be void but without prejudice, in a case within subsection (2)(a) above, to the service of a further notice to owner under section 63 of this Act on the person making the declaration.

This subsection applies whether or not the relevant notice to owner was duly served in accordance with that section on the person making the declaration.

(4) In any case within subsection (2)(c) above—

    (a) no proceedings shall be taken, after the statutory declaration is served until the end of the period of twenty-one days following the date of that declaration, for enforcing payment of the sum registered, and

    (b) where before the end of that period a notice is served by or on behalf of the chief officer of police on the person making the declaration asking him to provide a new statutory statement of ownership to that chief officer of police before the end of the period of twenty-one days from the date on which the notice is served, no such proceedings shall be taken until the end of the period allowed for response to that notice.

(5) Where in any case within subsection (2)(c) above—

    (a) no notice is served by or on behalf of the chief officer of police in accordance with subsection (4) above, or

    (b) such a notice is so served and the person making the declaration provides a new statutory statement of ownership in accordance with the notice,

then—

        (i) the registration and any proceedings taken before the declaration was served for enforcing payment of the sum registered shall be void, and

        (ii) the case shall be treated after the time mentioned in subsection (6) below as if the person making the declaration had given notice requesting a hearing in respect of the alleged offence as stated in the declaration.

(6) The time referred to in subsection (5) above is—

    (a) in a case within paragraph (a) of that subsection, the end of the period of twenty-one days following the date of the statutory declaration,

    (b) in a case within paragraph (b) of that subsection, the time when the statement is provided.

(7) In any case where notice is served by or on behalf of the chief officer of police in accordance with subsection (4) above, he must cause the clerk of the relevant court to be notified of that fact immediately on service of the notice.

(8) References in this section to the relevant notice to owner are to the notice to owner relating to the fixed penalty concerned.

Provisions supplementary to sections 72 and 73

    74.—(1) In any case within section 72(2)(b) or 73(2) of this Act—

    (a) section 127(1) of the Magistrates' Courts Act 1980 (limitation of time), and

    (b) section 331(1) of the Criminal Procedure (Scotland) Act 1975 (statutory offences time limit),

shall have effect as if for the reference to the time when the offence was committed or (as the case may be) the time when the contravention occurred there were substituted a reference to the date of the statutory declaration made for the purposes of section 72(1) or, as the case may be, 73(1).

(2) Where, on the application of a person who has received notice of the registration of a sum under section 71 of this Act for enforcement against him as a fine, it appears to the relevant court (which for this purpose may be composed of a single justice) that it was not reasonable to expect him to serve, within twenty-one days of the date on which he received the notice, a statutory declaration to the effect mentioned in section 72(2) or, as the case may be, 73(2) of this Act, the court may accept service of such a declaration by that person after that period has expired.

(3) A statutory declaration accepted under subsection (2) above shall be taken to have been served as required by section 72(1) or, as the case may be, section 73(1) of this Act.

(4) For the purposes of sections 72(1) and 73(1) of this Act, a statutory declaration shall be taken to be duly served on the clerk of the relevant court if it is delivered to him, left at his office, or sent in a registered letter or by the recorded delivery service addressed to him at his office.

(5) In sections 72, 73 and this section—

   (a) references to the relevant court are—

      (i) in the case of a sum registered under section 71 of this Act for enforcement as a fine in a petty sessions area in England and Wales, references to any magistrates' court acting for that area, and

      (ii) in the case of a sum registered under that section for enforcement as a fine by a court of summary jurisdiction in Scotland, references to that court,

   (b) references to the clerk of the relevant court, where that court is a magistrates' court, are references to a clerk to the justices for the petty sessions area for which that court is acting, and

   (c) references to proceedings for enforcing payment of the sum registered are references to any process issued or other proceedings taken for or in connection with enforcing payment of that sum.

(6) For the purposes of sections 72, 73 and this section, a person shall be taken to receive notice of the registration of a sum under section 71 of this Act for enforcement against him as a fine when he receives notice either of the registration as such or of any proceedings for enforcing payment of the sum registered.

(7) Nothing in the provisions of sections 72 or 73 or this section is to be read as prejudicing any rights a person may have apart from those provisions by virtue of the invalidity of any action purportedly taken in pursuance of this Part of this Act which is not in fact authorised by this Part of this Act in the circumstances of the case; and, accordingly, references in those provisions to the registration of any sum or to any other action taken under or by virtue of any provision of this Part of this Act are not to be read as implying that the registration or action was validly made or taken in accordance with that provision.

General restriction on proceedings

78.—(1) Proceedings shall not be brought against any person for the offence to which a fixed penalty notice relates until the end of the suspended enforcement period.   **B16–50**

(2) Proceedings shall not be brought against any person for the offence to which a fixed penalty notice relates if the fixed penalty is paid in accordance with this Part of this Act before the end of the suspended enforcement period.

Statements by constables

B16–51   79.—(1) In any proceedings a certificate that a copy of a statement by a constable with respect to the alleged offence (referred to in this section as a "constable's witness statement") was included in or given with a fixed penalty notice or a notice under section 54(3) of this Act given to the accused on a date specified in the certificate shall, if the certificate purports to be signed by the constable or authorised person who gave the accused the notice, be evidence of service of a copy of that statement by delivery to the accused on that date.

(2) In any proceedings a certificate that a copy of a constable's witness statement was included in or served with a notice to owner served on the accused in the manner and on a date specified in the certificate shall, if the certificate purports to be signed by any person employed by the police authority for the police area in which the offence to which the proceedings relate is alleged to have been committed, be evidence of service in the manner and on the date so specified both of a copy of that statement and of the notice to owner.

(3) Any address specified in any such certificate as is mentioned in subsection (2) above as being the address at which service of the notice to owner was effected shall be taken for the purposes of any proceedings in which the certificate is tendered in evidence to be the accused's proper address, unless the contrary is proved.

(4) Where a copy of a constable's witness statement is included in or served with a notice to owner served in any manner in which the notice is authorised to be served under this Part of this Act, the statement shall be treated as duly served for the purposes of section 9 of the Criminal Justice Act 1967 (proof by written statement) notwithstanding that the manner of service is not authorised by subsection (8) of that section.

(5) In relation to any proceedings in which service of a constable's witness statement is proved by certificate under this section—

  (a) that service shall be taken for the purposes of subsection (2)(c) of that section (copy of statement to be tendered in evidence to be served before hearing on other parties to the proceedings by or on behalf of the party proposing to tender it) to have been effected by or on behalf of the prosecutor, and

  (b) subsection (2)(d) of that section (time for objection) shall have effect with the substitution, for the reference to seven days from the service of the copy of the statement, of a reference to seven days from the relevant date.

(6) In subsection (5)(b) above "relevant date" means—

  (a) where the accused gives notice requesting a hearing in respect of the offence in accordance with any provision of this Part of this Act, the date on which he gives that notice, and

  (b) where a notice in respect of the offence was given to the accused under section 54(4) of this Act but no fixed penalty notice is given in respect of it, the last day for production of the notice under section 54(5) at a police station in accordance with that section.

(7) This section does not extend to Scotland.

Certificates about payment

B16–52   80. In any proceedings a certificate—

  (a) that payment of a fixed penalty was or was not received by a date specified in the certificate, by the fixed penalty clerk, or

(b) that a letter containing an amount sent by post in payment of a fixed penalty was marked as posted on a date so specified,

shall, if the certificate purports to be signed by the fixed penalty clerk, be evidence (and, in Scotland, sufficient evidence) of the facts stated.

Documents signed by the accused

81.—(1) Where— **B16–53**
   (a) any person is charged with a fixed penalty offence, and
   (b) the prosecutor produces to the court a document to which this subsection applies purporting to have been signed by the accused,
the document shall be presumed, unless the contrary is proved, to have been signed by the accused and shall be evidence (and, in Scotland, sufficient evidence) in the proceedings of any facts stated in it tending to show that the accused was the owner, the hirer or the driver of the vehicle concerned at a particular time.

   (2) Subsection (1) above applies to any document purporting to be—
   (a) a notice requesting a hearing in respect of the offence charged given in accordance with a fixed penalty notice relating to that offence, or
   (b) a statutory statement of any description defined in Schedule 4 to this Act or a copy of a statement of liability within the meaning of section 66 of this Act provided in response to a notice to owner.

Accounting for fixed penalties: England and Wales

82.—(1) In England and Wales, sums paid by way of fixed penalty for an **B16–54** offence shall be treated for the purposes of section 61 (application of fines and fees) of the Justices of the Peace Act 1979 as if they were fines imposed on summary conviction for that offence.

   (2) Where, in England and Wales, a justices' clerk for a petty sessions area comprised in the area of one responsible authority (within the meaning of section 59 of that Act) discharges functions in connection with a fixed penalty for an offence alleged to have been committed in a petty sessions area comprised in the area of another such authority—
   (a) that other authority must make to the first-mentioned authority such payment in connection with the discharge of those functions as may be agreed between them or, in default of such agreement, as may be determined by the Secretary of State, and
   (b) any such payment between responsible authorities shall be taken into account in determining for the purposes of subsection (4) of that section the net cost to those authorities respectively of the functions referred to in subsection (1) of that section.

   (3) Subsection (2) above does not apply to functions discharged in connection with a fixed penalty on or after the registration of a sum determined by reference to the penalty under section 71 of this Act.

Powers of court where clerk deceived

83.—(1) This section applies where— **B16–55**

 (a) in endorsing the counterpart of any person's licence under section 57 of this Act, the fixed penalty clerk is deceived as to whether endorsement under that section is excluded by section 61(2) of this Act by virtue of the fact that the licence holder would be liable to be disqualified under section 35 of this Act if he were convicted of the offence, or

 (b) in endorsing the counterpart of any person's licence under section 77 of this Act the clerk of court specified in the conditional offer (within the meaning of that section) is deceived as to whether he is required by section 76(5) of this Act to return the licence and its counterpart without endorsing the counterpart by virtue of the fact that the licence holder would be liable to be disqualified under section 35 of this Act if he were convicted of the offence.

(2) If—

 (a) the deception constituted or was due to an offence committed by the licence holder, and

 (b) the licence holder is convicted of that offence,

the court by or before which he is convicted shall have the same powers and duties as it would have had if he had also been convicted by or before it of the offence of which particulars were endorsed under section 57 or, as the case may be, 77 of this Act.

Regulations

B16–56 **84.** The Secretary of State may by regulations make provision as to any matter incidental to the operation of this Part of this Act, and in particular—

 (a) for prescribing any information or further information to be provided in any notice, notification, certificate or receipt under section 52(1), 54(4), 56, 59(1), 60(1), 63(2), 70(2) and (3)(b), 73(4)(b), 75(2) and (3) or 76(5) and (6) of this Act or in any official form for a statutory statement mentioned in Schedule 4 to, or a statement under section 66(2) of, this Act,

 (b) for requiring any such official form to be served with any notice served under section 63 or 73(4) of this Act, and

 (c) for prescribing the duties of justices' clerks or (as the case may be) clerks of courts of summary jurisdiction and the information to be supplied to them.

Service of documents

B16–57 **85.**—(1) Subject to any requirement of this Part of this Act with respect to the manner in which a person may be provided with any such document, he may be provided with the following documents by post (but without prejudice to any other method of providing him with them), that is to say—

 (a) any of the statutory statements mentioned in Schedule 4 to this Act, and

 (b) any of the documents mentioned in section 66(2) of this Act.

(2) Where a notice requesting a hearing in respect of an offence is permitted by a fixed penalty notice or notice to owner relating to that offence to be given by post, section 7 of the Interpretation Act 1978 (service of documents by post) shall apply as if that notice were permitted to be so given by this Act.

(3) A notice to owner may be served on any person—

(a) by delivering it to him or by leaving it at his proper address, or

(b) by sending it to him by post,

and where the person on whom such a notice is to be served is a body corporate it is duly served if it is served on the secretary or clerk of that body.

(4) For the purposes of this Part of this Act and of section 7 of the Interpretation Act 1978 as it applies for the purposes of subsection (3) above the proper address of any person in relation to the service on him of a notice to owner is—

(a) in the case of the secretary or clerk of a body corporate, that of the registered or principal office of that body or the registered address of the person who is or was the registered keeper of the vehicle concerned at the time of service, and

(b) in any other case, his last known address at the time of service.

(5) In subsection (4) above, "registered address", in relation to the registered keeper of a vehicle, means the address recorded in the record kept under the Vehicle Excise and Registration Act 1994 with respect to that vehicle as being that person's address.

Functions of traffic wardens

86.—(1) An order under section 95(5) of the Road Traffic Regulation Act 1984 may not authorise the employment of a traffic warden to discharge any function under this Part of this Act in respect of an offence if the offence appears to the traffic warden to be an offence involving obligatory endorsement unless that offence was committed while the vehicle concerned was stationary. **B16–58**

(2) In so far as an order under that section authorises the employment of traffic wardens for the purposes of this Part of this Act, references in this Part of this Act to a constable or, as the case may be, to a constable in uniform include a traffic warden.

Guidance on application of Part III

87. The Secretary of State must issue guidance to chief officers of police for police areas in respect of the operation of this Part of this Act with the objective so far as possible of working towards uniformity.

Interpretation

89.—(1) In this Part of this Act— **B16–59**

"authorised person" has the meaning given by section 54(9) of this Act,

"chief constable" means, in Scotland in relation to any conditional offer, the chief constable for the area in which the conditional offer has been issued,

"chief officer of police" (except in the definition of "authorised person") means, in relation to any fixed penalty notice, notice to owner or conditional offer, the chief officer of police for the police area in which the fixed penalty offence in question is alleged to have been committed,

"court of summary jurisdiction" has the same meaning as in section 462(1) of the Criminal Procedure (Scotland) Act 1975, "driver" except in section 62 of this Act means, in relation to an alleged fixed penalty offence, the person by whom, assuming the offence to have been committed, it was committed,

"justices' clerk" means the clerk to the justices for a petty sessions area,

"petty sessions area" has the same meaning as in the Magistrates' Courts Act 1980, and

"proceedings", except in relation to proceedings for enforcing payment of a sum registered under section 71 of this Act, means criminal proceedings.

(2) In this Part of this Act—

(a) references to a notice requesting a hearing in respect of an offence are references to a notice indicating that the person giving the notice wishes to contest liability for the offence or seeks a determination by a court with respect to the appropriate punishment for the offence,

(b) references to an offence include an alleged offence, and

(c) references to the person who is or was at any time the registered keeper of a vehicle are references to the person in whose name the vehicle is or was at that time registered under the Vehicle Excise and Registration Act 1994.

Index to Part III

B16–60   **90.** The expressions listed in the left hand column below are respectively defined or (as the case may be) fall to be construed in accordance with the provisions of this Part of this Act listed in the right-hand column in relation to those expressions.

Expression	*Relevant provision*
Authorised person	Section 54(9)
Conditional offer	Section 75(3)
Fixed penalty	Section 53
Fixed penalty clerk	Section 69(4) and 75(4)
Fixed penalty notice	Section 52
Fixed penalty offence	Section 51
Notice to owner	Sections 63(2) and 66(4)
Notice requesting a hearing in respect of an offence	Section 89(2)
Offence	Section 89(2)
Official form	Section 68(4)
Owner	Section 68(1)
Period allowed for response to a notice to owner	Section 63(5)
Proper address, in relation to the service of a notice to owner	Section 85(4)
Registered keeper	Section 89(2)
Statutory statement of facts	Part II of Schedule 4
Statutory statement of hiring	Part I of Schedule 4
Statutory statement of ownership	Part I of Schedule 4
Suspended enforcement period	Section 52(3)(a)
Time of the alleged offence	Section 63(3)

Penalty for breach of regulations

B16–61   **91.** If a person acts in contravention of or fails to comply with—

(a) any regulations made by the Secretary of State under the Road Traffic Act 1988 other than regulations made under section 31, 45 or 132,
(b) any regulations made by the Secretary of State under the Road Traffic Regulation Act 1984, other than regulations made under section 28, Schedule 4, Part III of Schedule 9 or Schedule 12,

and the contravention or failure to comply is not made an offence under any other provision of the Traffic Acts, he shall for each offence be liable on summary conviction to a fine not exceeding level 3 on the standard scale.

General interpretation

98.—(1) In this Act—   **B16–62**

"disqualified" means disqualified for holding or obtaining a licence and "disqualification" is to be construed accordingly,

"drive" has the same meaning as in the Road Traffic Act 1988,

"licence" means a licence to drive a motor vehicle granted under Part III of that Act and "counterpart", in relation to such a licence, has the same meaning as in that Part of that Act,

"provisional licence" means a licence granted by virtue of section 97(2) of that Act,

"the provisions connected with the licensing of drivers" means sections 7, 8, 22, 25 to 29, 31, 32, 34 to 48, 96 and 97 of this Act,

"road"—

(a) in relation to England and Wales, means any highway and any other road to which the public has access, and includes bridges over which a road passes, and

(b) in relation to Scotland, means any road within the meaning of the Roads (Scotland) Act 1984 and any other way to which the public has access, and includes bridges over which a road passes,

"the Road Traffic Acts" means the Road Traffic Act 1988, the Road Traffic (Consequential Provisions) Act 1988 (so far as it reproduces the effect of provisions repealed by that Act) and this Act, and

"the Traffic Acts" means the Road Traffic Acts and the Road Traffic Regulation Act 1984.

(2) Sections 185 and 186 of the Road Traffic Act 1988 (meaning of "motor vehicle" and other expressions relating to vehicles) apply for the purposes of this Act as they apply for the purposes of that Act.

(3) In the Schedules to this Act—

"RTRA" is used as an abbreviation for the Road Traffic Regulation Act 1984, and

"RTA" is used as an abbreviation for the Road Traffic Act 1988 or, if followed by "1989," the Road Traffic (Driver Licensing and Information Systems) Act 1989.

(4) Subject to any express exception, references in this Act to any Part of this Act include a reference to any Schedule to this Act so far as relating to that Part.

Sections 1 etc.   SCHEDULE 1

OFFENCES TO WHICH SECTIONS 1, 6, 11 AND 12(1) APPLY

1.—(1) Where section 1, 6, 11 or 12(1) of this Act is shown in column 3 of this   **B16–63**

Schedule against a provision of the Road Traffic Act 1988 specified in column 1, the section in question applies to an offence under that provision.

(2) The general nature of the offence is indicated in column 2.

1A. Section 1 also applies to—

(a) an offence under section 16 of the Road Traffic Regulation Act 1984 consisting in the contravention of a restriction on the speed of vehicles imposed under section 14 of that Act,

(b) an offence under subsection (4) of section 17 of that Act consisting in the contravention of a restriction on the speed of vehicles imposed under that section, and

(c) an offence under section 88(7) or 89(1) of that Act (speeding offences).

2. Section 6 also applies—

(a) to an offence under section 67 of this Act,

(b) in relation to Scotland, to an offence under section 173 of the Road Traffic Act 1988 (forgery, etc., of licences, test certificates, certificates of insurance and other documents and things), and

(c) to an offence under section 1(5) of the Road Traffic (Driver Licensing and Information Systems) Act 1989.

3. Section 11 also applies to—

(a) any offence to which section 112 of the Road Traffic Regulation Act 1984 (information as to identity of driver or rider) applies except an offence under section 61(5) of that Act,

(b) any offence which is punishable under section 91 of this Act,

(bb) an offence under paragraph 3 of Schedule 1 to the Road Traffic (Driver Licensing and Information Systems) Act 1989, and

(c) any offence against any other enactment relating to the use of vehicles on roads.

4. Section 12(1) also applies to—

(a) any offence which is punishable under section 91 of this Act,

(aa) an offence under paragraph 3(1) of Schedule 1 to the Road Traffic (Driver Licensing and Information Systems) Act 1989, and

(b) any offence against any other enactment relating to the use of vehicles on roads.

(1) Provision creating offence	(2) General nature of offence	(3) Applicable provisions of this Act
RTA section 1	Causing death by dangerous driving.	Section 11 of this Act.
RTA section 2	Dangerous driving.	Sections 1, 11 and 12(1) of this Act.
RTA section 3	Careless, and inconsiderate, driving.	Sections 1, 11 and 12(1) of this Act.
RTA section 3A	Causing death by careless driving when under influence of drink or drugs.	Section 11 of this Act
RTA section 4	Driving or attempting to drive, or being in charge of a mechanically propelled vehicle, when unfit to drive through drink or drugs.	Sections 11 and 12(1) of this Act.
RTA section 5	Driving or attempting to drive, or being in charge of a motor vehicle, with excess alcohol in breath, blood or urine.	Sections 11 and 12(1) of this Act.

(1) Provision creating offence	(2) General nature of offence	(3) Applicable provisions of this Act
RTA section 6	Failing to provide a specimen of breath for a breath test.	Sections 11 and 12(1) of this Act.
RTA section 7	Failing to provide specimen for analysis or laboratory test.	Sections 11 and 12(1) of this Act.
RTA section 12	Motor racing and speed trials.	Sections 11 and 12(1) of this Act.
RTA section 14	Driving or riding a motor vehicle in contravention of regulations requiring wearing of seat belts.	Sections 11 and 12(1) of this Act.
RTA section 15	Driving motor vehicle with child not wearing seat belt.	Sections 11 and 12(1) of this Act.
RTA section 19	Prohibition of parking of heavy commercial vehicles on verges and footways.	Sections 11 and 12(1) of this Act.
RTA section 22	Leaving vehicles in dangerous positions.	Sections 1, 11 and 12(1) of this Act.
RTA section 23	Carrying passenger on motor-cycle contrary to section 23.	Sections 11 and 12(1) of this Act.
RTA section 23	Carrying passenger on bicycle contrary to section 24.	Sections 11 and 12(1) of this Act.
RTA section 25	Tampering with motor vehicles.	Section 11 of this Act.
RTA section 26(1)	Holding or getting onto vehicle in order to be carried.	Section 11 of this Act.
RTA section 26(2)	Holding onto vehicle in order to be towed.	Sections 11 and 12(1) of this Act.
RTA section 28	Dangerous cycling.	Sections 1, 11 and 12(1) of this Act.
RTA section 29	Careless, and inconsiderate, cycling.	Sections 1, 11 and 12(1) of this Act.
RTA section 30	Cycling when unfit through drink or drugs.	Sections 11 and 12(1) of this Act.
RTA section 32	Unauthorised or irregular cycle racing, or trials of speed.	Sections 11 and 12(1) of this Act.
RTA section 33	Unauthorised motor vehicle trial on footpaths or bridleways.	Sections 11 and 12(1) of this Act.
RTA section 34	Driving motor vehicles elsewhere than on roads.	Sections 11 and 12(1) of this Act.
RTA section 35	Failing to comply with traffic directions.	Sections 1, 11 and 12(1) of this Act.
RTA section 36	Failing to comply with traffic signs.	Sections 1, 11 and 12(1) of this Act.
RTA section 40A	Using vehicle in dangerous condition etc.	Sections 11 and 12(1) of this Act.
RTA section 41A	Breach of requirement as to brakes, steering-gear or tyres.	Sections 11 and 12(1) of this Act.
RTA section 41B	Breach of requirement as to weight: goods and passenger vehicles.	Sections 11 and 12(1) of this Act.
RTA section 42	Breach of other construction and use requirements.	Sections 11 and 12(1) of this Act.
RTA section 47	Using, etc., vehicle without required test certificate being in force.	Sections 11 and 12(1) of this Act.

(1) Provision creating offence	(2) General nature of offence	(3) Applicable provisions of this Act
RTA section 53	Using, etc., goods vehicle without required plating certificate or goods vehicle test certificate being in force, or where Secretary of State is required by regulations under section 49 to be notified of an alteration to the vehicle or its equipment but has not been notified.	Sections 11 and 12(1) of this Act.
RTA section 63	Using, etc., vehicle without required certificate being in force showing that it, or a part fitted to it, complies with type approval requirements applicable to it, or using, etc., certain goods vehicles for drawing trailer when plating certificate does not specify maximum laden weight for vehicle and trailer, or using, etc., goods vehicle where Secretary of State has not been but is required to be notified under section 48 of alteration to it or its equipment.	Sections 11 and 12(1) of this Act.
RTA section 71	Driving, etc., vehicle in contravention of prohibition on driving it as being unfit for service or overloaded, or refusing, neglecting or otherwise failing to comply with a direction to remove a vehicle found overloaded.	Sections 11 and 12(1) of this Act.
RTA section 78	Failing to comply with requirement about weighing motor vehicle or obstructing authorised person.	Sections 11 and 12(1) of this Act.
RTA section 87(1)	Driving otherwise than in accordance with a licence.	Sections 11 and 12(1) of this Act.
RTA section 87(2)	Causing or permitting a person to drive otherwise than in accordance with a licence.	Section 11 of this Act.
RTA section 92(10)	Driving after making false declaration as to physical fitness.	Sections 6, 11 and 12(1) of this Act.
RTA section 94(3)	Failure to notify to Secretary of State of onset of, deterioration in, relevant or prospective disability.	Section 6 of this Act.
RTA section 94(3A)	Driving after such a failure.	Sections 6, 11 and 12(1) of this Act.
RTA section 94A	Driving after refusal of licence under section 92(3) or revocation under section 93.	Sections 6, 11 and 12(1) of this Act.
RTA section 99	Driving licence holder failing when his licence is revoked, to surrender it and its counterpart or when his particulars become incorrect, to surrender licence and counterpart and give particulars.	Section 6 of this Act.
RTA section 103(1)(a)	Obtaining driving licence while disqualified.	Section 6 of this Act.

(1) Provision creating offence	(2) General nature of offence	(3) Applicable provisions of this Act
RTA section 103(1)(b)	Driving while disqualified.	Sections 6, 11 and 12(1) of this Act.
RTA section 114(1)	Failing to comply with conditions of LGV or PCV driver's licence.	Sections 11 and 12(1) of this Act.
RTA section 114(2)	Causing or permitting a person under 21 to drive LGV or PCV in contravention of conditions of that person's licence.	Section 11 of this Act.
RTA section 143	Using motor vehicle, or causing or permitting it to be used, while uninsured or unsecured against third party risks.	Sections 6, 11 and 12(1) of this Act.
RTA section 163	Failing to stop vehicle when required by constable.	Sections 11 and 12(1) of this Act.
RTA section 164(6)	Failing to produce driving licence and counterpart etc. or to state date of birth.	Sections 11 and 12(1) of this Act.
RTA section 165(3)	Failing to give constable certain names and addresses or to produce certificate of insurance or certain test and other like certificates.	Sections 11 and 12(1) of this Act.
RTA section 165(6)	Supervisor or learner driver failing to give constable certain names and addresses.	Section 11 of this Act.
RTA section 168	Refusing to give, or giving false, name and address in case of reckless, careless or inconsiderate driving or cycling.	Sections 11 and 12(1) of this Act.
RTA section 170	Failure by driver to stop, report accident or give information or documents.	Sections 11 and 12(1) of this Act.
RTA section 171	Failure by owner of motor vehicle to give police information for verifying compliance with requirement of compulsory insurance or security.	Sections 11 and 12(1) of this Act.
RTA section 174(1) or (5)	Making false statements in connection with licences under this Act and with registration as an approved driving instructor; or making false statement or withholding material information in order to obtain the issue of insurance certificates, etc.	Section 6 of this Act.
RTA section 175	Issuing false documents.	Section 6 of this Act.

SCHEDULE 2

Prosecution and Punishment of Offences

Part I

Offences under the Traffic Acts

Section 9 etc.

Offences under the Road Traffic Regulation Act 1984

(1) Provision creating offence	(2) General nature of offence	(3) Mode of prosecution	(4) Punishment	(5) Disqualification	(6) Endorsement	(7) Penalty points
RTRA section 5	Contravention of traffic regulation order.	Summarily.	Level 3 on the standard scale.			
RTRA section 8	Contravention of order regulating traffic in Greater London.	Summarily.	Level 3 on the standard scale.			
RTRA section 11	Contravention of experimental traffic order.	Summarily.	Level 3 on the standard scale.			
RTRA section 13	Contravention of experimental traffic scheme in Greater London.	Summarily.	Level 3 on the standard scale.			
RTRA section 16(1)	Contravention of temporary prohibition or restriction.	Summarily.	Level 3 on the standard scale.	Discretionary if committed in respect of a speed restriction.	Obligatory if committed in respect of a speed restriction.	3–6 or 3 (fixed penalty)
RTRA section 16C(1)	Contravention of prohibition or restriction relating to relevant event.	Summarily.	Level 3 on the standard scale.			

Provision	Offence	Mode of prosecution	Punishment	Disqualification	Endorsement	Penalty points
RTRA section 17(4)	Use of special road contrary to scheme or regulations.	Summarily.	Level 4 on the standard scale.	Discretionary if committed in respect of a motor vehicle otherwise than by unlawfully stopping or allowing the vehicle to remain at rest on a part of a special road on which vehicles are in certain circumstances permitted to remain at rest.	Obligatory if committed as mentioned in the entry in column 5.	3–6 or 3 (fixed penalty) if committed in respect of a speed restriction, 3 in any other case.
RTRA section 18(3)	One-way traffic on trunk road.	Summarily.	Level 3 on the standard scale.			
RTRA section 20(5)	Contravention of prohibition or restriction for roads of certain classes.	Summarily.	Level 3 on the standard scale.			
RTRA section 25(5)	Contravention of pedestrian crossing regulations.	Summarily.	Level 3 on the standard scale.	Discretionary if committed in respect of a motor vehicle.	Obligatory if committed in respect of a motor vehicle.	3
RTRA section 28(3)	Not stopping at school crossing.	Summarily.	Level 3 on the standard scale.	Discretionary if committed in respect of a motor vehicle.	Obligatory if committed in respect of a motor vehicle.	3
RTRA section 29(3)	Contravention of order relating to street playground.	Summarily.	Level 3 on the standard scale.	Discretionary if committed in respect of a motor vehicle.	Obligatory if committed in respect of a motor vehicle.	2

SCHEDULE 2, PART I—*cont.*

Offences under the Road Traffic Regulation Act 1984

(1) Provision creating offence	(2) General nature of offence	(3) Mode of prosecution	(4) Punishment	(5) Disqualification	(6) Endorsement	(7) Penalty points
RTRA section 35A(1)	Contravention of order as to use of parking place.	Summarily.	(a) Level 3 on the standard scale in the case of an offence committed by a person in a street parking place reserved for disabled persons' vehicles or in an off-street parking place reserved for such vehicles, where that person would not have been guilty of that offence if the motor vehicle in respect of which it was committed had been a disabled person's vehicle. (b) Level 2 on the standard scale in any other case.			
RTRA section 35A(2)	Misuse of apparatus for collecting charges or of parking device or connected apparatus.	Summarily.	Level 3 on the standard scale.			
RTRA section 35A(5)	Plying for hire in parking place.	Summarily.	Level 2 on the standard scale.			

458

RTRA section 43(5)	Unauthorised disclosure of information in respect of licensed parking place.	Summarily.	Level 3 on the standard scale.
RTRA section 43(10)	Failure to comply with term or conditions of licence to operate parking place.	Summarily.	Level 3 on the standard scale.
RTRA section 43(12)	Operation of public off-street parking place without licence.	Summarily.	Level 5 on the standard scale.
RTRA section 47(1)	Contraventions relating to designated parking	Summarily.	(a) Level 3 on the standard scale in the case of an offence committed by a person in a street parking place reserved for disabled persons' vehicles where that person would not have been guilty of that offence if the motor vehicle in respect of which it was committed had been a disabled person's vehicle. (b) Level 2 in any other case.
RTRA section 47(3)	Tampering with parking meter.	Summarily.	Level 3 on the standard scale.
RTRA section 52(1)	Misuse of parking device.	Summarily.	Level 2 on the standard scale.

SCHEDULE 2, PART I—*cont.*

Offences under the Road Traffic Regulation Act 1984

(1) Provision creating offence	(2) General nature of offence	(3) Mode of prosecution	(4) Punishment	(5) Disqualification	(6) Endorsement	(7) Penalty points
RTRA section 53(5)	Contravention of certain provisions of designation orders.	Summarily.	Level 3 on the standard scale.			
RTRA section 53(6)	Other contraventions of designation orders.	Summarily.	Level 2 on the standard scale.			
RTRA section 61(5)	Unauthorised use of loading area.	Summarily.	Level 3 on the standard scale.			
RTRA section 88(7)	Contravention of minimum speed limit.	Summarily.	Level 3 on the standard scale.			
RTRA section 89(1)	Exceeding speed limit.	Summarily.	Level 3 on the standard scale.	Discretionary.	Obligatory.	3–6 or 3 (fixed penalty)
RTRA section 104(5)	Interference with notice as to immobilisation device.	Summarily.	Level 2 on the standard scale.			
RTRA section 104(6)	Interference with immobilisation device.	Summarily.	Level 3 on the standard scale.			
RTRA section 105(5)	Misuse of disabled person's badge (immobilisation devices).	Summarily.	Level 3 on the standard scale.			
RTRA section 108(2) (or that subsection as modified by section 190(2) and (3)).	Non-compliance with notice (excess charge).	Summarily.	Level 5 on the standard scale.			
RTRA section 108(3) (or that subsection as modified by section 109(2) and (3)).	False response to notice (excess charge).	Summarily.	Level 5 on the standard scale.			

Provision	Offence	Mode of prosecution	Punishment	Disqualification	Endorsement	Penalty points
RTRA section 112(4)	Failure to give information as to identity of driver.	Summarily.	Level 3 on the standard scale.			
RTRA section 115(1)	Mishandling or faking parking documents.	(a) Summarily. (b) On indictment	(a) The statutory maximum. (b) 2 years.			
RTRA section 115(2)	False statement for procuring authorisation.	Summarily.	Level 4 on the standard scale.			
RTRA section 116(1)	Non-delivery of suspect document or article.	Summarily.	Level 3 on the standard scale.			
RTRA section 117	Wrongful use of disabled person's badge.	Summarily.	Level 3 on the standard scale.			
RTRA section 129(3)	Failure to give evidence at inquiry.	Summarily.	Level 3 on the standard scale.			
RTA section 1	Causing death by dangerous driving.	On indictment.	10 years.	Obligatory.	Obligatory.	3–11
RTA section 2	Dangerous driving.	(a) Summarily. (b) On indictment	(a) 6 months or the statutory maximum or both. (b) 2 years or a fine or both.	Obligatory	Obligatory	3–11
RTA section 3	Careless, and inconsiderate, driving.	Summarily.	Level 4 on the standard scale.	Discretionary.	Discretionary.	3–9
RTA section 3A	Causing death by careless driving when under influence of drink or drugs.	On indictment.	10 years or a fine or both.	Obligatory.	Obligatory.	3–11
RTA section 4(1)	Driving or attempting to drive when unfit to drive through drink or drugs.	Summarily.	6 months or level 5 on the standard scale or both.	Obligatory.	Obligatory.	3–11

461

SCHEDULE 2, PART I—*cont.*

Offences under the Road Traffic Regulation Act 1984

(1) Provision creating offence	(2) General nature of offence	(3) Mode of prosecution	(4) Punishment	(5) Disqualification	(6) Endorsement	(7) Penalty points
RTA section 4(2)	Being in charge of a mechanically propelled vehicle when unfit to drive through drink or drugs.	Summarily.	3 months or level 4 on the standard scale or both.	Discretionary.	Obligatory.	10
RTA section 5(1)(a)	Driving or attempting to drive with excess alcohol in breath, blood or urine.	Summarily.	6 months or level 5 on the standard scale or both.	Obligatory.	Obligatory	3–11
RTA section 5(1)(b)	Being in charge of a motor vehicle with excess alcohol in breath, blood or urine.	Summarily.	3 months or level 4 on the standard scale or both.	Discretionary.	Obligatory.	10
RTA section 6	Failing to provide a specimen of breath for a breath test.	Summarily.	Level 3 on the standard scale.	Discretionary.	Obligatory	4
RTA section 7	Failing to provide specimen for analysis or laboratory test.	Summarily.	(a) Where the specimen was required to ascertain ability to drive or proportion of alcohol at the time offender was driving or attempting to drive, 6 months or level 5 on the standard scale or both.	(a) Obligatory in case mentioned in column 4(a)	Obligatory.	(a) 3–11 in case mentioned in column 4(a).

462

Provision creating the offence	General nature of offence	Mode of prosecution	Punishment — (b) In any other case, 3 months or level 4 on the standard scale or both.	Disqualification — (b) Discretionary in any other case.	(Endorsement)	Penalty points — (b) 10 in any other case.
RTA section 12	Motor racing and speed trials on public ways.	Summarily.	Level 4 on the standard scale.	Obligatory.	Obligatory.	3–11
RTA section 13	Other unauthorised or irregular competitions or trials on public ways.	Summarily.	Level 3 on the standard scale.			
RTA section 14	Driving or riding in a motor vehicle in contravention of regulations requiring wearing of seat belts.	Summarily.	Level 2 on the standard scale.			
RTA section 15(2)	Driving motor vehicle with child in front not wearing seat belt.	Summarily.	Level 2 on the standard scale.			
RTA section 15(4)	Driving motor vehicle with child in rear not wearing seat belt.	Summarily.	Level 1 on the standard scale.			
RTA section 15A(3) or (4)	Selling etc. in certain circumstances equipment as conducive to the safety of children in motor vehicles.	Summarily.	Level 3 on the standard scale.			
RTA section 16	Driving or riding motor cycles in contravention of regulations requiring wearing of protective headgear.	Summarily.	Level 2 on the standard scale.			

SCHEDULE 2, PART I—*cont.*

Offences under the Road Traffic Regulation Act 1984

(1) Provision creating offence	(2) General nature of offence	(3) Mode of prosecution	(4) Punishment	(5) Disqualification	(6) Endorsement	(7) Penalty points
RTA section 17	Selling, etc., helmet not of the prescribed type as helmet for affording protection for motor cyclists.	Summarily.	Level 3 on the standard scale.			
RTA section 18(3)	Contravention of regulations with respect to use of headworn appliances on motor cycles.	Summarily.	Level 2 on the standard scale.			
RTA section 18(4)	Selling, etc., appliance not of prescribed type as approved for use on motor cycles.	Summarily.	Level 3 on the standard scale.			
RTA section 19	Prohibition of parking of heavy commercial vehicles on verges, etc.	Summarily.	Level 3 on the standard scale.			
RTA section 21	Driving or parking on cycle track.	Summarily.	Level 3 on the standard scale.			
RTA section 22	Leaving vehicles in dangerous positions.	Summarily.	Level 3 on the standard scale.	Discretionary if committed in respect of a motor vehicle.	Obligatory if committed in respect of a motor vehicle.	3
RTA section 22A	Causing danger to road-users.	(a) Summarily. (b) On indictment.	(a) 6 months or the statutory maximum or both. (b) 7 years or a fine or both.			

				Discretionary.	Obligatory	3
RTA section 23	Carrying passenger on motor-cycle contrary to section 23.	Summarily.	Level 3 on the standard scale.			
RTA section 24	Carrying passenger on bicycle contrary to section 24.	Summarily.	Level 1 on the standard scale.			
RTA section 25	Tampering with motor vehicles.	Summarily.	Level 3 on the standard scale.			
RTA section 26	Holding or getting on to vehicle, etc., in order to be towed or carried.	Summarily.	Level 1 on the standard scale.			
RTA section 27	Dogs on designated roads without being held on lead.	Summarily.	Level 1 on the standard scale.			
RTA section 28	Dangerous cycling.	Summarily.	Level 4 on the standard scale.			
RTA section 29	Careless, and inconsiderate, cycling.	Summarily.	Level 3 on the standard scale.			
RTA section 30	Cycling when unfit through drink or drugs.	Summarily.	Level 3 on the standard scale.			
RTA section 31	Unauthorised or irregular cycle racing or trials of speed on public ways.	Summarily.	Level 1 on the standard scale.			
RTA section 32	Contravening prohibition on persons under 14 driving electrically assisted pedal cycles.	Summarily.	Level 2 on the standard scale.			
RTA section 33	Unauthorised motor vehicle trial on footpaths or bridleways.	Summarily.	Level 3 on the standard scale.			

SCHEDULE 2, PART I—*cont.*

(1) Provision creating offence	(2) General nature of offence	(3) Mode of prosecution	(4) Punishment	(5) Disqualification	(6) Endorsement	(7) Penalty points
		Offences under the Road Traffic Regulation Act 1984				
RTA section 34	Driving motor vehicles elsewhere than on roads.	Summarily.	Level 3 on the standard scale.			
RTA section 35	Failing to comply with traffic directions.	Summarily.	Level 3 on the standard scale.	Discretionary, if committed in respect of a motor vehicle by failure to comply with a direction of a constable or traffic warden.	Obligatory if committed as described in column 5.	3
RTA section 36	Failing to comply with traffic signs.	Summarily.	Level 3 on the standard scale.	Discretionary, if committed in respect of a motor vehicle by failure to comply with an indication given by a sign specified for the purposes of this paragraph in regulations under RTA section 36.	Obligatory if committed as described in column 5.	3
RTA section 37	Pedestrian failing to stop when directed by constable regulating traffic.	Summarily.	Level 3 on the standard scale.			

466

RTA section 40A	Using vehicle in dangerous condition etc.	Summarily.	(a) Level 5 on the standard scale if committed in respect of a goods vehicle or a vehicle adapted to carry more than eight passengers. (b) Level 4 on the standard scale in any other case.	Discretionary.	Obligatory	3
RTA section 41A	Breach of requirement as to brakes, steering-gear or tyres.	Summarily.	(a) Level 5 on the standard scale if committed in respect of a goods vehicle or a vehicle adapted to carry more than eight passengers. (b) Level 4 on the standard scale in any other case.	Discretionary.	Obligatory	3
RTA section 41B	Breach of requirement as to weight: goods and passenger vehicles.	Summarily.	Level 5 on the standard scale.			
RTA section 42	Breach of other construction and use requirements.	Summarily.	(a) Level 4 on the standard scale if committed in respect of a goods vehicle or a vehicle adapted to carry more than eight passengers. (b) Level 3 on the standard scale in any other case.			

Schedule 2, Part I—*cont.*

Offences under the Road Traffic Regulation Act 1984

(1) Provision creating offence	(2) General nature of offence	(3) Mode of prosecution	(4) Punishment	(5) Disqualification	(6) Endorsement	(7) Penalty points
RTA section 47	Using, etc., vehicle without required test certificate being in force.	Summarily.	(a) Level 4 on the standard scale in the case of a vehicle adapted to carry more than eight passengers. (b) Level 3 on the standard scale in any other case.			
Regulations under RTA section 49 made by virtue of section 51(2)	Contravention of requirement of regulations (which is declared by regulations to be an offence) that driver of goods vehicle being tested be present throughout test or drive, etc., vehicle as and when directed.	Summarily.	Level 3 on the standard scale.			
RTA section 53(1)	Using, etc., goods vehicle without required plating certificate being in force.	Summarily.	Level 3 on the standard scale.			
RTA section 53(2)	Using, etc., goods vehicle without required goods vehicle test certificate being in force.	Summarily.	Level 4 on the standard scale.			

RTA section 53(3)	Using, etc., goods vehicle where Secretary of State is required by regulations under section 49 to be notified of an alteration to the vehicle or its equipment but has not been notified.	Summarily.	Level 3 on the standard scale.
Regulations under RTA section 61 made by virtue of subsection (4).	Contravention of requirement of regulations (which is declared by regulations to be an offence) that driver of goods vehicle being tested after notifiable alteration be present throughout test and drive, etc., vehicle as and when directed.	Summarily.	Level 3 on the standard scale.
RTA section 63(1)	Using, etc., goods vehicle without required certificate being in force showing that it complies with type approval requirements applicable to it.	Summarily.	Level 4 on the standard scale.
RTA section 63(2)	Using, etc., certain goods vehicles for drawing trailer when plating certificate does not specify maximum laden weight for vehicle and trailer.	Summarily.	Level 3 on the standard scale.

SCHEDULE 2, PART I—*cont.*

Offences under the Road Traffic Regulation Act 1984

(1) Provision creating offence	(2) General nature of offence	(3) Mode of prosecution	(4) Punishment	(5) Disqualification	(6) Endorsement	(7) Penalty points
RTA section 63(3)	Using, etc., goods vehicle where Secretary of State is required to be notified under section 59 of alteration to it or its equipment but has not been notified.	Summarily.	Level 3 on the standard scale.			
RTA section 64	Using goods vehicle with unauthorised weights as well as authorised weights marked on it.	Summarily.	Level 3 on the standard scale.			
RTA section 65	Supplying vehicle or vehicle part without required certificate being in force showing that it complies with type approval requirements applicable to it.	Summarily.	Level 5 on the standard scale.			
RTA section 67	Obstructing testing of vehicle by examiner on road or failing to comply with requirements of RTA section 67 or Schedule 2.	Summarily.	Level 3 on the standard scale.			

RTA section 68	Obstructing inspection, etc., of vehicle by examiner or failing to comply with requirement to take vehicle for inspection.	Summarily.	Level 3 on the standard scale.
RTA section 71	Driving, etc., vehicle in contravention of prohibition on driving it as being unfit for service, or refusing, neglecting or otherwise failing to comply with direction to remove a vehicle found overloaded.	Summarily.	Level 5 on the standard scale.
RTA section 74	Contravention of regulations requiring goods vehicle operator to inspect, and keep records of inspection of, goods vehicles.	Summarily.	Level 3 on the standard scale.
RTA section 75	Selling, etc., unroadworthy vehicle or trailer or altering vehicle or trailer so as to make it unroadworthy.	Summarily.	Level 5 on the standard scale.
RTA section 76(1)	Fitting of defective or unsuitable vehicle parts.	Summarily.	Level 5 on the standard scale.
RTA section 76(3)	Supplying defective or unsuitable vehicle parts.	Summarily.	Level 4 on the standard scale.

SCHEDULE 2, PART I—*cont.*

(1) Provision creating offence	(2) General nature of offence	(3) Mode of prosecution	(4) Punishment	(5) Disqualification	(6) Endorsement	(7) Penalty points
		Offences under the Road Traffic Regulation Act 1984				
RTA section 76(8)	Obstructing examiner testing vehicles to ascertain whether defective or unsuitable part has been fitted, etc.	Summarily.	Level 3 on the standard scale.			
RTA section 77	Obstructing examiner testing condition of used vehicles at sale rooms, etc.	Summarily.	Level 3 on the standard scale.			
RTA section 78	Failing to comply with requirement about weighing motor vehicle or obstructing authorised person.	Summarily.	Level 5 on the standard scale.			
RTA section 81	Selling, etc., pedal cycle in contravention of regulations as to brakes, bells, etc.	Summarily.	Level 3 on the standard scale.			
RTA section 83	Selling, etc., wrongly made tail lamps or reflectors.	Summarily.	Level 5 on the standard scale.			
RTA section 87(1)	Driving otherwise than in accordance with a licence.	Summarily.	Level 3 on the standard scale.	Discretionary in a case where the offender's driving would not have been in accordance with any licence that could have been granted to him.	Obligatory in the case mentioned in column 5.	3–6

RTA section 87(2)	Causing or permitting a person to drive otherwise than in accordance with a licence.	Summarily.	Level 3 on the standard scale.			
RTA section 92(7C)	Failure to deliver licence revoked by virtue of section 92(7A) and counterpart to Secretary of State.	Summarily.	Level 3 on the standard scale.	Discretionary.	Obligatory.	3–6
RTA section 92(10)	Driving after making false declaration as to physical fitness.	Summarily.	Level 4 on the standard scale.			
RTA section 93(3)	Failure to deliver revoked licence and counterpart to Secretary of State.	Summarily.	Level 3 on the standard scale.			
RTA section 94(3)	Failure to notify Secretary of State of onset of, or deterioration in relevant or prospective disability.	Summarily.	Level 3 on the standard scale.			
RTA section 94(3A)	Driving after such a failure.	Summarily.	Level 3 on the standard scale.	Discretionary.	Obligatory.	3–6
RTA section 94A	Driving after refusal of licence under section 92(3) or revocation under section 93.	Summarily.	6 months or level 5 on the standard scale or both.	Discretionary.	Obligatory.	3–6
RTA section 96	Driving with uncorrected defective eyesight, or refusing to submit to test of eyesight.	Summarily.	Level 3 on the standard scale.	Discretionary.	Obligatory.	3

Schedule 2, Part I—*cont.*

Offences under the Road Traffic Regulation Act 1984

(1) Provision creating offence	(2) General nature of offence	(3) Mode of prosecution	(4) Punishment	(5) Disqualification	(6) Endorsement	(7) Penalty points
RTA section 99(5)	Driving licence holder failing when his licence is revoked, to surrender it and its counterpart or, when his particulars become incorrect, to surrender licence and counterpart and give particulars.	Summarily.	Level 3 on the standard scale.			
RTA section 103(1)(a)	Obtaining driving licence while disqualified.	Summarily.	Level 3 on the standard scale.			
RTA section 103(1)(b)	Driving while disqualified.	(a) Summarily, in England and Wales. (b) Summarily, in Scotland. (c) On indictment, in Scotland.	(a) 6 months or level 5 on the standard scale or both. (b) 6 months or the statutory maximum or both. (c) 12 months or a fine or both.	Discretionary.	Obligatory.	6
RTA section 109	Failing to produce to court Northern Ireland driving licence and counterpart.	Summarily.	Level 3 on the standard scale.			

RTA section 114	Failing to comply with conditions of LGV or PCV licence, or causing or permitting person under 21 to drive LGV or PCV in contravention of such conditions.	Summarily.	Level 3 on the standard scale.
RTA section 118	Failing to surrender revoked or suspended LGV or PCV licence and counterpart.	Summarily.	Level 3 on the standard scale.
Regulations made by virtue of RTA section 120(5)	Contravention of provision of regulations (which is declared by regulations to be an offence) about LGV or PCV drivers' licences.	Summarily.	Level 3 on the standard scale.
RTA section 123(4)	Giving of paid driving instruction by unregistered and unlicensed persons or their employers.	Summarily.	Level 4 on the standard scale.
RTA section 123(6)	Giving of paid instruction without there being exhibited on the motor car a certificate of registration or a licence under RTA Part V.	Summarily.	Level 3 on the standard scale.

SCHEDULE 2, PART I—*cont.*

Offences under the Road Traffic Regulation Act 1984

(1) Provision creating offence	(2) General nature of offence	(3) Mode of prosecution	(4) Punishment	(5) Disqualification	(6) Endorsement	(7) Penalty points
RTA section 135	Unregistered instructor using title or displaying badge, etc., prescribed for registered instructor, or employer using such title, etc., in relation to his unregistered instructor or issuing misleading advertisement, etc.		Summarily.	Level 4 on the standard scale.		
RTA section 136	Failure of instructor to surrender to Registrar certificate or licence.	Summarily.	Level 3 on the standard scale.			
RTA section 137	Failing to produce certificate of registration or licence as driving instructor.	Summarily.	Level 3 on the standard scale.			
RTA section 143	Using motor vehicle while uninsured or unsecured against third-party risks.	Summarily.	Level 5 on the standard scale.	Discretionary.	Obligatory.	6–8
RTA section 147	Failing to surrender certificate of insurance or security to insurer on cancellation or to make statutory declaration of loss or destruction.	Summarily.	Level 3 on the standard scale.			

RTA section 154	Failing to give information, or wilfully making a false statement, as to insurance or security when claim made.	Summarily.	Level 4 on the standard scale.
RTA section 163	Failing to stop motor vehicle or cycle when required by constable.	Summarily.	Level 3 on the standard scale.
RTA section 164	Failing to produce driving licence and counterpart etc. or to state date of birth, or failing to provide the Secretary of State with evidence of date of birth, etc.	Summarily.	Level 3 on the standard scale.
RTA section 165	Failing to give certain names and addresses or to produce certain documents.	Summarily.	Level 3 on the standard scale.
RTA section 168	Refusing to give, or giving false name and address in case of reckless, careless or inconsiderate driving or cycling.	Summarily.	Level 3 on the standard scale.
RTA section 169	Pedestrian failing to give constable his name and address after failing to stop when directed by constable controlling traffic.	Summarily.	Level 1 on the standard scale.

SCHEDULE 2, PART I—*cont.*

Offences under the Road Traffic Regulation Act 1984

(1) Provision creating offence	(2) General nature of offence	(3) Mode of prosecution	(4) Punishment	(5) Disqualification	(6) Endorsement	(7) Penalty points
RTA section 170(4)	Failing to stop after accident and give particulars or report accident.	Summarily.	Six months or level 5 on the standard scale or both.	Discretionary.	Obligatory.	5–10
RTA section 170(7)	Failure by driver, in case of accident involving injury to another, to produce evidence of insurance or security or to report accident.	Summarily.	Level 3 on the standard scale.			
RTA section 171	Failure by owner of motor vehicle to give police information for verifying compliance with requirement of compulsory insurance or security.	Summarily.	Level 4 on the standard scale.			
RTA section 172	Failure of person keeping vehicle and others to give police information as to identity of driver, etc., in the case of certain offences.	Summarily.	Level 3 on the standard scale.	Discretionary, if committed otherwise than by virtue of subsection (5) or (11).	Obligatory, if committed otherwise than by virtue of subsection (5) or (11).	3
RTA section 173	Forgery, etc., of licences, test certificates, certificates of insurance and other documents and things.	(a) Summarily. (b) On indictment.	(a) The statutory maximum. (b) 2 years.			

Provision	Mode of trial	Punishment	Disqualification
RTA section 174	Making certain false statements, etc., and withholding certain material information.	Summarily.	Level 3 on the standard scale.	
RTA section 175	Issuing false documents.	Summarily.	Level 4 on the standard scale.	
RTA section 177	Impersonation of, or of person employed by, authorised examiner.	Summarily.	Level 3 on the standard scale.	
RTA section 178	Taking, etc., in Scotland a motor vehicle without authority or, knowing that it has been so taken, driving it or allowing oneself to be carried in it without authority.	(a) Summarily.	(a) 3 months or the statutory maximum or both.	Discretionary.
		(b) On indictment.	(b) 12 months or a fine or both.	
RTA section 180	Failing to attend, give evidence or produce documents to, inquiry held by Secretary of State, etc.	Summarily.	Level 3 on the standard scale.	
RTA section 181	Obstructing inspection of vehicles after accident.	Summarily.	Level 3 on the standard scale.	
RTA Schedule 1 paragraph 6	Applying warranty to equipment, protective helmet, appliance or information in defending proceedings under RTA section 15A, 17 or 18(4) where no warranty given, or applying false warranty.	Summarily.	Level 3 on the standard scale.	

SCHEDULE 2, PART I—*cont.*

(1) Provision creating offence	(2) General nature of offence	(3) Mode of prosecution	(4) Punishment	(5) Disqualification	(6) Endorsement	(7) Penalty points
			Offences under this Act			
Section 25 of this Act.	Failing to give information as to date of birth or sex to court or to provide Secretary of State with evidence of date of birth, etc.	Summarily.	Level 3 on the standard scale.			
Section 26 of this Act.	Failing to produce driving licence and counterpart to court making order for interim disqualification	Summarily.	Level 3 on the standard scale.			
Section 27 of this Act.	Failing to produce licence and counterpart to court for endorsement on conviction of offence involving obligatory endorsement or on committal for sentence, etc., for offence involving obligatory or discretionary	Summarily.	Level 3 on the standard scale.			

Section 62 of this Act.	disqualification when no interim disqualification ordered. Removing fixed penalty notice fixed to vehicle.	Summarily.	Level 2 on the standard scale.
Section 67 of this Act.	False statement in response to notice to owner.	Summarily.	Level 5 on the standard scale.

Offences under the Road Traffic (Driver Licensing and Information Systems) Act 1989 (RTA)

RTA 1989 s.1(5)	Failure of holder of existing HGV or PSV driver's licence to surrender it upon revocation or surrender of his existing licence under Part III of RTA.	Summarily.	Level 3 on the standard scale.
RTA 1989, Schedule 1, para.3.	Failing to comply with conditions of existing HGV driver's licence, or causing or permitting person under 21 to drive HGV in contravention of such conditions.	Summarily.	Level 3 on the standard scale.

481

SCHEDULE 2, PART I—*cont.*

Offences under the Road Traffic (Driver Licensing and Information Systems) Act 1989 (RTA)

(1) Provision creating offence	(2) General nature of offence	(3) Mode of prosecution	(4) Punishment	(5) Disqualification	(6) Endorsement	(7) Penalty points
RTA 1989, Schedule 1, para. 8(2)	Contravention of provision of regulations (which is declared by regulations to be an offence) about existing HGV or PSV drivers' licences.	Summarily.	Level 3 on the standard scale.			
RTA 1989, Schedule 1, para. 10(4)	Taking PSV test before applying for licence or within prescribed period afterwards.	Summarily.	Level 3 on the standard scale.			
RTA 1989, Schedule 1, para. 10(5)	Taking PSV test after refusal of licence.	Summarily.	Level 3 on the standard scale.			

Offences under this Act (continued)

PART II

OTHER OFFENCES

(1) Offence	(2) Disqualification	(3) Endorsement	(4) Penalty points
Manslaughter or, in Scotland, culpable homicide by the driver of a motor vehicle.	Obligatory.	Obligatory	3–11
An offence under section 12A of the Theft Act 1968 (aggravated vehicle-taking).	Obligatory.	Obligatory.	3–11
Stealing or attempting to steal a motor vehicle.	Discretionary.		
An offence or attempt to commit an offence in respect of a motor vehicle under section 12 of the Theft Act 1968 (taking conveyance without consent of owner etc., or, knowing it has been so taken, driving it or allowing oneself to be carried in it).	Discretionary.		
An offence under section 25 of the Theft Act 1968 (going equipped for stealing, etc.) committed with reference to the theft or taking of motor vehicles.	Discretionary.		

SCHEDULE 3   **Section 51**

FIXED PENALTY OFFENCES

(1) Provision creating offence	(2) General nature of offence
Offences under the Greater London Council (General Powers) Act 1974 (c. 24)	
Section 15 of the Greater London Council (General Powers) Act 1974.	Parking vehicles on footways, verges, etc.
Offences under the Highways Act 1980 (c.66)	
Section 137 of the Highways Act 1980.	Obstructing a highway, but only where the offence is committed in respect of a vehicle.
Offences under the Road Traffic Regulation Act 1984 (c.27)	
RTRA section 5(1)	Using a vehicle in contravention of a traffic regulation order outside Greater London.
RTRA section 8(1)	Breach of traffic regulation order in Greater London.
RTRA section 11	Breach of experimental traffic order.
RTRA section 13	Breach of experimental traffic scheme regulations in Greater London.
RTRA section 16(1)	Using a vehicle in contravention of temporary prohibition or restriction of traffic in case of execution of works, etc.
RTRA section 17(4)	Wrongful use of special road.
RTRA section 18(3)	Using a vehicle in contravention of provision for one-way traffic on trunk road.
RTRA section 20(5)	Driving a vehicle in contravention of order prohibiting or restricting driving vehicles on certain classes of roads.
RTRA section 25(5)	Breach of pedestrian crossing regulations, except an offence in respect of a moving motor vehicle other than a contravention of regulation 8 of the "Zebra" Pedestrian Crossings Regulations 1971 or of regulation 16 or 17 of the "Pelican" Pedestrian Crossings Regulations and General Directions 1987.
RTRA section 29(3)	Using a vehicle in contravention of a street playground order.
RTRA section 35A(1)	Breach of an order regulating the use, etc., of a parking place provided by a local authority, but only where the offence is committed in relation to a parking place provided on a road.
RTRA section 47(1)	Breach of a provision of a parking place designation order and other offences committed in relation to a parking place designated by such an order, except any offence of failing to pay an excess charge within the meaning of section 46.

(1) Provision creating offence	(2) General nature of offence

Offences under the Road Traffic Regulation Act 1974 (c.27)—cont.

RTRA section 53(5)	Using vehicle in contravention of any provision of a parking place designation order having effect by virtue of section 53(1)(*a*) (inclusion of certain traffic regulation provisions).
RTRA section 53(6)	Breach of a provision of a parking place designation order having effect by virtue of section 53(1)(*b*) (use of any part of a road for parking without charge).
RTRA section 88(7)	Driving a motor vehicle in contravention of an order imposing a minimum speed limit under section 88(1)(*b*).
RTRA section 89(1)	Speeding offences under RTRA and other Acts.

Offences under the Road Traffic Act 1988 (c.52)

RTA section 14	Breach of regulations requiring wearing of seat belts.
RTA section 15(2)	Breach of restriction of carrying children in the front of vehicles.
RTA section 15(4)	Breach of restriction on carrying children in the rear of vehicles.
RTA section 16	Breach of regulations relating to protective headgear for motor cycle drivers and passengers.
RTA section 19	Parking a heavy commercial vehicle on verge or footway.
RTA section 22	Leaving vehicle in dangerous position.
RTA section 23	Unlawful carrying of passengers on motor cycles.
RTA section 34	Driving motor vehicle elsewhere than on a road.
RTA section 35	Failure to comply with traffic directions.
RTA section 36	Failure to comply with traffic signs.
RTA section 40A	Using vehicle in dangerous condition etc.
RTA section 41A	Breach of requirement as to brakes, steering-gear or tyres.
RTA section 41B	Breach of requirement as to weight: goods and passenger vehicles.
RTA section 42	Breach of other construction and use requirements.
RTA section 87(1)	Driving vehicle otherwise than in accordance with requisite licence.
RTA section 163	Failure to stop vehicle on being required by constable in uniform.

Offences under the Vehicle Excise and Registration Act 1994 (c.22)

Section 33 of the Vehicle Excise and Registration Act 1994	Using or keeping a vehicle on a public road without licence being exhibited in manner prescribed by regulations.
Section 42 of that Act	Driving or keeping a vehicle without required registration mark.
Section 43 of that Act	Driving or keeping a vehicle with registration mark obscured etc.

SCHEDULE 4   **Section 68**

STATUTORY STATEMENTS

PART I

STATUTORY STATEMENT OF OWNERSHIP OR HIRING

B16–66   1.—(1) For the purposes of Part III of this Act, a statutory statement of ownership is a statement on an official form signed by the person providing it and stating whether he was the owner of the vehicle at the time of the alleged offence and, if he was not the owner of the vehicle at that time, whether—
(a) he was never the owner, or
(b) he ceased to be the owner before, or became the owner after, that time, and in a case within paragraph (b) above, stating, if the information is in his possession, the name and address of the person to whom, and the date on which, he disposed of the vehicle or (as the case may be) the name and address of the person from whom, and the date on which, he acquired it.
(2) An official form for a statutory statement of ownership shall—
(a) indicate that the person providing the statement in response to a notice to owner relating to an offence may give notice requesting a hearing in respect of the offence in the manner specified in the form, and
(b) direct the attention of any person proposing to complete the form to the information provided in accordance with paragraph 3(3) below in any official form for a statutory statement of facts.
2.—(1) For the purposes of Part III of this Act, a statutory statement of hiring is a statement on an official form, signed by the person providing it, being a person by whom a statement of liability was signed, and stating—
(a) whether at the time of the alleged offence the vehicle was let to him under the hiring agreement to which the statement of liability refers, and
(b) if it was not, the date on which he returned the vehicle to the possession of the vehicle-hire firm concerned.
(2) An official form for a statutory statement of hiring shall—
(a) indicate that the person providing the statement in pursuance of a notice relating to an offence served under section 63 of this Act by virtue of section 66 of this Act may give notice requesting a hearing in respect of the offence in the manner specified in the form, and
(b) direct the attention of any person proposing to complete the form to the information provided in accordance with paragraph 3(3) below in any official form for a statutory statement of facts.
(3) In sub-paragraph (1) above "statement of liability," "hiring agreement" and "vehicle-hire firm" have the same meanings as in section 66 of this Act.

PART II

STATUTORY STATEMENT OF FACTS

B16–67   3.—(1) For the purposes of Part III of this Act, a statutory statement of facts is a statement on an official form, signed by the person providing it, which—

(a) states that the person providing it was not the driver of the vehicle at the time of the alleged offence, and

(b) states the name and address at the time when the statement is provided of the person who was the driver of the vehicle at the time of the alleged offence.

(2) A statutory statement of facts has effect as a notice given by the driver requesting a hearing in respect of the offence if it is signed by the person identified in the statement as the driver of the vehicle at the time of the alleged offence.

(3) An official form for a statutory statement of facts shall indicate—

(a) that if a person identified in the statement as the driver of the vehicle at the time of the alleged offence signs the statement he will be regarded as having given notice requesting a hearing in respect of the offence,

(b) that the person on whom the notice to owner relating to the offence is served may not give notice requesting a hearing in respect of the offence on his own account if he provides a statutory statement of facts signed by a person so identified, and

(c) that if the fixed penalty is not paid before the end of the period stated in the notice to owner as the period for response to the notice, a sum determined by reference to that fixed penalty may be registered without any court hearing for enforcement as a fine against the person on whom the notice to owner is served, unless he has given notice requesting a hearing in respect of the offence,

but that, in a case within paragraph (c) above, the sum in question may not be so registered if the person on whom the notice to owner is served provides a statutory statement of facts as mentioned in paragraph (b) above until two months have elapsed from the end of the period so stated without service of a summons or, in Scotland, complaint in respect of the offence on the person identified in that statement as the driver of the vehicle.

ROAD TRAFFIC ACT 1991

(1991 c. 40)

Offences of dangerous driving

1. [*Amends the Road Traffic Act 1988 by substituting therein ss.1, 2 and 2A.*]   **B17–01**

Careless, and inconsiderate, driving

2. [*Amends the Road Traffic Act 1988 by substituting therein a new s.3.*]

Causing death by careless driving when under influence of drink or drugs

3. [*Inserts s.3A in the Road Traffic Act 1988.*]

Driving under influence of drink or drugs

4. [*Amends s.4 of the Road Traffic Act 1988.*]

Disapplication of sections 1 to 3 of the Road Traffic Act 1988 for authorised motoring events

B17–02   **5.** [*Inserts s.13A in the Road Traffic Act 1988.*]

Causing danger to road-users

6. [*Inserts s.22A in the Road Traffic Act 1988.*]

Cycling offences

7. [*Amends the Road Traffic Act 1988 by substituting therein a new s.28.*]

Construction and use of vehicles

8. [*Amends the Road Traffic Act 1988 by inserting therein s.40A and substituting ss.41A, 41B and 42.*]

Vehicle examiners

B17–03   **9.**—(1) *Repeals s.7 of the Public Passenger Vehicles Act 1981 and s.68(1), (2) of the Road Traffic Act 1988 and further amends the 1988 Act by inserting therein s.66A.*

(2) Any reference in any Act, or in any instrument made under any Act, to a certifying officer or public service vehicle examiner appointed under the Public Passenger Vehicles Act 1981 or to an examiner appointed under section 68(1) of the Road Traffic Act 1988 shall, so far as may be appropriate in consequence of the preceding provisions of this section, be construed as a reference to an examiner appointed under section 66A of the Road Traffic Act 1988.

Testing vehicles on roads

10. [*Amends s.67 of the Road Traffic Act 1988.*]

Inspection of vehicles

11. [*Repeals s.8(1), (2) of the Public Passenger Vehicles Act 1981 and amends the Road Traffic Act 1988 by substituting therein a new s.68.*]

Power to prohibit driving of unfit vehicles

12. [*Repeals s.9 of the Public Passenger Vehicles Act 1981 and amends the Road Traffic Act 1988 by substituting therein a new s.69.*]

488

Power to prohibit driving of overloaded vehicles

13. [*Amends s.70 of the Road Traffic Act 1988.*]

Unfit and overloaded vehicles: offences

14. [*Amends the Road Traffic Act 1988 by substituting therein a new s.71.*]

Removal of prohibitions

15. [*Amends the Road Traffic Act 1988 by substituting therein a new s.72 and inserting s.72A.*]

Supply of unroadworthy vehicles etc.

16. [*Amends s.75 of the Road Traffic Act 1988.*]

Requirement of licence

17. [*Amends ss.87, 97 and 98 of the Road Traffic Act 1988.*]

Physical fitness

18. [*Amends ss.92 and 94 of the Road Traffic Act 1988 and inserts s.94A therein.*]

Effects of disqualification

19. [*Amends the Road Traffic Act 1988 by substituting therein s.103.*]

Exception from requirement of third-party insurance

20. [*Amends s.144 of the Road Traffic Act 1988.*]

Information as to identity of driver, etc.

21. [*Amends the Road Traffic Act 1988 by substituting therein s.172.*]

Amendment of Schedule 1 to the Road Traffic Offenders Act 1988

22. Schedule 1 to this Act, which amends Schedule 1 to the Road Traffic Offenders Act 1988 (procedural requirements applicable in relation to certain offences), shall have effect.

Speeding offences etc.: admissibility of certain evidence

23. [*Amends the Road Traffic Offenders Act 1988 by substituting therein a new s.20.*]

Alternative verdicts

24. [*Amends the Road Traffic Offenders Act 1988 by substituting therein a new s.24.*]

Interim disqualification

25. [*Amends the Road Traffic Offenders Act 1988 by substituting therein a new s.26.*]

Amendment of Schedule 2 to the Road Traffic Offenders Act 1988

26. Schedule 2 to this Act, which amends Schedule 2 to the Road Traffic Offenders Act 1988 (prosecution and punishment of offences), shall have effect.

Penalty points to be attributed to offences

27. [*Amends the Road Traffic Offenders Act 1988 by substituting therein s.28.*]

Penalty points to be taken into account on conviction

28. [*Amends the Road Traffic Offenders Act 1988 by substituting therein s.29.*]

Disqualification for certain offences

29. [*Amends s.34 of the Road Traffic Offenders Act 1988.*]

Courses for drink-drive offenders

30. [*Amends the Road Traffic Offenders Act 1988 by inserting therein ss.34A to 34C.*]

Experimental period for section 30

31.—(1) Subject to the following provisions, no order shall be made under section 34A of the Road Traffic Offenders Act 1988 after the end of 1997 or such later time as may be specified in an order made by the Secretary of State.

(2) At any time before the restriction imposed by subsection (1) above has taken effect, the Secretary of State may by order provide that it shall not do so.

(3) In this section "the experimental period" means the period beginning when section 30 above comes into force and ending—

(a) when the restriction imposed by subsection (1) above takes effect, or

(b) if the Secretary of State makes an order under subsection (2) above, on a date specified in the order (being a date falling before the time when the restriction imposed by subsection (1) above would otherwise have taken effect).

(4) During the experimental period—

(a) no order shall be made under section 34A of the Road Traffic Offenders Act 1988 by virtue of a person's conviction under section 3A of the Road Traffic Act 1988, and

(b) no order shall be made under section 34A of the Road Traffic Offenders Act 1988 except by a magistrates' court acting for a petty sessions area (or in Scotland, a sheriff court for a district or a stipendiary magistrate for a commission area) which is for the time being designated for the purposes of this section.

(5) In relation to orders made under section 34A during the experimental period, that section shall have effect with the omission of subsection (6) and section 34B shall have effect as if references to the supervising court were references to the court which made the order.

(6) The power to designate an area or district for the purposes of this section shall be exercisable by the Secretary of State by order, and includes power to revoke any designation previously made.

(7) An order under subsection (6) above shall specify the period for which an area or district is designated, and may—

(a) specify different periods for different areas or districts, and

(b) extend or abridge any period previously specified.

(8) The power to make an order under subsection (1) above shall not be exercisable after the end of 1997, and no more than one order may be made under that subsection.

(9) Any power of the Secretary of State to make orders under this section shall be exercisable by statutory instrument, and—

(a) no order shall be made under subsection (1) or (2) above unless a draft of it has been laid before and approved by resolution of each House of Parliament, and

(b) any statutory instrument containing an order under subsection (6) above shall be subject to annulment in pursuance of a resolution of either House.

Disqualification until test is passed

32. [*Amends the Road Traffic Offenders Act 1988 by substituting therein a new s.36.*] **B17–10**

Short periods of disqualification

33. [*Amends s.37 of the Road Traffic Offenders Act 1988.*]

Conditional offer of fixed penalty

34. [*Amends the Road Traffic Offenders Act 1988 by substituting therein ss.75 to 77.*]

Disabled persons' badges

35. [*Amends s.21 of the Chronically Sick and Disabled Persons Act 1970 and s.117 of the Road Traffic Regulation Act 1984.*]

Forfeiture of vehicles

B17–11 **36.** [*Amends s.43 of the Powers of Criminal Courts Act* 1973.]

Forfeiture of vehicles: Scotland

37. [*Amends ss.223 and 436 of the Criminal Procedure (Scotland) Act* 1975.]

Disqualification where vehicle used for assault

38. [*Amends s.44 of the Powers of Criminal Courts Act* 1973.]

Disqualification in Scotland where vehicle used to commit offence

39. [*Amends the Criminal Procedure (Scotland) Act* 1975 *by inserting therein ss.223A and 436A.*]

Power to install equipment for detection of traffic offences

B17–12 **40.**—(1) [*Amends the Highways Act* 1980 *by inserting therein s.95A.*]
(2) [*Amends the Roads (Scotland) Act* 1984 *by inserting therein s.49A.*]

Variation of charges at off-street parking places

41. [*Inserts s.35C into the Road Traffic Regulation Act* 1984.]

Variation of charges at designated parking places

42. [*Inserts s.46A into the Road Traffic Regulation Act* 1984.]

Permitted and special parking areas outside London

B17–13 **43.**—(1) Schedule 3 shall have effect for the purpose of making provision with respect to areas outside London corresponding to that made with respect to London, and areas within London, under sections 63 to 79 of this Act.
(2) In this section "London" has the same meaning as it has in Part II of this Act.

Parking attendants

B17–14 **44.**—(1) After section 63 of the Road Traffic Regulation Act 1984, there shall be inserted—

"Parking attendants

Parking attendants
63A.—(1) A local authority may provide for the supervision of parking places within their area by individuals to be known as parking attendants.

492

(2) Parking attendants shall also have such other functions in relation to stationary vehicles as may be conferred by or under any other enactment.

(3) A parking attendant shall be—
   (a) an individual employed by the authority; or
   (b) where the authority have made arrangements with any person for the purposes of this section, an individual employed by that person to act as a parking attendant.

(4) Parking attendants in Greater London shall wear such uniform as the Secretary of State may determine when exercising prescribed functions, and shall not exercise any of those functions when not in uniform.

(5) In this section 'local authority' and 'parking place' have the meanings given by section 32(4) of this Act."

(2) In section 35 of that Act (provisions as to use of parking places provided under section 32 or 33), subsection (9) shall be omitted.

Variable speed limits

45. [*Amends s.84 of the Road Traffic Regulation Act* 1984.]   **B17–15**

Tramcars and trolley vehicles

46.—(1) [*Amends the Road Traffic Regulation Act* 1984 *by inserting therein* s.141A].

(2) [*Amends the Road Traffic Act* 1988 *by inserting therein s.*193A.]

Applications for licences to drive hackney carriages etc.

47. [*Amends ss.*51 *and* 59 *of the Local Government (Miscellaneous Provisions) Act* 1976.]

Minor and consequential amendments

48. Schedule 4 to this Act, which makes minor amendments and amendments consequential on the preceding provisions of this Act, shall have effect.

Omission of enactments not brought into force

49. [*Amends Sched.* 2 *to the Road Traffic (Consequential Provisions) Act* 1988.]

Section 48   SCHEDULE 4

MINOR AND CONSEQUENTIAL AMENDMENTS

The Transport Act 1968 (c. 73)

1. In section 82(8) of the Transport Act 1968 (powers of entry and inspec-   **B17–16**
tion), for the words "section 68 of the Road Traffic Act 1988" there shall be substituted the words "section 66A of the Road Traffic Act 1988".

2. In section 99(8) of that Act (inspection of records), for the words from "a certifying" to "1988" there shall be substituted the words "an examiner appointed under section 66A of the Road Traffic Act 1988".

The Chronically Sick and Disabled Persons Act 1970 (c. 44)

3. In section 20(1) of the Chronically Sick and Disabled Persons Act 1970, in paragraph (b) (certain invalid carriages to be treated as not being motor vehicles for the purposes of the Road Traffic Act 1988 etc.)—
- (a) after the words "Road Traffic Act 1988" there shall be inserted the words ", except section 22A of that Act (causing danger to road users by interfering with motor vehicles etc.),", and
- (b) at the end of the paragraph there shall be added the words "and sections 1 to 4, 163, 170 and 181 of the Road Traffic Act 1988 shall not apply to it".

The Road Traffic (Foreign Vehicles) Act 1972 (c. 27)

6. In section 1 of the Road Traffic (Foreign Vehicles) Act 1972 (power to prohibit driving of foreign goods vehicle) in subsection (6)(a) for sub-paragraphs (i) to (iii) there shall be substituted the words "section 40A of the Road Traffic Act 1988 (using vehicle in dangerous condition etc.) or regulations under section 41 of that Act (construction, weight, equipment etc. of motor vehicles and trailers),".

7. In section 2(3B) of that Act (provisions supplementary to section 1) for "72(9)" there shall be substituted "72A".

8. In section 7(1) of that Act (interpretation)—
- (a) in the definition of "examiner", for the words following "means" there shall be substituted the words "an examiner appointed under section 66A of the Road Traffic Act 1988, or a constable authorised to act for the purposes of this Act by or on behalf of a chief officer of police", and
- (b) in the definition of "official testing station" for "72(8)" there shall be substituted "72A".

9. In Schedule 2 to that Act (provisions relating to vehicles and their driving) after the entry relating to section 100 of the Transport Act 1968 there shall be inserted the following entry—

"Section 40A of the Road Traffic Act 1988.	To create offence of using motor vehicle or trailer in dangerous condition etc."

The International Road Haulage Permits Act 1975 (c. 46)

10. In section 1(9) of the International Road Haulage Permits Act 1975 in the definition of "examiner" for the words "section 68(1)" there shall be substituted the words "section 66A".

The Highways Act 1980 (c. 66)

11. In section 42 of the Highways Act 1980 (power of district councils to maintain certain highways) in subsection (2)(c)(ii) for the words "under section 84 of that Act imposing a special limit" there shall be substituted the words "made by virtue of section 84(1)(a) of that Act imposing a speed limit".

12. In each of sections 90A(1) and 90B(1) of that Act (construction of road humps) at the beginning of paragraph (b) there shall be inserted the words "(whether or not the highway is subject to such a limit)".

13. In section 90F(2) of that Act (interpretation) for the definition of "statutory" there shall be substituted—

"statutory speed limit" means a speed limit having effect by virtue of an enactment other than section 84(1)(b) or (c) of the Road Traffic Regulation Act 1984 (temporary and variable speed limits)."

The Public Passenger Vehicles Act 1981 (c. 14)

14. In section 6(1)(a) of the Public Passenger Vehicles Act 1981 (certificates of fitness etc.), for the words "a certifying officer" there shall be substituted the words "an examiner appointed under section 66A of the Road Traffic Act 1988".

15. In section 10(2) of that Act (approval of type vehicle), for the words "the certifying officer" there shall be substituted the words "an examiner appointed under section 66A of the Road Traffic Act 1988".

16.—(1) Section 51 of that Act (appeals to Secretary of State) shall be amended as follows.

(2) In subsection (1) for the words "a certifying officer" there shall be substituted the words "an examiner".

(3) In subsection (4) for the words "the certifying officer" in each place where they occur there shall be substituted the words "the examiner".

The Criminal Justice Act 1982 (c. 48)

17. In Part II of Schedule 1 to the Criminal Justice Act 1982 (offences excluded from Secretary of State's power to make orders concerning the early release of prisoners)—

(a) in the entry relating to section 1 of the Road Traffic Act 1988, for the word "reckless" there shall be substituted the word "dangerous", and

(b) after that entry there shall be inserted—

"Section 3A (causing death by careless driving when under the influence of drink or drugs)."

The Transport Act 1982 (c. 49)

18.—(1) Section 9 of the Transport Act 1982 (private sector vehicle testing: the testing and surveillance functions) shall be amended as follows.

(2) Under the cross-heading "Functions under the 1988 Act"—

(a) for the paragraph beginning "The power of entry", there shall be substituted—

"The power of entry, inspection and detention of vehicles under section 68, but only in relation to vehicles brought to the place of inspection in pursuance of a direction given by a vehicle examiner or a constable under subsection (3) of that section.",

(b) in the following paragraph, after "69" there shall be inserted "69A,", and for the word "goods vehicles" there shall be substituted the words "vehicles".

(3) Under the cross-heading "Functions under the 1981 Act", the paragraph beginning "Any functions under section 9" shall be omitted.

19.—(1) Section 10 of that Act (private sector vehicle testing: supplementary) shall be amended as follows.

(2) For subsection (3) there shall be substituted—

"(3) The words "or an authorised inspector" shall be inserted—

(a) in sections 51(1)(b) and 61(2)(a) of the 1988 Act, after the words "a vehicle examiner", and

(b) in section 6(1)(a) and 10(2) of the 1981 Act, after the words "Act 1988"; and the words "or authorised inspector" shall be inserted after the word "examiner" wherever occurring in section 69 of the 1988 Act."

(3) In subsection (6) for "68(3)" there shall be substituted "68(1)", and for "(4)" there shall be substituted "(3)".

(4) In subsection (9), in subsection (2A) to be inserted in section 20 of the Public Passenger Vehicles Act 1981, for the words "public service vehicle examiner" there shall be substituted the words " an examiner appointed under section 66A of the Road Traffic Act 1988".

(5) In subsection (10) for the words from "certifying officer" to "goods vehicles examiner" there shall be substituted the words "vehicle examiner".

20. For section 20 of that Act (substitution of new section for section 72 of the 1988 Act) there shall be substituted—

"Amendment of section 72 of 1988 Act

20. In section 72 of the 1988 Act (removal of prohibitions) after the word 'constable' in each place where it occurs in subsections (1), (5) and (7), there shall be inserted the words 'or authorised inspector'.

21. For section 21(4) of that Act (amendments with respect to appeals) there shall be substituted—

'(4) In section 51 of that Act (appeals to the Secretary of State)—

(a) in subsection (1), after the word 'examiner' there shall be inserted the words 'or an authorised inspector';

(b) after subsection (1) there shall be inserted the following subsections—

'(1A) A person aggrieved by the refusal of the prescribed testing authority to approve a vehicle as a type vehicle under section 10 of this Act or by the withdrawal by that authority under that section of such approval may appeal to the Secretary of State.

(1B) On any appeal under subsection (1A) above, the Secretary of State shall cause an examination of the vehicle concerned to be made by an officer of the Secretary of State appointed by him for the purpose and shall make such determination on the basis of the examination as he thinks fit.';

and

(c) in subsection (4) after the word 'examiner' in both places where it occurs there shall be inserted the words 'prescribed testing authority or authorised inspector concerned'."

22.—(1) Section 24 of that Act (falsification of documents) shall be amended as follows.

(2) In subsection (2) for paragraph (a) there shall be substituted—

"(a) in subsection (4) after the words 'of this Act' there shall be inserted the words 'or an authorised inspector appointed under section 8 of the Transport Act 1982';".

(3) In subsection (4), in section 66A(2) to be inserted in the Public Passenger Vehicles Act 1981, for the words "a certifying officer, a public service vehicle examiner" there shall be substituted the words "an examiner appointed under section 66A of the Road Traffic Act 1988".

23. In section 26 of that Act (interpretation) for the definition of "goods vehicle examiner" there shall be substituted—

" 'vehicle examiner' means an examiner appointed under section 66A of the 1988 Act."

The Road Traffic Regulation Act 1984 (c. 27)

24. In section 9 of the Road Traffic Regulation Act 1984 (experimental traffic orders) in subsection (1)(b), as substituted by the New Roads and Street Works Act 1991, for the words "83(2) or 84" there shall be substituted the words "or 83(2) or by virtue of section 84(1)(a)".

25. In section 17(2) of that Act (traffic regulation on special roads) at the end there shall be added—

"(d) include provisions having effect in such places, at such times, in such manner or in such circumstances as may for the time being be indicated by traffic signs in accordance with the regulations."

26. In section 44 of that Act (control of off-street parking outside Greater London) in subsection (5) for the words "under section 84" there shall be substituted the words "made by virtue of section 84(1)(a)".

27. In section 49 of that Act (supplementary provisions as to designation orders and designated parking places), after subsection (4) there shall be inserted the following subsection—

"(4A) A constable, or a person acting under the instructions (whether general or specific) of the chief officer of police, may suspend the use of a parking place designated under section 45 of this Act for not more than 7 days in order to prevent or mitigate congestion or obstruction of traffic, or danger to or from traffic, in consequence of extraordinary circumstances."

28. In section 51 of that Act (parking devices), in subsection (5) the words "being not less than 2 years" shall be omitted.

29. In section 65 of that Act (powers and duties of highway authorities as to placing of traffic signs) after subsection (1) there shall be inserted—

"(1A) The power to give general directions under subsection (1) above includes power to require equipment used in connection with traffic signs to be of a type approved in accordance with the directions."

30. In section 85 of that Act (traffic signs for indicating speed restrictions) in subsections (1) and (2)(a) the words "the prescribed" shall be omitted.

31.—(1) Section 96 of that Act (additional powers of traffic wardens) shall be amended as follows.

(2) In subsection (2) at the end of paragraph (b) there shall be inserted—

"(bb) in this Act—

(i) section 100(3) (which relates to the interim disposal of vehicles removed under section 99); and

(ii) sections 104 and 105 (which relate to the immobilisation of illegally parked vehicles);".

(3) At the end of that section there shall be added—

"(4) Where an order has been made pursuant to subsection (2)(bb)(i) above, in section 100(3) of this Act the words "chief officer of the police force to which the constable belongs" shall be deemed to include a reference to a chief officer of police under whose direction a traffic warden acts.

(5) Any order made under section 95(5) of this Act may make different provision for different cases or classes of case, or in respect of different areas."

32. At the end of section 99 of that Act (removal of vehicles illegally parked) there shall be inserted—

"(6) For the purposes of this section, the suspension under section 13A or 49 of this Act of the use of a parking place is a restriction imposed under this Act."

33. In section 103 of that Act (supplementary provision as to removal of vehicles), for subsection (3) there shall be substituted—

"(3) Regulations made under sections 99 to 102 of this Act may make different provision for different cases or classes of case or in respect of different areas."

34.—(1) Section 104 of that Act (immobilisation of vehicles illegally parked) shall be amended as follows.

(2) In subsection (3) for the word "constable" there shall be substituted the words "person authorised to give such a direction by the chief officer of police within whose area the vehicle in question was found".

(3) In subsection (12) there shall be added at the end "or classes of case or in respect of different areas".

35. At the end of section 104 of that Act (immobilisation of vehicles illegally parked) there shall be inserted—

"(12A) For the purposes of this section, the suspension under section 13A or 49 of this Act of the use of a parking place is a restriction imposed under this Act."

36.—(1) Section 105 of that Act (exemptions from section 104) shall be amended as follows.

(2) In subsection (6)(a), for words from "either" to "use) of" there shall be substituted the words "in accordance with regulations under".

(3) In subsection (6)(b), for "117(2)(b)" there shall be substituted "117(1)(b)".

37. In paragraph 13 of Schedule 9 to that Act (consent of Secretary of State before local authority make certain orders), after sub-paragraph (1)(d)(ii) there shall be inserted—

"(iii) a provision imposing a prohibition by virtue of paragraph (b) or (c) of that subsection, or".

The Roads (Scotland) Act 1984 (c. 54)

38.—(1) In section 36 of the Roads (Scotland) Act 1984 (construction of road humps by roads authority) at the beginning of paragraph (b) there shall be inserted the words "(whether or not the road is subject to such a limit)".

(2) In section 40 of that Act (interpretation of sections 36 to 39) at the end of the definition of "statutory" there shall be added the words "other than section 84(1)(b) or (c) of the Road Traffic Regulation Act 1984 (temporary and variable speed limits)".

The Police and Criminal Evidence Act 1984 (c. 60)

39. In Part II of Schedule 5 to the Police and Criminal Evidence Act 1984 (serious arrestable offences)—

(a) in the entry relating to section 1 of the Road Traffic Act 1988, for the word "reckless" there shall be substituted the word "dangerous", and

(b) after that entry there shall be inserted—

"Section 3A (causing death by careless driving when under the influence of drink or drugs)."

The Coroners Act 1988 (c. 13)

40. In section 16 of the Coroners Act 1988 (adjournment of inquest in certain cases) in subsection (1)(a)(ii) for the words from "section" to "driving)" there shall be substituted the words "section 1 or 3A of the Road Traffic Act 1988 (dangerous driving or careless driving when under the influence of drink or drugs)".

41. In section 17 of that Act (supplementary provisions) in subsections (1)(b) and (2)(b) for the words from "section" to "driving)" there shall be substituted the words "section 1 or 3A of the Road Traffic Act 1988 (dangerous driving or careless driving when under the influence of drink or drugs)".

The Road Traffic Act 1988 (c. 52)

42. In section 7 of the Road Traffic Act 1988 (provision of specimens for analysis)—
    (a) in subsection (1) for the words "section 4" there shall be substituted the words "section 3A, 4", and
    (b) in subsection (3)(c) for the words "section 4" there shall be substituted the words "section 3A or 4".

43. In section 10 of that Act (detention of persons affected by alcohol or a drug) in subsections (1) and (2) for the words "motor vehicle" in each place where they occur there shall be substituted the words "mechanically propelled vehicle".

44. In section 11(1) of that Act (interpretation), for "4" there shall be substituted "3A".

45. In section 12 of that Act (motor racing on public ways), in subsection (2) for the words "public highway" there shall be substituted the word "highway".

46. In section 13 of that Act (regulation of motoring events on public ways), in subsection (4) for the words "public highway" there shall be substituted the word "highway".

47. In section 14 of that Act (seat belts: adults) in subsection (2)(b)(i) for the word "addresses" there shall be substituted the word "addressees".

48. In section 22 of that Act (leaving vehicles in dangerous positions) for the words "be likely to cause danger" there shall be substituted the words "involve a danger of injury".

49. In section 31 of that Act (regulation of cycle racing on public ways) for subsection (6) there shall be substituted—
    "(6) In this section "public way" means, in England and Wales, a highway, and in Scotland, a public road but does not include a footpath."

50.—(1) Section 41 of that Act (regulation of construction, weight, equipment and use of vehicles) shall be amended as follows.
(2) In subsection (2) at the end of paragraph (e) there shall be added the words "by means of the fixing of plates or otherwise) and the circumstances in which they are to be marked,".
(3) In subsection (2) after paragraph (j) there shall be inserted—
    "(jj) speed limiters,".
(4) After subsection (4) there shall be inserted—
    "(4A) Regulations under this section with respect to speed limiters may include provision—
        (a) as to the checking and sealing of speed limiters by persons authorised in accordance with the regulations and the making of charges by them,
        (b) imposing or providing for the imposition of conditions to be complied with by authorised persons,
        (c) as to the withdrawal of authorisations."

51. In section 44(1) of that Act (authorisation of use on roads of special vehicles not complying with regulations under section 41) for the words from "and nothing" to "prevent" there shall be substituted the words "and sections 40A to 42 of this Act shall not apply in relation to".

52.—(1) Section 45 of that Act (tests of satisfactory condition of vehicles) shall be amended as follows.

(2) In subsection (1), for the words "prescribes statutory requirements" onwards there shall be substituted the words "following requirements are complied with, namely—

    (a) the prescribed statutory requirements relating to the construction and condition of motor vehicles or their accessories or equipment, and

    (b) the requirement that the condition of motor vehicles should not be such that their use on a road would involve a danger of injury to any person."

(3) In subsection (3), for paragraph (b) there shall be substituted—

    "(b) examiners appointed under section 66A of this Act".

53. In section 46(a) of that Act (regulations as to authorisation of examiners), after the words "of examiners" there shall be inserted the words "in accordance with subsection (3)(a) of that section".

54.—(1) Section 49 of that Act (tests of satisfactory condition of goods vehicles and determination of plated weights etc.) shall be amended as follows.

(2) In subsection (1), for the words following paragraph (b) there shall be substituted the words "or

    (c) for the purpose of ascertaining whether the condition of the vehicle is such that its use on a road would involve a danger of injury to any person,

    or for any of those purposes."

(3) In subsection (2)(b), after the word "requirements" there shall be inserted the words "and the requirement that the condition of the vehicle is not such that its use on a road would involve a danger of injury to any person".

(4) In subsection (4), in the definition of "goods vehicle test", after the word "requirements" there shall be inserted the words ", or the requirement that the condition of the vehicle is not such that its use on a road would involve a danger of injury to any person,".

55.—(1) Section 50 of that Act (appeals against determinations) shall be amended as follows.

(2) In subsection (1) for the words "an area" onwards there shall be substituted the words "the Secretary of State".

(3) Subsections (2) and (3) shall be omitted.

56.—(1) Section 73 of that Act (provisions supplementary to section 69 to 72) shall be amended as follows.

(2) For subsection (1) there shall be substituted—

    "(1) Where it appears to a person giving a notice under section 69(6) or 70(2) of this Act that the vehicle concerned is an authorised vehicle, he must as soon as practicable take steps to bring the contents of the notice to the attention of—

        (a) the traffic commissioner by whom the operator's licence was granted for the vehicle, and

        (b) the holder of the licence if he is not in charge of the vehicle at the time when the notice is given.

    (1A) Where it appears to a person giving a notice under section 69(6) or 70(2) of this Act that the vehicle concerned is used under a PSV operator's licence, he must as soon as practicable take steps to bring the contents of the notice to the attention of—

        (a) the traffic commissioner by whom the PSV operator's licence was granted for the vehicle, and

        (b) the holder of the licence if he is not in charge of the vehicle at the time when the notice is given.

    (1B) In a case not within subsection (1) or subsection (1A) above, a person giving a notice under section 69(6) or 70(2) of this Act must as soon as practicable take steps to bring the contents of the notice to the attention of the owner of the vehicle if he is not in charge of it at the time when the notice is given.

(1C) A person giving a notice to the owner of a vehicle under section 72(7) of this Act must as soon as practicable take steps to bring the contents of the notice to the attention of any other person—

(a) who was the person to whom the previous notice under section 69(6) or 70(2) was given and was then the owner of the vehicle, or

(b) to whose attention the contents of the previous notice were brought under this section."

(3) Subsection (2) shall be omitted.

(4) In subsection (4) at the end there shall be added the words "; and "PSV operator's licence" has the same meaning as in the Public Passenger Vehicles Act 1981".

57. In subsection (1)(a) of section 74 of that Act (operator's duty to inspect goods vehicles) after the word "whether" there shall be inserted the words "the following requirements are complied with, namely—

(i)";

and for the words "are complied with" there shall be substituted the words "and

(ii) the requirement that the condition of the vehicle is not such that its use on a road would involve a danger of injury to any person".

58.—(1) Section 76 of that Act (fitting and supply of defective or unsuitable vehicle parts) shall be amended as follows.

(2) In subsection (1), after the words "to the vehicle" there shall be inserted the words "involve a danger of injury to any person or".

(3) In subsection (2)(b)(ii), after the words "its use" there shall be inserted the words "on a road", and at the end there shall be added the words "and would not involve a danger of injury to any person."

(4) At the end of each of subsection (3), (5)(b)(ii) and (6)(a) there shall be added the words "or involve a danger of injury to any person".

59.—(1) Section 79 of that Act (provisions relating to weighing of motor vehicles) shall be amended as follows.

(2) In subsection (2)—

(a) for "68(1)" there shall be substituted "66A";

(b) for the words from "vehicles of" to "vehicles generally" there shall be substituted the words "goods vehicles, public service vehicles, and vehicles which are not public service vehicles but are adapted to carry more than eight passengers,".

(3) In subsection (3)—

(a) for the words from "vehicles of" to "vehicles generally" there shall be substituted the words "such vehicles", and

(b) for the words "a certifying officer," there shall be substituted the word "an".

60. In section 84(2) of that Act (remuneration of examiners), for the words from "goods" to "73" there shall be substituted the words "examiners appointed under section 66A".

61. In section 85 of that Act (interpretation of Part II)—

(a) in the definition of "official testing station" for "72(8)" there shall be substituted "72A", and

(b) after the definition of "prescribed" there shall be inserted—
"public service vehicle" has the same meaning as in the Public Passenger Vehicles Act 1981,".

62. In section 86 of that Act (index to Part II), in the table, after the entry for "Prescribed" there shall be inserted—

"Public service vehicle   Section 85"

and after the entry for "Type approval requirements" there shall be inserted—

"Vehicle examiner   Section 66A".

63. In section 89 of that Act (tests of competence to drive) at the end of subsection (3)(a) there shall be inserted the words "and section 36 of the Road Traffic Offenders 1988 (disqualification),".

64. In section 115(3) of that Act (revocation or suspension of large goods vehicle or passenger-carrying vehicle driver's licences) for the words "subsection (1)(a) above" there shall be substituted the words "this section or section 117 of this Act".

65.—(1) Section 117 of that Act (disqualification on revocation of large goods vehicle or passenger-carrying vehicle driver's licences) shall be amended as follows.

(2) In subsection (1), for the words "for the purposes of that paragraph" there shall be substituted the words "in pursuance of section 115(3)".

(3) After subsection (2) there shall be inserted—
"(2A) Regulations may make provision for the application of subsections (1) and (2) above, in such circumstances and with such modifications as may be prescribed, where a person's large goods vehicle or passenger-carrying vehicle driver's licence is treated as revoked by virtue of section 37(1) of the Road Traffic Offenders Act 1988 (effect of disqualification by order of a court)."

66. In section 152 of that Act (duties of insurers etc.: exceptions) at the end of subsection (2) there shall be added the words "and, for the purposes of this section, "material" means of such a nature as to influence the judgment of a prudent insurer in determining whether he will take the risk and, if so, at what premium and on what conditions."

67. In section 163(1) of that Act (power of police to stop vehicles) for the words "motor vehicle" there shall be substituted the words "mechanically propelled vehicle".

68.—(1) Section 164 of that Act (power of constable to require production of driving licence etc.) shall be amended as follows.

(2) In subsection (1), after the word "constable" wherever it occurs there shall be inserted the words "or vehicle examiner".

(3) In subsection (2), for the words "Such a person" there shall be substituted the words "A person required by a constable under subsection (1) above to produce his licence".

(4) In subsection (3), after the word "constable" there shall be inserted the words "or vehicle examiner".

(5) In subsection (5) for the words "section 27 of the Road Traffic Offenders Act 1988" there shall be substituted the words "section 26 or 27 of the Road Traffic Offenders Act 1988 or section 44 of the Powers of Criminal Courts Act 1973 or section 223A or 436A of the Criminal Procedure (Scotland) Act 1975."

(6) In subsection (6) for the words "and (8)" there shall be substituted the words "to (8A)".

(7) After subsection (8) there shall be inserted—
"(8A) Subsection (8) above shall apply in relation to a certificate of com-

502

pletion of a training course for motor cyclists as it applies in relation to a licence."

(8) At then end of subsection (11) there shall be added the words "and "vehicle examiner" means an examiner appointed under section 66A of this Act."

69.—(1) Section 165 of that Act (powers of constables to obtain names and addresses of drivers etc.) shall be amended as follows.

(2) In subsection (1), after the word "constable" wherever it occurs there shall be inserted the words "or vehicle examiner".

(3) In subsection (5), after the word "constable" wherever it occurs there shall be inserted the words "or vehicle examiner".

(4) At the end of subsection (7) there shall be added the words "and "vehicle examiner" means an examiner appointed under section 66A of this Act."

70. In section 166 of that Act (powers of certain officers as respects goods vehicles etc.) for the words from the beginning to the end of paragraph (d) there shall be substituted the words "A person authorised for the purpose by a traffic commissioner appointed under the Public Passenger Vehicles Act 1981,".

71. In section 168 of that Act (offence of failing to give name and address in relation to certain offences) in paragraph (a) for the words "motor vehicle" there shall be substituted the words "mechanically propelled vehicle".

72.—(1) Section 170 of that Act (duty of driver to stop, report accident and give information or documents) shall be amended as follows.

(2) In subsections (1) to (3) for the words "motor vehicle" in each place where they occur there shall be substituted the words "mechanically propelled vehicle".

(3) In subsection (5) for the words "the vehicle" there shall be substituted the words "a motor vehicle".

(4) In subsection (7) for the word "five" there shall be substituted the word "seven".

73.—(1) Subsection (2) of section 173 of that Act (offences of forgery etc.) shall be amended as follows.

(2) After paragraph (c) there shall be inserted—

"(cc) any seal required by regulations made under section 41 of this Act with respect to speed limiters,".

(3) In paragraph (d) for the words from the beginning to "Part II of this Act)" there shall be substituted the words "any plate containing particulars required to be marked on a vehicle by regulations under section 41 of this Act".

(4) After paragraph (d) there shall be inserted—

"(dd) any document evidencing the appointment of an examiner under section 66A of this Act,".

(5) After paragraph (f) there shall be inserted—

"(ff) any certificate provided for by regulations under section 97(3A) of this Act relating to the completion of a training course for motor cyclists,".

(6) After paragraph (l) there shall be added—

"and

(m) a certificate of the kind referred to in section 34B(1) of the Road Traffic Offenders Act 1988."

74.—(1) Section 176 of that Act (power to seize documents etc.) shall be amended as follows.

(2) In subsection (4), for the words from "a certifying" to "68(1)" there shall be substituted the words "an examiner appointed under section 66A".

(3) In subsection (5)(a), for the words "for the purposes of sections 68 to 72" there shall be substituted the words "under section 66A".

75. In section 177 of that Act (impersonation of, or of person employed by, authorised examiner) after the words "a person authorised" there shall be inserted the words "in accordance with regulations made under section 41 of this Act with respect to the checking and sealing of speed limiters or a person authorised".

76. In section 181 of that Act (provisions as to accident inquiries) in subsections (1) and (2) for the words "motor vehicle" in each place where they occur there shall be substituted the words "mechanically propelled vehicle".

77. In section 183(3) of that Act (Crown application), for the words from "68" to "1981" there shall be substituted the words "66A of this Act".

78.—(1) Section 192 of that Act (interpretation) shall be amended as follows.

(2) In subsection (1), in the definition of "road"—

  (a) after the word " "road" " there shall be inserted "(a)", and

  (b) at the end there shall be inserted—

        "and

      (b) in relation to Scotland, means any road within the meaning of the Roads (Scotland) Act 1984 and any other way to which the public has access, and includes bridges over which a road passes,".

(3) In subsection (1), in the definition of "trolley vehicle" for the words "and moved by" there shall be substituted the word "under", and at the end there shall be added the words "(whether or not there is in addition a source of power on board the vehicle)".

(4) In subsection (2) the word " 'road' " shall be omitted.

79. [...]

The Road Traffic Offenders Act 1988 (c. 53)

80. In section 1 of the Road Traffic Offenders Act 1988 (requirement of warning etc. of prosecution of certain offences), in subsection (1) for the words "where a person" to "convicted unless" there shall be substituted the words "a person shall not be convicted of an offence to which this section applies unless".

81. For subsections (4) to (6) of section 2 of that Act (requirement of warning of prosecution: supplementary) there shall be substituted—

    "(4) Failure to comply with the requirement of section 1(1) of this Act in relation to an offence is not a bar to the conviction of a person of that offence by virtue of the provisions of—

        (a) section 24 of this Act, or

        (b) any of the enactments mentioned in section 24(6);

        but a person is not to be convicted of an offence by virtue of any of those provisions if section 1 applies to the offence with which he was charged and the requirement of section 1(1) was not satisfied in relation to the offence charged."

82. In section 5 of that Act (exemption from Licensing Act offence) for the words "section 4" there shall be substituted the words "section 3A, 4".

83. In section 7 of that Act (duty of accused to provide licence) for the words "obligatory endorsement" there shall be substituted the words "obligatory or discretionary disqualification".

84. In section 11(1) of that Act (evidence by certificate as to driver, user or owner) for the words "motor vehicle" in each place where they occur there shall be substituted the words "mechanically propelled vehicle".

85. In section 12 of that Act (proof of identity of driver) after subsection (3) there shall be added—

    "(4) In summary proceedings in Scotland for an offence to which section 20(2) of the Road Traffic Act 1988 applies, where—

        (a) it is proved to the satisfaction of the court that a requirement under section 172(2) of the Road Traffic Act 1988 to give information as to the identity of a driver on a particular occasion to which the complaint relates has been served on the accused by post, and

    (b) a statement in writing is produced to the court, purporting to be signed by the accused, that the accused was the driver of that vehicle on that occasion,

that statement shall be sufficient evidence that the accused was the driver of the vehicle on that occasion."

86. In section 14 of that Act (use of records kept by operators of goods vehicles) after the word "proceedings" there shall be inserted the words "for an offence under section 40A of the Road Traffic Act 1988 or".

87.—(1) Section 15 of that Act (use of specimens in proceedings for offences under sections 4 and 5 of the Road Traffic Act 1988) shall be amended as follows.

(2) In subsection (1) for the words "section 4 or 5 of the Road Traffic Act 1988 (motor vehicles: drink and drugs)" there shall be substituted the words "section 3A, 4 or 5 of the Road Traffic Act 1988 (driving offences connected with drink or drugs)", and for the words "sections 4 to 10" there shall be substituted the words "sections 3A to 10".

(3) In subsection (2) after the word "cases" there shall be inserted the words "(including cases where the specimen was not provided in connection with the alleged offence)".

(4) For subsection (3) there shall be substituted—

    "(3) That assumption shall not be made if the accused proves—

      (a) that he consumed alcohol before he provided the specimen and—

        (i) relation to an offence under section 3A, after the time of the alleged offence, and

        (ii) otherwise, after he had ceased to drive, attempt to drive or be in charge of a vehicle on a road or other public place, and

      (b) that had he not done so the proportion of alcohol in his breath, blood or urine would not have exceeded the prescribed limit and, if it is alleged that he was unfit to drive through drink, would not have been such as to impair his ability to drive properly."

88.—(1) Section 17 of that Act (provisions as to proceedings for certain offences in connection with the construction and use of vehicles) shall be amended as follows.

(2) In subsection (1) for the words "section 42(1) of the Road Traffic Act 1988 (contravention" there shall be substituted the words "section 40A, 41A, 41B or 42 of the Road Traffic Act 1988 (using vehicle in dangerous condition or contravention".

(3) In subsection (3) after the word "requirements" there shall be inserted the words ", or so that it has ceased to be excessive,".

89. In section 21(3) of that Act (evidence of one witness sufficient in Scotland in relation to certain offences) for the words "or 36" there shall be substituted the words ", 36 or 172."

90.—(1) Section 23 of that Act (alternative verdicts in Scotland) shall be amended as follows.

(2) In subsection (1)—

    (a) for the words "motor vehicle" there shall be substituted the words "mechanically propelled vehicle"; and

(b) for the word "reckless" there shall be substituted the word "dangerous".

(3) Subsection (2) shall be omitted.

91.—(1) Section 27 of that Act (production of licence) shall be amended as follows.

(2) In subsection (1), for the words from "endorsement" to "Act" there shall be substituted the words "or discretionary disqualification, and a court proposes to make an order disqualifying him or an order under section 44 of this Act, the court must, unless it has already received them,".

(3) Subsection (2) shall be omitted.

(4) In subsection (3), after the words "as required" there shall be inserted the words "under this section or section 44 of the Powers of Criminal Courts Act 1973, or section 223A or 436A of the Criminal Procedure (Scotland) Act 1975".

92.—(1) Section 30 of that Act (modification of penalty points where fixed penalty also in question) shall be amended as follows.

(2) In subsection (1)(a) for the words "obligatory or discretionary disqualification" there shall be substituted the words "obligatory endorsement".

(3) In subsection (2)—

(a) the words "Subject to section 28(2) of this Act" shall be omitted,

(b) in paragraph (a) for "28(1)" there shall be substituted "28", and

(c) in paragraph (b) at the end there shall be added the words "(except so far as they have already been deducted by virtue of this paragraph)".

(4) Subsection (3) shall be omitted.

93. In section 31(1) of that Act (court may take particulars endorsed on licence into account) for the words "obligatory endorsement" there shall be substituted the words "obligatory or discretionary disqualification".

94. In section 32(1) of that Act (court in Scotland may take extract from licensing records into account) for the words "obligatory endorsement" there shall be substituted the words "obligatory or discretionary disqualification".

95.—(1) Section 35 of that Act (disqualification for repeated offences) shall be amended as follows.

(2) In subsection (1)(a) for the words "involving obligatory or discretionary disqualification" there shall be substituted the words "to which this subsection applies".

(3) After subsection (1) there shall be inserted—

"(1A) Subsection (1) above applies to—

(a) an offence involving discretionary disqualification and obligatory endorsement, and

(b) an offence involving obligatory disqualification in respect of which no order is made under section 34 of this Act."

(4) In subsection (2) for the words "was imposed" there shall be substituted the words "was for a fixed period of 56 days or more and was imposed".

(5) In subsection (3) for the words "involving obligatory of [*sic*] discretionary disqualification" there shall be substituted the words "to which subsection (1) above applies".

(6) In subsection (5) for the words following "1973" there shall be substituted the words "or section 223A or 436A of the Criminal Procedure (Scotland) Act 1975 (offences committed by using vehicles) or a disqualification imposed in respect of an offence of stealing a motor vehicle, an offence under section 12 or 25 of the Theft Act 1968, an offence under section 178 of the Road Traffic Act 1988, or an attempt to commit such an offence".

(7) After subsection (5) there shall be inserted—

"(5A) The preceding provisions of this section shall apply in relation to a conviction of an offence committed by aiding, abetting, counselling, procuring, or inciting to the commission of, an offence involving obligatory disqualification as if the offence were an offence involving discretionary disqualification."

96. In section 37(3) of that Act (driver disqualified until test is passed entitled to provisional licence) for "36(1)" there shall be substituted "36".

97. After section 41 of that Act there shall be inserted—

"Suspension of disqualification pending determination of applications under section 34B

41A.—(1) Where a person makes an application to a court under section 34B of this Act, the court may suspend the disqualification to which the application relates pending the determination of the application.

(2) Where a court exercises its power under subsection (1) above it must send notice of the suspension to the Secretary of State.

(3) The notice must be sent in such manner and to such address, and must contain such particulars, as the Secretary of State may determine."

98. In section 42 of that Act (removal of disqualification) after subsection (5) there shall be inserted—

"(5A) Subsection (5)(a) above shall apply only where the disqualification was imposed in respect of an offence involving obligatory endorsement; and in any other case the court must send notice of the order made under this section to the Secretary of State.

(5B) A notice under subsection (5A) above must be sent in such manner and to such address, and must contain such particulars, as the Secretary of State may determine."

99.—(1) Section 45 of that Act (effect of endorsement) shall be amended as follows.

(2) In subsection (5)(b), for sub-paragraph (ii) there shall be substituted—

"(ii) an order is made for the disqualification of the offender under section 35 of this Act".

(3) In subsection (6) for the word "reckless" in both places where it occurs there shall be substituted the word "dangerous".

(4) In subsection (7), for paragraph (a) there shall be substituted—

"(a) section 3A, 4(1) or 5(1)(a) of that Act (driving offences connected with drink or drugs), or".

100.—(1) Section 47 of that Act (supplementary provisions as to disqualifications and endorsements) shall be amended as follows.

(2) In subsection (2), for the words from "and, if it" to "disqualified, must" there shall be substituted the words ", and where a court orders the holder of a licence to be disqualified for a period of 56 days or more it must,".

(3) In subsection (3), for the words "any such order" there shall be substituted the words "an order for the endorsement of a licence or the disqualification of a person".

101. For section 48 of that Act (exemption from disqualification and endorsement for offences against construction and use regulations) there shall be substituted—

"Exemption from disqualification and endorsement for certain construction and use offences

48.—(1) Where a person is convicted of an offence under section 40A of the Road Traffic Act 1988 (using vehicle in dangerous condition etc.) the court must not—

(a) order him to be disqualified, or

507

(b) order any particulars or penalty points to be endorsed on the counterpart of any licence held by him,

if he proves that he did not know, and had no reasonable cause to suspect, that the use of the vehicle involved a danger of injury to any person.

(2) Where a person is convicted of an offence under section 41A of the Road Traffic Act 1988 (breach of requirement as to brakes, steering-gear or tyres) the court must not—

(a) order him to be disqualified, or

(b) order any particulars or penalty points to be endorsed on the counterpart of any licence held by him,

if he proves that he did not know, and had no reasonable cause to suspect, that the facts of the case were such that the offence would be committed.

(3) In relation to licences which came into force before 1st June 1990, the references in subsections (1) and (2) above to the counterpart of a licence shall be construed as references to the licence itself."

102. For section 53 of that Act there shall be substituted—

"Amount of fixed penalty

53.—(1) The fixed penalty for an offence is—

(a) such amount as the Secretary of State may by order prescribe, or

(b) one half of the maximum amount of the fine to which a person committing that offence would be liable on summary conviction,

whichever is the less.

(2) Any order made under subsection (1)(a) may make different provision for different cases or classes of case or in respect of different areas."

103.—(1) Section 54 of that Act (power to give fixed penalty notices on the spot or at a police station exercisable only if offender would not if convicted be liable to disqualification under section 35) shall be amended as follows.

(2) In subsection (1), after the word "where", there shall be inserted the words "in England and Wales".

(3) After subsection (9) there shall be added—

"(10) In determining for the purposes of subsections (3)(b) and (5)(a) above whether a person convicted of an offence would be liable to disqualification under section 35, it shall be assumed, in the case of an offence in relation to which a range of numbers is shown in the last column of Part I of Schedule 2 to this Act, that the number of penalty points to be attributed to the offence would be the lowest in the range."

104. In section 61 of that Act (fixed penalty notice mistakenly given) after subsection (5) there shall be added—

"(6) In determining for the purposes of subsection (1) above whether a person convicted of an offence would be liable to disqualification under section 35, it shall be assumed, in the case of an offence in relation to which a range of numbers is shown in the last column of Part I of Schedule 2 to this Act, that the number of penalty points to be attributed to the offence would be the lowest in the range."

105. In section 69(4) of that Act (references to fixed penalty clerk) after the words "of this Act" there shall be inserted the words "(except in sections 75 to 77)".

106. At the end of section 86(1) of that Act (functions of traffic wardens) there shall be added the words "unless that offence was committed while the vehicle concerned was stationary."

107.—(1) Section 89 of that Act (interpretation), shall be amended as follows.

(2) After the definition of "authorised person" there shall be inserted—
" 'chief constable' means, in Scotland in relation to any conditional offer, the chief constable for the area in which the conditional offer has been issued."

(3) In the definition of "chief officer of police" for the words "or notice to owner" there shall be substituted the words ", notice to owner or conditional offer".

108. In section 90 of that Act (index to Part III)—
(a) in the entry relating to the expression "Conditional offer", for the words "Section 75(4)" there shall be substituted the words "Section 75(3)"; and
(b) at the end of the entry relating to the expression "Fixed penalty clerk" there shall be added the words "and 75(4)".

109. In section 92 of that Act (persons in public service of Crown) after "16" there shall be inserted "20".

110. In section 93(2) of that Act (persons subject to service discipline) for "4" there shall be substituted "3A".

111.—(1) In subsection (1) of section 98 of that Act (interpretation), in paragraph (b) of the definition of "road", for the words "has the same meaning as in the Roads (Scotland) Act 1984" there shall be substituted the words "means any road within the meaning of the Roads (Scotland) Act 1984 and any other way to which the public has access, and includes bridges over which a road passes,".

(2) At the end of subsection (2) of that section there shall be added the word "Act".

112.—(1) Schedule 3 to the Road Traffic Offenders Act 1988 (fixed penalty offences) shall be amended as follows.

(2) After the entry relating to section 36 of the Road Traffic Act 1988 there shall be inserted—

"RTA section 40A	Using vehicle in dangerous condition etc.
RTA section 41A	Breach of requirement as to brakes, steering-gear or tyres.
RTA section 41B	Breach of requirement as to weight: goods and passenger vehicles."

(3) In the entry relating to section 42 of the Road Traffic Act 1988, for the words in column 2 there shall be substituted the words "Breach of other construction and use requirements".

(4) In the entry relating to section 87(1) of the Road Traffic Act 1988, in column 2 for the word "without" there shall be substituted the words "otherwise than in accordance with".

113. In Schedule 5 to the Road Traffic Offenders Act 1988 (conditional offer of fixed penalty in relation to certain offences in Scotland), in the entry relating to section 87(2) of the Road Traffic Act 1988, in column (2) for the word "without" there shall be substituted the words "otherwise than in accordance with".

The Road Traffic (Consequential Provisions) Act 1988 (c. 54)

114. In section 8(3) of the Road Traffic (Consequential Provisions) Act 1988 (commencement) for the words from the beginning to the end of paragraph (c) there shall be substituted the words "Paragraph 15 to 20 of Schedule 2 to this Act".

SCHEDULE 5 **Section 52**

THE TRAFFIC DIRECTOR FOR LONDON

Status

B17–17   1. The Traffic Director for London shall be a corporation sole.

2. The Director shall not be regarded as the servant or agent of the Crown or as enjoying any status, immunity or privilege of the Crown; and the Director's property shall not be regarded as property of, or held on behalf of, the Crown.

Tenure of office

3.—(1) Subject to the following provisions of this paragraph, the Director shall hold and vacate office in accordance with the terms of his appointment.

(2) The Director shall be appointed for a term not exceeding five years.

(3) At the end of a term of appointment the Director shall be eligible for re-appointment.

(4) The Director may at any time resign his office by notice in writing addressed to the Secretary of State.

(5) The Secretary of State may remove the Director from office—

    (a) if a bankruptcy order has been made against him, or his estate has been sequestrated or he has made a composition or arrangement with, or granted a trust deed for, his creditors; or

    (b) if satisfied that he is otherwise unable or unfit to discharge his functions.

(6) The Director's terms of appointment may provide for his removal from office (without assigning cause) on notice from the Secretary of State of such length as may be specified in those terms, subject, if those terms so provide, to compensation of such amount as the Secretary of State may, with the approval of the Treasury, determine.

Remuneration etc.

4.—(1) There shall be paid to the Director such remuneration and such travelling and other allowances as the Secretary of State may determine.

(2) In the case of any such holder of the office of Director as may be determined by the Secretary of State, there shall be paid such pension, allowances or gratuities to or in respect of him, or such payments towards the provision of a pension, allowances or gratuities to or in respect of him, as may be so determined.

(3) If the Secretary of State determines that there are special circumstances which make it right that a person ceasing to hold office as Director should receive compensation, there may be paid to him a sum by way of compensation of such amount as the Secretary of State may determine.

(4) Sub-paragraph (3) above does not apply in the case of a person who receives compensation by virtue of paragraph 3(6) above.

(5) The approval of the Treasury shall be required for the making of a determination under this paragraph.

Staff

5.—(1) The Director shall act only with the approval of the Secretary of State, given with the approval of the Treasury, in determining—

    (a) the number of persons to be employed by him;

(b) the remuneration, allowances and gratuities to be paid to or in respect of such persons; and

(c) any other terms and conditions of their service.

(2) Anything authorised or required by or under any enactment to be done by the Director may be done by any person employed by him who has been authorised by the Director, whether generally or specially, for that purpose.

(3) Employment by the Director shall be included among the kinds of employment to which a scheme under section 1 of the Superannuation Act 1972 may apply; and, accordingly, in Schedule 1 to that Act (in which those kinds of employment are listed) at the end of the list of "Other Bodies" there shall be inserted—

"Employment by the Traffic Director for London."

(4) The Director shall pay to the Treasury, at such times as the Treasury may direct, such sums as the Treasury may determine in respect of the increase in the sums payable out of money provided by Parliament under that Act attributable to sub-paragraph (3) above.

(5) Where an employee of the Director who is (by reference to that employment) a participant in a scheme under section 1 of that Act, becomes a holder of the office of Director, the Treasury may determine that his term of office shall be treated for the purposes of the scheme as employment by the Director (whether or not any benefits are payable to or in respect of him by virtue of paragraph 4(2) above).

Financial provisions

6. The remuneration of the Director and any other payments made under paragraph 3(6) or 4 above to or in respect of him shall be paid out of grants made by the Secretary of State under section 80(2) of this Act.

Accounts

7.—(1) The Director shall keep accounts and shall prepare a statement of accounts in respect of each financial year.

(2) The accounts shall be kept, and the statement shall be prepared, in such form as the Secretary of State may, with the approval of the Treasury, direct.

(3) The accounts shall be audited by persons appointed in respect of each financial year by the Secretary of State.

(4) No person shall be qualified to be appointed as auditor under this paragraph unless he is—

(a) a member of a body of accountants established in the United Kingdom and for the time being recognised for the purposes of Part II of the Companies Act 1989; or

(b) a member of the Chartered Institute of Public Finance and Accountancy;

but a firm may be appointed as auditor under this paragraph if each of its members is qualified to be so appointed.

(5) In this paragraph, and in paragraph 8 below, "financial year" means—

(a) the period beginning with the day on which the first person to hold the office of Director takes office and ending with the following 31st March; and

(b) each subsequent period of twelve months ending with 31st March.

Annual report etc.

8.—(1) As soon as possible after the end of each financial year, the Director shall submit to the Secretary of State an annual report on the discharge in that year of his functions.

(2) Each report shall contain a copy of the statement of accounts prepared and audited under paragraph 7 above in respect of that financial year.

(3) The Secretary of State shall lay a copy of the Director's annual report before each House of Parliament.

(4) The Director shall provide the Secretary of State with such information relating to his property and the discharge and proposed discharge of his functions as the Secretary of State may require; and for that purpose shall—

  (a) permit any person authorised in that behalf by the Secretary of State to make copies of any accounts or other documents; and
  (b) give such explanation as may be required of any such accounts or documents.

Evidence

9. A document purporting to be duly executed under the seal of the Director or to be signed on the Director's behalf shall be received in evidence and, unless the contrary is proved, be deemed to be so executed or signed.

Public records

10. In Schedule 1 to the Public Records Act 1958, in Part II of the Table in paragraph 3 the following entry shall be inserted at the appropriate place—
    "Traffic Director for London".

The Parliamentary Commissioner

11. In the Parliamentary Commissioner Act 1967, in Schedule 2 (departments and authorities subject to investigation), the following entry shall be inserted at the appropriate place—
    "Traffic Director for London."

Parliamentary disqualification

12.—(1) In the House of Commons Disqualification Act 1975, in Part III of Schedule 1 (other disqualifying offices), the following entry shall be inserted at the appropriate place—
    "Traffic Director for London."

(2) The same entry shall be inserted at the appropriate place in Part III of Schedule 1 to the Northern Ireland Assembly Disqualification Act 1975.

SCHEDULE 6   **Section 66(7)**

Parking Penalties

The notice to owner

1.—(1) Where—
  (a) a penalty charge notice has been issued with respect to a vehicle under section 66 of this Act; and
  (b) the period of 28 days for payment of the penalty charge has expired without that charge being paid,
the London authority concerned may serve a notice ("a notice to owner") on the person who appears to them to have been the owner of the vehicle when the alleged contravention occurred.

(2) A notice to owner must state—
  (a) the amount of the penalty charge payable;
  (b) the grounds on which the parking attendant who issued the penalty charge notice believed that a penalty charge was payable with respect to the vehicle;
  (c) that the penalty charge must be paid before the end of the period of 28 days beginning with the date on which the notice to owner is served;
  (d) that failure to pay the penalty charge may lead to an increased charge being payable;
  (e) the amount of that increased charge;
  (f) that the person on whom the notice is served ("the recipient") may be entitled to make representations under paragraph 2 below; and
  (g) the effect of paragraph 5 below.

(3) The Secretary of State may prescribe additional matters which must be dealt with in any notice to owner.

Representations against notice to owner

2.—(1) Where it appears to the recipient that one or other of the grounds mentioned in sub-paragraph (4) below are satisfied, he may make representations to that effect to the London authority who served the notice on him.

(2) Any representations under this paragraph must be made in such form as may be specified by the London authorities, acting through the Joint Committee.

(3) The authority may disregard any such representations which are received by them after the end of the period of 28 days beginning with the date on which the notice to owner was served.

(4) The grounds are—
  (a) that the recipient—
    (i) never was the owner of the vehicle in question;
    (ii) had ceased to be its owner before the date on which the alleged contravention occurred; or
    (iii) became its owner after that date;
  (b) that the alleged contravention did not occur;
  (c) that the vehicle had been permitted to remain at rest in the parking place by a person who was in control of the vehicle without the consent of the owner;
  (d) that the relevant designation order is invalid;
  (e) that the recipient is a vehicle-hire firm and—
    (i) the vehicle in question was at the material time hired from that firm under a vehicle hiring agreement; and
    (ii) the person hiring it had signed a statement of liability acknowledging his liability in respect of any penalty charge notice fixed to the vehicle during the currency of the hiring agreement;
  (f) that the penalty charge exceeded the amount applicable in the circumstances of the case.

(5) Where the ground mentioned in sub-paragraph (4)(a)(ii) above is relied on in any representations made under this paragraph, those representations must include a statement of the name and address of the person to whom the vehicle was disposed of by the person making the representations (if that information is in his possession).

(6) Where the ground mentioned in sub-paragraph (4)(a)(iii) above is relied on in any representations made under this paragraph, those representations must include a statement of the name and address of the person from whom the vehicle was acquired by the person making the representations (if that information is in his possession).

(7) It shall be the duty of an authority to whom representations are duly made under this paragraph—
  (a) to consider them and any supporting evidence which the person making them provides; and
  (b) to serve on that person notice of their decision as to whether they accept that the ground in question has been established.

Cancellation of notice to owner

3.—(1) Where representations are made under paragraph 2 above and the London authority concerned accept that the ground in question has been established they shall—
  (a) cancel the notice to owner; and
  (b) state in the notice served under paragraph 2(7) above that the notice to owner has been cancelled.

(2) The cancellation of a notice to owner under this paragraph shall not be taken to prevent the London authority concerned serving a fresh notice to owner on another person.

(3) Where the ground that is accepted is that mentioned in paragraph 2(4)(e) above, the person hiring the vehicle shall be deemed to be its owner for the purposes of this Schedule.

Rejection of representations against notice to owner

4. Where any representations are made under paragraph 2 above but the London authority concerned do not accept that a ground has been established, the notice served under paragraph 2(7) above ("the notice of rejection") must—
  (a) state that a charge certificate may be served under paragraph 6 below unless before the end of the period of 28 days beginning with the date of service of the notice of rejection—
    (i) the penalty charge is paid; or
    (ii) the person on whom the notice is served appeals to a parking adjudicator against the penalty charge;
  (b) indicate the nature of a parking adjudicator's power to award costs against any person appealing to him; and
  (c) describe in general terms the form and manner in which an appeal to a parking adjudicator must be made,
and may contain such other information as the authority consider appropriate.

Adjudication by parking adjudicator

5.—(1) Where an authority serve notice under sub-paragraph (7) of paragraph 2 above, that they do not accept that a ground on which representations were made under that paragraph has been established, the person making those representations may, before—
  (a) the end of the period of 28 days beginning with the date of service of that notice; or
  (b) such longer period as a parking adjudicator may allow,
appeal to a parking adjudicator against the authority's decision.

(2) On an appeal under this paragraph, the parking adjudicator shall consider the representations in question and any additional representations which are made by the appellant on any of the grounds mentioned in paragraph 2(4) above and may give the London authority concerned such directions as he considers appropriate.

(3) It shall be the duty of any authority to whom a direction is given under sub-paragraph (2) above to comply with it forthwith.

Charge certificates

6.—(1) Where a notice to owner is served on any person and the penalty charge to which it relates is not paid before the end of the relevant period, the authority serving the notice may serve on that person a statement (a "charge certificate") to the effect that the penalty charge in question is increased by 50 per cent.

(2) The relevant period, in relation to a notice to owner, is the period of 28 days beginning—

   (a) where no representations are made under paragraph 2 above, with the date on which the notice to owner is served;

   (b) where—

      (i) such representations are made;

      (ii) a notice of rejection is served by the authority concerned; and

      (iii) no appeal against the notice of rejection is made,

     with the date on which the notice of rejection is served; or

   (c) where there has been an unsuccessful appeal against a notice of rejection, with the date on which notice of the adjudicator's decision is served on the appellant.

(3) Where an appeal against a notice of rejection is made but is withdrawn before the adjudicator gives notice of his decision, the relevant period in relation to a notice to owner is the period of 14 days beginning with the date on which the appeal is withdrawn.

Enforcement of charge certificate

7. Where a charge certificate has been served on any person and the increased penalty charge provided for in the certificate is not paid before the end of the period of 14 days beginning with the date on which the certificate is served, the authority concerned may, if a county court so orders, recover the increased charge as if it were payable under a county court order.

Invalid notices

8.—(1) This paragraph applies where—

   (a) a county court makes an order under paragraph 7 above;

   (b) the person against whom it is made makes a statutory declaration complying with sub-paragraph (2) below; and

   (c) that declaration is, before the end of the period of 21 days beginning with the date on which notice of the county court's order is served on him, served on the county court which made the order.

(2) The statutory declaration must state that the person making it—

   (a) did not receive the notice to owner in question;

   (b) made representations to the London authority concerned under paragraph 2 above but did not receive a rejection notice from that authority; or

   (c) appealed to a parking adjudicator under paragraph 5 above against the rejection by that authority of representations made by him under paragraph 2 above but had no response to the appeal.

(3) Sub-paragraph (4) below applies where it appears to a district judge, on the application of a person on whom a charge certificate has been served, that it would be unreasonable in the circumstances of his case to insist on him serv-

ing his statutory declaration within the period of 21 days allowed for by sub-paragraph (1) above.

(4) Where this sub-paragraph applies, the district judge may allow such longer period for service of the statutory declaration as he considers appropriate.

(5) Where a statutory declaration is served under sub-paragraph (1)(c) above—

(a) the order of the court shall be deemed to have been revoked;
(b) the charge certificate shall be deemed to have been cancelled;
(c) in the case of a declaration under sub-paragraph (2)(a) above, the notice to owner to which the charge certificate relates shall be deemed to have been cancelled; and
(d) the district judge shall serve written notice of the effect of service of the declaration on the person making it and on the London authority concerned.

(6) Service of a declaration under sub-paragraph (2)(a) above shall not prevent the London authority serving a fresh notice to owner.

(7) Where a declaration has been served under sub-paragraph (2)(b) or (c) above, the London authority shall refer the case to the parking adjudicator who may give such direction as he considers appropriate.

Offence of giving false information

9.—(1) A person who, in response to a notice to owner served under this Schedule, makes any representation under paragraph 2 or 5(2) above which is false in a material particular and does so recklessly or knowing it to be false in that particular is guilty of an offence.

(2) Any person guilty of such an offence shall be liable on summary conviction to a fine not exceeding level 5 on the standard scale.

Service by post

10. Any charge certificate, or notice under this Schedule—

(a) may be served by post; and
(b) where the person on whom it is to be served is a body corporate, is duly served if it is sent by post to the secretary or clerk of that body.

SCHEDULE 7   **Section 81**

MINOR AND CONSEQUENTIAL AMENDMENTS IN RELATION TO LONDON

The Tribunals and Inquiries Act 1971 (c. 62)

B17–19   1. […]

The Greater London Council (General Powers) Act 1974 (c. xxiv)

2. In section 15 of the Greater London Council (General Powers) Act 1974 (parking on footways etc.) in subsection (12)(b) for the words "under section 84" there shall be substituted the words "made by virtue of section 84(1)(a)".

The Road Traffic Regulation Act 1984 (c. 27)

3. In section 7 of the Road Traffic Regulation Act 1984 (provisions supplementary to section 6), in subsection (6) for the words "Secretary of State for the Home Department" there shall be substituted the words "the Com-

missioner of Police for any police area in which is situated any road or part of a road to which the order is to relate".

4. In that Act, after section 13 there shall be inserted—

"Temporary suspension

Temporary suspension of provisions under s.6 or 9 orders

13A.—(1) The Commissioner of Police of the Metropolis or the Commissioner of Police for the City of London may temporarily suspend the operation of any provision of an order made under section 6 or 9 of this Act so far as that provision relates to any road or part of a road in Greater London which is within his area, in order to prevent or mitigate congestion or obstruction of traffic, or danger to or from traffic in consequence of extraordinary circumstances.

(2) Subject to subsection (3) below, the period of suspension under subsection (1) above shall not continue for more than 7 days.

(3) If the Secretary of State gives his consent to the period of suspension being continued for more than 7 days, the suspension shall continue until the end of such period as may be specified by the Secretary of State in giving his consent."

5.—(1) Section 55 of that Act (financial provisions relating to designation orders) shall be amended as follows.

(2) In subsection (1), for the words from "designated" to the end there shall be substituted the words "for which they are the local authority and which are—

    (a) in the case of the council of a London borough and the Common Council of the City of London, parking places on the highway; and

    (b) in the case of any other authority, designated parking places."

(3) After subsection (3) there shall be inserted—

"(3A) The council of each London borough and the Common Council of the City of London shall, after each financial year, report to the Secretary of State on any action taken by them, pursuant to subsection (2) or (3) above, in respect of any deficit or surplus in their account for the year.

(3B) The report under subsection (3A) above shall be made as soon after the end of the financial year to which it relates as is reasonably possible."

(4) In subsection (4)(c), the words from "to the council" to "City of London" shall be omitted.

6.—(1) Section 105 of that Act (exemptions from provisions relating to immobilisation of vehicles) shall be amended as follows.

(2) In subsection (2) after the words "of any vehicle" there shall be inserted the words "found otherwise than in Greater London".

(3) After subsection (2) there shall be inserted—

"(2A) The exemption under subsection (1)(b) above shall not apply in the case of any vehicle found in Greater London if the meter bay in which it was found was not authorised for use as such at the time when it was left there."

(4) In subsection (3) for the words "subsection (2)(a)" there shall be substituted the words "subsections (2)(a) and (2A)".

7. In section 122 of that Act (exercise of functions by local authorities) there shall be added at the end—

"(3) The duty imposed by subsection (1) above is subject to the provisions of Part II of the Road Traffic Act 1991."

The Local Government Act 1985 (c. 51)

8.—(1) For paragraph 5 of Schedule 5 to the Local Government Act 1985 (designation of routes in London) there shall be substituted—

"5.—(1) For the purpose of facilitating the movement of traffic in Greater London, the Secretary of State may by order designate a road in that area.

(2) Before doing so, he shall consult—

    (a) the council of the London borough in which the road is;

    (b) the council of any other London borough or of any county where there is a road which he considers is likely to be affected by the designation; and

    (c) such other persons (if any) as he considers it appropriate to consult.

(3) No council of a London borough shall exercise any power under the Highways Act 1980 or the Road Traffic Regulation Act 1984 in a way which will affect, or be likely to affect, a designated road unless the requirements of sub-paragraph (4) below have been satisfied.

(4) The requirements are that—

    (a) the council concerned has given notice to the Director, in such manner as he may require, of its proposal to exercise the power in the way in question; and

    (b) either—

      (i) the Director has approved the proposal; or

      (ii) the period of one month beginning with the date on which he received notice of the proposal has expired without his having objected to it.

(5) The Secretary of State may by an instrument in writing exclude any power from the application of this paragraph to the extent specified in the instrument.

(6) Any such instrument may, in particular, exclude a power as respects—

    (a) all or any of the London boroughs;

    (b) all or any of the designated roads; or

    (c) the exercise of the power in such manner or circumstances as may be specified in the instrument.

(7) This paragraph does not apply to the exercise of a power under section 14 or sections 32 to 38 of the 1984 Act in relation to a road which is not a designated road.

(8) If the council of a London borough exercises any power in contravention of this paragraph, the Director may take such steps as he considers appropriate to reverse or modify the effect of the exercise of that power.

(9) Any reasonable expenses incurred by the Director in taking any steps under sub-paragraph (8) shall be recoverable by him from the council as a civil debt.

(10) In this paragraph—

'designated road' means a road designated under this paragraph; and 'Director' means the Traffic Director for London."

9.—(1) Paragraph 6 of that Schedule (guidance as to exercise of traffic powers) shall be amended as follows.

(2) In sub-paragraph (5) for the words "summarily as a civil debt" there shall be substituted the words "as a debt due to the Crown".

(3) After sub-paragraph (6), there shall be inserted—

"(7) Sub-paragraphs (3) to (6) above shall not apply in relation to the exercise of any power, by the council of a London borough, in complying with the duty imposed on them by section 57(1) of the Road Traffic Act 1991 (implementation of local plans)."

10. In paragraph 10(6) of that Schedule (recovery of sums expended by the Secretary of State in connection with traffic control systems) for the words "summarily as a civil debt" there shall be substituted the words "as a debt due to the Crown".

11. In paragraph 11 of that Schedule (recovery of sums expended by the Secretary of State to obtain information) for the words "summarily as a civil debt" there shall be substituted the words "as a debt due to the Crown".

The New Roads and Street Works Act 1991 (c. 22)

12. In section 64 of the New Roads and Street Works Act 1991 (traffic-sensitive streets), after subsection (3) there shall be added—

"(4) Where any council of a London borough or the Common Council of the City of London are asked by the Traffic Director for London to designate a street as a traffic-sensitive street and they decline to do so, the Director may appeal to the Secretary of State who may direct that the street be designated."

CRIMINAL JUSTICE ACT 1991

(1991 c. 53)

Custodial sentences

1.—(1) This section applies where a person is convicted of an offence pun-   **B18–01**
ishable with a custodial sentence other than one fixed by law.

(2) Subject to subsection (3) below, the court shall not pass a custodial sentence on the offender unless it is of the opinion—

(a) that the offence, or the combination of the offence and one or more offences associated with it, was so serious that only such a sentence can be justified for the offence; or

(b) where the offence is a violent or sexual offence, that only such a sentence would be adequate to protect the public from serious harm from him.

(3) Nothing in subsection (2) above shall prevent the court from passing a custodial sentence on the offender if he refuses to give his consent to a community sentence which is proposed by the court and requires that consent.

(4) Where a court passes a custodial sentence, it shall be its duty—

(a) in a case not falling within subsection (3) above, to state in open court that it is of the opinion that either or both of paragraphs (a) and (b) of subsection (2) above apply and why it is of that opinion; and

(b) in any case, to explain to the offender in open court and in ordinary language why it is passing a custodial sentence on him.

(5) A magistrates' court shall cause a reason stated by it under subsection (4) above to be specified in the warrant of commitment and to be entered in the register.

2.—(1) This section applies where a court passes a custodial sentence other   **B18–02**
than one fixed by law.

(2) The custodial sentence shall be—

    (a) For such a term (not exceeding the permitted maximum) as in the opinion of the court is commensurate with the seriousness of the offence, or the combination of the offence and one or more offences associated with it; or

    (b) where the offence is a violent or sexual offence, for such longer term (not exceeding that maximum) as in the opinion of the court is necessary to protect the public from serious harm from the offender.

(3) Where the court passes a custodial sentence for a term longer than is commensurate with the seriousness of the offence, or the combination of the offence and one or more offences associated with it, the court shall—

    (a) state in open court that it is of the opinion that subsection (2)(b) above applies and why it is of that opinion; and

    (b) explain to the offender in open court and in ordinary language why the sentence is for such a term.

(4) A custodial sentence for an indeterminate period shall be regarded for the purposes of subsections (2) and (3) above as a custodial sentence for a term longer than any actual term.

B18–03   3.—(1) Subject to subsection (2) below, a court shall obtain and consider a pre-sentence report before forming any such opinion as is mentioned in subsection (2) of section 1 or 2 above.

(2) Subsection (1) above does not apply if, in the circumstances of the case, the court is of the opinion that it is unnecessary to obtain a pre-sentence report.

(2A) In the case of an offender under the age of eighteen years, save where the offence or any other offence associated with it is triable only on indictment, the court shall not form such an opinion as is mentioned in subsection (2) above or subsection (4A) below unless there exists a previous pre-sentence report obtained in respect of the offender and the court has had regard to the information contained in that report, or, if there is more than one such report, the most recent report.

(3) In forming any such opinion as is mentioned in subsection (2) of section 1 or 2 above a court—

    (a) shall take into account all such information about the circumstances of the offence or (as the case may be) of the offence and the offence or offences associated with it (including any aggravating or mitigating factors) as is available to it; and

    (b) in the case of any such opinion as is mentioned in paragraph (b) of that subsection, may take into account any information about the offender which is before it.

(4) No custodial sentence shall be invalidated by the failure of a court to obtain and consider a pre-sentence report before forming an opinion referred to in subsection (1) above but any court on an appeal against such a sentence—

    (a) shall, subject to subsection (4A) below, obtain a pre-sentence report if none was obtained by the court below; and

    (b) shall consider any report obtained by it or by that court.

(5) In this part "pre-sentence report" means a report in writing which—

    (a) with a view to assisting the court in determining the most suitable method of dealing with an offender, is made or submitted by a probation officer or by a social worker of a local authority social services department; and

(b) contains information as to such matters, presented in such manner, as may be prescribed by rules made by the Secretary of State.

4.—(1) Subject to subsection (2) below, in a any case where section 3(1)   **B18–04**
above applies and the offender is or appears to be mentally disordered, the court shall obtain and consider a medical report before passing a custodial sentence other than one fixed by law.

(2) Subsection (1) above does not apply if, in the circumstances of the case, the court is of the opinion that it is unnecessary to obtain a medical report.

(3) Before passing a custodial sentence other than one fixed by law on an offender who is or appears to be mentally disordered, a court shall consider—
    (a) any information before it which relates to his mental condition (whether given in a medical report, a pre-sentence report or otherwise); and
    (b) the likely effect of such a sentence on that condition and on any treatment which may be available for it.

(4) No custodial sentence which is passed in a case to which subsection (1) above applies shall be invalidated by the failure of a court to comply with that subsection, but any court on an appeal against such a sentence—
    (a) shall obtain a medical report if none was obtained by the court below; and
    (b) shall consider any such report obtained by it or by that court.

(5) In this section—
    "duly approved", in relation to a registered medical practitioner, means approved for the purposes of section 12 of the Mental Health Act 1983 ("the 1983 Act") by the Secretary of State as having special experience in the diagnosis or treatment of mental disorder;
    "medical report" means a report as to an offender's mental condition made or submitted orally or in writing by a registered medical practitioner who is duly approved.

(6) Nothing in this section shall be taken as prejudicing the generality of section 3 above.

5.—(1) For subsection (2) of section 22 (suspended sentences of imprison-   **B18–05**
ment) of the Powers of Criminal Courts Act 1973 ("the 1973 Act") there shall be substituted the following subsections—

    "(2) A court shall not deal with an offender by means of a suspended sentence unless it is of the opinion—
        (a) that the case is one in which a sentence of imprisonment would have been appropriate even without the power to suspend the sentence; and
        (b) that the exercise of that power can be justified by the exceptional circumstances of the case.

    (2A) A court which passes a suspended sentence on any person for an offence shall consider whether the circumstances of the case are such as to warrant in addition the imposition of a fine or the making of a compensation order."

(2) The following shall cease to have effect, namely—
    (a) sections 28 and 29 of the 1973 Act (extended sentences of imprisonment for persistent offenders); and
    (b) section 47 of the Criminal Law Act 1977 (sentence of imprisonment partly served and partly suspended).

Community sentences

B18–06   6.—(1) A court shall not pass on an offender a community sentence, that is to say, a sentence which consists of or includes one or more community orders, unless it is of the opinion that the offence, or the combination of the offence and one or more offences associated with it, was serious enough to warrant such a sentence.

(2) Subject to subsection (3) below, where a court passes a community sentence—

   (a) the particular order or orders comprising or forming part of the sentence shall be such as in the opinion of the court is, or taken together are, the most suitable for the offender; and

   (b) the restrictions on liberty imposed by the order or orders shall be such as in the opinion of the court are commensurate with the seriousness of the offence, or the combination of the offence and one or more offences associated with it.

(3) In consequence of the provision made by section 11 below with respect to combination orders, a community sentence shall not consist of or include both a probation order and a community service order.

(4) In this Part "community order" means any of the following orders, namely—

   (a) a probation order;

   (b) a community service order;

   (c) a combination order;

   (d) a curfew order;

   (e) a supervision order; and

   (f) an attendance centre order.

B18–07   7.—(1) In forming any such opinion as is mentioned in subsection (1) or 2(b) of section 6 above, a court shall take into account all such information about the circumstances of the offence or (as the case may be) of the offence and the offence or offences associated with it (including any aggravating or mitigating factors) as is available to it.

(2) In forming any such opinion as is mentioned in subsection (2)(a) of that section, a court may take into account any information about the offender which is before it.

(3) Subject to subsection (3A) below a court shall obtain and consider a pre-sentence report before forming an opinion as to the suitability for the offender of one or more of the following orders, namely—

   (a) a probation order which includes additional requirements authorised by Schedule 1A to the 1973 Act;

   (b) a community service order;

   (c) a combination order; and

   (d) a supervision order which includes requirements imposed under section 12, 12A, 12AA, 12B or 12C of the Children and Young Persons Act 1969 ("the 1969 Act").

(3A) Subsection (3) above does not apply if, in the circumstances of the case, the court is of the opinion that it is unnecessary to obtain a pre-sentence report.

(3B) In the case of an offender under the age of eighteen years, save where the offence or any other offence associated with it is triable only on indictment, the court shall not form such an opinion as is mentioned in subsection (3A) above or subsection (5) below unless there exists a previous pre-sentence report obtained in respect of the offender and the court has had regard to the information contained in that report, or, if there is more than one such report, the most recent report.

(4) No community sentence which consists of or includes such an order as is mentioned in subsection (3) above shall be invalidated by the failure of a court to obtain and consider a pre-sentence report before forming an opinion referred to in that subsection, but any court an appeal against such a sentence—

(a) shall, subject to subsection (5) below obtain a pre-sentence report if none was obtained by the court below; and

(b) shall consider any such report obtained by it or by that court.

(5) Subsection (4)(a) above does not apply if the court is of the opinion—

(a) that the court below was justified in forming an opinion that it was unnecessary to obtain a pre-sentence report; or

(b) that, although the court below was not justified in forming that opinion, in the circumstances of the case at the time it is before the court, it is unnecessary to obtain a pre-sentence report.

Probation and community service orders

8.—(1) For section 2 of the 1973 Act there shall be substituted the following section—   **B18–08**

"Probation

2.—(1) where a court by or before which a person of or over the age of sixteen years is convicted of an offence (not being an offence for which the sentence is fixed by law) is of the opinion that the supervision of the offender by a probation officer is desirable in the interests of—

(a) securing the rehabilitation of the offender; or

(b) protecting the public from harm from him or preventing the commission by him of further offences,

the court may make a probation order, that is to say, an order requiring him to be under the supervision of a probation officer for a period of not less than six months nor more than three years.

For the purposes of this subsection the age of a person shall be deemed to be that which it appears to the court to be after considering any available evidence.

(2) A probation order shall specify the petty sessions area in which the offender resides or will reside; and the offender shall, subject to paragraph 12 of Schedule 2 to the Criminal Justice Act 1991 (offenders who change their residence), be required to be under the supervision of a probation officer appointed for or assigned to that area.

(3) Before making a probation order, the court shall explain to the offender in ordinary language—

(a) the effect of the order (including any additional requirements proposed to be included in the order in accordance with section 3 below);

(b) the consequences which may follow under Schedule 2 to the Criminal Justice Act 1991 if he fails to comply with any of the requirements of the order; and

(c) that the court has under that Schedule power to review the order on the application either of the offender or of the supervising officer,

and the court shall not make the order unless he expresses his willingness to comply with its requirements.

(4) The court by which a probation order is made shall forthwith give copies of the order to a probation officer assigned to the court, and he shall give a copy—

(a) to the offender;

(b) to the probation officer responsible for the offender's supervision; and

(c) to the person in charge of any institution in which the offender is required by the order to reside.

(5) The court by which such an order is made shall also, except where it itself acts for the petty sessions area specified in the order, send to the clerk to the justices for that area—

(a) a copy of the order; and

(b) such documents and information relating to the case as it considers likely to be of assistance to a court acting for that area in the exercise of its functions in relation to the order.

(6) An offender in respect of whom a probation order is made shall keep in touch with the probation officer responsible for his supervision in accordance with such instructions as he may from time to time be given by that officer and shall notify him of any change of address.

(7) The Secretary of State may by order direct that subsection (1) above shall be amended by substituting, for the minimum or maximum period specified in that subsection as originally enacted or as previously amended under this subsection, such period as may be specified in the order.

(8) An order under subsection (7) above may make in paragraph 13(2)(a)(i) of Schedule 2 to the Criminal Justice Act 1991 any amendment which the Secretary of State thinks necessary in consequence of any substitution made by the order."

(2) Section 13 of that Act (effect of probation and discharge) shall cease to have effect so far as relating to offenders placed on probation.

(3) For the purpose of rearranging Part I of that Act in consequence of the amendments made by subsections (1) and (2) above, that Part shall have effect subject to the following amendments, namely—

(a) after section 1 there shall be inserted as sections 1A to 1C the provisions set out in Part I of Schedule 1 to this Act;

(b) sections 7 and 9 (which are re-enacted with minor modifications by sections 1A and 1B) shall cease to have effect;

(c) sections 8 and 13 (which, so far as relating to discharged offenders, are re-enacted with minor modifications by sections 1B and 1C) shall cease to have effect so far as so relating; and

(d) immediately before section 11 there shall be inserted the following cross heading—

"Probation and discharge"

B18–09   9.—(1) For sections 3 to 4B of the 1973 Act there shall be substituted the following section—

3.—(1) Subject to subsection (2) below, a probation order may in addition require the offender to comply during the whole or any part of the probation period with such requirements as the court, having regard to the circumstances of the case, considers desirable in the interests of—

(a) securing the rehabilitation of the offender; or

(b) protecting the public from harm from him or preventing the commission by him of further offences.

(2) Without prejudice to the power of the court under section 35 of this Act to make a compensation order, the payment of sums by way of damages for injury or compensation for loss shall not be included among the additional requirements of a probation order.

(3) Without prejudice to the generality of subsection (1) above, the additional requirements which may be included in a probation order shall include the requirements which are authorised by Schedule 1A to this Act."

(2) After Schedule 1 to that Act there shall be inserted as Schedule 1A the provisions set out in Part II of Schedule 1 to this Act.

10.—(1) In subsection (1) of section 14 of the 1973 Act (community service orders in respect of offenders), the words "instead of dealing with him in any other way" shall cease to have effect. **B18–10**

(2) In subsection (1A) of that section, for paragraph (b) there shall be substituted the following paragraph—
"(b) not more than 240·"

(3) For subsections (2) and (2A) of that section there shall be substituted the following subsections—

"(2) A court shall not make a community service order in respect of any offender unless the offender consents and the court, after hearing (if the court thinks it necessary) a probation officer or social worker of a local authority social services department, is satisfied that the offender is a suitable person to perform work under such an order.

(2A) Subject to paragraphs 3 and 4 of Schedule 3 to the Criminal Justice Act 1991 (reciprocal enforcement of certain orders) a court shall not make a community service order in respect of an offender unless it is satisfied that provision for him to perform work under such an order can be made under the arrangements for persons to perform work under such orders which exist in the petty sessions area in which he resides or will reside."

(4) In section 15(1) of that Act (obligations of persons subject to community service orders), for paragraph (a) there shall be substituted the following paragraph—
"(a) keep in touch with the relevant officer in accordance with such instructions as he may from time to time be given by that officer and notify him of any change of address;".

11.—(1) Where a court by or before which a person of or over the age of sixteen years is convicted of an offence punishable with imprisonment (not being an offence for which the sentence is fixed by law) is of the opinion mentioned in subsection (2) below, the court may make a combination order, that is to say, an order requiring him both— **B18–11**
(a) to be under the supervision of a probation officer for a period specified in the order, being not less than twelve months nor more than three years; and
(b) to perform unpaid work for a number of hours so specified, being in the aggregate not less than 40 nor more than 100.
The opinion referred to in subsection (1) above is that the making of a combination order is desirable in the interests of—
(a) securing the rehabilitation of the offender; or

(b) protecting the public from harm from him or preventing the commission by him of further offences.

(3) Subject to subsection (1) above, part I of the 1973 Act shall apply in relation to combination orders—

    (a) in so far as they impose such a requirement as is mentioned in paragraph (a) of that subsection, as if they were probation orders; and

    (b) in so far as they impose such a requirement as is mentioned in paragraph (b) of that subsection, as if they were community service orders.

Curfew orders

B18–12

12.—(1) Where a person of or over the age of sixteen years is convicted of an offence (not being an offence for which the sentence is fixed by law), the court by or before which he is convicted may make a curfew order, that is to say, an order requiring him to remain, for periods specified in the order, at a place so specified.

(2) A curfew order may specify different places or different periods for different days, but shall not specify—

    (a) periods which fall outside the period of six months beginning with the day on which it is made; or

    (b) periods which amount to less than 2 hours or more than 12 hours in any one day.

(3) The requirements in a curfew order shall, as far as practicable, be such as to avoid—

    (a) any conflict with the offender's religious beliefs or with the requirements of any other community order to which he may be subject; and

    (b) any interference with the times, if any, at which he normally works or attends school or other educational establishment.

(4) A curfew order shall include provision for making a person responsible for monitoring the offender's whereabouts during the curfew periods specified in the order; and a person who is made so responsible shall be of a description specified in an order made by the Secretary of State.

(4A) A court shall not make a curfew order unless the court has been notified by the Secretary of State that arrangements for monitoring the offender's whereabouts are available in the area in which the place proposed to be specified in the order is situated and the notice has not been withdrawn.

(5) Before making a curfew order, the court shall explain to the offender in ordinary language—

    (a) the effect of the order (including any additional requirements proposed to be included in the order in accordance with section 13 below);

    (b) the consequences which may follow under Schedule 2 to this Act if he fails to comply with any of the requirements of the order; and

    (c) that the court has under that Schedule power to review the order on the application either of the offender or of the supervising officer,

and the court shall not make the order unless he expresses his willingness to comply with its requirements.

(6) Before making a curfew order, the court shall obtain and consider information about the place proposed to be specified in the order (including information as to the attitude of persons likely to be affected by the enforced presence there of the offender).

(7) The Secretary of State may by order direct—

    (a) that subsection (2) above shall have effect with the substitution, for any period there specified, of such period as may be specified in the order; or

(b) that subsection (3) above shall have effect with such additional restrictions as may be so specified.

13.—(1) Subject to subsection (2) below, a curfew order may in addition include requirements for securing the electronic monitoring of the offender's whereabouts during the curfew periods specified in the order.   **B18–13**

(2) A court shall not make a curfew order which includes such requirements unless the court—

(a) has been notified by the Secretary of State that electronic monitoring arrangements are available in the area in which the place proposed to specified in the order is situated; and

(b) is satisfied that the necessary provision can be made under those arrangements.

(3) Electronic monitoring arrangements made by the Secretary of State under this section may include entering into contracts with other persons for the electronic monitoring by them of offenders' whereabouts.

Orders: supplemental

14.—(1) Schedule 2 to this Act (which makes provision for dealing with failures to comply with the requirements of certain community orders, for amending such orders and for revoking them with or without the substitution of other sentences) shall have effect.   **B18–14**

(2) Sections 5, 6, 16 and 17 of, and Schedule 1 to, the 1973 Act (which are superseded by Schedule 2 to this Act) shall cease to have effect.

15.—(1) The Secretary of State may make rules for regulating—   **B18–15**

(a) the supervision of persons who are subject to probation orders;

(b) the arrangements to be made under Schedule 3 to the 1973 Act for persons who are subject to community service orders to perform work under those orders and the performance by such persons of such work;

(c) the monitoring of the whereabouts of persons who are subject to curfew orders (including electronic monitoring in cases where arrangements for such monitoring are available); and

(d) without prejudice to the generality of paragraphs (a) to (c) above, the functions of the responsible officers of such persons as are mentioned in those paragraphs.

(2) Rules under subsection (1)(b) above may in particular—

(a) limit the number of hours of work to be done by a person on any one day;

(b) make provision as to the reckoning of hours worked and the keeping of work records; and

(c) make provision for the payment of travelling and other expenses in connection with the performance of work.

(3) In this Part "responsible officer" means—

(a) in relation to an offender who is subject to a probation order, the probation officer responsible for his supervision;

(b) in relation to an offender who is subject to a community service order, the relevant officer within the meaning of section 14(4) of the 1973 Act; and

(c) in relation to an offender who is subject to a curfew order, the person responsible for monitoring his whereabouts during the curfew periods specified in the order.

(4) This section shall apply in relation to combination orders—

(a) in so far as they impose such a requirement as is mentioned in paragraph (a) of subsection (1) of section 11 above, as if they were probation orders; and

(b) in so far as they impose such a requirement as is mentioned in paragraph (b) of that subsection, as if they were community service orders.

B18–16 16. Schedule 3 to this Act shall have effect for making provision for and in connection with—

(a) the making and amendment in England and Wales of community orders relating to persons residing in Scotland or Northern Ireland; and

(b) the making and amendment in Scotland or Northern Ireland of corresponding orders relating to persons residing in England and Wales.

Financial penalties

B18–17 17.—(1) In section 37 (standard scale of fines) of the Criminal Justice Act 1982 ("the 1982 Act") and section 289G of the Criminal Procedure (Scotland) Act 1975 (corresponding Scottish provision), for subsection (2) there shall be substituted the following subsection—

"(2) The standard scale is shown below—

Level on the scale	Amount of fine
1	£200
2	£500
3	£1,000
4	£2,500
5	£5,000".

(2) Part I of the Magistrates' Courts Act 1980 ("the 1980 Act") shall be amended as follows—

(a) in section 24(3) and (4) (maximum fine on summary conviction of young person for indictable offence) and section 36(1) and (2) (maximum fine on conviction of young person by magistrates' court), for "£400" there shall be substituted "£1,000";

(b) in section 24(4) (maximum fine on summary conviction of child for indictable offence) and section 36(2) (maximum fine on conviction of child by magistrates' court), for "£100" there shall be substituted "£250"; and

(c) in section 32(9) (maximum fine on summary conviction of offence triable either way), for "£2,000" there shall be substituted "£5,000";

and in section 289B(6) of the Criminal Procedure (Scotland) Act 1975 (interpretation), in the definition of "prescribed sum", for "£2,000" there shall be substituted "£5,000".

(3) Schedule 4 to this Act shall have effect as follows—

(a) in each of the provisions mentioned in column 1 of Part I (the general description of which is given in column 2), for the amount specified in column 3 there shall be substituted the amount specified in column 4;

(b) in each of the provisions mentioned in column 1 of Part II (the general description of which is given in column 2), for the amount specified in column 3 there shall be substituted the level on the standard scale specified in column 4;

(c) in each of the provisions mentioned in column 1 of Part III (the general description of which is given in column 2), for the amount specified in column 3 there shall be substituted a reference to the statutory maximum;

(d) the provisions set out in Part IV shall be substituted for Scheule 6A to the 1980 Act (fines that may be altered under section 143); and

(e) [...]

Fixing of fines

18.—(1) Before fixing the amount of any fine to be imposed on an offender who is an individual, a court shall inquire into his financial circumstances.   **B18–18**

(2) The amount of any fine fixed by a court shall be such as, in the opinion of the court, reflects the seriousness of the offence.

(3) In fixing the amount of any fine to be imposed on an offender (whether an individual or other person), a court shall take into account the circumstances of the case including, among other things, the financial circumstances of the offender so far as they are known, or appear, to the court.

(4) Where—

(a) an offender has been convicted in his absence in pursuance of section 11 or 12 of the Magistrates' Courts Act 1980 (non-appearance of the accused),

(b) an offender—

(i) has failed to comply with an order under section 20(1) below; or

(ii) has otherwise failed to co-operate with the court in its inquiry into his financial circumstances, or

(c) the parent or guardian of an offender who is a child or young person—

(i) has failed to comply with an order under section 20(1B) below; or

(ii) has otherwise failed to co-operate with the court in its inquiry into its financial circumstances,

and the court considers that it has insufficient information to make a proper determination of the financial circumstances of the offender, it may make such determination as it thinks fit.

(5) Subsection (3) above applies whether taking into account the financial circumstances of the offender has the effect of increasing or reducing the amount of the fine.

Remission of fines

21.—(1) This section applies where a court has, in fixing the amount of a fine, determined the offender's financial circumstances under section 18(4) above.   **B18–19**

(2) If, on subsequently inquiring into the offender's financial circumstances, the court is satisfied that had it had the results of that inquiring when sentencing the offender it would—

(a) have fixed a smaller amount; or

(b) not have fined him,

it may remit the whole or any part of the fine.

(3) Where under this section the court remits the whole or part of a fine after a term of imprisonment had been fixed under section 82(5) of the Magistrates' Court Act 1980 (issue of warrant of commitment for default) or section 31 of the Powers of Criminal Courts Act 1973 (powers of Crown Court in relation to fines), it shall reduce the term by the corresponding proportion.

(4) in calculating any reduction required by subsection (3) above, any fraction of a day shall be ignored.

Effect of previous convictions and of offending while on bail

B18–20   29.—(1) In considering the seriousness of any offence, the court may take into account any previous convictions of the offender or any failure of his to respond to previous sentences.

(2) In considering the seriousness of any offence committed while the offender was on bail, the court shall treat the fact that it was committed in those circumstances as an aggravating factor.

(3) A probation order or conditional discharge order made before 1st October 1992 (which, by virtue of section 2 or 7 of the Powers of Criminal Courts Act 1973, would otherwise not be a sentence for the purposes of this section) is to be treated as a sentence for those purposes.

(4) A conviction in respect of which a probation order or an order discharging the offender absolutely or conditionally was made before that date (which by virtue of section 13 of that Act, would otherwise not be a conviction for those purposes) is to be treated as a conviction for those purposes.

(5) A conditional discharge order made after 30th September 1992 (which, by virtue of section 1A of the Powers of Criminal Courts Act 1973, would otherwise not be a sentence for the purposes of this section) is to be treated as a sentence for those purposes.

(6) A conviction in respect of which an order discharging the offender absolutely or conditionally was made after 30th September 1992 (which, by virtue of section 1C of the Powers of Criminal Courts Act 1973, would otherwise not be a conviction for those purposes) is to be treated as a conviction for those purposes.

AGGRAVATED VEHICLE-TAKING ACT 1992

(1992 c. 11)

New offence of aggravated vehicle-taking

B19–01   1.— [*Amends the Theft Act 1968 by inserting therein section 12A.*]

Offence to be tried only summarily if value of damage is small

B19–02   2.—(1) In Schedule 2 to the Magistrates' Courts Act 1980 (offences for which the value involved is relevant to the mode of trial) after paragraph 2 there shall be inserted the following paragraph—

"3. Offences under section 12A of the Theft Act 1968 (aggravated vehicle-taking) where no allegation is made under subsection (1)(b) other than of damage, whether to the vehicle or other property or both.	The total value of the damage alleged to have been caused.	(1) In the case of damage to any property other than the vehicle involved in the offence, as for the corresponding entry in paragraph 1 above, substituting a reference to the time of the accident concerned for any reference to the material time. (2) In the case of damage to the vehicle involved in the offence— (a) if immediately after the vehicle was recovered the damage was capable of repair— (i) what would probably then have been the market price for the repair of the damage, or (ii) what the vehicle would probably have cost to buy in the open market immediately before it was unlawfully taken, whichever is the less; or (b) if immediately after the vehicle was recovered the damage was beyond repair, what the vehicle would probably have cost to buy in the open market immediately before it was unlawfully taken."

(2) In the Magistrates' Courts Act 1980, at the end of section 22 (which introduces Schedule 2) there shall be added the following subsection—

"(12) Subsection (8) of section 12A of the Theft Act 1968 (which determines when a vehicle is recovered) shall apply for the purposes of paragraph 3 of Schedule 2 to this Act as it applies for the purposes of that section."

(3) In section 33 of the Magistrates' Courts Act 1980 (maximum penalties on summary conviction in pursuance of section 22)—

(a) in subsection (1), at the beginning of paragraph (a) there shall be inserted the words "subject to subsection (3) below"; and

(b) after subsection (2) there shall be inserted the following subsection—

"(3) Paragraph (a) of subsection (1) above does not apply to an offence under section 12A of the Theft Act 1968 (aggravated vehicle-taking)".

Obligatory disqualification

3.—(1) In Schedule 2 to the Road Traffic Offenders Act 1988 (punishment of   **B19–03**

offences, etc.), in Part II (disqualification, endorsement and penalty points for offences under Acts other than the Traffic Acts) after the entry relating to man-slaughter and culpable homicide there shall be inserted the following entry—

"An offence under	Obligatory.	Obligatory.	3-11".
section 12A of the			
Theft Act 1968			
(aggravated			
vehicle-taking).			

(2) In section 34 of the Road Traffic Offenders Act 1988 (disqualification for certain offences), after subsection (1) (obligatory disqualification except for special reasons) there shall be inserted the following subsection—

"(1A) Where a person is convicted of an offence under section 12A of the Theft Act 1968 (aggravated vehicle-taking), the fact that he did not drive the vehicle in question at any particular time or at all shall not be regarded as a special reason for the purposes of subsection (1) above."

Short title, commencement and extent

B19–04   **4.**—(1) This Act may be cited as the Aggravated Vehicle-Taking Act 1992.
(2) This Act shall come into force on such day as the Secretary of State may by order made by statutory instrument appoint, and different days may be so appointed for different purposes.
(3) This Act extends to England and Wales only.

TRANSPORT AND WORKS ACT 1992

(1992 c. 42)

PART II

SAFETY OF RAILWAYS ETC

CHAPTER I

OFFENCES INVOLVING DRINK OR DRUGS

Transport systems to which Chapter I applies

B20–01   **26.**—(1) This Chapter applies to transport systems of any of the following kinds—
   (a) a railway;
   (b) a tramway;
   (c) a system which uses another mode of guided transport and is specified for the purposes of this Chapter by an order made by the Secretary of State.

(2) This Chapter shall not apply to a transport system unless it is used, or is intended to be used, wholly or partly for the carriage of members of the public.

(3) The power to make orders under this section shall be exercisable by statutory instrument, which shall be subject to annulment in pursuance of a resolution of either House of Parliament.

Principal offences

Offences involving drink or drugs on transport systems

27.—(1) If a person works on a transport system to which this Chapter **B20–02** applies—
  (a) as a driver, guard, conductor or signalman or in any other capacity in which he can control or affect the movement of a vehicle, or
  (b) in a maintenance capacity or as a supervisor of, or look-out for, persons working in a maintenance capacity,
when he is unfit to carry out that work through drink or drugs, he shall be guilty off an offence.

(2) if a person works on a transport system to which this Chapter applies—
  (a) as a driver, guard, conductor or signalman or in any other capacity in which he can control or affect the movement of a vehicle, or
  (b) in a maintenance capacity or as a supervisor of, or look-out for, persons working in a maintenace capacity,
after consuming so much alcohol that the proportion of it in his breath, blood or urine exceeds the prescribed limit, he shall be guilty of an offence.

(3) For the purposes of this section, a person works on a transport system in a maintenance capacity if his work on the system involves maintenance, repair or alteration of—
  (a) the permanent way or other means of guiding or supporting vehicles,
  (b) signals or any other means of controlling the movement of vehicles, or
  (c) any means of supplying electricity to vehicles or to the means of guiding or supporting vehicles,
or involves coupling or uncoupling vehicles or checking that they are working properly before they are used on any occasion.

(4) For the purposes of subsection (1) above, a person shall be taken to be unfit to carry out any work if his ability to carry out that work properly is for the time being impaired.

Offences by operators of transport systems

28.—(1) If a person commits an offence under section 27 above, the respon- **B20–03** sible operator shall also be guilty of an offence.

(2) In this section "the responsible operator" means—
  (a) in a case where the transport system on which the offence under section 27 above is committed has only one operator, that operator;
  (b) in a case where the transport system on which the offence under section 27 above is committed has more than one operator, whichever of them is responsible for the work giving rise to the offence.

(3) No offence is committed under subsection (1) above if the responsible operator has exercised all due diligence to prevent the commission on the transport system of any offence under section 27 above.

(4) If a person commits an offence under section 27 above in the course of his employment with a person other than the responsible operator, his employer shall (without prejudice to any liability of that operator under subsection (1) above) also be guilty of an offence.

(5) No offence is committed under subsection (4) above if the employer has exercised all due diligence to prevent the commission on the transport system by any of his employees of any offence under section 27 above.

Police powers etc

Breath tests

B20–04
29.—(1) Where a constable in uniform has reasonable cause to suspect—
  (a) that a person working on a transport system to which this Chapter applies in any capacity mentioned in section 27(1) and (2) above has alcohol in his body, or
  (b) that a person has been working on a transport system to which this Chapter applies in any capacity mentioned in section 27(1) and (2) above with alcohol in his body and still has alcohol in his body,
he may require that person to provide a specimen of breath for a breath test.

(2) Where an accident or dangerous incident occurs on a transport system to which this Chapter applies, a constable in uniform may require a person to provide a specimen of breath for a breath test if he has reasonable cause to suspect that—
  (a) at the time of the accident or incident that person was working on the transport system in a capacity mentioned in section 27(1) and (2) above, and
  (b) an act or omission of that person while he was so working may have been a cause of the accident or incident.

(3) In subsection (2) above "dangerous incident" means an incident which in the constable's opinion involved a danger of death or personal injury.

(4) A person may be required under subsection (1) or subsection (2) above to provide a specimen either at or near the place where the requirement is made or, if the requirement is made under subsection (2) above and the constable making the requirement thinks fit, at a police station specified by the constable.

(5) A person who, without reasonable excuse, fails to provide a specimen of breath when required to do so in pursuance of this section shall be guilty of an offence.

Powers of arrest and entry

B20–05
30.—(1) A constable may arrest a person without warrant if he has reasonable cause to suspect that that person is or has been committing an offence under section 27(1) above.

(2) A constable may arrest a person without warrant if—
  (a) as a result of a breath test under section 29 above he has reasonable cause to suspect that the proportion of alcohol in that person's breath or blood exceeds the prescribed limit, or

(b) that person has failed to provide a specimen of breath for a breath test when required to do so in pursuance of section 29 above and the constable has reasonable cause to suspect that he has alcohol in his body.

(3) For the purpose of arresting a person under subsection (1) above, a constable may enter (if need be by force) any place where that person is or where the constable, with reasonable cause, suspects him to be.

(4) A constable may, for the purpose of—

(a) requiring a person to provide a specimen of breath under section 29(2) above in the case of an accident which the constable has reasonable cause to suspect involved the death of, or injury to, another person, or

(b) arresting a person in such a case under subsection (2) above,

enter (if need be by force) any place where that person is or where the constable, with reasonable cause, suspects him to be.

Provision of specimens for analysis

31.—(1) In the course of an investigation into whether a person has committed an offence under section 27 above, a constable may require him—   **B20–06**

(a) to provide two specimens of breath for analysis by means of a device of a type approved by the Secretary of State, or

(b) to provide a specimen of blood or urine for a laboratory test.

(2) A requirement under this section to provide specimens of breath shall only be made at a police station.

(3) A requirement under this section to provide a specimen of blood or urine shall only be made at a police station or at a hospital; and it shall not be made at a police station unless subsection (4) below applies.

(4) This subsection applies if—

(a) the constable making the requirement has reasonable cause to believe that for medical reasons a specimen of breath cannot be provided or should not be required,

(b) at the time the requirement is made, either a device (or reliable device) of the type mentioned in subsection (1)(a) above is not available at the police station or it is for any other reason not practicable to use such a device there, or

(c) the suspected offence is one under section 27(1) above and the constable making the requirement has been advised by a medical practitioner that the condition of the person required to provide the specimen might be due to a drug.

(5) A person may be required to provide a specimen of blood or urine in pursuance of this section notwithstanding that he has already provided or been required to provide two specimens of breath.

(6) If the provision of a specimen other than a specimen of breath may be required in pursuance of this section, the question whether it is to be a specimen of blood or a specimen of urine shall be decided by the constable making the requirement; but if a medical practitioner is of the opinion that for medical reasons a specimen of blood cannot or should not be taken, the specimen shall be a specimen of urine.

(7) A specimen of urine shall be provided within one hour of the requirement for its provision being made and after the provision of a previous specimen of urine.

(8) A person who, without reasonable excuse, fails to provide a specimen when required to do so in pursuance of this section shall be guilty of an offence.

(9) A constable shall, on requiring a person to provide a specimen in pursuance of this section, warn him that a failure to provide it may render him liable to prosecution.

Choice of specimens of breath

B20–07   **32.**—(1) Of any two specimens of breath provided by a person in pursuance of section 31 above, the one with the lower proportion of alcohol in the breath shall be used and the other shall be disregarded.

(2) But if the specimen with the lower proportion of alcohol contains no more than 50 microgrammes of alcohol in 100 millilitres of breath, the person who provided it may claim that it should be replaced by such specimen as may be required under section 31(6) above and, if he then provides such a specimen, neither specimen of breath shall be used.

(3) The Secretary of State may by regulations substitute another proportion of alcohol in the breath for that specified in subsection (2) above.

(4) The power to make regulations under this section shall be exercisable by statutory instrument; and no such regulations shall be made unless a draft of the instrument containing them has been laid before, and approved by a resolution of, each House of Parliament.

Protection for hospital patients

B20–08   **33.**—(1) While a person is at a hospital as a patient, he shall not be required to provide a specimen of breath for a breath test or to provide a specimen for a laboratory test unless the medical practitioner in immediate charge of his case has been notified of the proposal to make the requirement; and—

(a) if the requirement is then made, it shall be for the provision of a specimen at the hospital, but

(b) if the medical practitioner objects on the ground specified in subsection (2) below, the requirement shall not be made.

(2) The ground on which the medical practitioner may object is that the requirement or the provision of a specimen or (in the case of a specimen of blood or urine) the warning required under section 31(9) above would be prejudicial to the proper care and treatment of the patient.

(3) A person shall not be arrested under section 30(2) above while he is at a hospital as a patient.

Evidence in proceedings for offences under section 27

Use of specimens in proceedings

B20–09   **34.**—(1) In proceedings for any offence under section 27 above—

(a) evidence of the proportion of alcohol or any drug in a specimen of breath, blood or urine provided by the accused shall be taken into account, and

(b) it shall be assumed that the proportion of alcohol in the accused's breath, blood or urine at the time of the alleged offence was not less than in the specimen.

(2) That assumption shall not be made if the accused proves—

(a) that he consumed alcohol before he provided the specimen and after he had stopped work on the occasion of the alleged offence, and

(b) that, had he not done so, the proportion of alcohol in his breath, blood or urine would not have exceeded the prescribed limit and, where the offence alleged is an offence of being unfit to carry out the work in question through drink, would not have been such as to impair his ability to carry out that work properly.

(3) Where, at the time a specimen of blood or urine was provided by the accused, he asked to be provided with such a specimen, evidence of the proportion of alcohol or any drug found in the specimen shall not be admissible in the proceedings on behalf of the prosecution unless—

(a) the specimen in which the alcohol or drug was found is one of two parts into which the specimen provided by the accused was divided at the time it was provided, and

(b) the other part was supplied to the accused.

Documentary evidence as to specimens

35.—(1) In proceedings for any offence under section 27 above, evidence of the proportion of alcohol in a specimen of breath may be given by the production of a document (or documents) purporting to be—   **B20–10**

(a) a statement automatically produced by the device by which the proportion of alcohol in the specimen was measured, and

(b) a certificate signed by a constable (which may but need not be contained in the same document as the statement) that the specimen was provided by the accused at the date and time shown in the statement.

(2) In such proceedings, evidence of the proportion of alcohol or a drug in a specimen of blood or urine may be given by the production of a document purporting to be a certificate signed by an authorised analyst identifying the specimen and stating the proportion of alcohol or drug found in it.

(3) In such proceedings, evidence that a specimen of blood was taken from the accused with his consent by a medical practitioner may be given by the production of a document purporting to be a certificate to that effect signed by the practitioner.

(4) A document such as is mentioned in subsection (1) above shall be admissible in evidence on behalf of the prosecution in pursuance of this section only if a copy of it either was handed to the accused when the document was produced or was served on him not later than seven days before the hearing.

(5) A document such as is mentioned in subsection (2) or (3) abovve shall be admissible in evidence on behalf of the prosecution in pursuance of this section only if a copy of it was served on the accused not later than seven days before the hearing.

(6) A document purporting to be a certificate (or so much of a document as purports to be a certificate) shall not be admisssible in evidence on behalf of the prosecution in pursuance of this section if the accused, not later than three days before the hearing or within such futher time as the court may in special circumstances allow, has served notice on the prosecutor requiring the attendance at the hearing of the person by whom the document purports to be signed.

(7) In this section "served" means served personally or sent by registered post or recorded delivery service.

(8) In subsection (2) above "authorised analyst" means—

(a) any person possessing the qualifications prescribed by regulations made under section 76 of the Food Act 1984 or section 27 of the Food and Drugs (Scotland) Act 1956 as qualifying persons for appointment as public analysts under those Acts, or

(b) any other person authorised by the Secretary of State to make analyses for the purposes of this section.

Penalties

Penalties

B20–11   **36.**—(1) A person guilty of any offence under this Chapter other than an offence under section 29(5) above shall be liable on summary conviction to imprisonment for a term not exceeding six months, to a fine not exceeding level 5 on the standard scale or to both.

(2) A person guilty of an offence under section 29(5) above shall be liable on summary conviction to a fine not exceeding level 3 on the standard scale.

Miscellaneous and supplementary

Special provision for Scotland

B20–12   **37.**—(1) Section 30(3) and (4) above shall not extend to Scotland, and nothing in those subsections shall affect any rule of law in Scotland concerning the right of a constable to enter any premises for any purpose.

(2) In proceedings for any offence under section 27 above in Scotland—

(a) a document produced in evidence on behalf of the prosecution in pursuance of section 35 above and, where the person by whom the document was signed is called as a witness, the evidence of that person, shall be sufficient evidence of the facts stated in the document, and

(b) a written execution purporting to be signed by the person who handed to or served on the accused or the prosecutor a copy document or notice under section 35 above, together with, where appropriate, a post office receipt for the relevant registered or recorded delivery letter, shall be sufficient evidence of the handing or service of the copy document or notice.

Interpretation of Chapter I

B20–13   **38.**—(1) In this Chapter—

"breath test" means a preliminary test for the purpose of obtaining, by means of a device of a type approved by the Secretary of State, an indication whether the proportion of alcohol in a person's breath or blood is likely to exceed the prescribed limit;

"drug" includes any intoxicant other than alcohol;

"fail" includes refuse;

"hospital" means an institution which provides medical or surgical treatment for in-patients or out-patients.

(2) In this Chapter "the prescibed limit" means, as the case may require—

(a) 35 microgrammes of alcohol in 100 millilitres of breath,

(b) 80 milligrammes of alcohol in 100 millilitres of blood, or

(c) 107 milligrammes of alcohol in 100 millilitres of urine,
or such other proportion as may be prescribed by regulations made by the
Secretary of State.

(3) For the purposes of this Chapter, it is immaterial whether a person who
works on a transport system does so in the course of his employment, under a
contract for services, voluntarily or otherwise.

(4) For the purposes of this Chapter, a person does not provide a specimen
of breath for a breath test or for analysis unless the specimen—

(a) is sufficient to enable the test or the analysis to be carried out, and
(b) is provided in such a way as to enable the objective of the test or analysis to be satisfactorily achieved.

(5) For the purposes of this Chapter, a person provides a specimen of blood
if and only if he consents to its being taken by a medical practitioner and it is
so taken.

(6) The power to make regulations under subsection (2) above shall be exercisable by statutory instrument; and no such regulations shall be made unless
a draft of the instrument containing them has been laid before, and approved
by a resolution of, each House of Parliament.

Amendment of scope of offences involving drink or drugs under Road Traffic Act 1988

39.—(1) The following section shall be inserted in the Road Traffic Act 1988 **B20–14**
after section 192—

"Tramcars and other guided vehicles: drink and drugs

192A.—(1) Sections 4 to 11 of this Act shall not apply (to the extent
that apart from this subsection they would) to vehicles on any transport
system to which Chapter I of Part II of the Transport and Works Act
1992 (offences involving drink or drugs on railways, tramways and certain other guided transport systems) applies.

(2) Subject to subsection (1) above, the Secretary of State may by regulations provide that sections 4 to 11 of this Act shall apply to vehicles on
a system of guided transport specified in the regulations with such
modifications as he considers necessary or expedient.

(3) Regulations under subsection (2) above may make different provision for different cases.

(4) In this section—
"guided transport" means transport by vehicles guided by means
external to the vehicles (whether or not the vehicles are also capable of being operated in some other way), and
"vehicle" includes mobile traction unit."

Consequential amendment

40. In section 17 of the Railway Regulation Act 1842 (punishment of persons **B20–15**
employed on railways guilty of misconduct) the words "who shall be found
drunk while so employed upon the said railway" shall be omitted.

CRIMINAL JUSTICE ACT 1993

(1993 c. 36)

Miscellaneous

Fixing of fines

B21–01   65.—(1) The following section shall be substituted for section 18 of the Criminal Justice Act 1991 (fixing of certain fines by reference to units)—

"Fixing of fines

18.—(1) Before fixing the amount of any fine, a court shall inquire into the financial circumstances of the offender.

(2) The amount of any fine fixed by a court shall be such as, in the opinion of the court, reflects the seriousness of the offence.

(3) In fixing the amount of any fine, a court shall take into account the circumstances of the case including, among other things, the financial circumstances of the offender so far as they are known, or appear, to the court.

(4) Where—

(a) an offender has been convicted in his absence in pursuance of section 11 or 12 of the Magistrates' Courts Act 1980 (non-appearance of accused),

(b) an offender—

(i) has failed to comply with an order under section 20(1) below; or

(ii) has otherwise failed to co-operate with the court in its inquiry into his financial circumstances, or

(c) the parent or guardian of an offender who is a child or young person—

(i) has failed to comply with an order under section 20(1B) below; or

(ii) has otherwise failed to co-operate with the court in its inquiry into his financial circumstances,

and the court considers that it has insufficient information to make a proper determination of the financial circumstances of the offender, it may make such determination as it thinks fit.

(5) Subsection (3) above applies whether taking into account the financial circumstances of the offender has the effect of increasing or reducing the amount of the fine.".

(2) Section 19 of the Act of 1991 (fixing of fines in cases to which the unit fines system did not apply) shall cease to have effect.

(3) The further amendments made by Schedule 3 shall have effect.

(4) The amendments made by this section and that Schedule shall apply in relation to offenders convicted (but not sentenced) before the date on which this section comes into force as they apply in relation to offenders convicted after that date.

Powers of courts to deal with offenders

66.—(1) In section 1 of the Criminal Justice Act 1991 (restrictions on   **B12–02**
imposing custodial sentences), the following shall be substituted for subsection (2)(a)—

> "(a) that the offence, or the combination of the offence and one or more offences associated with it, was so serious that only such a sentence can be justified for the offence; or".

(2) In section 2 of the Act of 1991 (length of custodial sentences), in subsections (2)(a) and (3), for the word "other" there shall be substituted "one or more".

(3) In section 3 of the Act of 1991 (procedural requirements for custodial sentences), in subsection (3)(a), the words "or (as the case may be) of the offence and the offence or offences associated with it," shall be inserted after the word "offence".

(4) In section 6 of the Act of 1991 (restrictions on imposing community sentences)—

(a) in subsection (1), for the words "other offence" there shall be substituted "or more offences"; and

(b) in subsection (2)(b), for the word "other" there shall be substituted "one or more".

(5) In section 7 of the Act of 1991 (procedural requirements for community sentences), in subsection (1), the words "or (as the case may be) of the offence and the offence or offences associated with it," shall be inserted after the word "offence".

(6) For section 29 of the Act of 1991 (effect of previous convictions) there shall be substituted—

"Effect of previous convictions and of offending while on bail

29.—(1) In considering the seriousness of any offence, the court may take into account any previous convictions of the offender or any failure of his to respond to previous sentences.

(2) In considering the seriousness of any offence committed while the offender was on bail, the court shall treat the fact that it was committed in those circumstances as an aggravating factor.

(3) A probation order or conditional discharge order made before 1st October 1992 (which, by virtue of section 2 or 7 of the Powers of Criminal Courts Act 1973, would otherwsie not be a sentence for the purposes of this section) is to be treated as a sentence for those purposes.

(4) A conviction in respect of which a probation order or conditional discharge order was made before that date (which, by virtue of section 13 of that Act, would otherwise not be a conviction for those purposes) is to be treated as a conviction for those purposes.".

(7) In subsection (1) of section 12D of the Children and Young Persons Act 1969 (duty of court to state in certain cases that requirement is in place of custodial sentence), in paragraph (ii)(a) for the words "other offence" there shall be substituted "or more offences".

(8) In section 38 of the Magistrates' Courts Act 1980 (committal for sentence on summary trial of offence triable either way), in subsection (2)(a), for the word "other" there shall be substituted "one or more".

(9) The amendments made by this section shall apply in relation to offenders convicted (but not sentenced) before the date on which this section comes into force as they apply in relation to offenders convicted after that date.

Penalty for causing death by dangerous driving or by careless driving

B21–03   67.—(1) In Part I of Schedule 2 to the Road Traffic Offenders Act 1988 (prosecution and punishment of offences), in the entries relating to section 1 of the Road Traffic Act 1988 (causing death by dangerous driving) and section 3A of that Act (causing death by careless driving while under influence of drink or drugs), in column 4, for "5 years" there shall be substituted "10 years".

SCHEDULE 3   Section 65(3)

FINANCIAL PENALTIES

Increases in certain maximum fines

B21–04   1.—(1) In section 17 of the Criminal Justice Act 1991 (increases in certain maximum fines), subsection (3)(e) shall cease to have effect.

(2) In Schedule 4 to that Act (increase of certain maxima) Part V shall cease to have effect.

Statements as to offenders' financial circumstances

2.—(1) In section 20 of the Act of 1991 (statements as to offenders' means) the following shall be substituted for subsection (1)—

"(1) Where a person has been convicted of an offence, the court may, before sentencing him, make a financial circumstances order with respect to him.

(1A) Where a magistrates' court has been notified in accordance with section 12(2) of the Magistrates' Courts Act 1980 that a person desires to plead guilty without appearing before the court, the court may make a financial circumstances order with respect to him.

(1B) Before exercising its powers under section 55 of the Children and Young Persons Act 1933 against the parent or guardian of any person who has been convicted of an offence, the court may make a financial circumstances order with respect to the parent or (as the case may be) guardian.

(1C) In this section "a financial circumstances order " means, in relation to any person, an order requiring him to give to the court, within such period as may be specified in the order, such a statement of his financial circumstances as the court may require.".

(2) In subsections (2) and (3) of section 20 of the Act of 1991, for the words "an order under subsection (1) above" there shall be substituted "a financial circumstances order".

(3) Section 20(5) of the Act of 1991 shall cease to have effect.

Remission of fines

3. The following section shall be substitued for section 21 of the Act of 1991 (remission of fines)—

"Remission of fines

21.—(1) This section applies where a court has, in fixing the amount of a fine, determined the offender's financial circumstances under section 18(4) above.

(2) If, on subsequently inquiring into the offender's financial circumstances, the court is satisfied that had it had the results of that inquiry when sentencing the offender it would—

(a) have fixed a smaller amount; or

(b) not have fined him,

it may remit the whole or any part of the fine.

(3) Where under this section the court remits the whole or part of a fine after a term of imprisonment has been fixed under section 82(5) of the Magistrates' Courts Act 1980 (issue of warrant of commitment for default) or section 31 of the Powers of Criminal Courts Act 1973 (powers of Crown Court in relation to fines), it shall reduce the term by the corresponding proportion.

(4) In calculating any reduction required by subsection (3) above, any fraction of a day shall be ignored.".

Default in paying unit fines

4. Section 22 o the Act of 1991 (default in paying fines fixed under section 18 of that Act) shall cease to have effect.

Responsibility of parents and guardians

5. In section 57 of the Act of 1991 (responsibility of parent or guardian for financial penalties), the following shall be substituted for subsections (3) and (4)—   **B21–05**

"(3) For the purposes of any order under that section made against the parent or guardian of a child or young person—

(a) sections 18 and 21 above; and

(b) section 35(4)(a) of the 1973 Act (fixing amount of compensation order),

shall have effect (so far as applicable) as if any reference to the financial circumstances of the offender, or (as the case may be) to the means of the person against whom the compensation order is made, were a reference to the financial circumstances of the parent or guardian.

(4) For the purposes of any such order made against a local authority (as defined for the purposes of the Children Act 1989)—

(a) section 18(1) above, and section 35(4)(a) of the 1973 Act, shall not apply, and

(b) section 18(3) above shall apply as if the words from "including" to the end were omitted.".

Other amendments

6.—(1) In section 15 of the Children and Young Persons Act 1969 (variation and discharge of supervision orders), the following subsection shall be substituted for subsection (7)—   **B21–06**

"(7) A fine imposed under subsection (3) or (4) above shall be deemed, for the purposes of any enactment, to be a sum adjudged to be paid by a conviction.".

(2) In section 27 of the Powers of Criminal Courts Act 1973 (breach of requirement of suspended sentence supervison order), the following subsection shall be substituted for subsection (4)—

"(4) A fine imposed under subsection (3) above shall be deemed, for the purposes of any enactment, to be a sum adjudged to be paid by a conviction.".

(3) In section 97 of the Magistrates' Courts Act 1980 (maximum fine for refusal to give evidence), the following subsection shall be substituted for subsection (5)—

"(5) A fine imposed under subsection (4) above shall be deemed, for the purposes of any enactment, to be a sum adjudged to be paid by a conviction.".

(4) In section 12 of the Contempt of Court Act 1981 (maximum fine for contempt in face of magistrates' court), the following subsection shall be substituted for subsection (2A)—

"(2A) A fine imposed under subsection (2) above shall be deemed, for the purposes of any enactment, to be a sum adjudged to be paid by a conviction.".

(5) In section 14 of that Act (maximum fine for contempt in an inferior court), the following subsection shall be substituted for the subsection (2A) inserted by the Criminal Justice Act 1991—

"(2A) A fine imposed under subsection (2) above shall be deemed, for the purposes of any enactment, to be a sum adjudged to be paid by a conviction.".

(6) In section 58 of the Criminal Justice Act 1991 (binding over of parent or guardian), the following subsection shall be substituted for subsection (4)—

"(4) A fine imposed under subsection (2)(b) above shall be deemed, for the purposes of any enactment, to be a sum adjudged to be paid by a conviction.".

(7) In paragraph 6 of Schedule 2 to the Criminal Justice Act 1991 (miscellaneous supplemental provisions), the following sub-paragraph shall be substituted for sub-paragraph (2)—

"(2) A fine imposed under paragraph 3(1)(a) or 4(1)(a) above shall be deemed, for the purposes of any enactment, to be a sum adjudged to be paid by a conviction.".

VEHICLE EXCISE AND REGISTRATION ACT 1994

(1994 c. 22)

PART III

OFFENCES

Offence of using or keeping unlicensed vehicle

Penalty for using or keeping unlicensed vehicle

B22–01   29.—(1) If a person uses, or keeps, on a public road a vehicle (not being an exempt vehicle) which is unlicensed he is guilty of an offence.

(2) For the purposes of subsection (1) a vehicle is unlicensed if no vehicle licence or trade licence is in force for or in respect of the vehicle.

(3) A person guilty of an offence under subsection (1) is liable on summary conviction to an excise penalty of—

(a) level 3 on the standard scale, or

(b) five times the amount of the vehicle excise duty chargeable in respect of the vehicle,

whichever is the greater.

(4) Where a vehicle for which a vehicle licence is in force is transferred by the holder of the licence to another person, the licence is to be treated for the purposes of subsection (2) as no longer in force unless it is delivered to the other person with the vehicle.

(5) Where—

(a) an application is made for a vehicle licence for any period, and

(b) a temporary licence is issued pursuant to the application,

subsection (4) does not apply to the licence applied for if, on a transfer of the vehicle during the currency of the temporary licence, the temporary licence is delivered with the vehicle to the transferee.

(6) The amount of the vehicle excise duty chargeable in respect of a vehicle is to be taken for the purposes of subsection (3)(b) to be an amount equal to the annual rate of duty applicable to the vehicle at the date on which the offence was committed.

(7) Where in the case of a vehicle kept (but not used) on a public road that annual rate differs from the annual rate by reference to which the vehicle was at that date chargeable under section 2(2) to (4), the amount of the vehicle excise duty chargeable in respect of the vehicle is to be taken for those purposes to be an amount equal to the latter rate.

(8) In the case of a conviction for a continuing offence, the offence is to be taken for the purposes of subsections (6) and (7) to have been committed on the date or latest date to which the conviction relates.

Additional liability for keeper of unlicensed vehicle

30.—(1) Where the person convicted of an offence under section 29 is the   **B22–02** person by whom the vehicle in respect of which the offence was committed was kept at the time at which it was committed, the court shall (in addition to any penalty which it may impose under that section) order him to pay the amount specified in subsection (2).

(2) The amount referred to in subsection (1) is an amount equal to one-twelfth of the annual rate of vehicle excise duty appropriate to the vehicle for each month, or part of a month, in the relevant period (within the meaning of section 31).

(3) In relation to any month or part of a month in the relevant period, the reference in subsection (2) to the annual rate of vehicle excise duty appropriate to the vehicle is a reference to the annual rate applicable to it at the beginning of that month or part.

(4) A vehicle is to be taken for the purposes of this section to have belonged throughout the relevant period to the description of vehicle to which it belonged for the purposes of vehicle excise duty at—

(a) the date on which the offence was committed, or

(b) if the prosecution so elect, the date when a vehicle licence for it was last issued,

except so far as it is proved to have fallen within some other description for the whole of any month or part of a month in that period.

(5) In the case of a conviction for a continuing offence, the offence is to be taken for the purposes of this section to have been committed on the date or latest date to which the conviction relates.

Relevant period for purposes of section 30

31.—(1) For the purposes of section 30 the relevant period is the period—
  (a) ending with the date on which the offence was committed, and
  (b) beginning as provided by subsections (2) to (4).

(2) Subject to subsection (4), if the person convicted has before the date of the offence notified the Secretary of State of his acquisition of the vehicle in accordance with regulations made by the Secretary of State, the relevant period begins with—
  (a) the date on which the notification was received by the Secretary of State, or
  (b) the expiry of the vehicle licence last in force for the vehicle,
whichever is the later.

(3) Subject to subsection (4), in any other case the relevant period begins with—
  (a) the expiry of the vehicle licence last in force for the vehicle before the date on which the offence was committed, or
  (b) if there has not at any time before that date been a vehicle licence in force for the vehicle, the date on which the vehicle was first kept by the person convicted.

(4) Where—
  (a) the person convicted has been ordered to pay an amount under section 30 on the occasion of a previous conviction for an offence in respect of the same vehicle, and
  (b) that offence was committed after the date specified in subsection (2) or (3) as the date with which the relevant period begins,
the relevant period instead begins with the month immediately following that in which the earlier offence was committed.

(5) Where the person convicted proves—
  (a) that throughout any month or part of a month in the relevant period the vehicle was not kept by him, or
  (b) that he has paid the duty due (or an amount equal to the duty due) in respect of the vehicle for any such month or part of a month,
any amount which the person is ordered to pay under section 30 is to be calculated as if that month or part of a month were not in the relevant period.

(6) Where a person has previously been ordered under section 36 to pay an amount for a month or part of a month in the case of a vehicle, any amount which he is ordered to pay under section 30 in the case of the vehicle is to be calculated as if no part of that month were in the relevant period.

(7) In this section references to the expiry of a vehicle licence include a reference to—
  (a) its surrender, and
  (b) its being treated as no longer in force for the purposes of subsection (2) of section 29 by subsection (4) of that section.

(8) In the case of a conviction for a continuing offence, the offence is to be taken for the purposes of this section to have been committed on the date or latest date to which the conviction relates.

Other offences relating to licences

Not exhibiting licence

33.—(1) A person is guilty of an offence if—   **B22–04**
   (a) he uses, or keeps, on a public road a vehicle in respect of which vehicle excise duty is chargeable, and
   (b) there is not fixed to and exhibited on the vehicle in the manner prescribed by regulations made by the Secretary of State a licence for, or in respect of, the vehicle which is for the time being in force.
  (2) A person guilty of an offence under subsection (1) is liable on summary conviction to a fine not exceeding level 1 on the standard scale.
  (3) Subsection (1)—
   (a) has effect subject to the provisions of regulations made by the Secretary of State, and
   (b) is without prejudice to section 29.

Other offences

Forgery and Fraud

44.—(1) A person is guilty of an offence if he forges, fraudulently alters,   **B22–05**
fraudulently lends or fraudulently allows to be used by another person anything to which subsection (2) applies.
  (2) This subsection applies to—
   (a) a vehicle licence,
   (b) a trade licence,
   (c) a document in the form of a licence which is issued in pursuance of regulations under this Act in respect of a vehicle which is an exempt vehicle under paragraph 19 of Schedule 2,
   (d) a registration mark,
   (e) a registration document, and
   (f) a trade plate (including a replacement trade plate).
  (3) A person guilty of an offence under this section is liable—
   (a) on summary conviction, to a fine not exceeding the statutory maximum, and
   (b) on conviction on indictment, to imprisonment for a term not exceeding two years or to a fine or (except in Scotland) to both.

Other definitions

62.—(1) In this Act, unless the context otherwise requires—   **B22–06**
  "axle", in relation to a vehicle, includes—
   (a) two or more stub axles which are fitted on opposite sides of the longitudinal axis of the vehicle so as to form a pair in the case of two stub axles or pairs in the case of more than two stub axles,
   (b) a single stub axle which is not one of a pair, and
   (c) a retractable axle,
   ("stub axle" meaning an axle on which only one wheel is mounted),
  "built-in road construction machinery", in relation to a vehicle, means road construction machinery built in as part of, or permanently attached to, the vehicle,

"business" includes the performance by a local or public authority of its functions,

"disabled person" means a person suffering from a physical or mental defect or disability,

"exempt vehicle" means a vehicle in respect of which vehicle excise duty is not chargeable,

"farmer's goods vehicle" means a goods vehicle registered under this Act in the name of a person engaged in agriculture and used on public roads solely by him—

  (a) for the purpose of the conveyance of the produce of, or of articles required for, the agricultural land which he occupies, and

  (b) for no other purpose except a purpose not involving the conveyance of goods or burden for hire or reward or for or in connection with a trade or business,

"goods vehicle" means a vehicle constructed or adapted for use and used for the conveyance of goods or burden of any description, whether in the course of trade or not,

"motor dealer" means a person carrying on the business of selling or supplying vehicles,

"motor trader" means—

  (a) a manufacturer or repairer of, or dealer in, vehicles, or

  (b) any other description of person who carries on a business of such description as may be prescribed by regulations made by the Secretary of State,

and a person is treated as a dealer in vehicles if he carries on a business consisting wholly or mainly of collecting and delivering vehicles, and not including any other activities except activities as a manufacturer or repairer of, or dealer in, vehicles,

"public road"—

  (a) in England and Wales and Northern Ireland, means a road which is repairable at the public expense, and

  (b) in Scotland, has the same meaning as in the Roads (Scotland) Act 1984,

"registration mark" is to be construed in accordance with section 23(1),

"relevant right" is to be construed in accordance with section 27(3)(a) and (b),

"right of retention" is to be construed in accordance with section 26(1) and (2)(a),

"rigid goods vehicle" means a goods vehicle which is not a tractive unit,

"road construction machinery" means a machine or device suitable for use for the construction or repair of roads and used for no purpose other than the construction or repair of roads at the public expense,

"road construction vehicle" means a vehicle—

  (a) which is constructed or adapted for use for the conveyance of built-in road construction machinery, and

  (b) which is not constructed or adapted for the conveyance of any other load except articles and material used for the purposes of such machinery,

"showman's goods vehicle" means a showman's vehicle which—

  (a) is a goods vehicle, and

  (b) is permanently fitted with a living van or some other special type of body or superstructure forming part of the equipment of the show of the person in whose name the vehicle is registered under this Act,

"showman's vehicle" means a vehicle—
  (a) registered under this Act in the name of a person following the business of a travelling showman, and
  (b) used solely by him for the purposes of his business and for no other purpose,

"temporary licence" is to be construed in accordance with section 9(1),

"tractive unit" means a goods vehicle to which a semi-trailer may be so attached that—
  (a) part of the semi-trailer is superimposed on part of the goods vehicle, and
  (b) when the semi-trailer is uniformly loaded, not less than twenty per cent of the weight of its load is borne by the goods vehicle,

"trade licence" is to be construed in accordance with section 11,

"vehicle" means a mechanically propelled vehicle,

"vehicle excise duty" is to be construed in accordance with section 1(1),

"vehicle licence" is to be construed in accordance with section 1(2), and

"vehicle tester" means a person, other than a motor trader, who regularly in the course of his business engages in the testing on roads of vehicles belonging to other persons.

(2) For the purposes of this Act and any other enactment relating to the keeping of vehicles on public roads, a person keeps a vehicle on a public road if he causes it to be on such a road for any period, however short, when it is not in use there.

CRIMINAL JUSTICE AND PUBLIC ORDER ACT 1994

(1994 c. 33)

Secure training orders

Secure training orders

1.—(1) Subject to section 8(1) of the Criminal Justice Act 1982 and section 53(1) of the Children and Young Persons Act 1933 (sentences of custody for life and long term detention), where—   **B23–01**
  (a) a person of not less than 12 but under 15 years of age is convicted of an imprisonable offence; and
  (b) the court is satisfied of the matters specified in subsection (5) below,
the court may make a secure training order.

(2) A secure training order is an order that the offender in respect of whom it is made shall be subject to a period of detention in a secure training centre followed by a period of supervision.

(3) The period of detention and supervision shall be such as the court determines and specifies in the order, being not less than six months nor more than two years.

(4) The period of detention which the offender is liable to serve under a secure training order shall be one half of the total period specified by the court in making the order.

(5) The court shall not make a secure training order unless it is satisfied—

    (a) that the offender was not less than 12 years of age when the offence for which he is to be dealt with by the court was committed;

    (b) that the offender has been convicted of three or more imprisonable offences; and

    (c) that the offender, either on this or a previous occasion—

        (i) has been found by a court to be in breach of a supervision order under the Children and Young Persons Act 1969, or

        (ii) has been convicted of an imprisonable offence committed whilst he was subject to such a supervision order.

(6) A secure training order is a custodial sentence for the purposes of sections 1 to 4 of the Criminal Justice Act 1991 (restrictions etc. as to custodial sentences).

(7) Where a court makes a secure training order, it shall be its duty to state in open court that it is of the opinion that the conditions specified in subsection (5) above are satisfied.

(8) In this section "imprisonable offence" means an offence (not being one for which the sentence is fixed by law) which is punishable with imprisonment in the case of a person aged 21 or over.

(9) For the purposes of this section, the age of a person shall be deemed to be that which it appears to the court to be after considering any available evidence.

(10) This section shall have effect, as from the day appointed for each of the following paragraphs, with the substitution in subsections (1) and (5)—

    (a) of "14" for "12";

    (b) of "13" for "14";

    (c) of "12" for "13";

but no substitution may be brought into force on more than one occasion.

Secure training orders: supplementary provisions as to detention

B23–02   2.—(1) The following provisions apply in relation to a person ("the Offender") in respect of whom a secure training order ("the order") has been made under section 1.

(2) Where accommodation for the offender at a secure training centre is not immediately available—

    (a) the court may commit the offender to such place and on such conditions—

        (i) as the Secretary of State may direct, or

        (ii) as the Secretary of State may arrange with a person to whom this sub-paragraph applies,

    and for such period (not exceeding 28 days) as the court may specify or until his transfer to a secure training centre, if earlier;

    (b) if no such accommodation becomes or will become available before the expiry of the period of the committal the court may, on application, extend the period of committal (subject to the restriction referred to in paragraph (a) above); and

    (c) the period of detention in the secure training centre under the order shall be reduced by the period spent by the offender in such a place.

(3) The power conferred by subsection (2)(b) above may, subject to section 1(4), be exercised from time to time and the reference in subsection (2)(b) to the

expiry of the period of the committal is, in the case of the initial extension, a reference to the expiry of the period of the committal under subsection (2)(a) above and, in the case of a further extension, a reference to the expiry of the period of the previous committal by virtue of this subsection.

(4) Where the circumstances of the case require, the Secretary of State may transfer the offender from a secure training centre to such other place and on such conditions—

    (a) as the Secretary of State may direct, or

    (b) as the Secretary of State may arrange with a person to whom this paragraph applies;

and the period of detention in the secure training centre under the order shall be reduced by the period spent by the offender in such a place.

(5) The persons to whom subsections (2)(a)(ii) and (4)(b) apply are local authorities, voluntary organisations and persons carrying on a registered childrens' home.

(6) Where the Secretary of State is satisfied that exceptional circumstances exist which justify the offender's release on compassionate grounds he may release the offender from the secure training centre; and the offender shall, on his release, be subject to supervision for the remainder of the term of the order.

(7) A person detained in pursuance of directions or arrangements made for his detention shall be deemed to be in legal custody.

(8) In this section "local authority", "voluntary organisation" and "registered children's home" have the same meaning as in the Children Act 1989.

Supervision under secure training order

3.—(1) The following provisions apply as respects the period of supervision   **B23–03** of a person ("the offender") subject to a secure training order.

(2) The offender shall be under the supervision of a probation officer, a social worker of a local authority social services department or such other person as the Secretary of State may designate.

(3) The category of person to supervise the offender shall be determined from time to time by the Secretary of State.

(4) Where the supervision is to be provided by a social worker of a local authority social services department, the social worker shall be a social worker of the local authority within whose area the offender resides for the time being.

(5) Where the supervision is to be provided by a probation officer, the probation officer shall be an officer appointed for or assigned to the petty sessions area within which the offender resides for the time being.

(6) The probation committee or local authority shall be entitled to recover from the Secretary of State the expenses reasonably incurred by them in discharging their duty under this section.

(7) The offender shall be given a notice from the Secretary of State specifying—

    (a) the category of person for the time being responsible for his supervision; and

    (b) any requirements with which he must for the time being comply.

(8) A notice under subsection (7) above shall be given to the offender—

    (a) before the commencement of the period of supervision; and

    (b) before any alteration in the matters specified in subsection (7)(a) or (b) comes into effect.

(9) The Secretary of State may by statutory instrument make rules for regulating the supervision of the offender.

(10) The power to make rules under subsection (9) above includes power to make provision in the rules by the incorporation by reference of provisions contained in other documents.

(11) A statutory instrument made under subsection (9) above shall be subject to annulment in pursuance of a resolution of either House of Parliament.

(12) The sums required by the Secretary of State for making payments under subsection (6) shall be defrayed out of money provided by Parliament.

Breaches of requirements of supervision of persons subject to secure training orders

B23–04   4.—(1) Where a secure training order has been made as respects an offender and it appears on information to a justice of the peace acting for a relevant petty sessions area that the offender has failed to comply with requirements under section 3(7)(b) the justice may issue a summons requiring the offender to appear at the place and time specified in the summons before a youth court acting for the area or, if the information is in writing and on oath, may issue a warrant for the offender's arrest requiring him to be brought before such a court.

(2) For the purposes of this section a petty sessions area is a relevant petty sessions area in relation to a secure training order—

(a) if the secure training centre is situated in it;

(b) if the order was made by a youth court acting for it; or

(c) if the offender resides in it for the time being.

(3) If it is proved to the satisfaction of the youth court before which an offender appears or is brought under this section that he has failed to comply with requirements under section 3(7)(b) that court may—

(a) order the offender to be detained in a secure training centre for such period, not exceeding the shorter of three months or the remainder of the period of the secure training order, as the court may specify, or

(b) impose on the offender a fine not exceeding level 3 on the standard scale.

(4) Where accommodation for an offender in relation to whom the court decides to exercise their powers under subsection (3)(a) above is not immediately available, paragraphs (a), (b) and (c) of subsection (2) and subsections (5), (7) and (8) of section 2 shall apply in relation to him as they apply in relation to an offender in respect of whom a secure training order is made.

(5) For the purposes of this section references to a failure to comply include references to a contravention.

Provision etc. of secure training centres

B23–05   5.—(1) Section 43 of the Prison Act 1952 (which enables certain institutions for young offenders to be provided and applies provisions of the Act to them) shall be amended as follows.

(2) In subsection (1), after paragraph (c), there shall be inserted the following paragraph, preceded by the word "and"—

> "(d) secure training centres, that is to say places in which offenders not less than 12 but under 17 years of age in respect of whom secure training orders have been made under section 1 of the

Criminal Justice and Public Order Act 1994 may be detained and given training and education and prepared for their release".

(3) After subsection (4), there shall be inserted the following subsection—
"(4A) Sections 16, 22 and 36 of this Act shall apply to secure training centres and to persons detained in them as they apply to prisons and prisoners.".

(4) In subsection (5), for the words "such centres" there shall be substituted the words "centres of the descriptions specified in subsection (4) above".

(5) After subsection (5), there shall be inserted the following subsection—

"(5A) The other provisions of this Act preceding this section, except sections 5, 5A, 6(2) and (3), 12, 14, 19, 25, 28 and 37(2) and (3) above, shall apply to prisons and prisoners, but subject to such adaptations and modifications as may be specified in rules made by the Secretary of State.".

Management of secure training centres

6.—(1) Section 47 of the Prison Act 1952 (rules for the regulation and management of prisons and certain institutions for young offenders) shall be amended as follows.   **B23–06**

(2) In subsection (1), for the words between "remand centres" and "respectively", there shall be substituted the words ", young offender institutions or secure training centres".

(3) After subsection (4), there shall be inserted the following subsection—

"(4A) Rules made under this section shall provide for the inspection of secure training centres and the appointment of independent persons to visit secure training centres and to whom representations may be made by offenders detained in secure training centres.".

(4) In subsection (5), for the words betweeen "remand centre" and "not" there shall be substituted the words ", young offender institution or secure training centre".

Contracting out of secure training centres

7.—(1) The Secretary of State may enter into a contract with another person for the provision or running (or the provision and running) by him, or (if the contract so provides) for the running by sub-contractors of his, of any secure training centre or part of a secure training centre.   **B23–07**

(2) While a contract for the running of a secure training centre or part of a secure training centre is in force the centre or part shall be run subject to and in accordance with the Prison Act 1952 and in accordance with secure training centre rules subject to such adaptations and modifications as the Secretary of State may specify in relation to contracted out secure training centres.

(3) Where the Secretary of State grants a lease or tenancy of land for the purposes of any contract under this section, none of the following enactments shall apply to it, namely—
   (a) Part II of the Landlord and Tenant Act 1954 (security of tenure);
   (b) section 146 of the Law of Property Act 1925 (restrictions on and relief against forfeiture); and

(c) section 19 of the Landlord and Tenant Act 1927 and the Landlord and Tenant Act 1988 (covenants not to assign etc.).

In this subsection "lease or tenancy" includes an underlease or sub-tenancy.

(4) In this section—

(a) the reference to the Prison Act 1952 is a reference to that Act as it applies to secure training centres by virtue of section 43 of that Act; and

(b) the reference to secure training centre rules is a reference to rules made under section 47 of that Act for the regulation and management of secure training centres.

Officers of contracted out secure training

B23–08   8.—(1) Instead of a governor, every contracted out secure training centre shall have—

(a) a director, who shall be a custody officer appointed by the contractor and specially approved for the purposes of this section by the Secretary of State; and

(b) a monitor, who shall be a Crown servant appointed by the Secretary of State;

and every officer of such a secure training centre who performs custodial duties shall be a custody officer who is authorised to perform such duties or an officer of a directly managed secure training centre who is temporarily attached to the secure training centre.

(2) The director shall have such functions as are conferred on him by the Prison Act 1952 as it applies to secure training centres and as may be conferred on him by secure training centre rules.

(3) The monitor shall have such functions as may be conferred on him by secure training centre rules and shall be under a duty—

(a) to keep under review, and report to the Secretary of State on, the running of the secure training centre by or on behalf of the director; and

(b) to investigate, and report to the Secretary of State on, any allegations made against custody officers performing custodial duties at the secure training centre or officers of directly managed secure training centres who are temporarily attached to the secure training centre.

(4) The contractor and any sub-contractor of his shall each be under a duty to do all that he reasonably can (whether by giving directions to the officers of the secure training centre or otherwise) to facilitate the exercise by the monitor of all such functions as are mentioned in or imposed by subsection (3) above.

Powers and duties of custody officers employed at contracted out secure training centres

B23–09   9.—(1) A custody officer performing custodial duties at a contracted out secure training centre shall have the following powers, namely—

(a) to search in accordance with secure training centre rules any offender who is detained in the secure training centre; and

(b) to search any other person who is in or who is seeking to enter the secure training centre, and any article in the possession of such a person.

(2) The powers conferred by subsection (1)(b) above to search a person shall

not be construed as authorising a custody officer to require a person to remove any of his clothing other than an outer coat, headgear, jacket or gloves.

(3) A custody officer performing custodial duties at a contracted out secure training centre shall have the following duties as respects offenders detained in the secure training centre, namely—

(a) to prevent their escape from lawful custody;

(b) to prevent, or detect and report on, the commission or attempted commission by them of other unlawful acts;

(c) to ensure good order and discipline on their part; and

(d) to attend to their wellbeing.

(4) The powers conferred by subsection (1) above, and the powers arising by virtue of subsection (3) above, shall include power to use reasonable force where necessary.

Intervention by Secretary of State in management of contracted out secure training centres

10.—(1) This section applies where, in the case of a contracted out secure training centre, it appears to the Secretary of State— **B23–10**

(a) that the director has lost, or is likely to lose, effective control of the secure training centre or any part of it; and

(b) that the making of an appointment under subsection (2) below is necessary in the interests of preserving the safety of any person, or of preventing serious damage to any property.

(2) The Secretary of State may appoint a Crown servant to act as governor of the secure training centre for the period—

(a) beginning with the time specified in the appointment; and

(b) ending with the time specified in the notice of termination under subsection (4) below.

(3) During that period—

(a) all the functions which would otherwise be exercisable by the director or monitor shall be exercisable by the governor;

(b) the contractor and any sub-contractor of his shall each do all that he reasonably can to facilitate the exercise by the governor of those functions; and

(c) the officers of the secure training centre shall comply with any directions given by the governor in the exercise of those functions.

(4) Where the Secretary of State is satisfied—

(a) that the governor has secured effective control of the secure training centre or, as the case may be, the relevant part of it; and

(b) that the governor's appointment is no longer necessary for the purpose mentioned in subsection (1)(b) above,

he shall, by a notice to the governor, terminate the appointment at a time specified in the notice.

(5) As soon as practicable after making or terminating an appointment under this section, the Secretary of State shall give a notice of the appointment, or a copy of the notice of termination, to the contractor, any sub-contractor of his, the director and the monitor.

Contracted out functions at directly managed secure training centres

11.—(1) The Secretary of State may enter into a contract with another person **B23–11**

for any functions at a directly managed secure training centre to be performed by custody officers who are provided by that person and are authorised to perform custodial duties.

(2) Section 9 shall apply in relation to a custody officer performing contracted out functions at a directly managed secure training centre as it applies in relation to such an officer performing custodial duties at a contracted out secure training centre.

(3) In relation to a directly managed secure training centre, the reference in section 13(2) of the Prison Act 1952 (legal custody of prisoners) as it applies to secure training centres to an officer of the prison shall be construed as including a reference to a custody officer performing custodial duties at the secure training centre in pursuance of a contract under this section.

(4) Any reference in subsections (1), (2) and (3) above to the performance of functions or custodial duties at a directly managed secure training centre includes a reference to the performance of functions or such duties for the purposes of, or for purposes connected with, such a secure training centre.

Escort arrangements and officers

B23–12   12.—(1) The provisions of Schedule 1 to this Act (which make provision for escort arrangements for offenders detained at a secure training centre) shall have effect.

(2) The provisions of Schedule 2 to this Act shall have effect with respect to the certification of custody officers.

(3) In this Part, "custody officer" means a person in respect of whom a certificate is for the time being in force certifying—
  (a) that he has been approved by the Secretary of State for the purpose of performing escort functions or custodial duties or both in relation to offenders in respect of whom secure training orders have been made; and
  (b) that he is accordingly authorised to perform them.

Protection of custody officers at secure training centres

B23–13   13.—(1) Any person who assaults a custody officer—
  (a) acting in pursuance of escort arrangements;
  (b) performing custodial duties at a contracted out secure training centre; or
  (c) performing contracted out functions at a directly managed secure training centre,
shall be liable on summary conviction to a fine not exceeding level 5 on the standard scale or to imprisonment for a term not exceeding six months or to both.

(2) Any person who resists or wilfully obstructs a custody officer—
  (a) acting in pursuance of escort arrangements;
  (b) performing custodial duties at a contracted out secure training centre; or
  (c) performing contracted out functions at a directly managed secure training centre,
shall be liable on summary conviction to a fine not exceeding level 3 on the standard scale.

(3) For the purposes of this section, a custody officer shall not be regarded as acting in pursuance of escort arrangements at any time when he is not readily

identifiable as such an officer (whether by means of a uniform or badge which he is wearing or otherwise).

Wrongful disclosure of information relating to offenders detained at secure training centres

14.—(1) A person who—   **B23–14**
   (a) is or has been employed (whether as a custody officer or otherwise) in pursuance of escort arrangements or at a contracted out secure training centre; or
   (b) is or has been employed to perform contracted out functions at a directly managed secure training centre,
commits an offence if he discloses, otherwise than in the course of his duty or as authorised by the Secretary of State, any information which he acquired in the course of his employment and which relates to a particular offender detained at a secure training centre.
  (2) A person guilty of an offence under subsection (1) above shall be liable—
   (a) on conviction on indictment, to imprisonment for a term not exceeding two years or a fine or both;
   (b) on summary conviction, to imprisonment for a term not exceeding six months or a fine not exceeding the statutory maximum or both.

Interpretation of sections 7 to 14

15. In sections 7 to 14—   **B23–15**
   "contracted out functions" means any functions which, by virtue of a contract under section 11, fall to be performed by custody officers;
   "contracted out secure training centre" means a secure training centre or part of a secure training centre in respect of which a contract under section 7(1) is for the time being in force;
   "the contractor", in relation to a contracted out secure training centre, means the person who has contracted with the Secretary of State for the provision or running (or the provision and running) of it;
   "custodial duties" means custodial duties at a secure training centre;
   "directly managed secure training centre" means a secure training centre which is not a contracted out secure training centre;
   "escort arrangements" means the arrangements specified in paragraph 1 of Schedule 1 to this Act;
   "escort functions" means the functions specified in paragraph 1 of Schedule 1 to this Act;
   "escort monitor" means a person appointed under paragraph 2(1)(a) of Schedule 1 to this Act;
   "secure training centre rules" has the meaning given by section 7(4)(b); and
   "sub-contractor", in relation to a contracted out secure training centre, means a person who has contracted with the contractor for the running of it or any part of it.

Custodial sentences for young offenders

Long term detention of young offenders

16.—(1) Section 53 of the Children and Young Persons Act 1933 (which pro-   **B23–16**

vides for the long term detention of children and young persons for certain grave crimes) shall be amended as follows.

(2) In subsection (1), for the words after "conditions" there shall be substituted—

"—

(a) as the Secretary of State may direct, or
(b) as the Secretary of State may arrange with any person.".

(3) In subsection (2), for the words from the beginning to the words "and the court" there shall be substituted the following—

"(2) Subsection (3) below applies—
(a) where a person of at least 10 but not more than 17 years is convicted on indictment of—
(i) any offence punishable in the case of an adult with imprisonment for fourteen years or more, not being an offence the sentence for which is fixed by law, or
(ii) an offence under section 14 of the Sexual Offences Act 1956 (indecent assault on a woman);
(b) where a young person is convicted of—
(i) an offence under section 1 of the Road Traffic Act 1988 (causing death by dangerous driving), or
(ii) an offence under section 3A of the Road Traffic Act 1988 (causing death by careless driving while under influence of drink or drugs).
(3) Where this subsection applies, then, if the court".

(4) For the words from "as the" in subsection (3) to the end of the section there shall be substituted—

"—

(a) as the Secretary of State may direct, or
(b) as the Secretary of State may arrange with any person.
(4) A person detained pursuant to the directions or arrangements made by the Secretary of State under this section shall, while so detained, be deemed to be in legal custody.".

Maximum length of detention for young offenders

B23–17   17.—(1) Section 1B of the Criminal Justice Act 1982 (maximum length of detention in young offender institution for offenders aged 15, 16 or 17 years) shall be amended as follows.

(2) In subsection (2)(b), for the words "12 months" there shall be substituted the words "24 months".

(3) In subsection (4), for the words "12 months" there shall be substituted the words "24 months".

(4) In subsection (5), for the words, "12 months" in both places where they occur there shall be substituted the words "24 months".

Sentencing: guilty pleas

Reduction in sentences for guilty pleas

B23–18   48.—(1) In determining what sentence to pass on an offender who has pleaded guilty to an offence in proceedings before that or another court a court shall take into account—

    (a) the stage in the proceedings for the offence at which the offender indicated his intention to plead guilty, and

    (b) the circumstances in which this indication was given.

    (2) If, as a result of taking into account any matter referred to in subsection (1) above, the court imposes a punishment on the offender which is less severe than the punishment it would otherwise have imposed, it shall state in open court that it has done so.

VARIOUS TRUNK ROADS (PROHIBITION OF WAITING) (CLEARWAYS) ORDER 1963

(S.I. 1963 No. 1172)

Interpretation

3.—(1) In this Order the following expressions have the meanings hereby **C1–01** respectively assigned to them:—

"the Act of 1960" means the Road Traffic Act, 1960;

"main carriageway", in relation to a trunk road, means any carriageway of that road used primarily by through traffic and excludes any lay-by;

"lay-by", in relation to a main carriageway of a trunk road, means any area intended for use for the waiting of vehicles, lying at a side of the road and bounded partly by a traffic sign consisting of a yellow dotted line on the road, or of a white dotted line and the words "lay-by" on the road, authorised by the Minister under subsection (2) of section 51 of the Act of 1960, and partly by the outer edge of that carriageway on the same side of the road as that on which the sign is placed;

"verge" means any part of a road which is not a carriageway.

(2) The Interpretation Act, 1889, shall apply for the interpretation of this Order as it applies for the interpretation of an Act of Parliament, and as if for the purposes of section 38 of that Act this Order were an Act of Parliament and the Orders revoked by Article 2 were Acts of Parliament thereby repealed.

Prohibition of waiting on main carriageways

4. Save as provided in Article 5 of this Order no person shall, except upon **C1** the direction or with the permission of a police constable in uniform, cause or permit any vehicle to wait on any of those main carriageways forming part of trunk roads which are specified in Schedule 1 to this Order.

Exceptions to Article 4

5. Nothing in Article 4 of this Order shall apply— **C**

(a) so as to prevent a vehicle waiting on any main carriageway specified in Schedule 1 to this Order for so long as may be necessary to enable the vehicle, if it cannot be used for such purpose without waiting on that carriageway, to be used in connection with any building operation or demolition, the removal of any obstruction or potential obstruction to traffic, the maintenance, improvement or reconstruction of the road comprising that carriageway, or the erection, laying, placing, maintenance, testing, alteration, repair or removal of any structure, works, or apparatus in, on, under or over that road;

(b) to a vehicle being used for fire brigade, ambulance or police purposes;

(c) to a vehicle being used for the purpose of delivering or collecting postal packets as defined in section 87 of the Post Office Act, 1953;

(d) so as to prevent a vehicle being used by or on behalf of a local authority from waiting on any main carriageway specified in Schedule 1 to this Order for so long as may be necessary to enable the vehicle if it cannot be used for such a purpose without waiting on that carriageway, to be used for the purpose of the collection of household refuse from, or the clearing of cesspools at, premises situated on or adjacent to the road comprising that carriageway;

(e) to a vehicle waiting on any main carriageway specified in Schedule 1 to this Order while any gate or other barrier at the entrance to premises to which the vehicle requires access or from which it has emerged is opened or closed, if it is not reasonably practicable for the vehicle to wait otherwise than on that carriageway while such gate or barrier is being opened or closed;

(f) to a vehicle waiting in any case where the person in control of the vehicle:—
    (i) is required by law to stop;
    (ii) is obliged to do so in order to avoid an accident; or
    (iii) is prevented from proceeding by circumstances outside his control and it is not reasonably practicable for him to drive or move the vehicle to a place not on any main carriageway specified in Schedule 1 to this Order.

Restriction of waiting on verges, etc.

C1–04   **6.** No person shall cause or permit any vehicle to wait on any verge or lay-by immediately adjacent to a main carriageway specified in Schedule 1 to this Order for the purpose of selling goods from that vehicle unless the goods are immediately delivered at or taken into premises adjacent to the vehicle from which sale is effected.

USE OF INVALID CARRIAGES ON HIGHWAYS REGULATIONS 1970

(S.I. 1970 No. 1391)

Commencement, citation and interpretation

C2–01   **1.**—(1) These Regulations shall come into operation on the 29th September 1970, and may be cited as the Use of Invalid Carriages on Highways Regulations 1970.

(2) The Interpretation Act 1889 shall apply for the interpretation of these Regulations as it applies for the interpretation of an Act of Parliament.

Prescribed requirements and conditions for purposes of section 20(1) of the said Act of 1970

C2–02   **2.** The requirements with which an invalid carriage (within the meaning of subsection (2) of the said section 20) must comply, and the conditions in

accordance with which it must be used, in order that the modifications of the statutory provisions mentioned in subsection (1) of that section shall have effect in the case of the vehicle (being modifications of certain statutory provisions which relate to the use of vehicles on footways and roads) shall be—

(a) that the vehicle is being used by a person for whose use it was constructed or adapted, being a person suffering from some physical defect or disability, or by some other person for the purposes only of taking the vehicle to or bringing it away from any place where work of maintenance or repair is to be or has been carried out to the vehicle; and

(b) the requirements (subject to the exceptions specified in relation thereto) as set out in Regulations 3 to 6 below.

Unladen weight

3. The unladen weight of an invalid carriage (that is to say, its weight inclusive of the weight of water, fuel or accumulators used for the purpose of the supply of power for its propulsion and of loose tools, but exclusive of the weight of any other load or of a person carried by the vehicle) shall not exceed 250 lbs.   **C2–03**

Limit of speed

4. An invalid carriage which is mechanically propelled shall be so constructed as to be incapable of exceeding a speed of 4 miles per hour on the level under its own power.

Brakes

5.—(1) Subject to paragraph (3) below, an invalid carriage which is mechanically propelled shall be equipped with an efficient braking system so designed and constructed—   **C2–04**

(a) that the application of the brakes shall bring the vehicle to rest within a reasonable distance; and

(b) that its braking force, when the vehicle is not being propelled or is left unattended—

(i) can at all times be maintained in operation by direct mechanical action without the intervention of any hydraulic, electric or pneumatic device, and

(ii) when so maintained in operation by direct mechanical action, is capable of holding the vehicle stationary on a gradient of at least 1 in 5 without the assistance of stored energy.

(2) Every part of the braking system and of the means of operation thereof fitted to the vehicle shall be maintained in good and efficient working order and be properly adjusted.

(3) The requirements of paragraph (1) above shall be deemed to be complied with in the case of a vehicle which is not equipped with such a braking system as is mentioned in that paragraph if the vehicle is so designed and constructed that by the appropriate use of its means of propulsion and transmission gear it can be brought to rest within a reasonable distance and held stationary on a gradient of at least 1 in 5.

Lighting

C2–05   6.—(1) Subject to paragraph (3) below, an invalid carriage when on the carriageway of any road shall during the hours of darkness carry—

    (a) one lamp showing to the front a white light visible from a reasonable distance;

    (b) one lamp showing to the rear a red light visible from a reasonable distance; and

    (c) one unobscured and efficient red reflector facing to the rear.

(2) Every such lamp shall be kept properly trimmed, lighted, and in a clean and efficient condition, and every such lamp and reflector shall be attached to the vehicle in such position and manner, and shall comply with such conditions with respect thereto, as are specified in the Schedule to these Regulations.

(3) The foregoing provisions of this Regulation shall not apply in relation to a vehicle when it is on the carriageway of a road for the purpose only of crossing that carriageway in the quickest manner practicable in the circumstances.

(4) In this Regulation,—

    (a) "road" means any highway and any other road to which the public has access not being (in either case) a footway within the meaning of section 20(2) of the said Act of 1970, and

    (b) "hours of darkness" means the time between half-an-hour after sunset and half-an-hour before sunrise.

SCHEDULE   **(see Regulation 6)**

Conditions as to Lamps and Reflectors

C2–06   1. The lamp showing a white light to the front shall be fixed on the centre line or off side of the vehicle.

2. The lamp showing a red light to the rear shall be so fixed that—

    (a) its lateral position is on the centre line or off side of the vehicle,

    (b) its longitudinal position is not more than 20 inches from the extreme rear of the vehicle,

    (c) the maximum height from the ground of the highest part of the illuminated area of the lamp is 3 feet 6 inches, and

    (d) the minimum height from the ground of the lowest part of the said area is 12 inches, and shall be marked—

        (i) with the specification number of the British Standard for Cycle Rear Lamps, namely, BS 3648, and

        (ii) with the name, trade mark or other means of identification of the manufacturer of the lamp.

3. The reflector shall be so fixed that—

    (a) its lateral position is on the centre line or off side of the vehicle,

    (b) its longitudinal position is not more than 20 inches from the extreme rear of the vehicle,

    (c) the maximum height from the ground of the highest part of the reflecting area of the reflector is 3 feet 6 inches, and

    (d) the minimum height from the ground of the lowest part of the said area is 12 inches, and shall be marked—

(i) with the specification number of the British Standard for Reflex Reflectors for Vehicles, namely, AU 40 followed by a marking "LI" or "LIA" and with the registered trade name or trade mark of the manufacturer of the reflector, or

(ii) with an approval mark (that is to say, a marking designated as an approval mark by the Motor Vehicles (Designation of Approval Marks) (No. 2) Regulations 1964 incorporating the roman numeral I.

VEHICLE AND DRIVING LICENCES RECORDS (EVIDENCE) REGULATIONS 1970

(S.I. 1970 No. 1997)

Matters prescribed for s.27(3) of the Act

3. The following matters are prescribed for the purposes of section 27(3) of **C3–01** the Act—

(1) in connection with the licensing of drivers under Part II of the Road Traffic Act 1960—

(a) a document being, forming part of, or submitted in connection with, an application for a driving licence;

(b) a driving licence;

(c) a certificate of competence to drive;

(d) the conviction of an offence specified in Part I or Part II of Schedule 1 to the Road Traffic Act 1962 or of an offence treated as so specified by virtue of section 5 of the Road Safety Act 1967 of any person or any order made by the Court as a result of any such conviction;

(2) in connection with the licensing and registration of mechanically propelled vehicles under the 1962 Act—

(a) a document being, forming part of, or submitted in connection with, an application for—

(i) a vehicle licence;

(ii) a trade licence;

(iii) a repayment of duty under section 9 of the 1962 Act or the recovery of underpayments or overpayments of duty under section 11 of that Act;

(b) a vehicle licence, trade licence, registration book or registration mark;

(c) a document containing a declaration and particulars such as are prescribed under the 1962 Act in relation to vehicles exempted from duty under that Act;

(d) the conviction of an offence under the 1962 Act of any person;

(3) in connection with the examination of a goods vehicle under regulations under section 9 of the Road Safety Act 1967—

(a) an application for an examination of a vehicle under the said regulations;

(b) a notifiable alteration made to a vehicle and required by the said regulations to be notified to the Secretary of State;

(c) a plating certificate, goods vehicle test certificate, notification of the refusal of a goods vehicle test certificate, Ministry plate, Ministry test date disc or certificate of temporary exemption.

ROAD VEHICLES (REGISTRATION AND LICENSING) REGULATIONS 1971

(S.I. 1971 No. 450)

Interpretation

C4–01   **3.**—(1) In these Regulations, unless the context otherwise requires, the following expressions have the meanings hereby respectively assigned to them, that is to say:—

"the Act" means the Vehicles (Excise) Act 1971;

"agricultural machine" has the same meaning as in Schedule 3 to the Act;

"bicycle" means a mechanically propelled bicycle (including a motor scooter, a bicycle with an attachment for propelling it by mechanical power and a mechanically propelled bicycle used for drawing a trailer or sidecar) not exceeding 8 hundredweight in weight unladen;

"hours of darkness" means the time between half-an-hour after sunset and half-an-hour before sunrise;

"invalid vehicle" means a mechanically propelled vehicle (including a cycle with an attachment for propelling it by mechanical power) which does not exceed ten hundredweight in weight unladen and is adapted and used or kept on a road for an invalid or invalids;

"owner" in relation to a vehicle means the person by whom the vehicle is kept [...] and the expression "ownership" shall be construed accordingly;

"pedestrian controlled vehicle" means a mechanically propelled vehicle with three or more wheels which does not exceed 8 hundredweight in weight unladen and which is neither constructed nor adapted for use nor used for the carriage of a driver or passenger;

"prescribed" means, in relation to any declaration or particulars, prescribed by the Road Vehicles (Excise) (Prescribed Particulars) Regulations 1966, as amended by the Road Vehicles (Excise) (Prescribed Particulars) (Amendment) Regulations 1969 and by the Road Vehicles (Excise) (Prescribed Particulars) (Amendment) Regulations 1970;

"register" means the record kept by or on behalf of the Secretary of State of the mechanically propelled vehicles registered by him in pursuance of section 19 of the Act or which in accordance with the provisions of these Regulations are required to be registered with him;

"road" has the same meaning as in section 257 of the Road Traffic Act 1960;

"trade licence" has the meaning assigned to it by section 16 of the Act;

"trade plates" has the meaning assigned thereto in Regulation 31 of these Regulations;

"tricycle" means a mechanically propelled tricycle (including a motor scooter and a tricycle with an attachment for propelling it by mechanical power) not exceeding 8 hundredweight in weight unladen and not being a pedestrian controlled vehicle;

"valeting" means the thorough cleaning of a vehicle prior to its first registration by the Secretary of State including removing wax and grease from the exterior, engine and interior, and "valeted" shall be construed accordingly;

"works truck" means a mechanically propelled vehicle designed for use in private premises and used on a road only in delivering goods from or to such premises to or from a vehicle on a road in the immediate neighbourhood, or in passing from one part of any such premises to another or to other private premises in the immediate neighbourhood or in connection with road works while at or in the immediate neighbourhood of the site of such works.

(2) Any reference in these Regulations to any enactment shall be construed as a reference to that enactment as amended by or under any subsequent enactment.

(3) The Interpretation Act 1889 shall apply for the interpretation of these Regulations as it applies for the interpretation of an Act of Parliament, and as if for the purposes of section 38 of that Act these Regulations were an Act of Parliament and the Regulations revoked by Regulation 2 of these Regulations were Acts of Parliament thereby repealed.

Exclusion for electrically assisted pedal cycles

3A. The provisions of Parts II and III of these Regulations do not apply to an   **C4–02**
electrically assisted pedal cycle for the time being prescribed for the purposes of section 103 of the Road Traffic Regulation Act 1967 and section 193 of the Road Traffic Act 1972.

Notification of change of ownership

12.—(1) On a change of ownership of a mechanically propelled vehicle the   **C4–03**
previous owner of the vehicle shall deliver the registration book issued in respect of the vehicle and may deliver any current licence issued in respect of the vehicle to the new owner and shall notify in writing forthwith the change of ownership to the Secretary of State stating the registration mark of the vehicle, its make and class and the name and address of the new owner.

(2) Upon acquiring the vehicle the new owner shall—

(a) if he intends to use or keep the vehicle upon public roads otherwise than under a trade licence, forthwith insert his name and address in the appropriate part of the registration book and deliver it to the Secretary of State;

(b) if he does not intend to use or keep the vehicle upon public roads, forthwith notify the Secretary of State in writing that he is the owner of the vehicle, and he shall state in such notification the registration mark of the vehicle, its make and class, the name and address of the previous owner and the fact that he does not intend to use or keep the vehicle on public roads;

(c) if he intends to use the vehicle upon public roads solely under a trade licence at the expiration of three months from the date when he became the owner of the vehicle or, if a further change of ownership occurs, on the date of that change, whichever is the sooner, notify the Secretary of State in writing of his name and address and those of the previous owner.

Notification of change of address of owner

C4–04   **13.** If the owner of a mechanically propelled vehicle changes his address he shall forthwith enter particulars of his new address in the space provided in the registration book issued in respect of the vehicle and send the book to the Secretary of State.

Exhibition of licences

C4–05   **16.**—(1) Every licence issued under the Act and in force for a mechanically propelled vehicle, excepting a tramcar, shall be fixed to and exhibited on the vehicle in accordance with the provisions of this Regulation at all times while the vehicle is being used or kept on a public road:

Provided that when such a licence is delivered up with an application for a new licence to any post office authorised for the time being to issue vehicle licences in accordance with arrangements for that purpose made between the Post Office and the Secretary of State, no licence shall be required to be fixed to and exhibited on the vehicle until the new licence is obtained, when that licence shall be deemed to be the licence in force for the vehicle for the purposes of this Regulation.

(2) Each such licence shall be fixed to the vehicle in a holder sufficient to protect the licence from any effects of the weather to which it would otherwise be exposed.

(3) The licence shall be exhibited on the vehicle:—

(a) in the case of an invalid vehicle, tricycle or bicycle, other than a case specified in sub-paragraph (b) or (c) of this paragraph, on the near side of the vehicle in front of the driving seat so that all the particulars thereon are clearly visible by daylight from the near side of the road;

(b) in the case of a bicycle drawing a side-car or to which a side-car is attached when the bicycle is being kept on a public road, on the near side of the handlebars of the bicycle or on the near side of the side-car in front of the driving seat so that all the particulars thereon are clearly visible by daylight from the near side of the road;

(c) in the case of any vehicle fitted with a glass windscreen in front of the driver extending across the vehicle to its near side, on or adjacent to the near side [...] of the windscreen, so that all particulars thereon are clearly visible by daylight from the near side of the road;

(d) in the case of any other vehicle, if the vehicle is fitted with a driver's cab containing a near side window, on such window, or on the near side of the vehicle in front of the driver's seat or towards the front of the vehicle in the case of a pedestrian controlled vehicle and not less than 2 feet 6 inches and not more than 6 feet above the surface of the road, so that in each case all the particulars thereon are clearly visible by daylight from the near side of the road.

C4–06   **19.**—(1) Save as provided in paragraph (2) below, no person shall use or cause or permit to be used on a road during the hours of darkness any motor vehicle unless every letter and number of the registration mark displayed on the back of—

(a) the motor vehicle if it is not drawing a trailer, or

(b) the trailer if the motor vehicle is drawing one trailer, or

(c) the rearmost trailer if the motor vehicle is drawing more than one trailer,

is illuminated so as to be easily legible in the absence of fog from every part of the relevant area, the diagonal of the square governing that area being—

(i) 15 metres in the case of a bicycle, an invalid vehicle and a pedestrian controlled vehicle, and

(ii) 18 metres in the case of any other vehicle.

(2) The provisions of paragraph (1) above do not apply in respect of:—

(a) a works truck; or

(b) a vehicle which is not required to be fitted with a rear registration plate.

Trailers

22.—(1) Subject to paragraph (3) of this Regulation, where one or more trailers are attached to a mechanically propelled vehicle the owner of the vehicle shall ensure that there is displayed on the trailer or rearmost trailer (as the case may be) the registration mark of the mechanically propelled vehicle, and that such registration mark is fixed to and displayed on the trailer as if the trailer were a vehicle of the same class or description as the mechanically propelled vehicle.   **C4–07**

(2) Where the registration mark of a mechanically propelled vehicle is fixed to and displayed on a trailer attached to it in accordance with the foregoing paragraph, the requirements of these Regulations as to the fixing to and display of a registration mark on the back of a mechanically propelled vehicle shall not apply to the vehicle drawing the trailer.

(3) Where the mechanically propelled vehicle is a restricted vehicle, the registration mark fixed to and displayed on the trailer in accordance with paragraph (1) of this Regulation may, instead of being that of the vehicle to which the trailer is attached, be that of any other restricted vehicle belonging to the owner of the vehicle to which the trailer is attached, and in such a case the duty in the said paragraph (1) as to fixing and display shall apply as if the other restricted vehicle were the vehicle to which the trailer was attached.

(4) In this Regulation "restricted vehicle" means a vehicle mentioned in section 7(1) of the Act or paragraph 2(1) of Schedule 3 thereto.

"ZEBRA" PEDESTRIAN CROSSINGS REGULATIONS 1971

(S.I. 1971 No. 1524)

Interpretation

3.—(1) In these Regulations, unless the context otherwise requires, the fol-   **C5–01**

lowing expressions have the meanings hereby respectively assigned to them:—

"the appropriate Secretary of State" means, in relation to a crossing established on a road in England excluding Monmouthshire, the Secretary of State for the Environment, in relation to a crossing established on a road in Scotland, the Secretary of State for Scotland, and, in relation to a crossing established on a road in Wales or Monmouthshire, the Secretary of State for Wales;

"appropriate authority" means, in relation to a crossing on a trunk road, the appropriate Secretary of State, and in relation to any other crossing the local authority in whose scheme submitted and approved under section 21 of the Act of 1967 the crossing is for the time being included;

"carriageway" does not include that part of any road which consists of a street refuge or central reservation, whether within the limits of a crossing or not;

"central reservation" means any provision, not consisting of a street refuge, made in a road for separating one part of the carriageway of that road from another part of that carriageway for the safety or guidance of vehicular traffic using that road;

"crossing" means a crossing for foot passengers established either—

(a) by a local authority in accordance with the provisions for the time being in force of a scheme submitted and approved under section 21 of the Act of 1967, or

(b) in the case of a trunk road, by the appropriate Secretary of State in the discharge of the duty imposed on him by section 22 of the Act of 1967;

but does not include a "Pelican" crossing within the meaning of the "Pelican" Pedestrian Crossings Regulations 1969. [See now the "Pelican" Pedestrian Crossings Regulations 1987];

"dual-carriageway road" means a length of road on which a part of the carriageway thereof is separated from another part thereof by a central reservation;

"give-way line" has the meaning assigned to it by paragraph 2 of Schedule 3;

"one-way street" means any road in which the driving of all vehicles otherwise than in one direction is prohibited at all times;

"stud" means a mark or device on the carriageway, whether or not projecting above the surface thereof;

"zebra controlled area" means, in relation to a zebra crossing, the area of the carriageway in the vicinity of the crossing and lying on both sides of the crossing or only one side of the crossing, being an area the presence and limits of which are indicated in accordance with Schedule 3;

"zebra crossing" means a crossing the presence and limits of which are indicated in accordance with the provisions of Schedule 2;

"uncontrolled zebra crossing" means a zebra crossing at which traffic is not for the time being controlled by a police constable in uniform or by a traffic warden.

(2) Any reference in these Regulations to a numbered Regulation or Schedule is a reference to the Regulation or Schedule bearing that number in these Regulations except where otherwise expressly provided.

(3) Any reference in these Regulations to any enactment shall be construed as a reference to that enactment as amended by any subsequent enactment.

(4) The Interpretation Act 1889 shall apply for the interpretation of these Regulations as it applies for the interpretation of an Act of Parliament, and as if for the purposes of section 38 of that Act these Regulations were an Act of Parliament and the Regulations revoked by Regulation 2 were Acts of Parliament thereby repealed.

Zebra crossings

4.—(1) The provisions of Part I of Schedule 2 shall have effect for regulating   **C5–02**
the manner in which the presence and limits of a crossing are to be indicated by marks or studs on the carriageway for the purpose of constituting it a zebra crossing.

(2) The provisions of Part II of Schedule 2 shall have effect as respects the size, colour and type of the traffic signs which are to be placed at or near a crossing for the purpose of constituting it a zebra crossing.

Zebra controlled areas and give-way lines

5.—(1) Subject to paragraph (3) of this Regulation, the provisions of Schedule 3 shall have effect as respects the size, colour and type of the traffic signs which shall be placed in the vicinity of a zebra crossing for the purpose of constituting a zebra controlled area in relation to that crossing and of indicating the presence and limits of that area.

(2) A give-way line (included among the said signs) shall, where provided, also convey to vehicular traffic proceeding towards a zebra crossing the position at or before which a driver of a vehicle should stop it for the purpose of complying with Regulation 8.

(3) Where the appropriate authority is satisfied in relation to a particular area of carriageway in the vicinity of a zebra crossing that, by reason of the layout of, or character of, the roads in the vicinity of the crossing, the application of such a prohibition as is mentioned in Regulation 10 or 12 to that particular area or the constitution of that particular area as a zebra controlled area by placing of traffic signs in accordance with Schedule 3 would be impracticable, it shall not be necessary for that area to be constituted a zebra controlled area but, if by virtue of this paragraph it is proposed that no area, on either side of the limits of a zebra crossing (not on a trunk road), is to be constituted a zebra controlled area by November 30, 1973, a notice in writing shall be sent by the appropriate authority before the date of the appropriate Secretary of State stating the reasons why it is proposed that no such area should be so constituted.

Variations in dimensions shown in Schedule 3

6. Any variations in a dimension specified in the diagram in Schedule 3 or   **C5–03**
otherwise specified in that Schedule shall be treated as permitted by these Regulations if the variation—
   (a) in the case of a dimension of 300 millimetres or more, does not exceed 20 per cent of that dimension; or

(b) in the case of a dimension of less that 300 millimetres, where the actual dimension exceeds the dimension so specified, does not exceed 30 per cent of the dimension so specified, and where the actual dimension is less than the dimension so specified, does not exceed 10 per cent of the dimension so specified.

Precedence of pedestrians over vehicles

C5–04 8. Every foot passenger on the carriageway within the limits of an uncontrolled zebra crossing shall have precedence within those limits over any vehicle and the driver of the vehicle shall accord such precedence to the foot passenger, if the foot passenger is on the carriageway within those limits before the vehicle or any part thereof has come on to the carriageway within those limits.

For the purpose of this Regulation, in the case of such crossing on which there is a street refuge or central reservation the parts of the crossing which are situated on each side of the street refuge or central reservation as the case may be shall each be treated as a separate crossing.

Prohibition against the waiting of vehicles and pedestrians on zebra crossings

C5–05 9.—(1) The driver of a vehicle shall not cause the vehicle or any part thereof to stop within the limits of a zebra crossing unless either he is prevented from proceeding by circumstances beyond his control or it is necessary for him to stop in order to avoid an accident.

(2) No foot passenger shall remain on the carriageway within the limits of a zebra crossing longer than is necessary for the purpose of passing over the crossing with reasonable despatch.

Prohibition against overtaking at zebra crossings

C5–06 10. The driver of a vehicle while it or any part of it is in a zebra controlled area and it is proceeding towards the limits of an uncontrolled zebra crossing in relation to which that area is indicated (which vehicle is in this and the next succeeding Regulation referred to as "the approaching vehicle") shall not cause the vehicle, or any part of it—

(a) to pass ahead of the foremost part of another moving motor vehicle, being a vehicle proceeding in the same direction wholly or partly within that area, or

(b) subject to the next succeeding Regulation, to pass ahead of the foremost part of a stationary vehicle on the same side of the crossing as the approaching vehicle, which stationary vehicle is stopped for the purpose of complying with Regulation 8.

For the purposes of this Regulation—

(i) the reference to another moving motor vehicle is, in a case where only one other motor vehicle is proceeding in the same direction in a zebra controlled area, a reference to vehicle, and, in a case where more than one other motor vehicle is so proceeding, a reference to such one of those vehicles as is nearest to the limits of the crossing;

(ii) the reference to a stationary vehicle is, in a case where only one other vehicle is stopped for the purpose of complying with Regulation 8, a reference to that vehicle and, in a case where more than one other vehicle is stopped for the purpose of complying with that Regulation, a reference to such one of those vehicles as is nearest to the limits of the crossing.

11.—(1) For the purposes of this Regulation, in the case of an uncontrolled zebra crossing, which is on a road, being a one-way street, and on which there is a street refuge or central reservation, the parts of the crossing which are situated on each side of the street refuge or central reservation as the case may be shall each be treated as a separate crossing. **C5–07**

(2) Nothing in paragraph (b) of the last preceding Regulation shall apply so as to prevent the approaching vehicle from passing ahead of the foremost part of a stationary vehicle within the meaning of that paragraph, if the stationary vehicle is stopped for the purpose of complying with Regulation 8 in relation to an uncontrolled zebra crossing which by virtue of this Regulation is treated as a separate crossing from the uncontrolled zebra crossing towards the limits of which the approaching vehicle is proceeding.

Prohibition on stopping in areas adjacent to zebra crossings

12.—(1) For the purposes of this Regulation and the next two following Regulations, the expression "vehicle" shall not include a pedal bicycle not having a sidecar attached thereto, whether additional means of propulsion by mechanical power are attached to the bicycle or not. **C5–08**

(2) Save as provided in Regulations 14 and 15, the driver of a vehicle shall not cause the vehicle or any part thereof to stop in a zebra controlled area.

14. A vehicle shall not by Regulation 12 or 13 be prevented from stopping in any length of road on any side thereof— **C5–09**
   (a) if the driver has stopped for the purpose of complying with Regulation 8 or Regulation 10(b);
   (b) if the driver is prevented from proceeding by circumstances beyond his control or it is necessary for him to stop in order to avoid an accident;
   (c) for so long as may be necessary to enable the vehicle, if it cannot be used for such purpose without stopping in that length of road, to be used for fire brigade, ambulance or police purposes or in connection with any building operation, demolition or excavation, the removal of any obstruction to traffic, the maintenance, improvement or recon-struction of that length of road, or the laying, erection, alteration, repair or cleaning in or near to that length of road of any traffic sign or sewer or of any main, pipe or apparatus for the supply of gas, water or electricity, or at any telegraph or telephone wires, cables, posts or supports.

15. A vehicle shall not by Regulation 12 be prevented from stopping in a zebra controlled area— **C5–10**
   (a) if the vehicle is stopped for the purpose of making a left or right turn;
   (b) if the vehicle is a public service vehicle, being a stage carriage or an express carriage being used otherwise than on an excursion or tour within the meaning of section 159(1) of the Transport Act 1968, and the vehicle is waiting, after having proceeded past the zebra crossing in

relation to which the zebra controlled area is indicated, for the purpose of enabling persons to board or alight from the vehicle.

Regulation 4 SCHEDULE 2

MANNER OF INDICATING PRESENCE AND LIMITS OF ZEBRA CROSSINGS

PART I

Studs and Marks

C5–11   **1.**—(1) Every crossing and its limits shall be indicated by two lines of studs placed across the carriageway in accordance with the following provisions of this paragraph.

(2) Each line formed by the outside edges of the studs shall be so separated from the other line so formed that no point on one line shall be less than 2.4 metres nor more than 5 metres or such greater distance (not being more than 10.1 metres) as the appropriate Secretary of State may authorise in writing in the case of any particular crossing from the nearest point on the other line:

Provided that the preceding provisions of this sub-paragraph shall be regarded as having been complied with in the case of any crossing which for the most part complies with those provisions notwithstanding that those provisions may not be so complied with as respects the distance from one or more points on one line to the nearest point on the other line, so long as the general indication of the lines is not thereby materially impaired.

(3) The studs of which line is constituted shall be so placed that the distance from the centre of any one stud to the centre of the next stud in the line is not less than 250 millimetres nor more than 715 millimetres, and a distance of nor more than 1.3 metres is left between the edge of the carriageway at either end of the line and the centre of the stud nearest thereto:

Provided that the preceding provisions of this sub-paragraph shall be regarded as having been complied with in the case of any line where most of the studs constituting it comply with those provisions notwithstanding that those provisions may not be complied with as respects one or more such studs, so long as the general indication of the line is not thereby materially impaired.

(4) Studs shall not be fitted with reflecting lenses and shall be—

    (a) white, silver or light grey in colour;

    (b) square or circular in plan, the sides of a square stud not being less than 95 millimetres nor more than 110 millimetres in length and the diameter of a circular stud not being less than 95 millimetre nor more than 110 millimetres, and

    (c) so fixed that they do not project more than 16 millimetres above the carriageway at their highest points nor more than 7 millimetres at their edges.

2. A crossing or its limits shall be deemed to have ceased to be indicated in accordance with the preceding provisions of the Part of this Schedule by reason only of the discoloration of temporary removal or displacement of one or more studs in any line so long as the general indication of the line is not thereby materially impaired.

(3) Without derogation from the provisions of the preceding paragraphs of this Part of this Schedule, every crossing shall be further indicated in accordance with the following provisions of this Part and of Part II of this Schedule.

(4).—(1) The carriageway shall be marked within the limits of every such crossing with a pattern of alternate black and white stripes:

Provided that where the colour of the surface may itself be utilised for providing stripes which would otherwise be required to be black.

(2) Every stripe shall—

(a) extend along the carriageway from one line formed by the inside edges of the studs or form a part of the crossing which is not more than 155 millimetres from that line to the other line so formed or to a part of the crossing which is not more than 155 millimetres from that line; and

(b) be of a width of not less than 500 millimetres or of such smaller width not being less than 380 millimetres as in the case of any particular crossing the appropriate authority may consider necessary having regard to the layout of the carriageway and, in the case of the first stripe at each end of the crossing, not more than 1.3 metres, or in the case of any other stripe, not more than 715 millimetres or of such greater width not being more than 840 millimetres as in the case of any particular crossing the appropriate authority may consider necessary having regard to the layout of the carriageway.

(3) The preceding provisions of this paragraph of this paragraph shall be regarded as having been complied with in the case of any crossing which for the most part complies with those provisions notwithstanding that those provisions may not be complied with as respects one or more stripes and a crossing shall not be deemed to have ceased to be indicated in accordance with those provisions by reason only of the imperfection, discoloration or partial displacement of one or more of the stripes, so long as the general appearance of the pattern of stripes is not materially impaired.

PART II

Traffic Signs

1. The traffic signs which are to be placed at or near a crossing for the purpose of constituting it and indicating it as a zebra crossing shall consist of globes in relation to which the following provisions in this Part of this Schedule are complied with.

2.—(1) At or near each end of every crossing there shall be placed, and in the case of a crossing on which there is a street refuge or central reservations there may be placed on the refuge or reservation, in accordance with the following provisions of this paragraph globes mounted on posts or brackets.

(2) Globes shall be—

(a) yellow in colour;

(b) not less than 275 millimetres nor more than 335 millimetres in diameter; and

(c) so mounted that the height of the lowest part of the globe is not less than 2.1 metres nor more than 3.1 metres above the surface of the ground in the immediate vicinity.

(3) Globes shall be illuminated by a flashing light or, where the appropriate Secretary of State so authorises in writing in the case of any particular crossing, by a constant light.

(4) Where globes are mounted on or attached to posts specially provided for the purpose, every such post shall, in so far as it extends above ground level, be coloured black and white in alternative horizontal bands, the lowest band visible to approaching traffic being coloured black and not less than 275 millimetres nor more than 1 metre in width and each other band being not less than 275 millimetres nor more than 335 millimetres in width:

Provided that nothing in this sub-paragraph shall apply to any container fixed on any such post which encloses the apparatus for providing the illumination of a globe.

3. A crossing shall not be deemed to have ceased to be indicated in accordance with the preceding provisions of this Part of this Schedule by reason only of—

    (a) the imperfection, discoloration or disfigurement of any of the globes, posts or brackets, or

    (b) the failure of the illumination of any of the globes;

Provided that this sub-paragraph shall not apply unless at least one globe is illuminated in accordance with the provisions of sub-paragraph (3) of the last preceding paragraph.

4. Subject to paragraphs 5 and 6, a globe may be fitted with—

    (a) a backing board designed to improve the conspicuity of the globe;

    (b) a shield designed to prevent or reduce light from the globe shining into adjacent properties; or

    (c) such a board and shield.

5. If a backing board or shield is fitted to a globe it shall—

    (a) be firmly secured;

    (b) not prevent any driver of a vehicle proceeding towards the zebra crossing in question from seeing the globe; and

    (c) not constitute a danger to any user of the road.

6. Any backing board shall be coloured black and may have a white border.

Regulation 5   SCHEDULE 3

MANNER OF INDICATING ZEBRA CONTROLLED AREA AND PROVISION AS TO PLACING OF GIVE-WAY LINE

PART I

Traffic Signs

C5–12   1. Subject to the provisions of Regulation 5(3), the traffic signs which are to be placed on a road in the vicinity of a zebra crossing for the purpose of constituting a zebra controlled area lying on both sides of the limits of the crossing or on only one side of such limits and indicating the presence and limits of such an area shall consist of a pattern of lines of the size and type shown in the diagram in Part II of this Schedule and so placed as hereinafter provided.

2. A pattern of lines shall, subject as hereinafter provided, consist of:—

    (a) a transverse white broken line (hereinafter referred to as a "give-way line") placed on the carriageway 1 metre from and parallel to the nearer line of studs indicating the limits of the crossing and shall extend across the carriageway in the manner indicated in the said diagram; and

(b) two or more longitudinal white broken lines (hereinafter referred to as "zig-zag lines") placed on the carriageway or, where the road is a dual carriageway road, on each part of the carriageway, each zig-zag line containing not less than eight nor more than eighteen marks and extending away from the crossing at a point 150 millimetres from the nearest part of the give-way line on the same side of the crossing to a point 150 millimetres from the nearest part of a terminal line of the size and type shown in the said diagram (hereinafter referred to as a "terminal line").

3. Where the appropriate authority is satisfied in relation to a particular area of carriageway in the vicinity of a zebra crossing that by reason of the layout of, or character of, the roads in the vicinity of the crossing it would be impracticable to lay the pattern of lines as shown in the diagram in Part II of this Schedule and in accordance with the preceding paragraph any of the following variations as respects the pattern shall be permitted—

(a) the number of marks contained in each zig-zag line may be reduced from eight to not less than two;

(b) a mark contained in a zig-zag line may be varied in length so as to extend for a distance not less than 1 metre and less than 2 metres, but where such a variation is made as respects a mark each other mark in each zig-zag line shall be of the same or substantially the same length as that mark, so however that the number of marks in each zig-zag line shall not be more than eight nor less than two.

4. The angle of the give-way line (if any) in relation to and its distance from the nearer line of studs indicating the limits of a crossing may be varied, if the appropriate authority is satisfied that such variation is necessary having regard to the angle of the crossing in relation to the edge of the carriageway at the place where the crossing is situated.

5. Where by reason of Regulation 5(3) an area of carriageway in the vicinity of a zebra crossing is not constituted a zebra controlled area by the placing of a pattern of lines as provided in the foregoing provisions of this Schedule, a give-way line shall nevertheless be placed on the carriageway as previously provided in this Schedule unless the appropriate authority is satisfied that by reason of the position of that crossing it is impracticable so to place the line.

6. Each mark contained in a give-way line or in a zig-zag line and each terminal line may be illuminated by the use of reflecting material.

7. A zebra controlled area or its limits shall not be deemed to have ceased to be indicated in accordance with the provisions of this Schedule by reason only of the imperfection, discoloration or partial displacement of either a terminal line or one or more of the marks comprised in a give-way line or a zig-zag line, so long as the general indication of any such line is not thereby materially impaired.

PART II—DIAGRAM

Pattern of lines on one or both sides of a crossing indicating zebra controlled area.

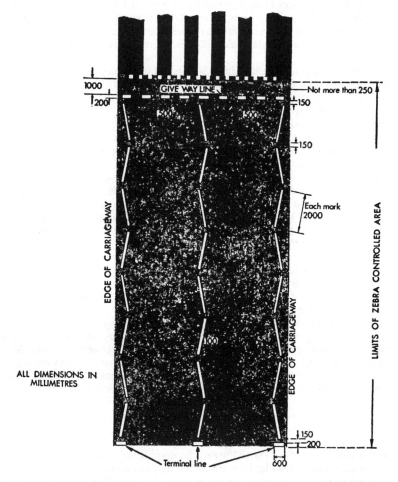

Note: Each zig-zag line need not contain the same number of marks.

MOTOR VEHICLES (THIRD PARTY RISKS) REGULATIONS 1972

(S.I. 1972 No. 1217)

Interpretation

C6–01   **4.**—(1) In these Regulations, unless the context otherwise requires, the following expressions have the meanings hereby respectively assigned to them:—

"the Act" means the Road Traffic Act 1972;

"company" means an authorised insurer within the meaning of Part VI of the Act or a body of persons by whom a security may be given in pursuance of the said Part VI;

"motor vehicle" has the meaning assigned to it by sections 190, 192 and 193 of the Act, but excludes any invalid carriage, tramcar or trolley vehicle to which Part VI of the Act does not apply;

"policy" means a policy of insurance in respect of third party risks arising out of the use of motor vehicles which complies with the requirements of Part VI of the Act and includes a covering note;

"security" means a security in respect of third party risks arising out of the use of motor vehicles which complies with the requirements of Part VI of the Act;

"specified body" means—

(a) any of the local authorities referred to in paragraph (a) of section 144(2) of the Act; or

(b) a Passenger Transport Executive established under an order made under section 9 of the Transport Act 1968, or a subsidiary of that Executive, being an Executive or subsidiary to whose vehicles section 144(2)(a) of the Act has been applied; or

(c) the London Transport Executive or a wholly-owned subsidiary of that Executive referred to in paragraph (e) of section 144(2) of the Act.

(2) Any reference in these Regulations to a certificate in Form A, B, C, D, E or F shall be construed as a reference to a certificate in the form so headed and set out in Part 1 of the Schedule to these Regulations which has been duly made and completed subject to and in accordance with the provisions set out in Part 2 of the said Schedule.

(3) Any reference in these Regulations to any enactment shall be construed as a reference to that enactment as amended by any subsequent enactment.

(4) The Interpretation Act 1889 shall apply for the interpretation of these Regulations as it applies for the interpretation of an Act of Parliament, and as if for the purposes of section 38 of that Act these Regulations were an Act of Parliament and the Regulations revoked by Regulation 2 of these Regulations were Acts of Parliament thereby repealed.

Issue of certificates of insurance or security

5.—(1) A company shall issue to every holder of a security or of a policy other than a covering note issued by the company:—   **C6–02**

(a) in the case of a policy or security relating to one or more specified vehicles a certificate of insurance in Form A or a certificate of security in Form D in respect of each such vehicle;

(b) in the case of a policy or security relating to vehicles other than specified vehicles such number of certificates in Form B or Form D as may be necessary for the purpose of complying with the requirements of section 162(1) of the Act and of these Regulations as to the production of evidence that a motor vehicle is not being driven in contravention of section 143 of the Act:

Provided that where a security is intended to cover the use of more than ten motor vehicles at one time the company by whom it was issued may, subject to the consent of the Secretary of State, issue one certificate only, and where such consent has been given the holder of the security may issue duplicate copies of such certificate duly authenticated by him up to such number and subject to such conditions as the Secretary of State may determine.

(2) Notwithstanding the foregoing provisions of this Regulation, where as respects third party risks a policy or security relating to a specified vehicle extends also to the driving by the holder of other motor vehicles, not being specified vehicles, the certificate may be in Form A or Form D, as the case may be, containing a statement in either case that the policy or security extends to such driving of other motor vehicles. Where such a certificate is issued by a company they may, and shall in accordance with a demand made to them by the holder, issue to him a further such certificate or a certificate in Form B.

(3) Every policy in the form of a covering note issued by a company shall have printed thereon or on the back thereof a certificate of insurance in Form C.

6. Every certificate of insurance or certificate of security shall be issued not later than four days after the date on which the policy or security to which it relates is issued or renewed.

Production of evidence as alternatives to certificates

7. The following evidence that a motor vehicle is not or was not being driven in contravention of section 143 of the Act may be produced in pursuance of section 162 of the Act as an alternative to the production of a certificate of insurance or a certificate of security:—

> (1) a duplicate copy of a certificate of security issued in accordance with the proviso to sub-paragraph (b) of paragraph (1) of Regulation 5 of these Regulations;
>
> (2) in the case of a motor vehicle of which the owner has for the time being deposited with the Accountant-General of the Supreme Court the sum for the time being specified in section 144(1) of the Road Traffic Act 1988, a certificate in Form E signed by the owner of the motor vehicle or by some person authorised by him in that behalf that such sum is on deposit;
>
> (3) in the case of a motor vehicle owned by a specified body, a police authority or the Receiver for the metropolitan police district, a certificate in Form F signed by some person authorised in that behalf by such specified body, police authority or Receiver as the case may be that the said Motor Vehicle is owned by the said specified body, police authority or Receiver.

(4) in the case of a vehicle normally based in the territory other than the United Kingdom and Gibraltar of a member State of the Communities or of Austria, Czechoslovakia, Finland, the German Democratic Republic, Hungary, Norway, Sweden or Switzerland, a document issued by the insurer of the vehicle which indicates the name of the insurer, the number or other identifying particulars of the insurance policy issued in respect of the vehicle and the period of the insurance cover. In this paragraph the territory of the state in which a vehicle is normally based is—

> (a) the territory of the state in which the vehicle is registered, or
>
> (b) in cases where no registration is required for the type of vehicle, but

the vehicle bears an insurance plate or distinguishing sign analogous to a registration plate, the territory of the state in which the insurance plate or the sign is issued, or

(c) in cases where neither registration plate nor insurance plate nor distinguishing sign is required for the type of vehicle, the territory of the state in which the keeper of the vehicle is permanently resident.

8. Any certificate issued in accordance with paragraph (2) or (3) of the preceding Regulation shall be destroyed by the owner of the vehicle to which it relates before the motor vehicle is sold or otherwise disposed of.   **C6–04**

Return of certificates to issuing company

12.—(1) The following provisions shall apply in relation to the transfer of a   **C6–05**
policy or security with the consent of the holder to any other person:—

(a) the holder shall, before the policy or security is transferred, return any relative certificates issued for the purposes of these Regulations to the company by whom they were issued; and

(b) the policy or security shall not be transferred to any other person unless and until the certificates have been so returned or the company are satisfied that the certificates have been lost or destroyed.

(2) In any case where with the consent of the person to whom it was issued a policy or security is suspended or ceases to be effective, otherwise than by effluxion of time, in circumstances in which the provisions of section 147(4) of the Act (relating to the surrender of certificates) do not apply, the holder of the policy or security shall within seven days from the date when it is suspended or ceases to be effective return any relative certificates issued for the purposes of these Regulations to the company by whom they were issued and the company shall not issue a new policy or security to the said holder in respect of the motor vehicle or vehicles to which the said first mentioned policy or security related unless and until the certificates have been returned to the company or the company are satisfied that they have been lost or destroyed.

(3) Where a policy or security is cancelled by mutual consent or by virtue of any provision in the policy or security, any statutory declaration that a certificate has been lost or destroyed made in pursuance of section 147(4) (which requires any such declaration to be made within a period of seven days from the taking effect of the cancellation) shall be delivered forthwith after it has been made to the company by whom the policy was issued or the security given.

(4) The provisions of the last preceding paragraph shall be without prejudice to the provisions of paragraph (c) of subsection (2) of section 149 of the Act as to the effect for the purposes of that subsection of the making of a statutory declaration within the periods therein stated.

MOTOR VEHICLES (COMPULSORY INSURANCE) (NO. 2) REGULATIONS 1973

(S.I. 1973 No. 2143)

6.—(1) Any person appointed by the Secretary of State for the purpose (in   **C7–01**

this Regulation referred to as an "appointed person") may require a person having custody of any vehicle, being a vehicle which is normally based in the territory of a state other than a relevant foreign state which is not a member of the Communities or in the non-European territory of a member state or in Gibraltar, when entering Great Britain to produce evidence that any loss or injury which may be caused by such a vehicle is covered throughout the territory in which the treaty establishing the European Economic Community is in force, in accordance with the requirements of the laws of the various member states on compulsory insurance against civil liability in respect of the use of vehicles.

(2) An appointed person may, if no such evidence is produced or if he is not satisfied by such evidence, prohibit the use of the vehicle in Great Britain.

(3) Where an appointed person prohibits the use of a vehicle under this Regulation, he may also direct the driver to remove the vehicle to such place and subject to such conditions as are specified in the direction; and the prohibition shall not apply to the removal of the vehicle in accordance with the direction.

(4) Any person who—

   (a) uses a vehicle or causes or permits a vehicle to be used in contravention of a prohibition imposed under paragraph (2) of this Regulation, or

   (b) refuses, neglects or otherwise fails to comply in a reasonable time with a direction given under paragraph (3) of this Regulation,

shall be guilty of an offence and shall be liable on summary conviction to a fine not exceeding £50.

(5) Section 181 of the Road Traffic Act 1972 shall apply for the purposes of an offence under this Regulation as if such an offence were an offence under that Act to which that section had been applied by column 7 of Part 1 of Schedule 4 to that Act.

(6) A prohibition under paragraph (2) of this Regulation may be removed by an appointed person if he is satisfied that appropriate action has been taken to remove or remedy the circumstances in consequence of which the prohibition was imposed.

7.—(1) Where a constable in uniform has reasonable cause to suspect the driver of a vehicle of having committed an offence under the preceding Regulation, the constable may detain the vehicle, and for that purpose may give a direction, specifying an appropriate person and directing the vehicle to be removed by that person to such place and subject to such conditions as are specified in the direction; and the prohibition shall not apply to the removal of the vehicle in accordance with that direction.

(2) Where under paragraph (1) of this Regulation a constable—

   (a) detains a motor vehicle drawing a trailer, or

   (b) detains a trailer drawn by a motor vehicle,

then, for the purpose of securing the removal of the trailer, he may also (in a case falling within sub-paragraph (a) above) detain the trailer or (in a case falling within sub-paragraph (b) above) detain the motor vehicle; and a direction under paragraph (1) of this Regulation may require both the motor vehicle and the trailer to be removed to the place specified in the direction.

(3) A vehicle which, in accordance with a direction given under paragraph (1) of this Regulation, is removed to a place specified in the direction shall be detained in that place, or in any other place to which it is removed in accordance with a further direction given under that paragraph, until a constable (or, if the place is in the occupation of the Secretary of State, the Secretary of State) authorised the vehicle to be released on being satisfied—

   (a) that the prohibition (if any) imposed in respect of the vehicle under the preceding Regulation has been removed, or that no such prohibition was imposed, or

   (b) that appropriate arrangements have been made for removing or remedying the circumstances in consequence of which any such prohibition was imposed, or

   (c) that the vehicle will be taken forthwith to a place from which it will be taken out of Great Britain to a place not in the European territory other than Gibraltar of a member state of the Communities and not in the territory of a relevant foreign state.

(4) Any person who—

   (a) drives a vehicle in accordance with a direction given under this Regulation, or

   (b) is in charge of a place at which a vehicle is detained under this Regulation,

shall not be liable for any damage to, or loss in respect of, the vehicle or its load unless it is shown that he did not take reasonable care of the vehicle while driving it or, as the case may be, did not, while the vehicle was detained in that place, take reasonable care of the vehicle or (if the vehicle was detained there with its load) did not take reasonable care of its load.

(5) In this Regulation "appropriate person"—

   (a) in relation to a direction to remove a motor vehicle, other than a motor vehicle drawing a trailer, means a person licensed to drive vehicles of the class to which the vehicle belongs, and

   (b) in relation to a direction to remove a trailer, or to remove a motor vehicle drawing a trailer, means a person licensed to drive vehicles of a class which, when the direction is complied with, will include the motor vehicle drawing the trailer with that direction.

8. Nothing in section 145(2) (policies to be issued by authorised insurers)   **C7–03**
and section 147(1) (policies to be of no effect unless certificates issued) of the Road Traffic Act 1972 shall apply in the case of an insurance policy which is issued elsewhere than in the United Kingdom in respect of a vehicle normally based in the territory other than the United Kingdom and Gibraltar of a member State of the Communities or of a relevant foreign state.

MOTOR VEHICLES (INTERNATIONAL CIRCULATION) ORDER 1975

(S.I. 1975 No. 1208)

Documents for drivers and vehicles going abroad

   1.—(1) Subject to the following provisions of this Article, the Minister of   **C8–01**
Transport may issue to a person resident in the United Kingdom a driving permit in any of the forms A, B and C in Schedule 1 to this Order for use outside the United Kingdom.

(1A) A permit shall be issued to a person only for vehicles of a class or classes in respect of which that person either—

   (a) holds a full licence, or has held and is entitled to obtain such licence and is authorised to drive by virtue of section 84(4) of the Road Traffic

Act 1972 or any corresponding Northern Ireland provision (licence applied for or surrendered for correction of particulars, etc.); or

(b) holds a provisional licence, or has held and is entitled to obtain such a licence and is authorised to drive as mentioned in paragraph (a) above, and has passed the test of competence to drive or a test which is a sufficient test;

and in this paragraph "full licence" means a licence (granted under Part III of the Road Traffic Act 1972 or Part I of the Road Traffic Act (Northern Ireland) 1970) other than a provisional licence, and "provisional licence" and "test of competence to drive" have the same meaning as in the said Part III or the said Part I, and "test of competence which is a sufficient test" has the same meaning as in the said Part III.

(1B) A permit in form A shall not be used to any person who is under 18 years of age unless the permit is restricted to the driving of motor cycles or invalid carriages, or both.

(1C) A permit in form B shall not be issued to any person who is under 18 years of age.

(1D) A permit in form C shall be limited in its period of validity to three years, or, if shorter—

(a) the unexpired period of the permit holder's current United Kingdom driving licence; or

(b) where the permit holder is authorised to drive by virtue of section 84(4) of the Road Traffic Act 1972 or any corresponding Northern Ireland provision (licence applied for or surrendered for correction of particulars, etc.) the remainder of the period for which he is so authorised together with the period of validity of any licence granted while he is so authorised.]

(2) The Secretary of State may issue for use outside the United Kingdom a document in the form D in Schedule 1 to this Order for any motor vehicle registered under the Vehicles (Excise) Act 1971, or in Northern Ireland under the Vehicles (Excise) Act (Northern Ireland) 1972.

(3) The Secretary of State may issue for use outside the United Kingdom with any such motor vehicles or any trailer a document certifying—

(a) the weight of the maximum load which it is to be permitted to carry, and

(b) the permissible maximum weight, that is to say, the weight of the vehicle when ready for the road and carrying the maximum load so specified.

(4) The Secretary of State may assign to any trailer an identification mark to be carried on the trailer outside the United Kingdom.

(5) The Secretary of State may assign to a motor vehicle to which the Decision of 1957 of the Council of the Organisation for European Economic Co-operation applies, an identification mark in the form of such a trade plate as may be required to be carried on such a vehicle under the provisions of section 1 of the Regulation attached to that Decision.

In this paragraph, "the Decision of 1957 of the Council of the Organisation for European Economic Co-operation" means the decision of the Council of the Organisation for European Economic Co-Operation concerning the International Circulation of Hired Private Road Motor Vehicles adopted by that Council at its 369th Meeting, in June, 1957.

(6) The Secretary of State may charge a fee for any document issued under this Article or for the assignment of any identification mark under this Article, and the fee shall be of the amount specified in relation thereto in Schedule 2 to this Order.

(7) The Secretary of State may for the purpose of his functions under this Article carry out [...] examinations of vehicles.

(8) The Secretary of State may delegate any of his functions under this Article (including any power of charging fees and the carrying out of [...] examinations) to any body concerned with motor vehicles or to any Northern Ireland Department.

(9) Sections 173 and 174 of the Road Traffic Act 1988 (forgery of documents, etc., false statements and withholding material information) and Article 174 of the Road Traffic (Northern Ireland) Order 1981 (false statements in connection with forgery of, and fraudulent use of, documents, etc.) shall apply to a Convention driving permit as they apply to licences under that Act or under that Order.

(10) Section 13 of the Road Traffic Offenders Act 1988 and Article 190 of the said Order of 1981 (admissibility of records as evidence) shall apply to records maintained by the Secretary of State in connection with his functions under this Article, or by a body or Northern Ireland department to which in accordance with paragraph (8) of this Article he has delegated the function in connection with which the records are maintained, as that section or that Article apply to records maintained in connection with functions under that Act or under that Order, and the powers conferred by section 13(5) of the said Act of 1988 and Article 190(4) of the said Order of 1981 to prescribe a description of matter which may be admitted as evidence under that section or under that Article shall have effect in relation to the application of that section and that Article by this Article.

Visitors' driving permits

2.—(1) Subject to the provisions of this Article, it shall be lawful for a person resident outside the United Kingdom who is temporarily in Great Britain and holds—　　**C8–02**

(a) a Convention driving permit, or

(b) a domestic driving permit issued in a country outside the United Kingdom, or

(c) a British Forces (BFG) driving licence,

during a period of twelve months from the date of his last entry into the United Kingdom to drive, or, except in the case of a holder of a British Forces (BFG) driving licence, for any person to cause or permit such a person to drive, in Great Britain a motor vehicle of any class other than a large goods vehicle or a passenger-carrying vehicle which he is authorised by that permit or that licence to drive, notwithstanding that he is not the holder of a driving licence under Part III of the Road Traffic Act 1988.

(2) Subject to the provisions of this Article, it shall be lawful for a person resident outside the United Kingdom who is temporarily in Great Britain and holds—

(a) a Convention driving permit, or

(b) a domestic driving permit issued in a country outside the United Kingdom,

during a period of twelve months from the date of his last entry into the United Kingdom to drive, or for any person to cause or permit such a person to drive, in Great Britain—

(i) in the case of any such person who is resident in a Member State of the European Economic Community, any large goods vehicle or passenger-carrying vehicle; and

(ii) in the case of any other such person, a large goods vehicle or passenger-carrying vehicle brought temporarily into Great Britain,

which he is authorised by that permit to drive, notwithstanding that he is not the holder of a large goods vehicle driver's licence or a passenger-carrying vehicle driver's licence.

(3) Subject to the provisions of this Article, it shall be lawful for a person resident outside the United Kingdom who is temporarily in Great Britain and holds a British Forces (BFG) public service vehicle driving licence during a period of twelve months from the date of his last entry into the United Kingdom to drive, or for any person to cause or permit such a person to drive, in Great Britain—

(a) in the case of any such person who is resident in a Member State of the European Economic Community, any passenger-carrying vehicle, and

(b) in the case of any other such person, a passenger-carrying vehicle brought temporarily into Great Britain,

which he is authorised by that licence to drive, notwithstanding that he is not the holder of a passenger-carrying vehicle driver's licence.

(4) Nothing in the preceding provisions of this Article shall authorise any person to drive, or any person to cause or permit any person to drive, a vehicle of any class at a time when he is disqualified by virtue of section 101 of the Road Traffic Act 1988 (persons under age) for holding or obtaining a driving licence authorising him to drive vehicles of that class, but in the case of any such person as is mentioned in paragraph (1), (2) or (3) of this Article, who is driving a vehicle which—

(a) in the case of a person not resident in a Member State of the European Economic Community, is brought temporarily into Great Britain, and

(b) is within the class specified in the first column of paragraph 6 of the Table in subsection (1) of that section, and

(c) is either a vehicle registered in a Convention country or a goods vehicle in respect of which that person holds a certificate of competence which satisfies the international requirements,

the second column of that paragraph, in its application for the purposes of this paragraph, shall have effect as if for "21" there were substituted "18."

In this paragraph the following expressions have the meanings respectively assigned to them:—

"the international requirements" means—

(i) in relation to a person who is driving a goods vehicle on a journey to which Council Regulation (EEC) No. 3820/85 of 20th December 1985, on the harmonisation of certain social legislation relating to road transport applies, the requirements of Article 5(1)(b) (minimum ages for goods vehicle drivers) of that Regulation;

(ii) in relation to a person who is driving a goods vehicle on a journey to which the European Agreement concerning the work of crews engaged in International Road Transport (AETR) signed at Geneva on 25th March 1971 applies, the requirements of Article 5(1)(b) (conditions to be fulfilled by drivers) of that Agreement;

"Convention country" means a country which is not a Member State of the European Economic Community nor a party to the aforementioned European Agreement but is a party to the Convention on Road Traffic concluded at Geneva in the year 1949, or the International Convention relative to Motor Traffic concluded at Paris in the year 1926.

(5) This Article shall not authorise a person to drive a motor vehicle of any class if, in consequence of a conviction or of the order of a court, he is disquali-

fied for holding or obtaining a driving licence under Part III of the Road Traffic Act 1988.

(6) The Secretary of State may by order contained in a statutory instrument withdraw the right conferred by paragraph (1)(b), (1)(c) or (2)(b) or (3) of this Article, or any two or more of those rights either in the case of all domestic driving permits, British Forces (BFG) driving licences, or British Forces (BFG) public service vehicle driving licences or in the case of such permits or licences of a description specified in the order or held by persons of a description so specified.

(7) In this Article—

> "Convention driving permit" means a driving permit in the form A in Schedule 1 to this Order issued under the authority of a country outside the United Kingdom, whether or not that country is a party to the Convention on Road Traffic concluded at Geneva in the year 1949, or a driving permit in the form B in the said Schedule issued under the authority of a country outside the United Kingdom which is a party to International Convention relative to Motor Traffic concluded at Paris in the year 1926 but not to the Convention of 1949;

> "domestic driving permit" in relation to a country outside the United Kingdom means a document issued under the law of that country and authorising the holder to drive motor vehicles, or a specified class of motor vehicles, in that country, and includes a driving permit issued by the armed forces of any country outside the United Kingdom for use in some other country outside the United Kingdom;

> "British Forces (BFG) driving licence" means a driving licence issued in Germany to members of the British Forces or of the civilian component thereof or to the dependants of such members by the British authorities in that country in such a form and in accordance with such licensing system as may from time to time be approved by those authorities; and "British Forces (BFG) public service vehicle driving licence" means any such driving licence authorising the driving of public service vehicles of any class;

> "dependants" in relation to such a member of the British Forces or the civilian component thereof, means any of the following persons, namely:—

> (a) the wife or husband of that member; and

> (b) any other person wholly or mainly maintained by him or in his custody, charge or care, and

> "public service vehicle" has the same meaning as in the Public Passenger Vehicles Act 1981 and "large goods vehicle", "passenger-carrying vehicle", "large goods vehicle driver's licence" and "passenger-carrying vehicle driver's licence" have the same meaning as in Part IV of the Road Traffic Act 1988.

(8) The provisions of this Article which authorise the holder of a permit or a licence to drive a vehicle during a specified period shall not be construed as authorising the driver of a vehicle at a time when the permit or the licence has ceased to be valid.

3.—(1) It shall be lawful—   **C8–03**

> (a) for a member of a visiting force of a country to which Part I of the Visiting Forces Act 1952 for the time being applies who holds a driving permit issued under the law of any part of the sending country or issued by the service authorities of the visiting force, or

(b) for a member of a civilian component of such a visiting force who holds such a driving permit, or

(c) for a dependant of any such member of a visiting force or of a civilian component thereof who holds such a driving permit,

to drive, or for any person to cause or permit any such person to drive, in Great Britain a motor vehicle of any class which he is authorised by that permit to drive, notwithstanding that he is not the holder of a driving licence under Part III of the Road Traffic Act 1988.

(2) This Article shall not authorise a person to drive a motor vehicle of any class if, in consequence of a conviction or of the order of a court, he is disqualified for holding or obtaining a driving licence under Part III of the Road Traffic Act 1988.

(3) Nothing in this Article shall authorise any person to drive, or any person to cause or permit any other person to drive, a vehicle of any class at a time when he is disqualified by virtue of section 101 of the Road Traffic Act 1988 (persons under age), for holding or obtaining a driving licence authorising him to drive vehicles of that class.

(4) The interpretative provisions of the Visiting Forces Act 1952 shall apply for the interpretation of this Article and "dependant", in relation to a member of any such visiting force or a civilian component thereof, means any of the following persons namely—

(a) the wife or husband of that member; and

(b) any other person wholly or mainly maintained by him or in his custody, charge or care.

Excise exemption and documents for vehicles brought temporarily into Great Britain

5.—(1) The next following paragraph shall apply to a vehicle brought temporarily into Great Britain by a person resident outside the United Kingdom if the person bringing that vehicle into Great Britain—

(a) satisfies a registration authority that he is resident outside the United Kingdom and that the vehicle is only temporarily in Great Britain, and

(b) complies with any regulations made under paragraph (4) of this Article.

(2) A vehicle to which this paragraph applies shall be exempt from any duty of excise under the Excise Act to the following extent:—

(a) a vehicle which would, but for this Order, be chargeable with excise duty under section 1 of the Excise Act and Schedule 1, 2 or 5 thereto, and in respect of which relief from customs duty has been afforded by virtue of Parts IV or V of the Customs and Excise Duties (Personal Reliefs for Goods Temporarily Imported) Order 1983, shall be exempted from excise duty for such period as relief from customs duty shall continue to be afforded in respect of that vehicle;

(b) a vehicle which would, but for this Order, be chargeable with excise duty under section 1 of the Excise Act and Schedule 2 thereto, and which is exempt from customs duty by virtue of the Temporary Importation (Commercial Vehicles and Aircraft) Regulations 1961 shall be exempt from excise duty for such period from the date of importation as that vehicle may remain so exempt from customs duty;

(c) a vehicle in so far as it is not excluded from the charge of duty under the Excise Act by virtue of Council Regulation (EEC) No. 4059/89 of 21st December 1989 and which, if used for the conveyance of goods or burden, would, but for this Order, be chargeable with excise duty under section 1 of the Excise Act and Schedule 3 or 4 thereto, and which is exempt from customs duty by virtue of the Temporary Importation (Commercial Vehicles and Aircraft) Regulations 1961 shall be exempt from excise duty for such period as that vehicle may remain so exempt from customs duty.

(3) A vehicle registered in the Isle of Man and brought temporarily into Great Britain by a person resident outside the United Kingdom shall be exempt from any duty of excise under the Excise Act for a period not exceeding one year from the date of importation, if the person bringing that vehicle into Great Britain—

    (a) satisfies a registration authority that he is resident outside the United Kingdom and that the vehicle is only temporarily in Great Britain, and

    (b) complies with any regulations made under paragraph (4) of this Article.

(4) The Secretary of State may by regulations provide—

    (a) for the furnishing to a registration authority by a person who imports a vehicle to which either of the two last preceding paragraphs applies of such particulars as may be prescribed, and

    (b) for the recording by a registration authority of any particulars which the Secretary of State may by the regulations direct to be recorded, and for the manner of such recording, and for the making of any such particulars available for use by such person as may be specified in the regulations on payment, in such cases as may be so specified, of such fee as may be prescribed, and;

    (c) for the production to a registration authority of prescribed documents, and

    (d) for the registration of vehicles which by virtue of this Article are exempt from excise duty and for the assignment of registration marks to, and for the issue of registration cards for, such vehicles.

(5) The following provisions of the Excise Act, that is to say:—

    (a) paragraphs (d) and (e) of section 23(1) as substituted by virtue of section 39(1) of, and paragraph 20 of Part I of Schedule 7 to, the Excise Act (which enable the Secretary of State to make regulations as respects registration books for vehicles in respect of which excise licences are issued), and

    (b) paragraph (f) of the said section 23(1) (which enables the Secretary of State to make regulations as to the display on a vehicle of registration mark assigned to it), and

    (c) section 26(1) (which relates to forgery of licences, registration marks or registration documents),

shall apply in relation to a registration card issued, or a registration mark assigned, in pursuance of this Article as they apply in relation to a registration book or registration document issued, or a registration mark assigned, under the Excise Act.

(6) If regulations under this Article provide for the assignment of a registration mark on production of some document relating to a vehicle which is exempt from excise duty by virtue of this Article, then paragraph (d) of the said section 23(1) shall apply in relation to that document so as to authorise the Secretary of State to make regulations under that section requiring the production of that document for inspection by persons of classes prescribed by regulations made under that section.

(7) Paragraphs (d) and (f) of the said section 23(1), and section 26(1) of the Excise Act shall, in Great Britain, apply in like manner in relation to a regis-

tration card issued, or a registration mark assigned, in pursuance of provisions corresponding to paragraph (4) of this Article in Northern Ireland.

(8) In relation to a motor vehicle brought temporarily into Great Britain by a
person resident outside the United Kingdom, reference in section 19 of the
Excise Act and in the said section 23(1) thereof to registration marks shall,
where appropriate, include references to nationality signs.

(9) In this Article—

"the Excise Act" means the Vehicles (Excise) Act 1971;

"the date of importation," in relation to a vehicle, means the date on
which that vehicle was last brought into the United Kingdom;

"registration authority" means the Automobile Association, the Royal
Automobile Club, the Royal Scottish Automobile Club, or the Secretary of State;

and references to registration marks shall, where appropriate, include reference to nationality signs.

Article 4   SCHEDULE 3

VISITORS' DRIVING PERMITS

C8–05   1. In this Schedule "driving permit" means a driving permit which by virtue
of this Order authorises a person to drive a motor vehicle without holding a
driving licence under Part III of the Road Traffic Act 1972, "Convention driving permit" has the meaning assigned to it by article 2(7) of this Order and
"driving licence" means a driving licence under the said Part III.

2.—(1) A court by whom the holder of a driving permit is convicted shall—

(a) if in consequence of the conviction or of the order of the court he is
disqualified for holding or obtaining a driving licence, or

(b) if the court orders particulars of the conviction to be endorsed on any
driving licence held by him,

send particulars of the conviction to the Secretary of State.

(2) A court shall in no circumstances enter any particulars in a driving
permit.

3.—(1) The holder of a driving permit disqualified in consequence of a conviction or of the order of a court for holding or obtaining a driving licence
shall, if so required by the court, produce his driving permit within five days,
or such longer time as the court may determine, and the court shall forward it
to the Secretary of State.

(2) The Secretary of State on receiving a permit forwarded under the foregoing sub-paragraph, shall—

(a) retain the permit until the disqualification ceases to have effect or until
the holder leaves Great Britain, whichever is the earlier;

(b) send the holder's name and address, together with the particulars of
the disqualification, to the authority by whom the permit was issued;
and

(c) if the permit is a Convention driving permit, record the particulars of
the disqualification on the permit.

(3) A person failing to produce a driving permit in compliance with this
paragraph shall be guilty of an offence which shall be treated for the purposes
of section 177 of the Road Traffic Act 1972 and of Part I of Schedule 4 thereto as

an offence against the provision specified in column 1 of that Part as section 101(4) and he shall be liable to be prosecuted and punished accordingly.

4.—(1) A court, on ordering the removal under section 95(1) of the said Act of a disqualification for holding or obtaining a driving licence, shall, if it appears that particulars of the disqualification have been forwarded to the Secretary of State under paragraph 2 of this Schedule, cause particulars of the order also to be forwarded to him [...].

(2) The Secretary of State, on receiving particulars of a court order removing such a disqualification, shall—

  (a) in the case of a permit on which particulars of a disqualification were entered in accordance with paragraph 3(2)(c) of this Schedule, enter on the permit particulars of the order removing the disqualification;

  (b) send the particulars of the order to the authority by whom the permit was issued; and

  (c) return the permit to the holder.

5.—(1) In the following provisions of the Road Traffic Act 1972, references to a driving licence shall include references to a driving permit.

(2) The said provisions are—

  (a) subsections (1) and (4) of section 161 (which, as amended by paragraph 19 of Schedule 6 to the Road Traffic Act 1974, authorises a police constable to require the production of a driving licence and in certain cases statement of date of birth by a person who is, or in certain circumstances has been, driving a vehicle),

  (b) subsection (2) of section 164 (which authorises a police constable to arrest a driver committing certain offences unless the driver gives his name and address or produces his driving licence), and

  (c) subsections (1) and (2) of section 169 (which relate to the use of a driving licence by a person other than the holder and to forgery of such a licence).

MOTOR VEHICLES (INTERNATIONAL CIRCULATION) (AMENDMENT) ORDER 1980

(S.I. 1980 No. 1095)

Citation and commencement

1. This Order may be cited as the Motor Vehicles (International Circulation) (Amendment) Order 1980 and shall come into operation—   **C9–01**

  (a) for all purposes of paragraph (1) of Article 10 on the first day of the month following that in which the Order is made, and

  (b) for all other purposes, on the date on which the Convention on Road Traffic concluded at Vienna in 1968 is first in force in respect of the United Kingdom, which date shall be notified in the London, Edinburgh and Belfast Gazettes.

2.–4. [*These articles amend the Motor Vehicles (International Circulation) Order 1975 (S.I. 1975 No. 1208) and are incorporated therein.*]   **C9–02**

5.–8. [*Revoked by the Motor Vehicles (International Circulation) (Amendment) Order* 1989 *(S.I.* 1989 *No.* 993).]

9. [*This article amends the Motor Vehicles (International Circulation) Order* 1975 *(S.I.* 1975 *No.* 1208) *and is incorporated therein.*]

10. [*Paras.* (2)–(4) *revoked by the Motor Vehicles (International Circulation) (Amendment) Order* 1989 *(S.I.* 1989 *No.* 993). *The remainder of the article amends the Motor Vehicles (International Circulation) Order* 1975 *(S.I.* 1975 *No.* 1208) *and is incorporated therein.*]

VEHICLE LICENCES (DURATION AND RATE OF DUTY) ORDER 1980

(S.I. 1980 No. 1183)

Interpretation and application

C10–01   **2.**—(1) In this Order "the Act of 1971" means the Vehicles (Excise) Act 1971.
(2) This Order shall, save in the case of licences for periods of seven consecutive days, apply only to vehicle licences issued to run from 1st October 1980 or from the beginning of any subsequent month.

Commencement and duration of licences

C10–02   **3.**—Vehicle licences (other than licences for one calendar year) may be taken out—
   (a) in the case of any vehicle licence, for any period of twelve months running from the beginning of the month in which the licence first has effect;
   (b) in the case of any vehicle the annual rate of duty applicable to which exceeds £18, for any period of six months running from the beginning of the month in which the licence first has effect;
   (c) in the case of a goods vehicle which is authorised to be used on roads by virtue of an order made under section 42(1) of the Road Traffic Act 1972, and the unladen weight of which exceeds eleven tons, for any period of seven consecutive days.

Rate of duty

C10–03   **4.**—The duty payable on a vehicle licence for a vehicle of any description shall—
   (a) if the licence is taken out for a period of twelve months, be paid at the annual rate of duty applicable to vehicles of that description under section 1 of the Act of 1971;
   (b) if the licence is taken out for a period of six months, be paid at a rate

equal to one half of the said annual rate plus ten per cent of that amount;

(c) if the licence is taken out for a period of seven consecutive days, be paid at a rate equal to one fifty-second of the said annual rate plus ten per cent of that amount;

and in computing the rate of duty in accordance with paragraph (b) or paragraph (c) above, any fraction of 5p shall be treated as 5p if it exceeds 2.5p and shall otherwise be disregarded.

MOTORWAYS TRAFFIC (ENGLAND AND WALES) REGULATIONS 1982

(S.I. 1982 No. 1163)

Interpretation

3.—(1) In these Regulations, the following expressions have the meanings   **C11–01** hereby respectively assigned to them:—

(a) "the 1984 Act" means the Road Traffic Regulation Act 1984;

(b) "carriageway" means that part of a motorway which—

  (i) is provided for the regular passage of vehicular motor traffic along the motorway; and

  (ii) where a hard shoulder is provided, has the approximate position of its left-hand or near-side edge marked with a traffic sign of the type shown in diagram 1012.1 in Schedule 1 to the Traffic Signs Regulations and General Directions 1981;

(c) "central reservation" means that part of a motorway which separates the carriageway to be used by vehicles travelling in one direction from the carriageway to be used by vehicles travelling in the opposite direction;

(d) "excluded traffic" means traffic which is not traffic of Classes I or II;

(e) "hard shoulder" means a part of the motorway which is adjacent to and situated on the left hand side or near side of the carriageway when facing in the direction in which vehicles may be driven in accordance with Regulation 6, and which is designed to take the weight of a vehicle;

(f) "motorway" means any road or part of a road to which these Regulations apply by virtue of Regulation 4;

(g) "verge" means any part of a motorway which is not a carriageway, a hard shoulder, or a central reservation.

(2) A vehicle shall be treated for the purposes of any provision of these Regulations as being on any part of a motorway specified in that provision if any part of the vehicle (whether it is at rest or not) is on the part of the motorway so specified.

(3) Any provision of these Regulations containing any prohibition or restriction relating to the driving, moving or stopping of a vehicle, or to its remaining at rest, shall be construed as a provision that no person shall use a motorway by driving, moving or stopping the vehicle or by causing or permitting it to be driven or moved, or to stop or remain at rest, in contravention of that prohibition or restriction.

(4) In these Regulations references to numbered classes of traffic are references to the classes of traffic set out in Schedule 4 to the Highways Act 1980.

Application

4. Subject to section 17(5) of the 1984 Act, these Regulations apply to every special road or part of a special road which can be used only by traffic of Class I or II.

Vehicles to be driven on the carriageway only

C11–02　　**5.** Subject to the following provisions of these Regulations, no vehicle shall be driven on any part of a motorway which is not a carriageway.

Direction of driving

6.—(1) Where there is a traffic sign indicating that there is no entry to a carriageway at a particular place, no vehicle shall be driven or moved onto that carriageway at that place.

(2) Where there is a traffic sign indicating that there is no left or right turn into a carriageway at a particular place, no vehicle shall be so driven or moved as to cause it to turn to the left or (as the case may be) to the right into that carriageway at that place.

(3) Every vehicle on a length of carriageway which is contiguous to a central reservation, shall be driven in such a direction that the central reservation is at all times on the right hand or off side of the vehicle.

(4) Where traffic signs are so placed that there is a length of carriageway (being a length which is not contiguous to a central reservation) which can be entered at one end only by vehicles driven in conformity with paragraph (1) of this Regulation, every vehicle on that length of carriageway shall be driven in such a direction only as to cause it to proceed away from that end of that length of carriageway towards the other end thereof.

(5) Without prejudice to the foregoing provisions of this Regulation, no vehicle which—

　　(a) is on a length of carriageway on which vehicles are required by any of the foregoing provisions of this Regulation to be driven in one direction only and is proceeding in or facing that direction, or

　　(b) is on any other length of carriageway and is proceeding in or facing one direction,

shall be driven or moved so as to cause it to turn and proceed in or face the opposite direction.

Restriction on stopping

C11–03　　**7.**—(1) Subject to the following provisions of this Regulation, no vehicle shall stop or remain at rest on a carriageway.

(2) Where it is necessary for a vehicle which is being driven on a carriageway to be stopped while it is on a motorway—

　　(a) by reason of a breakdown or mechanical defect or lack of fuel, oil or water, required for the vehicle; or

　　(b) by reason of any accident, illness or other emergency; or

(c) to permit any person carried in or on the vehicle to recover or move any object which has fallen onto a motorway; or

(d) to permit any person carried in or on the vehicle to give help which is required by any other person in any of the circumstances specified in the foregoing provisions of this paragraph,

the vehicle shall, as soon and in so far as is reasonably practicable, be driven or moved off the carriageway on to, and may stop and remain at rest on, any hard shoulder which is contiguous to that carriageway.

(3) (a) A vehicle which is at rest on a hard shoulder shall so far as is reasonably practicable be allowed to remain at rest on that hard shoulder in such a position only that no part of it or of the load carried thereby shall obstruct or be a cause of danger to vehicles using the carriageway.

(b) A vehicle shall not remain at rest on a hard shoulder for longer than is necessary in the circumstances or for the purposes specified in paragraph (2) of this Regulation.

(4) Nothing in the foregoing provisions of this Regulation shall preclude a vehicle from stopping or remaining at rest on a carriageway while it is prevented from proceeding along the carriageway by the presence of any other vehicle or any person or object.

Restrictions on reversing

8. No vehicle on a motorway shall be driven or moved backwards except in so far as it is necessary to back the vehicle to enable it to proceed forwards or to be connected to any other vehicle.   **C11–04**

Restriction on the use of hard shoulders

9. No vehicle shall be driven or stop or remain at rest on any hard shoulder except in accordance with paragraphs (2) and (3) of Regulation 7.

Vehicles not to use the central reservation or verge

10. No vehicle shall be driven or moved or stop or remain at rest on a central reservation or verge.

Vehicles not to be driven by learner drivers

11.—(1) No motor vehicle shall be driven on a motorway by a person who is authorised to drive that vehicle only by virtue of his being the holder of a provisional licence under section 97(2) of the Road Traffic Act 1988, unless, since the date of coming into force of the said provisional licence that person has passed a test prescribed under section 89 of that Act sufficient to entitle him under that Act to be granted a licence, other than a provisional licence, authorising him to drive that vehicle on a road.   **C11–05**

(2) Paragraph (1) above does not apply to a large goods vehicle or to a passenger-carrying vehicle.

(3) In this regulation, "large goods vehicle" and "passenger-carrying vehicle" have the meanings given by section 121 of the Road Traffic Act 1988.

Restriction on use of right hand or off side lane

C11–06   **12.**—(1) This Regulation applies to—

(a) a goods vehicle having a maximum laden weight exceeding 7.5 tonnes;

(b) a motor vehicle constructed solely for the carriage of passengers and their effects the overall length of which exceeds 12 metres;

(c) a motor vehicle drawing a trailer; and

(d) a vehicle which is a motor tractor, a light locomotive or a heavy locomotive.

(2) Subject to the provisions of paragraph (3) below, no vehicle to which this Regulation applies shall be driven or moved or stop or remain at rest on the right hand or offside lane of a length of carriageway which has three or more traffic lanes at any place where all the lanes are open for use by traffic proceeding in the same direction.

(3) The prohibition contained in paragraph (2) above shall not apply to a vehicle while it is being driven on any right hand or offside lane such as is mentioned in that paragraph in so far as it is necessary for the vehicle to be driven to enable it to pass another vehicle which is carrying or drawing a load of exceptional width.

(4) Nothing in this regulation shall have effect so as to require a vehicle to change lane during a period when it would not be reasonably practicable for it to do so without involving danger of injury to any person or inconvenience to other traffic.

(5) In this Regulation—

"goods vehicle" and "maximum laden weight" have the same meanings as in Schedule 6 to the 1984 Act, and

"overall length" has the meaning given by regulation 3(2) of the Road Vehicles (Construction and Use) Regulations 1986.

Restrictions affecting animals carried in vehicles

C11–07   **14.** The person in charge of any animal which is carried by a vehicle using a motorway shall, so far as is practicable, secure that—

(a) the animal shall not be removed from or permitted to leave the vehicle while the vehicle is on a motorway, and

(b) if it escapes from, or it is necessary for it to be removed from, or permitted to leave, the vehicle—

(i) it shall not go or remain on any part of the motorway other than a hard shoulder, and

(ii) it shall whilst it is not on or in the vehicle be held on a lead or otherwise kept under proper control.

Use of motorway by excluded traffic

C11–08   **15.**—(1) Excluded traffic is hereby authorised to use a motorway on the occasions or in the emergencies and to the extent specified in the following provisions of this paragraph, that is to say—

(a) traffic of Classes III or IV may use a motorway for the maintenance, repair, cleaning or clearance of any part of a motorway or for the erection, laying, placing, maintenance, testing, alteration, repair or removal of any structure, works or apparatus in, on, under or over any part of a motorway;

    (b) pedestrians may use a motorway—

        (i) when it is necessary for them to do so as a result of an accident or emergency or of a vehicle being at rest on a motorway in any of the circumstances specified in paragraph (2) of Regulation 7, or

        (ii) in any of the circumstances specified in sub-paragraphs (b), (d), (e) or (f) of paragraph (1) of Regulation 16.

(2) The Secretary of State may authorise the use of a motorway by any excluded traffic on occasion or in emergency or for the purpose of enabling such traffic to cross a motorway or to secure access to premises abutting on or adjacent to a motorway.

(3) Where by reason of any emergency the use of any road (not being a motorway) by any excluded traffic is rendered impossible or unsuitable the Chief Officer of Police of the police area in which a motorway or any part of a motorway is situated, or any officer of or above the rank of superintendent authorised in that behalf by that Chief Officer, may—

    (a) authorise any excluded traffic to use that motorway or that part of a motorway as an alternative road for the period during which the use of the other road by such traffic continues to be impossible or unsuitable, and

    (b) relax any prohibition or restriction imposed by these Regulations in so far as he considers it necessary to do so in connection with the use of that motorway or that part of a motorway by excluded traffic in pursuance of any such authorisation as aforesaid.

Exceptions and relaxations

16.—(1) Nothing in the foregoing provisions of these Regulations shall pre-   **C11–09** clude any person from using a motorway otherwise than in accordance with the provisions in any of the following circumstances, that is to say—

    (a) where he does so in accordance with any direction or permission given by a constable in uniform or with the indication given by a traffic sign;

    (b) where, in accordance with any permission given by a constable, he does so for the purpose of investigating any accident which has occurred on or near a motorway;

    (c) where it is necessary for him to do so to avoid or prevent an accident or to obtain or give help required as the result of an accident or emergency, and he does so in such manner as to cause as little danger or inconvenience as possible to other traffic on a motorway;

    (d) where he does so in the exercise of his duty as a constable or as a member of a fire brigade or of an ambulance service;

    (e) where it is necessary for him to do so to carry out in an efficient manner—

        (i) the maintenance, repair, cleaning, clearance, alteration or improvement of any part of a motorway, or

        (ii) the removal of any vehicle from any part of a motorway, or

        (iii) the erection, laying, placing, maintenance, testing, alteration, repair or removal of any structure, works or apparatus in, on, under or over any part of a motorway, or

    (f) where it is necessary for him to do so in connection with any inspection, survey, investigation or census which is carried out in accordance with any general or special authority granted by the Secretary of State.

(2) Without prejudice to the foregoing provisions of these Regulations, the Secretary of State may relax any prohibition or restriction imposed by these Regulations.

PROSECUTION OF OFFENCES ACT 1985 (SPECIFIED PROCEEDINGS) ORDER 1985

(S.I. 1985 No. 2010)

C12–01   **2.**—(1) Subject to paragraphs (2) and (3) below, proceedings for the offences mentioned in the Schedule to this Order are hereby specified for the purposes of section 3 of the Prosecution of Offences Act 1985 (which, amongst other things, places a duty on the Director of Public Prosecutions to take over the conduct of all criminal proceedings, other than specified proceedings, instituted on behalf of a police force).

(2) Where a summons has been issued in respect of an offence mentioned in the Schedule to this Order, proceedings for that offence cease to be specified when the summons is served on the accused unless the documents described in paragraphs (a) and (b) of section 12(1) of the Magistrates' Courts Act 1980 [*as amended*] (pleading guilty by post etc.) are served upon the accused with the summons.

(3) Proceedings for an offence cease to be specified if at any time a magistrates' court begins to receive evidence in those proceedings, and for the purpose of this paragraph nothing read out before the court under section 12(4) of the Magistrates' Courts Act 1980 shall be regarded as evidence.

SCHEDULE 1

OFFENCES PROCEEDINGS FOR WHICH ARE SPECIFIED BY ARTICLE 2(1)

C12–02   1. Fixed penalty offences within the meaning of section 27(5) of the Transport Act 1982.

2. The offence under section 8(1) of the Vehicles (Excise) Act 1971.

3. The offences under sections 18, 20, 21, 30(1) and (2), 33(2), 33AA(3), 40(5)(b), 44(1), 84(2), 143, 161(4) and (5), 162(1), 164(1) and 168(3) of the Road Traffic Act 1972.

4. All offences under the Road Traffic Regulation Act 1984 other than those under sections 35(5), 43(5) and (12), 47(3), 52(1), 108(3), 115(1) and (2), 116(1) and 129(3) and paragraph 6(3) of Schedule 12 or those mentioned in paragraph 1 above.

5. The offences arising by contravention of Regulations 3(9) (involving a pedal cycle) and 4(27), (28) and (30) of the Royal and other Parks and Gardens Regulations 1977 (S.I. 1977 No. 217).

REMOVAL AND DISPOSAL OF VEHICLES REGULATIONS 1986

(S.I. 1986 No. 183)

Interpretation

2. In these Regulations, unless the contrary intention appears, the following   **C13–01**
expressions have the meanings hereby assigned to them respectively, that is to
say:—
>   "the 1978 Act" means the Refuse Disposal (Amenity) Act 1978;
>   "the 1984 Act" means the Road Traffic Regulation Act 1984;
>   "motor vehicle" has the meaning assigned to it in section 11(1) of the
>   1978 Act;
>   "road", in England and Wales, means any highway and any other road
>   to which the public has access and, in Scotland, has the meaning
>   assigned to it in section 151 of the Roads (Scotland) Act 1984;
>   "vehicle", in relation to any matter prescribed by these Regulations for
>   the purposes of any provision in sections 3 and 4 of the 1978 Act,
>   means a motor vehicle, and in relation to any matter prescribed by
>   these Regulations for the purposes of any provision in sections 99
>   and 101 of the 1984 Act has the meaning assigned to it in section 99(5)
>   of that Act, and, in relation to any matter prescribed by these Regu-
>   lations for the purposes of section 99 of the 1984 Act, any reference to
>   a vehicle which has been permitted to remain at rest or which has
>   broken down includes a reference to a vehicle which has been per-
>   mitted to remain at rest or which has broken down before the coming
>   into force of these Regulations.

Power of constable to require removal of vehicles from roads

3.—(1) Except as provided by regulation 7 of these Regulations, this regu-   **C13–02**
lation applies to a vehicle which—
>   (a) has broken down, or been permitted to remain at rest, on a road in
>   such a position or in such condition or in such circumstances as to
>   cause obstruction to persons using the road or as to be likely to cause
>   danger to such persons, or
>   (b) has been permitted to remain at rest or has broken down and remained
>   at rest on a road in contravention of a prohibition or restriction con-
>   tained in, or having effect under, any of the enactments mentioned in
>   Schedule 1 to these Regulations.

(2) A constable may require the owner, driver or other person in control or
in charge of any vehicle to which this regulation applies to move or cause to be
moved the vehicle and any such requirement may include a requirement that
the vehicle shall be moved from that road to a place which is not on that or any
other road, or that the vehicle shall not be moved to any such road or to any
such position on a road as may be specified.

(3) A person required to move or cause to be moved a vehicle under this regulation shall comply with such requirement as soon as practicable.

Power of constable to remove vehicles

C13–03   4. Except as provided by regulation 7 of these Regulations, where a vehicle—

    (a) is a vehicle to which regulation 3 of these Regulations applies, or

    (b) having broken down on a road or on any land in the open air appears to a constable to have been abandoned without lawful authority, or

    (c) has been permitted to remain at rest on a road or on any land in the open air in such a position or in such condition or in such circumstances as to appear to a constable to have been abandoned without lawful authority,

then, subject to the provisions of sections 99 and 100 of the 1984 Act, a constable may remove or arrange for the removal of the vehicle, and, in the case of a vehicle which is on a road, he may remove it or arrange for its removal from that road to a place which is not on that or any other road, or may move it or arrange for its removal to another position on that or another road.

Power of traffic warden to remove vehicles

C13–04   4A.—(1) Except as provided by regulation 7 of these Regulations, a traffic warden may, subject to sections 99 and 100 of the 1984 Act, remove or arrange for the removal of a vehicle to which regulation 3 of these Regulations applies to a place which is not on that or any other road, or may move it or arrange for its removal to another position on that or another road.

    (2) This regulation applies only in respect of

    (a) a vehicle which is on a road in, and

    (b) its removal in and to a place in,

England or Wales.

Power of local authority to remove certain vehicles

C13–05   5.—(1) Except as provided by regulation 7 of these Regulations, where a vehicle (other than a motor vehicle which a local authority have a duty to remove under section 3 of the 1978 Act)—

    (a) having broken down on a road or on any land in the open air in the area of a local authority, appears to them to have been abandoned without lawful authority, or

    (b) has been permitted to remain at rest on a road or on any land in the open air in the area of a local authority in such a position or in such condition or in such circumstances as to appear to them to have been abandoned without lawful authority,

the local authority may, subject to the provisions of sections 99 and 100 of the 1984 Act, remove or arrange for the removal of the vehicle to a place which is not on any road.

    (2) In this regulation "local authority" means, in the case of a vehicle situate at a place—

    (a) in England, the council of the district or of the London borough, or the Common Council of the City of London;

    (b) in Scotland, the regional or islands or district council; or

    (c) in Wales, the council of the district,

within whose area is situate that place.

Powers of parking attendants to remove vehicles

5A.—(1) Except as provided by regulation 7 of these Regulations where, in   **C13–06**
the area of a particular local authority, a vehicle—
  (a) has been permitted to remain at rest or has broken down and remained
      at rest on a road in Greater London in contravention of a prohibition or
      restriction having effect under—
     (i) section 6 of the 1984 Act so far as it designates any parking place;
         or
     (ii) section 9 of the 1984 Act so far as the order designates any parking
          place in an area in respect of which section 65 of the Road Traffic
          Act 1991 is in force;
     (iii) section 46 of the 1984 Act so far as the order relates to a parking
           place in such an area;
  (b) has been permitted to remain at rest or has broken down and remained
      at rest on a road outside Greater London in contravention of a prohib-
      ition or restriction contained in an order under section 46 of the 1984
      Act in circumstances in which an offence would have been committed
      in respect of the vehicle but for paragraph 1(4)(b) of Schedule 3 to the
      1991 Act (permitted parking areas); or
  (c) has been permitted to remain at rest or has broken down and remained
      at rest on a road in contravention of a statutory prohibition or restric-
      tion in circumstances in which an offence would have been committed
      with respect to the vehicle but for section 76(3) of, or paragraph 1(4)(a)
      or 2(4) of Schedule 3 to, the Road Traffic Act 1991 (permitted parking
      areas or special parking areas),
a parking attendant acting on behalf of the local authority may, subject to the
provisions of sections 99 and 100 of the 1984 Act, remove or arrange for the
removal of the vehicle from the road to a place which is not on that or any
other road, or may move it or arrange for its removal to another position on
that or another road.
  (2) Sub-paragraphs (ii) and (iii) of paragraph (1)(a) and paragraph (1)(b)
above shall not apply in relation to a vehicle if—
  (a) not more than 15 minutes have elapsed since the end of any period for
      which the appropriate charge was duly paid at the time of parking; or
  (b) not more than 15 minutes have elapsed since the end of any unexpired
      time (in respect of another vehicle) which is available at the relevant
      parking meter at the time of parking.
  (3) This regulation applies only in respect of—
  (a) a vehicle which is on a road in, and
  (b) its removal in and to a place in,
England or Wales.
  (4) In this regulation—
      "local authority" has the same meaning as in section 100 of the 1984
          Act; and
      "parking meter" has the same meaning as in section 46(2)(a) of that Act.

Method of removing vehicles

6. Any person removing or moving a vehicle under regulation 4, 4A or 5 of   **C13–07**
these Regulations may do so by towing or driving the vehicle or in such other
manner as he may think necessary and may take such measures in relation to
the vehicle as he may think necessary to enable him to remove or move it as
aforesaid.

Exception for Severn Bridge

C13–08   **7.** Regulations 3, 4, 4A and 5 of these Regulations shall not apply in relation to any vehicle while on the central section of the specified carriageways (as defined in section 1 of the Severn Bridge Tolls Act 1965) of a road which crosses the Rivers Severn and Wye.

Period before which notice must be affixed to a vehicle in certain cases before removing it for destruction

C13–09   **10.** For the purposes of section 3(5) of the 1978 Act and section 99(4) of the 1984 Act, the period before the commencement of which a notice must be caused to be affixed to a vehicle by an authority who propose to remove it, before they remove it, being a vehicle which in the opinion of the authority is in such a condition that it ought to be destroyed, shall be seven days.

Regulation 3   SCHEDULE 1

CERTAIN ENACTMENTS BY OR UNDER WHICH ARE IMPOSED PROHIBITIONS
OR RESTRICTIONS ON THE WAITING OF VEHICLES ON ROADS

C13–10   Section 62 of the Roads (Scotland) Act 1984 (which permits a roads authority in Scotland to regulate traffic on its roads).

Section 52 of the Metropolitan Police Act 1839 and section 22 of the local Act of the second and third year of the reign of Queen Victoria, chapter 94 (relating to the prevention of obstruction in streets in London).

Section 21 of the Town Police Clauses Act 1847 (relating to the prevention of obstruction in streets in England and Wales elsewhere than in London).

Section 2 of the Parks Regulation (Amendment) Act 1926 (authorising the making of regulations as to Royal Parks).

Section 22 of the Road Traffic Act 1972 (which makes it an offence to fail to conform to the indications given by certain traffic signs).

Section 1 of the 1984 Act (which authorises the making of orders regulating traffic on roads outside Greater London), and, as respects Scotland, paragraph 7 of Schedule 10 to the 1984 Act (which provides that any byelaw made under section 104 of the Roads and Bridges (Scotland) Act 1878, or paragraphs (1) and (3) of section 385 of the Burgh Police (Scotland) Act 1892, which was in force at the commencement of the Road Traffic Regulation Act 1967, shall continue in force and have effect as if it were an order made under section 1 of the 1984 Act).

Section 6 of the 1984 Act (authorising the making of orders regulating traffic on roads in Greater London).

Section 9 of the 1984 Act (authorising the making of experimental traffic orders).

Section 12 of the 1984 Act (relating to experimental traffic schemes in Greater London).

Section 14 of the 1984 Act (which provides for the restriction or prohibition of the use of roads in consequence of the execution of works).

Section 17 of the 1984 Act (authorising the making of regulations with respect to the use of special roads).

Section 25 of the 1984 Act (authorising the making of regulations for crossings for foot passengers).

Sections 35 and 45 to 49 of the 1984 Act (relating to parking places for vehicles.)

Section 57 of the 1984 Act (relating to the provision of parking places in England and Wales for bicycles and motor cycles).

Sections 66 and 67 of the 1984 Act (which empower the police to place traffic signs relating to the local traffic regulations and temporary signs for dealing with traffic congestion and danger).

Any enactment contained in any local Act for the time being in force, and any byelaw having effect under any enactment for the time being in force, being an enactment or byelaw imposing or authorising the imposition of a prohibition or restriction similar to any prohibition or restriction which is or can be imposed by or under any of the above-mentioned enactments.

ROAD VEHICLES (CONSTRUCTION AND USE) REGULATIONS 1986

(S.I. 1986 No. 1078)

Length

7.—(1) Subject to paragraphs (2) to (6), the overall length of a vehicle or com-   **C14–01**
bination of vehicles of a class specified in an item in column 2 of the Table shall
not exceed the maximum length specified in that item in column 3 of the
Table, the overall length in the case of a combination of vehicles being calculated in accordance with regulation 81(g) and (h).

TABLE

(regulation 7(1))

1	2	3
Item	Class of vehicle	Maximum length (metres)
	Vehicle Combinations	
1	A motor vehicle drawing one trailer, where the combination of vehicles does not meet the requirements of paragraph (5A) and the trailer is not a semi-trailer.	18
1A	A motor vehicle drawing one trailer where the combination meets the requirements of paragraph (5A) and the trailer is not a semi-trailer.	18.35
2	An articulated bus.	18
3	An articulated vehicle the semi-trailer of which does not meet the requirements of and is not a low loader.	15.5

1	2	3
Item	Class of vehicle	Maximum length (metres)
3A	An articulated vehicle, the semi-trailer of which meets the requirements of paragraph (6) and is not a low loader.	16.5
3B	An articulated vehicle, the semi-trailer of which is a low loader.	18]
	Motor vehicles	
4	A wheeled motor vehicle.	12
5	A track-laying motor vehicle.	9.2
	Trailers	
6	An agricultural trailed appliance manufactured on or after 1st December 1985.	15
7	A semi-trailer manufactured on or after 1st May 1983 which does not meet the requirements of paragraph (6) and is not a low loader.	12.2
7A	A composite trailer drawn by— (a) a goods vehicle being a motor vehicle having a maximum gross weight exceeding 3500kg; or (b) an agricultural motor vehicle	14.04
8	A trailer (not being a semi-trailer or composite trailer) with at least 4 wheels which is— (a) drawn by a goods vehicle being a motor vehicle having a maximum gross weight exceeding 3500 kg; or (b) an agricultural trailer.	12
9	Any other trailer not being an agricultural trailed appliance or a semi-trailer.	7

(2) In the case of a motor vehicle drawing one trailer where—
  (a) the motor vehicle is a showman's vehicle as defined in paragraph 7 of Schedule 3 to the 1971 Act; and
  (b) the trailer is used primarily as living accommodation by one or more persons and is not also used for the carriage of goods or burden which is not needed for the purpose of such residence in the vehicle.
item 1 in the Table applies with the substitution of 22 m for 18 m and item 1A in the Table does not apply.
  (3) Items 1, 1A, 3, 3A and 3B of the Table do not apply to—
  (a) a vehicle combination which includes a trailer which is constructed and normally used for the conveyance of indivisible loads of exceptional length, or
  (b) a vehicle combination consisting of a broken down vehicle (including an articulated vehicle) being drawn by a motor vehicle in consequence of a breakdown or,
  (c) an articulated vehicle, the semi-trailer of which is a low loader manufactured before 1st April 1991.
  (3A) Items 6, 7, 7A, 8 and 9 of the Table do not apply to—
  (a) a trailer which is constructed and normally used for the conveyance of indivisible loads of exceptional length,

(b) a broken down vehicle (including an articulated vehicle) which is being drawn by a motor vehicle in consequence of a breakdown, or

(c) a trailer being a drying or mixing plant designed for the production of asphalt or of bituminous or tar macadam and used mainly for the construction, repair or maintenance of roads, or a road planing machine so used.

(3B) Furthermore item 7 does not apply to—

(a) a semi-trailer which is a car transporter,

(b) a semi-trailer which is normally used on international journeys any part of which takes place outside the United Kingdom.

(4) Where a motor vehicle is drawing—

(a) two trailers, then only one of those trailers may exceed an overall length of 7 m;

(b) three trailers, then none of those trailers shall exceed an overall length of 7 m.

(5) Where a motor vehicle is drawing—

(a) two or more trailers; or

(b) one trailer constructed and normally used for the conveyance of indivisible loads of exceptional length—

then—

(i) the overall length of that motor vehicle shall not exceed 9·2 m; and

(ii) the overall length of the combination of vehicles, calculated in accordance with regulation 81(g) and (h), shall not exceed 25·9 m, unless the conditions specified in paragraphs 1 and 2 of Schedule 12 have been complied with.

(5A) The requirements of this paragraph, in relation to a combination of vehicles, are that at least one of the vehicles in the combination is not a goods vehicle or, if both vehicles in the combination are goods vehicles that—

(a) the maximum distance measured parallel to the longitudinal axis of the combination of vehicles from the foremost point of the loading area behind the driver's cab to the rear of the trailer, less the distance between the rear of the motor vehicle and the front of the trailer, does not exceed 15.65 m; and

(b) the maximum distance measured parallel to the longitudinal axis of the combination of vehicles from the foremost point of the loading area behind the driver's cab to the rear of the trailer does not exceed 16 m;

but sub-paragraph (a) shall not apply if both vehicles in the combination are car transporters.

(6) The requirements of this paragraph, in relation to a semi-trailer, are that—

(a) the longitudinal distance from the axis of the king pin [...] to the rear of the semi-trailer does not exceed—

(i) 12·5 m in the case of a car transporter, or

(ii) 12 m in any other case; and

(b) no point in the semi-trailer forward of the transverse plane passing through the axis of the king pin [...] is more than—

(i) 4·19 m from the axis of the king pin, in the case of a car transporter, or

(ii) 2·04 m from the axis of the king pin, in any other case.

(6A) For the purposes of paragraph (5A)—

(a) where the forward end of the loading area of a motor vehicle is bounded by a wall, the thickness of the wall shall be regarded as part of the loading area; and

(b) any part of a vehicle designed primarily for use as a means of attaching another vehicle to it and any fitting designed for use in connection with any such part shall be disregarded in determining the distance between the rear of a motor vehicle and the front of a trailer being drawn by it.

(7) For the purpose of paragraph (6) the longitudinal distance from the axis of the king pin to the rear of a semi-trailer is the distance between a transverse plane passing through the axis of the king pin and the rear of the semi-trailer.

(7A) Where a semi-trailer has more than one king-pin or is constructed so that it can be used with a king-pin in different positions, references in this regulation to a distance from the king-pin shall be construed as the distance from the rearmost king-pin or, as the case may be, the rearmost king-pin position.

(7B) For the purposes of paragraphs (5A), (6) and (7)—
  (a) a reference to the front of a vehicle is a reference to the transverse plane passing through the extreme forward projecting points of the vehicle; and
  (b) a reference to the rear of a vehicle is a reference to the transverse plane passing through the extreme rearward projecting points of the vehicle,

inclusive (in each case) of all parts of the vehicle, of any receptacle which is of a permanent character and accordingly strong enough for repeated use, and any fitting on, or attached to the vehicle but exclusive of—
  (i) the things set out in sub-paragraph (i) of the definition of "overall length" in the Table in regulation 3(2), and
  (ii) in the case of a semi-trailer, the things set out in sub-paragraph (ii)(a) of that definition.

(8) Where a broken down articulated vehicle is being towed by a motor vehicle in consequence of a breakdown—
  (a) paragraph (5) shall have effect in relation to the combination of vehicles as if sub-paragraph (b) were omitted, and
  (b) for the purposes of paragraph (4) and of paragraph (5) as so modified, the articulated vehicle shall be regarded as a single trailer.

(9) No person shall use or cause or permit to be used on a road, a trailer with an overall length exceeding 18·65 m unless the requirements of paragraphs 1 and 2 of Schedule 12 are complied with.

Width

C14–02   8.—(1) Save as provided in paragraph (2), the overall width of a vehicle of a class specified in an item in column 2 of the Table shall not exceed the maximum width specified in column 3 in that item.

TABLE

(regulation 8(1))

1	2	3
Item	Class of vehicle	Maximum width (metres)
1	A locomotive, other than an agricultural motor vehicle.	2.75
2	A refrigerated vehicle.	2.60
3	Any other motor vehicle.	2.5
4	A trailer drawn by a motor vehicle having maximum gross weight (determined as provided in Part I of Schedule 8 to these Regulations) exceeding 3500 kg.	2.5
5	An agricultural trailer.	2.5
6	An agricultural trailed appliance.	2.5
7	Any other trailer dawn by a vehicle other than a motor cycle.	2.3
8	A trailer drawn by a motor-cycle.	1.5

(2) Paragraph (1) does not apply to a broken down vehicle which is being drawn in consequence of the breakdown.

(3) No person shall use or cause or permit to be used on a road a wheeled agricultural motor vehicle drawing a wheeled trailer if, when the longitudinal axes of the vehicles are parallel but in different vertical planes, the overall width of the two vehicles, measured as if they were one vehicle, exceeds 2·5 metres.

(4) In this regulation "refrigerated vehicle" means any vehicle which is specially designed for the carriage of goods at low temperature and of which the thickness of each of the side walls, inclusive of insulation, is at least 45 mm.

Height

9.—(1) The overall height of a bus shall not exceed 4·57 m.   **C14–03**

(2) Save as provided in paragraph (3), no person shall use or cause or permit to be used on a road any semi-trailer if—

(a) any part of the structure of the vehicle is more than 4·2 m from the ground when the vehicle is on level ground; and

(b) the total laden weight of the semi-trailer and the vehicle by which it is drawn exceeds 35,000 kg.

(2A) Save as provided by paragraph (3), no person shall use or cause or permit to be used on a road a motor vehicle drawing a trailer (other than a semi-trailer) if—

(a) any part of the structure of any of the vehicles in the combination is more than 4.2 m from the ground when the vehicles are on level ground; and

(b) the total laden weight of the vehicles in the combination exceeds 35,000 kg.

(3) For the purpose of paragraphs (2) and (2A) the structure of a vehicle includes any detachable structure attached to the vehicle for the purpose of containing any load, but does not include any load which is not a detachable structure or any sheeting or other readily flexible means of covering or securing a load.

The provisions of paragraphs (2) and (2A) do not apply in respect of any vehicle while it is being loaded or unloaded.

Indication of overall travelling height

C14–04   10.—(1) This regulation applies to every motor vehicle which is—

(a) constructed or adapted so as to be capable of hoisting and carrying a skip;

(b) carrying a container;

(c) drawing a trailer or semi-trailer carrying a container;

(d) engineering plant;

(e) carrying engineering equipment; or

(f) drawing a trailer or semi-trailer carrying engineering equipment.

(2) No person shall use or cause or permit to be used on a road a vehicle to which this regulation applies if the overall travelling height exceeds 3·66 m unless there is carried in the vehicle in the manner specified in paragraph (3) a notice clearly indicating in feet and inches and in figures not less than 40 mm tall, the overall travelling height.

(3) The notice referred to in paragraph (2) shall be attached to the vehicle in such a manner that it can be read by the driver when in the driving position.

(4) In this regulation—

"overall travelling height" means not less than and not above 25 mm more than the distance between the ground and the point on the motor vehicle, or on any trailer drawn by it, or on any load being carried by or any equipment which is fitted to the said motor vehicle or trailer, which is farthest from the ground, and for the purpose of determining the overall travelling height—

(a) the tyres of the motor vehicle and of any trailer which it is drawing shall be suitably inflated for the use to which the vehicle or combination of vehicles is being put; and

(b) the surface under the motor vehicle and any trailer which it is drawing and any load which is being carried on and any equipment which is fitted to any part of the said vehicle or combination of vehicles and which projects beyond any part of the said vehicle or combination of vehicles shall be reasonably flat; and

(c) any equipment which is fitted to the motor vehicle or any trailer which it is drawing shall be stowed in the position in which it is to proceed on the road;

"skip" means an article of equipment designed and constructed to be carried on a road vehicle and to be placed on a road or other land for the storage of materials, or for the removal and disposal of rubble, waste, household or other rubbish or earth.

Overhang

C14–05   11.—(1) The overhang of a wheeled vehicle of a class specified in an item in column 2 of the Table shall not, subject to any exemption specified in that item in column 4, exceed the distance specified in that item in column 3.

(2) In the case of an agricultural motor vehicle the distance measured horizontally and parallel to the longitudinal axis of the rear portion of the vehicle between the transverse planes passing through the rearmost point of the vehicle and through the centre of the rear or the rearmost axle shall not exceed 3 m.

TABLE

(regulation 11(1))

1	2	3	4
Item	Class of vehicle	Maximum overhang	Exemptions
1	Motor tractor	1·83 m.	(a) a track-laying vehicle (b) an agricultural motor vehicle
2	Heavy motor car and motor car	60% of the distance between the transverse plane which passes through the centre or centres of the foremost wheel or wheels and the transverse plane which passes through the foremost point from which the overhang is to be measured as provided in regulation 3(2).	(a) a bus (b) a refuse vehicle (c) a works truck (d) a track-laying vehicle (e) an agricultural motor vehicle (f) a motor car which is an ambulance (g) a vehicle designed to dispose of its load to the rear, if the overhang does not exceed 1·15 m (h) a vehicle first used before 2nd January 1933 (i) a vehicle first used before 1st January 1966 if— 　(i) the distance between the centres of the rearmost and foremost axles does not exceed 2·29 m, and 　(ii) the distance specified in column 3 is not exceeded by more than 76 mm (j) heating plant on a vehicle designed and mainly used to heat the surface of a road or other similar surface in the process of construction, repair or maintenance shall be disregarded.

Minimum ground clearance

C14–07 12.—(1) Save as provided in paragraph (2), a wheeled trailer which is—
(a) a goods vehicle; and
(b) manufactured on or after 1st April 1984,
shall have a minimum ground clearance of not less than 160 mm if the trailer has an axle interspace of more than 6 m but less than 11·5 m, and a minimum ground clearance of not less than 190 mm if the trailer has an axle interspace of 11·5 m or more.

(2) Paragraph (1) shall not apply in the case of a trailer—
(a) which is fitted with a suspension system with which, by the operation of a control, the trailer may be lowered or raised, while that system is being operated to enable the trailer to pass under a bridge or other obstruction over a road provided that at such times the system is operated so that no part of the trailer (excluding any wheel) touches the ground or is likely to do so; or
(b) while it is being loaded or unloaded.

(3) In this regulation—
"axle interspace" means—
(a) in the case of a semi-trailer, the distance between the point of support of the semi-trailer at its forward end and, if it has only one axle, the centre of that axle or, if it has more than one axle, the point halfway between the centres of the foremost and rearmost of those axles; and
(b) in the case of any other trailer, the distance between the centre of its front axle or, if it has more than one axle at the front, the point halfway between the centres of the foremost and rearmost of those axles, and the centre of its rear axle or, if it has more than one axle at the rear, the point halfway between the centre of the foremost and rearmost of those axles; and
"ground clearance" means the shortest distance between the ground and the lowest part of that portion of the trailer (excluding any part of a suspension, steering or braking system attached to any axle, and wheel and any air skirt) which lies within the area formed by the overall width of the trailer and the middle 70 per cent of the axle interspace, such distance being ascertained when the trailer—
(a) is fitted with suitable tyres which are inflated to a pressure recommended by the manufacturer, and
(b) is reasonably horizontal and standing on ground which is reasonably flat.

Turning circle—buses

C14–08 13.—(1) This regulation applies to a bus first used on or after 1st April 1982.

(2) Every vehicle to which this regulation applies shall be able to move on either lock so that no part of it projects outside the area contained between concentric circles with radii of 12 m and 5·3 m.

(3) When a vehicle to which this regulation applies moves forward from rest, on either lock, so that its outermost point describes a circle of 12 m radius, no part of the vehicle shall project beyond the longitudinal plane which, at the beginning of the manoeuvre, defines the overall width of the vehicle on the side opposite to the direction in which it is turning by more than—
(a) 0·8 m if it is a rigid vehicle; or
(b) 1·2 m if it is an articulated bus.

(4) For the purpose of paragraph (3) the two rigid portions of an articulated bus shall be in line at the beginning of the manoeuvre.

Braking systems of certain vehicles first used on or after 1st April 1983

15.—(1) Save as provided in paragraphs (2), (3) except sub-paragraph (b)(ii) **C14–09** and (4), the braking system of every wheeled vehicle of a class specified in an item in column 2 of the Table which in the case of a motor vehicle, is first used on or after 1st April, 1983 or which, in the case of a trailer, is manufactured on or after 1st October 1982, shall comply with the construction, fitting, and performance requirements specified in Annexes I, II and VII to Community Directive 79/489, and if relevant, Annexes III, IV, V, VI and VIII to that Directive, in relation to the category of vehicles specified in that item in column 3.

Provided that it shall be lawful for any vehicle of such a class which, in the case of a motor vehicle, was first used before 1st April 1983 or, in the case of a trailer, was manufactured before 1st October 1982 to comply with the said requirements instead of complying with regulations 16 and 17.

(1A) Save as provided in paragraphs (2), (3)(b) and (c), (3A) and (5), the braking system of every wheeled vehicle of a class specified in an item in column 2 of the Table which in the case of a motor vehicle,] is first used on or after the relevant date or which, in the case of a trailer, is manufactured on or after the relevant date shall comply with the construction, fitting and performance requirements specified in Annexes I, II and VII to Community Directive 85/647, and if relevant, Annexes III, IV, V, VI, VIII, X, XI and XII to that Directive, in relation to the category of vehicles specified in that item in column 3.

Provided that it shall be lawful for any vehicle of such a class which, in the case of a motor vehicle, was first used before the relevant date or which, in the case of a trailer, was manufactured before the relevant date, to comply with the said requirements instead of complying with paragraph (1), or with regulations 16 and 17.

(1B) In paragraph (1A), the relevant date in relation to a vehicle of a class specified in item 1 or 2 of the Table is 1st April 1990, in relation to a vehicle specified in item 4 of that Table is 1st April 1992, in relation to a vehicle in items 7, 8, 9 or 10 of that Table is 1st October 1988 and in relation to a vehicle of any other class is 1st April 1989.

(1C) Save as provided in paragraphs (2), (3)(b) and (c), (3A) and (5), the braking system of every wheeled vehicle of a class specified in an item in column 2 of the Table which in the case of a motor vehicle is first used on or after 1st April 1992 or in the case of a trailer is manufactured on or after 1st October 1991 shall comply with the construction, fitting and performance requirements specified in Annexes I, II and VII to Community Directive 88/194, and if relevant, Annexes III, IV, V, VI, VIII, X, XI, and XII to that Directive, in relation to the category of vehicles specified in that item in column 3.

Provided that it shall be lawful for any vehicle of such a class which, in the case of a motor vehicle was first used before 1st April 1992 or which, in the case of a trailer, was manufactured before 1st October 1991, to comply with the said requirements instead of complying with paragraph (1) or (1A), or with regulations 16 and 17.

TABLE

(regulation 15(1))

1	2	3
Item	Class of vehicle	Vehicle Category in the Community Directive
1	Passenger vehicles and dual-purpose vehicles which have 3 or more wheels except— (a) dual-purpose vehicles constructed and adapted to carry not more than 2 passengers exclusive of the driver; (b) motor-cycles with side-car attached; (c) vehicles with 3 wheels, an unladen weight not exceeding 410 kg, a maximum design speed not exceeding 50 km/h and an engine capacity not exceeding 50 cc; (d) buses	M1
2	Buses having a maximum gross weight which does not exceed 5000 kg.	M2
3	Buses having a maximum gross weight which exceeds 5000 kg.	M3
4	Dual-purpose vehicles not within item 1; and goods vehicles, having a maximum gross weight which does not exceed 3500 kg, and not being motorcycles with a sidecar attached.	N1
	Goods vehicles with a maximum gross weight which—	
5	exceeds 3500 kg but does not exceed 12,000 kg.	N2
6	exceeds 12,000 kg.	N3
	Trailers with a maximum total design axle weight which—	
7	does not exceed 750 kg.	O1
8	exceeds 750 kg but does not exceed 3500 kg.	O2
9	exceeds 3500 kg but does not exceed 10,000 kg.	O3
10	exceeds 10,000 kg.	O4

(2) The requirements specified in paragraphs (1), (1A) and (1C) do not apply to—

(a) an agricultural trailer or agricultural trailed appliance that is not, in either case, drawn at a speed exceeding 20 mph;
(b) a locomotive;
(c) a motor tractor;
(d) an agricultural motor vehicle unless it is first used after 1st June 1986 and is driven at more than 20 mph;
(e) a vehicle which has a maximum speed not exceeding 25 km/h;
(f) a works trailer;
(g) a works truck;
(h) a public works vehicle;

(i) a trailer designed and constructed, or adapted, to be drawn exclusively by a vehicle to which sub-paragraph (b), (c), (e), (g) or (h) of this paragraph applies;

(j) a trailer mentioned in regulation 16(3)(b), (d), (e), (f) and (g); or

(k) a vehicle manufactured by Leyland Vehicles Limited and known as the Atlantean Bus, if first used before 1st October 1984.

(3) The requirements specified in paragraphs (1), (1A) and (1C) shall apply to the classes of vehicles specified in the Table so that—

(a) in item 3, the testing requirements specified in paragraphs 1.5.1 and 1.5.2 of Annex II to Community Directives 79/489, 85/647 and 88/194 shall apply to every vehicle specified in that item other than—
   (i) a double-decked vehicle first used before 1st October 1983, or
   (ii) a vehicle of a type in respect of which a member state of the European Economic Community has issued a type approval certificate in accordance with Community Directive 79/489, 85/647 or 88/194.

(b) in items 2 and 3—
   (i) the requirements specified in paragraph 1.1.4.2 of Annex II to the said Community Directive 79/489; and
   (ii) sub-note (2) to paragraph 1.17.2 of Annex I to Community Directive 85/647 or 88/194,
   shall not apply;

(c) in items 1, 2, 3, 4, 5 and 6, in the case of vehicles constructed or adapted for use by physically handicapped drivers, the requirement in paragraph 2.1.2.1 of Annex I to Community Directive 79/489 that the driver must be able to achieve the braking action mentioned in that paragraph from his driving seat without removing his hands from the steering control shall be modified so as to require that the driver is able to achieve that action while continuing to steer the vehicle; and

(d) in items 1, 4, 5, 6, 7, 8, 9 and 10 the requirement specified in paragraph 1.1.4.2 of Annex II to Community Directive 79/489 shall not apply to a vehicle first used (in the case of a motor vehicle) or manufactured (in the case of a trailer) before the relevant date as defined in paragraph (1B) if either—
   (i) following a test in respect of which the fee numbered 26024/26250 to 26257, prescribed in Schedule 1 to the Motor Vehicles (Type Approval and Approval Marks) (Fees) Regulations 1990 is payable, a document is issued by the Secretary of State indicating that, at the date of manufacture of the vehicle, the type to which it belongs complies with the requirements specified in Annex 13 to the ECE Regulation 13.03, 13.04, 13.05 or 13.06; or
   (ii) as a result of a notifiable alteration to the vehicle, within the meaning of regulation 3 of the Plating and Testing Regulations, a fitment has been approved as complying with the requirements mentioned in sub-paragraph (i).

(3A) The requirements specified in paragraph (1A) shall apply to a road tanker subject to the exclusion of paragraph 4.3 of Annex X to Community Directive 85/647.

(4) Instead of complying with paragraph (1) of this regulation, a vehicle to which this regulation applies may comply with ECE Regulation 13.03, 13.04, 13.05 or 13.06.

(5) Instead of complying with paragraph (1A) of this regulation, a vehicle to which this regulation applies may comply with ECE Regulation 13.05 or 13.06.

(5A) Instead of complying with paragraph (1C) of this regulation, a vehicle to which this regulation applies may comply—

(a) in the case of a trailer manufactured before the 1st April 1992, with ECE Regulation 13.05 or 13.06; or

(b) in the case of any vehicle not falling within sub-paragraph (a), with ECE Regulation 13.06.

(6) In paragraph (3A) the expression "road tanker" means any vehicle or trailer which carries liquid fuel in a tank forming part of the vehicle or trailer other than that containing the fuel which is used to propel the vehicle, and also includes any tank with a capacity exceeding 3m³ carried on a vehicle.

(7) In this regulation, and in relation to the application to any vehicle of any provision of Community Directive 85/647 or 88/194, the definitions of "semi-trailer", "full trailer" and "centre-axle trailer" set out in that Directive shall apply and the meaning of "semi-trailer" in column 2 of the Table in regulation 3(2) shall not apply.

Braking systems of vehicles to which regulation 15 does not apply

C14–11   **16.**—(1) Save as provided in paragraphs (2) and (3), this regulation applies to every vehicle to which regulation 15 does not apply.

(2) Paragraph (4) of this regulation does not apply to a vehicle which complies with regulation 15 by virtue of the proviso to regulation 15(1), (1A) or (1C), or which complies with Community Directive 79/489, 85/647 or 88/194 or ECE Regulation 13.03, 13.04, 13.05 or 13.06.

(3) This regulation does not apply to the following vehicles, except in the case of a vehicle referred to in (a) insofar as the regulation concerns parking brakes (requirements 16 to 18 in Schedule 3)—

(a) a locomotive first used before 2nd January 1933, propelled by steam, and with an engine which is capable of being reversed;

(b) a trailer which—

(i) is designed for use and used for street cleansing and does not carry any load other than its necessary gear and equipment;

(ii) has a maximum total design axle weight that does not exceed 750 kg;

(iii) is an agricultural trailer manufactured before 1st July 1947 drawn by a motor tractor or an agricultural motor vehicle if the trailer—

(A) has a laden weight not exceeding 4070 kg; and

(B) is the only trailer being drawn; and

(C) is drawn at a speed not exceeding 10 mph; or

(iv) is drawn by a motor cycle in accordance with regulation 84;

(c) an agricultural trailed appliance;

(d) an agricultural trailed appliance conveyor;

(e) a broken down vehicle;

(f) before 1st October 1986—

(i) a trailer with an unladen weight not exceeding 102 kg which was manufactured before 1st October 1982; and

(ii) a gritting trailer; or

(g) on or after 1st October 1986, a gritting trailer with a maximum gross weight not exceeding 2000 kg.

(4) Save as provided in paragraph (7), a vehicle of a class specified in an item in column 2 of the Table shall comply with the requirements shown in column 3 in that item, subject to any exemptions or modifications shown in column 4 in that item, reference to numbers in column 3 being references to the requirements so numbered in Schedule 3.

TABLE   **C14–12**

(regulation 16(4))

1	2	3	4
Item	Class of vehicle	Requirements in Schedule 3	Exemptions or modifications
	Motor cars		
1	First used before 1st January 1915.	3, 6, 7, 13, 16	Requirements 13 and 16 do not apply to a motor car with less than 4 wheels.
2	First used on or after 1st January 1915 but before 1st April 1938.	1, 4, 6, 7, 9, 16	A works truck within items 1 to 11 is not subject to requirements 1, 2, 3 or 4 if it is equipped with one braking system with one means of operation.
3	First used on or after 1st April 1938 and being either a track-laying vehicle or a vehicle first used before 1st January 1968.	1, 4, 6, 7, 8, 9, 16	
4	Wheeled vehicles first used on or after 1st January 1968.	1, 4, 6, 7, 8, 9, 15, 18	
	Heavy motor cars		
5	First used before 15th August 1928.	1, 6, 16	
6	First used on or after 15th August 1928 but before 1st April 1938.	1, 4, 6, 7, 8, 16	
7	First used on or after 1st April 1938 and being either a track-laying vehicle or a vehicle first used before 1st January 1968.	1, 4, 6, 7, 8, 9, 16	
8	Wheeled vehicles first used on or after 1st January 1968.	1, 4, 6, 7, 8, 9, 15, 18	
	Motor cycles		
9	First used before 1st January 1927.	3, and, in the case of three-wheeled vehicles, 16	
10	First used on or after 1st January 1927 but before 1st January 1968.	2, 7, and, in the case of three-wheeled vehicles, 16	
11	First used on or after 1st January 1968 and not being a motor cycle to which paragraph (5) applies.	2, 7, and, in the case of three-wheeled vehicles, 18	

1	2	3	4
Item	Class of vehicle	Requirements in Schedule 3	Exemptions or modifications
	Locomotives		
12	Wheeled vehicles first used before 1st June 1955.	3, 6, 12, 16	
13	Wheeled vehicles first used on or after 1st June 1955 but before 1st January 1968.	3, 4, 6, 7, 8, 9, 18	
14	Wheeled vehicles first used on or after 1st January 1968.	3, 4, 6, 7, 8, 9, 18	
15	Track-laying vehicles.	3, 6, 16	
	Motor tractors		
16	Wheeled vehicles first used before 14th January 1931 and track-laying vehicles first used before 1st April 1938.	3, 4, 6, 7, 16	Industrial tractors within items 16 to 19 are subject to requirement 5 instead of requirement 4.
17	Wheeled vehicles first used on or after 14th January 1931 but before 1st April 1938.	3, 4, 6, 7, 9, 16	
18	Wheeled vehicles first used on or after 1st April 1938 but before 1st January 1968.	3, 4, 6, 7, 8, 9, 16	
19	Wheeled vehicles first used on or after 1st January 1968.	3, 4, 6, 7, 8, 9, 18	
20	Track-laying vehicles first used on or after 1st April 1938.	3, 4, 6, 7, 8, 16	
	Wheeled agricultural motor vehicles not driven at more than 20 mph		
21	First used before 1st January 1968.	3, 4, 6, 7, 8, 16	
22	First used on or after 1st January 1968 but before 9th February 1980.	3, 4, 6, 7, 8, 18	
23	First used on or after 9th February, 1980.	3, 5, 6, 7, 8, 18	
	Invalid carriages		
24	Whenever first used.	3, 13	
	Trailers		
25	Manufactured before 1st April 1938.	3, 10, 14, 17	
26	Manufactured on or after 1st April, 1938 and being either a track-laying vehicle, an agricultural trailer or a vehicle manufactured before 1st January 1968.	3, 8, 10, 14, 17	Agricultural trailers are not subject to requirement 8.

1	2	3	4
Item	Class of vehicle	Requirements in Schedule 3	Exemptions or modifications
27	Wheeled vehicles manufactured on or after 1st January 1968, not being an agricultural trailer.	3, 4, 8, 11, 15, 18	Trailers equipped with brakes which come into operation on the overrun of the vehicle are not subject to requirement 15.

Provided that wheeled agricultural motor vehicles not driven at more than 20 mph are excluded from all items other than items 21 to 23.

(5) Subject to paragraphs (5B) and (6), braking system of a motor cycle to which this regulation applies and which is—

(a) of a class specified in an item in column 2 of the Table below; and

(b) first used on or after 1st April 1987 and before 22nd May 1995;

shall comply with ECE Regulation 13.05, 78 or 78.01 in relation to the category of vehicles specified in that item in column 3.

(5A) Subject to paragraph (6), the braking system of a motor cycle to which this regulation applies and which is—

(a) of a class specified in an item in column 2 of the Table below; and

(b) first used on or after 22nd May 1995;

shall comply with ECE Regulation 78.01 in relation to the category of vehicles specified in that item in column 3.

TABLE   **C14–13**

(regulation 16(5) and (5A))

1	2	3
Item	Class of Vehicle	Vehicle Category in ECE Regulations
1	Vehicles (without a sidecar attached) with two wheels, an engine capacity not exceeding 50 cc and a maximum design speed not exceeding 50 km/h.	L1
2	Vehicles with three wheels (including two-wheeled vehicles with a sidecar attached) and with an engine capacity not exceeding 50 cc and a maximum design speed not exceeding 50 km/h.	L2
3	Vehicles with two wheels (without a sidecar attached) and with— (a) an engine capacity exceeding 50 cc, or (b) a maximum design speed exceeding 50 km/h.	L3
4	Vehicles with two wheels, a sidecar attached and— (a) an engine capacity exceeding 50 cc, or (b) a maximum design speed exceeding 50 km/h.	L4

(5B) In relation to a motor cycle with two wheels manufactured by Piaggio Veicoli Europei Societa per Azione and known as the Cosa 125, the Cosa 125E, the Cosa L125, the Cosa LX125, the Cosa 200, the Cosa 200E, the Cosa L200 or the Cosa LX200, paragraph (5) shall have effect as if ECE Regulation 13.05 were modified by—

(a) the omission of paragraph 4.4 (approval marks), and

(b) in paragraph 5.3.1.1, (independent braking devices and controls), the omission of the word "independent" in the first place where it appears,

but this paragraph shall not apply to a motor cycle first used on or after 1st July 1991.

(6) Paragraph (5) does not apply to a works truck or to a vehicle constructed or assembled by a person not ordinarily engaged in the business of manufacturing vehicles of that description.

(7) Instead of complying with the provisions of paragraph (4) of this Regulation an agricultural motor vehicle may comply with Community Directive 76/432.

Vacuum or pressure brakes warning devices

C14–14   17.—(1) Save as provided in paragraph (2), every motor vehicle which is equipped with a braking system which embodies a vacuum or pressure reservoir or reservoirs shall be equipped with a device so placed as to be readily visible to the driver of the vehicle and which is capable of indicating any impending failure of, or deficiency in, the vacuum or pressure system.

(2) The requirement specified in paragraph (1) does not apply in respect of—

(a) a vehicle to which paragraph (1), (1A) or (1C) of regulation 15 applies, or which complies with the requirements of that regulation, of Community Directives 79/489, 85/647 or 88/194 or of ECE Regulation 13.03, 13.04, 13.05 or 13.06;

(b) an agricultural motor vehicle which complies with Community Directive 76/432;

(c) a vehicle with an unladen weight not exceeding 3050 kg propelled by an internal combustion engine, if the vacuum in the reservoir or reservoirs is derived directly from the induction system of the engine, and if, in the event of a failure of, or deficiency in, the vacuum system, the brakes of that braking system are sufficient under the most adverse conditions to bring the vehicle to rest within a reasonable distance; or

(d) a vehicle first used before 1st October 1937.

Maintenance and efficiency of brakes

C14–15   18.—(1) Every part of every braking system and of the means of operation thereof fitted to a vehicle shall be maintained in good and efficient working order and be properly adjusted.

(1A) Without prejudice to paragraph (3), where a vehicle is fitted with an anti-lock braking system ("the ABS"), then while the condition specified in paragraph (1B) is fulfilled, any fault in the ABS shall be disregarded for the purposes of paragraph (1).

(1B) The condition is fulfilled while the vehicle is completing a journey at the beginning of which the ABS was operating correctly or is being driven to a place where the ABS is to undergo repairs.

(2) Paragraph (3) applies to every wheeled motor vehicle except—

(a) an agricultural motor vehicle which is not driven at more than 20 mph;

(b) a works truck; and

(c) a pedestrian-controlled vehicle.

(3) Every vehicle to which this paragraph applies and which is a class specified in an item in column 2 of Table I shall, subject to any exemption shown for that item in column 4, be so maintained that—

(a) its service braking system has a total braking efficiency not less than that shown in column 3(a) for that item; and

(b) if the vehicle is a heavy motor car, a motor car first used on or after 1st January 1915 or a motor-cycle first used on or after 1st January 1927, its secondary braking system has a total braking efficiency not less than that shown in column 3(b) for those items.

Provided that a reference in Table I to a trailer is a reference to a trailer required by regulations 15 or 16 to be equipped with brakes.

TABLE I   **C14–16**

(regulation 18(3))

1	2	3	4
Item	Class of vehicle	Efficiencies (%) (a) (b)	Exemptions
1	A vehicle to which regulation 15 applies or which complies in all respects other than its braking efficiency with the requirements of that regulation or with Community Directives 79/489, 85/647 or 88/194 or with ECE Regulation 13.03, 13.04, 13.05 or 13.06— (a) when not drawing a trailer; (b) when drawing a trailer	 50 25 45 25	a motor cycle.
2	A vehicle, not included in item 1 and not being a motor cycle, which is first used on or after 1st January 1968— (a) when not drawing a trailer; (b) when drawing a trailer manufactured on or after 1st January 1968; (c) when drawing a trailer manufactured before 1st January 1968	 50 25 50 25 40 15	
3	Goods vehicles first used on or after 15th August 1928 but before 1st January 1968 having an unladen weight exceeding 1525 kg being—		

621

1	2	3	4
Item	Class of vehicle	Efficiencies (%) (a) (b)	Exemptions
	(a) rigid vehicles with 2 axles not con-structed to form part of an articu-lated vehicle—		
	(i) when not drawing a trailer	45 20	
	(ii) when drawing a trailer	40 15	
	(b) other vehicles, including vehicles constructed to form part of an articulated vehicle, whether or not drawing a trailer	40 15	
4	Vehicles not included in items 1 to 3—		(a) a bus;
	(a) having at least one means of oper-ation applying to at least 4 wheels;	50 25	(b) an articulated vehicle;
	(b) having 3 wheels and at least one means of operation applying to all 3 wheels and not being a motor cycle with sidecar attached—		(c) a vehicle con-structed or adapted to form part of an articulated vehicle;
	(i) when not drawing a trailer	40 25	(d) a heavy motor car which is a goods vehicle first used before 15th August 1928.
	(ii) in the case of a motor cycle when drawing a trailer	40 25	
	(c) other		
	(i) when not drawing a trailer	30 25	
	(ii) in the case of a motor cycle when drawing a trailer.	30 25	

(4) A goods vehicle shall not be deemed to comply with the requirements of paragraph (3) unless it is capable of complying with those requirements both at the laden weight at which it is operating at any time and when its laden weight is equal to—

    (a) if a plating certificate has been issued and is in force for the vehicle, the design gross weight shown in column (3) of that certificate or, if no such weight is so shown, the gross weight shown in column (2) of that certificate; and

    (b) in any other case, the design gross weight of the vehicle.

Provided that in the case of a goods vehicle drawing a trailer, references in this paragraph to laden weight refer to the combined laden weight of the drawing vehicle and the trailer and references to gross weight and design gross weight are to be taken as references to train weight and design train weight respectively.

(5) The brakes of every agricultural motor vehicle which is first used on or after 1st June 1986 and is not driven at more than 20 mph, and of every agricul-tural trailer manufactured on or after 1st December 1985 shall be capable of achieving a braking efficiency of not less than 25 per cent when the weight of the vehicle is equal to the total maximum axle weights which the vehicle is designed to have.

(6) Every vehicle or combination of vehicles specified in an item in column 2 of Table II shall be so maintained that its brakes are capable, without the assistance of stored energy, of holding it stationary on a gradient of at least the percentage specified in column 3 in that item.

TABLE II

C14–17

(regulation 18(6))

1	2	3
Item	Class of vehicle or combination	Percentage gradient
1	A vehicle specified in item 1 of Table I— (a) when not drawing a trailer (b) when drawing a trailer	16 12
2	A vehicle to which requirement 18 in Schedule 3 applies by virtue of regulation 16.	16
3	A vehicle, not included in item 1, drawing a trailer manufactured on or after 1st January 1968 and required, by regulation 15 or 16, to be fitted with brakes.	16

(7) For the purpose of this regulation the date of manufacture of a trailer which is a composite trailer shall be deemed to be the same as the date of manufacture of the semi-trailer which forms part of the composite trailer.

(8) A vehicle which is subject to, and which complies with the requirements in, item 1 in Tables I and II shall not be treated as failing, by reason of its braking efficiency, to comply with regulation 15 or with Community Directives 79/489, 85/647 or 88/194 or ECE Regulation 13.03, 13.04, 13.05 or 13.06.

Application of brakes of trailers

19. Where a trailer is drawn by a motor vehicle the driver (or in the case of a locomotive one of the persons employed in driving or tending the locomotive) shall be in a position readily to operate any brakes required by these Regulations to be fitted to the trailer as well as the brakes of the motor vehicle unless a person other than the driver (or in the case of a locomotive a person other than one of the persons employed in driving or tending the locomotive) is in a position and competent efficiently to apply the brakes of the trailer.   **C14–18**

Provided that this regulation shall not apply to a trailer which—
  (a) in compliance with these Regulations, is fitted with brakes which automatically come into operation on the overrun of the trailer; or
  (b) […] is a broken down vehicle being drawn, whether or not in consequence of a breakdown, in such a manner that it cannot be steered by its own steering gear.

General requirement as to wheels and tracks

20. Every motor cycle and invalid carriage shall be a wheeled vehicle, and   **C14–19**

every other motor vehicle and every trailer shall be either a wheeled vehicle or a track-laying vehicle.

Diameter of wheels

C14–20 **21.** All wheels of a wheeled vehicle which are fitted with tyres other than pneumatic tyres shall have a rim diameter of not less than 670 mm.

Provided that this regulation does not apply to—

(a) a motor vehicle first used on or before 2nd January 1933;

(b) a trailer manufactured before 1st January 1933;

(c) a wheel fitted to a motor car first used on or before 1st July 1936, if the diameter of the wheel inclusive of the tyre is not less than 670 mm;

(d) a works truck or works trailer;

(e) a refuse vehicle;

(f) a pedestrian-controlled vehicle;

(g) a mobile crane;

(h) an agricultural trailed appliance;

(i) a broken down vehicle which is being drawn by a motor vehicle in consequence of the breakdown; or

(j) an electrically propelled goods vehicle the unladen weight of which does not exceed 1270 kg.

Springs and resilient material

C14–21 **22.**—(1) Save as provided in paragraphs (3) and (4), every motor vehicle and every trailer shall be equipped with suitable and sufficient springs between each wheel and the frame of the vehicle.

(2) Save as provided in paragraphs (3) and (4), in the case of a track-laying vehicle—

(a) resilient material shall be interposed between the rims of the weight-carrying rollers and the road surface so that the weight of the vehicle, other than that borne by any wheel, is supported by the resilient material; and

(b) where the vehicle is a heavy motor car, motor car, or trailer it shall have suitable springs between the frame of the vehicle and the weight-carrying rollers.

(3) This regulation does not apply to—

(a) a wheeled vehicle with an unladen weight not exceeding 4070 kg and which is—

(i) a motor tractor any unsprung wheel of which is fitted with a pneumatic tyre;

(ii) a motor tractor used in connection with railway shunting and which is used on a road only when passing from one railway track to another in connection with such use;

(iii) a vehicle specially designed, and mainly used, for work on rough ground or unmade roads and every wheel of which is fitted with a pneumatic tyre and which is not driven at more than 20 mph;

(iv) a vehicle constructed or adapted for, and being used for, road sweeping and every wheel of which is fitted with either a pneumatic tyre or a resilient tyre and which is not driven at more than 20 mph;

(b) an agricultural motor vehicle which is not driven at more than 20 mph;

(c) an agricultural trailer, or an agricultural trailed appliance;
(d) a trailer used solely for the haulage of felled trees;
(e) a motor cycle;
(f) a mobile crane;
(g) a pedestrian-controlled vehicle all the wheels of which are equipped with pneumatic tyres;
(h) a road roller;
(i) a broken down vehicle; or
(j) a vehicle first used on or before 1st January 1932.
(4) Paragraphs (1) and (2)(b) do not apply to a works truck or a works trailer.

Wheel loads

23.—(1) Subject to paragraph (2) this regulation applies to—   **C14–22**
(a) a semi-trailer with more than 2 wheels;
(b) a track-laying vehicle with more than 2 wheels; and
(c) any other vehicle with more than 4 wheels.
(2) This regulation does not apply to a road roller.
(3) Save as provided in paragraphs (4) and (5), every vehicle to which this regulation applies shall be fitted with a compensating arrangement which will ensure that under the most adverse conditions every wheel will remain in contact with the road and will not be subject to abnormal variations of load.
(4) Paragraph (3) does not apply in respect of a steerable wheel on which the load does not exceed—
(a) if it is a wheeled vehicle, 3560 kg; and
(b) if it is a track-laying vehicle, 2540 kg.
(5) In the application of paragraph (3) to an agricultural motor vehicle, wheels which are in line transversely on one side of the longitudinal axis of the vehicle shall be regarded as one wheel.

Tyres

24.—(1) Save as provided in paragraph (2), every wheel of a vehicle of a   **C14–23**
class specified in an item in column 2 of the Table shall be fitted with a tyre of a type specified in that item in column 3 which complies with any conditions specified in that item in column 4.
(2) The requirements referred to in paragraph (1) do not apply to a road roller and are subject, in the case of any item in the Table, to the exemptions specified in that item in column 5.

TABLE

(regulation 24(1))

1	2	3	4	5
Item	Class of vehicle	Type of Tyre	Conditions	Exemptions
1	Locomotives not falling in item 6	Pneumatic or resilient		
2	Motor tractors not falling in item 6	Pneumatic or resilient	No re-cut pneumatic tyre shall be fitted to any wheel of a vehicle with an unladen weight of less than 2540 kg unless the diameter of the rim of the wheel is at least 405 mm	
3	Heavy motor cars not falling in item 6	Pneumatic		The following, if every wheel not fitted with a pneumatic tyre is fitted with a resilient tyre— (a) a vehicle mainly used for work on rough ground; (b) a tower wagon; (c) a vehicle fitted with a turn table fire escape; (d) a refuse vehicle; (e) a works truck; (f) a vehicle first used before 3rd January 1933.
4	Motor cars not falling in item 6	Pneumatic	No re-cut tyre shall be fitted to any wheel of a vehicle unless it is— (a) an electrically propelled goods vehicle or, (b) a goods vehicle with an unladen weight	The following, if every wheel not fitted with a pneumatic tyre is fitted with a resilient tyre— (a) a vehicle mainly used for work on rough ground; (b) a refuse vehicle;

1	2	3	4	5
Item	Class of vehicle	Type of Tyre	Conditions	Exemptions
			of at least 2540 kg and the diameter of the rim of the wheel is at least 405 mm.	(c) a works truck; (d) a vehicle with an unladen weight not exceeding— (i) 1270 kg if electrically propelled; (ii) 1020 kg in any other case; (e) a tower wagon; (f) a vehicle fitted with a turntable fire escape; (g) a vehicle first used before 3rd January 1933.
5	Motor cycles	Pneumatic	No re-cut tyre shall be fitted	The following, if every wheel not fitted with a pneumatic tyre is fitted with a resilient tyre— (a) a works truck; (b) a pedestrian-controlled vehicle
6	Agricultural motor vehicles which are not driven at more than 20 mph	Pneumatic or resilient	The same as for item 2	The requirement in column 3 does not apply to a vehicle of which— (a) every steering wheel is fitted with a smooth-soled tyre which is not less than 60 mm wide where it touches the road; and (b) in the case of a wheeled vehicle, every driving wheel is fitted with a smooth-soled tyre which— (i) is not less than 150 mm wide if the unladen weight of the vehicle exceeds 3050 kg, or 76 mm wide in

1	2	3	4	5
Item	Class of vehicle	Type of Tyre	Conditions	Exemptions
				any other case, and either (ii) is shod with diagonal cross-bars not less than 76 mm wide or more than 20 mm thick extending the full breadth of the tyre and so arranged that the space between adjacent bars is not more than 76 mm; or (iii) is shod with diagonal cross-bars of resilient material not less than 60 mm wide extending the full breadth of the tyre and so arranged that the space between adjacent bars is not more than 76 mm.
7	Trailers	Pneumatic	Except in the case of a trailer mentioned in paragraph (d) of column 5, no re-cut tyre shall be fitted to any wheel of a trailer drawn by a heavy motor car or a motor car if the trailer— (a) has an unladen weight not exceeding— (i) if it is a living van, 2040 kg; or (ii) in any other case, 1020 kg; or, (b) is not constructed or adapted to carry any load, other than plant or other special	(a) an agricultural trailer manufactured before 1st December 1985; (b) an agricultural trailed appliance; (c) a trailer used to carry water for a road roller being used in connection with road works; (d) the following if every wheel which is not fitted with a pneumatic tyre is fitted with a resilient tyre— (i) a works trailer; (ii) a refuse vehicle;

1	2	3	4	5
Item	Class of vehicle	Type of Tyre	Conditions	Exemptions
			appliance which is a permanent or essentially permanent fixture and has a gross weight not exceeding 2290 kg	(iii) a trailer drawn by a heavy motor car every wheel of which is not required to be fitted with a pneumatic tyre; (iv) a broken down vehicle; or (v) a trailer drawn by a vehicle which is not a heavy motor car or a motor car.

(3) Save as provided in paragraph (4) a wheel of a vehicle may not be fitted with a temporary use spare tyre unless either—
    (a) the vehicle is a passenger vehicle (not being a bus) first used before 1st April 1987; or
    (b) the vehicle complies at the time of its first use with ECE Regulation 64 or Community Diective 92/23.

(4) Paragraph (3) does not apply to a vehicle constructed or assembled by a person not ordinarily engaged in the trade or business of manufacturing vehicles of that description.

Tyre loads and speed ratings

25.—(1) Save as provided in paragraphs (3), (4) and (7A) any tyre fitted to the axle of a vehicle—   **C14–25**
    (a) which is a class of vehicle specified in an item in column 2 of Table I; and
    (b) in relation to which the date of first use is as specified in that item in column 3 of that Table;
shall comply with the requirements specified in that item in column 4 of that Table.

TABLE I

(regulation 25(1))

1	2	3	4
Item	Class of vehicle	Date of first use	Requirements
1	Vehicles which are of one or more of the following descriptions, namely— (a) goods vehicles, (b) trailers,	Before 1st April 1991	The requirements of paragraphs (5) and (6)

1	2	3	4
Item	Class of vehicle	Date of first use	Requirements
	(c) buses, (d) vehicles of a class mentioned in column 2 in Table III		
2	Vehicles which are of one or more of the following descriptions— (a) goods vehicles (b) trailers (c) buses, (d) vehicles of a class mentioned in column 2 in Table III, and do not fall within item 3 below	On or after 1st April 1991	The require-ments of para-graphs (5), (6) and (7)
3	Vehicles of a class mentioned in para-graph (2)	On or after 1st April 1991	The require-ments of para-graph (5).

(2) The classes of vehicle referred to in item 3 in column 2 of Table I are—

(a) engineering plant;

(b) track-laying vehicles;

(c) vehicles equipped with tyres of speed category Q;

(d) works trucks; and

(e) motor vehicles with a maximum speed not exceeding 30 mph, not being vehicles of a class specified in—

(i) items 2 and 3 of Table II; or

(ii) paragraph (7A) or sub-paragraphs (a) to (d) of this paragraph;

or trailers while being drawn by such vehicles.

(3) Paragraph (1) shall not apply to any tyre fitted to the axle of a vehicle if the vehicle is—

(a) broken down or proceeding to a place where it is to be broken up; and

(b) being drawn by a motor vehicle at a speed not exceeding 20 mph.

(4) Where in relation to any vehicle first used on or after April 1, 1991 a tyre supplied by a manufacturer for the purposes of tests or trials of that tyre is fitted to an axle of that vehicle, paragraph (7) shall not apply to that tyre while it is being used for those purposes.

(5) The requirements of this paragraph are that the tyre, as respects strength, shall be designed and manufactured adequately to support the maximum permitted axle weight for the axle.

(6) The requirements of this paragraph are that the tyre shall be designed and manufactured adequately to support the maximum permitted axle weight for the axle when the vehicle is driven at the speed shown in column 3 in Table II in the item in which the vehicle is described in column 2 (the lowest relevant speed being applicable to a vehicle which is described in more than one item).

TABLE II

(regulation 25(6))

1	2	3	4	
Item	Class of vehicle	Speed (mph)	Variation to the load-capacity index expressed as a percentage.	
			Tyres marked in accordance with ECE Regulation 30, 30.01 or 30.02 and relevant car tyres	Tyres marked in accordance with ECE Regulation 54 and relevant commercial vehicle tyres
1	A vehicle of a class for which maximum speeds are prescribed by Schedule 6 to the 1984 Act other than an agricultural motor vehicle	The highest speed so prescribed	Single wheels: none Dual wheels: 95.5%	None
2	An electrically propelled vehicle used as a multi-stop local collection and delivery vehicle and having a maximum speed of not more than 25 mph	The maximum speed of the vehicle	None	150%
3	An electrically propelled vehicle used as a multi-stop collection and delivery vehicle and having a maximum speed of more than 25 mph and not more than 40 mph	The maximum speed of the vehicle	None	130%
4	An electrically propelled vehicle used only within a radius of 25 miles from the permanent base at which it is normally kept and having a maximum speed of more than 40 mph and not more than 50 mph	The maximum speed of the vehicle		
5	A local service bus	50	None	110%
6	A restricted speed vehicle	50	None	The relevant % variation specified in Annex 8 to ECE Regulation 54 or Appendix 8

1	2	3	4	
Item	Class of vehicle	Speed (mph)	Variation to the load-capacity index expressed as a percentage.	
			Tyres marked in accordance with ECE Regulation 30, 30.01 or 30.02	to Annex II to Community Directive 92/23 Tyres marked in accordance with ECE Regulation 54
7	A low platform trailer, an agricultural motor vehicle, an agricultural trailer, an agricultural trailed appliance or an agricultural trailed appliance conveyor	40	None	The relevant % variation specified in Annex 8 to ECE Regulation 54 or Appendix 8 to Annex II to Community Directive 92/23
8	A municipal vehicle	40	None	115%
9	A multi-stop local collection and delivery vehicle if not falling within the class of vehicle described in items 2 or 3 above	40	None	115%
10	A light trailer or any trailer equipped with tyres of speed category F or G	60	Single wheels: 110% Dual wheels: 105%	The relevant variation specified in Annex 8 to ECE Regulation 54 or Appendix 8 to Annex II to Community Directive 92/23
11	A trailer not falling in items 6–10	60	Single wheels: none Dual wheels: 95.5%	None
12	A motor vehicle not falling in items 1–11	70	Single wheels: none Dual wheels: 95.5%	None

(7) The requirement of this paragraph is that the tyre when first fitted to the vehicle was marked with a designated approval mark or complied with the requirements of ECE Regulation 30, 30.01, 30.02 or 54, but this requirement shall not apply to a retreaded tyre.

(7A) The requirements of paragraphs (6) and (7) shall not apply to a vehicle of a class specified in an item in column 2 of Table III while it is being driven or drawn at a speed not exceeding that specified in that item in column 3 of that Table.

TABLE III

(regulation 25(7A))

C14–27

1	2	3
Item	Class of vehicle	Speed (mph)
1	Agricultural motor vehicles	20
2	Agricultural trailers	20
3	Agricultural trailed appliances	20
4	Agricultural trailed appliance conveyors	20
5	Works trailers	18

(8) A vehicle of a class described in column 2 in Table II first used on or after 1st April 1991 shall not be used on a road—

    (a) in the case where there is no entry in column 4 specifying a variation to the load-capacity index expressed as a percentage, if the load applied to any tyre fitted to the axle of the vehicle exceeds that indicated by the load-capacity index; or

    (b) in the case where there is such an entry in column 4, if the load applied to any tyre fitted to the axle of the vehicle exceeds the variation to the load-capacity index expressed as a percentage.

(9) In this regulation—

    "designated approval mark" means the marking designated as an approval mark by regulation 5 of the Approval Marks Regulations and shown at item 33 in schedule 4 to those Regulations (that item being a marking relating to Community Directive 92/23);

    "dual wheels" means two or more wheels which are to be regarded as one wheel by virtue of paragraph 7 of regulation 3 in the circumstances specified in that paragraph;

    "load-capacity index" has the same meaning as in paragraph 2.28 of Annex II to Community Directive 92/23 or paragraph 2.29 of ECE Regulation 30.02 or paragraph 2.27 of ECE Regulation 54;

    "local bus service" means a bus being used in the provision of a local service as defined in section 2 of the Transport Act 1985;

    "municipal vehicle" means a motor vehicle or trailer limited at all times to use by a local authority, or a person acting in pursuance of a contract with a local authority, for road cleansing, road watering or the collection and disposal of refuse, night soil or the contents of cesspools, or the purposes of the enactments relating to weights and measures or the sale of food and drugs;

633

"multi-stop local collection and delivery vehicle" means a motor vehicle or trailer used for multi-stop collection and delivery services to be used only within a radius of 25 miles from the permanent base at which it is normally kept;

"single wheels" means wheels which are not dual wheels; and

"speed category" has the same meaning as in paragraph 2.29 of Annex II to Community Directive 92/23 or paragraph 2.28 of ECE Regulation 54.

(9A) For the purposes of this regulation, a tyre is a "relevant care tyre" if—

(a) it has been marked with a designated approval mark; and

(b) the first two digits of the approval number comprised in the mark are "02".

(9B) For the purposes of this regulation, a tyre is a "relevant commercial vehicle tyre" if—

(a) it has been marked with a designated approval mark, and

(b) the first two digits of the approval number comprised in the mark are "00".

(10) In this regulation any reference to the first use shall, in relation to a trailer, be construed as a reference to the date which is 6 months after the date of manufacture of the trailer.

Mixing of tyres

C14–28   26.—(1) Save as provided in paragraph (5) pneumatic tyres of different types of structure shall not be fitted to the same axle of a wheeled vehicle.

(2) Save as provided in paragraphs (3) or (5), a wheeled motor vehicle having only two axles each of which is equipped with one or two single wheels shall not be fitted with—

(a) a diagonal-ply tyre or a bias-belted tyre on its rear axle if a radial-ply tyre is fitted on its front axle; or

(b) a diagonal-ply tyre on its rear axle if a bias-belted tyre is fitted on the front axle.

(3) Paragraph (2) does not apply to a vehicle to an axle of which there are fitted wide tyres not specially constructed for use on engineering plant or to a vehicle which has a maximum speed not exceeding 30 mph.

(4) Save as provided in paragraph (5) pneumatic tyres fitted to—

(a) the steerable axles of a wheeled vehicle; or

(b) the driven axles of a wheeled vehicle, not being steerable axles, shall all be of the same type of structure.

(5) Paragraphs (1), (2), and (4) do not prohibit the fitting of a temporary use spare tyre to a wheel of a passenger vehicle (not being a bus) unless it is driven at a speed exceeding 50 mph.

(6) In this regulation—

"axles" includes—

(i) two or more stub axles which are fitted on opposite sides of the longitudinal axis of the vehicle so as to form—

(a) a pair in the case of two stub axles; and

(b) pairs in the case of more than two stub axles; and

(ii) a single stub axle which is not one of a pair;

"a bias-belted tyre" means a pneumatic tyre, the structure of which is such that the ply cords extend to the bead so as to be laid at alternate angles of substantially less than 90 degrees to the peripheral line of the tread, and are constrained by a circumferential belt comprising two or more layers of substantially inextensible cord material laid at alternate angles smaller than those of the ply cord structure;

"a diagonal-ply tyre" means a pneumatic tyre, the structure of which is such that the ply cords extend to the bead so as to be laid at alternate angles of substantially less than 90 degrees to the peripheral line of the tread, but not being a bias-belted tyre;

"a driven axle" means an axle through which power is transmitted from the engine of a vehicle to the wheels on that axle;

"a radial-ply tyre" means a pneumatic tyre, the structure of which is such that the ply cords extend to the bead so as to be laid at an angle of substantially 90 degrees to the peripheral line of the tread, the ply cord structure being stabilised by a substantially inextensible circumferential belt;

"stub axle" means an axle on which only one wheel is mounted; and

"type of structure", in relation to a tyre, means a type of structure of a tyre of a kind defined in the foregoing provisions of this paragraph.

Condition and maintenance of tyres

27.—(1) Save as provided in paragraphs (2), (3) and (4), a wheeled motor vehicle or trailer a wheel of which is fitted with a pneumatic tyre shall not be used on a road, if—   **C14–29**

(a) the tyre is unsuitable having regard to the use to which the motor vehicle or trailer is being put or to the types of tyres fitted to its other wheels;

(b) the tyre is not so inflated as to make it fit for the use to which the motor vehicle or trailer is being put;

(c) the tyre has a cut in excess of 25 mm or 10% of the section width of the tyre, whichever is the greater, measured in any direction on the outside of the tyre and deep enough to reach the ply or cord;

(d) the tyre has any lump, bulge or tear caused by separation or partial failure of its structure;

(e) the tyre has any of the ply or cord exposed;

(f) the base of any groove which showed in the original tread pattern of the tyre is not clearly visible;

(g) either—

(i) the grooves of the tread pattern of the tyre do not have a depth of at least 1 mm throughout a continuous band measuring at least three-quarters of the breadth of the tread and round the entire outer circumference of the tyre; or

(ii) if the grooves of the original tread pattern of the tyre did not extend beyond three-quarters of the breadth of the tread, any groove which showed in the original tread pattern does not have a depth of at least 1 mm; or

(h) the tyre is not maintained in such condition as to be fit for the use to which the vehicle or trailer is being put or has a defect which might in any way cause damage to the surface of the road or damage to persons on or in the vehicle or to other persons using the road.

(2) Paragraph (1) does not prohibit the use on a road of a motor vehicle or trailer by reason only of the fact that a wheel of the vehicle or trailer is fitted with a tyre which is deflated or not fully inflated and which has any of the defects described in sub-paragraph (c), (d) or (e) of paragraph (1), if the tyre

and the wheel to which it is fitted are so constructed as to make the tyre in that condition fit for the use to which the motor vehicle or trailer is being put and the outer sides of the wall of the tyre are so marked as to enable the tyre to be identified as having been constructed to comply with the requirements of this paragraph.

(3) Paragraph (1)(a) does not prohibit the use on a road of a passenger vehicle (not being a bus) by reason only of the fact that a wheel of the vehicle is fitted with a temporary use spare tyre, unless the vehicle is driven at a speed exceeding 50 mph.

(4) (a) Nothing in paragraph (1)(a) to (g) applies to—
    (i) an agricultural motor vehicle that is not driven at more than 20 mph;
    (ii) an agricultural trailer;
    (iii) an agricultural trailed appliance; or
    (iv) a broken down vehicle or a vehicle proceeding to a place where it is to be broken up, being drawn, in either case, by a motor vehicle at a speed not exceeding 20 mph.
  (b) Nothing in paragraph (1)(f) and (g) applies to—
    (i) a three-wheeled motor cycle the unladen weight of which does not exceed 102 kg and which has a maximum speed of 12 mph; or
    (ii) a pedestrian-controlled works truck.
  (c) Nothing in paragraph (1)(g) applies to a motorcycle with an engine capacity which does not exceed 50 cc.
  (d) With effect from 1st January 1992, paragraph 1(f) and (g) shall not apply to the vehicles specified in sub-paragraph (e) of this paragraph but such vehicles shall comply with the requirements specified in sub-paragraph (f) of this paragraph.
  (e) The vehicles mentioned in sub-paragraph (d) are—
    (i) passenger vehicles other than motor cycles constructed or adapted to carry no more than 8 seated passengers in addition to the driver;
    (ii) goods vehicles with a maximum gross weight which does not exceed 3500 kg; and
    (iii) light trailers not falling within sub-paragraph (ii);
    first used on or after 3rd January 1933.
  (f) The requirements referred to in sub-paragraph (d) are that the grooves of the tread pattern of every tyre fitted to the wheels of a vehicle mentioned in sub-paragraph (e) shall be of a depth of at least 1·6 mm throughout a continuous band comprising the central three-quarters of the breadth of tread and round the entire outer circumference of the tyre.

(5) A recut pneumatic tyre shall not be fitted to any wheel of a motor vehicle or trailer if—
  (a) its ply or cord has been cut or exposed by the recutting process; or
  (b) it has been wholly or partially recut in a pattern other than the manufacturer's recut tread pattern.

(6) (a) In this regulation—
    "breadth of tread" means the breadth of that part of the tyre which can contact the road under normal conditions of use measured at 90 degrees to the peripheral line of the tread;
    "original tread pattern" means in the case of—
    a re-treaded tyre, the tread pattern of the tyre immediately after the tyre was re-treaded;
    a wholly recut tyre, the manufacturer's recut tread pattern;
    a partially recut tyre, on that part of the tyre which has been recut, the

manufacturer's recut tread pattern, and on the other part, the tread
pattern of the tyre when new, and

any other tyre, the tread pattern of the tyre when the tyre was new.

"tie-bar" means any part of a tyre moulded in the tread pattern of the
tyre for the purpose of bracing two or more features of such tread
pattern;

"tread pattern" means the combination of plain surfaces and grooves
extending across the breadth of the tread and round the entire outer
circumference of the tyre but excludes any—

(i) tie bars or tread wear indicators;

(ii) features which are designed to wear substantially before the rest
of the pattern under normal conditions of use; and

(iii) other minor features; and

"tread wear indicator" means any bar, not being a tie-bar, projecting
from the base of a groove of the tread pattern of a tyre and moulded
between two or more features of the tread pattern of a tyre for the
purpose of indicating the extent of the wear of such tread pattern.

(b) The references in this regulation to grooves are references—

if a tyre has been recut, to the grooves of the manufacturer's recut
tread pattern; and if a tyre has not been recut, to the grooves which
showed when the trye was new.

(c) A reference in this regulation to first use shall, in relation to a trailer, be
construed as a reference to the date which is 6 months after the date of
manufacture of the trailer.

Tracks

28.—(1) Every part of every track of a track-laying vehicle which comes into   **C14–30**
contact with the road shall be flat and have a width of not less than 12.5 mm.

(2) The area of the track which is in contact with the road shall not at any
time be less than 225 cm² in respect of every 1000 kg of the total weight which
is transferred to the road by the tracks.

(3) The tracks of a vehicle shall not have any defect which might damage the
road or cause danger to any person on or in the vehicle or using the road, and
shall be properly adjusted and maintained in good and efficient working
order.

Silencers—general

54.—(1) Every vehicle propelled by an internal combustion engine shall be   **C14–31**
fitted with an exhaust system including a silencer and the exhaust gases from
the engine shall not escape into the atmosphere without first passing through
the silencer.

(2) Every exhaust system and silencer shall be maintained in good and
efficient working order and shall not after the date of manufacture be altered
so as to increase the noise made by the escape of exhaust gases.

(3) Instead of complying with paragraph (1) a vehicle may comply with
Community Directive 77/212, 81/334, 84/372 or 84/424 or, in the case of a
motor cycle other than a moped, 78/1015.

(4) In this regulation "moped" has the meaning given to it in paragraph (5)
of Schedule 9.

Noise limits—general

C14–32   **55.**—(1) Save as provided in paragraph (2) and regulation 59, this regulation applies to every wheeled motor vehicle having at least three wheels and first used on or after 1st October 1983 which is—

(a) a vehicle, not falling within sub-paragraph (b) or (c), with or without bodywork;

(b) a vehicle not falling within sub-paragraph (c) which is—
   (i) engineering plant;
   (ii) a locomotive other than an agricultural motor vehicle;
   (iii) a motor tractor other than an industrial tractor or an agricultural motor vehicle;
   (iv) a public works vehicle;
   (v) a works truck; or
   (vi) a refuse vehicle; or

(c) a vehicle which—
   (i) has a compression ignition engine;
   (ii) is so constructed or adapted that the driving power of the engine is, or by appropriate use of the controls can be, transmitted to all wheels of the vehicle; and
   (iii) falls within category I.1.1., I.1.2, or I.1.3 specified in Article 1 of Community Directive 77/212.

(2) This regulation does not apply to—

(a) a motorcycle with a sidecar attached;

(b) an agricultural motor vehicle which is first used before 1st June 1986 or which is not driven at more than 20 mph;

(c) an industrial tractor;

(d) a road roller;

(e) a vehicle specially constructed, and not merely adapted, for the purposes of fighting fires or salvage from fires at or in the vicinity of airports, and having an engine power exceeding 220 kW;

(f) a vehicle which runs on rails; or

(g) a vehicle manufactured by Leyland Vehicles Ltd. and known as the Atlantean Bus, if first used before 1st October 1984.

(3) Save as provided in paragraphs (4) and (5), every vehicle to which this regulation applies shall be so constructed that it complies with the requirements set out in item 1, 2, 3 or 4 of the Table; a vehicle complies with those requirements if—

(a) its sound level does not exceed the relevant limit specified in column 2(a), (b) or (c), as the case may be, in the relevant item when measured under the conditions specified in column 3 in that item and by the method specified in column 4 in that item using the apparatus prescribed in paragraph (6); and

(b) in the case of a vehicle referred to in paragraph 1(a) (other than one having less than four wheels or a maximum speed not exceeding 25 km/h) or 1(c), the device designed to reduce the exhaust noise meets the requirements specified in column 5 in that item.

(4) Save as provided in paragraph (5), paragraph (3) applies to every vehicle to which this regulation applies and which is first used on or after 1st April 1990, unless it is equipped with 5 or more forward gears and has a maximum power to maximum gross weight ratio not less than 75 kW per 1000 kg, and is of a type in respect of which a type approval certificate has been issued under the Type Approval (Great Britain) Regulations as if, for the reference to items 1, 2, 3 or 4 of the Table there were substituted a reference to item 4 of the Table.

(5) Paragraph (4) does not apply to a vehicle in category 5.2.2.1.3 as defined

in Annex I to Directive 84/424 and equipped with a compression ignition engine, a vehicle in category 5.2.2.1.4 as defined in that Annex, or a vehicle referred to in paragraph 1(b) unless it is first used on or after 1st April 1991.

(6) The apparatus prescribed for the purposes of paragraph 3(a) and regulation 56(2)(a) and Schedule 7A is a sound level meter of the type described in Publication No. 179 of the International Electrotechnical Commission, in either its first or second edition, a sound level meter complying with the specification for Type 0 or Type 1 in Publication No. 651 (1979) "Sound Level Meters" of the International Electrotechnical Commission, or a sound level meter complying with the specifications of the British Standard Number BS 5969:1981 which came into effect on 29th May 1981.

(7) Instead of complying with the preceding provisions of this regulation a vehicle may comply at the time of its first use with Community Directive 77/212, 81/334, 84/372 or 84/424.

TABLE

(regulation 55(3))

1	2			3	4	5
	Limits of sound level					
Item	(a) Vehicle referred to in paragraph (1)(a)	(b) Vehicle referred to in paragraph (1)(b)	(c) Vehicle referred to in paragraph (1)(c)	Conditions of measurement	Method of measurement	Requirements for exhaust device
1	Limits specified in paragraph 1.1 of the Annex to Community Directive 77/212.	89dB(A)	82dB(A)	Conditions specified in paragraph 1.3 of the Annex to Community Directive 77/212.	Method specified in paragraph 1.4.1. of the Annex to Community Directive 77/212.	Requirements specified in heading 11 of the Annex to Community Directive 77/212 (except paragraphs 112 and 11.5).
2	Limits specified in paragraph 5.2.2.1 of Annex I to Community Directive 81/334.	89dB(A)	82dB(A)	Conditions specified in paragraph 5.2.2.3 of Annex I to Community Directive 81/334.	Method specified in paragraph 5.2.2.4 of Annex I to Community Directive 81/334. Interpretation of results as specified in paragraph 5.2.2.5 of that Annex.	Requirements specified in section 3 and paragraphs 5.1 and 5.3.1 of Annex I to Community Directive 81/334.

| 3 | Limits specified in paragraph 5.2.2.1 of Annex 1 to Community Directive 84/372 | 89dB(A) | 82bB(A) | Conditions specified in paragraph 5.2.2.3 of Annex I to Community Directive 84/372. | Method specified in paragraph 5.2.2.4 of Annex I to Community Directive 84/372, except that vehicles with 5 or more forward gears and a maximum power to maximum gross weight ratio not less than 75 kW per 1000 kg may be tested in 3rd gear only. Interpretation of results as specified in paragraph 5.2.2.5 of that Annex. | Requirements specified in section 3 and paragraphs 5.1 and 5.3.1 of Annex I to Community Directive 84/372. |

TABLE

(regulation 55(3))—*cont.*

1	2			3	4	5
	Limits of sound level					
	(a) Vehicle referred to in paragraph (1)(a)	(b) Vehicle referred to in paragraph (1)(b)	(c) Vehicle referred to in paragraph (1)(c)	Conditions of measurement	Method of measurement	Requirements for exhaust device
Item						
4	Limits specified in paragraph 5.2.2.1 of the Annex I to Community Directive 84/424.	Vehicles with engine power— —less than 75 kW —84dB(A) —not less than 75 kW —86dB(A)	Limits specified in paragraph 5.2.2.1 of Annex I to Community Directive 84/424.	Conditions specified in paragraph 5.2.3 of Annex I to Community Directive 84/424.	Method specified in paragraph 5.2.2.4 of Annex I to Community Directive 84/424, except that vehicles with 5 or more forward gears and a maximum power to maximum gross weight ratio not less than 75 kW per 1000 kg may be tested in 3rd gear only. Interpretation of results as specified in paragraph 5.2.5 of that Annex.	Requirements specified in section 3 and paragraphs 5.1 and 5.3.1 of Annex I to Community Directive 84/424.

Noise limits—agricultural motor vehicles and industrial tractors

56.—(1) Save as provided in regulation 59, this regulation applies to every **C14–34** wheeled vehicle first used on or after 1st April 1983 being an agricultural motor vehicle or an industrial tractor, other than—

(a) an agricultural motor vehicle which is first used on or after 1st June 1986 and which is driven at more than 20 mph; or

(b) a road roller.

(2) Every vehicle to which this regulation applies shall be so constructed—

(a) that its sound level does not exceed—

(i) if it is a vehicle with engine power of less than 65kW, 89 dB(A);

(ii) if it is a vehicle with engine power of 65kW or more, and first used before 1st October 1991, 92 dB(A); or

(iii) if it is a vehicle with engine power of 65kW or more, and first used on or after 1st October 1991, 89 dB(A),

when measured under the conditions specified in paragraph I.3 of Annex VI of Community Directive 74/151 by the method specified in paragraph I.4.1 of that Annex using the apparatus prescribed in regulation 55(6); and

(b) that the device designed to reduce the exhaust noise meets the requirements specified in paragraph II.1 of that Annex and, if fibrous absorbent material is used, the requirements specified in paragraphs II.4.1 to II.4.3 of that Annex.

Noise limits—construction requirements relating to motor cycles

57.—(1) Subject to regulation 59, this regulation applies to every motor **C14–35** vehicle first used on or after 1st April 1983 which is—

(a) a moped; or

(b) a two-wheeled motor cycle, whether or not with sidecar attached, which is not a moped.

(2) A vehicle to which this regulation applies shall be so constructed that it meets—

(a) if it is first used before 1st April 1991, the requirements of item 1 or 2 of the Table in Part I of Schedule 7A;

(b) if it is first used on or after that date, the requirements of item 2 of that Table.

(3) Instead of complying with paragraph (2), a vehicle first used before 1st April 1991 may comply at the time of its first use with Community Directive 78/1015, 87/56 or 89/235.

(4) Instead of complying with paragraph (2), a vehicle first used on or after 1st April 1991 may comply at the time of its first use with Community Directive 87/56 or 89/235.

(5) In this regulation "moped" has the meaning given to it in paragraph 5 of Schedule 9.

Exhaust systems—motor cycles

57A.—(1)Any original silencer forming part of the exhaust system of a **C14–36** vehicle to which regulation 57 applies, being a vehicle first used before 1st February 1996, shall—

(a) be so constructed that the vehicle meets the requirements specified in paragraph 3 (other than sub-paragraphs 3.2 and 3.3) of Annex I to Community Directive 78/1015 and be marked in accordance with sub-paragraph 3.3 of that Annex; or

(b) be so constructed that the vehicle meets the requirements specified in paragraph 3 (other than sub-paragraphs 3.2 and 3.3) of Annex I to Community Directive 89/235 and be marked in accordance with sub-paragraph 3.3 of that Annex.

(2) Any original silencer forming part of the exhaust system of a vehicle to which regulation 57 applies, being a vehicle first used on or after 1st February 1996, shall be so constructed that the vehicle meets the requirements specified in paragraph 3 (other than sub-paragraphs 3.2 and 3.3) and Annex I to Community Directive 89/235 and be marked in accordance with sub-paragraph 3.3 of that Annex.

(3) A vehicle fitted with an original silencer may—

(a) if the vehicle is first used before 1st February 1996, instead of complying with paragraph (1), comply at the time of first use with Community Directive 78/1015, 87/56 or 89/235; or

(b) if the vehicle is first used on or after that date, instead of complying with paragraph (2), comply at the time of first use with Community Directive 89/235.

(4) Where any replacement silencer forms part of the exhaust system of a vehicle to which regulation 57 applies, being a vehicle first used on or after 1st January 1985, the first requirement or the second requirement as set out below must be met in respect of the silencer.

(5) In order for the requirement to be met in respect of a silencer forming part of the exhaust system of a vehicle (in this paragraph referred to as "the vehicle in question")—

(a) if the vehicle in question is first used before 1st April 1991, the silencer must be so constructed that, were it to be fitted to an unused vehicle of the same model as the vehicle in question, the unused vehicle would meet—

   (i) the requirements of item 1 or 3 of the Table in Part I of Schedule 7A; and

   (ii) the requirements specified in paragraph 3 (other than sub-paragraphs 3.2 and 3.3) of Annex I to Community Directive 78/1015 or 89/235,

   and the silencer must be marked in accordance with sub-paragraph 3.3 of Annex I to Community Directive 78/1015 or 89/235;

(b) if the vehicle in question is first used on or after 1st April 1991 but before 1st February 1996, the silencer must be so constructed that, were it to be fitted to an unused vehicle of the same model as the vehicle in question, the unused vehicle would meet—

   (i) the requirements of item 3 of the Table in Part I of Schedule 7A; and

   (ii) the requirements specified in paragraph 3 (other than sub-paragraphs 3.2 and 3.3) of Annex I to Community Directive 78/1015 or 89/235,

   and the silencer must be marked in accordance with sub-paragraph 3.3 of Annex I to Community Directive 78/1015 or 89/235;

(c) if the vehicle in question is first used on or after 1st February 1996, the silencer must be so constructed that, were it to be fitted to an unused vehicle of the same model as the vehicle in question, the unused vehicle would meet—

   (i) the requirements of item 3 of the Table in Part I of Schedule 7A; and

 (ii) the requirements specified in paragraph 3 (other than sub-paragraphs 3.2 and 3.3) of Annex I to Community Directive 89/235,
 and the silencer must be marked in accordance with sub-paragraph 3.3
 of Annex I to that Directive.

(6) In order for the second requirement to be met in respect of a silencer
forming part of the exhaust system of a vehicle (in Part II of Schedule 7A
referred to as "the vehicle in question")—

 (a) if the vehicle is first used before 1st April 1991, the silencer must meet
   the requirements of paragraph 2, 3 or 4 of Part II of Schedule 7A; or
 (b) if the vehicle is first used on or after that date, the silencer must meet
   the requirements of paragraph 4 of Part II of Schedule 7A.

(7) Any requirements specified in paragraph (5) or in Part II of Schedule 7A
relating to the silencer were it to be fitted to an unused vehicle of the same
model as the vehicle in question (as defined in that paragraph or in paragraph
(6) for the purposes of that Part, as the case may be) shall be deemed to be met
if they are met by the silencer as fitted to the vehicle in question at the time that
it is first fitted.

(8) For the purposes of this regulation, Community Directive 89/235 shall
have effect as if—

 (a) in Annex I, for sub-paragraph 3.4.1, there were substituted—
   "3.4.1. After removal of the fibrous material, the vehicle must
   meet the relevant requirements."; and
  for sub-paragraph 3.4.3 there were substituted—
   "3.4.3. After the exhaust system has been put into a normal state
   for road use by one of the following conditioning methods, the
   vehicle must meet the relevant requirements:";
 (b) references in Annex I as so modified to a vehicle meeting the relevant
   requirements were—
   (i) in relation to an original silencer, references to a vehicle meeting
    the requirements of item 2 of the Table in Part I of Schedule 7A;
    and
   (ii) in relation to a replacement silencer, references to a vehicle meet-
    ing the requirements of item 3 of that Table;
 (c) in Annex II there were omitted sub-paragraphs 3.1.2, 3.4 and 3.5 and in
   sub-paragraph 3.2—
   (i) the words "and the name referred to in 3.1.2", and
   (ii) the words after "legible".

(9) In relation to a replacement silencer which is—

 (a) fitted to a vehicle before 1st February 1997; and
 (b) clearly and indelibly marked with the name or trade mark of the
   manufacturer of the silencer and with that manufacturer's part number relating to it,
paragraphs (5) and (6) of this regulation and Parts II and III of Schedule 7A
shall have effect as if they contained no reference to a silencer being marked.

(10) For the purposes of this regulation, a silencer forming part of the
exhaust system of a vehicle shall not be regarded as being marked in accordance with sub-paragraph 3.3 of Annex I to Community Directive 78/1015 or
89/235, paragraph (9) of this regulation or any paragraph of Part II of Schedule 7A if the marking is so obscured by any part of the vehicle that it cannot
easily be read.

(11) Until 1st February 1996, for the purposes of paragraph (6), a vehicle first
used on or after 1st April 1991 shall be treated as a vehicle first used before 1st
April 1991.

(12) Part III of Schedule 7A shall have effect for the purpose of exempting
certain silencers from the provisions of paragraph (4).

(13) No person shall use a motor cycle on a road or cause or permit such a vehicle to be so used if any part of the exhaust system has been indelibly marked by the manufacturer of that part with the words "NOT FOR ROAD USE" or words to that effect.

(14) In this regulation—

"original silencer", in relation to a vehicle, means a silencer which was fitted to the vehicle when it was manufactured;

"replacement silencer", in relation to a vehicle, means a silencer fitted to the vehicle, not being an original silencer; and

"trade mark" has the same meaning as in the Trade Marks Act 1938.

Noise limits—maintenance requirements relating to motor cycles

C14–37   **57B.**—(1) No person shall use or cause or permit to be used on a road a motor cycle to which regulation 57 applies if the three conditions specified below are all fulfilled.

(2) The first condition is fulfilled if the vehicle does not meet the noise limit requirements.

(3) The second condition is fulfilled if—

(a) any part of the vehicle is not in good and efficient working order, or

(b) the vehicle has been altered.

(4) The third condition is fulfilled if the noise made by the vehicle would have been materially less (so far as applicable)—

(a) were all parts of the vehicle in good and efficient working order, or

(b) had the vehicle not been altered.

(5) For the purposes of this regulation, a vehicle meets the noise limit requirements if—

(a) in the case of a vehicle first used before 1st April 1991 and not fitted with a replacement silencer, it meets the requirements of item 1 or 2 of the Table in Part I of Schedule 7A;

(b) in the case of a vehicle first used before 1st April 1991 and fitted with a replacement silencer, it meets the requirements of item 1 or 3 of that Table;

(c) in the case of a vehicle first used on or after 1st April 1991 and not fitted with a replacement silencer, it meets the requirements of item 2 of that Table;

(d) in the case of a vehicle first used on or after 1st April 1991 and fitted with a replacement silencer, it meets the requirements of item 3 of that Table.

(6) In this regulation, "replacement silencer" has the same meaning as in regulation 57A.

Noise limits—vehicles not subject to regulations 55 to 57, first used on or after 1st April 1970

C14–38   **58.**—(1) Save as provided in paragraph (2) and in regulation 59, every wheeled motor vehicle which was first used on or after 1st April 1970 and which is not subject to regulations 55, 56 or 57 shall be so constructed that the sound level (A weighting) in decibels does not exceed the maximum permitted level shown in column 2 of the Table for the relevant class of vehicle shown in column 1, when the noise emitted by it is measured under the specified conditions using the prescribed apparatus.

(2) A vehicle to which this regulation applies is not required to comply with paragraph (1) if at the time of its first use it complied with Community Direc-

tive 70/157, 73/350 or 77/212 or, in the case of an agricultural motor vehicle, 74/151, or if it is—

   (a) a road roller;

   (b) a vehicle specially constructed, and not merely adapted, for the purposes of fighting fires or salvage from fires at or in the vicinity of airports, and having an engine power exceeding 220 kW;

   (c) a vehicle propelled by a compression ignition engine and which is of a type in respect of which a type approval certificate has been issued under the Type Approval (Great Britain) Regulations;

   (d) a motorcycle first used on or after 1st October 1980, with an engine capacity not exceeding 50 cc which complies with the requirements of item 1 or 2 of the Table in Part I of Schedule 7A; or

   (e) an agricultural motor vehicle manufactured on or after 7th February 1975 which complies with the requirements specified in regulation 56(2).

(3) The definition of sound level (A weighting) in decibels contained in clause 2 of the British Standard Specification for Sound Level Meters published by the British Standards Institution on 7th September 1962 under the number BS 3539: 1962, as amended by Amendment Slip No. 1, numbered AMD22 and published on 1st July 1968, applies for the purposes of this regulation.

(4) In this regulation, "the specified conditions" means the method described by the British Standard Method for the Measurement of Noise Emitted by Motor Vehicles published on 24th June 1966 under the number BS 3425:1966.

(5) In this regulation "the prescribed apparatus" means a noise meter—

   (a) which is in good working order and complies with the requirements laid down for vehicle noise meters in Part I of the said British Standard Specification numbered BS 3539:1962, as amended by the said Amendment Slip No. 1;

   (b) which has, not more than 12 months before the date of the measurement made in accordance with paragraph (1), undergone all the tests for checking calibration applicable in accordance with the Appendix to the said British Standard Specification; and

   (c) in respect of which there has been issued by the National Physical Laboratory, the British Standards Institution or the Secretary of State a certificate recording the date on which as a result of those tests the meter was found to comply with the requirements of clauses 8 and 9 of the said British Standard Specification.

TABLE

C14–39

(regulation 58(1))

1	2	3
Item	Class of vehicle	Maximum permitted sound level in dB(A)
1	Motor cycle of which the cylinder capacity of the engine does not exceed 50 cc	77
2	Motor cycle of which the cylinder capacity of the engine exceeds 50 cc but does not exceed 125 cc	82

1	2	3
Item	Class of vehicle	Maximum permitted sound level in dB(A)
3	Motor cycle of which the cylinder capcity of the engine exceeds 125 cc.	86
4	Goods vehicle to which regulation 66 applies and which is equipped with a plate complying with the requirements of regulation 66 and showing particulars of a maximum gross weight of more than 3560 kg	89
5	Motor car not being a goods vehicle of the kind described in item 4 above	85
6	Motor tractor	89
7	Locomotive	89
8	Agricultural motor vehicle	89
9	Works truck	89
10	Engineering plant	89
11	Passenger vehicle constructed for the carriage of more than 12 passengers exclusive of the driver	89
12	Any other passenger vehicle	85
13	Any other vehicle	85

Exceptions to regulations 55 to 58

C14–40   59.—Regulations 55, 56, 57, 57A, 57B and 58 do not apply to a motor vehicle which is—
  (a) proceeding to a place where, by previous arrangement—
      (i) noise emitted by it is about to be measured for the purpose of ascertaining whether or not the vehicle complies with such of those provisions as apply to it; or
      (ii) the vehicle is about to be mechanically adjusted, modified or equipped for the purpose of securing that it so complies; or
  (b) returning from such a place immediately after the noise has been so measured.

Radio interference suppression

C14–41   60.—(1) Save as provided in paragraph (2), every wheeled motor vehicle first used on or after 1st April 1974 which is propelled by a spark ignition engine shall comply at the time of its first use with Community Directive 72/245 or ECE Regulation 10 or 10.01 or, in the case of an agricultural motor vehicle, Community Directive 75/322.
    (2) This regulation does not apply to a vehicle constructed or assembled by a person not ordinarily engaged in the trade or business of manufacturing

vehicles of that description, but nothing in this paragraph affects the application to such vehicles of the Wireless Telegraphy (Control of Interference from Ignition Apparatus) Regulations 1973.

Emission of smoke, vapour, gases, oily substances etc

61.—(1) Subject to paragraph (4), every vehicle shall be constructed and   **C14–42**
maintained so as not to emit any avoidable smoke or avoidable visible vapour.

(2) Every motor vehicle using solid fuel shall be fitted with—
   (a) a tray or shield to prevent ashes and cinders from falling onto the road; and
   (b) an efficient appliance to prevent any emission of sparks or grit.

(3) Subject to paragraph (4) and to the exemptions specified in an item in column 4 of Table I, every wheeled vehicle of a class specified in that item in column 2 shall be constructed so as to comply with the requirements specified in that item in column 3.

(3A) A motor vehicle to which an item in Table II applies shall be so constructed as to comply with the requirements relating to conformity of production models set out in the provisions specified in that item in column (4) of that Table.

(3B) Instead of complying with paragraph (1) a vehicle may comply with a relevant instrument.

(3C) Instead of complying with such provisions of items 1, 2 and 3 in Table I as apply to it, a vehicle may at the time of its first use comply with a relevant instrument.

(4) For the purposes of paragraphs (3B) and (3C), a reference to a vehicle complying with a relevant instrument is a reference to a vehicle complying—
   (a) if it is propelled by a compression ignition engine, with Community Directive 72/306 (or, in the case of an agricultural vehicle, 77/537) or ECE Regulation 24.01, 24.02 or 24.03; or
   (b) if it is propelled by a spark ignition engine, with an instrument mentioned in column (4)(a) of Table II.

(5) No person shall use, or cause or permit to be used, on a road any motor vehicle—
   (a) from which any smoke, visible vapour, grit, sparks, ashes, cinders or oily substance is emitted if that emission causes, or is likely to cause, damage to any property or injury or danger to any person who is, or who may reasonably be expected to be, on the road;
   (b) which is subject to the requirement in item 2 of Table I (whether or not it is deemed to comply with that requirement by virtue of paragraph (4)), if the fuel injection equipment, the engine speed governor or any other parts of the engine by which it is propelled have been altered or adjusted so as to increase the emission of smoke; or
   (c) which is subject to the requirement in item 1 of Table I if the device mentioned in column 2 in that item is used while the vehicle is in motion.

(6) No person shall use, or cause or permit to be used, on a road a motor vehicle to which item 3 of Table I applies unless it is so maintained that the means specified in column 3 of that item are in good working order.

(7) Subject to paragraphs 7A, 7B, 7C, 7D, (8), (9) and (10), no person shall use, or cause or permit to be used, on a road a motor vehicle to which an item in Table II applies if, in relation to the emission of the substances specified in column (6) of the item, the vehicle does not comply with the requirements

649

relating to conformity of production models specified in column (4) unless the
following conditions are satisfied in respect to it—

(a) the failure to meet those requirements in relation to the emission of
those substances does not result from an alteration to the propulsion
unit or exhaust system of the vehicle,

(b) neither would those requirements be met in relation to the emission of
those substances nor would such emissions be materially reduced if
maintenance work of a kind which would fall within the scope of a
normal periodic service of the vehicle were to be carried out on the
vehicle, and

(c) the failure to meet those requirements in relation to such emissions
does not result from any device designed to control the emission of
carbon monoxide, hydrocarbons, oxides of nitrogen or particulates fitted to the vehicle being other than in good and efficient working order.

(7A) In relation to a vehicle to which Part III of schedule 1B of the Type
Approval (Great Britain) Regulations applies, item 8 of Table II shall have
effect as if for the entry in column (3) there were substituted "31st December
1993".

(7B) In relation to a vehicle to which Part III of Schedule 1B of the Type
Approval for Goods Vehicles Regulations applies, item 9 of Table II shall have
effect as if for the entry in column (3) there were substituted "1st October
1994".

(7C) In relation to a vehicle to which neither the Type Approval for Goods
Vehicles Regulations nor the Type Approval (Great Britain) Regulations
applies, and which was one among the first specified number of relevant
vehicles to have been manufactured, item 9 of Table II shall have effect as if for
the entry in column (3) there were substituted "1st October 1994".

(7D) For the purposes of paragraph (7C) above, in relation to a vehicle ("the
vehicle in question"),—

(a) "specified number " is 10 per cent. of the total number of vehicles to
which neither the Type Approval for Goods Vehicles Regulations nor
the Type Approval (Great Britain) Regulations applies that were
both—

　(i) manufactured by the manufacturer of the vehicle in question; and

　(ii) registered under the Vehicles (Excise) Act 1971 during the period
beginning with 1st October 1992 and ending with 30th September
1993;

or 50 whichever is the greater; and

(b) a "relevant vehicle" is a vehicle which—

　(i) is not subject to either the Type Approval for Goods Vehicles
Regulations or the Type Approval (Great Britain) Regulations;

　(ii) was manufactured by the manufacturer of the vehicle in question
on or after 1st April 1991 and before 1st October 1993;

　(iii) was in the territory of a member State at some time before 1st
October 1993;

　(iv) was in existence on 1st October 1993; but

　(v) had not been registered under the Vehicles (Excise) Act 1971
before 1st October 1993.

(8) Paragraph (7) shall not apply to a vehicle first used before 26th June 1990.

(9) Where—

(a) a vehicle is fitted with a device of the kind referred to in sub-paragraph
(c) of paragraph (7),

(b) the vehicle does not comply with the requirements specified in that
paragraph in respect to it, and

(c) the conditions specified in sub-paragraphs (a) and (b) of that paragraph are satisfied in respect to the vehicle,

nothing in paragraph (7) shall prevent the vehicle being driven to a place where the device is to be repaired or replaced.

(10) Where a vehicle was constructed or assembled by a person not ordinarily engaged in the business of manufacturing motor vehicles of that description, the date on which it is first used shall, for the purposes of paragraphs (3A), (7), (8) and (9), be regarded as being the 1st January immediately preceding the date of manufacture of the engine by which it is propelled.

However, the date on which a vehicle is first used shall not, by virtue of the foregoing provisions of this paragraph, be regarded in any circumstances as being later than the date on which it would otherwise have been regarded as being first used had those provisions been omitted.

(10A) Without prejudice to paragraphs (1) and (7) no person shall use, or cause or permit to be used on a road, a vehicle first used on or after 1st August 1975 and propelled by a four-stroke spark ignition engine, unless the vehicle is in such a condition that, when the engine is idling—

    (a) the carbon monoxide content of the exhaust emissions from the engine does not exceed—

        (i) in the case of a vehicle first used on or after 1st August 1983, 4.5%; or

        (ii) in any other case, 6%;

    of the total exhaust emissions from the engine by volume; and

    (b) the hydrocarbon content of those emissions does not exceed 0.12% of the total exhaust emissions from the engine by volume.

(10B) Paragraph (10A) does not apply to—

    (a) a vehicle if at the date that the engine was manufactured, that engine was incapable of meeting the requirements specified in that paragraph;

    (b) a vehicle being driven to a place where it is to undergo repairs;

    (c) a vehicle which was constructed or assembled by a person not ordinarily engaged in the business of manufacturing motor vehicles of that description;

    (d) an exempt vehicle within the meaning given by paragraph (12)(a) above;

    (e) a goods vehicle with a maximum gross weight exceeding 3,500 kg;

    (f) engineering plant, an industrial tractor, or a works truck;

    (g) [...]

    (h) a vehicle first used before 1st August 1987 if the engine is a rotary piston engine; and for the purposes of this paragraph "the engine", in relation to a vehicle, means the engine by which it is propelled.

(10C) For the purposes of this regulation—

    (a) any rotary piston engine shall be deemed to be a four-stroke engine; and

    (b) "rotary piston engine" means an engine in which the torque is provided by means of one or more rotary pistons and not by any reciprocating piston.

(11) In this regulation, a reference to a vehicle to which an item in Table II applies is a reference to a vehicle which—

    (a) is of a class specified in that item in column (2) of that Table,

    (b) is first used on or after the date specified in that item in column (3) of that Table, and

    (c) is not exempted by the entry in that item in column (5) of that Table and for the purposes of determining whether a vehicle is a vehicle to which item 8, 9 or 10 in that Table applies, regulation 4(2) shall be disregarded.

(12) In Table II—

  (a) "exempt vehicle" means—

    (i) a vehicle with less than 4 wheels,

    (ii) a vehicle with a maximum gross weight of less than 400 kg,

    (iii) a vehicle with a maximum speed of less than 25 km/h, or

    (iv) an agricultural motor vehicle;

  (b) "direct injection" means a fuel injection system in which the injector communicates with an open combustion chamber or the main part of a divided combustion chamber;

  (c) "indirect injection" means a fuel injection system in which the injector communicates with the subsidiary part of a divided combustion chamber;

  (d) a reference in column (5) to a vehicle complying with an item is a reference to a vehicle that complies with the provisions specified in that item in column (4) whether the vehicle is or is not within the class of vehicles to which that item applies and any instrument mentioned in that item shall for the purposes of the reference have effect as if it applied to the vehicle in question (whether it would otherwise have done so or not).

TABLE

(regulation 63(1))

1	2	3	4
Item	Class of vehicle	Requirements	Exemptions
1	Vehicles propelled by a compression ignition engine and equipped with a device designed to facilitate starting the engine by causing it to be supplied with excess fuel.	Provision shall be made to ensure the device cannot readily be operated by a person inside the vehicle.	(a) a works truck; (b) a vehicle on which the device is so designed and maintained that— (i) its use after the engine has started cannot cause the engine to be supplied with excess fuel, or (ii) it does not cause any increase in the smoke or visible vapour emitted from the vehicle.
2	Vehicles first used on or after 1st April 1973 and propelled by a compression ignition engine.	The engine of the vehicle shall be of a type for which there has been issued by a person authorised by the Secretary of State a type test certificate in accordance with the British Standard Specification for the Performance of Diesel Engines for Road Vehicles published on 19th May 1971 under number BS AU 141a: 1971. In the case of an agricultural motor vehicle (other than one which is first used after June 1, 1986 and is driven at more than 20 mph), an industrial tractor, a works truck or engineering plant, for the purposes of that Specification as to the exhaust gas opacity, measurements shall	(a) a vehicle manufactured before 1st April 1973 and propelled by an engine known as the Perkins 6.354 engine; (b) a vehicle propelled by an engine having not more than 2 cylinders and being an agricultural motor vehicle (other than one which is first used on or after June 1, 1986 and which is driven at more than 20 mph), an industrial tractor, a works truck or engineering plant.

TABLE

(regulation 63(1))—*cont.*

1	2	3	4
Item	Class of vehicle	Requirements	Exemptions
		be made with the engine running at 80% of its full load over the speed range from maximum speed down to the speed at which maximum torque occurs as declared by the manufacturer of the vehicle for those purposes.	
3	Vehicles first used on or after January 1, 1972 and propelled by a spark ignition engine other than a 2-stroke engine.	The engine shall be equipped with means sufficient to ensure that, while the engine is running, any vapours or gases in the engine crank case, or in any other part of the engine to which vapours or gases may pass from that case, are prevented, so far as is reasonably practicable, from escaping into the atmosphere otherwise than through the combustion chamber of the engine.	(a) a two-wheeled motor cycle with or without a sidecar attached; (b) [. . .] (c) a vehicle to which any item in Table II applies.

TABLE II

(regulation 61(3A) and (7))

(1) Item	(2) Class of Vehicle	(3) Date of First Use	(4) Design, construction and equipment requirements		(5) Vehicles exempted from requirement	(6) Emitted Substances
			(a) Instrument	(b) Place in instrument where requirements are stated		
1	Vehicles propelled by a spark ignition engine.	1st October 1982.	Community Directive 78/665, or ECE Regulation 15.03.	Annex 1, paragraphs 3 and 5. Paragraphs 5, 8 and 11.	(a) A vehicle whose maximum gross weight exceeds 3500 kg; (b) A vehicle which complies with the requirements of item 2, 4, 5, 8 or 11; (c) A vehicle whose maximum speed is less than 50 km/h; (d) An exempt vehicle.	Carbon monoxide, hydrocarbons and oxides of nitrogen.
2	All vehicles.	1st April 1991.	Community Directive 83/351, or ECE Regulation 15.04.	Annex I, paragraphs 5, 7 and 8. Paragraphs 5, 8 and 12.	(a) A vehicle propelled by a compression ignition engine and whose maximum gross weight exceeds 3500 kg; (b) A vehicle which complies with the requirements of item 4, 5, 8 or 11; (c) A vehicle within the meaning given by Article 1 of Community Directive 88/77 and which complies with the requirements of item 6, 9 or 10;	Carbon monoxide, hydrocarbons and oxides of nitrogen.

TABLE II

(regulation 61(3A) and (7))—*cont.*

(1) Item	(2) Class of Vehicle	(3) Date of First Use	(4) Design, construction and equipment requirements		(5) Vehicles exempted from requirement	(6) Emitted Substances
			(a) Instrument	(b) Place in instrument where requirements are stated		
					(d) An industrial tractor, works truck or engineering plant; (e) A vehicle whose maximum speed is less than 50 km/h; (f) An exempt vehicle.	
3	Industrial tractors, works trucks and engineering plant propelled in each case by a compression ignition engine.	1st April 1993.	ECE Regulation 49.	Paragraphs 5 and 7.	A vehicle which complies with the requirements of item 6, 9, 10 or 11.	Carbon monoxide, hydrocarbons and oxides of nitrogen.
4	Passenger vehicles which— (a) are constructed or adapted to carry not more than 5 passengers excluding the driver, and	1st April 1991.	Community Directive 88/76.	Annex I, paragraphs 5, 7 and 8.	(a) A vehicle which complies with the requirements of item 2, 8 or 11; (b) A vehicle whose maximum speed is less than 50 km/h; (c) An exempt vehicle.	Carbon monoxide, hydrocarbons and oxides of nitrogen.

	Description	Date	Directive/Regulation	Paragraphs	Vehicle meaning	Pollutants
	(b) have a maximum gross weight of not more than 2500 kg, not being off-road vehicles					
5	Vehicles which are not of a description specified in this column in item 4 but which— (a) are propelled by a spark ignition engine, and have a maximum gross weight of not more than 2000 kg, or	1st April 1992.	Community Directive 88/76 or ECE Regulation 83.	Annex I, paragraphs 5, 7 and 8. Paragraphs 5, 8 and 13.	(a) A vehicle within the meaning given by Article 1 of Community Directive 88/77 and which complies with the requirements of item 6, 9 10 or 11; (b) An industrial tractor, works truck or engineering plant; (c) A vehicle whose maximum speed is less than 50 km/h; (d) A vehicle which complies with the requirements of item 8; (e) An exempt vehicle.	Carbon monoxide, hydrocarbons and oxides of nitrogen.
	(b) are propelled by a compression ignition engine and have a maximum gross weight of more than 3500 kg.	1st April 1991.				
6	All vehicles propelled by compression ignition engines.	1st April 1991.	Community Directive 88/77, or ECE Regulation 49.01.	Annex I, paragraphs 6, 7 and 8 Paragraphs 5, 6 and 7.	(a) A vehicle whose maximum gross weight is less than 3500 kg, and which complies with the requirements of item 2;	Carbon monoxide, hydrocarbons and oxides of nitrogen.

(1) Item	(2) Class of Vehicle	(3) Date of First Use	(4) Design, construction and equipment requirements		(5) Vehicles exempted from requirement	(6) Emitted Substances
			(a) Instrument	(b) Place in instrument where requirements are stated		
					(b) A vehicle which complies with the requirements of items 4, 5, 8, 9, 10 or 11; (c) A fire appliance which is first used before 1st October 1992; (d) An industrial tractor, works truck or engineering plant; (e) An exempt vehicle.	
7	Passenger vehicles which— (a) are constructed or adapted to carry not more than 5 passengers excluding the driver, (b) have a maximum gross weight of not more than 2500 kg, and (c) are propelled by a compression ignition engine of the indirect injection type.	1st April 1991.	Commmunity Directive 88/436.	Annex I, paragraphs 5, 7 and 8, as far as they relate to particulate emissions.	(a) A vehicle which complies with the requirements of item 8 or 11; (b) A vehicle whose maximum speed is less than 50 km/h; (c) An off-road vehicle.	Particulates.
			(d) An exempt vehicle.			

8	All vehicles.	31st December 1992.	Community Directive 91/441. or ECE Regulation 83.01	Annex I, paragraphs 5, 7 and 8. Paragraphs 5, 8 and 13	(a) A vehicle within the meaning given by Article 1 of Community Directive 88/77 and which— (i) complies with the requirements of item 6 and is first used before 1st October 1993, or (ii) complies with the requirements of item 9, 10 or 11; (b) An industrial tractor, works truck or engineering plant; (c) A vehicle whose maximum speed is less than 50 km/h; (d) An exempt vehicle	Carbon monoxide, hydrocarbons and oxides of nitrogen.
9	All vehicles propelled by a compression ignition engine.	1st October 1993	Community Directive 91/542 or ECE Regulation 49.02	Annex I, paragraphs 6, 7 and 8 (excluding line B in the Tables in sub-paragraphs 6.2.1 and 8.3.1.1). Paragraphs 5, 6 and 7 (excluding line B in the Tables in sub-paragraphs 5.2.1 and 7.4.2.1).	(a) A vehicle which complies with the requirements of item 8, 10 or 11; (b) An industrial tractor, works truck or engineering plant; (c) An exempt vehicle.	Carbon monoxide, Hydrocarbons, oxides of nitrogen and particulates.

(1) Item	(2) Class of Vehicle	(3) Date of First Use	(4) Design, construction and equipment requirements		(5) Vehicles exempted from requirement	(6) Emitted Substances
			(a) Instrument	(b) Place in instrument where requirements are stated		
10	All vehicles propelled by a compression ignition engine.	1st October, 1996	Community Directive 91/542	Annex I, paragraphs 6, 7 and 8 (excluding line A in the Tables in sub-paragraphs 6.2.1 and 8.3.1.1).	(a) A vehicle which complies with the requirements of item 8 or 11; (b) An industrial tractor, works truck or engineering plant; (c) An exempt vehicle.	Carbon monoxide, hydrocarbons, oxides of nitrogen and particulates.
			ECE Regulation 49.02	Paragraphs 5, 6 and 7 (excluding line A in the Tables in sub-paragraphs 5.2.1 and 7.4.2.1).		
11	All vehicles.	1st October 1994	Community Directive 93/59	Annex I, paragraphs 5, 7 and 8.	(a) A vehicle within the meaning given by Article 1 of Community Directive 88/77 and which complies with the requirements of items 9 or 10; (b) An industrial tractor, works truck or engineering plant; (c) Vehicles whose maximum speed is less than 50 km/h; (d) An exempt vehicle.	Carbon monoxide, hydrocarbons, oxides of nitrogen and particulates."

Closets etc.

62.—(1) No wheeled vehicle first used after 15th January 1931 shall be   **C14–46** equipped with any closet or urinal which can discharge directly on to a road.

(2) Every tank into which a closet or urinal with which a vehicle is equipped empties, and every closet or urinal which does not empty into a tank, shall contain chemicals which are non-inflammable and non-irritant and provide an efficient germicide.

Wings

63.—(1) Save as provided in paragraph (4), this regulation applies to—   **C14–47**
  (a) invalid carriages;
  (b) heavy motor cars, motor cars and motor cycles, not being agricultural motor vehicles or pedestrian-controlled vehicles;
  (c) agricultural motor vehicles driven at more than 20 mph; and
  (d) trailers.

(2) Subject to paragraphs (3) and (5), every vehicle to which this regulation applies shall be equipped with wings or other similar fittings to catch, so far as practicable, mud or water thrown up by the rotation of its wheels or tracks.

(3) The requirements specified in paragraph (2) apply, in the case of a trailer with more than two wheels, only in respect of the rearmost two wheels.

(4) Those requirements do not apply in respect of—
  (a) a works truck;
  (b) a living van;
  (c) a water cart;
  (d) an agricultural trailer drawn by a motor vehicle which is not driven at a speed in excess of 20 mph;
  (e) an agricultural trailed appliance;
  (f) an agricultural trailed appliance conveyor;
  (g) a broken down vehicle;
  (h) a heavy motor car, motor car or trailer in an unfinished condition which is proceeding to a workshop for completion;
  (i) a trailer used for or in connection with the carriage of round timber and the rear wheels of any heavy motor car or motor car drawing a semi-trailer so used; or
  (j) a trailer drawn by a motor vehicle the maximum speed of which is restricted to 20 mph or less under Schedule 6 to the 1984 Act.

(5) Instead of complying with paragraph (2) a vehicle may comply with Community Directive 78/549.

Spray suppression devices

64.—(1) Save as provided in paragraph (2), this regulation applies to every   **C14–48** wheeled goods vehicle which is—
  (a) a motor vehicle first used on or after 1st April 1986 having a maximum gross weight exceeding 12,000 kg;
  (b) a trailer manufactured on or after 1st May 1985 having a maximum gross weight exceeding 3500 kg; or
  (c) a trailer, whenever manufactured, having a maximum gross weight exceeding 16,000 kg and 2 or more axles.

(2) This regulation does not apply to—
  (a) a motor vehicle so constructed that the driving power of its engine is,

or can by use of its controls be, transmitted to all the wheels on at least one front axle and on at least one rear axle;
  (b) a motor vehicle of which no part which lies within the specified area is less than 400 mm vertically above the ground when the vehicle is standing on reasonably flat ground;
  (c) a works truck;
  (d) a works trailer;
  (e) a broken down vehicle;
  (f) a motor vehicle which has a maximum speed not exceeding 30 mph;
  (g) a vehicle of a kind specified in sub-paragraph (b), (c), (d), (e), (f), (g), (h), (j), (k), (o) or (p) of regulation 51(2);
  (h) a vehicle specially designed, and not merely adapted, for the carriage and mixing of liquid concrete; or
  (i) a vehicle which is being driven or towed to a place where by previous arrangement a device is to be fitted so that it complies with the require-ments specified in paragraph (3).

(2A) This regulation shall not apply to a vehicle fitted with a spray-sup-pression system in accordance with the requirements of Annex III of Com-munity Directive 91/226 if the spray suppression devices with which the vehicle is equipped are legibly and permanently marked with a designated approval mark.

(3) A vehicle to which this regulation applies and which is of a class speci-fied in an item in column 2 of the Table shall not be used on a road on or after the date specified in column 3 in that item, unless it is fitted in relation to the wheels on each of its axles, with such containment devices as satisfy the tech-nical requirements and other provisions about containment devices specified in the British Standard Specification, provided that in the case of a contain-ment device fitted before 1st January 1985 the said requirements shall be deemed to be complied with if that containment device substantially con-forms to those requirements.

C14–49   TABLE

                                   (regulation 64(3))

1	2	3
Item	Class of vehicle	Date
1	A trailer manufactured before 1st January 1975	1st October 1987
2	A trailer manufactured on or after 1st January 1975 but before 1st May 1985	1st October 1986
3	A trailer manufactured on or after 1st May 1985	1st May 1985
4	A motor vehicle	1st April 1986

(4) In this regulation—
    "the British Standard Specification" means—
      (a) in relation to a containment device fitted before 1st May 1987, Part 1a of the amended Specification and Part 2 of the original Specifi-cation; and
      (b) in relation to a containment device fitted on or after 1st May 1987, Part 1a and Part 2a of the amended Specification;
    "designated approval mark" means the marking designated as an

approval mark by regulation 5 of the Approval Marks Regulations and shown at item 30 in Schedule 4 to those Regulations;

"the original Specification" means the British Standard Specification for Spray Reducing Devices for Heavy Goods Vehicles published under the reference BS AU 200: Part 1: 1984 and BS AU 200: Part 2: 1984;

"the amended Specification" means the original Specification as amended and published under the reference BS AU 200: Part 1a: 1986 and BS AU 200: Part 2a: 1986;

"containment device" means any device so described in the original Specification or the amended Specification;

"the specified area" means the area formed by the overall length of the vehicle and the middle 80% of the shortest distance between the inner edges of any two wheels on opposite sides of the vehicle (such distance being ascertained when the vehicle is fitted with suitable tyres inflated to a pressure recommended by the manufacturer, but excluding any bulging of the tyres near the ground).

(5) Nothing in this regulation derogates from any requirement specified in regulation 63.

Maintenance of spray suppression devices

65.—Every part of every containment device with which a vehicle is required to be fitted by the provisions of regulation 64 shall at all times when the vehicle is on a road be maintained free from any obvious defect which would be likely to affect adversely the effectiveness of the device. **C14–50**

Maximum permitted laden weight of a vehicle

75.—(1) Save as provided in paragraph (2), the laden weight of a vehicle of a class specified in an item in column 2 of the Table shall not exceed the maximum permitted laden weight specified in that item in column 3. **C14–51**

(2) The maximum permitted laden weight of a vehicle first used before 1st June 1973 which falls in item 1 or 2 shall not be less than would be the case if the vehicle fell in item 9.

TABLE **C14–52**

(regulation 75(1))

1	2	3
Item	Class of vehicle	Maximum permitted laden weight (kg)
1	A wheeled heavy motor car or motor car which is not described in items 2, 4 or 5 and which complies with the relevant braking requirement. See regulation 78(3) to (6) in relation to buses	The weight determined in accordance with Part I of Schedule 11

1	2	3
Item	Class of vehicle	Maximum permitted laden weight (kg)
1A	A wheeled heavy motor car or motor car which is not described in item 2, 4 or 5, which complies with the relevant braking requirement and in which— (a) every driving axle not being a steering axle is fitted with twin tyres; and (b) either every driving axle is fitted with road friendly suspension or no axle has an axle weight exceeding 9,500 kg.	The weight determined in accordance with Part IA of Schedule II.
2	A wheeled heavy motor car or motor car (not being an agricultural motor vehicle) which forms part of an articulated vehicle and which complies with the relevant braking requirement	The weight specified in column (5) in Part II of Schedule 11 in the item which is appropriate having regard to columns (2), (3) and (4) in that Part
3	A wheeled trailer, including a composite trailer, but not including a semi-trailer, which is drawn by a motor tractor, heavy motor car or motor car which complies with the relevant braking requirement, other than a trailer described in items 6, 7, 8 or 11	As for item 1
4	An articulated bus (see regulation 78(3) to (5))	27,000
5	A wheeled agricultural motor vehicle	As for item 1, but subject to a maximum of 24,390
6	A balanced agricultural trailer, as defined in paragraph (4), which is not described in items 8, 11 or 16	As for item 1, but subject to a maximum of 18,290
7	An unbalanced agricultural trailer, as defined in paragraph (4) which is not described in items 8, 11 or 16	18,290 inclusive of the weight imposed by the trailer on the drawing vehicle
8	A wheeled trailer manufactured on or after 27th February 1977 and fitted with brakes which automatically come into operation on the overrun of the trailer (whether or not it is fitted with any other brake), except an agricultural trailer which is being drawn by an agricultural motor vehicle, which complies with the requirements specified in items 3, 14 and 17 of Schedule 3 and of which the brakes can be applied either by the driver of the drawing vehicle or by some other person on that vehicle or on the trailer	3,500

1	2	3
Item	Class of vehicle	Maximum permitted laden weight (kg)
9	A wheeled heavy motor car or motor car not described in items 1, 2, 4 or 5— (a) with not more than 4 wheels (b) with more than 4 but not more than 6 wheels (c) with more than 6 wheels	 14,230 20,330 24,390
10	A wheeled trailer not described in items 3, 6, 7, 8, or 11 having less than 6 wheels, and not forming part of an articulated vehicle; and an agricultural trailed appliance	 14,230
11	A trailer manufactured before 27th February 1977 and having no brakes other than— (i) a parking brake and (ii) brakes which come into operation on the overrun of the trailer	 3,560
12	A wheeled locomotive, not described in item 5, which is equipped with suitable and sufficient springs between each wheel and the vehicle's frame and with a pneumatic tyre or a tyre of soft or elastic material fitted to each wheel— (a) if having less than 6 wheels (b) if having 6 wheels (c) if having more than 6 wheels	 22,360 26,420 30,490
13	A track-laying locomotive with resilient material interposed between the rims of the weight-carrying rollers and the road so that the weight of the vehicle (other than that borne by any wheels and the portion of the track in contact with the road) is supported by the resilient material	 22,360
14	A locomotive not described in items 5, 12 or 13	20,830
15	A track-laying heavy motor car or motor car	22,360
16	A track-laying trailer	13,210

(3) The maximum total weight of all trailers, whether laden or unladen, drawn at any one time by a locomotive shall not exceed 40,650 kg.

(3A) Nothing in item 1 or 1A of the Table shall prevent a vehicle being used on a road if—

    (a) a plating certificate in respect of the vehicle was in force immediately before 1st January 1993; and

    (b) the laden weight of the vehicle does not exceed the weight shown in that certificate as being the weight not to be exceeded in Great Britain.

(4) In this Part of these Regulations and Schedule 11—

    "air spring" means a spring operated by means of air or other compressible fluid under pressure;

    "air suspension" means a suspension system in which at least 75 per cent. of the spring effect is caused by an air spring.

    "balanced agricultural trailer" means an agricultural trailer the whole of the weight of which is borne by its own wheels; and

    "unbalanced agricultural trailer" means an agricultural trailer of which some, but not more than 35 per cent, of the weight is borne by the drawing vehicle and the rest of the weight is borne by its own wheels.

(5) For the purposes of this Part of these Regulations and Schedule 11, an axle shall be regarded as fitted with a road friendly suspension if its suspension is—

    (a) an air suspension, or

    (b) a suspension, not being an air suspension, which is regarded as being equivalent to an air suspension for the purposes of Community Directive 92/7.

(6) For the purposes of this Part of these Regulations and Schedule 11, an axle shall be regarded as fitted with twin tyres if it would be regarded as fitted with twin tyres for the purposes of Community Directive 92/7.

Maximum permitted laden weight of a vehicle and trailer, other than an articulated vehicle

C14–53   76.—(1) The total laden weight of a motor vehicle and the trailer or trailers (other than semi-trailers) drawn by it shall not, in a case specified in an item in column 2 of the Table, exceed the maximum permitted train weight specified in that item in column 3.

(1A) This regulation is subject to Schedule 11A (exemptions relating to combined transport operations).

(2) In this regulation, the expressions "road friendly suspension", "twin tyres" and "unbalanced agricultural trailer" shall be construed in accordance with regulation 75(4), (5) and (6).

TABLE

(regulation 76(1))

1	2	3
Item	Vehicle combination	Maximum permitted laden weight (kg)
1	A wheeled trailer which is drawn by a wheeled motor tractor, heavy motor car (not being in any case an agricultural motor vehicle) where— (a) the combination has a total of 4 axles and is being used for international transport; and (b) the drawing vehicle is a vehicle which was first used on or after 1st April 1973 and complies with the relevant braking requirement	35,000
1A	A wheeled trailer which is drawn by a wheeled motor tractor, heavy motor car or motor car (not being in any case an agricultural motor vehicle), where the combination has a total of 4 axles and the following conditions are satisfied in relation to the drawing vehicle, namely— (a) it was first used on or after 1st April 1973; (b) it complies with the relevant braking requirement; (c) every driving axle not being a steering axle is fitted with twin tyres; and (d) every driving axle is fitted with road friendly suspension	35,000
1AA	A wheeled trailer which is drawn by a wheeled motor tractor, heavy motor car or motor car (not being in any case an agricultural motor vehicle), where the combination has a total of 5 or more axles and the following conditions are satisfied in relation to the drawing vehicle, namely— (a) it was first used on or after 1st April 1973 (b) it complies with the relevant braking requirement (c) every driving axle not being a steering axle is fitted with twin tyres; and (d) either every driving axle is fitted with road friendly suspension or no axle has an axle weight exceeding 8,500 kg	38,000

1	2	3
Item	Vehicle combination	Maximum permitted laden weight (kg)
1B	A wheeled trailer, not being part of a combination described in items 1, 1A or 1AA which is drawn by a wheeled motor tractor, heavy motor car or motor car (not being in any case an agricultural motor vehicle), where— (a) the trailer is fitted with power-assisted brakes which can be operated by the driver of the drawing vehicle and are not rendered ineffective by the non-rotation of its engine; and (b) the drawing vehicle is equipped with a warning device so placed as to be readily visible to the driver of the vehicle and which is capable of indicating any impending failure of, or deficiency in, the vacuum or pressure system	32,250
1C	A wheeled trailer, which is of a description specified in item 8 in the Table of regulation 75 drawn by a wheeled motor tractor, heavy motor car or motor car (not being in any case an agricultural motor vehicle), the drawing vehicle being a vehicle which— (a) was first used on or after 1st April 1973; and (b) complies with the relevant braking requirement	29,500
2	A wheeled agricultural motor vehicle drawing a wheeled unbalanced agricultural trailer, if the distance between the rearmost axle of the trailer and the rearmost axle of the drawing vehicle does not exceed 2.9 m	20,000
3	A wheeled trailer or trailers drawn by a wheeled heavy tractor, heavy motor car, motor car or agricultural motor vehicle, not being a combination of vehicles mentioned in items 1, 1A, 1AA, 1B, 1C or 2	24,390

1	2	3
Item	Vehicle combination	Maximum permitted laden weight (kg)
4	A track-laying trailer drawn by a motor tractor, heavy motor car or motor car, whether wheeled or track-laying and a wheeled trailer drawn by a track-laying vehicle being a motor tractor, heavy motor car or motor car	22,360

Maximum permitted laden weight of an articulated vehicle

77.—(1) Except as provided in paragraph (2), the laden weight of an articu-   **C14–55**
lated vehicle of a class specified in an item in column 2 of the Table shall not
exceed the weight specified in column 3 in that item.

TABLE

(regulation 77(1))

1	2	3
Item	Class of vehicle	Maximum permitted laden weight (kg)
1	An articulated vehicle which complies with the relevant braking requirement	Whichever is the lower of— (a) the weight specified in column (3) of Part III of Schedule 11 in the item in which the spacing between the rearmost axles of the motor vehicle and the semi-trailer is specified in column (2), (b) if the vehicle is of a description specified in an item in column (2) of Part IV of Schedule 11, the weight specified in column (3) of that item
2	An articulated vehicle which does not comply with the relevant braking requirement if the trailer has— (a) less than 4 wheels (b) 4 wheels or more	 20,330 24,390

(2) This regulation does not apply to an agricultural motor vehicle, an agricultural trailer or an agricultural trailed appliance.

(2A) This regulation is subject to Schedule 11A (exemptions relating to combined transport operations).

(3) In Part IV of Schedule 11, "road friendly suspension" and "twin tyres"
shall be construed in accordance with regulation 75(5) and (6).

Maximum permitted wheel and axle weights

C14–56   **78.**—(1) The weight transmitted to the road by one or more wheels of a vehicle as mentioned in an item in column 2 of the Table shall not exceed the maximum permitted weight specified in that item in column 3.

(2) The Parts of the Table have the following application—

(a) Part I applies to wheeled heavy motor cars, motor cars and trailers which comply with the relevant braking requirement and to wheeled agricultural motor vehicles, agricultural trailers and agricultural trailed appliances; items 1(b) and 2 also apply to buses;

(b) Part II applies to wheeled heavy motor cars, motor cars and trailers which do not fall in Part I;

(c) Part III applies to wheeled locomotives; and

(d) Part IV applies to track-laying vehicles.

C14–57

Table

(regulation 78(1))

Part I

(wheeled heavy motor cars, motor cars and trailers which comply with the relevant braking requirement and wheeled agricultural motor vehicles, agricultural trailers and agricultural trailed appliances; and, in respect of items 1(b) and 2, buses)

1	2	3
Item	Wheel criteria	Maximum permitted laden weight (kg)
1	Two wheels in line transversely each of which is fitted with a wide tyre or with two pneumatic tyres having the centres of their areas of contact with the road not less than 300 mm apart, measured at right angles to the longitudinal axis of the vehicle—	
	(a) if the wheels are on the sole driving axle of a motor vehicle not being a bus,	10,500
	(b) if the vehicle is a bus which has 2 axles and of which the weight transmitted to the road surface by its wheels is calculated in accordance with regulation 78(5),	10,500
	(c) in any other case	10,170
2	Two wheels in line transversely otherwise than as mentioned in item 1	9,200

1	2	3
Item	Wheel criteria	Maximum permitted laden weight (kg)
3	More than two wheels in line transversely— (a) in the case of a vehicle manufactured before 1st May 1983 where the wheels are on one axle of a group of closely spaced axles, (b) in the case of a vehicle manufactured on or after 1st May 1983, (c) in any other case	10,170 10,170 11,180
4	One wheel not transversely in line with any other wheel— (a) if the wheel is fitted as described in item 1, (b) in any other case	5,090 4,600

PART II

(wheeled heavy motor cars, motor cars and trailers not falling in Part I)

1	2	3
Item	Wheel criteria	Maximum permitted laden weight (kg)
5	More than two wheels transmitting weight to a strip of the road surface on which the vehicle rests contained between two parallel lines at right angles to the longitudinal axis of the vehicle— (a) less than 1.02 m apart, (b) 1.02 m or more apart but less than 1.22 m apart, (c) 1.22 m or more apart but less than 2.13 m apart	11,180 16,260 18,300
6	Two wheels in line transversely	9,200
7	One wheel, where no other wheel is in the same line transversely	4,600

PART III

(wheeled locomotives)

1	2	3
Item	Wheel criteria	Maximum permitted laden weight (kg)
8	Two wheels in line transversely (except in the case of a road roller, or a vehicle with not more than four wheels first used before 1st June 1955)	11,180
9	Any two wheels in the case of a wheeled locomotive having not more than four wheels first used before 1st June 1955 (not being a road roller or an agricultural motor vehicle which is not driven at more than 20 mph)	Three quarters of the total weight of the locomotive

PART IV

(track laying vehicles)

1	2	3
Item	Wheel criteria	Maximum permitted laden weight (kg)
10	The weight of a heavy motor car, motor car or trailer transmitted to any strip of the road surface on which the vehicle rests contained between two parallel lines 0.6 m apart at right angles to the longitudinal axis of the vehicle	10,170
11	Two wheels in line— (a) heavy motor cars or motor cars with 2 wheels, (b) heavy motor cars or motor cars with more than 2 wheels	8,130 7,630
12	One wheel, where no other wheel is in the same line transversely, on a heavy motor car or a motor car	4,070

(3) In the case of an articulated bus, or, subject to paragraph (4), of a bus first used before 1st April 1988, the laden weight, for the purposes of regulation 75, and the weight transmitted to the road surface by wheels of the vehicle, for the purposes of items 1 and 2 of the Table in this regulation, shall be calculated

with reference to the vehicle when it is complete and fully equipped for service with—
   (a) a full supply of water, oil and fuel; and
   (b) weights of 63.5 kg for each person (including crew)—
      (i) for whom a seat is provided in the position in which he may be seated; and
      (ii) who may by or under any enactment be carried standing, the total of such weights being reasonably distributed in the space in which such persons may be carried, save that in the case of a bus (not being an articulated bus) only the number of such persons exceeding 8 shall be taken into account.

(4) The weights for the purposes referred to in paragraph (3) may, in the case of a bus to which that paragraph applies, be calculated in accordance with paragraph (5) instead of paragraph (3).

(5) In the case of a bus first used on or after 1st April 1988, the weights for the purposes referred to in paragraph (3) shall be calculated with reference to the vehicle when it is complete and fully equipped for service with—
   (a) a full supply of water, oil and fuel;
   (b) a weight of 65 kg for each person (including crew)—
      (i) for whom a seat is provided, in the position in which he may be seated; and
      (ii) who may by or under any enactment be carried standing, the total of such weights being reasonably distributed in the space in which such persons may be so carried, save that in the case of a bus (not being an articulated bus) only the number of such persons exceeding 4 shall be taken into account;
   (c) all luggage space within the vehicle but not within the passenger compartment loaded at the rate of 100 kg per m³ or 10 kg per person mentioned in sub-paragraph (b) above, whichever is the less; and
   (d) any area of the roof of the vehicle constructed or adapted for the storage of luggage loaded with a uniformly distributed load at the rate of 75 kg per m².

(6) Regulation 75 shall not apply to a two axle bus if—
   (a) its laden weight as calculated in accordance with paragraph (5) does not exceed 17,000 kg; and
   (b) the distance between the two axles is at least 3.0 m.

Maximum permitted weights for certain closely-spaced axles, etc.

79.—(1) This regulation applies to— **C14–61**
   (a) a wheeled motor vehicle which complies with the relevant braking requirement;
   (b) a wheeled trailer which is drawn by such a motor vehicle; and
   (c) an agricultural motor vehicle, an agricultural trailer and an agricultural trailed appliance.

(2) Save as provided in paragraph (5), where a vehicle to which this applies is of a description specified in an item in column 2 of Part V of Schedule 11 and has two closely-spaced axles, the total weight transmitted to the road surface by all the wheels of those axles shall not exceed the maximum permitted weight specified in column 3 of that item.

(3) Save as provided in paragraph (5) where a vehicle to which this regulation applies is of a description specified in an item in column 2 of Part VI of Schedule 11 and has three closely-spaced axles, the total weight transmitted to

the road surface by all the wheels of those axles shall not exceed the weight specified in column 3.

(4) Save as provided by paragraph (5), where a vehicle is fitted with four or more closely-spaced axles, the weight transmitted to the road surface by all the wheels of those axles shall not exceed 24,000 kg.

(5) Nothing in paragraphs (2), (3) or (4) of this regulation shall apply so as to prevent a vehicle first used before 1st June 1973 from being used on a road at a weight as respects those axles at which it could be used if it fell within item 5 in the Table in regulation 78 and nothing in those paragraphs shall prevent a vehicle beig used on a road if—

(a) a plating certificate in respect of the vehicle was in force immediately before 1st January 1993; and

(b) no axle has an axle weight exceeding the weight shown in that certificate as being the weight not to be exceeded in Great Britian for that axle.

(6) In Parts V and VI of Schedule 11, "air-suspension", "road friendly suspension" and "twin tyres" shall be construed in accordance with regulations 75(4), (5) and (6).

Over-riding weight restrictions

80.—(1) Subject to paragraph (2), (2A), (2B) and (2C), no person shall use, or cause or permit to be used, on a road a vehicle—

(a) fitted with a plate in accordance with regulation 66, but for which no plating certificate has been issued, if any of the weights shown on the plate is exceeded;

(b) for which a plating certificate has been issued, if any of the weights shown in column (2) of the plating certificate is exceeded; or

(c) required by regulation 68 to be fitted with a plate, if the maximum gross weight referred to in paragraph (2)(c) of that regulation is exceeded.

(2) Where any two or more axles are fitted with a compensating arrangement in accordance with regulation 23 the sum of the weights shown for them in the plating certificate shall not be exceeded. In a case where a plating certificate has not been issued the sum of the weights referred to shall be that shown for the said axles in the plate fitted in accordance with regulation 66.

(2A) Paragraph (1) shall not apply to a vehicle for which a plating certificate has been issued in the form set out in Schedule 10A or 10C where—

(a) the vehicle is being used for international transport; and

(b) none of the weights shown in column (3) of the plating certificate is exceeded.

(2B) Where both a train weight and a maximum train weight are shown in column (2) of a plating certificate issued for a motor vehicle, paragraph (1)(b) in so far as it relates to train weights shall not apply to the motor vehicle if—

(a) the motor vehicle is a wheeled heavy motor car drawing a wheeled trailer and the requirements set out in Part III of Schedule 11A are for the time being fulfilled; or

(b) the motor vehicle is comprised in an articulated vehicle and the requirements set out in Part III of Schedule 11A are for the time being fulfilled,

and the train weight of the motor vehicle does not exceed the maximum train weight shown in column (2) of the certificate.

(3) Nothing in regulations 75 to 79 shall permit any such weight as is men-

tioned in the preceding provisions of this regulation to be exceeded and nothing in this regulation shall permit any weight prescribed by regulations 75 to 79 in relation to the vehicle in question to be exceeded.

Maintenance and use of vehicle so as not to be a danger, etc.

100.—(1) A motor vehicle, every trailer drawn thereby and all parts and accessories of such vehicle and trailer shall at all times be in such condition, and the number of passengers carried by such vehicle or trailer, the manner in which any passengers are carried in or on such vehicle or trailer, and the weight, distribution, packing and adjustment of the load of such vehicle or trailer shall at all times be such, that no danger is caused or is likely to be caused to any person in or on the vehicle or trailer or on a road.

C14–63

Provided that the provisions of this regulation with regard to the number of passengers carried shall not apply to a vehicle to which the Public Service Vehicles (Carrying Capacity) Regulations 1984 apply.

(2) The load carried by a motor vehicle or trailer shall at all times be so secured, if necessary by physical restraint other than its own weight, and be in such a position, that neither danger nor nuisance is likely to be caused to any person or property by reason of the load or any part thereof falling or being blown from the vehicle or by reason of any other movement of the load or any part thereof in relation to the vehicle.

(3) No motor vehicle or trailer shall be used for any purpose for which it is so unsuitable as to cause or be likely to cause danger or nuisance to any person in or on the vehicle or trailer or on a road.

Parking in darkness

101.—(1) Save as provided in paragraph (2) no person shall, except with the permission of a police officer in a uniform, cause or permit any motor vehicle to stand on a road at any time between sunset and sunrise unless the near side of the vehicle is as close as may be to the edge of the carriageway.

C14–64

(2) The provisions of paragraph (1) do not apply in respect of any motor vehicle—
  (a) being used for fire brigade, ambulance or police purposes or for defence purposes (including civil defence purposes) if compliance with those provisions would hinder or be likely to hinder the use of the vehicle for the purpose for which it is being used on that occasion;
  (b) being used in connection with—
     (i) any building operation or demolition;
     (ii) the repair of any other vehicle;
     (iii) the removal of any obstruction to traffic;
     (iv) the maintenance, repair or reconstruction of any road; or
     (v) the laying, erection, alteration or repair in or near to any road of any sewer, main, pipe or apparatus for the supply of gas, water or electricity, of any telecommunication apparatus as defined in Schedule 2 to the Telecommunications Act 1984 or of the apparatus of any electric transport undertaking,
  if, in any case, compliance with those provisions would hinder or be likely to hinder the use of the vehicle for the purpose for which it is being used on that occasion;

675

    (c) on any road in which vehicles are allowed to proceed in one direction only;

    (d) standing on a part of a road set aside for the parking of vehicles or as a stand for hackney carriages or as a stand for buses or as a place at which such vehicles may stop for a longer time than is necessary for the taking up and setting down of passengers where compliance with those provisions would conflict with the provisions of any order, regulations or byelaws governing the use of such part of a road for that purpose; or

    (e) waiting to set down or pick up passengers in accordance with regulations made or directions given by a chief officer of police in regard to such setting down or picking up.

Passengers on motor cycles

C14–65   **102.** If any person in addition to the driver is carried astride a two-wheeled motor cycle on a road (whether a sidecar is attached to it or not) suitable supports or rests for the feet shall be available on the motor cycle for that person.

Obstruction

103. No person in charge of a motor vehicle or trailer shall cause or permit the vehicle to stand on a road so as to cause any unnecessary obstruction of the road.

Driver's control

104. No person shall drive or cause or permit any other person to drive, a motor vehicle on a road if he is in such a position that he cannot have proper control of the vehicle or have a full view of the road and traffic ahead.

Opening of doors

105. No person shall open, or cause or permit to be opened, any door of a vehicle on a road so as to injure or endanger any person.

Reversing

C14–66   **106.** No person shall drive, or cause or permit to be driven, a motor vehicle backwards on a road further than may be requisite for the safety or reasonable convenience of the occupants of the vehicle or other traffic, unless it is a road roller or is engaged in the construction, maintenance or repair of the road.

Leaving motor vehicles unattended

107.—(1) Save as provided in paragraph (2), no person shall leave, or cause or permit to be left, on a road a motor vehicle which is not attended by a person licensed to drive it unless the engine is stopped and any parking brake with which the vehicle is required to be equipped is effectively set.

(2) The requirement specified in paragraph (1) as to the stopping of the engine shall not apply in respect of a vehicle—
   (a) being used for ambulance, fire brigade or police purposes; or
   (b) in such a position and condition as not to be likely to endanger any person or property and engaged in an operation which requires its engine to be used to—
      (i) drive machinery forming part of, or mounted on, the vehicle and used for purposes other than driving the vehicle; or
      (ii) maintain the electrical power of the batteries of the vehicle at a level required for driving that machinery or apparatus.
(3) In this regulation "parking brake" means a brake fitted to a vehicle in accordance with requirement 16 or 18 in Schedule 3.

Securing of suspended implements

108. Where a vehicle is fitted with any apparatus or appliance designed for   **C14–67** lifting and part of the apparatus or appliance consists of a suspended implement, the implement shall at all times while the vehicle is in motion on a road and when the implement is not attached to any load supported by the appliance or apparatus be so secured either to the appliance or apparatus or to some part of the vehicle that no danger is caused or is likely to be caused to any person on the vehicle or on the road.

Television sets

109.— (1) No person shall drive, or cause or permit to be driven, a motor   **C14–68** vehicle on a road, if the driver is in such a position as to be able to see, whether directly or by reflection, a television receiving apparatus or other cinematographic apparatus used to display anything other than information—
   (a) about the state of the vehicle or its equipment;
   (b) about the location of the vehicle and the road on which it is located;
   (c) to assist the driver to see the road adjacent to the vehicle; or
   (d) to assist the driver to reach his destination.
(2) In this regulation "television receiving apparatus" means any cathode ray tube carried on a vehicle and on which there can be displayed an image derived from a television broadcast, a recording or a camera or computer.

SCHEDULE 2
(see regulation 3)

COMMUNITY DIRECTIVES AND ECE REGULATIONS

TABLE 1

Community Directives

1	2	3				4	
		Community Directives				Item No. in Schedule 1 to—	
Item	Reference No	(a) Date	(b) Official Journal Reference	(c) Subject matter	(d) Previous Directives included	(a) The Type Approval (Great Britain) Regulations	(b) The Type Approval for Goods Vehicles Regulations
1	70/157	6.2.70	L42, 23.2.70, p. 16	The permissible sound level and the exhaust system of motor vehicles			
2	70/220	20.3.70	L76, 6.4.70, p. 1	Measures to be taken against air pollution by gases from spark ignition engines of motor vehicles			
3	70/221	20.3.70	L76, 6.4.70, p. 23	Liquid fuel tanks and rear protective devices for motor vehicles and their trailers			
4	70/388	27.7.70	L176, 10.8.70, p. 12	Audible warning devices for motor vehicles		10	
5	71/127	1.3.71	L68, 22.3.71, p. 1	The rear-view mirrors of motor vehicles			
6	71/320	[26.7.71]	L202, 6.9.71, p. 37	The braking devices of certain			

categories of motor vehicles and their trailers

No.	Directive	Date	Reference	Subject	Relates		
7	72/245	20.6.72	L152, 6.7.72, p. 15	The suppression of radio interference produced by spark ignition engines fitted to motor vehicles		2A	5A
8	72/306	2.8.72	L190, 20.8.72, p. 1	The emission of pollutants from diesel engines for use in vehicles		5	3
9	73/350	7.11.73	L321, 22.11.73, p. 33	The permissible sound level and the exhaust system of motor vehicles	70/157		4A
10	74/132	11.2.74	L74, 19.3.74, p. 7	The braking devices of certain categories of motor vehicles and their trailers	71/320		
11	74/151	4.3.74	L84, 28.3.74, p. 25	Parts and characteristics of agricultural motor vehicles (see Note 1)			
12	74/290	28.5.74	L159, 15.6.74, p. 61	Measures to be taken against air pollution by gases from spark ignition engines for motor vehicles	70/220		
13	74/346	25.6.74	L191, 15.7.74, p. 1	Rear view mirrors for agricultural motor vehicles (see Note 1)			
14	74/347	25.6.74	L191, 15.7.74, p. 5	Field of vision and windscreen wipers for agricultural motor vehicles (see Note 1)			
15	74/483	17.9.74	L266, 2.10.74, p. 4	External projections of motor vehicles		19	
16	75/322	20.5.75	L147, 9.6.75, p. 28	Suppression of radio interference from spark ignition engines of agricultural motor vehicles (see Note 1)			
17	75/443	26.6.75	L196, 26.7.75, p. 1	Reverse and speedometer equipment of motor vehicles		20	

1	2	3				4	
		Community Directives				Item No. in Schedule 1 to—	
Item	Reference No	(a) Date	(b) Official Journal Reference	(c) Subject matter	(d) Previous Directives included	(a) The Type Approval (Great Britain) Regulations	(b) The Type Approval for Goods Vehicles Regulations
18	75/524	25.7.75	L236, 9.9.75, p. 3	The braking devices of certain categories of motor vehicles and their trailers	71/320 as amended by 74/132	13A	
19	76/114	18.12.75	L24, 30.1.76, p. 1	Statutory plates and inscriptions for motor vehicles and trailers		12A	
20	76/115	18.12.75	L24, 30.1.76, p. 6	Anchorage for motor vehicle seat belts			
21	76/432	6.4.76	L122, 8.5.76, p. 1	Braking devices of agricultural vehicles (see Note 1)			
22	77/102	30.11.76	L32, 3.2.77, p. 32	Measures to be taken against air pollution by gases from spark ignition engines of motor vehicles	70/220 as amended by 74/290		
23	77/212	8.3.77	L66, 12.3.77, p. 33	The permissible sound level and the exhaust system of motor vehicles	70/157 as amended by 73/350	14B	4B, 4C, 4D
24	77/537	28.6.77	L220, 29.8.77, p. 38	Emission of pollution from diesel engines for agricultural motor vehicles (see Note 1)			
25	77/541	28.6.77	L220, 29.8.77, p. 95	Seat belts and restraint systems for motor vehicles		12A	
26	77/649	27.9.77	L267, 19.10.77, p. 1	Field of vision of motor vehicle drivers			

27	78/318	21.12.77	L81, 28.3.78, p. 49	Wiper and washer systems of motor vehicles	76/114	22	
28	78/507	19.5.78	L155, 13.6.78, p. 31	Statutory plates and inscriptions for motor vehicles and trailers			
29	78/549	12.6.78	L168, 26.6.78, p. 45	Wheel guards of motor vehicles			
30	78/665	14.7.78	L223, 14.8.78, p. 48	Measures to be taken against air pollution by gases from spark ignition engines of motor vehicles	70/220 as amended by 74/290 and 77/102	4B, 4C	2
31	78/1015	23.11.78	L349, 13.12.78, p. 21	The permissible sound level and exhaust system of motorcycles	74/483	19A	
32	79/488	18.4.79	L128, 26.5.79, p. 1	External projections of motor vehicles			
33	78/489	18.4.79	L128, 26.5.79, p. 12	The braking devices of certain categories of motor vehicles and their trailers	71/320 as amended by 74/132 and 75/524	13B	6, 6C
34	79/490	18.4.79	L128, 26.5.79, p. 22	Liquid fuel tanks and rear under-run protection	70/221		
35	79/795	20.7.79	L239, 22.9.79, p. 1	The rear-view mirrors of motor vehicles	71/127	10A	
36	79/1073	22.11.79	L331, 27.12.79, p. 20	Field of vision and windscreen wipers for agricultural motor vehicles	74/347		
37	80/780	22.7.80	L229, 30.8.80, p. 49	Rear view mirrors for motor cycles			
38	80/1269	16.12.80	L375, 31.12.80, p. 46	The engine power of motor vehicles			
39	81/334	13.4.81	L131, 18.5.81, p. 6	The permissible sound level and exhaust system of motor vehicles	70/157 as amended by 73/350 and 77/212	14C	4B, 4C, 4D
40	81/575	29.7.81	L209, 29.7.81, p. 30	Anchorage for motor vehicle seat belts	76/115	12A	
41	81/576	29.7.81	L209, 29.7.81, p. 32	Seat belts and restraint systems for motor vehicles	77/541	12A	

681

| 1 | 2 | 3 Community Directives | | | | 4 Item No. in Schedule 1 to— | |
Item	Reference No	(a) Date	(b) Official Journal Reference	(c) Subject matter	(d) Previous Directives included	(a) The Type Approval (Great Britain) Regulations	(b) The Type Approval for Goods Vehicles Regulations
42	81/643	29.7.81	L231, 15.8.81, p. 41	Field of vision of motor vehicle drivers	77/649		
43	82/318	2.4.82	L139, 19.5.82, p. 9	Anchorages for motor vehicle seat belts	76/115 as amended by 81/575	12A	
44	82/319	2.4.82	L139, 19.5.82, p. 17	Seat belts and restraint systems for motor vehicles	77/541 as amended by 81576	12A	
45	82/890	17.12.82	L378, 31.12.82, p. 45	Agricultural motor vehicles			
46	83/351	16.6.83	L197, 20.7.83, p. 1	Air pollution by gases from positive ignition engines of motor vehicles	70/220 as amended by 74/290, 77/102 and 78/665	4C	
47	84/372	3.7.84	L196, 26.7.84, p. 47	The permissible sound level and exhaust system of motor vehicles	70/157 as amended by 73/350, 77/212 and 81/334		
48	84/424	3.9.84	L238, 6.9.84, p. 31	The permissible sound level and exhaust system of motor vehicles	70/157 as amended by 73/350, 77/212, 81/334 and 84/372		

No.	Directive	Date	Official Journal reference	Subject matter	Directives amended	Ref	
48A	85/3	19.12.84	L2, 3.1.85, p. 14	The weights dimensions and other technical characteristics of certain road vehicles		10B	
49	85/205	18.2.85	L90, 29.3.85, p. 1	Mirrors	71/127 as amended by 79/795		
49A	85/210	20.3.85	L96, 3.4.85, p. 25	The lead content of petrol]			
50	85/647	23.12.85	L380, 31.12.85, p. 1	The braking devices of certain motor vehicles and their trailers	71/320 as amended by 74/132, 75/524 and 79/489		
50A	86/360	24.7.86	L217, 5.8.86, p. 19	The weights, demensions and other technical characteristics of certain road vehicles	85/3		
51	86/562	6.11.86	L327, 27.11.86, p. 49	Mirrors	71/127 as amended by 79/795 and 85/205	4D 2B	
51A	87/56	18.12.86	L24, 27.1.87, p. 42	The permissible sound level and exhaust system of motorcycles	78/1015		
52	88/76	31.12.87	L36, 9.2.88, p. 1	Measures to be taken against air pollution by gases from the engines of motor vehicles	70/220 as amended by 74/290, 77/102, 78/665 and 83/351		
53	89/297	13.4.89	L124, 5.5.89, p. 1	Lateral protection (side guards) of certain motor vehicles and their trailers			
54	88/77	3.12.87	L36, 9.2.88, p. 33	Measures to be taken against the emission of gaseous pollutants from diesel engines for use in vehicles		4E	2D

1	2	3 Community Directives				4 Item No. in Schedule 1 to—	
Item	Reference No	(a) Date	(b) Official Journal Reference	(c) Subject matter	(d) Previous Directives included	(a) The Type Approval (Great Britain) Regulations	(b) The Type Approval for Goods Vehicles Regulations
54A	88/194	24.3.88	L92, 9.4.88, p. 47	The braking devices of certain categories of motor vehicles and their trailerrs	71/320 as amended by 74/132, 75/524, 79/489 and 85/647		
54B	88/321	16.5.88	L147, 14.6.88, p. 77	Mirrors	71/127 as amended by 79/795, 85/205 and 86/562		
55 55A	88/195 88/366	24.3.88 17.5.88	L92, 9.4.88, p. 50 L181, 12.7.88, p. 40	Engine power of motor vehicles Field of vision of motor vehicle drivers	80/1269 77/649 as amended by 81/643		
55A	88/218	11.4.88	L98, 15.4.88, p. 48	The weights dimensions and other technical characteristics of certain road vehicles	85/3 as amended by 86/360		
56	88/436	16.6.88	L214, 6.8.88, p. 1	Measures to be taken against air pollution by gases from engines of motor vehicles (restriction of particulate pollution emissions from diesel engines)	70/220 as amended by 74/290, 77/102, 78/665, 83/351 and 88/76	27	
56A	89/235	13.3.89	L98, 11.4.89, p. 1	The permissible sound level and exhaust systems of motor cycles	78/1015 as amended by 87/56		

56AA	89/338	27.4.89	L142, 25.5.89, p. 3	The weights dimensions and other technical characteristics of certain road vehicles	85/3 as amended by 86/360 and 88/218	
57	89/458	18.7.89	L226, 3.8.89, p. 1	Measures to be taken against air pollution by emissions from motor vehicles	70/220 as amended by 74/290, 77/102, 78/665, 83/351, 88/76 and 88/436	
57A	89/460	18.7.89	L226, 3.8.89, p. 5	The weights dimensions and other technical characteristics of certain road vehicles	85/3 as amended by 86/360, 88/218 and 89/338	
57B	89/461	18.7.89	L226, 3.8.89, p. 7	The weights dimensions and other technical characteristics of certain road vehicles	85/3 as amended by 86/360, 88/218, 89/338 and 89/460	
58	90/628	30.10.90	L341, 6.12.90, p. 1	Safety belts and restraint systems of motor vehicles	77/541 as amended by 81/576 and 82/319	
59	90/269	30.10.90	L341, 6.12.90, p. 14	Anchorages for motor vehicle safety belts	76/115 as amended by 81/575 and 82/318	12A
60	90/630	30.10.90	L341, 6.12.90, p. 20	Field of vision of motor vehicle drivers	77/649 as amended by 81/643 and 88/366	12A

1	2	3				4	
		Community Directives				Item No. in Schedule 1 to—	
Item	Reference No	(a) Date	(b) Official Journal Reference	(c) Subject matter	(d) Previous Directives included	(a) The Type Approval (Great Britain) Regulations	(b) The Type Approval for Goods Vehicles Regulations
60A	91/60	4.2.91	L37, 9.2.91, p. 37	The weights dimensions and other technical characteristics of certain road vehicles	85/3 as amended by 86/360, 88/218 and 89/338, 89/460 and 89/641		
61	91/226	27.3.91	L103, 23.4.91, p. 5	Spray-suppression systems of certain categories of motor vehicles and their trailers			
62	92/7	10.2.91	L57, 2.3.92, p. 29	The weights dimensions and other technical characteristics of certain road vehicles	85/3 as amended by 86/360, 88/218, 89/338, 89/338, 89/460 and 89/641		
63	91/441	26.6.91	L242, 30.8.91, p. 1	Measures to be taken against air pollution by emissions from motor vehilces	70/220 as amended by 74/290, 77/102, 78/665, 83/351, 88/76, 88/436 and 89/458	4G	2F

					88/77	4H	2G
64	91/542	1.10.91	L295, 25.10.91, p. 1	Measures to be taken against the emission of gaseous pollutants from diesel engines for use in vehicles			
65	92/22	31.3.92	L129, 14.5.92, p. 11	Safety glazing and glazing materials on motor vehicles and their trailers			
66	92/23	31.3.92	L129, 14.5.92, p. 95	Tyres of motor vehicles and their trailers and their fitting			

NOTE 1. This item is to be interpreted as including reference to the amendments made by Community Directive 82/890 (item 45).

TABLE II

ECE REGULATIONS

1	2	3				4	
		ECE Regulations				Item No. in Schedule 1 to—	
Item	Reference No.	(a) Number	(b) Date	(c) Subject matter	(d) Date of amendment	(a) The Type Approval (Great Britain) Regulations	(b) The Type Approval for Goods Vehicles Regulations
1	10	10	17.12.68	Radio interference suppression	—	2	5
2	10.01	10	17.12.68	Radio interference suppression	19.3.78	2A	5A
3	13.03	13	29.5.69	Brakes	4.1.79	13C, 13D	6A, 6B, 6D
4	13.04	13	29.5.69	Brakes	11.8.81	13C, 13D	6A, 6B, 6D
4A	13.05	13	29.5.69	Brakes	26.11.84	—	—
4B	13.06	13	29.5.69	Brakes	22.11.90	—	—
5A	14	14	30.1.70	Anchorages for seat belts	—	12A	—
6	14.01	14	30.1.70	Anchorages for seat belts	28.4.76	12A	—
6A	14.02	14	30.1.70	Anchorages for seat belts	22.11.84	12A	2
7	15.03	15	11.3.70	Emission of gaseous pollutants	6.3.78	4B	2
8	15.04	15	11.3.70	Emission of gaseous pollutants	20.10.81	4C	—
9	16.03	16	14.8.70	Seat belts and restraint systems	9.12.79	12A	3
10	24.01	24	23.8.71	Emission of pollutants by a diesel engine	11.9.73	5	3A
11	24.02	24	23.8.71	Emission of pollutants by a diesel engine	11.2.80	5A	—
12	24.03	24	23.8.71	Emission of pollutants by a diesel engine	20.4.86	—	—
13	26.01	26	28.4.72	External projections	11.9.73	19	—

			Subject			
13A	30	30	1.4.75	Pneumatic tyres for motor vehicles and their trailers	—	17, 17A	—
13B	30	30.01	1.4.75	Pneumatic tyres for motor vehicles and their trailers	25.9.77	17, 17A	—
13C	30.02	30	1.4.75	Pneumatic tyres for motor vehicles and their trailers	5.10.87	17, 17A	—
14	34	34	25.7.75	Prevention of fire risks	—	—	—
15	34.01	34	25.7.75	Prevention of fire risks	18.1.79	—	—
16	36	36	12.11.75	Construction of public service vehicles	—	—	—
17	39	39	11.7.78	Speedometers	—	20	—
18	43	43	15.9.80	Safety glass and glazing materials	—	15B	—
19	43.01	43	15.9.80	Safety glass and glazing materials	12.11.82	15B	—
20	44	44	1.2.81	Child restraints	1.2.84	—	—
21	44.01	44	1.2.81	Child restraints	30.5.88	—	—
21A	46.01	46	21.10.84	Mirrors	—	—	—
21B	49	49	15.4.82	Emissions of gaseous pollutants	—	—	—
21AA	49.01	49	14.5.90	Emissions of gaseous pollutants	30.12.92	—	—
21AB	49.02	49	15.4.82	Emissions of gaseous pollutants	—	—	—
21C	54	54	1.3.83	Pneumatic tyres for commercial vehicles and their trailers	—	17A	—
22	64	64	1.8.85	Vehicles with temporary-use spare wheels/tyres	—	—	—
23	78	78	15.10.88	Brakes	—	—	—
24	78.01	78	15.10.88	Brakes	22.11.90	—	—
25	83	83	5.11.89	Emissions of gaseous pollutants	—	4F	2H
26	83.01	83	5.11.89	Emissions of gaseous pollutants	30.12.92	4K	2F

(see regulation 16)   SCHEDULE 3

BRAKING REQUIREMENTS

1. The braking requirements referred to in regulation 16(4) are set out in the Table and are to be interpreted in accordance with paragraphs 2 to 5 of this Schedule.

TABLE

(Schedule 3)

Number	Requirement
1	The vehicle shall be equipped with— (a) one efficient braking system having two means of operation; (b) one efficient split braking system having one means of operation; or (c) two efficient braking systems each having a separate means of operation, and in the case of a vehicle first used on or after 1st January 1968, no account shall be taken of a multi-pull means of operation unless, at first application, it operates a hydraulic, electric or pneumatic device which causes the application of brakes with total braking efficiency not less than 25%.
2	The vehicle shall be equipped with— (a) one efficient braking system having two means of operation; or (b) two efficient braking systems each having a separate means of operation.
3	The vehicle shall be equipped with an efficient braking system.
4	The braking system shall be so designed that in the event of failure of any part (other than a fixed member or a brake shoe anchor pin) through or by means of which the force necessary to apply the brakes is transmitted, there shall still be available for application by the driver brakes sufficient under the most adverse conditions to bring the vehicle to rest within a reasonable distance. The brakes so available shall be applied to— (a) in the case of a track-laying vehicle, one track on each side of the vehicle; (b) in the case of a wheeled motor vehicle, one wheel if the vehicle has 3 wheels and otherwise to at least half the wheels; and (c) in the case of a wheeled trailer, at least one wheel if it has only 2 wheels and otherwise at least 2 wheels. This requirement applies to the braking systems of both a trailer and the vehicle by which it is being drawn except that if the drawing vehicle complies with regulation 15, Community Directive 78/489, 85/647 or 88/194 or ECE Regulation 13.03, 13.04 13.05 or 13.06, the requirement applies only to the braking system of the drawing vehicle. It does not apply to vehicles having split braking systems (which are subject to regulation 18(3)(b)) or to road rollers. (The expressions 'part' and 'half the wheels' are to be interpreted in accordance with paragraphs (3) and (4) respectively).
5	The braking system shall be so designed and constructed that, in the event of the failure of any part thereof, there shall still be available for application by the driver a brake sufficient under the most adverse conditions to bring the vehicle to rest within a reasonable distance.

Number	Requirement
6	The braking system of a vehicle, when drawing a trailer which complies with regulation 15, Community Directive 79/489, 85/647 or 88/194 or ECE Regulation 13.03, 13.04, 13.05 or 13.06, shall be so constructed that, in the event of a failure of any part (other than a fixed member or brake shoe anchor pin) of the service braking system of the drawing vehicle (excluding the means of operation of a split braking system) the driver can still apply brakes to at least one wheel of the trailer, if it has only 2 wheels, and otherwise to at least 2 wheels, by using the secondary braking system of the drawing vehicle. (The expression "part" is to be interpreted in accordance with paragraph 3).
7	The application of any means of operation of a braking system shall not affect or operate the pedal or hand lever of any other means of operation.
8	The braking system shall not be rendered ineffective by the non-rotation of the engine of the vehicle or, in the case of a trailer, the engine of the drawing vehicle (steam-propelled vehicles, other than locomotives and buses, are excluded from this requirement).
9	At least one means of operation shall be capable of causing brakes to be applied directly, and not through the transmission gear, to at least half the wheels of the vehicle. This requirement does not apply to a works truck with an unladen weight not exceeding 7370 kg, or to an industrial tractor; and it does not apply to a vehicle with more than 4 wheels if— (a) the drive is transmitted to all wheels other than the steering wheels without the interposition of a differential driving gear or similar mechanism between the axles carrying the driving wheels; and (b) the brakes applied by one means of operation apply directly to 2 driving wheels on opposite sides of the vehicle; and (c) the brakes applied by another means of operation act directly on all the other driving wheels. (The expression "half the wheels" is to be interpreted in accordance with paragraph (4)).
10	The brakes of a trailer shall come into operation automatically on its overrun or, in the case of a track-laying trailer drawn by a vehicle having steerable wheels at the front or a wheeled trailer, the driver of, or some other person on, the drawing vehicle or on the trailer shall be able to apply the brakes on the trailer.
11	The brakes of a trailer shall come into operation automatically on its overrun or the driver of the drawing vehicle shall be able to apply brakes to all the wheels of the trailer, using the means of operation which applies the service brakes of the drawing vehicle.
12	The brakes of the vehicle shall apply to all wheels other than the steering wheels.
13	The brakes of the vehicle shall apply to at least 2 wheels.
14	The brakes of the vehicle shall apply in the case of a wheeled vehicle to at least 2 wheels if the vehicle has no more than 4 wheels and to at least half the wheels if the vehicle has more than 4 wheels; and in the case of a track-laying vehicle to all the tracks.

Number	Requirement
15	The brakes shall apply to all the wheels.
16	The parking brake shall be so designed and constructed that— (a) in the case of a wheeled heavy motor car or motor car, its means of operation is independent of the means of operation of any split braking system with which the vehicle is fitted; (b) in the case of a motor vehicle other than a motor cycle or an invalid carriage, either— (i) it is capable of being applied by direct mechanical action without the intervention of any hydraulic, electric or pneumatic device; or (ii) the vehicle complies with requirement 15; and (c) it can at all times when the vehicle is not being driven or is left unattended be set so as— (i) in the case of a track-laying vehicle, to lock the tracks; and (ii) in the case of a wheeled vehicle, to prevent the rotation of at least one wheel in the case of a three wheeled vehicle and at least two wheels in the case of a vehicle with more than three wheels.
17	The parking brake shall be capable of being set so as effectively to prevent two at least of the wheels from revolving when the trailer is not being drawn.
18	The parking brake shall be so designed and constructed that— (a) in the case of a motor vehicle, its means of operation (whether multi-pull or not) is independent of the means of operation of any braking system required by regulation 18 to have a total braking efficiency of not less than 50 per cent.; and (b) in the case of a trailer, its brakes can be applied and released by a person standing on the ground by a means of operation fitted to the trailer; and (c) in either case, its braking force, when the vehicle is not being driven or is left unattended (and in the case of a trailer, whether the braking force is applied by the driver using the service brakes of the drawing vehicle or by a person standing on the ground in the manner indicated in sub-paragraph (b)) can at all times be maintained in operation by direct mechanical action without the intervention of any hydraulic, electric or pneumatic device and, when so maintained, can hold the vehicle stationary on a gradient of at least 16 per cent. without the assistance of stored energy.

2. For the purposes of requirement 3 in the Table, in the case of a motor car or heavy motor car propelled by steam and not used as a bus, the engine shall be deemed to be an efficient braking system with one means of operation if the engine is capable of being reversed and, in the case of a vehicle first used on or after 1st January 1927, is incapable of being disconnected from any of the driving wheels of the vehicle except by the sustained effort of the driver.

3. For the purpose of requirements 4 and 6 in the Table, in the case of a wheeled motor car and of a vehicle first used on or after 1st October 1938 which is a locomotive, a motor tractor, a heavy motor car or a track-laying motor car, every moving shaft which is connected to or supports any part of a braking system shall be deemed to be part of the system.

4. For the purpose of [requirements 4, 9 and 14] in the Table, in determining whether brakes apply to at least half the wheels of a vehicle, not more than one front wheel shall be treated as a wheel to which brakes apply unless the vehicle is—

    (a) a locomotive or motor tractor with more than 4 wheels;

    (b) a heavy motor car or motor car first used before 1st October 1938;

    (c) a motor car with an unladen weight not exceeding 1020 kg;

    (d) a motor car which is a passenger vehicle but is not a bus;

    (e) a works truck;

    (f) a heavy motor car or motor car with more than 3 wheels which is equipped in respect of all its wheels with brakes which are operated by one means of operation; or

    (g) a track-laying vehicle.

5. In this Schedule a "multi-pull means of operation" means a device forming part of a braking system which causes the muscular energy of the driver to apply the brakes of that system progressively as a result of successive applications of that device by the driver.

"PELICAN" PEDESTRIAN CROSSINGS REGULATIONS AND GENERAL DIRECTIONS 1987

(S.I. 1987 No. 16)

Citation and commencement

1. This Instrument may be cited as the "Pelican" Pedestrian Crossings Regulations and General Directions 1987 and shall come into force on 18th February 1987.   **C15–01**

Revocation

2. The "Pelican" Pedestrian Crossings Regulations and General Directions 1969 and the "Pelican" Pedestrian Crossings (Amendment) Regulations and General Directions 1979 are hereby revoked.   **C15–02**

Interpretation

3.—(1) In this Instrument—

    (a) any reference to a numbered regulation is a reference to the regulation bearing that number in the Regulations contained in Part II of this Instrument; and

    (b) except where otherwise stated, any reference to a numbered Schedule is a reference to the Schedule to the Regulations contained in Part II of this Instrument bearing that number.

(2) In this Instrument the following expressions have the meanings hereby respectively assigned to them—

    "the 1984 Act" means the Road Traffic Regulation Act 1984;

    "the 1969 Regulations" means the "Pelican" Pedestrian Crossing Regulations 1969;

"appropriate authority" means, in relation to a trunk road, the appropriate Secretary of State and, in relation to any other road, the local authority who established the crossing;

"appropriate Secretary of State" means, in relation to a crossing established or to be established on a road in—

(a) England, the Secretary of State for Transport;

(b) Scotland, the Secretary of State for Scotland; or

(c) Wales, the Secretary of State for Wales;

"carriageway" means—

(a) where it is in a highway, a way constituting or comprised in the highway being a way over which the public have a right of way for the passage of vehicles; and

(b) where it is in any other road to which the public has access, that part of the road to which vehicles have access,

but does not, in either case, include any central reservation (whether within the limits of a crossing or not);

"central reservation" means any provision which separates one part of a carriageway from another part of that carriageway, and includes a refuge for pedestrians;

"crossing" means a crossing for pedestrians established either·

(a) in the case of any road other than a trunk road, by a local authority under the provisions of section 23 of the 1984 Act; or

(b) in the case of a trunk road, by the appropriate Secretary of State in discharge of the duty imposed on him by section 24 of the 1984 Act;

"indicator for pedestrians" means the traffic sign of that description prescribed by regulation 2(1) and Schedule 1;

"one-way street" means any road on which the driving of vehicles otherwise than in one direction is prohibited at all times;

"pedestrian" means a foot passenger;

"pedestrian light signals" means the traffic signs of that description prescribed by regulation 2(1) and Schedule 1;

" 'Pelican' crossing" means a crossing—

(a) at which there are traffic signs of the size, colour and type prescribed, or treated as if prescribed, by regulation 2(1) and Schedule 1; and

(b) the presence and limits of which are indicated, or are treated as indicated, in accordance with regulation 2(2) and Schedule 2;

" 'Pelican' controlled area" means, in relation to a "Pelican" crossing, the area of the carriageway in the vicinity of the crossing and lying on both sides of the crossing or only one side of the crossing, the presence and limits of which are indicated, or are treated as indicated, in accordance with regulation 3 and Schedule 2;

"primary signal" means the traffic sign prescribed as a vehicular light signal by regulation 2(1) and Schedule 1 erected on or near the carriageway facing traffic approaching the "Pelican" crossing and sited between the stop line and the line of studs indicating the limits of the crossing in accordance with Schedule 2 nearest to the stop line;

"refuge for pedestrians" means an area of a carriageway to which vehicles do not have access and on which pedestrians may wait after crossing one part of that carriageway and before crossing the other part;

"secondary signal" means the traffic sign prescribed as a vehicular light signal by regulation 2(1) and Schedule 1 erected on or near the carriageway facing traffic appoaching the "Pelican" crossing but sited beyond the furthest edge of the "Pelican" crossing as viewed from the direction of travel of such traffic;

"stop line" means, in relation to the driver of a vehicle approaching a "Pelican" crossing, the transverse white line which is parallel to the limits of the crossing as indicated in accordance with Schedule 2 and on the same side of the crossing as the driver;

"stud" means any mark or device on the carriageway, whether or not projecting above the surface thereof;

"a system of staggered crossings" means two "Pelican" crossings provided on a road where there is a central reservation in the road, each separately constituted as a "Pelican" crossing, one such crossing being on one side of the central reservation and the other such crossing being on the other side and which together do not form a straight line across the road.

(3) Any reference in this Instrument to a vehicular light signal is—

    (a) where a primary signal has been erected without a secondary signal, a reference to the light signal displayed by both the primary signal; and

    (b) where a secondary signal has been erected as well as a primary signal, a reference to the light signal displayed by both the primary signal and the secondary signal or by either the primary signal operating without the secondary signal or by the secondary signal operating without the primary signal.

PART II

REGULATIONS

Citation

1. The Regulations contained in this Part of this Instrument may be cited as the "Pelican" Pedestrian Crossings Regulations 1987.   **C15–03**

"Pelican" crossings

2.—(1) The provisions of Schedule 1 shall have effect as respects the size, colour and type of the traffic signs which are to be placed at or near a crossing for the purpose of constituting it a "Pelican" crossing.   **C15–04**

(2) The provisions of Schedule 2 shall have effect for regulating the manner in which the presence and limits of a crossing are to be indicated for the purposes of constituting it a "Pelican" crossing.

(3) Any crossing which, immediately before the coming into operation of these Regulations, was constituted as a "Pelican" crossing in accordance with the 1969 Regulations shall, notwithstanding the revocation of those Regulations, be treated as constituted in accordance with these Regulations for so long as the traffic signs situated at or near it and the manner in which its presence and limits are indicated comply with the 1969 Regulations.

"Pelican" controlled areas

3.—(1) The provisions of Schedule 2 shall have effect as respects the size,   **C15–05**

colour and type of the traffic signs which shall be placed in the vicinity of a "Pelican" crossing for the purpose of constituting a "Pelican" controlled area in relation to that crossing and of indicating the presence and limits of that area.

(2) A stop line shall indicate to vehicular traffic proceeding towards a "Pelican" crossing the position at which a driver of a vehicle shall stop it for the purposes of complying with regulations 16 and 17.

(3) Where the appropriate authority is satisfied in relation to a particular area of carriageway in the vicinity of the "Pelican" crossing that, by reason of the layout or character of the roads in the vicinity of the crossing, the application of such a prohibition as is mentioned in any of regulations 12, 13, 14, 19 and 20 to that particular area or the constitution of that particular area as a "Pelican" controlled area by the placing of traffic signs in accordance with Schedule 2 would be impracticable, it shall not be necessary for that area to be constituted a "Pelican" controlled area but if, by virtue of this paragraph, it is proposed that no area, on either side of the limits of a "Pelican" crossing (not on a trust road), is to be constituted a "Pelican" controlled area by 18th February 1989, a notice in writing shall be sent by the appropriate authority to the appropriate Secretary of State stating the reasons why it is proposed that no such area should be constituted.

(4) Where immediately before the coming into operation of these Regulations, the approach for vehicular traffic to a "Pelican" crossing has been indicated by a pattern of studs placed and white lines marked on the carriageway in accordance with the provisions of paragraph 3 of Schedule 2 to the 1969 Regulations, then, notwithstanding the revocation effected by article 2 of Part I of this Instrument, that approach may until 18th February 1989 continue to be so indicated for so long as the said pattern of studs and white lines does not lie within a "Pelican" controlled area or in the vicinity of such an area on the same side of the crossing as that pattern.

Variations in dimensions

4.—(1) Any variation in—

> (i) a dimension (other than as to the height of a letter) specified in any of the diagrams in Parts II and III of Schedule 1; or
>
> (ii) a dimension as to the height of a letter specified in the diagram in Part III of that Schedule,

shall be treated as permitted by these Regulations if the variation—

> (a) in the case of a dimension of less than 10 millimetres, does not exceed 1 millimetre;
>
> (b) in the case of a dimension of 10 millimetres or more but less than 50 millimetres, does not exceed 10 per cent. of that dimension;
>
> (c) in the case of a dimension of 50 millimetres or more but less than 300 millimetres, does not exceed 7½ per cent. of that dimension; or
>
> (d) in the case of a dimension of 300 millimetres or more, does not exceed five per cent. of that dimension.

(2) Any variation in a dimension specified in any of the diagrams in Schedule 2 shall be treated as permitted by these Regulations if the variation—

> (a) in the case of a dimension of 300 millimetres or more, does not exceed 20 per cent. of that dimension; or
>
> (b) in the case of a dimension of less than 300 millimetres, where the actual dimension exceeds the dimension so specified, does not exceed 30 per cent. of the dimension so specified, and where the actual dimension is

less than the dimension so specified, does not exceed 10 per cent. of the dimension so specified.

Box for housing equipment

5. Apparatus designed to control or to monitor, or to control and monitor,   C15–07
the operation of the vehicular light signals and pedestrian light signals may be housed in one or more boxes attached to the post or other structure on which such signals are mounted.

Additional traffic signs

6. In addition to the traffic signs prescribed in regulation 2(1) and Schedule   C15–08
1, the traffic signs specified in diagrams 610, 611, 612, 613 and 616 in Schedule 1 to the Traffic Signs Regulations 1981 may be placed at or near a "Pelican" crossing.

Significance of traffic signs

7. Regulations 8 to 10 are made under section 64 of the 1984 Act and shall   C15–09
have effect for the purpose of prescribing the warnings, information, require-ments and prohibitions which are to be conveyed to traffic by the traffic signs of the size, colour and type prescribed by regulations 2(1) and 6 and Schedule 1.

Significance of vehicular light signals

8.—(1) The vehicular light signal at a "Pelican" crossing shall convey the   C15–10
following information, requirements and prohibitions—
   (a) the steady green light shall convey the information that vehicular traf-fic may proceed across the crossing;
   (b) except as provided in sub-paragraph (d) below, the steady amber light shall convey the prohibition that vehicular traffic shall not proceed beyond the stop line, or, if the stop line is not for the time being visible, beyond the post or other structure on which is mounted the primary signal facing such traffic on the side of the carriageway on which vehicles approach the crossing except in the case of any vehicle which when the steady amber light is first shown is so close to the stop line, post or structure that it cannot safely be stopped before passing the line, post or structure;
   (c) except as provided in sub-paragraph (d) below, the red light shall con-vey the prohibition that vehicular traffic shall not proceed beyond the stop line, or, if the stop line is not for the time being visible, beyond the post or other structure on which is mounted the primary signal facing such traffic on the side of the carriageway on which vehicles approach the crossing;
   (d) on any occasion when a vehicle is being used for fire brigade, ambu-lance or police purposes and observance of the prohibitions conveyed by the steady amber and red lights (as specified in sub-paragraphs (b) and (c) above respectively) would be likely to hinder the use of the vehicle for the purpose in question, then sub-paragraphs (b) and (c)

above shall not apply to that vehicle. In the circumstances described in the preceding part of this sub-paragraph, the steady amber light and the red light shall each convey the information that the vehicle may only proceed beyond the stop line or (as the case may be) the post or other structure if the driver—

  (i) accords precedence to any pedestrian who is on that part of the carriageway which lies within the limits of the crossing or on a central reservation which lies between two crossings which do not form a system of staggered crossings; and

  (ii) subject to sub-paragraph (i) above, does not proceed in such a manner or at such a time as is likely to cause danger to any other vehicle approaching or waiting at the crossing, or in such a manner as to compel the driver of any such vehicle to change its speed or course in order to avoid an accident; and

(e) the flashing amber light shall convey the information that vehicular traffic may proceed across the crossing but that every pedestrian if he is on the carriageway or a central reservation within the limits of that crossing (but not if he is on a central reservation which lies between two crossings which form a system of staggered crossings) before any part of a vehicle has entered those limits, has the right of precedence within those limits over that vehicle, and the requirement that the driver of a vehicle shall accord such precedence to any such pedestrian.

(2) Vehicular traffic passing the vehicular light signal in accordance with the foregoing provisions of this regulation shall proceed with due regard to the safety of other users of the road and subject to the direction of any police constable in uniform or traffic warden who may be engaged in the regulation of traffic.

Significance of pedestrian traffic signals

C15–11 **9.** The pedestrian traffic signal at a "Pelican" crossing shall convey to pedestrians the warnings and information specified in the following paragraphs of this regulation.

(2) The pedestrian light signal shall convey to pedestrians the following warnings and information—

(a) the red light shall convey to a pedestrian the warning that he should not in the interests of safety use the crossing;

(b) the steady green light shall convey to a pedestrian the information that he may use the crossing and drivers of vehicles may not cause their vehicles to enter the limits of the crossing; and

(c) the flashing green light shall convey—

  (i) to a pedestrian who is already on the crossing when the flashing green light is first shown the information that he may continue to use the crossing, and that if he is on the carriageway or on a central reservation within the limits of that crossing (but not if he is on a central reservation which lies between two crossings which form part of a system of staggered crossings) before any part of a vehicle has entered those limits he has the right of precedence within those limits over that vehicle; and

  (ii) to a pedestrian who is not already on the crossing when the flashing green light is first shown the warning that he should not in the interests of safety start to cross the carriageway.

(3) When the word "WAIT" shown by the indicator for pedestrians is

illuminated it shall convey to a pedestrian the same warning as that conveyed by the red light shown by the pedestrian light signal, that is to say, that he should not in the interests of safety use the crossing.

(4) Any audible signal emitted by any device for emitting audible signals provided in conjunction with the steady green light for pedestrians, and any tactile signal made by any device for making tactile signals similarly provided, shall convey to a pedestrian the same information as that conveyed by the steady green light, that is to say, that he may use the crossing and drivers of vehicles may not cause their vehicle to enter the limits of the crossing.

Significance of additional traffic signs

10. The traffic signs referred to in regulation 6 shall convey the information, prohibitions or requirements mentioned in relation thereto in the captions to the diagrams in Schedule 1 to the Traffic Signs Regulations 1981 mentioned in that regulation.   **C15–12**

Movement of traffic and precedence of pedestrians

11. Regulations 12 to 20 are made under section 25 of the 1984 Act and shall have effect with respect to the movement of traffic (including pedestrians) and the precedence of pedestrians over vehicles at and in the vicinity of a "Pelican" crossing.   **C15–13**

Prohibition on stopping in areas adjacent to "Pelican" crossings

12.—(1) For the purposes of this regulation and the next two following regulations, the expression "vehicle" shall not include a pedal bicycle not having a sidecar attached thereto, whether additional means of propulsion by mechanical power are attached to the bicycle or not.   **C15–14**

(2) Save as provided in regulations 13 and 14, and subject to regulation 15, the driver of a vehicle shall not cause the vehicle or any part thereof to stop in a "Pelican" controlled area.

13. A vehicle shall not by regulation 12 be prevented from stopping in any length of road on any side thereof—   **C15–15**

    (a) if the driver has stopped for the purpose of complying with regulation 16, 17 or 19(b);

    (b) if the driver is prevented from proceeding by circumstances beyond his control or it is necessary for him to stop in order to avoid an accident; or

    (c) for so long as may be necessary to enable the vehicle, if it cannot be used for such purpose without stopping in that length of road, to be used for fire brigade, ambulance or police purposes or in connection with any building operation, demolition or excavation, the removal of any obstruction to traffic, the maintenance, improvement or reconstruction of that length of road, or the laying, erection, alteration, repair or cleaning in or near to that length of road of any sewer or of any main, pipe or apparatus for the supply of gas, water or electricity, or of any telecommunication apparatus kept installed for the purposes of a telecommunications code system or of any other telecommunication apparatus lawfully kept installed in any position.

14.—(1) A vehicle shall not by regulation 12 be prevented from stopping in a "Pelican" controlled area—   **C15–16**

    (a) if the vehicle is stopped for the purposes of making a left or right turn; or

    (b) if the vehicle is a public service vehicle being used—

        (i) in the provision of a service which is a local service within the meaning of the Transport Act 1985; or

        (ii) to carry passengers for hire or reward at separate fare otherwise than in the provision of a local service,

but excluding in each case any such vehicle being used on an excursion or tour, and the vehicle is waiting, after having proceeded past the "Pelican" crossing in relation to which the "Pelican" controlled area is indicated, in order to take up or set down passengers.

(2) In sub-paragraph (b) of paragraph (1) of this regulation "local service" and "excursion or tour" have respectively the same meanings as in the Transport Act 1985.

Saving for crossings constituted in accordance with 1969 Regulations

C15–17   **15.** In relation to any crossing which, immediately before the coming into operation of these Regulations, was constituted as a "Pelican" crossing in accordance with the 1969 Regulations, for a period of two years commencing on the date these Regulations come into operation regulations 12, 13 and 14 shall not apply and regulation 9 of the 1969 Regulations shall, notwithstanding the repeal of those Regulations, continue to have effect but only for so long during that period as the crossing remains so constituted.

Prohibition against the proceeding of vehicles across a "Pelican" crossing

C15–18   **16.** When the vehicular traffic light signal is showing a red light, the driver of a vehicle shall not cause the vehicle or any part thereof to proceed beyond the stop line, or, if that line is not for the time being visible, beyond the post or other structure on which is mounted the primary signal facing the driver on the side of the carriageway on which vehicles approach the crossing.

Precedence of pedestrians over vehicles on a "Pelican" crossing

C15–19   **17.** When the vehicular traffic light signal at a "Pelican" crossing is showing a flashing amber light, every pedestrian, if he is on the carriageway, or a central reservation within the limits of that crossing (but not if he is on a central reservation which lies between two crossings which form part of a system of staggered crossings) before any part of the vehicle has entered those limits, shall have precedence within those limits over that vehicle and the driver of a vehicle shall accord such precedence to any such pedestrian.

Prohibition against the waiting of vehicles and pedestrians on a "Pelican" crossing

C15–20   **18.**—(1) The driver of a vehicle shall not cause the vehicle or any part thereof to stop within the limits of a "Pelican" crossing unless either he is prevented from proceeding by circumstances beyond his control or it is necessary for him to stop in order to avoid an accident.

(2) No pedestrian shall remain on the carriageway within the limits of a "Pelican" crossing longer than is necessary for the purpose of passing over the crossing with reasonable dispatch.

Prohibition against overtaking at a "Pelican" crossing

19. The driver of a vehicle while it or any part of it is in a "Pelican" con-   **C15–21** trolled area and it is proceeding towards the limits of a "Pelican" crossing in relation to which the area is indicated (hereinafter referred to as "the approaching vehicle" shall not cause that vehicle, or any part of it—

  (a) to pass ahead of the foremost part of another moving motor vehicle being a vehicle proceeding in the same direction wholly or partly within that area; or

  (b) subject to the next succeeding regulation, to pass ahead of the foremost part of a stationary vehicle on the same side of the crossing as the approaching vehicle, which stationary vehicle is stopped for the purpose of complying with regulation 16 or 17.

For the purposes of this regulation—

  (i) the reference to another moving motor vehicle is, in a case where only one other motor vehicle is proceeding in the same direction in a "Pelican" controlled area, a reference to that vehicle, and, in a case where more than one other motor vehicle is so proceeding, a reference to such one of those vehicles as is nearest to the limits of the crossing; and

  (ii) the reference to a stationary vehicle is, in a case where only one other vehicle is stopped for the purpose of complying with regulation 16 or 17, a reference to that vehicle, and, in a case where more than one other vehicle is stopped for that purpose, a reference to such one of those vehicles as is nearest to the limits of the crossing.

20. Nothing in paragraph (b) of regulation 19 shall apply so as to prevent the approaching vehicle from passing ahead of the foremost part of a stationary vehicle within the meaning of that paragraph, if the stationary vehicle is stopped for the purpose of complying with regulation 16 or 17 in relation to a "Pelican" crossing which is a separate crossing from the "Pelican" crossing towards the limits of which the approaching vehicle is proceeding.

Regulation 2(1)   SCHEDULE 1

THE SIZE, COLOUR AND TYPE OF TRAFFIC SIGNS AT A
"PELICAN" CROSSING

PART I

Traffic signs

1. The traffic signs which are to be placed at or near a crossing for the pur-   **C15–22** pose of constituting it a "Pelican" crossing shall consist of a combination of—

  (a) vehicular light signals;
  (b) pedestrian light signals; and
  (c) indicators for pedestrians,

of the size, colour and type prescribed by the following provisions of this

Schedule, together with any additional traffic signs placed at or near the crossing pursuant to regulation 6.

Vehicular light signals

  2. The vehicular light signals shall be as follows—

(a) three lights shall be used, one red, one amber, and one green;

(b) the lamps showing the aforesaid lights shall be arranged vertically, the lamp showing the red light being the uppermost and that showing the green light the lowermost;

(c) each lamp shall be separately illuminated and the effective diameter of the lens thereof shall be not less than 195 millimetres nor more than 220 millimetres;

(d) the height of the centre of the amber lens from the surface of the carriageway in the immediate vicinity shall, in the case of signals placed at the side of the cariageway or on a central reservation, be not less than 2.4 metres nor more than 4 metres and, in the case of signals placed elsewhere and over the carriageway, no less than 6.1 metres nor more than 9 metres;

(e) the centres of the lenses of adjacent lamps shall be not less than 305 millimetres nor more than 360 millimetres apart;

(f) the lamp showing the amber light shall be capable of showing a steady light or a flashing light such that it flashes at a rate of not less than 70 nor more than 90 flashes per minute; and

(g) no lettering or symobls shall be used upon the lens.

Pedestrian light signals

  3.—(1) The pedestrian light signals shall be of the size, colour and type shown in the diagrams in Part II of this Schedule.

(2) The height of the lower edge of the container enclosing the light signals from the surface of the carriageway in the immediate vicinity shall be not less than 2.1 metres nor more than 2.6 metres.

(3) The said signals shall be so designed that—

(a) the red figure shown in the said diagrams can be internally illuminated by a steady light;

(b) the green figure shown in the said diagrams can be internally illuminated by a steady light or by a flashing light at a rate of not less than 70 nor more than 90 flashes per minute; and

(c) when one signal is illuminated the other signal is not illuminated.

(4) A device for emitting audible signals may be provided for use when the green figure is illuminated by a steady light.

Indicator for pedestrians

  4.—(1) The indicator for pedestrians shall be of the size, colour and type shown in the diagram in Part III of this Schedule.

(2) The indicator for pedestrians shall be so designed and constructed that "WAIT" as shown on the diagram can be illuminated and that there is incorporated in the indicator a device, which may be a push button or pressure pad and which is hereinafter in ths Schedule referred to as "a push button", which can be used by pedestrians with the effect hereinafter described.

(3) The instruction for pedestrians shown in the diagram may be internally illuminated.

(4) A device for making tactile signals may be provided for use when the green figure shown in the diagram is illuminated by a steady light.

Sequence of signals

5.—(1) The vehicular light signals and pedestrian light signals and the indi-   **C15–26**
cators for pedestrians when they are placed at or near any crossing shall be so designed and constructed that—

(a) before the signals and indicators are operated by the pressing of a push button or as described in paragraph 6 of this Schedule the vehicular light signal shows a steady green light, the pedestrian light signal shows a red light, the word "WAIT" in the indicator for pedestrians is not illuminated, any device for making tactile signals is inactive, and any device for emitting audible signals is silent;

(b) when a push button is pressed—

(i) after the expiration of the vehicle period but before the vehicular light signals are showing a steady amber light, the signals and indicators, unless they are working as described in paragraph 6 of this Schedule, are caused to show lights in the sequences speci-fied in descending order in column 1 in the case of vehicular light signals, in column 2 in the case of pedestrian light signals and in column 3 in the case of the indicators for pedestrians, of either Part IV or Part V of this Schedule;

(ii) when the vehicular light signals are showing a steady amber light or a red light when the signal to pedestrians shows a red or steady green light, there is no effect;

(iii) when the pedestrian light signals are showing a flashing green light, the word "WAIT" in each of the indicators for pedestrians is illuminated immediately and the signals and indicators are caused to show lights in the sequence specified in sub-paragraph (i) of this paragraph at the end of the next vehicle period; and

(iv) after the pedestrian light signals have ceased to show a flashing green light and before the end of the next vehicle period, the word "WAIT" in each of the indicators for pedestrians is illuminated immediately and the signals and indicators are caused to show lights in the sequence specified in sub-paragraph (i) of this para-graph at the end of the vehicle period;

(c) the periods during which lights are shown by the signals and the indicators, commence and terminate in relation to each other as shown in either Part IV or Part V of this Schedule as if each horizontal line therein represented one moment in time, subsequent moments occurring in descending order, but the distances between the horizontal lines do not represent the lengths of the periods during which the lights shown by the signals and the indicator are, or are not, lit.

(2) Where a device for emitting audible signals has been provided pursuant to paragraph 3(4) of this Schedule, it shall be so designed and constructed that a pulsed sound is emitted throughout every period when the pedestrian light signals are showing a steady green light, and at the same time the vehicular light signals are showing a red light, but only during such periods and at no

other times, save that such a device need not operate during the hours of darkness.

(3) Where a device for making tactile signals has been provided pursuant to paragraph 4(4) of this Schedule, it shall be so designed and constructed that a regular movement perceptible to touch by pedestrians is made throughout every period when the pedestrian light signals are showing a steady green light, and at the same time the vehicular light signals are showing a red light, but only during such periods and at no other times.

(4) In this paragraph "vehicle period" means such a period as may be fixed from time to time in relation to a "Pelican" crossing, which commences when the vehicular light signals cease to show a flashing amber light and during which the vehicular traffic light signals show a green light.

Operation by remote control

C15–27   6. The vehicular light signals, pedestrian light signals, indicators for pedestrians, any device for making tactile signals, and any device for emitting audible signals, when they are place at or near any crossing may also be so designed and constructed that they can by remote control be made to operate—

(a) as if a push button has been pressed; and
(b) so that the pressing of a push button has no effect, other than causing the word "WAIT" in each of the indicators for the pedestrians to be illuminated, until normal operation is resumed.

C15–28

SCHEDULE 1

PART IV

SEQUENCE OF OPERATION OF VEHICULAR AND PEDESTRIAN LIGHT SIGNALS AND INDICATOR FOR PEDESTRIANS (BUT NOT THE AUDIBLE SIGNALS)

Sequence of vehicular traffic light signals	Sequence of pedestrian signals	
	Pedestrian light signals	Indicator for pedestrians
(1)	(2)	(3)
Green light	Red light	The word "WAIT" is illuminated
Amber light		
Red light		
	Green light	The word "WAIT" is not illuminated
Flashing amber light	Flashing green light	The word "WAIT" is illuminated
	Red light	
Green light		

SCHEDULE 1   **C15–29**

PART V

ALTERNATIVE SEQUENCE OF OPERATION OF VEHICULAR AND PEDESTRIAN
LIGHT SIGNALS AND INDICATOR FOR PEDESTRIANS (BUT NOT THE AUDIBLE
SIGNALS)

Sequence of vehicular traffic light signals	Sequence of pedestrian signals	
(1)	Pedestrian light signals (2)	Indicator for pedestrians (3)
Green light	Red light	The word "WAIT" is illuminated
Amber light		
Red light		
	Green light	The word "WAIT" is not illuminated
Flashing amber light	Flashing green light	The word "WAIT" is illuminated
	Red light	
Green light		

Regulation 2(2)   SCHEDULE 2

THE MANNER OF INDICATING THE PRESENCE AND LIMITS OF
A "PELICAN" CROSSING AND "PELICAN" CONTROLLED AREA

General

1. In this Schedule, and except where otherwise stated, any reference to a   **C15–30**
numbered diagram is a reference to the diagram bearing that number in this
Schedule.

2.—(1) Every crossing which is a "Pelican" crossing on a road which is not a
one-way street shall have its limits indicated, subject to the following provisions of this Schedule, by the pattern of studs on or in and lines on the carriageway in the manner shown—

    (a) in diagram 1 where there is no central reservation;
    (b) in diagram 2 where there is a central reservation, but the crossing does
        not form part of a system of staggered crossings; and
    (c) in diagram 3 where the crossing forms part of a system of staggered
        crossings.

(2) Every crossing which is a "Pelican" crossing on a road which is a one-
way street shall have its limits indicated, subject to the following provisions of
this Schedule, by the pattern of studs on or in and lines on the carriageway in
the manner shown—

705

(a) in diagram 4 where there is no central reservation;

(b) in diagram 5 where there is a central reservation but the crossing does not form part of a system of staggered crossings; and

(c) in diagram 6 where the crossing forms part of a system of staggered crossings.

Manner of indicating the limits of the crossing

C15–31   3. The limits of a "Pelican" crossing shall be indicated by two lines of studs in the positions shown, and in accordance with the measurements in, the diagram corresponding to the type of crossing.

4. The two lines of studs indicating the limits of the crossing need not be at right angles to the edge of the carriageway, but shall form straight lines and shall as near as is reasonably practicable be parallel to each other.

Manner of indicating a "Pelican" controlled area and provision as to placing the stop line

C15–32   5. Subject to paragraph 8 of this Schedule, the presence and limits of a "Pelican" controlled area shall be indicated by the pattern of lines placed in the positions shown, and in accordance with the measurements, in the diagram corresponding to the type of crossing, and in accordance with the provisions of paragraphs 6 and 7 of this Schedule.

6. Where the crossing is on a road which is not a one-way street the pattern of lines shall consist of—

(1) a stop line placed on the carriageway parallel to the nearer row of studs indicating the limits of the crossing and extending, in the manner indicated in the appropriate diagram, across the part of the carriageway used by vehicles approaching the crossing from the side on which the stop line is placed;

(2) two or more longitudinal white broken lines (hereinafter referred to as "zig-zag lines") placed on the carriageway or, where the road is a dual-carriageway road, on each part of the carriageway, each zig-zag line containing not less than eight nor more than 18 marks and extending away from the crossing in the manner indicated in the appropriate diagram;

(3) subject to sub-paragraph (4) of this paragraph, where a central reservation is provided the road marking shown in diagram 1040.1 in Schedule 2 to the Traffic Signs Regulations 1981 may be placed on the carriageway between the zig-zag lines on the approaches to the central reservation;

(4) where a central reservation is provided connecting crossings which form part of a system of staggered crossings, the road markings mentioned in sub-paragraph (3) of this paragraph shall be placed on the carriageway in the manner indicated in diagram 3.

7. Where the crossing is on a road which is a one-way street the pattern of lines shall consist of:

(1) a stop line placed parallel to the nearer row of studs indicating the limits of the crossing and extending—

(a) in the case of a crossing of type shown in diagram 4 or 5, from one edge of the carriageway to the other; and

    (b) in the case of a crossing of the type shown in diagram 6, from the
edge of the carriageway to the central reservation;

    (2) two or more zig-zag lines placed on the carriageway, each containing
not less than eight and not more than 18 marks, and extending away from
the crossing;

    (3) subject to sub-paragraph (4) of this paragraph, where a central reservation is provided the road marking shown in diagram 1041 in Schedule 2
to the Traffic Signs Regulations 1981 may be placed on the carriageway
between the zig-zag lines on the approaches to the central reservation;
and

    (4) where a central reservation is provided connecting crossings which
form part of a system of staggered crossings, the road markings mentioned
in sub-paragraph (3) of this paragraph shall be placed on the carriageway
in the manner indicated in diagram 6.

8.—(1) Where the appropriate authority is satisfied in relation to a particular area of carriageway in the vicinity of a "Pelican" crossing that by reason of
the layout of, or character of, the roads in the vicinity of the crossing it would
be impracticable to lay the pattern of lines as shown in the diagrams in, and in
accordance with paragraphs 5 to 7 of, this Schedule any of the following variations as respects the pattern shall be permitted— **C15–33**

    (a) the number of marks contained in each zig-zag line may be reduced
        from eight to not less than two; and

    (b) a mark contained in a zig-zag line may be varied in length so as to
        extend for a distance not less than 1 metre and less than 2 metres, but
        where such a variation is made as respects a mark each other mark in
        each zig-zag line shall be of the same or substantially the same length
        as that mark, so however that the number of marks in each zig-zag line
        shall not be more than eight nor less than two.

    (2) The angle of the stop line in relation to the nearer line of studs indicating
the limits of a crossing may be varied, if the appropriate authority is satisfied
that such variation is necessary having regard to the angle of the crossing in
relation to the edge of the carriageway at the place where the crossing is
situated.

    (3) The maximum distance of 3 metres between the stop line and the nearer
line of studs indicating the limits of the crossing shown in the diagrams in this
Schedule may be increased to such greater distance, not in any case exceeding
10 metres, as the appropriate authority may decide.

    (4) Where by reason of regulation 3(3) an area of carriageway in the vicinity
of a "Pelican" crossing is not constituted a "Pelican" controlled area by the
placing of a pattern of lines as provided in the foregoing provisions of this
Schedule, a stop line shall nevertheless be placed on the carriageway as previously provided in this Schedule.

Colour and dimensions of road markings and studs

9. The road markings shown in the diagrams in this Schedule shall be white
in colour, and may be illuminated by reflecting material. **C15–34**

10.—(1) The studs shown in the diagrams shall be either white, silver or
light grey in colour and shall not be fitted with reflective lenses.

    (2) The said studs shall be either circular in shape with a diameter of not
more than 110 millimetres or less than 95 millimetres or square in shape
with each side being not more than 110 millimetres or less than 95 millimetres.

    (3) Any stud which is fixed or embedded in the carriageway shall not pro-

ject more than 18 millimetres above the carriageway at its highest point nor more than 6 millimetres at its edges.

11. Where in any diagram in this Schedule a dimension or measurement is indicated in brackets against a dimension or measurement not indicated in brackets any dimension or measurement indicated in brackes may be treated as an alternative to the dimension or measurement not so indicated.

Supplementary

12. The foregoing provisions of this Schedule shall be regarded as having been complied with in the case of any pattern of studs or white lines if most of the studs or lengths of white lines comply notwithstanding that one or more studs or some of the lengths of white lines may not comply with those provisions by reason of discoloration, temporary removal, displacement or for some other reason so long as the general appearance of the pattern of studs or white lines is not thereby materially impaired.

PART III

GENERAL DIRECTIONS

Citation

1. The Directions contained in this Part of this Instrument may be cited as the "Pelican" Pedestrian Crossings General Directions 1987.

Number and manner of placing of vehicular light signals

2.—(1) There shall be placed at a "Pelican" crossing which is on a road which is not a one-way street and which is of the type specified in column 1 of Part I of the Table below, the vehicular light signals facing each direction of traffic specified in relation thereto in column 2 of Part I of the said Table.

(2) There shall be placed at a "Pelican" crossing which is on a one-way street and which is of a type specified in column 1 of Part II of the said Table the vehicular light signals specified in relation thereto in column 2 of Part II of the said Table.

(3) The vehicular light signals referred to in paragraphs (1) and (2) shall be placed as primary signals or secondary signals as specified in column 2 of the said Table.

(4) One or more additional vehicular light signals may be placed either as a primary signal or as a secondary signal on the side of, or over, the carriageway or on any central reservation.

(5) Every vehicular light signal placed at a "Pelican" crossing pursuant to the provisions of this direction shall face the stream of traffic which it is intended to control.

TABLE   **C15–36**

PART I

PELICAN CROSSING ON ROADS WHICH ARE NOT ONE-WAY STREETS

(1) *Type of crossing*	(2) *Vehicular light signals required facing each direction of traffic*
Crossing on a road without a central reservation.	One primary signal on the side of the carriageway nearest to the direction of vehicular traffic and one secondary signal on the side of the carriageway furthest away from the direction of vehicular traffic.
Crossing on a road with a central reservation which does not form part of a system of staggered crossings.	One primary signal on the side of the carriageway nearest to the direction of vehicular traffic and one secondary signal on the central reservation.
Crossing which forms part of a system of staggered crossings.	One primary signal on the side of the carriageway nearest to the direction of vehicular traffic and one primary signal on the central reservation.

PART II

PELICAN CROSSINGS ON ROADS WHICH ARE ONE-WAY STREETS

(1) *Type of crossing*	(2) *Vehicular light signals required*
Crossing on a road without a central reservation.	One primary signal on the side of the carriageway.
Crossing on a road with a central reservation which does not form part of a system of staggered crossings.	One primary signal on the side of the carriageway and one secondary signal on the central reservation.
Crossing which forms part of a system of staggered crossings.	One primary signal on the side of the carriageway and one primary signal on the central reservation.

Number and manner of placing of pedestrian light signals and indictors for pedestrians

3.—(1) At least one pedestrian light signal and at least one indicator for ped-   **C15–37**
estrians shall be placed at each end of a "Pelican" crossing.

(2) Where there is a central reservation in a crossing, one or more additional indicators for pedestrians shall be placed on the central reservation.

(3) Each pedestrian light signal at either end of the crossing shall be so placed as to be clearly visible to any person who is about to use the crossing at the other end of the crossing.

(4) Each indicator for pedestrians shall be so placed that the push button in the indicator is readily accessible to pedestrians who wish to press it.

Additional traffic signs

C15–38   4. The traffic signs specified in diagrams 610 and 611 in Schedule 1 to the Traffic Signs Regulations 1981 shall be placed only on a central reservation in a crossing, or on a central reservation which lies between two crossings which form part of a system of staggered crossings.

Colouring of containers and posts

5.—(1) The containers of the vehicular light signals and of the pedestrian light signals shall be coloured black and may be mounted with a backing board and if so mounted the backing board shall be coloured black and may have a white border not less than 45 millimetres nor more than 55 millimetres in width which may be of a reflective material.

(2) Where a vehicular light signal, a pedestrian light signal or an indicator for pedestrians is mounted on a post specially provided for the purpose, that part of the post which extends above ground level shall be coloured grey and may have one white band not less than 140 millimetres nor more than 160 millimetres in depth, the lower edge of the band being not less than 1.5 metres nor more than 1.7 metres above the level of the surface of the ground in the immediate vicinity.

(3) Any box attached to a post or other structure on which pedestrian light signals or vehicular light signals are mounted and housing apparatus designed to control, or to monitor, or to control and monitor, the operation of such signals shall be coloured grey, yellow or black, or a combination of any of those colours.

Approval for mechanisms and sequence adjustments

C15–39   6.—(1) Vehicular light signals, pedestrian light signals and indicators for pedestrians may be placed at or near any "Pelican" crossing only if the apparatus (including the content of all instructions stored in, or executable by, it) used to secure that the signals and indicators comply with the relevant provisions of the Regulations is of a type approved in writing by or on behalf of the Secretary of State.

(2) Such signals may be retained in place notwithstanding the subsequent withdrawal of any approval relating to any such apparatus.

Special cases

7. Nothing in these Directions shall be taken to limit the power of the Secretary of State by any special direction to dispense with, add to or modify any of the requirements of the Directions in relation to any particular case.

MOTOR VEHICLES (DRIVING LICENCES) REGULATIONS 1987

(S.I. 1987 No. 1378)

Citation and commencement

1. These Regulations may be cited as the Motor Vehicles (Driving Licences)   **C16–01**
Regulations 1987 and shall come into force on 3rd September 1987.

Revocation and saving

2. The Regulations specified in Schedule 1 are hereby revoked but, subject   **C16–02**
as hereinafter provided, any reference in any application or appointment
made, notice or approval given, licence, certificate or other documents
granted or issued or other thing done under the said Regulations to any provision of the Regulations revoked by these Regulations, whether specifically
or by means of a general description, shall, unless the context otherwise
requires, be construed as a reference to the corresponding provision of these
Regulations.

Interpretation

3.—(1) In these Regulations, unless the context otherwise requires, the fol-   **C16–03**
lowing expressions have the meanings hereby respectively assigned to them,
that is to say:—
    "1972 Act" means the Road Traffic Act 1972;
    "1981 Act" means the Public Passenger Vehicles Act 1981;
    "1985 Act" means the Transport Act 1985;
    "appropriate driving test" and "extended driving test" have the same
        meaning as in section 36 of the Road Traffic Offenders Act 1988;
    "category" in relation to a class of motor vehicles means a category of
        motor vehicles of the classes specified in the second column of
        Schedule 3, and a category identified by a letter means the category
        corresponding to the letter in the first column of that Schedule;
    "controlled by a pedestrian" in relation to a vehicle means that the
        vehicle either—
    (a) is constructed or adapted for use under such control; or
    (b) is constructed or adapted for use either under such control or un-
        der the control of a person carried on it but is not for the time
        being in use under, or proceeding under, the control of a person
        carried on it;
    "disability" includes disease;
    "full licence" means a licence other than a provisional licence;
    "kerbside weight" means the weight of a vehicle when it carries—
    (a) in the case of a motor vehicle—
        (i) no person; and
        (ii) a full supply of fuel in its tank, an adequate supply of other

711

liquids incidental to its propulsion and no load other than the tools and equipment with which it is normally equipped; or

(b) in the case of a trailer, no person and is otherwise unladen;

"licence" means a licence to drive a motor vehicle granted under Part III of the 1972 Act other than a large goods vehicle or passenger-carrying vehicle driver's licence as defined in section 110(2) of the Road Traffic Act 1988;

"licensing authority" means the Secretary of State;

"maximum authorised mass" has the same meaning—

(a) in relation to goods vehicles as "permissible maximum weight" in section 108(1) of the Road Traffic Act 1988, and

(b) in relation to any other vehicle or trailer as "maximum gross weight" in regulation 3(2) of the Road Vehicles (Construction and Use) Regulations 1986;

"maximum speed" means the speed which a vehicle is incapable, by reason of its construction, of exceeding on the level under its own power when fully laden;

"moped" means—

(a) in the case only of motor cycles which are first used on or after 1st August 1977, a motor cycle (not being a motor vehicle of category K) which has a maximum speed which does not exceed 30 miles per hour, a kerbside weight which does not exceed 250 kilograms, and, if propelled by an internal combustion engine, an engine the cylinder capacity of which does not exceed 50 cubic centimetres, or

(b) in the case only of motor cycles which are first used before 1st August 1977, a motor cycle which has an engine with a cylinder capacity not exceeding 50 cubic centimetres and is equipped with pedals by means of which the cycle is capable of being propelled;

"provisional licence" means a licence granted by virtue of section 88(2) of the 1972 Act;

"test" means a test of competence to drive conducted under section 85 of the 1972 Act and includes an extended driving test;

"vehicle propelled by electrical power" means a vehicle of which the motive power is solely derived from any electrical storage battery carried on the vehicle and not connected to any source of power when the vehicle is in motion;

"vehicle with automatic transmission" means a vehicle in which the driver is not provided with any means whereby he may, independently of the use of the accelerator or the brakes, vary gradually the proportion of power being produced by the engine which is transmitted to the road wheels of the vehicle.

(2) In determining for the purpose of these Regulations when a motor cycle is first used, the date of such first use shall be taken to be such date as is the earliest of the undermentioned relevant dates applicable to that cycle—

(a) in the case of a motor cycle registered under the Roads Act 1920, the Vehicles (Excise) Act 1949, the Vehicles (Excise) Act 1962 or the Vehicles (Excise) Act 1971, the relevant date is the date on which it was first so registered; and

(b) in each of the following cases:—

(i) in the case of a motor cycle which is being or has been used under a trade licence as defined in section 16 of the Vehicles (Excise) Act 1971 (otherwise than for the purposes of demonstration or testing or of being delivered from premises of the manufacturer by whom it was made, or of a distributor of vehicles or dealer in vehicles to premises of a distributor of vehicles, dealer in vehicles or purchaser thereof, or to premises of a person obtaining possession thereof under a hiring agreement or hire purchase agreement);

(ii) in the case of a motor cycle which belongs or has belonged to the Crown and which is or was used or appropriated for use for naval, military or air force purposes;

(iii) in the case of a motor cycle which belongs or has belonged to a visiting force or a headquarters or defence organisation to which in each case the Visiting Forces and International Headquarters (Application of Law) Order 1965 applies;

(iv) in the case of a motor cycle which has been used on roads outside Great Britain and has been imported into Great Britain; and

(v) in the case of a motor cycle which has been used otherwise than on roads after being sold or supplied by retail and before being registered,

the relevant date is the date of manufacture of the cycle.

In this paragraph "sold or supplied by retail" means sold or supplied otherwise than to a person acquiring solely for the purpose of re-sale or re-supply for a valuable consideration.

(3) The provisions of paragraph 6 of Schedule 9 to the Road Vehicles (Construction and Use) Regulations 1986 shall apply for determining for the purposes of the definition of "moped" in paragraph (1), whether the maximum speed of a motor cycle does not exceed 30 mph.

(4) Except where otherwise expressly provided, any reference in these Regulations to a numbered regulation or Schedule is a reference to the regulation or Schedule bearing that number in these Regulations, and any reference to a numbered paragraph is a reference to the paragraph bearing that number in the regulation in which the reference occurs.

Minimum ages for holding or obtaining licences

4.—(1) Subsection (1) of section 96 of the 1972 Act (which specifies the minimum age for holding or obtaining a licence to drive certain classes of motor vehicles) shall have effect as if in the Table in that subsection—   **C16–04**

(a) in item 2, the age of 17 were substituted for the age of 16 in relation to all motor cycles other than—

   (i) mopeds;

   (ii) motor cycles which are mowing machines; or

   (iii) motor cycles which are vehicles controlled by a pedestrian;

(b) in item 3, the age of 16 were substituted for the age of 17 in the case of a person to whom an award of a mobility allowance has been made in pursuance of section 37A of the Social Security Act 1975 provided that where the award was made before he attained the age of 16 it is in force when he attains that age;

(c) in item 4, in relation to an agricultural tractor which—

   (i) is so constructed that the whole of its weight is transmitted to the road surface by means of wheels;

   (ii) has an overall width not exceeding 2.45 metres;

   (iii) is chargeable with duty under section 1 of the Vehicles (Excise) Act 1971 by reference to paragraph 1 of Schedule 3 to that Act as being an agricultural machine or, by virtue of the provisions of section 7(1) of that Act, is not chargeable with duty thereunder; and

      (iv) is driven without a trailer attached to it, other than a trailer which has an overall width not exceeding 2.45 metres and which is either a two-wheeled or close-coupled four-wheeled trailer,

the age of 16 were substituted for the age of 17, but in the case of a person who has not passed the test of competence prescribed under section 85(2) of the 1972 Act to drive such a tractor, only while taking, proceeding to or returning from, such a test;

(d) in item 6, the age of 17 were substituted for the age of 21 in relation to a road roller falling within that item if the roller—

      (i) is propelled otherwise than by steam;

      (ii) has an unladen weight not exceeding 11,690 kilograms, and

      (iii) is not constructed or adapted for the conveyance of a load other than the following articles, that is to say, water, fuel, accumulators and other equipment used for the purpose of propulsion, loose tools, loose equipment and objects such as are mentioned in paragraph (3) below,

and if no wheel of the roller is fitted with a pneumatic, soft or elastic tyre;

(e) in item 6, the age of 18 were substituted for the age of 21 in the case of a person employed by a Health Authority or, in Scotland, the Common Services Agency when driving a vehicle for the purposes of an ambulance service of such an Authority or of that Agency;

(f) in item 6, the age of 18 were substituted for the age of 21 in the case of a person who fulfils the conditions—

      (i) that he is employed by a registered employer, and

      (ii) that he is a registered employee of such an employer,

in relation to any vehicle (other than a road roller) which is a heavy goods vehicle (hgv) of a class or a large goods vehicle (lgv) of a category to which his training agreement applies and is owned or operated by his employer or by a registered hgv or lgv training establishment;

(g) in item 6, the age of 18 were substituted for the age of 21 in relation to a large passenger vehicle where—

      (i) the driver of the vehicle is not engaged in the carriage of passengers and either holds a licence to drive a public service vehicle granted under section 22 of the 1981 Act or a passenger-carrying vehicle driver's licence, is undergoing a test of his ability to drive a passenger-carrying vehicle in pursuance of regulations for the time being in force under section 89 of the Road Traffic Act 1988, or is acting under the supervision of a person who holds such a licence; or

      (ii) the driver is engaged in the carriage of passengers—

          (a) on a regular service over a route which does not exceed 50 kilometres; or

          (b) on a national transport operation when the vehicle used is constructed and equipped to carry not more than 17 persons including the driver,

and the vehicle is operated under a PSV operator's licence granted under section 12 of the 1981 Act, a permit granted under section 19 of the 1985 Act or a community bus permit granted under section 22 of that Act, and in each case the driver holds a licence to drive the vehicle granted under section 22 of the 1981 Act or a passenger-carrying vehicle driver's licence;

(h) in items 5 and 6, the age of 17 were substituted for the ages of 18 and 21 respectively in the case of members of the armed forces of the Crown in relation to any vehicle when being used in the course of urgent work of national importance in accordance with an order of the Defence Council in pursuance of the Defence (Armed Forces) Regulations 1939 which were continued permanently in force in the form set out in Part C of Schedule 2 to the Emergency Laws (Repeal) Act 1959 by section 2 of the Emergency Powers Act 1964;

(i) in items 5 and 6, the age of 17 were substituted for the ages of 18 and 21 respectively in the case of a member of the armed forces of the Crown when receiving instruction in the driving of large goods vehicles of any category in preparation for a test of competence under section 89 of the Road Traffic Act 1988 to drive vehicles of that category, or when taking, proceeding to, or returning from any such test.

(2) For the purposes of paragraph (1)(c) any implement fitted to a tractor shall be deemed to form part of the tractor notwithstanding that it is not a permanent or essentially permanent fixture, and in that paragraph—

(i) "overall width", in relation to a vehicle, means the width of the vehicle measured between vertical planes parallel to the longitudinal axis of the vehicle and passing through the extreme projecting points thereof exclusive of any driving mirror and so much of the distortion of any tyre as is caused by the weight of the vehicle; and

(ii) "close-coupled", in relation to wheels on the same side of a trailer, means fitted so that at all times while the trailer is in motion they remain parallel to the longitudinal axis of the trailer and that the distance between the centres of their respective areas of contact with the road surface does not exceed 840 millimetres.

(3) For the purposes of paragraph 1(d) the unladen weight of a vehicle shall be treated as including the weight of any object for the time being attached to the vehicle, being an object specially designed to be so attached for the purpose of temporarily increasing the vehicle's gross weight.

(4) In paragraph 1(f) and in this paragraph—

"heavy goods vehicle" has the same meaning as in Part I of Schedule 1 to the Road Traffic (Driver Licensing and Information Systems) Act 1989;

"large goods vehicle", "passenger-carrying vehicle" and "passenger-carrying vehicle driver's licence" have the same meaning as in Part IV of the Road Traffic Act 1988;

"registered" means registered for the time being by the Training Committee in accordance with the relevant provisions of the training scheme;

"the Training Committee" means the committee which has been established by the employers' associations and the trade unions in the road goods transport industry with a constitution approved by the Secretary of State and which is known as the National Joint Training Committee for Young HGV Drivers in the Road Goods Transport Industry or the National Joint Training Committee for Young LGV Drivers in the Road Goods Transport Industry;

"the training scheme" means the scheme which has been established by the Training Committee with the approval of the Secretary of State for training young drivers of hgvs or lgvs and which provides for—

(a) the registration by the Training Committee of employers who are willing and able to provide hgv or lgv driver training for persons employed by them;

715

(b) the registration by the Training Committee of persons operating establishments for providing hgv or lgv driver training;

(c) a syllabus for hgv or lgv driver training; and

(d) the registration by the Training Committee of individual employees who are undergoing, or are to undergo, hgv or lgv driver training in the service of a registered employer in accordance with a form of agreement approved by the Training Committee;

and "training agreement", in relation to an individual who is undergoing, or is to undergo, such training as aforesaid, means his agreement therefore with his registered employer in pursuance of the training scheme.

(5) In paragraph (1)(g), "large passenger vehicle" means a motor vehicle which is constructed solely to carry passengers and their effects and is adapted to carry more than nine persons inclusive of the driver and expressions used which are also used in the Community Drivers' Ages and Hours of Work Regulation have the same meaning as in that instrument.

(6) In paragraph (5), "the Community Drivers' Ages and Hours of Work Regulation" means Council Regulation (EEC) 3820/85 as read with regulation 4 of the Community Drivers Hours and Recording Equipment (Exemptions and Supplementary Provisions) Regulations 1986.

Applications for the grant of licences

C16–05   5.—(1) Applications for the grant of a licence may be received and dealt with at any time within two months before the date on which the grant of the licence is to take effect.

(2) For the purposes of section 89(1)(f) of the Road Traffic Act 1988 the period of normal residence in Great Britain or, as the case may be, the United Kingdom, during which the holder of an exchangeable licence shall be eligible for the grant of a licence is five years.

Refusal of a provisional licence for group D

C16–06   6.—(1) Notwithstanding anything in section 88 of the 1972 Act and subject to paragraph (2), the licensing authority shall refuse to grant a provisional licence authorising the driving of a motor cycle of a class included in category A if the applicant has held such a licence and the licence applied for would come into force—

(a) except in the circumstances specified in sub-paragraph (b) of this paragraph, within the period of one year beginning at the end of the period for which the previous licences authorised (or would, if not surrendered or revoked, have authorised) the driving of such a motor cycle; or

(b) where the licence would be for a period of less than two years and the previous licence was surrendered or revoked, within the period of two months beginning on the date of such surrender or revocation.

(2) Paragraph (1) shall not apply—

(a) where the previous licence was granted before 1st October 1982;

(b) where the applicant appears to the Secretary of State to be a person suffering from a relevant or prospective disability within the meaning of section 87 of the 1972 Act; or

(c) where the previous licence was surrendered or revoked in pursuance of section 89(2) or (3) of the 1972 Act.

Fees for licences

7. The fee payable for a licence granted on or after 1st February 1992 shall be, in the case of a licence of a description and in certain instances granted in particular circumstances, specified in column (1) of the Table in this regulation, the fee specified in relation to that licence in column (2) of that Table.

(1) *Description of Licence*	(2) *Fee*
(1) A licence (except a licence falling in paragraph (2) below) granted to a person—	
(a) who has not held a licence before, or	
(b) whose last licence was a full licence granted before 1st January 1976, or	
(c) whose last licence was a full licence which expired before 31st December 1978, or	
(d) whose last licence was a provisional licence granted before 1st October 1982.	£21
(2) A full licence granted in exchange for a full Northern Ireland licence or to a person who has held a full Northern Ireland licence which was granted on or after 1st January 1976.	£6
(3) A full or provisional licence granted in exchange for a subsisting licence or in place of a licence revoked pursuant to section 99(3) of the Road Traffic Act 1988 except—	
(a) where the licence granted is a first full licence granted in exchange for a provisional licence, or	
(b) where the licence is issued pursuant to section 118(4) of the Road Traffic Act 1988, or	
(c) where the subsisting or revoked licence is surrendered pursuant to section 99(3) or (4) of the Road Traffic Act 1988 and the Secretary of State is required to grant a new licence free of charge.	£6
(4) A provisional licence (except a licence falling in paragraph (1) above or (7) or (9) below) which authorises the driving of vehicles of any class in category A save where such a licence is granted in place of a licence which was revoked pursuant to section 93 or 94 of the Road Traffic Act 1988.	£6
(5) A full or provisional licence (except a licence falling in paragraph (1)(a) above) granted to a person on or after that person's 70th birthday except where that person has been granted a licence falling within this paragraph within the previous 3 years and, on the grant of that licence, paid the prescribed fee for it.	£6
(6) The first licence (except a licence falling in paragraph (1) above or (7) or (8) below) granted to a person after the expiration of a period of disqualification imposed on him by an order of the court—	
(a) in the circumstances prescribed under section 94(4) of the Road Traffic Act 1988 but irrespective of the date when the order of the court was made;	£20
(b) otherwise than in the circumstances prescribed under section 94(4) of that Act.	£12
(7) The first provisional licence (except a licence falling in paragraph (1) above) granted to a person after he has been disqualified by an order of the court made pursuant to section 36 of the Road Traffic Offenders Act 1988 whether or not the court also made an order pursuant to section 34 or 35 of that Act—	

(1) *Description of Licence*	(2) *Fee*
(a) in the circumstances prescribed under section 94(4) of the Road Traffic Act 1988 but irrespective of the date when the order of the court was made;	£20
(b) otherwise than in the circumstances prescribed under section 94(4) of that Act.	£12
(8) The first full licence granted to a person after he has passed a driving test which he was required to take by an order of the court made pursuant to section 36 of the Road Traffic Offenders Act 1988 except where the person has never held a full licence.	£6
(9) A duplicate licence.	£6

Duration of provisional licences

C16–08   8.—(1) Subject to paragraph (2), for the purposes of subsection (1A) of section 89 of the 1972 Act there is hereby prescribed—

    (a) a motor cycle of a class falling within category A;

    (b) a period of two years; and

    (c) in relation to a licence granted to the holder of a previous licence which was surrendered, revoked or treated as being revoked, the circumstances—

        (i) that the licence would come into force within the period of one year beginning on the date the previous licence was surrendered, revoked, or treated as being revoked; and

        (ii) that the licence when granted would be for a period of one month or more.

(2) Paragraph (1) shall not apply in the case of a licence granted in pursuance of section 89(1)(aa) or (4) of the 1972 Act.

Conditions attached to provisional licences

C16–09   9.—(1) Subject to paragraphs (2), (3), (4) and (5), the holder of a provisional licence shall comply with the following conditions in relation to motor vehicles of a class which he is authorised to drive by virtue of the provisional licence, that is to say he shall not drive or ride such a motor vehicle—

    (a) otherwise than under the supervision of a qualified driver who is present with him in or on the vehicle;

    (b) unless a distinguishing mark in the form set out in Schedule 2 is displayed on the vehicle in such manner as to be clearly visible to other persons using the road from within a reasonable distance from the front and from the back of the vehicle;

    (c) while it is being used to draw a trailer; and

    (d) in the case of a motor bicycle not having attached thereto a side-car, while carrying on it another person;

Provided that where the holder of a provisional licence has passed a test which authorises him to be granted a full licence to drive or ride a particular class of vehicles the above-mentioned conditions shall cease to apply in relation to the driving or riding (as the case may be) by him of motor vehicles of that class.

(2) The condition specified in paragraph (1)(a) shall not apply when the holder of the provisional licence—

(a) is undergoing a test [...];
(b) is driving a vehicle (not being a motor car) constructed to carry only one person and not adapted to carry more than one person;
(c) is driving a vehicle the unladen weight of which does not exceed 815 kilograms, being a vehicle propelled by electrical power, constructed or adapted to carry only one person and constructed or adapted for the carriage of goods or burden of any description;
(d) is driving a road roller the unladen weight of which does not exceed 3050 kilograms, being a vehicle constructed or adapted for the carriage of goods or burden of any description;
(e) is riding a motor bicycle, whether or not having attached thereto a side-car; or
(f) is driving a motor vehicle on a road in an exempted island.

(3) The condition specified in paragraph (1)(c) shall not apply when the holder of the provisional licence is driving an agricultural tractor, nor shall it prevent the holder of a provisional licence from driving an articulated vehicle.

(4) The condition specified in paragraph (1)(d) shall not apply when the holder of the provisional licence is riding a pedal cycle of the tandem type to which additional means of propulsion by mechanical power are attached.

(5) Any holder of a provisional licence need not comply with this regulation during any period in which—
(a) he is treated, by virtue of regulation 25, for the purposes of section 84(1) and (2) of the 1972 Act as the holder of a licence; or
(b) he is entitled by virtue of article 2(1) of the Motor Vehicles (International Circulation) Order 1975
to drive motor vehicles of a class which he is authorised to drive by virtue of the provisional licence.

(6) In this regulation—
"exempted island" means any island outside the mainland of Great Britain from which motor vehicles, unless constructed for special purposes, can at no time be conveniently driven to a road in any other part of Great Britain by reason of the absence of any bridge, tunnel, ford or other way suitable for the passage of such motor vehicles but this expression "exempted island" does not include any of the following islands, namely, the Isle of Wight, St. Mary's (Isles of Scilly), the islands of Arran, Barra, Bute, Great Cumbrae, Islay, the island which comprises Lewis and Harris, Mainland (Orkney), Mainland (Shetland), Mull, the island which comprises North Uist, Benbecula and South Uist, Skye and Tiree;
"leg disability" means a disability which consists solely of any one or more of following—
(a) the absence of a leg or legs;
(b) the deformity of a leg or legs; or
(c) the loss of use of a leg or legs;
and references to a leg include references to a foot or part of a leg or foot, and the reference to loss of use, in relation to a leg, includes a reference to a deficiency of movement or power in the leg;
"qualified driver" means a person who holds—
(i) a full licence authorising him to drive as a full licence holder a motor vehicle of the same class as the vehicle being driven by the holder of the provisional licence; or
(ii) in the case only of the supervision of the driver of a motor car by a person whose licence is limited, in pursuance of an application in that behalf by him or under section 87(4)(ii) of the 1972 Act solely on account of a leg disability to motor vehicles of a particular construction or design or class, a full licence authorising him so to

drive motor cars of a class falling within the same category as the motor car being driven by the holder of the provisional licence and who, in either such case except in the case of a member of the armed forces of the Crown acting in the course of his duties, is at least 21 years of age and has held the licence referred to above for at least 3 years.

Restricted provisional licences

C16–10   10. A provisional licence shall be restricted so as to authorise only the driving of motor vehicles of a class included in category K in any case where the applicant is unable to read in good daylight at a distance of 20.5 metres (with the aid of glasses or contact lenses if worn) a registration mark which is fixed to a motor vehicle and comprises letters and figures 79.4 millimetres high.

Full licences not carrying provisional entitlement

C16–11   11.—(1) Section 88(4) of the 1972 Act shall not apply in the case of a licence which—
  (a) is limited to vehicles of a particular construction or design whether pursuant to an application in that behalf by the holder of the licence or pursuant to section 87(4)(ii) of the 1972 Act; or
  (b) authorises its holder to drive vehicles of a class included in category K only.
  (2) Section 88(4) of the 1972 Act in its application to a full licence granted on or after 1st October 1982 which does not authorise the driving of a vehicle of a class included in category B, B plus E, B1, C1, C1 plus E, D1, D1 plus E or P shall have effect subject to the limitation that it shall not authorise the holder of such a licence to drive any motor cycle of a class included in category A subject to the same conditions as if he were authorised by a provisional licence to drive the last mentioned vehicles.

Signature of licences

C16–12   12. Every person to whom a licence is granted shall forthwith sign it in ink with his usual signature.

Lost or defaced licences

C16–13   13.—(1) If the holder of a licence—
  (a) satisfies the licensing authority that—
      (i) the licence or its counterpart has been lost or defaced; and
      (ii) the holder is entitled to continue to hold the licence; and
  (b) pays the fee prescribed by regulation 7,
the licensing authority shall, on surrender of any licence or counterpart that has not been lost, issue to him a duplicate licence and counterpart and shall endorse upon the counterpart any particulars endorsed upon the original licence or counterpart as the case may be and the duplicates so issued shall have the same effect as the originals.
  (2) If at any time while a duplicate licence is in force the original licence is found, the person to whom the original licence was issued, if it is in his pos-

session, shall return it to the licensing authority, or if it is not in his possession, but he becomes aware that it is found, shall take all reasonable steps to obtain possession of it and if successful shall return it as soon as may be to the licensing authority.

(3) The obligation in paragraph (2) shall apply in respect of the counterpart of a licence as if for the words "original licence" in each place where they occur there were substituted the words "original counterpart."

Persons by whom tests may be conducted

14.—(1) Subject to paragraph (2) tests may be conducted—
  (a) by examiners appointed by the licensing authority;
  (b) by the Secretary of State for Defence, in so far as concerns the testing of persons in the service of the Crown under his department;
  (c) in England and Wales, by the chief officer of any fire brigade maintained in pursuance of the Fire Services Act 1947 or, in Scotland, by the firemaster of such a brigade, in so far as concerns the testing of members of any such brigade or of persons employed in the driving of motor vehicles for the purposes of any such brigade;
  (d) by any chief officer of police in so far as concerns the testing:—
    (i) of members of a police force; or
    (ii) of persons employed in the driving of motor vehicles for police purposes by a police authority or by the Receiver for the Metropolitan Police District;
  (e) by the Commissioner of Police of the Metropolis in so far as concerns the testing of any person who is the holder of or is an applicant for a licence to drive a motor cab by virtue of the Metropolitan Public Carriage Act 1869; and
  (f) by any person appointed for the purpose by the licensing authority under the provisions of regulation 15.

(2) Where a person is disqualified until he passes the appropriate driving test, that test shall be conducted either by—
  (a) an examiner appointed by the licensing authority; or
  (b) the Secretary of State for Defence if the person who has been disqualified is in the service of the Crown under the Ministry of Defence and agrees to be tested by the Secretary of State for Defence.

15.—(1) Any person may apply to the licensing authority to be appointed to
conduct tests of persons (other than persons who have been disqualified until they pass the appropriate driving test) employed or proposed to be employed by him as drivers, and the licensing authority may, if he is satisfied that—
  (a) the number of drivers of motor vehicles ordinarily employed by the applicant exceeds 250;
  (b) proper arrangements will be made by the applicant for the conduct of such tests in accordance with these Regulations; and
  (c) proper records of such tests and the results thereof will be kept by the applicant,
grant the application subject to any special conditions which he may think fit to impose.

(2) The licensing authority may at any time revoke an appointment made by him under this regulation and the authority to conduct tests shall thereupon cease.

17. Any person appointed by sub-paragraph (b), (c), (d), (e) or (f) of paragraph (1) or (b) of paragraph (2) of regulation 14 to conduct tests may, subject to the approval of the licensing authority, authorise suitable persons to act as examiners of those who submit themselves for a test.

Appointments for tests and notice of cancellation thereof

18.—(1) A person who desires to take a test to be conducted by an examiner appointed under paragraph (1)(a) or (2)(a) (as the case may be) of regulation 14 shall apply for an appointment for such a test to the licensing authority.

(2) An applicant for such an appointment as aforesaid shall, when making the application, pay to the licensing authority such fee in respect of the test as is prescribed and the licensing authority shall make any arrangements necessary for the taking of the test.

(3) For the purposes of paragraph (b) of section 86 of the 1972 Act (which section specifies the only circumstances in which a fee paid on application for an appointment for a test may be repaid) notice cancelling an appointment for such a test as is mentioned in paragraph (1) shall be given to the clerk to the licensing authority not less than ten clear days (excluding Saturdays, Sundays, any bank holiday, Christmas Day or Good Friday) before the date of the appointment.

(4) In paragraph (3) "bank holiday" means a day which is, or is to be, observed as a bank holiday or a holiday under the Bank and Financial Dealings Act 1971, either generally or in the locality in which the applicant is due to take his test.

Fees in respect of tests

19.—(1) The following provisions of this regulation shall apply in the case of a person who submits himself for a test other than an extended driving test or applies for an appointment for a test other than an extended driving test.

(2) No fee shall be payable—
    (a) in respect of a test conducted by a person appointed under paragraph (1)(b), (c), (d) or (f) of regulation 14;

(3) Subject to paragraph (3B) below, the fee payable in respect of a test to be commenced between the hours of 0830 and 1630 on Monday to Friday (inclusive of both those days) by an examiner appointed under paragraph (1)(a) of regulation 14 is—
    (a) in the case of a test for the grant of a licence authorising a person to drive a motor vehicle in category A or category P, £35; and
    (b) in the case of any other test not specified in regulation 15 of the Motor Vehicles (Driving Licences) (Large Goods and Passenger-Carrying Vehicles) Regulations 1990, £27.50.

(3A) Subject to paragraph (3B) below, the fee payable in respect of a test to be conducted at any other time by an examiner appointed under paragraph (1)(a) of regulation 14 is—
    (a) in the case of a test for the grant of a licence authorising a person to drive a motor vehicle in category A or category P, £46.50; and
    (b) in the case of any other test not specified in regulation 15 of the Motor Vehicles (Driving Licences) (Large Goods and Passenger-Carrying Vehicles) Regulations 1990, £37.50.

(3B) No fee is payable in respect of a test taken in an invalid carriage.

(5) The fee payable in respect of a test to be conducted by a person appointed by paragraph (1)(e) of regulation 14 is £27.50 and that fee shall be paid to that person to be retained by him as remuneration.

19A.—(1) The following provisions of this regulation shall apply in the case **C16–19** of a person who submits himself for an extended driving test or applies for an appointment for such a test.

(2) No fee shall be payable in respect of a test to be conducted by the Secretary of State for Defence.

(3) The fee payable in respect of a test to be conducted on a day other than a Saturday by an examiner appointed under paragraph (2)(a) of regulation 14 is—

> (a) in the case of a test to drive a motor vehicle in category A or category P, £70; and
> (b) in the case of any other test, £55,

save that no fee is payable in respect of a test to be taken in an invalid carriage.

(4) The fee payable in respect of a test to be conducted on a Saturday by an examiner appointed under paragraph (2)(a) of regulation 14 is—

> (a) in the case of a test to drive a motor vehicle in category A or category P, £92; and
> (b) in the case of any other test, £77.50,

save that no fee is payable in respect of a test to be taken in an invalid carriage.

Nature of tests

20.—(1) Subject to paragraph (5), except where a person is disqualified until **C16–20** he passes an extended driving test the test which a person is required to pass before a licence can be granted to him authorising him to drive a motor vehicle of a class included in any particular category shall be a test carried out on a vehicle (other than a vehicle of a class included in category B plus E, C1 plus E or D1 plus E) of that class which satisfies the person conducting the test:—

> (a) that the person taking the test is fully conversant with the contents of the Highway Code;
> (b) generally that the person taking the test is competent to drive, without danger to and with due consideration for other users of the road, the vehicle on which he is tested; and
> (c) that the person taking the test is able to comply with such of the additional requirements specified in Schedule 4 as are referred to in the third column of Schedule 3 in relation to the category which includes the class of vehicle on which he is tested.

(2) Subject to paragraphs (3) to (5), the extended driving test which a person disqualified under section 36 of the Road Traffic Offenders Act 1988 following conviction of an offence involving obligatory disqualification or following disqualification under section 35 of that Act is required to pass before a licence can be granted to him authorising him to drive a motor vehicle of a class included in any particular category shall be a test—

> (a) carried out on a vehicle (other than a vehicle of a class included in category B plus E, C1 plus E or D1 plus E) of that class which satisfies the person conducting the test as to the matters set out in sub-paragraphs (a)–(c) of paragraph (1); and

(b) during which the person being tested is required to drive for a minimum of 60 minutes.

(3) Where a person who is disqualified until he passes the appropriate driving test passes such a test on a vehicle of a class included in any particular category the disqualification shall be deemed to have expired in relation to—

(a) all classes of vehicle included in that particular category unless—

    (i) the test is passed on a vehicle with automatic transmission and that particular category is B, C1 or D1, in which case the disqualification shall be deemed to have expired only in relation to such classes of vehicle included in that particular category with automatic transmission, or

    (ii) the test is passed on an invalid carriage, in which case the disqualification shall be deemed to have expired only in relation to such classes of vehicle included in that particular category as are invalid carriages, or

    (iii) the test is passed on a vehicle which is adapted to meet the particular needs of the person tested, in which case the disqualification shall be deemed to have expired only in relation to such classes of vehicle included in that particular category as are so adapted; and

(b) all classes of vehicle included in any other category which is referred to in the fourth column of Schedule 3 as being an additional category in relation to that particular category unless—

    (i) the test is passed on a vehicle with automatic transmission and the additional category is B, C1, D1, B plus E, C1 plus E or D1 plus E, in which case the disqualification shall be deemed to have expired only in relation to such classes of vehicle included in the additional category with automatic transmission, or

    (ii) the test is passed on an invalid carriage, or

    (iii) the test is passed on a vehicle which is adapted to meet the particular needs of the person tested, in which case the disqualification shall be deemed to have expired only in relation to such classes of vehicle included in the additional category as are so adapted.

(4) Where a person who is disqualified until he passes the appropriate driving test passes such a test on a vehicle of a class included in category B, C1 or D1 the disqualification shall be deemed to have expired in relation to all classes of vehicle included in category C, C plus E, D, and D plus E.

(5) Where a person passes a test on a vehicle of a class included in any particular category he shall be deemed for the purposes of the Road Traffic Act 1988 and of these Regulations competent to drive—

(a) all classes of vehicle included in that particular category unless—

    (i) the test is passed on a vehicle with automatic transmission and that particular category is B, C1 or D1, in which case he shall be deemed for those purposes competent to drive only such classes of vehicle included in that particular category with automatic transmission, or

    (ii) the test is passed on an invalid carriage, in which case he shall be deemed for those purposes competent to drive only such classes of vehicle included in that particular category as are invalid carriages, or

    (iii) the test is passed on a vehicle which is adapted to meet the particular needs of the person tested, in which case he shall be deemed for those purposes competent to drive only such classes

of vehicle included in that particular category as are so adapted; and
  (b) all classes of vehicle included in any other category which is referredto in the fourth column of Schedule 3 as being an additional category in relation to that particular category unless—
     (i) the test is passed on a vehicle with automatic transmission and the additional category is B, C1, D1, B plus E, C1 plus E or D1 plus E, in which case he shall be deemed for those purposes competent to drive only such classes of vehicle included in the additional category with automatic transmission, or
    (ii) the test is passed on an invalid carriage, or
    (iii) the test is passed on a vehicle which is adapted to meet the particular needs of the person tested, in which case he shall be deemed for those purposes competent to drive only such classes of vehicle included in the additional category as are so adapted.

Production of vehicle for test etc.

21.—(1) A person submitting himself for a test shall—   **C16–21**
  (a) provide for the purposes of the test a motor vehicle (not being a motor vehicle of a class included in category B plus E, C1 plus E or D1 plus E), which—
     (i) is suitable for the purposes of the test; and
    (ii) is not fitted with a device designed to permit a person other than the driver to operate the accelerator, unless any pedal or lever by which the device is operated and any other parts which it may be necessary to remove to make the device inoperable by such a person during the test have been removed;
  (b) sign on the Driving Test Report Form produced to him by the examiner before the test commences, a declaration that there is in force, in relation to the use of the vehicle provided for the purposes of the test, a policy of insurance which complies with the requirements of Part VI of the Road Traffic Act 1988,
  (bb) produce evidence of his identity to the satisfaction of the examiner in the form of—
     (i) a licence to drive a motor vehicle granted under Part III or IV of the Road Traffic Act 1988 or under the 1981 Act bearing his signature,
    (ii) a Northern Ireland licence bearing his signature,
    (iii) a British external licence bearing his signature,
    (iv) a British Forces licence, bearing his signature,
    (v) a driving permit issued by the service authorities of a visiting force specified in Article 3 of the Motor Vehicles (International Circulation) Order 1975 bearing his signature,
    (vi) a Convention driving permit as defined in Article 2(7) of that Order bearing his signature,
    (vii) an exchangeable licence bearing his signature,
    (viii) any other document falling within the definition of "domestic driving permit" in that Article which bears the holder's name in the roman alphabet, his photograph and his signature,
    (ix) a passport bearing his signature, or
    (x) an identity card issued by his employer which bears the holder's name in the roman alphabet, his photograph and his signature;

(c) except when the test is for a motor bicycle, allow to travel in the vehicle mentioned in paragraph (1)(a) during the test—
  (i) the person authorised to conduct the test; and
  (ii) any person authorised by the licensing authority to attend the test for the purpose of supervising it or otherwise; and
(d) when the test is for a motor bicycle, allow the attendance of—
  (i) the person authorised to conduct the test; and
  (ii) any person authorised by the licensing authority for the purpose of supervising the test or otherwise.
(2) Where a person submitting himself for a test fails—
  (a) to produce a vehicle which complies with sub-paragraph (a) of paragraph (1); or
  (b) to comply with any of the provisions of sub-paragraphs (b), (bb), (c) and (d) of that paragraph,
the examiner may refuse to conduct the test.

Evidence of results of tests

C16–22　　22.—(1) A person who passes a test shall be furnished with a certificate to that effect in the form (adapted as the case may require) set out in Part I of Schedule 6.

(2) A person who fails to pass a test shall be furnished with a statement to that effect in the form (adapted as the case may require) set out in Part II of Schedule 6.

(3) [...]

(4) An applicant for a licence who before the licence is granted is required to satisfy the licensing authority that he has passed a test shall at the time when he applies for the licence deliver the certificate furnished to him under paragraph (1) to the licensing authority for retention.

(5) [...]

Period of ineligibility for a subsequent test

C16–23　　23.—(1) Subject to the provisions of section 85(3) of the 1972 Act the period during which a person who has submitted himself for a test and failed to pass that test shall be ineligible to submit himself for another test on a vehicle of a class included in the same [category] shall be one month.

(2) [...]

Persons by whom approved training courses may be provided

C16–24　　23A.—(1) Approved training courses for motor cyclists may be provided—
  (a) by the Secretary of State for Defence, in so far as concerns the training of persons in the service of the Crown under his department;
  (b) in England and Wales, by the chief officer of any fire brigade maintained in pursuance of the Fire Services Act 1947 or, in Scotland, by the firemaster of such a brigade, in so far as concerns the training of members of any such brigade or of persons employed in the driving of motor vehicles for the purposes of any such brigade;
  (c) by any chief officer of police, in so far as concerns the training of members of a police force or of persons employed in the driving of motor vehicles for police purposes by a police authority; and
  (d) by any person approved for the purpose by the licensing authority.

(2) Any person may apply to the licensing authority to be approved to provide an approved training course for motor cyclists under sub-paragraph (d) of paragraph (1) above, and the licensing authority may, if satisfied that—

(a) proper arrangements will be made by the applicant for the conduct of the course in accordance with these Regulations; and

(b) proper records of the course and results thereof will be kept by the applicant,

grant the application subject to any conditions which it thinks fit to impose.

(3) Subject to paragraphs (4) to (10) below, a person who provides an approved training course for motor cyclists in pursuance of paragraph (1) above may authorise motor cycle instructors to conduct the motor cycle training on his behalf.

(4) A motor cycle instructor may be authorised under paragraph (3) above if and only if—

(a) he satisfies the conditions set out in sub-paragraphs (a), (b) and (c) of paragraph (5) below, in which case, on being authorised, he shall be known as a certified instructor; or

(b) he satisfies the conditions set out in sub-paragraphs (a) and (c) of paragraph (5) below, in which case, on being authorised, he shall be known as an assistant instructor.

(5) The conditions referred to in paragraph (4) above are that—

(a) he holds a full licence to drive vehicles in category A; and

(b) he has held that licence for a period of, or for periods amounting to, at least 2 years; and

(c) either—

(i) he has completed successfully the licensing authority's assessment course for motor cycle instructors, or

(ii) he has been trained by a motor cycle instructor who has completed such a course successfully.

(6) Subject, in the case of a certified instructor, to paragraphs (7) to (9) below, and in the case of an assistant instructor, to paragraphs (7) and (8) below—

(a) a certified instructor shall be entitled to conduct the training of motor cyclists and, provided he has completed successfully the licensing authority's assessment course for motor cycle instructors, to train other motor cycle instructors to conduct the training of motor cyclists; and

(b) an assistant instructor shall be entitled to conduct the training of motor cyclists save that he shall not be entitled to conduct the training of motor cyclists in practical on-road riding skills.

(7) Certified and assistant instructors shall not be entitled to conduct any training until—

(a) the person giving the authorisation under paragraph (3) above has notified the licensing authority of the authorisation in writing; and

(b) the licensing authority has approved the authorisation in writing.

(8) Where the licensing authority does not approve an authorisation given under paragraph (3) above that authorisation shall be of no effect.

(9) A certified instructor shall not be entitled to conduct training as a certified instructor unless there is in force in respect of him a certificate, which shall be renewable every four years, issued by the licensing authority and obtained by the person who has authorised him under paragraph (3) above, in the form set out in Schedule 7.

(10) An assistant instructor who, subsequent to his authorisation under paragraph (3) above, satisfies the condition set out in sub-paragraph (b) of paragraph (5) above, shall become a certified instructor on satisfying the con-

dition, but he shall not be entitled to conduct training as a certified instructor unless paragraph (9) above is satisfied.

(11) When conducting motor cycle training a certified instructor shall carry with him the certificate issued in respect of him by the licensing authority.

(12) A person who is approved to provide an approved training course for motor cyclists in pursuance of sub-paragraph (d) of paragraph (1) above and who satisfies the conditions set out in sub-paragraphs (a), (b) and (c) of paragraph (5) above shall, in relation to training conducted by himself, be deemed for the purposes of this Part of these Regulations to be a certified instructor, and shall be entitled to conduct training as a certified instructor provided there is in force in respect of him a certificate, renewable every four years and issued to him by the licensing authority, in the form set out in Schedule 7, and he complies with paragraph (11) above.

(13) A person who is approved to provide an approved training course for motor cyclists in pursuance of sub-paragraph (d) of paragraph (1) above and who satisfies the conditions set out in sub-paragraphs (a) and (c) of paragraph (5) above shall, in relation to training conducted by himself, be deemed for the purposes of this Part of these Regulations to be an assistant instructor and shall be entitled to conduct the training of motor cyclists save that he shall not be entitled to conduct the training of motor cyclists in practical on-road riding skills.

(14) The licensing authority may at any time by notice in writing—

    (a) withdraw an approval made under sub-paragraph (d) of paragraph (1) above; or

    (b) revoke an authorisation given under paragraph (3) above.

(15) Where the licensing authority withdraws an approval made under sub-paragraph (d) of paragraph (1) above, the approval and the authority of any person to act as a certified or assistant instructor on behalf of the person whose approval has been withdrawn shall cease forthwith; and where the licensing authority revokes an authorisation given under paragraph (3) above, the authority of the person whose authorisation is revoked to act as a certified or assistant instructor, as the case may be, shall cease forthwith.

(16) Where the licensing authority withdraws an approval made under sub-paragraph (d) of paragraph (1) above, the person whose approval is withdrawn shall, within 28 days from the date of that withdrawal, return to the licensing authority all certificates which were supplied to him under paragraphs (9) and (12) above and all forms for certificates which were supplied to him under regulation 23B(5) below.

(17) Where the licensing authority revokes an authorisation given under paragraph (3) above in respect of a certified instructor, or where a certified instructor authorised under paragraph (3) above ceases to conduct training on behalf of the person who authorised him, the certified instructor shall return to the person who authorised him the certificate he was required to carry under paragraph (11) above as soon as is reasonably practicable; and, on receiving it, the person who authorised him shall return that certificate to the licensing authority immediately.

Nature and approval of training courses

23B.—(1) A training course for motor cyclists shall comprise the elements A to E set out in Schedule 8 and shall be approved by the licensing authority.

(2) Before any practical training is given to motor cyclists on an approved training course the requirements of paragraphs 1 and 2 of Schedule 8 must be fulfilled.

(3) To complete an approved training course successfully, a motor cyclist must satisfy the person who provides the course of each of the following in sequence, commencing with sub-paragraph (a)—

  (a) that he has fulfilled the requirements set out in paragraph 3 of Schedule 8; and
  (b) that he can execute the manoeuvres set out in paragraph 4 of Schedule 8; and
  (c) that the requirements of paragraph 5 of Schedule 8 are fulfilled; and
  (d) that he rides safely on roads in a variety of road traffic situations, including as many as practicable of those set out in paragraph 6 of Schedule 8.

(4) On the successful completion of an approved training course a motor cyclist shall be issued with a certificate of completion signed on behalf of the person providing the course by a certified instructor, who may be the person providing the course, on a form supplied by the licensing authority as prescribed in Schedule 9.

(5) Forms for certificates evidencing the successful completion of an approved training course shall be supplied by the licensing authority to those authorised to provide approved training courses pursuant to paragraph (1) of regulation 23A above at a charge of £5.00 per form.

23C. When, during an approved training course, motor cyclists are receiv-   **C16–26**
ing practical on site training or are undertaking practical on site riding there shall be no more than 4 motor cyclists in the charge of any one certified or assistant instructor at any one time; and when, during such a course, motor cyclists are undertaking practical on-road riding there shall be no more than 2 motor cyclists in the charge of any one certified instructor at any one time.

Exemptions and Transitional and Supplementary Provisions

23D.—(1) For the purposes of regulations 23E, 23F, 23G and 23H below—   **C16–27**
  "provisional licence holder" means a person who holds a valid provisional licence under which he drives and which, subject to section 97(3) of the Road Traffic Act 1988, authorises him to drive a vehicle of a class included in category A or category P; and
  "provisional entitlement holder" means a person who holds and drives under a valid licence which, not being a provisional or full licence to drive a vehicle of a class included in category A or category P, authorises him (by virtue of section 98(2) of the Road Traffic Act 1988) to drive a class of vehicle in one of those categories as if he were a provisional licence holder.

(2) For the purposes of regulation 23G below "exempted island" means an island outside the mainland of Great Britain other than—

  (a) the Isle of Wight, Lewis and Harris, North Uist, Benbecula and South Uist, Mainland Orkney, Mainland Shetland and Skye; and
  (b) an island from which motor vehicles, not constructed for special purposes, can at some time be conveniently driven to a road in any part of the mainland of Great Britain because of the presence of a bridge, tunnel, ford, or other way suitable for the passage of such motor vehicles.

23E.—(1) A person who was a provisional licence holder immediately   **C16–28**
before 1st December 1990 shall be exempt from the restriction imposed by section 97(3)(e) of the Road Traffic Act 1988 during the validity of that licence and if that licence has been exchanged for a full licence entitling him to drive a vehicle of a class included in category B and he has not, after that exchange,

been disqualified until he passes the appropriate driving test, section 98(3)(c) of the Road Traffic Act 1988 shall not apply to him.

(2) A provisional licence holder who has passed Part I of the test for motor bicycles shall be exempt from the restriction imposed by section 97(3)(e) and from the requirement imposed by section 89(2A) of the Road Traffic Act 1988 for the period during which the certificate furnished to him under regulation 22(1) is valid.

(3) Section 98(3)(c) of the Road Traffic Act 1988 shall not apply to a person who was a provisional entitlement holder immediately before 1st December 1990 [unless he has been disqualified until he passes the appropriate driving test] or to a provisional entitlement holder who has passed Part I of the test for motor bicycles for the period during which the certificate furnished to him under regulation 22(1) is valid.

(4) A provisional entitlement holder who has passed Part I of the test for motor bicycles shall be exempt from the requirement imposed by section 89(2A) of the Road Traffic Act 1988 for the period during which the certificate furnished to him under regulation 22(1) is valid.

(5) A person who is disqualified until he passes the appropriate driving test shall be exempt from the restriction imposed by section 97(3)(e) and the requirement imposed by section 89(2A) of the Road Traffic Act 1988 if, before the date on which he is disqualified, he has passed a test to drive a vehicle of a class included in category A or on a vehicle of a class included in category P.

C16–29   **23F.** A person who was a provisional licence or provisional entitlement holder immediately before 1st December 1990 and who applies to take and takes a test of competence to drive a vehicle of a class included in category P or a motor bicycle fitted with a side-car on or before 31st May 1991 shall be exempt from the requirement imposed by section 89(2A) of the Road Traffic Act 1988.

C16–30   **23G.**—(1) A provisional licence or provisional entitlement holder who is resident on an exempted island shall be exempt from the requirement imposed by section 89(2A) of the Road Traffic Act 1988 in respect of a test of competence to drive a vehicle of a class included in category A or category P taken, or to be taken, on an island, whether or not that island is an exempted island.

(2) A provisional licence holder who is resident on an exempted island shall be exempt from the restriction imposed by section 97(3)(e) of the Road Traffic Act 1988 when he satisfies either of the conditions set out in paragraph (4) below.

(3) Section 98(3)(c) of the Road Traffic Act 1988 shall not apply to a provisional entitlement holder who is resident on an exempted island when he satisfies either of the conditions set in paragraph (4) below.

(4) The conditions referred to in paragraphs (2) and (3) above are—
  (a) that the holder is driving on an exempted island, whether or not he is also resident on that island; or
  (b) that the holder is driving on a non-exempted island for the purpose of getting to or from an approved training course or to a place where he is to take, or from a place where he has taken, a test of competence to drive a vehicle of a class included in category A or category P.

C16–31   **23H.** Without prejudice to regulations 23F and 23G(1) above a person who, immediately before 1st December 1990, is a provisional licence or provisional entitlement holder may take Part I of the test for motor bicycles instead of an approved training course if, but for this provision, he would be required to take an approved training course, provided he takes Part I of the test for motor bicycles on or before 31st May 1991.

Disabilities

24.—(1) The following disabilities are prescribed for the purposes of section   **C16–32**
87(1) of the 1972 Act—

(a) epilepsy;

(b) severe mental handicap;

(c) liability to sudden attacks of disabling giddiness or fainting, other than such attacks falling within paragraph (1)(d);

(d) liability to sudden attacks of disabling giddiness or fainting which are caused by any disorder or defect of the heart as a result of which the applicant for the licence or, as the case may be, the holder of the licence has a device implanted in his body, being a device which, by operating on the heart so as to regulate its action, is designed to correct the disorder or defect; and

(e) inability to read in good daylight (with the aid of glasses or contact lenses if worn) a registration mark fixed to a motor vehicle and containing letters and figures 79.4 millimetres high at a distance of—

    (i) 20.5 metres, in any case except that mentioned below; or

    (ii) 12.3 metres, in the case of an applicant for a licence authorising the driving of vehicles of a class included in category K only.

(2) Epilepsy is prescribed for the purposes of section 87(3)(b) of the 1972 Act and an applicant for a licence suffering from epilepsy shall satisfy the following conditions, namely that he shall—

(a) have been free from any epileptic attack during the period of one year immediately preceding the date when the licence is granted; or

(b) have had an epileptic attack whilst asleep more than three years before the date when the licence is granted and shall have had attacks only whilst asleep between the date of that attack and the date when the licence is granted;

and that the driving of a vehicle by him in accordance with the licence is not likely to be a danger to the public.

(3) The disability prescribed in paragraph (1)(d) is prescribed for the purpose of section 87(3)(b) of the 1972 Act and an applicant for a licence suffering from that disability shall satisfy the conditions that—

(a) the driving of a vehicle by him in pursuance of the licence is not likely to be a source of danger to the public; and

(b) he has made adequate arrangements to receive regular medical supervision by a cardiologist (being a supervision to be continued throughout the period of the licence) and is conforming to those arrangements.

(4) The following disability is prescribed for the purposes of paragraphs (a) and (c) of section 87(3) of the 1972 Act namely, a disability which is not progressive in nature and which consists solely of any one or more of the following:—

(a) the absence of one or more limbs;

(b) the deformity of one or more limbs; and

(c) the loss of use of one or more limbs.

(5) The disability prescribed in paragraph (1)(e) is prescribed for the purposes of section 87A(2)(b) of the 1972 Act.

(6) (a) In paragraph (1)(b), the expression "severe mental handicap" means a state of arrested or incomplete development of mind which includes severe impairment of intelligence and social functioning.

(b) In paragraph (3)(b), the expression "cardiologist" means a registered medical practitioner who specialises in disorders or defects of the heart and who, in that connection, holds a hospital appointment.

(c) In paragraph (4), references to a limb include references to a part of a limb, and the reference to loss of use, in relation to a limb, includes a reference to a deficiency of limb movement or power.

(7) Subject to paragraph (8), the circumstances prescribed for the purposes of subsection (5) of section 94 of the Road Traffic Act 1988, under subsection (4) of that section, are that the person who is an applicant for, or holder of, a licence—

(a) has been disqualified by an order of a court by reason that the proportion of alcohol in his breath, blood or urine exceeded the limit prescribed by virtue of section 5 of the Road Traffic Act 1988 by at least two and a half times or that he failed, without reasonable excuse, to provide a specimen when required to do so pursuant to section 7 of that Act; or

(b) has been disqualified by an order of a court on two or more occasions within any period of 10 years by reason that the proportion of alcohol in his breath, blood or urine exceeded the limit prescribed by virtue of section 5 of the Road Traffic Act 1988 or that he was unfit to drive through drink contrary to section 4 of that Act.

(8) In paragraph (7)(a) the order of the court shall have been made on or after 1st June 1990 and in paragraph (7)(b) at least the last such order shall have been made on or after 1st June 1990.

Persons who become resident in Great Britain

C16–33   25.—(1) A person who becomes resident in Great Britain shall during the period of one year after he becomes so resident be treated for the purposes of section 84(1) and (2) of the 1972 Act as the holder of a licence authorising him to drive motor vehicles of the classes which he is authorised to drive by any permit of which he is a holder, if he satisfies the conditions specified in paragraph (2).

(2) The conditions mentioned in paragraph (1) are that:—

(a) the person who becomes resident shall be the holder of a permit which is for the time being valid; and

(b) he is not disqualified for holding or obtaining a licence in Great Britain.

(3) The following enactments relating to licences or licence holders shall apply in relation to permits or the holders of permits (as the case may be) subject to modifications in accordance with the following provisions:—

(a) section 47(2) of the Road Traffic Offenders Act 1988 (which relates to the powers and duties of a court when it orders a disqualification or an endorsement) shall apply in relation to the holder of a permit, only where the court has ordered him to be disqualified and as if for the words "send the licence" onwards there were substituted the words "send the permit," on its being produced to the court, to the Secretary of State who shall keep the permit until the disqualification has expired or been removed or the person entitled to the permit leaves Great Britain and in any case has made a demand in writing for its return to him;

(b) section 7 of the Road Traffic Offenders Act 1988 (production of licence and counterpart to court) shall apply as if the references to a licence were references to a permit and as if the words after paragraph (c) thereof were omitted;

(c) section 27(1), (2) and (3) of the Road Traffic Offenders Act 1988 (production of licence and counterpart) shall apply as if the references to a licence were references to a permit, but with the omission—
  (i) of any reference to the counterpart of a licence,
  (ii) in subsection (1) of the words ", before making any order under section 44 of this Act,", and
  (iii) in subsection (3) of the words ", unless he satisfies the Court that he has applied for a new licence and has not received it";

(d) section 42(5) of the Road Traffic Offenders Act 1988 (which relates to the duty of a court when it orders a disqualification to be removed) shall apply in relation to the holder of a permit as if for the words "endorsed on the counterpart of the licence" onwards there were substituted the words "notified to the Secretary of State";

(e) section 164(1), (6) and (8) of the Road Traffic Act 1988 (which authorise a police constable to require the production of a licence and its counterpart) shall apply as if the references to a licence were references to a permit and any reference to a counterpart of a licence were omitted; and

(f) section 173 of the Road Traffic Act 1988 (forgery of documents, etc.) shall apply as if the reference in paragraph (a) of subsection (2) of that section to any licence under any Part of that Act were a reference to a permit and the reference, in the case of a licence to drive, to any counterpart were omitted.

(4) In this regulation "permit" means a "domestic driving permit" a "Convention driving permit" or a "British Forces (BFG) driving licence" as defined in article 2(6) of the Motor Vehicles (International Circulation) Order 1975 not being a domestic driving permit or a British Forces (BFG) driving licence in the case of which any order made, or having effect as if made, by the Secretary of State is for the time being in force under article 2(5) of that Order.

Statement of date of birth

26. The circumstances in which a person specified in section 161(1) of the **C16–34** 1972 Act shall, on being required by a police constable, state his date of birth are as follows:—

(1) where that person fails to produce forthwith for examination his licence on being required to do so by a police constable under that section; or

(2) where, on being so required, that person produces a licence—
  (a) which the police constable in question has reason to suspect—
    (i) was not granted to that person;
    (ii) was granted to that person in error; or
    (iii) contains an alteration in the particulars entered on the licence (other than as described in paragraph (b) below) made with intent to deceive; or
  (b) in which the driver number has been altered, removed or defaced; or

(2A) where that person is a person specified in subsection (1)(d) of that section and the police constable has reason to suspect that he is under 21 years of age.

(3) In paragraph (2), "driver number" means the number described as the driver number in the licence.

Learner motor cycles

27. For the purposes of section 88(2)(c) of the 1972 Act (provisional licence **C16–35**

not to authorise the driving of certain motor cycles) the first use of a motor cycle shall be taken to have occurred on the date of first use as determined in accordance with paragraph (2) of regulation 3.

Invalid carriages

C16–36   28. For the purposes of Part III of the 1972 Act and all regulations made thereunder the maximum weight specified in section 190(5) of that Act (which defines the expression "invalid carriage" for the purposes of the Act) shall be varied from 254 kilograms to 510 kilograms.

Entitlement to categories

C16–37   29.—(1) Subject to paragraphs (2) and (3), the categories of vehicles specified in the second column of the table in Schedule 3 are hereby designated as groups for the purposes of section 89(1)(a) and (b) of the Road Traffic Act 1988.

(2) In the case of a person who has passed a test in a vehicle with automatic transmission of a class included in category B, C1 or D1 or who has held a licence restricted to vehicles with automatic transmission of any such class, the categories of vehicles designated as groups by paragraph (1) are, in the case of categories B, C1 and D1, restricted to vehicles of any class with automatic transmission.

(3) In the case of a person who has passed a test in an invalid carriage, the categories of vehicles designated as groups by paragraph (1) are restricted to invalid carriages in such categories.

Effect of changes in classification of vehicles by reason of changed definition of "moped"

C16–38   30.—(1) In licences (whether full or provisional) issued before 1st April 1977—

(a) any reference to motor vehicles of group E shall be construed as a reference to motor vehicles of new group E;

(b) any reference to motor vehicles of group L shall be construed as reference to motor vehicles of new group L;

(c) any reference to motor vehicles of any other group the constitution of which was affected by the amendments made by the Motor Vehicles (Driving Licences) (Amendment) Regulations 1976 shall be construed as references to motor vehicles of the group in question as so amended in constitution; and

(d) any reference to a moped shall be construed by reference to the revised definition of "moped".

(2) In relation to an application for the grant of a licence by a person who—

(a) before 1st August 1977 held a licence granted under Part III of the 1972 Act, or under any enactment which that Part replaced, or under a relevant external law (as defined in section 85(1) of the 1972 Act) to drive motor vehicles of a class included in old group E; or

(b) before that date passed a test to drive motor vehicles of a class included in old group E or a test which by virtue of regulation 20(6) is regarded as a test to drive such motor vehicles,

and in relation to any licence issued in pursuance of such applications, the licence which he held, or the test which he passed, before that date shall for the purposes of section 85(1) and (4) of the 1972 Act (restrictions on grant of licences etc.) be regarded as a licence or test (as the case may be) to drive vehicles of a class included in new group E.

(3) A person whose entitlement to the grant of a licence to drive vehicles of new group E is preserved by this regulation may, not withstanding anything in section 84(1) and (2) of the 1972 Act (drivers of motor vehicles to have driving licences), at any time pending the grant of such a licence to him drive, and be employed in driving, such vehicles if—

(a) his application in accordance with section 88(1)(a) of the 1972 Act (provisions as to grant of licences), together with the fee prescribed under that section, for the grant of such a licence has been received by the Secretary of State;

(b) he satisfies the requirements of subsection (1)(b) and (c) of that section;

(c) he is not disqualified by reason of age or otherwise for obtaining the licence;

(d) he is not a person to whom the Secretary of State is required by section 87(2) of the 1972 Act (requirements as to physical fitness of drivers) to refuse to grant the licence;

(e) in the case of a person on whom notice under subsection (4) of that section, or any enactment which that provision replaced, has been served, the vehicles are of the particular construction and design or class specified in the notice; and

(f) he complies, in relation to that driving, with such of the conditions specified in regulation 8(1) as will apply to the driving of those vehicles by him under the authority of that licence, when granted.

(4) In this regulation, reference to "old group" and "new group" followed by a letter are references respectively to the group in question as constituted before and after the coming into operation of the Motor Vehicles (Driving Licences) (Amendment) Regulations 1976, and the reference to the revised definition of "moped" is a reference to the definition of that word in regulation 3(1), which was inserted in regulation 3(1) of the Motor Vehicles (Driving Licences) Regulations 1976 by the said amendment Regulations.

Effect of changes in classification of vehicles by reason of changed weight limit for motor tricycles

31.—(1) In licences (whether full or provisional) issued before the date of   **C16–39** reclassification any reference to motor vehicles of a group identified by a letter shall be construed for all purposes on and after that date as a reference to motor vehicles of the new group as well as the old group identified by that letter.

(2) In relation to an application for the grant of a licence coming into force on or after the date of re-classification by a person who—

(a) before that date held a licence granted under Part III of the 1972 Act, or under any enactment which that Part III replaced, or under a relevant external law (as defined in section 85(1) of the 1972 Act) to drive motor vehicles of a class included in an old group; or

(b) before that date passed a test to drive motor vehicles of a class included in an old group or a test which by virtue of regulation 20(6) is regarded as a test to drive such vehicles,

and in relation to any licence issued in pursuance of such an application, the licence which he held, or the test which he passed, before that date shall, for the purposes of section 85(1) and (4) of the 1972 Act (restrictions on the grant of licences etc.), be regarded as a licence or test, as the case may be, to drive vehicles of a class included in the new group as well as the old group identified by the same letter.

(3) In this regulation references to "old group" and "new group" are references respectively to the group in question as constituted before and after the date of re-classification and "the date of re-classification" refers respectively to 12th August 1981 when the weight limit for motor tricycles in group C was increased to 425 kilograms unladen and 2nd September 1985 when that weight limit was increased to 450 kilograms unladen.

Effect of changes in classification of vehicles by reason of deletion of group M

C16–40   **32.**—(1) The deletion of group M in Schedule 3 by regulation 9(e) of the Motor Vehicles (Driving Licences) (Amendment) (No. 4) Regulations 1982 shall not affect—

    (a) any entitlement of a holder of a licence for vehicles of a class included in that group granted before the date of coming into operation of the said regulation 9(e) to drive vehicles of that class, and vehicles of any other class included in that group, in pursuance of the licence; or

    (b) any such licence ceasing to be in force whether before or after that date, or any right that the person who held the licence would have had to the grant of a further licence on or after that date authorising him to drive such vehicles.

(2) In licences (whether full or provisional) issued before the date of coming into operation of regulation 9(e) of the Motor Vehicles (Driving Licences) (Amendment) (No. 4) Regulations 1982 any reference to groups A or B shall be construed for all purposes on and after that date as a reference to the groups as prescribed in these Regulations on and after that date.

Effect of change in classification from groups to categories

C16–41   **33.**—(1) Subject to paragraph (4) below in licences (whether full or provisional) issued before 1st June 1990 any reference (including a reference construed in accordance with regulations 30, 31 and 32) to motor vehicles of a group specified in column (1) of the table in this regulation shall be construed as a reference to motor vehicles of the category specified opposite thereto in column (2) of that table and licences to drive vehicles of a class included in such a group shall authorise the holder to drive motor vehicles of a class included in that category in addition to motor vehicles of a class included in that group.

(2) A person who before 1st June 1990 has passed or is regarded as having passed a test to drive motor vehicles of a class included in a group specified in column (1) of the table in this regulation shall also be regarded as having passed a test to drive motor vehicles of a class included in the category specified opposite thereto in column (2) of that table.

(3) In this regulation "group" has the same meaning as it had in these Regulations before they were amended by the Motor Vehicles (Driving Licences) (Amendment) Regulations 1990.

(4) Paragraph (1) above shall not authorise a person to drive motor vehicles used for the carriage of passengers with more than 16 seats in addition to the driver's seat on or after 1st October 1992.

TABLE

(1) *Group*	(2) *Category*
A	B
B	B, limited to vehicles with automatic transmission
C	B1
D	A
E	P
F	F
G	G
H	H
J	B1, limited to invalid carriages
K	K
L	L
M	Trolley vehicles used for the carriage of passengers, with more than 16 seats in addition to the driver's seat
N	N.

Effect of change in classification on entitlement to drive large buses

34.—(1) [...]

(2) A person who holds a licence on or after 1st June 1990 to drive vehicles in categories B and D1 and who held on 31st May 1990 a licence entitling him to drive vehicles of a class included in group A or B or was entitled on that date to drive such vehicles by virtue of section 88(1) of the Road Traffic Act 1988, may also drive motor vehicles used for the carriage of passengers, with more than 16 seats in addition to the driver's seat, other than for hire and reward.

(4) The provisions of section 98(2) of the Road Traffic Act 1988 shall not apply so far as to confer on a person who holds a full licence to drive motor vehicles of certain classes only, entitlement to drive a motor vehicle used for the carriage of passengers, with more than 16 seats in addition to the driver's seat.

(5) A person may not drive a vehicle by virtue of this regulation if he could not, by reason of the provisions of section 101 of the Road Traffic Act 1988, lawfully hold a licence to drive such a vehicle.

(6) Paragraph (2) above shall cease to have effect on 1st October 1992.

C16–42

Effect of change in classification on entitlement to heavy goods vehicles to which Part IV of the Road Traffic Act 1988 does not apply

35. The holder of a licence to drive vehicles in categories B and C1 may also drive a heavy goods vehicle of any of the classes listed in regulation 29 of the Heavy Goods Vehicles (Drivers' Licences) Regulations 1977.

C16–43

REMOVAL, STORAGE AND DISPOSAL OF VEHICLES (PRESCRIBED SUMS AND CHARGES ETC.) REGULATIONS 1989

(S.I. 1989 No. 744)

C17–01   **1.**—(1) These Regulations may be cited as the Removal, Storage and Disposal of Vehicles (Prescribed Sums and Charges etc.) Regulations 1989 and shall come into force on 1st June 1989.

(2) The Removal, Storage and Disposal of Vehicles (Charges) Regulations 1985 are hereby revoked.

C17–02   **2.**—(1) In these Regulations "the Act of 1978" means the Refuse Disposal (Amenity) Act 1978 and "the Act of 1984" means the Road Traffic Regulation Act 1984.

(2) For the purposes of the provisions of regulation 3 below relating to storage, each period of 24 hours therein referred to shall be reckoned from noon on the first day after removal during which the place at which the vehicle is stored is open for the claiming of vehicles before noon.

C17–03   **3.**—(1) The prescribed sum for the purposes of section 4(5) of the Act of 1978 and section 101(4) and (4A)(b)(ii) of the Act of 1984 shall be:—

(a) in respect of removal, £105; and

(b) in respect of storage, £12 for each period of 24 hours or a part thereof during which the vehicle is in the custody of the authority;

(2) The prescribed sum for the purposes of section 4(6) of the Act of 1978 and section 101(5) and (5A)(b)(ii) of the Act shall be:

(a) in respect of removal, £105; and

(b) in respect of storage, £12 for each period of 24 hours or a part thereof during which the vehicle is in the custody of the authority;

(c) in respect of disposal, £50.

(3) The prescribed charge for the purposes of section 5(1)(a) of the Act of 1978 and section 102(2)(a) of the 1984 Act shall, in respect of removal, be £105.

(4) The prescribed scale by reference to which charges shall be ascertained in respect of storage for the purposes of section 5(1)(b) of the Act of 1984 shall be £12 for each period of 24 hours or a part thereof during which the vehicle is in the custody of the chief officer of a police force or the authority as the case may be.

(5) The prescribed manner for determining the charges recoverable in respect of disposal for the purposes of section 5(1)(c) of the Act of 1978 and section 102(2)(c) of the Act of 1984 shall be by reference to a single charge of £50.

MOTOR CARS (DRIVING INSTRUCTION) REGULATIONS 1989

(S.I. 1989 No. 2057)

PART I

Citation and commencement

1. These Regulations may be cited as the Motor Cars (Driving Instruction)   **C18–01**
Regulations 1989 and shall come into force on 1st December 1989.

Interpretation

2.—(1) In these Regulations—   **C18–02**

"the Act" means the Road Traffic Act 1988;

"continued ability and fitness test" means the test of continued ability
and fitness to give instruction in the driving of motor cars referred to
in section 125(5) of the Act and the nature of which is prescribed in
regulation 8;

"driving ability and fitness test" means the practical test of ability and
fitness to drive referred to in section 125(3)(a) of the Act and the
nature of which is prescribed in regulation 5;

"examination" means the examination of ability to give instruction in
the driving of motor cars referred to in section 125(3)(a) of the Act;

"examiner," in relation to part of the examination or the continued ability and fitness test, means an officer of the Secretary of State
appointed to conduct that part of the examination or that test;

"instructional ability and fitness test" means the practical test of ability
and fitness to give instruction in the driving of motor cars referred to
in section 125(3)(a) of the Act and the nature of which is prescribed in
regulation 6 of these Regulations;

"licence" means a licence to give driving instruction granted under section 129 of the Act;

"the register" has the meaning given by section 123(1)(a) of the Act;

"the Registrar" means the officer of the Secretary of State by whom the
register is, on behalf of the Secretary of State, compiled and maintained; and

"written examination" means the written examination referred to in
section 125(3)(a) of the Act and the nature of which is prescribed in
regulation 4 of these Regulations.

(2) In these regulations a reference to a part of the examination is a reference
to one of the three parts of the examination set out in regulation 3(2).

PART II

General provisions

3.—(1) A person who desires to submit himself for any part of the examin-   **C18–03**
ation shall supply the Registrar with such particulars as the Secretary of State
may determine.

(2) The examination shall consist of—
  (a) the written examination,
  (b) the driving ability and fitness test, and
  (c) the instructional ability and fitness test.

(3) Where a person has passed the written examination (whether before or after these Regulations are made) he shall not be eligible to take it again during the following two years.

(4) Subject to the provisions of this regulation, a person shall be regarded as having passed the examination only if the following conditions are fulfilled in his case—

  (a) he has passed the three parts of the examination in the order set out in paragraph (2) above;
  (b) he passed the driving ability and fitness test—
      (i) before 1st December 1989; or
      (ii) on his first or second attempt after the 30th November 1989; or
      (iii) on his first, second or third attempt after he had passed the written examination.
  (c) within two years after passing the written examination and having passed the driving ability and fitness test he made an application to take the instructional ability and fitness test;
  (d) he passed the instructional ability and fitness test—
      (i) before 1st December 1989; or
      (ii) on his first or second attempt after 30th November 1989; or
      (iii) on his first, second or third attempt after he had passed the written examination,
  and on a date appointed by the Registrar in respect of an application made in accordance with sub-paragraph (c).

(5) For the purposes of this regulation and regulation 9—

  (a) where a person has commenced the driving ability and fitness test or the instructional ability and fitness test and does not complete the test, the person shall be treated as having failed the test in question unless the Registrar is satisfied that the person had a reasonable excuse for not completing that test;
  (b) subject to sub-paragraph (c), a reference to the passing of the written examination or the driving ability and fitness test (including paragraph (4)(a)) shall, in relation to a person who has passed that examination or test (as the case may be) on more than one occasion, be read as a reference to the last of those occasions;
  (c) if a person takes the written examination on an occasion when he is not eligible to take it he shall not in any circumstances be regarded as having passed on that occasion.

(6) For the purposes of this regulation a person shall be deemed to have made an application on the date that his application and the fee prescribed by these Regulations are received by the Registrar.

Written examination

C18–04   4. The written examination shall consist of a theoretical examination, in which the candidate is required to answer from his own knowledge, on all or any of the following subjects—

  (a) the principles of road safety generally and their application in particular circumstances;
  (b) the techniques of driving a motor car correctly, courteously and safely,

including control of the vehicle, road procedure, recognising hazards, taking proper action with respect to hazards, dealing properly with pedestrians and other road users and the use of safety equipment;

(c) the tuition required to instruct a pupil on the matters set out in sub-paragraph (b), the correction of the pupil's errors, the manner of the instructor, the relationship between instructor and pupil and simple vehicle adaptation for disabled drivers;

(d) the theory of learning and the theory and practice of teaching and assessment;

(e) the Highway Code and other matters in the booklet in which it is published;

(f) the booklet "Your Driving Test" (D.L. 68) issued by the Department of Transport and published by HM Stationery Office;

(g) the interpretation of the reasons for failure appended to the Statement of Failure to pass the test of competence prescribed by regulation 22(2) of the Motor Vehicles (Driving Licences) Regulations 1987,

(h) knowledge, adequate to the needs of driving instruction, of the mechanism and design of a motor car; and

(j) the book "The Driving Manual," issued by the Department of Transport and published by HM Stationery Office.

Driving ability and fitness test

5.—(1) The driving ability and fitness test shall consist of tests of eyesight   **C18–05** and driving technique and the candidate shall be required to reach the qualifying standard in both tests on the same occasion.

(2) The test of eyesight shall be a test of the candidate's ability to read in good daylight, a motor vehicle registration mark containing letters and figures 79.4 millimetres in height at a distance of 27.5 metres (with the aid of glasses or contact lenses if worn).

(3) The test of driving technique shall be a test in which the candidate is required to satisfy the examiner that he has an adequate knowledge of the principles of good driving and road safety and that he can apply them in practice.

(4) A candidate taking the test of driving technique shall in particular be required to satisfy the examiner on—

(a) his expert handling of controls;

(b) his use of correct road procedure;

(c) his anticipation of the actions of other road users and taking of appropriate action;

(d) his sound judgment of distance, speed and timing; and

(e) his consideration for the convenience and safety of other road users.

(5) The candidate taking the test of driving technique shall be required to demonstrate his ability to perform all or any of the following manoeuvres—

(a) moving away straight ahead or at an angle;

(b) overtaking, meeting or crossing the path of other vehicles and taking an appropriate course;

(c) turning right hand and left hand corners;

(d) stopping the vehicle as in an emergency;

(e) driving the vehicle backwards and whilst so doing entering limited openings to the right and to the left;

(f) turning the vehicle around in the road to face in the opposite direction by the use of forward and reverse gears; and

(g) passing close to the kerb using forward and reverse gears.

Instructional ability and fitness test

6.—(1) The instructional ability and fitness test shall be a test in which the candidate is required to demonstrate his knowledge and ability by giving practical driving instruction to an examiner as if the examiner were—

(a) a novice or partly-trained pupil, and then

(b) a pupil who is at about driving test standard.

(2) The candidate shall, in respect of one or both of those levels as the examiner shall specify, instruct the examiner in such of the following subjects as the examiner shall specify as the basis of the instruction—

(a) explaining the controls of the vehicle,

(b) moving off,

(c) making normal stops,

(d) reversing, and while doing so entering limited openings to the right or to the left,

(e) turning to face the opposite direction, using forward and reverse gears,

(f) parking close to the kerb, using forward and reverse gears,

(g) using mirrors and explaining how to make an emergency stop,

(h) approaching and turning corners,

(j) judging speed, and making normal progress,

(k) road positioning,

(l) dealing with road junctions,

(m) dealing with cross roads,

(n) dealing with pedestrian crossings,

(o) meeting, crossing the path of, overtaking and allowing adequate clearance for, other vehicles and other road users, and

(p) giving correct signals.

(3) The candidate's knowledge and ability shall be assessed on—

(a) the method, clarity, adequacy and correctness of his instruction,

(b) the observation and correction of the examiner's driving errors, and

(c) his manner generally.

Motor car to be provided for practical part of examination

7.—(1) A candidate for the driving ability and fitness test or the instructional ability and fitness test shall provide, at his own expense, a motor car for the purposes of that test, in respect of which the following conditions are satisfied.

(2) The vehicle must have four wheels and be either—

(a) constructed solely for the carriage of passengers and their effects and fitted with a rigid roof, with or without a sliding panel, or

(b) a dual purpose vehicle as defined in regulation 3(2) of the Road Vehicles (Construction and Use) Regulations 1986.

(3) The vehicle must—

(a) have a readily adjustable driving seat and a seat for a forward-facing front passenger,

(b) have a steering wheel on its off-side,
(c) be provided with a means whereby the driver may, independently of the use of the accelerator or the brakes, gradually vary the proportion of the power being produced by the engine which is transmitted to the road wheels; and
(d) be otherwise suitable for the purposes of the test.

(4) The vehicle must not, during the conduct of any driving ability and fitness test, carry the distinguishing mark referred to in regulation 9(1)(b) of the Motor Vehicles (Driving Licences) Regulations 1987 or anything resembling such a distinguishing mark.

(5) In the case of a vehicle provided for the purposes of an instructional ability and fitness test, there must be in force in relation to the use of the vehicle a policy of insurance that—

(a) complies with the requirements of section 145 of the Act in relation to candidate as driver of the vehicle,
(b) complies with the requirements of that section in relation to the examiner as the driver of the vehicle as if the section applied to persons in the public service of the Crown, and
(c) insures the examiner as driver of the vehicle in respect of liability for damage to the vehicle during the test,

and throughout the test there shall be displayed in a conspicuous manner on the front and on the back of the vehicle distinguishing marks in the form referred to in regulation 9(1)(b) of the Motor Vehicles (Driving Licences) Regulations 1987.

PART III

Nature of test and provision of a motor car

8.—(1) The following provisions shall have effect where a person is   **C18–08** required to undergo the continued ability and fitness test.

(2) The test shall consist of the attendance of the examiner, while the person is giving instruction to a pupil or pupils.

(3) Unless the examiner otherwise directs, the test shall be carried out in a motor car on a road while the examiner is in the vehicle and a pupil is under instruction.

(4) The candidate shall be assessed on his instructional ability, and, in particular, in respect of the following qualities—

(a) his method, clarity, adequacy and correctness of instruction;
(b) his observation and proper correction of the pupil's errors;
(c) his manner, patience and tact in dealing with the pupil; and
(d) his ability to inspire confidence.

(5) Where the test is to be conducted in a motor car, the person shall provide a motor car which is a passenger vehicle and which is suitable for such a test.

PART IV

Additional conditions to be satisfied for the grant of a licence

9.—(1) To the conditions as to which the Registrar is required to be satisfied   **C18–09** for the grant of a licence under section 129 of the Act, there are added the following conditions which shall have effect subject to paragraph (3) below and to regulation 3(5).

(2) The additional conditions are—

(a) that the person has passed the driving ability and fitness test after passing the written examination;

(b) that he passed the driving ability and fitness test—
  (i) before 1st December 1989; or
  (ii) on his first or second attempt after 30th November 1989; or
  (iii) on his first, second or third attempt after he had passed the written examination;

(c) that he made the application within two years after passing the written examination;

(d) that—
  (i) he has not failed instructional ability and fitness test more than twice since he passed the written examination; or
  (ii) he has not failed the instructional ability and fitness test more than once since 30th November 1989.

(3) A person shall be deemed to have made an application on the date that his application and the fee prescribed by these Regulations are received by the Registrar.

Duration of licences

C18–10   10. Subject to sections 129(6) and 130 of the Act, a licence shall remain in force for a period of six months from the date of issue.

Conditions subject to which licences are granted

C18–11   11.—(1) A licence shall be granted subject to the following conditions—

(a) the holder may give instruction in the driving of a motor car only from the establishment identified in the licence; and

(b) the holder may give instruction in the driving of a motor car only if, at the time he gives such instruction, the number of approved driving instructors for whom that establishment is their principal place of work as a driving instructor is not less than the number of persons who hold a licence in which that establishment is identified.

(2) A licence, other than a licence which comes into force upon the expiry of a licence previously issued to the same person, shall also be subject to the following conditions—

(a) the holder must, for at least one fifth of the total time he spends giving instruction during the first three months' the licence is in force, receive direct supervision from an approved driving instructor;

(b) the holder must maintain in respect of each working day during the first three months the licence is in force a record of the time he spends giving instruction in the driving of a motor car, giving the particulars set out in Part I of Schedule 1 to these Regulations, and
  (i) he must continue to maintain such a record when any records previously maintained by him are being retained by or on behalf of the Secretary of State after they have been delivered pursuant to sub-paragraph (d) below, but
  (ii) he need not maintain such a record after he has complied with sub-paragraph (e) below;

(c) the record must be signed each day by the holder and by any approved driving instructor under whose direct personal supervision the holder has given instruction;

(d) the holder must on request produce all records maintained by him under this regulation to an officer authorised by the Secretary of State or (if he so required) deliver them to him for retention; and

(e) the holder must, deliver those records (other than any that have been delivered to an officer authorised by the Secretary of State pursuant to paragraph (d) and not returned) to the Registrar during the seven day period which ends three months after the licence came into force.

(3) A licence granted to a person to whom a licence has not previously been issued shall be subject to the following conditions, in addition to any conditions to which it is subject by virtue of paragraphs (1) and (2) above, that is to say—

(a) the holder must, before the end of the period which ends five weeks after the licence comes into force, have received training in the giving of practical driving instruction including all the matters set out in Part II of Schedule 1 to these Regulations for periods amounting in the aggregate to not less than 40 hours; and

(b) the holder must before the end of that five week period deliver to the Registrar, as evidence that he has received the training referred to in sub-paragraph (a), a statement—

(i) giving the particulars set out in Part III of Schedule 1 to these Regulations,

(ii) containing a declaration signed by the holder that the training has been received, and

(iii) containing a declaration, signed by each person who has given the training, that he has given the training stated to have been given by him;

and any relevant training received by the holder not more than 12 months before the date that the licence comes into force shall count as training for the purposes of this paragraph.

Form of licences

12. A licence shall be in the form set out in, and contain the particulars required by, Schedule 2 to these Regulations.

Part V

Fees

13. The fee to be paid by a person who applies in respect of a matter mentioned in an item in column 2 of the Table below shall be the amount specified in that item in column 3 of that Table. **C18–12**

TABLE

(1) Item No.	(2) Matter in respect of which application is made	(3)
1	Submission to written examination	£50
2	Submission to driving ability and fitness test	£55
3	Submission to instructional ability and fitness test	£55
4	Retention of name in the register	£180
5	A licence	£85
6	Entry to the register following the passing of the examination	£180
7	Entry to the register without passing the examination by virtue of sections 125(7) or 126(3) of the Act.	£180

Official title of registered person and certificate of registration

C18–13   14.—(1) The official title for use by persons whose names are in the register shall be "Department of Transport Approved Driving Instructor."

(2) The certificate for issue to persons whose names are in the register as evidence of their names being therein shall be in the form set out in Schedule 3 to these Regulations.

Form of badge

C18–14   15. The badge for use by persons whose names are in the register as evidence of their names being therein shall be in the form set out in Schedule 4 to these Regulations.

Exhibition of certificate of registration or licence

C18–15   16. The prescribed manner of fixing to and exhibiting on a motor car a certificate or a licence for the purposes of section 123(2) of the Act is the manner specified in paragraph (2).

(2) The certificate or licence shall be—

(a) fixed to and immediately behind the front windscreen of the motor car on its nearside edge, and

(b) exhibited so that the particulars on the back of the certificate or licence are clearly visible in daylight from outside the motor car and the particulars on the front of the certificate or licence are clearly visible from the front nearside seat of the vehicle, where fitted.

(3) The prescribed form of certificate for the purposes of section 123(2) is a certificate in the form set out in Schedule 3 to these Regulations.

Revocations and transitional provisions

C18–16   17.—(1) The Regulations specified in Part I of Schedule 5 to these Regulations are revoked.

(2) Part II of Schedule 5 contains transitional provisions relating to applications for the entry of a person's name in the register and for the grant of a licence made before 1st December 1989.

Regulation 11   SCHEDULE 1

LICENCE CONDITIONS

PART I

PARTICULARS OF WHICH A RECORD IS TO BE KEPT BY CERTAIN LICENCE HOLDERS DURING FIRST THREE MONTHS THAT A LICENCE IS IN FORCE

1. The name of the holder of the licence.
2. The number of the licence.
3. The name of the establishment from which the holder of the licence has given instruction.
4. The name of the person under whose direct personal supervision the holder of the licence has given instruction.
5. In respect of each working day—
   (a) the date;
   (b) the total number of hours spent giving instruction from the establishment; and
   (c) the periods spent under the direct personal supervision of the person referred to in paragraph 4 above.

PART II

MATTERS TO BE INCLUDED IN PRACTICAL DRIVING INSTRUCTION TRAINING

1. Explaining the controls of the vehicle, including the use of dual controls.
2. Moving off.
3. Making normal stops.
4. Reversing, and while doing so entering limited openings to the right or to the left.
5. Turning to face the opposite direction, using forward and reverse gears.
6. Parking close to the kerb, using forward and reverse gears.
7. Using mirrors and explaining how to make an emergency stop.
8. Approaching and turning corners.
9. Judging speed and making normal progress.
10. Road positioning.
11. Dealing with road junctions.
12. Dealing with cross roads.
13. Dealing with pedestrian crossings.
14. Meeting, crossing the path of, overtaking and allowing adequate clearance for, other vehicles and other road users.
15. Giving correct signals.
16. Comprehension of traffic signs, including road markings and traffic control signals.
17. Method, clarity, adequacy and correctness of instruction.

18. Observation and correction of driving errors committed by pupils and general manner.

Part III

Particulars to be Given in Statement to Registrar

1. The name and address of the holder of the licence.

2. The number of the licence.

3. The name and address of the establishment where the training has been given.

4. The name and address of the person or persons who have given the training.

5. The matters included in the training.

6. The dates on which the training has been given.

7. The number of hours of training spent on each of the matters.

MOTOR VEHICLES (DRIVING LICENCES) (AMENDMENT) REGULATIONS 1990

(S.I. 1990 No. 842)

C19–01   *These regulations amend the Motor Vehicles (Driving Licences) Regulations 1987 (S.I. 1987 No. 1378) and are incorporated therein.*

They give effect, with permitted derogations and in respect of motor vehicles other than heavy goods and public service vehicles, to the system of classification for motor vehicles set out in Article 3 of Council Directive (EEC) No. 80/1263 of December 4, 1980 on the introduction of a Community driving licence. The principal amendments are as follows:

(a) *changes are made in respect of the entitlement to drive motor vehicles used for the carriage of passengers, other than for hire and reward, with more than 16 seats in addition to the driver's seat. A person who is already the holder of an ordinary driving licence continues to have entitlement to drive such vehicles. New licence holders only have provisional entitlement and must have applied for a public service vehicle driver's licence. A person who has a public service vehicle driver's licence to drive such vehicles for hire and reward may also drive them other than for hire and reward.*

(b) *the 1987 Regulations are also amended so as to prohibit a learner motor cyclist carrying any pillion passenger even is he is a qualified driver.*

(c) *a separate fee for a licence granted to persons who have been convicted of certain drinking and driving offences is prescribed. This is set at £20. such persons, if disqualified on or after November 1, 1988, would previously have paid £5 for the grant of a new licence on the expiry of that period of disqualification. The £5 fee remains in respect of those disqualified for other offences.*

(d) *additional circumstances under which the Secretary of State may require a person to submit himself for a medical examination regarding his fitness to drive are prescribed. The Secretary of State need not pay the fees involved in such prescribed circumstances, which relate to disqualifications after drinking and driving offences.*

(e) *where the appropriate references are added to the counterparts of licences so as*

748

to reflect amendments to the Road Traffic Act 1988 and the Road Traffic Offenders Act 1988 brought about by the Driving Licences (Community Driving Licence) Regulations 1990 (S.I. 1990 No. 114).

FIXED PENALTY OFFENCES ORDER 1992

(S.I. 1992 No. 345)

1. The Order may be cited as the Fixed Penalty Offences Order 1992 and shall come into force on 1st April 1992.   **C20–01**

2. The offence under section 15(4) of the Road Traffic Act 1988 of driving a motor vehicle in contravention of section 15(3) of that Act shall be a fixed penalty offence and, in consequence, the entry in Schedule 3 to the Road Traffic Offenders Act 1988 relating to the Road Traffic Act 1988 shall be modified by the insertion, after the entry relating to section 15(2) of the Road Traffic Act 1988, of the words "RTA section 15(4)" in column (1) and "Breach of restriction on carrying children in the rear of vehicles" in column (2).

FIXED PENALTY ORDER 1992

(S.I. 1992 No. 346)

1.—(1) This Order may be cited as the Fixed Penalty Order 1992 and shall come into force on 1st April 1992.   **C21–01**

(2) This Order applies in relation to a fixed penalty offence alleged to have been committed on or after 1st April 1992.

(3) This Order shall not extend to Scotland.

2. The fixed penalty for an offence shown in column (1) of the Schedule to this Order shall be the amount shown opposite thereto in column (2).   **C21–02**

Article 2   SCHEDULE

(1) *Offence*	(2) *Fixed Penalty*
(a) A fixed penalty offence other than one in paragraph (b), (c) or (d) below;	£20.00
(b) A fixed penalty parking offence committed in London before the day on which the first priority route order comes into force and such an offence committed on or after that day in London otherwise than on a red route;	£30.00
(c) A fixed penalty parking offence committed in London on a red route on or after the day on which the first priority route order comes into force;	£40.00
(d) A fixed penalty offence involving obligatory endorsement	£40.00

In this Schedule:

"fixed penalty parking offence" means:

   (i) an offence under the Road Traffic Regulation Act 1984 which is a fixed penalty offence, which does not involve obligatory endorsement and which is committed in respect of a stationary vehicle;

   (ii) an offence under section 15(1) of the Greater London Council (General Powers) Act 1974;

   (iii) an offence under section 137(1) of the Highways Act 1980;

   (iv) an offence under section 19 of the Road Traffic Act 1988; or

   (v) an offence under section 42 of the Road Traffic Act 1988 consisting in the causing of an unnecessary obstruction of a road in breach of regulation 103 of the Road Vehicles (Construction and Use) Regulations 1986;

   or, in the case of paragraph (b) above,

   (vi) an offence under the Parks Regulation Acts 1872 and 1926 consisting in the failure to comply with, or acting in contravention of, regulation 4(30) of the Royal and other Parks and Gardens Regulations 1977;

"London" means the areas which, under section 76(1) of the London Government Act 1963, comprise the Metropolitan Police District together with the City of London, the Inner Temple and the Middle Temple;

"red route" means a length of road—

   (1) to which, for the time being, a traffic sign lawfully placed on the road relates bearing the words, "Red Route", with or without any other word or any sign or other indication, or

   (2) on which, for the time being, a traffic sign consisting of a red line or mark has been lawfully placed, or

   (3) to which, for the time being, such traffic sign as is referred to in paragraph (1) above relates and on which, for the time being, such traffic sign as is referred to in paragraph (2) above has been lawfully placed;

"the first priority route order" means the first order made under section 50 of the Road Traffic Act 1991;

"traffic sign" means a traffic sign for the purposes of section 64(1) of the Road Traffic Regulation Act 1984 which conveys any restriction or prohibition under an order made under the said Act of 1984.

VEHICLES (CHARGES FOR RELEASE FOR IMMOBILISATION DEVICES) REGULATIONS 1992

(S.I. 1992 No. 386)

C22–01   **1.**—(1) These Regulations may be cited as the Vehicles (Charges for Release from Immobilisation Devices) Regulations 1992 and shall come into force on 1st April 1992.

(2) The Vehicles (Charges for Release from Immobilisation Devices) Regulations 1991 are hereby revoked.

2. For the purposes of section 104(4) of the Road Traffic Regulation Act 1984, the charge in respect of the release of a vehicle from an immobilisation device shall be £38.

ROAD TRAFFIC OFFENDERS (PRESCRIBED DEVICES) ORDER 1992

(S.I. 1992 No. 1209)

1.This Order may be cited as the Road Traffic Offenders (Prescribed **C23–01**
Devices) Order 1992 and shall come into force on 1st July 1992.
2. A device designed or adapted for measuring by radar the speed of motor vehicles is a prescribed device for the purposes of section 20 of the Road Traffic Offenders Act 1988.

MOTOR CARS (DRIVING INSTRUCTION) (AMENDMENT) REGULATIONS 1992

(S.I. 1992 No. 1621)

These regulations amend the Motor Cars (Driving Instruction) Regulations 1989 **C24–01**
(S.I. 1989 No. 2057) and are incorporated therein.
They increase from £50 to £54 the fees payable for the driving ability and fitness test and the instructional ability and fitness test. The fee for the retention or entry of a person's name in the register is increased from £170 to £180.

ROAD TRAFFIC OFFENDERS (PRESCRIBED DEVICES) (NO. 2) ORDER 1992

(S.I. 1992 No. 2843)

1. This Order may be cited as the Road Traffic Offenders (Prescribed **C25–01**
Devices) (No. 2) Order 1992 and shall come into force on 1st January 1993.
2. A device designed or adapted for recording by photographic or other image recording means the position of motor vehicles in relation to light signals is a prescribed device for the purposes of section 20 of the Road Traffic Offenders Act 1988.

MOTOR VEHICLES (WEARING OF SEAT BELTS BY CHILDREN IN FRONT SEATS) REGULATIONS 1993

(S.I. 1993 No. 31)

Citation, commencement and revocations

C26–01   1.—(1) These Regulations may be cited as the Motor Vehicles (Wearing of Seat Belts by Children in Front Seats) Regulations 1993 and shall come into force on 2nd Febraury 1993.

(2) The Motor Vehicles (Wearing of Seat Belts by Children) Regulations 1982 are hereby revoked.

General interpretation

C26–02   2.—(1) In these Regulations—

"the Act" means the Road Traffic Act 1988;

"Construction and Use Regulations" means the Road Vehicles (Construction and Use) Regulations 1986;

"front seat", in relation to a vehicle, means a seat which is wholly or partially in the front of the vehicle and "rear seat", in relation to a vehicle, means any seat which is not a front seat (see also regulation 4);

maximum laden weight" has the meaning given by Part IV of Schedule 6 to the Road Traffic Regulation Act 1984;

"medical certificate" has the meaning given in Schedule 1 to these Regulations;

"restraint system" means a system combining a seat fixed to the structure of the vehicle by appropriate means and a seat belt for which at least one anchorage point is located on the seat structure;

"seat belt", except in this Regulation, includes a child restraint and references to wearing a seat belt shall be construed accordingly;

"disabled person's belt", "lap belt", "seat", and "three point belt" have the meanings given by regulation 47(8) of the Construction and use Regulations.

(2) Without prejudice to section 17 of the Interpretation Act 1978, a reference to a provision of the Construction and Use Regulations is a reference to that provision as from time to time amended or as from time to time re-enacted with or without modification.

(3) In these Regulations—

"child" means a person under the age of 14 years;

"large child" means a child who is not a small child; and

"small child" means a child who is—

(a) aged under 12 years; and

(b) under 150 centimetres in height.

(4) In these Regulations, "adult belt" means a seat belt in respect of which one or more of the following requirements is satisfied, namely that—

(a) it is a three-point belt which has been marked in accordance with regulation 47(7) of the Construction and Use Regulations;

(b) it is a lap belt which has been so marked;

(c) it is a seat belt that falls within regulation 47(4)(c)(i) or (ii) of those Regulations;

(d) it is a seat belt fitted in a relevant vehicle ("the vehicle in question") and comprised in a restraint system—

   (i) of a type which has been approved by an authority of another member State for use by all persons who are either aged 13 years or more or of 150 centimetres or more in height, and

   (ii) in respect of which, by virtue of such approval, the requirements of the law of another member State corresponding to these Regulations would be met were it to be worn by persons who are either aged 13 years or more or of 150 centimetres or more in height when travelling in the vehicle in question in that State.

(5) In these Regulations, "child restraint" means a seat belt or other device in respect of which the following requirements are satisfied, namely that—

   (a) it is a seat belt or any other description of restraining device for the use of a child which is—

      (i) designed either to be fitted directly to a suitable anchorage or to be used in conjunction with an adult belt and held in place by the restraining action of that belt, and

      (ii) marked in accordance with regulation 47(7) of the Construction and use Regulations; or

   (b) it is a seat belt consisting of or comprised in a restraint system fitted in a relevant vehicle ("the vehicle in question"), being a restraint system—

      (i) of a type which has been approved by an authority of another member State for use by a child, and

      (ii) in respect of which, by virtue of such approval, the requirements of the law of that State corresponding to these Regulations would be met were it to be worn by a child when travelling in the vehicle in question in that State.

(6) Subject to paragraph (7), for the purposes of these Regulations, a seat shall be regarded as provided with an adult belt if an adult belt is fixed in such a position that it can be worn by an occupier of that seat.

(7) A seat shall not be regarrded as provided with an adult belt if the belt—

   (a) has an inertia reel mechanism which is locked as a result of the vehicle being, or having been, on a steep incline, or

   (b) does not comply with the requirements of regulation 48 of the Construction and Use Regulations.

(8) For the purposes of these Regulations, a seat shall be regarded as provided with a child restraint if a child restraint is—

   (a) fixed in such a position that it can be worn by an occupier of that seat, or

   (b) elsewhere in or on the vehicle but—

      (i) could readily be fixed in such a position without the aid of tools, and

      (ii) is not being worn by a child for whom it is appropriate and who is occupying another seat.

(9) For the purposes of these Regulations, a seat belt is appropriate—

   (a) in relation to a child aged under 3 years, if it is a child restraint of a description prescribed for a child of his height and weight by regulation 5;

   (b) in relation to a child aged 3 years or more, if it is a child restraint of a description prescribed for a child of his height and weight by regulation 5 or is an adult belt; or

(c) in relation to a person aged 14 years or more, if it is an adult belt.

(10) Unless the context otherwise requires, in these Regulations—

(a) any reference to a numbered regulation is a reference to the regulation bearing that number in these Regulations; and

(b) a numbered paragraph is a reference to the paragraph bearing that number in the regulation or Schedule in which the reference appears.

Interpretation of references to relevant vehicles

C26–03   3.—(1) In these Regulations, "relevant vehicle" means—

(a) a passenger car,

(b) a light goods vehicle, or

(c) a small bus.

(2) For the purposes of this regulation—

"light goods vehicle" means a goods vehicle which—

(a) has four or more wheels,

(b) has a maximum design speed exceeding 25 kilometres per hour,

(c) has a maximum laden weight not exceeding 3.5 tonnes;

"passenger car" has the same meaning as in section 15 of the Act;

"small bus" means a motor vehicle which—

(a) is constructed or adapted for use for the carriage of passengers and is not a goods vehicle,

(b) has more than 8 seats in addition to the driver's seat,

(c) has four or more wheels,

(d) has a maximum design speed exceeding 25 kilometres per hour,

(e) has a maximum laden weight not exceeding 3.5 tonnes, and

(f) is not constructed or adapted for the carriage of standing passengers.

Interpretation of references to the front of a vehicle

C26–04   4.—(1) This regulation has effect for the purpose of defining in relation to a vehicle what part of the vehicle is to be regarded as the front of the vehicle for the purposes of section 15(1) of the Act and these Regulations.

(2) Subject to paragraph (3), every part of the vehicle forward of the transverse vertical plane passing through the rearmost part of the driver's seat shall be regarded as the front of the vehicle; and accordingly no part of the vehicle of the rear of that plane shall be regarded as being in the front of the vehicle.

(3) Where a vehicle has a deck which is above the level of the driver's head when he is in the normal driving position, no part of the vehicle above that level shall be regarded as being in the front of the vehicle.

Description of seat belts to be worn by children

C26–05   5.—(1) For a child of any particular height and weight travelling in a particular vehicle, the description of seat belt described for the purposes of section 15(1) of the Act to be worn by him is—

(a) if he is a small child and the vehicle is a relevant vehicle, a child restraint of a description specified in sub-paragraph (a) or (b) of paragraph (2);

(b) if he is a small child and the vehicle is not a relevant vehicle, a child restraint of a description specified in sub-paragraph (a) of paragraph (2);

(c) if he is a large child, a child restraint of a description specified in sub-paragraph (a) of paragraph (2) or an adult belt.

(2) The descriptions of seat belt referred to in paragraph (1) are—

(a) a child restraint with the marking required under regulation 47(7) of the Construction and use Regulations if the marking indicates that it is suitable for his weight and either indicates that it is suitable for his height or contains no indication as respects height;

(b) a child restraint which would meet the requirements of the law of another member State corresponding to these Regulations were it to be worn by that child when travelling in that vehicle in that State.

Vehicles to which section 15(1) of the Act does not apply

6.—Two-wheeled motor cycles with or without sidecars are exempt from the prohibition in section 15(1) of the Act.

Exemptions

7.—(1) The prohibition in section 15(1) of the Act shall not apply in relation to—   **C26–06**

(a) a small child aged 3 years or more if a seat belt of a description prescribed by regulation 5 for a small child of his height and weight is not available for him in the front or rear of the vehicle and he is wearing an adult belt;

(b) a child for whom there is a medical certificate;

(c) a child aged under 1 year in a carry cot provided that the carry cot is restrained by straps;

(d) a disabled child who is wearing a disabled person's belt; or

(e) a child riding in a motor car first used before 1st January 1965 if—

(i) the vehicle has no rear seat, and

(ii) apart from the driver's seat, no seat in the vehicle is provided with a seat belt which is appropriate for that child,

and for the purposes of this paragraph, the date on which a vehicle is first used shall be determined in accordance with regulation 3(3) of the Construction and Use Regulations.

(2) The prohibition in section 15(1) of the Act shall not apply in relation to a child riding in a vehicle which—

(a) is being used to provide a local service within the meaning of the Transport Act 1985; and

(b) is neither a motor car nor a passenger car.

(3) The prohibition in section 15(1) of the Act shall not apply in relation to a large child if no appropriate seat belt is available for him in the front of the vehicle.

(4) For the purposes of this regulation, a reference to a seat belt being available shall be construed in accordance with Schedule 2.

Regulation 2(1)   SCHEDULE 1

MEANING OF "MEDICAL CERTIFICATE"

PART I

C26–07   **1.**—(1) Subject to paragraph 2, in these Regulations, "medical certificate", in relation to a person driving or riding in a vehicle, means—

    (a) a valid certificate signed by a medical practitioner to the effect that it is inadvisable on medical grounds for him to wear a seat belt, or

    (b) a valid certificate to such effect issued by the authority having power to issue such a certificate under the law of another member State corresponding to these Regulations.

    2. A certificate shall not be regarded as a medical certificate in relation to a person driving or riding in a vehicle for the purposes of these Regulations unless—

    (a) it specifies its period of validity and bears the symbol shown in Part II of this Schedule; or

    (b) the person is aged under 14 years and the vehicle is not a relevant vehicle.

    3. Paragraph 2 does not apply in relation to a certificate issued before 1st January 1995.

PART II

(see paragaph 2(a) in Part I of this Schedule)

Regulation 7(4)   SCHEDULE 2

INTERPRETATION OF REFERENCE TO AVAILABILITY OF SEAT BELTS

C26–08   **1.** For the purposes of these Regulations, in relation to a child riding in a vehicle,—

    (a) if any front seat in the vehicle (other than the driver's seat) is provided with an adult belt, that belt shall be regarded as being available for him in the front of the vehicle unless the requirements of paragraph 2 are satisfied in relation to that person, that seat and that belt; and

    (b) if any rear seat in the vehicle is provided with an adult belt, that belt shall be regarded as being available for him in the rear of the vehicle unless the requirements of paragraph 2 are satisfied in relation to that person, that seat and that belt.

    2. The requirements of this paragraph are satisfied in relation to a particular child ("the child in question") and a particular seat ("the relevant seat") provided with a particular seat belt ("the relevant belt") if—

(a) another person is wearing the relevant belt;

(b) another child is occupying the relevant seat and wearing a child restraint which is an appropriate child restraint for that child;

(c) another person, being a person holding a medical certificate, is occupying the relevant seat;

(d) a disabled person (not being the child in question) is occupying the relevant seat and wearing a disabled person's belt;

(e) by reason of his disability, it would not be practicable for the child in question to wear the relevant belt;

(f) the child in question is prevented from occupying the relevant seat by the presence of a carry cot which is restrained by straps and in which there is a child aged under 1 year;

(g) the child in question is prevented from occupying the relevant seat by the presence of a child restraint which could not readily be removed without the aid of tools; or

(h) the relevant seat is specially designed so that—

    (i) its configuration can be adjusted in order to increase the space in the vehicle available for goods or personal effects, and

    (ii) when it is so adjusted the seat cannot be used as such,

and the configuration is adjusted in the manner dscribed in sub-paragraph (i) above and it would not be reasonably practicable for the goods and personal effects being carried in the vehicle to be so carried were the configuration not so adjusted.

3. Paragraphs 2(b) and (d) shall not apply unless the presence of the other person renders it impracticable for the child in question to wear the relevant belt.

4. Paragraph 2(f) shall not apply if it would be reasonably practicable for the carry cot to be carried in any other part of the vehicle where it could be restrained by straps so as to render it practicable for the child in question to wear the relevant belt.

5. Paragraph 2(g) shall not apply if the child restraint is appropriate for the child in question.

MOTOR VEHICLES (WEARING OF SEAT BELTS) REGULATIONS 1993

(S.I. 1993 No. 176)

PART I

INTRODUCTION

Citation, commencement and revocations

1.—(1) These Regulations may be cited as the Motor Vehicles (Wearing of Seat Belts Regulations 1993 and shall come into force on 2nd Febraury 1993.   **C27–01**

(2) The Regulations set out in Schedule 3 to these Regulations are hereby revoked.

General interpretation

2.—(1) In these Regulations—

"the Act" means the Road Traffic Act 1988;

"the Construction and Use Regulations" means the Road Vehicles (Construction and Use) Regulations 1986;

"licensed hire car" has the meaning given by section 13(3) of the Transport Act 1985;

"licensed taxi" has the meaning given by section 13(3) of the Transport Act 1985;

"maximum laden weight" has the meaning given by Part IV of Schedule 6 to the Road Traffic Regulation Act 1984;

"medical certificate" has the meaning given in Schedule 1 to these Regulations;

"passenger car" has the same meaning as in section 15 of the Act;

"private hire vehicle" means a motor vehicle which has no more than 8 seats in addition to the driver's seat, other than a licensed taxi or a public service vehicle (within the meaning of the Public Passenger Vehicles Act 1981), which is provided for hire with the services of a driver for the purposes of carrying passengers and which displays a sign pursuant to either section 21 of the Vehicles (Excise) Act 1971 or section 48(2) of the Local Government (Miscellaneous Provisions) Act 1976 or any similar enactment;

"rear seat" in relation to a vehicle means a seat not being the driver's seat, a seat alongside the driver's seat or a specified passenger seat;

"restraint system" means a system combining a seat fixed to the structure of the vehicle by appropriate menas and a seat belt for which at least one anchorage point is located to the seat structure;

"seat belt" except in this regulation, includes a child restraint and references to wearing a seat belt shall be construed accordingly;

"trade licence" has the meaning given by section 38(1) of the Vehicles (Excise) Act 1971;

"disabled persons's belt", "lap belt", "seat", "specified passenger seat" and "three point belt" have the meanings given by regulation 47(8) of the Construction and use Regulations.

(2) Without prejudice to section 17 of the Interpretation Act 1978, a reference to a provision in any subordinate legislation (within the meaning of that Act) is a reference to that provision as from time to time amended or as from time to time re-enacted with or without modification.

(3) In these Regulations—

"child" means a person under the age of 14 years;

"large child" means a child who is not a small child; and

"small child" means a child who is—

(a) aged under 12 years; and

(b) under 150 centimetres in height.

(4) In these Regulations, "adult belt" means a seat belt in respect of which one or more of the following requirements is satisfied, namely that—

(a) it is a three-point belt which has been marked in accordance with regulation 47(7) of the Construction and use Regulations;

(b) it is a lap belt which has been so marked;

(c) it is a seat belt that falls within regulation 47(4)(c)(i) or (ii) of those Regulations;

(d) it is a seat belt fitted in a relevant vehicle ("the vehicle in question") and comprised in a restraint system—

(i) of a type which has been approved by an authority of another member State for use by all persons who are either aged 13 years or more or of 150 centimetres or more in height, and

(ii) in respect of which, by virtue of such approval, the requirements of the law of another member State corresponding to these Regulations would be met were it to be worn by persons who are either aged 13 years or more or of 150 centimetres or more in height when travelling in the vehicle in question in that State.

(5) In these Regulations, "child restraint" means a seat belt or other device in respect of which the following requirements are satisfied, namely that—

(a) it is a seat belt or any other description of restraining device for the use of a child which is—
   (i) designed either to be fitted directly to a suitable anchorage or to be used in conjunction with an adult belt and held in place by the restraining action of that belt, and
   (ii) marked in accordance with regulation 47(7) of the Construction and Use Regulations; or

(b) it is a seat belt consisting of or comprised in a restraint system fitted in a relevant vehicle ("the vehicle in question"), being a restraint system—
   (i) of a type which has been approved by an authority of another member State for use by a child, and
   (ii) in respect of which, by virtue of such approval, the requirements of the law of that State corresponding to these Regulations would be met were it to be worn by a child when travelling in the vehicle in question in that State.

(6) Subject to paragraph (7), for the purposes of these Regulations, a seat shall be regarded as provided with an adult belt if an adult belt is fixed in such a position that it can be worn by an occupier of that seat.

(7) A seat shall not be regarded as provided with an adult belt if the belt—

(a) has an inertia reel mechanism which is locked as a result of the vehicle being, or having been, on a steep incline, or

(b) does not comply with the requirements of regulation 48 of the Construction and Use Regulations.

(8) For the purposes of these Regulations, a seat belt is appropriate—

(a) in relation to a child aged under 3 years, if it is of a description prescribed for a child of his height and weight by regulation 8;

(b) in relation to a child aged 3 years or more, if it is a child restraint of a description prescribed for a child of his height and weight by regulation 8 or is an adult belt; or

(c) in relation to a person aged 14 years or more, if it is an adult belt.

(9) For the purposes of these Regulations, any reference to a seat belt being available shall be construed in accordance with Schedule 2 to these Regulations.

(10) Unless the context otherwise requires, in these Regulations—

(a) any reference to a numbered regulation is a reference to the regulation bearing that number in these Regulations; and

(b) a numbered paragraph is a reference to the paragraph bearing that number in the regulation or Schedule in which the reference appears.

Interpretation of references to relevant vehicles

3.—(1) In these Regulations, "relevant vehicle" means—   **C27–03**

(a) a passenger car,

(b) a light goods vehicle, or

    (c) a small bus.

    (2) For the purposes of this regulation—

       "light goods vehicle" means a goods vehicle which—

         (a) has four or more wheels,

         (b) has a maximum design speed exceeding 25 kilometres per hour,

         (c) has a maximum laden weight not exceeding 3.5 tonnes, and

       "small bus" means a motor vehicle which—

         (a) is constructed or adapted for use for the carriage of passengers and is not a goods vehicle,

         (b) has more than 8 seats in addition to the driver's seat,

         (c) has four or more wheels,

         (d) has a maximum design speed exceeding 25 kilometres per hour,

         (e) has a maximum laden weight not exceeding 3.5 tonnes, and

         (f) is not constructed or adapted for the carriage of standing passengers.

PART II

ADULTS IN THE FRONT OR REAR OF A VEHICLE

General

C27–04   4. This Part of these Regulations has effect for the purpose of section 14 of the Act.

Requirement for adults to wear adult belts

C27–05   5.—(1) Subject to the following provisions of these Regulations, every person—

      (a) driving a motor vehicle (other than a two-wheeled motor cycle with or without a sidecar);

      (b) riding in a front seat of a motor vehicle (other than a two-wheeled motor cycle with or without a sidecar); or

      (c) riding in a rear seat of a motor car or a passenger car which is not a motor car;

shall wear an adult belt.

    (2) Paragraph (1) does not apply to a person under the age of 14 years.

Exemptions

C27–06   6.—(1) The requirements of regulation 5 do not apply to—

      (a) a person holding a medical certificate;

      (b) a person using a vehicle constructed or adapted for the delivery of goods or mail to consumers or addressees, as the case may be, while engaged in making local rounds of deliveries or collections;

      (c) a person driving a vehicle while performing a manoeuvre which includes reversing;

      (d) a qualified driver (within the meaning given by regulation 9 of the Motor Vehicles (Driving Licences) Regulations 1987, who is supervising the holder of a provisional licence (within the meaning of Part III of the Act) while that holder is performing a manoeuvre which includes reversing;

      (e) a person by whom, as provided in the Motor Vehicles (Driving

Licences) Regulations 1987, a test of competence to drive is being conducted and his wearing a seat belt would endanger himself or any
other person;
 (f) a person driving or riding in a vehicle while it is being used for fire
brigade or police purposes or for carrying a person in lawful custody
(a person who is being so carried being included in this exemption);
 (g) the driver of—
   (i) a licensed taxi while it is being used for seeking hire, or answer-
ing a call for hire, or carrying a passenger for hire, or
   (ii) a private hire vehicle while it is being used to carry a passenger
for hire;
 (h) a person riding in a vehicle, being used under a trade licence, for the
purpose of investigating or remedying a mechanical fault in the
vehicle;
 (j) a disabled person who is wearing a disabled person's belt; or
 (k) a person riding in a vehicle while it is taking part in a procession
organised by or on behalf of the Crown.
 (2) Without prejudice to paragraph (1)(k), the requirements of regulation 5
do not apply to a person riding in a vehicle which is taking part in a procession
held to mark or commemorate an event if either—
 (a) the procession is one commonly or customarily held in the police area
or areas in which it is being held, or
 (b) notice in respect of the procession was given in accordance with section 11 of the Public Order Act 1986.
 (3) The requirements of regulation 5 do not apply to—
 (a) a person driving a vehicle if the driver's seat is not provided with an
adult belt;
 (b) a person riding in the front of a vehicle if no adult belt is available for
him in the front of the vehicle;
 (c) a person riding in the rear of a vehicle if no adult belt is available for
him in the rear of the vehicle.

PART III

CHILDREN IN THE REAR OF A VEHICLE

General

7. This Part of these Regulations has effect for the purpose of section 15(3) **C27–07**
and (3A) of the Act.

Description of seat belts to be worn by children

8.—(1) For a child of any particular height and weight travelling in a particular vehicle, the description of seat belt prescribed for the purposes of section 15(3) of the Act to be worn by him is—
 (a) if he is a small child and the vehicle is a relevant vehicle, a child
restraint of a description specified in sub-paragraph (a) or (b) of paragraph (2);
 (b) if he is a small child and the vehicle is not a relevant vehicle, a child
restraint of a description specified in sub-paragraph (a) of paragraph
(2);

(c) if he is a large child, a child restraint of a description specified in sub-paragraph (a) of paragraph (2) or an adult belt.
(2) The descriptions of seat belt referred to in paragraph (1) are—
(a) a child restraint with the marking required under regulation 47(7) of the Construction and use Regulations if the marking indicates that it is suitable for his weight and either indicates that it is suitable for his height or contains no indication as respects height;
(b) a child restraint which would meet the requirements of the law of another member State corresponding to these Regulations were it to be worn by that child when travelling in that vehicle in that State.

Vehicles to which section 15(3) and (3A) of the Act do not apply

C27–08   9. The following classes of vehicles are exempt from the prohibition in section 15(3) and (3A) of the Act, that is to say—
(a) vehicles which are neither motor cars nor passenger cars;
(b) licensed taxis and licensed hire cars in which (in each case) the rear seats are separated from the driver by a fixed partition.

Exemptions

C27–09   10.—(1) The prohibitions in section 15(3) and (3A) of the Act do not apply in relation to—
(a) a small child aged 3 years or more if a seat belt of a description prescribed by regulation 8 for a small child of his height and weight is not available in the front or rear of the vehicle and he is wearing an adult belt;
(b) a child for whom there is a medical certificate;
(c) a child aged under 1 year in a carry cot provided that the carry cot is restrained by straps; or
(d) a disabled child who is wearing a disabled person's belt.
(2) The prohibition in section 15(3) of the Act does not apply in relation to a small child in a passenger car if no appropriate seat belt is available for him in the front or in the rear of the vehicle.
(3) The prohibition in section 15(3) of the Act does not apply in relation to a small child in a vehicle other than a passenger car if no appropriate seat belt is available for him in the rear of the vehicle.
(4) The prohibition in section 15(3) of the Act does no apply in relation to a large child in any vehicle if no appropriate seat belt is available for him in the rear of the vehicle.
(5) The prohibition in section 15(3A) of the Act does not apply in relation to a child if no appropriate seat belt is available for him in the front of the vehicle.

Regulation 2(1)   SCHEDULE 1

MEANING OF "MEDICAL CERTIFICATE"

Part I

C27–10   1.—(1) Subject to paragraph 2, in these Regulations, "medical certificate", in relation to a person driving or riding in a vehicle, means—

(a) a valid certificate signed by a medical practitioner to the effect that it is inadvisable on medical grounds for him to wear a seat belt, or

(b) a valid certificate to such effect issued by the authority having power to issue such a certificate under the law of another member State corresponding to these Regulations.

2. A certificate shall not be regarded as a medical certificate in relation to a person driving or riding in a vehicle for the purposes of these Regulations unless—

(a) it specifies its period of validity and bears the symbol shown in Part II of this Schedule; or

(b) the person is aged under 14 years and the vehicle is not a relevant vehicle.

3. Paragraph 2 does not apply in relation to a certificate issued before 1st January 1995.

PART II

(see paragaph 2(a) in Part I of this Schedule)

Regulation 2(9)   SCHEDULE 2

INTERPRETATION OF REFERENCES TO AVAILABILITY OF SEAT BELTS

1. For the purposes of these Regulations, in relation to a person aged 14 **C27–11** years or more riding in a vehicle,—

(a) if any front seat in the vehicle (other than the driver's seat) is provided with an adult belt, that belt shall be regarded as being available for him in the front of the vehicle unless the requirements of paragraph 3 are satisfied in relation to that person, that seat and that belt; and

(b) if any rear seat in the vehicle is provided with an adult belt, that belt shall be regarded as being available for him in the rear of the vehicle unless the requirements of paragraph 3 are satisfied in relation to that person, that seat and that belt.

2. For the purposes of these Regulations, in relation to a child riding in a vehicle,—

(a) if any front seat in the vehicle (other than the driver's seat) is provided with an appropriate seat belt, that belt shall be regarded as an appropriate seat belt available for him in the front of the vehicle unless the requirements of paragraph 3 are satisfied in relation to that child, that seat and that belt; and

(b) if any rear seat in a vehicle is provided with an appropriate seat belt, that belt shall be regarded as an appropriate seat belt available for him in the rear of the vehicle unless the requirements of paragraph 3 are satisfied in relation to that child, that seat and that belt.

3. The requirements of this paragraph are satisfied in relation to a particular person ("the person in question") and a particular seat ("the relevant seat") provided with a particular seat belt ("the relevant belt") if—

(a) another person is wearing the relevant belt;

(b) a child is occupying the relevant seat and wearing a child restraint which is an appropriate child restraint for that child;

(c) another person, being a person holding a medical certificate, is occupying the relevant seat;

(d) a disabled person (not being the person in question is occupying the relevant seat and wearing a disabled person's belt;

(e) by reason of his disability, it would not be practicable for the person in question to wear the relevant belt;

(f) the person in question is prevented from occupying the relevant seat by the presence of a carry cot which is restrained by straps and in which there is a child aged under 1 year;

(g) the child in question is prevented from occupying the relevant seat by the presence of a child restraint which could not readily be removed without the aid of tools; or

(h) the relevant seat is specially designed so that—

    (i) its configuration can be adjusted in order to increase the space in the vehicle available for goods or personal effects, and

    (ii) when it is so adjusted the seat cannot be used as such,

and the configuration is adjusted in the manner described in sub-paragraph (i) and it would not be reasonably practicable for the goods and personal effects being carried in the vehicle to be so carried were the configuration not so adjusted.

4. Paragraph 3 shall have effect in relation to regulation 10(5) as if sub-paragraphs (a) to (d) of that paragraph were omitted.

5. Paragraph 3(b) and (d) shall not apply unless the presence of the other person renders it impracticable for the person in question to wear the relevant belt.

6. Paragraph 3(f) shall not apply if it would be reasonably practicable for the carry cot to be carried in any other part of the vehicle where it could be restrained by straps so as to render it practicable for the person in question to wear the relevant belt.

7. Paragraph 3(g) shall not apply if—

(a) the person in question is a child; and

(b) the child restraint is appropriate for him.

8. A child restraint shall be regarded as provided for a seat for the purposes of this Schedule if—

(a) it is fixed in such a position that it can be worn by an occupier of that seat, or

(b) it is elsewhere in or on the vehicle but—

    (i) it could readily be fixed in such a position without the aid of tools, and

    (ii) it is not being worn by a child for whom it is appropriate and who is occupying another seat.

ROAD TRAFFIC OFFENDERS (PRESCRIBED DEVICES) ORDER 1993

(S.I. 1993 No. 1698)

1. This Order may be cited as the Road Traffic Offenders (Prescribed   **C28–01**
Devices) Order 1993 and shall come into force on 9th August 1993.
2. The following devices are prescribed devices for the purpose of section 20
of the Road Traffic Offenders Act 1988—
  (a) a device designed or adapted for recording a measurement of the
      speed of motor vehicles activated by means of sensors or cables on or
      near the surface of the highway;
  (b) a device designed or adapted for recording a measurement of the
      speed of motor vehicles activated by means of a light beam or beams.

TRAFFIC SIGNS REGULATIONS AND GENERAL DIRECTIONS 1994

(S.I. 1994 No. 1519)

Part I

The Traffic Signs Regulations 1994

SECTION 1

PRELIMINARY

Citation and commencement

1. This Part of this Instrument—   **C29–01**
  (a) may be cited—
      (i) as the Traffic Signs Regulations 1994, and
      (ii) together with Part II below, as the Traffic Signs Regulations and
           General Directions 1994; and
  (b) shall come into force on 12th August 1994.

Revocations

2. The Instruments specified in Appendix 2 to this Instrument, so far as they   **C29–02**

765

consist of or comprise regulations, are hereby revoked except that for the purposes of the Traffic Signs (Welsh and English Language Provisions) Regulations 1985 the revocations of the Regulations marked with an asterisk in Appendix 2 shall have no effect.

Savings

3.—(1) Subject to paragraph (2), any traffic sign which immediately before the coming into force of these Regulations is placed on or near any road shall be treated as prescribed by these Regulations, notwithstanding any provisions of these Regulations to the contrary, provided that—
  (a) it is a sign prescribed, or to be treated as if prescribed, by the 1981 Regulations; and
  (b) it continues to comply with those Regulations,
as if those Regulations had not been revoked.
  (2) Paragraph (1) shall cease to have effect—
  (a) on 1st January 1996 in relation to any road markings shown in diagrams RM 2 to RM 29 in the Second Schedule to the Traffic Signs Regulations 1957 in relation to the sign shown in diagram 623 in Schedule 1 and any road markings shown in diagrams 1005 to 1008, 1013, 1015, 1016, 1027, 1028, 1030, 1031 and 1034 to 1039 in Schedule 2 to the Traffic Signs Regulations 1964; and
  (b) on 1st January 1999 in relation to any sign shown in any of the diagrams 508, 509, 537.1, 537.2, 537.3, 537.4, 542.1, 542.2, 554 (when varied to "Ice" or "Snowdrifts"), 556.3, 556.4, 577, 603, 605.1 and 622.2A (when varied to indicate a 16.5 tonne maximum gross weight prohibition) in Schedule 1 and diagrams 1016.1, 1018, 1020 and 1021 in Schedule 2 to the 1981 Regulations; and
  (c) on 1st January 2005 in relation to any sign shown in any of the diagrams 403 to 405, 412A to 418, 422 to 433, 435 to 459, 468 to 472, and 474 to 495 in the First Schedule to the Traffic Signs Regulations 1957, in diagrams 742, 746, 837, and 838 in Schedule 1 to the Traffic Signs Regulations 1964, and in diagrams 626.1, 627, 628.1, 641, 642.1, 653, 734.7, 739.3, 742.1, 742.2, 742.3, 742.4, 742.5, 742.6, 747, 748, 749, 750, 751, 752, 752.1, 753, 753.1, 758, 759, 837.1, 838.1 and 905 in Schedule 1 to the 1981 Regulations; and
  (d) on 1st January 2015 in relation to any sign shown in diagrams 728.1, 728.2, 729, 729.1, 729.2, 729.3, 730, 730.1, 732, 732.1, 732.2, 733, 733.1, 734.1, 734.2, 734.3, 734.4, 734.5, 734.6, 734.8, 734.9, 734.10, 736, 736.1, 737.1, 760 and 761 in Schedule 1 to the 1981 Regulations.
  (3) A sign which is of the size, colour and type shown in diagram 701, 702, 702.1, 703, 703.1, 703.2, 703.3, 704, 705, 706, 707, 708, 709, 710, 710.1, 711.1, 712, 712.1, 713, 714, 715, 716, 717, 718, 718.1, 718.2, 718.3, 719, 719.1, 719.2, 719.3A, 719.4, 720, 721.1, 722, 723, 724, 724.1, 724.2, 725, 726, 727, 727.2, 728, 728.1, 728.2, 728.3, 729, 729.1, 729.2, 729.3, 730, 730.1, 732, 732.1, 732.2, 732.4, 732.5, 733, 733.1, 734.1, 734.2, 734.3, 734.4, 734.5, 734.6, 734.7, 734.8, 734.9, 734.10, 735.1, 735.2, 736, 736.1, 737.1, 739, 739.1, 739.2, 739.3, 739.4, 739.5, 741, 741.1 or 905 in Schedule 1 to the 1981 Regulations may be erected on or near a road after the coming into force of these Regulations, notwithstanding that it is not of the size, colour and type shown in any diagram in these Regulations, provided that the design or manufacture of the sign had begun before the coming into force of these Regulations.

Interpretation—general

4. In these Regulations unless the context otherwise requires—　　**C29–04**
　　"the 1984 Act" means the Road Traffic Regulation Act 1984;
　　"the 1988 Act" means the Road Traffic Act 1988;
　　"the 1981 Regulations" means the Traffic Signs Regulations and General Directions 1981;
　　"articulated vehicle" means a motor vehicle with a trailer so attached to it as to be partially superimposed upon it;
　　"automatic half-barrier level crossing" means a level crossing where barriers are installed to descend automatically across part of the road when a railway vehicle or tramcar approaches and the operation of the barriers is monitored remotely from the crossing;
　　"automatic barrier crossing (L)" means a level crossing where barriers are installed to descend automatically across part of the road when a railway vehicle or tramcar approaches and the driver of the railway vehicle or tramcar is required to monitor the operation of the barriers when the railway vehicle or tramcar is at or near the crossing;
　　"automatic open crossing (L)" means a level crossing without automatic barriers where light signals are so installed as to be operated automatically by a railway vehicle or tramcar approaching the crossing and the driver of the railway vehicle or tramcar is required to monitor the operation of the light signals when the railway vehicle or tramcar is at or near the crossing;
　　"automatic open crossing (R)" means a level crossing without automatic barriers where light signals are so installed as to be operated automatically by a railway vehicle or tramcar approaching the crossing and the operation of the light signals is monitored remotely from the crossing;
　　"automatic level crossing" means an automatic half-barrier level crossing, an automatic barrier crossing (L), an automatic open crossing (L) or an automatic open crossing (R);
　　"central reservation" means—
　　　(a) any land between the carriageways of a road comprising two carriageways; or
　　　(b) any permanent work (other than a traffic island) in the carriageway of a road,
　　which separates the carriageway or, as the case may be, the part of the carriageway which is to be used by traffic moving in one direction from the carriageway or part of the carriageway which is to be used (whether at all times or at particular times only) by traffic moving in the other direction;
　　"contra-flow" means a part of a carriageway of a road where—
　　　(a) traffic is authorised to proceed in the opposite direction to the usual direction of traffic on that part; or
　　　(b) a specified class of traffic is authorised to proceed in the opposite direction to other traffic on that carriageway;
　　"cycle lane" means a part of the carriageway of a road which—
　　　(a) starts with the marking shown in diagram 1009; and
　　　(b) is separated from the rest of the carriageway—
　　　　(i) if it may not be used by vehicles other than pedal cycles, by the marking shown in diagram 1049; or
　　　　(ii) if it may be used by vehicles other than pedal cycles, by the marking shown in diagram 1004 or 1004.1;

"dual carriageway road" means a road which comprises a central reservation;

"enactment" includes any Act or subordinate legislation as defined in section 21(1) of the Interpretation Act 1978;

"excursion or tour" has the meaning given in section 137(1) of the Transport Act 1985;

"goods vehicle" means a motor vehicle or trailer constructed or adapted for use for the carriage or haulage of goods or burden of any description;

"hours of darkness" means the time between half an hour after sunset and half an hour before sunrise;

"level crossing" means a place where a road is crossed by a railway or a tramway on a reserved track on the level;

"local bus" means a public service vehicle used for the provision of a local service not being an excursion or tour;

"local service" has the meaning given in section 2 of the Transport Act 1985;

"major road" means the road at a road junction into which there emerges vehicular traffic from a minor road;

"manually operated" means a change from one sign to another or one signal aspect to another set in process by an operator;

"maximum gross weight" means—

(a) in the case of a motor vehicle not drawing a trailer or in the case of a trailer, its maximum laden weight;

(b) in the case of an articulated vehicle, its maximum laden weight (if it has one) and otherwise the aggregate maximum laden weight of all the individual vehicles forming part of that articulated vehicle; and

(c) in the case of a motor vehicle (other than an articulated vehicle) drawing one or more trailers, the aggregate maximum laden weight of the motor vehicle and the trailer or trailers drawn by it,

and the foregoing references to the maximum laden weight of a vehicle (including a vehicle which is a trailer) are references—

(i) in the case of a vehicle as respects which a gross weight not to be exceeded in Great Britain is specified in construction and use requirements (as defined by section 41(8) of the 1988 Act), to the weight so specified, or

(ii) in the case of a vehicle as respects which no such weight is so specified, to the weight which the vehicle is designed or adapted not to exceed when in normal use and travelling on a road laden.

"minor road" means a road on which, at its junction with another road, there is placed the sign shown in diagram 601.1 or 602 or the road marking shown in diagram 1003;

"mobile road works" means works on a road carried out by or from a vehicle or vehicles which move slowly along the road or which stop briefly from time to time along that road;

"motorway" means a special road—

(a) which in England or Wales (save as otherwise provided by or under regulations made under, or having effect as if made under, section 17 of the 1984 Act) can only be used by traffic of Class I or II as specified in Schedule 4 to the Highways Act 1980; or

(b) which in Scotland can only be used by traffic of Class I or Class II as specified in Schedule 3 to the Roads (Scotland) Act 1984;

"non-primary route" means a route, not being a primary route or a motorway or part of a primary route or of a motorway;

"passenger vehicle" means a vehicle constructed or adapted for the carriage of passengers and their effects;

"pedal cycle" means a unicycle, bicycle, tricycle, or cycle having four or more wheels, not being in any case mechanically propelled unless it is an electrically assisted pedal cycle of such class as is to be treated as not being a motor vehicle for the purposes of the 1984 Act;

"pedestrian zone" means an area—
(a) which has been laid out to improve amenity for pedestrians; and
(b) to which the entry of vehicles is prohibited or restricted;

"Pelican crossing" means a pedestrian crossing which conforms to The "Pelican" Pedestrian Crossings Regulations and General Directions 1987;

"plate" means a sign which by virtue of general directions given in exercise of the power conferred by section 65 of the 1984 Act must always be placed in combination or in conjunction with another sign and which is supplementary to that other sign;

"police vehicle" means a vehicle being used for police purposes or operating under the instructions of a chief officer of police;

"primary route" means a route, not being a route comprising any part of a motorway, in respect of which the Secretary of State—
(a) in the case of a trunk road is of the opinion, and
(b) in any other case after consultation with the traffic authority for the road comprised in the route is of the opinion,
that it provides the most satisfactory route for through traffic between places of traffic importance;

"principal road" means a road for the time being classified as a principal road—
(a) by virtue of section 12 of the Highways Act 1980 (whether as falling within subsection (1) or classified under subsection (3)), or
(b) by the Secretary of State under section 11(1) of the Roads (Scotland) Act 1984;

"public service vehicle" has the meaning given in section 1 of the Public Passenger Vehicles Act 1981;

"retroreflecting material" means material which reflects a ray of light back towards the source of that light;

"road maintenance vehicle" means a vehicle which—
(a) in England and Wales is specially designed or adapted for use on a road by or on behalf of a highway authority for the purposes of the Highways Act 1980 for the purposes of road maintenance; or
(b) in Scotland is specially designed or adapted for use on a road by or on behalf of a roads authority for the purposes of the Roads (Scotland) Act 1984 for the purposes of road maintenance;

"road marking" means a traffic sign consisting of a line or mark or legend on a road;

"route" includes any road comprised in a route;

"scheduled express service" means a service provided by a public service vehicle—
(a) used to carry passengers for hire or reward at separate fares otherwise than in the provision of a local service; and
(b) which is operated in accordance with a timetable;

"school bus" means a vehicle constructed or adapted to carry 12 or more passengers and being used to carry persons to or from a school as defined in section 114(1) of the Education Act 1944 and, in Scotland, as defined in the Education (Scotland) Act 1980;

"sign" means a traffic sign;

"stud" means a prefabricated device fixed or embedded as a mark in the carriageway of a road;

"taxi" means—

   (a) in England and Wales, a vehicle licensed under—

      (i) section 37 of the Town Police Clauses Act 1847; or

      (ii) section 6 of the Metropolitan Public Carriage Act 1869;

or under any similar enactment; and

   (b) in Scotland, a taxi licensed under section 10 of the Civic Government (Scotland) Act 1982;

"taxi rank" means an area of carriageway reserved for use by taxis waiting to pick up passengers;

"temporary statutory provision" means—

   (a) a provision having effect under section 9 (experimental traffic orders), section 12 (experimental traffic schemes in Greater London) or section 14 (temporary restriction of traffic on roads) of the 1984 Act or under a provision referred to in section 66 (traffic signs for giving effect to local traffic regulations) of that Act;

   (b) a prohibition, restriction or requirement indicated by a traffic sign placed pursuant to section 67 (emergencies and temporary obstructions) of the 1984 Act; or

   (c) a provision having effect under section 62 (temporary prohibition or restriction of traffic etc on roads for reasons of safety or public convenience) of the Roads (Scotland) Act 1984;

"terminal sign" means a sign placed in accordance with direction 8 or 9 of the Traffic Signs General Directions 1994;

"tourist attraction" means a permanently established excursion destination which—

   (a) is recognised by a local authority, the English Tourist Board, the Scottish Tourist Board or the Wales Tourist Board;

   (b) caters primarily for visitors to the area in which the attraction is located rather than for local residents;

   (c) is open to the public without prior booking during its normal opening hours; and

   (d) does not have retailing or catering as its main purpose;

"Tourist Information Centre" means a staffed information service centre recognised and supported by the English, Scottish or Wales Tourist Board;

"Tourist Information Point" means a display of tourist information approved by a regional, area or local tourist board;

"traffic lane" means, in relation to a road, a part of the carriageway having, as a boundary which separates it from another such part, a road marking of the type shown in diagram 1004, 1004.1, 1005, 1005.1, 1008, 1008.1, 1010, 1013.1, 1013.3, 1040, 1040.2, or 1049;

"tramcar" has the meaning given in section 141A(4) of the 1984 Act;

"trolley vehicle" has the meaning given in section 141A(4) of the 1984 Act;

"trunk road" as respects England and Wales has the meaning given in section 329(1) of the Highways Act 1980 and as respects Scotland in section 151(1) of the Roads (Scotland) Act 1984;

"unladen vehicle" has the meaning given in Schedule 18;

"variable message sign" has the meaning given in regulation 46(1);

"with-flow lane" means a traffic lane reserved for a specified class of traffic proceeding in the same direction as general traffic in an adjoining traffic lane; and "works bus" means a vehicle constructed or adapted to carry 12 or more passengers (excluding the driver) which has been provided by an employer for the purpose of carrying persons employed by him or on his behalf to or from their place of employment and is being used for that purpose.

Interpretation of "speed limit"

5.—(1) In these Regulations "speed limit" means—   **C29–05**
   (a) a maximum or minimum limit of speed on the driving of vehicles on a road—
     (i) imposed by an order under section 14 of the 1984 Act (temporary prohibition or restriction of traffic on roads);
     (ii) imposed by regulations under section 17 of the 1984 Act (traffic regulation on special roads);
     (iii) arising by virtue of the road being restricted for the purposes of section 81 of the 1984 Act (general speed limit for restricted roads);
     (iv) imposed by an order under section 84 of the 1984 Act (speed limits on roads other than restricted roads);
     (v) imposed by an order under section 88 of the 1984 Act (temporary speed limits); or
     (vi) imposed by or under a local Act; or
   (b) a maximum limit of speed on the driving of vehicles on a road advised by a traffic authority,
and "maximum speed limit" and "minimum speed limit" should be construed accordingly.

(2) In these regulations "national speed limit" means any prohibition imposed on a road by the 70 miles per hour, 60 miles per hour and 50 miles per hour (Temporary Speed Limit) Order 1977 or by regulation 3 of the Motorways (Speed Limit) Regulations 1974.

References in the Regulations

6. In these Regulations, unless it is expressly provided otherwise or the   **C29–06**
context otherwise requires—
   (a) a reference to a numbered regulation is a reference to the regulation so numbered in these Regulations;
   (b) a reference to a numbered paragraph is a reference to the paragraph so numbered in the regulation in which the reference occurs;
   (c) a reference to a sub-paragraph followed by a number or letter is a reference to the sub-paragraph bearing that number or letter in the paragraph in which the reference occurs;
   (d) a reference to a numbered diagram is a reference to the diagram so numbered in a Schedule to these Regulations;
   (e) a reference to a sign or road marking shown in a diagram in a Schedule to these Regulations means a sign or road marking of the size, colour and type shown in that diagram and prescribed by these Regulations and includes a reference to that sign or road marking as varied in accordance with these Regulations;
   (f) a reference to the information, warning, requirement, restriction, prohibition or speed limit conveyed by a sign shown in a diagram includes a reference to that information, warning, requirement,

restriction, prohibition or speed limit, however expressed, as varied
to accord with any variation of the diagram made in accordance with
these Regulations; and

(g) in any provision which includes a table, references to a table or to a
numbered table are to the table or as the case may be to the table so
numbered in that provision.

Interpretation of Schedules 1 to 12

C29–07   7.—(1) In any untitled table under or beside any diagram (in this paragraph referred to as "the diagram") in Schedules 1 to 12—

(a) in item 1 any regulations which are specified are regulations in these
Regulations in which a specific reference is made to the diagram;

(b) in item 2 any directions which are specified are directions in the Traffic Signs General Directions 1994 in which a specific reference is made
to the diagram;

(c) in item 3 any diagrams which are specified are diagrams in the Schedules to these Regulations which show signs which may or must be
placed in conjunction or in combination with the sign shown in the
diagram;

(d) in item 4 any item which is specified is an item in Schedule 16 which
specifies permitted variants to the diagram; and

(e) in item 5 any item which is specified is an item in Schedule 17 which
specifies the illumination requirements for the sign shown in the
diagram.

(2) The table entitled "Table of combinations" under or beside any diagram in Part III of Schedule 12 indicates the manner in which the sign shown
in that diagram may be varied in accordance with paragraphs (6) to (8) of
regulation 17.

(3) Dimensions indicated on any diagram shown in Schedules 1 to 12 are
expressed in millimetres unless otherwise specified.

SECTION 2

GENERAL PROVISIONS

Authorisations by the Secretary of State

C29–08   8. Nothing in these Regulations shall be taken to limit the powers of the
Secretary of State under section 64 of the 1984 Act to authorise the erection or
retention of traffic signs of a character not prescribed by these Regulations.

Temporary obstructions

C29–09   9. Nothing in these Regulations shall have effect so as to authorise any persons not otherwise authorised to do so to place on or near a road any object or device for warning traffic of a temporary obstruction.

Application of section 36 of the Road Traffic Act 1988 to signs and disqualification for offences

10.—(1) Section 36 of the 1988 Act shall apply to—   **C29–10**
  (a) the signs shown in any of the diagrams 601.1, 602, 606, 610, 611.1, 614, 616, 626.2, 629.2, 629.2A, 784, 953, 953.1 and 7023 and to the sign shown in diagram 602 when placed in combination with that shown in diagram 778 or 778.1;
  (b) the red light signal when displayed by the light signals prescribed by regulation 30 or by regulation 32;
  (c) the road markings shown in diagram 1013.1 or 1013.3 insofar as those markings convey the requirements specified in regulation 26;
  (d) the road marking shown in diagram 1003 insofar as that marking conveys the requirements specified in regulation 25;
  (e) the road markings shown in diagrams 1043, 1044 and 1045;
  (f) the light signals prescribed by regulation 30(2) as varied in accordance with regulation 31 when they are displaying the green arrow signals shown in diagrams 3000.4, 3000.6, 3002, 3003, 3004, 3005, 3006, 3007, 3008, 3009.1, 3011.1 and 3011.2 insofar as they convey the restrictions specified in paragraphs (1)(f) and (1)(g) of regulation 33; and
  (g) the light signal shown in diagram 3013.1.
  (2) The signs hereby specified for the purposes of column 5 of the entry in Schedule 2 to the Road Traffic Offenders Act 1988 relating to offences under section 36 of the 1988 Act are—
  (a) the signs shown in diagrams 601.1 and 616;
  (b) the signs shown in diagrams 629.2 and 629.2A;
  (c) the sign shown in diagram 784;
  (d) the red light signal when displayed by the light signals prescribed by regulation 30 or by regulation 32;
  (e) the road markings shown in diagram 1013.1 or 1013.3 insofar as those markings convey the requirements specified in regulation 26(2); and
  (f) the light signals prescribed by regulation 30(2) when they are displaying the green arrow signals shown in diagrams 3000.4, 3000.6, 3002, 3003, 3004, 3005, 3006, 3007, 3008, 3009.1, 3011.1 and 3011.2 insofar as they convey the restrictions specified in paragraphs (1)(f) and (1)(g) of regulation 33.

Signs, markings and signals to be of the sizes, colours and types shown in the diagrams

11.—(1) Subject to the provisions of these Regulations, a sign for conveying   **C29–11** information or a warning, requirement, restriction, prohibition or speed limit of the description specified under a diagram in Schedules 1 to 7, Part II of Schedule 10 and Schedule 12 to traffic on roads shall be of the size, colour and type shown in the diagram.
  (2) The signs shown in diagrams 515.1, 515.1A, 515.2, 1012.2, 1012.3, 1049.1 and 7102 shall be of the size, colour and type shown in the two parts of those diagrams.

(3) In Schedule 6, a road marking shown in a diagram as a horizontal line shall be laid transversely, and a marking shown as a vertical line shall be laid longitudinally, to the flow of traffic, except so far as the nature of the diagram or the caption to the diagram indicates that it may or should be laid in another direction.

(4) The road marking shown in diagram 1055 shall be white, silver or light grey in colour.

Variations of dimensions

C29–12   **12.**—(1) Where any diagram in Schedules 1 to 12 specifies a dimension for an element of a sign together with a dimension for that element in brackets, the dimensions so specified shall, subject to paragraph (2), be alternatives.

(2) Subject to paragraphs (3) and (4), where alternative dimensions are specified for more than one element of a sign, the dimensions chosen for each element must correspond with one another so that the shape and proportions of the sign are as shown in the diagram.

(3) Paragraph (2) does not apply to the road marking shown in diagram 1009 and the respective lengths of the lines comprised in that sign and of the gaps between them may be either—

    (a) 600 and 300 millimetres, in which case the width of the lines may be 100, 150 or 200 millimetres; or

    (b) 300 and 150 millimetres, in which case the width of the lines shall be 100 millimetres.

(4) Paragraph (2) does not apply to the road markings shown in diagrams 1013.3, 1035, 1036.1, 1036.2, 1037.1, 1040, 1040.2, 1040.4 and 1041.

(5) Where any diagram in Schedules 1 to 12 specifies a maximum and a minimum dimension for an element of a sign, the dimension chosen for that element shall, subject to the footnote to Table 1, be not more than the maximum and not less than the minimum.

(6) Where maximum and minimum dimensions are specified for more than one element of a sign, the dimensions chosen for each element must correspond with one another so that the shape and proportions of the sign are as shown in the diagram.

(7) Where a sign shown in diagram 606, 607, 609, 610, 611, 611.1, 612, 613, 614, 616, 636, 638, 642, 643, 644 or 645 is placed temporarily on a road by a constable or a person acting under the instructions (whether general or specific) of the chief officer of police for the purposes of indicating a temporary statutory provision, any dimension in the diagram for the diameter of a roundel, or for the sign may be reduced so long as any dimension shown in the diagram for the diameter of a roundel or for the measurement horizontally of the sign is at least 200 millimetres, and the height of any lettering is at least 20 millimetres.

(8) Any sign shown in diagrams 960, 960.1, 7201, 7202, 7203, 7203.1, 7204, 7205, 7206, 7207, 7210, 7211, 7212, 7213, 7214, 7215, 7216, 7217, 7218, 7220, 7221, 7230, 7231, 7232, 7233, 7234, 7235, 7236, 7237, 7238, 7239, 7240, 7250, 7251, 7252, 7253, 7254, 7255, 7256 or in a diagram in Schedule 7 (other than diagrams 2032, 2130, 2208, 2708, 2711, 2712, 2713, 2714, 2715, 2922, 2923 and 2932) shall be of such dimensions as, having regard to the character of the road and the speed of the vehicular traffic generally using it, are necessary to accommodate any place name, route symbol or number, arrow, indication of distance, symbol or any other indication which, in accordance with these

Regulations, may be shown on the sign and which it is appropriate to show for the purpose for which that sign is placed on the road.

(9) Any sign shown in a diagram in Part III of Schedule 12 shall be of such dimensions as, having regard to the character of the road and the speed of traffic generally using it, are necessary to accommodate the route symbols or arrows appropriate to the number of traffic lanes and the nature of the road works in relation to which the sign is placed.

(10) Any dimension (not being an angle or specified as a maximum or minimum) specified in these Regulations shall be treated as permitted by these Regulations if it is varied in accordance with the following Tables, subject, in the case of Tables 1 and 2, to the Notes to those Tables.

TABLE I

Diagrams in Schedules 1 to 5, 7, 10 and 12—Height of letters or numbers   **C29–13**

(1) Item	(2) Dimensions shown in diagrams	(3) Permitted variations
1.	100 millimetres or more	Up to 5 per cent of the dimension
2.	Less than 100 millimetres	Up to 7.5 per cent of the dimension

NOTE: Where the height of letters or numbers is expressed as a range within maximum and minimum dimensions the permitted variations indicated in this Table shall apply to those dimensions shown as the maximum and minimum.

TABLE II

Diagrams in Schedule 6—All dimensions   **C29–14**

(1) Item	(2) Dimensions shown in diagrams	(3) Permitted variations
1.	3 metres or more	(i) Up to 15 per cent of the dimension where the varied dimension is greater than the specified dimension; or
		(ii) Up to 10 per cent of the dimension where the varied dimension is less than the specified dimension.
2.	300 millimetres or more, but less than 3 metres	(i) Up to 20 per cent of the dimension where the varied dimension is greater than the specified dimension; or
		(ii) Up to 10 per cent of the dimension where the varied dimension is less than the specified dimension.

(1) Item	(2) *Dimensions shown in diagrams*	(3) *Permitted variations*
3.	10 millimetres or more but less than 300 millimetres	(i) Up to 30 per cent of the dimension where the varied dimension is greater than the specified dimension; or (ii) Up to 10 per cent of the dimension where the varied dimension is less than the specified dimension.
4.	Less than 10 millimetres	(i) Up to 2 millimetres more than the dimension where the varied dimension is greater than the specified dimension; or (ii) Up to 1 millimetre less than the dimension where the varied dimension is less than the specified dimension.

NOTE: Where a dimension denoting the length or width of a road marking is varied in accordance with this Table, and there is a space between two parts of the marking, the dimensions of that space may be varied as required to accommodate the variation of the length or width of the marking, provided that the character of the marking is maintained.

TABLE III

C29–15 All dimensions other than those in Tables I and II

(1) Item	(2) *Dimensions shown in diagrams*	(3) *Permitted variations*
1.	300 millimetres or more	Up to 5 per cent of the dimension
2.	50 millimetres or more, but less than 300 millimetres	Up to 7.5 per cent of the dimension
3.	Less than 50 millimetres	Up to 10 per cent of the dimension

(11) Any variation of any angle specified in any diagram in Schedule 1, 6 or 8, except diagrams 1043 and 1044, shall be treated as permitted by these Regulations if the variation does not exceed 5 degrees.

(12) Where—

(a) overall dimensions are given for a sign shown in any diagram in the Schedules to these Regulations; and

(b) the legend on that sign is varied in accordance with regulation 17 and with item 4 of the table appearing under or beside that diagram,

the overall dimensions or the number of lines filled by the legend, or both, may be varied so far as necessary to give effect to the variation of the legend.

Proportions and form of letters, numerals, symbols and other characters

13.—(1) Subject to paragraphs (2), (3) and (5)—   **C29–16**
  (a) all letters, numerals and other characters incorporated in the signs or
     parts of the signs shown in the diagrams in Schedules 1 to 5, 7, 10 and
     12 which have a red, blue, brown, black or green background (other
     than those incorporated in the bottom panel of diagram 674, dia-
     grams 973, 973.1, 2401, 2402, 2403, 2607, 2610, 2620.1, 2610.2, the top
     panels of diagrams 2919 and 2920, the petrol price display in diagram
     2919, and diagrams 5001.1, 5001.2, 5003, 5003.1, 5005 and 5005.1, the
     top and bottom panels of diagram 7008 and the words "National
     Trust for Scotland" used in conjunction with the symbol shown in
     diagram T303 in Part IV of Schedule 14) and the signs shown in dia-
     grams 2714 and 2715 shall have the proportions and form shown in
     Part I of Schedule 13; and
  (b) all letters, numerals and other characters incorporated in the signs or
     the parts of signs shown in the diagrams in Schedules 1 to 5, 7, 10 and
     12 which have a white, yellow or orange background (other than
     those incorporated in the bottom panel of diagram 674, diagrams 973,
     973.1, 2401, 2402, 2403, 2610, 2610.1, 2610.2, 2714, 2715, the top panels
     of diagrams 2919 and 2920, and the top and bottom panels of diagram
     7008) shall have the proportions and form shown in Part II of Sched-
     ule 13.

(2) Letters and numerals used for the purpose of indicating a route number
on any sign shown in a diagram in Part X of Schedule 7 (other than those
incorporated in diagram 2913 and 2914) shall have the proportions and form
shown in Part III of Schedule 13, except where a route number is indicated in
brackets on a sign shown in diagram 2904, 2904.1, 2906, 2908 or 2909 in which
case those letters and numerals shall have the proportions and form shown
in either Part I or Part III of Schedule 13 as appropriate.

(3) Letters and numerals used for the purpose of indicating a route number
on any sign shown in a diagram in Part III of Schedule 12 when used on a
motorway shall have the proportions and form shown in Part IV of Schedule
13.

(4) Subject to and within the limits of any dimension specified as a maximum or minimum in diagrams 973, 973.1, 2401, 2402, 2403, 2607, 2610,
2610.1, 2610.2, the top panels of diagrams 2919 and 2920, the petrol price display in diagram 2919, and the top and bottom panels of diagram 7008 any
letters or numerals or other characters incorporated in those diagrams may
have proportions and form other than the proportions and form shown in
Schedule 13.

(5) All letters, numerals, symbols and other characters incorporated in
variable message signs shall have the general proportions and form shown in
Part V of Schedule 13 where the construction or method of operation of the
sign does not permit the use of letters, numerals and other characters of the
proportions and form shown in Part I, II, III or IV of Schedule 13 or of symbols shown in diagrams in Schedules 1 to 5, 10 or 12.

(6) All letters, numerals and other characters incorporated in the road
markings shown in the diagrams in Schedule 6 shall have the proportions
and form shown in Part VI of Schedule 13.

(7) Symbols incorporated in signs for the purpose of indicating diversion
routes to be followed in an emergency shall have the proportions and form
shown in Part VII of Schedule 13.

(8) Symbols incorporated in signs for the purpose of indicating the type of a tourist attraction shall have the proportions and form shown in Schedule 14.

Signs attached to vehicles

C29–17   **14.**—(1) A sign attached to a vehicle of the description and in the position on that vehicle specified in an item in column (2) of the Table, when the vehicle is on a road which is subject to a maximum speed limit specified in column (3) of that item, shall be of the size, colour and type shown in one of the diagrams specified in column (4) of that item.

TABLE

(1) Item	(2) Description of vehicle, and position	(3) Maximum speed limit	(4) Diagram numbers
1.	Road maintenance vehicle, on the front	30 m.p.h. or under	610, 7001 and 7001.1
2.	Road maintenance vehicle, on the rear	30 m.p.h. or under	610, 7001, 7001.1, 7401, 7401.1, 7402, 7403 and 7404
3.	Road maintenance vehicle, on the rear	More than 30 m.p.h.	7401, 7401.1, 7402, 7403 and 7404
4.	Police vehicle, on the front or the rear	70 m.p.h. or under	829.1, 829.2, 829.3 and 829.4

(2) The operating requirements for the lamps that form part of the signs shown in diagrams 7401, 7402 and 7403 are that—
   (a) the lamps shall be illuminated only when the signs are being used in accordance with the Table; and
   (b) each lamp shall show an intermittent amber light at a rate of flashing of not less than 60 nor more than 90 flashes per minute, and in such a manner that the lights of one horizontal pair are always shown when the lights of the other horizontal pair are not shown.

SECTION 3

WARNING, REGULATORY AND INFORMATORY TRAFFIC SIGNS

Sign shown in diagram 610 and its significance

C29–18   **15.**—(1) Except as provided in paragraphs (2) and (3), the requirement conveyed by the sign shown in diagram 610 shall be that vehicular traffic passing the sign must keep to the left of the sign where the arrow is pointed downwards to the left, or to the right of the sign where the arrow is pointed downwards to the right.

(2) On an occasion where a vehicle is being used for fire brigade, ambulance or police purposes and the observance of the requirement specified in paragraph (1) would be likely to hinder the use of that vehicle for one of those purposes then, instead of that requirement, the requirement conveyed by the sign in question shall be that the vehicle shall not proceed beyond that sign in such a manner or at such a time as to be likely to endanger any person.

(3) The requirement specified in paragraph (1) does not apply to a tramcar or trolley vehicle.

Signs shown in diagrams 601.1, 602, 778, 778.1 and 784 and their significance

16.—(1) The requirements conveyed to vehicular traffic on roads by a sign shown in the diagram specified in column (2) of an item in the Table are specified in column (3) of that item. **C29–19**

TABLE

(1) Item	(2) Diagram number	(3) Requirements
1.	601.1	(a) Every vehicle shall stop before crossing the transverse line shown in diagram 1002.1 or, if that line is not clearly visible, before entering the major road in respect of which the sign shown in diagram 601.1 has been provided; and (b) no vehicle shall cross the transverse line shown in diagram 1002.1 or, if that line is not clearly visible, enter the major road in respect of which the sign shown in diagram 601.1 has been provided, so as to be likely to endanger the driver of or any passenger in any other vehicle or to cause that driver to change the speed or course of his vehicle in order to avoid an accident.
2.	602	No vehicle shall cross the transverse line shown in diagram 1003 nearer to the major road at the side of which that line is placed, or if that line is not clearly visible, enter that major road, so as to be likely to endanger the driver of or any passenger in any other vehicle or to cause that driver to change the speed or course of his vehicle in order to avoid an accident.
3.	602 when placed in combination with 778 or 778.1	No vehicle shall cross the transverse line shown in diagram 1003 nearer to the level crossing at the side of which that line is placed, or if that line is not clearly visible, enter that level crossing, so as to be likely to endanger the driver of or any passenger in any railway vehicle or tramcar or to cause that driver to change the speed of his vehicle in order to avoid an accident.

(1) Item	(2) Diagram number	(3) Requirements

4.	784	No abnormal transport unit shall proceed onto or over an automatic half-barrier level crossing or an automatic open crossing (R) unless—
		  (a) the driver of the unit has used a telephone provided at or near the crossing for the purpose of obtaining from a person, authorised in that behalf by the railway or tramway authority, permission for the unit to proceed;
		  (b) that permission has been obtained before the unit proceeds; and
		  (c) the unit proceeds in accordance with any terms attached to that permission.
		Provided that sub-paragraphs (b) and (c) above shall not apply if—
		  (i) on the use by the driver of the telephone placed at or near the crossing he receives an indication for not less than two minutes that the telephone at the other end of the telephone line is being called, but no duly authorised person answers it, or he receives no indication at all due to a fault or malfunction on the telephone; and
		  (ii) the driver then drives the unit on to the crossing with the reasonable expectation of crossing it within times specified in a railway or tramway notice at that telephone as being times between which railway vehicles or tramcars do not normally travel over than crossing.

(2) In this regulation—
> "abnormal transport unit" means—
>> (a) a motor vehicle or a vehicle combination—
>>> (i) the overall length of which, inclusive of the load (if any) on the vehicle or the combination, exceeds 55 feet; or
>>> (ii) the overall width of which, inclusive of the load (if any) on the vehicle or the combination, exceeds 9 feet 6 inches; or
>>> (iii) the maximum gross weight of which exceeds 38 tonnes; or
>> (b) a motor vehicle, or a vehicle combination, which in either case is incapable of proceeding, or is unlikely to proceed, over an automatic railway level crossing at a speed exceeding 5 miles per hour;
> "driver" in relation to an abnormal transport unit, means where that unit is a single motor vehicle the driver of that vehicle and, where that unit is a vehicle combination, the driver of the only or the foremost motor vehicle forming part of that combination; and
> "vehicle combination" means a combination of vehicles made up of one or more motor vehicles and one or more trailers all of which are linked together when travelling.

Permitted variants

17.—(1) Where the circumstances in which a sign shown in a diagram in a

Schedule (other than Schedule 6) to these Regulations is to be placed so require or where appropriate in those circumstances, the form of the sign shall or may be varied—

(a) in the manner (if any) allowed or required in item 4 of the untitled table below or beside the diagram; or

(b) in the manner allowed or required in column (3) of an item in Schedule 16, if the diagram is one whose number is given in column (2) of that item.

(2) A symbol in the form of a prescribed sign to which direction 7 of the Traffic Signs General Directions 1994 applies shall not be incorporated in a sign in accordance with item 31 of Schedule 16, except in circumstances where it could be placed as a sign in accordance with that direction.

(3) A symbol incorporated as mentioned in paragraph (2) shall or may be varied in the same manner as the sign which the symbol represents or from which it is derived.

(4) In each of the signs shown in diagrams 780, 780.1 and 780.2 the safe height shown on the sign shall be varied where necessary so that it is between 1½ and 2 feet (450 to 600 millimetres) less than the height of the lowest part of the overhead wire, of which the sign gives warning, over the highest part of the surface of the carriageway beneath that wire.

(5) Where a sign shown in a diagram in Schedule 7 indicates a road or a route, and that road or route is temporarily closed, there may be affixed to the sign or to that part of the sign where that road or route is indicated, in order to cancel temporarily the indication, a board coloured red and displaying in white lettering the words "Road temporarily closed" or "Route temporarily closed".

(6) In this paragraph and paragraphs (7) and (8)—

(a) "combination sign" means a sign shown in diagram 7201, 7210, 7211, 7212, 7213, 7214, 7215, 7216, 7217, 7218, 7220, 7221, 7230, 7231, 7232, 7233, 7234, 7235, 7236, 7237, 7238, 7239 or 7240;

(b) "panel" means a sign shown in diagram 7260, 7261, 7262, 7263, 7264, 7270, 7271, 7272, 7273, 7274 or 7275 when used as part of a combination sign and references to a panel whose number is shown in a Table of combinations are to a sign shown in a diagram having a number so shown;

(c) "permitted combination" means one of the combinations specified in paragraph (8);

(d) "the table" in relation to a combination sign means the Table of combinations appearing below or beside the diagram in which that sign is shown;

(e) "top panel" means a panel shown at the top of a combination sign and "bottom panel" means a panel shown at the bottom of such a sign.

(7) If and only if the top and bottom panels of the sign as varied together constitute a permitted combination, a combination sign may be varied in the following ways—

(a) by substituting for the top panel or, where a top panel is not shown, by adding as a top panel, a panel whose number is shown in item (1) of the table;

(b) by substituting for the bottom panel or, where a bottom panel is not shown by adding as a bottom panel, a panel whose number is shown in item (2) of the table;

(c) if the word "none" appears in item (1) of the table, by omitting the top panel;

(d) if the word "none" appears in item (2) of the table, by omitting the bottom panel.

(8) Each of the following is a permitted combination—

(a) a top panel whose number appears in item (1) of a column in the table and a bottom panel whose number appears in item (2) of the same column;

(b) a top panel whose number appears in item (1) of a column in the table and, if the word "none" appears in item (2) of the same column, no bottom panel;

(c) a bottom panel whose number appears in item (2) of a column in the table and, if the word "none" appears in item (1) of the same column, no top panel;

(d) if the word "none" appears in both items of the same column of the table, no top panel and no bottom panel.

(9) Where the form of a sign is varied in accordance with these Regulations, the information, warning, requirement, restriction, prohibition or speed limit conveyed to traffic by the sign is varied to accord with the form of the sign as varied.

Illumination of signs

C29–21   **18.**—(1) Subject to paragraph (2), every sign shown in a diagram whose number is indicated in column (2) of an item in Schedule 17 shall be illuminated in the manner and at the times described in column (3) of that item.

(2) Where a sign shown in a diagram whose number is indicated in column (2) of an item in Schedule 17 is placed for the purpose of conveying to vehicular traffic a warning, information, prohibition, restriction or requirement which applies only at certain times, the sign shall be illuminated in accordance with that Schedule only during those times.

(3) Where a sign shown in a diagram whose number is indicated in column (2) of an item in Schedule 17 is illuminated by means of external lighting, then that means of lighting shall be fitted to—

(a) the sign; or

(b) the structure on which the sign is mounted or which is otherwise specially provided,

except that if a sign is mounted on a bridge, tunnel or similar structure over a road the means of lighting may alternatively be mounted separately in a manner such as to illuminate the face of the sign effectively.

C29–22   **19.**—(1) Nothing in this regulation shall apply to the signs shown in diagrams 560, 561, 776, 781, 5001.1, 5001.2, 5003, 5003.1, 5005 and 5005.1.

(2) Subject to the provisions of regulation 18 and paragraph (1), any sign shown in a diagram in Schedules 1 to 5, 7, 10 and 12—

(a) when placed as part of a road works scheme must, and

(b) in other situations may,

be illuminated by the use of retroreflecting material in accordance with the following provisions of this regulation.

(3) Subject to paragraph (4), where retroreflecting material is used on any part of a sign shown in a diagram, all other parts of that sign shall also be illuminated by means of retroreflecting material.

(4) No retroreflecting material shall be applied to—

(a) any part of a sign coloured black;

(b) that part of the sign shown in diagram 605.2 which is coloured fluorescent yellow, unless the retroreflecting material is applied to that part in horizontal strips with a gap between each strip, or unless the retroreflecting material is itself also fluorescent;

(c) that part of a sign shown in diagram 2714 or 2715 which is coloured orange,

and in this paragraph the work "part", in relation to a sign, means any part of that sign which is uniformly coloured and bounded by parts of a different colour.

Illumination of plates

20.—(1) Where a plate is placed in combination with a sign shown in a dia-   **C29–23**
gram in Schedules 1 to 5 or 12, and that sign is illuminated in accordance with regulation 18, the plate shall, subject to paragraph (2), be illuminated by the same means as the sign.

(2) Paragraph (1) shall not apply where the means of lighting provided for the illumination of the sign adequately illuminates the plate.

Illumination of signs shown in diagrams 560 and 561

21.—(1) The signs shown in diagrams 560 and 561 shall not be illuminated   **C29–24**
by the fitting of a means of internal or external lighting.

(2) A sign shown in a diagram whose number appears in column (2) of an item in the Table and having the dimension specified in column (3) of that item shall be illuminated by either of the methods prescribed in paragraph (3) which are shown in column (4) of the item, and by no other method.

TABLE

(1) Item	(2) Diagram number	(3) Dimension	(4) Method of illumination
1.	560	150 millimetres diameter	Paragraph 3(a) or (b)
2.	560	75 millimetres or more but less than 150 millimetres diameter	Paragraph 3(c) or (d)
3.	561	180 square centimetres area	Paragraph 3(b) or (e)

(3) The prescribed methods of illumination are—

(a) the use of 14 circular reflectors of the corner cube type, each reflector having a diameter of 22 millimetres;

(b) the use of retroreflecting material extending over the whole surface of the sign;

(c) the use of a single circular reflector of the corner cube type extending over the whole surface of the sign;

(d) the use of reflectors consisting of bi-convex lenses extending over the whole surface of the sign; and

(e) the use of a single rectangular reflector of the corner cube type extending over the whole surface of the sign.

Buses and coaches

C29–25   **22.**—(1) In the signs shown in the permitted variants of diagrams 618.1, 618.2, 618.3, 618.3A, 620 and 820, in diagrams 877, 954, 954.1, 954.2, 954.3, 970, 973, 973.1, 974, 975, 1025, 1025.1, 1025.2 and 1025.3 and in the permitted variant of diagram 1028.2 the expressions "bus", "buses" and "buses and coaches" have the meanings given in paragraphs (2) and (3).

(2) "Buses" in the signs referred to in paragraph (1) means—
>(a) before 1st January 1997—
>>(i) public service vehicles used for the provision of local services or scheduled express services;
>>(ii) school buses; or
>>(iii) works buses; and
>(b) after 31st December 1996—
>>(i) motor vehicles constructed or adapted to carry more than 8 passengers (exclusive of the driver); and
>>(ii) local buses not so constructed or adapted;

and "bus" shall be construed accordingly.

(3) The expression "buses and coaches" referred to in paragraph (1) means until 31st December 1996 vehicles constsructed or adapted to carry 12 or more passengers (exclusive of the driver).

Bus lanes

C29–26   **23.**—(1) In the sign shown in diagram 962, 962.2, 963, 963.2, 964, 1048 or 1048.1 the expression "bus lane" has the meaning given in paragraphs (2) and (3).

(2) Before 1st January 1997 "bus lane" in the signs referred to in paragraph (1) means a traffic lane reserved for—
>(a) public service vehicles used in the provision of local services or scheduled express services;
>(b) school buses;
>(c) works buses; and
>(d) pedal cycles and taxis where indicated on the sign shown in diagram 958 or 959 and pedal cycles where indicated on the sign shown in diagram 960, 962.2, 963.2 or 1048.1.

(3) After 31st December 1996 "bus lane" in the signs referred to in paragraph (1) means a traffic lane reserved for—
>(a) motor vehicles constructed or adapted to carry more than 8 passengers (exclusive of the driver);
>(b) local buses not so constructed or adapted; and
>(c) pedal cycles and taxis where indicated on the sign shown in diagram 958 or 959 and pedal cycles where indicated on the sign shown in diagram 960, 962.2, 963.2 or 1048.1.

Bus symbols

C29–27   **24.**—(1) Before 1st January 1997 the symbol representing a bus ("the bus symbol") in the sign or the permitted variant of the sign shown in a diagram whose number is indicated in column (2) of an item in the Table refers to the vehicles indicated in column (3) of that item.

TABLE

(1) Item	(2) Diagram number	(3) Vehicles
1.	952	All motor vehicles constructed or adapted to carry more than 12 passengers (exclusive of the driver), except— (a) public service vehicles used in the provision of local services; (b) scheduled express services; (c) school buses; or (d) works buses.
2.	953, the permitted variant of 953.1 with the bus symbol, the permitted variants of 958 and 959 without the legend "local", 960, 962, 962.2, 963, 963.2 and 970	(a) Public service vehicles used in the provision of local services; (b) scheduled express services; (c) school buses; or (d) works buses.
3.	(a) The permitted variants of 640.2A, 665 and 666 with the bus symbol; (b) 969 and 2106; (c) the permitted variants of 958 and 959 with the legend "& coaches" placed on the symbol; and (d) the permitted variants of diagrams 832.3, 832.4, 832.5, 832.6 and 832.7	All motor vehicles constructed or adapted to carry 12 or more passengers (exclusive of the driver).
4.	972	Public service vehicles used in the provision of excursions or tours.

(2) After 31st December 1996 the bus symbol when incorporated into any sign refers to—

    (a) motor vehicles constructed or adapted to carry more than 8 passengers (exclusive of the driver); or

    (b) local buses not so constructed or adapted.

(3) In the signs shown in diagrams 953, the permitted variant of 953.1, 958, 959 and 960 the word "local" on the bus symbol indicates that the road or the traffic lane on or near which the sign has been placed shall be used only by local buses.

SECTION 4

ROAD MARKINGS

Road marking shown in diagram 1003 and its significance

25.—(1) The requirements conveyed to vehicular traffic on roads by the road marking shown in diagram 1003 shall be as follows. **C29–28**

(2) Except as provided by paragraphs (3) and (4), the requirement conveyed by the transverse lines shown in diagram 1003, whether or not they are placed in conjunction with the sign shown in diagram 602 or 1023, shall be that no vehicle shall proceed past such one of those lines as is nearer the major road into that road in a manner or at a time likely to endanger the driver of or any passenger in a vehicle on the major road or to cause the driver of such a vehicle to change its speed or course in order to avoid an accident.

(3) Wherever the transverse lines are placed in conjunction with the sign shown in diagram 602, and that sign is at the same time placed in combination with the sign shown in diagram 778 or 778.1 at a level crossing, then the requirement shall be that no vehicle shall proceed past such one of those lines as is nearer the level crossing in a manner or at a time likely to endanger the driver of or any passenger in a railway vehicle or tramcar, or to cause that driver to change the speed of his vehicle in order to avoid an accident.

(4) Wherever the transverse lines are placed in advance of a point in the road where the width of the carriageway narrows significantly, then the requirement shall be that no vehicle shall proceed past such one of these lines as is nearer to the point of narrowing in a manner or at a time likely to endanger the driver of or any passenger in a vehicle that is proceeding in the opposite direction to the first-mentioned vehicle, or to necessitate the driver of such a vehicle to change its speed or course in order to avoid an accident.

Road markings shown in diagrams 1013.1 and 1013.3 and their significance

26.—(1) A road marking for conveying the requirements specified in paragraph (2) and the warning specified in paragraph (5) shall be of the size, colour and type shown in diagram 1013.1 or 1013.3.

(2) The requirements conveyed by the road marking mentioned in paragraph (1) shall be that—

    (a) subject to paragraph (3), no vehicle shall stop on any length of road along which the marking has been placed at any point between the ends of the marking; and

    (b) subject to paragraph (4), every vehicle proceeding on any length of road along which the marking has been so placed that, as viewed in the direction of travel of the vehicle, a continuous line is on the left of a broken line or of another continuous line, shall be so driven as to keep the first-mentioned continuous line on the right hand or off side of the vehicle.

(3) Nothing in paragraph (2)(a) shall apply—

    (a) so as to prevent a vehicle stopping on any length of road so long as may be necessary for any of the following purposes—

       (i) to enable a person to board or alight from the vehicle,

      (ii) to enable goods to be loaded on to or to be unloaded from the vehicle,

     (iii) to enable the vehicle to be used in connection with—

        (a) any building operation or demolition;

        (b) the removal of any obstruction to traffic;

        (c) the maintenance, improvement or reconstruction of that length of road; or

        (d) the laying erection, alteration or repair in or near that length of road of any sewer or of any main, pipe or apparatus for

the supply of gas, water or electricity, or of any telecommunications apparatus as defined in paragraph 1(1) of Schedule 2
to the Telecommunications Act 1984,
if the vehicle cannot be used for such a purpose without stopping
on the length of road;
(b) so as to prevent a vehicle stopping in a lay-by;
(c) to a vehicle for the time being used for fire brigade, ambulance or
police purposes;
(d) to a pedal bicycle not having a sidecar attached thereto, whether
additional means of propulsion by mechanical power are attached to
the bicycle or not;
(e) to a vehicle stopping in any case where the person in control of the
vehicle is required by law to stop, or is obliged to do so in order to
avoid an accident, or is prevented from proceeding by circumstances
outside his control;
(f) to anything done with the permission or at the direction of a constable
in uniform or in accordance with the direction of a traffic warden; or
(g) to a vehicle on a road with more than one traffic lane in each direction.
(4) Nothing in paragraph (2)(b) shall be taken to prohibit a vehicle from
being driven across, or so as to straddle, the continuous line referred to in that
paragraph, if it is safe to do so and if necessary to do so—
(a) to enable the vehicle to enter, from the side of the road on which it is
proceeding, land or premises adjacent to the length of road on which
the line is placed, or another road joining that road;
(b) in order to pass a stationary vehicle;
(c) owing to circumstances outside the control of the driver;
(d) in order to avoid an accident;
(e) in order to pass a road maintenance vehicle which is in use, is moving
at a speed not exceeding 10 miles per hour, and is displaying to the
rear the sign shown in diagram 610 or 7403;
(f) in order to pass a pedal cycle moving at a speed not exceeding 10 miles
per hour;
(g) in order to pass a horse that is being ridden or led at a speed not
exceeding 10 miles per hour; or
(h) for the purposes of complying with any direction of a constable in uniform or a traffic warden.
(5) The warning conveyed by the road marking mentioned in paragraph (1)
shall be that no vehicle while travelling next to a broken line placed on the left
of a continous line, as viewed in the direction of travel of the vehicle, should
cross or straddle the first-mentioned line unless it is seen by the driver of the
vehicle to be safe to do so.

Permitted variants

27. Where the circumstances in which a road marking shown in a diagram   **C29–30**
in Schedule 6 is to be placed so require or where appropriate in those circumstances, the form of the marking shall or may be varied as follows—
(a) in the manner (if any) allowed or required in item 4 of the untitled
table below or beside the diagram; or
(b) in the manner allowed or required in column (3) of an item in Sched-

ule 16, if the diagram is one whose number is given in column (2) of that item.

(2) In the road marking shown in diagram 1035, route numbers, place names and the direction in which any arrow-head points shall be varied to accord with the circumstances but the words "turn left", "ahead" or "turn right" shall not be included in the marking.

(3) Where the form of a road marking is varied in accordance with this regulation, the information, warning, requirement, restriction, prohibition or speed limit conveyed by the marking is varied to accord with the form of marking as varied.

Illumination of road markings

28.—(1) Subject to paragraph (2) a road marking shown in diagram 1001, 1002.1, 1003, 1003.1, 1003.3, 1003.4, 1004, 1004.1, 1005, 1005.5, 1008, 1008.1, 1009, 1010, 1012.1, 1012.2, 1012.3, 1013.1, 1013.3, 1014, 1022, 1023, 1024, 1024.1, 1036.1, 1036.2, 1037.1, 1039, 1040, 1040.2, 1040.3, 1040.4, 1040.5, 1041, 1042, 1046, 1049, 1060, 1060.1, 1061 or 1061.1 shall be illuminated with retroreflecting material.

(2) Paragraph (1) shall not apply to a road marking shown in diagram 1003, 1023 or 1049 when varied for use on a cycle track as defined in the Highways Act 1980 or the Roads (Scotland) Act 1984.

(3) Subject to paragraph (4), studs incorporating reflectors or retroreflecting material and so spaced as to form a single line of studs not less than 3 nor more than 4.5 metres apart shall be fitted—

(a) between the two lines constituting the marking shown in diagram 1013.1 unless that marking—
  (i) is placed on an automatic level crossing;
  (ii) is placed on a length of the road situated within 90 metres of the transverse stop line shown in diagram 1001 provided in association with any such crossing; or
  (iii) is so placed that the continuous lines shown in version B of diagram 1013.1 are more than 175 millimetres apart and are separated by an area of cross-hatching so shown;
(b) between the two continuous parallel lines forming part of the marking shown in diagram 1013.3.

(4) Where the marking shown in diagram 1013.1 is placed in any of the cases referred to in paragraphs (i), (ii) and (iii) of paragraph (3)(a) then the studs mentioned in paragraph (3) shall be fitted either in opposite pairs within the width of each of the two lines or in a single line between them.

(5) Subject to the foregoing provisions of this regulation, and to paragraph (6), any road marking may be illuminated with retroreflecting material, and studs incorporating reflectors or retroreflecting material may be used with a road marking shown in diagram 1004, 1004.1, 1005, 1005.1, 1008, 1008.1, 1009, 1010, 1012.1, 1012.2, 1012.3, 1025.2, 1025.3, 1035, 1040, 1040.2, 1040.3, 1040.4, 1040.5, 1041 or 1042 in such a manner that any such stud shall not be fitted to any part of the marking coloured white or yellow but shall be applied to the surface of the carriageway in the gaps between parts of the marking.

(6) In the case of a road marking shown in diagram 1012.1, 1012.2, 1012.3 or 1042 the studs shall, if fitted, be applied to the surface of the carriageway at the side of and adjacent to the line shown in the diagram.

(7) Reflectors or retroreflecting material incorporated in studs shall be white except that in the case of studs used with a road marking shown in

diagram 1009, 1010, 1012.1, 1012.2, 1012.3, 1025.2, 1025.3, 1040.3, 1041 or 1042 the reflectors or retroreflecting material shall reflect—

    (a) red light where the near side edge of a carriageway is indicated to drivers of approaching vehicles, or when placed in conjunction with the markings shown in diagrams 1041 and 1042 to indicate the off side edge of a carriageway;

    (b) amber light to indicate the off side edge of a carriageway which is contiguous to a central reservation or to traffic cones or cylinders at road works or the road marking shown in diagram 1040.3, or which carries traffic in one direction only; and

    (c) green light when placed in conjunction with a road marking shown in diagram 1009, 1010, 1025.2 or 1025.3 where the edge of any part of the carriageway available for through traffic at a road junction, a lay-by or a parking place is so indicated to drivers of approaching vehicles.

  (8) The colour of the parts of the stud other than the reflectors or retroreflecting material shall either be the same as the reflectors or retroreflecting material, or be white, or be a natural metallic finish or other neutral colour, or shall be fluorescent green/yellow in the case of studs placed temporarily at road works.

Height of road markings and size of studs

  29.—(1) The size and shape of a stud incorporating reflectors or retroreflecting material shall be such that the part which is visible above the surface of the road can be contained within—   **C29–32**

    (a) an overall length in the direction of travel of traffic of not less than 35 millimetres and not exceeding 250 millimetres; and

    (b) an overall width of not less than 84 millimetres and not exceeding 230 millimetres.

  (2) No road marking or stud shall project above the surface of the adjacent carriageway more than 6 millimetres at any point except—

    (a) a depressible stud, which shall not project above that surface more than 25 millimetres at its highest point, whether depressed or not;

    (b) a non-depressible stud, which shall not project above that surface more than 20 millimetres at its highest point;

    (c) the road marking shown in diagram 1003.4, which shall not project above that surface more than 125 millimetres at its highest point or 6 millimetres at its perimeter;

    (d) the road marking shown in diagram 1012.2, the raised ribs on which shall project above the surface of the remainder of the marking by 11 millimetres; or

    (e) the road marking shown in diagram 1012.3, the raised ribs on which shall project above the surface of the remainder of the marking by 8 millimetres; and

    (f) the road marking shown in diagram 1049.1, the height of which above the surface of the adjacent carriageway shall be within the range of dimensions indicated on the second part of that diagram illustrating the cross-section of the marking.

  (3) In this regulation, the expression "depressible stud" means a stud so fitted that the height by which it, or part of it, projects above the surface of the adjacent carriageway is apt to be reduced when pressure is applied to the stud from above; and "non-depressible stud" and "depressed" shall be construed accordingly.

SECTION 5

LIGHT SIGNALS AND WARNING LIGHTS

Use of different types of light signals

C29–33   **30.**—(1) Light signals used for the control of vehicular traffic shall be of the size, colour and type prescribed in paragraph (2), (3), (5), (7) or (9).

(2) Subject to regulation 31, light signals used to control vehicular traffic at road junctions, at places where the headroom or the width of the road is permanently restricted, or at places where pedestrians cross the road (other than Pelican crossings) shall be of the size, colour and type shown in diagram 3000, 3000.3, 3000.4, 3000.5 or 3000.6 and be illuminated in the sequence prescribed in paragraph (4).

(3) Light signals used to control vehicular traffic consisting solely of pedal cycles shall be of the size, colour and type shown in diagram 3000.2 and be illuminated in the sequence prescribed in paragraph (4).

(4) The sequence of illumination of the lights shown by the signals prescribed in paragraphs (2) and (3) shall be as follows—

   (a) red,
   (b) red and amber together,
   (c) green,
   (d) amber,

provided that where the light signals are varied as prescribed in regulation 31, the green arrow shown in diagram 3000.4 or 3000.6 and shown as a permitted variant of diagram 3000.3 or 3000.5 or one of the green arrows shown as a permitted variant of diagram 3000.3, 3000.4 or 3000.6 may be illuminated while any of the lights referred to in sub-paragraphs (a) (b) (c) and (d) are illuminated.

(5) Light signals used to control vehicular traffic entering or proceeding along a motorway or dual carriageway road shall be—

   (a) of the size, colour and type shown in diagram 6031.1 or 60322.1; and
   (b) operated as prescribed in paragraph (6).

(6) The operating requirements for the light signals prescribed in paragraph (5) are that—

   (a) each lamp shall show an intermittent red light at a rate of flashing of not less than 60 nor more than 90 flashes per minute, and in such a manner that the lights of one vertical pair are always shown when the lights of the other vertical pair are not shown; and
   (b) the red cross or the white symbol shown in diagram 6031.1 or 6032.1 shall be illuminated by a steady light when the red lights are flashing.

(7) Light signals used to control traffic at level crossings, swinging or lifting bridges, tunnels, airfields or in the vicinity of premises used regularly by fire, police or ambulance service vehicles shall be—

   (a) of the size, colour and type shown in diagram 3014; and
   (b) illuminated in the sequence prescribed in paragraph (8).

(8) The sequence for the illumination of the light signals prescribed in paragraph (7) shall be as follows—

   (a) a single steady amber light,
   (b) two intermittent red lights, each of which will be shown at a rate of flashing of not less than 60 nor more than 90 flashes per minute, and

in such a manner that one light is always shown when the other light is not shown.

(9) Light signals used to control tramcars shall—

(a) be of the size, colour and type shown in diagram 3013; and

(b) display the aspects shown in diagrams 3013.1, 3013.2, 3013.3, 3013.4 and 3013.5 in the sequence prescribed in paragraph (10).

(10) The sequence for the illumination of the light signals prescribed in paragraph (9) shall be as follows—

(a) the horizontal line shown in diagram 3013.1,

(b) the vertical line shown in diagram 3013.2 or either of the diagonal lines shown in diagram 3013.3 or 3013.4,

(c) the central circle shown in diagram 3013.5.

(11) When the light signals prescribed in paragraph (9) ("tram signals") are affixed to the light signals mentioned in paragraph (2) ("standard signals") in the manner shown in diagram 3000.3, 3000.4, 3000.5 or 3000.6 their aspect may be such that they convey to the driver of a tramcar a significance (within the meaning of regulation 33) which is different from that conveyed at the same time to the drivers of other vehicular traffic by the aspect of the standard signals to which the tram signals are affixed.

Permitted variants of green arrow light signals

31.—(1) A lens or lenses of the size and colour shown in either diagram 3001   **C29–34** or 3001.1 which, when illuminated, shows a green arrow—

(a) may be substituted for the lens showing the green light in the light signals referred to in regulation 30(2) using any of the methods shown in diagram 3003, 3005, 3006, 3011.1 or 3011.2; or

(b) may be affixed to the light signals referred to in regulation 30(2) or to those signals as altered in accordance with sub-paragraph (a) using any of the methods shown in diagram 3000.4, 3000.6, 3002, 3004, 3005, 3006, 3007, 3008, 3009.1, 3011.1 or 3011.2.

(2) The direction of the arrow prescribed as the permitted variant of diagram 3000.3 and shown in diagram 3000.4 may be varied so that the head of the arrow points to any position on the 90° arc shown in diagram 3002 or 3004.

(3) The direction of the arrow prescribed as the permitted variant of diagrams 3000 and 3000.5 and shown in diagram 3000.6 may be varied so that the head of the arrow points to any position on the 180° arc shown in diagram 3003 or 3009.1.

(4) The direction of any arrow prescribed as a permitted variant of diagrams 3000.3 and 3000.4 where the arrow is substituted for the green light may be varied so that the head of the arrow points to any position on the 90° arcs shown in diagram 3005 or 3006, provided that there is a difference of not less than 45° between the directions in which paired arrows point.

(5) The direction of either of the green arrows included in diagram 3000.4, where the sign shown in that diagram has been varied by the substitution of a green arrow for the tram signal aspect, may be varied so that the head of the arrow points to any position on the 45° arcs shown in diagram 3007 or 3008 provided that there is a difference of not less than 45° between the directions in which paired arrows point.

(6) The direction of either of the green arrows included in diagram 3000.6, where the sign shown in that diagram has been varied by the substitution of a green arrow for the tram signal aspect, may be varied so that—

(a) when the arrows are illuminated and extinguished simultaneously,

the head of the upper arrow may point in any direction on the 135° arc
and the head of the lower arrow may point in any direction on either of
the two 45° arcs shown in diagram 3011.1, provided that there is a difference of not less than 45° between the directions in which the two
arrows point; and

(b) when the arrows are illuminated and extinguished independently, the
head of either of the arrows may point in any direction on the two 180°
arcs shown in diagram 3011.2, provided that there is a difference of not
less than 45° between the directions in which the arrows point.

Portable light signals

C29–35   32. Portable light signals—
(a) shall be of the size, colour and type shown in diagram 3000.1; and
(b) shall be illuminated in the sequence prescribed by regulation 30(4).

Significance of light signals

C29–36   33.—(1) The significance of the light signals prescribed in paragraphs (2)
and (3) of regulation 30 and in regulation 32 shall be as follows—
(a) except as provided in sub-paragraphs (b), (f) and (g) the red signal
shall convey the prohibition that vehicular traffic other than tramcars
shall not proceed beyond the stop line;
(b) when a vehicle is being used for fire brigade, ambulance or police purposes and the observance of the prohibition conveyed by the red signal in accordance with sub-paragrtaph (a) would be likely to hinder
the use of that vehicle for the purpose for which it is being used, then
sub-paragraph (a) shall not apply to the vehicle, and the red signal
shall convey the prohibition that that vehicle shall not proceed beyond
the stop line in a manner or at a time likely to endanger any person or
to cause the driver of any vehicle proceeding in accordance with the
indications of light signals operating in association with the signals
displaying the red signal to change its speed or course in order to
avoid an accident;
(c) except as provided in sub-paragraph (f), the red-with-amber signal
shall denote an impending change to green or a green arrow in the
indication given by the signals but shall convey the same prohibition
as the red signal;
(d) the green signal shall indicate that vehicular traffic other than tramcars
may proceed beyond the stop line and proceed straight on or to the left
or to the right;
(e) the amber signal shall, when shown alone, convey the same prohibition as the red signal, except that, as respects any vehicle other than a
tramcar which is so close to the stop line that it cannot safely be stopped without proceeding beyond the stop line, it shall convey the same
indication as the green signal or green arrow signal which was shown
immediately before it;
(f) save as provided in sub-paragraph (g), the green arrow signal shall
indicate that vehicular traffic other than tramcars may, notwithstanding any other indication given by the signals, proceed beyond the stop
line only in the direction indicated by the arrow for the purpose

of proceeding in that direction through the junction controlled by those signals; and

(g) where more than one green arrow is affixed to light signals in accordance with regulation 31(1)(b), vehicular traffic other than tramcars may, notwithstanding any other indication given by the signals, proceed beyond the stop line only in the direction indicated by any one of the green arrows for the purpose of proceeding in that direction through the junction controlled by those signals.

(2) Vehicular traffic proceeding beyond a stop line in accordance with paragraph (1) shall proceed with due regard to the safety of other road users and subject to any direction given by a constable in uniform or a traffic warden or to any other applicable prohibition or restriction.

(3) The significance of the light signals prescribed in regulation 30(5) shall be as follows—

(a) when placed beside the carriageway of a road, they shall convey the prohibition that vehicular traffic (other than vehicles being used in the circumstances described in paragraph (1)(b)) shall not proceed beyond the signals; and

(b) when displayed on a gantry over the carriageway, they shall convey the prohibition that vehicular traffic (other than vehicles being used in the circumstances described in paragraph (1)(b)) proceeding in the traffic lane immediately below the signals shall not proceed beyond them in that lane,

and for the purposes of this paragraph light signals which are mounted on a post situated beside the carriageway but which are projected over it or part of it shall be treated as light signals placed beside the carriageway of that road.

(4) The significance of the light signals prescribed in regulation 30(7) shall be as follows—

(a) the amber signal shall convey the prohibition that traffic shall not proceed beyond the stop line on the carriageway, except for a vehicle which is so close to the stop line that it cannot safely be stopped without proceeding beyond the stop line; and

(b) the intermittent red signals shall convey the prohibition that traffic shall not proceed beyond the stop line.

(5) The significance of the light signals prescribed in regulation 30(9) shall be as follows—

(a) the aspect shown in diagram 3013.1 shall convey the prohibition that a tramcar shall not proceed beyond the stop line;

(b) the aspect shown in diagram 3013.2 shall indicate that a tramcar may proceed beyond the stop line and proceed straight ahead;

(c) the aspect shown in diagram 3013.3 shall indicate that a tramcar may proceed beyond the stop line and proceed to the left;

(d) the aspect shown in diagram 3013.4 shall indicate that a tramcar may proceed beyond the stop line and proceed to the right; and

(e) the aspect shown in diagram 3013.5 shall convey the prohibition that a tramcar shall not proceed beyond the stop line except that, as respects a tramcar which is so close to the stop line that it cannot safely be stopped without proceeding beyond the stop line, it shall convey the same indication as the aspect which was shown immediately before it.

(6) In this regulation—

(a) "primary signals" means light signals erected on or near the carriageway of a road and sited near either one or both ends of the stop line, or if there is no stop line, sited at either or both edges of the carriageway or part of the carriageway which is in use by traffic approaching and controlled by the signals;

(b) "secondary signals" means light signals erected on or near the carriageway facing traffic approaching from the direction of the primary signals but sited beyond those signals as viewed from the direction of travel of such traffic;

(c) "stop line" in relation to light signals means the road marking shown in diagram 1001 placed on a carriageway in conjunction with those light signals being either primary signals alone, or secondary signals alone or both primary and secondary signals and, where no stop line is provided or the stop line is not visible, references in the preceding paragraphs of this regulation to the stop line are—

(i) in a case where the sign shown in diagram 7011 is placed in conjunction with the light signals, to be treated as references to that sign; and

(ii) in any other case, to be treated as references to the post or other structure on which the primary signals are mounted; and

(d) any reference to light signals, to the signals or to a signal of a particular colour is, where secondary signals have been placed, a reference to the light signals displayed by both the primary and secondary signals or, as the case may be, by the primary signals operating without the secondary signals or by the secondary signals operating without the primary signals.

Light signals for lane control of vehicular traffic

C29–37   **34.**—(1) A light signal placed above the carriageway and facing the direction of oncoming vehicular traffic used for the control of that traffic proceeding along the traffic lane over which those signals have been placed shall be of the size, colour and type shown in diagram 5001.1, 5001.2, 5003, 5003.1, 5005 or 5005.1.

(2) The height of the centre of each light signal from the surface of the carriageway in the immediate vicinity shall be not less than 5.5 metres nor more than 9 metres.

(3) The signals prescribed by this regulation shall be so designed that—

(a) the red cross shown in diagram 5003 or 5003.1 ("the red cross") can be internally illuminated in such a manner as to show a steady red light;

(b) the green arrow shown in diagram 5001.1 or 5001.2 ("the downward green arrow") can be internally illuminated in such a manner as to show a steady green light;

(c) the white arrow shown in diagram 5005 or 5005.1 ("the diagonal white arrow") can be internally illuminated in such a manner as to show a steady white light; and

(d) whenever one of the signals referred to in sub-paragraphs (a) to (c) is illuminated neither of the other signals referred to in those sub-paragraphs shall be illuminated when placed over the same traffic lane.

(4) The significance of the light signals prescribed in this regulation shall be as follows—

(a) the red cross shall convey to vehicular traffic proceeding in the traffic lane above which it is displayed the prohibition that such traffic shall not proceed beyond the red cross in the traffic lane until that prohibition is cancelled by a display over that traffic lane of the downward green arrow or diagonal white arrow or by a display over that traffic lane or beside the carriageway of the traffic sign shown in diagram 5015 or 6001;

(b) the downward green arrow shall convey to vehicular traffic proceeding in the traffic lane above which it is displayed the information that such traffic may proceed or continue to do so in the lane beneath the arrow; and

(c) the diagonal white arrow shall convey to vehicular traffic proceeding in the traffic lane above which it is displayed the warning that such traffic should move into the adjacent traffic lane in the direction indicated by the arrow as soon as traffic conditions permit.

Warning signal for motorways and dual carriageway roads

35.—(1) A traffic sign for conveying the warning specified in paragraph (2)   **C29–38** to vehicular traffic on a motorway or a dual carriageway road shall be a light signal of the size, colour and type shown in diagram 6023.

(2) The warning conveyed by the light signal shall be that—

(a) there is a hazard ahead on the motorway or dual carriageway road; and

(b) drivers should drive at a speed which does not exceed 30 miles per hour until they are certain that the hazard has been passed or removed.

(3) When the light signal prescribed by this regulation is operated, each lamp shall show an intermittent amber light at a rate of flashing of not less than 60 nor more than 90 flashes per minute and in such a manner that one light is always shown when the other light is not shown.

Matrix signs for motorways and dual carriageway roads

36.—(1) In this regulation "matrix sign" means a sign shown in a diagram in   **C29–39** Part I of Schedule 11 for conveying to traffic on motorways and dual carriageway roads information or a warning, requirement, restriction, prohibition or speed limit—

(a) relating to or arising out of temporary hazardous conditions on or near the motorway or dual carriageway road; and

(b) specified under a diagram contained in Part I of that Schedule.

(2) A matrix sign shall be a light signal and shall be of the size, colour and type prescribed by this regulation and shown in a diagram in Part I of Schedule 11.

(3) Where a matrix sign is placed beside the carriageway of a road the warning, requirement, restriction, prohibition or speed limit conveyed by the sign shall apply to all vehicular traffic facing that sign and proceeding along the carriageway beside which the sign is placed.

(4) For the purposes of this regulation a sign which is mounted on a post situated beside the carriageway but is projected over it or part of it shall be treated as a sign placed beside the carriageway of that road.

(5) Where a matrix sign mounted on a gantry or other structure is so placed that a traffic lane of the carriageway passes directly beneath it, the warning,

requirement, restriction, prohibition or speed limit conveyed by the sign shall apply only to vehicular traffic facing that sign and proceeding along the traffic lane passing directly beneath it.

(6) The legend or symbol in a matrix sign shall be displayed by means of white or off-white light and except in the case of the sign shown in diagram 6012 shall be accompanied by the four lamps prescribed in paragraph (7).

(7) The four lamps mentioned in paragraph (6)—

(a) shall be of the size, colour and type shown in diagram 6022 when placed beside the carriageway or in diagram 6021 when mounted on a gantry or other structure over the carriageway; and

(b) when a matrix sign other than the one shown in diagram 6012 is displayed, each lamp shall show an intermittent amber light at a rate of flashing of not less than 60 nor more than 90 flashes per minute and in such a manner that one horizontal pair of lights is always shown when the lights of the other horizontal pair of lights is not shown.

Light signals for pedestrians

C29–40　　37.—(1) Light signals for conveying to pedestrians the information mentioned in paragraph (3) shall be of the size, colour and type shown in diagram 4002.

(2) The signals shall be so designed that—

(a) the red figure shown in diagram 4002 ("the red signal") can be internally illuminated by a steady light;

(b) the green figure shown in diagram 4002 ("the green signal") can be internally illuminated by a steady light;

(c) when one signal is illuminated the other signal is not illuminated; and

(d) the green signal is and remains illuminated only for so long as there is conveyed to vehicular traffic a requirement, prohibition or restriction against entering that part of the carriageway across which the light signals for pedestrians are facing, being a requirement, prohibition or restriction indicated by—

(i) the light signals prescribed in paragraphs (2), (3) or (9) of regulation 30;

(ii) the light signals prescribed in regulation 30(2) varied in accordance with regulation 31 as respects the direction of the green arrow; or

(iii) a traffic sign shown in diagram 606, 612, 613 or 616.

(3) The period during which, in the interests of safety, pedestrians—

(a) should not cross the carriageway shall be shown by the red signal during such time as it is illuminated; and

(b) may cross the carriageway shall be shown by the green signal during such time as it is illuminated by the steady light.

(4) Any audible sign emitted by any device for emitting audible signals provided in conjunction with the green signal, and any tactile signal made by any device for making tactile signals similarly provided, shall convey to pedestrians the information mentioned in paragraph (3)(b).

(5) A sign of the size, colour and type shown in diagram 4003 shall during such time as the word "WAIT" is illuminated indicate to pedestrians the warning mentioned in sub-paragraph (a) of paragraph (3).

C29–41　　38.—(1) Light signals conveying to pedestrians at level crossings the prohibition mentioned in paragraph (2) shall be of the size, colour and type shown in diagram 4006 and so designed that—

(a) the red figure shown in diagram 4006 is internally illuminated by an intermittent red light which is shown at a rate of flashing of not less than 60 nor more than 90 flashes per minute; and

(b) the red figure is illuminated only when the intermittent red lights prescribed in regulation 30(8)(b) are illuminated.

(2) The red figure when illuminated in the manner described in paragraph (1) shall convey the prohibition that pedestrians shall not proceed beyond the transverse road marking shown in diagram 1003.2 on the footway or diagram 1001 on the carriageway.

School crossing patrol signs and warning lights

39.—(1) A sign which is exhibited by a school crossing patrol for the purpose of stopping any vehicle in accordance with section 28 of the 1984 Act shall be of the size, colour and type shown in diagram 605.2.   **C29–42**

(2) A sign for conveying a warning to vehicular traffic, which is approaching a place in a road where children on their way to or from school or on their way from one part of a school to another cross or seek to cross that road ("a crossing place"), that the crossing place lies ahead and is being patrolled by a school crossing patrol or is otherwise in use by such children—

(a) shall be a light signal of the size, colour and type shown in diagram 4004, each lamp of which when operated shall show an intermittent amber light at a rate of flashing of not less than 60 nor more than 90 flashes per minute and in such a manner that one light is always shown when the other light is not shown; and

(b) may be erected on or near part of the road in advance of a crossing place in relation to oncoming traffic.

Cattle crossing signs and warning lights

40.—(1) A sign of the size, colour and type shown in diagram 4005 may be erected on or near a road in advance of a place in that road where cattle under the supervision of a herdsman on their way from one part of a farm to another cross the road ("a cattle crossing") to convey to oncoming traffic the warning specified in paragraph (2).   **C29–43**

(2) The warning conveyed by the sign shall be that—

(a) a cattle crossing lies ahead and may be in use; and

(b) traffic should be prepared to stop.

(3) When the sign is operated, each lamp shall show an intermittent amber light at a rate of flashing of not less than 60 nor more than 90 flashes per minute and in such a manner that one light is always shown when the other light is not shown.

SECTION 6

MISCELLANEOUS TRAFFIC SIGNS

Certain temporary signs

41.—(1) A temporary sign shall be of such size, colour and type as is specified in this regulation.   **C29–44**

(2) The shape of a temporary sign shall be—
  (a) rectangular;
  (b) rectangular but with the corners rounded; or
  (c) pointed at one end but otherwise rectangular in accordance with (a) or (b).

(3) A temporary sign may incorporate—
  (a) wording;
  (b) numerals;
  (c) arrows or chevrons;
  (d) any appropriate symbol taken from any diagram in any Schedule; and
  (e) the arms, badge or other device of a traffic authority, police authority or an organisation representative of road users,
and shall be of a size appropriate to the circumstances in which it is placed.

(4) Every letter and numeral incorporated in a temporary sign other than any letter incorporated in the sign in accordance with paragraph (3)(e) shall be not less than 40 nor more than 350 millimetres in height, and every arrow so incorporated shall be not less than 250 nor more than 1000 millimetres in length.

(5) Every letter, numeral, arrow, chevron or symbol, other than a sign shown in a diagram in Schedules 1 to 5 when used as a symbol, incorporated in a temporary sign shall be—
  (a) black on a background of white or of yellow;
  (b) white on a blue background;
  (c) blue on a white background;
  (d) if the sign conveys information or warnings of the kind mentioned in sub-paragraphs (c) or (d) of paragraph (7), white on a red background, except where it is placed on a motorway when it shall be black on a yellow background; or
  (e) if the sign is a variable message sign, yellow on a black background or black on a yellow background, except when the sign is not in use when it shall display a plain black or grey face.

(6) No temporary sign shall convey to traffic any information, warning, requirement, restriction or prohibition of a description which can be conveyed either by a sign shown in a diagram in Schedules 1 to 12 or by a sign so shown placed in combination or in conjunction with another sign so shown in such a diagram.

(7) In this regulation "temporary sign" means a sign placed temporarily on or near a road for conveying to traffic—
  (a) information as respects deviations or alternative traffic routes;
  (b) information as respects the route which may conveniently be followed on the occasion of a sports meeting, exhibition or other public gathering which in each case it is anticipated will attract a considerable volume of traffic;
  (c) information as to the date from which works are to be executed on or near a road;
  (d) information or warnings as to the avoidance of any temporary hazards occasioned by works being executed on or near a road, by adverse weather conditions or other natural causes, by the failure of street lighting or by malfunction of or damage to any apparatus, equipment or facility used in connection with the road or anything situated on, near or under it or by damage to the road itself; or
  (e) requests for information by the police in connection with a road traffic accident.

Flashing beacons

42.—(1) A beacon—   **C29–45**
  (a) showing an intermittent amber light and placed in combination with a temporary sign within the meaning of regulation 41 or the sign shown in diagram 562, 610, 7001, 7009, 7010, 7012, 7013, 7019, 7020, 7021 or 7022, and in compliance with the requirements in paragraph (2); or
  (b) showing an intermittent blue light and placed by a constable or a person acting under instructions (whether general or specific) of the chief officer of police in combination with a sign shown in diagram 606, 609, 610, 616, 633, 829.1, 829.2, 829.3, 829.4 or 7105, and in compliance with (c) and (d) of the requirements in paragraph (2),
shall convey the warning that drivers of vehicles should take special care.
  (2) The requirements mentioned in paragraph (1) are—
  (a) the peak intensity of light emitted by the lens or lenses of each such beacon shall be—
      (i) if the period between individual flashes does not exceed ¼ of a second, not less than 100 candela on the principal axis of the relevant lens;
      (ii) if the period between individual flashes exceeds ¼ of a second, not less than 2000 candela on the principal axis; or
      (iii) if the period between the cessation of a double flash and the start of the succeeding double flash exceeds ¼ of a second, not less than 1000 candela on the principal axis;
  (b) each lens shall be of such a shape and size that the perimeter of its area projected horizontally onto a vertical plane shall be capable of lying wholly inside a square having sides of 200 millimetres in length and wholly outside a square having sides of 100 millimetres in length;
  (c) the height of the centre of the lenses from the surface of the carriageway in the immediate vicinity shall be not less than 800 nor more than 1500 millimetres; and
  (d) the rate of flashing shall be not less than 40 nor more than 150 individual or double flashes per minute.

Road danger lamps

43.—(1) A lamp showing a steady or intermittent amber light which—   **C29–46**
  (a) conforms to British Standard Specification BS3143: Part 1: 1985 amended by Amendment No. 1 dated February 1985; or BS3143: Part 2: 1990; or an equivalent specification of a European Economic Area State; and
  (b) is illuminated separately and by a single source of light.
shall indicate to traffic the limits of a temporary obstruction of the road and in this regulation is called a "road danger lamp".
  (2) The height of the centre of each lens of a road danger lamp from the surface of the road in the immediate vicinity of the lamp shall not exceed 1500 millimetres where the speed limit on the road is 40 miles per hour or less, or 1200 millimetres where the speed limit on the road is more than 40 miles per hour.
  (3) Where a road danger lamp which shows an intermittent light is placed—
  (a) within 50 metres of a street lamp lit by electricity on a road subject to a speed limit of 40 miles per hour or less, the lamp shall operate in such a way that the rate of flashing shall be not less than 40 nor more than 150 flashes per minute; and

(b) on roads other than those mentioned in sub-paragraph (a), the rate of flashing shall be not less than 900 flashes per minute.

Cones, delineators and cylinders

C29–47   44.—(1) The sign shown in diagram 7101 shall, subject to paragraph (2), consist of a conically shaped device made of rubber or flexible plastic material of which—

(a) the base is coloured red, black, grey or brown;

(b) the base is a polygon having not more than eight sides, which would be contained wholly within a circle with a diameter of three quarters of the height of the device; and

(c) the part of the device coloured white is illuminated with white retro-reflecting material,

and information about the manufacture of the sign required in order to comply with British Standard Specification BS 873: Part 8: 1985 or an equivalent specification of a European Economic Area State, occupying an area not exceeding 30 square centimetres, may be indicated on the part of the sign coloured white in characters not exceeding 5 millimetres in height, at least 90 per cent of the remaining area of white colour shall be illuminated with white retroreflecting material, and the part of the device coloured red may be illuminated with red retroreflecting material.

(2) A rotating device which is red and not illuminated by means of retro-reflecting material and which displays one or more of the signs shown in diagram 560 or 561, which shall be coloured amber, intermittently while rotating and constantly while static, may be mounted on top of the sign shown in diagram 7101.

(3) The sign shown in diagram 7102 shall consist of a device made of rubber or flexible plastic material of which—

(a) the base is coloured red, black, grey or brown, except that a white line 100 millimetres wide at an angle of not more than 60° to the road surface and illuminated with retroreflecting material may be marked on one side of the base at right angles to the face of the device;

(b) the base has a maximum width (measured parallel to the face of the device) of three quarters of the height of the device, a minimum length of three quarters of the height of the device and is no more than 70 millimetres high at the outermost edge; and

(c) the part of the device coloured white is illuminated with white retro-reflecting material,

and information about the manufacture of the sign required in order to comply with British Standard Specification BS 873: Part 8: 1985 or an equivalent specification of a European Economic Area State, occupying an area not exceeding 30 square centimetres, may be indicated on the part of the sign coloured white in characters not exceeding 5 millimetres in height and, if only one side of the device is illuminated in accordance with this paragraph, the reverse side shall be coloured red or grey in material which is not retroreflecting, and the part of the device coloured red may be illuminated with red retroreflecting material.

(4) The sign shown in diagram 7103 shall consist of a cylindrically shaped device made of rubber or flexible plastic material and—

(a) the part of the device coloured white shall be illuminated with white retroreflecting material; and

(b) information about the manufacture of the sign required in order to comply with British Standard Specification BS 873: Part 8: 1985 or an equivalent specification of a European Economic Area State, occupying an area not exceeding 30 square centimetres, may be indicated on the part of the sign coloured white in characters not exceeding 5 millimetres in height, and at least 90 per cent of the remaining area of white colour shall be illuminated with white retroreflecting material; and

(c) the part of the device coloured red may be illuminated with red retroreflecting material.

Refuge indicator lamps

45. A lamp in the form of an illuminated spherical globe for conveying the warning that drivers of vehicles are approaching a street refuge may be placed subject to the following conditions—   **C29–48**

(a) the globe shall be white;

(b) the globe shall have a diameter of not less than 290 nor more than 310 millimetres; and

(c) the height of the centre of the globe above the surface of the carriageway in the immediate vicinity shall be not less than 3800 millimetres nor more than 5000 millimetres.

Variable message signs

46.—(1) A device may display at different times—   **C29–49**

(a) a sign shown in a diagram in Schedules 1 to 5, 7, 11 or 12;

(b) a legend of a type shown in Schedule 15 in accordance with the provisions of that Schedule; or

(c) a blank grey or a blank black face,

and in these Regulations such a device is referred to as a "variable message sign".

(2) A variable message sign shall be of a size appropriate to display the messages referred to in sub-paragraphs (a) and (b) of paragraph (1), having regard to the normal speed of traffic on the road on or near which the sign is situated.

(3) If the construction or method of operation of a variable message sign prevents the sign from being displayed in the colours shown for it in the appropriate diagram in Schedules 1 to 5, 7, Part I of Schedule 11 or Schedule 12, a black legend or symbol on a white or yellow background may be displayed as a white, off-white or yellow legend or symbol on a dark background, provided that any red triangle or red circle forming part of the sign is retained.

(4) When a variable message sign displays the sign shown in diagram 670, any sign shown in a diagram in Part I of Schedule 11 other than diagram 6012, or a legend of the type shown in Schedule 15, it may also display four lamps of the size, colour and type specified in regulation 36(7), save that the rate of flashing shall be not less than 60 nor more than 150 flashes per minute and the distance between the lamps shall be varied to accord with the overall size of the variable message sign.

(5) The display of a blank black or grey face on a variable message sign accompanied by four flashing lamps of the kind mentioned in paragraph (4) shall indicate to drivers that they should take special care.

(6) A variable message sign which displays alternately the signs shown in diagrams 7023 and 7024 shall be manually operated.

Appendix B

FIXED PENALTY CHECKLISTS

Procedure where Fixed Penalty Notice is given to the driver: offence endorsable

1. Constable in uniform has reason to believe a fixed penalty offence is or has been committed and requests to see the driving licence of the person concerned.

2. If the driver produces his licence, go to 3.
   If the driver fails to produce his licence, go to 6.

3. If the driver would not be liable to disqualification as a "totter" if convicted of the offence, go to 4.
   If he would be liable to disqualification as a "totter" if convicted of the offence, go to 7.

4. A fixed penalty notice is issued.
   If it is paid within the suspended enforcement period (SEP), go to 5.
   If it is not paid within the SEP, go to 8.

5. Fixed penalty clerk endorses and returns the licence to the driver.

6. Constable issues a provisional fixed penalty notice, ordering the driver to produce his licence at the police station within seven days.
   If he does so, go to 3.
   If he does not, go to 7.

7. The driver is reported for prosecution.

8. If a hearing is requested within the SEP, summary proceedings commence.
   If a hearing is not requested within the SEP, go to 9.

9. A registration certificate is issued, sum registered in default, and the sum in default is enforced as a fine and the fixed penalty clerk endorses the driving licence and returns it.

Procedure where Fixed Penalty Notice affixed to the vehicle: offence not endorsable

1. Constable in uniform or authorised traffic warden has reason to believe in the case of any stationary vehicle that a fixed penalty offence is being or has on that occasion been committed in respect of it, and issues a fixed penalty notice, and the notice is attached to the vehicle.

2. If the fixed penalty is paid within the suspended enforcement period (SEP), no further action.
   If the fixed penalty is not paid within the SEP, then go to 3.

3. If a hearing is requested within the SEP summary proceedings follow.
   If a hearing is not requested within the SEP, the police serve notice on the person who appears to be the owner, go to 4.

4. If the fixed penalty is paid within the response period to the notice to owner, no further action.
   If the fixed penalty is not paid within the response period to the notice to owner, go to 5.

5. If a hearing is requested within the response period to the notice to owner, then summary proceedings follow.
   If a hearing is not requested within the response period to the notice to owner, go to 6.

6. If there is no response to the notice to owner, the sum is registered and enforced as a fine against the person serviced with the notice.
   If there is a response, go to 7.

7. If the person served with the notice to owner is not the owner, and supplies a statutory statement of ownership to that effect in response and within the time allowed, then not liable for the offence.
   If the person served with the notice to owner was the owner, but not the driver, go to 8.

8. If the statutory statement of ownership does not identify the actual driver, the sum is registered and enforced as a fine against the person served with the notice.
   If the statutory statement of ownership does identify the actual driver, go to 9.

9. If the fixed penalty is paid by the actual driver, no further action.
If a summons is issued on the actual driver within two months of
the response period, then summary proceedings will follow.
If a summons is not served on the actual driver within two
months, the sum is registered and enforced as a fine against the
person served with the notice to owner.

Procedure where Fixed Penalty Notice is given to the driver: offence not endorsable

1. Constable in uniform or authorised traffic warden has reason to
believe a driver is committing or has committed a fixed penalty
offence and issues a fixed penalty notice.

2. If the fixed penalty is paid within the suspended enforcement
period (SEP), no further action.

3. If it is not paid then:
   (a) If a hearing is requested within the SEP summary proceedings
   follow.

   (b) If no hearing is requested within the SEP, a registration certificate is issued, sum registered in default, and the sum in
   default is enforced as a fine.

Procedure where fixed penalty notice neither given to the driver nor affixed to the vehicle: endorsable and non-endorsable offences

1. Where a constable has reason to believe that a fixed penalty
offence has been committed, and no fixed penalty notice has been
given to the driver or attached to the vehicle, then go to 2.

2. A notice of the fixed penalty offence may be sent to the driver by or
on behalf of the Chief Officer of the Police, go to 3.

3. If the person who is sent the fixed penalty notice responds within
28 days and pays the fixed penalty, go to 4.
If the person who is sent the fixed penalty notice does not respond
within 28 days nor pays the fixed penalty, then summary proceedings follow.

4. If the driver would be liable to disqualification as a "totter" if convicted of the offence, then summary proceedings will follow.
    If he would not be liable to disqualification as a "totter" if convicted of the offence, then the fixed penalty clerk endorses and returns the driving licence.

Appendix C

BREATH/BLOOD/URINE CHART

Prescribed limit. If a blood specimen was provided by the defendant the prescribed limit is 80 mg. of alcohol in 100 ml. of blood; if a urine specimen, 107 mg. of alcohol in 100 ml. of urine; if breath, 35 μg. of alcohol in 100 ml. of breath.

| | Alcohol | |
Breath (μg./ml.)	Blood (mg./ml.)	Urine (mg./ml.)
35	80	107
36	83	110
37	85	113
38	87	116
39	90	119
40	92	122
41	94	125
42	97	129
43	99	132
44	101	135
45	103	138
46	106	141
47	108	144
48	110	147
49	113	150
50	115	153
51	117	156
52	120	159
53	122	162
54	124	165
55	126	168
56	129	171
57	131	174
58	133	177
59	136	181
60	138	184
61	140	187
62	143	190
63	145	193
64	147	196
65	149	199
66	152	202
67	154	205
68	156	208
69	159	211
70	161	214
71	163	217
72	166	220
73	168	223
74	170	226
75	172	230
76	175	233
77	178	236
78	180	239
79	182	242
80	184	245

Appendix D

TABLE OF METABOLIC LOSSES FOR BREATH ANALYSES WITH TIME

Breath (μg.%)	15 min	30 min	45 min	60 min	75 min	90 min
35	33	31	30	28	26	25
40	38	36	35	33	31	30
45	43	41	40	38	36	35
50	48	46	45	43	41	40
55	53	51	50	48	46	45
60	58	56	55	53	51	50
65	63	61	60	58	56	55
70	68	66	65	63	61	60
75	73	71	70	68	66	65
80	78	76	75	73	71	70
85	83	81	80	78	76	75
90	88	86	85	83	81	80
95	93	91	90	88	86	85
100	98	96	95	93	91	90
105	103	101	100	98	96	95
110	108	106	105	103	101	100
115	113	111	110	108	106	105
120	118	116	115	113	111	110
125	123	121	120	118	116	115
130	128	126	125	123	121	120
135	133	131	130	128	126	125
140	138	136	135	133	131	130
145	143	141	140	138	136	135
150	148	146	145	143	141	140
155	153	151	150	148	146	145
160	158	156	155	153	151	150
165	163	161	160	158	156	155
170	168	166	165	163	161	160
175	173	171	170	168	166	165

This table has been drawn up to aid persons who wish to compare breath and blood analysis, when the samples have been taken at different times.

When compiling the table, the following assumptions were made:

(a) The subject has fully absorbed all of the alcohol consumed into his bloodstream.

(b) The average metabolic rate of alcohol destruction by the body is 15mg./100ml./hour in the blood, and 6.5 μg./100ml./hour in the breath.

(c) The blood/breath ratio is 2300:1.

Each pair of numbers shows equivalent breath and blood concentrations, and each row is calculated to show how these values will decrease with the elapse of time in steps of 15 minutes.

TABLE OF METABOLIC LOSSES FOR BLOOD ANALYSES WITH TIME

Blood (mg.%)	15 min	30 min	45 min	60 min	75 min	90 min
80	76	72	68	65	61	57
92	88	84	80	77	73	69
103	99	95	91	88	84	80
115	111	107	103	100	96	92
126	122	118	114	111	107	103
138	134	130	126	123	119	115
149	145	141	137	137	130	126
161	157	153	149	146	142	138
172	168	164	160	157	153	149
184	180	176	172	169	165	161
195	191	187	183	180	176	172
207	203	199	195	192	188	184
218	214	210	206	203	199	195
230	226	222	218	215	211	207
241	237	233	229	226	222	218
253	249	245	241	238	234	230
264	260	256	252	249	245	241
276	272	268	264	261	257	253
287	283	279	275	272	268	264
299	295	291	287	284	280	276
310	306	302	298	295	291	287
322	318	314	310	307	303	299
333	329	325	321	318	314	310
345	341	337	333	330	326	322
356	352	348	344	341	337	333
368	364	360	356	353	349	345
379	375	371	367	364	360	356
391	387	383	379	376	372	368
402	398	394	390	387	383	379

This table has been drawn up to aid persons who wish to compare breath and blood analysis, when the samples have been taken at different times.

When compiling the table, the following assumptions were made:
- (*a*) The subject has fully absorbed all of the alcohol consumed into his bloodstream.
- (*b*) The average metabolic rate of alcohol destruction by the body is 15mg./100ml./hour in the blood, and 6.5µg/100ml./hour in the breath.
- (*c*) The blood/breath ratio is 2300:1.

Each pair of numbers shows equivalent breath and blood concentrations, and each row is calculated to show how these values will decrease with the elapse of time in steps of 15 minutes.

For example, after 60 minutes have elapsed, a breath concentration of 70µg/100ml. will, on average, drop to 63µg/100ml., and the corresponding blood concentration of 161mg./100ml. will drop to 146mg./100ml.

Appendix E

CHART OF OFFENCES WITH PENALTIES

Offences under the Road Traffic Regulation Act 1984

(1) Provision creating offence	(2) General nature of offence	(3) Mode of prosecution	(4) Punishment	(5) Disqualification	(6) Endorsement	(7) Penalty points
R.T.R.A., s.17(4)	Use of special road contrary to scheme or regulations	Summarily	Level 4 on the standard scale	Discretionary if committed in respect of a motor vehicle otherwise than by unlawfully stopping or allowing the vehicle to remain at rest on a part of a special road on which vehicles are in certain circumstances permitted to remain at rest	Obligatory if committed as mentioned in the entry in column 5	3–6, (fixed penalty) for speed restriction 3 in any other case
R.T.R.A., s.25(5)	Contravention of pedestrian crossing regulations	Summarily	Level 3 on the standard scale	Discretionary if committed in respect of a motor vehicle	Obligatory if committed in respect of a motor vehicle	3
R.T.R.A., s.28(3)	Not stopping at school crossing	Summarily	Level 3 on the standard scale	Discretionary if committed in respect of a motor vehicle	Obligatory if committed in respect of a motor vehicle	3

(1) Provision creating offence	(2) General nature of offence	(3) Mode of prosecution	(4) Punishment	(5) Disqualification	(6) Endorsement	(7) Penalty points
R.T.R.A., s.29(3)	Contravention of order relating to street playground	Summarily	Level 3 on the standard scale	Discretionary if committed in respect of a motor vehicle	Obligatory if committed in respect of a motor vehicle	2
R.T.R.A., s.30(5)	As above (greater London)	Summarily	Level 3 on the standard scale	Discretionary if committed in respect of a motor vehicle	Obligatory if committed in respect of a motor vehicle	2
R.T.R.A., s.89(1)	Exceeding speed limit	Summarily	Level 3 on the standard scale	Discretionary	Obligatory	3–6 or 3 (fixed penalty)
R.T.A., s.1	Causing death by dangerous driving	On indictment	10 years and/or unlimited fine	Obligatory two years and driving test	Obligatory	3–11
R.T.A., s.2	Dangerous driving	(a) Summarily (b) On indictment	(a) 6 months or the statutory maximum or both (b) 2 years or a fine or both	Obligatory 12 months and driving test	Obligatory	3–11
R.T.A., s.3	Careless and inconsiderate driving	Summarily	Level 4 on the standard scale	Discretionary	Obligatory	3–9
R.T.A., s.3A	Causing death by careless driving when under influence of drink or drugs	On indictment	10 years or a fine or both	Obligatory	Obligatory	3–11

R.T.A., s.4(1)	Driving or attempting to drive when unfit to drive through drink or drugs	Summarily	6 months or level 5 on the standard scale or both. Forfeiture of vehicle	Obligatory	Obligatory	3–11
R.T.A., s.4(2)	Being in charge of a mechanically propelled vehicle when unfit to drive through drink or drugs	Summarily	3 months or level 4 on the standard scale or both. Forfeiture of vehicle	Discretionary	Obligatory	10
R.T.A., s.5(1)(a)	Driving or attempting to drive with excess alcohol in breath, blood or urine	Summarily	6 months or level 5 on the standard scale or both	Obligatory	Obligatory	3–11
R.T.A., s.5(1)(b)	Being in charge of a motor vehicle with excess alcohol in breath, blood or urine	Summarily	3 months or level 4 on the standard scale or both	Discretionary	Obligatory	10
R.T.A., s.6	Failing to provide a specimen of breath for a breath test	Summarily	Level 3 on the standard scale. Forfeiture of vehicle	Obligatory	Obligatory	4

(1) Provision creating offence	(2) General nature of offence	(3) Mode of prosecution	(4) Punishment	(5) Disqualification	(6) Endorsement	(7) Penalty points
R.T.A., s.7	Failing to provide specimen for analysis or laboratory test	Summarily	(a) Where the specimen was required to ascertain ability to drive or proportion of alcohol at the time offender was driving or attempting to drive, 6 months or level 5 on the standard scale or both (b) In any other case, three months or level 4 on the standard scale or both	(a) Obligatory in case mentioned in column 4(a) (b) Discretionary in any other case	Obligatory	(a) 3–11 in case mentioned in column 4(a) (b) 10 in any other case
R.T.A., s.12	Motor racing and speed trials on public ways	Summarily	Level 4 on the standard scale	Obligatory	Obligatory	3–11
R.T.A., s.22	Leaving vehicles in dangerous positions	Summarily	Level 3 on the standard scale	Discretionary if committed in respect of a motor vehicle	Obligatory if committed in respect of a motor vehicle	3

R.T.A., s.22A	Causing danger to road users	(a) Summarily (b) On indictment	(a) 6 months or the statutory maximum or both (b) 7 years or a fine or both		
R.T.A., s.23	Carrying passenger on motor-cycle contrary to section 23	Summarily	Level 3 on the standard scale	Discretionary	Obligatory	3
R.T.A., s.35	Failing to comply with traffic directions	Summarily	Level 3 on the standard scale	Discretionary if committed in respect of a motor vehicle by failure to comply with a direction of a constable or traffic warden	Obligatory if committed as described in column 5	3
R.T.A., s.36	Failing to comply with traffic signs	Summarily	Level 3 on the standard scale	Discretionary, if committed in respect of a motor vehicle by failure to comply with an indication given by a sign specified for the purposes of this paragraph in regulations under R.T.A., s.36	Obligatory if committed as described in column 5	3

(1) Provision creating offence	(2) General nature of offence	(3) Mode of prosecution	(4) Punishment	(5) Disqualification	(6) Endorsement	(7) Penalty points
R.T.A., s.41A	Breach of requirement as to brakes, steering-gear or tyres	Summarily	(a) Level 5 on the standard scale if committed in respect of a goods vehicle or a vehicle adapted to carry more than eight passengers (b) Level 5 on the standard scale in any other case	Discretionary	Obligatory	3
R.T.A., s.87(1)	Driving otherwise than in accordance with a licence	Summarily	Level 3 on the standard scale	Discretionary in a case where the offender's driving would not have been in accordance with any licence that could have been granted to him	Obligatory in the case mentioned in column 5	3–6
R.T.A., s.96	Driving with uncorrected defective eyesight, or refusing to submit to test of eyesight	Summarily	Level 3 on the standard scale	Discretionary	Obligatory	3

R.T.A., s.103(1)(b)	Driving while disqualified	(a) Summarily, in England and Wales (b) Summarily, in Scotland (c) On indictment in Scotland	(a) 6 months or level 5 on the standard scale or both (b) 6 months or the statutory maximum or both (c) 12 months or a fine or both	Discretionary	Obligatory	6
R.T.A., s.143	Using motor vehicle while uninsured or unsecured against third party risks	Summarily	Level 5 on the standard scale	Discretionary	Obligatory	6–8
R.T.A., s.170(4)	Failing to stop after accident and give particulars or report accident	Summarily	6 months or level 5 on the standard scale or both	Discretionary	Obligatory	5–10
R.T.A., s.178	Taking etc. in Scotland a motor vehicle without authority or, knowing that it has been so taken, driving it or allowing oneself to be carried in it without authority	(a) Summarily (b) On indictment	(a) 3 months or the statutory maximum or both (b) 12 months or a fine or both	Discretionary		

		Other Offences	
(1) *Offence*	*(2)* *Disqualification*	*(3)* *Endorsement*	*(4)* *Penalty points*
(1) Manslaughter or, in Scotland, culpable homicide by the driver of a motor vehicle.	Obligatory	Obligatory	3–11
(2) An offence under section 12A of the Theft Act 1968 (aggravated vehicle-taking).	Obligatory	Obligatory	3–11
(3) Stealing or attempting to steal a motor vehicle.	Discretionary		
(4) An offence in respect of a motor vehicle under section 12 of the Theft Act 1968 (taking conveyance without consent of owner etc. or, knowing it has been so taken, driving it or allowing oneself to be carried in it).	Discretionary		
(5) An offence under section 25 of the Theft Act 1968 (going equipped for stealing etc.) committed with reference to the theft or taking of motor vehicles.	Discretionary		

Appendix F

MAGISTRATES' ASSOCIATION'S SUGGESTIONS FOR ROAD TRAFFIC OFFENCE PENALTIES

HOW TO USE THE "SUGGESTIONS"

For the general approach, please refer to the main introduction, noting that it cannot be emphasised too strongly that **THE LIST IS NOT A TARIFF**.

The recommended approach for serious road-traffic offences is to use scales based on seriousness indicators. These suggestions offer a starting point based on an average offence without aggravating factors. However, please note that suggested starting points are now based on a **NOT GUILTY** plea to allow a DISCOUNT of up to a third to be given for a prompt guilty plea.

The seriousness of offences differs widely, especially in cases of careless driving, and many road traffic offences are more hazardous when speeds are higher. Experience has proved that drinking and driving offences account for very many accidents, injuries and deaths. The Court of Appeal has consistently upheld higher penalties for offenders with higher alcohol figures, and it is suggested that penalties and especially periods of disqualification should reflect this. When fixing the size of a fine where an order of disqualification is also made, it should be remembered that the impact of disqualification varies from offender to offender and disqualification will frequently itself entail a very heavy financial burden.

The level of penalties must not become out of proportion compared to the level of fines for common criminal offences such as thefts from shops and assaults.

Variable Penalty Points

Variable penalty points offences imply greater variations in sentence. The fine will give a result adjusted to the financial circumstances of the offender but the penalty points chosen should correspond to the seriousness of the offence.

The Multiple Offender

Where on one occasion an offender is convicted of a large number of offences it is suggested that the court should also take an overall view and initially decide upon the maximum total amount of the fines which it is appropriate to impose for all the offences, even though this total may prove to be considerably less than the figure which would result from adding together all the suggested penalties involved.

Companies

When fining companies the position will depend on the financial standing of the company.

T. R. P. Rudin
SECRETARY

Twelfth Edition
September 1993

The Magistrates' Association
28 Fitzroy Square, London W1P 6DD

IMPORTANT

These suggestions may be reproduced for the use of benches provided the front page is included.

**THIS IS NOT A TARIFF and these Suggestions are to be used only as a starting point
Allow a discount of about a third for a timely guilty plea**

SUGGESTIONS FOR COURTS' ASSESSMENT OF PENALTIES FOR MAIN TRAFFIC OFFENCES

The maximum standard levels are at present:

Level 1 – £200
Level 2 – £500
Level 3 – £1,000
Level 4 – £2,500
Level 5 – £5,000

D   Must disqualify at least 12 months (unless special reasons) and endorse.
(If disqualifying for a lengthy period, or if driving skill suspect, consider disqualifying until test passed)

E   Must endorse (unless special reasons) and may disqualify

MD May disqualify – no power to endorse or assign penalty points
The maximum penalties for "goods vehicles" also apply to "vehicles adapted to carry more than eight passengers". (See offences 7, 8, 9, 21 and 41, 42 and 43)

†   Fixed penalty offences
◆   Refer to Guidelines

825

**THIS IS NOT A TARIFF and these Suggestions are to be used only as a starting point
Allow a discount of about a third for a timely guilty plea**

OFFENCE	PENALTY POINTS	MAXIMUM PENALTY	COMMENTS	FINE
ACCIDENT				
1.◆ Failing to stop	5–10	Level 5 E and/or six months prison	**Refer to Guidelines:** Should disqualify if serious	£360
2.◆ Failing to report to the police	5–10	Level 5 E and/or six months prison	**Refer to Guidelines:** Should disqualify if serious	£360
ALCOHOL Over 35µg breath: 80mg blood: 107mg urine				
3. Drunken driving or driving with excess alcohol	(3–11)	Level 5 D and/or six months prison	**See Excess Alcohol chart on page 51**	
4. Refusing evidential specimen (driving)	(3–11)	Level 5 D and/or six months prison	D 18 months	£720
5. In charge drunk or with excess alcohol or refusing evidential specimen	10	Level 4 E and/or 3 months prison		£360
6. Refusing roadside breath test	4	Level 3 E		£180

DEFECTS

7.† Brakes	3	Level 4 E but for goods vehicles etc. Level 5 E	Consider degree of responsibility Driver £120 LGV/HGV Owner £300 LGV/HGV Driver £210
8.† Steering	3	Level 4 E but for goods vehicles etc. Level 5 E	Consider degree of responsibility Driver £120 LGV/HGV Owner £300 LGV/HGV Driver £210
9.† Tyres (NB. Suggested penalty refers to each tyre)	3	Level 4 E but for goods vehicles etc. Level 5 E	Consider degree of responsibility Driver £120 LGV/HGV Owner £300 LGV/HGV Driver £210

DISQUALIFIED

10.◆ By court order	6	Level 5 E and/or six months prison	**Refer to Guidelines**: Entry point for this offence is CUSTODY

DOCUMENTS

11. Failing to produce	–	Level 3	£60

DOUBLE WHITE LINES

12.† Failing to comply with system	3	Level 3 E	£120

THIS IS NOT A TARIFF and these Suggestions are to be used only as a starting point
Allow a discount of about a third for a timely guilty plea

OFFENCE	PENALTY POINTS	MAXIMUM PENALTY	COMMENTS	FINE
DRIVING				
13.◆ Dangerous	(3–11)	Level 5 D and/or six months prison	**Refer to Guidelines:** Entry point for this offence is COMMUNITY PENALTY	
			Disqualify for at least the compulsory twelve months and order retest	
14.◆ Careless or inconsiderate	3–9	Level 4 E	**Refer to Guidelines:** *Always* consider degree of carelessness	£180
HELMET				
15.† No safety helmet	–	Level 2		£60
INSURANCE				
16.◆ No insurance	6–8	Level 5 E		£540 £660
			LGV/PCV or taxi-cabs	

In fixing the fine regard should be had as to whether the offence was deliberate or inadvertent, whether the offender was misled or any other mitigating circumstances and whether the "user" or "permitter" was responsible for the offence. **IF DELIBERATE THE COURT SHOULD DISQUALIFY**. In any event the court must have regard to the amount of the insurance premium.

LICENCE OFFENCES AND LEARNER DRIVERS

	3–6 where endorsable	Level 3 in some cases E		
17.† Driving not in accordance with a licence	3–6 where endorsable	Level 3 in some cases E	see below	
eg.				
† no licence where could not be covered	3–6	Level 3 E	£150	
† no licence where could be covered	–	Level 3	£30	
† under age	3–6	Level 3 E	£120	
† unsupervised in car	3–6	Level 3 E	£120	Consider disqualification
† learner motor cyclist with passenger	3–6	Level 3 E	£90	Consider disqualification
† no "L" plates	3–6	Level 3 E	£60	
18.† No excise licence	–	Level 3 or 5 times annual duty (whichever greater)		Actual duty loss plus penalty of approximately twice that amount or £120 whichever greater
19. No operator's licence	–	Level 4	£450	

LIGHTS

20.† Driving without lights	–	Level 3	£90

THIS IS NOT A TARIFF and these Suggestions are to be used only as a starting point
Allow a discount of about a third for a timely guilty plea

LOADS
21.† Construction & Use: Condition/Load etc. – danger of injury by:

OFFENCE	PENALTY POINTS	MAXIMUM PENALTY	COMMENTS		FINE
† condition of vehicle or of accessories or equipment	3	Level 4 E but for goods vehicles etc. Level 5 E	Ordinary vehicle-driver/owner LGV/HGV Driver LGV/HGV Owner	but consider degree of responsibility	£180 £300 £600
† purpose of use	3	Level 4 E but for goods vehicles etc. Level 5 E	Ordinary vehicle-driver/owner LGV/HGV Driver LGV/HGV Owner	but consider degree of responsibility	£180 £300 £600
† number or manner of carriage of passengers	3	Level 4 E but for goods vehicles etc. Level 5 E	Ordinary vehicle-owner LGV/HGV Driver LGV/HGV Owner	but consider degree of responsibility	£180 £300 £600
† weight, position or distribution of load	3	Level 4 E but for goods vehicles etc. Level 5 E	Ordinary vehicle-owner LGV/HGV Driver LGV/HGV Owner	but consider degree of responsibility	£180 £300 £600

Offence	Points	Level	Category	Penalty
† insecure load	3	Level 4 but for goods vehicles etc. Level 5 E	Non-LGV/HGV Owner/Driver	£150 but consider degree of responsibility
			Non-LGV/HGV Commercial	£180
			LGV/HGV Driver	£360
			LGV/HGV Owner	£750
† overloading or exceeding maximum axle weight – commercial vehicle	–	Level 5	Non-LGV/HGV Driver	£180 but consider degree of responsibility
			Non-LGV/HGV Owner	£360
			LGV/HGV Driver	£360
			LGV/HGV Owner	£750

Suggestion refers to conviction on each charge. In addition, for overloading add £30 for each 1% of overload (ignoring the first 10%) but always have regard to commercial gain and damage to roads.

OWNERSHIP/DRIVER

22. Not supplying details of driver	3	Level 3 E	£210
Not notifying DVLA etc.	–	Level 3	£150

PARKING

23.† Dangerous position	3	Level 3 E	£90
24.† On zig-zags by pedestrian crossing	3	Level 3 E	£90
25.† Obstruction	–	Level 3	£60
26.† Stopping on Clearway	–	Level 3	£90

THIS IS NOT A TARIFF and these Suggestions are to be used only as a starting point
Allow a discount of about a third for a timely guilty plea

OFFENCE	PENALTY POINTS	MAXIMUM PENALTY	COMMENTS	FINE
PEDESTRIAN OR SCHOOL CROSSING				
27.† Offences other than parking (†certain offences only)	3	Level 3 E	Consider disqualification	£90
SEAT BELTS				
28.† Not wearing	–	Level 2		£60
29.† Driving with a child not wearing	–			
† (front)		Level 2		£60
† (back)		Level 1		£30
SPEEDING				
30.† Exceeding speed limit	3–6	Level 3 E	Consider disqualification if 30 m.p.h. over limit	SEE TABLE OF BANDS ON PAGE 50
SPEED LIMITERS				
31.† Speed Limiter not fitted	–			Driver £300 Owner £420
32.† Speed Limiter not being used or not correctly calibrated	–			Driver £150 Owner £210

TACHOGRAPH

33. No tachograph or not used as required	–	Level 5	£240
34. Tachograph falsification	–	Level 5	£360

TAKEN VEHICLES

35.◆ Aggravated Vehicle Taking	(3–11)	Level 5 must disqualify at least 12 months and/or 6 months prison	**Refer to Guidelines:** Entry point for this offence is CUSTODY
36.◆ Taking vehicle without consent	–	Level 5 may disqualify only and/or 6 months prison	**Refer to Guidelines:** Entry point for this offence is COMMUNITY PENALTY
37. Carried in taken vehicle	–	Level 5 may disqualify and/or 6 months prison	Consider custody/community penalty £300

TEST CERTIFICATE

38. No test certificate	–	Level 3 but for goods vehicles and vehicles adapted to carry more than 8 passengers Level 4	Ordinary vehicles £90 / 3.5 tonnes or over GVW £120 / LGV and PCV £180 / Trailers (but dependent on size) £90

TRAFFIC LIGHTS

39.+ Failing to comply with	3	Level 3 E	£90

**THIS IS NOT A TARIFF and these Suggestions are to be used only as a starting point
Allow a discount of about a third for a timely guilty plea**

OFFENCE	PENALTY POINTS	MAXIMUM PENALTY	COMMENTS	FINE	
TRAFFIC OR POLICE SIGNS					
40.† Failing to comply with (except traffic lights or double white lines)	3	Level 3 (power to disqualify, endorse, test in some cases)	Endorse where required	£90	
VEHICLE OFFENCES under the Construction and Use Regulations not shown elsewhere					
41.† Loss of wheel	3	Level 4 E but for goods vehicles etc. Level 5	in all cases consider degree of responsibility	Driver £420 / Owner £600	
42.† Exhaust emission	—	Level 3 but for goods vehicles etc. Level 4	in all cases consider degree of responsibility	Driver £90 / Owner £150	
43.† Other offences	—	Level 3 but for goods vehicles etc. Level 4	in all cases consider degree of responsibility	Driver £60 / Owner £90	

MOTORWAY OFFENCES

DRIVING

44.† Driving in reverse	3	Level 4 E	On main motorway	£360
			On sliproad	£120
45.† Driving in wrong direction	3	Level 4 E	Consider disqualification	On main motorway £600
				On sliproad £180
46.† Driving off carriageway	3	Level 4 E	Central reservation	£180
			Hard shoulder	£150
47.† Driving on sliproad against "No entry sign"	3	Level 4 E		£180
48.† Making U-Turn	3	Level 4 E	Consider disqualification	£480

LEARNERS

49.† Learner driver or excluded vehicle	3	Level 4 E		£180

THIS IS NOT A TARIFF and these Suggestions are to be used only as a starting point
Allow a discount of about a third for a timely guilty plea

OFFENCE	PENALTY POINTS	MAXIMUM PENALTY	COMMENTS	FINE
SPEEDING				
50.† Exceeding speed limit	3–6	Level 4 E*	Consider disqualification if 30 m.p.h. over limit	SEE TABLE OF BANDS BELOW
*Level 3E in respect of goods and other vehicles restricted to a lower limit				
STOPPING				
51.† Stopping on hard shoulder	–	Level 4		On main motorway £120 / On sliproad £60
THIRD LANE				
52.† Vehicle over 7.5 tonnes or drawing trailer in third lane	3	Level 4 E		£300
WALKING				
53.† Walking on motorway	–	Level 4		On main motorway or sliproad £90 / On hard shoulder or verge £60

†SPEEDING – TABLE OF BANDS

Penalty Points: 3 – 6

Maximum penalty: see numbers 30 and 50 above

Guideline for speeding, but consider scene of offence and more for heavy vehicles/LGVs/PCVs

MILES OVER LIMIT	SUGGESTED VARIABLE	PENALTY POINTS	SUGGESTED FINE
1–14	A fixed penalty will often have been offered	3	£90
15–19	A fixed penalty will often have been offered	4	£120
20–24	A fixed penalty will often have been offered	5	£150
25–29	A fixed penalty may have been offered	6	£180
	Equivalent to 100 m.p.h. on the motorway – Consider disqualification		
30–34	Disqualify for 7 days	6	£210
35–39	Disqualify for 14 days	6	£240

Above this speed – 40 miles or more over the limit (e.g. 70 m.p.h. in a 30 m.p.h. area – 110 m.p.h. on the motorway – sharp increase in penalty and disqualification (minimum 21 days).

Appendix G

SHORTEST STOPPING DISTANCES

Miles per hour	Thinking distance		Braking distance		Overall stopping distance	
	metres	feet	metres	feet	metres	feet
20	6	20	6	20	12	40
30	9	30	14	45	23	75
40	12	40	24	80	36	120
50	15	50	38	125	53	175
60	18	60	55	180	73	240
70	21	70	75	245	96	315
80	24	80	98	320	122	400
90	27	90	124	405	151	495
100	33	100	153	500	186	600

Appendix H

SPEED AND DISTANCE CHART

Miles per hour	Feet per second	Feet per minute	Metres per second	Metres per minute
20	29	1,740	9	530
30	44	2,640	13	805
40	59	3,540	18	1,079
50	73	4,380	22	1,335
60	88	5,280	27	1,609
70	103	6,180	31	1,884
80	117	7,020	36	2,140
90	132	7,920	40	2,424
100	146	8,760	45	2,670

Appendix I

ENDORSEMENT CODE

Aiding, abetting, counselling or procuring
Offences as coded below, but with zero changed to 2,
e.g. UT 40 becomes UT 42

Causing or permitting
Offences as coded below, but with zero changed to 4,
e.g. IN 10 becomes IN 14.

Inciting
Offences as coded below, but with zero changed to 6,
e.g. DD 30 becomes DD 36.

Periods of time
Periods of time are signified as follows: D = days; M = months;
Y = years.

Code   Accident offences
AC 10   Failing to stop after an accident.
AC 20   Failing to give particulars or to report an accident within 24 hours.
AC 30   Undefined accident offence.

Disqualified driver
BA 10   Driving while disqualified.
BA 20   Driving while disqualified by reason of age.
BA 30   Attempting to drive whilst disqualified by order of court.

Careless driving
CD 10   Driving without due care and attention.
CD 20   Driving without reasonable consideration for other road users.
CD 30   Driving without due care and attention or without reasonable consideration for other road users (primarily for use by Scottish courts).
CD 40   Causing death by careless driving when unfit through drink.
CD 50   Causing death by careless driving when unfit through drugs.
CD 60   Causing death by careless driving with alcohol above the limit.

CD 70 Causing death by careless driving and failing to provide a specimen for analysis.

Construction and use offences

CU 10 Using a vehicle with defective brakes.

CU 20 Causing or likely to cause danger by reason of use of unsuitable vehicle or using a vehicle with parts or accessories (excluding brakes, steering or tyres) in a dangerous condition.

CU 30 Using a vehicle with defective tyres.

CU 40 Using a vehicle with defective steering.

CU 50 Causing or likely to cause danger by reason of load or passengers.

CU 60 Undefined failure to comply with Construction and Use Regulations.

Reckless driving/dangerous driving

DD 30 Reckless driving.

DD 40 Dangerous driving.

DD 60 Manslaughter or culpable homicide while driving a vehicle.

DD 70 Causing death by reckless driving

DD 80 Causing death by dangerous driving.

Drink or drugs

DR 10 Driving or attempting to drive with blood alcohol level above limit.

DR 20 Driving or attempting to drive while unfit through drink or drugs.

DR 30 Driving or attempting to drive then refusing to supply a specimen for laboratory testing.

DR 40 In charge of a vehicle while blood alcohol level above limit.

DR 50 In charge of a vehicle while unfit through drink or drugs.

DR 60 In charge of a vehicle then refusing to supply a specimen for laboratory testing.

DR 70 Failing to provide specimen for breath test (roadside).

Insurance offences

IN 10 Using a vehicle uninsured against third party risks.

Licence offences

LC 10 Driving without a licence.

LC 20 Driving otherwise than in accordance with a licence.

LC 30 Driving after making a false declaration about fitness when applying for a licence.

LC 40 Driving a vehicle having failed to notify a disability.

LC 50 Driving after a licence has been revoked or refused on medical grounds.

Miscellaneous offences

MS 10 Leaving a vehicle in a dangerous position.

MS 20 Unlawful pillion riding.

MS 30 Playstreet offences.

MS 40 Driving with uncorrected defective eyesight or refusing to submit to a test. (Obsolete code, see now MS 70 and MS 80.)

MS 50 Motor racing on the highway.

MS 60 Offences not covered by other codes.

MS 70 Driving with uncorrected defective eyesight.

MS 80 Refusing to submit to eyesight test.

MS 90 Failure to give information as to identity of driver.

Motorway offences

MW 10 Contravention of Special Road Regulations (excluding speed limits).

Criminal use of vehicle

NE 99 Use of vehicle for purpose of committing crime (Crown Court only).

Pedestrian crossings

PC 10 Undefined contravention of Pedestrian Crossing Regulations (primarily for use by Scottish courts).

PC 20 Contravention of Pedestrian Crossing Regulations with moving vehicle.

PC 30 Contravention of Pedestrian Crossing Regulations with stationary vehicle.

Provisional licence offences

PL 10 Driving without "L" plates.

PL 20 Not accompanied by a qualified person.

PL 30 Carrying a person not qualified.

PL 40 Drawing an unauthorised trailer.

PL 50 Undefined failure to comply with conditions of a provisional licence.

Speed limits

SP 10 Exceeding goods vehicle speed limit.

SP 20 Exceeding speed limit for type of vehicle (excluding goods or passenger vehicles).

SP 30 Exceeding statutory speed limit on a public road.

SP 40 Exceeding passenger vehicle speed limit.

SP 50 Exceeding speed limit on a motorway.

SP 60 Undefined speed limit offence.

Traffic directions and signs
TS 10 Failing to comply with traffic light signals.
TS 20 Failing to comply with double white lines.
TS 30 Failing to comply with a "Stop" sign.
TS 40 Failing to comply with directions of a constable or traffic warden.
TS 50 Failing to comply with a traffic sign (excluding "Stop" signs, traffic lights or double white lines).
TS 60 Failing to comply with a school crossing patrol sign.
TS 70 Undefined failure to comply with a traffic direction or sign.

Theft or unauthorised taking
UT 10 Taking and driving away a vehicle without consent or an attempt thereat (primarily for use by Scottish courts).
UT 20 Stealing or attempting to steal a vehicle.
UT 30 Going equipped for stealing or taking a vehicle.
UT 40 Taking or attempting to take a vehicle without consent; driving or attempting to drive a vehicle knowing it to have been taken without consent, allowing oneself to be carried in or on a vehicle knowing it to have been taken without consent.

Special codes
TT 99 Disqualification for accumulating 12 or more penalty points.

Sentence code

The sentence is represented by four characters, *e.g.* G 02 Y (probation order two years). The first letter indicates the nature of the sentence, the middle two numbers (0 always precedes what would otherwise be a single figure) and the final letter indicates the period of the sentence, if any, as hours (H), days (D), months (M), or years (Y). Apart from the special code TT 99 which indicates a disqualification under the penalty points procedure there is no code to represent disqualification because this appears in a special column on the licence. In the case of an absolute discharge there is no period so the code J 000 is used.

The first letter of the code indicates the sentence as follows:
A imprisonment
B detention in a place approved by the Secretary of State
C suspended sentence of imprisonment
E conditional discharge
F bound over
G probation
H supervision order (juvenile court)

J absolute discharge
K attendance centre
L detention centre
M community service order
P youth custody
S compensation
T hospital or guardianship order
W care order
X total period of partially suspended sentence, *i.e.* period sentence served and period sentence suspended.

Appendix J
SAMPLE PRINTOUTS

(i) Camic Breath Analyser

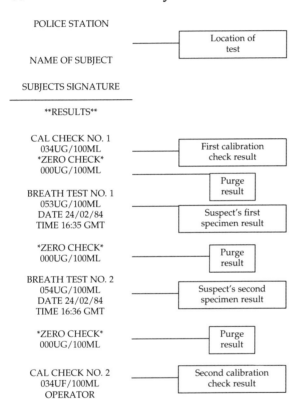

POLICE STATION

        ———— Location of test

NAME OF SUBJECT

SUBJECTS SIGNATURE
————————————————

RESULTS

CAL CHECK NO. 1
  034UG/100ML ———— First calibration check result
  ZERO CHECK
  000UG/100ML ————

        Purge result

BREATH TEST NO. 1
  053UG/100ML
  DATE 24/02/84 ———— Suspect's first specimen result
  TIME 16:35 GMT

  ZERO CHECK
  000UG/100ML ———— Purge result

BREATH TEST NO. 2
  054UG/100ML ———— Suspect's second specimen result
  DATE 24/02/84
  TIME 16:36 GMT

  ZERO CHECK
  000UG/100ML ———— Purge result

CAL CHECK NO. 2
  034UF/100ML ———— Second calibration check result
  OPERATOR

I CERTIFY THAT IN THIS
STATEMENT READING 1
RELATES TO THE FIRST
SPECIMEN OF BREATH
PROVIDED BY THE SUBJECT
NAMED ABOVE AND
READING 2 TO THE
SECOND, AT THE DATE
AND TIME SHOWN HEREIN

————————————————

CAMIC

849

(ii) Lion Intoximeter 3000

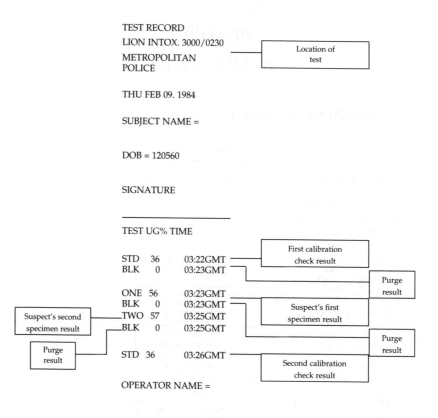

TEST RECORD

LION INTOX. 3000/0230 ——— [Location of test]

METROPOLITAN POLICE

THU FEB 09. 1984

SUBJECT NAME =

DOB = 120560

SIGNATURE

TEST UG% TIME

STD   36   03:22GMT ——— [First calibration check result]

BLK   0   03:23GMT

[Purge result]

ONE 56   03:23GMT ——— [Suspect's first specimen result]

BLK   0   03:23GMT

TWO 57   03:25GMT

BLK   0   03:25GMT

[Purge result]

[Suspect's second specimen result]

[Purge result]

STD 36   03:26GMT ——— [Second calibration check result]

OPERATOR NAME =

I CERTIFY THAT IN THIS
STATEMENT READING 1
RELATES TO THE FIRST
SPECIMEN OF BREATH
PROVIDED BY THE
SUBJECT NAMED
ABOVE AND READING
2 TO THE SECOND, AT
THE DATE AND TIME
SHOWN HEREIN

SIGNATURE

Appendix K

PROSECUTING A ROAD TRAFFIC LIST IN THE MAGISTRATES' COURT

1. Check files against list; some files may be delivered at court.
2. Check the offences, their elements and their penalties and ensure that there is an accurate summary of the facts supported by evidence which makes out the offences.

A. Proving Case in Absence of the Defendant
(non-imprisonable offences only)

3. Prove issue and service of summons (or adjournment notice if appropriate):
   (a) Confirm copy of summons held by clerk or in file
   (b) confirm certificate of postal service on summons completed
   (c) check that there is no indication that postal service failed, *e.g.* returned summons, or that personal service was carried out.
   IF no issue of summons: request second summons and service.
   IF no proof of service: request adjournment for postal/personal service.
   IF service has been impossible: case/file to be marked "Not served."
4. Prove service of section 9 statements:
   (*a*) Check certificate of postal service within time limit (usually orange certificate stuck to copy of statements) and no response from defendant requiring witnesses to attend
   (*b*) check that there is no indication that postal service failed, *e.g.* returned statements.
   IF service of statements too late/not proven: *either*: seek adjournment for witnesses to attend checking dates against calendar *or*: prove case in absence if witnesses present (see 6 below).
5. State intention to prove in absence and open case (very briefly if at all). If there are alternative charges, *e.g.* using without insurance/driving licence/test certificate and failing to produce such, withdraw the latter or offer no evidence if pleas have been entered; alternatively if correct documents produced at court proceed only with failing to produce.

6. Prosecution case: read statements stating who made, when and that statutory declaration signed;
   or call witnesses to give evidence: witness takes oath, identified, obtain leave to refer to notes if appropriate, gives evidence in chief, bench may question, release.
7. Close prosecution case.
8. Verdict of court. Prosecution application for costs/compensation.
9. Clerk may read any mitigation submitted by defendant. Assist court in sentencing:
   (a) Check whether driving licence (DL) or printout (PO) held on file or by clerk (may be delivered at court);
   (b) check whether points from current offences will render defendant a "totter";
   (c) check whether court likely to consider disqualification, *e.g.* for excess speed (clerk will be able to advise on court policy);
   IF no DL/PO: seek adjournment to obtain;
   IF disqualification possible: seek adjournment for defendant to attend;
   (d) hand up DL/PO and be prepared to explain any previous offences.
10. Record sentence, fine, costs, penalty points, etc. in correct position of file cover.
11. Record time any witnesses released.

B. PROVING CASE IN PRESENCE OF ACCUSED
(after not guilty plea)

12. If prosecution witnesses present: proceed with trial, ensuring to note times witnesses released.
    IF not: adjourn for witnesses to attend
    or: prove service of section 9 statements and proceed as at 5 and 6 above (court may accede to defendant's wish that prosecution witnesses attend even though no response made to section 9 statements).

C. SENTENCING IN ABSENCE OF DEFENDANT AFTER NO/NOT GUILTY PLEA
(usually arises when case previously proved in absence and then adjourned to obtain DL/PO).

13. Check that DL/PO held.
    IF not: seek further adjournment to obtain.

14. Outline case: check that facts do support offence
    IF not: request court to nullify previous finding and withdraw charge/offer no evidence.
15. Proceed as at 9 and 10 above.

D. Sentencing in Absence of Defendant after Guilty Plea by Post

16. Service of summons proved by defendant's response. If plea is equivocal: adjourn for not guilty hearing/clearer plea.
17. Proceed as at 13, 14, 15 above.
    BUT outline of case MUST be limited to facts stated on summons to which the defendant has pleaded guilty.

E. Sentencing in Presence of Defendant
(usually when case previously proved in absence and then adjourned for defendant to attend as disqualification being considered).

18. Confirm defendant is present.
    IF Not: request warrant be issued (usually backed for bail).
19. Proceed as at 14 above.

INDEX

855

SHORTEST STOPPING DISTANCES

Miles per hour	Thinking distance		Braking distance		Overall stopping distance	
	metres	feet	metres	feet	metres	feet
20	6	20	6	20	12	40
30	9	30	14	45	23	75
40	12	40	24	80	36	120
50	15	50	38	125	53	175
60	18	60	55	180	73	240
70	21	70	75	245	96	315
80	24	80	98	320	122	400
90	27	90	124	405	151	495
100	33	100	153	500	186	600

ALTERNATIVE VERDICTS

Offence charged	Alternative
Section 1 (causing death by dangerous driving)	Section 2 (dangerous driving) Section 3 (careless, and inconsiderate, driving)
Section 2 (dangerous driving)	Section 3 (careless, and inconsiderate, driving)
Section 3A (causing death by careless driving when under influence of drink or drugs)	Section 3 (careless, and inconsiderate, driving) Section 4(1) (driving when unfit to drive through drink or drugs) Section 5(1)(a) (driving with excess alcohol in breath, blood or urine) Section 7(6) (failing to provide specimen)
Section 4(1) (driving or attempting to drive when unfit to drive through drink or drugs)	Section 4(2) (being in charge of a vehicle when unfit to drive through drink or drugs)
Section 5(1)(a) (driving or attempting to drive with excess alcohol in breath, blood or urine)	Section 5(1)(b) (being in charge of a vehicle with excess alcohol in breath, blood or urine)
Section 28 (dangerous cycling)	Section 29 (careless, and inconsiderate, cycling)